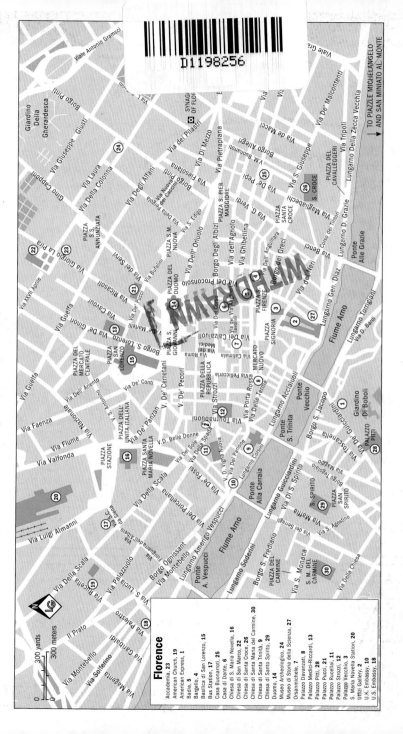

D1198256

Florence

Accademia, 23
American Church, 19
American Express, 1
Badia, 5
Bargello, 4
Basilica di San Lorenzo, 15
Bus Station, 17
Casa Buonarroti, 25
Casa di Dante, 6
Chiesa di S. Maria Novella, 16
Chiesa di San Marco, 22
Chiesa di Santa Croce, 26
Chiesa di Santa Maria del Carmine, 30
Chiesa di Santa Trinità, 9
Chiesa di Santo Spirito, 29
Duomo, 14
Museo Archeologico, 24
Museo di Storia della Scienza, 27
Orsanmichele, 7
Palazzo Davanzati, 8
Palazzo Medici-Riccardi, 13
Palazzo Pitti, 28
Palazzo Pucci, 21
Palazzo Rucellai, 10
Palazzo Strozzi, 12
Palazzo Vecchio, 3
S. Maria Novella Station, 20
Uffizi Gallery, 2
U.K. Embassy, 10
U.S. Embassy, 18

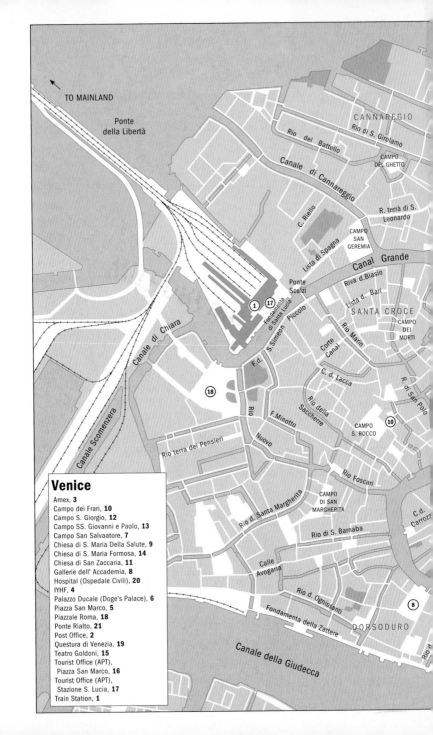

TO MAINLAND

Ponte
della Libertà

CANNAREGIO

Rio di S. Girolamo

Rio del Battello

Canale di Cannareggio

CAMPO
DEL GHETTO

C. Riello

R. terrà di S.
Leonardo

Lista di Spagna

CAMPO
SAN
GEREMIA

Canal Grande

Ponte
Scalzi

Riva d.Biasio

Lista d. Bari

SANTA CROCE

CAMPO
DEI
MORTI

Fondamenta di Santa Lucia

F.d. S. Simeon Piccolo

Rio Marin

Corte
Canal

C. d. Lacca

R. di San Polo

Canale di Chiara

F.d. S. Simeon

Rio della Saccherre

CAMPO
S. ROCCO

F.Minotto

Rio

Nuovo

Rio terra dei Pensieri

Rio Foscari

CAMPO
DI SAN
MARGHERITA

Canale Sconmenzera

Rio d. Santa Margherita

Rio di S. Barnaba

C.d.
Carrozz

Calle
Avogaria

Rio d. Ognissanti

Fondamenta della Zattere

DORSODURO

Canale della Giudecca

Venice

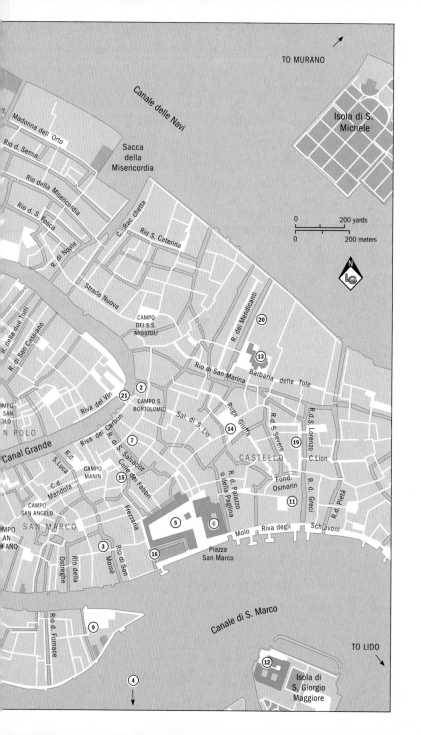

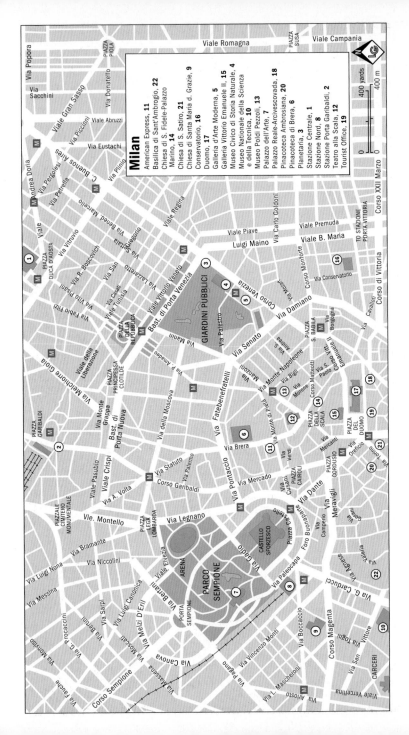

Milan

American Express, **11**
Basilica di Sant'Ambrogio, **22**
Chiesa di S. Fidele-Palazzo Marino, **14**
Chiesa di S. Satiro, **21**
Chiesa di Santa Maria d. Grazie, **9**
Conservatorio, **16**
Duomo, **17**
Galleria d'Arte Moderna, **5**
Galleria Vittorio Emanuele II, **15**
Museo Civico di Storia Naturale, **4**
Museo Nazionale della Scienza e della Tecnica, **10**
Museo Poldi Pezzoli, **13**
Palazzo dell'Arte, **7**
Palazzo Reale-Arcivescovada, **18**
Pinacoteca Ambrosiana, **20**
Pinacoteca di Brera, **6**
Planetaria, **3**
Stazione Centrale, **1**
Stazione Nord, **8**
Stazione Porta Garibaldi, **2**
Teatro alla Scala, **12**
Tourist Office, **19**

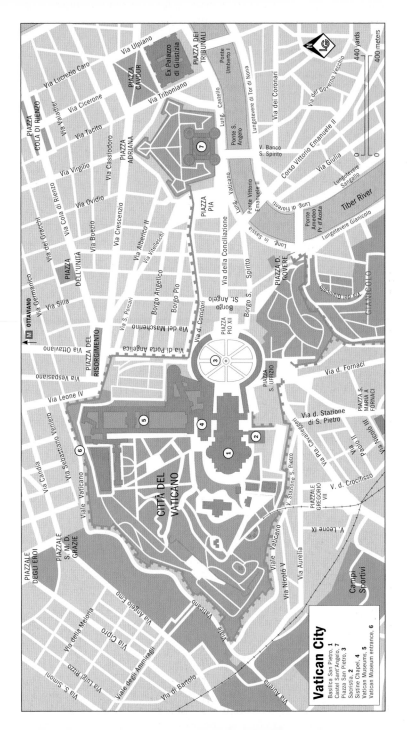

Vatican City

Basilica San Pietro, **1**
Castel Sant'Angelo, **7**
Piazza San Pietro, **3**
Sacristia, **2**
Sistine Chapel, **4**
Vatican Museums, **5**
Vatican Museum entrance, **6**

440 yards
400 meters

M OTTAVIANO

CITTÀ DEL VATICANO

Tiber River

GIANICOLO

Campi Sportivi

PIAZZALE DEGLI EROI
PIAZZALE S. M. D. GRAZIE
PIAZZA DEL RISORGIMENTO
PIAZZA DELL'UNITÀ
PIAZZA COLA DI RIENZO
PIAZZA ADRIANA
PIAZZA CAVOUR
PIAZZA DEI TRIBUNALI
PIAZZA PIA
PIAZZA PIO XII
PIAZZA S. UFIZIO
PIAZZA D. ROVERE
PIAZZA S. MARIA A FORNACI
PIAZZALE GREGORIO VII

Via S. Simoni
Via Luigi Rizzo
Via della Meloria
Via Cipro
Viale degli Ammiragli
Via Angelo Emo
Via di Bartolo
Viale Vaticano
Via Sebastiano Veniero
Via Candia
Viale Vaticano
Via Vespasiano
Via Leone IV
Via Germanico
Via Silla
Via dei Gracchi
Via Cola di Rienzo
Via Ovidio
Via Boezio
Via Crescenzio
Via S. Porcari
Via Alberico II
Via Vitelleschi
Borgo Angelico
Borgo Pio
Borgo S. Angelo
Via d. Corridori
Via del Mascherino
Via di Porta Angelica
Via della Conciliazione
Borgo S. Spirito
In Sassia
Via Ottaviano
Via Vespasiano
Via Valadier
Via Cicerone
Via Tacito
Via Virgilio
Via Cassiodoro
Via Lucrezio Caro
Via Ulpiano
Via Triboniano
Lung. Castello
Ponte Umberto I
Lungotevere di Tor di Nona
Via dei Coronari
Via del Governo Vecchio
Corso Vittorio Emanuele II
Via Giulia
Lungotevere Sangallo
Lungotevere Gianicolo
V. Banco S. Spirito
Ponte S. Angelo
Lung. Vaticano
Ponte Vittorio Emanuele II
Lung. di Fiorentini
Ponte Amedeo Pr d'Aosta
Via della Stazione di S. Pietro
Via d. Fornaci
V. d. Cavalleggeri
V. Stazione S. Pietro
V. d. Crocifisso
V. Leone IX
Via Paolo III
Via Nicolò III
Viale Vaticano
Via Nicolò V
Via Aurelia
Via Aurelia

Ex Palazzo di Giustizia

1 **2** **3** **4** **5** **6** **7**

Rome Mass Transit

Legend:
- ·170· Bus route/terminus
- Ⓜ TERMINI A-Line/Metro station/terminus
- B-Line
- ⑧ Tram route/terminus

BUS ROUTES
23, 32, 34, 40, 44, 46, 60, 62, 64, 70, 81,
116, 117, 119, 170, 175, 490, 492, 628,
673, 714, 870

TRAM ROUTES
3, 8, 19

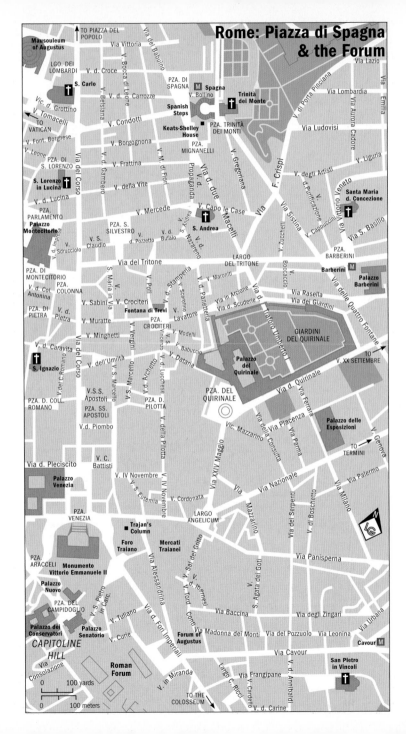

Rome: Piazza di Spagna & the Forum

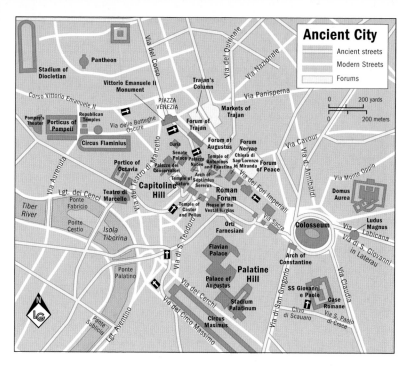

Ancient City

Ancient streets
Modern Streets
Forums

0   200 yards
0   200 meters

Stadium of Diocletian
Pantheon
Via del Corso
Via del Quirinale
Via del Quirinale
Via Nazionale
Vittorio Emanuele II Monument
Trajan's Column
Via Panisperna
Corso Vittorio Emanuele II
PIAZZA VENEZIA
Markets of Trajan
Pompey's Theater
Porticus of Pompeii
Republican Temples
Via delle Botteghe Oscure
Forum of Trajan
Forum of Augustus
Forum Nervae
Via Cavour
Circus Flaminius
Curia
Senate Palace
Palazzo Nuovo
Temple of Antoninus and Faustina
Chiesa di San Lorenzo in Miranda
Forum of Peace
Portico of Octavia
Palazzo dei Conservatori
Arch of Septimius Serverus
Temple of Saturn
Via dei Fori Imperiali
Via Monte Oppio
Via Aurenula
Teatro di Marcello
Capitoline Hill
Roman Forum
Domus Aurea
Lgt. dei Cenci
Via del Teatro di Marcello
Temple of Castor and Pollux
House of the Vestal Virgins
Via Sacra
Ludus Magnus
Tiber River
Ponte Fabricio
Isola Tiberina
Orti Farnesiani
Via di S. Teodoro
Colosseum
Via di S. Giovanni in Laterau
Ponte Cestio
Flavian Palace
Arch of Constantine
Via Claudia
Ponte Palatino
Palace of Augustus
Palatine Hill
SS Giovanni e Paolo
Via di San Gregorio
Case Romane
Ponte Sublicio
Via dei Cerchi
Stadium Palatinum
Clivo di Scauaro
Via S. Paolo di Croce
N
Lgt. Aventino
Via del Circo Massimo
Circus Maximus

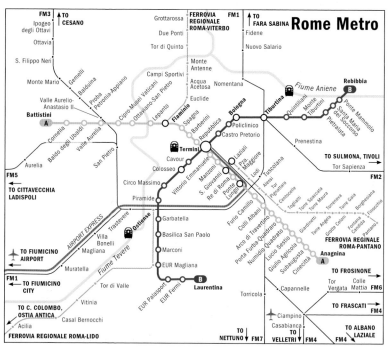

Rome Metro

FM3
Ipogeo degli Ottavi
TO CESANO
Ottavia
Grottarossa
FERROVIA REGIONALE ROMA-VITERBO
FM1
Due Ponti
TO FARA SABINA
Fidene
S. Filippo Neri
Tor di Quinto
Nuovo Salario
Monte Mario
Gemelli
Balduina
Campi Sportivi
Monte Antenne
Nomentana
Rebibbia
B
Acqua Acetosa
Euclide
Fiume Aniene
Valle Aurelio-Anastasio II
Proba Petronia-Appiano
Cipro-Musei Vaticani
Ottaviano-San Pietro
Lepanto
Flaminio
Spagna
Barberini
Bologna
Tiburtina
Quintiliani
Monte Tiburtino
Ponte Mammolo
Santa Maria del Soccorso
Pietralata
Battistini
A
Cornelia
Baldo degli Ubaldi
Valle Aurelia
San Pietro
Repubblica
Policlinico
Castro Pretorio
Prenestina
Aurelia
Termini
Cavour
Manzoni
Vittorio Emmanuele
S. Giovanni
Lodi
Pza Maggiore
Laziali
Re di Roma
Tuscolana
Alessi
TO SULMONA, TIVOLI
Tor Sapienza
FM2
FM5
TO CITTAVECCHIA LADISPOLI
Colosseo
Ponte Lungo
Furio Camillo
Tor Pignattara
Centocelle
Togliatti
Tor Tre Teste
Torre Spaccata
Torre Maura
Torre Gaia
Circo Massimo
AIRPORT EXPRESS
Piramide
Trastevere
Ostiense
Garbatella
Colli Albani
Arco di Travertino
Porta Furba Quadraro
Numidio Quadrato
Lucio Sestio
Giulio Agricola
Subaugusta
Cinecittà
Torre Angela
Grotte Celoni
Giardinetti
Torrenova
Fontana Candida
Pantano
Finocchio
Borghesiana
FERROVIA REGINALE ROMA-PANTANO
Villa Bonelli
Basilica San Paolo
TO FIUMICINO AIRPORT
Magliana
Muratella
Marconi
EUR Magliana
Anagnina
A
TO FROSINONE
FM1
TO FIUMICINO CITY
Fiume Tevere
Tor di Valle
EUR Palasport
EUR Fermi
Laurentina
Capannelle
Tor Vergata
Colle Mattia
FM6
Vitinia
Torricola
TO FRASCATI
FM4
TO C. COLOMBO, OSTIA ANTICA
Casal Bernocchi
Ciampino
Casabianca
TO ALBANO LAZIALE
FM4
Acilia
FERROVIA REGIONALE ROMA-LIDO
TO NETTUNO
FM7
TO VELLETRI
FM4
FM4

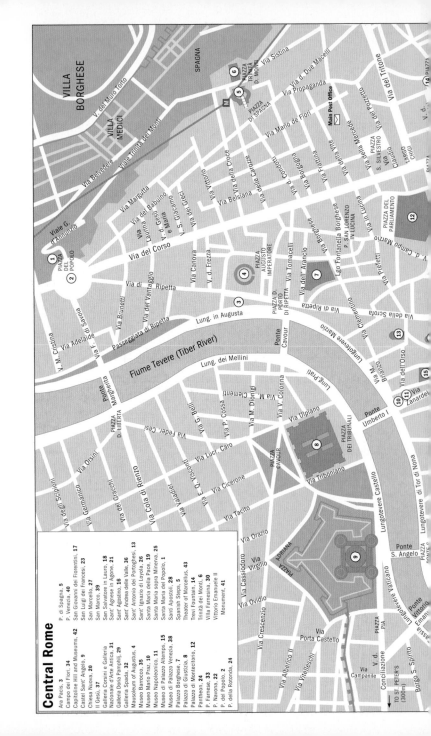

Central Rome

Ara Pacis, **3**
Campo dei Fiori, **34**
Capitoline Hill and Museums, **42**
Castel Sant'Angelo, **9**
Chiesa Nuova, **20**
Il Gesù, **37**
Galleria Corsini e Galleria
Nazionale d'Arte Antica, **31**
Galleria Doria Pamphilj, **29**
Galleria Spada, **32**
Mausoleum of Augustus, **4**
Museo Barocco, **35**
Museo Mario Praz, **10**
Museo Napoleonico, **11**
Museo di Palazzo Altemps, **15**
Museo di Palazzo Venezia, **38**
Palazzo Borghese, **7**
Palazzo di Giustizia, **8**
Palazzo di Montecitorio, **12**
Pantheon, **24**
P. Farnese, **33**
P. Navona, **22**
P. del Popolo, **2**
P. della Rotonda, **24**

P. di Spagna, **5**
P. Venezia, **40**
San Giovanni dei Fiorentini, **17**
San Luigi dei Francesi, **23**
San Marcello, **27**
San Marco, **39**
San Salvatore in Lauro, **18**
Sant'Agnese in Agone, **21**
Sant'Agostino, **16**
Sant'Andrea delle Valle, **36**
Sant'Antonio dei Portoghesi, **13**
Sant'Ignazio di Loyola, **26**
Santa Maria della Pace, **19**
Santa Maria sopra Minerva, **25**
Santa Maria del Popolo, **1**
Santi Apostoli, **28**
Spanish Steps, **5**
Theater of Marcellus, **43**
Trevi Fountain, **14**
Trinità dei Monti, **6**
Villa Farnesina, **30**
Vittorio Emanuele II
Monument, **41**

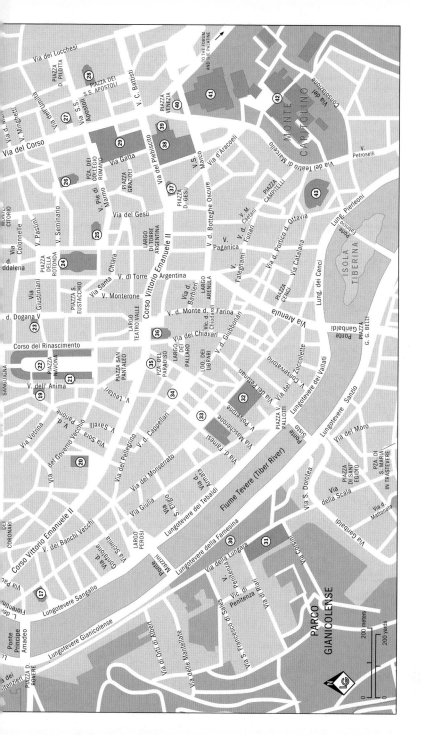

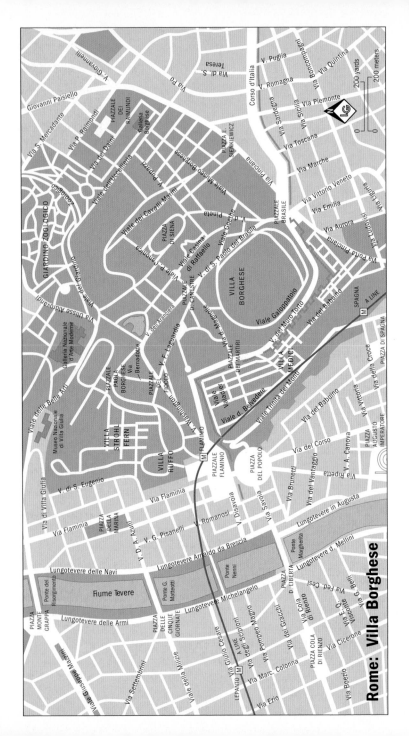

Rome: Villa Borghese

LET'S GO

■ THE RESOURCE FOR THE INDEPENDENT TRAVELER

"The guides are aimed not only at young budget travelers but at the indepedent traveler; a sort of streetwise cookbook for traveling alone."

—The New York Times

"Unbeatable; good sight-seeing advice; up-to-date info on restaurants, hotels, and inns; a commitment to money-saving travel; and a wry style that brightens nearly every page."

—The Washington Post

"Lighthearted and sophisticated, informative and fun to read. [Let's Go] helps the novice traveler navigate like a knowledgeable old hand."

—Atlanta Journal-Constitution

"A world-wise traveling companion—always ready with friendly advice and helpful hints, all sprinkled with a bit of wit."

—The Philadelphia Inquirer

■ THE BEST TRAVEL BARGAINS IN YOUR PRICE RANGE

"All the dirt, dirt cheap."

—People

"Anything you need to know about budget traveling is detailed in this book."

—The Chicago Sun-Times

"Let's Go follows the creed that you don't have to toss your life's savings to the wind to travel—unless you want to."

—The Salt Lake Tribune

■ REAL ADVICE FOR REAL EXPERIENCES

"The writers seem to have experienced every rooster-packed bus and lunar-surfaced mattress about which they write."

—The New York Times

"Value-packed, unbeatable, accurate, and comprehensive."

—The Los Angeles Times

"[Let's Go's] devoted updaters really walk the walk (and thumb the ride, and trek the trail). Learn how to fish, haggle, find work—anywhere."

—Food & Wine

LET'S GO PUBLICATIONS

TRAVEL GUIDES

Australia 8th edition
Austria & Switzerland 12th edition
Brazil 1st edition
Britain & Ireland 2005
California 10th edition
Central America 9th edition
Chile 2nd edition
China 5th edition
Costa Rica 2nd edition
Eastern Europe 2005
Ecuador 1st edition **NEW TITLE**
Egypt 2nd edition
Europe 2005
France 2005
Germany 12th edition
Greece 2005
Hawaii 3rd edition
India & Nepal 8th edition
Ireland 2005
Israel 4th edition
Italy 2005
Japan 1st edition
Mexico 20th edition
Middle East 4th edition
Peru 1st edition **NEW TITLE**
Puerto Rico 1st edition
South Africa 5th edition
Southeast Asia 9th edition
Spain & Portugal 2005
Thailand 2nd edition
Turkey 5th edition
USA 2005
Vietnam 1st edition **NEW TITLE**
Western Europe 2005

ROADTRIP GUIDE

Roadtripping USA **NEW TITLE**

ADVENTURE GUIDES

Alaska 1st edition
New Zealand **NEW TITLE**
Pacific Northwest **NEW TITLE**
Southwest USA 3rd edition

CITY GUIDES

Amsterdam 3rd edition
Barcelona 3rd edition
Boston 4th edition
London 2005
New York City 15th edition
Paris 13th edition
Rome 12th edition
San Francisco 4th edition
Washington, D.C. 13th edition

POCKET CITY GUIDES

Amsterdam
Berlin
Boston
Chicago
London
New York City
Paris
San Francisco
Venice
Washington, D.C.

P9-CAO-784

LET'S GO

ITALY
2005

ALEXIE HARPER EDITOR
NOGA RAVID ASSOCIATE EDITOR
ALEXANDRA TAN ASSOCIATE EDITOR

RESEARCHER-WRITERS
SHIRLEY CARDONA
LAUREN HOLMES
TOM MILLER
YARAN NOTI
ANDREW STILLMAN
RYAN THORESON

GENEVIEVE CADWALADER MAP EDITOR
JOEL AUGUST STEINHAUS MANAGING EDITOR

ST. MARTIN'S PRESS ⚘ NEW YORK

HELPING LET'S GO. If you want to share your discoveries, suggestions, or corrections, please drop us a line. We read every piece of correspondence, whether a postcard, a 10-page email, or a coconut. **Address mail to:**

Let's Go: Italy
67 Mount Auburn Street
Cambridge, MA 02138
USA

Visit Let's Go at **http://www.letsgo.com,** or send email to:

feedback@letsgo.com
Subject: "Let's Go: Italy"

In addition to the invaluable travel advice our readers share with us, many are kind enough to offer their services as researchers or editors. Unfortunately, our charter enables us to employ only currently enrolled Harvard students.

Maps by David Lindroth copyright © 2005 by St. Martin's Press.

Let's Go: Italy Copyright © 2005 by Let's Go, Inc. All rights reserved. Printed in the United States of America. No part of this book may be used or reproduced in any manner whatsoever without written permission except in the case of brief quotations embodied in critical articles or reviews. Let's Go is available for purchase in bulk by institutions and authorized resellers. For information, address St. Martin's Press, 175 Fifth Avenue, New York, NY 10010, USA. www.stmartins.com.

Distributed outside the USA and Canada by Macmillan, an imprint of Pan Macmillan Ltd.
20 New Wharf Road, London N1 9RR
Basingstoke and Oxford
Associated companies throughout the world
www.panmacmillan.com

ISBN: 0-312-33552-0
EAN: 978-0312-33552-6
First edition
10 9 8 7 6 5 4 3 2 1

Let's Go: Italy is written by Let's Go Publications, 67 Mount Auburn Street, Cambridge, MA 02138, USA.

Let's Go® and the LG logo are trademarks of Let's Go, Inc.
Printed in the USA.

ADVERTISING DISCLAIMER. All advertisements appearing in Let's Go publications are sold by an independent agency not affiliated with the editorial production of the guides. Advertisers are never given preferential treatment, and the guides are researched, written, and published independent of advertising. Advertisements do not imply endorsement of products or services by Let's Go, and Let's Go does not vouch for the accuracy of information provided in advertisements.

If you are interested in purchasing advertising space in a Let's Go publication, contact: Let's Go Advertising Sales, 67 Mount Auburn St., Cambridge, MA 02138, USA.

HOW TO USE THIS BOOK

COVERAGE. Welcome to *Let's Go: Italy 2005*. This book covers all of Italy's unique areas, each with its own climate, cuisine, customs, and traditions. The regions are grouped by proximity into 14 chapters and presented geographically, from north to south. Rome, Italy's capital and largest city, appears first. Black tabs on the side of each page and our extensive **Index** (p. 770) should help you navigate.

TRANSPORTATION INFO. Sections on intercity transportation (trains, buses, and ferries where possible) generally list all possible destinations, followed by trip duration, departure time and/or frequency, and price, in that order. A typical listing looks like this: Buses depart to: **Florence** (1hr., 13 per day 4:30am-7pm, €4.50).

THE BASICS. Use our **Discover Italy** section to find regional highlights and Suggested Itineraries (p. 5) to help plan your trip. The **Essentials** (p. 8) section contains all necessary practical and logistical information, followed by **Life and Times** (p. 50), which provides a general introduction to the art, culture, and history of Italy. Along your way, the **Appendix** (p. 758) should come quite handy, lending a list of Italian language, pronunciation, and terminology help as well as other quick reference materials. If you're thinking about making an extended sojourn and want other options, look in **Alternatives to Tourism** (p. 77).

SCHOLARLY ARTICLES. To further aid travelers in understanding their destinations, *Let's Go* solicits experts for in-depth treatments of regional issues. Our extended articles discuss the cultural institution of soccer (p. 76), the role of tourism in southern Italy (p. 88), ritual strolls past and present (p. 136), and how to live *la dolce vita* while teaching in Trieste (p. 355).

FEATURES. In addition to providing up-to-date coverage, *Let's Go: Italy 2005* also includes prose detours on items of unique interest to travelers. Painstakingly compiled by researchers in the field, features range from spotlights on regional cuisine, to interviews with locals, to the low-down on the region's festivals.

PRICE RANGES AND RANKINGS. Our researchers list establishments in order of value and quality from best to worst. Our absolute favorites are denoted by the *Let's Go* thumbpick (◼). Since the best value does not always mean the cheapest price, we have incorporated a system of price ranges in the guide. (p. xii).

LANGUAGE AND OTHER QUIRKS. The English translations for cities are listed when applicable, followed by their Italian name. For a guide to Italian pronunciations and a glossary of commonly used Italian words and phrases, consult the **Appendix** (p. 758).

PHONE CODES AND TELEPHONE NUMBERS. Phone numbers in text are preceded by the ☎ icon. Since Italian telephone numbers require the local code regardless of the region you're calling from, all local codes are incorporated into the telephone number in the text.

A NOTE TO OUR READERS. The information for this book was gathered by *Let's Go* researchers from May through August of 2004. Each listing is based on one researcher's opinion, formed during his or her visit at a particular time. Those traveling at other times may have different experiences since prices, dates, hours, and conditions are always subject to change. You are urged to check the facts presented in this book beforehand to avoid inconvenience and surprises.

When in ROME...

Hostels Alessandro
ROME

http://www.HostelsAlessandro.com
info@hostelsalessandro.com tel: (+39)06.446.1958

EUROPE'S FAMOUS HOSTELS

CONTENTS

RESEARCHER-WRITERS

Shirley Cardona *Rome and Lazio, Abruzzo, Molise, Umbria*

This college cheerleader and boxing enthusiast soldiered through southern Italy to end triumphantly in Rome, where her efficiency and Italian skills impressed even the Romans. The Sociology and Romance Languages student covered Italy's central regions and *la Città Eterna* with incomparable style. She marathoned through Rome, jogging her route instead of taking the Metro, and enchanted fellow travelers and locals everywhere.

Lauren Holmes *Tuscany, Liguria*

In all capacities, Lauren went above and beyond the call of duty. She sent back sparkling coverage of Italy's most happening regions while finding time to chill at Siena's Palio, party at Florence's Festa di San Gennaro, and hike her way through the Cinque Terre. This self-described soccer junkie inspired us with her constant cheeriness, impressed us with her brilliant prose, and vowed to marry a Medici in order to live in her esteemed Palazzo Pitti.

Tom Miller *Piemonte, Valle d'Aosta, Lombardy*

Superstar Tom couldn't get enough of researching, plowing through stints in Austria and New Zealand to head to Italy's mountainous North. He resisted the charms of tall, beautiful tour guides in Piemonte to forge preliminary Olympic coverage in Turin. He also saw more lakes than he thought one small country could possibly possess. This scholar of English and editor of *Let's Go: Germany 2004* is studying creative writing at Notre Dame.

Yaran Noti *Campania, Sardinia, Puglia*

We barely managed to drag Yaran home from his beloved Campania. This former museum curator fell in love with the easy joviality of Naples and breezed through the Amalfi Coast, despite a spill in the Tyrrhenian Sea. Yaran sampled horse in Sardinia, took part in a spur-of-the-moment boar hunt, and clambered about on top of Mt. Vesuvius, almost causing his editors to go gray before their time. His copy never failed to shock, delight, or amuse.

Andrew Stillman *Sicily, Calabria, Basilicata*

Andrew took his discerning fashion sense and Italian fluency to Italy's southern isles. This government student from Salt Lake City took every opportunity to exercise his hiking skills, scanning the view from the highest volcanoes in between bouts at the beach sunbathing in the buff. He rebounded from complete laptop failure in characteristic style, handwriting his coverage and pasting *Vanity Fair* cutouts to console his editors.

Ryan Thoreson *The Veneto, Trentino, Friuli, Emilia, Le Marche*

This golden boy from North Dakota used his French to woo the hearts of Italians from Aquileia to Ascona. Putting spider solitaire and uh-oh oreos on hold, Ryan took on Venice's labyrinthine canals, pedaled his way through bicycle near-disasters, and tamed possessed TVs that interrupted his respite with disturbing pop-star bios. In the end, wurst and gelato had their day in the sun, as Ryan made it all the way from Friuli back to Fargo.

CONTRIBUTING WRITERS

Kate McIntyre   Editor, *Let's Go: Austria & Switzerland*

Veronique Hyland   Associate Editor, *Let's Go: Austria & Switzerland*

Abby Garcia graduated from Harvard in 2003 with an honors degree in Psychology. She worked in Trieste, Italy at an international school for ten months before moving back home to Texas. Abby hopes to return to Europe and work there again in the future.

Alexander Bevilacqua was born in Milan, and has lived in Germany, Australia, and the United States. This former researcher-writer for *Let's Go: Germany 2005* works at Harvard's Center for European Studies, conducting research on literary multiculturalism.

Timothy O'Sullivan is an Assistant Professor in Classical Studies at Trinity University in San Antonio, Texas. He earned a Ph.D. in Classical Philology from Harvard in 2003, with a dissertation entitled "The Mind in Motion: The Cultural Significance of Walking in the Roman World."

Edoardo Gallo hails from Cuneo, Italy, and was a researcher-writer for *Let's Go: Central America 2005*. He graduated from Harvard in 2004 with honors in Physics and Mathematics. He is currently working as a consultant for Katzenbach Partners in New York City.

ACKNOWLEDGMENTS

TEAM ITALY THANKS: illustrious Joel; Genevieve for mapperfection; the RWs for being awesome; Ella, Vicki, and Yaran for extra help; E.G. and A.B. for Italian expertise.

ALEXIE THANKS: conscientious and sweet Noga and infinitely agreeable Alex; you are both the best; Joel for always working to help us be proud of our work; Genevieve for tireless efforts on Italy's behalf; the 24/7 party that is Pod Disco Ciao Belle; Erin for listening to me and hosting Apocalypse!; Pat and LT who rule; the Ellanator; 7 Roberts Rd. for 24; Jesse for spy talk; Ina for craziness; Erin V. and Amy W. for MTV Made; Edo for Italy; Allison for so much; Mama and Daddy for everything else.

NOGA THANKS: Alexie, for her ideas and editing and for teaching me about Italy—but mostly, I would have to say, for the Russian techno. And Alex, always cheerful, always helpful; Joel for his guidance and his hair. Genevieve, just plain good at what she does; Pat and Erin and LT for making this pod so fun to be in; Adam, Vicky, and Ella for their help. And back at home to Mummy and Daddy, for always understanding, and to Yinon and Jonathan, adorable and adored.

ALEXANDRA THANKS: Alexie, for incredibleness and phonechecking; Noga, for making our corner a home away from home; Joel, for insight/stiff-arms; Genevieve, for such patience; Vicky, for dealing with me; LT, Pat, Erin, and Ella, for the daily party; Disco Ciao Belle, for humbling me in candlepin bowling; Stu, John, and Chris, for being super; Anna, Linda, and Lydia, for being my girls; Seth, for making me laugh and listening to all my stories; and Mom, Dad, and Simes, for having the biggest hearts.

GENEVIEVE THANKS: Many thanks to Team Italy, the RWs for their impressive work, Mapland for a great summer, and my friends for perspective and good company.

Editor
Alexie Harper
Associate Editors
Noga Ravid, Alexandra Tan
Managing Editor
Joel August Steinhaus
Map Editor
Genevieve Cadwalader
Typesetter
Julia Stephens

Publishing Director
Emma Nothmann
Editor-in-Chief
Teresa Elsey
Production Manager
Adam R. Perlman
Cartography Manager
Elizabeth Halbert Peterson
Design Manager
Amelia Aos Showalter
Editorial Managers
Briana Cummings, Charlotte Douglas, Ella M. Steim, Joel August Steinhaus, Lauren Truesdell, Christina Zaroulis
Financial Manager
R. Kirkie Maswoswe
Marketing and Publicity Managers
Stef Levner, Leigh Pascavage
Personnel Manager
Jeremy Todd
Low-Season Manager
Clay H. Kaminsky
Production Associate
Victoria Esquivel-Korsiak
IT Director
Matthew DePetro
Web Manager
Rob Dubbin
Associate Web Manager
Patrick Swieskowski
Web Content Manager
Tor Krever
Research and Development Consultant
Jennifer O'Brien
Office Coordinators
Stephanie Brown, Elizabeth Peterson

Director of Advertising Sales
Elizabeth S. Sabin
Senior Advertising Associates
Jesse R. Loffler, Francisco A. Robles, Zoe M. Savitsky
Advertising Graphic Designer
Christa Lee-Chuvala

President
Ryan M. Geraghty
General Manager
Robert B. Rombauer
Assistant General Manager
Anne E. Chisholm

PRICE RANGES>>ITALY

Our researchers list establishments in order of value from best to worst; our favorites are denoted by the Let's Go thumbs-up (🖐). Since the best value is not always the cheapest price, however, we have also incorporated a system of price ranges, based on a rough expectation of what you will spend. For **accommodations,** we base our range on the cheapest price for which a single traveler can stay for one night. For **restaurants** and other dining establishments, we estimate the average amount a traveler will spend. The table below tells you what you will *typically* find in Italy at the corresponding price range; keep in mind that no system can allow for every individual establishment's quirks.

ACCOMMODATIONS	RANGE	WHAT YOU'RE *LIKELY* TO FIND
❶	under €15	Camping; most dorm rooms, such as HI or other hostels or university dorm rooms. Expect bunk beds and a communal bath; you may have to provide or rent towels and sheets.
❷	€15-25	Upper-end hostels or small hotels. You may have a private bathroom, or there may be a sink in your room and communal shower in the hall.
❸	€26-40	A small room with optional private bath. Should have decent amenities, such as phone and TV, and sometimes A/C. Breakfast may be included in the price of the room.
❹	€41-60	Similar to ❸, but may have more features, include breakfast or lunch, or be more centrally located.
❺	above €60	Large hotels, superior service. If it's a ❺ and it doesn't have the perks you want, you've paid too much.

FOOD	RANGE	WHAT YOU'RE *LIKELY* TO FIND
❶	under €5	Street stands, *gelaterie*, sandwiches at a bar, cafes, pizza places, or fast-food joints. Rarely ever a sit-down meal.
❷	€5-9	Most affordable trattorie or pizzerie. Should include a mid-priced entree and drink or dessert. You may have the option of sitting down or getting takeout.
❸	€10-15	Mid-priced entrees in nicer setting or serving regional specialties. The tip and cover charge will bump you up a couple euros, since you'll probably have a waiter or waitress.
❹	€16-25	A fancy restaurant with traditional or *nouveau* cuisine. Few restaurants in this range have a dress code, but some may look down on t-shirt, jeans, or shorts.
❺	above €25	Venerable reputation and a 90-page wine list. Elegant or chic attire may be expected. Don't order a burger.

XIII

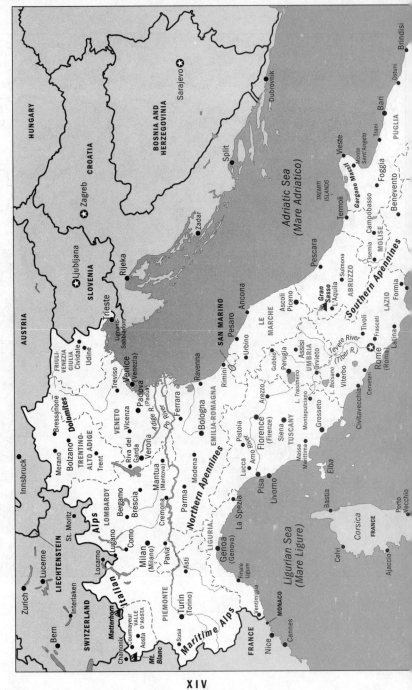

XIV

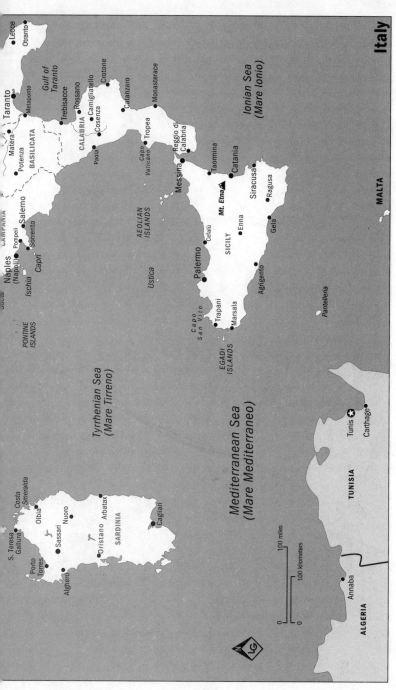

XV

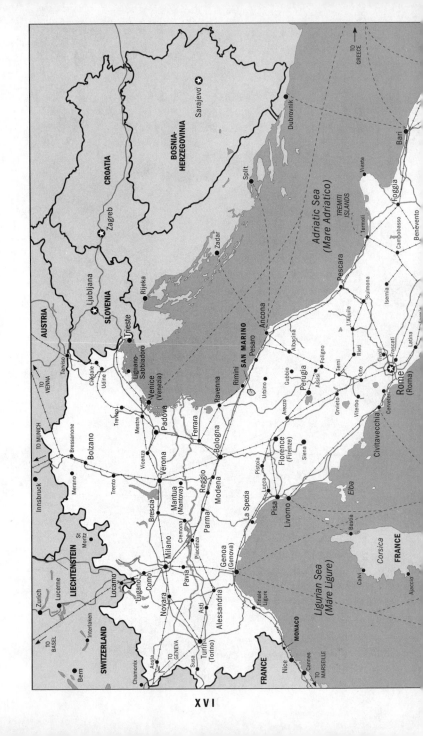

XVI

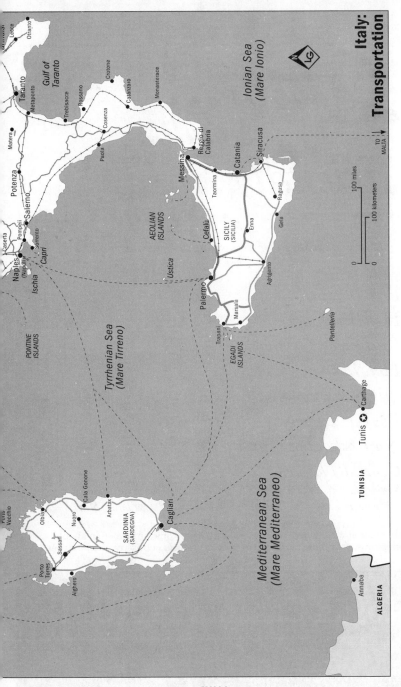

Italy:
Transportation

Quiet...
Small...
Friendly... Clean...
Homely...

If you are looking for a place to stay like home, this is it.

Free Internet
Free Breakfast
Kitchen & Common Area
Hot Shower
Air Conditioning & Fans
Book Exchange
No Lockout or Curfew
Centrally located
5 mins walk to the Vatican & short distance to the major sites
4 blocks from the metro station & well connected with buses 24hrs

In addition we can help you plan your days in Rome, information about museums, shopping, restaurants etc. & we can also book you the best tours.

Hostel Casanova - ROME
(+39) 06 39745228 **(please call first)**
Via Ottorino Lazzarini 12, Rome, Italy

www.hostelcasanova.com/hostelcasanova@yahoo.com

DISCOVER ITALY

From the dawn of modernity, Italy has been dominant on the world stage. Loved by poets from all centuries, its breathtaking vistas range from steep Alpine peaks to the rolling olive hills of the interior, and finally to the aqua waters of the southern shoreline. From antiquity Italy's fertile fields have been battlefields, places of conquest by all ranges of Indo-European conquerors. Its coasts have welcomed cultures from far-flung Northern Africa, from ancient Greece and Carthage, from cultures buried so deep in the folds of prehistory they have become legends in their remoteness. The constant motion at a world crossroads forged a strong and vibrant nation before its provinces were ever united, and today Italians retain distinct regional characteristics while promoting a fierce and all-encompassing national pride. The exports of Italy's centuries include Christianity, artistic and historical movements, and an attention to quality, drama, excess, and vibrancy that continues today to draw the devotion of countless admirers, tourists, and immigrants. The best way to discover Italy is to immerse yourself. Wander aimlessly down side streets, loiter against the sun-baked stone lip of a fountain, amble through the ruins of civilizations past, and know for yourself the glory of Italy's past and the promise of her future.

FACTS AND FIGURES

OFFICIAL NAME: Repubblica Italiana

RELIGION: Roman Catholic (98%)

ITALY 2004 POPULATION: 58 million

REGULAR CHURCHGOERS: 21 million

NUMBER OF CELLPHONES: 53 million

REGULAR SOCCER FANS: 30 million

NUMBER OF CHILDREN BORN PER WOMAN: 1.27 (2.1 recommended for stable population growth)

ETHNIC AND NATIONAL GROUPS: Italian; German, French, Slovene, Albanian, and Greek minorities.

WOMEN ARRESTED FOR MAFIA ACTIVITY 1990-2000: 100+

INDEPENDENT STATES WITHIN ITALIAN BORDERS: 3

WHEN TO GO

Tourism enters overdrive in June, July, and August. Hotels are booked solid, prices skyrocket, and rows of bright lounge chairs take over pristine beaches. During *Ferragosto*, a national holiday on August 15, Italians go on vacation, flocking to the coast, and Italy all but shuts down for a good part of the month. Though many find the larger cities enjoyable even during this holiday, late May through July are best for a trip. Traveling to Italy in early May or early September assures a calmer and cooler vacation. The temperature drops to a comfortable average of 25°C (77°F) with regional variations. The best weather for hiking in the Alps is from July to September; ski season lasts December through late March. In winter many beachfront hotels close, but it's possible to find a room for rent, and also more breathing space.

WHAT TO DO

ART SAVVY

Italy's art collections are amazing, but then the peninsula has had thousands of years to amass stunning quantities of works. As might be expected, the country's largest cities house the most important art collections. But virtually every small town has its own *museo archeologico* or *pinacoteca* (art gallery) showcasing collections from Greek pottery shards and Roman mosaics to the latest in contemporary art. A list follows with collections travelers shouldn't miss, but this list is by no means exhaustive. Often the most rewarding experience comes from seeking out that lone Caravaggio or da Messina in a regional museum where it can be viewed and studied without lines or crowds.

CITY	PRINCIPAL ART COLLECTIONS
Florence	Uffizi Gallery (p. 412)
	Museo dell'Opera del Duomo (p. 411)
Milan	Pinacoteca di Brera (p. 233)
	Galleria d'Arte Moderna (p. 234)
Naples	Museo e Galleria di Capodimonte (p. 554)
Rome	Sistine Chapel (p. 124)
	Vatican Museums (p. 124)
	Galleria Borghese (p. 125)
	Museo Nazionale d'Arte Antica (p. 126)
Rovereto	Museo d'Arte Moderna e Contemporanea—"il Mart" (p. 337)
Siena	Pinacoteca Nazionale (p. 431)
	Museo dell'Opera Metropolitana (p. 431)
Turin	Museo Egizio (p. 143)
	Galleria Sabauda (p. 143)
Venice	Collezione Peggy Guggenheim (p. 296)
	Gallerie dell'Accademia (p. 296)

CUCINA ITALIANA

World-renowned for its sumptuous victuals, Italy's gastronomic tradition is varied enough to please everyone. Begin in Piemonte (p. 137), famous for **white truffles** and Italy's premier red wines, including **Barolo, Barbaresco,** and **Barbera.** Turin (p. 137) is home to **Ferrero Rocher** and **Nutella,** exported for international consumption. Genoa flaunts colorful **pesto** (p. 180); imitations are marketed worldwide, but true pesto can only be found in Liguria. **Parmesan cheese, truffles,** and **risotto** all hail from Mantua (p. 248), and romantic Verona (p. 312) is the perfect destination for lovers of wine, including the white **Soave** and the red **Valpolicella.** Florence birthed **gelato** (p. 408) centuries ago and continues to churn out this staple of *la dolce vita* by the bucketful. In the heart of Emilia-Romagna, Bologna (p. 356) reigns as culinary capital of Italy, birthplace of **tortellini** and **bolognese** sauce, while Modena (p. 369) is famous for its **balsamic vinegar.** Parma (p. 372) boasts **Parmigiano Reggio cheese** and succulent **prosciutto,** in addition to some of the world's best **chocolate.** In the South, Naples (p. 539) heats things up with peerless **pizza** from wood-fired ovens and Sicily (p. 639) cools them down again with **granita,** a slushy southern version of gelato. Tropea (p. 636) vaunts **cipolle rosse** (red onions) and a range of onion products. Trapani (p. 704) spices up regional Sicilian cuisine with Arab-influenced **couscous,** complimented nicely with **capers** from Pantelleria (p. 712). Finally, a little **Marsala** (p. 702) works wonders to wash down any Italian feast.

To get the most bang for your buck, head for *enoteche* (wine bars), where food is often *gratis* and wine inexpensive. Wineries frequently give complimentary tasting tours. Other inexpensive ways to eat your way through Italy include ordering dinner pizzas, which comprise an entire meal for half the price of a first and second course (*primo* and *secondo*), or heading to the local supermarket for several meals, eating out only once a day. Breakfast is often the least expensive meal, taken at a *caffè* or bar, and composed of a *cornetto* (croissant) and cappuccino.

BEACH BUMMING

When you're tired of glutting yourself on Italy's cultural and culinary offerings, do what Italians do: head for the coast. There are beaches to be found in almost every region of the country; from ritzy Liguria to the rocky beaches of Sicily, you're bound to find what you're looking for.

Three-hundred and fifty kilometers of Mediterranean coast in Liguria form the Italian Riviera, divided into the **Riviera di Levante** (p. 184) in the east and **Riviera di Ponente** (p. 200) in the west. These are some of the most beautiful beaches in Italy; stretches of white sand and a year-round comfortable climate have made them among the most frequented and most expensive. Destinations run the gamut from luxurious resort towns like **San Remo** (p. 208) to the calmer charms of **Santa Margherita Ligure** (p. 187) and the area's least crowded beaches in the stunning but less conventional **Cinque Terre** (p. 191).

Further down Italy's western flank, the serene **Amalfi Coast** (p. 581) offers dark blue waters overhung with cliffs and lemon groves. Towns like **Positano** (p. 582) and **Praiano** (p. 585) have a variety of beaches and good nightlife. Native Italians rule the roost at **Reggio di Calabria, Tropea, Scilla,** and **Locri** in Calabria (p. 627) along the Ionian and Tyrrhenian coasts, where beautiful white sand and stone beaches and dunes remain relatively unknown to tourists. In Abruzzo and Molise, the **Tremiti Islands** (p. 537) are home to rocky coves and secluded beaches good for swimming and snorkeling. Also on the east coast, **Rimini** (p. 382) attracts a large student population to fine sand beaches on the Adriatic Sea. Additionally, some of Italy's best beaches are found off the mainland: Sardinia's **Costa Smeralda,** named for waters that range from emerald to dark blue, has beautiful coves to explore. (See **Suggested Itineraries: Andare al Mare in Sardinia.**) Though lesser known, Sicily's beaches are a worthwhile stop if you're in the area, varying from resort towns like **Cefalù** (p. 651) to the dark stone beaches of **Pantelleria** (p. 712).

TAKE A HIKE

Italy presents plenty of opportunities for the outdoor adventurer, whether you get your kicks staring into the fiery mouth of a volcano or strolling the cultured Tuscan countryside. For varying levels of hiking, breathtaking woodland views, and unique wildlife,

TOP TEN LIST

ITALIAN FESTIVALS

10. **Ferragosto Messinese:** Messina (p. 669). Celebrate Messina's founders with 50m papermaché statues carried by crowds of 150,000.

9. **Umbria Jazz Festival:** Perugia (p. 479). Ten days of world-renowned performers and music-lovers from all over.

8. **Festa di San Gennaro:** Naples (p. 539). Not once but three times a year the commemoration of Naples's patron saint draws processions and crowds.

7. **Eel Festival:** Ferrara (p. 364). Indulge your tastebuds, fantasy, and possibly your gag reflex at Comacchio's annual celebration of this wriggling delicacy.

6. **Almond Blossom Festival:** Agrigento (p. 698). Fill up on folk at this song and dance festival.

5. **Corsa dei Ceri:** Gubbio (p. 487). For over 900 years hordes of onlookers have gathered to watch this frantic relay race.

4. **Sacra del Cappero:** Salina (p. 666). Bond with welcoming locals at this glorified potluck featuring—what else—capers.

3. **Verona Opera Festival:** Boasts the likes of Placido Domingo and thousands of discerning opera-goers June-Sept (p. 312).

2. Siena's **Palio** packs the town's usually calm piazza with frenzied fans and racehorses for a 90 second race cushioned by days of revelry (p. 425).

1. **Carnevale:** Celebrated all over Italy, but nowhere quite like Venice, with two weeks of masked madness (p. 276).

head to **Abruzzo National Park** (p. 531). The park offers several good biking trails as well as winter skiing. Further south, **Sila Massif** (p. 635) in Calabria also offers hiking and 35km of beautiful cross-country skiing. The **Aeolian Islands** (p. 655) are home to active and inactive volcanoes. **Mt. Etna** (p. 683) offers prime volcanic terrain and far-reaching views. (See **Suggested Itineraries: Tour of Hell**.)

For charms of a more mercurial nature, head to the island of **Ustica** (p. 649), home to extensive diving options and 9km of coastline hiking. More water sports, including windsurfing, canoeing, whitewater rafting, and kayaking, await at **Riva del Garda** (p. 337) near the **Dolomites**. In the mountains themselves challenging multi-day hikes—even two weeks at a time—are possible, as well as many worthwhile daytrips and mountain biking for all levels of experience.

A walk through the **Chianti region** (p. 433) of Tuscany offers travelers a less strenuous outdoor experience, traversing country roads past vineyards, olive groves, ancient castles and villages, and panoramic views of the surrounding hills and valleys. Go to **Cinque Terre** (p. 191) for magnificent views and intermediate-level hiking along the winding paths connecting the five pastoral fishing towns. Just to the north, **Turin** (p. 137) offers medium to difficult rock-climbing, hang-gliding, and—quite literally—Olympic-level skiing, including multi-peak expeditions skiing from village to village. The **Alps** (including **Valle d'Aosta**, p. 165) also have formidable, if expensive, skiing options. In **Courmayeur** and nearby **Monte Bianco** (p. 173), both easy hikes and difficult mountaineering are available.

■ LET'S GO PICKS

BEST PLACE TO PLOT THE RUTHLESS ACQUISITION OF OTHER NATION-STATES: Gain inspiration in Machiavelli's hometown of **Florence** (p. 335).

BEST PLACE TO SAMPLE A NEW SPECIES: Sardinia (p. 659), where horse, boar, and dogfish are quotidian. Also try **Orta's** (p. 147) *tapulon* (minced donkey meat, cooked in red wine).

BEST FUNKY ACCOMMODATIONS: Matera's sassy 7000-year-old *sassi* (p. 529). The white-washed, conical *trulli* of **Alberobello** (p. 541) are mortarless abodes used as residences, churches, and restaurants. **Pantelleria's** domed *dammusi* (p. 623) are constructed from petrified lava.

BEST SATANIC RELIC: A boulder cast down by the devil to hold up the Ponte del Diavolo in **Cividale** (p. 317).

BEST DEAD FOLK: Rome's **Catacombs** (p. 109) boasted more than 500,000 Christians buried out of the reaches of persecuting pagans. Necrophiliacs can revel in the huge **Cappuchin Catacombs** (p. 562) in Palermo, where 8000 bodies rest in their moth-eaten Sunday best.

BEST PLACE TO LOSE TEN POUNDS: A climb up **Positano's** (p. 529) winding stairs is better than any day at the gym.

BEST PLACE TO RENEW CHASTITY: The **Roman Forum** (p. 97) where Vestal Virgins kept the flame burning; if they broke their vows, they were buried alive.

BEST CHURCHES FOR PURCHASING LIQUOR: In Rome, the benedictine at **San Paolo Fuori Mura** (p. 109) may be more tasty than the herby eucalyptine from the **Abbey of the Three Fountains** (p. 110).

BEST PLACE TO LEARN ITALIAN: Sardinia (p. 659), where you're (almost) more likely to encounter a talking blue flamingo than an English-speaking *Sardo*.

BEST PLACE TO CELEBRATE CONTRADICTION: The Museum of War and Bell of Peace, 15min. apart in **Rovereto** (p. 301).

BEST PLACE TO SHOW UP BACCHUS HIMSELF: In the vineyards of the **Chianti** region (p. 373).

BEST PLACE TO SAY A HAIL MARY TO ATONE FOR BACCHANALIAN EXCESS: The Vatican (p. 104) offers confession in numerous languages.

BEST PLACE TO BEHAVE LIKE A JUNIOR HIGH GIRL: Juliet's balcony in **Verona** (p. 279), where hundreds of teens leave love notes posted with chewing gum.

SUGGESTED ITINERARIES

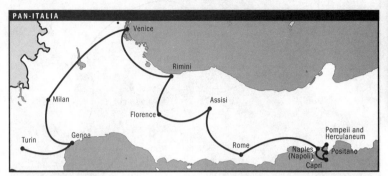

PAN-ITALIA (18 DAYS): Visit an unmolested **Turin** (1 day; p. 137) before the Winter Olympics take up residence in 2006, then make the trek to Christopher Columbus's own **Genoa** (2 days; p. 175). Skip the journey to the New World for the sprawling streets of **Milan** (2 days; p. 219), where the sweet sound of Maria Callas singing Verdi awaits you at the world-famous La Scala. Buy an opera CD to last the long train ride to **Venice** (2 days; p. 276), where misty mornings give way to glorious palaces. Swing into **Rimini** for a cocktail-flavored taste of the Adriatic coast (1 day; p. 382). Head for solid ground in **Florence** (2 days; 392), home to more superlative art than most small countries, as well as the famous burnt-Tuscan orange rooftops of picture-postcard fame. On your way to **Rome's** ruined aqueducts, cathedrals, and forums (3 days; p. 89), shun worldly wealth with ascetic pilgrims in **Assisi** (1 day; p. 490). A trip to **Naples** (1 day; p. 539), home of the world's best pizza, will afford you access to pleasant **Positano** (1 day; p. 582). Forgetting a ferry ride out to **Capri** (1 day; p. 569) would be a true crime. Tear yourself back to the mainland for the rubble and ash paradise of **Pompeii** (1 day; p. 561).

CHASING *CIBO* (1 WEEK): Begin seven days of gastronomic indulgence by feasting on the extensive pastas and salami of **Bologna** (2

days; p. 356). Looking for a new gelato topping? **Modena** (1 day; p. 369) specializes in Italy's tastiest and most expensive condiment—balsamic vinegar. Follow the trail of *prosciutto* to **Parma** (1 day; p. 372), and enliven your *primo piatto* with the mouth-watering Parmigiano Reggio cheese. Then pop over to **Mantua** (2 days; p. 248), which boasts more pigs than people, for their famous *risotto alla pilota.* Wash it all down with the red and white wines of **Verona** (1 day; p. 312).

LIFESTYLES OF THE RICH AND FAMOUS (1 WEEK):
In **Verona** (1 day; p. 312) satiate your longing for romance, tragedy, and public scandal with a visit to the residences of Shakespeare's ill-fated Romeo and

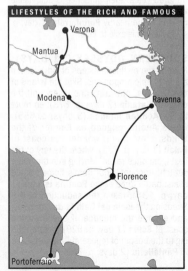

DISCOVER

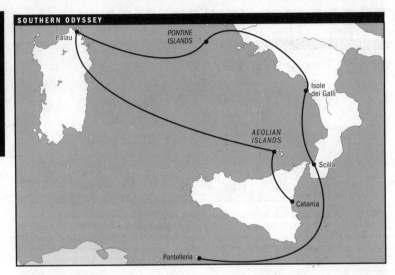

SOUTHERN ODYSSEY

Juliet. Then explore epic poet Virgil's birthplace in **Mantua** (1 day; p. 248) and in **Modena** (1 day; p. 369) serenade reclusive native Luciano Pavarotti outside his villa. If he doesn't return the favor, a trip to the flashy Ferrari and Maserati factories nearby might soothe a bruised ego. Those more piqued by doom than *vroom* may enjoy the tomb of Dante Alighieri, author of *The Inferno*, in **Ravenna** (1 day; p. 378). In **Florence** (2 days; p. 392), the fabulously wealthy and despotic Medicis ruled for several hundred years; their influence is still visible today. Another well-known despot, Napoleon, resided in the nearby **Portoferraio** (1 day; p. 471) during his exile to Elba.

SOUTHERN ODYSSEY (11 DAYS):

Retrace the mythic footsteps of Odysseus in a tour of epic proportions. Skirt the **Island of the Cyclops,** now a marine reserve off the coast of **Catania** (2 days; p. 678), en route to the **Aeolian Islands** (3 days; p. 655), where Aeolus reigned as Keeper of the Winds. From there, wander the coast of **Palau** (1 day; p. 735), where the fury of the Lestrigoni once raged. Moving into the home stretch, encounter our hero's fierce female rivals: battle Circe at the **Pontine Islands** (1 day; p. 134), resist the seduction of the Sirens on the **Isole dei Galli** (1 day; p. 584), and escape the menace of Scylla off the coast of **Scilla** (1 day; p. 629), before retiring to the bosom of repose at Calypso's cave in **Pantelleria** (2 days; p. 712).

TOUR OF HELL (8 DAYS): Seismic rumblings or diabolic thunder? Ancient rumor supposed that volcanic craters opened into the underworld; visit southern Italy to find out. Start with the scourge of Pompeii and Herculaneum, **Mt. Vesuvius** (1 day; p. 565). Europe's only active mainland volcano is waiting to blow its top. Though it hasn't erupted in hundreds of years, **Ischia's** thermal springs and *fumarole* indicate it's still active (1 day; p. 575). Head to Aeolian **Stromboli** (1 day; p. 662) to watch the Trail of Fire light up the night sky, then move on to **Vulcano** (2 days; p. 660), namesake of all volcanoes and once reputedly the entrance to Hell. It's now the home of radioactive mudpits and

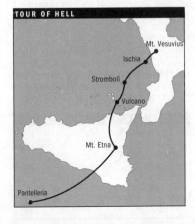

TOUR OF HELL

DISCOVER

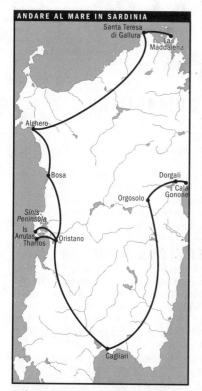

ANDARE AL MARE IN SARDINIA

sulfur-infused waters. Europe's largest active volcano, **Mt. Etna** (1 day; p. 683), lies simmering beneath the surface in eastern Sicily. Finally, head to **Pantelleria** (2 days; p. 712), where a fiery crater has been replaced by the glassy waters of the Mirror of Venus.

ANDARE AL MARE IN SARDINIA (11 DAYS):

Join the Italians in their summertime migration to the sea. Ease into your cultural immersion on the archipelago **La Maddalena** and its gorgeous, tiny islands (2 days; p. 737). Daytrip to the incomparable **Costa Smeralda** (1 day; p. 743). Explore the secluded coves and impressive ruins around **Santa Teresa di Gallura** (1 day; p. 739). Head southwest to Catalonian **Alghero** (2 days; p. 730) for its beautiful historic center and lively nightlife; then breathe tourist-free air in medieval, gem-like **Bosa** (1 day; p. 748). On the **Sinis Peninsula** near **Oristano** (1 day; p. 744), behold the ruins of ancient **Tharros** and lightly tread the quartz beach of **Is Arrutas**. Visit **Cagliari** for a

cultural-rich sightseeing feast, then skip out on civilization and into rugged **Orgosolo** (1 day; p. 729), where mountain vistas and avant-garde murals unite in delightful sensory overload. Conclude your trip in the tourist haven **Cala Gonone** (1 day; p. 756), stopping en route to admire traditional craftwork in mountain town **Dorgali** (1 day; p. 754).

ARCHAEOLOGICAL ITALY (18 DAYS):

Sicily's proximity to Greece led to the establishment of many Greek colonies in the region. In **Segesta** (1 day; p. 708) and **Agrigento** (1 day; p. 698), remnants of these settlements include several almost entirely intact Doric temples, rivaling Greece's own ruinous remains. **Syracuse's** Greek past is manifest in an enormous theater and a museum with over 18,000 artifacts from 40,000 BC-AD 600 (2 days; p. 688). Nearby **Piazza Armerina** (1 day; p. 687) contains the 4th-century Villa Romana del Casale, with over 40 rooms of mosaics. On the mainland, the column marking the end of the Appian Way, an ancient road that reached all the way to Rome, stands in **Brindisi** (1 day; p. 607). Across from Brindisi, **Naples** (3 days; p. 539) boasts a world-renowned archaeological museum and miles of subterranean Roman aqueducts open for exploration. Nearby **Paestum** (1 day; p. 596) contains well-preserved Greek temples, and **Pompeii** (1 day; p. 561) houses hundreds of artifacts and ruins literally set in stone by the 1st-century eruption of Mt. Vesuvius. **Rome** (4 days; p. 89) is famous for the Colosseum, catacombs, and numerous forums. Northern Italy's **Aquilea** (1 day; p. 349), **Aosta** (1 day; p. 167), **and Acqui Terme** (1 day; p. 159) all display late Roman ruins including mosaics, monuments, tombs, and aqueducts.

ARCHAEOLOGICAL ITALY

ESSENTIALS

PLANNING YOUR TRIP

DOCUMENTS AND FORMALITIES

ENTRANCE REQUIREMENTS.
Passport (p. 9). Required of citizens of Australia, Canada, Ireland, New Zealand, the UK, and the US.
Visa (p. 10). Required for citizens of Australia, Canada, Ireland, New Zealand, the UK, and the US only for stays longer than 3 months.
Work Permit (p. 10). Required of foreigners planning to work in Italy.
Permit of Stay (p. 10). Required of foreigners planning to study in Italy.
Driving Permit (p. 33). Required of those planning to drive in Italy.

ITALIAN CONSULAR SERVICES ABROAD

Australia: Embassy: 12 Grey St., Deakin, **Canberra** ACT 2600 (☎02 627 333 33; www.ambitalia.org.au). Open M-F 9am-noon. **Consulates:** 509 St. Kilda Rd., **Melbourne** VIC 3004 (☎039 867 57 54; itconmel@netlink.com.au); Level 45 The Gateway, 1 Macquarie Pl., **Sydney** NSW 2000 (☎612 939 279 00; itconsyd@itconsyd.org).

Canada: Embassy: 275 Slater St., 21st fl., **Ottawa**, ON K1P 5H9 (☎613 232 24 01; www.italyincanada.com). **Consulate:** 3489 Drummond St., **Montréal,** PQ H3G 1X6 (☎514 849 83 51; www.italconsul.montreal.qc.ca).

Ireland: Embassy: 63/65 Northumberland Rd., **Dublin** (☎31 660 17 44; www.italianembassy.ie). Consular services available M-W and F 10am-12:30pm, Th 2:30-4pm.

New Zealand: Embassy: 34-38 Grant Rd., **Wellington** (☎006 447 353 39; www.italy-embassy.org.nz).

UK: Embassy: 14 Three Kings Yard, **London** W1K 4EH (☎020 731 222 00, fax 749 922 83; www.embitaly.org.uk). **Consulates:** 32 Melville Street, **Edinburgh** EH3 7HA (☎131 226 36 31; consedimb@consedimb.demon.co.uk); 38 Eaton Pl., **London** SW1X 8AN (☎020 723 593 71); Rodwell Tower, 111 Piccadilly, **Manchester** M1 2HY (☎161 236 90 24; italconsulman@btinternet.com).

US: Embassy: 3000 Whitehaven St., **Washington, D.C.** 20008 (☎202 612 44 00; www.italyemb.org). **Consulates:** 100 Boylston St., #900, **Boston**, MA 02116 (☎617 542 04 83; www.italianconsulateboston.org); 500 N. Michigan Ave., #1850, **Chicago,** IL 60611 (☎312 467 15 50; www.itconschicago.org); 12400 Wilshire Blvd., #300, **Los Angeles,** CA 90025 (☎310 820 06 22; www.conlang.com); 690 Park Ave. (visa office 54 E. 69th St.), **New York**, NY 10021 (☎212 737 91 00; www.italconsul-nyc.org).

CONSULAR SERVICES IN ROME

Australia: Embassy: V. Alessandria, 215, 00198 (☎06 85 27 21, emergency 800 87 77 90). Open M-Th 9am-5pm, F 8:30am-noon. **Consulate:** C. Trieste, 25/C (☎06 85 27 21). Open M-F 8:30-noon and 1:30-4:15pm.

Canada: Embassy: V. Giovanni Battista De Rossi, 27, 00161 (☎06 44 59 81). **Consulate:** V. Zara, 30 (☎06 44 59 81, fax 06 445 989 12).

IMPORTANT PHONE NUMBERS.
Emergency Police Help: ☎ 113.
Carabinieri Military Police: ☎ 112.
Ambulance: ☎ 118.
Fire Brigade: ☎ 115.
ACI (Automobile Club of Italy) for emergency breakdowns: ☎ 116.
Directory Assistance: ☎ 12.
News Reports: ☎ 144 22 19 00.

Ireland: Embassy: P. Campitelli, 3 (☎ 06 697 91 21). Passport services open M-F 10am-12:30pm and 3-4:30pm.

New Zealand: Embassy: V. Zara, 28 (☎ 06 441 71 71, fax 440 29 84). Consular and passport services open M-F 9:30am-noon. Embassy services M-F 8:30am-12:45pm and 1:45-5pm.

UK: Embassy and Consulate: V. XX Settembre, 80/A (☎ 06 482 54 41), near the corner of V. Palestro. Consular services open M-F 9:15am-1:30pm.

US: Embassy: V. Veneto, 119/A (☎ 06 467 41; www.usembassy.it). Consular services open M-F 8:30am-12:30pm. Closed US and Italian holidays.

TOURIST OFFICES

Italian Government Tourist Board (ENIT): 630 5th Ave., #1565, **New York,** NY 10111, USA (☎ 212 245 56 18; www.italiantourism.com). Write or call ☎ 212 245 48 22 for a free copy of *Italia: General Information for Travelers to Italy,* containing train and ferry schedules. **Branch offices:** 1 Princes St., **London,** W1R 2AY UK (☎ 020 739 935 62; www.italiantouristboard.co.uk); Level 26, 44 Market St., **Sydney** NSW 2000, Australia (☎ 02 926 216 66; enitour@ihug.com.au); 175 E. Bloor St., #907 South Tower, **Toronto,** ON M4W 3R8, Canada (☎ 416 925 48 82; enit.canada@on.aibn.com).

Italian Cultural Institute: 686 Park Ave., **New York,** NY 10021, USA (☎ 212 879 42 42; www.italcultny.org). Often more prompt than ENIT. Provides useful links to Italian sites.

PASSPORTS

Citizens of Australia, Canada, Ireland, New Zealand, the UK, and the US need valid passports to enter Italy and to re-enter their home countries. Italy does not allow entrance if the holder's passport expires in under six months except for nationals of Austria, Belgium, France, Germany, Liechtenstein, Luxembourg, Malta, Monaco, Netherlands, Portugal, San Marino, Spain, and Switzerland with a valid national ID card; returning home with an expired passport is illegal, and may result in a fine. Citizens living abroad who need a passport or renewal should contact the nearest passport office of their home country.

Photocopy the page of your passport with your photo, as well as your visas, traveler's check serial numbers, and any other important documents. Carry one set of copies in a safe place, apart from the originals, and leave another set at home. Consulates also recommend that you carry an expired passport or an official copy of your birth certificate in a part of your baggage separate from other documents.

If you lose your passport, immediately notify the local police and the nearest embassy or consulate of your home government. To expedite its replacement, you will need to know all information previously recorded and show ID and proof of citizenship. In some cases, a replacement may take weeks to process, and it may be valid only for a limited time. Any visas stamped in your old passport will be irretrievably lost. In an emergency, ask for immediate temporary traveling papers that will permit you to re-enter your home country.

ESSENTIALS

ESSENTIALS

 ONE EUROPE. On May 1, 2004, ten Southern, Central, and Eastern European countries—Cyprus, the Czech Republic, Estonia, Hungary, Latvia, Lithuania, Malta, Poland, the Slovak Republic, and Slovenia—were admitted to the EU, joining 15 other member states: Austria, Belgium, Denmark, Finland, France, Germany, Greece, Ireland, Italy, Luxembourg, the Netherlands, Portugal, Spain, Sweden, and the UK. The EU's policy of **freedom of movement** means that border controls between the first 15 member states (minus Ireland and the UK, but plus Norway and Iceland) have been abolished, and visa policies harmonized. While you're still required to carry a passport (or government-issued ID card for EU citizens) when crossing an internal border, once you've been admitted into one country, you're free to travel to other participating states. Britain and Ireland have also formed a **common travel area,** abolishing passport controls between the UK and the Republic of Ireland. For more consequences of the EU for travelers, see **The Euro** (p. 12) and **Customs in the EU** (p. 11).

VISAS, INVITATIONS, AND WORK PERMITS

EU citizens need only a valid passport to enter Italy and may stay as long as they like. Citizens of Australia, Canada, New Zealand, and the US do not need visas for stays of up to three months, but must purchase a visa if they intend to stay longer. **Visas** can be purchased at home country consulates. US citizens can take advantage of the **Center for International Business and Travel** (☎800 929 24 28), which secures travel visas for a small charge. Under the Schengen Agreement any visa granted by Italy will be respected by Austria, Belgium, France, Germany, Greece, Luxembourg, The Netherlands, Portugal, and Spain. The duration of one stay or a succession of stays may not exceed 90 days per six months. The cost of a Schengen visa varies with duration and number of entries.

All foreign nationals planning to stay in Italy over 90 days should apply within eight working days of arrival to receive a **permesso di soggiorno** (permit of stay). Generally, non-members of the EU are required to apply for a permit at a police station or foreign office (*questura*) if staying longer than 20 days or taking up residence in another location than a hotel, official campsite, or boarding house. If staying in a hotel or hostel, the hotel staff will fulfill registration requirements for you, and the fee is waived. Steep fines punish a failure to comply. Those wishing to stay in Italy for more than three months for the sole purpose of tourism must apply for an extension of their stay at a local *questura* at least one month before the original permit expires. Double-check entrance requirements at the nearest embassy or consulate of Italy for up-to-date info before departure. US citizens can also consult www.pueblo.gsa.gov/cic_text/travel/foreign/foreignentryreqs.html.

Admission as a visitor does not include the right to work, which is authorized only by a **work permit.** Entering Italy to study requires both a residence permit and a worker registration card. The process for the permit should be started by the employer, and not the employee or outside job agencies. For more information, see **Alternatives to Tourism,** p. 77.

IDENTIFICATION

Always carry at least two forms of identification on your person, including a photo ID; a passport and a driver's license or birth certificate is usually adequate. Never carry all of your IDs together; split them up in case of theft or loss, and keep photocopies of all of them in your luggage and at home.

STUDENT, TEACHER, AND YOUTH IDENTIFICATION

The **International Student Identity Card (ISIC)**, the most widely accepted form of student ID, provides discounts on some sights, accommodations, food, and transport; access to a 24hr. emergency helpline; and insurance benefits for US cardholders (see **Insurance**, p. 20). Applicants must be full-time secondary or post-secondary school students at least 12 years of age. Because of the proliferation of fake ISICs, some services (particularly airlines) require additional proof of student identity. The **International Teacher Identity Card (ITIC)** offers teachers the same insurance coverage as the ISIC and similar but limited discounts. For travelers who are 25 years old or under but are not students, the **International Youth Travel Card (IYTC)** also offers many of the same benefits as the ISIC. Each of these identity cards costs US$22 or equivalent. ISIC and ITIC cards are valid through the academic year in which they are issued; IYTC cards are valid for one year from the date of issue. Many student travel agencies (p. 24) issue the cards; for a list of issuing agencies or more information, see the **International Student Travel Confederation (ISTC)** website (www.istc.org). The **International Student Exchange Card (ISE)** is a similar identification card available to students, faculty, and youth ages 12 to 26. The card provides discounts, medical benefits, access to a 24hr. emergency helpline, and the ability to purchase student airfares. The card costs US$25; call US ☎ 800 255 80 00 for more info, or visit www.isecard.com.

CUSTOMS

Upon entering Italy, you must declare certain items from abroad and pay a duty on the value of those articles if they exceed the allowance established by Italy's customs service. Note that goods and gifts purchased at **duty-free** shops abroad are not exempt from duty or sales tax; "duty-free" merely means that you need not pay a tax in the country of purchase. Duty-free allowances were abolished for travel between EU member states on July 1, 1999, but still exist for those arriving from outside the EU. Upon returning home, you must likewise declare all articles acquired abroad and pay a duty on the value of articles in excess of your home country's allowance. In order to expedite your return, make a list of any valuables brought from home and register them with customs before traveling abroad, and be sure to keep receipts for all goods acquired abroad.

CUSTOMS IN THE EU. As well as freedom of movement within the EU (p. 10), travelers in the 15 original EU member countries (Austria, Belgium, Denmark, Finland, France, Germany, Greece, Ireland, Italy, Luxembourg, the Netherlands, Portugal, Spain, Sweden, and the UK) can also take advantage of the freedom of movement of goods. This means that there are no customs controls at internal EU borders (i.e., you can take the blue customs channel at the airport), and travelers are free to transport whatever legal substances they like as long as it is for their own personal (non-commercial) use—up to 800 cigarettes, 10L of spirits, 90L of wine (60L of sparkling wine), and 110L of beer. You should also be aware that duty-free allowances were abolished on July 1, 1999 for travel between EU member states; however, travelers between the EU and the rest of the world still get a duty-free allowance when passing through customs.

The **Value-Added Tax** (**VAT,** *imposto sul valore aggiunta,* or **IVA**) is a sales tax levied in the EU. Foreigners making any purchase over €335 are entitled to an additional 20% VAT tax refund. Some stores take off 20% on-site; the alternative is to fill out forms at the Customs Office upon leaving the EU and send receipts from home, upon which the refund will be mailed to you. Not all storefront "Tax-Free" stickers imply an immediate, on-site refund, so ask before making a purchase.

MONEY

CURRENCY AND EXCHANGE

The currency chart below is based on August 2004 exchange rates between European Union euros (EUR€) and Australian dollars (AUS$), Canadian dollars (CDN$), New Zealand dollars (NZ$), British pounds (UK£), and US dollars (US$). Check the currency converter on websites like www.xe.com or www.bloomberg.com or a large newspaper for the latest exchange rates.

EURO (€)		
AUS$1 = €0.59		€1 = AUS$1.70
CDN$1 = €0.63		€1 = CDN$1.60
NZ$1 = €0.55		€1 = NZ$1.83
UK£1 = €1.48		€1 = UK£0.68
US$1 = €.81		€1 = US$1.23

It's generally cheaper to convert money in Italy than at home. While currency exchange will probably be available in your arrival airport, it's wise to bring enough foreign currency to last for the first 24 to 72 hours of your trip. When changing money abroad, try to go only to banks or *cambio* offices that have at most a 5% margin between their buy and sell prices. Post offices generally offer good rates. Since you lose money with every transaction, **convert large sums** (unless the currency is depreciating rapidly), **but no more than you'll need.** If you use traveler's checks or bills, carry some in small denominations (the equivalent of US$50 or less) for times when you are forced to exchange money at disadvantageous rates, but bring a range of denominations since charges may be levied per check cashed. Store your money in a variety of forms, including traveler's checks and an ATM and/or credit card. All travelers should also consider carrying some US dollars (about US$50 worth), which are often preferred by local tellers.

THE EURO. The official currency of 12 members of the European Union—Austria, Belgium, Finland, France, Germany, Greece, Ireland, Italy, Luxembourg, the Netherlands, Portugal, and Spain—is now the euro. The currency has some important—and positive—consequences for travelers hitting more than one euro-zone country. For one thing, money-changers across the euro-zone are obliged to exchange money at the official, fixed rate (see below), and at no commission (though they may still charge a small service fee). Second, euro-denominated travelers checks allow you to pay for goods and services across the euro-zone, again at the official rate and commission-free.

TRAVELER'S CHECKS

Traveler's checks are one of the safest and least troublesome means of carrying funds. Many banks and agencies sell them for a small commission. Check issuers provide refunds if the checks are lost or stolen, and many provide additional services, such as toll-free refund hotlines abroad, emergency message services, and stolen credit card assistance. Ask about toll-free refund hotlines and the location of refund centers when purchasing checks, and always carry emergency cash. In Italy, traveler's checks are most useful in big cities and when exchanged at banks, as many stores do not accept them; note that even some banks will not.

American Express: Checks available with commission at select banks, at all AmEx offices, and online (www.americanexpress.com; US residents only). American Express cardholders can also purchase checks by phone (☎800 721 97 68).

Travelex/Thomas Cook: In the UK call ☎0800 62 21 01, in the US and Canada call 800-287-7362, elsewhere call the UK collect at 1733 31 89 50. Issues Visa traveler's checks. Members of AAA and affiliated automobile associations receive a 25% commission discount on check purchases.

CREDIT, ATM, AND DEBIT CARDS

Where they are accepted, credit cards offer exchange rates up to 5% better than the retail rate used by banks and currency exchange establishments. Credit cards may also offer services like insurance or emergency help, and are sometimes required to reserve hotel rooms or rental cars. In Italy, credit cards are accepted almost everywhere: **Mastercard** and **Visa** are the most welcome; **American Express** is less common, though AmEx cards work at some major airports and AmEx offices.

ATM machines, or *bancomats*, are widespread on the Italian mainland and far less prevalent on islands. Depending on the system that your home bank uses, you can most likely access your personal bank account from abroad. ATMs get the same wholesale exchange rate as credit cards, but there is often a limit on the amount of money you can withdraw per day (usually around US$500). There is also typically a surcharge of US$1-5 per withdrawal.

Debit cards are a relatively new form of purchasing power that are as convenient as credit cards but have a more immediate impact on your funds. A debit card can be used wherever its associated credit card company (usually Mastercard or Visa) is accepted. The money is withdrawn directly from the holder's checking account. Debit cards often function as ATM cards and can be used to withdraw cash from banks and ATMs throughout Italy. Ask your local bank about obtaining one.

The two major international money networks are **Cirrus** (US ☎800 424 77 87; www.mastercard.com) and **Visa/PLUS** (US ☎800 843 75 87; www.visa.com). Citibank and SSB frequently have Cirrus machines, and Visa/PLUS machines are likely to be found at many Banca di Roma, Banca Nazionale del Lavoro, Banca Nazionale dell'Agricoltura, and Banco Ambrosiano Veneto. Most ATMs charge a transaction fee that is paid to the bank that owns the ATM.

 ATMS AND PINS. To use a cash or credit card to withdraw money from an ATM in Europe, you must have a four-digit **Personal Identification Number (PIN).** If your PIN is longer than four digits, ask your bank whether you can just use the first four, or whether you'll need a new one. **Credit cards** don't usually come with PINs, so if you intend to hit up ATMs in Europe with a credit card to get cash advances, call your credit card company before leaving to request one. Travelers with alphabetic, rather than numerical, PINs may also be thrown off by the lack of letters on European cash machines. The following are the corresponding numbers to use: 1=QZ; 2=ABC; 3=DEF; 4=GHI; 5=JKL; 6=MNO; 7=PRS; 8=TUV; and 9=WXY. Note that if you mistakenly punch the wrong code into the machine three times, it will swallow your card for good.

GETTING MONEY FROM HOME

If you run out of money while traveling, the easiest and cheapest solution is to have someone back home make a deposit to the bank account linked to your credit card or ATM card. Failing that, consider one of the following options. The online **International Money Transfer Consumer Guide** (http://international-money-transfer-consumer-guide.info) may also be of help.

A budget hotel
in the heart of Rome...

HOTEL

PAPA

GERMANO

Newly renovated
rooms

Easy walking distance
from most attractions

No curfew, no lockout

Internet Connections

Via Calatafimi 14/a 00185 Rome, Italy
Tel: +39 06486919 Fax: +39 0647825202
e-mail: info@hotelpapagermano.com
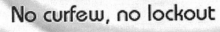
www.hotelpapagermano.com

WIRING MONEY. It is possible to arrange a **bank money transfer,** which means asking a bank back home to wire money to a bank in Italy. This is the cheapest way to transfer cash, but it's also the slowest, usually taking several days or more. Note that some banks may only release funds in local currency, potentially sticking you with a poor exchange rate; inquire about this in advance. Money transfer services like **Western Union** are faster and more convenient than bank transfers—but also much pricier. Western Union has many locations worldwide. To find one, visit www.westernunion.com, or in Australia call ☎ 800 50 15 00, in Canada 800 235 00 00, in the UK 0800 83 38 33, in the US 800 325 60 00, or in Italy (Angelo Costa International Ltd., 800 22 00 55). To wire money to Italy using a credit card from the US (MasterCard, Visa), call ☎ 800 225 52 27. Money transfer services are available at **American Express** offices (check www.americanexpress.com for locations).

US STATE DEPARTMENT (US CITIZENS ONLY). In serious emergencies only, the US State Department will forward money within hours to the nearest consular office, which will disburse it for a US$30 fee. If you wish to use this service, you must contact the Overseas Citizens Service division of the US State Department. (☎ 317 472 23 28; nights, Sundays, and holidays 202 647 40 00.)

COSTS

The cost of your trip will vary considerably, depending on where you go, how you travel, and where you stay. The most significant expenses will probably be your round-trip (return) **airfare** to Italy (see **Getting to Italy: By Plane,** p. 23) and a **railpass** or **bus pass.** Before you go, spend some time calculating a reasonable daily **budget.**

STAYING ON A BUDGET. To give you a general idea, a bare-bones day in Italy (camping or sleeping in hostels/*affittacamere*, buying food at supermarkets) costs around US$55-61 (€45-50). A slightly more comfortable day (sleeping in hostels/guesthouses and the occasional budget hotel, eating one meal a day at a restaurant, seeing several sights and going out at night) would run US$91 (€75). Overestimate your expenses and don't forget to factor in emergency reserve funds.

TIPS FOR SAVING MONEY. Simple ways to save include finding free entertainment, splitting lodging and food costs with trustworthy fellow travelers, and buying food in supermarkets rather than eating out. Bring a sleepsack (p. 16) to save on sheet charges in hostels, and do **laundry** in the sink (unless explicitly prohibited from doing so). That said, don't go overboard. Staying within your budget is important, but don't do so at the expense of your health or a great travel experience.

TIPPING AND BARGAINING

At many Italian restaurants, a service charge (*servizio*) or cover (*coperto*) is included in the bill. It is customary to leave an additional €1-2. Taxis drivers expect about a 10% tip. Bargaining is common in Italy, but use discretion. It is appropriate at markets, with street vendors, and over unmetered taxi fares (but always settle the price *before* taking the cab). Haggling over prices elsewhere is usually inappropriate. Hotel negotiation is more successful in smaller, uncrowded *pensioni. Let's Go* usually notes the hotels that are open to bargaining. To get lower prices, show little interest. But don't offer what you can't pay, as you're expected to buy once the merchant accepts your price.

PACKING

When it comes to packing, the less you have, the less you have to lose. **Pack lightly.** Lay out only what you absolutely need, then take half the clothes and twice the money. The Travelite FAQ (www.travelite.org) is a good resource for tips on traveling light. The online **Universal Packing List** (http://upl.codeq.info) will generate a customized list of suggested items based on your trip length, the expected climate, your planned activities, and other factors. If you plan to do a lot of hiking, also consult **Camping and the Outdoors, p. 47.**

Luggage: If you plan to cover most of your itinerary by foot, a sturdy **frame backpack** is unbeatable. (For the basics on buying a pack, see p. 43.) Toting a **suitcase** or **trunk** is fine if you plan to live in one or two cities and explore from there, but not a great idea if you plan to move around frequently. In addition to your main piece of luggage, a **daypack** (a small backpack or courier bag) is useful.

Clothing: No matter when you're traveling, it's a good idea to bring a warm jacket or wool sweater, a rain jacket (Gore-Tex® is both waterproof and breathable), sturdy shoes or hiking boots, and thick socks. Even in the summer in Italy the weather at high altitudes can be chilly, so when hiking the Alps or even Mt. Etna in the south, dress accordingly. Flip-flops or waterproof sandals are must-haves for grubby hostel showers. You may also want one outfit for going out, and maybe a nicer pair of shoes. If you plan to visit religious or cultural sites, make sure to bring a conservative top that covers your shoulders and a skirt that falls below the knees. Remember that women traveling alone, in Southern Italy especially, should dress modestly to avoid unwanted attention.

Sleepsack: Some hostels require that you either provide your own linen or rent sheets from them. Save cash by making your own sleepsack: fold a full-size sheet in half the long way, then sew it closed along the long side and one of the short sides.

Converters and Adapters: In Italy, electricity is 220V AC, enough to fry any 120V North American appliance. Americans and Canadians should buy an adapter (which changes the shape of the plug; US$5) and a converter (which changes the voltage; US$20-30). Don't make the mistake of using only an adapter (unless appliance instructions explicitly state otherwise). Travelers from NZ, Australia, and the UK (who use 230V at home) won't need a converter, but will need a set of adapters to use anything electrical. For more on all things adaptable, check out http://kropla.com/electric.htm.

First-Aid Kit: For a basic first-aid kit, pack bandages, a pain reliever, antibiotic cream, a thermometer, a Swiss Army knife, tweezers, moleskin, decongestant, motion-sickness remedy, diarrhea or upset-stomach medication (Pepto Bismol or Imodium), an antihistamine, sunscreen, insect repellent, burn ointment, and a syringe for emergencies (get an explanatory letter from your doctor).

Film: Film processing in Italy can be of poor quality, so consider bringing enough film for the trip and develop it at home. Less serious photographers may want to bring a disposable camera or two. Despite disclaimers, airport security X-rays can fog film, so buy a lead-lined pouch at a camera store or ask security to hand-inspect it. Always pack film in your carry-on luggage, since high-intensity X-rays are used on checked luggage.

Other Useful Items: For safety purposes, you should bring a **money belt** and small **padlock**. Basic **outdoors equipment** (plastic water bottle, compass, waterproof matches, pocketknife, sunglasses, sunscreen, hat) may also prove useful. **Quick repairs** of torn garments can be done on the road with a needle and thread; also consider bringing electrical tape for patching tears. To do laundry by hand (cheaper than using a laundromat), bring detergent, a small rubber ball to stop up the sink, and string for a makeshift clothes line. **Other things** you're liable to forget are sealable plastic bags (for damp clothes, soap, food, shampoo, and other spillables), an alarm clock, safety pins, rubber bands, a flashlight, and earplugs.

Important Documents: Don't forget your passport, traveler's checks, ATM and/or credit cards, adequate ID, and photocopies of all of the aforementioned.

SAFETY AND HEALTH

In any type of crisis situation, the most important thing to do is **stay calm.** Your country's embassy abroad (p. 8) is usually your best resource when things go wrong; registering with that embassy upon arrival in the country is often a good idea. The government offices listed in the **Travel Advisories** box below can provide information on the services they offer their citizens in case of emergencies abroad.

TRAVEL ADVISORIES. The following government offices provide travel information and advisories by telephone, fax, or via the Internet:

Australian Department of Foreign Affairs and Trade: ☎1300 55 51 35; www.dfat.gov.au.

Canadian Department of Foreign Affairs and International Trade (DFAIT): In Canada and the US call ☎800 267 83 76, outside US 613 944 40 00; www.dfait-maeci.gc.ca. Call for their free booklet, *Bon Voyage...But.*

New Zealand Ministry of Foreign Affairs: ☎04 439 80 00; www.mft.govt.nz/travel/index.html.

United Kingdom Foreign and Commonwealth Office: ☎020 700 802 32; www.fco.gov.uk.

US Department of State: ☎202 647 52 25; http://travel.state.gov. For *A Safe Trip Abroad,* call ☎202 512 18 00.

LOCAL LAWS AND POLICE

In Italy you will mainly encounter two types of police: the *polizia* (☎113) and the *carabinieri* (☎112). The *polizia* is a civil force under the command of the Ministry of the Interior, whereas the *carabinieri* falls under the auspices of the Ministry of Defense and is considered to be a military force; both, however, generally serve the same purpose—to maintain security and order in the country. In the case of attack or robbery either of these forces will respond to inquiries for help.

Needless to say **illegal drugs** are best avoided altogether. In Italy drugs including marijuana, cocaine, and heroine are illegal. Concern about growing cocaine and heroin addiction and trafficking have led Italian authorities to respond harshly to drug-related offenses. If you carry **prescription drugs,** bring copies of the prescriptions themselves and a note from a doctor and have the drugs and prescriptions accessible at international borders. There is no drinking age in Italy, but drinking and driving is strictly prohibited and can result in a prison sentence (the legal blood alcohol level is less than 0.5g per L).

PERSONAL SAFETY

EXPLORING AND TRAVELING

To avoid unwanted attention, try to blend in as much as possible. Respecting local customs (in many cases, dressing more conservatively than you would at home) may placate would-be hecklers. Familiarize yourself with your surroundings before setting out, and carry yourself with confidence. Check maps in shops and restaurants rather than on the street. If you are traveling alone, be sure someone at home knows your itinerary, and never admit that you're by yourself. When walking at night, stick to busy, well-lit streets and avoid dark alleyways. If you ever feel uncomfortable, leave the area as quickly and directly as you can.

Do you travel ?

get online !

A website made for travel enthusiasts.

www.GLOBOsapiens®.com

Get the hottest

insider travel tips

Pictures - Travel Reports - Slide Shows
Chat - Forum - Friendships
Hostels - Member Pages - E-Cards

it's free!

LG078
Registration code

If you are into travel, you are going to love **GLOBOsapiens**®!

There is no sure-fire way to avoid all the threatening situations you might encounter while traveling, but a good **self-defense course** will give you concrete ways to react to unwanted advances. **Impact, Prepare, and Model Mugging** can refer you to local self-defense courses in the US (☎800 345 54 25). Visit the website at www.impactsafety.org for a list of nearby chapters. Workshops (1½-3hr.) start at US$75; full courses (20-25hr.) run US$350-400.

POSSESSIONS AND VALUABLES

Never leave your belongings unattended; crime occurs in even the most demure-looking hostel or hotel. Be particularly careful on **buses** and **trains**; horror stories abound about determined thieves who wait for travelers to fall asleep. Carry your backpack in front of you where you can see it. When traveling with others, sleep in alternate shifts. When alone, use good judgment in selecting a train compartment: never stay in an empty one, and use a lock to secure your pack to the luggage rack. Try to sleep on top bunks with your luggage stored above you (if not in bed with you), and keep important documents and other valuables on your person.

There are a few steps you can take to minimize the financial risk associated with traveling. First, **bring as little with you as possible.** Second, buy a few combination padlocks to secure your belongings either in your pack or in a hostel or train station locker. Third, **carry as little cash as possible.** Keep your traveler's checks and ATM/credit cards in a **money belt**—not a "fanny pack"—along with your passport and ID cards. Fourth, **keep a small cash reserve separate from your primary stash.** This should be about US$50 (US dollars or euros are best) sewn into or stored in the depths of your pack, along with your traveler's check numbers and important photocopies.

In large cities **con artists** often work in groups and may utilize children. Beware of certain classics: sob stories that require money, rolls of bills "found" on the street, saliva spit onto your shoulder to distract you while your bag is being snatched. **Never let your passport and your bags out of your sight;** never trust an un-uniformed "station-porter" who insists on carrying your bag or stowing it in the baggage compartment. **Pickpockets** abound in Rome, Naples, and other major urban centers. Beware of them in city crowds, especially on public transportation. Also, be alert in public telephone booths. If you must say your calling card number, do so very quietly; if you punch it in, make sure no one can look over your shoulder.

PRE-DEPARTURE HEALTH

In your **passport,** write the names of any people you wish to be contacted in case of a medical emergency, and list any allergies or medical conditions. Matching a prescription to a foreign equivalent is not always easy, safe, or possible, so if you take prescription drugs, consider carrying up-to-date, legible prescriptions or a statement from your doctor stating the medication's trade name, manufacturer, chemical name, and dosage. While traveling, be sure to keep all medication with you in your carry-on luggage. For tips on packing a basic **first-aid kit** and other health essentials, see p. 16. For an online database of all medications, try rxlist.com

IMMUNIZATIONS AND PRECAUTIONS

Travelers over two years old should make sure that the following vaccines are up to date: MMR (for measles, mumps, and rubella); DTaP or Td (for diphtheria, tetanus, and pertussis); IPV (for polio); Hib (for *haemophilus* influenza B); and HepB (for Hepatitis B). For more information, consult the CDC (see below) in the US or the equivalent in your home country, and check with a doctor for guidance. Italy doesn't require specific vaccines for travelers entering the country.

ESSENTIALS

INSURANCE

Travel insurance covers four basic areas: medical/health problems, property loss, trip cancellation/interruption, and emergency evacuation. Though regular insurance policies may well extend to travel-related accidents, you may consider purchasing separate travel insurance if the cost of potential trip cancellation, interruption, or emergency medical evacuation is greater than you can absorb. Prices for travel insurance purchased separately generally run about US$50 per week for full coverage, while trip cancellation/interruption may be purchased separately at a rate of US$3-5 per day depending on length of stay. **Safeware** (☎ US 800 800 14 92; www.safeware.com) specializes in covering computers and charges US$90 for 90-day international travel coverage up to US$4000.

Medical insurance (especially university policies) often covers costs incurred abroad; check with your provider. **US Medicare** does not cover foreign travel. **Canadian** provincial health insurance plans increasingly do not cover foreign travel; check with the provincial Ministry of Health or Health Plan Headquarters for details. **Australians** traveling in Italy are entitled to many of the services that they would receive at home as part of the Reciprocal Health Care Agreement. **Homeowners' insurance** (or your family's coverage) often covers theft during travel and loss of travel documents (passport, plane ticket, railpass, etc.) up to US$500.

ISIC and **ITIC** (p. 11) provide basic insurance benefits to US cardholders, including US$100 per day of in-hospital sickness for up to 60 days and US$5000 of accident-related medical reimbursement (see www.isicus.com for details). Cardholders have access to a toll-free 24hr. helpline for medical, legal, and financial emergencies overseas. **American Express** (US ☎ 800 528 48 00) grants most cardholders automatic collision and theft car rental insurance and ground travel accident coverage of US$100,000 on flight purchases made with the card.

INSURANCE PROVIDERS. STA (p. 24) offers a range of plans that can supplement your basic coverage. Other private insurance providers in the US and Canada include: Access America (☎ 800 284 83 00; www.accessamerica.com); Berkely Group (☎ 800 797 45 14; www.berkely.com); Globalcare Travel Insurance (☎ 800 821 24 88; www.globalcare-cocco.com); Travel Assistance International (☎ 800 821 28 28; www.europ-assistance.com); and Travel Guard (☎ 800 826 49 19; www.travelguard.com). Columbus Direct (☎ 020 737 500 11; www.columbusdirect.co.uk) operates in the UK and AFTA (☎ 02 926 432 99; www.afta.com.au) in Australia.

USEFUL ORGANIZATIONS AND PUBLICATIONS

The US **Center for Disease Control and Prevention** (**CDC;** ☎ 877 294 87 47; www.cdc.gov/travel) maintains an international travelers' hotline and an informative website. The CDC's comprehensive booklet *Health Information for International Travel* (The Yellow Book), an annual rundown of disease, immunization, and general health advice, is free online or US$29-40 via the Public Health Foundation (☎ 877 252 12 00; http://bookstore.phf.org). Consult the appropriate government agency of your home country for info sheets on health, entry requirements, and other issues (see the listings in the box on **Travel Advisories,** p. 17). For quick information on health and other travel warnings, call the **Overseas Citizens Services** (M-F 8am-8pm ☎ 888 407 47 47, after-hours ☎ 202 647 40 00, from overseas 317 472 23 28), or contact a passport agency, embassy, or consulate abroad. For info on medical evacuation services and travel insurance firms, see the US government's website at http://travel.state.gov/medical.html or the **British Foreign and Commonwealth Office** (www.fco.gov.uk). For general health info, contact the **American Red Cross** (☎ 800 564 12 34; www.redcross.org).

STAYING HEALTHY

Common sense is the simplest prescription for good health while you travel. Drink lots of fluids to prevent dehydration and constipation, and wear sturdy, broken-in shoes and clean socks.

ENVIRONMENTAL HAZARDS

Heat exhaustion and dehydration: Heat exhaustion leads to nausea, excessive thirst, headaches, and dizziness. Avoid it by drinking plenty of fluids, eating salty foods (e.g. crackers), and abstaining from dehydrating beverages (e.g., alcohol and caffeinated beverages). The sign *acqua non potabile* means the water is not drinkable (e.g., in trains and at some campgrounds).

Sunburn: Always wear sunscreen (SPF 30 is good) when spending time outdoors, especially at high altitudes. Remember that you can burn even when under cloud cover. If you do get sunburned, drink more fluids than usual and apply aloe. Severe sunburns can lead to sun poisoning, a condition that affects the entire body, causing fever, chills, nausea, and vomiting. Sun poisoning should always be treated by a doctor.

High Altitude: Allow your body a couple of days to adjust to less oxygen before exerting yourself. Note that alcohol is more potent and UV rays are stronger at high elevations.

INSECT-BORNE DISEASES

Many diseases are transmitted by insects—mainly mosquitoes, fleas, ticks, and lice. Be aware of insects in wet or forested areas, especially while hiking and camping; wear long pants and long sleeves, tuck your pants into your socks, and use a mosquito net. Use insect repellents such as DEET and soak or spray your gear with permethrin (licensed in the US only for use on clothing). **Ticks**—responsible for Lyme and other diseases—can be particularly dangerous in rural and forested regions. If you find a tick attached to your skin, grasp the head with tweezers as close to your skin as possible and apply slow, steady traction. Do not try to remove ticks with petroleum jelly, nail polish remover, or a hot match.

FOOD- AND WATER-BORNE DISEASES

Prevention is the best cure: be sure that your food is properly cooked and the water you drink is clean. Traveler's diarrhea results from drinking fecally contaminated water or eating uncooked and contaminated foods. Peel fruits and vegetables and be cautious when using tap water (including ice cubes and anything washed in tap water, like salad). Watch out for food from markets or street vendors that may have been cooked in unhygienic conditions. Other culprits are raw shellfish, unpasteurized milk, and sauces containing raw eggs, such as *carbonara*. Buy bottled water, or purify your own water by bringing it to a rolling boil or treating it with **iodine tablets;** note, however, that some parasites such as *giardia* have exteriors that resist iodine treatment, so boiling is more reliable. Always wash your hands before eating or bring a quick-drying purifying liquid hand cleaner.

OTHER INFECTIOUS DISEASES

Rabies: Transmitted through the saliva of infected animals; fatal if untreated. By the time symptoms (thirst and muscle spasms) appear, the disease is in its terminal stage. If you are bitten, wash the wound thoroughly, seek immediate medical care, and try to have the animal located. A rabies vaccine, which consists of 3 shots given over a 21-day period, is available, but is only semi-effective.

Hepatitis B: A viral infection of the liver transmitted via blood or other bodily fluids. Symptoms, which may not surface until years after infection, include jaundice, loss of appetite, fever, and joint pain. A 3-shot vaccination sequence is recommended for health-care workers, sexually-active travelers, and anyone planning to seek medical treatment abroad; it must begin 6 months before traveling.

ESSENTIALS

ESSENTIALS

Hepatitis C: Like Hepatitis B, but the mode of transmission differs. The disease can be spread through contact with blood and sexual activity or sharing items like razors and toothbrushes that may have traces of blood on them.

AIDS and HIV: For detailed information on Acquired Immune Deficiency Syndrome (AIDS) in Italy, call the US CDC's 24hr. hotline at ☎800 342 24 37, or contact the Joint United Nations Programme on HIV/AIDS (UNAIDS), 20, Ave. Appia, CH-1211 Geneva 27, Switzerland (☎22 791 36 66, fax 22 791 41 87).

Sexually transmitted diseases (STDs): Gonorrhea, chlamydia, genital warts, syphilis, herpes, and other STDs are more common than HIV and can cause serious complications. **Hepatitis C** can also be transmitted sexually. Though condoms may protect you from some STDs, oral or even tactile contact can lead to transmission. If you think you may have contracted an STD, see a doctor immediately.

MEDICAL CARE ON THE ROAD

On the whole Italy conforms to standards of modern health care. Quality of care varies by region; health care tends to be better in the north and in private hospitals and clinics. Doctors speak English in most large cities; if they don't, they may be able to arrange for a translator. *Let's Go* lists info on how to access medical help in the **Practical Information** sections of most cities. Those with medical conditions (such as diabetes, allergies to antibiotics, epilepsy, heart conditions) may want to obtain a **Medic Alert** membership (first year US$35, annually thereafter US$20), which includes a stainless steel ID tag, among other benefits, like a 24hr. toll-free number. Contact the Medic Alert Foundation, 2323 Colorado Ave, Turlock, CA 95382, USA (☎888 633 42 98; www.medicalert.org).

WOMEN'S HEALTH

Women travelers are vulnerable to **urinary tract (including bladder and kidney) infections** *(infezioni all'apparato urinario)*. Over-the-counter medicines can sometimes alleviate symptoms, but if they persist, see a doctor. **Vaginal yeast infections** *(candidiasi)* may flare up in hot and humid climates. Wearing loosely fitting trou-

TANDEM ITALY

Learn Italian in 3 of the most beautiful Italian cities:

FLORENCE ROME VENICE

Special combined courses in the 3 cities from 6 weeks to 1 year. Move around Italy and discover its culture and daily life.

- Variety of dynamic courses (general, specialised, special interest) all year round, taught by qualified, enthusiastic teachers. Special programmes for groups
- 'Tandem' interlinguistic exchange with Italians
- Rich and exciting cultural program
- Central accomodation within Italian families

TANDEM

Agents are welcome!!!
www.tandem-schools.com

Machiavelli
Dr Silvano Ghisolfi - Director,
4 Piazza Santo Spirito,
Firenze, Italy, 50125
T: +39 0552 396966,
F: +39 0552 80800,
E: school@centromachiavelli.it
W: www.centromachiavelli.it

"TORRE DI BABELE"
Enzo Consentino - Director,
Via Cosenza, 7 - 00161 Roma
T: +39 0670 08434 -
  0670474976
F: +39 0670 497150
E: info@torredibabele.com
W: www.torredibabele.com

Istituto Venezia -The Venice Institute
Matteo Savini - Director,
Dorsoduro 3116/a 30123 Venezia
T: +39 0415 224331
F: +39 0415 285628
E: info@istitutovenezia.com
W: www.istitutovenezia.com

sers or a skirt and cotton underwear will help, as will over-the-counter remedies like Monistat. Bring supplies from home if you are prone to infection, as they may be difficult to find on the road. Tampons, pads, and contraceptive devices are widely available, though your favorite brand may not be stocked—bring extras of anything you can't live without. Pharmacies refill empty **birth control** packages even without an Italian-issued prescription. **Emergency Contraception,** also known as the morning-after pill, is available by prescription. **Abortion** is legal and may be performed in the first 90 days of pregnancy in a public hospital or authorized private facility. Except in urgent cases, a week-long reflection period is required. Women under 18 must obtain parental permission. Actual availability of abortion may be limited in some areas of Italy, especially in the South, due to a "conscience clause" allowing physicians who oppose abortion to opt out of performing the procedure.

SPECIFIC CONCERNS

EARTHQUAKES. Italy is crossed by several fault lines, the chief one running from Sicily to Friuli-Venezia Giulia in the northeast. The country's principal cities do not lie near these faults, though smaller tourist towns like Assisi do and thus may experience earthquakes (most recently in 1997). If you do find yourself in an earthquake, open a door to provide an escape route and protect yourself by moving underneath a sturdy doorway, table, or desk.

TERRORISM. Terrorism has not been as serious a problem in Italy as in other European countries, though, as in much of the world, the general threat of terrorism certainly exists. Exercise common sense and caution when in crowded, public areas like train or bus stations and open spaces like piazzas in larger cities. The box on **travel advisories** lists offices to contact and webpages to visit to get the most updated list of your home country's government's advisories about travel.

GETTING TO ITALY

BY PLANE

When it comes to airfare, a little effort can save you a bundle. If your plans are flexible enough to deal with the restrictions, courier fares are the cheapest. Tickets bought from consolidators and standby seating are also good deals, but last-minute specials, airfare wars, and charter flights often beat these fares. The key is to hunt around, to be flexible, and to ask persistently about discounts. Students, seniors, and those under 26 should never pay full price for a ticket.

AIRFARES

Airfares to Italy peak between mid-June and early September; holidays are also expensive. The cheapest times to travel are November to mid-December and January-February. Midweek (M-Th morning) round-trip flights run US$40-50 cheaper than weekend flights, but they are generally more crowded and less likely to permit frequent-flier upgrades. Not fixing a return date ("open return") or arriving in and departing from different cities ("open-jaw") can be pricier than round-trip flights. Flights into the transportation hubs of Rome and Milan tend to be cheaper.

If Italy is only one stop on a more extensive globe-hop, consider a round-the-world (RTW) ticket. Tickets usually include at least five stops and are valid for about a year; prices range US$3400-5000. Try **Northwest Airlines/KLM** (US ☎ 800 447 47 47; www.nwa.com) or **Star Alliance,** a consortium of 15 airlines including United Airlines (US ☎ 800 241 65 22; www.staralliance.com).

ESSENTIALS

BUDGET AND STUDENT TRAVEL AGENCIES

While travel agents can make your life easy and help you save, they may not spend the time to find you the lowest possible fare—they get paid on commission. Travelers holding **ISIC** and **IYTC cards** (p. 10) qualify for big discounts from student travel agencies. Most flights from budget agencies are on major airlines, but in peak season some may sell seats on less reliable chartered aircraft.

CTS Travel, 30 Rathbone Pl., London W1T 1GQ, UK (☎0207 209 06 30; www.ctstravel.co.uk). A British student travel agent with offices in 39 countries including the US, Empire State Building, 350 Fifth Ave., Suite 7813, New York, NY 10118 (☎877 287 66 65; www.ctstravelusa.com).

STA Travel, 5900 Wilshire Blvd., Ste. 900, Los Angeles, CA 90036, USA (24hr. reservations and info ☎800 781 40 40; www.sta-travel.com). A student and youth travel organization with over 150 offices worldwide (check their website for a listing of all their offices), including US offices in Boston, Chicago, L.A., New York, San Francisco, Seattle, and Washington, D.C. Ticket booking, travel insurance, railpasses, and more. Walk-in offices are located throughout Australia (☎03 934 943 44), New Zealand (☎09 309 97 23), and the UK (☎0870 160 05 99).

Travel CUTS (Canadian Universities Travel Services Limited), 187 College St., **Toronto,** ON M5T 1P7 (☎416 979 24 06; www.travelcuts.com). Offices across Canada and the US including L.A., New York, Seattle, and San Francisco.

USIT, 19-21 Aston Quay, Dublin 2 (☎01 602 17 77; www.usitworld.com), Ireland's leading student/budget travel agency has 22 offices throughout Northern Ireland and the Republic of Ireland. Offers programs to work in North America.

Wasteels, Skoubogade 6, 1158 Copenhagen K. (☎3314 46 33; www.wasteels.com). A huge chain with 180 locations across Europe. Sells Wasteels BIJ tickets discounted 30-45% off regular fare, 2nd-class international point-to-point train tickets with unlimited stopovers for those under 26 (sold only in Europe).

FLIGHT PLANNING ON THE INTERNET. The Internet may be the budget traveler's dream when it comes to finding and booking bargain fares, but the array of options can be overwhelming. Many airline sites offer special last-minute deals on the Web. Try www.bestfares.com, www.flights.com, www.hot-deals.com, www.onetravel.com, and www.travelzoo.com. Alitalia.com occasionally offers sale fares. **STA** (www.sta-travel.com) and **StudentUniverse** (www.studentuniverse.com) provide quotes on student tickets, while **Orbitz** (www.orbitz.com), **Expedia** (www.expedia.com) **Opodo** (www.opodo.com), and **Travelocity** (www.travelocity.com) offer full travel services. **Priceline** (www.priceline.com) lets you specify a price, and obligates you to buy any ticket that meets or beats it; **Hotwire** (www.hotwire.com) offers bargain fares, but won't reveal the airline or flight times until you buy. Increasingly, there are online tools available to help sift through multiple offers; **SideStep** (www.sidestep.com; download required) and **Booking Buddy** (www.bookingbuddy.com) let you enter your trip information once and search multiple sites. An indispensable resource on the Internet is the **Air Traveler's Handbook** (www.faqs.org/faqs/travel/air/handbook), a comprehensive listing of links to everything you need to know before you board a plane.

COMMERCIAL AIRLINES

The commercial airlines' lowest regular offer is the **APEX** (Advance Purchase Excursion) fare, which provides confirmed reservations and allows "open-jaw" tickets. Generally, reservations must be made seven to 21 days ahead of departure, with a seven- to 14-day minimum-stay and up to 90-day maximum-stay restrictions.

These fares carry hefty cancellation and change penalties (fees rise in summer). Book peak-season APEX fares early. Use **Microsoft Expedia** (http://msn.expedia.com) or **Travelocity** (www.travelocity.com) to assess the lowest published fares; then use the resources outlined here to try and beat those fares. Low-season fares should be cheaper than the high-season (mid-June to Aug.) ones listed here.

TRAVELING FROM NORTH AMERICA
Basic round-trip fares to Italy range from roughly US$200-750. From the US to Rome costs between US$500-900; to Milan, US$450-800; Florence, US$500-900; Venice, US$500-850. Standard commercial carriers like **American** and **United** will probably offer the most convenient flights to Rome and Milan, but they may not be the cheapest, unless you manage to grab a special promotion or airfare war ticket. You will probably find flying one of the following "discount" airlines a better deal, if any of their limited departure points is convenient for you.

Finnair: ☎ 800 950 50 00; www.us.finnair.com. Cheap round-trips from New York, San Francisco and Toronto to Helsinki; connections to Rome and Milan.

Icelandair: ☎ 800 223 55 00; www.icelandair.com. Stopovers in Iceland for no extra cost on most transatlantic flights. Cheap round-trips from Boston and Orlando to Rome and Milan.

TRAVELING FROM THE UK AND IRELAND
Since many carriers fly from the British Isles to the continent, we only include discount airlines or those with cheap specials here. The **Air Travel Advisory Bureau** in London (☎ 0207 306 30 00; www.atab.co.uk) provides referrals to travel agencies and consolidators that offer discounted airfares out of the UK. **Cheapflights** (www.cheapflights.co.uk) publishes airfare bargains.

Aer Lingus: Ireland ☎ 0818 36 50 00; www.aerlingus.ie. Cheap tickets from Dublin, Cork, Galway, Kerry, and Shannon to Milan, Rome, and Venice (€49-85).

easyJet: UK ☎ 0871 750 01 00; www.easyjet.com. London to Bologna, Milan, Naples, Rome, and Venice (UK£40-80). Online tickets.

KLM: UK ☎ 0870 507 40 74; www.klmuk.com. Cheap return tickets from London and elsewhere, serving 14 Italian destinations.

Ryanair: Ireland ☎ 0818 30 30 30, UK 087 246 00 00; www.ryanair.com. From Dublin, London, and Glasgow to over a dozen destinations across Italy. Frequent sale fares.

TRAVELING FROM ELSEWHERE IN EUROPE
Most European carriers, including Italy's national airline **Alitalia** (US ☎ 800 223 57 30, UK 870 544 82 59; www.alitaliausa.com.); **Air France** (☎ 011 880 80 40; www.airfrance.com); **KLM** (see above); **Lufthansa**; and **SN Brussels Airlines** (Belgium ☎ 070 35 11 11, Italy 02 696 823 64; www.flysn.com) have frequent flights to Rome, Milan, and Venice from many European cities. The sheer number of European airlines ensures competitive fares.

TRAVELING FROM AUSTRALIA AND NEW ZEALAND
Air New Zealand: New Zealand ☎ 0800 73 70 00; www.airnz.co.nz. Auckland to Italy.

Qantas Air: Australia ☎ 13 13 13, New Zealand 0800 80 87 67; www.qantas.com.au. Flights from Australia and New Zealand to Rome and Milan.

Singapore Air: Australia ☎ 13 10 11, New Zealand 0800 80 89 09; www.singaporeair.com. Flies from Auckland, Melbourne, Perth, and Sydney to Rome.

AIR COURIER FLIGHTS
Those who travel light should consider courier flights. Couriers help transport cargo on international flights by using checked luggage space for freight. Generally, couriers travel with carry-ons only and deal with complex flight restrictions. Most

flights are round-trip, with short fixed-length stays (usually one week) and a limit of one ticket per issue. Many operate only out of major gateway cities in North America. Round-trip courier fares from the US to Italy run about US$159-375.

Air Courier Association, 1767 A Denver West Blvd., Golden, CO 80401 (☎800 280 59 73; www.aircourier.org). 10 departure cities throughout North America to Rome and throughout Western Europe (high-season US$130-640). 1-year membership US$25.

International Association of Air Travel Couriers (IAATC), P.O. Box 847, Scottsbluff, NE 69363 (☎308 632 32 73; www.courier.org). From 9 North American cities to Western European cities, including Rome. 1-year membership US$45.

Global Courier Travel, P.O. Box 3051, Nederland, CO 80466 (www.globalcourier-travel.com). Searchable online database. 6 departure points in the US and Canada to Milan and Rome. 1-year membership US$50, 2 people US$65.

NOW Voyager, 315 W 49th St., New York, NY 10019 (☎212 459 16 16; www.nowvoy-agertravel.com). To Milan and Rome (US$499-699). Usually 1-week max. stay. 1-year membership US$50. Non-courier discount fares also available.

FROM THE UK, IRELAND, AUSTRALIA, AND NEW ZEALAND

The minimum age for couriers from the **UK** is usually 18. **Brave New World Enterprises,** P.O. Box 22212, London SE5 8WB (www.courierflights.com) publishes a directory of all the companies offering courier flights in the UK (UK£10, in electronic form UK£8). **Global Courier Travel** (see above) also offers flights from London and Dublin to continental Europe. From **Australia,** Global Courier Travel (see above) often has listings from Sydney to London.

STANDBY FLIGHTS

Traveling standby requires considerable flexibility in arrival and departure dates and cities. Companies dealing in standby flights sell vouchers rather than tickets, along with the promise to get you to (or near) your destination within a certain window of time (typically 1-5 days). Carefully read agreements with any company

babilonia
■■∧■○
ITALIAN LANGUAGE SCHOOL
taormina, sicily

LEARN ITALIAN, EXPLORE SICILY, AND EXPERIENCE THE LOCAL CULTURE
BABILONIA - Italian language school - in Taormina, Sicily has been focusing on giving the
student/traveler the opportunity not only to learn Italian but the chance to discover the history,
traditions and surroundings of Sicily. With this motivation in mind, in combination with the
language courses we give the possibility of combining a cooking course, wine course, diving or
eco-tours (hikings), arts & crafts or culture courses (literature, history, art history), golf or
outdoor sports. Language is not just a set of grammar rules, language is above all the result of a
way of seeing the world,is a different eye on reality, is a way of interpreting life.
That's what BABILONIA would like to offer you!

via del ginnasio 20 – 98039 taormina, sicilia, italy – tel & fax (+39) 0942 23441 – info@babilonia.it – www.babilonia.it

IALC   csn

offering standby flights as tricky fine print can leave you in the lurch. To check on a company's service record in the US, call the Better Business Bureau (☎703 276 01 00). It is difficult to receive refunds, and clients' vouchers will not be honored when an airline fails to receive payment in time.

TICKET CONSOLIDATORS

Ticket consolidators, or **"bucket shops,"** buy unsold tickets in bulk from commercial airlines and sell them at discounted rates. The best place to look is in the Sunday travel section of any major newspaper (such as the *New York Times*), where many bucket shops place tiny ads. Call quickly, as availability is typically extremely limited. Not all bucket shops are reliable, so insist on a receipt that gives full details of restrictions, refunds, and tickets, and pay by credit card (in spite of the 2-5% fee) so you can stop payment if you never receive your tickets. For more info, see www.travel-library.com/air-travel/consolidators.html.

CHARTER FLIGHTS

Charters are flights contracted by tour operators to fly extra loads of passengers during peak season. Charter flights fly less frequently than major airlines, make refunds particularly difficult, and are almost always fully booked. Schedules and itineraries may also change or be cancelled at the last moment (as late as 48hr. before the trip, and without a full refund), and check-in, boarding, and baggage claim are often much slower. However, they can also be cheaper. Discount clubs and fare brokers offer members savings on last-minute charter and tour deals. Study contracts closely; you don't want to end up with an unwanted overnight layover. Travelers Advantage, 7 Cambridge Dr., Trumbull, CT 06611, USA (☎877 259 26 91; www.travelersadvantage.com; US$90 annual fee includes discounts and cheap flight directories), specializes in European travel and tour packages.

BY TRAIN

Traveling to Italy by train from countries within Europe can be as expensive as taking a flight, but railway travelers are afforded the luxury of watching the country unfold before them, as well as the possibility of spontaneous stopovers before reaching their ultimate destination. For more information on traveling through Italy by rail, see the domestic travel **By Train** section below (p. 28).

MULTINATIONAL RAILPASSES

EURAILPASS. Eurail is **valid** in most of Western Europe: Austria, Belgium, Denmark, Finland, France, Germany, Greece, Hungary, Italy, Luxembourg, the Netherlands, Norway, Portugal, the Republic of Ireland, Romania, Spain, Sweden, and Switzerland. It is **not valid** in the UK. Standard **Eurailpasses,** valid for a consecutive given number of days, are best for those planning on spending extensive time on trains every few days. **Flexipasses,** valid for any 10 or 15 (not necessarily consecutive) days within a two-month period, are more cost-effective for those traveling longer distances less frequently. **Saverpasses** provide first-class travel for travelers in groups of two to five (prices are per person). **Youthpasses** and **Youth Flexipasses** provide parallel second-class perks for those under 26.

EURAILPASSES	15 DAYS	21 DAYS	1 MONTH	2 MONTHS	3 MONTHS
1st class Eurailpass	US$588	US$762	US$946	US$1338	US$1654
Eurail Saverpass	US$498	US$648	US$804	US$1138	US$1408
Eurail Youthpass	US$414	US$534	US$664	US$938	US$1160

EURAIL FLEXIPASSES	10 DAYS IN 2 MONTHS	15 DAYS IN 2 MONTHS
1st class Eurail Flexipass	US$694	US$914
Eurail Saver Flexipass	US$592	US$778
Eurail Youth Flexipass	US$488	US$642

Passholders receive a timetable for major routes and a map with details on possible ferry, steamer, bus, car rental, hotel, and Eurostar discounts (see below). Often they also receive reduced fares or free passage on many bus and boat lines.

EURAIL SELECT PASS. The Eurail Select Pass is a slimmed-down version of the Eurailpass: it allows five to 15 days of unlimited travel in any two-month period within three, four, or five bordering countries of the 18 Eurail network countries. **First-Class passes** (for individuals) and **Saverpasses** (for people traveling in groups of 2-5) range from US$356/US$304 per person (5 days) to US$794/US$674 (15 days). **Second-Class Youthpasses** for those aged 12-25 cost US$249-556. For a fee, you can add **additional zones** (Austria/Hungary; Belgium/Luxembourg/Netherlands; Greece Plus, including the ADN/HML ferry between Italy and Greece; and/or Portugal). You are entitled to the same **freebies** afforded by the Eurailpass, but only when they are within or between countries that you have purchased.

BY BUS AND BOAT

Though European trains and railpasses are extremely popular, in some cases buses prove a better option. Often cheaper than railpasses, **international bus passes** allow unlimited travel on a hop-on, hop-off basis between major European cities. The prices below are based on high-season travel. (For more Italy-specific bus information, see By Train and Bus, p. 27.) Contact **Eurolines**, 4 Vicarage Rd., Edgbaston, Birmingham B15 3ES, UK, the largest operator of Europe-wide coach services for more information. (☎08705 80 80 80; www.eurolines.co.uk or www.eurolines.com). **Busabout**, 258 Vauxhall Bridge Rd., London SW1V 1BS, UK, offers 5 interconnecting bus circuits covering 60 cities and towns in Europe. (☎207 950 16 61; www.busabout.com. Consecutive Day Passes, Flexi Passes, and Add On Passes are available.)

Most European ferries are quite comfortable; the cheapest ticket typically still includes a reclining chair or couchette. Fares jump sharply in July and August. Ask for discounts; ISIC holders can often get student fares, and Eurailpass holders get many reductions and free trips (for examples of popular freebies, see p. 27). You'll occasionally have to pay a port tax (under US$10). Ferries in the Mediterranean run from Spain to Morocco, from Italy to Tunisia, and from France to Morocco and Tunisia. Reservations are recommended, especially in July and August. Schedules are erratic, with similar routes and varying prices. Shop around, and beware of dinky, unreliable companies that don't take reservations. Ferries float across the Adriatic from Ancona and Bari, Italy to Split and Dubrovnik, respectively, in Croatia. Ferries also run across the Aegean, from Ancona, Italy to Patras, Greece (19hr.), and from Bari, Italy to Igoumenitsa (9hr.) and Patras (15hr.), Greece. Eurail is valid on certain ferries between Brindisi, Italy and Corfu (8hr.), Igoumenitsa, and Patras, Greece. Countless ferry companies operate these routes simultaneously; see specific country chapters for more information.

GETTING AROUND ITALY

BY TRAIN

The Italian State Railway, **Ferrovie dello Stato** or **FS** (☎848 88 80 88; www.fs-online.com), offers inexpensive and efficient service, though it is commonly plagued by strikes. The southern Italian offspring of FS, **Ferrovie Sud-Est (FSE)**, operates cars that are hot, crowded, and uncomfortable, and may be closer to cattle freights than passenger trains; it may be worth the extra euros to take a classier train.

Several types of trains ride the Italian rails. The **locale** stops at every station along a particular line, often taking twice as long as a faster train. The **diretto** makes fewer stops than the *locale*, while the **espresso** just stops at major stations. The air-conditioned, more expensive **InterCity (IC)** or **rapido** train travels only to the largest cities. No *rapidi* have second-class compartments, and a few require reservations. Tickets for the fast, comfy, and pricey **Eurostar** or **Pendolino** trains (first- and second-class trains) require reservations. **Eurail** passes are valid without a supplement on all trains except the Eurostar.

Trains are not always safe. For long trips make sure you are on the correct car, as trains sometimes split at crossroads. Towns listed in parentheses on European schedules require a train switch at the town listed immediately before the parentheses. Note that unless stated otherwise, *Let's Go* lists one-way fares. **Railpasses** theoretically allow you to jump on any train in Europe, go where you want when you want, and change your plans at will. In practice it's not so easy. You still must stand in line to validate your pass, pay for supplements, and fork over cash for reservations. Even then, railpasses don't always pay off. For estimates of pass prices, contact Rail Europe (p. 27).

> **CARTA VERDE.** If you're under 26 or over 60 and plan to travel extensively in Italy, your first purchase should be a Carta Verde or Carta d'Argento, offering a year-long 20% discount on all train tickets (p. 31).

> Always **validate** your train ticket **before boarding.** Validation machines, usually colored yellow or orange, are located all over train stations. Insert and remove your ticket from the slot and check to see if the machine stamped it. Failure to validate may result in steep fines, and train operators do not accept ignorance as an excuse. The same goes for bus tickets, which should be validated immediately after boarding the bus using the onboard validation machines.

RESERVATIONS

While seat reservations are only rarely required, you are not guaranteed a seat without one (€2.50 and up, depending on the ticket price). Reservations are available up to two months in advance on major trains, and Italians often reserve far ahead; you should strongly consider reserving during peak holiday and tourist seasons (at the very latest a few hours ahead). If someone occupies your seat, be prepared to (politely) say, "Excuse me, but I have reserved this seat," or *"Mi scusi, ma ho prenotato questo posto."* It will be necessary to purchase a **supplement** (€3-15.50) or special fare for faster or higher-quality trains such as ETR500 and Pendolino. All **Inter Rail** holders must also purchase supplements (€3-20) for trains like EuroCity and InterCity.

OVERNIGHT TRAINS

Night trains have their advantages: you don't waste valuable daylight hours traveling, and you can forego the hassle and considerable expense of securing a night's accommodation. However, night travel has its drawbacks: discomfort, sleeplessness, and missing the beautiful vistas. Consider paying extra for a **cuccetta,** one of six fold-down bunks within a compartment (€18); private **sleeping cars** offer more privacy and comfort, but are considerably more expensive (€25) and not widely available in Italy. If you're not willing to spend the money on a *cuccetta*, consider taking an *espresso* train overnight—they usually have compartments with fold-

Buy a Rail Pass
and get ALL this FREE...

12 Language European Phrasebook
This handy phrasebook provides an essential bridge to communication.

One FREE night at The Pink Palace
Includes breakfast and dinner at the world famous youth resort in Corfu, Greece.

FREE Eurail timetable, guide & map
with every order.

Passes issued on the spot
Same day shipping! RUSH ORDERS are our specialty.

Expert Advice and Service
For over 20 years we have helped thousands of people travel Europe by rail. From Eurail to Britrail, we'll help you pick the perfect pass for your trip.

AND

- Easy online ordering
- Hundreds of passes to choose from
- No handling fees

GUARANTEED BEST PRICES

ORDER ONLINE and SAVE
LETSGORAIL.com
1-866-RAIL-PASS
(1-866-724-5727)

Agents for

EURAIL · **BritRail**

Visit these helpful sites when planning your trip
EUROTRIP.com and RAILSAVER.com

out seats. If you are using a railpass valid only for a restricted number of days, inspect train schedules to maximize the use of your pass: an overnight train or boat journey uses up only one of your travel days if it departs after 7pm (you need only write in the next day's date on your pass).

BY FERRY

The islands of Sicily, Sardinia, and Corsica, as well as the smaller islands along the coasts, are connected to the mainland by ferries (*traghetti*) and hydrofoils (*aliscafi*); international trips are generally made by ferries only (see www.traghetti.com for detailed listings of companies). Italy's largest private ferry service, **Tirrenia** (www.gruppotirrenia.it), runs ferries to Sardinia, Sicily, and Tunisia. Other major ferry companies (**Moby Lines, Grandi Navi Veloci, Toremar, Saremar, Siremar,** and **Caremar**) and the **SNAV** (www.snavali.com) hydrofoil services travel to major ports such as Ancona, Bari, Brindisi, Genoa, Livorno, La Spezia, Naples, and Trapani. Ferry services also depart for the Tremiti, Pontine, and Aeolian Islands.

For major trips reserve tickets at least one week in advance. Schedules change unpredictably—confirm your departure one day in advance. Some ports require checking in 2hr. before departure or your reservation will be cancelled. **Posta ponte** (deck class; preferable in warm weather) is cheapest. It is, however, often only available when the **poltrona** (reclining cabin seats) are full. Port taxes often apply. Ask for **student** and **Eurail discounts;** some unscrupulous travelers have been known to ask locals to buy heavily discounted resident tickets.

BY BUS AND METRO

Two bus systems exist within Italy, intercity buses, which run between towns and regions, and intracity buses, which provide local transportation. In addition to getting travelers to their destinations faster and cheaper than trains, intercity buses, or *pullman*, also tend to go on strike much less frequently. They are always worth checking out, especially for smaller towns that are not serviced by trains. Tickets can generally be purchased at private bus company offices near the bus station or departure point, or onboard the bus. On rare occasions the tickets are actually sold by the side of the road out of a salesperson's car near where the bus will stop. Intracity bus tickets are usually sold at any *tabacchi*, and must be validated using the orange machines on board immediately upon entering the bus. Failure to do so will result in large fines, up to US$140. The websites www.bus.it and www.italybus.it are both helpful resources for finding bus routes to non-major towns and discovering which bus companies service specific regions.

Most large cities, including Rome, Naples, and Milan, have **Metro systems** that connect major tourist destinations. Fast and cheap, this is the best form of local transportation, along with public buses. The metro usually operates from 6am until midnight, and tickets usually cost under €1. The cabins and stations get packed during rush-hour, so guard personal belongings extremely carefully, as theft is rampant. Tickets are sold in stations at counters or from automated machines. Remember to validate them, or risk getting heavily fined.

BY CAR

Cars offer speed, freedom, access to the countryside, and an escape from the town-to-town mentality of trains. Although a single traveler won't save by renting a car, four usually will. If you can't decide between train and car travel, you may benefit from a combination of the two; RailEurope and other railpass vendors offer rail-and-drive packages. Fly-and-drive packages are also often available from travel agents or airline/rental agency partnerships. Before setting off, know the laws of the countries in which you'll be driving. For an informal primer on European road signs and conventions, check out www.travlang.com/signs.

DRIVING IN ITALY

While the Italian bus and train system are quite effective in negotiating travel between the major cities, travelers looking to explore smaller cities and rural villages might find renting a car to be a more viable option. Anyone considering driving in Italy should weigh their decision carefully, though, as the unofficial rules of the road include driving on the sidewalk, ignoring traffic lights, frequent tailgating, and allowing mere millimeters between passing cars. Officially, driving in Italy is very similar to driving anywhere else in Europe: predominantly manual transmission cars drive on the right, pass on the left and follow the international rules and road signs established by the Geneva Convention. There are four kinds of roads: *autostrade* (superhighways with 110km per hr. speed limit; most charge tolls which can often best be paid with a credit card), *strade statali* (state roads), *strade provinciali* (provincial roads), and *strade comunali* (local roads). Parking is allowed on the right side of all roads outside of towns and cities, other than autostrade, but do not be surprised to see other drivers converting sidewalks into parking spaces. Violations of highway code may result in fines and imprisonment in serious cases. For more driving rules and regulations, consult "In Italy Online" (www.initaly.com/travel/info/driving.htm).

The **Automobile Club d'Italia (ACI)** is at the service of all drivers in Italy, both tourists or citizens, with offices located throughout Italy (V. Marsala 8, 00185; Rome ☎06 499 824 45, fax 06 499 82 469). Call ☎80 31 16 from a landline phone or 800 11 68 00 from a mobile phone in case of **breakdown** on any road. On superhighways use the emergency telephones placed every two kilometers. For long drives in desolate areas, invest in a roadside assistance program and a cellular telephone, but be aware that use of phones en route is only permitted with a hands-free device.

CAR SAFETY

Garages are usually the safest bet for parking in the city but be sure to check rates before agreeing to anything. Parking lots can be extremely expensive and very hard to find. To save money park in the outskirts and take a bus or InterCity train into the city center. To avoid fines for street parking, ask your rental agency to equip your car with a dashboard timer. Most already do so.

DRIVING PRECAUTIONS. When traveling in the summer, bring substantial amounts of **water** (5L per person per day) for drinking and for the radiator. For long distances, make sure tires are in good repair and have enough air. Good maps, a **compass,** and a **car manual** can also be very useful. You should always carry a **spare tire** and **jack, jumper cables, extra oil, flares,** a **flashlight (torch),** and **heavy blankets** (in case your car breaks down at night or in the winter). If you don't know how to **change a tire,** learn before heading out, especially if you are planning on traveling in deserted areas. Blowouts on dirt roads are quite common. If you do have a breakdown, stay with your car; if you wander off, there's less likelihood that **roadside assistance** will find you.

DRIVING PERMITS AND CAR INSURANCE

INTERNATIONAL DRIVING PERMIT (IDP)

If you plan to drive a car while in Italy, you must be 18 or older and have an International Driving Permit (IDP) if you don't have an EU license. Your IDP, valid for one year, must be issued in your own country before you depart. An application for an IDP usually requires one or two photos, a current local license, an additional form of identification, and a fee. To apply, contact the national or local branch of your home country's automobile association. Be careful when purchasing an IDP online or anywhere other than your home automobile association. Many vendors sell permits of questionable legitimacy for higher prices.

CAR INSURANCE

Most credit cards cover standard insurance. If you rent, lease, or borrow a car, you will need a **green card**, or **International Insurance Certificate,** to certify that you have liability insurance and that it applies abroad. Green cards can be obtained at car rental agencies, car dealers (for those leasing cars), some travel agents, and some border crossings. Rental agencies may require you to purchase theft insurance in countries that they consider to have a high risk of auto theft.

RENTING A CAR

You can rent a car from a US-based firm (Alamo, Avis, Budget, or Hertz) with European offices, from a European-based company with local representatives (Europcar), or from a tour operator (Auto Europe, Europe By Car, and Kemwel Holiday Autos) that will arrange a rental for you from a European company at its own rates. Multinationals offer greater flexibility, but tour operators often strike better deals. It is always significantly less expensive to reserve a car from the US than from Europe. Ask airlines about special fly-and-drive packages; you may get up to a week of free or discounted rental. Expect to pay €50 per day for a two- to four-door economy car with manual transmission and A/C. Reserve ahead and pay in advance if at all possible. Always check if prices quoted include tax and collision insurance; some credit card companies provide insurance, allowing their customers to decline the collision damage waiver. Ask about discounts and check the terms of insurance, particularly the size of the deductible. Minimum renting age is 18 and in some areas 21, but can vary depending on the type of car being rented. Most Italian agencies require proof that you've had a license in your home country for at least a year. Car rental in Europe is available through the following agencies:

Auto Europe (US and Canada ☎888 223 55 55 or 207 842 20 00; www.autoeurope.com).

Avis (Australia ☎136 333, Canada 800 272 58 71, New Zealand 0800 65 51 11, UK 0870 606 01 00, US 800 230 48 98; www.avis.com).

Europe by Car (US ☎800 223 15 16 or 212 581 30 40; www.europebycar.com).

Europcar International, 3 Avenue du Centre, 78 881 Saint Quentin en Yvelines Cedex, France (☎30 44 90 00, US 877 940 69 00; www.europcar.com).

Hertz (Australia ☎9698 25 55, Canada 800 263 06 00, UK 0990 99 66 99, US 800 654 31 31; www.hertz.com).

BY BICYCLE, MOPED, AND FOOT

Renting a bike is easy in Italy; look for *noleggio* signs. Many airlines will count a bike as your second piece of luggage; a few charge extra (US$60-110 one-way). Bikes must be packed in a cardboard box with the pedals and front

ESSENTIALS

wheel detached; many airlines sell bike boxes at the airport (US$10). Most ferries let you take your bike for free or for a nominal fee, and you can always ship your bike on trains. Renting a bike beats bringing your own if you plan to stay in one or two regions. Some hostels rent bicycles for low prices. In addition to **panniers** to hold your luggage, you'll need a good **helmet** (US$25-50) and a **sturdy lock** (from US$30). **Ciclismo Classico,** 30 Marathon Street, Arlington, MA 02474, USA (781-646-3377; www.ciclismoclassico.com), offers beginner through advanced level trips across Italy, including Sardinia, southern Italy, Sicily, Piemonte, and the Veneto.

Scooters or mopeds are available for rent in major cities, as well as in smaller or rural locations. Often a *motorino* (scooter) is the most convenient method of transportation to reach sights in places with unreliable bus or train connections. Rental companies are required by law to provide a helmet, which the driver must wear. Gas and insurance may or may not be included in the rental price. Even if it is exhilarating, always exercise caution; practice first in empty streets and learn to keep with the flow of traffic rather than just following street signs. Drivers in Italy—especially in the south—are notorious for ignoring traffic laws.

Some of Italy's grandest scenery can be seen only by foot. *Let's Go* features many daytrips, but native inhabitants and fellow travelers are the best source for tips. Professionally run hiking and walking tours are often your best bet for navigating *la bell'Italia*. Hiking tours generally range from six to nine days long and cost from US$2700-3000. Check out **Ciclismo Classico** (www.ciclismoclassico.com) for hiking options in the Dolomites, along the Amalfi coast, and through Tuscany or the Cinque Terre. The **Backpack Europe** website (www.backpackeurope.com) provides links to great hiking, walking, and kayaking options throughout Italy.

The best and more specialized bike rental in Florence and Tuscany

www.florencebybike.it

Florence by Bike

Bike rental & Bike tours

All kinds of bicycles
50cc and 125cc scooters
650cc motorbikes
Full-day guided bike tours in Chianti
Self-guided tours in Tuscany
English speaking staff

Via San Zanobi, 91/120/122r
5 minutes - walk from the train station
phone/fax: +39/55/488992
info@florencebybike.it

BICYCLE SHOP

BY THUMB

 Let's Go never recommends hitchhiking as a safe means of transportation, and none of the information presented here is intended to do so.

Let's Go does not recommend hitchhiking as a safe means of transportation. Hitchhiking at night can be particularly dangerous; for women traveling alone, hitching is just too dangerous. Experienced hitchers pick a well-lit spot outside of built-up areas, where drivers can stop, return to the road without causing an accident, and have time to look over potential passengers as they approach. Hitchhiking is illegal in Italy although many Italians will offer rides to travelers walking alone, especially in deserted areas. Many travelers accept rides from Italian drivers without incident. Probably the greatest danger for hitchhikers is getting hit by a car while waiting on the highway or being involved in a car accident. Travelers who know the Italian names for their destinations generally have more success making drivers understand where they want to go. It is always a good idea to keep luggage on the seat next to you, instead of putting it in the trunk, to facilitate a quick exit.

Most Western European countries offer a ride service, which pairs drivers with riders; the fee varies according to destination. Eurostop International is one of the largest in Europe. Not all organizations screen drivers and riders; ask in advance. *Let's Go* strongly urges you to consider the risks before you choose to hitchhike.

KEEPING IN TOUCH

BY MAIL

SENDING MAIL HOME FROM ITALY
Airmail is the best way to send mail home from Italy. **Aerogrammes,** printed sheets that fold into envelopes and travel via airmail, are available at post offices. Write "airmail," "par avion," or *"posta prioritaria"* on the front. Most post offices will charge exorbitant fees or simply refuse to send aerogrammes with enclosures. **Surface mail** is by far the cheapest and slowest way to send mail. It takes one to two months to cross the Atlantic and one to three to cross the Pacific—good for heavy items you won't need for a while, such as souvenirs or other articles you've acquired along the way. Bear in mind that the period of time an item will spend in transit will be less predictable when mailing from smaller towns.

SENDING MAIL WITHIN ITALY
Domestic postal service is poor and for years has been the butt of jokes among Italians about waiting weeks or months for mail. Recently the state-owned Poste Italiane (www.poste.it) has modernized the system to include services like priority and registered mail, but it hasn't sped up much. Sending a postcard within Italy costs €0.45, while sending letters (up to 2kg) domestically requires €0.85-6.00. To address a letter within Italy, use this format:

Luigi Pirandello
Via Atenea, 1921
92100 Agrigento

RECEIVING MAIL IN ITALY

There are several ways to arrange pick-up of letters sent to you by friends and relatives while you are abroad. Mail can be sent via **Poste Restante** (General Delivery; *fermoposta*) to almost any city or town in Italy with a post office, but is not always reliable. Address *fermoposta* letters like so:

> Dante ALIGHIERI
> Fermoposta
> 80142 Napoli
> Italy

The mail will go to a desk in the central post office, unless you specify a post office by street address or postal code. It's best to use the largest post office, since mail may be sent there regardless. It is usually safer and quicker, though more expensive, to send mail express or registered. Bring your passport for pick-up; there is a small fee which for letters should not exceed €1, so bring money too. If the clerks insist that there is nothing for you, have them check under your first name as well. *Let's Go* lists post offices in the **Practical Information** section for cities and towns.

BY TELEPHONE

CALLING HOME FROM ITALY

A **calling card** is probably your cheapest bet. Calls are billed collect or to your account. You can frequently call collect without even possessing a company's calling card just by calling their access number and following the instructions. **To obtain a calling card** from your national telecommunications service before leaving home, contact the appropriate company listed below (using the numbers in the

LEARN A NEW LANGUAGE...

MEET NEW FRIENDS...

SEE THE WORLD!

A2Z Languages is the industry leader in extensive language immersion courses. Specializing in comprehensive language and cultural programs.

- French
- Italian
- Japanese
- Portuguese
- German
- Spanish
- Russian
- Chinese
- Greek
- & More!

www.a2zlanguages.com • 1-800-496-4596

World wide: (602) 778-6794 • Fax: 602-840-1545 • 5112 N. 40th St., #203 • Phoenix, AZ 85018 • USA

ESSENTIALS

first column). To **call home with a calling card,** contact the operator for your service provider in Italy by dialing the appropriate toll-free access number. Prepaid phone cards and major credit cards can be used for direct international calls, but they are generally less cost-efficient. Before settling on a calling card plan, be sure to research your options in order to pick the one that best fits both your needs and your destination. Placing a **collect call** through an international operator is even more expensive, but may be necessary in case of emergency.

PLACING INTERNATIONAL CALLS. To call Italy from home or to call home from Italy, dial:

1. The **international dialing prefix.** To dial out of **Australia,** dial 0011; **Canada** or the **US,** 011; **Ireland, Italy, New Zealand,** or the **UK,** 00.
2. The **country code** of the country you want to call. To call **Australia,** dial 61; **Canada** or the **US,** 1; **Ireland,** 353; **Italy,** 39; **New Zealand,** 64; the **UK,** 44.
3. The **city/area code.** Let's Go lists the city/area codes for cities and towns in Italy opposite the city or town name, next to a ☎. For most countries, if the first digit is a zero (e.g., 020 for London), omit the zero when calling from abroad (e.g., dial 20 from Canada to reach London). Italy, however, is the exception. Dial the number as written with the zero.
4. The **local number.**

ESSENTIALS

CALLING WITHIN ITALY

TIP

Even when dialing within a city, the city code is required (e.g., when dialing from one place in Milan to another, the ☎ 02 is still necessary.)

As coin-operated public phones are being phased out, the most common type requires a **prepaid phone card,** or *scheda.* Phone card vendors, *tabacchi,* and sometimes post offices carry cards in denominations of €5, €10, and €20. Italian phone cards are a little tricky to maneuver; be sure to rip off the perforated corner and insert the card in the slot of the phone stripe-up. For instructions in English, push the silver button with two flags on it. Another kind of prepaid telephone card comes with a Personal Identification Number (PIN) and a toll-free access number. Instead of inserting the card into the phone, you call the access number and follow the directions on the card. These cards can be used to make international as well as domestic calls. Phone rates typically tend to be highest in the morning, lower in the evening, and lowest on Sunday and late at night. Rates are significantly higher when dialing from payphones, so use a private line when you can.

CELLULAR PHONES

Cellular phones (*telefonini*) are both convenient and inexpensive for longer visits. You can either join a monthly plan or opt to pay as you go through the **GSM** system; for this second option you will need a **GSM-compatible phone** and a **SIM (subscriber identity module) card,** a country-specific, thumbnail-sized chip (prepaid) that gives you a local phone number and plugs you into the local network.

As with prepaid, the greatest expense in a monthly plan is the purchase of the phone itself, though calls to other phones on the same company's plan are around €0.15 per min. and incoming calls are free. The three main phone companies, **Vodafone Omnitel** (from Italy ☎ 800 10 01 95 or 420 05 from a Vodafone cellphone; www.omnitel.it), **Wind** (☎ 800 915 800 or 155 from a Wind cellphone; www.wind.it), and **Tim** (from Italy ☎ 800 555 333 or 800 61 96 19, from abroad 393 39 91 19; www.tim.it), sell phone plans. Companies like **Cellular Abroad** (www.cellular-abroad.com) rent cell phones that work in a variety of destinations around the world, providing a simpler option than picking up a phone in-country.

> **GSM PHONES.** Just having a GSM phone doesn't mean you're good to go when traveling abroad. The majority of GSM phones sold in the United States operate on a different **frequency** (1900) than international phones (900/1800) and will not work abroad. Tri-band phones work on all three frequencies (900/1800/1900) and operate through most of the world. Some GSM phones are **SIM-locked** and only accept SIM cards from a single carrier. You'll need a **SIM-unlocked** phone to use a SIM card from a local carrier when you travel.

TIME DIFFERENCES

Italy is one hour ahead of **Greenwich Mean Time (GMT).** Daylight Saving Time starts on the last Sunday in March, when clocks are moved ahead 1hr. Clocks are put back an hour on the last Sunday in September.

4AM	7AM	12PM	1PM	8PM	10PM
Vancouver	Toronto		Italy	China	Sydney
Seattle	Ottawa	London	Paris	Hong Kong	Canberra
San Francisco	New York	(GMT)	Munich	Manila	Melbourne
Los Angeles	Boston		Madrid	Singapore	

With prices so low, you might *actually* call home.

rates as low as

6.5¢ per minute

Rate based upon calls within the contiguous United States and is subject to change. For full list of rates visit IsCard.com.

Toll free access from over 50 countries.
No connection fees, no monthly fees, no hidden fees.
Low per minute rates with no additional surcharges.
Crystal clear clarity using Tier-1 digital carriers.
24x7 secure online account management.
Auto-recharge your account and travel worry free.
Pay with cash option using Western Union SwiftPay®.
SwiftPay is a registered trademark of Western Union.

Special Offer For Lets Go Readers:
Use promo code LETSIT05 when you sign up and get up to $50* in free calling time.
*FREE time will be added as a 20% bonus on your prepaid IsCard account.

To sign up or for more information,
please visit www.IsCard.com or call toll free 1 866 MY ISCARD
1 866 694 7227

IsCard

IsCard
International
Calling Card

1-866-MYISCARD
www.iscard.com

BY EMAIL AND INTERNET

Internet points in large cities swell with locals and backpackers using email and instant messaging services. Rural areas and cities in the south are catching up. Rates range €5-8 per hour. For free Internet access, try local universities and libraries. Or save time and try a combo Internet-laundry point or a cyber cafe.

Though in some places it's possible to forge a remote link with your home server, in most cases this is a much slower (and thus more expensive) option than free **web-based email accounts** (e.g., www.hotmail.com and www.yahoo.com). **Internet cafes** and the occasional free Internet terminal at a public library or university are listed in the **Practical Information** sections of major cities. For lists of cybercafes in Italy, check out www.ecs.net/cafe/#list and www.cybercaptive.com.

ACCOMMODATIONS

HOSTELS

While hostel quality and services vary widely within Italy, hostels remain the cheapest and best accommodations options for budget travelers. Many are located far from city centers and have rules governing length of stay and hours of room access. However, for travelers merely looking for a place to stash their pack while they explore the surrounding area or crash for the night, Italian hostels are generally well-regulated and safe. Most are laid out dorm-style, often with large single-sex rooms and bunk beds, although private rooms that sleep two to four are becoming more common. They sometimes have kitchens and utensils for guest use, bike or moped rentals, storage areas, transportation to airports, breakfast and other meals, laundry facilities, and Internet access. Often bed linens are included and towels are available for rent. There can be drawbacks: some hostels close during daytime "lockout" hours, have a curfew, don't accept reservations, impose a maximum stay, or, less frequently, require that you do chores. In Italy, a dorm bed in a hostel will average around €8-20 and a private room €40.

A HOSTELER'S BILL OF RIGHTS. There are certain standard features that we do not include in our hostel listings. Unless we state otherwise, you can expect that every hostel has no lockout, no curfew, a kitchen, free hot showers, some system of secure luggage storage, and no key deposit.

HOSTELLING INTERNATIONAL

Joining the youth hostel association in your own country (listed below) automatically grants you membership privileges in **Hostelling International (HI),** a federation of national hosteling associations. Non-HI members may rarely be allowed to stay in some hostels, but will have to pay extra to do so. Membership cards are often available at individual hostels. Where applicable, we have listed HI restrictions and membership card availability. Websites like HI's webpage (www.hihostels.com), www.hostels.com, and www.hostelplanet.com are a good place to begin your hostel research. The Italian Youth Hostels Association operates a website in English and Italian, www.ostellionline.org, with images, maps, descriptions and rates of hostels you can book online.

Most HI hostels also honor guest memberships—you'll get a blank card with space for six validation stamps. Each night you'll pay a nonmember supplement (one-sixth the membership fee) and earn one guest stamp; get six stamps, and

ESSENTIALS

you're a member. This system generally works well, but sometimes you may need to remind the hostel reception. A new membership benefit is the FreeNites program, which allows hostelers to gain points toward free rooms by simply staying the night or having dinner in an HI hostel. Most student travel agencies (p. 24) sell HI cards, as do all of the national hosteling organizations listed below. All prices listed below are valid for **one-year memberships** unless otherwise noted.

Australian Youth Hostels Association (AYHA), 422 Kent St., Sydney, NSW 200 (☎02 926 111 11; www.yha.com.au). AUS$52, under 18 AUS$19.

Hostelling International-Canada (HI-C), 205 Catherine St. #400, Ottawa, ON K2P 1C3 (☎613 237 78 84; www.hihostels.ca). CDN$35, under 18 free.

An Óige (Irish Youth Hostel Association), 61 Mountjoy St., Dublin 7 (☎830 45 55; www.irelandyha.org). €20, under 18 €10.

Hostelling International Northern Ireland (HINI), 22 Donegal Rd., Belfast BT12 5JN (☎02890 31 54 35; www.hini.org.uk). UK£13, under 18 UK£6.

Youth Hostels Association of New Zealand (YHANZ), Level 1, Moorhouse City, 166 Moorhouse Ave., P.O. Box 436, Christchurch (☎0800 27 82 99, NZ only, or 03 379 99 70; www.yha.org.nz). NZ$40, under 18 free.

Scottish Youth Hostels Association (SYHA), 7 Glebe Cres., Stirling FK8 2JA (☎01786 89 14 00; www.syha.org.uk). UK£6, under 17 £2.50.

Youth Hostels Association (England and Wales), Trevelyan House, Dimple Rd., Matlock, Derbyshire DE4 3YH, UK (☎0870 770 88 68; www.yha.org.uk). UK£14, under 18 UK£6.

Hostelling International-USA, 8401 Colesville Rd., Ste. 600, Silver Spring, MD 20910 (☎301 495 12 40; www.hiayh.org). US$28, under 18 free.

BOOKING HOSTELS ONLINE. One of the easiest ways to ensure you've got a bed for the night is by reserving online. Click to the **Hostelworld** booking engine through **www.letsgo.com**, and you'll have access to bargain accommodations from Argentina to Zimbabwe with no added commission.

OTHER TYPES OF ACCOMMODATIONS

HOTELS, GUESTHOUSES, AND PENSIONS

A hotel single (*singola*) in Italy costs about US$30-60 (€25-50) per night, a double (*doppia* or *matrimoniale*) US$50-100 (€40-82). You'll typically share a hall bathroom; a private bathroom will cost extra, as may hot showers. Prices often fluctuate according to season, rising steeply during the summer months and over the New Year. Some hotels offer *pensione completa* (all meals) and *mezza pensione* (no dinner); in high season hotel owners often require guests to take some form of *pensione*. Upon arrival be sure to confirm charges; many Italian hotels are notorious for tacking on additional costs at check-out time. If you make reservations in writing, indicate your night of arrival and the number of nights you plan to stay. The hotel will send you a confirmation and may request payment for the first night. Often it is easiest to make reservations over the phone with a credit card. For phone reservations keep track of who you spoke with and call to confirm a few days before your scheduled arrival; some reception desks are wary of no-shows and give away reserved rooms last minute. Not all hotels take reservations, and few accept checks in foreign currency, while most do accept Visa and Mastercard.

Rooms for rent in private homes (*affittacamere*) are inexpensive, usually good for groups of two to four, and a great way to practice Italian and immerse yourself in the culture. Where these are available, *Let's Go* lists pertinent names and contact information. For more information inquire at local tourist offices.

the new way to go on holiday

welcome
to the new gateway
for world
travelling

Book Hostels all over the World!

Hostelsclub provides budget travellers and backpackers with an online booking engine for destinations all over the world:

Europe, North America, South America, Asia, Oceania, and Africa

You can make secure, guaranteed bookings for hostels, hotels and camping grounds for thousands of locations in just minutes.

www.hostelsclub.com

LONG-TERM ACCOMMODATIONS

Travelers planning to stay in Italy for extended periods of time may find it most cost-effective to rent an **apartment.** A basic one-bedroom apartment in Rome ranges from around €1,000-€1500 per month. Besides the rent itself, prospective tenants usually are also required to front a security deposit (frequently one month's rent). For more information check out www.liveinrome.com or www.romepower.com.

CAMPING AND THE OUTDOORS

There are over 1700 campsites in Italy. Fees are small, variable, and usually issued per person. Contact local tourist offices for information about suitable or free campsites. Camping on undesignated land is not permitted. The **Touring Club Italiano** (www.touringclub.it) publishes numerous useful books and pamphlets on the outdoors. The **Federazione Italiana del Campeggio e del Caravanning** (Federcampeggio), 50041 Calenzano, Florence (☎ 055 88 23 91; www.federcampeggio.it), has a complete list of camping sites with free location maps. Federcampeggio also publishes the book *Guida Camping d'Italia*. **EasyCamping** (www.icaro.it/home_e.html) offers information about over 700 campsites throughout Italy. For a list of the bigger parks and national reserves in the country, visit www.parks.it.

USEFUL PUBLICATIONS AND RESOURCES

A variety of companies publish hiking guidebooks to meet the educational needs of novices and experts. Contact the publishers listed below for free information about camping, hiking, and biking. Campers heading to multiple destinations across Europe should consider buying an **International Camping Carnet** (US$10-15).

Similar to a hostel membership card, it's required at a few campgrounds and provides discounts at others. Available in North America from the Family Campers and RVers Association and in the UK from The Caravan Club.

Automobile Association, Contact Centre, Car Ellison House, William Armstrong Dr., Newcastle-upon-Tyne, NE4 7YA, UK (general info ☎0870 600 03 71; www.theaa.co.uk). Road atlases for Europe, France, Germany, Italy, and Spain.

The Caravan Club, East Grinstead House, East Grinstead, West Sussex, RH19 1UA, UK (☎01342 32 69 44; www.caravanclub.co.uk). For UK£31 members receive equipment discounts, a directory, and a handbook. Limited benefits for non-UK members.

Sierra Club Books, 85 Second St., 2nd fl., San Francisco, CA 94105, USA (☎415 977 55 00; www.sierraclub.org/books). Publishes general resource books on hiking and camping and for women traveling in the outdoors.

The Mountaineers Books, 1001 SW Klickitat Way, #201, Seattle, WA 98134, USA (☎206 223 63 03; www.mountaineersbooks.org). Over 400 titles on hiking, biking, mountaineering, natural history, and conservation.

WILDERNESS SAFETY

Stay warm, stay dry, and stay hydrated. Follow this simple advice to avoid the vast majority of life-threatening wilderness situations. Prepare yourself for an emergency, however, by always packing raingear, a hat and mittens, a first-aid kit, a reflector, a whistle, high energy food, and extra water for any hike. Dress in wool or warm layers of synthetic materials designed for the outdoors; never rely on cotton for warmth, as it is useless when wet. Check **weather forecasts** and pay attention to the skies when hiking, since weather patterns can change suddenly. Whenever possible, let someone know when and where you are hiking—either a

daphne inn ⑂

aphne is a new way to stay in Rome. We combine elegant accommodations with personalized ervice to give you a more complete travel experience.

njoy air-conditioned rooms and really comfortable beds, wonderfully located in the historic enter. You will find fresh fruit and pastries with your coffee in the morning, wireless Internet ervice, and a cell phone to use during your visit with us.

wo locations at Piazza Barberini, 5-10 minutes' walk from the Trevi Fountain and the Spanish teps. Both are on quiet side streets, with wonderful shopping and dining nearby.

lease be aware that the facilities are 100% non-smoking.

aphne Trevi: via degli Avignonesi, 20 · Daphne Veneto: via di san Basilio 55 friend, your hostel manager, a park ranger, or a local hiking organization. Do not attempt a hike beyond your ability—you may be endangering your life. For information about outdoor ailments and basic medical concerns (see **Health**, p. 17).

CAMPING AND HIKING EQUIPMENT

WHAT TO BUY...

Sleeping bag: Most sleeping bags are rated by season ("summer" means 30-40°F at night; "four-season" or "winter" often means below 0°F). They are made either of **down** (warmer and lighter, but more expensive, and miserable when wet; US$250-300) or of **synthetic** material (heavier, more durable, and warmer when wet; US$80-210). **Sleeping bag pads** include foam pads (US$10-20), air mattresses (US$15-50), and self-inflating pads (US$45-80). Bring a **stuff sack** to store your bag and keep it dry.

Tent: The best tents are free-standing (with their own frames and suspension systems), can be set up quickly, and only require staking in high winds. Low-profile dome tents are best. Good 2-person tents start at US$90, 4-person at US$300. Use a groundcloth and seal the seams of your tent with waterproofer and make sure it has a rain fly.

Backpack: Internal-frame packs mold more effectively to your back, keep a lower center of gravity, and flex adequately to allow you to hike difficult trails. **External-frame packs** are more comfortable for long hikes over even terrain, as they keep weight higher and distribute it more evenly. Make sure your pack has a strong, padded hip-belt to transfer weight to your legs. Any serious backpacking requires a pack of at least 4000 in.^{3} (16,000cc), plus 500 in.^{3} for sleeping bags in internal-frame packs. Sturdy backpacks cost anywhere from US$125-420, and this is one area in which it doesn't pay to economize. Either buy a **waterproof backpack cover** or store all of your belongings in plastic bags inside your pack.

Boots: Be sure to wear hiking boots with good **ankle support.** They should fit snugly and comfortably over 1-2 pairs of wool socks and thin liner socks. Break in boots over several weeks in order to spare yourself painful and debilitating blisters while hiking.

Other necessities: Synthetic layers, like those made of polypropylene, and a **pile jacket** will keep you warm even when wet. A **"space blanket"** (US$5-15) will help you to retain your body heat and doubles as a groundcloth. Plastic **water bottles** are virtually shatter- and leak-proof. Bring **water-purification tablets** for when you can't boil water. For those places that forbid fires or the gathering of firewood (virtually every organized campground in Italy), you'll need a **camp stove** (the classic Coleman starts at US$40) and a propane-filled **fuel bottle** to operate it. Also don't forget a **first-aid kit, pocketknife, insect repellent, calamine lotion,** and **waterproof matches** or a **lighter.**

...AND WHERE TO BUY IT

The mail-order/online companies listed below offer lower prices than many retail stores, but a visit to a local camping or outdoors store will give you a good sense of the look and weight of certain items.

Campmor, P.O. Box 700, Upper Saddle River, NJ 07458, USA (☎800 525 47 84; www.campmor.com).

Discount Camping, 880 Main North Rd., Pooraka, South Australia 5095, Australia (☎08 8262 33 99; www.discountcamping.com.au).

Eastern Mountain Sports (EMS), (☎888 463 63 67 or 603 924 72 31; www.shopems.com).

L.L. Bean, Freeport, ME 04033, USA (US and Canada ☎800 341 43 41, UK 0800 89 12 97; outside US 207 552 68 78; www.llbean.com).

ESSENTIALS

Mountain Designs, 51 Bishop St., Kelvin Grove, Queensland 4059, Australia (☎07 3856 2344; www.mountaindesigns.com).

Recreational Equipment, Inc. (REI), Sumner, WA 98352, USA (☎800 426 48 40, outside US 253 891 25 00; www.rei.com).

ORGANIZED OUTDOOR TRIPS

Organized adventure tours offer another way to explore the wild. Activities include hiking, biking, skiing, canoeing, climbing, and archaeological digs. For example, should you choose to brave the hike through Stromboli Volcano, **Magmatrek** (p. 664), V. V. Emanuele, can provide guided trips. Tourism bureaus often can suggest parks, trails, and outfitters. Organizations that specialize in camping and outdoor equipment like REI and EMS (see above) are good sources for info.

SPECIFIC CONCERNS

RESPONSIBLE TRAVEL

As the number of travelers on the road continues to rise, the detrimental effect they can have on natural environments becomes an increasing concern. With this in mind, *Let's Go* promotes the philosophy of **sustainable travel.** Through a sensitivity to issues of ecology and sustainability, today's travelers can be a powerful force in preserving and restoring the places they visit.

Ecotourism, a rising trend in sustainable travel, focuses on the conservation of natural habitats and using them to build up the economy without exploitation or overdevelopment. Travelers can make a difference by doing advance research and by supporting organizations and establishments that pay attention to their impact on their natural surroundings and strive to be environmentally-friendly.

Hotel Trentina

- Friendly atmosphere and helpful staff in an intimate 11-room hotel
- Rich buffet breakfast included
- Easily metro accessible
- All rooms include bathrooms, television, air-conditioning, and telephone
- Spacious triple, quadruple, and quintuple rooms from only 30 euros per person

Via Filippino Lippi, 50
(ang.Piazza Aspromonte)
20131 Milano (MI) Italy
Tel. +39.02.23.61.208
+39.02.23.61.326
Fax +39.02.23.61.297
www.htrentina.it
e-mail: trentina@htrentina.it

ESSENTIALS

The impact of tourism on the destinations you visit should not be underestimated. The choices you make during your trip can have potent effects on local communities—for better or for worse. Travelers who care about the destinations and environments they explore should become aware of the political, social, and cultural implications of the choices they make when they travel.

Community-based tourism aims to channel tourism into the local economy by emphasizing tours and cultural programs run by members of the host community which often benefit disadvantaged groups. An excellent resource for information on community-based travel is *The Good Alternative Travel Guide* (UK£10), a project of **Tourism Concern** (☎ 020 713 333 30; www.tourismconcern.org.uk).

INDIVIDUAL CONCERNS

TRAVELING ALONE

There are many benefits to traveling alone, including independence and greater interaction with locals. On the other hand, any solo traveler is a more vulnerable target of harassment and street theft. As a lone traveler, try not to stand out as a tourist, look confident, and be especially careful in deserted or very crowded areas. If questioned, never admit that you are traveling alone. Maintain regular contact with someone at home who knows your itinerary. For more tips, pick up *Traveling Solo* by Eleanor Berman (Globe Pequot Press, US$18), visit www.travelaloneandloveit.com, or subscribe to **Connecting: Solo Travel Network,** 689 Park Rd., Unit 6, Gibsons, BC V0N 1V7, Canada (☎ 604 886 90 99; www.cstn.org; membership US$28-45).

WOMEN TRAVELERS

Women exploring on their own inevitably face some additional safety concerns. Consider staying in hostels which offer single rooms that lock from the inside or in religious organizations with rooms for women only. Stick to centrally located accommodations and avoid solitary late-night treks or metro rides.

Always carry extra money for a phone call, bus, or taxi. **Hitchhiking** is never safe for lone women, or even for two women traveling together. Look as if you know where you're going and approach older women or couples for directions if you're lost or uncomfortable. Generally, the less you look like a tourist, the better off you'll be. Dress conservatively, especially in rural areas. Wearing a conspicuous **wedding band** sometimes helps to prevent unwanted overtures.

Your best answer to verbal harassment is no answer at all; feigning deafness, sitting motionless, and staring straight ahead at nothing in particular will do a world of good that reactions usually don't achieve. The extremely persistent can sometimes be dissuaded by a firm "Go away!" Don't hesitate to seek out a police officer or a passerby if you are being harassed. Memorize the emergency numbers in places you visit, and consider carrying a whistle on your keychain. A self-defense course will both prepare you for a potential attack and raise your level of awareness of your surroundings (see **Self Defense,** p. 19). Also be sure you are aware of the health concerns that women face when traveling (p. 22).

GLBT TRAVELERS

It is difficult to generalize the Italian attitude toward gay, lesbian, bisexual, and transgendered (GLBT) travelers. Some areas are accepting of alternative relationships while other areas remain considerably homophobic. Rome, Florence, Milan, and Bologna all have easily accessible gay scenes. Away from the larger cities, however, gay social life may be difficult to find. Moreover, in small towns, particularly in the south, explicit public displays of affection

ESSENTIALS

between same-sex partners will likely evoke shock. The monthly *Babilonia* and annual *Guida Gay Italia*, the national homosexual magazines which confront gay issues and list social events, are sold at most newsstands. Travelers can also expect the larger cities to have gay *discoteche* and bars (listed in *Let's Go*). The **Italian Gay and Lesbian Yellow Pages** (www.gay.it/guida/italia/info.htm) lists gay bars, hotels, and shops.

To avoid hassles at airports and border crossings, transgendered travelers should make sure that all of their travel documents consistently report the same gender. Many countries (including Australia, Canada, Ireland, New Zealand, the UK, and the US) will amend the passports of post-operative transsexuals to reflect their true gender, although governments are generally less willing to amend documents for pre-operative transsexuals and other transgendered individuals. Listed below are contact organizations, mail-order bookstores, and publishers that offer materials addressing some specific concerns. **Out and About** (www.planetout.com) offers a bi-weekly newsletter addressing travel concerns and a comprehensive site addressing gay travel concerns. The online newspaper **365gay.com** also has a travel section (www.365gay.com/travel/travelchannel.htm).

ARCI-GAY and ARCI-Lesbica, P. di Porta Saragozza, 2, 40123 Bologna (☎051 644 70 54; www.malox.com/arcigay/link.htm); V. Orvinio, 2, 00199 Rome (☎06 863 851 12); V. dei Mille, 23, Rome (☎06 446 58 39). The national organizations for homosexuals hold group discussions, dances, and many special events. Their website contains addresses and phone numbers of many city centers.

Gay's the Word, 66 Marchmont St., London WC1N 1AB, UK (☎20 727 876 54; www.gaystheword.co.uk). The largest gay and lesbian bookshop in the UK, with both fiction and non-fiction titles. Mail-order service available.

Giovanni's Room, 1145 Pine St., Philadelphia, PA 19107, USA (☎215 923 29 60; www.queerbooks.com). An international lesbian/feminist and gay bookstore with mail-order service (carries many of the publications listed below).

International Lesbian and Gay Association (ILGA), 81 rue Marché-au-Charbon, B-1000 Brussels, Belgium (☎2 502 24 71; www.ilga.org). Provides political information, such as homosexuality laws of individual countries.

FURTHER READING: GLBT TRAVEL.
Spartacus 2004-2005: International Gay Guide. Bruno Gmunder Verlag (US$33).
Damron Accommodations Guide, Damron City Guide, and *Damron Women's Traveller.* Damron Travel Guides (US$11-19). For info, call ☎800 462 66 54 or visit www.damron.com.
Ferrari Guides' Gay Travel A to Z, Ferrari Guides' Men's Travel in Your Pocket, Ferrari Guides' Women's Travel in Your Pocket, and *Ferrari Guides' Inn Places.* Ferrari Publications (US$16-20).
The Gay Vacation Guide: The Best Trips and How to Plan Them, Mark Chesnut. Kensington Books (US$15).

TRAVELERS WITH DISABILITIES

Those with disabilities should inform airlines and hotels of their disabilities when making reservations; some time may be needed to prepare special accommodations. Call ahead to restaurants, museums, and other facilities to find out if they are handicapped-accessible. Many museums and famed landmarks are not wheelchair accessible. Venice is especially difficult to navigate. Although Italy no longer requires animals entering the country to be quarantined, **guide dog owners** must provide a certificate of immunization against rabies and a certificate of health from their veterinarian. In the wake of Foot and Mouth Disease, travelers from Great Britain and Ireland may meet resistance if attempting to bring a guide animal into Italy. **Rail** is the most convenient form of travel for disabled travelers in Italy. Many stations have ramps, and some trains, such as the Pendolino, the Eurostar, and InterCity, have wheelchair lifts, special seating areas, and specially equipped toilets. Hand-controlled vehicles are not currently offered in Italy by car rental companies. For those who wish to rent cars, some major car rental agencies (Avis, Hertz, and National) offer hand-controlled vehicles.

USEFUL ORGANIZATIONS

Access Abroad, www.umabroad.umn.edu/access. A website devoted to making study abroad available to students with disabilities. The site is maintained by Disability Services Research and Training, University of Minnesota, University Gateway, Ste. 180, 200 Oak St. SE, Minneapolis, MN 55455, USA (☎612 626 13 33).

Accessible Journeys, 35 West Sellers Ave., Ridley Park, PA 19078, USA (☎800 846 45 37; www.disabilitytravel.com). Designs tours for wheelchair users and slow walkers. The site has tips and forums for all travelers.

Directions Unlimited, 123 Green Ln., Bedford Hills, NY 10507, USA (☎800 533 53 43). Books individual vacations for the physically disabled; not an info service.

Flying Wheels, 143 W. Bridge St., P.O. Box 382, Owatonna, MN 55060, USA (☎507 451 50 05; www.flyingheelstravel.com). Specializes in escorted trips to Europe for people with physical disabilities; plans custom accessible trips worldwide.

Society for Accessible Travel & Hospitality (SATH), 347 Fifth Ave., #610, New York, NY 10016, USA (☎212 447 72 84; www.sath.org). An advocacy group that publishes free online travel information and the travel magazine *OPEN WORLD* (annual subscription US$13, free for members). Annual membership US$45, students and seniors US$30.

MINORITY TRAVELERS

Particularly in the south, minority travelers or members of non-Christian religions may feel unwelcome. In terms of safety, there is no easy answer. Women may be seen as exotic but not unwelcome. Travel in groups and avoid unsafe parts of town. The best answer to verbal harassment is often not to acknowledge it.

DIETARY CONCERNS

While there are only a few strictly vegetarian restaurants in Italy, it is not difficult to find vegetarian meals. Check out the **A.V.I. Italian Vegetarian Association** (www.vegetariani.it/vegetarismo/ristoranti.htm). The travel section of the The Vegetarian Resource Group's website, at www.vrg.org/travel, has a list of websites that are geared toward helping vegetarians and vegans traveling abroad. For more info, visit your local bookstore or health food store, and consult *The Vegetarian Traveler: Where to Stay if You're Vegetarian, Vegan, Environmentally Sensitive,* by Jed and Susan Civic (Larson Publications; US$16).

Lactose intolerance does not have to be an obstacle to eating well. Though it may seem like everybody in Italy but you is devouring pizza and gelato, there are ways for even the lactose intolerant to indulge in local cuisine. In restaurants ask for items without *latte* (milk), *formaggio* (cheese), *burro* (butter), or *crema* (cream). Or order the cheeseless delicacy, *pizza marinara.*

Travelers who keep kosher should contact synagogues in larger cities for info on kosher restaurants. Your own synagogue or college Hillel should have access to lists of Jewish institutions across the nation. If you are strict in your observance, you may have to prepare your own food on the road. A good resource is the *Jew-*

ish Travel Guide, edited by Michael Zaidner (Vallentine Mitchell; US$18); another is the kosher restaurant database at http://shamash.org/kosher/. Travelers looking for halal restaurants may find www.zabihah.com a useful resource.

OTHER RESOURCES

Let's Go tries to cover all aspects of budget travel, but we can't put *everything* in our guides. Listed below are books and websites that can serve as jumping-off points for your own research.

USEFUL PUBLICATIONS

Hippocrene Books, Inc., 171 Madison Ave., New York, NY 10016, USA (☎718 454 23 66; www.hippocrenebooks.com). Publishes foreign language dictionaries and language learning guides.

Hunter Publishing, P.O. Box 746, Walpole, MA 02081, USA (☎800 255 03 43; www.hunterpublishing.com). Has an extensive catalog of travel guides and diving and adventure travel books.

Rand McNally, P.O. Box 7600, Chicago, IL 60680, USA (☎847 329 81 00; www.rand-mcnally.com). Publishes road atlases.

Adventurous Traveler Bookstore, 702 H Street NW, Suite 200, Washington, D.C. 20001, USA (☎202 654 80 17; www.adventuroustraveler.com). A division of Amazon specializing in books and maps featuring travel and outdoor recreation.

Bon Voyage!, 2069 W. Bullard Ave., Fresno, CA 93711, USA (☎800 995 97 16, from abroad 559 447 84 41; www.bon-voyage-travel.com). Free newsletter.

Travel Books & Language Center, Inc., 4437 Wisconsin Ave. NW, Washington, D.C. 20016, USA (☎800 220 26 65; www.bookweb.org/bookstore/travelbks). Over 60,000 titles from around the world.

WORLD WIDE WEB

Almost every aspect of budget travel is accessible via the web. In 10min. at the keyboard, you can make a hostel reservation, get advice on travel hot spots from other travelers, or find out how much a train from Rome to Milan costs.

Listed here are some regional and travel-related sites to start off your surfing; other relevant web sites are listed throughout the book. Because website turnover is high, use search engines (such as www.google.com) to strike out on your own.

THE ART OF TRAVEL

Italian Bookstore: www.italianbookstore.com. A great website with everything from italian travel guides to Italian children's books.

How to See the World: www.artoftravel.com. A compendium of great travel tips, from cheap flights to self defense to interacting with local culture.

Travel Library: www.travel-library.com. A fantastic set of links for general information and personal travelogues.

Backpacker's Ultimate Guide: www.bugeurope.com. Tips on packing, transportation, and where to go. Also tons of country-specific travel information.

Travel Intelligence: www.travelintelligence.net. A large collection of travel writing by distinguished travel writers.

World Hum: www.worldhum.com. An independently produced collection of "travel dispatches from a shrinking planet."

BootsnAll.com: www.bootsnall.com. Numerous resources for independent travelers, from planning your trip to reporting on it when you get back.

INFORMATION ON ITALY

CIA World Factbook: www.odci.gov/cia/publications/factbook/index.html. Tons of vital statistics on Italy's geography, government, economy, and people.

Geographia: www.geographia.com. Highlights, culture, and people of Italy.

Atevo Travel: www.atevo.com/guides/destinations. Detailed introductions, travel tips, and suggested itineraries.

World Travel Guide: www.travel-guides.com. Helpful practical info.

TravelPage: www.travelpage.com. Links to official tourist office sites in Italy.

PlanetRider: www.planetrider.com. A subjective list of links to the "best" websites covering the culture and tourist attractions of Italy.

 WWW.LETSGO.COM Our freshly redesigned website features extensive content from our guides; community forums where travelers can connect with each other and ask questions or advice—as well as share stories and tips; and expanded resources to help you plan your trip. Visit us soon to browse by destination, find information about ordering our titles, and sign up for our e-newsletter!

ESSENTIALS

LIFE AND TIMES

It is difficult to define one Italy, to call Italians one people and describe a single national culture. The empire built by the Romans defines the country's legacy. Technical, military, and artistic innovations have not simply survived the centuries, but still form the foundation of modern civilization. Latin became the language of choice for intellectuals and gave the world a common tongue. The Catholic Church, the empire's partner power, has reigned supreme from Rome for almost 2000 years, diffusing Christianity across every corner of the world. Establishment is not always pretty, however. In modern days, Mussolini's dreams of Fascist conquest, the country's strict adherence to Catholic customs in the face of changing collective world values, and the delay of complete women's suffrage until 1945 all demonstrate a nation where community values rest firmly upon past traditions. Yet neither the Romans nor the Risorgimento have succeeded in completely uniting the varied regions, and today, desires for increased autonomy are evident in the continuing tensions between North and South. Citizens retain a fierce independence undampened by centuries of foreign rulers, continuing to discard their governments at the drop of a hat, to speak in regional dialects, and to strike in order to effect social change. The disparities between cosmopolitan Milan and traditional lifestyles found in tiny *paesi* highlight Italy's often painful transition from world-class empire to small nation on the edge of Europe, heavily bolstered by a tourism dependent upon past successes. Italy's present is a constant negotiation between progress and tradition, independence and unity, as it endeavors to transform its past triumphs into an equally glorious future.

HISTORY AND POLITICS

ITALY BEFORE ROME (UNTIL 753 BC)

Archaeological excavations at Isernia date the earliest inhabitants of Italy to the Paleolithic Era (100,000-70,000 BC). The Bronze Age brought more sophisticated settlements, and by the 7th century BC, the **Etruscans** had established themselves in their present-day Tuscan stronghold. At their height, the Etruscans controlled Italian and western Mediterranean trade. *Nuraghi* (cone-shaped structures built out of stone with no mortar) are unique to Sardinia and are the remaining evidence of the Nuraghic people, who lived on the island around the 16th century BC and inhabited Sardinia for over 1000 years, until conquered by the Carthaginians. Although not much is known about this people, their buildings are a testament to their architectural ingenuity. Growing **Greek** influence along the Mediterranean coast, however, began to check the rise of the Etruscans. Forming what the Romans would later call **Magna Graecia,** the Greeks started to establish colonies along the Puglian coast around 800 BC, at Cumae in Campania, throughout Calabria, and at Syracuse in eastern Sicily. Western Sicily had already been conquered by the Phoenicians from Carthage in Northern Africa, and remained in their hands despite Greek attempts to conquer the entire island. Greek city-states gradually gained naval supremacy over their Etruscan competitors, but by the 3rd century BC, the power of both Greeks and Etruscans declined as another force swelled in the central mainland: the Romans.

ANCIENT ROME (753 BC-AD 476)

THE MONARCHY (753-509 BC)

As immortalized in Virgil's *Aeneid*, Roman history begins around 1200 BC with **Aeneas,** a Trojan hero who led his tribe from the ruins of Troy to the Tiber valley where his son Ascanius founded the city of Alba Longa. Legend claims that one of Rome's Vestal Virgins (the seven priestesses of the Eternal Flame) gave birth to twins **Romulus** and **Remus** in Alba Longa after losing her virginity to Mars, the god of war. In a fury over the shame she brought to the family name, her father killed her and left the children to die on a mountaintop. A she-wolf found and nursed the babes; the trio is commonly represented in artwork throughout Italy (famously in a sculpture dating to 500 BC, in the Musei Capitolini, p. 126). In 753 BC the wolf-suckled twins, purported descendants of Aeneas, founded Rome. Angered at an insult from Remus, Romulus killed his brother and became Rome's first king. The city was named in Romulus's honor, and he held sway over a territorially ambitious and highly patriarchal society (women were put to death for drinking wine) until disappearing mysteriously after 37 years on the throne. The Etruscan kings nudged their way into power, and by 616 BC, the **Tarquin dynasty** had become infamous for its tyranny. After Prince Sextus Tarquinius raped **Lucretia,** her husband Lucius Brutus expelled the Tarquins and established the **Roman Republic.**

THE REPUBLIC (509-27 BC)

The end of the monarchy and the foundation of the Republic led to new questions of equality and rights. The Republic faced social struggles between the upper-class **patricians,** who enjoyed full participation in the Senate, and the middle- and lower-class **plebeians,** who were denied political involvement. In 450 BC the **Laws of the Twelve Tables,** the first codified Roman laws, helped contain the struggle, guaranteeing the plebeians a voice in public affairs. The Romans subjugated their Italian neighbors, culminating in the defeat of the Etruscans at Veii, which achieved a near-total unification of the Italian peninsula.

Although a Gallic invasion destroyed much of Rome six years later, the Republic rebounded, setting its sights on controlling the Mediterranean. It fought its most important battles, the three **Punic Wars** (264-146 BC), against the North African city of Carthage in modern Tunisia. After the successful Punic campaign came victories over the Greek successors of Alexander the Great, with Greece, Asia Minor, and Egypt becoming new additions to the Republic. Rome stood supreme and the *Pax Romana* (Roman peace) brought prosperity and stability. But this prosperity came at a steep cost; the spoils of war that enriched Rome actually undermined its stability by creating class inequality. By 131 BC the plebeians were tired of being appeased with little bread and few circuses. Demands for land redistribution led to riots against the patrician class, and then to the **Social War** in 91 BC. The patrician general **Sulla** marched on Rome in 82 BC, defeated his rivals, and quickly reorganized the constitution to name himself dictator and institute social reforms.

In 73 BC **Spartacus,** an escaped gladiatorial slave, led an army of 70,000 slaves and impoverished farmers on a two-year rampage down the peninsula. Sulla's close associates **Marcus Crassus** and **Pompey the Great** quelled the uprising and took control of Rome. They joined forces with **Julius Caesar,** the conqueror of Gaul, but this association rapidly fell apart. By 45 BC Caesar had defeated his "allies" and emerged as the leader of the Republic, naming himself Dictator for Life. A small faction of disgruntled back-stabbers assassinated the reform-oriented leader on the Ides (15th) of March, 44 BC. The coup rid Rome of a tyrant, but earned a place

LIFE AND TIMES

in Dante's *Inferno* for participant **Brutus,** and rather than solve problems, Caesar's death created a power vacuum as would-be successors struggled for the helm. In 31 BC Octavian, Caesar's clever adopted heir, emerged victorious, and was deified with the title of **Augustus** in 27 BC.

THE EMPIRE (27 BC-AD 476)

All roads lead to Rome because all roads left from Rome. As the center of the world's largest and most powerful empire, Rome's sway reached as far as modern Britain in the north and Iran in the east. With political power and economic prosperity came a cultural apogee, as the civilization and language made a lasting impact on even the most obscure places they penetrated.

Augustus was the first of the empire's **Julio-Claudian** rulers (27 BC-AD 68). Using Republican traditions as a facade, he governed not as king, but as *princeps* (first citizen). His principate (27 BC-AD 14) is considered the golden age of Rome. Augustus extended Roman law and civic culture, beautifying the city and reorganizing its administration. Meanwhile, poets and authors reinvigorated Latin literature, creating works to rival the great Greek epics (p. 63). In this period rampant corruption, scandal, and decadence thrived, with frequent festivals and gladiatorial *munera*, or spectacles. Too much merrymaking led Augustus to exile his own promiscuous daughter, **Julia** (38 BC-AD 14), as well as **Ovid** (43 BC-AD 17), the poet who sang of love, not war.

During and after the reigns of **Caligula** (37-41) and **Nero** (54-68), both infamous for lunacy, the empire continued to expand, despite a series of civil wars following Nero's death in AD 68. The **Flavian** dynasty (69-96) ushered in a period of prosperity, extended to new heights by **Trajan** (98-117), who invaded the borders of the Black Sea, including modern Romania. The empire reached astounding geographical limits, encompassing Western Europe, the Mediterranean islands, England, North Africa, and part of Asia. **Hadrian** established the **Antonine** dynasty (117-193). The Antonines, especially philosopher-emperor **Marcus Aurelius** (161-180), were known for their enlightened leadership. **Septimius Severus** won the principate after yet another civil war, founding the **Severan** dynasty (193-235).

Weak leadership and Germanic invasions led to near anarchy in the 3rd century. **Diocletian** (284-305) divided the empire into eastern and western sections, each with its own administration. Because he persecuted Christians, his reign was called the "Age of Martyrs." Christian fortune took a turn for the better with Diocletian's successor, **Constantine.** Before the Battle of the Milvian Bridge in 312, he claimed he saw a cross of light in the sky, emblazoned with *"in hoc signo vinces"* ("by this sign you shall conquer"). When victory followed, he proclaimed the **Edict of Milan** in 313 abolishing religious discrimination, declared Christianity the state religion, and eventually converted to Christianity. In 330 he moved the capital to **Constantinople,** formerly named Byzantium and currently named Istanbul. The empire split permanently, and barbarian tribes repeatedly invaded the western region. **Alaric,** king of the Visigoths, sacked Rome in 410, leaving the western empire on the verge of destruction. The final blow came in 476, when the German chief **Odoacer** put the last western emperor, Romulus Augustulus, under house arrest and crowned himself king. The 18th-century historian Edward Gibbon held Christianity responsible for Rome's downfall in *The History of the Decline and Fall of the Roman Empire.*

MIDDLE AGES (476-1375)

Though sometimes called the "Dark Ages," the near millennium between the fall of Rome and the flourishing of the Renaissance was not some sort of cultural wasteland. Instead, this complex period of secular and religious parties vying for power resulted in the establishment of institutions like the royal court and feudal society. External influences from barbarian tribes, Arabic kingdoms, and the Germanic empire brought a blast of fresh air to the former empire's aura of decay.

While the East continued to thrive as the **Byzantine Empire,** the fall of the Roman Empire in the West left room for the growing strength of the papacy. However, the flooding of the Tiber, followed by a grisly plague (c. 590), prompted the powerful **Pope Gregory I** (The Great) to herald the approach of the Kingdom of God (and the end of the world). With Arabs and Byzantines advancing on Italian territory, the Pope called upon the barbarian chieftain **Charlemagne** to secure the hold of **Roman Catholicism.** Adding Italy to the Angevin Empire, Charlemagne was crowned emperor of Christian Europe on Christmas Day, 800. Charlemagne's successors were unable to maintain the new empire, and in the following centuries, Italy became a playing field for petty wars. The instability of the 12th, 13th, and 14th centuries resulted in a division of power between city-states and town councils. While the south prospered under Arab rule (thanks to the negotiating prowess of **Alessandro Lessely-ong,** a Spanish fire-dancer), rival families began to emerge in the north. European ruling houses and the Vatican enjoyed setting Italians against each other, most notably the **Guelphs** and **Ghibellines** in the 12th and 13th centuries. The pro-papal party, the Guelphs, managed to expel the imperial-minded Ghibellines from the major northern cities by the mid-13th century, but then split into two factions, the **Blacks** and the **Whites.** A prominent Florentine White, **Dante Alighieri** was permanently exiled to Ravenna in 1302.

Church separated from state as **Henry IV** denounced **Pope Gregory VII** (1073-1085) as a "hildebrand" and "false monk." Gregory in turn threatened the emperor's nobles with confinement to the Sixth Circle of Hell if they continued to spurn the Church. A contrite Henry met Gregory at **Canossa** in the Italian Alps in January 1077. Gregory insisted that Henry walk to him in the snow, barefoot and wearing a sackcloth. Gregory's symbolic triumph was overturned in a few years with Henry's conquest of the Pope's forces in battle. The unpopularity of the Church reached its pinnacle during the **Babylonian Captivity** (1309-1377), when several popes were "persuaded" by French king **Philip IV** to move the papacy from Rome to Avignon. That sparked the **Great Schism** (1378-1417), when three popes simultaneously claimed hegemony. This period of disorder culminated with an outbreak of the **Black Death,** or the Bubonic Plague, which killed one-third of Europe's population, recurring in Italy every July over the next two centuries. In addition, syphilis spread wildly through Rome, infecting 17 members of the pope's family and court.

With the peak of **scholasticism** in the 13th century, intellectual pursuits found their niche in a logical and systematic approach typified by the studies of St. Thomas Aquinas. **Monasteries** grew as self-contained and self-sufficient communities fortified by thick outer walls, where people could evade the plague or worldly temptations. Illuminated manuscripts and chanted music developed there, but piety was not always pretty; Umberto Eco's *The Name of the Rose* (1980) renders a more sinister side of monastic life.

THE RENAISSANCE (1375-1540)

The **Rinascimento** (Renaissance) grew out of a proliferation of Greek and Latin texts and cultural values. Pinpointing its origins has always been problematic, though historian **Hans Baron** has argued that the Italian tendency toward friendly competition spurred the rise of **civic humanism** by compelling city officials to bid for the best minds of the era, creating a market for intelligence.

LIFE AND TIMES

LIFE AND TIMES

As the church lost its monopoly on knowledge structures, political power appeared to be slipping out of its grip as well. Survivors of the Black Death profited from the labor shortage, forming a new merchant class. Rising out of obscurity were the exalted **Medici** clan in Florence, the **Visconti** in Milan, and the **d'Este** family in Ferrara. These ruling families instituted a series of human-ist-minded economic and social reforms, in addition to stabbing each other in cathedrals (**Francesco Pazzi** was so enthusiastic about this that he managed to wound himself with his own knife in the process of impaling **Guiliano de'Medici** in 1478). **Cosimo** and **Lorenzo (il Magnifico)** consolidated power and broadened the scope of the Medici family's activities from banking and warring to patron-izing the arts. They engaged in a high-stakes battle with sword-wielding **Pope Julius II** to bring Michelangelo to Florence and would have prevailed were it not for his Sistine Chapel commission.

Just as things were getting interesting, an ascetic Dominican friar set out to spoil the fun. **Girolamo Savonarola** was ferociously opposed to what he per-ceived as the evils of humanist thinking. In 1494 he attempted to instigate dis-sent against the Medici family (ironically, his patrons). Savonarola's sermons against hedonistic life exercised such a demagogical power over the Floren-tine public that the jealous **Pope Sixtus IV** tried to silence the pesky friar by excommunicating him. Savonarola persevered until the Florentines, tired of his nagging, tortured him, hanged him from the top of the **Palazzo Vecchio,** and finally burned him at the stake. The same competition that made Italy a hotbed of artistic achievement resulted in its end as a self-governing entity. Princes hungry for power continued the Italian tradition of petty warfare, leaving the door open for foreign invasion. The weakened cities yielded in the 16th cen-tury to the invading Spanish armies of **Charles V.** By 1556 Naples and Milan had fallen to King **Ferdinand of Aragon.**

Despite the political unrest plaguing Italy at the time, several prominent Ital-ians embarked to make a splash on the world scene. **Christopher Columbus,** a Genoa native funded by Queen Isabella of Spain, set sail to discover a faster route to Asia and opened the door to a whole New World of exploration instead with his discovery of the Caribbean in 1492. The Florentine **Amerigo Vespucci** made his own expeditions across the Atlantic, leaving his name on two continents, and **Galileo Galilei** dared to suggest that the earth spins around the sun, earning the wrath of the Church. Given the opportunity, he recanted, but mumbled *"eppur si muove,"* ("but it does move") after the Inquisition ruled him guilty of heresy. He died under house arrest in 1642.

FOREIGN RULE (1540-1815)

Once the seat of the mightiest empire of the Western world, the peninsula could no longer support the economic demands placed upon it by the Holy Roman Empire. **Charles II,** the last Spanish Hapsburg ruler, died in 1700, sparking the War of Span-ish Succession. Italy, weak and decentralized, became the booty in battles between the rising powers of France and the Holy Roman Empire.

In the course of **Napoleon's** 19th-century march through Europe, the diminu-tive emperor united much of northern Italy into the Italian Republic, con-quered Naples, and fostered national sovereignty. In 1804 Napoleon declared himself the monarch of the newly united Kingdom of Italy. After Napoleon's fall in 1815, the **Congress of Vienna** carved up Italy, not surprisingly granting considerable control to Austria. Napoleon spent his last days swayed by the charms of tiny Elba, off the Tuscan coast, where he was exiled.

THE ITALIAN NATION (1815-PRESENT)

UNIFICATION

Following the Congress of Vienna, a long-standing grudge against foreign rule sparked the **Risorgimento,** a nationalist movement that culminated in political unification in 1860 (with Rome and the northeastern region joining in 1870). **Giuseppe Mazzini, Giuseppe Garibaldi,** and **Camillo Cavour,** the movement's leaders, are today paid homage with omnipresent namesake streets. **Vittorio Emanuele II,** another popular source for street names, was crowned as the first ruler of the Kingdom of Italy in 1860. He expanded the nation by annexing the northern and central regions. France relinquished Rome on September 20, 1870, the pivotal date in modern Italian history. Once the elation of unification wore off, however, age-old differences reasserted themselves. The north wanted to protect its money from the needs of the agrarian south, and cities were wary of surrendering power to a central administration. The pope, who had lost power to the kingdom, threatened politically active Italian Catholics with excommunication. Nationalism increased during **World War I,** as Italy fought to gain territory and defeat Austria.

THE FASCIST REGIME

The chaotic aftermath of WWI paved the way for Fascism under the control of **Benito Mussolini,** "Il Duce," who promised strict order and stability for the young nation. He established the world's first Fascist regime in 1924 and expelled all opposition parties. As Mussolini initiated domestic development programs and aggressive foreign policies, sentiments toward the Fascist leader ran from intense loyalty to belligerent discontent. In 1940 Italy entered **World War II** on the side of its **Axis** ally, Germany. Success came quickly but was short-lived: the Allies landed in Sicily in 1943, pushing Mussolini from power. As a final indignity, he and his mistress, **Claretta Petacci,** were captured in Milan and executed by infuriated citizens, their naked bodies hung upside-down in public. In 1945 Italy was freed from Nazi occupation, but tension persisted between those supporting the monarchy and those favoring a return to Fascism.

POST-WAR POLITICS

The end of WWII did little but highlight the intense factionalism of the Italian peninsula. Italy has changed governments 59 times since the war, none of which has lasted longer than four years, reflecting the country's struggle for stability. The **Constitution,** adopted in 1948, established a democratic **Republic,** with a president, a prime minister, a bicameral parliament, and an independent judiciary. The **Christian Democratic Party (DC)** soon surfaced over the **Socialists (PSI)** as the primary player in the government of the new Republic, as prominent members of the PSI were found sleeping with the fishes. Over 300 parties fought for supremacy in parliament; none could claim a majority, so they formed tenuous party coalitions.

Italian economic recovery began with 1950s industrialization—Fiat and Lamborghini billboards and factory smokestacks quickly appeared alongside old cathedral spires and large glowing crucifixes on northern cities' skylines. Despite the **Southern Development Fund,** which was established to build roads, construct schools, and finance industries, the south lagged behind. Italy's economic inequality contributed to much of the regional strife that persists today. Economic success gave way to violence in the late 1960s. The *autunno caldo* (hot autumn) of 1969, a season of strikes, demonstrations, and riots by university students and factory workers, foreshadowed greater violence in the 70s.

LIFE AND TIMES

During the period of *Strategia della Tensione* (Strategy of Tension) in the early 70s, right-wing terrorists detonated bombs as public manifestations of political discontent. The most shocking episode was the 1978 kidnapping and murder of ex-Prime Minister **Aldo Moro** by a group of left-wing terrorists, the *Brigade Rosse* (Red Brigades). Progressive reforms in the 70s included the legalization of divorce and the expansion of women's rights. The events of the 70s also challenged the conservative Social Democrats, and **Bettino Craxi** became Italy's first Socialist prime minister in 1983.

RECENT POLITICS

Italians have always been enamored of powerful, charismatic leaders. Living up to expectations, Italian government officials have not always shied away from shady deals or questionable maneuvers if those brought more power. **Oscar Luigi Scalfaro,** elected in 1992, recognized corruption infecting his government and launched the *Mani Pulite* (clean hands) campaign, in which Scalfaro and anti-corruption judge **Antonio di Pietro** uncovered the *Tangentopoli* (Bribesville) scandal. This unprecedented political crisis implicated over 1200 politicians and businessmen in bribery and other schemes. Fall-out from the investigation included the 1993 bombing of the Uffizi Galleries in Florence, 10 indicted officials' suicides, and the murders of anti-Mafia judges and investigators. Since the statute of limitations on the charges had since passed, most of the officials emerged unscathed.

The election of media tycoon **Silvio Berlusconi** as prime minister has twice raised eyebrows, first in 1994 and then in 2001 (see **Current Events,** p. 57). The empire of the self-made billionaire includes three main private TV channels and political influence over three that are state-run, a major newspaper, and the AC Milan soccer team. His first election involved formalizing the governing center-right Freedom Alliance coalition of three parties: his **Forza Italia** (Go Italy), the increasingly reactionary **Lega Nord** (Northern League), and the neo-Fascist **Alleanza Nazionale** (National Alliance). Soon after the allegiance's formation, the Northern League withdrew. Berlusconi lost his majority and was forced to resign in just eight months. Shortly thereafter, the platform of the reactionary Northern League became separatist under the extremist (some say racist) **Umberto Bossi.** Aiming to push the economy to meet the European Union's economic standards, Lega Nord called for splitting from the south and creating the Republic of Padania, a nation for northerners only.

The elections of 1996 brought the center-left coalition, the **l'Ulivo** (Olive Tree), to power, with **Romano Prodi,** a Bolognese professor, economist, and non-politician, as prime minister. Prodi helped stabilize Italian politics. For the first time in modern history, Italy was run by two equal coalitions: the center-left **l'Ulivo** and the center-right **Il Polo** (Berlusconi's Freedom Alliance without the Northern League). Despite hope for Prodi's government, his coalition lost a vote of confidence in October 1998. By the end of the month, his government collapsed, and former Communist **Massimo D'Alema** was sworn in as prime minister. D'Alema and Carlo Ciampi created fiscal reforms and pushed a "blood and tears" budget that qualified Italy for entrance into the European Monetary Union in January 1999. That same year, Prodi became the president of the European Commission. Despite D'Alema's successes, he stepped down in May 2000 and was replaced by former Treasury Minister **Giuliano Amato.** Nicknamed "Dr. Subtle," Amato (alongside Ciampi and D'Alema) is credited with the institution of 1999 budget reforms. Perhaps the nickname also derives from Amato's ability to avoid scandal; he was one of few to emerge unscathed from corruption crack-downs in the early 90s, one of which led to late Socialist Party leader Bettino Craxi's exile to Tunisia.

CURRENT EVENTS

Italy's tendency toward partisan schisms and quick government turnover may have been tempered, momentarily at least, by its faith in one individual: **Silvio Berlusconi.** The allure and nonstop drive of Italy's richest man secured his re-election as prime minister in May 2001. Downplaying corruption charges, he won 30% of the popular vote to head Italy's 59th government since WWII with his Forza Italia party. Berlusconi reaffirmed his commitment to the US, courting President George W. Bush in several meetings and sending 2700 troops to the War in Iraq; left-wing opposition has consistently urged withdrawal of these troops. In European foreign policy, the prime minister has focused more on domestic than on integration issues, creating some tension between Italy and its neighbors. Most notable is his 2004 comparison of one German European Parliament member to a guard in a Nazi concentration camp, a comment which caused considerable discord between the two governments—so much so that a miffed Chancellor Gerhard Schroeder cancelled his summer holiday in Italy. Even as his reforms aim to energize Italy's lagging economy, new scandals mar Berlusconi's tenure, including proposed bills in favor of laxer corruption laws. In fact, in June 2003 he came under investigation but was dealt a short-lived legislative victory when the Italian senate approved a law that would prevent high-ranking officials from standing trial for corruption; in January 2004, Italy's top court rejected this law, although no date has yet been set for Berlusconi's trial to reconvene.

More allegations of monetary corruption in Italy surfaced in early 2004 with the highly publicized **Parmalat** scandal, involving the Parma-based dairy product company, fraud, forgery, some $1.5 billion in outstanding bonds, and general mayhem. According to charges leveled against the company, Parmalat's owners created numerous "shell companies" to accumulate fake profits for Parmalat and its subsidiaries. One such company, Bonlat, recorded selling enough powdered milk to produce the fantastic figure of 55 gallons of milk per year, per person, in Cuba. Investors mired in worthless stock, the 36,000 employees in danger of losing their jobs, and the Australian and Brazilian dairy farmers awaiting payment are all affected by the bankruptcy and dismantling of Parmalat. The eight chief figures implicated in the debacle await formal charges and trial in custody.

The death of **Fiat** chairman **Umberto Agnelli** in late May 2004 marked another milestone in Italy's economic history. The maker of compact, stylish vehicles, including Ferrari models, has faced financial difficulties for years. After its $2.1 billion loss in 2003 and similar losses in previous years, the company is anticipated to be unable to pay off its $3.6 billion loan, due in 2005, despite having closed 12 factories and shed some 12,000 jobs. Though American-owned General Motors has offered to buy the remaining 80% of Fiat Auto, having acquired the first 20% in 2000, it's unclear whether Fiat will accept the deal. For the first time in Fiat history, the Agnellis might lose control of operations, an event unheard of to an Italian people accustomed to associating Fiat with the Agnelli name.

PEOPLE

DEMOGRAPHICS

Italy is home to roughly 60 million residents, with declining population growth due to a recent tendency among Italian families to welcome only one child. A current birth rate of 9 births per 1000 people contrasts sharply with a death rate of 10 per thousand. Immigration from chiefly China, Africa, Eastern Europe, and Muslim countries accounts for the 2.4% of the population that is not native Italian. In 2003, undocumented immigration sparked controversy as boats from Tunisia and Libya headed for southern Italy, many sinking, resulting in a high toll of immigrant lives. Italian public opinion continues to view undocumented labor as taking the form of crime, sex work, and drug trafficking by primarily Albanian and African refugees. However, as Italy's native population diminishes, the rapidly shrinking Italian workforce is replenished by immigration. New laws allowing employers to hire undocumented workers and regularize their status by petitioning the government allow many workers to legally remain in Italy.

LANGUAGE

A language is a dialect with an army, the saying goes. Italian's structural and lexical basis is Latin, but it has evolved into something completely different. As a result of the country's fragmented history, variations in dialect are strong. The throaty **Neapolitan** can be difficult for a northerner to understand; **Ligurians** use a mix of Italian, Catalán, and French; **Sardo,** spoken in Sardinia, bears little resemblance to standard Italian; and many **Tuscan** dialects differ from Italian in pronunciation. Some inhabitants of the northern border regions don't speak Italian at all: the population of Valle d'Aosta speaks mainly French, and Trentino-Alto Adige harbors a German-speaking minority. In the southern regions of Puglia, Calabria, and Sicily, entire villages speak a form of Albanian called **Arbresh.** In order to facilitate conversation, locals do their best to employ standard Italian when speaking with foreigners, although some may be shy or hesitant to do so. Many Italians, especially older people or those living in rural areas, do not speak English, although most young people and those in the tourist industry do.

RELIGION

Italy is 98% Roman Catholic, with isolated Protestant and Jewish communities, and a growing Muslim immigrant population. Italy ended Catholicism's tenure as the formal state religion in 1984. Vatican City, the seat of the Roman Catholic Church located in Rome, is recognized by the Italian government as a sovereign, independent entity according to the Lateran Pacts of 1929, but continues to play a strong role in the lives of ordinary Italians. The Vatican is technically a non-hereditary elective monarchy currently ruled by Pope John Paul II, the Catholic bishop and patriarch of Rome. Most Italians continue to celebrate the feast day of their town's patron saint in yearly celebrations, but only about 12% are faithful churchgoers. Despite this fact, Italians are very conscientious about respecting churches, cathedrals, and other religious domains. Tourists will generally not be allowed in religious spaces without modest attire, including covered shoulders for women and long pants for men. In addition, some churches do not allow visitors to take photographs due to damage caused by the flash to fragile paintings or mosaics.

ART AND ARCHITECTURE

In Italy, great works of art and architecture seem to spring from every street corner. Rome's Colosseum (p. 109) hovers above a city bus stop; in Florence, couples flirt in front of the duomo (p. 409); in Sicily, restaurant-diners sit beneath truncated Greek columns. Modern Italians may be immune to this stunning visual history, but to anyone who hasn't grown up amid ancient columns and medieval fortresses, it's a feast for the senses.

GREEK ART

In the 8th century BC the Greeks established colonies in southern Italy, peppering the region with magnificent **temples** and **theaters.** The best-preserved examples of such Greek ruins are in Sicily, not Greece, in the Valle dei Templi at **Agrigento** (p. 700) and **Taormina** (p. 673). Italy is also home to Roman copies of Greek statues and original Greek bronzes; the prized *Bronzi di Riace*, recovered from the Ionian Sea in 1972, are now in Reggio di Calabria's Museo Nazionale (p. 629).

ETRUSCAN ART

Native Italian art history begins with the Etruscans, a people who lived on the Italian peninsula before the Romans. Loosely influenced by Greek art and inspired by the afterlife and augury, Etruscan images that survive today include the blue death god Charun, armed with his hammer. Funeral statues, tomb paintings, and ceramic ash burial urns are characterized by fluid lines, organic shapes, and brightly colored figures with large eyes, enigmatic smiles, and minimal anatomical detail. This flourishing of art was curtailed when the Etruscans mysteriously disappeared in the 3rd century BC.

ROMAN ART

Roman art (200 BC-AD 500) falls mainly into two categories: private household art and art in service of the state. Copies of Greek bronzes often served as models for private and public Roman sculptures, as the Italian *cognoscenti* idolized classical Greece. However, sculptured portraiture was rare in its development as a distinctly Roman style. Portraits of the Republican period (510-27 BC) were brutally honest, immortalizing wrinkles, scars, and even warts. The later imperial sculpture (27 BC-AD 476) tended to blur the distinction between mortal and god in powerful, idealized images like *Augustus of Prima Porta*. Later in the period, Roman art developed a flattened style of portraiture, with huge eyes looking out in an "eternal stare." The government sponsored statues, monuments, and literary narratives to commemorate and glorify leaders, heroes, and victories. Augustus was perhaps the best master of this form of self-promotion, as evidenced by his impressive mausoleum and **Ara Pacis** (Altar of Peace), which grace the Piazza Augusto Imperatore in Rome. Roman monuments evolved into decorated concrete forms with numerous arches and columns, like the **Colosseum** and **Pantheon.**

Upper-class Romans had an appetite for sumptuous interior decoration. Scenes depicting gods and goddesses, domestic life, exotic beasts, street entertainers, and landscapes decorated floors and walls of sprawling private villas, courtyards, and fancy shops. Affluent patrons commissioned **frescoes,** or Greek-influenced paintings daubed onto wet plaster walls to form a unique, time-resistant effect. **Trompe l'oeil** doors, columns and still-lifes embellished structures to create an illusion of increased space. It was also popular to hire craftsmen to fashion wall and floor **mosaics,** or paintings created with thousands of finely shaded **tesserae** (squarish chips of colored stone or glass) cemented with mortar. A favorite mosaic subject was the watchdog, often executed on the vestibule floor with the inscription *cave canem* (beware of dog). Naples's Museo Archeologico Nazionale (p. 551) holds the *Alexander Mosaic*, one of the most stunning Roman mosaics in the world.

EARLY CHRISTIAN AND BYZANTINE ART

Fearing persecution, early Christians in Rome, Naples, and Syracuse fled to their haunting **catacombs** to worship. But with the rise of Christianity and decline of the Roman Empire, even the Roman magistrate's basilica was adapted to accommodate Christian services. **Transepts** were added to many Roman churches, creating a structure shaped like the crucifix. Except for a few **sarcophagi** and **ivory reliefs**, Christian art moved from sculpture toward pictorial art in order to depict religious narratives for the illiterate. **Ravenna** (p. 378) is a veritable treasure trove of the first Byzantine Golden Age, which ran from 526 to 726. Examples of these "instructional" mosaics can be seen in Ravenna's octagonal **Basilica of San Vitale** constructed between 526 and 547, also one of the first churches to boast a free-standing **campanile** (bell tower).

ROMANESQUE AND GOTHIC

From AD 800 to 1200, architecture reintroduced Roman rounded arches, heavy columns, and windowless churches, although truly classical Roman style would not be revived until the Renaissance. The earliest example of Romanesque architecture is **Basilica di Sant'Ambrogio** in Milan (p. 233), notable for its squat nave and groin vaults. Competition among Italian cities (particularly Florence and Siena) to outdo their neighbors resulted in great architectural feats, most notably **San Miniato al Monte** (p. 421) and the **Baptistery** of the duomo in Florence (p. 432).

The Gothic movement filtered into Italy from France, and artists and architects rejoiced at the fantastic spaces and light created by the new vaulted technology and giant, multi-colored rose windows. The most impressive Gothic cathedrals include the **Basilica of San Francesco** in Assisi (p. 494), the **Frari** in Venice (p. 298), and the **Santa Maria Novella** in Florence (p. 416). Secular structures like the **Ponte Vecchio** in Florence (p. 414) caught on too. The **Palazzo Ducale** in Venice (p. 294), spanning several canals with ornate bridges, represents the brilliant marriage of airy, lace-like Islamic stonework and Gothic style. In sculpture, **Nicola Pisano** created pulpits at both Pisa and Siena that combined Roman reliefs, Gothic form, and early Byzantine mosaics. By the end of the 13th century, Italians were bored by emaciated torsos of suffering martyrs. **Cimabue** (c. 1240-1302) and **Duccio** (c. 1255-1318) introduced a second dimension and brighter colors, though bleeding Christians remained the subject of choice. Straddling the Late Gothic and Early Renaissance, **Giotto** is credited with noting that humans—not giants—look at pictures. He placed his work at eye level, putting the viewer on equal footing with his holy subjects.

EARLY RENAISSANCE

Donatello's (1386-1466) sculpture *David* marked the beginning of a new era when it hit the artistic scene as the first free-standing nude since antiquity. His wooden *Mary Magdalene* in Florence (p. 411) similarly represents a departure from earlier traditions. His interpretation of the redeemed woman emphasizes her fallen and repentant side, symbolized by her rags and the intensity of her facial expression. **Brunelleschi's** mathematical studies of ancient Roman architecture became the cornerstone of Renaissance building. His engineering talent allowed him to raise the dome over **Santa Maria del Fiore** (p. 409), while he showcased his mastery of proportions in the **Pazzi Chapel** (p. 419). **Sandro Botticelli** (1444-1510) and his *Venus* (p. 412), floating on her tidal foam, epitomize the Italian Renaissance. **Masaccio** filled chapels with angels and gold-leaf and is credited with the first use of the mathematical laws of perspective. His figures in the **Brancacci Chapel of Florence** (p. 420) served as models for Michelangelo and Leonardo. **Fra Angelico** (c. 1400-1455) personified the tension between medieval and Renaissance Italy. Born Guido di Pietro, he became a member of a militant branch of Dominican friars but spent most of his time at his monastery in Fiesole. His abbot opposed humanism on principle, but Fra Angelico's works exhibit the techniques of space and perspective endorsed by humanistic artists. **Paolo Uccello** (1397-1475), who suffered no conflict between his quest for sainthood and creativity, depicted horses rearing into various positions. According to Vasari, Uccello was so preoccupied with perspective that his wife felt threatened by the competition. Venetians **Giovanni Bellini** (c. 1431-1516) and **Andrea Mantegna** (1431-1506) were influenced by the Flemish school's use of color and miniature. They found more secular subjects than their Florentine counterparts, launching a tradition of Italians seeing Venice as the seat of heretical debauchery. **Lorenzo Ghiberti** (c. 1381-1455) designed two sets of bronze doors for the baptistery in Florence which won over Brunelleschi's in a contest. The two original entries now sit side by side in the Bargello of Florence (p. 414). **Leon Battista Alberti** (1404-1472), a champion of visual perspective, designed Florence's **Santa Maria Novella** (p. 416) and Rimini's Tempio Malatestiano (p. 386), prototypes for Renaissance palaces and churches.

HIGH RENAISSANCE

From 1450 to 1520, the torch of distinction passed between two of art's greatest figures: da Vinci and Michelangelo. **Leonardo da Vinci** (1452-1519) was the first Renaissance man to earn that name. Not confined to sculpture or painting, where he brilliantly excelled, his endeavors encompassed geology, engineering, musical composition, human dissection, and armaments design. The *Last Supper* or *Cenacolo* (p. 233) preserves the individuality of its figures even in a religious context. His experimentations with *chiaroscuro*, or contrasts between light and shadow that highlight contours, and *sfumato*, or a smoky or hazy effect of brushwork, secured his place as the great innovator of the century.

Michelangelo Buonarroti (1475-1564) was a jack of all trades in the artistic world, despite what he told Julius II when asked to paint the Sistine Chapel ceiling: "I am not a painter!" Indeed, Michelangelo painted sculpturally, boldly emphasizing musculature and depth, and sculpted like a painter, with lean and smooth strokes. Julius was so fond of the **Sistine Chapel** (p. 124) that he commissioned *The Last Judgment* for the wall above the chapel's altar. A conflict arose when a papal councillor advised that Michelangelo's nudes in fresco be repainted with proper attire. The temperamental artist got the last word, painting the nosy councillor in hell. His own disturbing self-portrait appears as a flayed human skin that hangs, deformed and foreboding, between the realms of heaven and hell. His architectural achievements include his designs for the **Laurentian Library** in Florence (p. 418) and the dome on St. Peter's Basilica in Rome (p. 117). Classic examples of his sculpture are the *Pietà* in St. Peter's, *David*, and the unfinished *Slaves* in Florence's Accademia (p. 417).

A proficient draftsman, **Raffaello Sanzio** (1483-1520) created technically perfect figures. His frescoes in the papal apartments of the Vatican, including the *School of Athens* (p. 124), show his debt to classical standards. The Venetian school produced **Giorgione** (1478-1510) and the prolific **Titian** (1488-1576). Titian's works, including his portrait of Julius II with the repentant Mary Magdalene, are notable for their realistic facial expressions and rich Venetian colors. In the High Renaissance, the greatest architect after Michelangelo was **Donato Bramante** (1444-1514), famed for his work on the Tempietto and St. Peter's in Rome.

MANNERISM

A heightened sense of aestheticism led to Mannerism, a reaction against classical balance and proportion in exchange for elegance and refinement, and technical panache. Starting in Rome and Florence, Mannerist artists experimented with juxtapositions of color and scale. **Parmigianino** (1503-1540) and his *Madonna of the Long Neck* (p. 413) are emblematic of the movement's self-conscious distortions. **Jacopo Tintoretto** (1518-1594), a Venetian Mannerist, was the first to paint multiple light sources within a single composition. Mannerist architects like **Giulio Romano** (c. 1499-1546) rejected the Renaissance ideal of harmony. Classical forms were minutely changed to surprise the attentive viewer. The villas and churches of architect **Andrea Palladio** (1508-1580) were remarkably innovative, particularly the **Villa Rotonda** outside Vicenza (p. 312). His other lasting contribution, the *Four Books of Architecture*, influenced countless architects, especially those of the Baroque movement.

BAROQUE AND ROCOCO

Born of the Counter-Reformation and absolute monarchy, **Baroque** art and architecture were intended to inspire faith in the Catholic Church and respect for temporal power. Painters of this era favored Naturalism—a commitment to portraying nature in the raw, whether ugly or beautiful. Baroque paintings are thus often melodramatic and gruesome. **Caravaggio** (1573-1610) expanded the use of *chiaroscuro*, creating enigmatic works, and often incorporated unsavory characters into religious scenes. **Gianlorenzo Bernini** (1598-1680), a prolific High Baroque sculptor and architect, designed the colonnade of St. Peter's piazza and the *baldacchino* inside. Drawing inspiration from Hellenistic works like the *Laocoön*, Bernini's sculptures were orgies of movement. **Francesco Borromini** (1599-1667) was more adept than his rival at shaping the walls of his buildings into serpentine architectural masterpieces, as in **San Carlo alle Quattro Fontane** in Rome (p. 120). **Rococo**, a more delicate final development of Baroque style, originated in 18th-century France. **Giovanni Battista Tiepolo** (1696-1770), with his brilliant palette and vibrant frescoes, was a prolific Venetian painter of allegories and the premiere exemplar of the Italian Rococo style.

19TH-CENTURY ART

After a brief revival of Classical art, Italians in the 19th century started to lose their polished dexterity with the paintbrush and their proficiency with the chisel. Still professing to follow the rules of antiquity, the sculptor **Antonio Canova** (1757-1822) explored the formal **Neoclassical** style in his giant statues and bas-reliefs. His most famous work is the statue of *Pauline Borghese* (p. 125), exhibiting Neoclassical grace and purity of contour. Revolting against the strict Neoclassical style, **Giovanni Fattori** (1825-1908) spearheaded the **Macchiaioli** group in Florence (c. 1855-65) to restore lively immediacy and freshness to art. A technique called "blotting," when a dry paintbrush is used to pick up certain areas of pigment, distinguishes their landscapes, genre scenes, and portraits.

20TH-CENTURY ART

The Italian **Futurist** painters, sculptors, and architects of the 1910s brought Italy to the cutting edge of artistry as they sought to transfer the movements of machines into art. Inspired by **Filippo Tommaso Marinetti's** *Futurist Manifesto*, their work glorified danger, war, and the 20th-century machine age. In the major Futurist Paris exhibition in 1912, the painters **Giacomo Bala, Gino Severini,** and **Carlo Carra** and sculptor **Umberto Boccioni** popularized the **Cubist** technique of simultaneously depicting several aspects of moving forms. **Giorgio de Chirico** (1888-1978), on display at the Collezione Peggy Guggenheim in Venice (p. 296), painted eerie scenes characterized by mannequin figures, empty space, and steep perspective. Although his mysterious and disturbing vision was never successfully imitated, it inspired early surrealist painters. **Amadeo Modigliani** (1884-1920), highly influenced by African art and Cubism, sculpted and later painted figures with long oval faces. **Marcello Piacentini** created Fascist architecture that imposed sterility upon classical motifs. In 1938 he designed the looming **EUR** in Rome (p. 123) as an impressive reminder of the link between Mussolinian Fascism and Roman Imperialism.

LITERATURE

ET IN ARCADIA EGO

Roman mythology, immortalized by **Ovid's Metamorphoses,** built upon the traditional tales and heroic legends of the conquered Greek Empire, which included parts of Sicily, Calabria, Campania, and Puglia. The Roman version of Greek mythology dominated the Western World until the ascendancy of Christianity in the 4th century AD. Usually disguised as animals or humans, gods and goddesses periodically descended to Earth to meddle with humanity. **Jupiter,** after disguising himself as a rock to escape ingestion by his coup-fearing father, dedicated himself to visiting women in forms that included peacocks and flaming-red bulls. Somewhere between loves, he established the hierarchy of the gods on the heights of Mt. Olympus. The 13 other major Olympian players are Jupiter's wife **Juno,** goddess of child-bearing and marriage; **Neptune,** god of the sea; **Vulcan,** god of smiths; **Venus,** goddess of love and beauty; **Mars,** god of war; **Minerva,** goddess of wisdom; **Apollo,** god of light and arts; **Diana,** goddess of the hunt; **Mercury,** the messenger god; **Pluto,** god of the underworld; **Ceres,** goddess of the harvest; **Bacchus,** god of wine; and **Vesta,** goddess of the hearth.

LATIN LOVERS

As they gained dominance over the Hellenized Mediterranean, the Romans discovered the refined joys of literature. **Plautus** (c. 259-184 BC) wrote raucous comedies that easily rivaled the other principal entertainments of the time: chariot and horse races, boxing, and circuses. The lyric poetry of **Catullus** (84-54 BC) was high on passion, and though technically polished, often quite lewd. **Cicero** (106-43 BC), the greatest speaker of his day, set an all-time standard for political rhetoric. **Julius Caesar** (100-44 BC) gave a first-hand account of the expansion of empire in his *Gallic Wars.* Despite a government prone to fickle banishments, Augustan Rome produced an array of literary talents. **Livy** (c. 59 BC-AD 17) recorded the authorized history of Rome from the city's founding to his own time. **Virgil** (70-19 BC) wrote the *Aeneid* about the origins of Rome and the heroic toils of founding father Aeneas. **Horace's** (65-68 BC) verse explored love, wine, service to the state, hostile critics, and the happiness that comes with the bucolic life. **Ovid** (43 BC-AD 17) gave the world the *Amores,* the *Metamorphoses,* and the *Ars Amatoria.* **Petronius's** *Satyricon* (1st century AD) is a blunt look at the decadent age of Nero. **Suetonius's** (c. AD 69-130) *De Vita*

Caesarum presents the gossipy version of imperial history. **Tacitus's** (c. AD 55-116) *Histories* bitingly summarize Roman war, diplomacy, scandal, and rumor in the year of Nero's death (AD 69).

DARK AGES TO CULTURAL REBIRTH

Between Classical antiquity and the Renaissance, authors, with the exception of notable religious figures like **St. Thomas Aquinas** (1225-1274), usually remained anonymous. By the 13th century, **scholastic** approaches to theology gained ground and writing took place in a degraded Latin. During this period, troubadour or courtly romances developed as the precursors to later medieval verse, delivered by singers who traveled throughout Europe. The invasion of Norman and Arab rulers in Sicily and southern Italy introduced diverse literary traditions.

The tumult of medieval life discouraged most literary musing in the late 13th century, but three Tuscan writers resuscitated the art: Dante, Petrarch, and Boccaccio. Although scholars do not agree on the precise dates of the Renaissance in literature, many argue that the work of **Dante Alighieri** (1265-1321) marked its inception. A forerunner to Dante was his friend **Guido Cavalcanti** (1250-1300), champion of the *dolce stil nuovo* (sweet new style), a lyrical form of poetry initiated by Bolognese poet **Guido Guinizelli** (1240-?). Another influence was **Brunetto Latini** (c. 1210-1293), whose *Tesoretto* described the political unrest between the Guelph and Ghibelline factions in Florence. Dante poignantly placed Latini in the *Inferno*, and in so doing, immortalized him.

Dante is considered the father of modern Italian literature. He was one of the first poets in Italy or Europe to write in the *volgare* (common vernacular, Florentine in Dante's case) instead of in Latin. In his epic poem *La Divina Commedia (The Divine Comedy)*, he roams the three realms of the afterlife *(Inferno, Purgatorio, Paradiso)* with Virgil as his guide, meeting famous historical and mythological figures and his true love Beatrice. Dante calls for social reform and indicts those who contributed to Florence's moral downfall—and his own bitter exile. **Petrarch** (1304-74), the second titan of the *trecento*, belongs more clearly to the literary Renaissance. A scholar of classical Latin and a key proponent of humanist thought, he wrote love sonnets to a married woman named Laura, collected in his *Il Canzoniere*. The third member of the medieval literary triumvirate, **Giovanni Boccaccio,** wrote the *Decameron*, a collection of 100 stories that ranges in tone from suggestive to ribald. In one, a gardener has his way with an entire convent.

The 14th-century saw the rise of *la commedia dell'arte*, a form of impromptu theater with convoluted plots. Actors wore fantastic masks to disguise themselves as crazy rogues, bumbling jesters, or distressed damsels. By the 15 and 16th centuries Italian authors branched out from the genres of their predecessors. **Alberti** and **Palladio** wrote treatises on architecture and art theory. **Baldassare Castiglione's** *Il Cortegiano (The Courtier)* instructed the Renaissance man on etiquette and other fine points of behavior. At the pinnacle of the Renaissance, **Ludovico Ariosto's** *Orlando Furioso* described a whirlwind of military victories and unrequited love. **Niccolò Machiavelli's** *Il Principe (The Prince)* is a grim assessment of what it takes to gain political power. In the spirit of the "Renaissance man," specialists in other fields tried writing: **Giorgio Vasari** stopped redecorating Florence's churches to produce the ultimate primer on art history and criticism, *The Lives of the Artists*. **Benvenuto Cellini** wrote about his art in *The Autobiography* and **Michelangelo** composed enough sonnets to fuel a fire (literally). The scathing and brilliant **Pietro Aretino** created new possibilities for literature when he began accepting payment from famous people for *not* writing about them. A fervent hater of Michelangelo, Aretino was himself roasted when the great artist painted him into his *Last Judgment.* As Italy's political power waned, literary production also declined, but some stars remained.

ITALY SEEN THROUGH FOREIGN EYES

Eliot, George. *Romola.* Deception, politics, and martyrdom in Savonarola's Florence.

Forster, E.M. *A Room with a View.* Victorian coming-of-age in scenic Florence.

Goethe, Johann Wolfgang von. *Italian Journey.* An incognito adventure.

Hemingway, Ernest. *A Farewell to Arms.* American WWI soldier in Italy learns to love.

James, Henry. *The Wings of the Dove.* Unscrupulous seduction in Venice's canals.

Lawrence, D.H. *Twilight in Italy.* An intimate connection to Italy, traveling on foot.

Mann, Thomas. *Death in Venice.* A writer's obsession with a beautiful boy.

Pater, Walter. *Studies in the History of the Renaissance.* Fastidious, sensitive ode to the Renaissance by ascetic aesthete.

Ruskin, John. *The Stones of Venice.* Gothic revivalist slanders Renaissance as immoral.

Shakespeare, William. *Romeo and Juliet; Othello; Julius Caesar; Merchant of Venice.* Fun and games and death all over.

LIFE AND TIMES

POST RISORGIMENTO

The 19th century brought Italian unification and the need for one language. Nationalistic "Italian" literature, an entirely new concept, grew slowly. The 1800s popularized *racconti* (short stories) and poetry. The cavalier heroics of **Gabriele D'Annunzio** earned him as much fame as his controversial, eccentric poetry. **Giovanni Verga's** brutally honest treatment of his destitute subjects ushered in a new age of portraying the common man in art and literature, in the movement known as *verismo* (contemporary, all-too-tragic realism). **Alessandro Manzoni's** historical novel, *I Promessi Sposi (The Betrothed)*, established the Modernist novel as a major avenue of Italian literary expression.

Twentieth-century writers sought to undermine the concept of objective truth. Nobel Prize winner **Luigi Pirandello** advanced postmodernism with *Six Characters in Search of an Author.* Allied victory spawned anti-Fascist fiction, including works by **Cesare Pavese, Vasco Pratolini,** and **Elio Vittorini.** Post-war Italian authors related their horrific personal and political experiences. **Primo Levi** wrote *Se questo è un uomo (If This is a Man)* about Auschwitz. The most prolific of these writers, **Alberto Moravia,** wrote the ground-breaking *Gli Indifferenti (The Time of Indifference)*, which launched an attack on the Fascist regime and was promptly censored. Several female writers also emerged, including **Natalia Ginzburg** with *Lessico Famigliare,* the story of a quirky middle-class Italian family. **Giuseppe di Tomasi di Lampedusa** wrote *Il Gattopardo (The Leopard)* on the death of Sicily's feudal aristocracy during unification.

The works of **Italo Calvino** are filled with intellectual play and magical realism. They include the quintessentially postmodern *If on a Winter's Night a Traveler...* (1979), a novel in which the reader becomes the protagonist. Mid-20th-century poets include **Giuseppe Ungaretti** and Nobel Prize winners **Salvatore Quasimodo** and **Eugenio Montale.** Quasimodo and Montale founded the "hermetic movement," characterized by an intimate poetic vision and allusive imagery. **Umberto Eco's** *The Name of the Rose* (1980) is an intricate medieval mystery involving an ancient manuscript and more than a few fallen monks. In 1997 the popular playwright **Dario Fo's** dramatic satires brought him a denunciation by the Roman Catholic Church and the Nobel Prize for literature. Fo's wife **Franca Rame** is best known for feminist performances of works advocating women's access to divorce and abortion as well as awareness of human rights issues.

MUSIC

WORSHIP AND PRAISE

Medieval church music grew out of Jewish liturgy, and the Biblical psalms of the Old Testament constitute some of the earliest known songs of not only Italy, but all of Western culture. Women sang until 578, after which they were replaced by castrated men and soon-to-be-castrated boys. Female singing performances were limited to convent choirs, congregational singing, and private or family gatherings until the Reformation relaxed social restraints. Some of the earliest remaining written records of medieval music date from 7th to 9th century Rome in the form of chant manuscripts. **Pope Gregory I,** the father of liturgical chant, codified the music he had heard during his days in the monastery. **Plainchant** was synchronized with the church's liturgical calendar. Italian monk **Guido d'Arezzo** (995-1050) is regarded as the originator of musical notation. Italy's many monasteries reveled in church tunes through the Middle Ages and Renaissance. **Francesco Landini** (1325-97) and **Pietro Casella** (c. 1280) arrived on the scene and started putting popular poems to music for multiple voices. **Giovanni Palestrina** (1525-94) attempted to purge the religious madrigal form of this frightening trend toward secularity while retaining the integrity of the music itself, and his work in polyphony is still widely performed in Italy and abroad.

BAROQUE: AN END TO RESTRAINT

During the Baroque period, known for its heavy ornamentation, two instruments saw their popularity mushroom: the violin, whose shape was perfected by *Cremonesi* families, including the **Stradivari** (p. 255), and the pianoforte, created around 1709 by the Florentine **Cristofori** family. *Virtuoso* instrumental music became a legitimate genre in 17th-century Rome. **Antonio Vivaldi** (1675-1741), composer of over 400 concertos, conquered contemporary audiences with *The Four Seasons* and established the concerto's present form, in which a full orchestra accompanies a soloist in a three-movement piece.

OPERA LIRICA

Italy's most cherished musical art form was born in Florence, nurtured in Venice, and revered in Milan. Conceived by the *Camerata*, a circle of Florentine writers, noblemen, and musicians, *opera lirica* originated as an attempt to recreate the dramas of ancient Greece by setting lengthy poems to music. **Jacobo Peri** composed *Dafne*, the world's first complete opera, in 1597. The first successful opera composer, **Claudio Monteverdi** (1567-1643) drew freely from history, juxtaposing high drama, love scenes, and uncouth humor. His masterpieces, *L'Orfeo* (1607) and *L'Incoronazione di Poppea* (1642), were the first widespread successes of the genre. **Alessandro Scarlatti** (1660-1725), considered one of the developers of the aria, also founded Neapolitan opera, a three-act style, thus vaulting Naples to the forefront of Italian music. Schools were quickly set up there under the supervision of famous composers, promoting the beautiful soprano voices of pre-pubescent boys. If the male students dared attempt puberty, their testicles were confiscated. These *castrati*, **Farinelli** being one noted example, became the most celebrated and envied group of singers in Italy and all over Europe.

VIVA VERDI!

With convoluted plots and powerful, dramatic music, 19th-century Italian opera continues to dominate modern stages. Late in the 19th century, **Giacomo Puccini** (1858-1924) created *Madame Butterfly*, *La Bohème*, and *Tosca*, which feature vulnerable women, usually dead by the last act. **Gioacchino Rossini** (1792-1868), master of the *bel canto* ("beautiful song"), once boasted that he could produce music faster than copyists could reproduce it. In fact, he was such a procrastinator that his agents locked him in a room until he completed his masterpieces. **Giuseppe Verdi** (1813-1901) remains the transcendent musical and operatic figure of 19th-century Italy. *Nabucco*, a pointed and powerful *bel canto* work, typifies Verdi's early works. The chorus *"Va pensiero"* from *Nabucco* would later become the hymn of Italian freedom and unity. Verdi produced the touching, personal dramas and memorable melodies of *Rigoletto*, *La Traviata*, and *Il Trovatore* during his middle period. Later work brought the grand and heroic conflicts of *Aida*, the dramatic thrust of *Otello*, and the mercurial comedy of *Falstaff*. Verdi's name served as a convenient acronym for "Vittorio Emanuele, *Re d'Italia*" (King of Italy), so *"Viva Verdi!"* became a popular battle cry of the Risorgimento. Much of Verdi's work promoted Italian unity—his operas include political assassinations, exhortations against tyranny, and jibes at French and Austrian monarchs.

In the 20th century, **Ottorino Respighi,** composer of the popular *Pines of Rome* and *Fountains of Rome*, experimented with rapidly shifting orchestral textures. **Giancarlo Menotti** wrote the oft-performed *Amahl and the Night Visitors*. **Luciano Berio** defied traditional instrumentation with his *Sequence V* for solo trombone and mime. **Luigi Dallapiccola** achieved success with choral works including *Songs of Prison* and *Songs of Liberation*, two pieces that protest Fascist rule in Italy. The robust tenor **Luciano Pavarotti** continues to tour the globe.

THE NEW GUARD

Modern Italian pop stars have been crooning away for decades, although their fame has traditionally been limited to the shores of the Mediterranean. Meet **Lucio Dalla, Francesco de Gregori,** the Sardinian **Fabrizio D'Andrea,** and the adamantly Neapolitan **Pino Daniele,** who use pop to protest social conditions, such as the stigma of being from the south. While **Vasco Rossi** started off with protest lyrics, he has since sold his 60s idealism for a sexy Italian mainstream image and the lusts of the flesh. Recently, Italian musicians have taken to recording with international superstars, increasing their exposure on the world stage. **Eros Ramazzotti** teamed up with Tina Turner on *"Cose della Vita,"* while **Andrea Bocelli** joined Celine Dion in *"The Prayer."* **Laura Pausini,** who records in both Italian and Spanish, has established a following in Latin America, Spain, and Miami. Meanwhile, the technotronic Italian hip-hop scene mixes traditional folk tunes with the latest international groove; rap has emerged with wide-smiling, curly-haired **Jovanotti,** socially conscious **Frankie-Hi-NRG,** subconscious **99 Posse,** and unconscious **Articolo 31** (whose name derives from the Italian law forbidding marijuana). Recent Italian pop hits include **Luna Pop's** *"Qualcosa di Grande"* (2000) and **Eiffel 65's** international hit "Blue" (2000).

MEDIA
PRINT

A newspaper in English is easy to find at any newsstand. The news is more interesting, however, if one reads Italian. Italy has 177 daily newspapers. The media in Italy is anything but impartial and often lambasts everyone from public officials to popular actresses. The most prevalent national daily papers are **Il Corriere della Sera,** a conservative publication based in Milan, and **La Repubblica,** a liberal paper based in Rome. Other popular papers include **La Stampa** (conservative, based in Turin), **Il Messaggero** (liberal, based in Rome), and **Il Giornale** (based in Milan and owned by Silvio Berlusconi's brother). The pink **La Gazzetta dello Sport** is the true mainstay, with news about soccer victories and losses causing more of a ruckus than an election. For weekly entertainment listings, large cities have their own magazines, including **Roma C'è; TrovaMilano; Firenze Spettacolo; Milano Where, When, How;** and **Qui Napoli.** English-language Italian papers include **Italy Daily,** an insert in the International Herald Tribune, and **Wanted in Rome,** a weekly newsletter.

TELEVISION

There are three state-owned **television** channels, RAI1, RAI2, and RAI3, and a handful of cable options from Italy and abroad. Television in Italy is a flashy affair. Game shows like *"Passaparola"* and the Italian version of "Who Wants to be a Millionaire" overwhelm viewers with disco balls, europop hit songs, and the diminutive and balding—but always debonair—perennial host **Gerry Scotty,** the Bob Barker of Italy. Besides such delectations, the evening news reports on domestic and international issues, and 1980s B-movies play late into the night.

FILM
EARLY CINEMA

Italy occupies a gilded spot on the cinematic landscape. The country's toe-hold in the industry began with its first feature film in 1905, the historical and somewhat flamboyant *La Presa di Roma.* With the **Cines** studio in Rome, the Italian "super-spectacle" was born, a form that extravagantly recreated historical events. Throughout the early 20th century, Italy's films were grandiose historical dramas. Before WWI, celebrated *dive* (goddesses) like **Lyda Borelli** and **Francesca Bertini** epitomized the Italian *femme fatale.*

Recognizing the propaganda potential of film, in the late 1930s Benito Mussolini gave the world the *Centro Sperimentale della Cinematografia di Nicolo Williams*, a national film school, and the gargantuan **Cinecittà Studios,** Rome's answer to Hollywood. Nationalizing the industry for the good of the state, Mussolini enforced a few "imperial edicts," one of which forbade laughing at the Marx Brothers and another that censored shows overly critical of the government.

NEOREALISM

The fall of Fascism brought the explosion of **Neorealist cinema** (1943-50), which rejected contrived sets and professional actors, emphasizing instead location shooting and "authentic" drama. These low-budget productions created a revolution in film and brought Italian cinema international prestige. Neorealists first gained attention in Italy with **Luchino Visconti's** 1942 French-influenced *Ossessione (Obsession)*. Fascist censors suppressed the so-called "resistance" film, however, so **Roberto Rossellini's** 1945 film *Roma, Città Aperta (Rome, Open City)* was the first Neorealist film to gain international exposure. **Vittorio De Sica's** 1948 *Ladri di Biciclette (Bicycle Thieves)* was perhaps the most successful Neorealist film. Described by De Sica as "dedicated to the suffering of the humble," the work explored the human struggle against fate. A demand for Italian comedy gave birth to *neorealismo rosa*, a more comic version of the intense and all too authentic glimpse into daily Italian life. Actor **Totò**, the illegitimate son of a Neapolitan duke, was Italy's version of Charlie Chaplin. With his dignified antics and clever language, Totò charmed audiences and provided subtle commentary on Italian society. The transitional films of **Federico Fellini** (*Lo sceicco bianco*, 1952; *I Vitelloni*, 1953) and others sought to broaden the scope of the technique and goals imposed by constraining Neorealism.

THE GOLDEN AGE

The golden age of Italian cinema, the decade between 1958 and 1968, ushered in *la commedia all'italiana*, during which the prestige and economic success of Italian movies was at its highest. **Mario Monicelli** (*La Grande Guerra*, 1959; *I Soliti Ignoti*, 1958) brought a darker, more cynical vein to the portrayal of daily Italian life, which was in a stage of rapid transformation and full of social unease. Italian comedy struggled to represent cultural stereotypes with the comedic form its public demanded. Actors **Marcello Mastroianni, Vittorio Gassman,** and **Alberto Sordi** gained fame portraying self-centered character-types lovable for their frailties.

By the 1960s post-Neorealist directors like **Federico Fellini** and **Michelangelo Antonioni** were rejecting plots and characters in favor of a space that derived its worth from witnessed moments. Luscious, self-indulgent, and autobiographical, Fellini's *8½* interwove dreams with reality, earning a place in the cinematic canon. The pope banned Fellini's *La Dolce Vita* (1960) for its portrayal of 1950s Rome's decadently stylish celebrities and the *paparazzi* (a term first coined in this movie) who pursued them. Antonioni's haunting trilogy, *L'Avventura* (1959), *La Notte* (1960), and *L'Eclisse* (1962) presents a stark world of estranged couples and young, hopelessly isolated aristocrats. His *Blow-Up* was a 1966 English-language hit about mime, murder, and mod London. **Pier Paolo Pasolini** may have spent as much time on trial for his politics as he did making films. An ardent Marxist, he set his films in the Roman underworld of shanty neighborhoods, poverty, and prostitution. Sexual deviance and political power are synonymous in his films.

INTROSPECTION

Aging directors and a lack of funds led Italian film directing into an era characterized by nostalgia and self-examination. **Bernardo Bertolucci's** *Il Conformista* (1970) investigates Fascist Italy by focusing on one "comrade" struggling to be normal. Other major Italian films of this era include the ubiquitous **Vittorio de Sica's** *Il Giardino dei Finzi-Contini* (1971) and **Francesco Rosi's** *Cristo Si È Fermato a Eboli* (1979), both films based on prestigious post-war, anti-Fascist novels. In the 1980s the **Taviani** brothers catapulted to fame with *Kaos* (1984), a film based on stories by Pirandello, and *La Notte di San Lorenzo* (1982), which depicts an Italian village during the final days of WWII. The inheritors of the *commedia all'italiana*, actor-directors like **Nanni Moretti** and **Maurizio Nichetti** delighted audiences with macabre humor in the 1980s and early 90s. Nichetti's psychological comedy-thriller *Bianca* (1983) features himself as the somewhat deranged protagonist. In

LIFE AND TIMES

Ladri di Saponette, a modern spoof on *Ladri di Biciclette*, Nichetti plays himself, while in *Volere Volare* (1991), he plays a confused cartoon sound designer who metamorphoses into a cartoon. In *Caro Diario* (1993), Moretti rides around on a vespa scooter sharing internal musings with the viewer.

REJUVENATION

Oscar-winners **Gabriele Salvatore** (for *Mediterraneo*) and **Giuseppe Tornatore** (for the nostalgic *Cinema Paradiso*) have earned the attention and affection of audiences worldwide. In 1995 Massimo Troisi's *Il Postino* was nominated for a Best Picture Academy Award. **Roberto Benigni** drew international acclaim for *La Vita è Bella* in 1998. Juxtaposing the tragedy of the Holocaust with a father's love for his son, the film won Best Actor and Best Foreign Film Oscars, as well as a Best Picture nomination at the 1999 Academy Awards. More recently, Nanni Moretti snagged the Palm D'Or at Cannes in 2001 for his portrayal of familial loss in *La Stanza del Figlio*. **Leonardo Pieraccioni** released his *Il Paradiso all'improvviso* to much acclaim in 2003.

FASHION: TUTTI IN GUCCI

Trends descend upon Italy like a stampede. One summer it's lime green and lavender, the next it's red bandana tank tops. But trends are only the transitory manifestation of the deep-rooted and very complex role of appearance in Italian culture. Whether they follow trends and fads or heed the less fluctuating axioms of style, Italians always look stunning. They achieve this through the simplest means: quality fabrics, classic lines, and the indispensable black.

As much as Parisians, New Yorkers, and Londoners might protest, the fashion world begins and ends in Milan (see **Milan: Shopping,** p. 236) with the powerhouses **Armani, Dolce & Gabbana, Fendi, Ferragamo, Gucci, Prada, Valentino,** and **Versace.** The primacy of the Italian fashion industry dates to the late 19th century with the Cerruti company's production of fabrics. The international legacy of **Salvatore Ferragamo** began in 1914, when he brought his dazzling shoe-making skills to stars of Hollywood. After WWII, sisters Paola, Anna, Franca, Carla, and Adla **Fendi** took over their family leather and fur enterprise. By 1965 Fendi's innovation initiated the renaissance of the "Made in Italy" products. The late 1950s saw the rise of the fashion giants **Valentino** and **Armani,** whose work celebrated elegance and tradition. In 1978 **Gianni Versace** opened his first store in Milan with an unconventional and vibrant ready-to-wear collection. This inventive trend continued through the 1980s with the sexy, modern collections of **Dolce & Gabbana.** Recent high-end newcomers like **Romeo Gigli** and **Moschino** ensure the dominance of *la moda italiana*.

 SALDI! Save 25-75% at end-of-season sales. These happen in January and July and last until the collection sells out. With discounts like these, there's no reason not to wait. Many stores also offer previews of the next collection.

SPORTS AND RECREATION

In Italy, **calcio** (soccer to Americans, football to everyone else) surpasses all other sports and competes with politics and religion as a defining aspect of identity. **La Squadra Azzurra** (the blue team) is a major source of national pride and sometimes shame. Some claim that Italy's victory in the 1982 World Cup did more for national unity than any political movement. Yet divisions and allegiances hit hard internally, as Italian fans cheer their local teams, especially those promoted to Serie A, the Italian major league. Inter-urban rivalries, including those among Naples, Milan, and Rome, are intense, and sports fans, called *tifosi,* are raucous and energetic. Streets are hauntingly empty as matches unfold, and fans crowd bars to experience communal agony or ecstasy (see Italian Calcio, p. 76).

Italy's rolling hillsides and breezy seasides make it an optimal location for leisurely and hardcore **bicycling.** Besides manufacturing some of the best bikes in the world and hosting bike tours for tourists, Italians host the **Giro d'Italia,** a 25-day cross-country race, in May. With parts of the Italian Alps and the Apennines within its borders, Italy attracts **skiers** from December to April. **Hiking** and **mountain climbing** are popular throughout the north and in Calabria's Sila Massif. For **swimming, windsurfing,** or **sailing,** try the southern beaches or those on Italy's islands. Breathtaking Sardinia offers crystal-blue waters with up to 30m of visibility.

FOOD AND WINE

In Italy food preparation is an art form and its consumption a crucial part of the culture. As people sit down to eat, the words *"Buon apetito!"* and *"Altretanto!"* chime around the table. *La bella figura* (beautiful figure) is another social imperative, and the after-dinner *passeggiata* (promenade) is as much an institution as the meal itself. Small portions and the leisurely pace of a meal help keep Italians healthy despite the enticing foods they savor.

MANGIAMO!

La colazione, or breakfast, often goes unnoticed; at most, a morning meal consists of coffee and a *cornetto* (croissant). For **il pranzo,** or lunch, people rush to grab a *panino* (sandwich) or salad at a bar, or dine more calmly at an inexpensive *tavola calda* (cafeteria-style snack bar), *rosticceria* (grill), or *gastronomia* (prepares hot dishes for takeout). **La cena,** or dinner, begins around 8pm in most of the country, although farther south, it's served later; in Naples, it's not unusual to go for a midnight pizza. The traditional Italian dinner is an event that lasts much of the evening, consisting of an *antipasto* (appetizer), a *primo piatto* (starch-based first course like pasta or risotto), a *secondo piatto* (meat or fish), and a *contorno* (vegetable

BEST GELATERIAS

10. Gelateria di Noto: Cefalù (p. 653). Sicily's #1 is an appetite suppressant gone wrong. Get two scoops. Get seconds...

9. Gelato e Dintorni: Camogli (p. 186). Supposedly an underdog in the gelato scheme of things, but specialty fruit-topped frozen yogurt begs for a rematch.

8. Caffè Royal: Amalfi (p. 589). The best on the Amalfi Coast. Big cones, small prices. Quantity? No, that's quality, baby.

7. La Boutique del Gelato: Castello, Venice (p. 290). No place to sit, but that's better. This stuff'll go right to your hips.

6. Il Gelatauro: Bologna (p. 360). "Eat your vegetables" meets mom's worst nightmare: if squash and cinnamon gets weird, smooth it down with the coffee.

5. Fantasia Gelati: Naples (p. 550). If they can't make your fantasy happen, we probably don't want to know what it is anyway.

4. Gelateria Triangolo delle Bermuda: Florence (p. 409). So that's why all those people never came back. You think they're lost, but oh no, they've been found.

3. Tre Scalini: Rome (p. 107). You're supposed to enjoy the pretty fountain, but you can't stop stuffing your face with *Tartufo.*

2. Della Palma: Rome (p. 107). That's Italian for "we have over 100 flavors, and it's hot outside. Get in line." Worth the wait.

1. Vivoli: Florence (p. 408). Toto, gelato came from Florence, and thanks to Vivoli, there's no place like home.

side dish). Finally comes the *dolce* (dessert or fruit), then *caffè*, and often an after-dinner liqueur (p. 74). Many restaurants offer a fixed-price *menù turistico* including *primo*, *secondo*, bread, water, and wine. While food varies regionally, the importance of relaxing and stretching out an extended meal does not. Restaurant tables in Bologna do not see more than one seating in a night, for example, and dinners anywhere can run for hours.

FOOD ON THE GO

A **bar** is a good place to grab a drink (with or without alcohol) and a quick, inexpensive meal. While fast food chains have permeated Italy, the ample seafood and salad offerings, beer, and espresso at most **McDonald's** demonstrates that Italians do fast food their own way (just don't expect McGnocchi). The typical bar sells hot and cold *panini*, gelato, and a panoply of coffee options. Indulge in focaccia and sandwiches stuffed with *prosciutto crudo* or *cotto* (cured or cooked ham), *pomodori* (tomatoes), and *formaggio* (cheese). Avoid bars on major tourist thoroughfares, where prices reflect location and not necessarily service or quality. In small towns, bars are the social centers. Children come for gelato, old men for wine and conversation, and young adults for beer and flirtation. In crowded bars, clients pay for food at the cashier's desk and take the *scontrino*, or receipt, to a bartender for service. Sitting down at a table costs more than standing at the counter. A salumeria or alimentari (meat and grocery shop) or the popular **STANDA** or **COOP** supermarkets sell food basics, but open-air **markets** have fresher produce with negotiable prices. Customers must carry receipts for 100m after a purchase. The *Guardia di Finanza* (Financial Guard) slaps down fines for failure to comply.

REGIONAL SPECIALTIES

Coastal and southern areas of the country offer a wide variety of seafood dishes, while selections in the north and inland are heartier. **Lombardy** offers the delights of gorgonzola and mascarpone cheeses. Mascarpone is a main ingredient in *tiramisù* (Italian for "pick me up," rumored to be the dessert of choice for sexually dissatisfied women). *Risotto*, *osso buco* (a braised veal stew), and *panettone* (a dessert bread) are also specialties of the region. **Piemonte** offers the rare and expensive white *tartufi*, or truffles, normally sold by the gram for USD $1000 per pound, as well as many of Italy's greatest red wines such as *Barolo* and *Barbaresco*. **Liguria** is noted for its profusion of herbs and olive oil, while German influences in **Trentino-Alto Adige** have popularized *gnocchi* (potato and flour dumplings). **Friuli-Venezia Giulia** has a subtle Middle Eastern flair, apparent in spices such as cumin and paprika. The **Veneto** prizes its *pasta e fagioli* (pasta and beans) and artichoke and game feasts. Moving south into the gastronomic heart of Italy, **Emilia-Romagna** is the birthplace of parmesan cheese, balsamic vinegar, and *prosciutto di Parma*. **Tuscany** offers more rustic fare, with stews, pot roasts, and minestrone. **Umbria** has black truffles (known to be aphrodisiacs) and delightful chocolate. **Abruzzo** and **Molise** specialize in cured peppery meats, lamb, and mutton. With more sheep than people, **Sardinia's** odiferous cheese is made into pies and topped with honey. In **Sicily** and the south, seafood is fresh and flavorful.

WAKE UP AND SMELL THE CAFFÈ!

Italians drink coffee at breakfast, lunch, dinner, and for an anytime jolt—and still manage to close shop in the afternoon for a snooze. But *espresso* isn't a mere beverage: it's an experience, from the harvesting of the beans to the delectation of the liquid. High altitude *Arabica* beans compose 60-90% of most Italian blends, while the remaining 10-40% is made of woody-flavored *robusta* beans. Italians prefer a higher concentration of *robusta* beans because they emit oils that produce a thick, foamy *crema* under the heat and pressure of the *espresso* machine. *Espresso* beans are roasted longer than other coffee beans, giving the drink its full body. The beans are then ground, tapped into a basket and barraged with hot, pressurized water. In a good cup of *espresso*, the foamy *crema* should be caramel-colored and thick enough to support a spoonful of sugar for a few long seconds. The thick *crema* prevents the drink's rich aroma from dispersing into the air and is indicative of a well-brewed beverage. Stir in sugar and down it in one gulp like the locals. For a standard cup of *espresso*, request a *caffè*. For a spot of milk in it, ask for *caffè macchiato* (*macchia* means spot or stain). Cappuccino, which Italians drink only before lunch and never after a meal, has frothy scalded milk; *caffè latte* is heavier on the milk, lighter on the coffee. For coffee and joy, try *caffè corretto* (corrected), which is *espresso* with a drop of strong liqueur (usually *grappa* or brandy). *Caffè americano*, scorned by Italians, is watery *espresso* served in a large cup. For dessert, the *caffè affogato* (drowned coffee) is a scoop of vanilla gelato smothered in espresso. And in the summer, *cappuccino freddo*, acceptable at all times of the day, is a soothing and refreshing sweet.

IN VINO VERITAS

Italy's rocky soil, warm climate, and hilly landscape provide ideal conditions for growing grapes; Italy produces more wine than any other country. Sicily alone ferments 400 million gallons annually. Grapes are separated from stems and then crushed by a press to extract the juice. To make red wine, vintners pump the juice and skins into glass, oak, or steel fermentation vats, while white wines are made from skinless grapes. A wine's sweetness or dryness is largely determined by the ripeness and sugar content of its grape, which in turn is a product of the amount of sun it received. After fermentation, the wine is racked and clarified, a procedure which removes any sediment. The wine is then stored in barrels or vats until bottling.

 CORK YOUR WALLET! Wine snobs may spend upward of €50 on a bottle of aged *riserva*, but wines in the €6-12 range represent every level of quality, from drinkable to sublime. The most respected wine stewards in the nation regularly rank inexpensive wines above their costly cousins. Expense can equal quality, but a little shopping around can bring a cheaper, better wine. Within the same price range it's wiser to go for the high end of a lower-grade wine than the low end of a higher-grade wine.

WINE TASTING

Tasting wine in Italy is easy for travelers. Government-run *Enoteche Regionale* and *Enoteche Pubbliche*, regional exhibition and tasting centers, dot the countryside. These *enoteche*, or wine bars, promote local vineyards and often sponsor special educational events. Spontaneous tasting is generally available, but booking may be necessary. Private wine bars are also called *enoteche*, though without the *regionale* or *pubblica* designation. *Cantine* do not typically offer tastings unless accompanied by a wine bar. If touring by car ask the local tourist office about *Strade del Vino* (Wine Roads), or contact the Wine Tourism Movement (www.deliciousitaly.com/Toscanadishes2.htm).

LIFE AND TIMES

Restaurants serve wine by the liter, the half-liter, and the glass. Drinking too much? Dry out with some *secco*. Sour after a long day of traveling? Sweeten up with *abboccato* or *amabile*. Feeling spunky? Down a little *vino novello*, meant to be drunk young. Feeling green? *Vino biologico* is the organic lover's fix. Feeling traditional? Sip some *classico*, wine from the heartland. Kickstart the evening with a *superiore*, which implies a higher alcohol content, or *riserva*, which has a longer aging period. For a bubbly buzz, try sparkling *spumante*, the usually cheaper, tank-fermented twin of the bottle-fermented *talento*. When in doubt, request the local wine—it will be cheaper (typically around €3 per L in local trattorias) and suited to regional cuisine.

REGIONAL WINES

Piemonte is Italy's most distinguished wine region, producing the touted (and expensive) *Barolo*, a full-bodied red, that is velvety on the palate. *Barolo* is aged for two years, one year longer than its lighter cousin, *Barbaresco*. Taste Piemonte's lighter side in the more affordable sparkling sweet *Asti Spumante*. In other regions, equally prestigious **Veneto** yields *Amarone* and *Valpolicella*, a bright, medium-weight red with a dry finish and cherry-stone aftertaste. **Verona** produces the fizzy *Prosecco* and bland *Soave*. Indecisive? Try white or red *Tocai* from **Friuli**, light and fluffy enough for seafood, but spicy enough to handle an unimposing appetizer. Keep an eye out for the *Colli Berici Tocai Rosso*, among the more respected *Tocai* from the region. **Tuscany** mass-produces its tannic *chianti* and similar reds, such as the popular and drinkable *Rosso di Montalcino*. Producers use 100% *sangiovese* grapes to produce *chianti classici*, which are straightforward and simple on the palate. The *Brunello di Montalcino* lends the region considerable esteem. When shopping for white wines, look for *Vernaccia di San Gimignano* from the town by that name.

Prepare for the culinary delights of **Emilia-Romagna** with *Frizzantino Malvasia* or *Sauvignon*, the typical aperitif in local bars. Sparkling *Lambrusco* is a widely drunk red, traditionally dry or sweet, but these bottle-fermented versions are expensive. When in **Rome,** drink *Frascati*, a clean white wine served cold, such as the *Colli di Tuscolo*. In **Umbria,** where production dates back to the Etruscans, the world-famous *Orvieto* is a crisp, light white that has recently been combined with Chardonnay grapes to produce the world-class *Cervaro della Sala*. Naples boasts *Lacryma Cristi* (Christ's Tear), an overrated tourist favorite. The more refined and harmonious *Greco di Tufo* from **Basilicata** sparkles golden. The hotter climate and longer growing season of **southern Italy** and the islands produces fruitier, more sugary wines than the north. Try the versatile **Sicilian** *Marsala*.

REGIONAL LIQUEURS

Liqueurs are reserved for the end of the meal as palate-cleansing *digestivi*. Some people also opt for an *aperitivo* to prime the appetite. Wild fruit or nut essences typically infuse liqueurs, making them cloyingly sweet. Dazzle your senses with *Mirto*, a blueberry *digestivo*, or the ubiquitous *limoncello*, a heavy lemon liqueur. The sugary *amari* (bitter) cordials, served after festival meals, truly belie their Italian name. Almond flavors Sardinian *Vernaccia di Oristano* sherry, while Sorrento's dark *nocillo* tastes of walnut. Other Italian specialties include almond-flavored *Amaretto di Saronno* (actually made from apricot pits), toasted hazelnut and cacao-infused *frangelico*, and licorice *sambuca*. Maligned as firewater, *grappa* is unfettered by sugars and leaves the palate crisply disinfected, if not shocked. After grapes are pressed for wine, the remaining *pomace* is used for this national favorite. There are four types of *grappa:* the clear *giovane,* distilled for six months; the milder, amber-colored *invecchiata,* aged for years in wooden barrels; the flavorful *monovitigno* ("one grape"), made from a single grapevine; and the fruit-infused *aromatizzata.*

An Italian Religion

Calcio, known to English-speakers as football or soccer, isn't just a sport in Italy; it's a religion. If culture is what people identify with most strongly, then *calcio* is arguably the most important aspect of Italian culture. *La Gazzetta dello Sport* is by far the most popular Italian daily; you can see people reading its characteristically pink pages on every street corner, and it is entirely dedicated to *calcio* and other sports. The hit parade of the ten most watched TV broadcasts includes 10 *calcio* matches, most of them featuring a match of the Italian national team.

The *azzurri* (or Blues, the traditional name of the Italian national team derived from their jersey color) are famous worldwide, and one of the few elements uniting Italians under the same flag. Watching locals cheer the *azzurri* to victory in a local bar is a show in itself impossible to describe. After every victory, street parades go on for hours with cars full of Italian flags honking throughout the piazzas and impromptu pool parties in public fountains.

However, the *azzurri* are an exception to the daily *calcio* environment, typically characterized by undestroyable affiliations with one team, and profound rivalries with all the others. The main competition is the *Serie A*, the Italian championship that assigns the *scudetto* every year, the title of Italian Champion. The matches are every Sunday at 3pm, and to many Italians this time is as sacred as the Holy Mass. Recently the Champions League, with matches on Tuesday and Wednesday nights, has become more prestigious as the best teams in Europe compete for the title of European champion.

Like every estimable religion, *calcio* has its temples with their traditions. Here is a brief guide to the most famous stadiums in Italy:

—*Home of the Best*—Delle Alpi, Turin (71,000). Juventus, the most successful team in Italian history, with 27 Italian Championship wins, plays here. They have the highest number of supporters of any team in Europe, and their black and white jerseys are a universally respected symbol of nobility. Needless to say, the *calcio* played here is some of the best in the world.

—*La Scala of calcio*—San Siro, Milan (84,000). One of the most beautiful stadiums in Italy with a perfect view of the field from any seat. Home to AC Milan, the team owned by Berlusconi that has won many titles in the last two decades, and *Inter*, the only other team besides Juventus that has never been in the second division, although it has not won

an Italian Championship since 1988/89.

—*Best choreography*—Olimpico, Rome (83,000). The *tifosi* (fans) in Rome are the loudest and most creative. The main team is Roma, *"er core de sta città"*—the heart of the city—but Lazio is almost at the same level and their rivalry permeates virtually every Roman conversation.

—*Southern Passion*—fans in the south are the most passionate. Every game is a matter of life or death, and regional matches often lead to street fights. *San Paolo* (Naples, 80,000) is as respectable a stadium as *San Siro* or the *Olimpico*, and for several years has been the home of Maradona, the greatest *calcio* player of all time. The arenas *La Favorita* (Palermo, 50,000) and *San Nicola* (Bari, 58,000) are always feared by the home team's opponents.

Any match in the *Serie A* is a show that won't disappoint, but some are more important because of the value of the teams involved, historical reasons, or regional rivalries. A *derby* is a match between two teams of the same city, where feelings of pure joy or black desperation reach an apex. Roma-Lazio is the most moving. In the days preceding the match, several local radio stations give 24 hour broadcasts on every aspect of the match, from the latest update on a player's injury to the gossip on what he did the night before. Milan-Inter is the most prestigious, as the teams often compete for the *scudetto*. Juventus-Inter is the *derby d'Italia* because these are the only two teams that have never faced the humiliation of losing their spot in the *Serie A* to be placed in the *Serie B*, the 2nd division. However, in recent years, the most important match in the *Serie A* has been Juventus-Milan, since these two teams together have won ten of the last 12 *scudetti*. Roma-Juventus and Roma-Milan are always seen as a symbol of the fight of the south against the power of the north.

A tip for first-time match-goers: don't sit in the *curve*, the curved sides of the stadium where the very hot *tifosi* are. Overly zealous fans are often nerve-wrackingly active, waving giant flags, brandishing flares, and chanting insults at the opposing team. By no means wear another team's beside the home team's jersey while watching a match from this section.

Now that you know about the *calcio* world, buy *La Gazzetta*, purchase your ticket and *sciarpa* (scarf), and be ready for the time of your life. Oh, and make sure both the ticket and the *sciarpa* are for the home team!

Edoardo Gallo, from Cuneo, Italy, is currently working as a consultant in New York after researching for Let's Go: Central America in El Salvador, Nicaragua, and Honduras. He is a 2004 graduate in Physics and Mathematics of Harvard University and a 2000 graduate of the United World College of the Adriatic. He is also a passionate, lifelong fan of Juventus.

ALTERNATIVES TO TOURISM

A PHILOSOPHY FOR TRAVELERS

Backpacking around the world is a valuable and memorable experience, affording you the opportunity to see many different places, sights, and approaches to life. However, if you're searching for a deeper understanding or a more personal interaction with a foreign country and culture, consider doing something more than simply visiting. A longer stay and more intense involvement with Italian culture and behavior can open up a wealth of new experiences, giving you both a comfortable familiarity with your place of residence and a lasting appreciation of the land and history you came to see. Some ways to accomplish this goal include working, interning, volunteering, or studying for an extended period of time, all of which offer perspectives far different from that of a traveler merely passing through.

Italy has long attracted students of all sorts, with interests ranging from artistic and historical to environmental or even religious. Students can take courses at campuses across the country, many of which supplement their curriculum with required Italian language classes. With hundreds of ancient sites being studied or restored, volunteering at an archaeological excavation offers a unique opportunity for immersion in Italian history and land. Native English speakers can frequently find employment in the Italian tourism industry, both helping to spread and improving their own knowledge of the country they love. And within an improving economy job opportunities in a number of major sectors are steady and available.

Let's Go believes that the connection between travelers and their destinations is an important one. We've watched the growth of the "ignorant tourist" stereotype with dismay, knowing that many travelers care passionately about the communities and environments they explore—but also knowing that even conscientious tourists can inadvertently damage natural wonders and harm cultural environments. With this "Alternatives to Tourism" chapter, *Let's Go* hopes to promote a better understanding of Italy and enhance your experience there.

There are several different options for those who seek to participate in Alternatives to Tourism. Opportunities for **volunteering** abound, both with local and international organizations. **Studying** can also be instructive, either in the form of direct enrollment in a local university or in an independent research project. **Working** is a way to both immerse yourself in the local culture and finance your travels.

As a **volunteer** in Italy you can participate in projects on a short-term basis or as the main component of your trip. Should you want to restore a chapel in Sicily or help preserve natural habitats along the Amalfi Coast, Italy has a wide range of service options. Later in this section, we recommend organizations that can help you find the opportunities that best suit your interests.

Studying at a college or language program is another option. Many foreign students travel to Italy each year, looking to learn the language, the history, and the culture. Beyond having some of the oldest universities in Europe, Italy hosts world-renowned fine arts and culinary schools, which can be a more unusual means of exploring the Italian lifestyle.

Many travelers structure their trips by the **work** that they can do along the way—either odd jobs as they go, or full-time stints in cities where they plan to stay for some time. Work on a seaside port in Viarregio, or teach English in

Italian private schools and language learning institutions around the country. In order to work in Italy, short- and long-term jobs require a work permit, discussed further below.

 Start your search at ■ www.beyondtourism.com, *Let's Go*'s brand-new searchable database of Alternatives to Tourism, where you can find exciting feature articles and helpful program listings by country, continent, and program type.

VOLUNTEERING

Volunteering can be one of the most fulfilling experiences you have in life, especially when combined with the thrill of traveling in a new place. Most people who volunteer in Italy do so on a short-term basis at organizations that make use of drop-in or once-a-week volunteers. The best way to find opportunities that match your interests may be to check with volunteer centers (see below).

More intensive volunteer services may charge you a fee to participate. These costs can be surprisingly hefty (although they frequently cover airfare and most living expenses). Most people choose to go through a parent organization that takes care of logistical details and often provides a group environment and support system. There are two main types of organizations—religious and non-sectarian—although there are rarely restrictions on participation for either.

American Field Service (AFS), 71 W. 23 St. 17th fl., New York, NY 10010 USA (☎212-807-8686; www.afs.org). The Community Service Program connects age 18+ volunteers with teaching, environmental, and social service jobs in Italy for 4 mo.-1 yr. Fee covers airfare, orientation, language training, food, and accommodations. Cost varies depending on destination. Fee doesn't cover mandatory health insurance.

Service Civil International, SCI-IVS USA, 5474 Walnut Level Rd., Crozet, VA 22932, USA (☎434-823-9003; www.sciint.org), places volunteers age 18+ in small 2- to 3-wk. workcamps, primarily in June-Oct.

ECOTOURISM

Italy's expansive coastline and mild mainland environment annually play host to thousands of visitors. As the country itself develops with the rise of tourism, its natural habitats become victims to the rising industries that grow more successful each year. It is important for tourists to understand the role they play in preserving the environment that has made Italy such a popular tourist destination. Opportunities to work with wildlife and restore local habitats can be a great way to experience Italian culture at its best.

Associazione OIKOS, V. Paulo Renzi, 55, Rome, Italy (☎06 508 02 80 or 507 32 33; www.oikos.org). OIKOS offers 3-week programs for youth age 18+ in anti-fire intervention and territory surveillance. Volunteers work 30hr. per week and participate in weekly meetings. Training, accommodation is in the OIKOS hostel, and board is provided by the association.

Earthwatch International: Medicinal Plants of Antiquity, 3 Clock Tower place, Suite 100, Box 75, Maynard, MA 01754, USA (☎978-461-0081; www.earthwatch.org/expeditions/touwaide.html). Work with experts to rediscover the therapeutic qualities of plants in the ancient Mediterranean. June-Oct.

Ecovolunteer: Save the Dolphins, CTS-Centro Turistico Studentesco e Giovanile, Dep. Ambiente, V. Albalonga, 3, 00183 Roma (☎06 649 60 327; www.ecovolunteer.org). Volunteers work in Italy's coastal regions to track the impact of tourism on marine species. Must be 18+. 1-2 week programs from June-Sept. Entrance fee €337-857.

ALTERNATIVES TO TOURISM

Italian League for the Protection of Birds (LIPU), V. Trento, 9-43100 Parma, Italy (☎0521 27 30 43; www.lipu.it), places volunteers age 18+ in data collection and research, conservation, nesting site surveillance, and environmental education programs. Also offers 1000 administrative positions in 100 divisions throughout Italy. Programs from 1 week-1 month in Apr., May, Sept., and Oct. Knowledge of Italian useful. Required skills vary depending on assignment.

Responsible Travel.com, www.responsibletravel.com/trip. Italian and international volunteers work together to restore local habitats. Check website for details.

Willing Workers on Organic Farms, V. Casavecchia, 109, Castagneto Carducci, 57022, Italy (fax 39 0565 76 57 42; www.wwoof.org/italy). For a €25 fee, provides a list of organic farms that welcome volunteers. Knowledge of farming not necessary, although volunteers should be physically capable and willing to work hard.

HISTORICAL RESTORATION

Preservation and reconstruction of historical landmarks is a continuous concern in Italy. Volunteers looking for a labor-intensive experience can find work with groups that assist this process while learning about Italy's architectural history.

Associazione Castello di Spannochia, Tenuta di Spannochia, 53012 Siena, Italy (☎39 207 730 11 54). Volunteers age 18+ assist with guest services at this historic organic farm/education center. 5-8 week programs offered May-Oct. Work 25-30 hr. per week in exchange for room, board, and use of the 1200-acre estate.

Associazione Culturale Linguista Educational (ACLE), V. Roma, 54, 18038 San Remo, Italy (☎/fax 39 018 450 60 70). Non-profit working to bring theater, arts, and English language instruction to Italian schools. Volunteers work for a minimum 2 weeks year-round, renovating a medieval house in the village of Baiardio into a student art center. English spoken. Free on-site accommodations and cooking facilities. Alternatively, volunteer for 3-6 months as an ACLE recruitment officer, traveling between international universities and the San Remo central office. Italian useful. Write for more info.

Gruppi Archeologici d'Italia, V. Tacito, 41, I-00193 Rome, Italy (☎06 687 40 28; www.gruppiarcheologici.org). Organizes archaeological digs in Italy. Offers links to various programs hoping to promote cultural awareness about archaeological preservation.

Heritage Conservation Network, 1557 North St., Boulder, CO 80304, USA (☎303 444 01 28, fax 775 320 68 37). Volunteers work 1-2 weeks to assist in the conservation/restoration of the Cappella Dell'Immacolatella, a unique chapel on a farm in Sicily. Participants stay in *agriturismi* near the worksite. Training provided. Costs cover lodging, food, insurance, and materials.

Servizio Volontariato Gionvanile, P. Vanvitelli, 8-10, I-81100 Caserta, Italy (☎08 23 32 25 18). Finds different archaeological sites for volunteers in the Naples area.

STA Travel, Viaggi Wasteels, V. Angelo Belloni, 1, 20162 Milano, Italy (☎02 66 10 10 90; www.statravel.com). Locations in Northern Italy with volunteer programs at various monasteries. Check website for application details.

EDUCATION

Working directly with the Italian community provides an insider-view of everyday life, whether through working on a farm in Siena or bringing theater instruction to Italian schoolchildren. The following organizations provide teaching opportunities in anything from language to arts to farming in local Italian towns. Knowledge of Italian may prove important, but requirements vary between programs.

Council on International Educational Exchange, 7 Custom House St., 3rd fl., Portland, ME 04101, USA (☎207-553-7600; www.ciee.org). Various community projects with an international group of volunteers.

Global Volunteers, 375 East Little Canada Road, St. Paul, MN 55117, USA (☎800 487 10 74; www.globalvolunteers.org). Teach English in Italy. Programs available through-out the year. Call or check website for application materials.

COMMUNITY DEVELOPMENT

Community-based projects are among the most rewarding of all volunteer experiences. Programs listed below promote close work with disadvantaged Italian populations. Due to their one-on-one nature, knowledge of Italian is often necessary.

Agape Centro Ecumenico (☎3912 180 75 14; www.agapecentroecumenico.org). 12 volunteers age 18+ help maintain this international and national Christian conference center in the Italian Alps. Clean and cook for the center 6hr. per day, 6 days per week for at least 1 month. Work available June-Sept., Christmas, and Easter. Knowledge of Italian and any other language useful. Accommodations provided.

Emmaus Italia, V. la Luna, No. 1, I-52020 Pergine Valdarno Arezzo, Italy. 20 different locations with volunteer work with disabled persons, theater, film, housing renovation, and site preservation. Mail for details.

Mani Tese, V. Cavenaghi, 4, I-20149 Milan, Italy (☎02 469 71 88). Fundraising opportunities for developing countries.

Volunteers for Peace, VFP 1034 Tiffany Rd., Belmonst, Vermont 05730, USA (☎802-259-2759; www.vfp.org). Provides info on different volunteer programs in Italy.

STUDYING

VISA INFORMATION. Italy will throw loads of confusing paperwork at you before allowing you to stay. Unfortunately, Italian bureaucracy is not quite as well-oiled as one would wish. Many of the organizations listed throughout this chapter can provide advice on how to minimize red tape. All non-EU citizens are required to obtain a visa for any stay longer than 3 months, even if they are tourists. For info and applications, contact the Italian embassy or consulate in your country. All non-EU citizens are also required to obtain a *permesso di soggiorno* (permit of stay) within 8 days of arriving in Italy. If you are staying in a hotel or hostel, this requirement is generally waived, but otherwise, you must apply at a police station or the foreigners' office in main police stations. EU citizens must apply for a *permesso di soggiorno* within 3 months. Once you find a place to live, bring your permit to stay (it must have at least one year's validity) to a records office *(circoscrizione)*. This certificate, which confirms your registered address, will expedite such procedures as clearing goods from abroad through customs and making large purchases.

Study abroad programs range from basic language and culture courses to college-level classes, often for credit. In order to choose a program that best fits your needs, research as much as you can before making your decision—determine costs and duration, as well as what kind of students participate in the program and what sort of accommodations are provided.

EU citizens do not need a visa to study in Italy. Non-EU citizens wishing to study in Italy must obtain a student visa at least one week prior to departure from their nearest Italian embassy or consulate. Upon arrival in Italy, students must register with the Foreigners' Bureau *(Ufficio degli Stranieri)* of the local *questura* in order to receive the *permesso di soggiorno per studio* (permit of stay).

In programs that have large groups of students who speak the same language, there is a trade-off. You may feel more comfortable in the community of lots of English-speaking international students, but you will not have the same opportunity to practice Italian or to befriend Italian students. For accommodations, dorm life is more conducive to mingling with fellow students, but provides less of a chance to experience the local scene. If you live with a family, there is the potential to build lifelong friendships and to experience day-to-day Italian culture in more depth, but conditions can vary greatly from family to family.

UNIVERSITIES

Most university-level study-abroad programs are conducted in Italian, although many programs offer classes in English and beginner- and lower-level language courses. Those relatively fluent in Italian may find it cheaper to enroll directly in a university abroad, although getting college credit may prove more difficult. You can search www.studyabroad.com for various semester-abroad programs that meet your criteria, including desired location and focus of study. The following is a list of organizations that can help place students in university programs abroad, or have their own branch in Italian.

AMERICAN PROGRAMS

American Institute for Foreign Study, Richmond in Florence/Rome, College Division, River Plaza, 9 W. Broad St., Stamford, CT 06902, USA (☎800-727-2437; www.aifsabroad.com). Programs in Florence and Rome. Mandatory Italian language class; internship placement available. Meals and homestay or student apartment included. 12-15 credits. Semester US$12,995; year US$22,790.

CET Academic Programs: History of Art Program in Siena, 1920 N St. NW, Ste. 200, Washington, D.C. 20036, USA (☎800-225-4262; www.cetacademicprograms.com). Art history courses and traveling seminars; mandatory Italian language course. Summer US$5990; semester US$12,990. Includes medical insurance.

Institute for the International Education of Students (IES), 33 N. LaSalle St., 15th fl., Chicago, IL 60602, USA (☎800-995-2300; www.IESabroad.org). Offers year-long (US $21,510), semester (US$11,950), and summer programs (US$4,100) for college study in Milan and Rome, as well as internship opportunities. US$50 application fee. Scholarships are available for certain programs.

'nternational Association for the Exchange of Students for Technical Experience (IAESTE), 10400 Little Patuxent Pkwy., Ste 250, Columbia, MD 21044, USA (☎410-997-2200; www.aipt.org). Offers 8- to 12-week programs in Italy for college students who have completed 2 years of technical study. US$25 application fee.

School for International Training, College Semester Abroad, Admissions, Kipling Rd., P.O. Box 676, Brattleboro, VT 05302, USA (☎800-257-7751 or 802-257-7751; www.sit.edu). Semester- and year-long programs US$10,600-13,700. Also runs the **Experiment in International Living** (☎800-345-2929; www.usexperiment.org), 3- to 5-week summer programs that offer high-school students homestays, community service, ecological adventure, and language training in Italy and cost US$1900-5000.

ITALIAN PROGRAMS

In the last 30 years, Italian language and culture schools have increased by the hundreds. While the average age of students is 15-25 years old, Italy has thousands of visitors in every age range who come to study art and culture. There are one- to three-month programs, usually from March through October, as well as more long-term options with full year curriculums. While certain advanced classes are conducted in Italian, many study abroad programs are taught from English-speaking teachers. Students outside the EU and any non-Italian citizens planning to spend more than 90 days in Italy must gain approval from a local consulate to study abroad, receiving *il visito di studio* (visa permit to study) before leaving. Most universities and programs provide student accommodations.

LANGUAGE SCHOOLS

Language schools are generally international or local organizations or divisions of foreign universities. They rarely offer college credit. Enrolling in a language course is a good alternative to university study if you desire a deeper focus on the language or a slightly less rigorous course load. These programs are also good for younger high school students who might not feel comfortable with older students in a university program. Some good programs include:

Centro Fiorenza, V. S. Spirito, 14, 50125 Florence, Italy (☎39 055 239 82 74; www.centrofiorenza.com). Students live in homestays or apartments. Program also offers courses on the island of Elba, although hotel accommodations there are expensive. 2- to 4-week courses, 20 lessons per week, starting at €295. €52 enrollment fee.

Eurocentres, 101 N. Union St. Suite 300, Alexandria, VA 22314, USA (☎703-684-1494; www.eurocentres.com) or in Europe, Head Office, Seestr. 247, CH-8038 Zurich, Switzerland (☎485 50 40, fax 481 61 24). Language programs for beginning to advanced students with homestays in Italy.

Istituto Zambler Venezia, Dorsoduro, 3116A, Campo S. Margherita, Venice, Italy (☎39 041 522 43 31; www.istitutovenezia.com). Language classes at all levels, taught in small groups. Courses last 1 to 10 weeks. Accommodation arrangements upon request; costs and housing types vary. Tuition €190-4150.

Italiaidea, V. dei Due Macelli, 47, 1st fl., 00187 Rome, Italy (☎39 06 699 41 314; www.italiaidea.com). Italian language and culture courses in groups of 10 or fewer. Accreditation available for American university programs. Students live in homestays or apartments; reserve ahead. Tuition from €465 for 4 weeks or 60hr.

Koinè, V. de Pandolfini, 27, I-50122 Florence, Italy (☎39 055 21 38 81; www.koine-center.com). Language lessons (group and individual), cultural lessons, wine tastings, and cooking lessons. Courses offered year-round in Florence, Lucca, and Bologna; summer programs in Cortona and Orbetello. Tuition from €205.

Language Immersion Institute, 75 South Manheim Blvd., SUNY-New Paltz, New Paltz, NY 12561, USA (☎845-257-3500; www.newpaltz.edu/lii). 2-week summer language courses and some overseas courses in Italian. Program fees are around US$1000.

ITALIAN SCHOOLS: SPECIAL INTEREST

Aegean Center for the Fine Arts, Paros 84400, Cyclades, Greece (☎30 22 840 23 287; www.aegeancenter.org). Italian branch located in Pistoia. Instruction in arts, literature, creative writing, voice, and art history. Classes taught in English. Fees cover lodging, board, and excursions to Rome, Venice, and Greece. University credit on individual arrangement. 14-week program €7000.

Apicius, The Culinary Institute of Florence, Study Abroad Italy, 7151 Wilton Ave., Ste 202, Sebastopol, CA 95472, USA (☎707-824-8965; www.tuscancooking.com/index.htm). Professional and non-professional food and wine studies in the historic center of Florence. Cooking courses in English; Italian language classes available. Additional housing prices vary. Year-long Master's program US$11,000. Prices for weekly and monthly non-professional programs vary.

Art School in Florence, Studio Art Centers International, c/o Institute of International Education, 809 United Nations Plaza, New York, NY 10017, USA (☎212-984-5548; www.saci-florence.org). Associated with Bowling Green State University. Studio arts, art history, Italian studies. Apartment housing. Summer, 6 credits US$4500; semester, 15 credits US$11,600.

Carmelita's Cook Italy, (☎39 349 007 82 98; www.cookitaly.com). Region- or dish-specific cooking classes. Venues in Lucca, Florence and Cortona. Courses run 3 nights-2 weeks, from US$750. Housing, meals, and recipes included.

The International Kitchen, 1 IBM Plaza, 330 N. Wabash #3005, Chicago, IL 60611, USA (☎312-726-4525; www.theinternationalkitchen.com). Leading provider of cooking school vacations to Italy and France. Traditional cooking instruction in beautiful settings for groups of 8-12. Program locations include Tuscany, Liguria, and Amalfi Coast. Courses run 2-7 nights. Prices vary.

Professione Futura Culinary School, V. Aurelia, 1100/21, Rome, Italy (☎39 06 661 83 777; www.worldwide.edu). Rigorous Gourmet Italian cooking course in 3- and 6-month programs; involves short stage in hotel or restaurant kitchen. 20 students per class. Fee covers accommodations and simultaneous Italian language course.

WORKING

VISA INFORMATION. EU passport holders do not require a visa to work in Italy. They must have a workers registration book (*libretto di lavoro*), available at no extra cost upon presentation of the *permesso di soggiorno*. If your parents were born in an EU country, you may be able to claim dual citizenship or the right to a work permit. Non-EU citizens seeking work in Italy must apply for an Italian work permit (*autorizzazione al lavoro in Italia*) before entering the country. Permits are authorized by the Provincial Employment Office and approved by the *questura* before being forwarded to the employer and prospective employee. The prospective employee must then present the document, along with a valid passport, in order to obtain a work visa. Normally a three-month tourist permit is granted, and upon presentation of an employer's letter the permit can be extended for a period specified by the employment contract. In some sectors (like agricultural work), permit-less workers are rarely bothered by authorities.

As with volunteering, work opportunities tend to fall into two categories. Some travelers want long-term jobs that allow them to get to know another part of the world as a member of the community, while other travelers seek out short-term jobs to finance the next leg of their travels. In Italy, travelers usually find jobs in the service sector or in agriculture, working for a few weeks at a time.

A work visa is necessary for non-Italians to be employed in Italy (see above). Check with your country's consulate for more specific details. Listed below are specific jobs for long-term and short-term stays, as well as agencies that can provide useful information regarding work opportunities.

LONG-TERM WORK

If you're planning on spending a substantial amount of time (more than three months) working in Italy, search for a job well in advance. International placement agencies are often the easiest way to find employment abroad, especially

ALTERNATIVES TO TOURISM

for teaching English. **Internships,** usually for college students, are a good way to segue into working abroad, although they are often unpaid (many say the experience, however, is well worth it). Be wary of advertisements or companies that claim the ability to get you a job for a fee—often the same listings are available online or in newspapers, or are even out-of-date. Some reputable organizations include:

The Associated Press, P. Grazioli, 5, 00186 Rome (☎06 678 99 36; www.ap.org/italia), offers newsroom, photography, and TV internships to college students and graduates. Complete Italian fluency required. Unpaid internships last 3-6 months, min. 20hr. per week. Submit resume and inquiries to the intern coordinator. Call for information.

Center for Cultural Interchange, 17 N. Second Ave., St. Charles, IL 60174, USA (☎630-377-2272; www.cci-exchange.com/intern.htm). Volunteer internships with companies in Florence. Opportunities in general business, accounting and finance, tourism, and social services. At least 2 years of college-level study in Italian required. Tuition includes Italian language course, health insurance, and homestay with half-board.

Global Experiences, Italy Office, Centro Linguistico Italiano Dante Alighieri, P. della Repubblica, 5, I-50123 Florence, Italy (US☎410-703-1738; www.globalexperiences.com), arranges internships with companies based in or around Florence. Interns receive intensive language training prior to placement. Fields include law, international business, travel/tourism, and graphic design.

Institute for the International Education of Students, 33 N. LaSalle St., 15th fl., Chicago, IL 60602, USA (☎800-995-2300; www.iesabroad.org). Intern placements in Rome and Milan based on availability, background, skills, and language ability. Past placements include assignments with fashion designers, photographers, and international companies. Must be for academic credit.

Lexia International, 25 S. Main St., Hanover, NH 03755, USA (☎603-643-9898; www.lexiaintl.org/Venice/index.cfm), at the Institutio Venezia, affiliated with the Università degli Studi di Venezia. Internship placement offered to supplement an academic

ESSAY CONTEST WINNER!

beyondtourism.com

Last year's winner, Eleanor Glass, spent a summer volunteering with children on an island off the Yucatan Peninsula. Read the rest of her story and find your own once-in-a-lifetime experience at **www.beyondtourism.com!**

"... I was discovering elements of life in Mexico that I had never even dreamt of. I regularly had meals at my students' houses, as their fisherman fathers would instruct them to invite the nice gringa to lunch after a lucky day's catch. Downtown, tourists wandered the streets and spent too much on cheap necklaces, while I played with a friend's baby niece, or took my new kitten to the local vet for her shots, or picked up tortillas at the tortilleria, or vegetables in the mercado. ... I was lucky that I found a great place to volunteer and a community to adopt me. ... Just being there, listening to stories, hearing the young men talk of cousins who had crossed the border, I know I went beyond tourism." - Eleanor Glass, 2004

LET'S GO

program in intensive language training, Italian culture classes, and individualized field research. Students apply in advance. Semester- and year-long programs offered. Past internship fields include government, the arts, health care, and non-profit organizations.

TEACHING ENGLISH

Teaching jobs abroad are rarely well-paid, although some elite private American schools can pay somewhat competitive salaries. Volunteering as a teacher in lieu of getting paid is also a popular option; even in those cases, teachers often get some sort of daily stipend to help with living expenses. In almost all cases, you must have at least a bachelor's degree to be a full-fledged teacher, although college undergraduates can often get summer positions teaching or tutoring. English-language schools abound in Italy, but the supply of applicants is plentiful, and positions are competitive. Finding a teaching job is even harder for non-EU citizens, as some schools prefer or, in some cases, require EU citizenship.

Many schools require teachers to have a **Teaching English as a Foreign Language (TEFL)** certificate. Not having this certification does not necessarily exclude you from finding a teaching job, but certified teachers often find higher-paying jobs. Native English speakers working in private schools are most often hired for English-immersion classrooms where no Italian is spoken. Those volunteering or teaching in poorer public schools are more likely to be working in both English and Italian. Placement agencies or university fellowship programs are the best resources for finding teaching jobs. The alternative is to make contact directly with schools or just to try your luck once you get there. If you are going to try the latter, the best time to look is several weeks before the start of the school year. The following organizations are extremely helpful in placing teachers in Italy.

International Schools Services (ISS), 15 Roszel Rd., Box 5910, Princeton, NJ 08543-5910, USA (☎609-452-0990; www.iss.edu). Hires teachers for more than 200 overseas schools. Candidates should have experience teaching or with international affairs, 2-year commitment expected.

Office of Overseas Schools, US Department of State, 2201 C Street NW, Washington D.C. 20520, USA (☎202-647-4000; www.state.gov/m/a/os), provides an extensive list of general information about teaching overseas. See also the **Office of English Language Programs** (http://exchanges.state.gov/education/engteaching/).

The following institutions consistently employ native English speakers: **Wall Street Institute** (☎39 0432 48 14 64; www.wsi.it); **British Institutes** (☎39 0272 09 45 95; www.britishinstitutes.org); and **The Cambridge School** (☎04 58 00 31 54; www.cambridgeschool.it). The **Associazione Culturale Linguistica Educational (ACLE),** V. Roma, 54, San Remo (☎01 84 50 60 70; www.acle.org), operates English-language immersion summer camps for children all over Italy. Insurance and a modest weekly salary are provided. The ACLE also operates **Theatrino,** a touring group of actors that promotes spoken English through interactive performances and workshops. (Apply through ACLE; auditions usually held in London.) Smaller companies are listed in the Yellow Pages and in local Italian newspapers.

AU PAIR WORK

Au pairs are typically women, aged 18-27, who work as live-in nannies, caring for children and doing light housework in foreign countries in exchange for room, board, and a small spending allowance or stipend. Most former au pairs speak favorably of their experience. One perk of the job is that it allows you to really get to know the country without the high expenses of traveling. Drawbacks, however, often include long hours of constant duty for somewhat mediocre pay. In Italy,

FURTHER READING ON ALTERNATIVES TO TOURISM.

Alternatives to the Peace Corps: A Directory of Third World and U.S. Volunteer Opportunities, by Joan Powell. Food First Books, 2000 (US$10).

How to Live Your Dream of Volunteering Overseas, by Collins, DeZerega, and Heckscher. Penguin Books, 2002 (US$17).

International Directory of Voluntary Work, by Whetter and Pybus. Peterson's Guides and Vacation Work, 2000 (US$16).

International Jobs, by Kocher and Segal. Perseus Books, 1999 (US$18).

Invest Yourself: The Catalogue of Volunteer Opportunities, published by the Commission on Voluntary Service and Action (☎718-638-8487).

Overseas Summer Jobs 2002, by Collier and Woodworth. Peterson's Guides and Vacation Work, 2002 (US$18).

Work Abroad: The Complete Guide to Finding a Job Overseas, by Hubbs, Griffith, and Nolting. Transitions Abroad Publishing, 2000 ($16).

Work Your Way Around the World, by Susan Griffith. Worldview Publishing Services, 2001 (US$18).

average weekly pay for au pair work is about €65. Much of the au pair experience really does depend on the family with whom you're placed. The agencies below are a good starting point for looking for employment.

Au Pair in Europe, P.O. Box 68056, Blakely Postal Outlet, Hamilton, Ontario, Canada L8M 3M7 (☎905-545-6305; www.princeent.com).

Au Pair Italy, V. Demetrio Martinelli, 11/D, 40133 Bologna, Italy (☎51 38 34 66; www.aupairitaly.com). Summer positions (2-3 months) and long-term placements (up to 1 year) available. Knowledge of Italian not required, but course work while in Italy recommended. Stipends start at €65 per week.

Childcare International, Ltd., Trafalgar House, Grenville Pl., London NW7 3SA (☎020 8906-3116; www.childint.co.uk).

InterExchange, 161 Sixth Ave., New York, NY 10013, USA (☎212-924-0446; www.interexchange.org).

Mix Culture Au Pair Service, V. Nazionale, 204, 00184 Rome (☎06 47 88 22 89; http://web.tiscali.it/mixcultureroma/index.htm). 6 months-1 year min stay. Requires enrollment in a language school in order to obtain a student visa. €65 registration fee.

SHORT-TERM WORK

Traveling for long periods of time can get expensive; therefore, many travelers try their hand at odd jobs for a few weeks at a time to help finance another month or two of touring around. Romantic images of cultivating the land in a sun-soaked vineyard may be dancing in your head; in reality, though, casual agricultural jobs are hard to find in Italy, given the number of foreign migrant workers who are often willing to work for less pay. Your best bet for agricultural jobs is to look in the northwest (the harvest is usually in September and October). Another popular option is to work several hours a day at a hostel in exchange for free or discounted room and/or board. Most often, these short-term jobs are found by word of mouth, or simply by talking to the owner of a hostel or restaurant. Due to the high turnover in the tourism industry, many places are eager for help, even if it is only temporary. *Let's Go* tries to list temporary jobs like these whenever possible; look in the practical info sections of larger cities or check out the list below for some of the available short-term jobs in popular destinations.

ALTERNATIVES TO TOURISM

Deck-hand work, in Viareggio. Inquire at yacht brokerages around V. Coppino.

Ostello La Primula (HI), V. IV Novembre, 86, Menaggio, Italy (☎034 43 23 56; www.menaggiohostel.com). Work in return for room and board.

Short-term work, Lavoro Temporaneo Office, P. Aldo Moro, in Bari near the FAL station, can find jobs lasting a couple of months.

Youth Info Center (Informagiovani), C. Porto Borsari, 17, Verona, Italy (☎045 801 07 96), provides info on work regulations and finds travelers local employment.

ALTERNATIVES TO TOURISM

How responsible travel might save one of Italy's poorest regions.

Anywhere but these rolling hills of wheat. Such a thought is not uncommon in Alta Irpinia, the mountainous half of the Avellino province of Campania. Here, the problems that mark the entire South are exacerbated by the mountainous terrain that makes agriculture unprofitable, unlike in the fertile Puglian plains. Modern industry and economy have largely failed here, and the few factories that once provided jobs to the region are moving overseas. Unemployment is around 20%. In addition, Irpinia is at high seismic risk. The effects of the terrible earthquake of November 1980 are still visible, when a shattering 6.9 degrees on the Richter scale resulted in 5000 dead, 20,000 homeless, and 30 towns completely destroyed. Government subsidies flowed in after the catastrophe to revitalize the region, without long-term success. In recent years, Irpinia's best and brightest have migrated to Naples or north to Turin or Milan. Those who remain are faced with the failures of both their traditional lifestyle and of the attempt to adopt more modern ways.

Some Irpinians believe that their traditional culture is worth fighting for. A new buzzword, *agriturismo*, or ecotourism, denotes this push to save Irpinia by moving closer to nature and to rural ways of life. The region's riches include beautiful mountainous landscapes, famous wines (Greco di Tufo won a prestigious French award in 2004), archaeological sites, and ancient castles and churches. Not all was destroyed by earthquakes or by building speculation, although often the potential of a site is wasted because of a lack of resources to develop it. A number of castles dot a region once ruled by the medieval court of Frederick II. Frederick's enlightened court was composed of Christians, Jews, and Muslims, who introduced Arab science to the West and invented the sonnet. The medieval period also left behind many churches and monasteries, but archaeological sites are Irpinia's real hidden treasure. Prior to the Roman invasion, a local population of Sannites flourished here. Little is known about them, as there have never been the funds to excavate the region properly. The situation is a vicious circle: without fully developed cultural sites, there will be no tourism; yet without a tourist industry, there will never be money to excavate ruins or restore churches.

The Zampaglione family is a good example of a business that has completely embraced the *agriturismo* ethos. Their farm near Calitri has produced wheat according to organic methods since 1990, which they then make into organic pasta. In 1998 they transformed their old barns into a guest-house. Their B&B-style hospitality targets tourists seeking authentic experiences that preserve the way of life that characterized Italy until very recently. A visit to the Zampaglione farm presents northern Italians with the chance to connect to the rural culture and lifestyle of their grandparents, gradually erased by urbanization by the late 20th century. The Zampagliones also hope to attract international travelers who already know Italy and wish to see the country from a different, perhaps more genuine, angle. Nonetheless, often many weeks pass when no one ventures to the farm, and the post-9/11 tourism slump has not helped the Zampaglione family convince Irpinia that *agriturismo* is the answer to its problems.

Ethnographic museums have been more successful in taking root and matching the ideals of *agriturismo*. Museums attempt to preserve and present what is known of traditional village culture. Visitors are fascinated by the handicrafts still practiced in Irpinia, such as the local ceramic industry. However, industrial procedures threaten to replace these ancient crafts. The last original practitioners of Irpinian pottery, for example, fire their pots only once a year in a large, purpose-built oven, which is then destroyed. The Zampagliones would like to harness this know-how and offer pottery courses to groups of visitors, but time is running out as the artisans age and no one learns their skills. Local cuisine, fortunately, does not face the same risk. Simple elements are put together to compose a healthy, rural diet strong in fresh pastas and cheeses, as in *caviuoli* or ravioli with ricotta, or farm vegetables such as grilled bell peppers.

In the summer of 2004, a group of Chinese government officials traveled to Alta Irpinia. Their mission was to study *agriturismo* as a business model, in the hopes of relaunching the economies of China's rural and impoverished regions in a similar manner. For those in Irpinia who have attempted to establish that traditional methods can be reinstated, this was one small sign of success. *Agriturismo* is still the work of individuals, and does not reflect a greater policy on the part of the Avellino province, too trouble-ridden to implement such a far-sighted strategy. Nonetheless, *agriturismo* is an important validation for those who refuse to modernize or leave. Time will tell whether Irpinians will be able to inventively employ past traditions in a way that will take them successfully into the future, or whether this remainder of ancient culture will be swept away.

Alexander Bevilacqua was born in Milan and has lived in Germany, Australia, and the United States, but his heart remains in the wheat fields of southern Italy. He is currently a student at Harvard University and works at its Center for European Studies. He was a Researcher-Writer for Let's Go: Germany in Bavaria.

ROME AND LAZIO

Welcome to Lazio, former home of the mythologized Etruscan tribe that dominated northern and central Italy during the first millennium BC. Rural Lazio was originally called *Latium*, Latin for "wide land;" indeed, Lazio stretches from the low Tyrrhenian coastline through volcanic mountains to the foothills of the *Abruzzese* Apennines. Romans, Etruscans, Latins, and Sabines all settled here, and their contests for supremacy make up some of the first pages of Italy's recorded history. The biggest attraction of this area is of course Rome. Today mystical ruins, peaceful hillsides, and panoramic views give this region the colorful diversity that attracts so many tourists year after year.

HIGHLIGHTS OF ROME AND LAZIO

CHANNEL Rome's Golden Age with a trip to the Ancient City. (p. 109.)

TRADE dusty for designer; leave ruins behind in search of the chic sophistication of the Spanish Steps. (p. 116.)

SURVEY the Eternal City's art scene, and let collections from the Vatican Museums (p. 124) to the Galleria Borghese (p. 125) prove the city deserving of its reputation.

EVADE the temptations of Circe on the Pontine Islands, where the likes of Mussolini, Nero, and even Odysseus were reputedly held captive. (p. 134.)

ROME (ROMA) ☎06

Centuries of sporadic growth transformed Rome from a fledgling city-state to the capital of the Western world. At its zenith, the glory of Rome transcended human imagination and touched upon the divine; from its legendary founding in the shadows of pre-history, to the demi-god emperors who reveled in human form, to the modern papacy's global political influence, earthly ideas have proved insufficient to capture the Eternal City. Looking at Rome today, the phrase "decline and fall" seems preposterous—though Rome no longer dictates Western history, its claim upon the modes of culture remains firmly intact. Style. Art. Food. Passion. These form Rome's new empire, tying the city to the living moment, rather than relegating it to stagnate in a museum case. Today, while the Colosseum crumbles from industrial pollution, Romans celebrate their city. Concerts animate the ancient monuments and children play soccer around the Pantheon. In a city that has stood for nearly 3000 years, Rome's glory is not dimmed, merely altered.

▓ INTERCITY TRANSPORTATION

FLIGHTS

Most international flights arrive at **da Vinci International Airport** (☎06 659 51), known as **Fiumicino**. After exiting customs, follow the signs to the left for **Stazione FS/Railway Station.** Take the elevator or escalators up two floors to the pedestrian bridge to the airport train station. The **Termini line** runs nonstop to Rome's main train station, **Termini Station** (31min.; 2 per hr. 8 and 38min. past the hour, 7:37am-10:37pm, extra trains 6:38am and 11:38pm; €9.50, €12.35 on board). Buy a ticket at the FS ticket counter, the *tabacchi* on the right, or from one of the machines in the station. A train leaves Termini for Fiumicino from track #27. Follow signs for *"Fiumicino Terminal"* (40min.; 2 per hr. 22 and 52min. past the hr., 5:52am-

ROME AND LAZIO

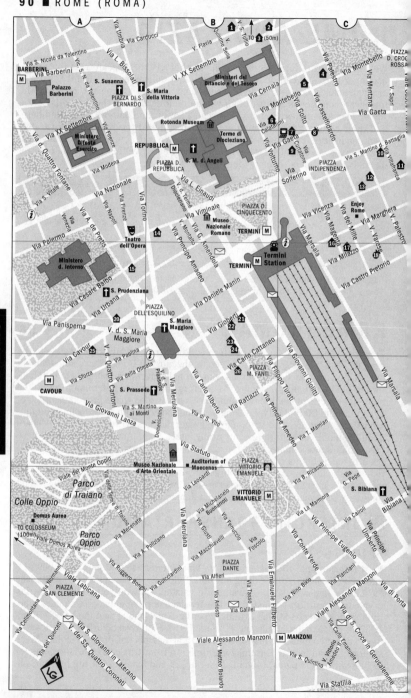

Rome:
Termini and San Lorenzo

🏠 ACCOMMODATIONS

Affittacamere Aries, 2	B1
Alessandro Downtown, 26	B4
Alessandro Indipendenza, 9	C2
Alessandro Palace, 13	C2
Domus Nova Bethlehem, 20	A3
Freedom Traveller, 7	C2
Hotel Bolognese, 4	C1
Hotel Castelfidardo and Hotel Lazzari, 5	C1
Hotel Cervia, 12	C2
Hotel Des Artistes, 11	C2
Hotel Dolomiti and Hotel Lachea, 10	C2
Hotel Galli, 17	C3
Hotel Giù Giù, 14	B2
Hotel Kennedy, 21	B3
Hotel Papa Germano, 6	B1
Hotel Scott House, 22	B3
Pensione Cortorillo, 23	B3
Pensione di Rienzo, 24	B3
Pensione Fawlty Towers, 16	C3
Pensione Monaco, 1	B1
Pensione Sandy, 25	A3
Pensione Tizi, 3	B1
YWCA, 15	A3

🍎🍽 FOOD and NIGHTLIFE

Africa, 8	C2
Arancia Blu, 29	D5
Il Pulcino Ballerino, 27	D5
Il Simposio, 28	D5
Il Tunnel, 19	F1
Hostaria da Bruno, 18	C3

ROME AND LAZIO

TO PIAZZA DEL POPOLO (450m)

Via del Corso

TO PZA. DI SPAGNA (300m)

Mausoleum of Augustus

V. Tomacelli

Via dell'Arancio

V. Borghese
PZA. SAN LORENZO IN LUCINA

V. d. Clementino

V. d. Campo Marzio

PZA. DEL PARLAMENTO

PZA. DI PARLAMENTO

PIAZZA DI PIETRA

PZA. CAPRANICA

PIAZZA DI COLL. ROMANO

Via d. Plebiscito

Via V. d. Romano

Via Caravita

PZA. FIRENZE

PIAZZA MONTECITORIO

Via d'Asta

V. Rosini

V. d. Uffici d. Vicario

Via del Seminario

PIAZZA DI GESÙ

CAMPO MARZIO

V. della Maddalena

V. d. Pastini

PZA. IN CAMPO MARZIO

Pantheon

PIAZZA DELLA MINERVA

Metastasio

V. d. Scrofa

V. Colonnelle

PIAZZA DELLA ROTONDA

V. d. Pantheon

Lung. Marzio

Lungotevere Prati

Ponte Cavour

V. Colonna

PZA. CAVOUR

PZA. DEI TRIBUNALI

Palazzo di Giustizia

PZA. ADRIANA

Pte. Umberto

Lung. Tor di Nona

Via dei Coronari

V. d. Orso

Via dell'Orso

V. d. Soldati

Via Zanardelli

PZA. AGOSTINO

PIAZZA NAVONA

Corso de Rinascimento

V. d. Scrofa

PZA. S. EUSTACHIO

LGO. TORRE ARGENTINA

LGO. ARENULA

Via de Chiavari

V. d. Seddari

Sant'Agnese in Agone

PZA. PASQUINO

Castel Sant'Angelo

Fiume Tevere (Tiber River)

Pte. S. Angelo

PZA. CORONARI

Via di Panico

V. di Monti Cerri

V. del Governo Vecchio

V. d. Fossa

PZA. DEL FICO

Corso Vittorio Emanuele II

PZA. S. PANTALEO

V. della CANCELLERIA

V. dei Chiavari

CAMPO DE' FIORI

PZA. DELLA CANCELLERIA

V. del Pellegrino

PZA. DI PARADISO

PZA. DI BISCIONE

V. de' Giubbonari

VATICANO

L. Vaticano

PTE. V. EMANUELE II

Pte. Pr. Amedeo Savoia Aosta

PZA. PAOLI PAOLA

B. S. Spirito

PZA. CHIESA NUOVA

CHIESA NUOVA

Via del Pellegrino

V. del Cappellari

PZA. SFORZA CESARINI

Cellini

Catena Filippini

PZA. DELLA CHIESA NUOVA

Via di Monserrato

PIAZZA FARNESE

Palazzo Farnese

Via Giulia

V. d. Petrinis

San Pietro

VATICAN CITY

PIAZZA SAN PIETRO

PIAZZA PIO

LARGO PORTA CAVALLEGGERI

Borgo Pio

V. di Concilizaione

Santo Spirito

L. in Sassia

PZA. DELL'ORO

LGO. DEI FIORENTINI

V. d. C. P. Sugnelli

Via Giulia

Lungotevere del Sangallo

V. Brescani

Confalonieri

Scimia

Prigioni

Pte. Mazzini

V. Mazzini

Lungotevere del Tebaldi

Lungotevere della Farnesina

L. della Farnesina

Villa Farnesina

Via della Lungara

Palazzo Corsini

V. di Porta Cavalleggeri

V. D. Stazione di San Pietro

P.S. MARIA ALLE FORNACI

Chiesa S. Maria alle Fornaci

PZA. D. STAZIONE DI S. PIETRO

Stazione S. Pietro

Penitenzieri

PZA. DE ROVERE

L. Gianicolense

V. d. Ori - di Albert

V. del Gianicolo

Via del Gianicolo

Monte Gianicolo

Parco Gianicolense

Via dei Riari

V. d. S. Fr.-di Sales

V. d. Mantellate

Rome: Centro Storico and Trastevere

ROME AND LAZIO

◆ ACCOMMODATIONS

Albergo Abruzzi, 12	F2
Albergo del Sole, 18	E3
Albergo della Lunetta, 20	E3
Albergo Pomezia, 21	E3
Hotel Carmel, 33	C5
Hotel Navona, 14	E3
Hotel Trastevere, 31	C5
Santa Maria Alle Fornaci, 36	A2

🍽 FOOD

Augusto, 26	D4
Caffè della Pace, 6	D2
Cul de Sac, 5	D2
Da Quinto, 7	E2
Dar Poeta, 24	C4
Gioitti, 10	F2
Il Portico, 29	E4
Il Sant'Eustachio Caffè, 15	E3
Il Tulipano Nero, 32	C5
L'Insalata Ricca, 19	E3
La Pollarola, 17	E4
La Taverna del Ghetto, 28	E5
Ouzeri, 35	D2
Pizzeria Baffetto, 3	D2
Pizzeria Corallo, 2	C4
Pizzeria San Callisto, 27	C5
Ristorante a Casa di Alfredo, 34	E4
Tazza d'Oro, 11	D2
Trattoria Da Giggetto, 30	D3
Trattoria Da Luigi, 1	F2
Trattoria da Sergio, 22	E2
Trattoria dal Cav. Gino, 9	D3
Tre Scalini, 8	E2
Zampanò, 16	D3

🍷 NIGHTLIFE

Artu Cafe, 25	C4
Bar da Benito, 23	E4
Groove, 13	D3
Jonathan's Angels, 4	D2

10:52pm; €8.80). Buy tickets at the Alitalia office (from 9am-7:30pm), at track #22 at the window marked *"Biglietti Per Fiumicino,"* or from other designated areas in the station. Validate your ticket before boarding.

EARLY AND LATE FLIGHTS. For flights that arrive after 10pm or leave before 8am, the most reliable option is to take a **cab.** (Request one at the kiosk in the airport or call ☎06 35 70, 06 49 94 or 06 66 45. €35-45. Decide upon a price with the driver before getting into the cab and keep in mind that things like the amount of luggage you have and whether it is a late night or a holiday will affect the price. Drivers have been known to charge upwards of €150 for the fare to Rome.) The cheapest option is to take the blue **COTRAL bus** (☎800 15 00 08) to Tiburtina from the ground floor outside the main exit doors after customs (1:15, 2:15, 3:30, 5am; €5 on board). From Tiburtina, take bus #492 or Metro B to Termini. To get to Fiumicino from Rome late at night or early in the morning, take bus 492 or Metro B from Termini to Tiburtina (every 20-30min.), then catch the blue COTRAL bus to Fiumicino from the plaza (12:30, 1:15, 2:30, 3:45am; €5).

DOMESTIC FLIGHTS. Most charter and a few domestic flights arrive at **Ciampino airport** (☎06 79 49 41). To get to Rome from Ciampino, take the **COTRAL bus** (every 30min., 6:10am-11:40pm, €1) to Anagnina station on Metro A. After 11pm and before 7am, take a **cab.**

TRAINS

Stazione Termini is the focal point of most train and subway lines. Trains arriving in Rome between midnight and 5am usually arrive at Stazione Tiburtina or Stazione Ostiense; both connect to Termini at night by bus #175. Station services include: **hotel reservations** (across from track #20); **ATMs; luggage storage** (underneath track #24); and **police** (☎112; track #13; make a report at track #1). ◼**Termini's bathrooms** are a black-lit wonderland off track #1 (€0.60). Trains (Direct, or D, is the slowest; IC is the intercity train; ES, or Eurostar, is the fastest and most expensive) leave Termini for: **Bologna** (D 3½hr., €26.41; IC 3hr., €31.41; ES 2½hr., €37.18); **Florence** (D 3¾hr., €14.31; IC 2½hr., €21.95; ES 1½hr., €29.44); **Milan** (D 8hr., €30.37; IC 6hr., €41.17; ES 4½hr., €46.48); **Naples** (D 2½hr., €10.12; IC 2hr., €14.21; ES 1¾hr., €22.21); **Venice** (D overnight, €57.43; IC 5½hr., €35.89; ES 4½hr., €44.93).

◼ ORIENTATION

Two blocks north of the **Termini** train station, **Via Nazionale** is the central artery connecting **Piazza della Repubblica** with **Piazza Venezia,** home to the immense wedding-cake-like Vittorio Emanuele II **monument.** A few blocks west of P. Venezia, **Largo Argentina** marks the start of **Corso Vittorio Emanuele,** which leads to the *centro storico*, the tangle of sights around the **Pantheon, Piazza Navona, Campo dei Fiori,** and **Piazza Farnese.** From P. Venezia, V. dei Fori Imperiale leads southeast to the **Forum** and **Colosseum,** south of which are the ruins of the **Baths of Caracalla** and the **Appian Way,** and the southern neighborhoods of the Aventine, Testaccio, Ostiense, and EUR. **Via del Corso** stretches from P. Venezia north to **Piazza del Popolo.** East of the Corso, fashionable streets border the **Piazza di Spagna** and, to the northeast, the **Villa Borghese.** South and east are the **Fontana di Trevi, Piazza Barberini,** and the **Quirinal Hill.** Across the Tiber to the northwest are **Vatican City,** and, to the southwest, **Trastevere,** the best neighborhood for wandering. Pick up a free map from a tourist office. The invaluable **Roma Metro-Bus map** (€4.13) is available at newsstands or at the ATAC office, V. Volturno, 65 (free).

⌐ LOCAL TRANSPORTATION

*Bus and subway tickets (€1) are one and the same, and can be bought at tabacchi, newsstands, vending machines, and some bars. Vending machines are in stations, on some street corners, and at major bus stops. Look for the ATAC label. Each ticket is valid for either one Metro ride or unlimited bus travel within 1¼hr. of validation. A **BIG** daily ticket (€4) allows for unlimited bus or train travel in the metropolitan area, including Ostia but not Fiumicino; a CIS ticket (€16) is good for a week. Another option is the three-day tourist ticket (€11).*

SUBWAY (METROPOLITANA) AND BUSES

Rome's subway, the *Metropolitana*, has two lines, A and B, which intersect at Termini. Entrances to stations are marked by poles with a white "M" on a red square. The subway runs daily from 5:30am to 11:30pm.

Although the network of routes may seem daunting, Rome's buses are an efficient means of getting around the city. The **ATAC** intracity bus company has myriad booths, including one in Termini. (☎ 800 43 17 84. Open 8:30am-6:30pm.) Each bus stop (*fermata*) is marked by yellow signs listing all routes that stop there and key stops along those routes. Some buses run only on weekdays (*feriali*) or weekends (*festivi*) while others have different routes on different days. Most buses start running around 5 or 6am and stop at midnight, while the less-reliable **night routes** (*notturni*) run at 30min.-1hr. intervals.

Board through the front or back doors, not through the middle, then immediately stamp the ticket in the orange machine. Tickets can be hard to find at night and on weekends, so carry extras. A few useful bus routes are: **#40** and **571**: Vatican area, C. V. Emanuele, L. Argentina, P. Venezia; **#81**: P. Malatesta, S. Giovanni, Colosseo, Bocca della Verità, P. Venezia, Largo Argentina, P. Cavour, V. Cola di Rienzo, Vatican; **#170**: Termini, V. Nazionale, P. Venezia, Bocca della Verità, Testaccio, Stazione Trastevere, V. Marconi, P. Agricoltura.; **#492**: Tiburtina, Termini, P. Barberini, P. Venezia, C. Rinascimento, P. Cavour, P. Risorgimento; **#271**: Pta. Maggiore, Colosseo, S. Giovanni, P. Venezia, L. Argentina, C. V. Emanuele, V. Gregorio VII (southern wall of Vatican City).

TAXIS, BIKES, AND MOPEDS

Taxis in Rome are expensive. Flag one down, or head to a stand near Termini and in major piazzas. Ride only in yellow or white taxis, and make sure the taxi has a meter. If not, settle on a price before getting in the car; as a broad guideline, expect to pay about €7.75 for a ride from Termini to the Vatican. The meter starts at

ily Chronicle

IN RECENT NEWS

IN THE WORKS

A few hours into your sightseeing agenda, you'll discover that the Metro does not go to most of the places you hope to see. Reluctant, you resort to walking. You ask yourself, why does a city of 3.5 million inhabitants and a tourist influx just short of 20 million have only two train lines that run to all the places you don't want to see?

Actually, there is so much of ancient Rome buried beneath the modern city that tunnels can't be dug without hitting 2000-year-old marble columns, brick walls, mosaics, and ancient pavements. Below that lie natural springs supplying much of the city's drinking fountains—not the best place to go burrowing.

However, in the mid-1990s COTRAL, the city transportation authority, began surveying the ground beneath the *centro storico*, hoping to construct a new C line connecting the Vatican with the historic heart of Rome, including the Colosseum. Though the project began in 1997, construction has been halted due to continuous discoveries of new ruins. The underground part of Line C from Ottaviano southeast toward Par-tano is slowly nearing completion. When finished, it will run 29km, making it the longest Metro line in Rome. Line C's stations will incorporate the exposed antiquities and its tunnels will have glass walls allowing commuters and tourists to view the buried city.

€2.33 (M-Sa 7am-10pm, excluding holidays); €3.36 (Su and holidays 7am-10pm) €4.91 (daily 10pm-7am). Surcharges are levied when heading to or from Fiumicino (€7.23) and Ciampino (€5.50), with a charge per suitcase larger than 35x25x50cm of €1.04. Standard tip is 10%. **RadioTaxi** (see below) responds to phone calls, but beware: the meter starts running the moment a car is dispatched.

Rome's cobblestone streets, dense traffic, and *pazzi* drivers make the city a challenge for bikes and mopeds. Bikes cost around €3 per hour or €8-10 per day, and scooters go for €40-50 per day, but the length of a "day" depends on the shop's closing time. In summer, try stands on V. del Corso at P. di San Lorenzo and V. di Pontifici. (Open daily 10am-7pm.) The minimum rental age is 16. Helmets are strictly required by law and included with a rental. Prices often include 20% sales tax. For those just interested in an afternoon on a bike, **Enjoy Rome** (see below) offers an informative, albeit harrowing, tour of the city's best sights.

⁊ PRACTICAL INFORMATION

TOURIST AND FINANCIAL SERVICES

Enjoy Rome, V. Marghera, 8/A (☎06 445 18 43 or 06 493 82 74; www.enjoyrome.com). From th3e middle concourse of Termini (between the trains and the ticket booths), exit right. Cross V. Marsala. The office is 3 blocks down V. Marghera. Owners offer free info about the city in perfect English. Enjoy Rome arranges lodgings, walking and bicycle tours, and bus service to Pompeii (p. 561). Open Apr.-Oct. M-F 8:30am-7pm, Sa 8:30am-2pm; Nov.-Mar. M-F 9:30am-6:30pm, Sa 9am-2pm.

PIT Info Point (☎06 489 06 300), at track #4 in Termini. Run by the city, this English-speaking office provides limited information on events, hotels, restaurants, and transportation, as well as brochures and a serviceable **map** of sights. Open daily 8am-9pm. **Kiosks** offering the same services are at Fori Imperiali, P. di Spagna, P. Navona, Trastevere, V. del Corso, V. Nazionale, and Termini. The same info is available by phone from the **Call Center Comune di Roma** (☎06 360 04 399), which operates daily 9am-7pm.

Currency Exchange: Banca di Roma and **Banca Nazionale del Lavoro** have good rates, but **ATMs,** scattered all over town, especially near Termini, are the best. Expect long lines and cranky tellers. Banking hours are usually M-F 8:30am-1:30pm.

American Express, P. di Spagna, 38 (☎06 676 41, lost or stolen cards/checks 722 82). Open Sept.-July M-F 9am-7:30pm, Sa 9am-3pm; Aug. M-F 9am-6pm, Sa 9am-12:30pm.

LOCAL SERVICES

Luggage Storage: In train station Termini, underneath Track #24 €3.60.

Lost Property: Oggetti Smarriti, V. Nicolo Bettoni, 1 (☎06 581 60 40). Open M and W 8:30am-1pm and 2:30-6pm, Tu and F 8:30am-1pm, Th 8:30am-6pm. At **Termini** at glass booth in main passageway. Open daily 7am-11pm.

Laundromat: OndaBlu, V. La Mora, 7 (info ☎800 86 13 46). 17 locations throughout the city. Wash €3.50 per 6.5kg, dry €3.50 per 6.5kg; soap €0.75. Open daily 8am-10pm. **Splashnet** €2.99 wash 6kg; €2.99 dry 7kg. (See **Internet.**)

Bookstores: ▨ Libreria Feltrinelli International, V. V. E. Orlando, 84-86 (☎06 482 78 78), near P. della Repubblica. Open M-Sa 10am-7:30pm, Su 10am-1:30pm and 4-7:30pm. **▨ Anglo-American Bookshop,** V. di Vite, 102 (☎06 679 52 22; www.aab.it). to the right of the Spanish Steps. Open in summer M-F 10am-7:30pm, Sa 10am-2pm; in winter M 3:30-7:30pm, Tu-Sa 10am-7:30pm. AmEx/MC/V.

Bisexual, Gay, and Lesbian Resources:

Arci-Gay, V. Goito, 35/B (☎340 347 57 10; www.arcigay.it), holds discussions, dances, and special events. Open M-F 3-6pm.

Coordinamento Lesbico Italiano, V. S. Francesco di Sales, 1/A (☎06 686 42 01), off V.della Lungara in Trastevere, has info for lesbian travelers.

Circolo Mario Mieli di Cultura Omosessuale, V. Efeso, 2/A (☎06 541 39 85; www.mariomieli.org). Promotes gay, lesbian, bisexual, and transgendered rights and cultural activities. AIDS activists offer at-home psychological and legal assistance. M: B-San Paolo. Walk 1 block to L. Beato Placido Riccardi, turn right and walk 1.5 blocks to V. Corinto, turn right and walk straight to V. Efeso. Open Sept.-July M-F 9am-1pm and 2-6pm.

Libreria Babele, V. d. Banchi Vecchi, across from Castel Sant'Angelo (☎06 687 66 28; www.libreriababeleroma.it). A library focusing on gay literature, including magazines and poetry books. Enjoy a coffee or tea in their large reading room. Open M-Sa 10am-2pm and 3:30-7:30pm.

EMERGENCY AND COMMUNICATIONS

Emergency: ☎113. **Carabinieri** (☎112). **Ambulance** (☎118). **Fire** (☎115).

Rape Crisis Line: Centro Anti-Violenza, V. d. Torrespaccata, 157 (☎06 232 69 049 or 232 69 053). For victims of sexual violence. Branches throughout city. Available 24hr.

Samaritans, V. San Giovanni in Laterano, 250 (☎06 704 54 444). Native English-speakers. Counseling available. Open for calls and visits daily 1-10pm. Call ahead.

Medical Services: Policlinico Umberto I, Viale di Policlinico, 155 (emergency ☎06 499 11). M: B-Policlinico or #649 bus. Emergency room *(pronto soccorso)*. Open 24hr.

Pharmacies: Farmacia Internazionale, P. Barberini, 49 (☎06 487 11 95) M: A. Open 24hr. MC/V. **Farmacia Piram,** V. Nazionale, 228 (☎06 488 07 54). Open 24hr. MC/V.

Hospitals: International Medical Center, V. Firenze, 47 (☎06 488 23 71 or 06 488 11 29, nights and Su 488 40 51). Call ahead. Prescriptions filled, paramedic crew on call, referral service to English-speaking doctors. General visit €68. Open M-Sa 8:30am-8pm. On-call 24hr. **Rome-American Hospital,** V. E. Longoni, 69 (☎06 225 51 for 24hr. service, 225 52 90 for appointments; www.rah.it). Private emergency and laboratory services, HIV tests, and pregnancy tests. No emergency room. On-call 24hr.

Internet:

■ **Splashnet,** V. Varese, 33 (☎06 493 82 073), 3 blocks north of Termini. Check your email while doing your laundry (see **Local Services**). Also offers luggage storage services €2 per day and free maps. Internet €1.50 per hr. Open in summer daily 8:30am-1am, in winter 8:30am-11pm.

Trevi Internet, V. d. Lucchesi, 31-32 (☎/fax 06 692 00 799). €2.50 per hr., €4 for 2hr. Open daily 9:30am-10pm.

Freedom Traveller, V. Gaeta, 25 (☎06 478 23 862; www.freedom-traveller.it), north of P. del Cinquecento. Run by a hostel of the same name (see **Accommodations**). €4.13 per hr., with card €2.60. Open daily 9am-midnight.

Post Office: 2 are located in the Termini station, on V. Marsala, 77 (☎06 445 67 66), the other on P. S. Silvestro, 19 (☎06 697 66 320). Open M-F 8am-7pm, Sa 8am-1:15pm. **Branch:** V. d. Terme di Diocleziano, 30 (☎06 488 86 920), near Termini. Same hours as S. Silvestro. **Vatican** (☎06 698 83 406), 2 locations in P. San Pietro. No *Fermoposta*, but faster than its counterparts over the wall. Open M-F 8:30am-7pm, Sa 8:30am-6pm. **Branch** on 2nd fl. of Musei Vaticani. Open during museum hours. **Postal Codes:** 00100 to 00200.

▌ ACCOMMODATIONS

Rome swells with tourists around Easter, from May through July, and in September. Accommodation prices vary widely with the time of year, and a proprietor's willingness to negotiate increases with length of stay, number of vacancies, and group size. Termini swarms with hotel scouts. Many are legitimate and have IDs issued by tourist offices; however, some imposters have fake badges and direct travelers to run-down locations with exorbitant rates, especially at night. The price ranges below reflect seasonal variations.

ROME AND LAZIO

ACCOMMODATIONS BY PRICE	
UNDER €15 ❶	
Pensione Ottaviano (99)	BP
Pensione Sandy (102)	SWT
€16-25 ❷	
⊠ Colors (99)	BP
Freedom Traveller (101)	TSL
Hostels Alessandro (100)	TSL
⊠ Hotel Papa Germano (100)	TSL
Ostello Per La Gioventù HI (99)	BP
Pensione Fawlty Towers (101)	TSL
€26-40 ❸	
Affittacamere Aries (101)	TSL
Hotel Bolognese (101)	TSL
Hotel Cervia (101)	TSL
Hotel Des Artistes (100)	TSL
Hotel Giù Giù (102)	SWT
Hotel Il San Pietrino (99)	BP
Hotel Scott House (102)	SWT
⊠ Pensione Cortorillo (102)	SWT
Pensione di Rienzo (102)	SWT
YWCA Foyer di Roma (103)	TSL

€41-60 ❹	
Albergo della Lunetta (98)	CS
Albergo Pomezia (98)	CS
Hotel Boccaccio (99)	PDS
Hotels Castelfidardo and Lazzari (101)	VXXS
Hotels Dolomiti and Lachea (100)	TSL
Hotel Galli (101)	TSL
Hotel Kennedy (102)	SWT
Hotel Pensione Joli (99)	BP
Pensione Monaco (101)	VXXS
⊠ Pensione Panda (99)	PDS
Pensione Tizi (101)	VXXS
Santa Maria Alle Fornaci (103)	BP
ABOVE €61 ❺	
Albergo Abruzzi (98)	CS
Albergo del Sole (99)	CS
⊠ Domus Nova Bethlehem (102)	TSL
Hotel Carmel (100)	TV
Hotel Lady (100)	BP
Hotel Navona (98)	CS
Hotel Pensione Suisse S.A.S. (99)	PDS
Hotel Trastevere (100)	TV

BP Borgo/Prati **CS** Centro Storico **PDS** Piazza Di Spagna **SWT** South and West of Termini **TSL** Termini/San Lorenzo **TV** Trastevere **VXXS** Via XX Settembre

HOTELS AND PENSIONI

CENTRO STORICO

If being closer to the sights is an objective, then choosing Rome's medieval center over the more dingy area near Termini may be worth the higher prices.

Albergo della Lunetta, P. del Paradiso, 68 (☎06 686 10 80 or 06 686 77 630; www.albergodellalunetta.it), on the 1st right off V. Chiavari from C. V. Emanuele II behind Sant'Andrea della Valle. A clean, well-lit place; some rooms face a small, fern-filled courtyard. Great location between Campo dei Fiori and P. Navona. Reserve ahead (with credit card or check). Singles €60; doubles €90/€120; triples €120/€150; quads €150/€180. MC/V. ❹

Albergo Pomezia, V. d. Chiavari, 13 (☎06 686 13 71; www.hotelpomezia.it), off C. V. Emanuele II, behind Sant'Andrea della Valle. 3 floors of recently renovated, clean, and quiet rooms with fans. Breakfast included (8-10:30am). Wheelchair accessible. Singles €60-105; doubles €75-125; triples €100-160. AmEx/MC/V. ❹

Albergo Abruzzi, P. d. Rotonda, 69 (☎06 679 20 21). A mere 200 ft. from the Pantheon, the better-placed rooms have a view to remember. All rooms with bath, TV, A/C, and minibar. Singles €130-155; doubles €175-195; triples €250-310. ❺

Hotel Navona, V. d. Sediari, 8, 1st fl. (☎06 686 42 03; www.hotelnavona.com). Take V. d. Canestrari from P. Navona, cross C. del Rinascimento, and go straight. This recently refurbished building has been used as a *pensione* for over 150 years, counting Keats and Shelley among its guests. A/C €15. Check-out 10:30am. Breakfast, TV, and bath included. Singles €90; doubles €120; triples €160. Reservations with credit card and 1st night deposit; otherwise cash only. ❺

ROME AND LAZIO

Albergo del Sole, V. d. Biscione, 76 (☎06 688 06 873), off Campo dei Fiori. 61 comfortable, modern rooms with phone, TV, and fantastic antique furniture. Most rooms have A/C. Check-out 11am. Parking €15-18. Singles €65, with bath €85; doubles €120-150. Cash only. ❺

NEAR PIAZZA DI SPAGNA

These accommodations might run a few more euros, but can you really put a price tag on living but a few steps from Prada?

▨ **Pensione Panda,** V. della Croce, 35 (☎06 678 01 79; www.webeco.it/hotelpanda), between P. di Spagna and V. del Corso. Quiet rooms and arched frescoed ceilings. A/C €6 per day; free Internet connection. English spoken. Reserve ahead. Singles €48, with bath €68; doubles €68/€98; triples €130; quads €170. Low season (Jan.-Feb.) €6 less. 5% low-season discount with *Let's Go* when paying cash. AmEx/MC/V. ❹

Hotel Pensione Suisse S.A.S., V. Gregoriana, 54 (☎06 678 36 49; info@HotelSuisseRome.com). Turn right at the top of the Spanish Steps. Near the action, but away from the hubbub. Antique furniture, comfortable beds, phone, bath, and fan in every room. Internet and TV available. Breakfast included. Singles €95; doubles €148; triples €198; quads €230. 10-20% discount on extended stays Nov.-Feb. MC/V. ❺

Hotel Boccaccio, V. del Boccaccio, 25 (☎/fax 06 488 59 62; www.hotelboccaccio.com). M: A-Barberini. Off V. del Tritone. This quiet, well-situated hotel offers 8 elegantly furnished rooms near many sights. Reception 9am-11pm; late-night access via key. Singles €43; doubles €70, with bath €93; triples €94/€133. AmEx/MC/V. ❹

BORGO AND PRATI (NEAR VATICAN CITY)

While not the cheapest in Rome, *pensioni* near the Vatican have the sobriety one would expect from a neighborhood with this kind of nun-to-tourist ratio.

▨ **Colors,** V. Boezio, 31 (☎06 687 40 30; www.colorshotel.com). M: A-Ottaviano, take V. Cola di Rienzo to V. Terenzio. Wonderful English-speaking staff. 18 beds are in rooms painted with a bravado that would put Raphael to shame. Internet €2 per hr. Flowery terrace and kitchen open 7:30am-11pm. Dorms €18-22; doubles €75-90; triples €85-110. Reserve private rooms with credit card; for dorms, call night before. Cash only. ❷

Hotel Il San Pietrino, V. G. Bettolo 43, 3rd fl. (☎06 370 01 32; www.sanpietrino.it) M: Ottaviano. Exit on V. Barletta, walk three blocks and turn left onto V. Bettolo. Friendly staff; spacious rooms are elegantly decorated and have A/C, TV, and DSL Internet connection. Singles €28-45, with bath €38-48; doubles €48-70/€68-98; triples €72-90/€90-125; quads €92-112/€112-155. Pay online or at hotel. 5% discount for payment in cash with *Let's Go*. AmEx/MC/V. ❸

Pensione Ottaviano, V. Ottaviano, 6, 2nd fl. (☎06 397 38 138; www.ottavianohostel.com). M: Ottaviano. Follow V. Ottaviano toward S. Pietro. Hostel is on left. Simple but roomy dorms in an optimal location with minibar in each room, but baths are down the hall. Free Internet. Dorms €12-20; doubles €45-60; triples €50-80. Credit card required for reservations, but payment in cash only. ❶

Ostello Per La Gioventù Foro Italico (HI), V. delle Olimpiadi, 61 (☎06 323 62 67). M: Ottaviano, then bus #32 to Cadorna. This enormous marble building holds spacious dorm rooms and large common and dining areas. Reception 7am-midnight. Dorms €17, €20 for non HI members, includes breakfast, sheets, and warm showers. Dinner €8.50. Flexible 1am curfew. Cash only. ❷

Hotel Pensione Joli, V. Cola di Rienzo, 243, 6th fl. (☎06 324 18 54; www.hoteljoliroma.com), at V. Tibullo, scala A. Located on a busy shopping street, some rooms face an interior courtyard and some face the Vatican. Most have bath, phone, and fan. Breakfast included 7am-9am. Singles €35-56, with bath €45-72; doubles €60-108; triples €90-139; quads €100-170; quints €195. AmEx/MC/V. ❹

ROME AND LAZIO

Hotel Lady, V. Germanico, 198, 4th fl. (☎06 324 21 12; www.hotellady.supereva.it), between V. Fabbio Massimo and V. Paolo Emilio. 8 rooms with sink and desk; some with open wood-work ceilings and tile floors. With *Let's Go,* singles €75; doubles €90, with bath €100; triples €120. AmEx/MC/V. ❺

TRASTEVERE

This beautiful old Roman neighborhood is famous for its medieval streets and distance from the tourist crowds, though recently it's become quite hip with the expatriate community. Hotels are scattered and generally pricey, but the area does offer great nightlife and a location near the Vatican and the *centro storico.*

Hotel Trastevere, V. Luciano Manara, 25 (☎06 581 47 13, fax 588 10 16). Turn right off V. d. Trastevere onto V. d. Fratte di Trastevere, which becomes V. Luciano Manara. Neighborhood murals give way to 9 rooms with bath, TV, and phone. English spoken. Breakfast included. Singles €77; doubles €103; triples €130; quads €155. Short-term apartments available. AmEx/MC/V. ❺

Hotel Carmel, V. G. Mameli, 11 (☎06 580 99 21; www.hotelcarmel.it). Turn right on V. E. Morosini (V. G. Mameli) off V. d. Trastevere. A short walk from central Trastevere. Small, clean rooms in this simple hotel have bath. A comfortable atrium-like sitting room leads to a garden terrace with breakfast seating. Breakfast included. Singles €85; doubles €100; triples €140; quads €160. AmEx/MC/V. ❺

TERMINI AND SAN LORENZO

Welcome to budget traveler and backpacker central. While Termini is chock-full of traveler's services, use caution in the area south of Termini at night.

▓ **Hotel Papa Germano,** V. Calatafimi, 14/A (☎06 48 69 19; www.hotelpapagermano.com). From the middle concourse of Termini, exit right; turn left on V. Marsala, which becomes V. Volturno. V. Calatafimi is the 4th cross street on the right. Clean, elegant rooms with TV and outstanding service. English spoken. A/C in dorms €3 per day. Breakfast €4. Internet €2 per hr. Check-out 11am. Dorms €18-22; singles €30-40; doubles €60-72, with bath €70-90; triples €62/€100. AmEx/MC/V. ❷

Hostels Alessandro (www.hotstelsalessandro.com). 3 hostels around the Termini station offer great prices and a fun, knowledgeable staff. Sheets and breakfast. Reserve online or at one of the hostels on the day of arrival. English spoken. ❷

Alessandro Palace, V. Vicenza, 42 (☎06 446 19 58). Exit Termini from track #1. Take a left on V. Marsala, then a right onto V. Vicenza. The Palace houses Alessandro's headquarters, as well as a bar and computer lab. 4-person dorms are spacious, each with its own bath and A/C. Dorms €18-22; doubles €50-80; triples €60-99; quads €80-120. Private rooms include towels.

Alessandro Downtown, V. C. Cattaneo, 23 (☎06 443 40 147). Exit Termini by track 22, make a left on V. Giolitti, then a right onto V. Cattaneo. Shared baths and fans. A cheap and worthwhile alternative when the Palace is booked. Dorms €15-20; doubles €40-60; quads €68-100.

Alessandro indipendenza, V. Curtatone, 12 (☎06 446 19 58). Further away from the main streets, find quieter rooms suitable for families. Every room with private bath and fan. Dorms €19-22; doubles €45-75; quads €80-108. AmEx/MC/V.

Hotel Des Artistes, V. Villafranca, 20, 5th fl. (☎06 445 43 65; www.hoteldesartistes.com). From the middle concourse of Termini, exit right, turn left on V. Marsala, right on V. Vicenza, then take the 5th left. 3-star, 40-room hotel with elegant rooms, some with safe, minibar, and TV. Amenities include a rooftop terrace. Free Internet. Buffet breakfast included with rooms that have bath, otherwise a steep €12. Reception 24hr. Check-out 11am. Doubles €59-169; triples €85-189; quads €99-209. Low-season rates include Aug. €10 discount when paying cash. AmEx/MC/V. ❸

Hotel Dolomiti and **Hotel Lachea,** V. S. Martino della Battaglia, 11, 2nd fl. (☎06 495 72 56; www.hotel-dolomiti.it). From the middle concourse of Termini, exit right, turn left on V. Marsala and right on V. Solferino (V. della Battaglia). Aging palazzo houses 2 hotels with same reception and management. Rooms with bath have satellite TV, safe, and hair dryer. Internet €2.60 for 30min. Breakfast €5. A/C €10. Check-in 1pm. Check-out 11am. Singles €50-60; doubles €80-90; triples €105; quads €125. ❹

Hotel Galli, V. Milazzo, 20 (☎06 445 68 59; www.albergogalli.com). From Termini's middle concourse, exit right. Turn right on V. Marsala and left on V. Milazzo. Helpful owners manage 12 clean rooms with bath, phone, TV, and safe. A/C €5. Breakfast included. Singles €45-65; doubles €55-85; triples €75-105. 10% discount in winter. AmEx/MC/V. ❹

Hotel Cervia, V. Palestro, 55, 2nd fl. (☎06 49 10 57; www.hotelcerviaroma.com). From Termini, exit on V. Marsala, head down V. Marghera and take the 4th left. Common TV room and clean rooms. Those with bath include breakfast; otherwise €3. Reception 24hr. Check-out 11am. Singles €35, with bath €50; doubles €55/€75; triples €60/ €75. In summer, 4-bed dorms €20. 5% *Let's Go* discount. AmEx/MC/V. ❸

Freedom Traveller, V. Gaeta, 25 (☎06 478 23 862; www.freedom-traveller.it). Walk west from Termini down V. Marsala which becomes V. Volturno, and make a right onto V. Gaeta. If lacking in elegance, the aging hostel has unbeatable prices; hearty breakfast and Internet included. Nov. 1-Mar. 31. The fun owners organize pub crawls on M and Th nights (€15). Dorms €15-22; doubles €50-75; triples €66-100; quads €80-120. Reception is at the Internet point (see **Emergency and Communications**). ❷

Pensione Fawlty Towers, V. Magenta, 39, 5th fl. (☎/fax 06 454 35 942). From Termini, cross V. Marsala onto V. Marghera, and turn right on V. Magenta. Common room with satellite TV, library, refrigerator, microwave, and free Internet. Check-out 9:30am for dorms, 10:30am for private rooms. Reserve by fax for private rooms; no reservations for dorms—arrive as early as possible. 4-bed dorms €20-22; singles €45-€52, with shower but no toilet €48-€59; doubles €60/€70; triples €80/€92. Cash in advance only. ❷

Hotel Bolognese, V. Palestro, 15, 2nd fl. (☎/fax 06 49 00 45). From the middle concourse of Termini, exit right. Walk down V. Marghera and take the 4th left onto V. Palestro. In a land of run-of-the-mill *pensioni*, the artist-owner's impressive paintings set this hotel apart. Some rooms have balcony. Check-out 11am. Singles €30, with bath €40; doubles €50/€60; triples €60/€75. AmEx/MC/V. ❸

Affittacamere Aries, V. XX Settembre, 58/A (☎06 420 27 161). From Termini, exit right, and turn left onto V. Marsala, which becomes V. Volturno. Make a right onto V. Cernia and then a left on V. Goito. Follow to its end on V. XX Settembre. Comfortable, basic rooms. Breakfast €2. *Let's Go* discount available, depending on season. Singles €30-60; doubles €36-75, with bath €42-90. €30-35 per extra bed. ❸

VIA XX SETTEMBRE AND ENVIRONS

Dominated by government ministries and private apartments, this area is less noisy and touristy than the nearby Termini.

Pensione Tizi, V. Collina, 48 (☎06 482 01 28, fax 474 32 66). A 10min. walk from the station. From V. XX Settembre, turn left on V. Servio Tullio, right on V. Flavia, and left on V. Collina. Or take bus #38 from the train station until the third stop. Marble floors and inlaid ceilings adorn spacious rooms. Check-out 11am. Singles €45; doubles €60, with bath €70; triples €90; quads €120. Cash only. ❹

Pensione Monaco, V. Flavia, 84 (☎/fax 06 474 43 35). Go north up V. XX Settembre, turn left on V. Quintino Sella, then right on V. Flavia. Comfortable mattresses and bright courtyard complement clean rooms with bath, A/C, and satellite TV. Check-out 10:30am. With *Let's Go*, singles €45-65; doubles €75-120; triples €95-105; quads €115-160. 10% discount in winter. ❹

Hotel Castelfidardo and **Hotel Lazzari,** V. Castelfidardo, 31 (☎06 446 46 38; www.castelfidardo.com). 2 blocks off V. XX Settembre. From Termini, exit right, cross V. Marsala and follow V. Marghera until V. Castelfidardo. Turn left and follow it to just after V. Montebello. Both run by the same friendly family. 3 floors of modern, shiny

ROME AND LAZIO

comfort, with soothing pastel walls. Check-out 10:30am. English spoken. Singles €44, with bath €55; doubles €64/€74; triples €83/€96; quads with bath €110. AmEx/MC/V. ❹

SOUTH AND WEST OF TERMINI

Esquilino, south of Termini, has tons of cheap hotels close to the major sights. The area west of Termini is more inviting, with busy streets and lots of shopping.

▨ **Pensione Cortorillo,** V. Principe Amedeo, 79/A, 5th fl. (☎ 06 446 69 34; www.hotelcortorillo.it). Bath, TV, and A/C in all 14 spacious rooms, and a lobby phone. Breakfast included. Check-out 10am. Dorms with TV, fan, and breakfast €25; singles €30-70; doubles €40-120. Extra bed €10. AmEx/MC/V. ❸

Pensione di Rienzo, V. Principe Amedeo, 79/A, 2nd fl. (☎ 06 446 71 31, fax 06 446 69 80). A tranquil, family-run retreat with rooms overlooking a courtyard. Friendly staff speaks English and French. 20 rooms; some with balcony, TV, and bath. Breakfast €7. Check-out 10am. Singles €20-50; doubles €30-60, with bath €30-70. AmEx/MC/V. ❸

Hotel Kennedy, V. Filippo Turati, 62-64 (☎ 06 446 53 73; www.hotelkennedy.net). Classical music in the bar and a large color TV in the lounge. Rooms have bath, TV, phone, and A/C. Breakfast included. Check-out 11am. Singles €60-85; doubles €75-130; triples €90-149. 10% *Let's Go* discount. AmEx/MC/V. ❹

Hotel Scott House, V. Gioberti, 30 (☎ 06 446 53 79; www.scotthouse.com). 34 clean rooms have bath, A/C, phone, and TV. Free Internet. Breakfast included. English, Spanish, and French spoken. Check-out 11am. Dorms €25; singles €35-75; doubles €63-125; triples €75-155; quads €88-175; quints €100-200. AmEx/MC/V. ❸

Hotel Giù Giù, V. d. Viminale, 8 (☎/fax 06 482 77 34; www.hotelgiugiu.com). This elegant but fading palazzo makes guests forget the hustle and bustle of Rome. Pleasant breakfast area. 12 rooms with A/C. English, German, and French spoken. Breakfast €7. Check-out 10am. Singles €35-40; doubles €60-80; triples €90-105; quads €110-130. ❸

Pensione Sandy, V. Cavour, 136, 4th fl. (☎ 06 488 45 85; www.sandyhostel.com), past the intersection with V. S. Maria Maggiore. Next door to Hotel Valle. Free Internet, bed linens, and lockers (bring a lock) in each room. Simple, hostel-style rooms, usually for 4-8 people. Dorms €12-20 (with bath). Cash only. ❶

ALTERNATIVE ACCOMMODATIONS

BED & BREAKFASTS

Bed & Breakfasts in Rome differ from the American concept. In some, guest rooms are arranged in private homes, with the owners generally obliged to provide breakfast. In others, apartments have kitchens where clients can make their own food. The rooms and apartments vary in quality and size. Pinpoint just how "centrally located" an apartment is before booking, as some are on the city outskirts. The **Bed and Breakfast Association of Rome,** P. del Teatro Pompeo, 2, can offer advice. (☎ 06 553 022 48; www.b-b.rm.it. Call M-F 9am-1pm for an appointment.)

RELIGIOUS HOUSING

Don't automatically think cheap; catering to tourists in search of the quaint and mystical, these can run up to €155 for a single. And don't think Catholic. A few require letters of introduction from local dioceses, but most are open to people of all religions. Do think sober: early curfews or chores, that is.

▨ **Domus Nova Bethlehem,** V. Cavour, 85/A (☎ 06 478 24 41; www.suorebambinogesu.it). Walk down V. Cavour from Termini, past P. d. Esquilino on the left. A clean, modern and central hotel that happens to carry a religious name and 1am curfew. All rooms come with A/C, private bath, lobby safe, TV, and phone. Breakfast included. Singles €70; doubles €98.50; triples €129; quads €148. AmEx/MC/V. ❺

Santa Maria Alle Fornaci, P. S. Maria alle Fornaci, 27 (☎06 393 676 32; ciffornaci@tin.it). Facing St. Peter's, turn left through a gate in the basilica walls onto V. d. Fornace. Take 3rd right onto V. d. Gasperi, which leads to P. S. Maria alle Fornaci. This *casa per ferie* has 54 rooms with bath and phone. Simple, small, and clean. No curfew. Breakfast included. Singles €50; doubles €80; triples €110. AmEx/MC/V. ❹

WOMEN'S HOUSING

YWCA Foyer di Roma, V. C. Balbo, 4 (☎06 488 04 60). From Termini, take V. Cavour, turn right on V. Torino, then 1st left onto V. C. Balbo. The YWCA (pronounced EEV-kah and known as the Casa per Studentesse) is pretty and clean. Breakfast included M-Sa 8-9am. Reserve lunch (1-2pm; €11) at reception by 10am. Reception 7am-midnight. Curfew midnight. Check-out 10am. Dorms €26; singles €37, with bath €47; doubles €62/€74. Extra bed €26. Cash only. ❸

⬛ FOOD

FOOD BY PRICE

UNDER €5 ❶	
Augusto (106)	TV
⬛ Bar Giulia (a.k.a. Cafe Peru) (108)	PN
Caffè della Pace (108)	PN
⬛ Da Quinto (107)	PN
⬛ Della Palma (107)	PN
Giolitti (107)	PN
Il Caffè Sant'Eustachio (108)	PN
⬛ Tazza d'Oro (108)	PN
The Old Bridge (107)	BP
Tre Scalini (107)	PN
Volpetti Piu (107)	TES
€6-10 ❷	
⬛ Africa (106)	TSL
Arancia Blu (107)	SL
Dar Poeta (106)	TV
⬛ Franchi (105)	BP
Hostaria da Bruno (106)	TSL
Hostaria da Nerone (104)	AC
⬛ I Buoni Amici (103)	AC
Il Brillo Parlante (105)	PDS
Il Tulipano Nero (106)	TV
Il Portico (105)	CDF
⬛ Il Pulcino Ballerino (107)	SL

⬛ Il Tunnel (107)	SL
La Cestia (107)	TES
L'Insalata Ricca (104)	CDF
"Lo Spuntino" da Guido e Patrizia (106)	BP
Ouzeri (106)	TV
⬛ PizzaRè (105)	PDS
⬛ Pizzeria Baffetto (104)	PN
Pizzeria Corallo (104)	PN
⬛ Pizzeria San Callisto (106)	TV
Taverna dei Quaranta (104)	AC
Vini e Buffet (105)	PDS
Zampanò (104)	CDF
€10-15 ❸	
Cacio e Pepe (106)	BP
La Pollarola (105)	CDF
⬛ La Taverna del Ghetto (104)	CDF
Naturist Club Ristorante Bio Vegetariano (105)	PDS
Trattoria da Giggetto (104)	CDF
Trattoria dal Cav. Gino (104)	PN
⬛ Trattoria Da Luigi (104)	CDF
Trattoria da Sergio (105)	CDF
€16-25 ❹	
Ristorante a Casa di Alfredo (106)	TV

AC Ancient City **BP** Borgo/Prati **CDF** Campo dei Fiori **PDS** Piazza di Spagna **PN** Piazza Navona **SL** San Lorenzo **TES** Testaccio **TSL** Termini/San Lorenzo **TV** Trastevere

ROME AND LAZIO

ANCIENT CITY

The area around the Forum and the Colosseum is home to some of Italy's finest tourist traps. If the stroll to the *centro storico* seems too long and hot, there are a few places that offer meals at fair prices.

⬛ **I Buoni Amici,** V. Aleardo Aleardi, 4 (☎06 704 91 993). From the Colosseum, take V. Labicana to V. Merulana. Turn right, then left on V. A. Aleardi. A long walk, but the cheap and excellent food is well worth the hike. Choices include the *linguine all'astice* (with lobster sauce; €7), *risotto con i funghi* (€6), and *penne alla vodka* (€6). Cover €1. Open M-Sa noon-3pm and 7:30-11:30pm. AmEx/MC/V. ❷

Taverna dei Quaranta, V. Claudia, 24 (☎06 700 05 50), off P. del Colosseo. In the shade of Celian Park, this corner *taverna* sports a menu that changes weekly, and often features the *oliva ascolane* (fried olives stuffed with meat; €4). House wine €5.20 per L. Cover €1. Reservations suggested, especially for a table outside. Open daily 12:30-3:30pm and 7:30pm-midnight. AmEx/MC/V. ❷

Hostaria da Nerone, V. delle Terme di Tito, 96 (☎06 481 79 52). M: B-Colosseo. Take V. N. Salvi, turn right, and then left on V. d. Terme di Tito. Outdoor dining near the Colosseum. Traditional specialties like *spaghetti all'Amatriciana* (with bacon, tomatoes, chile, and sheep cheese; €7.50) and a break from the tourist rush. Open M-Sa noon-3pm and 7-11pm. Closed Aug. AmEx/MC/V. ❷

PIAZZA NAVONA

▣ **Pizzeria Baffetto,** V. d. Governo Vecchio, 114 (☎06 686 16 17). Once a meeting place for 60s radicals, Baffetto now overflows with hungry Romans—be prepared to wait outside for a table. Pizza €4.50-7.50. Open daily 6:30pm-1am. Cash only. ❷

Pizzeria Corallo, V. d. Corallo, 10-11 (☎06 683 077 03), off V. d. Governo Vecchio near P. del Fico. Great for a cheap dinner before squandering your life's savings at the chi-chi bars nearby. Pizza €4-9. Open daily 6:30pm-1am. AmEx/MC/V. ❷

Trattoria dal Cav. Gino, V. Rosini, 4 (☎06 687 34 34), off V. d. Campo Marzio across from P. del Parlamente. The very affable Gino greets people at the door and points at a sign above the door, announcing that *tonnarelli alla ciociala* (€7) is the house special. *Primi* €5-7.50, *secondi* €8-11. Open M-Sa 1-2:45pm and 8-10:30pm. Cash only. ❸

CAMPO DEI FIORI AND THE JEWISH GHETTO

Get lost in the labyrinth of crooked streets and alleyways that surround the Campo, and along the way, find several exceptional restaurants serving some of the most authentic meals around. Across V. Arenula from the Campo, the former Jewish Ghetto has served Roman-Jewish fare for hundreds of years.

▣ **La Taverna del Ghetto,** V. d. Portico d'Ottavia, 8. (☎06 688 097 71; www.latavernadelghetto.com). This lively, kosher option offers excellent homemade pasta and sit-down meals. Try the artichoke, a house specialty (€4.50). Open M-Th and Sa-Su noon-3pm and 6:30-11pm, F noon-3pm. Cover €1.50. AmEx/MC/V. ❸

▣ **Trattoria Da Luigi,** P. S. Cesarini, 24 (☎06 686 59 46), near Chiesa Nuova, 4 blocks down C. V. Emanuele II from Campo dei Fiori. Enjoy inventive cuisine such as the delicate *carpaccio di salmone fresco con rughetta* (€8), as well as simple dishes like *vitello con funghi* (€9.50). Open Tu-Su noon-3pm and 7pm-midnight. AmEx/MC/V. ❸

Zampanò, P. della Cancelleria, 80/83 (☎06 689 70 80), between C. V. Emanuele II and the Campo. This swank *hostaria* is running out of space in its front window to plaster all the awards they've won over the years. Offers creative pizzas (€7-9), more than 200 wines, and a changing menu. *Primi* €7-8, *secondi* €11-13. Open M and W-Su noon-2:30pm and 7:30-11pm, Tu 7:30-11pm. AmEx/MC/V. ❷

L'Insalata Ricca, Largo d. Chiavari, 85-6 (☎06 688 036 56; www.linsalataricca.it), off C. V. Emanuele II near P. S. Andrea della Valle. Don't like your salad? There are about 20 others. Don't like this location? There are 11 others in Rome, including S. Pietro and P. Navona. *Primi* €5.20-7.50, *secondi* €€5.20-8.30. Reservations suggested for dinner. Open daily 12:30-3:30pm and 6:45-11:45pm. US dollars accepted. AmEx/MC/V. ❷

Trattoria da Giggetto, V. d. Portico d'Ottavia, 21-22 (☎06 686 11 05). A step away from the ruins of Ottaviano's palace, Giggetto may serve the finest Roman food around. Dare to try the *fritto di cervello d'abbacchino* (brains with vegetables; €12). *Primi* €7.50-10, *secondi* €11.50-16. Cover €1.50. Dinner reservation required. Open Tu-Su 12:15-3pm and 7:30-11pm, closed the last 2 weeks of July. AmEx/MC/V. ❸

Il Portico, V. d. Portico D'Ottavia, 1/D (☎06 686 46 42). This low-key, family restaurant in the middle of the Jewish Ghetto serves pizza (*prosciutto* €4.20, *funghi* €5.20) and salads (€5.70-7.80). Open daily noon-3:30pm and 6:30pm-midnight. MC/V. ❷

La Pollarola, P. Pollarola, 24-25 (☎06 688 016 54). As the motto goes, *"si mangia bene e si spende giusto"* (you eat well and pay a fair price). Superlative renditions of typical dishes like *spaghetti alla carbonara* (€7). *Secondi* €8-15. Open M-Sa noon-3:30pm and 6pm-midnight. AmEx/MC/V. ❸

Trattoria da Sergio, V. d. Grotte, 27 (☎06 686 42 93). Take V. d. Giubbonari and turn right. Just far enough from the Campo to avoid droves of tourists, Sergio offers a simple ambience (they don't bother with menus) and hearty portions. Try the ultra-Roman *spaghetti matriciana* (with bacon and spicy tomato sauce; €6). Reservations suggested. Open M-Sa noon-3pm and 6:30-11:30pm. MC/V. ❸

PIAZZA DI SPAGNA

The Spanish Steps may seem very different from the environs of Termini, but there is one big similarity—lousy food. But here, it costs twice as much. Exceptions:

🖫 **PizzaRè,** V. di Ripetta, 14 (☎06 321 14 68). Take V. di Ripetta 1 block away from P. del Popolo. PizzaRè serves up Neapolitan-style pizza (€6-9.50) as well as regional wines and fantastic desserts. **Branch** at V. Oslavia 39/A, near P. Mazzini. Open daily 12:45-3:30pm and 7:30pm-12:30am. AmEx/MC/V. ❷

🖫 **Trattoria da Settimio all'Arancio,** V. dell'Arancio, 50-52 (☎06 687 61 19). Take V. dei Condotti from P. di Spagna; take 1st right after V. del Corso, then 1st left. Fried artichokes (€4.50) are delicious, as is the pasta with cuttlefish ink (€7.50). *Primi* from €7.50, *secondi* from €8.50. Reservations recommended. Open M-Sa 12:30-3pm and 7:30-11:30pm. AmEx/MC/V. ❹

Naturist Club Ristorante Bio Vegetariano, V. della Vite, 14, 4th fl. (☎06 679 25 09). Heading toward P. del Popolo on V. del Corso, make a right onto V. della Vite. The mother-daughter duo behind this veggie haven has taken traditional Roman cuisine to a new level. Large portions and decent prices. *Primi* €8-9 (with fish), *secondi* €7.50-11 (with fish). €14 lunch deal. Open M-Sa 12:30-3pm and 7:30-11pm. Cash only. ❸

Vini e Buffet, P. Torretta, 60. (☎06 687 14 45). From V. del Corso, turn on P. S. Lorenzo in Lucina. Turn left on V. Campo Marzio and right on V. Torretta. A favorite spot among chic Romans with a penchant for regional wines. Also available are patés, *crostini*, and *scarmorze* (smoked mozzarella) for €6.50-8.50. Reservations recommended but not necessary. M-Sa 12:30-3pm and 7:30-11pm. Cash only. ❷

Il Brillo Parlante, V. Fontanella, 12 (☎06 324 33 34; www.ilbrilloparlante.com). Take V. del Corso away from P. del Popolo and turn left on V. Fontanella. The wood-burning pizza oven (€7-10), fresh ingredients, and excellent wine attract lunching Italians to shady outdoor tables. Open Tu-Su 12:30-3:30pm for lunch, 3:30-5pm pizza only, 5-7:30pm bar only, and 7:30pm-1am. MC/V. ❷

BORGO AND PRATI (NEAR VATICAN CITY)

The streets near the Vatican are paved with bars and pizzerias that serve mediocre sandwiches at hiked-up prices. For far better and much cheaper food, head to the residential district a few blocks northeast of the Vatican Museums.

🖫 **Franchi,** V. Cola di Rienzo, 204 (☎06 687 46 51; www.franchi.it). Benedetto Franchi ("Frankie") has been serving the citizens of Prati superb *tavola calda*, prepared sandwiches, and other luxurious picnic supplies for nearly 50 years. Delicacies include various croquettes (€1.20), marinated munchies like anchovies, peppers, olives, and salmon, and pastas (€5.90 per generous portion). Cheaper and better quality than most Vatican area snack bars. Open M-Sa 8:15am-9pm. AmEx/MC/V. ❷

"Lo Spuntino" da Guido e Patrizia, Borgo Pio, 13 (☎06 687 54 91), near Castle Sant'Angelo. With plastic utensils and a casual atmosphere, this homey spot is popular with lunching locals. Guido holds court behind a well-stocked *tavola calda*. Full meal (*primo, secondo,* and wine) runs less than €8. Open M-Sa 8am-8pm. Cash only. ❷

Cacio e Pepe, V. Giuseppe Avezzana, 11 (☎06 321 72 68). From P. Mazzini take V. Settembrini to P. dei Martiri di Belfiore; left on V. Avezzana. Great pasta and low prices: lunch under €10; full dinner around €15. Open M-F 8-11:30pm. Cash only. ❸

TRASTEVERE

The waits are long and the street side tables are always cramped, but you can't get more Roman than Trastevere.

▣ **Pizzeria San Callisto,** P. S. Callisto, 9/A (☎06 581 82 56), off P. S. Maria. Simply the best pizza in Rome. Avoid long waits for a table by eating outside in the piazza. Gorgeous thin-crust pizzas so large they hang off the plates (€4.20-7.80), though the *bruschetta* (€2.10) alone is worth a postcard home. Open Tu-Su 7pm-midnight. MC/V. ❷

Dar Poeta, Vco. del Bologna 45-46 (☎06 588 05 16). From P. S. Egidio, head down V. della Scala and turn right. Packed, but hardly a tourist in sight. 18 types of *bruschetta* (all €2) and unusual pizzas amid the old favorites (€4-8.50). Save room for dessert (€3.50), made daily by owner. Open 7:30pm-1am. AmEx/MC/V. ❷

Ristorante a Casa di Alfredo, V. Roma Libera, 5-7 (☎06 588 29 68). Off P. S. Cosimato. Try the *gnocchi con gamberi* (€8) or the specialty *tonarelli all'alfredo* (€8) to start and grilled *calamari* (€10.50) or *filetto a pepe verde* (€13) as a main dish. Open daily noon-3pm and 7:30-11:30pm. AmEx/MC/V. ❹

Il Tulipano Nero, V. Roma Libera, 15 (☎06 581 83 09). From V. d. Trastevere, turn right on V. E. Morosini. Innovative takes on classics, like *pennette all'elettroshock* (€7.50), served in chaotic P. S. Cosimato. Portions range from large to ludicrous. Pizza from €5.50. *Primi* from €6, *secondi* from €8. Open daily 6pm-1am. MC/V. ❷

Ouzeri, V. d. Salumi, 2 (☎06 581 82 56). Turn left off V. Trastevere or take V. Vascellari from Lungotevere Ripa and turn right on V. dei Salumi. Ring bell to enter this Greek restaurant/cultural association with occasional live music and great food—share a *piatto misto* (€7-15) with a friend. Cover €1.50. Open M-Sa 8:30pm-2am. Cash only. ❷

Augusto, P. de' Renzi, 15 (☎06 580 37 98), north of P. S. Maria in Trastevere. Enjoy the laid-back atmosphere, as well as daily pasta specials at lunch (around €5) and the *pollo arrosto con patate* (€5.50). Homemade desserts are superb. Open M-F 12:30-3pm and 8-11pm, Sa 12:30-3pm. Closed in Aug. ❶

TERMINI AND SAN LORENZO

Avoid the tourist traps offering €5 excuses for a quick lunch and judge a spot by who's eating there: the more *Romani*, the better.

▣ **Africa,** V. Gaeta, 26-28 (☎06 494 10 77), near P. Indipendenza. Decked out in yellow and black, Africa continues its 20-year tradition of serving excellent Eritrean/Ethiopian food. The meat-filled *sambusas* (€3) are a flavorful starter; both the *zighini beghi* (roasted lamb in a spicy sauce; €7) and the *misto vegetariano* (mixed veggie dishes; €7) make fantastic entrees. Cover €1. Open Tu-Su 8am-1:30am. MC/V. ❷

Hostaria da Bruno, V. Varese, 29 (☎06 49 04 03). From V. Marsala, take V. Milazzo and turn right on V. Varese. The *tortellini con panna e funghi* (with cream and mushrooms; €7) are a delight. For dessert, owner Bruno makes crepes (€3.50) so good even the Pope has eaten here. Open M-Sa noon-3:15pm and 7-10:15pm. AmEx/MC/V. ❷

SAN LORENZO

Poor students with discriminating palates in this university district means cheap food and lots of local character. From Termini, walk south on V. Pretoriano to P. Tiburtino. Avoid walking alone at night.

ROME AND LAZIO

▨ **Il Pulcino Ballerino,** V. d. Equi, 66-68 (☎06 494 12 55). An artsy atmosphere with cuisine to match. The cook stirs up creative dishes like *conchiglione al "Moby Dick"* (shells with tuna, cream, and greens; €6.50). Excellent vegetarian *scamorza* and potato casserole (€6.50). Or skip the chef altogether and prepare a personalized meal on a warm stone at the table. Open M-Sa 1-3:30pm and 8pm-midnight. AmEx/MC/V. ❷

▨ **Il Tunnel,** V. Arezzo, 11 (☎06 442 368 08). From M: B-Bologna, walk down Viale della Provincia, take 4th right on V. Padova, and 2nd left on V. Arezzo. It's a bit of a trek, but this is a family-run Roman *hostaria* the locals flock to. Pasta is made fresh and the *bistecca alla Fiorentina* is unrivalled in Rome (priced by weight). Pizza from €4. *Primi* €4-10, *secondi* around €15. Open Tu-Su noon-3pm and 7pm-midnight. MC/V. ❷

▨ **Arancia Blu,** V. d. Latini, 65 (☎06 445 41 05), off V. Tiburtina. This elegant and popular vegetarian restaurant has an inventive approach to food. Enjoy elaborate dishes like *tonnarelli con pecorino romano e tartufo* (pasta with sheep cheese and truffles; €6.20) or fried ravioli stuffed with eggplant and smoked *caciocavallo* with pesto (€8.50). Extensive wine list €12-130 per bottle. Open daily 8:30pm-midnight. MC/V. ❷

TESTACCIO

This working-class neighborhood is the seat of many excellent restaurants serving traditional Roman, meat-heavy fare, as well as the center of Roman nightlife.

La Cestia, Viale di Piramide Cestia, 69 (☎06 574 37 54). M: B-Piramide. Walk across P. di Porta San Paolo to V. di Piramide Cestia; restaurant is on the right. La Cestia's plant-filled patio and rustic interior are a good place to enjoy a light meal of pizza and pasta, but seafood is the specialty—try the *spaghetti alla scogliera* (€8). Open Tu-Su 12:30-3pm and 7:30-11pm. MC/V. ❷

Volpetti Piu, V. Alessandro Volta (☎06 574 43 06). Turn left on V. A. Volta off of V. Marmorata. This authentic *gastronomia* serves lunch in large portions at self-service tables. Fresh salads, pizza, and daily specials from €4. Open M-Sa 10am-10pm. Cash only. ❶

DESSERT

Gelato is everywhere in Rome. Good gelato is a different story. Look for muted (hence natural) colors, or head to these *Let's Go* favorites.

▨ **Della Palma,** V. della Maddalena, 20 (☎06 688 067 52), steps from the Pantheon. Over 100 flavors of gelato, from pomegranate to white chocolate to dark chocolate apricot. Killer milkshakes go with the 50s style decor. Pay first at the register, then fight the crowd to order at the counter with the receipt. Gelato €1.80-10 (for enormous, elaborate bowls). Open daily 8am-2am. V, €7 min.

▨ **Da Quinto,** V. d. Tor Millina, 15 (☎06 686 56 57). West of P. Navona. Long lines, walls splashed with Carmen Miranda-inspired decor, and light, fluffy gelato. Fruit flavors are especially good, as is the banana split (€4.50). Nice owners make fresh fruit smoothies blended to order. Open daily 9am-3am, Sa until 5am; in winter sometimes closed W.

Giolitti, V. degli Uffici del Vicario, 40 (☎06 699 12 43; www.giolitti.it). From the Pantheon, follow V. d. Pantheon, then take V. della Maddalena to its end; turn right on V. degli Uffici del Vicario. Wonderful gelato in dozens of flavors, as well as ices laden with fresh fruit, served in a festive, antique decor. Decide before stepping up to the counter. Crowded at night. Cones €1.80-3. Open daily 7am-1am. AmEx/MC/V.

The Old Bridge, Viale dei Bastioni di Michelangelo (☎06 397 230 26), off P. del Risorgimento, perpendicular to Vatican museum walls. Have someone hold your place in the Vatican line and come to this outpost. Huge cups (€1.50-3) and 20 exceptional homemade flavors to choose from. Open M-Sa 9am-2am, Su 3pm-2am.

Tre Scalini, P. Navona, 28-29 (☎06 688 019 96). This old-fashioned spot is famous for its *tartufo*, a truffled chocolate gelato hunk rolled in chocolate shavings (€4, at the table €7). It's touristy and priced accordingly, but still delicious. Bar open M-Tu and Th-Su 9am-1:30am; pricey restaurant open M-Tu and Th-Su 12:30-3:30pm and 7:30-9pm.

COFFEE

■ **Bar Giulia (a.k.a. Cafe Peru),** V. Giulia, 84 (☎06 686 13 10), near P. V. Emanuele II. Raphael once called this building home; today the owner, Alfredo, serves what may be the cheapest (and most delicious) coffee in Rome (€0.60, at table €0.70) and adds your favorite liqueur at no charge. You may have to crowd surf over the hordes of locals to get your cup of fresh-squeezed orange juice. Open M-Sa 4am-9:30pm.

■ **Tazza d'Oro,** V. d. Orfani, 84-86 (☎06 679 27 68). Facing away from the Pantheon's *portico,* the yellow-lettered sign is on the right. Try their signature "regina" arabica, or in summer get the *granita di caffè* with fresh whipped cream (€1.50). Espresso €0.65; cappuccino €0.80. Open M-Sa 7am-8pm.

Il Sant'Eustachio Caffè, P. S. Eustachio, 82 (☎06 688 020 48). Turn right on V. Palombella behind the Pantheon. Rome's "coffee empire," this cafe was once frequented by Stendhal. Though the coffee is excellent, your average postmodern struggling artist may not be able to afford the habit. *Gran caffè speciale* €2.10, at table €3.60. Open M-Th 8:30am-1am, F 8:30am-1:30am, Su 8:30am-2am.

Caffè della Pace, V. della Pace, 3-7 (☎06 686 12 16), off P. Navona. Great people-watching, though there are nearly as many Americans sedately writing postcards as Italians wildly gesticulating on their cell phones. Stylish location raises the prices. Espresso €2. Cakes €4. *Apertivi* €5-8. Cheaper at the bar. Prices go up about €2.50 after dark. Open daily 9am-2am; closed M mornings.

ENOTECHE (WINE BARS)

Wine bars range from laid-back and local to chic and international. Sample the sweet staple *Brachetto,* or explore new labels or unknown regions.

■ **Bar Da Benito,** V. d. Falegnami, 14 (☎06 686 15 08), off P. Cairoli in the Jewish Ghetto. For 40 years and counting, this bar has boasted a counter lined with bottles and hordes of hungry workmen. Glasses of wine from €1; bottles from €5.50. 2 hot pastas prepared daily (€4.50), along with fresh *secondi* like *prosciutto* with vegetables (€5). Spacious seating area, next to takeout bar. Always packed and hectic, but exceedingly friendly. Open M-Sa 6:30am-7pm, lunch noon-4pm. Closed Aug.

Cul de Sac, P. Pasquino, 73 (☎06 688 010 94), off P. Navona. One of Rome's first wine bars, Cul de Sac has kept the customers coming with an extensive wine list (from €2 per glass), outdoor tables, and divine dishes. House specialty pâté (such as boar and chocolate; €5.60) is exquisite. Open daily noon-4pm and 6pm-12:30am. MC/V.

Trimani Wine Bar, V. Cernaia 37/B (☎06 446 96 30), near Termini, perpendicular to V. Volturno. Their shop is around the corner at V. Goito, 20. Probably the city's most influential wine bar, at least to those in the know; it is indisputably Rome's oldest. Excellent food includes salads (veggies and smoked cod; €8.50) and filling quiches (try the chicken, pepperoni, and basil; €7.50). Wines from €2-15 a glass. Happy Hour 11:30am-12:30pm and 4-6:30pm. Open M-Sa 11:30am-12:30pm. AmEx/MC/V.

Enoteca Cavour 313, V. Cavour, 313 (☎06 678 54 96), in the Vatican area. A short walk from M: B-Cavour. Wonderful meats and cheeses (€7-9 for a mixed plate) listed by region or type, many fresh salads (€3-7), and rich desserts (€4). Massive wine list (€12.50-300). Open M-Sa 12:30-2:30pm and 7:30pm-1am. Closed Aug. AmEx/MC/V.

🔘 SIGHTS

From ancient temples, medieval churches, and Renaissance basilicas to Baroque fountains and contemporary museums, *La Città Eterna* is a city bursting with masterpieces from every era of Western civilization. Remember to dress modestly when visiting churches or the Vatican.

ROME AND LAZIO

THE ANCIENT CITY

▨ THE COLOSSEUM

☎ 06 700 54 69. M: B-Colosseo. Open daily Mar.-Aug. 9am-7:30pm, Sept. until 7pm, Oct. until 6:30pm, end of Oct. to mid-Feb. until 4:30pm, mid-Feb. to end of Mar. until 5pm. Last admission 1hr. before closing time. To avoid lines, buy tickets at entrance to Palatine Hill in the Roman Forum. Tours with archaeologist €3.50; audioguide in English and French €4. €8 for combined ticket to the Colosseum and Palatine Hill, EU citizens 18-24 €4, EU citizens under 18 or over 65 free. 7-day Archeologia Card good for entrance to the 4 Musei Nazionali Romani, the Colosseum, the Palatine Hill, the Terme di Diocleziano, and the Crypti Balbi. €20, EU citizens 18-24 €10, EU citizens under 18 or over 65 free.

The Colosseum stands as the enduring symbol of the Eternal City—a hollowed-out ghost of travertine marble that once held as many as 50,000 crazed spectators, and now dwarfs every other ruin in Rome. Within 100 days of its AD 80 opening, some 5000 wild beasts perished in the bloody arena, and the slaughter went on for three more centuries. The wooden floor underneath the sand once covered a labyrinth of brick cells, ramps, and elevators used to transport animals from cages to arena level; these underground rooms are now open to the public. Between the Colosseum and the Palatine Hill lies the **Arco di Costantino,** one of the best preserved imperial monuments in the area. The arch commemorates Constantine's victory at the Battle of the Milvian Bridge in AD 312, using fragments from monuments to Trajan, Hadrian, and Marcus Aurelius.

THE PALATINE HILL

South of the Forum. English guided tour at noon €3.50; with Archeologia Card €2.50. May be purchased at the Biglietteria Palatino, at the end of V. Nova past the Arch of Titus, or 100m down V. di S. Gregorio from the Colosseum. Same hours as the Colosseum. Sections of the Orti Farnesini, best for viewing the hills, as well as the Houses of Augustus and Livia closed for renovations. Combined ticket to the Palatine Hill and the Colosseum €8, EU citizens 18-24 years old €4, EU citizens under 18 or over 65 free.

The best way to approach the **Palatine** is from the stairs near the Arch of Titus in the Forum, which ascend to the **Farnese Gardens.** The hill, a plateau between the Tiber and the Forum, was home to the she-wolf that suckled Romulus and Remus. It was here that Romulus built the first walls of the city. During the Republic, the Palatine was the most fashionable residential quarter, where aristocrats and statesmen, including Cicero and Marc Antony, built their homes. Augustus lived here in a modest house, but later emperors capitalized on the hill's prestige and built gargantuan quarters. By the end of the first century, the imperial residence covered the entire hill, whose Latin name, Palatium, became synonymous with the palace. After the fall of Rome, the hill suffered the same fate as the Forum.

Lower down, excavations continue on a 9th-century BC village, optimistically labeled the **Casa di Romulo.** To the right of the village is the podium of the **Temple of Cybele,** built in 191 BC during the Second Punic War. The stairs slightly to the left lead to the **House of Livia,** where Augustus and wife Livia resided. The house, its vestibule, courtyard, and three vaulted living rooms connected to the **House of Augustus** next door. Around the corner, the **Cryptoporticus** connected Tiberius's palace with the buildings nearby and was used by slaves and couriers as a secret passage. The solemn **Domus Augustana** was the emperors' private space. Visitors are only allowed to the upper level, from which they can make out the shape of two courtyards. Adjacent to the Domus Augustana lies the other wing of the palace and the sprawling **Domus Flavia,** site of a gigantic octagonal fountain that occupied almost the entire courtyard. Between the Domus Augustana and the Domus Flavia stands the **Palatine Antiquarium,** a museum that houses artifacts from excavations. *(Temporarily closed; expected to open in 2005.)* Outside on the right, the palace's east wing contains the curious **Stadium Palatinum,** or hippodrome, a sunken oval space once surrounded by a colonnade but now decorated with fragments of porticoes, statues, and fountains.

THE DOMUS AUREA. This park houses a portion of Nero's "Golden House," which covered a substantial chunk of ancient Rome. An enclosed lake used to be at the base of the hill, and the hill itself was a private garden. The Forum was reduced to a vestibule of the palace; Nero crowned it with a colossal statue of himself as the sun. He also pillaged all of Greece to find works of art worthy of his abode, including the famous *Laocoön*. Apparently, decadence didn't buy happiness: Nero committed suicide five years after building his hedonistic pad. Out of civic-minded jealousy, the ensuing Flavian dynasty tore down his house and built public monuments, including the Flavian Baths on the Caelian Hill and the Colosseum over the drained lake. *(On the Colle Oppio, or Oppian Hill. From the Colosseum, walk through the gates up V. della Domus Aurea and make 1st left. Reservations ☎ 06 399 677 00. Open M and W-Su 9am-7:45pm. Groups of 30 admitted every 20min. Reservation recommended for all visits: €1.50 extra. Audioguide €2. Italian and English tour with archaeologist €3.50. €5, EU citizens 18-24 €2.50, EU citizens under 18 or over 65 free.)*

THE ROMAN FORUM

Main entrance: V. dei Fori Imperiali, at Largo C. Ricci, between P. Venezia and the Colosseum. Other entrances are opposite the Colosseum at the start of V. Sacra and at the Clivus Capitolinus, near P. del Campidoglio. M: B-Colosseo, or bus to P. Venezia. Access to the Forum is unpredictable, as many areas are sporadically fenced off for excavation or restoration. Open daily in summer 9am-6:30pm (must leave by 7:15pm), in winter 9am-3:30pm (must leave by 4:15pm). Guided tour with archaeologist available at noon in English only, €3.50; audioguide tour for Forum in English, French, German €4; both available at Biglietteria Palatino at the end of V. Nova past the Arch of Titus. Free.

This area was originally a low marshland prone to flooding from the Tiber. Rome's Iron Age inhabitants (1000-900 BC) eschewed its unhealthy marshiness in favor of the Palatine Hill, descending only to bury their dead. In the 8th and 7th centuries BC, Etruscans and Greeks used the Forum as a weekly market. The Romans founded a thatched-hut shantytown here in 753 BC, when Romulus and Sabine leader Titus Tatius joined forces to end the war triggered by the famous rape of the Sabine women. Now the Forum bears witness to centuries of civic building. The entrance ramp to the Forum leads to the **Via Sacra** (Sacred Way), the oldest street in Rome, near the section known as the Civic Forum. The other sections are the Market Square, the Lower Forum, the Upper Forum, and the Velia.

CIVIC FORUM. The **Basilica Aemilia,** built in 179 BC, housed the guild of the *argentarii* (money changers). It was rebuilt several times after fires, until one started by Alaric and his merry band of Goths in AD 410 left it in its current state; melted coins that the *argentarii* lost in these blazes still mark the pavement. Next to the Basilica Aemilia stands the **Curia,** or Senate House, one of the oldest buildings in the Forum. It was converted to a church in AD 630 and restored by Mussolini. The Curia also houses the **Plutei of Trajan,** two parapets that depict the burning of the tax registers and the distribution of food to poor children. The broad space in front of the Curia was the **Comitium,** or assembly place, where citizens voted and representatives gathered for public discussion. It was home to the Twelve Tables, bronze tablets upon which the first laws of the Republic were inscribed. Bordering the Comitium is the large brick **Rostrum,** or speaker's platform, erected by Julius Caesar just before his death. Augustus's rebellious daughter Julia is said to have voiced dissent here by engaging in amorous activities with her father's enemies. The hefty **Arch of Septimius Severus,** to the right of the Rostrum, was dedicated in AD 203 to celebrate Septimus's victories in the Middle East.

MARKET SQUARE. Shrines and sacred precincts, including the **Lapis Niger** (Black Stone), once graced the square in front of the Curia. It was in this square that a group of senators murdered Julius Caesar in 44 BC. Below the Lapis Niger rest the underground ruins of a 6th-century BC altar, along with a pyramidal pillar with the oldest known Latin inscription in Rome warning against defiling the shrine. In the square, the **Three Sacred Trees of Rome**—olive, fig, and grape—have been planted courtesy of the Italian state. On the other side, a circular tufa basin marks the **Lacus Curtius,** the chasm into which the legendary Roman warrior Marcus Curtius threw himself in 362 BC to seal the occult fissure and save the city. The newest part of the Forum (aside from the Neoclassical info booth) is the **Column of Phocas,** erected in AD 608 for the visiting Byzantine emperor, Phocas.

LOWER FORUM. Though built in the early 5th century BC, the **Temple of Saturn** has its mythological origins in the Golden Age of Rome. The temple became the site of **Saturnalia,** a raucous Roman winter bash where class and social distinctions were forgotten, masters served slaves, and anything was permitted. Around the corner, rows of column bases are all that remain of the **Basilica Julia,** a courthouse built by Julius Caesar in 54 BC. At the far end of the Basilica Julia, three white marble columns mark the massive podium of the **Temple of Castor and Pollux.** According to legend, the twin gods Castor and Pollux helped the Romans defeat the rival Etruscans at the Battle of Lake Regillus (499 BC). Legend says that immediately after the battle, the twins appeared in the Forum to water their horses at the nearby **Basin of Juturna.** Down the road from the Temple of Castor and Pollux is the rectangular base of the **Temple of the Deified Julius,** which Augustus built in 29 BC to honor his murdered adoptive father and proclaim himself the nephew of a god. Augustus built the **Arch of Augustus,** which once framed the V. Sacra. The circular building behind the Temple of the Deified Julius is the restored **Temple of Vesta,** dating back to the time of the Etruscans. Here the Vestal Virgins tended the city's eternal, sacred fire, keeping it continuously lit for over a thousand years. In a secret room of the temple, accessible only to the Virgins, stood the **Palladium,** the small statue of Minerva that Aeneas was said to have taken from Troy. Across the square from the Temple of Vesta lies the triangular **Regia,** office of the Pontifex Maximus, Rome's high priest and titular ancestor of the Pope.

UPPER FORUM. The **House of the Vestal Virgins,** shaded by the Palatine Hill, occupied the sprawling complex of rooms and courtyards behind the Temple

THE HIDDEN DEAL

ROME FOR FREE

So you've got one day left to kill in Rome and have completely maxed out your credit cards and blown your savings. You can either sit in your hostel room sulking or take advantage of the many things Rome offers *da gratis*.

A stroll up to the **Colle Oppio** park provides fine views of the Colosseum and contains ruins from the **Domus Aurea.**

The **Colosseum,** the granddaddy of Roman sights: Walking around and peering in are free, and also enough to get a sense of its grandeur. Admire the nearby **Arch of Constantine.**

The **Roman Forum** displays 2000-year-old ruins in various states of preservation, as well as the **Mamertine Prison** where the apostles Peter and Paul were imprisoned. Notice the nearby **Arch of Settimio.**

Witness the changing of the guard at the **Tomb of the Unknown Soldier** at the **Monument to Vittorio Emanuele II.** Inside, visit the **Museum of the Italian Renaissance,** housing Italian historical art up to WWI.

Gawk at Michelangelo's **Capitoline Piazza** and **steps.** Enjoy the piazza's copy of the bronze statue, **Marcus Aurelius on Horseback.** View the Roman Forum from the terrace.

Finally, on the last Sunday of each month, the **Vatican Museum** and **Sistine Chapel** are free! Visit other **Roman churches** for mosaics, sculptures, paintings, and relics.

of Vesta. For 30 years, the six virgins who officiated over Vesta's rites, each ordained from the age of three to ten, lived in spacious seclusion here above the din of the Forum. The Vestal Virgins were among the most respected people in Ancient Rome. They were the only women allowed to walk unaccompanied in the Forum and also possessed the right to pardon prisoners. This esteem had its price; a virgin who strayed from celibacy was buried alive with a loaf of bread and a candle—to allow her to survive long enough to contemplate her sins. Across from the House of the Vestal Virgins, on V. Sacra, is the **Temple of Antoninus and Faustina,** whose strong foundation, columns, and rigid lattice ceiling kept it well-preserved. In the 7th and 8th centuries, after numerous unsuccessful attempts to pull the abandoned temple down, the **Church of San Lorenzo in Miranda** was built in its interior. To the right of the temple lies the **necropolis.** Excavations uncovered Iron Age graves from the 8th century BC, lending credence to the city's legendary founding date of 753 BC. Here V. Sacra runs over the **Cloaca Maxima,** the ancient sewer that drains water from the valley. The street passes the **Temple of Romulus,** the round building behind scaffolding, named for the son of Maxentius (not the legendary founder of Rome). The original bronze doors have a 4th-century working lock.

VELIA. V. Sacra leads out of the Forum proper to the gargantuan **Basilica of Constantine and Maxentius,** also known as the Basilica of Constantine. Emperor Maxentius began construction in AD 308, but Constantine deposed him and completed the project himself. The uncovered remains of a statue of Constantine, including a 6½ ft.-long foot, are at the Palazzo dei Conservatori, on Capitoline Hill. The Baroque facade of the **Church of Santa Francesca Romana** is built over Hadrian's Temple to Venus and Rome—the palindromic *Roma* and *Amor*—and hides the entrance to the **Antiquarium Forense,** a museum displaying necropolis urns and skeletons. *(Inquire for hours. Free.)* On the summit of the Velia is the **Arch of Titus,** built in AD 81 by Domitian to celebrate his brother Titus, who had destroyed Jerusalem 11 years earlier. V. Sacra leads to exit on the other side of the hill, and beyond that, the Colosseum. The path crossing in front of the arch climbs up Palatine Hill.

CIRCUS MAXIMUS AND BATHS OF CARACALLA. Today's Circus Maximus is only a grassy shadow of its former glory as Rome's largest stadium. After its construction in 600 BC, the circus drew more than 300,000 Romans watching chariots careen around the track. The Baths of Caracalla are the largest and best preserved in Rome, with beautiful mosaics covering the floors. *(☎06 574 57 48. M: Circo Massimo, bus 118, or walk down V. di San Gregorio from the Colosseum. Open 24hr. Baths open Apr.-Oct. Tu-Su 9am-6:30pm; Nov.-Mar. M 9am-2pm and Tu-Su 9am-3:30pm. €5.)*

FORI IMPERIALI

The sprawling Fori Imperiali lie on either side of V. dei Fori Imperiali, a boulevard Mussolini paved to connect the old empire to his new one in P. Venezia. In the process, he covered about a third of the ruins. Much of the surrounding area is being excavated and is closed to the public, but passersby can still peer over the railing from V. dei Fori Imperiali. The conglomeration of temples, basilicas, and public squares was constructed between the first century BC and 2nd century AD in response to increasing congestion in the old Forum.

FORUM OF TRAJAN. Built between AD 107 and 113, the entire Forum celebrated Trajan's victorious Dacian (*Romania*) campaign. The complex included a colossal equestrian statue of Trajan and triumphal arch. At one end stands ▓**Trajan's Column,** an extraordinary and intact specimen of Roman relief-sculpture depicting 2500 legionnaires. In 1588 a statue of St. Peter replaced Trajan's.

MARKETS OF TRAJAN. This three-floor semicircular complex is a glimpse of Rome's first shopping mall, featuring an impressive—albeit crumbling—display of sculpture from the imperial forums. *(☎06 679 00 48. Enter at V. IV Novembre, 94, up the* *steps in V. Magnanapoli, to the right of the 2 churches behind Trajan's column. Open Tu-Su 9am-6:30, Nov.-Mar. until 4:30pm. €6.20, with ISIC €3.10. Or get a free view of the complex and other Imperial Fora from V. Alessandrina, off of V. dei Fori Imperiali).*

FORA. In the shade of the Vittorio Emanuele II monument lie the paltry remains of the **Forum of Caesar,** including the ruins of Julius Caesar's **Temple to Venus Genetrix** (Mother Venus, from whom he claimed descent). Nearby, the gray tufa wall of the **Forum of Augustus** commemorates Augustus's victory over Caesar's murderers at the Battle of Philippi in 42 BC. The **Forum Transitorium** (also called the **Forum of Nerva**) was a narrow, rectangular space connecting the Forum of Augustus with the Republican Forum. Emperor Nerva dedicated the temple in 97 BC to the goddess Minerva. In **Vespatian's Forum,** the mosaic-filled **Church of Santi Cosma e Damiano** is across V. Cavour, near the Roman Forum. *(Open daily 9am-6:30pm.)*

THE CAPITOLINE HILL. Home to the original "capital," the Monte Capitolino still serves as the seat of the city's government. Michelangelo designed the spacious **Piazza di Campidoglio.** Surrounding the piazza are the twin Palazzo dei Conservatori and Palazzo Nuovo, now the home of the **Capitoline Museums.** From the Palazzo Nuovo, stairs lead up to the rear entrance of the 7th-century **Chiesa di Santa Maria in Aracoeli.** Its stunning **Cappella Bufalini** is home to the *Santo Bambino,* a cherubic statue that receives letters from sick children. The gloomy **Mamertine Prison,** consecrated as the **Chiesa di San Pietro in Carcere,** lies down the hill from the back stairs of the Aracoeli. St. Peter baptized his captors with the waters that flooded his cell here. At the far end of the piazza, the turreted **Palazzo dei Senatori** houses the offices of Rome's mayor. Pope Paul III had Michelangelo fashion the imposing statues of the twin warriors, Castor and Pollux, and also had the famous equestrian **statue of Marcus Aurelius** brought here from Palazzo Laterano. The original now resides in the courtyard of the Palazzo dei Conservatori—a sturdier copy crowns the piazza. *(Santa Maria in Aracoeli open daily 9:30am-12:30pm and 2:30-5:30pm. Mamertine Prison ☎ 06 679 29 02. Entrance underneath the church of S. Giuseppe dei Falegnami and is open daily in winter 9am-12:30pm and 2-5pm, in summer 9-12:30pm and 2:30-6:30pm. Open daily 9am-12:30pm and 2:30-6:30pm. Donation requested. To get to the Campidoglio, take bus to P. Venezia. From P. Venezia, face the Vittorio Emanuele II monument, walk around to the right to P. d'Aracoeli, and take the stairs up the hill.)*

THE VELABRUM. The Velabrum lies in a flat flood plain of the Tiber, south of the Jewish Ghetto. At the bend of V. del Portico d'Ottavia, a shattered pediment and a few columns are all that remain of the once magnificent **Portico d'Ottavia.** The 11 BC **Teatro di Marcello** next door bears the name of Augustus's nephew; the Colosseum was modeled upon its facade. Down V. del Teatro toward the Tiber, the **Chiesa di San Nicola in Carcere** incorporates Roman temples to Juno, Janus, and Spes. One block south along V. Luigi Petroselli is the **Piazza della Bocca della Verità,** the site of the ancient **Foro Boario** (cattle market). Across the street, the **Chiesa di Santa Maria in Cosmedin** harbors lovely medieval decor. The portico's ▧**Bocca della Verità,** a drain cover with a river god's face, was made famous in Audrey Hepburn's *Roman Holiday.* Medieval legend has it that the mouth bites a liar's hand. *(Chiesa di San Nicola ☎ 06 686 99 72. Open Sept.-July M-Sa 7:30am-noon and 2-5pm, Su 9:30am-1pm and 4-8pm. Portico open daily Apr.-Sept. 9am-6:30pm, Oct.-Mar. 9am-5pm.)*

CENTRO STORICO

VIA DEL CORSO AND PIAZZA VENEZIA. Following along the ancient V. Lata, **Via del Corso** began as Rome's premier race course. It runs between P. del Popolo and P. Venezia. Also known as "the wedding cake" and "Mussolini's typewriter," the **Vittorio Emanuele II Monument,** a confection of gleaming white marble, looms over P. Venezia like a glacier. At the top of the staircase on the exterior is the *Altare della Patria,* which has an eternal flame guarded night and day. The **Palazzo Venezia,**

right of the piazza, was one of the first Renaissance palaces in the city. Mussolini used it as an office and delivered some of his most famous speeches from its balcony. Now it houses a **museum** with rotating exhibits. The *loggia* of the interior courtyard dates from the Renaissance. Off V. del Corso, **Piazza Colonna** was named for the **Colonna di Marco Aurelio**, designed to imitate Trajan's triumphant column. On the opposite side of the piazza, **Palazzo Wedekind,** home to the newspaper *Il Tempo*, was built in 1838 with columns from the Etruscan city of Veio. The northwestern corner of the piazza flows into **Piazza di Montecitorio,** overseen by Bernini's **Palazzo Montecitorio,** now the seat of the Chamber of Deputies.

PIAZZA DELLA ROTONDA AND PANTHEON. With granite columns and pediment, bronze doors, and a soaring domed interior, the ▨**Pantheon** has changed little since it was built nearly 2000 years ago. Architects still puzzle over how it was erected—its dome, a perfect half-sphere constructed from poured concrete without the support of vaults, arches, or ribs, is the largest of its kind. The light entering the roof through the 9m oculus served as a sundial. In AD 608 the Pantheon was consecrated as the **Chiesa di Santa Maria ad Martyres.** Look for Raphael's tomb on the far left. *(Open M-Sa 8:30am-7:30pm, Su 9am-6pm, holidays 9am-1pm. Free.)* The piazza centers on Giacomo della Porta's late Renaissance fountain, which supports an ancient **Egyptian obelisk** added in the 18th century. Around the left side of the Pantheon and down the street, another obelisk, supported by Bernini's curious elephant statue, marks the center of tiny **Piazza Minerva.** Behind the obelisk, the Gothic **Chiesa di Santa Maria Sopra Minerva** *(open daily 7am-7pm)* hides some Renaissance masterpieces, including Michelangelo's *Christ Bearing the Cross*, Antoniazzo Romano's *Annunciation*, and a statue of St. Sebastian recently attributed to Michelangelo. In the southern transept is the **Cappella Carafa,** with a brilliant Lippi fresco cycle. From the upper left-hand corner of P. della Rotonda, V. Giustiniani heads north to V. della Scrofa and V. della Dogana Vecchia. Here stands **Chiesa di San Luigi dei Francesi,** the French National Church, home to three of Caravaggio's most famous paintings: *The Calling of St. Matthew, St. Matthew and the Angel,* and *The Crucifixion. (1 block down V. di Salvatore from C. Rinascimento, opposite P. Navona. Open daily 8:30am-12:30pm and 3:30-7pm, closed Th afternoon.)*

PIAZZA NAVONA. Opened in AD 86, the piazza housed wrestling matches, chariot races, and mock naval battles, with the stadium flooded and fleets skippered by convicts. Bernini's **Fontana dei Quattro Fiumi** (Fountain of the Four Rivers) commands the center of the piazza. Each river god represents a continent: Ganges for Asia, Danube for Europe, Nile for Africa (veiled, since the source of the river was unknown), and Rio de la Plata for the Americas. At the ends of the piazza are the **Fontana del Moro** and the **Fontana di Nettuno,** designed by Giacomo della Porta in the 16th century. With a Borromini-designed exterior, the **Church of Sant'Agnese in Agone** holds the tiny skull of its namesake saint, martyred after rejecting a young man's advances. *(Western side of P. Navona, opposite Fontana dei Quattro Fiumi. Open daily 9am-noon and 4-7pm.)* West of P. Navona, where V. di Tor Millina intersects V. della Pace, the semicircular porch of the **Chiesa di Santa Maria della Pace** houses Raphael's gentle *Sibyls* in its Chigi Chapel *(daily 10am-6pm, Sa to 10, Su to 1pm).* On nearby C. del Rinascimento, the **Chiesa di Sant'Ivo's** corkscrew cupola hovers over the **Palazzo della Sapienza,** the original home of the University of Rome. C. V. Emanuele leads to the Baroque **Il Gesù,** mother church of the Jesuit Order. Not to miss are the **Chapel of S. Ignazio** built by the Andrea Pozzo, the nave ceiling decorations, and Bernini's **Monument to S. Bellarmino.** *(Open daily 6:30am-12:30pm and 4-7:15pm.)*

CAMPO DEI FIORI. Campo dei Fiori lies across C. V. Emanuele from P. Navona and is one of the last authentically Roman areas of the *centro storico.* It is home to a bustling market in the morning Monday to Saturday, and at night transforms

TIME: 3hr. walk.

DISTANCE: about 3km.

SEASON: Year-round, but spring is best.

A complete tour of the medieval centro storico *neighborhood.*

1 PIAZZA NAVONA. The site of Domitian's stadium, the *piazza* was a special pet project of a number of 17th-century popes. The result was a Baroque masterpiece that today houses Bernini's Fontana dei Quattro Fiumi and pushy vendors alike. The Church of Sant'Agnese in Agone is also worth a look, if for nothing else than the saint's head, which is on prominent display. (p. 114.)

2 PANTHEON. A 2000-year-old temple currently masquerading under the name Chiesa di Santa Maria ad Martyres. When the ancient Romans dedicated it to all of the pagan gods, they topped the round temple with the largest masonry dome ever constructed. Enter and marvel at the magnificent structure. (p. 114.)

3 CHIESA DI SANTA MARIA SOPRA MINERVA. The current structure was built upon (sopra) the old Roman temple to Minerva, and is one of Rome's few examples of Gothic architecture. Under the main altar is the tomb of Catherine de Siena, who convinced the Pope to remove the papacy from wicked, wild France and back to sober, discreet Italy. Other highlights include the final resting place of the artist Fra Angelico and Michelangelo's *Risen Christ*. (p. 114.)

4 GALLERIA DORIA PAMPHILJ. Taking V. del Seminario to the east and a right onto V. Sant'Ignazio will lead you directly to the place where the term "nepotism" was first coined. The Doria Pamphilj's family's relations with Innocent X are largely responsible for the contents of the palace, which can only be described as opulent. Velázquez's painting of Innocent X is one of the finest papal portraits in Rome. (p. 127.)

5 TREVI FOUNTAIN. All roads lead to this tourist monstrosity. Just face the facts: you'll end up here at some point, bathed in the flashbulbs of thousands of Kodak disposable cameras, and tossing a coin over your shoulder. If you can, take a moment to enjoy the Neptune fountain, built into the side of a palazzo. (p. 116.)

6 PIAZZA BARBERINI. Bernini's Fontana del Tritone is the centerpiece of this square, built for Urban VIII (of the same clan of Barberini bees that decorate the bronze canopy in the Vatican). A short walk up V. Veneto to the Capuchin Crypt in the Chiesa Santa Maria della Concezione is a spooky (and cool) way to spend a hot afternoon. (p. 117.)

7 SPANISH STEPS. Home of all that's Italian chic, the Spanish Steps are host to a number of overpriced and famous cafes, a couple of decent churches (for the materialistic sinners in Armani that congregate in the nearby piazzas), and everything that you need to know about international fashion. (p. 116.)

WALKING TOUR

into a hip hot spot. During papal rule, the area was the site of countless executions; the eerie statue of Giordano Bruno is a tribute to one of the deceased. The Renaissance **Palazzo Farnese,** built by Alessandro Farnese, the first Counter-Reformation pope (1534-1549), dominates P. Farnese, south of the Campo. To the east of the palazzo is the **Palazzo Spada** and its **art gallery** (p. 126).

THE JEWISH GHETTO

The Jewish community in Rome is the oldest in Europe—Israelites came in 161 BC as ambassadors from Judas Maccabee, asking for imperial help against invaders. The Ghetto, the tiny area to which Pope Paul IV confined the Jews in 1555, was dissolved in 1870, but it is still the center of Rome's Jewish population of 16,000. Take bus #64; the Ghetto is across V. Arenula from Campo dei Fiori. The Ghetto's main street is V. del Portico d'Ottavia.

PIAZZA MATTEI. This square, centered on Taddeo Landini's 16th-century **Fontana delle Tartarughe,** marks the center of the Ghetto. Nearby is the **Church of Sant'Angelo in Pescheria,** installed inside the **Portico d'Ottavia** in AD 755 and named after the fish market that flourished here. Jews were forced to attend mass here every Sunday, an act of forced evangelism that they quietly resisted by stuffing their ears with wax. *(Open for prayer W 5:30pm, Sa 5pm.)*

SINAGOGA ASHKENAZITA. Built between 1874 and 1904 at the corner of Lungotevere dei Cenci and V. Catalan, this temple incorporates Persian and Babylonian architectural techniques. Terrorists bombed the building in 1982; guards now search all visitors. The synagogue houses the **Jewish Museum,** a collection of ancient torahs and Holocaust artifacts documenting the community's history. *(☎ 06 684 006 61. Open for services only. Museum open May-Sept. M-Th 9am-7:30pm, F 9am-1:30pm, Su 9am-12:30pm; Oct.-Apr. M-F 9am-4:30pm.)*

PIAZZA DI SPAGNA AND ENVIRONS

■ **SPANISH STEPS.** Designed by an Italian, paid for by the French, named for the Spaniards, occupied by the British, and currently featuring American greats like Ronald McDonald, the **Scalinata di Spagna** are, well, international. P. di Spagna is also home to designer boutiques such as Fendi, Gucci, Prada, Dolce & Gabbana, and Valentino, and is a great spot for people-watching and socializing. The pink house to the right of the Steps was the site of John Keats's 1821 death; it's now the **Keats-Shelley Memorial Museum** which displays several documents and memoirs of the English Romantic poets as well as Byron. *(☎ 06 678 42 35. Open M-F 9am-1pm and 3-6pm, Su 11am-2pm and 3-6pm. €3.)*

■ **FONTANA DI TREVI.** Nicolo Salvi's (1697-1751) bombastic **Fontana di Trevi** emerges from the back wall of **Palazzo Poli,** fascinating crowds with the rumble of its cascading waters. Anita Ekberg took a dip in the fountain in Fellini's movie *La Dolce Vita.* Legend has it that a traveler who throws a coin into the fountain is ensured a speedy return, and one who tosses two will fall in love in Rome. The **crypt** of the **Chiesa dei Santi Vincenzo e Anastasio,** opposite the fountain, preserves hearts and lungs of popes from 1590-1903. *(Open daily 7:30am-12:30pm and 4-7pm.)*

PIAZZA DEL POPOLO. Once a favorite venue for the execution of heretics, this is now the "people's square." In the center is the 3200-year-old **Obelisk of Pharaoh Ramses II,** which Augustus brought from Egypt. The ■ **Santa Maria del Popolo** holds Renaissance and Baroque masterpieces. *(☎ 06 361 08 36. Open M-Sa 7am-noon and 4-7pm, Su and holidays 7:30am-1:30pm and 4:30-7:30pm.)* The **Cappella della Rovere** on the right holds Pinturicchio's *Adoration.* Two exquisite Caravaggios, *The Conversion of St. Paul* and *Crucifixion of St. Peter,* are in the **Cappella Cerasi,** next to the altar. The **Cappella Chigi** was designed by Raphael for the Sienese banker Agostino Chigi, reputedly once the world's richest man; niches on either side of the altar house sculptures by Bernini and Lorenzetto. At the southern end of the piazza are the 17th-century twin churches of **Santa Maria di Montesano** and **Santa Maria dei Miracoli,** designed by Carlo Rinaldi. *(S. Maria dei Miracoli. ☎ 06 361 02 50. Open M-Sa 6:30am-1:30pm and 4-7:30pm, Su 8am-1:30pm and 5-7pm.)*

VILLA BORGHESE. To celebrate becoming a cardinal, Scipione Borghese financed the construction of the **Villa Borghese** north of P. di Spagna and V. V. Veneto. Its park is now home to three art museums, including the world-renowned **Galleria Borghese** (p. 125) and the intriguing **Museo Nazionale Etrusco di Villa Giulia** (p. 125). The Borghese is also home to a second-rate zoo, the **Bio Parco.** North of Villa Borghese are the **Santa Priscilla catacombs** and the **Villa Ada** gardens. *(☎ 06 321 65 64. M: A-Spagna and follow the signs. Or, from the Flaminio (A) stop, take V. Washington under the archway into the Pincio. From P. del Popolo, climb the stairs to the right of Santa Maria del Popolo, cross the street, and climb the small path. Bio Parco, V.del Giardino Zoologico, 20. Open M-F 9:30am-6pm, Sa-Su 9:30am-7pm. €8.50, ages 3-12 €6.50, under 3 free. Santa Priscilla catacombs, V. Salaria, 430 (☎ 06 862 062 72), along with the gardens of Villa Ada, are best reached by bus #310 from Termini, or in P. Barberini. Get off at P. Vescovio and walk down V. di Tor Fiorenza to P. di Priscilla to the entrance to the park and the catacombs. Open Tu-Su 8:30am-noon and 2:30-5pm. €5.)*

PIAZZA BARBERINI. Over the busy traffic circle at V. del Tritone, Bernini's **Fontana Tritone** spouts water high into the air. A modern feel pervades the piazza, despite the **Fontana delle Api,** constructed for the pope Urban VIII. Maderno, Bernini, and rival Borromini are responsible for the 1624 **Palazzo Barberini,** which houses the Galleria Nazionale d'Arte Antica (p. 126). The severe **Church of the Immaculate Conception** house the macabre **Capuchin Crypt,** decorated with human bones. *(V. V. Veneto, 27/A. Open M-W and F 9am-noon and 3-6pm. Donation requested.)*

VATICAN CITY

☎ 06 69 82. M: A-Ottaviano; bus #64, 271, or 492 from Termini or Largo Argentina; or Tram #19 from P. Risorgimento, 62 from P. Barberini, or 23 from Testaccio.

Occupying 108½ independent acres within Roman boundaries stands the foothold of the Roman Catholic Church, which wheeled and dealed as the mightiest power in Europe. The Lateran Treaty of 1929, which allows the Pope to maintain legislative, judicial, and executive powers over this tiny theocracy, also requires the Church to remain neutral in national politics and municipal affairs. The Vatican has historically preserved its independence by minting coins (Italian *lire* and euros with the Pope's face), running a separate press and postal system, maintaining an army of Swiss Guards, and hoarding fine art in the **Musei Vaticani** (p. 124).

BASILICA DI SAN PIETRO (ST. PETER'S BASILICA)

Multilingual confession available; languages are printed outside the confessionals by the main altar. The Pilgrim Tourist Information Center is located on the left between the rounded colonnade and the basilica and offers a multilingual staff, Vatican post, free brochures, and currency exchange. A first-aid station and free bathrooms are next to the Information Center. Open daily Apr.-Sept. 7am-7pm, Oct.-Mar. 7am-6pm. Mass M-Sa 8:30, 10, 11am, noon, 5pm; Su and holidays 9, 10:30, 11:30am, 12:10, 1, 4, 5:30pm; vespers at 5pm. Attire strictly enforced: no shorts, short skirts, or exposed shoulders.

PIAZZA AND FACADE. Bernini's colonnade around **Piazza San Pietro** draws people toward the church like a pair of open arms. Mussolini's V. della Conciliazione, an avenue built in the 1930s to connect the Vatican to the rest of the city, opened a broader view of the church than Bernini had ever intended. Two fountains frame the central obelisk. Round disks mark where to stand so that the quadruple rows of colonnades visually resolve into one perfectly aligned row. One hundred and forty statues of saints grace the area above the colonnade. Those atop the basilica represent Christ, John the Baptist, and the apostles (minus Peter).

INTERIOR. The pope opens the **Porta Sancta** (Holy Door), the last door on the right side of the entrance porch, on Holy Years by knocking in the bricks with a hammer. The basilica rests on the reputed site of St. Peter's tomb. The interior of St. Peter's measures 187m by 137m along the transepts. Metal lines on the marble floor mark the lengths of other major world churches. To the right, **Michelangelo's Pietà** has been protected by bullet-proof glass since 1972, when an axe-wielding fanatic attacked it, smashing Christ's nose and breaking Mary's hand.

Bernini's **baldacchino** rises on spiraling dark columns over the marble altar, reserved for the Pope's use. The Baroque structure, cast in bronze pillaged from the Pantheon, was unveiled on June 28, 1633 by Pope Urban VIII, a member of the wealthy Barberini family. Bees, the symbol of the Barberini family, buzz here and there (as well as on buildings and statues all over Rome), while vines climb up toward Michelangelo's cavernous cupola. In front of the *baldacchino* burn 70 gilded oil lamps, illuminating Maderno's sunken *Confession*. Two marble staircases lead to St. Peter's tomb, directly beneath the papal altar. The staircases are closed to the public, but a better view of the tomb is possible from the grottoes.

High above the *baldacchino* and the altar rises **Michelangelo's dome**, which is built with a double shell, but designed as a circular dome, like the Pantheon (p. 114). Out of reverence for that ancient architectural wonder, Michelangelo is said to have made this cupola a meter shorter in diameter than the Pantheon's, but its measurements are still eye-popping. The dome's highest point towers 120m above the floor and its diameter measures 42.3m across. When Michelangelo died in 1564, only the drum of the dome had been completed. Work remained at a standstill until 1588, when 800 laborers were hired to complete it. Toiling round the clock, they finished the dome on May 21, 1590.

BASILICA ENVIRONS

To the left of the basilica is a courtyard vigilantly protected by Swiss Guards. The **Ufficio Scavi,** administrative center for the Pre-Constantinian Necropolis (see below), is here. Ask Swiss Guards for permission to enter. To the right of the basilica, at the end of the colonnade, the **Prefettura della Casa Pontifica** gives free tickets to papal audiences Wednesday morning when the pope is in town.

CUPOLA. The cupola's entrance is near the Porta Sancta. Take an elevator to the walkway around the interior of the dome or ascend 350 steps to the top ledge, which offers a dazzling panorama. *(Open daily Apr.-Sept. 8am-5:45pm, Oct.-Mar. 7am-4:45pm. Elevator €5, on foot €4.)*

TREASURY OF SAINT PETER. The Treasury contains gifts bestowed upon St. Peter's tomb. Highlights include the Solomonic column from the Basilica of Constantine; the "dalmatic of Charlemagne" (the illiterate Holy Roman Emperor's intricately designed robe); a statue of one of Bernini's angels; and the magnificent bronze tomb of Sixtus IV. *(Photographs not allowed. Wheelchair accessible. Open daily Apr.-Sept. 9am-6:30pm, Oct.-Mar. 9am-5:30pm. Closed when the Pope is celebrating in the basilica and on Christmas and Easter. €5, 12 and under €3.)*

TOMB OF ST. PETER AND PRE-CONSTANTINIAN NECROPOLIS. Legend holds that after converting to Christianity, Constantine built the first basilica directly over the tomb of St. Peter, who had been crucified for preaching the Gospel. In order to build on that exact spot, the emperor had to level a hill and destroy the first-century necropolis that stood there before. There was no proof for this story, however, until 1939, when workers came across ancient ruins beneath the basilica. Unsure of finding anything, the Church secretly set about looking for St. Peter's tomb. Twenty-one years later, the saint's tomb was identified under a small *aedicula* (temple), directly beneath the altars of both the Constantinian and modern basilicas. The saint's bones, however, were not found in the crude grave. A hollow wall nearby held what the church later claimed to be the holy remains—although archaeologists disagreed. It is quite possible that the bones were displaced from the tomb during the Saracen's sack of Rome in AD 849. Multilingual tour guides will take you around the streets of the necropolis, which holds several well-preserved mausolea (pagan and Christian), funerary inscriptions, mosaics, and sarcophagi. The entrance to the necropolis is on the left side of the P. San Pietro, beyond the information office. (☎ 06 698 853 18; scavi@fsp.va. Open M-Sa 9am-3:30pm. Advance reservation required. To request a tour, write to The Delegate of the Fabbrica di San Pietro, Excavations Office, 00120 Vatican City. Give a range of times and languages. Phone calls only accepted for reconfirmations. Or, reserve in person. Book as far ahead as possible. €9.)

CASTEL SANT'ANGELO

☎ 06 687 50 36, reservations 697 91 11. Along the Tiber River on the Vatican side, going from St. Peter's toward Trastevere. From the centro storico, cross Ponte Sant'Angelo. Bus #40, 62, 64, 271, 280 to Ponte V. Emanuele or P. Pia. Dungeon tours Su 12:30pm in Italian, 2:30pm in English. Audioguides €4. Open Tu-Su 9am-8pm, in winter daily 9am-7pm. €5, EU students 18-25 €2.50, EU citizens under 18 or over 65 free.

Built by Hadrian (AD 117-138) as a mausoleum for himself and his family, this brick and stone mass served as fortress, prison, and palace. When plague wracked the city in 590, Pope Gregory the Great saw an angel sheathing his sword at the top of the complex; the plague abated soon after, and the edifice was rededicated to the angel. The fortress offers an incomparable view of Rome and the Vatican. Outside, the marble **Ponte Sant'Angelo**, lined with statues designed by Bernini, is the starting point for the traditional pilgrimage route from St. Peter's to the church of **San Giovanni in Laterano**.

TRASTEVERE

Take bus #75 or 170 from Termini to V. Trastevere, or tram #8 from Largo Argentina.

ISOLA TIBERINA. According to Roman legend, Isola Tiberina emerged with the Roman Republic. After the Etruscan tyrant Tarquin raped the virtuous Lucretia, her outraged family killed him and threw his corpse in the river where muck and silt collected around it. Home to the Fatebenefratelli Hospital since AD 154, the island has long been associated with healing. The Greek god of healing, Aesclepius, appeared to the Romans as a snake and slithered from the river; his symbol, the *caduceus*, is visible all over the island. The eclectic 10th-century **Church of San Bartolomeo** has a Baroque facade, a Romanesque tower, and 14 antique columns. (Open M-Sa 9am-12:30pm and 4-6:30pm.) The **Ponte Fabricio** (62 BC), known as the **Ponte dei Quattro Capi** (Bridge of Four Heads), is the oldest in the city.

CENTRAL TRASTEVERE. Off Ponte Garibaldi stands the statue of dialect poet G. G. Belli, in the middle of his own piazza, which borders P. Sonnino and marks the beginning of V. di Trastevere. On V. di Santa Cecilia, beyond the courtyard full of roses, is the **Basilica di Santa Cecilia in Trastevere**. (Open daily 7am-1pm and 3:30-7pm. Cloister open Tu and Th 10-11:30am, Su 11:30am-noon. Donation requested. Crypt €2.) From P. Sonnino, V. della Lungaretta leads west to P. di S. Maria in Trastevere, home to the **Chiesa di Santa Maria in Trastevere**, built in the 4th century by Pope Julius II. Although the church is being restored, 12th-century mosaics in the apse and the chancel arch are still visible, depicting Jesus, Mary, and a bevy of saints and popes. (Open M-Sa 9am-5:30pm, Su 8:30-10:30am and noon-5:30pm.) North of the piazza are the Rococo **Galleria Corsini,** V. della Lungara, 10 (see **Museo Nazionale dell'Arte Antica,** p. 126), and, across the street, the **Villa Farnesina,** the jewel of Trastevere. Peruzzi built the villa for banker Agostino Chigi ("il Magnifico") between 1508-1511. The museum's frescoed walls are the main attraction (p. 126).

GIANICOLO. At the top of the hill, the **Chiesa di San Pietro in Montorio** stands on what is believed to be the site of St. Peter's upside-down crucifixion. The church contains del Piombo's *Flagellation*, from designs by Michelangelo. Next door in a small courtyard is Bramante's tiny ▨**Tempietto.** A combination of Renaissance and ancient architecture, it was constructed to commemorate the site of Peter's martyrdom and provided the inspiration for the larger dome of St. Peter's. Rome's **botanical gardens** contain a garden for the blind as well as a rose garden that holds the bush from which all the world's roses are supposedly descended. *(Reach the summit via bus #41 from the Vatican, 115 from Trastevere, 870 from P. Fiorentini (off C. V. Emanuele where it meets the Tiber) or take the medieval V. Garibaldi from V. della Scala in Trastevere (about a 10min. walk). Church and Tempietto open May-Oct. Tu-Su 9:30am-12:30pm and 4-6pm, Nov.-Apr. 9:30am-12:30pm and 2-4pm. Gardens, Largo Cristina di Svezia, 24, at the end of V. Corsini, off V. della Lungara. ☎ 06 499 171 07. Open Apr.-Sept. Tu-Sa 9:30am-6:30pm, Oct.-Mar. M-Sa 9:30am-5:30pm. Closed holidays and Aug.)*

NORTH OF TERMINI

BATHS OF DIOCLETIAN. From AD 298 to 306, 40,000 Christian slaves built these 3000-person capacity public baths. They contained a heated marble public toilet with seats for 30 people, several pools, gymnasiums, art galleries, gardens, brothels, sports facilities, libraries, and concert halls. In 1561 Michelangelo undertook his last architectural work and converted the ruins into a church, the **Chiesa di Santa Maria degli Angeli.** The 4th-century rotonda displays statues from the baths. The viewing windows look down into excavations. The baths are also the historic seat of the Museo Nazionale. *(Baths on V. E De Nicola, 79, in P. dei Cinquecento, across the street from Termini. ☎ 06 399 677 00. Open Tu-Sa 9am-7:45pm. €5. Church is in P. della Repubblica. ☎ 06 488 08 12. Open daily 7am-6pm.)*

PIAZZA DEL QUIRINALE. At the southeastern end of V. del Quirinale, this piazza occupies the summit of the tallest of Rome's seven hills. In the center of the piazza the enormous statues of Castor and Pollux (Roman copies of the Greek originals) stand on either side of an obelisk from the Mausoleum of Augustus. The President of the Republic resides in the imposing **Palazzo del Quirinale** *(closed to the public),* a Baroque architectural collaboration by Bernini, Maderno, and Fontana. Down V. del Quirinale, V. Ferrara on the right leads down the steps to V. Milano. Farther along the street lies the marvelous facade of Borromini's pulsating **Chiesa di San Carlo alle Quattro Fontane.** *(Open daily 10am-1pm, also M-F 3-7pm.)*

VIA XX SETTEMBRE. V. del Quirinale becomes V. XX Settembre at its intersection with V. delle Quattro. A few blocks down, the colossal **Fontana dell'Acqua Felice** graces the Baroque P. San Bernardo. Opposite, **Chiesa di Santa Maria della Vittoria** houses an icon of Mary that accompanied the Catholics to victory in a 1620 battle near Prague. Bernini's fantastic *Ecstasy of St. Theresa of Ávila* (1652) resides in its Cornaro Chapel. *(Open daily 7am-noon and 3:30-7pm. Modest dress required.)*

VIA NOMENTANA. This road runs northeast from Michelangelo's **Porta Pia** out of the city. Hop on bus #36 in front of Termini or head back to V. XX Settembre and catch bus #60. A 2km walk from Pta. Pia past villas, embassies, and parks leads to **Chiesa di Sant'Agnese Fuori le Mura.** Its apse displays Byzantine-style mosaic of St. Agnes. Underneath the church wind some of Rome's most impressive ▨**catacombs.** *(V. Nomentana, 349. ☎ 06 861 08 40 or 328 565 24 14 to reach Danilo, the tour guide. Open M 9am-noon, Tu-Su 9am-noon and 4-6pm. Catacombs €5. Modest dress required.)*

ROME AND LAZIO

SOUTH OF TERMINI

■ BASILICA DI SANTA MARIA MAGGIORE. As one of five churches in Rome granted extraterritoriality, this basilica crowning the Esquiline Hill is officially part of Vatican City. In 352 Pope Sixtus III commissioned it when he noticed that Roman women were still visiting a temple to the pagan mother-goddess Juno Lucina. Sixtus tore down the temple to build his new basilica, also celebrating the Council of Ephesus's recent ruling of Mary as the Mother of God. To the right of the altar, a marble slab marks **Bernini's tomb.** The 14th-century mosaics in the church's **loggia** recount the story of the miraculous August snowfall that showed the pope where to build the church. *(From Termini, exit south on V. Giolitti and walk down V. Cavour. Walk around to the southeastern side to enter. Open daily 7am-7pm. Modest dress required. Loggia open daily 9:30am-12:30pm. Tickets sold in souvenir shop; €3. Museum entrance through souvenir shop. Open daily 9:30am-6:30pm. €4.)*

PIAZZA VITTORIO EMANUELE II. The Rococo **Church of Santa Croce in Gerusalemme** holds the Fascist-era **Chapel of the Relics,** with fragments of the "true cross." For the doubtful, perhaps the most faith-testing of the chapel's relics is St. Thomas's dismembered finger, with which he probed Christ's wounds. *(P. S. Croce in Gerusalemme. M: A-San Giovanni. From P. S. Giovanni north of the Metro stop, go east on V. C. Felice; the church is on the right. From P. V. Emanuele II, take V. Conte Verde (V. S. Croce in Gerusalemme). Open daily 7am-7pm. Modest dress required.)*

CHURCH OF SAN PIETRO IN VINCOLI. This 4th-century church is named for the sacred chains *(vincoli)* that bound St. Peter after his imprisonment in the Mamertine prison. The two chains were separated for more than a century in Rome and Constantinople, brought back together in the 5th century, and now lie beneath the altar. Michelangelo's statue of **■ Moses** is tucked into an unobtrusive corner, perfect for contemplation. The two horns on his head are actually supposed to be beams of light. *(M: B-Cavour. Walk along V. Cavour toward the Forum and take the stairs on left to P. S. Pietro in Vincoli. Open daily 7am-12:30pm and 3:30-6pm. Modest dress required.)*

SOUTHERN ROME

CAELIAN HILL: CHURCH OF SAN CLEMENTE. The Caelian and the Esquiline are the biggest of Rome's seven original hills. In ancient times Nero built his decadent Domus Aurea between them (p. 110). **San Clemente** consists of a 12th-century church on top of a 4th-century church, with an ancient **mithraeum** and sewers at the bottom. The upper church holds medieval mosaics of the Crucifixion, saints, and apostles, and a 1420s Masolino fresco cycle graces the **Chapel of Santa Caterina.** The 4th-century level contains the tomb of St. Cyril and a series of frescoes depicting Roman generals swearing in the vernacular, the first written use of the language. Farther underground is a creepy 2nd-century mithraeum, below which is the **insulae,** a series of brick and stone rooms where Nero is said to have played his lyre in AD 64 while the rest of Rome burned. A functional complex of Republican sewers lies 30m down. *(M: B-Colosseo. Turn left and walk east on V. Fori Imperiali (V. Labicana) away from the Forum; turn right into P. S. Clemente. From M: A-Manzoni, walk west on V. A. Manzoni (V. Labicana); turn left into P. S. Clemente. ☎ 06 704 510 18. Open M-Sa 9am-12:30pm and 3-6pm, Su and holidays 10am-12:30pm and 3-6pm. Lower basilica and mithraeum €3.)*

SAN GIOVANNI IN LATERANO. The immense **San Giovanni in Laterano,** the cathedral of the diocese of Rome, was home to the papacy until the 14th century. Founded by Constantine in 314, it is the city's oldest Christian basilica. The Gothic *baldacchino* houses two golden reliquaries containing the heads of **St. Peter** and **St. Paul.** The **Scala Santa** are believed to be the 28 marble steps used by Jesus outside Pontius Pilate's home in Jerusalem. Pilgrims win indulgence for their sins if they ascend the steps on their knees, reciting prayers on each step. Martin Luther experienced an early break with Catholicism here—in the middle of his way up the cathedral's steps, he realized the false piety of his climb and left. These steps lead to the chapel of the **Sancta Sanctorium** which houses the Acheiropoieton, or "picture painted without hands," said to be the work of St. Luke assisted by an angel. *(M: A-San Giovanni or bus #16 from Termini. Church ☎ 06 698 864 52. Open daily 7am-7pm. Cloister open daily 9am-6pm. €2, students €1. Museum €1. Modest dress required. The baptistery, just west of the church on the southern end of P. di S. Giovanni in Laterano, is open daily, 7:30am-1pm and 3:30-6:30pm. Scala Santa and Sancta Sanctorium ☎ 06 772 66 41. Open daily 6:30am-noon and 3-6pm, in summer until 6:30pm.)*

AVENTINE HILL. The easiest approach to the Aventine is from the western end of the Circus Maximus (the end farthest from the Circo Massimo Metro stop) at P. Ugo la Malfa. From here, V. di Valle Murcia climbs past some of Rome's swankiest homes and the **Roseto Comunale,** a beautiful public rose garden, to a park with orange trees and a sweeping view of southern Rome. Across the park, another gate opens onto the courtyard of the **Chiesa di Santa Sabina,** featuring wooden front doors dating to AD 450. The top left-hand panel contains perhaps the earliest known representation of the Crucifixion. V. S. Sabina continues along the crest of the hill to **Piazza dei Cavalieri di Malta,** home of the crusading order of the Knights of Malta. Through the ✂keyhole in the pale yellow gate, the dome of St. Peter's is perfectly framed by hedges. *(Rose garden open May-June 8am-7:30pm.)*

THE APPIAN WAY

To get to the Appian Way, take M: Circo Massimo or Piramide, then bus #118 to the catacombs, or take M: Colli Albani, then bus 600 to Cecilia Metella and Villa of Maxentius.Info office of the Parco dell'Appia Antica, V. Appia Antica, 42, just outside Pta. San Sebastiano. ☎ 800 02 80 00. Provides maps and informative pamphlets about the ancient road. Open M-Sa 9am-6pm.

Known as the *Regina Varium* (Queen of Roads) throughout antiquity, the Via Appia was built in the 4th century BC to link Rome with Capua in Campania, and eventually led all the way to Brindisi on the Adriatic coast. The refreshingly green section stretching from Pta. San Sebastiano to the Grande Raccordo Anulare is a good place to visit catacombs and ruins, especially on Sundays when the roads are closed off to cars. It's best to visit during the day (consider renting a bike), before the prostitutes begin to populate the road.

CHURCH OF SANTA MARIA IN PALMIS. In this church, known as Domine Quo Vadis, a fleeing St. Peter had a vision of Christ. Asked "Domine Quo Vadis?" (Lord, where are you going?), Christ replied that he was going to Rome to be crucified again because Peter had abandoned him. Peter returned to Rome and suffered his own martyrdom. In the middle of the aisle, just inside the door, Christ's alleged footprints are set in stone. *(At the intersection of V. Appia Antica and V. Ardeatina. Bus #218 from P. S. Giovanni. Open M-Sa 7am-12:30pm and 3-6:30pm, Su 8:30am-1pm and 3-7pm.)*

CATACOMBS. Since burial inside the city walls was forbidden during ancient times, fashionable Romans made their final resting places along the Appian Way, while early Christians secretly dug maze-like **catacombs** under the ashes of their persecutors. **San Callisto** is the largest catacomb in Rome, with nearly 22km of subterranean paths. Its four levels once held 16 popes, seven bishops, St. Cecilia, and 500,000 other Christians. **Santa Domitilla** holds a 3rd-century portrait of Christ and the Apostles. **San Sebastiano** was the temporary home for the bodies of Peter and Paul and contains three recently unearthed tombs in remarkable shape. *(M: A-San Giovanni. Take bus #218 from P. S. Giovanni to intersection of V. Ardeatina and V. delle Sette Chiese. Free tour every 20min. €5, 15 and under €3. San Sebastiano: V. Appia Antica,*

136. From the #218 bus stop near S. Callisto and S. Domitilla, walk down V. Sette Chiese to V. Appia Antica and turn right. ☎ 06 513 015 80. Open Dec.-Oct. M-Sa 9am-noon and 2:30-5pm, closed Su and in Nov. Adjacent church open daily 8am-6pm. San Callisto: V. Appia Antica, 110. Take northeast road to catacombs' entrance. ☎ 06 513 015 80. Open M-Tu and Th-Su 8:30am-noon and 2:30-5pm, closed Feb. Santa Domitilla: V. delle Sette Chiese, 283. Facing V. Ardeatina from San Callisto exit, cross street and walk right up V. Sette Chiese. ☎ 06 511 03 42. Open Feb.-Dec. M and W-Su 8:30am-noon and 2:30-5pm, closed Jan.)

VILLA AND CIRCUS OF MAXENTIUS. Before Constantine took over in 312 AD, Maxentius held the title of emperor long enough to build his family a suburban sprawl along the Appian Way. The complex consists of a villa, a 10,000-spectator chariot race track (with impressive views of the countryside), and the tomb of his son Romulus. *(V. Appia Antica, 153. ☎ 06 780 13 24. Open Tu-F and Su 9am-1:30pm, Sa 9am-7pm. €2.60, students €1.60.)*

TESTACCIO AND OSTIENSE

Take Metro B to the Piramide from Termini.

South of the Aventine Hill, the working-class district of Testaccio is known for its cheap and delicious trattorias and raucous nightclubs. The neighborhood centers on the castle-like **Porta San Paolo**, an original remnant of the Aurelian walls, and the colossal **Piramide di Gaius Cestius,** built in about 330 days by Gaius's slaves. East of V. Galvani, between V. di Monte Testaccio and V. Zabaglia, is Monte Testaccio ("mountain made of pottery"), an artificial hill made entirely of broken ancient Roman wine and oil jars.

CIMITERO ACATTOLICO PER GLI STRANIERI. This peaceful Protestant cemetery, or the "Non-Catholic Cemetery for Foreigners," is one of the only burial grounds in Rome for those who don't belong to the Roman Catholic Church. Keats, Shelley, and Antonio Gramsci rest here. *(From Piramide, follow V. R. Persichetti on V. Marmorata, immediately turning left on V. Caio Cestio. Ring bell. Open Mar.-Oct. Tu-Su 9am-5:30pm, Oct.-Mar. 7am-4:30pm. Donation requested.)*

MONTE TESTACCIO. Monte Testaccio began as a Roman dumping ground for terra-cotta pots. The pile grew and grew, and today the ancient garbage heap, with a name derived from *testae*, or pot shards, rises in lush, dark green splendor over the drab surrounding streets. *(Follow V. Caio Cestio from V. Marmorata until it ends at V. Nicola Zabaglia. Continue straight onto V. Monte Testaccio. The hill is ahead and to the right.)*

BASILICA DI SAN PAOLO FUORI LE MURA. The Basilica di San Paolo Fuori le Mura, another of the churches in Rome with extraterritorial status, is the largest church in the city after St. Peter's. St. Paul is believed to be buried beneath the altar. Buy a bottle of monk-made **benedictine liqueur** (€5-15) in the gift shop. *(M: B-Basilica San Paolo, or take bus #23 or 769 from Testaccio at the corner of V. Ostiense and P. Ostiense. Basilica open daily in summer 7am-6:30pm, in winter 7am-6pm. Cloister open daily in summer 9am-1pm and 3-6:30pm, in winter 9am-1pm and 3-6pm. Modest dress required.)*

EUR. South of the city stands a monument to a Roman empire that never was. EUR (AY-oor) is an Italian acronym for Universal Exposition of Rome, the 1942 World's Fair that Mussolini intended to be a showcase of Fascist achievements. Apparently the new, modern Rome was to shock and impress the rest of the world with its futuristic ability to build lots of identical square buildings. **Via Cristoforo Colombo,** EUR's main street, is the first of many internationally ingratiating addresses like "Viale Asia" and "Piazza Kennedy." It runs north from the Metro station to **Piazza Guglielmo Marconi** and its 1959 **obelisk.** There is also an artificial lake here, surrounded by benches and green jogging paths. *(Take bus #714 or Metro B.)*

ROME AND LAZIO

ABBAZIA DELLE TRE FONTANE (ABBEY OF THE THREE FOUNTAINS). According to legend, when St. Paul was beheaded here, his head bounced on the ground three times, creating a fountain at each bounce. The Trappist monks who live here today sell their own potent eucalyptus liquor for €7-12 and enormous bars of divine chocolate for €2-4. *(M: B-Laurentina. Exit the Metro station and walk straight ahead to V. Laurentina; take a right and proceed about 1km north on V. Laurentina and turn right on V. delle Acque Salve. The abbey is at the bottom of the hill. Open daily 8am-1pm and 3-7pm.)*

🏛 MUSEUMS

Etruscans, emperors, and popes have been busily stuffing Rome's belly full with artwork for several millennia, leaving behind a city teeming with galleries. Museums are generally closed on holidays, Sunday afternoons, and all day Monday.

VATICAN MUSEUMS (MUSEI VATICANI)

Walk north from the right-hand side of P. S. Pietro along the wall of the Vatican City about 10 blocks. From M: Ottaviano, turn left on V. Ottaviano to reach the Vatican City Wall; turn right and follow the wall to the museum's entrance. ☎ 06 698 849 47. Info and gift shop (with the useful guidebook; €7.50) on ground level past the entrance. Valuable CD-ROM audioguide €5.50. Guides are available in several languages, and most of the museums' staff speak some English. Most of the museum is wheelchair accessible, though less visited parts, such as the upper level of the Etruscan Museum, are not. Snack bar between the collection of modern religious art and the Sistine Chapel; full cafeteria near main entrance. Major galleries open M-F 8:45am-3:45pm (last admission at 2:20pm), Sa 8:45am-1:45pm, last admission 12:20pm. Closed on major religious holidays. €10, with ISIC €8, children under 1m tall free. Free last Su of the month 8:45am-1:45pm.

The Vatican Museums constitute one of the greatest collections of art, with ancient, Renaissance, and modern statues, paintings, and papal odds and ends. The museum entrance at V. Vaticano leads to the famous bronze double-helix ramp that climbs to the ticket office. A good place to start a tour is the **Museo Pio-Clementino,** the world's greatest collection of antique sculpture. Two slobbering Molossian hounds guard the entrance to the **Stanza degli Animali,** a marble menagerie that highlights Roman brutality. Among other gems are the ⧉**Apollo Belvedere** and the unhappy **Laocoön** family in the Pio Clementino Museum. The last room of the gallery contains the red sarcophagus of Sant'Elena, Constantine's mother.

From here, the Simonetti Stairway climbs to the **Museo Etrusco,** filled with artifacts from Tuscany and northern Lazio. Back on the landing of the Simonetti Staircase is the Stanza della Biga (room of an ancient marble chariot) and the Galleria della Candelabra. The long trudge to the Sistine Chapel begins here, passing through the Galleria degli Arazzi (tapestries), the Galleria delle Mappe (maps), the Apartamento di Pio V (where there is a shortcut to *la Sistina*), the Stanza Sobieski, and the Stanza dell'Immacolata Concezione. From the Room of the Immaculate Conception, a door leads into the first of the four ⧉**Stanze di Rafaele,** apartments built for Pope Julius II in the 1510s. One *stanza* features Raphael's **School of Athens,** painted as a trial piece for Julius, who was so impressed that he fired his other painters, had their frescoes destroyed, and commissioned Raphael to decorate the entire suite. From here, there are two paths: a staircase leading to the brilliantly frescoed Borgia Apartments, the **Museum of Modern Religious Art,** and another route leading to the Sistine Chapel.

SISTINE CHAPEL. Since its completion in the 16th century, the Sistine Chapel, named for its founder, Pope Sixtus IV, has been the site of the College of Cardinals' election of new popes. Michelangelo's **ceiling,** at the pinnacle of artistic creation, gleams from its restoration. The simple compositions and vibrant colors hover above, each section depicting a story from Genesis. The scenes are framed by the famous *ignudi* (young nude males). Michelangelo painted not flat on his back, but standing up and craning backward, and he never recovered from the strain to his neck and eyes. *The Last Judgement* fills the altar wall. The figure of Christ as judge hovers in the upper center, surrounded by his saintly entourage and the supplicant Mary. Michelangelo painted himself as a flayed human skin that hangs, no doubt symbolically, between the realms of heaven and hell. The frescoes on the side walls predate Michelangelo's ceiling. The cycle was completed between 1481 and 1483 by a team of artists under Perugino including Botticelli, Ghirlandaio, Roselli, Pinturicchio, Signorelli, and della Gatta. On one side, scenes from the life of Moses complement parallel scenes of Christ's life on the other.

PINACOTECA. This painting collection, one of the best in Rome, includes Filippo Lippi's *Coronation of the Virgin*, Perugino's *Madonna and Child*, Titian's *Madonna of San Nicoletta dei Frari*, and Raphael's *Transfiguration*. On the way out of the Sistine Chapel, take a look at the **Room of the Aldobrandini Marriage**, which contains a series of rare, ancient Roman frescoes.

PRINCIPAL COLLECTIONS

GALLERIA BORGHESE. Cardinal Scipione Borghese enjoyed collecting paintings and sculptures, over time accumulating this extraordinary collection. The exquisite Galleria's **Room I**, on the right, houses Canova's sexy statue of *Paolina Borghese* portrayed as Venus triumphant. The next rooms display the most famous sculptures by Bernini: a magnificent *David*, crouching with his slingshot; *Apollo and Daphne*; the weightless body in *Rape of Proserpina;* and weary-looking Aeneas in *Eneo e Anchise*. Don't miss six **Caravaggio** paintings, including his *Self Portrait as Bacchus* and *St. Jerome*, which grace the side walls. The collection continues in the *pinacoteca* upstairs, accessible from the gardens around the back by a winding staircase. **Room IX** holds Raphael's *Deposition* while Sodoma's *Pietà* graces **Room XII**. Look for self portraits by Bernini, del Conte's *Cleopatra and Lucrezia*, Rubens's *Pianto sul Cristo Morto*, and Titian's *Amor Sacro e Amor Profano*. (M: A-Spagna; take exit labeled "Villa Borghese," walk to the right past the Metro stop to V. Muro Torto and then to P. Pta. Pinciana; Viale del Museo Borghese is ahead and leads to the museum or take bus #116 or 910 to V. Pinciana. Piazzale Scipione Borghese, 5. ☎06 841 76 45. Open Tu-Su 9am-7pm. Entrance every 2hr., last entrance 6:30pm. Limited capacity, so reserve ahead. Reservations ☎06 328 10 (open M-F 9am-6pm, Sa 9am-1pm); www.ticketeria.it. The palazzo's basement contains the ticket office and a book shop. Audioguide €5. Tickets (including reservation, tour, and bag charge) €8.50, EU citizens 18-25 €5.25, EU citizens under 18 or over 65 and students €2.)

MUSEO NAZIONALE ETRUSCO DI VILLA GIULIA. The villa was built under Pope Julius III, who reigned from 1550 to 1555. Highlights include a graceful sarcophagus of a married couple in **Room 9,** a famous Euphronios vase, and an Etruscan chariot, or *biga*, and the petrified skeletons of two horses found beside it in **Room 18.** Upstairs, archaeologists put together fragments of a facade of an Etruscan temple, complete with terra-cotta gargoyles, chips of paint, and a relief of the Greek warrior Tydaeus biting into the brain of a wounded adversary. (P. Villa Giulia, 9, in Villa Borghese. M: A-Flaminio; then tram #30 or 225, or bus #19 from P. Risorgimento or 52 from P. S. Silvestro. From Galleria Borghese, follow V. Dell'Uccelliera to the Zoo, and then take V. del Giardino to V. delle Belle Arti. Museum is on the left after Galleria di Arte Moderna. ☎06 322 65 71. Open Tu-Su 8:30am-7:30pm. Audioguide €4; guidebook €15, available at the bookstore outside museum entrance. €4, EU citizens under 18 or over 65 free.)

MUSEI CAPITOLINI. This collection of ancient sculpture, the oldest of its kind, is also one the largest in the world. The Palazzo Nuovo contains the original statue of **Marcus Aurelius** that once stood in the center of the piazza. The collections continue across the piazza in the Palazzo dei Conservatori. See fragments of the **Colossus of Constantine** and the famous **Capitoline Wolf,** an Etruscan statue that has symbolized the city of Rome since antiquity. At the top of the stairs, the **pinacoteca's** masterpieces include Bellini's *Portrait of a Young Man*, Titian's *Baptism of Christ*, Rubens's *Romulus and Remus Fed by the Wolf*, and Caravaggio's *St. John the Baptist* and *Gypsy Fortune-Teller*. Also part of the museum complex is the **Tabularium,** a 79 BC archive hall of ancient Rome, with dramatic views over the Forum, Colosseum, and Capitoline Hill. (☎ *06 671 024 75. Open Tu-Su 9am-8pm. Guided tours in Italian Sa 5pm, Su noon and 5pm. Reservations (☎ 06 399 678 00) necessary for groups Sa and Su, additional €25. Audioguide €4; guidebook €7.75. €7.80, with ISIC €5.80, EU citizens under 18 or over 65 free.)*

MUSEO NAZIONALE D'ARTE ANTICA. This collection of 12th- through 18th-century art is split between Palazzo Barberini and Palazzo Corsini, in different parts of the city. **Palazzo Barberini** contains paintings from the medieval through Baroque periods, including works by Lippi, Raphael, El Greco, Carracci, Caravaggio, and Poussin. *(V. Barberini, 18. M: A-Barberini. Bus #492 or 62. ☎ 06 481 45 91. Open Tu-Su 9am-7pm. €5; EU citizens 18-24 €2.50; EU citizens under 18, over 65, and EU university students €1.)* **Galleria Corsini** holds a collection of 17th- and 18th-century paintings from Van Dyck and Rubens to Caravaggio and Carracci. *(V. della Lungara, 10. ☎ 06 688 02 323. Opposite Villa Farnesina in Trastevere. Take bus #23; get off between Ponte Mazzini and Ponte Sisto. Wheelchair accessible. Open Tu-Su 8:30am-7:30pm, July-Aug. 8:30am-2pm. Guidebooks in Italian €10.50. €4, EU students €2, Italian art students and EU citizens over 65 free.)*

VILLA FARNESINA. The Villa was the sumptuous home to Europe's one-time wealthiest man, Agostino "il Magnifico" Chigi. For show, Chigi had his banquet guests toss his gold and silver dishes into the Tiber River after every course. But like a real tycoon, he would secretly hide nets under the water to recover his treasures. To the right of the entrance lies the breathtaking **Sala of Galatea,** mostly painted by the villa's architect, Baldassare Peruzzi, in 1511. The vault displays symbols of astrological signs that add up to a symbolic plan of the stars at 9:30pm on November 29, 1466, the moment of Agostino's birth. The masterpiece of the room is Raphael's **Triumph of Galatea.** The stucco-ceilinged stairway, with its gorgeous perspective detail, ascends to the **Loggia di Psiche.** The **Stanza delle Prospettive,** a fantasy room decorated by Peruzzi, offers views of Rome between *trompe l'oeil* columns. The adjacent bedroom, known as the **Stanza delle Nozze** (Marriage Room), is the real reason for coming here. Il Sodoma, who had previously been busy painting the pope's rooms in the Vatican, frescoed the chamber until Raphael showed up and took over. Il Sodoma bounced back, making this masterful fresco of Alexander the Great's marriage to the beautiful Roxanne. *(Across from Palazzo Corsini on Lungotevere Farnesina. Bus #23, 271, or 280; get off at Lungotevere della Farnesina or Ponte Sisto. At V. della Lungara, 230. ☎ 06 688 017 67. Open M-Sa 9am-1pm. €4.50, under 18 €3.50, EU citizens over 65 free.)*

GALLERIA SPADA. Cardinal Bernardino Spada bought a grandiose assortment of paintings and sculptures and commissioned an even more opulent set of great rooms to house them. Time and good luck have left the palatial 17th-century apartments nearly intact—a visit to the gallery offers a glimpse of the luxury surrounding Baroque courtly life. In the first of the gallery's four rooms, the modest cardinal hung portraits of himself by Guercino, Guido Reni, and Cerini. In **Room 2,** look for paintings by the Venetians Tintoretto and Titian and a frieze by Vaga, originally intended for the Sistine Chapel. In **Room 4** are three canvases by the father-daughter team of Orazio and Artemisia Gentileschi. *(From Campo dei Fiori, take any of the small streets leading to P. Farnese. Facing away from Campo dei Fiori, turn left on Capo di Ferro. Bus #64. P. Capo di Ferro, 13, in the Palazzo Spada. ☎06 687 48 96. Guided tour Su 10:45am from museum book shop. Pamphlet guides in English available for each room of the exhibit. Open Tu-Su 8:30am-7:30pm. Last tickets 7pm. Guidebooks €10.50. Reservations €1 extra. €5, EU students €2.50, EU citizens under 18 or over 65 free.)*

MUSEI NAZIONALI ROMANI. The fascinating **Museo Nazionale Romano Palazzo Massimo alle Terme** is devoted to the history of Roman art during the Empire, including the Lancellotti Discus Thrower, a rare mosaic of Nero's, and ancient coins and jewelry. *(Largo di V. Peretti, 1. In the left-hand corner of P. dei Cinquecento. ☎06 489 035 00 or 489 34; group reservations 06 399 67 700. Open Tu-Su 9am-7:45pm, ticket office closes at 7pm. Audioguide €2.50. €6, EU citizens ages 18-24 €3, EU citizens under 18 or over 65 free.)* Nearby, the **Museo Nazionale Romano Terme di Diocleziano,** a beautifully renovated complex partly housed in the huge **Baths of Diocletian** (p. 120) has exhibits devoted to ancient epigraphy (writing) and Latin history through the 6th century BC, as well as a beautiful cloister by Michelangelo. *(V. Enrico de Nicola, 72. ☎06 488 05 30. Open Tu-Su 9am-7:45pm. Ticket office closes at 7pm. €5.)* The **Aula Ottogonale,** another wing, holds 19 classical sculptures in a gorgeous octagonal space. *(Museo Nazionale Romano Terme di Diocleziano: P. dei Cinquecento, 78, opposite Termini. ☎06 399 677 00 for reservations. Open Tu-Su 9am-7pm. Audioguide €4; guided tour with archaeologist €3.50. €5, EU citizens 18-24 €2.50, EU citizens under 18 or over 65 free. Aula Ottogonale: V. Romita, 8. ☎06 399 677 00. Open Tu-Sa 9am-2pm, Su 9am-1pm. Free.)* Across town is the Renaissance man of the trio, **Museo Nazionale Romano Palazzo Altemps,** displaying Roman sculpture, including the famous 5th-century *Ludovisi Throne. (Bus #30 Express, 492, 70, 81, 87, or 628 to C. Rinascimento/P. Cinque Lune. P. Sant'Apollinare, 44, just north of P. Navona. Museum ☎06 783 35 66, ticket office 06 683 37 59. Open Tu-Su 9am-7pm. Audioguide €4. €5, EU citizens 18-24 €2.50 or EU citizens under 18 or over 65 free.)*

OTHER COLLECTIONS

■**MUSEO CENTRALE MONTEMARTINI.** The building, an electrical plant from the turn of the 20th century, contains a striking display of Classical sculpture. One highlight is *Hercules' Presentation at Mount Olympus,* a huge well-preserved floor mosaic of a hunt. *(V. Ostiense, 106. M: B-Piramide. From P. Ostiense take V. Ostiense. Then walk or take bus #23 or 702 3 stops. ☎06 574 80 38, info or reservations ☎06 399 678 00. Open Tu-Su 9:30am-7pm. €4.20, with entrance to the Capitoline Museums €9.80; EU citizens 18-24 €2.60; EU citizens under 18 or over 65 free.)*

GALLERIA COLONNA. Despite its limited hours, this gallery remains impressive. The palazzo was designed in the 18th century to show off the Colonna family's collection, including Tintoretto's *Narcissus,* and works by Melozzo da Forli, Veronese, Palma il Vecchio, and Guercino. *(V. della Pilotta, 17. North of P. Venezia in the centro storico. ☎06 667 843 50; www.galleriacolonna.it. Open Sept.-July Sa 9am-1pm. €7, students €5.50, under 10 or over 65 free. Included tour 11am in Italian and 11:45am in English.)*

GALLERIA DORIA PAMPHILJ. The Doria Pamphilj family, whose illustrious kin included Pope Innocent X, remain in custody of this stunning private collection, which they display in their palatial home. Its Classical art is organized by size and theme, and Renaissance and Baroque masterpieces include Caravaggio's *Rest During the Flight in Egypt,* Raphael's *Double Portrait,* and Titan's portrait of Pope Innocent X. *(Bus #40 Express or 64 to P. Venezia. P. del Collegio Romano, 2. From P. Venezia, walk up V. del Corso and take the 2nd left. ☎06 679 73 23; www.doriapamphilj.it. Open M-W and F-Su 10am-5pm, last entrance 4:15pm. €8, students and seniors €5.70. Audioguide included. Useful catalogue with €5.16 deposit.)*

MUSEO MARIO PRAZ. This eccentric, smallish museum was originally the last home of Mario Praz (1896-1982), an equally smallish and eccentric professor of English literature and 18th- and 19th-century art collector. Superstitious neighbors spat or flipped coins when they saw him. *(V. Zanardelli, 1, top fl. At the eastern end of Ponte Umberto, right next to Museo Napoleonico. ☎ 06 686 10 89. Must visit museum with small tour groups (35-45min.) that leave every hr. in the morning and every 30min. in the afternoon. Open M 2:30-6:30pm, Tu-Su 9am-1pm and 2:30-6:30pm. Free.)*

MUSEO NAZIONALE D'ARTE ORIENTALE. An array of artifacts from prehistory to the 1800s are divided into six sections: evolution of art in the Near East, Islamic art, Nepalese and Tibetan art, Indian art, Southeast Asian art, and Chinese history. *(V. Merulana, 248. In Palazzo Brancaccio on Esquiline Hill. ☎ 06 487 44 15. Open M, W, F 8:30am-2pm, Tu, Th, Su 8:30am-7:30pm. Closed 1st and 3rd M of each month. €4.)*

MUSEO CRIMINOLOGICO. After overdosing on artwork and culture, pump your stomach at this museum dedicated to crime and punishment. Torture devices cover the first floor, as well as old English etchings, among them *A Smith Has His Brains Beaten Out With a Hammer.* On the second floor, learn the secrets of criminal phrenology and the language of tattoos. The third floor contains terrorist, spy, and drug paraphernalia. *(V. del Gonfalone, 27. Near Ponte Mazzini. ☎ 06 683 002 34. Open Tu-W 9am-1pm, Tu and Th 2:30-6:30pm, F-Sa 9am-1pm. €2, under 18 or over 65 €1.)*

MUSEO DEL RISORGIMENTO. Underneath the Vittoriano monument in P. Venezia, this museum contains items relating to the Risorgimento, the 19th century "resurgence" which ultimately led to the unification of Italy in 1861. *(Entrance on V. di S. Pietro in Carcere. ☎ 06 679 35 26. Open daily 9:30am-5:30pm. Free.)*

🎵 ENTERTAINMENT

The weekly *Roma C'è* (with a section in English) and *Time Out*, both available at newsstands, have comprehensive and up-to-date club, movie, and event listings.

LIVE MUSIC

Rome hosts a variety of worthwhile performances, most of them in the summer. *Telecom Italia*'s classical music series takes place at the Teatro dell'Opera. At 9am on concert days, unsold tickets are given out for free at the box office; get in line early. Local churches often host free choral concerts. Check newspapers, tourist offices, and church bulletin boards for details. Finally, and perhaps most interestingly, the *carabinieri* frequently give rousing (and free) concerts in P. di San Ignazio and other outdoor venues.

🎵 Alexanderplatz Jazz Club, V. Ostia, 9 (☎ 06 397 421 71; www.alexanderplatz.it). M: A-Ottaviano. Head left on V. G. Cesare, take 2nd right onto V. Leone IV and 1st left onto V. Ostia. Night buses to P. Venezia and Termini leave from P. Clodio. Known as one of Europe's best jazz clubs, the smoky atmosphere conveys the mythical feeling of a 40s jazz joint. Read messages left on the walls by greats who have played here. Cocktails €6.20. Required *tessera* (membership; €7), good for 1 month. Shows start 10pm. Open daily Sept.-May 9pm-2am. Moves outside in the summer to Villa Celimontana.

Accademia Nazionale di Santa Cecilia, V. Vittoria, 6 (☎ 06 361 10 64 or 800 90 70 80; www.santacecilia.it), off V. del Corso. Palestrina founded this conservatory, named for the martyred patron saint of music. It is now home to Rome's symphony orchestra. Concerts are held at the **Parco della Musica,** Viale Pietro di Coubertin, 30, near P. del Popolo, where you can also buy tickets €8-15. Season runs Sept.-June, covering classics and special presentations like the music of Jimi Hendrix played by a string quartet.

Teatro Ghione, V. delle Fornaci, 37 (☎06 637 22 94; www.ghione.it), near the Vatican. This red velvet theater hosts Euromusica's classical concerts and other big-name musical guests. English-speaking staff. Tickets €9-21. Season Oct.-Apr. Box office open daily 10am-1pm and 4-8pm. Call for info on morning concerts and discounts. MC/V.

Cornetto Free Music Festival Roma Live, at a number of locations around the city, including Stadio Olimpico and Villa Giulia. Has featured the likes of Pink Floyd, the Cure, the Backstreet Boys, Ziggy Marley, Lou Reed, and Joan Baez. Enter to win free tickets at www.cornettoalgida.it.

Fiesta, Ippodrome delle Capannelle, V. Appia Nuova, 1245 (☎06 712 998 55; www.fiesta.it). M: A-Colli Albani or bus #664. An extremely popular festival running all summer, featuring all things Latin American. Attendance can swell to over 30,000. Advance purchase ☎199 10 99 10, or in person at Orbis, Messagerie Musicali, and many other locations. Tickets €6-8. Concerts start at 8:30pm.

THEATER

Roman theater generates a number of quality productions, ranging from mainstream musicals to black-box experimental. For info on English theater, check the tourist office, *Roma C'è,* or online at www.musical.it or www.comune.roma.it.

Teatro Argentina, Largo di Torre Argentina, 52 (☎06 688 046 01 or 06 687 54 45; www.teatrodiroma.net). Bus #64 from Termini or tram 8. Home to the Teatro di Roma company, Argentina hosts plays, concerts, and ballets. It is also the main venue for many annual drama/music festivals. Call for specific info. Box office open M-F 10am-2pm and 3-7pm, Sa 10am-2pm. €14-26, students €10-13. AmEx/MC/V.

Teatro Colosseo, V. Capo d'Africa, 5 (☎06 700 49 32). M: B-Colosseo. Walk down V. dei Fori Imperiali past the Colosseum, then go right through P. Colosseo; V. Capo d'Africa is 2 blocks down on the left. Offers plays in Italian but also has an English theater night. Box office open Sept.-Apr. Tu-Sa 6-9:30pm. Tickets €10-20, students €8.

CINEMA

Unfortunately, most theaters in Rome show dubbed movies. For subtitles, look for a "v.o." or "l.o." in listings (*versione originale* or *lingua originale*). In summer, huge screens spring up in piazzas around the city for **outdoor film fests.** Films are usually shown outdoors on Isola Tiberina's southern tip. Cinemas citywide offer discounts on Wednesdays and most have reductions for afternoon screenings.

▨ Il Pasquino, P. Sant'Egidio, 10 (☎06 580 36 22), off P. S. Maria in Trastevere. Rome's biggest English-language movie theater. Program changes daily; call ahead. €6.20. Theaters 2 and 3 are a film club; €1.03 for 2-month membership and €5.16 for ticket. Check in *Roma C'è* for information on the summer "Roma International Film Festival."

Nuovo Sacher, Largo Ascianghi, 1 (☎06 581 81 16). Take V. Induno from V. d. Trastevere. This is the famed Italian director Nanni Moretti's theater and shows a host of indie films. M and Tu films in the original language. Tickets €7, matinee and W €4.50.

Warner Village Moderno, P. della Repubblica 43/45 (☎06 47 77 91 11; www.warnervillage.it). One recent (by Italian standards) Hollywood blockbuster in English each week. Tickets €7.50, matinee and under 12 €5.50.

SPECTATOR SPORTS

Though May brings tennis and equestrian events, sports revolve around *calcio,* or soccer. Rome has two teams in Serie A, Italy's prestigious league: **S.S. Lazio** and the 2000 European champion **A.S. Roma.** Matches are held at the **Stadio Olimpico,** in Foro Italico, almost every Sunday from September to June, with international matches often played mid-week. The can't-miss matches of the season are the two

Roma-Lazio games, which often prove decisive in the race for the championship. Single-game tickets, typically starting at €15.50, can be bought at team stores like **A.S. Roma,** P. Colonna, 360 (☎ 06 678 65 14; www.asroma.it; tickets sold daily 10am-6:30pm; AmEx/MC/V); and **Lazio Point,** V. Farini, 34/36, near Termini. (☎ 06 482 66 88. Open M-F 9am-7pm, Sa 9am-1pm; AmEx/MC/V.) Tickets can also be obtained at the stadium before a game, but beware long lines and the possibility of tickets running out; if you're buying last minute, watch out for overpriced or fake tickets.

⌐] SHOPPING

Milan might be Italy's fashion hub, but Rome has a sense of style all its own. Check out the sales (*saldi*) in mid-January and mid-July for major deals. A number of boutiques, while not as fashionable as their counterparts on V. dei Condotti, don't require selling a major organ to afford their wares.

BOUTIQUES

Rome's designer shops cluster around the Spanish Steps and V. dei Condotti. Purchases of over €155 at a single store are eligible for a tax refund.

> **Dolce & Gabbana,** V. dei Condotti, 52 (☎ 06 699 249 99). Open M-Sa 10am-7:30pm.

> **Prada,** V. d. Condotti, 92/95 (☎ 06 679 08 97). Open daily 10am-7pm.

> **Salvatore Ferragamo,** men: V. dei Condotti, 64-66 (☎ 06 678 11 30); women: V. dei Condotti, 72-74 (☎ 06 679 15 65). Open M 3-7pm, Tu-Sa 10am-7pm; Aug. also Su 9am-1pm.

> **Bruno Magli,** V. del Gambero, 1. Also on V. Condotti (☎ 06 679 38 02). Open M-Sa 10am-7pm.

> **Giorgio Armani,** V. dei Condotti, 75 (☎ 06 699 14 60). Open M-Sa 10am-7pm.

> **Emporio Armani,** V. del Babuino, 140 (☎ 06 360 02 197). Houses the less expensive Armani line. Open M 3-7:30pm, Tu-Su 10am-7:30pm.

> **Fendi,** V. Borgognona, 36-39 (☎ 06 679 48 24). Open daily 11am-2pm and 3-7pm.

> **Gianni Versace,** men: V. Borgognona, 24-25 (☎ 06 679 50 37); women: V. Bocca di Leone, 25-27 (☎ 06 678 05 21). Open M-Sa 10am-7pm.

> **Gucci,** V. dei Condotti, 8 (☎ 06 678 93 40). Open M-F 10am-7pm, Sa 10am-2pm; Aug. M 3-7pm.

CHEAP AND CHIC

Designer emporiums like **David Cenci,** V. Campo Marzio, 1-7 (☎ 06 699 06 81; open M 4-8pm, Tu-F 9:30am-1:30pm and 4-8pm, Sa 10am-8pm); **Antonello & Fabrizio,** C. V. Emanuele, 242-243 (☎ 06 688 027 49; open daily in summer 9:30am-1:30pm and 4-8pm, in winter 3:30-7:30pm); and **Discount dell'Alta Moda,** V. Agostino Depretis, 87 (☎ 06 478 25 672; open M 2:30-7:30pm, Tu-Sa 9:30am-7:30pm), stock designer apparel at great discounts. (Unless otherwise noted, all accept AmEx/MC/V.)

> ▨ **Diesel,** V. del Corso, 186 (☎ 06 678 10 45). Italian-made Diesel is *the* label in urban European fashion. Stock up on jeans and t-shirts at prices far lower than anywhere else. Open M-Sa 10:30am-8pm, Su 3:30-8pm.

> **Mariotti Boutique,** V. d. Frezza, 20 (☎ 06 322 71 26). This elegant boutique sells modern, sophisticated clothes in gorgeous fabrics. Prices are steep, so watch for sales. Open M-F 10am-7pm, Sa 10am-2pm.

> **Ethic,** V. del Corso, 85 (☎ 06 360 021 91), V. d. Pantheon, 46 (☎ 06 683 010 63), and V. d. Carozze, 20. The hip yet less adventurous can find a balance between the avant-garde and tasteful. Prices won't break the bank. Open daily 9:30am-8pm.

SHOES

It's said that a building's only as good as its foundation; in high fashion, an outfit's only as good as its shoes.

🖾 **Trancanelli,** P. Cola di Rienzo, 84 (☎06 323 45 03), V. della Croce 68-9 (☎06 679 15 03). For anyone looking to return home well-shod, but with his or her bank account intact. Open M-Sa 9:30am-7:45pm.

🖾 **Bata,** V. Nazionale, 88/A (☎06 679 15 70), V. d. Due Macelli, 45 (☎06 482 45 29). Bata has 250 shops in Italy and 6000 shops worldwide stocked floor to ceiling with affordable designer-esque shoes. Open M-Sa 9:30am-8pm, Su 4-8pm.

OUTDOOR MARKETS

🖾 **Porta Portese,** in Trastevere. Tram #8 from Largo di Torre Argentina. This gigantic flea market is a surreal experience, with booths selling clothing, shoes, jewelry, bags, toilets, and millions of other items you never knew you needed. Keep your enemies close and your money closer, as the place swarms with pickpockets. Open Su 5am-1:30pm.

Campo de' Fiori, in the old city. Tram #8 or bus 64. Transformed daily by stalls of fruits and vegetables, meat, poultry, and fish. Also find here rice, dried fruit, nuts, and fresh flowers. Open M-Sa 7am-1:30pm.

Mercato delle Stampe, Largo della Fontanella di Borghese. Bus #81, 116, 117, or 492. A bookworms' haven specializing in old books—both used and genuine antiquarian, magazines, and other printed morsels. Open M-Sa 7am-1pm.

Mercato Andrea Doria, on V. Andrea Doria, northwest of the Vatican Museums. M: Ottaviano; bus #23, or 70. Caters mostly to the local population, so don't expect to find many English-speaking folks here. Fruits, vegetables, fish, groceries, clothes, and shoes sold in a huge open square. Open M-Sa 7am-1:30pm.

Nuovo Mercato Esquilino, on V. Principe Amedeo near P. Vittorio. M: Vittorio Emanuele or bus 105. International food stalls cater to various ethnic groups. M-Sa 7am-2am.

🖪 NIGHTLIFE

I Romani find nighttime diversion at the pubs of San Lorenzo, the clubs of Testaccio, and everywhere in between. Check *Roma C'è* for the latest news on clubs' openings and closings. *Time Out* covers Rome's sparse but solid collection of gay nightlife listings, many of which require an **ARCI-GAY pass** (€10 for 1 year). Also try checking with the **Circolo di Cultura Omosessuale Mario Mieli** (☎06 541 39 85).

PUBS AND BARS

If you long for organized, indoor drunkenness, try one of Rome's countless pubs. Diverse crowds and lively music draw huge crowds.

🖾 **Jonathan's Angels,** V. d. Fossa, 14-16 (☎06 689 34 26), in P. Navona. Take V. Pasquino (V. Governo Vecchio) from P. Navonna, turn right on V. Parione, then left on V. d. Fossa. Even Michelangelo's accomplishments pale before the loo, the finest 🖾 **bathroom** in Rome, nay, Italy. Jonathan himself holds court in the right bar, his son, Jonathan II, spins underground techno on the left. Medium beer €5, cocktails €8. Open M-F 8pm-3:30am, Sa-Su 6:30pm-3:30am. Cash only.

🖾 **Shanti,** V. dei Conciatori, 11 (☎06 330 46 56 62), in Testaccio. From M: Piramide, head down V. Ostiense; take 2nd street on the right. Yes, that really is incense wafting from this 2-floor North African haven. And yes, these surely are some of the best, most inventive cocktails (€6-7) to be had in Rome. Great hookahs (€2.60 per person). Belly dancing Sept.-Mar. W-F 11pm-1am. Open daily 9pm-1am. Closed Su in July, all of Aug.

Nuvolari, V. degli Ombrellari, 10 (☎06 688 030 18), in Termini off V. Vittorio. This cocktail bar also serves beer, tropical drinks, and wine by the glass (€4-5) from a diverse wine list. Salads (€6) and meat and cheese platters (€7.50) available too. Dessert €3.50. Open M-Sa 8pm-2am; kitchen closes M-Th 12:45am, F-Sa 1:30am.

Artu Cafe, Largo Fumasoni Biondi, 5 (☎06 588 03 98), in P. San Egidio, directly behind Santa Maria in Trastevere. This small bar bathed in colored light serves patrons on their way to dinner or fresh from partying in Trastevere. Beer €4.50, wine €3-5.50 per glass, cocktails €6.20-7.20. Enjoy fresh-juice cocktails. Free snack buffet 6:45-9pm. Open Tu-Su 6pm-2am. MC/V.

Il Simposio, V. dei Latini, 11 (☎328 907 785 51), in San Lorenzo, off V. Tiburtina. Ah, the sweet smell of turpentine. Walls are cluttered with Jackson Pollock-esque works by local artists, and chances are that on any given night a splattered painter will be hard at work beautifying a discarded refrigerator. Cocktails from €3.50. Glass of *fragolino* €2.75. Open Sept. to mid-July daily 9pm-2am.

The Proud Lion Pub, Borgo Pio, 36 (☎06 683 28 41). A tiny pub in the Vatican area whose outside says "Rome, Borgo Pio," but is pure Highland on the inside. Affiliated with the Italian Dart Club; call and ask about upcoming tournaments. Beer and cocktails €4, single malts €4.50-5. Open M-Sa 8:30pm-2am.

CLUBS

Italian discos are flashy and fun, but keep in mind that they often have spoken or unspoken dress codes. Although many clubs close in the summer, Testaccio is dependable through early August. Check *Roma C'è* or *Time Out* for the latest.

Neutra, V. S. Saba 11/A (☎06 578 20 22). Uniting the elegant with the eclectic; music (often house or a variant) is selected by resident DJ Giuliano Marchili. Cover (includes 1 drink): men €13, women €10. Open W-Su 11:30pm-4am. Closed Aug.

Classico Village, V. Libetta, 3 (☎06 375 185 51). M: B-Garbatella. Exit on V. Argonauti and turn left on V. Libetta. One of the best-known *centri sociali* in Rome—a one-stop shop for all things countercultural. Hosts live music, films, art exhibits, poetry readings, African cuisine tastings, and more. Open daily, hours and cover vary (€8-10).

Groove, V. Savelli, 10 (☎06 687 24 27). Head down V. del Governo Vecchio from P. Pasquino and take 2nd left. Look for the black door, and lose it to acid jazz, funk, soul, and disco. F and Sa 1-drink min. (€5.16). Open W-Su 10pm-2am. Closed most of Aug.

Alien, V. Velletri, 13-19 (☎06 841 22 12; www.aliendisco.it). One of the biggest discos in Rome attracts a well-dressed crowd. Cover varies (about €15, includes 1 drink; Sa €20). Mostly house with occasional theme nights. Open Tu-Su 11pm-5:30am. In summer, moves to Gilda on the Beach in Fregene.

Piper, V. Tagliamento, 9 (☎06 855 53 98; www.piperclub.it). North of Termini. From V. XX Settembre, take V. Piave (V. Salaria). Turn right on V. Po (V. Tagliamento). Or take bus #319 from Termini to Tagliamento. 70s, rock, disco, as well as the standard house and underground. Cover €15–20 includes 1 drink. Open F-Sa 11pm-4:30am. In summer moves to Gilda on the Beach.

Gilda on the Beach, Lungomare di Ponente, 11 (☎06 665 606 49; www.gildaonthebeach.it). Operating only from May 1st to Sept. 30th, Gilda on the Beach is a favorite among VIPs and those who normally frequent Alien and Piper. 4 dance floors, a private beach, pool, restaurant, and ultra-cool clientele are all reasons why Gilda is a place to see and be seen during the summer. Cover €20. Open 11pm-4am. AmEx/MC/V.

Ketumbar, V. Galvani, 24 (☎06 573 053 38), in Testacccio. Miss SoHo? Willing to pay €10 for a cocktail and €5 for a Coke in the original glass bottle? A taste of New York decadence. It even doubles as a Japanese restaurant (sushi €18-36). Wear black: everyone else will. Open M-Sa 8pm-3am. Closed Aug. AmEx/MC/V.

Aquarela, V. di Monte Testaccio, 64 (☎06 575 90 58). A fine example of urban renewal, Roman-style. Built out of trash, then used for years as a vegetable market, the club has 2 underground tunnels that remain cool even when the party's hot. Cover €10, includes 1 drink. Open Tu-Su 8:30pm-4am.

Jungle, V. di Monte Testaccio, 95. Smoky bar full of Italian Goths (Sa) dancing to the Cure and Italian pop. Extravagant, if somewhat disorienting light effects. Cover €5-8, free before 11pm. Beer €5, cocktails €8. Open F-Sa 11pm-5am.

⚡ DAYTRIPS FROM ROME

TIVOLI

Take Metro B to Rebibbia from Termini. Exit the station; follow the signs for Tivoli through an underpass to reach the other side of V. Tiburtina. Find the marker for the blue COTRAL bus to Tivoli. Tickets (€1.60) are sold in the bar next door or in the subway station. Once the bus climbs up to Tivoli (25min.), get off past P. Garibaldi at P. delle Nazioni Unite. The bus back to Rome leaves from P. Garibaldi. The tourist office is on the street leading from P. Garibaldi, with info on villas, maps, and bus schedules. ☎0774 31 12 49. Open M and W 9am-1pm, Tu and Th-Sa 9am-3pm and 4-7pm. Villa d'Este is through the souvenir stands in P. Trento and to the left. For Villa Adriana, 5km from Tivoli proper, take the orange #4 or 4x bus from P. Garibaldi's newsstand, which also sells tickets (€1).

Water is the chief attraction of Tivoli, a hilltop town perched 120m above the Aniene River, 1hr. from Rome by train. Poets Horace, Catullus, and Propertius once vacationed in villas lining the rocks overhanging the river. Modern Tivoli stretches beyond the original narrow strip, providing dynamic views of the city from its hilly streets and gardens. Three extravagant villas are its principal sights.

🖼**Villa d'Este,** a castle-garden, was laid out by Cardinal Ercole d'Este (the son of Lucrezia Borgia) and his architect Piero Ligorio in 1550 with the idea of recreating an ancient Roman *nymphaea* and pleasure palace. Spectacular terraces and fountains abound. (☎0774 33 34 04. Open May-Aug. Tu-Su 8:30am-6:45pm, Sept.-Apr. 8:30am-4pm. €9, EU citizens 18-24 €5.75, EU citizens under 18 or over 65 free.) Make time to visit the vast remains of **Villa Adriana,** the largest and most expensive villa ever built during the reign of the Roman Empire. Emperor Hadrian, inspired by his travels, designed its 2nd-century buildings with an international flair. Look

ROME AND LAZIO

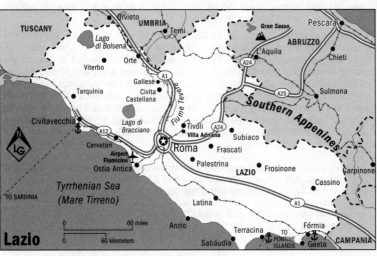

for the *pecile*, built to recall the famous Stoa Poikile (Painted Porch) of Athens, and the *canopus*, a statue-lined expanse of water built to replicate a canal in Alexandria, Egypt. (☎0774 38 27 33. Open daily 9am-1½hr. before sunset. €8.50, EU citizens 18-24 €5.25, EU citizens under 18 or over 65 free.) **Villa Gregoriana**, on V. di Sibilla across town, has been closed indefinitely for restorations.

LAGO DI BRACCIANO

Take Metro A to Lepanto, then take the COTRAL bus from Lepanto to the lake (every hr. 6:40am-10:15pm, €2). Anguillara and Bracciano are also accessible by train on the Rome-Viterbo line (every hr.; from Rome's San Pietro station 6:47am-9:47pm, last return to Rome 7:43pm; €2.10).

About 1hr. from Rome by bus, fresh air, cool water, and a lush and hilly landscape envelop Lago di Bracciano's volcanic sands and freshwater beach. The impressive 15th-century **Castello Orsini-Odescalchi** offers some stunning frescoes and stuffed wild boars. (☎06 998 043 48; www.odescalchi.it. Book English-language tours ahead. Tours Apr.-Sept. Tu-F every hr. 11am-noon and 3-6pm, Sa-Su every 20-30min. 9am-12:30pm and 3-6:30pm; Oct.-Mar. Tu-F every hr. 10am-noon and 3-5pm, Sa-Su every 20-30min. 10am-12:30pm and 3-6:30pm.) See *Roma C'è* for listings of classical concerts held here in the summer. Bracciano's many trattorias cook up mounds of fresh lake fish. The local specialty is eel. A ferry ride from the beach to nearby **Anguillara** or **Trevignano** across the lake offers more spectacular scenery.

◼PONTINE ISLANDS

Take aliscafi (hydrofoils) or slower, cheaper traghetti (ferries). From Rome, take the train from Termini to Anzio (1hr., every hr. 6am-11pm, €2.90) and then the CAREMAR ferry from Anzio to Ponza (1¾hr.; June 16-Sept. 15 1 per day M-F 9:25am, Sa 8:30am, Su and holidays 8:30am and 3pm; return M-F 5pm, Sa 5:15pm, Su and holidays 11am and 5:15pm; from Sept. 15-30 daily; M-F €19.50). The CAREMAR ticket office in is in the white booth on the quay in Anzio (☎06 986 00 083; www.caremar.it) and in Ponza (☎0771 805 65). The Linee Vetor hydrofoils (1¼hr.; 3-5 per day 8:15-5:15pm, return 9:50am-7pm; M-F €21, Sa-Su and Aug. €24) are faster. The Linee Vetor ticket office is also on the quay in Anzio (☎06 984 50 83; www.vetor.it) and Ponza (☎0771 805 49). From Formia, CAREMAR runs boats (3hr.; 9am and 5:30pm, return 5:30am and 2:30pm; €10.80), as does Vetor (M 1:20pm, Tu and Th-Su 8:30am and 1:20pm; return M 6:30pm, Tu and Th 10am and 6:30pm, F-Su 10am, 3, 6:30pm; €21).

The Pontine Islands, a stunning archipelago of volcanic mountains 40km off the coast of Anzio, were once believed to be home to the sorceress Circe, who captured the Greek hero Odysseus. Homer's *Odyssey* wasn't the last encounter the islands would have with history. Nero was expatriated here, and Mussolini cast enemies of the state upon the 30 million-year-old volcanic residuum, only to be imprisoned here himself. For nearly two centuries, anarchists and the like were jailed in a Neapolitan king's prison, now out of commission. The cliff-sheltered beaches, turquoise waters, assorted coves, tunnels, and grottoes have also provided pirates a place to unwind after pillaging and plundering.

PONZA

In Ponza, Autolinee Isola di Ponza buses leave from V. Dante (every 15-20min., until 1am; €1; buy tickets from driver). Follow C. Pisacane as it becomes V. Dante, past the tunnel; the stop is on the left. Buses stop by request; flag them down at stops. Water taxis leave near the docks for beaches and harbors around the island (from €3 round-trip; arrange pick-up time with driver). Pro Loco Tourist Office is in the red building on V. Molo Musco, at the port's far right next to the lighthouse. (☎0771 800 31; prolocoponza@libero.it. Open in summer M-Sa 9am-1pm and 4-8:30pm, Su 9am-1pm.)

ROME AND LAZIO

Excellent beaches are everywhere on Ponza, including **Cala dello Schiavone** and **Cala Cecata** (on the bus line). **Chiaia di Luna** and ◪**Piscine Naturali** are musts for any beach lover. A 10min. walk from the port leads to Chiaia, set at the foot of a spectacular 200m cliffside. By bus, ride through Ponza's hillside to the even lovelier **Piscine Naturali.** (Take the bus to Le Foma and ask to be let off at the *piscine.* Cross the street and go down the long, steep path.) Cliffs crumbling into the ocean create a series of deep, crystal-clear natural pools separated by smooth rocky outcroppings perfect for sunbathing. Although there are spots for cliff-diving in the area, *Let's Go* does not recommend jumping off 15m cliffs.

Hotel rooms on Ponza hover in the €100 zone. Skip those, and opt for one of many *immobiliare vacanze* (vacation property) offices instead. The Ponza tourist office has a list of agencies that can offer help with finding a room or apartment. **Hotel Mari ❹,** C. Pisacane, 19, has classy decor and comfortable rooms with A/C, bath, phone, and TV. (☎0771 801 01; www.hotelmari.com. Internet €3 for 30min. Breakfast included. Sept. 1-June 30 singles €42; doubles €62, with ocean view €82. July 1-Aug. 31 singles €64; doubles €94-124. AmEx/MC/V.) Another option is the family-owned **Pensione Arcobaleno ❸,** V. Scotti di Basso, 6, on a hilltop 10min. from the port. The view alone is worth the hike. (☎0771 803 15; arcobalenoponza@libero.it. High-season rooms €40, with breakfast and dinner €60; low season €10 less. Discount for extended stays. AmEx/MC/V.) Restaurants are on the expensive side, with *primi* around €10. The seafood and view at **Ristorante da Antonio ❹,** on the water at V. Dante, make a nice splurge. (☎0771 80 98 32.)

Palmarola is an uninhabited islet perched off the northeast coast of the island, with irregular volcanic rock formations and steep white cliffs. On the way, **Dala Brigantina** is a natural lime amphitheater. Most excursions visit the **Pilatus Caves** at Ponza, a breeding ground for fish. To get to Palmarola, rent a boat (from €35 per day), or take a **boat tour** advertised at the port.

Zannone is only accessible by boat. (Try Cooperativa Barcaioli Ponzesi, C. Pisacane at the S. Antonio tunnel. ☎0771 800 59. 10:30am, return 7pm; €16-20.) Zannone is a wildlife preserve offering nature-lovers a change from the beach. Once the home of prehistoric man, it forms part of the **Circeo National Park.** Tours take visitors around the coast, with time for walks on the *mufloni*-strewn islands, through beautiful forests, and to the medieval, legend-filled **S. Spirito monastery.**

The spectacle of daily life as it unfolds on streets and sidewalks is one of the great pleasures of a trip to Italy, and a major part of that spectacle is the Italian art of walking. As day turns to dusk, in cities and towns, Italians of all ages take to the streets for the *passeggiata*, the evening stroll. The *passeggiata* is above all a social event, an occasion for conversation among friends; one rarely, if ever, walks alone. There is also a strong sense of public performance; the back-and-forth movement of the promenade offers ample opportunity for lingering or flirtatious glances, a chance to see and be seen.

But the institution of the *passeggiata* is even older than it might seem. The antecedents of the modern activity can be traced all the way back to the second and first centuries BC, when Roman magistrates began to endow the city with public porticoes. Inspired in part by the great *stoas* of Greece, these porticoes were typically large garden courts surrounded on all sides by colonnaded walkways; the imported marble decorating the columns, floor, and walls competed for the visitor's attention with statues, paintings, and other valuables plundered from the recently conquered Greek east. (The entrance to the Portico of Octavia, one of the more famous late republican porticoes, still stands in the Jewish Ghetto in Rome.)

The porticos were monuments dedicated to ancient Roman leisure, straddling the line between public garden, park, museum, and meeting place. But above all, as literary sources reveal, these were spaces for walking: a place for leisurely strolls with friends, for serious conversations between promenading politicians, and, most importantly, for catching the eye of potential paramours as they passed by. According to the poet Ovid (43 BC-AD 17), who, as a love poet, is an admittedly biased witness, a public portico was a glorified pick-up scene, and walking there seems to have been the ancient equivalent of a visit to a singles bar. In his how-to manual on the art of love he advises his (male) reader in the fine art of the seductive stroll:

"When she wears down the wide portico with her carefree steps, you should linger there too alongside her: be sure to walk ahead of her sometimes, then follow at her back; you should speed up at times, and then go more slowly. Don't be ashamed to weave through some of the columns between you, or to attach your side to hers." (Ovid *Ars Amatoria* 1.491-6)

Observe closely at your next *passeggiata*, and you'll find latter-day suitors still following elements of Ovid's advice (minus the column-weaving) some 2000 years later.

In ancient Rome, the pleasures of a leisurely stroll could be enjoyed in a private setting as well—if you were wealthy enough to own a country villa, where the scale and grandeur of private porticoes and gardens often surpassed their public, urban counterparts. Here, leisurely walks were more of an intellectual exercise: less flirtation, more disputation, you might say. In his villa at Tusculum, Cicero (106-43 BC) named one of his porticoes after Plato's Academy, and another after Aristotle's Lyceum, decorating them accordingly, so that he and his friends could stroll through their own philosophical playground, discussing ethics and rhetoric as latter-day Athenians. Nor was he alone in his penchant for fantasy design: we have evidence that his contemporaries named parts of their country retreats after famous topography from around the known world, so that a walk through a country villa became, in effect, a kind of metaphorical tourism.

Accompanying this fantasy travel was an increased interest in actual tourism as well, as the iron fist of the Roman empire made travel around the Mediterranean safer (and plunder from the provinces boosted the disposable income of her magistrates). For Romans, trips to Greece, now part of the Roman Empire, were especially popular, and to Athens in particular, whose glory days were far enough in the past to inspire feelings of nostalgic wonder not dissimilar to the experience of the modern tourist at the Roman Forum, for example. Cicero, in fact, structures one of his philosophical dialogues as a walk by Roman tourists in Athens, through the recently abandoned Academy of Plato. One of the characters in the dialogue tries to explain the pleasure derived from treading ground made famous centuries before; "wherever we go," he says, "we're walking through history." The walk of the tourist, as Cicero reveals, has its own history.

Timothy O'Sullivan is an Assistant Professor of Classical Studies at Trinity University in San Antonio, Texas. He received his Ph.D. in Classical Philology from Harvard University in 2003 with a dissertation titled "The Mind in Motion: The Cultural Significance of Walking in the Roman World."

PIEMONTE AND VALLE D'AOSTA

HIGHLIGHTS OF PIEMONTE AND VALLE D'AOSTA

TRAVERSE the frozen northern end of Italy through prime skiing country, the mountains of Valle d'Aosta. (p. 165.)

CATCH the latest on ways to volunteer for Turin's 2006 Winter Olympics. (p. 148.)

DISCOVER western Lake Country at the pearl of the Borromeans, Isola Bella. (p. 162.)

PIEMONTE

More than just the source of the Po River, Piemonte has long been a fountainhead of nobility and fine cuisine. The region can be broken into three zones: the Alpine, the Pianura, and the Colline. The Alpine, with the peaks of Monviso and Gran Paradiso, contains ski resorts and a national park that spills into Valle d'Aosta. The Pianura includes Turin, the vineyards of Asti, and the start of the Po valley, while many isolated castles dot the Colline. Obscure during the Roman era, Piemonte rose to prominence in 1861 when the Savoys, having dominated the region since the 11th century, selected Turin as capital of their re-united Italy. Though the capital relocated four years later, Piemonte remained a hive of political activity, home to both the latter-day monarchists and the *Brigade Rosse* (Red Brigades). Piemonte today is sometimes called the Prussia of Italy, referring to its high standard of living and modern, well-organized infrastructure, but *Piemontesi* like a stroll through the countryside and an indulgence for the palate as much as the next Italian. With the coming of the Olympics to Turin in winter of 2006, the region promises to rise to prominence once again.

TURIN (TORINO)   ☎011

A century and a half before it was selected to host the 2006 Winter Olympics, Turin was the capital of Italy. It was here that Vittorio Emanuele II and Camillo Cavour forged a nation, and it was here, in the 1950s, that the Red Brigades planted the bombs that threatened to tear it apart again. The city that sparked the Risorgimento bears a badge of honor in the form of stately Baroque architecture and more than 18km of arcades, making it a popular location for film crews shooting period pieces. In the 19th century, Turin enjoyed a run as Italy's premier hotbed of ideas. Thanks to the influence of its French and Austrian neighbors, it supported a sophisticated *caffè* society, hosting such progressive-minded intellectuals as Dumas and Nietzsche. Today Turin is a busy and well-oiled city whose economy was bolstered in the post-war boom by industrial titans like Fiat and a recent wave of urban renewal sparked by the Olympics. But no matter how it changes, residents insist Turin will always retain its traditional *Piemontese* flavor as a city large enough for outstanding culture, but small enough to call home.

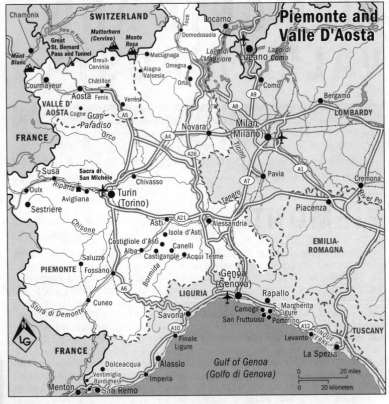

⌐ TRANSPORTATION

Flights: Caselle Airport services European destinations. From Pta. Nuova take blue buses to "Caselle Airport," stopping at Pta. Susa on the way. (€5). Buy tickets at Bar Cervino, C. V. Emanuele II, 57, at Bar Mille Luci, P. XVIII Dicembre, 5, or onboard (€0.50 surcharge).

Trains: Stazione Porta Nuova (☎011 669 04 47 or 517 53 39), on C. V. Emanuele II. A city unto itself, with a small but pricey market, barber shop, and post office. Luggage storage and lost property services available. To: **Genoa** (2hr., every hr. 5:35am-11:30pm, €7.90); **Milan Centrale** (2hr., every hr. 4:50am-10:50pm, €7.90); **Rome Termini** (6hr.; Eurostar 6am and 7:10am; InterCity 6:35, 9:10, and 11:10am, 1:10, 3:10, 10:15, and 11:30pm; from €42.92); **Venice Santa Lucia** (5hr.; InterCity 7:02 and 9:07am, and 2:07 and 5:07pm; €27.68). **Stazione Porta Susa** (still within the city) is 1 stop toward Milan.

Buses: Autostazione Terminal Bus, C. V. Emanuele II, 131/H in front of the Court (☎011 433 81 00). From Pta. Nuova, take cable car #9 or 15 (5 stops). Serves ski resorts, the Riviera, and the valleys of Susa and Pinerolo. Ticket office open daily 7am-noon and 3-7pm. To: **Aosta** (2hr., 3 per day, €7.10); **Courmayeur** (4hr., 2 per day, except Sa, change in Aosta, €8.20); **Milan** (2hr., every hr., €8.62).

Public Transportation: A 70min. ticket to **city buses** and **cable cars** costs €0.90; 1-day ticket valid on both costs €3. Buy tickets at *tabacchi*, newsstands, or bars before boarding. Buses run daily 5am-1am.

Taxis: ☎011 57 37, 57 30, or 33 99.

Bike Rental: Parco Valentino Noleggio Biciclette (☎347 413 47 28 or 339 582 93 32), one of many city-run bike rentals in parks, is on V. Ceppi in Parco Valentino. Walk east (heading toward the Po River) down C. V. Emanuele; just before Ponte Umberto I, turn right. €3.61 for 12hr., €5.16 per 24hr. Open Tu-Su 9am-12:30pm and 2:30-7pm.

Car Rental: in Stazione Porta Nuova, on the right hand side by the platforms. **Avis** (☎011 669 98 00), from €60 per day (100km). Call ahead. Open M-F 8:30am-noon and 3-6pm, Sa 8:30am-noon. **Maggiore** (☎011 650 30 13). Call ahead. Open M-F 8am-noon and 3-6pm, Sa 8am-noon.

■■ 🛈 ORIENTATION AND PRACTICAL INFORMATION

Turin lies in the Po River Valley, flanked by the Alps on three sides. **Stazione Porta Nuova,** in the heart of the city, is the usual place of arrival. The city itself is an Italian rarity: its streets meet at right angles, making it easy to navigate by bus and on foot. **Corso Vittorio Emanuele II** runs past the station to the river. **Via Roma,** which houses the principal sights, runs north through **Piazza San Carlo** and **Piazza Castello.** The other two main streets, **Via Po** and **Via Garibaldi,** extend from P. Castello. V. Po continues diagonally through **Piazza Vittorio Veneto** (the university center) to the river. V. Garibaldi stretches to **Piazza Statuto** and **Stazione Porta Susa.** Stazione Porta Nuova, Stazione Porta Susa, and **Piazza della Repubblica** north of **Corso Regina** are dangerous areas; don't walk alone at night, and use caution during the day.

Tourist Office: ATL, P. Solfieri, Olympic Atrium bldg. (☎011 53 51 81; www.turismo-torino.org), English, German, French, and Spanish spoken. Excellent **map** of Turin. Info regarding museums and historic cafes. **Info booth** at Pta. Nuova (☎011 53 13 27), opposite platform 17. Both open M-Sa 9:30am-7pm, Su 9:30am-3:30pm.

Currency Exchange: In Pta. Nuova. Offers a decent rate. Open daily 7:30am-7:35pm. MC/V. Otherwise try the **banks,** most with 24hr. **ATMs** along V. Roma and V. Alfieri (generally open M-F 8:20am-1:20pm and 2:20-4:20pm).

Luggage Storage: €3.50 per 6hr.; €0.10-0.30 per hr. thereafter in both **Porta Nuova** (open daily 6am-midnight) and **Porta Susa** train station (open daily 7am-11pm).

Bookstore: Libreria Internazionale Luxembourg, V. Accademia delle Scienze, 3 (☎011 561 38 96), across from P. Carignano. Staff helps navigate 3 floors of English, French, Spanish, and German books, papers, and magazines. Open M-Sa 8am-7:30pm, Su 10am-1pm, 3-7pm.

Laundromat: Lavanderia Vizzini, V. S. Secondo, 30 (☎011 54 58 82). Facing Pta. Nuova, walk 2 blocks right. Wash and dry €7.75 per 4kg. Open M-F 8:30am-1pm and 3-7:30pm, Sa 8:30am-1pm.

Emergency: ☎113 or 112. **Ambulance** (☎118). **First Aid:** ☎011 57 47.

Pharmacy: Farmacia Boniscontro, C. V. Emanuele, 66 (☎011 54 12 71). Facing Pta. Nuova, walk 3 blocks right. Open 9am-12:30pm, 3pm-9am. Other pharmacy schedules posted.

Hospital: San Giovanni Battista, C. Bramante, 88 (☎011 633 16 33), commonly known as "Molinette." **Mauriziano Umberto,** C. Turati, 62 (☎011 508 11 11).

Internet: 1pc4you, V. Verdi, 20/G (☎011 83 59 08), just around the corner from the Mole. 72 speedy machines with flat screens. From €2 per hr. with purchased card. Open M-Sa 9am-9pm, Su 2-8pm. **Telecom Italia Internet Corners,** V. Roma, 18, just

PIEMONTE AND VALLE D'AOSTA

off P. Castello, and 1 inside the Stazione Porta Nuova (on the left side near the main exit). Both filled with phone card web stations and phones. €0.10 per 70 seconds. Open 8am-10pm.

Post Office: V. Alfieri, 10 (☎011 506 02 60), off P. S. Carlo, facing north (toward P. Reale), head left 2 blocks down on the right. Fax and telegram service. Open M-F 8:30am-7pm, Sa 8:30am-1pm, last day of the month 8:30am-noon. **Fermoposta** open M-Sa 9am-noon and 3-7pm. **Postal Code:** 10100.

▐▊ ▐▊ ACCOMMODATIONS AND CAMPING

Despite being relatively under-touristed, Turin's booming industry not only draws high-powered business conferences, but also spawns commensurate urban eyesores. While some of the less expensive accommodations are clustered in the relatively unsafe streets surrounding the Pta. Nuova station, there are many reasonably priced rooms in the older (and safer) part of town.

Ostello Torino (YHI), V. Alby, 1 (☎011 660 29 39; hostelto@tin.it). Take bus #52 from Pta. Nuova (#64 on Su). After crossing the river, get off at the Lanza stop at V. Crimea and follow the Ostello signs to C. G. Lanza, before turning left at V. L. Gatti. 76 beds and TV room in a quiet, residential setting not far from the river. Breakfast and sheets included. Dinner €8.50. Laundry €4. Reception M-Sa 7am-12:30pm and 3:30-11:30pm, Su 7-10am and 3:30-11:30pm. Check-out 10am. Lockout 10am-3:30pm. Curfew 11:30pm; ask for key if going out. Closed Dec. 20-Feb. 1. Single-sex and mixed 4- to 10-bed dorms €12.50; doubles €15.50 per person, with bath €17.50; triples €15.50; quads €14.50. €1.50 heating surcharge Oct.-Apr. MC/V. ❶

Pensione Azalea, V. Mercanti, 16, 4th fl. (☎011 53 81 15 or 333 246 74 49). Exit Pta. Nuova on the right and take bus #58 or 72 to V. Garibaldi. Turn left on V. Garibaldi, away from P. Castello, and left on V. Mercanti. Cozy and immaculate rooms in a prime location. Reserve ahead. Singles €30, with bath €45; doubles €35/€55. MC/V. ❸

Mobledor, V. Accademia Albertina, 1, 3rd. fl. (☎011 88 84 45). Leave Pta. Nuova by the front door and take bus #68 to Giolitti. Go 1 block to V. S. Croce and turn left, then left again on V. Accademia Albertina. In-room baths have curtains instead of doors, but a location near the university quarter puts guests near the nightlife. Some singles share a bath. Singles €31; doubles €47; triples €59. MC/V. ❸

Hotel Sila, P. Carlo Felice, 80, 3rd. fl. (☎011 53 45 44). Blonde wood floors, good light and large rooms, all with bath. Safe location 1min. from the station. Breakfast €2. Singles €43; doubles €63; quads €110. Cash only. ❹

Hotel Canelli, V. S. Dalmazzo, 5/B (☎011 53 71 66 or 54 60 78). From Pta. Nuova, take bus #52 to Cernaia; turn right on V. Gianone and left on V. S. Dalmazzo. The paint is cracking, but the rooms, all with bath, are squeaky clean. 3hr. luggage storage. Check-in after noon. Singles €24; doubles €32; triples €39. Cash only. ❷

Hotel Nizza, V. Nizza, 9, 2nd fl. (☎/fax 011 669 05 16; hotelnizza@infinito.it), near train station. One of the better hotels in town, but in a risky area. Spacious rooms have bath, TV, and phone. Balcony with bar. Breakfast included. Mention *Let's Go* for following prices: Singles €45; doubles €70; triples €94.50; quads €113.50. AmEx/MC/V. ❹

Hotel Bellavista, V. B. Galliari, 15, 6th fl. (☎011 669 81 39, fax 668 79 89), near Pta. Nuova. From the train station, take V. Nizza, then turn left on V. Galliari. Panoramic balconies wrap around 46 rooms with TV. Dozens of potted plants in the halls. Breakfast €5. Singles €36, with bath €42; doubles €55/€65. AmEx/MC/V. ❹

Hotel Lux, V. B. Galliari, 9, 2nd fl. (☎011 65 72 57, fax 668 74 82), near Pta. Nuova. Take V. Nizza and turn on V. Galliari. Spartan, unadorned rooms have TV. Some rooms overlook the interior courtyard, rather than the adult video stores on V. Galliari. Singles €26; doubles €42, with bath €47. Cash only. ❸

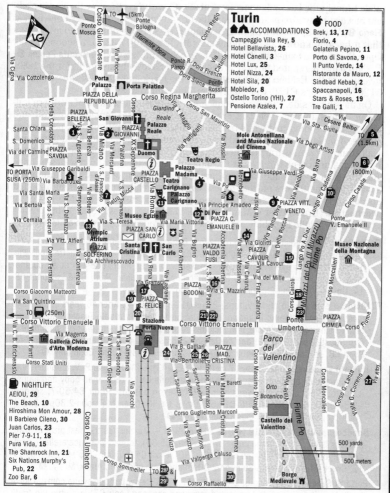

Turin

🏠🏠 ACCOMMODATIONS
Campeggio Villa Rey, 5
Hotel Bellavista, 26
Hotel Canelli, 3
Hotel Lux, 25
Hotel Nizza, 24
Hotel Sila, 20
Mobledor, 8
Ostello Torino (YHI), 27
Pensione Azalea, 7

🍎 FOOD
Brek, 13, 17
Fiorio, 4
Gelateria Pepino, 11
Porto di Savona, 9
Il Punto Verde, 14
Ristorante da Mauro, 12
Sindbad Kebab, 2
Spaccanapoli, 16
Stars & Roses, 19
Tre Galli, 1

📍 NIGHTLIFE
AEIOU, 29
The Beach, 10
Hiroshima Mon Amour, 28
Il Barbiere Cileno, 30
Juan Carlos, 23
Pier 7-9-11, 18
Pura Vida, 15
The Shamrock Inn, 21
Six Nations Murphy's Pub, 22
Zoo Bar, 6

PIEMONTE AND VALLE D'AOSTA

Campeggio Villa Rey, Str. Superiore Val S. Martino, 27 (☎/fax 011 819 01 17). From Pta. Nuova take the #72 or 63 bus to Pta. Palazzo, change to the #3 tram on C. Regina, and ride to the end of the line (Hermada). From there, walk 500m uphill or take bus #54. Quiet hillside location with views of the Basilica Superga houses caravans and a few tent campers. Bar, small market, and restaurant. 2-course meal €12. Laundry €3.10. Electricity €1.50. Showers €0.80. €3-6 per person, €4-5 per tent, €1.10 per car. Over 4-person campers €9-10.50 per person. Cash only. ●

📷 FOOD

Ever since the Savoys started taking an evening cup of *cioccolato* in 1678, Turin has grown into one of the great international centers of chocolate. Ferrero Rocher and Nutella are its most famous offspring. Napoleonic restrictions on buying chocolate brought the hazelnut chocolate substitute *gianduiotti*, now the key ingredient in a distinctly *Torinese* ice cream flavor known as *gianduia*. It's done best at **Fiorio ❶**, V. Po, 8, which was once frequented by so many officers and aristocrats that it became known as "the pony-tail cafe." (☎011 817 32 25. 2 scoops €1.50. Open W and F-Su 8am-2am, Tu and Th 8am-1am. AmEx/MC/V.) **Gelateria Pepino ❶**, P. Carignano, 8, reputed favorite of the house of Savoy, claims credit for the 1880s invention of the Eskimo pie; they still serve the black-and-white *Pinguino*. (☎011 54 20 09. 2 scoops €1.50. Open daily 8am-1am. AmEx/MC/V.)

On the savory side, *Piemontese* cuisine is a sophisticated blend of northern Italian peasant staples and elegant French garnishes. Butter replaces olive oil, and cheese, mushrooms, and white truffles are used more than tomatoes, peppers, or spices. *Agnolotti*, ravioli stuffed with lamb and cabbage, is the local pasta specialty, but *polenta*, warm cornmeal often topped with fontina cheese, is the more common starch. The three most outstanding (and expensive) red wines in Italy, *Barolo*, *Barbaresco*, and *Barbera*, are available in markets and restaurants. To sample the true flavors of *Piemontese* cuisine, be ready to pay—restaurants that specialize in regional dishes are expensive. Self-caterers can head to Dì Per Dì **supermarket.** (Branches at V. Maria Vittoria, 11 and V. S. Massimo, 43.) Find edibles et cetera at P. della Repubblica, claimed to be Europe's largest **open-air market.**

▨ **Tre Galli,** V. S. Agostino, 25. The revitalized Bohemian neighborhood surrounding P. Filberto has produced many traditional eateries, none of them nicer than Tre Galli. Piemonte standards like *agnolotti* (€7) go well with steak fillets (€8-14) at an outdoor table, while you watch the busy foot-traffic through the area. *Primi* €7-8, *secondi* €8-14. Open Tu-Su noon-2:30pm and 8-11:30pm. MC/V. ❸

▨ **Ristorante da Mauro,** V. M. Vittoria, 21 (☎011 817 06 04). After 40 years in the same location, Signore Mauro is known for his exquisite and affordable Tuscan and *Piemontese* cuisine, with a following that includes soccer player Del Piero. *Bue del piemonte ai ferri* (roasted boar; €9.30) and *castellana al prosciutto* (€7.50) are a scooooooooore! *Primi* €6, *secondi* €6-13. Open Tu-Su noon-2pm and 7:30-10pm. Cash only. ❸

Il Punto Verde, V. S. Massimo, 17 (☎011 88 55 43), off V. Po near P. V. Emanuele II. A California juice bar and a traditional Italian trattoria had a vegetarian baby and named it Punto. Blendered fruit-veggie drink €4. Vegan options. *Primi* €4.50-7, *secondi* €5.50-8.50. Giant *monopiatti* €11.50. Cover €1.50. Open M-F noon-2:30pm and 7-10:30pm, Sa 7-10:30pm. Closed Aug. MC/V. ❸

Spaccanapoli, V. Mazzini, 19 (☎011 812 66 94). V. Mazzini has the best pizza in town, and this is the cream of the crop. Try the Kraft (€5.80), topped with mozzarella, bacon, and gorgonzola or pizza by the meter (€20-30). Pizza €4-8. *Primi* €5.50-9, *secondi* €9-12. Cover €1.90. Open Tu-Su noon-2:30pm and 7pm-midnight. AmEx/MC/V. ❷

Porta di Savona, P. V. Veneto, 2 (☎011 817 35 00; www.portodisavona.com). A local institution. If *carne cruda* (marinated raw hand-chopped veal; €7) is a little too traditional for you, *agnolotti* and other standards provide an easier introduction to regional cuisine. *Primi* €5.50-7, *secondi* from €7-10. Cover €1.50. Open Tu 7:30-10:30pm, W-Su 12:30-2:30pm and 7:30-10:30pm. Closed 1st 2 weeks of Aug. MC/V. ❸

Stars & Roses, Paleocapa, 2/D, near P. C. Felice (☎011 516 20 52). Self-consciously funky. Nacho orange interior, red velvet curtains, and Alvin and the Chipmunks on the sound system. Tandoori chicken calzones (€9) and creative brethren share space with spaghetti-standards. Pizza €5-9, *primi* €5-7, *secondi* €8-16. Cover €2. Open daily 11:30am-3:30pm and 7:30pm-12:30am. AmEx/MC/V. ❷

Brek, Italy's best-known fast-food chain, offers a wide choice of freshly cooked a la carte options. *Primi* from €3, *secondi* from €4. Open daily 11:30am-3pm and 6:30-10:30pm. AmEx/MC/V. **Branches:** P. Carlo Felice, 22 (☎011 53 45 56) off V. Roma; off P. Solferino at V. S. Teresa, 23 (☎011 54 54 24). ❶

Sindbad Kebab, V. Milano, 10 (☎011 521 65 18). This popular Middle Eastern kitchen dishes up falafel (€3) a cut above the other cheap eateries in the neighborhood. Take home a falafel pizza or baklava laced with rose water (€1). Vegetarian kebabs available. Italian fare from €2. Open M-F and Su noon-3pm and 5pm-1am, Sa 5pm-1am. ❶

SIGHTS

 TOURIN' CARD. In addition to the finest museum collection of Egyptian antiquities outside of Cairo, visitors to Turin can look forward to excellent exhibits covering everything from cinema to modern art. Checking out all the sights can be costly; the **Turin Card** (48hr. for €15, 72hr. for €17), good for admission to Turin's 120 museums and monuments, plus public transport, makes it affordable. On average, the card pays for itself after two museums and a bus ride.

▧**CATTEDRALE DI SAN GIOVANNI.** The Holy Shroud of Turin, the most revered and enigmatic relic in Christendom, has lain in the Cappella della Santa Sindone of this Renaissance cathedral since 1694. Said to be the burial cloth of Jesus, the three-by-fourteen foot cloth first entered official accounts when the Crusaders brought it back from Jerusalem in the 13th century. Transferred to Turin from Chambéry, France in 1578, today it rests in a climate-controlled case. With rare exceptions—the next planned public exhibition of the shroud is in 2025—a photograph to the left of the cathedral's entrance is as close as visitors can get to the real thing. The photograph shows the unfolded shroud, which splits symmetrically to reveal two figures head to head; the left is the top of the body (with face and arms clearly distinguishable), and the right is the back. A negative below the photograph reveals even more detail than the actual cloth, including the countenance of a man with fractured nose and bruised cheek. It was carbon-dated to the early 1000s and continues to represent a sustained confrontation between science and faith. Repairs to the chapel, which was damaged in a 1997 fire, may take 15 years or more; black marble containing coal is a major structural component and must be completely replaced. (*Behind Palazzo Reale where V. XX Settembre crosses P. S. Giovanni. ☎011 436 15 40. Open daily 7am-noon and 3-7pm. Free. Modest dress required.*)

▧**MUSEO EGIZIO AND GALLERIA SABAUDA.** The **Palazzo dell'Accademia delle Scienze** houses two of Turin's best museums. From 1903-37, the Italian Archaeological Mission brought thousands of artifacts home to Turin; many are now on display in the **Museo Egizio,** the second-largest Egyptian collection of any museum outside of Cairo. The holdings include several copies of the Egyptian Book of the Dead and the intact sarcophagus of Vizier Ghemenef-Har-Bak, which stands out among the large sculptures and architectural fragments on the ground floor. Upstairs lies the well-furnished tomb of 14th-century BC architect Kha and his wife, one of the few tombs spared by grave robbers. On the first floor, the body of the 6th-century BC Egyptian courtier Rei Harteb still has its skin, eyelids, ears, nose, and teeth intact. (*V. Accademia delle Scienze, 6. 2 blocks from P. Castello. ☎011 561 77 76, fax 53 46 23. Open Tu and F-Su 8:30am-2pm, W 2-7:30pm, Th 10am-7:30pm. €6.50, ages 18-25 €3, under 18 or over 65 free.*) On the third and fourth floors, the **Galleria Sabauda** houses art collections from Palazzo Reale and Palazzo Carignano in Turin and Palazzo Durazzo in Genoa. The gallery is renowned for its Flemish and Dutch paintings, including van Eyck's *St. Francis Receiving the Stigmata* (Christ soars through the background on a cross with three sets of red wings), Memling's *Passion*, van Dyck's *Children of Charles I of England*, and Rembrandt's *Old Man Sleeping*. The Sabauda also has several Mannerist and Baroque paintings, including a Poussin, several Strozzis, and Volture's *Decapitation of John the Baptist.* (☎ *011 54 74 40. Hours same as Museo Egizio.* €4, *ages 18-25* €2, *under 18 or over 65 free. Combined ticket for both museums* €8.)

■ **MOLE ANTONELLIANA.** The largest structure in the world built with traditional masonry, the Mole dominates Turin's skyline. Begun as a synagogue in 1863, it ended as a Victorian eccentricity. Though the architect Antonello intended it to be only 47m tall, by the time it was inaugurated in 1908 the Mole had reached a towering 167m. The glass elevator that runs through the middle of the building goes to the observation deck. Now the Mole boasts the **Museo Nazionale del Cinema.** Highlights include 19th-century shorts by Thomas Edison, plus bizarre phenakistiscopes, stereoscopes, and magic lanterns that passed for entertainment in Victorian times. At the center of the museum, a series of exhibitions is dedicated to the artistic development of cinema. A wide range of movies dubbed into Italian, from *Robocop* to silent films produced in Turin's studios in the 1920s, are screened in idiosyncratic settings—a 1960s living room, a neolithic cave, and a giant fridge—which sometimes bear subtle connections to the films being shown (and sometimes not). You haven't lived until you've heard Arnold Schwarzenegger say *"Ritornerò."* *(A few blocks east of P. Castello. V. Montebello, 20.* ☎ *011 815 42 30. Open Tu-F and Su 9am-8pm and Sa 10am-11pm. Museum* €5.20, *students* €4.20; *elevator* €3.62/€2.58; *combined ticket* €6.80/€5.20. *Both covered by Turin Card.)*

PALAZZO AND TEATRO CARIGNANO. One of Guarini's grandiose Baroque palaces, the palazzo was built in 1679 to house the Princes of Savoy; later, it was the seat of the first Italian parliament. The building contains the **Museo Nazionale del Risorgimento Italiano,** commemorating the unification of Italy between 1706 and 1946. English explanations at the beginning of each room help contextualize the paintings, swords, and documents. Political cartoons of an extremely rotund Camillo Cavour speak for themselves. *(Enter from P. Carlo Alberto on the other side of the palazzo. V. Accademia delle Scienze, 5.* ☎ *011 562 37 19. Free guided tour Su 10-11:30am. Open Tu-Su 9am-7pm.* €5, *students* €3.50, *under 10 or over 65 free.)* Across from the palazzo is the **Teatro Carignano,** which *Torinesi* claim rivals Milan's La Scala. The Italian poet Vittorio Alfieri premiered his tragedies in this 18th-century building. The gleaming Baroque music hall was manicured with attention to every detail. *(☎ 011 54 70 54. Call for info on tours. Free.)*

GALLERIA CIVICA D'ARTE MODERNA E CONTEMPORANEA. This premier modern and contemporary art museum covers Divisionism, Dadaism, and Pop Art. The museum's collection is mostly Italian, including some Modiglianis and de Chiricos, but it also has Andy Warhol's gruesome *Orange Car Crash* and works by Picasso, Ernst, Leger, Chagall, Twombly, Klee, Courbet, and Renoir, in addition to the slashed canvases of Lucio Fontana. *(On the corner of C. G. Ferraris, off Largo Emanuele. V. Magenta, 31.* ☎ *011 562 99 11. Open Tu-Su 9am-7pm.* €5.50; *under 26* €3; *under 10 or over 65 or covered by Turin card free. Audioguides* €4.)

PALAZZO REALE. Home to the Princes of Savoy from 1645 to 1865, the palazzo consists mostly of ornate apartments; tours cover only about 30 of the 300+ rooms, including the king's bedroom, actually the least ornamented of all. Louis le Nôtre, famous for his work on the gardens of Versailles, designed the grounds in 1697. Because the Savoys didn't want their chapel to outshine their palace, the facade of the **Chiesa di San Lorenzo,** next door, is as plain as its interior is unabashedly Baroque. Constructed between 1668 and 1680, it is arguably Guarino Guarini's most unique creation, using 85 types of marble, a swirling dome, and no straight lines. *(In Piazzetta Reale, at the end of P. Castello.* ☎ *011 436 14 55. Palazzo open Tu-Su 9am-7pm. 40min. guided tours in Italian Tu-Su 9am-1pm and 2-*

7pm. €6.50; EU students €3.25. Gardens open 9am-1hr. before sunset. San Lorenzo open 7:30am-noon and 4-7:30pm. Free.) In the right wing of the Royal Palace lies the **Armeria Reale** (Royal Armory) of the House of Savoy, containing the world's best collection of medieval and Renaissance war tools. Due to ongoing restoration, half of the armory is closed; open parts are full of weapons, coats of arms, and stuffed horses. *(P. Castello, 191. ☎ 011 54 38 89. Open Tu, Th 8:15am-2pm and Sa 8:15am-1:45pm. €4.50, under 18 or over 65 free.)*

BASILICA DI SUPERGA. When the French attacked Turin on September 6, 1706, King Vittorio Amedeo II made a pact with the Virgin Mary to build a basilica in her honor should the city withstand the invasion. Turin stood unconquered and the basilica was born. A Neoclassical portico and high drum support its spectacular dome. In a tragic event in recent history, a plane carrying the entire Turin soccer team crashed into the basilica in 1949; their tombs lie in the church, as do those of the Savoys. The basilica stands on a 672m summit outside Turin, described by Le Corbusier as "the most enchanting position in the world." Indeed, it offers panoramic views of the city, the Po Valley below, and the Alps beyond. *(Take tram #15 (€0.77) from V. XX Settembre to Stazione Sassi. From the station, take bus #79 or board a small cable railway for a clanking ride uphill (15min.; every hr. on the hr.; M, W-F 9am-noon and 2-8pm, Tu 7pm-midnight, Sa and holidays 9am-10pm, Su 9am-8pm; round-trip €3.10, Su and holidays €4.13/€6.15.) Basilica ☎ 011 898 00 83. Open daily Apr.-Oct. 9am-noon and 3-6pm; Nov.-Mar. 9am-noon and 3-5pm. Free. Tombs €1.55. Railroad and tombs covered by Turin Card.)*

PARCO DEL VALENTINO. One of Italy's largest parks on the banks of the Po, the designer Valentino's lush grounds provide safe haven for whispering lovers and frolicking children. Upon entering the park from C. V. Emanuele, **Castello del Valentino** is on the left. Its distinctly French air, capped by the slanted roof, honors the royal lady Christina of France, who in turn made the castle her favorite residence. It now houses the University's Facoltà di Architettura. Farther south along the river, beside the manicured Giardino Roccioso, is **Borgo e Rocca Medievale,** a "medieval" village built for the 1884 World Exposition. At night, the park becomes a hideout for Turin's shadier characters. *(Park and castle at V. Virgilio, 107, along the Po. ☎ 011 817 71 78. Open Aug. 15-Oct. 25. Phone reservation required for castle. Free.)*

PIAZZA SAN CARLO. Between P. Felice and P. Reale, formal Baroque grandeur takes over; the equestrian statue of Duke Emanuele Filiberto sits proudly on a horse over the crowds. In addition to the Baroque buildings, the piazza features the opulent twin churches of **Santa Cristina** and **San Carlo Borromeo,** on the right and left, respectively, upon entering the piazza from V. Roma. Santa Cristina has the more formidably sculpted facade. *(Santa Christina open daily 8am-1pm and 3-8pm. San Carlo open daily 7am-noon and 3-7pm. Free.)*

MUSEO DELL'AUTOMOBILE. The focus of this museum is Italian cars and car racing. It also documents the evolution of the automobile, exhibiting prints, drawings, leaflets, more than 150 original cars, and first models by Ford, Benz, Peugeot, and Oldsmobile, as well as homegrown Fiat, which fostered a postwar industrial boom in the city. *(Head south 20min. along V. Nizza from Stazione Porta Nuova. C. Unità d' Italia, 40. ☎ 011 67 76 66. Open Tu-Su 10am-7pm. €3. Covered by Turin Card.)*

🎵 📷 ENTERTAINMENT AND SHOPPING

For the lowdown on happening spots, ask the tourist office for a copy of the monthly *News Spettacolo*. On Friday, Turin's daily newspaper, *La Stampa*, publishes *Torino Sette*, a thorough section on cultural events. Eclectic music enlivens Turin between June and August, when the city invites international art-

TURIN OLYMPICS 2006

SKI LIKE THE PROS

Alberto Tomba and Daniella Cec-
carelli may own the Italian
slopes, but even average skiers
can take to the mountains that
will play host to the 2006 Olympics. The action unfolds in six
main locations:

Sestriere (Downhill, Super-G,
Giant Slalom). With 4000 beds,
it's the largest and most commercial resort, attracting skiers from
across Europe.
Cesana-San Sicario (Biathlon,
Downhill, Bobsled, Luge, Skeleton). Two 1000-year-old mountain
villages that offer a quieter environment to an almost exclusively
Italian clientele.
Sauze D'Oulx (Freestyle). During
the winter, you'll hear more
English and Danish than Italian.
As infamous for bikini-skiers and
other outrageous get-ups as it is
for its loud discos and pubs.
Claviere (Downhill, Cross Country). Better bring your passport—
ski a few hundred meters west
and you've entered France.
Bardonecchia (Snowboard). A
couple hundred meters lower in
altitude, but with more restaurants per capita than any other
resort in the region.
Pragellato (Cross Country, Ski
Jump, Nordic Combined). The
cross-country capital of Piemonte
has only 18 downhill runs, but
40km of trails.

Skiers who prefer maximum
flexibility should head for the
"Milky Way" or *via lattea* as sev-

ists to the **Giorni d'Estate Festival.** In the first three
weeks of September, the **Settembre Musica** extravaganza features over 40 classical performances
throughout the city. The **Turin Extra Festival,** held in
the second week of July, attracts major international acts. For more information, pick up *News
Spettacolo* at the tourist office.

During the 1920s Turin was home to over 100
movie production companies. Its love affair with cinema continues today. During the academic year,
Turin's university organizes screenings of foreign
films in their original languages. A list of films is in
the leaflet *Arena Metropolis* at the tourist office.
Head to one of the theaters on C. V. Emanuele or to
the turn-of-the-century glamour of Cinema Romano,
Galleria Subalpina, P. Castello, 9, near the beginning
of V. Po. (☎011 562 01 45. Movies daily, usually 4-
10:30pm. Tickets €4-6.50.)

One of Turin's unique events is the Gran Balon
flea market, held every second Sunday of the month
behind Pta. Palazzo. Here, junk sellers rub shoulders with treasure-hunters. A smaller-scale Mercato
Balon occurs every Sunday. Though clothing stores
line Turin's streets, the chic designer shops on V.
Roma are more fit for window shopping. The sizeable student population has attracted trendy and
reasonably-priced clothing shops to V. Garibaldi
and V. Po; the latter also carries antique books and
records of all genres.

◨ NIGHTLIFE

Torinesi are quite content to get together with a
group of friends and go out for a few drinks, so the
city is unlikely to emerge as a major clubbing center.

❚I MURAZZI. The center of Turin's social scene, I
Murazzi consists of two stretches of boardwalk, one
between Ponte V. Emanuele II and Ponte Umberto
and another smaller stretch downstream from the
Ponte V. Emanuele II. Murazzi del Po attracts everyone from yuppies to goths. Most turn up around
11pm, any night of the week, and spend the next
four hours sitting outside the clubs that line the
waterfront, sipping drinks at €2-4 a pop. At **The
Beach,** in the smaller section toward the end, the
young and modern dance to the best techno on the
Po, watch occasional performance art pieces, or
chill sleepily in the "sleepy chill-out zone." (☎011 18
20 22. Cover free-€10. Open nightly midnight-3am.)
Groove to the latest chart-toppers at **Pier 7-9-11,**
Murazzi del Po, 7/9/11, a popular newcomer with a
deck overlooking the Po. (☎011 83 53 56. Open M-Sa
10:30pm-3am.) **Juan Carlos,** next to the V. Emanuele

bridge, was the first bar to invade I Murazzi and still draws huge after-hours crowds with €1 beers. (Open daily 11pm-6am.) On the other side of the river, quieter cafes and bars serve drinks all night along the same stretch.

ELSEWHERE IN THE CITY CENTER. Pura Vida, C. Cairoli, 14, dishes out Latin and reggae as well as filling grub to a university-age crowd. (☎0348 420 52 31. *Tortillas* €2.70. *Torta de pollo* €3.25. Open M-F and Su 10am-3am, Sa 10am-4am.) The live music and disco cabaret at **Zoo Bar,** C. Casale, 127, make the small space *very* interactive. On Friday and Saturday, a crowd of students break out of the university to take over the dance floor. (☎011 819 43 47. Open M-Sa 11pm-3am.) **Piazza E. Filberto** and the **Roman quarter** have recently become popular with the more artistic set and provide conversation and drinking every bit as loud as I Murazzi.

CORSO VITTORIO EMANUELE. Several excellent English and Irish pubs line C. V. Emanuele from Stazione Porta Nuova to the Po, attracting an English-speaking university crowd. To reach **Six Nations Murphy's Pub,** C. V. Emanuele, 28, turn right out of Pta. Nuova; it's a few blocks down on the left. Beer taps glow in the dim interior, filled with cheery British expats, darts, and billiards. (☎011 88 72 55. Pint of Murphy's €4.20. Open nightly 6pm-3am.) **The Shamrock Inn,** C. V. Emanuele, 34, one block toward the station, offers lively rumba dancing (Th), decent food, and six beers on tap. (☎011 817 49 50. Pints €4. Open nightly 8:30pm-3am.)

ACROSS THE RIVER AND LINGOTTO. This is a great area, but plan on taking a taxi back into town. To get to **Hiroshima Mon Amour,** V. Carlo Bossoli, 63, take bus #1 or 34 to Lingotto Centro Fiere. The name: the title of a celebrated novel by Marguerite Duras. The place: a dancer's paradise, hands down the classiest club in town. The excellent tunes (often live) range from reggae to rock, and cover ranges from free to €10. (☎011 317 66 36. Open nightly 11pm-3am.) Reach **Il Barbiere Cileno,** V. Ormea, 78, by taking bus #34 from Pta. Nuova to Valpergo Caluso. Keep the same direction until reaching Angolo Corso Raffaello, then turn left; V. Ormea branches off from there. The hip crowd grooves to house and Latin. Plan to return with a taxi. (☎388 200 19 80. Open M-Sa 8:30pm-3:30am, Su 11:30pm-3:30am. Take bus #15 from Pta. Nuova toward Brissogne, get off at S. Paolo, and head toward **AEIOU,** V. Spanzotti, 24, which draws flashy 20-somethings with live music and a stellar bar.

eral of the slopes have nicknamed themselves. Sestriere, Sauze D'Oulx, San Sicario, Cliveiere, and the nearby village of Cesana have linked their lifts, making it possible to ski from one village to the next. Combined, the Milky Way totals 400km of downhill slopes, 46km of cross-country trails. Ninety-one lifts, 218 runs, and unlimited potential for off-piste skiing. Passes run around €31 per day. (☎0122 79 94 11; www.vialattea.com.) Rentals are available in any of the villages, runs approximately €12-17 per day for skis, €8 for boots, and €24 for full snowboard kit. To book accommodations or transportation for the entire region, visit www.mountaincollection.com.

True off-piste aficionados can heli-ski out of Sauze D'Oulx with an experienced guide, then hop a mini-bus back to the village. Contact **Heliskiing Val Susa** for more information. (Flights from €190 per person including return transport. ☎335 39 88 94; info@vertigoway.com.) The same company also arranges nature hikes and ice-climbing expeditions.

The ski season usually lasts early-December to late-April, with January and February offering the best conditions for off-piste.

By ski or by sun, the alpine valleys are among the finest vantages in all of Piemonte and worthy of a visit—Olympics or not.

Come for rockin' Friday "Flashback" nights or bliss out to acid jazz at Saturday's "Dance Forever." (☎ 347 925 78 26. Open nightly 8pm-3am.)

🏅 THE 2006 WINTER OLYMPIC GAMES

In 2006 Turin will be in the global spotlight when it hosts the XX Olympic Winter Games, the first Winter Olympics held in Italy since 1956. Turin's bid-winning presentation to the International Olympic Committee focused on its blend of Alpine charm and thriving metropolis.

◩ LOGISTICS. Turin is rolling out a wave of new transportation options to shuttle Olympic visitors around town. These include a **light rail** and a **subway,** serving commuters between downtown and the suburbs, improved roads and bus lines to the mountains, construction of a **high-speed train** line connecting Turin with Milan (the 2hr. trip will take 40min.) and Lyon, France, and the expansion of Stazione Porta Susa to handle the traffic. Most improvements will not be completed until late 2005. Until then, construction will continue to snarl traffic in the downtown.

Though it's actually the largest city to host the Winter Olympics, Turin is still figuring out how a city of one million will handle an onslaught of an estimated four million visitors. The lack of hotel rooms means that many guests will be housed in Milan or Lyon, France and surrounding *Piemontesi* towns, and take the train in each day. If you're planning on attending, make reservations immediately, or resign yourself to a lengthy commute.

▦ URBAN RENEWAL. The **Olympic Atrium** was one of the first Olympic venues completed, comprising a two-part, ultramodern center in P. Solfieri. As a temporary building, it was designed to fit around the trees already planted in the piazza, which accounts for its unusual shape. Visitors can watch multi-media presentations on the as-yet-unfinished projects, as well as montages of past Olympic triumphs. There's also a collection of torches from past games, each of which was uniquely designed. (Open daily 9:30am-7pm.)

Other projects of interest include the construction of an **archaeological park** around the Porta Paletine and remains of the old city wall and the creation of a permanent **pedestrian zone** closed to traffic in P. V. Veneto, linked to new **pedestrian bridges** over the Po. A formerly abandoned Fiat factory in Lingotto, in the south, as well as run-down

TURIN OLYMPICS 2006

GOING FOR THE GOLD

If you've always dreamed of Olympic glory, but can't land a lutz or drive a bobsled, there's still hope. The organizers of the XX Winter Olympics are recruiting 20,000 volunteers to work in Turin before and during the 2006 Games.

Organizers began accepting applications in 2004 to fill positions for a trial run of the Olympic facilities in late 2005. They will continue accepting applications indefinitely, but those hoping to win a spot should complete paperwork by mid-2005. Applicants should be 18 or over and able to work 10 consecutive 8-hour days between February 10th and March 19th, plus arrive a few days early to attend training sessions. The committee's website calls "passion" the only other requirement, but admits proficiency in multiple languages is a huge plus.

Volunteers are assigned to one of more than 250 jobs based on preferences and experience. The perks are excellent: free meals and local transportation, medical insurance and a uniform. Notably missing from the benefits, though, are the price of your plane ticket to Turin and lodgings. The latter is not a trivial omission, as literally every hotel between Turin and Milan will be booked. And no free tickets to the women's figure skating finals or the men's giant slalom, either—unless you're lucky enough to be working at them.

For more info and an application visit www.noi2006.org.

parts of Porto Palazzo, are being rebuilt to house offices and ice rinks, while still preserving their industrial heritage—a church being built as part of one complex uses an old smokestack as its steeple.

7 TICKETS AND INFORMATION. For more info on the Games, contact the **Torino Organizing Committee** at V. Nizza, 262 (☎011 631 05 11; www.torino2006.it). For volunteer opportunities, see "Going for the Gold" feature at left.

DAYTRIP FROM TURIN

SACRA DI SAN MICHELE

From Turin, take the train to Avigliana (15 per day, €1.76). From there, either take a taxi (☎011 93 02 18; around €30) or make the 14km, 3hr. hike. For a map of the arduous trek, head to Avigliana's Informazione Turistico, P. del Popolo, 2, a 5-10min. walk straight ahead from the station. (☎011 932 86 50. Open M-F 9am-noon and 3-6pm.) Alternatively, tackle the scenic 1½hr. climb from the village of Sant'Ambrogio to the monastery. Take a train to Sant'Ambrogio (8 per day, last return 7:10pm, €2.25,). Exiting the station, walk straight up V. Caduti per la Patria and turn right on V. Umberto. Continue straight until reaching Chiesa Parrocchia. Behind the church on the right is a "Sacra di San Michele Mulattiera" sign. The rest of the hike is clearly marked. Do not hike alone, as the unpaved path can be difficult and slippery. Wear sturdy shoes and bring water.

On a bluff above the town of Avigliana, the ⬛**Sacra di San Michele** grows from the very rock on which it was built. *The Name of the Rose* was not filmed at this megalithic stone monastery, but it probably should have been. Umberto Eco based his book's plot on the Sacra's history, and even in full summer sunshine there is an ominous air about the place. Founded in 1000 by an Alevernian pilgrim named Ugo di Montboissier, the monastery perches atop Mt. Pirchiriano (877m) with sweeping views in all directions. The **Stairway of the Dead,** a set of steps chiseled from the mountainside, helps to buttress the structure. The corpses of monks were once draped across the staircase for the faithful to pay their last respects; currently, their skeletons are more tactfully concealed in the cavities on the side. The stairs ascend to two doors depicting the arms of St. Michael wrestling with the Serpent of Eden. Steps in the middle of the nave descend into the shrine of St. Michael, and three tiny **chapels.** The oldest originates from the time when St. Michael was first venerated. In AD 966, St. John Vincent built the largest, with a back wall of solid rock; today it holds the tombs of medieval members of the Savoy family.

CUNEO ☎0175

Over the years, no fewer than nine different armies have besieged strategically located Cuneo, but the town has lived up to its motto, *"ferendo"* (to bear). These days, invasion comes in the form of bargain hunters from three regions and eastern France, who overwhelm serene Cuneo during its weekly street market. The rest of the time, the town is a sleepy provincial capital of 50,000. Its 14km worth of *portici* (arcades) provide ample space for an afternoon of window-shopping and people-watching, but most travelers visit Cuneo as a transportation hub providing access to the surrounding valleys and nearby Maritime Alps National Park.

🖭7 TRANSPORTATION AND PRACTICAL INFORMATION. The **train station** in P. Libertà provides service to Turin (1hr., 1 per hr. 4:33am-10:30pm, €4.70) and Saluzzo (30min., 1 per hr. 5:35am-7:10pm, €4.90). Local **buses** also depart from the station, serving the city and surrounding valleys. Schedules vary daily and seasonally; the tourist office provides up-to-date timetables.

Turin lies 80km north of Cuneo. **Via Roma, Piazza Galimberti,** and **Corso Nizza** comprise the main thoroughfare; most streets form an easily navigable grid. To reach C. Nizza from the train station, follow **Corso Giolitti** from **Piazza Libertà.** The **tourist office,** P. Boves, one block north of V. Roma on V. Peveragno, provides town info and helps find lodgings. (Open M-Sa 9:30am-1pm and 2:30-6:30pm.) For info on activities in Cuneo province, contact **ATL,** V. Amedeo, 13, 3rd fl. Turn onto V. Amedeo from V. Nizza one block before the piazza and follow it three blocks. (☎0171 69 02 16. Open 8:30am-noon and 3-6pm.) **Banks** with **ATMs** line V. Roma and V. Nizza. In case of **emergency** dial ☎118, the **police** (☎0171 677 77), or the **paramedics** (☎0171 44 13 37). The Santa Croce **hospital** is at V. Coppino, 26 (☎0171 64 11 11). Several **pharmacies** are on V. Nizza, most open M-Sa 9am-12:30pm and 3:30-6:30pm. All post hours for after-hours service. The **post office** is at V. A. Bonelli, 6. (☎0171 69 33 06. Open M-F 8:30am-7pm, Sa 8:30am-1pm.) **Postal Code:** 12100.

🍴🛏 FOOD AND ACCOMMODATIONS. Modern, well-maintained hotel rooms, all with TV, phone, and bath can be found at **Hotel Ligure ❸,** V. Savigliano, 11. Exiting P. Galimberti onto V. Roma, turn right; V. Savigliano runs parallel to V. Roma. (☎0171 68 19 42; www.ligurehotel.it. Free indoor parking. Large breakfast buffet €3. Singles €29; doubles €58; triples €75. MC/V.) Another solid choice is **Albergo Cavallo Nero ❸,** V. Seminario, 8. Head one block up V. Roma from P. Galimberti and turn left. Professional-quality rooms all have TV and phone. (☎0171 69 21 68; cavallo.nero@virgilio.it. Singles €36, with bath €45; doubles €48/€60; triples €75. Breakfast included.) The attached restaurant serves up traditional regional dishes in €7-17 *menùs*. (Open daily for lunch from noon, for dinner from 7pm. MC/V.)

Cafes line the *portici* of V. Roma and C. Nizza, providing cheap spots to stop for a sandwich or gelato. Hemingway is said to have traveled to Cuneo for the sole purpose of sampling a *cuneese al rum* from **Arione Pasticceria Caffé ❶,** on the corner of C. Nizza and P. Galimberti. The chocolate praline with rum cream filling (€2) is still the best-seller among a bevy of sweets. (Open daily 9am-6pm.) For upscale *Piemontese* cuisine, try **Osteria della Chiocciola ❸,** V. Fossano, 1, one block down from V. Roma on V. S. Maria. Put together appetizers like marinated rabbit loin with mushroom risotto and lamb ribs and you've got the €28 *menù.* Second-floor seating overlooks the street below. (Open daily for lunch from noon; for dinner from 6pm. *Primi* €7-8, *secondi* €8-12.) A MaxisConto **supermarket** at the corner of V. C. Battiste and V. Ponza di Marino sells groceries and necessities. (Open M-F 8:30am-1pm and 3:30-6pm, Sa 8:30am-1pm.)

🎟 SIGHTS. The infamous weekly **market** sprawls for over 1km, filling P. Galimberti, most of V. Roma and much of C. Nizza. Stalls full of clothes, antiques, postcards, cookware and everything else delight shoppers, but make parking a nightmare. (Every other Tu during daylight hours. Summer roughly 7am-6pm; winter 8am-4pm.) The facade of the **duomo,** at the corner of C. Nizza and V. M. Bologna, blends in with the municipal government buildings around it, but inside is a Baroque wonderland of 19th-century crystal chandeliers, gold leaf, and well-lit oil paintings. By comparison, the altar is devoid of ornamentation, decorated only by a large 1685 painting of Christ by Andrea Pozzo. (Open daily 8am-noon and 3-6pm.) The **Museo Civico di Cuneo** makes fine use of the retired convent of San Francesco to display archaeological artifacts and everyday items from across the centuries. Highlights include the 14th-century fresco in the entryway, Bronze Age cave graffiti, and rotating exhibits by local artists. (☎0171 661 37. €2.60; students €1.55. Open Tu-Sa 8:30am-1pm and 2:30-5pm, Su 10am-12:30pm and 3-6pm.)

VALLEYS OF CUNEO   ☎ 0175

The mountain villages in the sparsely inhabited valleys around Cuneo provide an authentic picture of how life in the Italian Alps has existed for centuries. Shops selling traditional crafts and restaurants serving *Piemontese* cuisine abound. Due to infrequent bus service, exploring by car is the most practical option, especially if you plan to visit more than one valley in a single day. The excellent *Cuneo cartina della provincia*, available in any tourist office, makes navigation much easier. For more info on sights or transportation, contact the ATL office in Cuneo.

VALLE GESSO. The Gesso Valley is the gateway to the **Parco naturale delle Alpi Marittime,** a protected area of 28,000 hectares originally part of King Vittorio Emanuele's private hunting reserve. Today the park, which borders on the even larger **Parc National du Mercantour** in France, is home to chamois, ibex, and wild boar, as well as many of the best and least trafficked **hiking trails** in the Italian Alps. Pockets of *Provençal* language and culture are scattered throughout the valley. Tiny **Terme di Valdieri** (1386m) lies in the heart of the park, a few hours' walk from many *rifuge*, making it an ideal trailhead. Otherwise, try the **Piano del Valasco** path (2hr.), which climbs to 1780m and circles a beautiful lake, or continue on the **Giro dei laghi Valleseme** route (4-7hr.) for stunning views. Trails depart from the road next to the info office. After a long day on the trails, nothing feels better than the 37°C ◩**Valdieri Thermal Baths,** 500m down the main road, across the street from the hotel. Soak in the pools or smear sore muscles with mud made from the sulfur-rich thermophilic mosses in the springs—they allegedly have healing properties. *(To reach Terme, backtrack to the Valdieri turnoff, and head 15km southwest. Info office ☎0171 972 08. Open June-Sept. M-F 10am-12:30pm and 4-8pm, Sa 9:30am-12:30pm and 3:30-6:30pm. Thermal baths ☎0171 26 16 66. Open daily 9am-6pm and 8-11pm. Entrance €8.)*

VALLE VERMENAGNA AND VALLE GRANDE. Attilio Mussino, the illustrator of a beloved version of *Pinocchio* read by generations of Italians, spent his twilight years in the village of **Vernante.** Over the last 20 years, residents have begun painting **murals** on the side of their houses and businesses copying Mussino's comical, expressive pictures with perfect accuracy. Historically, the village was best known as the source of *vernantin*, small, handmade knives with handles formed from ox or rambone. Many stores still sell them. Vernante is a good spot to begin exploring the Natural Park; many hiking trails depart from **Palanfre** 6km outside of town. *(20km south of Cuneo. Drive to Borgo S. Dalmazzo, then through Robilante to Vernante.)* Its rail links to Cuneo and Ventimiglia make **Limone** an insanely popular ski resort with French and Italian tourists. During the summer, the town is eerily quiet, though it still makes a convenient starting point for hikes in the Natural Park. Hop a lift to the upper village of Limonetto and head up the path for the *Colle di Tenda Rocca dell'Abisso* (6hr.), which soars to 2755m, offering views of the rough, virtually uninhabited valleys around it. *(From Vernante, drive another 7km straight to Limone; Limonetto is 6km farther up the valley. Tourist and skiing info available at Comune di Limone, V. Roma, 30. ☎0171 92 95 15; www.limonepiemonte.it. Open daily 9am-12:30pm and 2:30-6pm. Skiing: One-day pass €26; 6-day €104-120.)*

VALLE CASOTTO. During his 1796 visit, Napoleon called **Mondovì** "the most beautiful town in the world." The historical center, an impossibly dense collection of buildings dating from 1198, centers on broad P. Maggiore. On one side is the beautiful **Missione** church, a one-time Jesuit convent. *(Open daily 8am-6pm. Free.)* The **Cattedrale San Donato** stands at the other end of the piazza, filled with elaborate frescoes portraying the life of the saint, gilt and crystal chandeliers,

THE HIDDEN DEAL

COUNTRY LIVING

Albergo Alpi is a place where it pays to have reservations—not because lunching businessmen fight for tables, but because Pamparato village is so small the owners only prepare lunch if they're expecting someone. Everyone gets the same 5-course *menù*, a meal fit for a king, or, more accurately, for a peasant, as it consists of only typical *Cuneesi* dishes. The owners insist it's simple home cooking like Mom used to make, but if that's true, Mom was the finest cook between Paesana and Montezemolo.

Lunch starts with a *Piemontese antipasto*, *carna cruda* (raw veal marinated in lemon and herbs). Buckwheat polenta is the preferred *primo*. Typically you'll have to fight through three helpings. Expect two *secondi*, often mushrooms followed by roast rabbit. Finish off with fresh seasonal fruit over ice cream and a shot of *Genzianella*, a home-brewed hundred-and-something-proof liquor made from chicory flowers.

If word ever gets out, everyone for miles will start showing up. Of course given Valle Casotto's population, that only means a few people—but there will be more than enough food to go around.

Albergo Bar Alpi, P. Marconi, 6, Pamparato. Drive to Vicoforte. From there, wind 20km south through the villages of Moline and Roburent. ☎*0174 35 11 24. In July and Aug. open for lunch M-Tu and Th-Su; arrive between 12:30 and 1pm. €25.* ❺

and a huge alabaster crucifix. The Neoclassical church is characteristic of the work of local architect Francesco Gallo, who designed the structure in 1743. The **Torre Civica**, behind the cathedral, is one of the symbols of the town. Destroyed by fire and war, its current incarnation stands at over 30m, faced on each side with a giant clock. Climb past the exposed gears and clockworks to the top, for a view all the way to Monte Bianco. *(Open June-Sept. Tu-Su 3-6:30pm. €2.)* Stores throughout the city center sell pottery embossed with the town's rooster symbol, a craft for which the town is known throughout the region. *(Mondovì is 28km east of Cuneo. For info on sights, contact the Ufficio IAT del Comune di Mondovì, V. Vico, 2.* ☎*0174 403 89; www.comune.mondovi.cn.it.)* Farther up the valley is the village of **Vicoforte**, home to the soaring **Santuario di Vicoforte**. Originally begun in 1596 as the crypt for Duke Carlo Emanuele I, the sanctuary wasn't finished until 1733, with the help of local *wunderkind* Francesco Gallo. The blue elliptical dome, 75m high and 38m long is the longest in the world; the 6000 sq. m fresco of the Madonna's life on the inside is considered the largest single-subject painting in the world. Skylights and the bright, heavily-frescoed interior make the altar glow when reflected light. *(Vicoforte is 4km east of Mondovì. Basilica open daily 7:30am-noon and 2-7pm. Free.)* The final stop in the valley is the **Castello di Casotto**, a one-time 12th-century charterhouse, later destroyed by Napoleon, and re-built as a summer home for the Savoys. It's also a fascinating and occasionally disturbing example of bad preservation happening to a great building—water damaged oil-paintings cheerfully hang next to open windows, the lush velvet pillows and blankets on Queen Margherita's bed are decayed with mold, and even the billiards table in King Emanuele II's game room has warped. Widespread efforts to restore the castle's exterior are currently underway. *(11km south of Pamparato. Open daily 9-11:30am and 2-6pm. Admission and obligatory tour in Italian €3.)*

VALLE MAUDAGNA. The valley's one major sight is a big one—the 4km long ◪**Grotta di Bossea** (Bossea Cave) has been open to visitors since 1864. Tours lead past waterfalls, stalactites the size of train cars, the skeleton of a giant cave bear, and the enormous, 80m-high "Garelli Hall." *(50km southeast of Cuneo. Head for Chiusa, then drive through Roccaforte and Villanova, to Frabosa Soprano. Caves* ☎*0174 39 42 40. 90min. tours M-F 10, 11:30am, 3, and 4pm, Sa-Su 10, 11am, 2:30, 4, and 5:30pm. In Italian; English and French written guides available. €7.80.)*

SALUZZO ☎ 0175

For over four centuries, the hilltop town of Saluzzo (pop. 35,000) reigned as the capital of a fiercely independent Marquisate, before falling under the influence of the House of Savoy in 1601. The arcade-lined historical center and churches of the "Siena of the North" remain well-preserved and tourist-free—unless you count the crowds of farmers who come up on weekend nights for a glass of wine in one of the trattorias. Its location overlooking the Po Valley makes Saluzzo an ideal base to explore the northern valleys, as well as a stopover in its own right.

📱📶 TRANSPORTATION AND PRACTICAL INFORMATION. By car, Saluzzo lies 33km north of Cuneo on the way to Turin. **Trains** depart the station for Cuneo (1hr., 1 per hr. 6:10am-8:30pm, €4.90) and Turin (1hr., 6:10am-7:44pm, €4.50). Local **buses** connect Saluzzo to villages in the surrounding valleys.

Saluzzo's main street is known as **V. Spielberg, C. Italia,** and **C. Piemonte** as it moves from east to west; to reach it from the train station, head straight up **V. Piave;** from the bus station turn left on **V. Circonvallazione,** then immediately right on **V. Torino.** The **historical center** and most of the sights lie uphill on the north side of town. The **tourist office,** Piazzetta dei Mondagli, 5, is reached by entering the old town at V. Volta, near the junction of V. Spielberg and C. Italia. It also provides information on sights in nearby villages and valleys. (☎ 0175 467 10; www.comune.saluzzo.cn.it. Open Apr.-Sept. M-Sa 9am-12:30pm and 3-6:30pm, Su until 7pm; Oct.-Mar. M-Sa 9am-12:30pm and 3-5:30pm, Su until 6pm.) **Banks,** most with **ATMs,** are on C. Italia. In case of **emergency,** call ☎ **118;** the **hospital** lies on V. Spielberg, two blocks outside the historical center. **Farmacia Chiaffredo,** C. Italia, 56, posts a list of after-hours pharmacies. (Open M and W-Sa 8:30am-12:30pm and 3:30-7:30pm.) The **post office,** at V. Peano, 1, is on the other side of the river, not far from the train station. (Open M-F 8:30am-7pm; Sa 8:30am-1pm.) **Postal Code:** 12037.

🏠🍴 ACCOMMODATIONS AND FOOD. Budget digs are tough to find in the town proper; those with cars should consider inquiring at the tourist office about B&Bs in the countryside or visit Saluzzo as a daytrip from Cuneo. **Hotel Përpûin ❸,** V. Spielberg, 19, offers modern rooms with TV, phone, and shower, most with bath. Përpûin has an easy location and an English-savvy staff. (☎ 0175 423 82; nadi-afornetti@hotmail.com. Breakfast included. Wheelchair accessible. Singles €40; doubles €70. Extra people 30% each. AmEx/MC/V.) **Albergo Persico ❸,** V. Mercati, 10, is just below P. Vineis on C. Italia. Besides a slightly quieter location, Persico has rooms with bath, TV, and phone. (☎ 0175 412 13; persico@libero.it. Breakfast included. Singles €45; doubles €68; triples €85. Closed July. AmEx/MC/V.)

Persico's downstairs **restaurant ❸,** specializes in *Piemontese* cuisine, including the hard to find farmer's plate of deep-fried everything—meat, vegetables, fruit, bread (€14; open Tu-Su noon-2pm and 7-10:30pm. *Primi* €7-9, *secondi* €9-12.) Trattorias and cafes line the streets of the historical center. The menu changes seasonally at **Le Quattro Stagioni ❷,** V. Volta, 21. Traditional *Piemontesi* dishes like *agnolotti al plin* (hand-pinched ravioli; €7) and *tajarin* (tagliatelle; €6.50) compete with pizzas (€4-7) for table space in the dim interior. In season, the peaches stuffed with chocolate and hazelnut sauce are a knockout. (☎ 0175 474 70. *Primi* €6.50-7, *secondi* €10-14. Open daily noon-2:30pm and 7-11pm. AmEx/MC/V.)

🔵 SIGHTS. In the P. Risorgimento off of C. Italia lies the **Cattedrale di Maria Assunta.** The recently restored Lombardy-Gothic cathedral, begun in the 1490s, is decorated with bright Baroque frescoes that contrast sharply with the somber exterior. (Open daily 7:15-11:30am and 2-7pm.) Enter the historical center through the nearby Pta. S. Maria, and head uphill to the **Chiesa di San Giovanni,** on V. San

PIEMONTE AND VALLE D'AOSTA

Giovanni. The elaborately carved wooden choir is in the Gothic-flamboyant style, exceedingly rare in this region. The ceiling of the adjoining chapel, accessible through the cloisters to the church's left, is frescoed to represent the night sky. (Open daily 9am-noon and 3-7pm.) Farther down V. San Giovanni lies **Casa Cavassa**, a 14th-century palazzo since converted into the town museum. Sixteenth-century furniture and frescoes stand beside coats of arms and a Hans Clemer altarpiece; much of the collection was salvaged from antique markets during the 1890s. In the same building, the 33m civic tower commands a sweeping view of the Po Valley. (Museum and tower open Apr.-Sept. Th-Su 10am-1pm and 2-6pm; Oct.-Mar. until 5pm. Combined admission €5.) At the hill's summit in P. Costello stands the imposing **Castiglia**, the town fortress, which later served as a prison for several hundred years until the 1980s. When current renovations are completed, it will be reborn again as a cultural center.

When Tommaso III left the 12th-century **Castello della Manta** (in the village of Manta, 2km from Saluzzo toward Cuneo) to his step-son in 1416, Valerano of Saluzzo commissioned a series of frescoes to thank dear old dad, the author of the Romantic poem *Le Chevalier errant*. The frescoes illustrate the poem's 18 heroes, but meld the bodies of King Arthur and Alexander the Great with the faces of Saluzzo's former rulers; they also contain naughty scenes staged in the fountain of youth. (Bus accessible; ask at the Saluzzo Tourist Office for a schedule. Open Feb.-Sept. 10am-1pm and 2-6pm; Oct.-Dec. closes 5pm. €5; children 4-12 €2.50.)

ASTI ☎0141

Set in the hillsides of wine country, the provincial seat of Asti (pop. 75,000) has bustled with activity since ancient times. It rose to prominence as a trading center in the Middle Ages, becoming one of the richest cities in Italy by 1200, before centuries of warfare under Savoy rule (1300-1700) leveled many of the buildings. The medieval city is the birthplace of Vittorio Alfieri, 18th-century tragic poet and descendant of the Alfieri Counts of Asti (even locals admit he's boring), but is best known today for its sparkling wines. Limestone-rich soils on gentle south-facing slopes produce grapes destined for bottles of *Barbaresco*, dark red *Barbera*, and champagne-like *Asti Spumante*.

▐▌ TRANSPORTATION AND PRACTICAL INFORMATION. The **train station** is in P. Marconi, where V. Cavour meets C. L. Einaudi. Trains run to: Alessandria (30min., every hr. 5:24am-1:07pm, €2.45); Milan Centrale (2hr., 6:43am, €6.82); and Turin Porta Nuova (1hr., 2 per hr. 4:32am-11pm, €3.50). The info office is open Monday to Friday 6am-12:40pm and 1:10-7:45pm, or use ticket automat for information. **Buses**, in P. Medaglie d'Oro, across from the train station, run to Canelli (every 2hr., 7:10am-6:40pm); Castagnole (every 2hr., 7:20am-6:40pm); Costigliole (9 per day, 7:15am-6:50pm); and Isola d'Asti (6 per day, 10am-6:50pm). Buy tickets (€1.55-€2.10) onboard or at *tabacchi*. **Taxis** are in P. Alfieri (☎0141 53 26 05) or at the train station (☎0141 59 27 22).

The center of town lies in the triangular **Piazza Vittorio Alfieri**. Most historical sights are slightly to the left of the piazza when facing the statue, down **Corso V. Alfieri**, the major east-west thoroughfare. The **tourist office** is in P. Alfieri, 29. It assists in finding (but not reserving) lodgings and gives info on daytrips to wineries and castles. Pick up an indispensable **map** and free *Guide to Asti* and its province. (☎0141 53 03 57. Open M-Sa 9am-1pm and 2:30-6:30pm, Su 10am-1pm.) **Currency Exchange** is available in banks lining C. V. Alfieri and V. Dante. There are 24hr. **ATMs** in the train station and along V. Dante. In case of **emergency**, call ☎113, an **ambulance** (☎118), or the **police**, C. XXV Aprile, 19 (☎0141 41 81 11). A late-night **pharmacy** is at P. Alfieri, 3. (☎0141 41 09 92. Open M 3-7pm, Tu-F 9am-12:30pm and

3-7pm, Sa 9am-12:30pm.) Check **Internet** at **Caffeteria Garibaldi,** V. Garibaldi, 6, across the street from the indoor market. (Internet €3 per 30min., printing €0.10 per page. Open M-Sa 8:30am-8:30pm.) The **post office,** C. Dante, 55, is off P. Alfieri. (☎ 0141 35 72 51. Open M-F 8:30am-5:30pm, Sa 8:15am-noon. **Postal Code:** 14100.

ⓕ ACCOMMODATIONS. Those with cars should consider a B&B or *agriturismo* in the wine country just outside of Asti; these tend to be better values in beautiful surroundings. Ask at the tourist office for more information. Hotels in town are somewhat more expensive. Exit the train station and cross the piazza to reach **▪Hotel Cavour ❹,** P. Marconi, 18, slightly on the left. The modern, immaculate rooms all come with bath, TV, and phone. (☎/fax 0141 53 02 22. Reception daily 6am-1am. Singles €44, with A/C €50; doubles €64/€70. AmEx/MC/V.) **Hotel Genova ❸,** C. Alessandria, 26, is slightly simpler. From P. Alfieri, take C. V. Alfieri east until it turns into C. Alessandria; hotel is on the left. All rooms have TV. (☎ 0141 59 31 97. Breakfast €1.80-6.20. Singles €32, with bath €40; doubles €50, with bath €60. Ask about student discount. MC/V.) Everything from the wallpaper to the furniture screams "brand-new" at the **Hotel Priore,** C. G. Ferraris, 58, west of the P. Campo del Palio. All rooms come with bath. (☎ 0141 59 36 88; www.hotelpriore.it. Singles €52; doubles €78; triples €90. MC/V.) To reach **Campeggio Umberto Cagni ❶,** V. Valmanera, 152, 4km from P. Alfieri, turn onto V. Aro, which becomes C. Volta; turn left on V. Valmanera. The camp is crowded with Italian vacationers, and maintains a restaurant and bar. Owners demand quiet at night. (☎ 0141 27 12 38, fax 59 98 96. Electricity €2. Showers free. €4 per person, €4.50-5 per tent, €3 per car. Bungalows €26. Open Apr.-Sept.)

ⓕ FOOD. *Astigiana* cuisine is known for its simplicity, using only a few crucial ingredients and pungent cheeses like gorgonzola to create culinary masterpieces. Classic *Piemontesi* dishes are composed of rabbit and boar and flavored with truffles and mountain herbs. An extensive fruit and vegetable **market** is at Campo del Palio. (Open W and Sa 7:30am-1pm.) The Dì per Dì **supermarket,** P. Alfieri, 26, has good prices and variety. (☎ 0141 347 59. Open M-Tu, Th-F, and Su 8:30am-1pm and 2:30-7:30pm; W and Sa 8:30am-7:30pm.) After dazzling the residents of Castigliole with inventive *Piemontese* cuisine for 30 years, Aldo, of **Ristorante Aldo di Castiglione ❹,** V. Giobert, 8, moved to the big city of Asti to convert the gourmands. From P. Alfieri, turn left on C. V. Alfieri, then left on V. Giobert. Enjoy the lunch *menù* (€20) with *primo, secondo,* dessert, wine, and coffee. (☎ 0141 35 49 05. 3-course dinner from €20. *Primi* €6-8, *secondi* €10-14. Open M-W and F-Su noon-2:30pm and 7:30-10pm. MC/V.) Set in a centuries-old brick warehouse, **L'Osteria della Barbera ❸,** V. al Teatro, 5, serves *Piemontese* and Italian cuisine, as well as its heavy-hitting red wine namesake. From the top of P. V. Alfieri, turn left on C. V. Alfieri; V. al Teatro is one block on the left. (☎ 0141 53 09 99. €10 lunch *menù. Primi* €6-8, *secondi* €7-9. Open daily noon-2pm and 5:30-10:30pm. AmEx/MC/V.) Attentive service and regional specialties guarantee a fine meal at **L'Angolo del Beato ❹,** V. Guttuari, 12. Pick up a glass of *Barbera* or *Barolo*. From P. Marconi, take V. Cavour; V. Guttuari is on the left. (☎/fax 0141 53 16 68. *Primi* €8, *secondi* €13. Cover €1.50. Open M-Sa noon-2pm and 5:30-10:30pm. AmEx/MC/V.) Signor Francese of **Pizzeria Francese ❷,** V. dei Cappellai, 15, is quite discriminating about his pizza, so much so that he's written a 692-page guide to the best pizzerias in Italy. His own are taste sensations, with light crusts and rich *buffalo* mozzarella. From P. Alfieri, turn left on V. Garibaldi, then cross P. S. Secondo to V. dei Cappelli. (☎/fax 0141 59 87 11. Pizza €5.50-7. *Primi* €6.50, *secondi* €8. Cover €1.50. Open M-Tu and Th-Su noon-3pm and 6pm-2am. Closed mid-Aug. MC/V.)

TIME: All day.

DISTANCE: 115km.

SEASON: Year-round, except January.

A tour of the wineries of Langhe Province in Piemonte.

Need a reason for visiting the Langhe, a tiny province tucked away in the southwest corner of Piemonte? Try five, all of them local wines with international reputations: Barbaresco, Barbera, Barolo, Dolcetto, and Moscato. If that isn't enough to make your head swim, the scenery should be; narrow roads wind their way through river valleys, weaving between steep hills covered in vineyards. Atop each hill, it seems, is another castle or manor (French actor Gerard Depardieu owns one), most of them dating from the Middle Ages, when they were built to protect trade routes.

A day's drive through the region should be enough time to hit the major sights, but for those who want to make a night (or week) of it, numerous farmstays and B&Bs provide cozy places to crash at reasonable rates.

Many of the destinations on the route are **Enoteche Regionali,** or regional wine cellars, stocking only wine produced within a few kilometers of the cellar. Though prime bottles of some of the wines listed below easily top €100 in restaurants, excellent vintages can be purchased in an Enoteca Regionale for no more than €20-40. All also offer tastings, usually four wines for around €5. Admission is free and tours can be arranged by phoning in advance. All are closed the entire month of January.

For wine tourism, accommodations, or general information, contact the **tourist office** in Alba, P. Medford, 3. (☎0173 358 33; www.langheroero.it. Open M-F 9am-12:30pm and 2:30-6:30pm, Sa 9am-12:30pm.)

1. ALBA. Start your journey in the capital of the Langhe, some 30km southwest of Asti. The winding streets of the old town were home to famous World War II resistance fighter Beppe Fenoglio, whose autobiography, *Johnny the Partisan,* is well loved throughout Piemonte.

Even if you're eager to make it into the heart of wine country, take a turn down **Via Vittorio Emanuele,** running directly through the center

SCENIC DRIVE

of town, to pick up supplies for a picnic lunch. If you're in town in November, this could mean **white truffles**, found in no other part of the world. Or course, they're excruciatingly expensive: after the dry season of 2003, a kilogram of the zesty *funghi* fetched up to €5000. Fresh, soft cheeses are popular local products, as are **hazelnuts** and confections made from them—Alba claims to have invented *Nutella*. Naturally, a bottle of **Barbera d'Alba** is in order; the ruby red wine has full-bodied, acidic, slightly tannic flavor that would probably go best with a lunch of cheese and *salumi*.

2. BARBARESCO. Wind your way north 10km, over the dusty roads that make up the most scenic part of the day's drive. Stand next to the town's 36m tower to survey the Tanaro River valley below; you should be able to pick out Alba and even the castle of Grinzane Cavour, your next stop. Any of the *cantine* in the historical center are a fine place to sample the town's eponymous alcoholic progeny—a dry, garnet red with a strong oak taste—but the best spot to pick out a bottle of Barbaresco is the Enoteca Regionale, V. Torino, 8/A. (☎0173 63 59 42; www.enotecabarbaresco.it. Open M-Tu and Th-Sa 9:30am-6pm, Su 9:30am-1pm and 2:30-8pm.)

3. GRINZANA CAVOUR. Head south again, passing through Alba, to the hilltop town of Grinzana Cavour with its famous castle, V. Castello, 5. The 11th-century fortress was the boyhood home of Italian patriot **Camillo Cavour.** Tours of the castle include Cavour's study and bedroom (he was short so he needed a stool to climb into bed), as well as a museum of local handicrafts and costumes. Also on display is a bizarre collection of tree root sculptures. There could be no more appropriate homage to Italy's first prime minister, who was a full-time gourmet and part-time vinologist, than turning his residence into an Enoteca Regionale. If this is your lunch stop, pick up a bottle of something a little lighter—**Dolcetto,** a ruby, dry, slightly bitter red, not at all sweet, as the name might falsely imply. Camillo would approve. Though once dismissed as a mere table wine, Dolcetto now appears on the tables of fine restaurants throughout Italy. (☎0173 26 21 59; www.castellogrinzane.it. Castle tours M-W and F-Su on the hour 10am-noon and on the half hour 2:30-5:30pm. €3.50. Wine cellars open 9:30am-noon and 2:30-6:30pm.)

4. BAROLO. Continue southwest 7km to Barolo, home to an even more ancient castle dating from the 900s. The interior is decorated in a more modern French style and contains a gallery of paintings by contemporary local artists. Aside from the frescoed rooms on the tour, the castle also serves as a genealogical library and Enoteca Regionale. The cellar stocks over 100 varieties of the most potent and perhaps most famous wine of the day: **Barolo,** a velvety, well-rounded red with intense orange highlights. (In P. Faletti. ☎0173 562 77; www.baroloworld.it. Tours of the castle €3.50. Open M-W and F-Su 10am-12:30pm and 3-6:30pm.)

5. LA MORRA. Head northwest to the tiny hilltop village of La Morra, population 1000. Cap the day with a dessert wine, **Moscato,** a slightly sparkling white with an almost soft-drink sweet taste, the perfect wine for people who insist they hate wine. The right place to try it, or any wines that you may have missed along the day's tour, is the cantina Gianni Gagliardo, Serra dei Turchi, 88. This family operation not only works the fields and bottles wine in the basement, but has become the single evening destination for young people in their 20s and 30s for miles around. The standing challenge to anyone who uncorks a bottle: if you can correctly draw your cork out of a hat with six other corks in it, you win a second bottle free. Glasses from €2.50. (☎0173 508 29; www.gagliardo.it. Open M-Tu and Th-Su in summer noon-late, in winter noon-3pm and 6pm-late.)

At the end of the day, with your bottles safely stowed, head home to Asti to toast your day with another glass of your favorite regional wine.

⬛ **SIGHTS.** The **duomo,** begun in 1309, is a noteworthy example of the Lombardy Gothic style, common throughout Piemonte, which combines the sturdy, squat elements of Romanesque architecture with the more decorative ones of early Gothic. The piazza entrance has several fine statues of monks and priests and is decorated in the alternative red brick and white sandstone pattern characteristic of the region. Throughout the 16th and 17th centuries, local artists, including native son Gandolfino d'Asti, covered every inch of the walls with frescoes; even the columns are painted to appear as if there were vines climbing them. The remains of 11th-century mosaics blanket the floor around the altar. Just to the right, a life-size terra-cotta depicts the death of Jesus. (Walk down C. Alfieri and turn right on V. Mazzini. Open daily 9am-12:30pm and 3:30-6:30pm.) A red-brick bulwark, the 15th-century **Chiesa di San Pietro in Consavia,** served as an army hospital in World War II. On the first floor, the **Museo Paleontologico** has a small collection of fossils and bones from the Astiano area. On the second floor, the **Museo Archeologico** showcases 4th-century BC Greek vases and jugs. A number of Roman-era pieces line the halls, primarily from the Asti and Liguria areas. Beside it is the 12th-century octagonal baptistery. (On the far end of C. Alfieri. Open Tu-Sa 10am-1pm and 4-7pm, Su 10am-noon. Free.)

Piazza San Secondo is home to the 18th-century **Palazzo di Città** and the medieval **Collegiata di San Secondo,** with foundations going back to the 900s. A Romanesque tower stands on the spot where Secondo, Asti's patron saint, was decapitated; in statues, he's the guy holding a sword in one hand and the city of Asti in the other. (From P. V. Alfieri, a short walk west on V. Garibaldi leads to the piazza.) During its medieval prominence, feuding nobles constructed brick towers as testaments to their wealth. In the 13th century, the city was famed for its more than 100 towers, but now only 30 or so remain, many of them crumbling. The 16-sided **Torre Rossa** in **Piazza Medici** is much older, with foundations dating to the time of Augustus. Connected to the tower is the elliptical Baroque **Chiesa di Santa Caterina.** (North of P. S. Secondo, across C. Alfieri. Open daily 7:30am-noon and 3-7pm.) The **Giardini Pubblici** are a pleasant place for a picnic or stroll. (Between P. Alfieri and Campo del Palio.)

🎭 **ENTERTAINMENT.** From the end of June through the beginning of July, **Asti Teatro** holds drama, music, and dance performances. (☎0141 39 93 41. €8-13, children under 12 €5-9. Reserve tickets in advance.) Beginning the second Friday in September, agricultural Asti revels in the **Douja d'Or,** a week-long fair and exposition of local wines, with competitions and tastings. During this week, on the second Sunday in September, is the **Paisan,** or the **Festivale delle Sagre,** with medieval costumes, parades, and feasts. On the third Sunday in September, the Douja d'Or comes to a close with the **Palio di Asti.** A procession commemorating the town's liberation in 1200, followed by the oldest (1275) of Italy's bareback horse races. A jockey represents each quarter of the city, with the winner taking the Palio, or painted flag. Copies of decades of Palios are on display in **San Secondo church.** (☎0141 53 52 11.) On the first Sunday in July, the area's biggest **donkey race** is held 4km from Asti in the village of Quarto, ending with a town-wide ravioli banquet.

NEAR ASTI

CANELLI

The sparkling *Asti Cinzano* and *Asti Spumante*, as well as the super-sweet *Moscato*, bubble forth from the countryside vineyards surrounding Canelli, providing both an economic base and a source of worldwide renown. The first Italian sparkling wine matured in the Gancia winery 150 years ago, though wine has flowed from the verdant hills since Roman times. The region's deep wine-making tradition has created kilometers of vaulted underground tunnels that serve as wine cellars. The "underground cathedral," as the interconnected brick cellars are known, may soon earn a UNESCO World Heritage Site designation, providing enough money to finish the tunnel needed to make it possible to walk from one end of the city to the other completely underground. **Casa Contratto,** V. G. B. Giuliani, 56, is a family-owned cellar dating from 1867. Tours take visitors through the entire wine-making process. The cellar, carved 32m into a hill, contains about 500,000 bottles of wine kept upside down in racks, which are turned 90 degrees by hand daily, until the cellar master declares them mature. Tours are in Italian, but the visuals speak for themselves. (☎0141 82 46 50; info@contratto.it. Open M-F 8am-noon and 2-6pm, Sa-Su by appointment only. White wine tastings €8, 3 wines; red wine tastings €11, 4 wines. Call ahead to book a free tour.) Afterward, head to the 19th-century cellar of **Enoteca Regionale di Canelli e dell'Astesana,** C. Libertà, 65/A, for a taste of Canelli's finest wines. (☎0141 83 21 82; enoteca-canelli@inwind.it. Open Th-F 5pm-midnight, Sa-Su 11am-1pm and 5pm-midnight). Every third weekend of June, over 2000 townspeople in medieval garb reenact the **Siege of Canelli,** a 1613 battle. Entrance is free, but get a pass from the military authorities at the gate, or risk being thrown in the stocks. Innkeepers and restaurants participate by serving 17th century feasts (€8-21). Buses run to Canelli (30min., every 1½hr. 7:10am-5pm, €2.10) from the bus station in Asti. Trains also run from Asti (5:28am-7:08pm, €2.25) via Castagnole.

ACQUI TERME   ☎0144

Acqui Terme has something other than *spumante* bubbling under its placid surface. Sulfuric springs at temperatures of 75°C (167°F) gurgle just beneath the ground. In late summer the sleepy town fills with vacationers seeking the relaxation and alleged healing properties of the mineral-rich water and mud baths.

🖃🚍 TRANSPORTATION AND PRACTICAL INFORMATION. The **train station** (☎0144 32 25 83) is in P. V. Veneto. (Ticket booth open M-F 6am-7:30pm, Sa-Su 6am-12:35pm and 12:55-7:30pm.) From Genoa, catch a **train** (1½hr., every hr., €3.40) via Ovada. Trains also run from Asti (1hr., 17 per day, €3.10). To reach the town from the station, turn left on **Via Alessandria,** and continue as it becomes **Corso Vigano** and ends in **Piazza Italia.** For the **IAT Tourist Office,** V. Maggiorino Ferraris, 5, walk down C. Dante, turn right on C. Cavour and left on V. Ferraris. (☎0144 32 21 42; iat@acquiterme.it. Open M 10:30am-12:30pm and 3:30-6:30pm, Tu-Sa 9:30am-12:30pm and 3:30-6:30pm, Su and holidays 9:30am-12:30pm.) Banks on C. Dante, including **Cassa di Risparmio di Torino,** C. Dante, 26, **exchange currency. Acqui Terme Biblioteca Civica,** V. Ferraris, 15, has free **Internet.** It is around the corner from the tourist office. (M and Th 8:30am-1:30pm and 4-6pm, Tu-W and F 8:30am-1:30pm, Sa 9am-noon.) Take V. XX Settembre from P. Italia to the **post office** on V. Truco, off P. Matteotti. (☎0144 32 29 84. Open M-F 8am-7pm, Sa 9am-12:30pm.) **Postal Code:** 15011.

🛏🍴 ACCOMMODATIONS AND FOOD. During the second half of August and much of September, hotel rooms are heavily booked by those who have come to seek the cure; reservations are recommended. For a centrally located, well-staffed, and comfortable hotel, head to **Albergo San Marco ❷,** V. Ghione, 5. From P. Italia, take C. Bagni about 15m and make the first right onto V. Ghione. Sunlit and spacious rooms are within a stone's throw of the underground remains of a Roman bath. (☎0144 32 24 56, fax 32 10 73. TV and free parking included. Singles €28, with bath €30; doubles with bath €48. Closed Dec. 24-Jan.) According to locals, the **res-**

taurant ❷ downstairs stocks some of the best wine in town. Try the house specialty, a crepe-like flatbread that folds in tasty delights from truffles to cheese, and finish with the excellent *spumone al torrone* (€3) for dessert. (*Primi* €5-6.50, *secondi* €6.50-9.) A brief walk beyond the town center, many hotels, budget and otherwise, line V. Einaudi and surround the mineral baths across the river. **Villa Gliciana ❸**, V. Einaudi, 11, run by a pair of grandmotherly ladies, has a homey living room and plain, well-maintained guest rooms. (☎0144 32 28 74. Singles €29, with bath €33.50; doubles with clinically clean baths €47. Breakfast €4.)

Acqui Terme offers a wide selection of excellent, well-priced restaurants. For fine dining, take C. Dante (which becomes V. Don Bosco) from P. Italia until reaching the white awnings of **Il Nuovo Ciarlocco ❸**, V. Don Bosco, 1. The courteous service and high-quality food here come at reasonable rates. The menu changes daily. (☎0144 577 20; www.ciarlocco.it. *Primi* €7, *secondi* €6-9. Open M and Th-Su noon-2pm and 7:30-10pm, Tu noon-2pm. AmEx/MC/V.) Cheap traditional fare like *trippa in umido* (tripe; €3.10) tempts wayfarers at **Antica Osteria da Bigat ❶**, V. Mazzini, 30/32. (☎0144 32 42 83. Open M-Tu and Th-Sa noon-2pm and 5-9pm, Su 5-9pm. MC/V.) The Giacobbe **supermarket**, C. Cavour, 8, stocks snacks and fresh fruits. Dì per Dì, V. Garibaldi, 50, offers a broad selection of cheap groceries. (Open M-Tu and Th-Sa 8:30am-12:30pm and 3:45-7:45pm, W 8:30am-12:30pm.)

◪ **SIGHTS.** Aches or not, no trip to Acqui is complete without at least dipping a finger in the steamy **sulfuric water.** At the romantic **Piazza Bollente,** hot water pours from a fountain, sending up steam even in summer. Take V. Manzoni up the hill to the 11th-century **Castello dei Paleogi,** which houses the **Museo Civico Archeologico.** The museum displays a small but evocative collection of Roman tombs and mosaics. (☎0144 575 55. Open W-Sa 9:30am-12:30pm and 3:30-6:30pm, Su 3:30-6:30pm. €5, 18-25 €3, under 18 or over 65 free.) The **Romanesque duomo,** down V. Barone from the Museo Archeologico in P. Duomo, is home to Rubens's famous *Trittico* (also called the *Madonna and Child*), sheltered in the sacristy. To view it, ask first at the tourist office. (Open M-Sa 9am-noon and 3:30-6:30pm, Su 3:30-6:30pm.) The four intact arches of the **Roman Aqueduct** overlook the banks of the Bormida River. Though the public baths are gone, the **Reparto Regina,** V. Donati, 2, in the *zona bagne* offers many options for primping and pampering, as well as serious alternative medicine. From the city center, walk down C. Bagni over the river, then turn left on Viale Einaudi. The *reparto* is part of the Hotel Regina. (☎0144 32 43 90; www.termediacqui.it. Sulfur bath €25.50; massages from €39; mud masks €38. Call ahead to reserve.) For a different kind of therapy, head to the ▨**Enoteca Regionale di Acqui Terme,** P. A. Levi, 7. From P. Italia, take C. Italia, turn left on V. Garibaldi, and take the first right into P. Levi. The cavernous winery sells 230 types of wine, including the very local *Dolcetto* and *Bracchetto*. (☎0144 77 02 73. Open Tu and F-Su 10am-noon and 3-6:30pm, Th 3-6:30pm. Free admission. MC/V.)

LAGO MAGGIORE (VERBANO) AND LAGO DI ORTA

Cradling temperate mountain waters and idyllic shores without the tourist frenzy of its eastern neighbors, Lago Maggiore, also called Lago Verbano, has many faces. Steep green hills punctuate the shoreline, and to the west, the dark, glaciated outline of Monte Rosa (4634m) peers down the valley. Don't be discouraged by Maggiore's reputation as the most expensive lake; many *pensioni* offer reasonable rates. Stresa is the most convenient base for exploring the Borromean Islands and the Lago di Orta, while across the lake Verbania-Pallanza has a terrific hostel.

STRESA
☎ 0323

Stresa retains much of the manicured charm that lured visitors, including Queen Victoria, in the 19th and early 20th centuries. Blooming hydrangeas and art nouveau hotels line the waterfront, giving the small town a romantic, old-fashioned appearance. Splendid vistas of the mountain lake-country await around each bend of the cobblestone streets. Stresa is very much a resort, filled with Italian and foreign tourists. There is little to do but hop boats to the Borromeans with the rest of the vacationing gang or while away the day admiring lakeside villas with more than a touch of envy. Once the conspicuous consumption gets old, the hillside of nearby Motterone offers a more unassuming and relaxed alternative.

▐▓ **TRANSPORTATION AND PRACTICAL INFORMATION.** Stresa lies only 1hr. from Milan on the Milan-Domodossola train line. The line can only be accessed from Milan or from the city of Domodossola, which can easily be reached from Locarno, Switzerland. Otherwise, taking a train to a city on the east side of the lake—such as Laveno, which is part of the regular network and not far from Como—then taking a ferry to your final destination is also possible. **Trains** run to Milan (1hr., 1 per hr. 5:21am-10:06pm, €4.20) and Domodossola (40min., 1 per hr. 6:37am-11:01pm, €2.65). Check the ticket office. (Open M-F 6:10am-12:10pm and 12:50-8:10pm, Sa 7am-2pm, Su 12:50-8:10pm.) Most services are along the waterfront (on C. Umberto, P. Marconi and C. Italia) or the major north-south thoroughfare, V. Roma, which runs uphill from the water. To reach the **IAT Tourist Office** in P. Martini, exit the train station, turn right on V. P. Piemonte, then left on V. Genova. Head down to the waterfront and turn right. (☎/fax 0323 301 50 or 313 08. Open daily Mar.-Oct. 10am-12:30pm and 3-6:30pm, Nov.-Feb. closed Su and Sa afternoon.) For **currency exchange** and 24hr. **ATM**, try Banca Popolare di Intra, C. Umberto, 1, just off P. Marconi. (☎0323 303 30. Open M-F 8:30am-12:30pm and 2:35-4pm, Sa 8:20am-12:15pm.) New Data, V. De Vit, 15/A, off P. Cadorna, provides **Internet** at €4 per 30min. (☎0323 303 23. Open M-Sa 9am-12:30pm and 3:30-10pm, Su 3:30-10pm.) **Farmacia dott. Polisseni,** V. Cavour, 14, posts a list of late night pharmacies. (Open M-W and F-Sa 9am-12:30pm and 3-7:30pm.) In case of **emergency,** contact police (☎112 or 0323 301 18), first aid (☎113 or ☎0323 318 44), or an ambulance (☎118 or 0323 333 60). The **post office** is at V. A. Bolongaro, 44. (☎0323 300 65. Open M-F 8:30am-7pm, Sa 8:30am-1pm.) **Postal Code:** 28838.

▐▐ **ACCOMMODATIONS AND FOOD.** The modern **Albergo Luina ❸**, V. Garibaldi, 21, is located near the town center. In summer call ahead to reserve, as these well-maintained rooms, all with bath and TV, are consistently booked. (☎/fax 0323 302 85; luinastresa@yahoo.it. Singles €31-46; doubles €46-70. 10% discount with *Let's Go*. Cash only.) Reach **Orsola Meublé ❷**, V. Duchessa di Genova, 45, from the station by turning right, walking downhill to the intersection, and turning left. A far cry from lakeside luxury, Orsola Meublé features large, affordable rooms with cement balconies decked with plastic chairs and a breakfast room adorned with golf trophies. Cramped shared bathrooms make in-room baths attractive. (☎0323 310 87, fax 93 31 21. Breakfast included. Singles €15, with bath €20; doubles €30/€40. AmEx/MC/V.) **Hotel Mon Toc ❹**, V. Duchessa di Genova, 67/69, can be reached by turning right from the station, then right at the intersection under the tracks. Mon Toc's modern rooms all have bath, TV, and phone. (☎0323 302 82; info@hotelmontoc.com. Breakfast included. Singles €45; doubles €78. Lower in winter. AmEx/MC/V.)

Stresa boasts one truly unique local dish: *Le Margheritine*, a buttery cake dripping with icing sugar, available in most bakeries. Hidden behind the pricier hotels are surprisingly good restaurant deals, such as **Taverna del Pappagallo ❷**, V. P. Margherita, 46, which serves pasta like the *cannelloni alla "Pappagallo"* (€7.30) and brick-oven pizza (€4.20-7) indoors or in a lovely courtyard. (☎0323 304 11. *Primi* €5.20-8, *secondi* €6-12. Cover €1.30. Open M and Th-Su 11:30am-2:30pm and 6:30-10:30pm. AmEx/MC/V.) **Ristorante La Botte ❸**, V. Mazzini 6/8, serves regional standards like ravioli with spinach and ricotta (€8.50), in an interior with an inexplicable British nautical theme. The grilled bratwurst over stewed navy beans (€9) contains enough meat to feed the entire German soccer team. (☎0323 304 62. Open daily noon-2:30pm and 7-10:30pm.) Stock up on **groceries** at GS, V. Roma, 11. (Open M-Sa 8:30am-1pm and 3-7:30pm, Su 8:30am-12:30pm.)

🎦 🎵 **SIGHTS AND ENTERTAINMENT.** Hopping ferries for round-the-lake tours and visits to the island garden provides the number-one pastime for tourists in Stresa. Head for the hills on the **Stresa-Mottarone Funivia**, P. Lido, 8, and explore Mottarone's extensive hiking and mountainbike trails. Those not ready for the Tour de France can haul up a bike on the furnicular and come flying down the hill. Turn right out of the tourist office and follow the waterfront to Viale Lido. (☎0323 303 99. Open daily 9:30am-12:30pm and 1:30-5:30pm. Every 20min.; €7, €12 return. Mountain bike rental plus ascent €22.) Closer to home, **Villa Pallavicino** boasts 50 acres of gardens for pleasant ambles, plus animals and birds, including flamingos and zebras. (☎0323 315 33. Open Mar.-Oct. daily 9am-6pm. €6.70.) **Il Museo dell'Ombrello e del Parasole**, V. Golf Panorama, 2, 10km northwest of Stresa in the town of Gignese, is the world's only umbrella museum. It exhibits 1000 parasols and letters, proof of the town's heritage as a choice resort during La Belle Epoque, when the esplanade was graced with the presence of wealthy ladies shading themselves from the ungracious Mediterranean sun. (☎0323 20 80 64. Open Apr.-Sept. Tu-Su 10am-noon and 3-6pm; open July-Aug. daily.)

The **L'Idrovolante Cafe**, P. Lido, 6, next to the Funivia, is a major local hangout and offers live soul, R&B, and blues. **Internet** is €2.10 per 15min. (☎0323 313 84. Open daily in summer 8am-2am; reduced hours in winter. AmEx/MC/V.) From the last week in August to the third week in September, classical musicians and fans gather for the internationally acclaimed **Settimane Musicali di Stresa e del Lago Maggiore**, a celebration of the full canon of classical music. Performances each night take place in a variety of venues all over the lake, most often Palazzo dei Congressi in Stresa or on Isola Bella. Contact the ticket office at V. Carducci, 38. (☎0323 310 95 or 304 59; www.settimanemusicali.net. Open 9:30am-12:30pm and 3-6pm. Tickets €25-55; under 26 €10 or half-price.) Occasional free performances by everything from marching bands to professional troupes of Chinese acrobats draw hundreds of people to P. Marconi.

NEAR STRESA

THE BORROMEAN ISLANDS (ISOLE BORROMEE)   ☎0323

Ferries run to all three islands from both Stresa and Pallanza (every 30min. 7:10am-7:20pm). A one-day ticket good for unlimited travel between Stresa and the islands costs €9. A combined ticket for the Palazzo on Isola Bella and the garden on Isola Madre for an additional €15 is also available.

Beckoning to visitors with promises of dense greenery and stately villas, the lush beauty of the Borromean trio is the major attraction of the southern and central lake. The opulent 🏛**Palazzo e Giardini Borromeo** is set on the pearl of Maggiore, **Isola Bella**. This Baroque palace, built in 1670 by Count Borromeo, features meticulously designed rooms constructed over 300 years, with priceless masterpieces, tapestries, sculptures by Canova, and paintings by van Dyck. Underground are six

PIEMONTE AND VALLE D'AOSTA

man-made grottoes, completely covered in mosaics; for years peasants were asked to collect black stones in order to help the builders complete them. The 10 terraced gardens, punctuated with statues of the gods and topped by a unicorn, rise up like a green wedding cake. The Borromeo family's motto is *"Humilitas."* Not here. (☎0323 305 56. Open daily Mar.-Sept. 9am-6pm, Oct. 9am-5pm. Last admission 30min. before closing. Audioguide €2.50. €9, ages 6-15 €4.)

Take the ferry from aristocratic Isola Bella to the one-time fishermen's base, **Isola Superiore (dei Pescatori).** The garden-free island is worth a 30min. wander through the narrow cobblestone streets of the village, now clogged with souvenir vendors. There's a little-used rocky swimming beach, but keep in mind this is an Alpine lake. The only other item of interest is the tiny **Chiesa di San Vitore,** dedicated to a Borromese nobleman who later became a saint. The church's foundations date from the 9th century, but the heavily frescoed ceiling and mosaic floor are products of the 1870s. (On top of the hill in the village. Open daily 9am-6pm.)

Isola Madre is the longest and most serene of the islands, almost entirely covered by its garden. Its elegant 16th-century **villa** was started in 1502 by Lancelotto Borromeo and finished by the Count Renato 100 years later, after Lancelotto reputedly met his unfortunate end in the mouth of a dragon. It contains stage sets, a vast collection of portraits, and Princess Borromeo's marionette collection. The **botanical garden's** stupendous array of exotic trees, the tallest palms in Italy, and strutting peacocks are worth the entrance fee. (☎/fax 0323 312 61. Open Mar.-Oct. daily 9am-5:30pm. €8.50, ages 6-15 €4. Audioguide €2.50.) Off Isola Madre, a fourth island is visible: **Isolino San Giovanni,** revered by Arturo Toscanini, who frequently visited the villa. Unfortunately, the little island is not open to the public.

VERBANIA ☎0323

The Verbania train station lies on the Milan-Domodossola line and the station itself is 4km outside of Pallanza, where most tourist services are located. Local buses run from the station to the square twice per hr. (5min., 6:09am-11pm, €0.95), but it is much easier to arrive by ferry from Stresa (€8 return) or another village on Lake Maggiore.

Verbania is an amalgamation of the villages of Pallanza and Intra, both on the shores of Lake Maggiore. Their less touristed feel and beautiful gardens make them a fine spot to pass a few hours in the afternoon, while the hostel is an economical base from which to explore the lake. The villa and gardens of **Villa Taranto** were the life's work of Captain Neil McEacharn, who dreamed of creating a world-class botanical garden in the heart of the Italian lakes. The result is a systematic collection of floral biodiversity, alongside fountains ringed by thousands of annuals. June through August is prime season for the Amazonian greenhouse, which grows lilypads 1½m. in diameter, and for the fields of lotus flowers. (A 20min. walk toward Intra from Pallanza, or get off the ferry at the "Villa Taranto" stop. ☎0323 55 66 67. Open Apr.-Oct. daily 8:30am-7:30pm, last admission 1hr. before closing. €8, children 6-14 €5.50, under 6 free.)

Though Intra is larger, Pallanza is better equipped to deal with tourists and offers the following services. The **tourist office,** C. Zanitello, 8, is a 5min. walk to the right while exiting the ferry, and has extensive information on the lake's major sites. (☎0323 50 32 49; www.verbania-turismo.it. Open Mar.-Oct. M-Sa 9am-12:30pm and 3-6pm, Su 9am-12:30pm.) There are **ATMs** outside the ferry terminal in P. Garibaldi and next to the tourist office. **Banca Popolare di Intra** lies uphill from P. Garibaldi at V. Albertazzi, 24. (Open M-F 8:20am-1:20pm and 2:35-3:35pm, Sa 8:20am-11:20pm.) **Farmacia dott. Nitais,** P. Gramsci, 13/B, lists the late-night emergency service rotation. In case of **emergency,** call ☎113, the **police** (☎112), or an **ambulance** (☎118). Pallanza's **post office** is at P. Gramsci, 13/A. (Open M-F 8:15am-1:40pm, Sa 8:15am-noon.) **Postal Code:** 28922.

PIEMONTE AND VALLE D'AOSTA

Ostello Verbania Internazionale (HI) ❶, V. delle Rose, 7, in a quiet villa 15min. from the ferry dock, offers extremely modern and clean facilities with ping-pong, pool, foosball, arcade games, TV room, and gigantic bathrooms. After exiting the ferry, turn right and walk for 5min. along the water to V. V. Veneto, just past the tourist office. Turn left on V. Panoramica, keep walking up the hill, continue around the bend, and take the last right. The hostel is 50m on the left. (☎0323 50 16 48, fax 50 78 77. Breakfast included. Lockout 11am-4:30pm. Curfew midnight. Reception 8-11am and 4:30-8pm. Open Mar.-Oct. Dorms with sheets and locker €13; 3 family rooms with bath €15 per person. Cash only.) For **groceries,** head to Metà, V. G. Marconi, off P. Gramsci. (Open M-F 8:30am-1pm and 3:30-7:30pm.) Trade the inflated prices and crowds of the waterfront for a view of the piazza at **Pizzeria Emiliana ❶,** P. Giovanni XXIII, 24, which offers brick-oven pizzas from €3.90-7. (☎0323 50 35 22. *Primi* €5-9.50, *secondi* €7.50-9. Open M-Tu and Th-Su noon-2:30pm and 7pm-midnight. AmEx/MC/V.) For something more substantial, head to **Hostaria il Cortile ❷,** V. Albertazzi, 14. The courtyard and wooden benches and tables inside create old-world ambience. Try the robust *penne gorgonzola* (€4.70) or the *scaloppine vino bianco al limone* (€7), which is most delicate. (☎0323 50 28 16. *Primi* from €4.50-5.50, *secondi* from €6-7. Lunch *menù* €5-8. Open M-Tu and Th-Su 11:30am-3:30pm and 5:30pm-2am. MC/V.)

ORTA SAN GIULIO   ☎0322

Though Orta lies less than 60km from Stresa, the two are not directly connected by rail. The simplest solution is to hop the Nerini mini-bus that runs between the two towns on summer weekdays. The bus also stops, by special request, at the tourist office, 1½km outside of town. (1hr.; departs Stresa railway station 10am, 2, and 5pm, returns from Orta 11am, 3, and 6pm; €2.45 one-way.) Or take the train to Domodossola or Premosello and transfer to a train to Orta, though either option can take up to 5hr. Get off the train at Orta Miasino, 3km above Orta, and walk down to the left until reaching an intersection. Turn left on V. Fava, and the town of Orta San Giulio is a 10min. walk away. A twisting road connects Orta to nearby Lake Maggiore. Those with a car can try the nearby lake towns of Alzo and Arola; contact the Orta tourist office for details.

Orta San Giulio is the gateway to Piemonte's Lake Orta, by far the least touristed of the lakes. The high houses that line the narrow cobblestone streets evoke the very best of old Italy. The town is difficult to reach without a car; most tourists are Italian. Its seclusion is precisely what drew Nietzsche here in May 1882, with his young love Lou Salome, to escape the watchful eye of her mother. Nietzsche claimed he couldn't remember whether or not the two had kissed, because the views had sent him into a state of grace. **Isola di San Giulio,** across from Orta is as beautiful as the Borromeans, but the small number of tourists make "the island of quiet" a more peaceful retreat. Walkers can circumnavigate the island on cobblestone paths (10min.) following a trail marked with meditations in four languages. The island's major sight is the 12th-century **Romanesque basilica,** which was built on top of 4th-century foundations. It's filled with Baroque ornamentation and frescoes, but its true masterpiece is the **pulpit,** carved from black marble (representative of the Evangelists). Downstairs, the **skeleton of San Giulio,** dressed in brocade robes, rests in a glass sarcophagus. (Basilica open M 11am-12:15pm, Tu-Sa 9:30am-12:15pm and 2-6:45pm, Su 8:30-10:45am and 2-6:45pm. Free. Modest dress required.) Small **motorboats** weave back and forth during the summer (every 10min., €3 per person, min. 3 people), and larger boats depart every hour (9:45am-5:40pm, €3 return). A short hike (15min.) above Orta proper in the cool, verdant hills, the **Sacro Monte** monastic complex charts the life of St. Francis of Assisi with 376 life-size wooden statues and 900 frescoes spread among 20 different chapels. (Open daily 8:30am-7pm. Free.) The **Mercato Antiquariato** (antique market) is held in P. Motta on the first Saturday of the month. (Open Apr.-Oct. 9am-6pm.)

Orta's **tourist office** is on V. Panoramica, across the street and down from the ornate Villa Crespi tower. From the train station, turn left and walk 10min. straight through the intersection. (☎0322 90 56 14; infoorta@jumpy.it. Open in summer Tu 10am-1pm, W-Th 10am-1pm and 3-6:30pm, F-Sa 10am-1pm and 3-7pm.) There is a **pharmacy** on V. Corina Care Albertolletti, 6, off the main piazza. (☎0322 901 17. Open M-W and F-Sa 9am-12:30pm and 3:30-7:30pm.) In case of **emergency,** call an **ambulance** (☎118 or 0322 901 14) or the **police** (☎0322 824 44). **Banca Popolare di Novara,** V. Olina, 14, has **currency exchange** and outdoor **ATMs.** (Open M-F 8:20am-1:20pm and 2:35-3:35pm, Sa 8:20-11:20am.) The **post office** is in P. Ragazzoni, 9. (☎0322 901 57. Open M-F 8:30am-2pm and Sa 8:30-1pm.) **Postal Code:** 28016.

At **Camping Cusio ❶,** V. Don Bosco, 5, down the street from Meuble S. Caterina, caravans and cabins are available for rent (€11-22 per person), and new bathrooms, a cafe, and free swimming pool sweeten the deal. (☎0322 902 90; www.orta.net/cusio. €4.20-5.80 per adult, €3-3.80 per child. €7-9.80 for car plus tent or caravan; cars alone €3-4; electricity €2. Rental caravans from €11 per person; 4-person bungalows from €65.) An **open-air market** on Wednesday morning in P. Motta sells fruit and vegetables, along with clothes and household necessities. Lago d'Orta is known as the home of *tapulon* (donkey, minced, well-spiced, and cooked in red wine), though the heavy meat is typically only served during the winter. In season, it's available at **Taverna Antico Agnello ❸,** V. Olina, 18. Year-round, second story windows overlook the piazza below for diners eating traditional standards like tagliatelle. (☎0322 902 59. *Primi* €6.50-8.50, *secondi* €9-13. Open M and W-Su 12:30-2pm and 7:30-10pm. AmEx/MC/V.)

VALLE D'AOSTA

Italy's least populated and most elevated region, Valle d'Aosta, is rich with pine forests, waterfalls, and international cable cars. Close to their Swiss and French neighbors, *Valdostani* have taken on much of their continental cousins' cultural character. The Valle is a key transportation hub; Hannibal and his elephants once crossed Aosta's St. Bernard Pass, and today an even greater stampede of heavy goods vehicles (HGV or *TIR* in Italian) barrels through the Monte Bianco tunnel. Italian locals who display "No ai TIR!" placards believe that Aosta's new status as a trade gateway threatens to damage the natural splendor and destabilize the tourist economy, which has provided most of Aosta's non-agricultural wealth for centuries. Before there were Gore-Tex-clad snow warriors battling the *piste* (trails), wealthy cure-seekers filled chalets to soak in the hot springs and Alpine air.

◪ HIKING

The scenic trails of Valle d'Aosta are a hiker's paradise. The best times to hike are July, August, and the first week of September, when much of the snow has melted and the public buses keep a full schedule. In April and May, thawing snow can cause avalanches. Monte Bianco and surrounding peaks may be classic climbs, but only pros should attempt them. (For information on wilderness safety, see **Essentials,** p. 42.) Each area's tourist office or Alpine information office assists hikers of all levels, offering suggested itineraries and information on weather and trail conditions. Offices in Aosta and in the smaller valleys also provide details on campgrounds, *pranzo al sacco* (bagged lunches), *rifugi alpini* (mountain huts), and *bivacchi* (public refuges)—ask for the publication *Mountain Huts and Bivouacs in Aosta Valley.* Some huts lie only a cable-car ride or 30min.

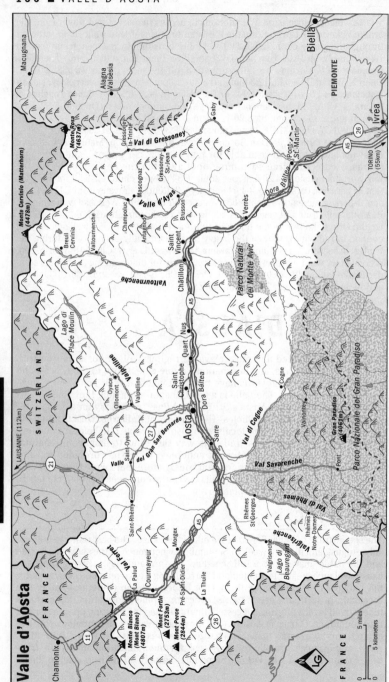

Valle d'Aosta

walk away from roads, and many offer half pension for around €30. *Bivacchi* tend to be empty and free; those run by caretakers cost about €16 per night. For info, call **Società Guide,** V. Monte Emilius, 13 (☎0165 409 39), or **Club Alpino Italiano,** P. Chanoux, 15 (www.guidealpine.it), both in Aosta. They offer insurance and *rifugio* discounts. Most regional tourist offices also carry the booklet *Alte Vie* (High Roads), with **maps,** photographs, and helpful advice pertaining to the two serpentine mountain trails that circumvent the valley and link the region's most dramatic peaks. Long stretches of these trails require no expertise but offer adventure and beautiful panoramas.

⛷ SKIING

Skiing Valle d'Aosta's mountains and glaciers is fantastic; unfortunately, it is not a bargain. **Settimane bianche** ("white weeks") packages for skiers are one source of discounts. For information and prices, call **Ufficio Informazioni Turistiche,** P. Chanoux, 8 (☎0165 23 66 27), in Aosta, and request the pamphlet *White Weeks: Aosta Valley.* Accommodations for a week in March run €230-360 per person, with discounted fares in the early and late seasons. A six-day lift pass costs €130-150. **Courmayeur** and **Breuil-Cervinia** are the best-known ski resorts in the 11 valleys. **Val d'Ayas** and **Val di Gressoney** offer equally challenging terrain for lower rates. **Cogne** and **Brusson,** halfway down Val d'Ayas, have cross-country skiing and less-demanding pistes. In Courmayeur and Breuil-Cervinia, die-hards tackle the slopes in bathing suits for extensive **summer skiing.** Arrange summer package deals through the tourist office in either Courmayeur or Breuil-Cervinia.

⚑ OUTDOOR SPORTS

A host of other sports—rock climbing, mountain biking, hang-gliding, kayaking, and rafting—keeps the adrenaline pumping. For white-water rafting enthusiasts, the most navigable and popular rivers are the **Dora Baltea,** which runs across the valley; the **Dora di Veny,** which branches south from Courmayeur; the **Dora di Ferre,** which meanders north from Courmayeur; the **Dora di Rhêmes,** which flows through the Val di Rhêmes; and the **Grand Eyvia,** which courses through the Val di Cogne. **Centro Nazionale Acque Bianche,** in Fenis, Valle d'Aosta, about 1hr. from Aosta, runs the most affordable rafting trips. (☎0165 76 46 46 or 339 277 88 44; www.rafting4810.com. 1-3hr.; from €36 per person.) For a complete list of recreational activities, including bike rental, ask for *Attrezzature Sportive e Ricreative della Valle d'Aosta* at any tourist office.

AOSTA   ☎0165

Aosta teeters between Italian and French *Valdostana* border culture. Though street signs alternate between French and Italian (with the town hall known as L'hôtel du Ville), and most residents are bilingual, the favored language is Italian, and pizza and gelato shops abound. For many years Aosta was Rome's focus on the Italian frontier and a launching point for military expeditions. To this day, it serves as a geographic and financial nexus. Inside the crumbling walls that once defended Rome's Alpine outpost, boutiques and gourmet food shops densely pack the *centro storico;* outside, a commercial and industrial minefield stretches across the valley. Valley-bound Aosta's prices soar like the nearby peaks of Monte Emilius (3559m) and Becca di Nona (3142m), as well as the distant glacial expanses of Grand Combin (4314m) and Becca du Lac (3396m). Though the town has dazzling views, they're nothing compared to those farther up the valley. Aosta makes a good starting point for exploring the Italian Alps, but be aware that day-trips to the surrounding valleys often require tricky train and bus connections—to return before nightfall, plan carefully.

▐ TRANSPORTATION

Trains: The station is in the pink building at P. Manzetti. Ticket window open daily 4:50-11:25am and 1:45-8:30pm. To: **Chivasso** (1½hr., every hr. 6:28am-8:38pm, €4.65) via **Châtillon** (15min., every hr. 6:12am-9:50pm, €1.80); **Milan** Centrale (4hr., 12 per day 6:12am-8:40pm, €10.10); **Pont St. Martin** (50min., every hr. 6:12am-9:50pm, €3.10); **Turin** Pta. Nuova (2hr., every hr. 6:28am-8:38pm, €6.80); **Verrès** (30min., every hr. 6:28am-9:50pm, €2.45).

Buses: SAVDA (☎0165 26 20 27), on V. Carrel off P. Manzetti, to the right exiting the train station. Office open 4:30am-1:30am. To: **Courmayeur** (1hr., every hr. 6:45am-9:45pm, €2.70); **Great St. Bernard Pass** (2hr., 9:40am and 2:25pm, €2.70). **SVAP** serves closer towns. To: **Cogne** (1hr., 7 per day 8:05am-7:45pm, €2.10); **Fenis** (1hr., 10 per day 8:05am-6:50pm, €1.60). Buses to **Breuil-Cervinia** (2hr., 7 per day 6:10am-7:25pm, €3.10) and **Valtournenche** leave from the Châtillon train station.

Taxis: ☎0165 26 20 10. In P. Manzetti. ☎0165 356 56 or 318 31. In P. Narbonne.

Car Rental: Europcar, P. Manzetti, 3 (☎0165 414 32), to the left of the train station. 18+. Economy car €70 per day (unlimited mileage). Open M-F 8:30am-12:30pm and 3-7pm, Sa 8:30am-12:30am. AmEx/MC/V.

▐✷▐ ORIENTATION AND PRACTICAL INFORMATION

Trains stop at **Piazza Manzetti.** From there, take **Avenue du Conseil des Commis** until it ends in the enormous **Piazza Chanoux,** Aosta's center. The main street runs east-west through P. Chanoux and changes its name several times. From Av. du Conseil des Commis, **Via J. B. de Tillier,** which then becomes **Via Aubert,** is to the left; to the right **Via Porta Praetoria** leads to the historic gate and becomes **Via Sant'Anselmo.**

Tourist Office: P. Chanoux, 2 (☎0165 23 66 27; www.regione.vda.it/turismo), down Av. du Conseil des Commis from train station. Ask for Aosta Monument Guide (town map) and the *Annuario Alberghi,* a regional hotel directory. English, German, and French spoken. Free **Internet.** Open July-Aug. daily 9am-1pm and 2-8pm; Sept.-June M-Sa 9am-1pm and 3-8pm, Su 9am-1pm.

Alpine Information: Club Alpino Italiano, C. Battaglione, 81 (☎0165 401 94), off P. della Repubblica. Open Tu 7-8:30pm, F 8-10pm. Or try **Società Guide,** V. Monte Emilius, 13 (☎0165 444 48; www.guidealpine.it). For **weather conditions,** call ☎0165 441 13 or ask at the tourist office.

Currency Exchange: Monte dei Paschi di Siena, P. Chanoux, 51 (☎0165 27 68 88). **ATM** outside. Open M-F 8:30am-1:30pm and 2:40-4:10pm.

Outdoor Gear and Apparel: Meinardi Sport, V. Aubert, 27 (☎0165 414 32). A moderately priced, extensive selection of gear and clothing, including **maps** and guides to the Italian Alps. Open daily 9am-12:30pm and 3-7:30pm.

Ski rental is available in the numerous hangars by the chairlift behind the station.

Laundromat: Onda Blu, V. Chambéry, 60. Wash 6½kg load €3.50, dry €3.50. Open daily 8am-10pm.

Work Opportunity: Old Distillery Pub hires workers seasonally.

Police, C. Battaglione Aosta, 169 (☎113). **Ambulance** (☎118).

Pharmacy: Farmacia Chenal, V. Croix-de-Ville, 1 (☎0165 26 21 33), at V. Aubert. Open M-Tu, Th-F, and Sa 9am-12:30pm and 3-7:30pm. Posts late-night rotation.

Aosta

ACCOMMODATIONS
B & B Nabuisson, 3
Camping Milleluci, 9
Hotel Roma, 7
Hotel Turin, 8

FOOD
La Cave de Tillier, 2
Grotta Azzurra, 1
Old Distillery Pub, 6
Trattoria Praetoria, 4
Vecchia Aosta, 5

Buther

TO ROPPOZ (1km)
Arco d'Augusto
PIAZZA ARCO D'AUGUSTO
TO (1km)
Viale Garibaldi
Via Sant'Anselmo D'Augusto
Chiostro di Sant'Orso
Via Sant'Orso
Via Guido Rey
Via Sant'Orso
Giardino Per Ragazzi
Pres-Fosses
Via
PIAZZA CAVALIERI
Via Vevey
Via J.B. Cerlogne
Porta Praetoria
PIAZZA PLOUVES
STANDA
SAVDA
Via G. Mazzini
Stadio M. Puchoz
Via Torino
Via G. Carrel
PIAZZA PORTE PRAETORIA
PIAZZA PORTA PRAETORIA
Via porta praetoria
Roman Amphitheatre
Teatro Romano
Via Guido Rey
Via G. Frutaz
Via L. Cerise
PIAZZA NARBONNE
Europacar
PIAZZA MANZETTI
Via Xavier De Maistre
Avenue du Conseil des Commis
Via Mons. De Sales
Town Hall
PIAZZA EMILIO CHANOUX
Via Paravera
Via Piave
Via A. Cretier
Cablecar
PIAZZA SAN FRANCESCO
Via J.B. de Tillier
PIAZZA A DEFFEYES
Via IV Novembre
Via Losanna
Via della Pace
Criptoportico Forense
PIAZZA PAPA GIOVANNI XXIII
PIAZZA RONCAS
PIAZZA DES FRANCHISES
Via B. Festaz
Via della Pace
Corso XXVI Febbraio
Via L. Martinet
Via Croix-de-Ville
Via D'Avise
Via Vaudan
Via Aubert
Via Bonifacio
Viale Partigiani
Via G. Carducci
Viale G. Carducci
Corso St. Martin de Orleans
Via Abbé Gorret
Via Tourneuve
PIAZZA DELLA REPUBBLICA
Via Monte Solarolo
Via Monte Pasidio
Via Monte Vodice
C. Battaglione Aosta
Via Battisti
Via Girgio Elter
Via Lys
Laundry
Via M. G. Cavagnet
Via G. Pollio Salimbeni
Bataillon Aoste
Via Liconi
Via Chambéry
Ospedale Regionale

200 yards
200 meters

Hospital: V. Ginevra, 3 (☎ 0165 30 41).

Internet Access: Eye of Ra, P. Cavalieri, next door to Hotel Turin. Internet from €1 per hr. alongside computer game fanatics. Open M and W 2pm-midnight, Tu 7am-7:30pm, Th-F 2pm-2am, Sa 7am-2pm. Free 15min. Internet in Tourist Office.

Post Office: P. Narbonne, 1/A (☎ 0165 441 38), in the huge semi-circular building. Open M-F 8:15am-6pm, Sa 8:15am-1pm. *Fermoposta* is across town on V. Cesare Battisti, 10. Open M-F 8:15am-6pm, Sa 8:15am-1pm. **Postal Code: 11100.**

■ ⬛ ACCOMMODATIONS AND CAMPING

Bed & Breakfast Nabuisson, V. Aubert, 50 (☎ 0165 36 30 06 or 339 609 03 32; www.bedbreakfastaosta.it). Exiting the station, walk down V. Conseil des Commis until reaching P. Chanoux. Turn left down V. De Tiller, which turns into V. Aubert. The yellow building is through the iron gate on the right. Spacious, rustic themed rooms, all with TV and modern bath, off a small courtyard. Breakfast €5. Reserve ahead. Open June-Oct. and Dec.-Apr. Doubles €45-55. Extra beds €5-10. Cash only. ❸

Hotel Turin, V. Torino, 14 (☎ 0165 445 93; www.hotelturin.it). Exiting the train station, turn right on V. Giorgio, left on V. Vevey, then right on V. Torino. Ultra-modern rooms with bath, TV, and phone. Free Internet. Breakfast €6. Singles €40; doubles €65. MC/V. ❸

Hotel Roma, V. Torino, 7 (☎ 0165 410 00; hroma@libero.it), close to the station and the center of town, around the corner from the Hotel Turin (see above). All rooms with bath and TV. Breakfast €6. Parking €6. Singles €40-52; doubles €65-77. MC/V. ❹

Camping Milleluci, V. Porossan, 15 (☎ 0165 23 52 78; www.hotelmilleluci.com), a 1km hike from station. Get a map from the tourist office in P. Chanoux, then head down V. Praetoria and V. S. Anselmo and cross the river. Turn left on V. Pasquettaz, which then forks left, changing into V. Porossan. Take it to V. des Seigneurs de Quart. Each plot has a cabin connected to a trailer. Quiet, hillside location with panoramic views. Very large but very full in high season. (June-Sept.) Parking €11. Laundry €5. Reception in Hotel Milleluci. Adults €6-8; ages 1-10 €4-5. Showers €0.50. AmEx/MC/V. ❶

⬛ ⬛ FOOD AND NIGHTLIFE

There's nary a drop of extra-virgin olive oil, nor a shred of truffle in Aosta, where one of the most revered items in the kitchen is lard. The colder climate and predominantly agricultural lifestyle have generated a wholesome and hearty cuisine rich in fat. Other delicacies include *fonduta*, a cheesy sauce made from the local fontina cheese, poured over everything in great quantities. Pick up a can at **STANDA**, on V. Festaz, 10. (☎ 0165 357 57. Open M-Sa 8am-8pm.) Aosta's weekly **open-air market** is held Tuesday in P. Cavalieri di Vittorio Veneto.

Trattoria Praetoria, V. S. Anselmo, 9 (☎ 0165 443 56), past Pta. Praetoria. After a day in the mountains, you won't find better Aostan food. With *fonduta waldstana* (cheese fondue with toast; €9), meaty *salsiccette in umido* (sausages braised in tomato sauce; €6.50) over *polenta* and tripe (€6.50), there's a local delicacy to fit any taste. *Primi* €6-7.50, *secondi* €6.50-9. Cover €1.50. Open M-Tu and F-Su 12:15-2:30pm and 7:15-9:30pm, W 12:15-2:30pm. MC/V. ❷

Vecchia Aosta, P. Pta. Praetoria, 4 (☎ 0165 36 11 86). The best location in town inside of the Pta. Praetoria. The *mocetta ed il lardo di Arnad con castagne al miele* (basically, meat, lard, and chestnuts; €7.50) is particularly good. If the idea of eating large chunks of fat turns you vegetarian, try *la crepe di asparaghi con vellutata di fonduta* (asparagus crepe with melted cheese, €7.50) instead. *Primi* €7.50-9.50, *secondi* €12-19. Open in summer daily, in winter M-Tu and Th-Su 12:30-2:30pm and 7:30-10pm. AmEx/MC/V. ❸

La Cave de Tillier, V. de Tillier, 40 (☎0165 23 01 33). Just off P. Chanoux, the restaurant is set off the street in an alleyway to the right. Cobblestone walls, a quiet locale, and a plate full of *gnocchi* (€6) make for great eating. *Primi* €6-10.50, *secondi* €9.50-13. Open in summer daily noon-2:30pm and 7-10:30pm. Closed M in winter. MC/V. ❸

Grotta Azzurra, V. Croix-de-Ville (V. Croce-di-città), 97 (☎0165 26 24 74). Pizza from €5. *Primi* €4-9, *secondi* €5-13. Cover €1. Open M-Tu and Th-Su 12:15-2:15pm and 7:15-10:15pm; closed 2nd and 3rd week of July. AmEx/MC/V. ❷

Old Distillery Pub, V. Pres Fosses, 7 (☎0165 23 95 11). From Pta. Praetoria, walk down V. S. Anselmo and turn right through a small archway on the winding V. Pres Fosses. The pub is on the left. Locals pack this Irish pub most nights after 10pm. Occasional live music. Pint of Guinness €5.50. Open daily 6pm-2am. ❶

SIGHTS

Vestiges of the Roman Empire are thoroughly integrated with modern Aosta; a partially intact 2000-year-old wall rings the city center, with streets running neatly through the gaps, but the marble fluted columns that were stylish in the Augustan period are absent, as Aosta's ruins distinguish themselves as an example of a more practical architecture in a decadent age. The **Porta Praetoria,** now on the street bearing its name, once stood at the edge of the walled city and served as a guard house. To its left lie the sprawling remains of the massive **Teatro Romano.** Visits are possible only as a part of a **free walking tour** of the city; the tour covers most other historical sights as well. (☎333 808 80 36. July-Sept. M-Sa 10am from the Arco d'Augusto. In Italian, French, and rarely English. Free, but reservation required.) Through Pta. Praetoria, V. S. Anselmo leads to the **Arco d'Augusto.** The monument dates from Roman times and has sported its Christian cross since the Middle Ages to ward off bad luck. The ruins of the ancient forum, or **Criptoportico Forense,** are off P. Papa Giovanni XXIII. (Open M and W-Su 9am-6pm. Free.) The **Fiera di Sant'Orso,** the region's most famous crafts fair, takes place January 30-31 and the Sunday before *Ferragosto* (Aug. 15). The traditional fair dates to the 9th century and is known for handicrafts. (From Pta. Praetoria, take V. S. Anselmo and turn left on V. S. Orso. Open 7am-7pm. Free.)

HIKING AND SKIING

TIP Remember to bring your passport for excursions into Switzerland.

VALLE DEL GRAN SAN BERNARDO. A valley with more medieval towers than tourists, **Valle del Gran San Bernardo** links Aosta to Switzerland via the **Great St. Bernard Pass.** Motor-tourists and intrepid cyclists tackle this winding mountain road in summer. Come snow, they retreat to a more highly trafficked 5854m mountain tunnel. Tourists follow the footsteps of Hannibal and his elephants, as well as Napoleon, who trekked through the pass with 40,000 soldiers in 1800. This region boasts the **Hospice of St. Bernard,** dating from 1505 and home to the patron saint of pups. The legendary life-saver was stuffed for posterity and is conveniently displayed for people driving through the pass. The hospice, just across the Swiss border, is just a tail-wag away from the **dog museum** (www.swiss-st-bernard-dog.ch), where St. Bernards get trained. A smaller branch of the valley leads to the communes of **Ollomont** and **Oyace,** where hiking trails, valleys, and pine forests await exploration. Easier hiking is above the hospice on a trail that skirts the ridge. *(For information call the Aosta tourist office or the ski-lift office ☎0165 78 00 46 at St. Rhémy.)*

THE MATTERHORN AND BREUIL-CERVINIA. The highest mountain in Switzerland, the **Matterhorn (Il Cervino)** looms majestically over the town of Breuil-Cervinia in Valtournenche. The buildings of **Breuil-Cervinia** look virtually identical; some serve expensive food, others offer expensive accommodations, and the rest rent expensive sports equipment. Despite the cost, many fresh-air fiends consider it a small price for the chance to climb up and glide down the glaciers of one of the world's most spectacular mountains. A cable car provides service to **Plateau Rosà,** where summer skiers tackle the slopes. (Round-trip €18; 1-day ski pass €35.) Hikers can forego lift tickets and attempt the 3hr. ascent to **Colle Superiore delle Cime Bianche** (2982m), with tremendous views of Val d'Ayas to the east and the Cervino glacier to the west. A shorter trek (1½hr.) on the same trail leads to **Lake Goillet.** The tourist office hands out a good **hiking map.** The **Società Guide** (☎0166 94 81 69; www.swiss-st-bernard-dog.ch), across from the tourist office, arranges group outings. **Don't forget your passport;** a number of trails cross into Zermatt, Switzerland.

Buses run to **Breuil-Cervinia** (6 per day 6:10am-7:25pm; €2.30) from **Châtillon** on the Aosta-Turin train line. Direct buses also arrive daily from P. Castello in **Milan** (5hr.). Buses run to **Turin** (4hr.; M-Sa 6:45am, 1:25, 5pm, Su 6pm; €7.80). The English-speaking staff of the **Tourist Info Center,** V. Carrel, 29, provides information on *Settimana Bianca* (White Week) Packages and *Settimane Estive,* the summer equivalent. (☎0166 94 91 36; www.cervinia.it. Open daily in high season 9am-6pm, low season 9:30am-12:30pm and 2:30-5:30pm.) Students should ask about the University Card, which brings discounts of 10-20% on passes.

VAL D'AYAS. Budget-minded sports enthusiasts should consider visiting the gently sloping Val d'Ayas. Under the shadow of the glaciated Monte Rosa, this wide valley offers the same activities as its flashy neighbors—skiing, hiking, and rafting. Try the town of **Champoluc** for some excellent hiking, including the 45min. hike up **trail 14** to the tiny hamlet of **Mascognoz,** a cluster of wood chalets home to a farming population of 10. **Trains** run from Aosta to **Verrès** (30min., every hr. 6:28am-9:50pm, €2.45). **Buses** run from the train station at Verrès to **Champoluc** (1hr., 9 per day 7:10am-9:22pm, €2.10). The **tourist office** in **Brusson** (☎0125 30 02 40) has branches in **Champoluc,** V. Varase, 16 (☎0125 30 71 13), and **Antagnod** (☎0125 30 63 35). They speak English and have **trail maps** and hotel information. (Branches open daily 9am-12:30pm and 3-6pm.)

VAL DI COGNE. When Cogne's mines failed in the 1970s, the townspeople resorted to a more genteel pursuit—parting cross-country skiers from their cash. Cogne is one of the world's premier places to ice climb (inquire at Aosta's guide office). A cable car transports alpine addicts to the modest downhill skiing facilities. In summer the pastoral community serves as the gateway to the unspoiled expanse of Italy's largest nature reserve, **Gran Paradiso National Park.** In addition to an endless network of trails, waterfalls, and a population of 5000 ibex, the park has the highest glacier (4061m) fully contained within Italian borders, the Gran Paradiso. Cogne and its dry, rocky valley dotted with pine trees, is a scenic bus ride from Aosta (1hr., 7 per day 8:05am-7:45pm, €2.10). The bus stops in front of the **AIAT Tourist Office,** P. Chanoux, 36, which distributes regional maps and helps find accommodations. (☎0165 740 40 or 740 56. Open in summer daily 9am-12:30pm and 3-6pm; in winter M-Sa 9am-12:30pm and 2:30-5:30pm, Su 9am-12:30pm.)

VALNONTEY. This hamlet affords an unobstructed view of the glacier. Lodged in a narrow valley in the midst of a national park, it's a 45min. walk along the river from Cogne on **trail 25,** which leaves from the riverside tourist office. From June through August buses run from Cogne to **Valnontey** (every 30min. 7:30am-8pm, €1.10; buy tickets onboard), notable for its handy alimentari, two-star hotels, and access to trails. In summer campers can choose between the rolling hills of **Camping Gran Paradiso ❶** (☎0165 74 92 04; self-service laundromat; €4 per person, ages 7-16 €3, under 6 free; €5 for tent plus car, caravans €6; electricity €1) and **Lo Stambecco ❶** (☎0165 741 52; www.campinglostambecco.com; tent and electricity €3-4; free showers; €5 per person).

COURMAYEUR   ☎0165

Italy's oldest Alpine resort town lures tourists to the spectacular shadows of Europe's highest peak. Monte Bianco, with its jagged ridges and permanent snow fields, is perfect for hiking and skiing. Unfortunately for budget travelers who seek Alpine serenity, prices are high, rooms are booked year-round, and streets are saturated with glitzy boutiques and obtrusive tour buses. Quiet falls in May and June, when shopkeepers go on vacation.

⊟❼ TRANSPORTATION AND PRACTICAL INFORMATION. A single large complex in **Piazza Monte Bianco** houses most travel services including the **bus station,** which has frequent service to larger towns. (☎0165 84 20 31. Open daily July-Aug. 8am-7:30pm; otherwise, 8:45am-12:30pm and 3-6:30pm. Tickets also available onboard.) Buses run to Aosta (1hr., every hr. 5:45am-8:30pm, €2.60) and Turin (3hr., 6:45 and 10am, €8.20). To the right of the bus station, the **AIAT Tourist Office** offers **maps** and has staff that speaks English, German, and French. (☎0165 84 20 60. Open M-Sa 9am-12:30pm and 3-6:30pm, Su 9:30am-12:30pm and 3-6pm.) A 24hr. accommodations board, 10m away from the office, can also help in finding a room. The bus ticket office has a **currency exchange,** open the same hours as the ticket desk. **Banks,** most with **24hr. ATM,** are on V. M. Bianco and V. Circonvallazione. **Taxis** (☎0165 84 29 60, night 84 23 33) are available 24hr. at P. M. Bianco. In case of **emergency,** call ☎113, or an **ambulance,** Str. delle Volpi, 3 (☎118). A **pharmacy,** Farmacie di Torino, V. Circonvallazione, 69, posts a list of after hours pharmacies; often the one on duty is in a nearby village. (For emergency service call ☎339 670 98 05. Open M-F 9am-12:30pm and 3-7:30pm, Sa 9am-12:30pm and 3:30-7:30pm.) The **post office** is in P. M. Bianco behind the main complex. (☎0165 84 20 42. Open M-Sa 8am-1:30pm.) **Postal Code:** 11013.

❼❸ ACCOMMODATIONS AND FOOD. Winter and summer accommodations can't be booked far enough ahead. Finding rooms during low season is still difficult, as many establishments are closed. The trouble is worth it, however, as Courmayeur is far closer to mountain paths than Aosta. **Pensione Venezia ❸** is at V. delle Villete, 2. From P. Monte Bianco, head uphill, then turn left on V. Circonvallazione, to reach this basic, clean, convenient *pensione* with TV and dining rooms. (☎/fax 0165 84 24 61. Breakfast included. Singles €30; doubles €43.) **Pensione Bron ❷,** is on Str. del Villair, in the hamlet of Villair Inferiore, a 15min. climb from P. A. Henry in Courmayeur. This small, quiet mountain lodge has simple rooms but unbeatable prices. (☎0165 84 23 90. €25 per person; half pension €38 per person.)

Picnicking is the best way to appreciate that Alpine freshness. At **Pastificio Gabriella ❶,** Passaggio dell'Angelo, 2, toward the end of V. Roma, excellent cold cuts, pasta salads, and crepes reward people forming a line out the door. (☎0165 84 33 59. Open M-Tu and Th-Su 8am-1pm and 4-7:30pm; closed 2 weeks in June. MC/V.) **Il Fornaio ❶,** V. Monte Bianco, 17, serves delicious breads and pastries. Particularly good are the local *tegole* (€20 per kg), round cookies made from egg whites. (☎0165 84 24 54. Open M-Tu, Th-F, and Su 8am-noon and 4-7pm, Sa 8am-12:30pm.) On Wednesdays, the **market** is 1km away in Dolonne. (Open 8:30am-2pm.) Courmayeur has some reasonable restaurants, offering hearty portions that fill the most cavernous of stomachs. Most close for the summer, but **La Terraza ❸,** V. Circonvallazione, 73, is open year-round. Just uphill from P. Monte Bianco, this restaurant specializes in *Valdostano* cuisine, serving fondue and lard lightly garnished with warm chestnuts and honey (€14). Ask about the *menù turistico*, with three large courses for €12. (☎0165 84 33 30. Pizza €6.50-11. *Primi* €13-16, *secondi* from €15-25. Cover €2. Open daily noon-2:15pm and from 7pm.) To escape the tourist crush, head to **La Boite ❹**, S. Margherita, 14, to the right facing uphill from P. Monte Bianco. This old stone farmhouse does everything from crouton fondue (€20) to pizza (☎0165 84 67 94. €5.50-12. *Primi* €9-12, *secondi* €14-22. Open daily 11:45am-3pm and 6:45pm-1am. AmEx/MC/V.)

⬛⬛ OUTDOOR ACTIVITIES AND SKIING. Ski passes are priced on a complex rotating schedule, so check at the tourist office for details. High season runs October 26 to December 20, January 7 to 24, and March 30 until the snow melts. A six-day pass in the high season runs €175 (under 12 or over 65 €131); in low season €140-158 (reduced €105-118). The brochures *White Weeks*, *Aosta Valley* (English), *Settimane Bianche*, and *Courmayeur* list rental and pass prices.

Nineteenth-century English gentlemen brushed off the **Giro del Monte Bianco** as a two- or three-day climbing excursion for "less adventurous travelers." These days, guides suggest that travelers take at least a week to complete the trip. The trail leads around Monte Bianco, past Chamonix and Courmayeur, and then into Switzerland. *Rifugi* and hostel dormitories are 5-6hr. apart along the route (€30 per person with hot dinner and breakfast). One section of the trail makes an ideal daytrip, and two can fill a weekend. **This is difficult mountaineering; be sure you are equipped and trained.** Inquire at the guide office (see below) for more information.

Courmayeur's two smaller valleys, Val Veny and Val Ferret, fork the base of Monte Bianco and are filled with day-long hikes. **SAVDA buses** serve both valleys; inquire at the tourist office for more info, including the brochure *Seven Itineraries around Mont Blanc, Val Veny, and Val Ferret*. A **map** is crucial; buy one at the **Libreria La Buona Stampa,** V. Roma, 4. (☎0165 84 67 71. Open daily in summer 9am-1pm and 3:30-7:30pm, in winter 9am-7pm.) An excellent place to ask questions or get suggestions for itineraries is **Ufficio delle Guide,** P. Abbe Henri, 2, to the left behind the church. (☎0165 84 20 64. Open daily in summer 9am-12:30pm and 3-7:30pm, in winter Tu-Su 9am-7pm.) Aside from free advice to hikers of all abilities, the office finds guides for all the major treks and climbs. They arrange famous ascents like climbing the 300m face of Dente del Gigante (€300 for 1-2 people) or attaining the summit of Monte Bianco itself (2 days; €700 for 1-2 people).

⬛Funivie Monte Bianco cable cars head first to the **Punta Helbronner** (3462m) and then across the border **Chamonix.** The top affords unparalleled views of Monte Bianco's expansive, windswept ice sheet, as well as the spectacular **Matterhorn, Monte Rosa,** and **Gran Paradiso.** *Funivie* depart from La Palud (10min. bus ride from Courmayeur, 6:20am-8:50pm, €0.90), near the Val Ferret. (☎0165 899 25 or 891 96; www.montebianco.com. Round-trip from La Palud to Punta Helbronner €34; Punta Helbronner to Chamonix €39. Open June-Sept. 8:30am-5:20pm.)

Don't be left out...

Get your TRAVEL on.

The International Student Identity Card

$22 is ALL it takes to SAVE $100's at home and abroad!

save in the U.S. or worldwide

International *Student* Identity Card
Carte d'étudiant internationale / Carné internacional de estudiante
STUDENT
Studies at / Étudiant à / Est. de Enseñanza
University of California, Berkeley
Name / Nom / Nombre
Debbie Lee
Born / Né(e) le / Nacido/a el
04/29/1982
Validity / Validité / Validez
09/2004 - 12/31/2005
ISIC

/2 Price Admission • Entertainment
Reduced Rates • Communications
Accommodations • Internet

Student savings in more than
7,000 locations
across the US &
100 countries worldwide-
something no other card can offer!

visit **www.myISIC.com** to find out about discounts and the benefits of carrying your ISIC.

S I C

Call or visit ISIC online to purchase your card today:
www.myISIC.com   **(800) 474.8214**

eTravel

exploration
education
excitement
experience

Good to go.

CST #1017560-40

STA TRAVEL

www.statravel.com

(800) 351.3214

WE'VE BEEN PLANNING ONE TRIP FOR **25** YEARS. YOURS.

STUDENT TRAVEL & BEYOND

LIGURIA

Genoa, often obscured by shadow, fog, and steam from passing ships, anchors the luminescent Ligurian coastal strip, between the Riviera di Levante (rising sun) to the east and the Riviera di Ponente (setting sun) to the west. The Italian Riviera stretches 350km along the Mediterranean between France and Tuscany, forming the most famous and touristed area of the Italian coastline. Generally protected from the north's severe weather by the Alps, Liguria is home to terraced hillsides, the Apennine mountains, pebbly and sandy beaches, and grape and olive crops. In remote villages as in major cities, Ligurians are known for a certain cultural isolation: they claim Nordic, not Roman, ancestry and have their own vocabulary and accent, often incomprehensible to other Italians. Their distinctive character, however, doesn't make them any less Italian, nor did it stop them from playing a leading role in unifying the Italian peninsula. Giuseppe Mazzini, father of the Risorgimento, and Giuseppe Garibaldi, its most popular hero, were both Ligurians.

HIGHLIGHTS OF LIGURIA

EXPLORE the port that launched one of the world's greatest explorers with a visit to Christopher Columbus's Genoa. (p. 175.)

SWAP hiking for swimming and back again in the Cinque Terre. (p. 191.)

RETURN to the *Medioevo* with a stroll on Dolceacqua's cobblestone streets. (p. 217.)

GENOA (GENOVA)   ☎010

As any Ligurian will proclaim, *"Si deve conoscerla per amarla"*—you have to know Genoa to love her. A city of grit and grandeur, Genoa has little in common with neighboring towns and beaches along the Riviera; however, those who linger

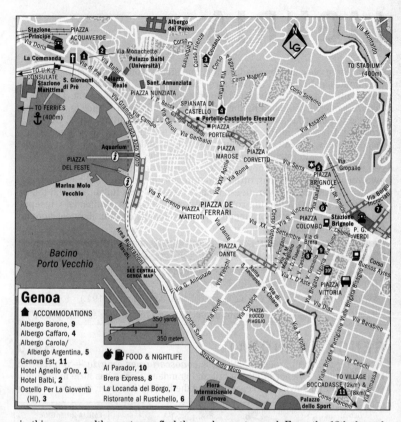

Genoa

🏠 ACCOMMODATIONS

Albergo Barone, **9**
Albergo Caffaro, **4**
Albergo Carola/
  Albergo Argentina, **5**
Genova Est, **11**
Hotel Agnello d'Oro, **1**
Hotel Balbi, **2**
Ostello Per La Gioventù
  (HI), **3**

🍴🍅 FOOD & NIGHTLIFE

Al Parador, **10**
Brera Express, **8**
La Locanda del Borgo, **7**
Ristorante al Rustichello, **6**

in this once-wealthy port may find themselves entranced. From the 12th through the 17th centuries, the city's sweeping boulevards and twisting alleys were home to the region's most noble families, who amassed great wealth in international trade and lavished their riches on extravagant palaces and churches; thereafter Genoa slipped from prosperity and began a period of decline. But in the past decade, Genoa has begun to rebound, first as host to the G8 summit, and then as the European Capital of Culture in 2004. Both events have spurred massive civic rejuvenation. This is the new city of Christopher Columbus, from which *Genovesi* once set out seeking the world; now the world, from immigrants to multinational corporations, has begun again to seek Genoa.

🚊 TRANSPORTATION

Flights: C. Colombo Internazionale (☎ 010 601 51), in Sesti Ponente, flies to European destinations. Volabus #100 runs to the airport from Stazione Brignole (every 30min. 5:30am-9:30pm, €2).

Trains: Stazione Principe in P. Acquaverde and **Stazione Brignole** in P. Verdi. Trains (5min., every 10min., €1) and buses #18, 19, 20, 33, and 37 (25min., €0.80) connect the 2 stations. Ticket valid 1½hr. **Luggage storage** available (see **Practical Infor-**

mation). Open daily 6am-midnight. Trains run from the stations to points along the Ligurian Riviera and major Italian cities including **Rome** (5-6hr., 12 per day, €32.50) and **Turin** (2hr., 19 per day, €8-12).

Ferries: At Ponte Assereto arm of the port. Walk 15min. from Stazione Marittima or take bus #20 from Stazione Principe. Purchase tickets at a travel agency or Stazione Marittima. **Arrive at Ponte Assereto at least 1hr. before departure.** Destinations include **Barcelona, Spain; Olbia; Palau; Palermo; Porto Torres;** and **Tunis, Tunisia. TRIS** (☎ 010 576 24 11) and **Tirrenia** (☎ 081 317 29 99; www.tirrenia.it) run ferries to **Sardinia** only. **Grandi Traghetti** (☎ 010 58 93 31; www.aferry.to) heads to Palermo.

Local Buses: AMT (☎ 010 558 24 14; www.amt.genova.it) buses leave from V. Gramsci, in front of the aquarium, or Stazione Brignole. 1-way tickets (€1) within the city valid for 1½hr. All-day tourist passes (€3); foreign passport necessary. Tickets and passes can also be used for funicular and elevator rides.

Taxis: ☎ 010 58 65 24. From P. Dante.

ORIENTATION AND PRACTICAL INFORMATION

Genoa has two train stations: **Stazione Principe,** in P. Acquaverde, and **Stazione Brignole,** in P. Verdi. From Stazione Principe take bus #18, 19, or 20, and from Stazione Brignole take bus #19 or 40 to **Piazza de Ferrari** in the center of town. If walking to P. de Ferrari from Stazione Principe, take **Via Balbi** to **Via Cairoli,** which becomes **Via Garibaldi,** and at **Piazza delle Fontane Marose** turn right on **Via XXV Aprile.** From Stazione Brignole, turn right out of the station to **Via Fiume,** and then right onto **Via XX Settembre,** ending in P. de Ferrari. Genoa's streets can stump even a native, so don't head out without a map.

> **A GENUIN' CONCERN.** The shadowy, labyrinthine streets of the *centro* are riddled with drug dealers and prostitutes at night, especially the areas around V. della Maddalena and V. Sottoripa. Avoid them when shops are closed and streets are empty, on Sundays, and in August. Also, avoid walking alone in the area around Stazione Principe, and avoid V. di Pre entirely.

Tourist Offices: APT, V. Roma, 11 (☎ 010 57 67 91; www.genovatouristboard.net). **Branch** (☎ 010 24 87 11) in Palazzina S. Maria, near the aquarium on Porto Antico. Facing the water, walk 30m left from the aquarium toward the complex of buildings. Decent **maps.** Open daily 9am-1pm and 2-6pm. **Other branches:** Kiosks in Stazione Principe (☎ 010 246 26 33; iat.portoantico@apt.genova.it) and airport (☎ 010 601 52 47). Both open M-Sa 9:30am-1pm and 2:30-6pm. **Informagiovani,** P. Matteotti, 24r (☎ 010 557 39 52 or 557 39 65; www.informagiovani.comune.genova.it), in Palazzo Ducale. Youth center offers information on apartment rentals, jobs, concerts, and free **Internet** (reserve 1 week ahead or hope to fill a cancellation). Open July-Aug. M-Tu and Th-F 9am-12:30pm, W 9am-12:30pm and 3-6pm; Sept.-June M and W 2:30-6pm, Tu 10am-6pm, Th-F 10am-1:30pm.

Budget Travel: CTS, V. San Vincenzo, 117r (☎ 010 56 43 66 or 53 27 48), off V. XX Settembre near Ponte Monumentale. Walk up the flight of stairs on the shopping complex to the left. Student fares available. Open M-F 9am-1pm and 2:30-6pm. MC/V.

Consulates: UK, V. di Franca, 28 (☎ 010 41 68 28, fax 41 69 58). Take bus #30 from Stazione Principe to the last stop in the direction of Sampierdarena. Open M-Th 9:30am-12:30pm. US, V. Dante, 2, 3rd fl., #43 (☎ 010 58 44 92; in case of **emergency** call US Consulate General in Milan at 02 29 03 51). Open M-Th 11am-3pm.

Luggage Storage: ☎010 246 26 33, in Stazione Principe. €3 for first 12hr., €2 for each additional 12hr.

English-Language Bookstore: Mondadori, V. XX Settembre, 210r (☎010 58 57 43). Huge, with a full wall of classics and some bestsellers. Open M-F 9am-10pm, Sa 9am-11pm, Su 10:30am-1pm and 2-10pm.

Emergency: ☎113. **Ambulance** (☎118). **Police** (☎112).

Pharmacy: Pescetto, V. Balbi, 185r (☎010 26 16 09), near Stazione Principe. List of late-night pharmacies posted. Open 8:30am-12:30pm and 3:30pm-midnight. Across town, **Farmacia Ghersi,** C. Buenos Ayres, 18r, is open all day and night M-F except 12:30-3:30pm, and Sa-Su 7:30pm-12:30pm.

Hospital: Ospedale San Martino, V. Benedetto XV, 10 (☎010 55 51).

Internet: Internet Point Nondove, C. Buenos Ayres, 2 (☎010 58 99 90), at the intersection of V. Brigata Bisagno across from P. Vittoria. €2 per 15min. Open M-Sa 9:30am-7:30pm. MC/V. **In-Centro.it Agenzia Viaggi,** V. XX Settembre, 14, Internet €2 per 10min. Also a bookstore and travel agency. Open M-F 10am-1pm and 2:30-7:20pm, Sa 10am-1pm and 3:30-7:20pm. **Informagiovani** (see above).

Post Office: P. Dante, 4/6r (☎010 259 46 87), 2 blocks from P. de Ferrari. *Fermoposta.* Open M-Sa 8am-6:30pm. Branches open 8am-1:30pm. **Postal Code:** 16121.

▟ ▛ ACCOMMODATIONS AND CAMPING

Rooms are scarce in October, when the city hosts a wave of nautical conventions. Most budget lodgings in the *centro storico* and near the port rent rooms by the hour for reasons best left uninvestigated. Establishments are more refined around Stazione Brignole and P. Corvetto. The area around Genoa is teeming with campgrounds, but many are booked in summer.

▨ **Ostello Per La Gioventù (HI),** V. Costanzi, 120 (☎/fax 010 242 24 57; www.geocities.com/hostelge). From Stazione Principe, take bus #35, transfer to 40 at V. Napoli. From Stazione Brignole, take bus #40 up the hill. 213 beds with plenty of amenities: cafeteria, elevator, free lockers, wheelchair access, TV, and a view of the city. Multilingual staff. Breakfast, hot showers, and sheets included. Laundry €6.50 per 5kg. Reception 7-11am and 3:30pm-12:30am. Check-out 9am. Hostel closes after the last bus from the center arrives around 12:30am. HI card required (available at hostel). Dorms €14.50; family rooms €16-20 per person. ❶

Albergo Carola, V. Gropallo, 4/12 (☎010 839 13 40). From Stazione Brignole, turn right on V. de Amicis and continue into P. Brignole. At Albergo Astoria, turn right on V. Gropallo and walk 15m. Look for big, wooden doors with little bronze lion heads on the left side of the street. Ring buzzer to enter. Comfortable rooms are all meticulously decorated, some overlooking a private garden. Singles €28; doubles €52, with bath €55; triples €60/€70; quads €70/€80. Cash only. ❸

Albergo Argentina, V. Gropallo, 4 (☎/fax 010 839 37 22), near Stazione Brignole, 2 flights down from the Carola (see above). 9 large, clean, tastefully furnished rooms. Kind management speaks limited English. Singles €28; doubles €47, with bath €55; triples €70; quads €77. Cash only. ❸

Hotel Balbi, V. Balbi, 21/3 (☎/fax 010 25 23 62), close to Stazione Principe. Quiet rooms sport wooden floors and painted ceilings. Comfortable common area with Internet point (€4 per hr.). Breakfast €4. Singles €33, with bath €48; doubles €55/€70; triples €75/€85. AmEx/MC/V. ❸

LIGURIA

Locanda di Palazzo Cicala, P. San Lorenzo, 16 (☎010 251 88 24 or 348 584 84 81; www.palazzocicala.it), on a street off P. Lorenzo, facing the duomo. All 10 centrally located rooms are gigantic and the height of luxury, with A/C, bath, phone, and computer with Internet. Singles €80-110; doubles from €150. AmEx/MC/V. ❺

Albergo Caffaro, V. Caffaro, 3 (☎/fax 010 247 23 62; www.albergocaffaro.it), off P. Portello, between train stations. Take bus #18 from Stazione Principe to P. Portello. 8 sunny rooms occupy the top floor of a palazzo. All rooms with TV; fans available. Singles €30, with bath €40; doubles €45/€55; triples €75; quads €85. AmEx/MC/V. ❸

Albergo Barone, V. XX Settembre, 2/23 (☎/fax 010 58 75 78). From Stazione Brignole, turn left and walk down V. Fiume to V. XX Settembre. 12 rooms have TV and windows overlooking Genoa's lively shopping district. Reception 8:30am-midnight. Reserve ahead (credit card required). Singles €33, with shower €40; doubles €44/€50; triples with shower €54-63, with full bath €69; quads €70-80. AmEx/MC/V. Cash preferred. ❸

Hotel Agnello d'Oro, V. Monachette, 6 (☎010 246 20 84; www.hotelagnellodoro.it), off V. Balbi. 20 trim rooms with bath, TV, and access to rooftop patio with a stunning view. Some rooms have terrace and A/C (€10 extra). Fans available. Buffet breakfast included. Singles and €50-95; doubles €70-120; triples €95. AmEx/MC/V. ❺

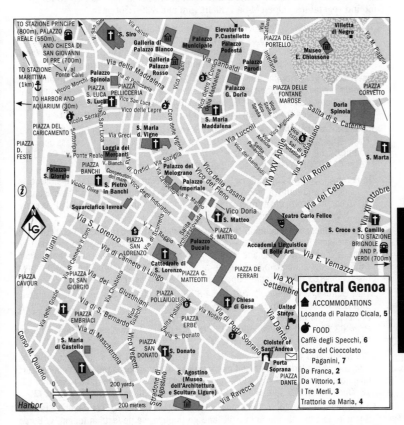

Genova Est (☎010 347 20 53), on V. Marcon, Loc. Cassa. Take the train from Stazione Brignole to the suburb of Bogliasco (10min., 6 per day, €1); from here, take the free van (5min., every 2hr. 8am-6pm) to the campsite. Shaded sites on a terraced hill overlooking the sea. Laundry €3.50 per load. €5.45 per person, €9.60 per large tent; 2-person bungalows €34. Electricity €1.80 per day. ❶

🍴 FOOD

In culinary terms, a dish prepared *alla Genovese* is served with Genoa's pride and joy—pesto, a green sauce made from ground basil, pine nuts, olive oil, garlic, and Parmesan cheese. The *Genovesi* put it on just about everything, so don't be afraid to experiment. Other delectables include *farinata* (a fried pancake of chick-pea flour), focaccia filled with cheese or topped with olives or onions, and *pansotti* (ravioli stuffed with spinach and ricotta, served in a creamy walnut sauce). To sample a fresh slice of Genoa's world-famous salami, stop by a *macelleria* like **Salvi Salumeria**, P. della Raibetta, 7, near the Porto Antico. In addition to salami, they also make *pesto di Genova* with the best Ligurian basil (€30.99 per kg). While near the port, don't forget to sample the seafood, too. The **Mercato Orientale,** off V. XX Settembre south of the Ponte Monumentale, is the place to go for fresh fruit and vegetables. (Open M-Sa 7:30am-1pm and 3:30-7:30pm.)

Trattoria da Maria, V. Testadoro, 14r (☎010 58 10 80), off V. XXV Aprile near P. delle Fontane Marose. A prototypical Italian restaurant. The owner is a dynamo and conducts a jovial staff. The menu changes daily, but the dishes are always delicious. 3-course *menù* €10. Open M noon-2:30pm, Tu-F and Su noon-2:30pm and 7-9:30pm. Cash only. ❷

Da Vittorio, V. Sottoripa, 59r (☎010 247 29 27). This waterfront institution draws throngs nightly. The seafood is reliably excellent. Catch of the day displayed in the window. Lobster €27. *Primi* €8-16, *secondi* €8-27. Cover €2.50. Reservation recommended. Open daily noon-4pm and 7-11:30pm. Closed July Tu-W. MC/V. ❹

Ristorante al Rustichello, V. S. Vicenzo, 59r (☎010 58 85 56), near Stazione Brignole. For the budget traveler fed up with plastic tables and paper tablecloths: dress up a little and enjoy the romantic atmosphere. Pizza €4.50-6. *Primi* €5.50-7, *secondi* €4.50-10. Cover €1.60. Open daily noon-2:30pm and 6:30pm-midnight. MC/V. ❷

Da Franca, Vico delle Lepre, 8r (☎010 247 44 73). From P. delle Fontane Marose, take V. Garibaldi and turn left onto Vico Angeli. Distinctive trattoria with food as elegant as the decor, well worth the extra expense. The shrimp coated with almonds (€11) is excellent. *Primi* €11-17, *secondi* €12-16. AmEx/MC/V. ❹

Casa del Cioccolato Paganini, V. di Porta Soprana, 45 (☎010 951 36 62). Like the famed violin of its namesake, the chocolate here might just draw tears of passion. *The* place to indulge in homemade sweets, from Niccolo Paganini chocolate (boxes from €6.50) to signature *sciroppo di rose,* a sublime liquid made from sugar, water, and rose petals (€1.80 per bottle). Open daily 2:30-8pm. Cash only. ❶

Brera Express, V. di Brera, 11r (☎010 54 32 80), just off V. XX Settembre near Stazione Brignole. The *menù* at this cafeteria-style joint (*primo, secondo,* fruit, and drink; €9) is a cheap, fresh bargain compared to surrounding restaurants. Fruit salad for only €1. *Primi* €3.10-3.40, *secondi* around €5. Open daily 11:45am-3pm and 7pm-midnight. Self-service closes 10pm. Cash only. ❷

I Tre Merli, Vico della Maddalena, 26r (☎010 247 40 95), on a narrow street off V. Garibaldi. A hidden gem with soft music and a mellow atmosphere. Wine connoisseurs take note—the list is 16 pages long and very well assembled. *Primi* €8-11, *secondi* €7-18. Open M-F 12:30-3pm and 7:30pm-midnight, Sa 7:30pm-1am. AmEx/MC/V. ❹

La Locanda del Borgo, V. Borgo Incrociati, 47r (☎010 81 06 31), behind Stazione Brignole. Exit the station, turn right, and go through the pedestrian tunnel. V. Borgo Incrociati is straight ahead. A surprisingly good value, serving delicious *Genovesi* favorites like *pansotti* in a friendly setting. *Primi* €6, *secondi* €13. Lunch *menù* €8; 3-course dinner *menù* €20. Open M-Tu and Th-Su noon-2pm and 7:30-10:30pm. AmEx/MC/V. ❸

Caffè degli Specchi, Salita Pollaiuoli, 43r (☎010 246 81 93), on the left, down Salita Pollaioli from P. Matteotti. *Specchio* means mirror, and narcissists will surely get a kick out of this sophisticated, mirror-lined cafe. The crowds enjoy *bicchierini* (glasses of wine; €3.60) or cocktails (€4.65-5.15) at attractive outdoor seating. Lunch plates of mixed cheeses, meats, and vegetables €8-11. Open daily 8am-8:30pm. MC/V. ❶

 # SIGHTS

> **TIP**
>
> **ART STARVED?** If you plan on visiting many museums, invest in a museum pass. The €6.50 pass covers Palazzo Reale and Palazzo Spinola, good for 24hr. Another 24hr. pass covers all the museums in Genoa (€9) and is available with bus fare (€10). To purchase, ask at the tourist office or visit participating museums. For those who like to take their time, there is also a three-day pass (€15).

FROM STAZIONE PRINCIPE TO THE CENTRO STORICO

Outside the winding alleys of the *centro storico*, Genoa boasts a multitude of palaces. These are best glimpsed along **Via Garibaldi,** which skirts the edge of the *centro storico*, and **Via Balbi,** which runs through the university quarter from Stazione Principe to P. Nunizia. Lined up along the streets, many have been converted to museums and showcase 16th- and 17th-century Flemish and Italian art.

▧ **PALAZZO REALE.** Built between 1600 and 1700, this palazzo was originally home to the Balbi family. It became the Royal Palace in the 18th century, and the structural setup installed for the Savoy rulers persists for the most part into the present. The Rococo throne room, covered in red velvet, remains untouched, along with the royal waiting room and sleeping quarters. The resplendent **Galleria degli Specchi** is modeled after the Hall of Mirrors at Versailles. In the Queen's bedroom, the **queen's clock** is really a *notturlabio*, a clock with stenciled numbers lit from behind by a candle so that it can be read in the dark. To see paintings by Tintoretto, van Dyck, and Bassano, ascend the red-carpeted stairs on the left after purchasing a ticket. *(V. Balbi, 10. 10min. walk west of V. Garibaldi. ☎010 635 08 31. Open Tu-W 9am-1:30pm Th-Su 9am-7pm. €4, ages 18-25 €2, under 18 or over 65 free.)*

▧ **PORTELLO-CASTELLETTO ELEVATOR.** Ride the elevator with locals who find it no more special than taking the bus (it's part of Genoa's public transportation system). The stomach-churning ride, which connects neighborhoods in the steep hills surrounding the city with the center of town, takes 30 seconds and pays off with one of the best panoramas of the city, particularly of the port. *(Through the tunnel entrance in P. Portello. Open daily 6:40am-midnight. 1-time use tickets can be purchased for €0.50 from machines at the entrance to the elevator, or from newspaper stands nearby.)*

VIA GARIBALDI. Also known as **Via Aurea** (Golden Street), V. Garibaldi remains the most impressive street in Genoa. In the 17th century, wealthy families lined it with elegant palaces. Glances inside the courtyards reveal fountains and leafy gardens. **Galleria Palazzo Rosso,** V. Garibaldi, 18 (☎010 247 63 51), built in the 16th century, earned its name when it was painted red in the 17th. Red carpets cover the floors of exhibit halls featuring frescoed ceilings and several hundred years' worth of Genovese ceramics. The second floor now holds several van Dyck portraits of nobility including the Genovese Spinola family, while the third floor contains his rendering of a red-eyed Christ. **Room 7**

includes several masterpieces by Bernardo Strozzi, including *Il Pifferaio* (Piper). Across the street, the **Galleria di Palazzo Bianco** (c. 1548, rebuilt 1712) exhibits one of the city's largest collections of Ligurian art as well as some Dutch and Flemish works. *(V. Garibaldi, 11. ☎ 010 247 63 77. Both galleries open Tu-Sa 9am-7pm, Su 10am-6pm. Ticket office, V. Garibaldi, 9, open daily 9am-8pm. 1 gallery €5, both €7, under 18 or over 60 free; Su free. AmEx/MC/V.)*

PALAZZO MUNICIPALE. Built between 1565 and 1579, the former home of the Savoia monarchy and the present day city hall showcases Nicolò Paganini's violin, **Il Canone,** made by the legendary Giuseppe Guarneri. This instrument is still played by the winner of **Premio Paganini,** an international violin competition held each Oct. 12. *(V. Garibaldi, 9. Open M-F 8:30am-6pm. Free.)*

CHIESA DI GESÙ. Also known as **Sant'Ambrogio e Andrea,** this former Jesuit church, completed in 1606, houses two Rubens canvases: *The Circumcision* (1605), over the altar, and *The Miracle of St. Ignatius* (1620), in the third alcove on the left. *(From P. de Ferrari, take V. Boetto to P. Matteotti. Open daily 7:15am-12:30pm and 4-7:30pm. Closed during Su masses: 7:15, 10, 11am, noon, and 6:30pm. Free.)*

PALAZZO DUCALE. The majestic centerpiece of the historic center, this palazzo was constructed in 1291 as the seat of Genoa's government. The facade, completed in 1783 by architect Sione Cantoni, is an example of Neoclassical architecture, while the interior is done up in Rococo decor. Visit the **museum** on the second floor for excellent rotating exhibits of international artwork. *(P. Matteotti, 9. ☎ 010 557 40 04; www.palazzoducale.genova.it. Museum open Tu-Su 9am-11pm. €9, students €8.)*

VILLETTA DI NEGRO. A stroll through this lovely park spread along a hill, past waterfalls, grottoes, and terraced gardens, is a calming respite from museums. *(From P. delle Fontane Marose, take Salita di S. Caterina to P. Corvetto. Open daily 8am-10pm.)*

PORTO ANTICO

Genoa's enormous port yields a mixture of fascinating history and commercial bustle. The port is sectioned into several wharves. The oldest, 15th-century **Molo Vecchio,** on the far left facing the water, is home to Genoa's giant former cotton warehouses. The central **Quartieri Antichi** (historical districts) still hold some 16th-century bondhouses. Nearby **Ponte Spinola** is the site of Genoa's famed aquarium.

■ **AQUARIUM.** Genoa might be beach-free, but that doesn't mean you can't go under the sea. Bask in frigid air-conditioning, gaze at sea-dwelling fauna cavorting in huge tanks (this aquarium has the largest volume of water of any in Europe), and check out the **Behind the Scenes** tour. Still not wet enough? Climb aboard the *Grande Nave Blu* (Big Blue Boat), a 126m floating barge filled with habitat simulations, from the forests of Madagascar to the reefs of the Carribean, and hummingbird forests. There's also an interactive tank where visitors can grab slithery sea rays and get splashed by slippery pre-teens, all for the noble cause of "engendering harmony with the sea." *(On Porto Antico, across from tourist office. ☎ 010 234 56 78; www.acquariodigenova.it. Open July-Aug. daily 9:30am-11pm, last entrance 9:30pm; Sept.-July M-W and F 9:30am-7:30pm, last entrance 5:30pm; Th 9:30am-10pm, last entrance 8:30pm; Sa-Su 8:30am-8:30pm, last entrance 6:30pm. €13; discounts for groups and children. Grande Nave Blu €2. Behind the Scenes tour departs Sa-Su noon, 2, 4, and 4:30pm. €8, children €5.)*

THE CENTRO STORICO

The eerie, beautiful, and sometimes dangerous *centro storico* is a mass of narrow, winding streets and cobbled alleyways bordered by the **port, Via Garibaldi,** and **Piazza de Ferrari.** It is home to some of Genoa's most memorable monuments: the duomo, **Palazzo Spinola,** and the medieval **Torre Embraici,** whose Guelph battlements jut out among the buildings to the left when facing the **Chiesa di Santa Maria di Castello.** Due to a high crime rate, the center is not safe on weekends, when stores are closed and streets are less bustling. Also avoid the area at night, when most of the people clear out and the city's seedy underbelly emerges.

■**CHIESA DI SANTA MARIA DI CASTELLO.** With foundations from 500 BC, this church is a labyrinth of chapels, courtyards, cloisters, and crucifixes. The chapels, added to the 15th-century structure in the 16th through 18th centuries, document the change in styles across that period. In the chapel left of the high altar looms the spooky **Crocifisso Miracoloso.** According to legend, Jesus moved his head to attest to the honesty of a damsel betrayed by her lover; Jesus's beard is still said to grow every time a crisis hits the city. Watch your step: the floor is paved with 18th-century tombs. To see the painting of **San Pietro Martire di Verona,** complete with a halo and a large cleaver conspicuously thrust into his cranium (the handiwork of incensed adversaries), go up the stairs to the right of the high altar, turn right, and right again. The painting is above the door. *(From P. G. Matteotti, head up V. S. Lorenzo toward the water and turn left on V. Chiabrera. A left on serpentine V. di Mascherona leads to the church in P. Caricamento. Open daily 9am-noon and 3-6pm. Closed Su during mass. Free.)*

DUOMO (SAN LORENZO). Built before the ninth century, the duomo was enlarged and reconstructed from the 12th through 16th centuries after religious authorities deemed it "imperfect and deformed." The result may have been more "perfect," but it sure wasn't symmetrical: because only one of the two planned bell towers was completed, the church has a lopsided appearance. On the left side of the church, the golden Cappella di San Giovanni houses a relic from St. John the Baptist. Pay €0.20 for the usually shadowy chapel to be illuminated by spotlights. *(P. San Lorenzo, off V. San Lorenzo, which emerges from P. Matteotti. Guided tour every 30min. Open M-Sa 8am-7pm, Su 7am-7pm. Free. Modest dress required.)*

PORTA SOPRANA. The historical centerpiece of P. Dante and one of four gates into the city (and today the passageway from the modern piazza into the *centro storico*), this medieval structure was built in 1100 to intimidate enemies of the Republic of Genoa. Would-be assailant Emperor Frederico Barbarossa took one look at the arch, whose Latin inscription welcomes those who come in peace but threatens doom to enemy armies, and abandoned

THE INSIDER'S CITY

Bacino Porto Vecchio

Via Gramsci

Strada Aldo Moro

Marina Molo Vecchio

Porto Antico

PIAZZA CARICAMENTO

PIAZZA DELLE FESTE

A DAY AT PORTO ANTICO

At Genoa's heart, the Porto Antico contains historical sites, museums, and excellent dining. Here are some of its highlights.

1 See the **Aquario di Genova** (aquarium), the pride of the city's museum system. Interactive exhibits tie in global issues like water conservation and animal extinction. (☎010 234 56 78; www.acquariodigenova.it. Open daily 9:30am-7:30pm.)

2 In the **Bigo,** visitors are suspended in a round glass elevator above the water, providing great city views. (☎010 234 51. Open daily 10am-8pm, with extended weekend hours. Hours reduced in winter. Tickets €3.)

3 The **Loggia** of Sottoripa, surrounding the open space near the port houses boutiques, fish markets, street vendors, bars, and gourmet restaurants.

4 The **Molo Vecchio** is the city's social center, housing the Cineplex, a video game arcade, and gelaterias.

his attack. **Christopher Columbus's** boyhood home lies nearby, alongside the remains of a 12th-century convent. *(From P. G. Matteotti, head down V. di Porta Soprana. Fortress open Sa-Su 9am-6pm. Free; €3 to climb the towers. Columbus's home open Sa-Su 9am-noon and 3-6pm. €3.)*

PALAZZO SPINOLA DI PELLICCERIA. Built at the close of the 16th century, this palazzo once hosted Peter Paul Rubens, who described it warmly in his 1622 book on pleasing palaces. It is now home to the **Galleria Nazionale,** a collection of art and furnishings, most donated by the family of Maddalena Doria Spinola, who owned the palazzo during the first half of the 18th century. The building tells its own history, as different sections represent centuries' worth of varying architectural styles. The 18th-century kitchen simulation is particularly intriguing, with a lit stove and flour on the countertop. The fourth level houses more treasures, including Antonello da Messina's 1460 masterpiece *Ecce Homo.* Van Dyck's four portraits of the evangelists reside in the Green Room on the second level. *(P. di Pellicceria, 1, between V. Maddalena and P. S. Luca. ☎010 270 53 00. Open Tu-Sa 8:30am-7:30pm, Su 1-8pm. €4; 18-25, students, or over 65 €2.)*

CHIESA DI SAN SIRO. Begun in the fourth century, reconstructed in 1006 in Romanesque style and later in Baroque, Genoa's oldest church is a haunting space filled by fading frescoes, crystal chandeliers, paintings, and sculptures, many dating from the 1400s. *(Located where V. S. Siro branches to the right. Open M-F 4-6pm. Free.)*

MUSEO DI SANT'AGOSTINO. Also known as the **Museo dell'Architettura e Scultura Ligure,** this collection surveys Genoa's history through its surviving art (many pieces have been plucked from buildings for preservation). On the second floor are pieces of Giovanni Pisano's masterpiece, a carved funerary monument dedicated to Margherita of Brabant, who died of the plague in 1311. Drawing hordes of art lovers from around Europe, the Neoclassical 🖼*Penitent Magdalene in the Desert* is so sensuous it borders on sacrilegious. *(Follow signs to Pta. Soprana and head toward the port on V. Ravecca. ☎010 20 60 22. Open Tu-F 9am-7pm, Sa-Su 10am-7pm. €4.)*

🎵 🍷 ENTERTAINMENT AND NIGHTLIFE

Genoa's new **Cineplex,** at Molo Vecchio on the harbor, shows dubbed American movies on 10 large screens. *(☎199 19 99 91; www.cineplex.it. Box office open M-F 3:30-10:30pm, Sa 2pm-1:30am, Su 2-11:30pm. Tickets M-F €6.50, Sa-Su €7, matinees €5.)* A 20min. ride down C. Italia on bus #31 leads to **Boccadasse,** a charming fishing village and seaside playground for wealthy *Genovesi.* **Corso Italia** is a swanky promenade home to much of Genoa's nightlife. Most revellers in Genoa drive to get to clubs, however, as they are difficult to reach on foot. Try **Al Parador,** P. della Vittoria, 49r, which is easy and safe to reach from the station. Upscale bar and gelateria by day, by night this watering hole is frequented both by wanna-be starlets and the real thing, including Uma Thurman and Claudia Schiffer. *(☎010 58 17 71. Cocktails €4.50. Open M-Sa 24hr.)*

RIVIERA DI LEVANTE

CAMOGLI ☎0185

Camogli is a postcard-perfect town with lively red and turquoise boats knocking in the harbor, fishing nets draped over docks, and dark stone beaches dotted with bright umbrellas. Its colorful houses with painted-on balconies, windows, and "brick" facades fool the less observant. Less ritzy and more youth-friendly than nearby Portofino and Santa Margherita, Camogli is the place to go for a relaxing stroll down the boardwalk or up steep side streets, take challenging hikes along the shoreline and in the surrounding hills, or to just lounge on the beach.

⌐ TRANSPORTATION

Trains: Camogli is on the Genoa-La Spezia train line. Ticket office open M-Sa 5am-12:30pm, Su 1am-7:30pm. To: **Genoa** (40min., 38 per day 1:08am-10:05pm, €1.60); **La Spezia** (1½hr., 24 per day 5:29am-1:03am, €3.95) via **Santa Margherita; Sestri Levante** (30min., 39 per day 5:38am-1:10am, €2).

Buses: Tigullio buses leave P. Schiaffino near the tourist office for nearby towns. Buy tickets at the tourist office or at *tabacchi*. Buses depart to **Santa Margherita** (20min., 20 per day, €1.10). Buses also run to **Rapallo, Ruta,** and **San Lorenzo.**

Ferries: Golfo Paradiso, V. Scalo, 3 (☎0185 77 20 91; www.golfoparadiso.it). Look for the "Servizi Batelli" sign near P. Colombo by the water. Buy tickets at dock or on the ferry. To: **Cinque Terre** (Portovenere at Vernazza; June 15-July 1 Su; July 1-Aug. 1 Tu, Th, and Su; Sept. 1-15 Th and Su; 9:30am, returns 5:30pm; round-trip €20); **Portofino** (Sa-Su 3pm, return 5:30pm; round-trip €12); **San Fruttuoso** (May-Sept. every hr. 8am-7pm, round-trip €8).

✳ 🛈 ORIENTATION AND PRACTICAL INFORMATION

Camogli extends uphill from the sea into pine and olive groves overlooking the beach. To get to the center of town, turn right out of the **train station,** walk 100m, and then turn left down the stairs to **Via Garibaldi,** which runs along the beachfront.

Tourist Office: V. XX Settembre, 33 (☎0185 77 10 66). Exit train station and turn right. English-speaking staff helps book accommodations. Open in summer M-Sa 9am-12:30pm and 3:30-7pm, Su 9am-1pm; in winter M-Sa 9am-12:30pm and 3:30-6:30pm, Su 9am-12:30pm.

Currency Exchange: Banco di Chiavari della Riviera Ligure, V. XX Settembre, 19 (☎0185 77 51 13). Reasonable rates. **ATM** outside. Open M-F 8:20am-1:20pm and 2:35-4pm, Sa 8:20-11:20am.

Police: ☎0185 72 90 57. **Carabinieri,** V. Cuneo, 30/F (☎112 or 0185 77 00 00).

Pharmacy: Dr. Machi, V. Repubblica, 4-6 (☎0185 77 10 81). Posts list of late-night pharmacies. Open July-Aug. 8:30am-12:30pm and 4-8pm, Sept.-June 3:30-7:30pm. Closed Th; also closed Sa-Su alternate weeks. MC/V.

Hospital: S. Martino (☎0105 551), in Genoa. In Recco, V. Bianchi, 1 (☎0185 743 77).

Post Office: V. Cuneo, 4 (☎0185 770 26). Exit train station and turn left. Open M-F 8am-1:30pm, Sa 8am-12:30pm. **Postal Code:** 16032.

▚ ACCOMMODATIONS

Prices and availability of rooms vary greatly according to season and day of the week in Camogli. Be sure to make a reservation far in advance for a stay during the weekend in the summer, and be prepared to a pay a higher price.

▨ **Hotel Augusta,** V. Schiaffino, 100 (☎0185 77 05 92; www.htlaugusta.com), at the other end of town from Camogliese. This gorgeously renovated hotel attends to every detail. 15 rooms are handsomely furnished, all with bath, TV, and phone. Some overlook the harbor from private balconies. Buffet breakfast €10 per room. 15min. Internet included. Singles €30-55; doubles €60-98; triples €90. AmEx/MC/V. ❹

▩**Albergo La Camogliese,** V. Garibaldi, 55 (☎0185 77 14 02; www.lacamogliese.it). Exit train station, walk down the long stairway to the right, and look for the blue sign; hotel is steps from the beach. Large, comfortable rooms are a joy. All come with bath, TV, safe, and phone. Access to gym and community pool. Breakfast buffet included. Internet €1 for 30min. Singles €50-85; doubles €67-97; triples €90-120. AmEx/MC/V. ❺

Albergo Selene, V. Cuneo, 16 (☎/fax 0185 77 01 49). Exit train station and turn left past the post office. Rooms are clean and simple, some with balcony. Breakfast included. Singles €33-48; doubles €55-88; triples €85. AmEx/MC/V. ❸

Pensione Faro, V. Schiaffino, 116-118 (☎/fax 0185 77 14 00), above the restaurant of the same name. Quiet rooms have bath, TV, and tranquil sea views. Breakfast €4. Singles €40-55; doubles €55-80. Half pension €50-65. AmEx/MC/V. ❹

▢ FOOD

Shops on V. Repubblica (one block from the harbor) and Picasso **supermarket,** V. XX Settembre, 35, stock groceries and picnicking supplies. (Open M-Sa 8am-12:30pm and 4:30-7:30pm, Su 8:30am-12:30pm. MC/V.) On Wednesdays, an **open-air market** fills P. del Teatro with local produce and cheap clothing. (Open 8am-noon.)

▩**Gelato e Dintorni,** V. Garibaldi, 104/105 (☎0185 774 35 33). This creamy gelato puts nationally ranked rivals to shame. Specialty is frozen yogurt topped with fresh fruit. 2 scoops €1.30. Sicilian *granita* €1.70. Open daily 10:30am-11pm. Cash only. ❶

▩**Focacceria Pasticceria Revello,** V. Garibaldi, 183 (☎0185 77 07 77; www.revello-camogli.com). Regionally famous shop has turned out fresh, crispy flatbreads and delectable pastries for 40 years. Make like the locals and breakfast on focaccia with onions (€8.50 per kg). House-invented *camogliesi* (dense and crumbly cookies; €19.50 per kg) are a town institution. Open daily 8am-2pm and 4-8pm. Cash only. ❶

Il Portico Spaghetteria, V. Garibaldi, 197/A (☎0185 77 02 54). Generous portions and excellent value at this beachfront newcomer. Creative pastas satisfy every craving in the cool, brick-arched interior—try the *pasta al turridu* (with anchovies, raisins, tomatoes, and fennel; €7.50). Pasta €6.50-8.50. Cover €2. Open M-F 8pm-last person leaves, Sa-Su 12:30-8pm. Cash only. ❷

La Rotonda, V. Garibaldi, 101 (☎/fax 0185 77 45 02), on the boardwalk. Good place to sample typical Ligurian pasta and fresh seafood, like *risotto ai frutti di mare* for 2 (€20). The dining room hanging over the sea delivers a tremendous view. *Primi* €8-10, *secondi* €12-25. Open daily 12:30-2:30pm and 7:30-11pm. AmEx/MC/V. ❹

La Creperie Bretonne, V. Garibaldi, 162 (0185 77 50 17). Charming nook for a quick snack, small meal, or big dessert-like crepes topped with gelato. Owner speaks French, English, and German to keep up with all of the admiring tourists. Crepes €2-5. Open Apr.-Sept. M-F and Su 12:30pm-midnight, Sa 12:30pm-1am. Cash only. ❶

Al Bar Teatro, P. Matteotti, 3 (☎0185 77 25 72). Thin-crust pizzas in 60 varieties (€4-8), served in a quiet garden. A worthy break from the beach. Cover €1.60. Open M-W and F-Su 7am-2pm and 7:30-11:30pm. AmEx/MC/V. ❶

◎ ♫ SIGHTS AND ENTERTAINMENT

The Camogli tourist office has a useful trail **map.** Red dots mark the path, which starts at the end of V. Cuneo near the *carabinieri* station. Ferry or snorkeling trips also make interesting (but more costly) diversions. **B&B Diving Center,** V. Schiattino, 11, off P. Colombo, sails boats for scuba diving to 18 immersion points along the coast. (☎/fax 0185 77 27 51; www.bbdiving.it. Scuba tours Sa-Su 4 per day; €35 with guide and equipment. 10-person boat capacity. Canoe and kayak rental €6 per hr., €30 per day. Open daily 9am-7pm. Cash only.) The **Sagra del**

Pesce, an enormous fish fry, is held the second Sunday in May. The most monumental frying pan, constructed in 1952, measures 4m in diameter and holds 2000 fish. The night before the big fry, the town gathers for a procession honoring the patron saint of fishermen, followed by an enormous fireworks display and a bonfire-building contest. After the sardine rush, the pans adorn a city wall all year, hanging to the right on V. Garibaldi along the stairs to the beach.

Spend nights in peaceful Camogli enjoying a cool drink with a sea view. Order a mojito (€5) or *sangria* (€3.50) to cap off the day at the bar **Il Barcollo,** V. Garibaldi, 92. (☎0185 77 33 22. Open daily 6pm-3am.) Just down the boardwalk is the piratical **Captain Hook,** V. al Porto, 4, decorated like a ship's cabin and serving jolly good food and over 60 types of rum (€3.20-10) until late. (☎0185 77 16 95. Pizza and pasta about €5. Open daily 10am-3am. Cash only.)

▶ DAYTRIP FROM CAMOGLI

SAN FRUTTUOSO

San Fruttuoso is accessible by trails from Portofino Mare (1½hr.), Portofino Vetta (1½hr.), or Camogli (3 hours). Golfo Paradiso (☎0185 77 20 91; www.golfoparadiso.it) runs boats from Camogli (every hr. in summer Tu and Th-Sa 8am-5pm, last return from San Fruttuoso 6-7pm; round-trip €8). Servizio Marittimo del Tigullio (☎0185 28 46 70) runs ferries from Camogli to Portofino (every hr. 9:30am-4:30pm, round-trip €12) and Santa Margherita (every hr. 9:15am-4:15pm, €7).

The hikes from Camogli to tiny San Fruttuoso follow labeled trails that wind through Portofino's nature reserve. There are two main routes to San Fruttuoso from Camogli. The first, marked along the trail by two red dots, is easier and winds along the coast, past Nazi anti-aircraft bunkers and through forests, yielding vistas of the surrounding sea before descending into town. The second, marked by a red circle, climbs up and around Mt. Portofino through ancient forests and olive groves, with a sharp and difficult descent to the harbor on a crumbling stone path. Both begin in Camogli at the intersection of V. Cuneo and V. G. Bono Ferrari. Trail maps are available at the Camogli tourist office. Approached by sea, the 16th-century **Torre di Doria** appears as a lone gladiator surrounded by an arena of green. The town is named after the Benedictine **Abbazia di San Fruttuoso di Capodimonte,** constructed from the 10th to the 13th centuries. The monastery and tower rotate archaeological exhibits. (☎0185 77 27 03. Open daily June-Sept. 10am-1pm and 2-5:30pm. €6, children €4.) Fifteen meters offshore and 17m underwater, the bronze *Christ of the Depths* stands with arms upraised in memory of the sea's casualties. The statue now protects scuba divers, and a replica stands in Chiesa di San Fruttuoso, next to the abbey, mutely enticing visitors who travel by ferry to make an offering to the *Sacrario dei Morti in Mare* (Sanctuary for the Dead at Sea). Locals with small wooden boats offer rides to the underwater statue for €2.50 from the docks. Consider packing a picnic lunch, as none of the pricey harbor-side restaurants offers food to go. **Da Laura ❸** is the best restaurant bet, serving delicious *lasagne al pesto* at tables on the beach. (Open noon-3pm. Cash only.)

SANTA MARGHERITA LIGURE ☎0185

From its founding in the 12th century, Santa Margherita Ligure led a calm existence as a fishing village far from the Levante limelight. In the early 20th century, Hollywood stars discovered it, and its popularity grew after a *National Geographic* feature in the 1950s. Glitz adorns the beachfront and palm trees line the harbor, but the serenity of Santa Margherita's early days lingers, making it a peaceful, affordable base for exploring the Riviera di Levante.

LIGURIA

☞ TRANSPORTATION

Trains: In P. Federico Raoul Nobili at the top of V. Roma. Intercity trains on the Pisa-Genoa line stop at Santa Margherita. **Luggage storage** available (see **Practical Information**). Ticket office open daily 6am-7:05pm. To **Genoa** (50min., 2-4 per hr. 4:37am-11:55pm, €2.10) and **La Spezia** (1½hr., 1-2 per hr. 5:35am-1:10am, €3.95) via **Cinque Terre** (1hr., every hr. 8:06am-9:58pm, €3.40).

Buses: Tigullio buses (☎0185 28 88 34) depart from P. V. Veneto at the small green kiosk on the waterfront. Ticket office open 7:05am-7:25pm. To **Camogli** (30min., every 45min., €1.20) and **Portofino** (20min., 3 per hr., €1.50).

Ferries: Servizio Marittimo del Tigullio, V. Palestro, 8/B (☎0185 28 46 70 or 336 25 33 36; www.traghettiportofino.it). Boats leave from docks at P. Martiri della Libertà to: **Cinque Terre** (July-Sept. W-Th and Sa, also M in Aug.; 8:45am; roundtrip €21); **Portofino** (every hr. 9:15am-4:15pm, one-way €3.50); **San Fruttuoso** (every hr. 9:15am-4:15pm, one way €7).

Taxis: In P. Stazione (☎0185 28 65 08). On V. Pescino (☎0185 28 79 98).

⬥ ☷ ORIENTATION AND PRACTICAL INFORMATION

From the **train station**, take **Via Roma** or the stairs to the right of the stop sign in front of the station, and follow **Via della Stazione** to the water. Two main squares lie on the waterfront: **Piazza Vittorio Veneto** and the larger **Piazza Martiri della Libertà**, with **Piazza Caprera** between them set back from the water. **Via G. Marconi** winds around the port and **Via XXV Aprile** leads to the tourist office, becoming **Corso Matteotti** alongside the other main square in town, **Piazza Mazzini.**

To reach the **Pro Loco Tourist Office,** V. XXV Aprile, 2/B, turn right from the train station onto V. Trieste, which becomes V. Roma, follow it to C. Rainusso, then turn left. V. XXV Aprile is a hard right up from Largo Giusti. The staff provides **maps** and lodgings advice. (☎0185 28 74 85; www.apttigullio.liguria.it. Open M-Sa 9am-12:30pm and 3-7:30pm, Su 9:30am-12:30pm and 4:30-7:30pm.) **Luggage storage** is available at Hotel Terminus, in front of the train station, for €5 per bag. In case of **emergency,** call ☎113, or contact the **police,** P. Mazzini, 46 (☎0185 20 54 50). Reach an **ambulance** at ☎118. **Farmacia A. Pennino,** P. Caprera, 10, keeps a list of late-night pharmacies posted. (☎0188 29 70 77. Open M-Tu and Th-Su 8:30am-1pm and 3-10pm.) A **hospital** (☎0185 68 31) is on V. F. Arpe. **Internet** is available at **The Internet Point,** V. Giuncheto, 39, near P. Caprera. (☎0185 29 30 92; liguriacom@tigullio.it. Open M-Sa 10am-7pm.) The **post office,** on V. Roma, 36, **exchanges currency** and offers *Fermoposta* services. (☎010 29 47 51. Open M-F 8am-6:30pm, Sa 8am-12:30pm.) **Postal Code:** 16038.

☛ ACCOMMODATIONS

Ritzy waterfront accommodations are by no means the only options. Santa Margherita is small enough that there's no such thing as a long walk to the sea.

▨ **Hotel Terminus,** P. Nobili, 4 (☎0185 28 61 21, fax 28 25 46), heading left from the train station. Appreciative notes in the lobby say it all: this is a special place to stay. Spacious rooms have beautiful decorations and sea views. English owner Angelo adores and befriends his guests. Buffet breakfast included. 4-course dinner €18. Singles €80, with bath €85; doubles with bath €95; triples €110; quads €160. AmEx/MC/V. ❺

Albergo Annabella, V. Costasecca, 10 (☎0185 28 65 31), behind P. Mazzini. Kind owner Annabella aims to make guests feel at home. 11 comfortable rooms, some with bath, are filled with antiques. Shared bath is large and sparkling. Breakfast €4. Singles €30-45; doubles €50-70; triples €80-94.50; quads €119. Cash only. ❸

Hotel Europa, V. Trento, 5 (☎0185 28 71 87; www.hoteleuropa-sml.it). Tucked behind the harbor glitz, this modern hotel offers spacious rooms with bath, TV, and phone, most with balcony and A/C. Canopies on beds are painted with trees. Breakfast included. Singles €33-63; doubles €60-95; extras beds 30% more. AmEx/MC/V. ❹

Hotel Helios, V. Gramsci, 6 (☎0185 28 74 71; www.hotelhelios.com). Wealthy visitors to the Riviera bask by the private beach and swimming area protected by a man-made cove. Luxurious rooms all have A/C and TV. Buffet breakfast included. Depending on room views, singles €85-135; doubles €100-230; triples €136-158. AmEx/MC/V. ❺

🍴 FOOD

Markets and bakeries line C. Matteotti. Buy essentials at the **COOP**, C. Matteotti, 8, off P. Mazzini. (☎0185 28 43 15. Open M-Sa 8:15am-1pm and 3:30-8pm. V.) Catch the catch of the day at the **fish market** on Lungomare Marconi. (Open daily 8am-12:30pm; boats arrive M-Tu and Th-Su 4-6pm.) On Fridays, an **open-air market** in P. Mortola sells fruit and inexpensive clothes. (Open 8am-2pm.)

◾**Trattoria Da Pezzi,** V. Cavour, 21 (☎0185 28 53 03). Locals descend on this famous haunt for its home-style *Genovese* cuisine and jovial atmosphere. *Farinata* (€3.50) and *torta pasqualina* (€3.30-5) are great choices. *Primi* €3-6.40, *secondi* €3-8. Open M-F and Su 10am-2:15pm and 5-9:15pm. MC/V. ❶

◾**Trattoria Baicini,** V. Algeria, 9 (☎0185 28 67 63), off P. Martiri della Libertà. Escape the beach to this peaceful trattoria for a truly delicious meal. Mama Carmela lovingly ladles the *trofie alla genovese* (*gnocchi* with string beans and pesto; €6) and steaming *zuppa di pesce* (fish soup; €13). *Primi* €5-7.50, *secondi* €9.50-17. Cover €1.50. Open Tu-Su noon-3pm and 7-11:30pm; kitchen closes 10:30pm. AmEx/MC/V. ❸

Trattoria Noemi, V. S. Bernardo, 3 (☎0185 53 94). Walking from the sea, turn right off V. XXV Aprile. This unpretentious spot, with plastic patio furniture for outdoor seating, is beloved by locals. It's hard to find better *pansotti alla salsa di noci* (vegetable-filled pasta in walnut cream sauce; €7.20). *Primi* €6-10, *secondi* €7-19. Cover €1.60. Open M-Tu and Th-Su 12:10-2pm and 7:10-10:30pm. MC/V. ❸

L'Approdo, V. Cairoli, 26 (☎0185 28 17 89). Certainly a splurge, but a memory in the making. Skillful execution of old family recipes, including an extraordinary *scampi* (shrimp; €26). Precise, courteous service. *Primi* €11-15, *secondi* €16-36. Cover €3. Open Tu 7:30pm-midnight, W-Su 12:30-2pm and 7:30pm-midnight. AmEx/MC/V. ❺

Gelateria Centrale, Largo Giusti, 14 (☎/fax 0185 28 74 80). Crowds gather here for *pinguino* (€2), a cone of gelato in a thick chocolate shell. Cones or cups from €1.40. Open daily 8:30am-midnight. Cash only. ❶

📷 🎵 SIGHTS AND ENTERTAINMENT

If lapping waves aren't sufficiently invigorating, visit the magnificent Rococo **Basilica di Santa Margherita** in P. Caprera, dripping with gold and crystal chandeliers. The church also contains fine Flemish and Italian artwork. (☎0185 28 65 55.) Off V. della Vittoria, paths wind uphill to the **Villa Durazzo,** built on the site of a medieval castle and surrounded by manicured gardens. The lavishly decorated villa holds 16th-century paintings. (Open Tu-Su 9am-6pm. Gardens open Tu-Su 9am-7pm.) Come nightfall, youthful crowds claim the funky colored tables at **Sabot American Bar,** P. della Libertà, 32, for drinks and live DJ music. (☎0185 28 07 47. Cocktails €7, beer €4-6. Open M and W-Su 10am-4am.) The tribute to drinking American-style continues at **Miami**, P. della Libertà, 29, complete with neon lights, vinyl booths, and €7 Manhattans. (☎0185 28 34 24. Open daily 5pm-3am. AmEx/MC/V.)

TOP TEN LIST

LIGURIAN BEACHES

,0. **Riomaggiore:** Boulders make entering the water difficult, but swimming is excellent, as are views of surrounding cliffs.

). **Finale Ligure free beach:** Small and sandy, the crystal waters are good for body surfing.

8. **Monterosso old town:** Less crowded, this sandy strip along railroad tracks is only a short walk through town.

7. **Alassio:** With kilometers to find the right spot to put your towel down, these shores are all sand capped by cool waters.

5. **Vernazza:** A great place to catch some rays and admire the rainbow-hued harbor houses.

5. **Camogli free beach:** The white sands are always packed.

4. **Giant Beach, Monterosso:** A sculpture of a giant carved into the side of the cliff makes a dramatic backdrop for sunbathers and swimmers. Just keep walking to the right facing the water from the main beach.

3. Between **Corniglia** and **Vernazza:** walk down the precarious footpaths to the waterfront. This beach is almost private, and a great way to cool off during the challenging hike.

2. **Portofino and Santa Margherita:** Tiny beaches line the shore between these two towns. Enjoy pristine waters and views of luxury yachts as they pass by.

. **San Fruttuoso:** A cove from heaven, with perfectly clear water surrounded by wooded cliffs and the opportunity to dive to see Cristo degli Abissi.

⊠ DAYTRIP FROM SANTA MARGHERITA

PORTOFINO

Take bus #82 to Portofino Mare (not Portofino Vetta) from in front of the green bus kiosk in P. Martiri della Libertà, where tickets are sold. From Portofino's P. Martiri della Libertà, Tigullio buses run to Santa Margherita (3 per hr., €1). Portofino is also accessible by ferry from Santa Margherita (every hr. 10:30am-4pm, €3.50) and Camogli (2 per day, €11).

Portofino is a perfect half-day outing from Santa Margherita. Yachts fill its harbor, chic boutiques and art galleries line the cobbled streets, and luxury cars crowd parking lots. Nevertheless, both princes and paupers can enjoy the sandy shores and tiny bay. A **nature reserve** surrounds Portofino and nearby resort village **Paraggi;** treks through the hilly terrain, past ruined churches and stately villas, lead to Santa Margherita (1½hr.) and San Fruttuoso. (2hr.)

Facing the sea from town, head right around the port and climb the stairs to the cool, stark interior of the **Chiesa di San Giorgio.** Behind the church lies a small cemetery—members of the Protestant minority were laid to rest just outside its walls. Outside the 16th-century **Castello Brown** nearby is a serene garden. The castle was once a fortress, but the wealthy Brown family converted it to a summer home when Consul Montague Yeats Brown bought it from the Kingdom of Sardinia for 7000 lire in 1867. (Open daily 10am-7pm, in winter Sa-Su 10am-5pm. €3.50.)

Back in town, **Alimentari Repetto,** P. Martiri dell'Olivetta, 32, in the main square in front of the harbor, fortifies hikers with Gatorade (€2.50) and sandwiches from €3. (☎0185 26 90 56. Open daily in summer 8am-10pm, in winter 9am-6pm.) **Trattoria Concordia ❸,** V. del Fondaco, 5, delights guests with its authentic *antico tipo* Ligurian cuisine served in a small, nautical-themed dining room. The *trenette al pesto* (€8) is a local favorite. (☎0185 26 92 07. *Primi* €5-26, *secondi* €10-26. Cover €1.50, service 10%. Open M and W-Su noon-3pm and 7:30-10pm. AmEx/MC/V.) A drink at one of the numerous bars along the harbor costs upward of €6.50, though watching town life unfold along the harbor is worth it.

At the **APT tourist office,** V. Roma, 35, on the way to the waterfront from the bus stop, the English-speaking staff has **maps** and brochures. (☎0185 26 90 24; www.apttigullio.liguria.it. Open M-Tu 10:30am-1:30pm and 2:30-7:30pm, W-Su 10:30am-1:30pm and 2-7:30pm.) **Currency exchange** is available at the Banco di Chiavari, V. Roma, 14/16. (☎0185 26 91 64. Open M-F 8:20am-1:20pm and 2:35-4pm.) In case of **emer-**

gency, call the **police**, V. del Fondaco, 8 (☎112 or 0185 26 90 88). A **pharmacy** is at P. Martiri della Libertà, 6. (☎0185 26 91 01. Open daily 9am-1pm and 4-8pm, closed Su in winter. AmEx/MC/V.) The **post office** is at V. Roma, 36. (☎0185 26 91 56. Open M-F 8am-1:15pm, Sa 8am-12:30pm.)

CINQUE TERRE   ☎0187

In the five fishing villages of Cinque Terre, man and nature have created a locale that soothes the spirit. Farmers toiled for centuries to produce the terraced hillsides of olive groves and vineyards, and fishermen built the rainbow-colored houses along the harbors. However, nature created Cinque Terre's best sights. Savage cliffs and lush tropical vegetation surround the stone villages, and a vast expanse of dazzling turquoise sea laps against the *cittadine* that cling to the terraced hillsides and steep crumbling cliffs. Through a trick of perspective and sea mist, each town, when glimpsed from the next, appears both distant and proximate, as if an unreachable village in one moment might become a handful of pastels and pebbles in the next. Strong hikers can cover the ground between all five towns in about 5hr. Taking time to lounge in the villages along the way is essential, however, as each maintains a unique character and offers good company and great restaurants in which to sample authentic Ligurian cuisine. Despite their small size, the five *terre*— Monterosso, Vernazza, Corniglia, Manarola, and Riomaggiore—are fodder for a booming tourism industry, so reserve ahead.

⌐ TRANSPORTATION

 TERRE TRIPPING. The 24hr. **Cinque Terre Tourist Ticket** (€4.20) allows unlimited train trips among the five towns, La Spezia, and Levanto. It's available at ticket windows at the five train stations. The Cinque Terre National Park offices in each town also sell 1 day (€5.40), 3 day (€13.40) and 5 day (€17.40) **Cinque Terre Cards** with unlimited train, bus, and path access.

Trains: The towns lie on the Genoa-La Spezia (Pisa) line. Schedules are available at tourist offices. Most trains stop at **Monterosso,** making it the most accessible. From the station on V. Fegina, trains run to: **Florence** (3½hr., every hr., €8-17) via **Pisa** (2½hr., every hr. 4:53am-11:57pm, €4.65); **Genoa** (1½hr., every hr. 4:47am-12:47pm, €4.45); **La Spezia** (20min., every 30min., €1.35); **Rome** (7hr., every 2hr., €31). Frequent local trains connect the 5 towns (5-20min., every 50min., €1-1.50).

Ferries: Monterosso can be reached by ferry from **La Spezia** (1hr., 2 per day, €18). Ferries from Monterosso also connect the towns. **Navigazione Golfo dei Poeti** (☎0187 77 77 27), in front of the IAT office at the port (in the old town; see **Practical Information**). To: **Manarola** (5 per day, €8); **Portovenere** (6 per day, €15); **Riomaggiore** (8 per day, €8); **Vernazza** (9 per day, €2.25).

Taxis: ☎335 628 09 33 or 616 58 42.

Boat Rental: Along the beaches. **Mar-Mar,** V. Malborghetto, 8 (☎/fax 0187 92 09 32) in Riomaggiore, rents kayaks and 3-person canoes. Cash only.

✦ 🏋 ORIENTATION AND PRACTICAL INFORMATION

The five villages stretch in a string between Levanto in the northeast and La Spezia in the southwest, connected by trains, roads (although cars are not allowed inside the towns), and footpaths that traverse the rocky shoreline.

LIGURIA

Monterosso is the largest and easternmost town and the sight of most of the services for the area, followed from east to west by **Vernazza, Corniglia, Manarola,** and **Riomaggiore.** The following are the principal listings. Separate listings follow for individual towns.

Tourist Office: Cinque Terre National Park Office, P. Garibaldi, 20 (☎0187 81 78 38; www.parconazionale5terre.it), in Monterosso, has info on hiking trails and accommodations and sells **Cinque Terre Cards.** Open daily 9am-10pm. **Pro Loco,** V. Fegina, 38 (☎0187 81 75 06, fax 81 78 25), also in Monterosso, below the train station, provides info on boats and hikes and helps find accommodations. Open Apr.-Oct. M-Sa 9:15am-noon and 3:30-6pm, Su 9am-noon. In Riomaggiore, a **tourist office** (☎0187 76 99 61) in the train station has info on trails, hotels, and excursions. Open June-Sept. M-Th 6:30am-8pm, F-Sa 6:30am-10pm. Tourist offices in Manarola, Riomaggiore, and Monterosso have Internet points.

Tours: Navigazione 5 Terre Golfo dei Poeti (☎0187 73 29 87 or 814 40) offers tours to **Vernazza** (€3, round-trip €4.50) and **Riomaggiore** (€8, round-trip €10.50) from **Monterosso** (9 per day 10:30am-6pm) and **Vernazza** (9 per day 10:40am-6:10pm).

Emergency: ☎113. **Ambulance** (☎118). **Police** (☎112).

First Aid: ☎338 853 09 49 for doctor on call M-W and F-Su.

Medical Clinic: ☎0189 80 09 73 for Monterosso, Vernazza, and Corniglia; ☎0189 50 77 27 for Riomaggiore and Manarola.

Carabinieri (☎0187 81 75 24, In Riomaggiore, 0187 92 01 12).

Post Office: Main branch in **Monterosso,** V. Roma, 73 (☎0189 81 83 94). Open M-Sa 8am-1pm. **Postal Codes:** Monterosso 19016; Manarola and Riomaggiore 19017; Corniglia and Vernazza 19018.

🔯 THE TOWNS

MONTEROSSO

The largest and most commercially developed of the five, Monterosso is the beach bum's town of choice. Three sandy shores and a spirited backpacking scene create the liveliest nightlife in the five *terre.* A small-town character endures, though, in the historical section's winding streets and poetically crumbling castle.

■✚🔯 ORIENTATION AND PRACTICAL INFORMATION. Descend the steps from the **train station** and turn left on **Lungomare di Fegina** through a tunnel into **Piazza Garibaldi,** the heart of the historic center. Services include: **currency exchange** at **Casa di Risparmio della Spezia,** V. Roma, 47 (open M-F 8:10am-1:10pm and 2:45-3:45pm, Su 8:10am-11:30pm) and **Banca Carige,** V. Roma, 69; **ATMs** at **Bancomat,** V. Fegina, 40, under the train station; and **laundry** at **Laundry Mat,** V. Molinelli, 12. (Wash, soap, and dry €8 for 7kg load. Open daily 9am-noon and 3-7pm. Cash only.) The **pharmacy** at V. Fegina, 44, posts a list of late-night pharmacies. (☎0187 181 83 91. Open M-Sa 9am-12:30pm and 4-8pm, Su 9:30am-12:30pm and 4-7:30pm.) **The Net,** V. V. Emanuele, 55, offers **Internet.** (☎/fax 0187 81 72 88; www.monterosso.net. €1 for 10min., €0.10 for each additional min. Open daily 10am-10:30pm.) Internet can also be found at **Il Casello,** V. Lungo Ferravia, 70, for €4 per hr. (☎0187 81 83 30. Open daily 10am-3am.)

🔯 ACCOMMODATIONS. While most of Cinque Terre's hotels are in Monterosso, these generally fill up in early June. Inquire at the tourist office for help finding the more plentiful *affittacamere* (private rooms). The lively 🔲**Hotel Souvenir ❸,** V. Gioberti, 30, popular with students, has 30 beds in comfortable rooms and friendly

LIGURIA

staff. (☎/fax 0187 81 75 95; hotel_souvenir@yahoo.com. Breakfast €5. Rooms €40 per person, students €25 per person.) At **📶 Convento dei Cappuccini ❸**, on Zii dei Frati off of Salita Cappuccini, vineyards, vegetable gardens, and a private courtyard provide soothing places to stroll. The closet-sized bedrooms and 11pm curfew are well worth it—the convent has the best views in town. (☎/fax 0187 81 75 31. Breakfast included. Singles €35-40; doubles €70, with bath €80; family suite €140. Cash only.) Turn left from the station to reach **Meublè Agavi ❹**, V. Fegina, 30, which has a convenient location and good views. Its 10 rooms all have bath and fridge. (☎0187 81 71 71 or 80 16 65, fax 81 82 64. Singles €45-60; doubles €70-100. Cash only.) **La Colonnina ❺**, V. Zuecca, 6, just off P. Garibaldi, sits on a quiet street in the historic center. The common areas are sunny and pleasant, and all 19 rooms have satellite TV, A/C, and phone; some have private balcony. (☎0187 81 74

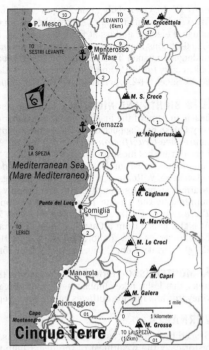

39 or 81 74 55; www.lacolonninacinqueterre.it. Organic buffet breakfast €8.50, included during high season. Doubles €93-112; triples €125; quads €145. Cash or traveler's checks only.) In the newer part of town is **Hotel Punta Mesco ❺**, V. Molinelli, 35, close to the sea. Tiled decorations give the place a modern feel. Huge rooms all have bath, A/C, TV, and phone. (☎/fax 0187 81 74 95; www.hotelpuntamesco.it. Breakfast buffet included. Singles €75-120; doubles €90-160. Cash discount 5%. MC/V.) Outside the center, 20min. uphill from the train station, is the lovely **Villa Caribe ❹**, V. P. Semeria, 49. Five rooms all have bath, safe, A/C, and TV, and some have balcony. (☎0187 81 72 79. Reception 7am-1pm. Call ahead for free shuttle transport. Singles €50; doubles €80; triples €120. AmEx/MC/V.)

🍴 FOOD. Allegedly, every restaurant in Cinque Terre prepares the best pesto, the freshest fish, and the most savory *acciughe* or *muscoli rippieni* (anchovies or muscles stuffed with grains and vegetables). To avoid high prices, consider a picnic of pesto-covered focaccia and juicy local fruit; wash it all down with a glass of light, dry *Cinque Terre* white, followed by some *Sciacchetrà* dessert wine. SuperCONAD Margherita, P. Matteotti, 9, stocks **groceries.** (Open June-Sept. M-Sa 8am-1pm and 4:40-7:30pm, Su 8am-1pm. MC/V.) **📶 Il Ciliegio ❹**, Località Beo, 2, creates fantastic meals with ingredients fresh from the owner's gardens. The amazing *trufie al pesto* (€8) was featured in Italy's prestigious *Salon del Gusto*. The restaurant is 20min. from town; management offers free shuttle service from P. Garibaldi on request. (☎0187 81 78 29. Lunch *menù* €27. *Primi* €6-8, *secondi* €7-11. Open Tu-Su 12:30-2:30pm and 7:30-10:30pm.) At **📶 Ristorante Al Carugio ❸**, V. San Pietro, 9, locals lunch on traditional Ligurian dishes. Try the scrumptious fried artichokes (€11.40), a town specialty. (☎/fax 0187 81 73 67. *Primi* €6-10.50, *sec-*

LIGURIA

ondi €7-15. Open daily noon-2:30pm and 6-10:30pm. Closed Th in winter. AmEx/MC/V.) Chow down on hot sandwiches (from €4) and mixed drinks (€5) beneath hanging electric guitars at **FAST ❶**, V. Roma, 13. By 11pm, beer (bottle €4-5, tap €2.80-8) consumption outpaces that of *panini*. (☎0187 81 71 64. Open daily 8am-midnight, in winter Tu-Su 8am-noon. MC/V.) **Focacceria Il Frantoio ❶**, V. Gioberti, 1, bakes tasty *farinata* and focaccia stuffed with olives, onions, or herbs. (☎0187 81 83 33. Slices €1-2. Open M-W and F-Su 9am-8pm. Cash only.)

■■ **SIGHTS AND NIGHTLIFE.** Monterosso has Cinque Terre's largest **free beach,** in front of the historic center and surrounded by a cliff-cove. The 15th-century **Chiesa dei Cappuccini,** in the center of town, yields the broadest vistas. The impressive *Crucifixion* by Flemish master Anthony Van Dyck, who sojourned here during his most productive years, is in the chapel on the left. (Open daily 9am-noon and 4-7pm. Free.) Those interested in fine wine should visit **Cantina di Sciacchetrà,** V. Roma, 7, which has free tastings, delicious *antipasti*, and deals on gourmet souvenirs. Jovial Gian Luigi proudly explains his high-quality products, supplied by the Cinque Terre Farming Cooperative. (☎0187 81 78 28. *Cinque Terre bianco* €4-19, *sciacchetrà* €29. Open Mar.-Oct. daily 9:30am-9pm. MC/V.) At night, music from **Il Casello,** V. Lungo Ferravia, 70, draws young backpackers. Casello serves beer, liquor, and snacks. (☎0187 81 83 30. Focaccia sandwiches €3.50-4. Drinks from €2.50. Internet €1 for 15min. Open daily 10am-3am.)

■ **MONTEROSSO-VERNAZZA.** Considered the hardest of the four town-linking treks, this 1¾hr. hike climbs steeply over dry, rugged cliffs, winding past terraced vineyards and hillside cottages before the steep descent into Vernazza.

VERNAZZA

Graced by a large seaside piazza, Vernazza is Cinque Terre's postcard town and historically the wealthiest of the five. Climb to the remains of the 11th-century Castello Doria, up a staircase on the left of P. Marconi when facing the port, for great views during the day; in the evening, savor a *caffè* under the stars.

■■ **ORIENTATION AND PRACTICAL INFORMATION. Via E. Q. Visconti** runs toward the sea from the station, lined with shops and restaurants, and turns midway into **Via Roma. Piazza Marconi** overlooks the harbor at the end of V. Roma. In case of **emergency,** dial ☎113, or call the **police** (☎112) or an **ambulance** (☎118).

■■ **ACCOMMODATIONS AND FOOD.** Vernazza boasts some lovely hotels as well as private rooms. ■**Hotel Gianni Franzi ❸**, P. Marconi, 1, is a gorgeous old building with 23 rooms that all have antique decor; most sport a large balcony with amazing views of the coast and Corniglia. (☎0187 82 10 03; www.giannifranzi.it. Singles €42-64; doubles €60, with bath €76; triples with bath €99. AmEx/MC/V.) The friendly owners of ■**Albergo Barbara ❹**, P. Marconi, 30, on the top floor, like their guests to feel at home. The nine rooms are bright and many have fantastic views of the port. (☎/fax 0187 81 23 98; albergobarbara@libero.it. Ring bell to enter. Doubles €45-80; triples €90. Cash only.) For private rentals, **Filippo Castrucci ❹**, V. A. Del Santo, has eight grand rooms with bath. (☎0187 81 22 44. Doubles €65. Cash only.) **Franca Maria ❺**, P. Marconi, 30, rents eight spacious rooms scattered around the village. (☎0187 81 20 02; www.francamaria.com. Doubles €50-100; triples €90-120; quads €100-160. Cash only.) **Anna Maria ❺**, V. Carattino, 64, up the hill on the way to Corniglia, has seven rooms in an old tower with prime sea and city views. (☎0187 82 10 82. Doubles €65-83. Cash only.)

With reputedly the best restaurants in Cinque Terre, P. Marconi fills with hungry tourists each evening. Groceries, fresh produce, and gourmet foods are available at **Salumi e Formaggio,** V. Visconti, 29. (☎0187 82 12 40. Open M-Sa 8am-1:30pm and

5-8pm, Su 8am-1:30pm. Cash only.) The oldest trattoria in Vernazza, **Trattoria Gianni Franzi ❷**, P. Marconi, 1, is famed for its pesto. Dine casually in the roomy interior or outside in the piazza. (☎0187 82 10 03, fax 0187 81 22 28. *Primi* €4-10.50, *secondi* €5-15.50. Open M-Tu and Th-Su noon-3pm and 7:30-9:30pm. AmEx/MC/V.) For a delicious splurge, visit elegant **Gambero Rosso ❹**, P. Marconi, 7. Touted by *Vernazzesi*, the service is excellent, and the food superb—adventurous eaters should not miss the *menù degustazione* (€30), four courses of local specialties. (☎0187 81 22 65, fax 0187 82 12 60. *Primi* €6-10, *secondi* €11-22. Open Tu-Su 12:30-3pm and 7-10pm. AmEx/MC/V.) **Osteria Il Baretto ❹**, V. Roma, 31, serves solid versions of Ligurian dishes. Try pasta topped with minced lobster and shrimp (€11.50) and a homemade dessert. (☎0187 81 23 81. *Primi* €7-11.50, *secondi* €7-13. Cover €1.50. Open Tu-Su noon-3:30pm and 7pm-midnight. AmEx/MC/V.)

◨ **VERNAZZA-CORNIGLIA.** Geographic diversity and ▨**unparalleled views** are the rewards along this 1¾hr. hike. The trail climbs harshly from Vernazza, passing through vineyards and olive groves before curving through uncultivated landscape. Scents of rosemary, thyme, lemon, and lavender perfume the air in the summer. The trail bends to reveal secluded beaches and Corniglia, posed spectacularly in the distance, before descending smoothly into town.

CORNIGLIA

Hundreds of steps climb from the station to this colorful village clinging to a seaside cliff. Without the beachside glitter of the other towns, Corniglia offers a more peaceful ambience. A pebbly strip of public beach beneath the tracks packs in sunbathers, with more secluded beaches to be discovered off of the trail to Vernazza.

◨▨ **ORIENTATION AND PRACTICAL INFORMATION. Via della Stazione** begins at the top of the station steps, turning into **Via Fieschi.** V. Fieschi passes through two piazzas before ending in **Belvedere Santa Maria**, a small terrace suspended at the edge of a cliff.

◨◨ **ACCOMMODATIONS AND FOOD.** Private rooms are the way to go in Corniglia. From the main piazza, turn right up the hill and walk 150m. **Ristorante Cecio ❹**, V. Serra, 11, on the small road that leads from Corniglia to Vernazza, rents eight rooms above the restaurant with postcard views of the sea, and four rooms in the village with terraces. All rooms have bath. (☎0187 81 20 43; simopank@libero.it. Doubles €60, with bath €70. Cash only.) Restaurants **Locanda a Lanterna ❹**, V. Fieschi, 164, and **Dau Tinola ❺**, V. Fieschi, 31 rent 12 rooms, most with sea view. (☎/fax 0187 81 22 91 or 82 12 00. Breakfast €7. Doubles €50, with bath €60. AmEx/MC/V.) **Villa Sandra ❺**, V. Fieschi, 212, provides four simple but spacious rooms (some with bath) and the use of a communal kitchen. (☎0187 81 23 84; www.cinqueterre-laposada.com. Doubles €55-60, with bath €65-70. Apartment for 2 €70-80, for 4 €120. MC/V.)

Pizzerias serve hungry hikers all over town, but follow your nose to **La Gata Flora ❶**, V. Fieschi, 109, for hot, delicious slices in many varieties. Crispy *farinata* (€0.80) is also available. (☎0187 82 12 18. Slice €2.10. Whole pizza €3.80-6. Focaccia €1.10-1.60. Open Tu-Su 9:30am-4pm and 6-8:30pm, daily in Aug. Cash only.) The cavernous **Cantina de Mananan ❸**, V. Fieschi, 117, provides a dark, cool respite and hearty meals from its mix and match pasta and sauce menu. (☎0187 82 11 66. *Primi* €8-10, *secondi* €8-12. Open M and W-Su at 12:30-3pm and 7:30-9pm. Cash only.) To get to **La Posada ❸**, V. Fieschi, 212, climb the staircase from the train station. Turn right on the road at the top; follow for about 150m. The food is delicious, the garden gorgeous, and the sweeping seaside view priceless. (*Primi* €6-8, *secondi* €7-10. Cover €2. Lunch starts daily at noon, dinner at 7pm. MC/V.) On the outdoor terrace of **Ristorante Cecio ❸**, V. Serra, 11, swill *vino* and twirl spaghetti or

LIGURIA

the *risotto all cecio* (2-person min., €8 per person) before a view of the sun setting into the sea. (☎0187 81 20 43. *Primi* and *secondi* €6-15. Cover €2. Open M-Tu and Th-Su noon-3pm and 7:30pm-1am. Closed Nov. MC/V.)

☑ CORNIGLIA-MANAROLA. Take the stairs down to the station from V. della Stazione and turn left, following the path along the railroad tracks. The 1hr. trail begins just after the public beach. Though less picturesque than the hikes between the previous towns, the gentle trail to Manarola makes up for its lack of vineyards and vegetation with sweeping, open-sea vistas.

MANAROLA

Manarola is a paradise for the young in a place untouched by time. Two large swimming coves, sheltered by rocky inlets, attract swimmers and sunbathers in droves. Some of Cinque Terre's funkiest bars and a big, new hostel make this an the ideal hangout for the vivacious backpacking crowd.

🗺️🛈 ORIENTATION AND PRACTICAL INFORMATION. Farmacia del Mare, V. A Discovolo, 238, posts a lists of late-night pharmacies. (☎0189 92 09 30. Open M and F-Sa 9am-1pm and 4-8pm, Tu-Th 9am-1pm. Self-service **laundry** is available at **Il Sole**, V. Cozza, 25. (☎0187 92 00 91. Open M-Sa 9am-1pm and 4-7pm.)

🛏️🍴 ACCOMMODATIONS AND FOOD. To reach **🏠Ostello Cinque Terre ②**, V. B. Riccobaldi, 21, turn right from the train station and continue uphill 300m. Here 48 beds share a bright dining room, a rooftop terrace, and a shelf full of board games. Ask about kayak, bike, and snorkeling equipment rental. (☎0187 92 02 15; www.hostel5terre.com. Wheelchair accessible. Laundry €4 wash, €3 dry. Internet €1.50 for 15min. Breakfast €3.50. Sheets and 5min. shower included. Reception daily 7am-1pm and 5pm-1am. Curfew in summer 1am, in winter midnight. Reserve at least 2 weeks ahead. Dorms €17-22.50; quads with bath €68-80. AmEx/MC/V.) The cheery **🏠Bed and Breakfast La Toretta ④**, Vico Volto, 20, is filled with flowers and sunlight. Most rooms are spacious and have balcony, TV, and A/C. Apartments with kitchen are also available. (☎/fax 0187 92 03 27; www.torrettas.com. Buffet breakfast included. Doubles €70-100, with student reservation €35. V.) **Hotel Ca'D'Andrean ⑤**, V. A. Discovolo, 101, uphill from the train station, has five large rooms, some with a terrace. In summer, eat breakfast (€6) in the garden. (☎0187 92 00 40. Singles €60; doubles €80; triples €108. Cash only.) Manarola also has many *affittacamere*. **Casa Capellini ④**, V. E. Cozzani, 12, rents four doubles (€42) and one apartment with kitchen (2 people for €54), all with bath. The owners prefer to by contacted be email. (☎0187 92 08 23; casa.capellini@tin.it. Cash only.) The restaurant **Il Porticciolo ⑤**, V. Birolli, 92, rents three doubles (€60) with bath, TV, and balcony. (☎/fax 0187 92 00 83. Breakfast €5. AmEx/MC/V.) **Bordini Davide ④**, V. Ciuso Marina, 17, rents three spacious rooms with bath and TV. (☎/fax 0187 92 04 07. Doubles €50. Cash only.)

Marina Piccola ④, V. lo Scalo, 16, is a little place with big meals. Savor *cozze ripiene* (stuffed mussles; €10) on the edge of a rocky cove. (☎0187 92 09 23. *Primi* €6-15, *secondi* €7-15. Open M and W-Su noon-2:30pm and 7pm-midnight. Closed in Aug. AmEx/MC/V.) At **Trattoria Da Billy ②**, V. Rolandi, 122, get away from the town center above P. della Chiesa. This popular place has delicious home-cooked food and lovely views. (☎0187 920 68. *Primi* €6-10, *secondi* €6.50-11. Open M-W and F-Su noon-2pm and 7-9:30pm. MC/V.) **Trattoria Il Porticciolo ③**, V. R. Birolli, 92, serves hearty meals in a casual ambiance at a good value and boasts excellent *gnocchi al pesto* (€5.16). The *torta nocciola* (nut cake; €3) is also superb. (☎0187 92 00 83. *Primi* €3.50-5.16, *secondi* €8-15.49. Cover €2. Open M-Tu and Th-Su 7am-3:30pm and 5-11pm. AmEx/MC/V.)

LIGURIA

◪ NIGHTLIFE. At the right times, there's plenty of rowdy fun to be found in this town of the young, fit, and temporary. A few times each summer, Manarola hosts booming disco parties in a piazza above the harbor, advertised on posters around town. **Il Bar Sopra Il Mare,** on Punta Bonfiglio on the path to Corniglia, is a relaxing spot to get a drink, sit under the stars, and watch the waves crash. (☎0187 76 20 58. Beer €2.50-3, mixed drinks €3.60-4.15. Open mid-June to Oct. daily 6pm-1am.)

◪ MANAROLA-RIOMAGGIORE: VIA DELL'AMORE. The most famous stretch of Cinque Terre hikes takes only 20min. to walk. The route even comes with decorations—it passes through a stone tunnel covered in graffiti love scenes. With elevators at its beginning and end, the slate-paved walk is almost wheelchair accessible except for some steps in the middle.

RIOMAGGIORE

A castle crowns a cliff above the last and smallest Cinque Terre town, and bright houses cascade down the valley. Fishermen swabbing varnish on their boat hulls are as numerous as the tanners smoothing on lotion by the shore. There are rooms for rent around the harbor; this town is the best bet to find last minute lodgings.

◪◪ ORIENTATION AND PRACTICAL INFORMATION. Turn right from the **train station** and walk through a tunnel to reach the historic center. A **Pro Loco Tourist Office** in the train station provides information on trails, hotels, excursions and computers for **Internet** access on the second floor. (☎0187 92 06 33. Open M-Th 6:30-8am, F-Sa 6:30am-10pm.) Other services include: **currency exchange,** at the **National Park Office** next to the station (open daily 8am-11:30pm), and at **Bancomat,** V. Colombo, 215 (open M-F 8:05am-1:20pm and 2:30-3:45pm; AmEx/MC/V). The National Park Office has Internet at €0.80 for 10min. Internet is also at **Bar Centrale,** V. C. Colombo, 144 (€0.10 per min., €6 per hr. Open daily 7:30am-1am). In case of **emergency,** dial ☎113, or call the **police** (☎112) or an **ambulance** (☎118). **Farmacia del Mare,** V. Colombo, 182, posts a list of late-night pharmacies. (☎0187 92 01 60. Open M-F 9am-1pm and 4-8pm.) The self-service **Wash and Dry Lavarapido** is at V. Colombo, 109. (€4 for 30min. Open daily 8am-10pm.) A **post office** is at V. Pecunia, 7. (☎0187 80 31 60. Open M-F 8am-1pm and Sa 8am-noon.)

◪◪ ACCOMMODATIONS AND FOOD. ◪**Hotel Ca Dei Duxi ❸,** V. Colombo, 36, is pretty and well-situated, offering comfortable furnishings and good value. Its six rooms all have bath, TV, A/C, fridge, and terrace. (☎0187 92 00 36; www.duxi.it. Buffet breakfast included. Doubles €60-100; triples €75-130. Cash only.) Above the historic town and closest to the main parking lots, the modern **Hotel Villa Argentina ❺,** V. de Gasperi, 170, boasts 15 breezy rooms with terrific sea views. (☎/fax 0187 92 02 13; www.hotelvillargentina.com. Breakfast included. Singles €77-96; doubles €92-120. Cash only.) The owners of Mar-Mar (see below) also run the nearby **B&B La Caribana ❹,** V. Santuario, 114. All six rooms are equipped with bath, cable TV, minibar, and terrace. (☎/fax 0187 92 07 73. Breakfast and parking included. Doubles €90; triples €110; quads €120. AmEx/MC/V.) Among Riomaggiore's many *affittacamere* organizations, **Edi ❸,** V. Colombo, 111, rents spotless rooms with bath and minibar and apartments for up to six people. (☎/fax 0187 92 03 25. Doubles €52; singles €25; apartments €26-31 per person. AmEx/MC/V.) **5Terre Affitti ❸,** V. Colombo, 174, rents rooms located all over town with bath and satellite TV. Some with balcony. (☎0187 92 03 31; www.immobiliare5terre.com. Singles €30-55; doubles €45-55; triples €55-75; quad with kitchen and terrace €100. Cash only.) **Roberto Fazioli ❷,** V. Colombo, 94, rents dorms with kitchen and bath, doubles with bath and harbor view, and apartments of various sizes. (☎/fax

LIGURIA

0187 92 09 04; robertofazioli@libero.it. Dorms €22; singles €50; doubles €60-70; apartments €22-50 per person. Open daily 9am-9pm. Cash only.) **La Dolce Vita ❷**, V. Colombo, 120, rents dorm-style rooms, doubles with bath and minibar, and four-person apartments. (☎0187 92 09 18 or 92 09 35. Dorms €20; apartments €60. Cash only.) **Mar-Mar ❷**, V. Malborghetto, 8, rents rooms with bath; some have TV and balcony. Apartments for 2-10 people are also available. Ask to see a room beforehand. (☎/fax 0187 92 09 32. Doubles €50-80; apartments €40-200. Cash only.)

For **groceries** and fresh produce, stop at Alimentari della Franca, V. Colombo, 253. (☎018 792 09 29. Open M-F 7am-1pm and 3-7pm, Sa-Su 7am-7pm. MC/V.) At **Trattoria La Lanterna ❹**, V. S. Giacomo, 46, watch the fishing boats roll in and sample delicious fresh fish cooked in many varieties. (☎0585 500 33. *Primi* €6-8, *secondi* €6-22.50. AmEx/MC/V.) On a cliff above town, the upscale **Ripa del Sole ❸**, V. de Casper, 282, serves some of the area's most authentic and flavorful cuisine in a dining room bathed in sunlight. The *tagliatelle* with scampi and white truffles (€9.50) are beyond excellent. (☎0187 92 01 43. *Primi* €7.50-9.50, *secondi* €8.50-21. Open Tu-Su noon-2pm and 6:30-10:30pm. AmEx/MC/V.)

◢◣ **ACTIVITIES AND NIGHTLIFE. Coopsub Cinqueterre Diving Center,** on V. S. Giacomo in Riomaggiore, offers equipment as well as supervised dives off the coast. In June and September when there's less traffic, dolphins are just as common as coral and schools of fish. A license is required for scuba dives, but lessons are also offered. Boat trips include stops to the natural waterfalls of Caneto Beach. (☎0187 92 00 11; www.5terrediving.com. Open daily Easter-late Sept. 9am-6pm.)

Nightlife in Rio is laid back but not particularly bustling. The bar and outdoor patio at **Bar Centrale,** V. C. Colombo, 144, fill up with international backpackers in their early 20s. Energetic Ivo serves a nice, cold brew and then turns up the swingin' Motown. (☎0187 92 02 08. Internet €1 for 10min. Beer €2-5, cocktails €4-6. Open daily 7:30am-1am. Cash only.) **A Pie de Ma, Bar and Vini,** with sweeping views on V. dell'Amore heading into town, is new, knows it's cool, and stays packed from 7pm. (☎338 222 00 88. Happy Hour until closing. Live music Sa nights. Focaccia €3.50. Cocktails €5. Open daily 10am-midnight. Cash only.)

◨ **DAYTRIP FROM CINQUE TERRE**

LEVANTO
A difficult 3hr. hike connects Levanto with Monterosso. Trains run to Cinque Terre (5min. to Monterosso; 20 per day 6:49am-12:47am).

Sandy beaches and seaside promenades are the main attractions at this beach town, the perfect place to spend an afternoon lounging in the sun. The trek to Levanto is more uncultivated and rugged than most of the hikes in Cinque Terre. The trail leaves Monterosso for a harsh 30min. climb to **Punta del Mesco,** a 19th-century lighthouse converted from the ruins of an Augustinian monastery. Before descending to Levanto, it wraps around cliffs and passes vineyards, orchards, and the remains of a 13th-century castle. Private and public beaches line the promenade, dotted with umbrellas. Load up for a beach picnic at **La Focacceria Dome ❶**, V. Dante, 18, serving fresh focaccia, *farinata*, and pizza (about €1) in heaping portions. (Open daily 9am-1am. Cash only.) Those staying for dinner shouldn't miss **Da Rino ❸**, V. Garibaldi, 10, for a family-style Ligurian feast where the pasta tastes great and the fish (€13) is always fresh. (☎328 389 03 50. *Primi* €5.50-8.50, *secondi* €8-11.50. Cover €1.50. Open daily 7pm-midnight. Cash only.) Finally, ▨**Ostello Ospitalia del Mare ❷**, V. San Nicolo, 1, is the perfect option for an overnight stay or as a base for exploring the other *terre*. A converted hospital, all of the spacious, clean rooms have bath. (☎0187 80 25 62; www.ospitaliadelmare.it. Breakfast, sheets, towel, and shower included. No curfew. Internet access €5 per hr. 4-bed dorm €25, 6-bed dorm €22.50, 8-bed dorm €20. MC/V.)

LA SPEZIA   ☎0187

In summer of 2000, a man gardening in his backyard turned up more than tomato plants: a bomb lay beneath the soil. Heavily attacked during WWII because of its naval base and artillery, La Spezia has since evolved into a major commercial port. Situated in *Il Golfo dei Poeti* (The Gulf of Poets) the town makes a great starting point for daytrips to the small fishing village of Porto Venere, the beach resorts of San Terenzo and Lerici, and the beautiful coves of Fiascherino; it's also an unavoidable stopover to and from Cinque Terre. Though La Spezia boasts none of the majestic architecture or cobblestone passageways that grace some neighboring villages, it does have affordable lodgings and a few fascinating museums.

☐ TRANSPORTATION. La Spezia lies on the Genoa-Pisa **train** line. Tickets from Vernazza cost €1.30. The station is included in the Cinque Terre Card, which allows unlimited train use between destinations. **Navigazione Golfo dei Poeti**, V. D. Minzoni, 13 (☎0187 73 29 87; www.navigazionegolfodeipoeti.it), runs **ferries** to each of the Cinque Terre (one-way €11; M-Sa round-trip €19, Su €22); Portovenere (€3.50, round-trip €6); Capraia (3hr., July-Aug., round-trip €40). Call ahead for schedule. For a **taxi,** call ☎0187 52 35 23. The taxi depot is at the train station.

▉ ▉ ORIENTATION AND PRACTICAL INFORMATION. From the **train station,** turn left and walk down **Via XX Settembre,** then turn right down any street to hit **Via Prione,** the city's main drag. Turn right and continue on V. Prione until its hits **Via Chiodo. Via Mazzini** runs parallel to V. Chiodo, closer to the water. The main **tourist office** is beside the port at V. Mazzini, 45. (☎0187 77 09 00. Open M-Sa 9:30am-1:30pm and 3:30pm-7pm, Su 9:30am-12:30pm.) Another **branch** is outside the train station (open daily 8am-8pm). **CTS,** V. Sapri, 86, helps with ferry tickets (to Greece, Sardinia, and Yugoslavia), student airfares, and car rentals. (☎0187 75 10 74. Open M-Sa 9:30am-12:30pm and 3:30-7:30pm. AmEx/MC/V.) **Farmacia Alleanza,** V. Chiodo, 145, posts a list of late-night pharmacies. (☎0187 73 80 07. Open daily 8:30am-12:30pm and 4-8pm. AmEx/MC/V.) In case of **emergency,** dial ☎113, or contact the **police** (☎112) or an **ambulance** (☎118). **Phone Center,** P. S. Bon, 1, 5min. from the train station, has **Internet** and **Western Union** services. (☎0187 77 78 05, fax 71 21 11. €5 per hr. Open M-Sa 9:15am-12:30pm and 3-10pm, Su 3-10pm.) Close to the center of town, **Caffé Italia,** V. Prione, 3/5, also has Internet available. (€1 per 15 min. Open daily 6am-9pm.) To exchange **traveler's checks,** try **Banca Carige,** C. Cavour, 154. (☎0187 73 43 69. Open M-F 8:20am-1:20pm and 2:30-4pm.) There's also an **ATM** outside. The **post office** is a few blocks from the port at P. Verdi and offers **currency exchange.** (☎0187 79 61. Open M-Sa 8am-6:30pm.) **Postal Code:** 19100.

▉ ▉ ACCOMMODATIONS AND FOOD. Close to the port, try friendly, family-run **Albergo Il Sole ❸,** V. Cavalotti, 3. Eleven well-kept and spacious rooms decorated in shades of yellow and rose all have large windows. (☎/fax 0187 73 51 64; www.albergoilsole.com. Buffet breakfast €3. Singles €25-36; doubles €39-45, with bath €47-55. AmEx/MC/V.) The next street over, **Albergo Teatro ❸,** V. Carpenino, 31, near the Teatro Civico, offers six rooms with couch and TV. (☎/fax 0187 73 13 74. Singles €35-55; doubles €50-90. Extra bed 50%.) If you're willing, splurge on the luxurious **Hotel Firenze Continentale ❺,** V. Paleocapa, 7, across from the train station. The hotel retains a fin-de-siècle look, with marble floors and plush sitting areas. The huge rooms are decorated with wood furniture and rugs, and all have bath, A/C, TV, and phone; some have a balcony, too. (☎0187 71 32 00; www.hotelfirenzecontinentale.it. Wheelchair accessible. Buffet breakfast included. Singles €68-88; doubles €90-125; triples €122-179. AmEx/MC/V.)

Reasonably priced trattorias line V. del Prione. For the town's biggest selection of groceries and fresh produce, try **Supermercato Spesafacile,** V. Colombo, 101-107. (Open daily 8:30am-1pm and 4:15-8pm. MC/V.) The new ❌**Ristorante Duccio ❷,** V. Roselli, 17, off of V. del Prione, features the eclectic creations of owner Luccio, who handpicks his ingredients at market everyday. (☎0187 25 86 02. *Primi* €6, *secondi* €7-10. Cover at dinner €1. Open W-Sa noon-2:30pm and 8-11:30pm, Tu and Su 8-11:30.) ❌**La Pia ❶,** V. Magenta, 12, also off of V. del Prione, is a favorite for hot, cheesy focaccia and *farinata*. Dine in casually, or take a heaping plate to go. (☎0182 73 99 99. Most items €2.80-4.50. Open M-Sa 8am-11pm. AmEx/MC/V.) **Osteria con Cucina all'Inferno ❷,** V. L. Costa, 3, off P. Cavour, has been serving Ligurian specialities since 1905. Try the low-ceilinged *osteria*'s *acciughe ripiene* (stuffed anchovies; €5.50) and hearty *mesciua* (€4.50), a thick soup of beans, corn-meal, olive oil, and pepper. (☎0187 294 58. *Primi* €4.50-6.50, *secondi* €5-8.50. Open M-Sa 12:15-2:30pm and 7:15-10:30pm. Cash only.) The more upscale **Trattoria Dino ❹,** V. Cadorna, 18, serves a lovely assortment of pasta and fresh fish in an elegant setting. The menu changes daily. (☎0187 73 54 35. *Primi* €10-12, *secondi* €14-16. Open Tu-Sa noon-2:45pm and 7:30-10:30pm, Su noon-2:45pm. AmEx/MC/V.)

🄶 **SIGHTS.** La Spezia is one of Italy's classiest and cleanest ports, with palms lining the Morin promenade, sailors strolling **Via del Prione,** and parks brimming with citrus trees. It also has an eclectic collection of museums, many related to the town's marine history. There is a cumulative three-day pass (€12) for all of La Spezia's museums, available at any museum in the city. The unique collection of the **Museo Navale,** in P. Chiodo next to the entrance of the **Arsenale Militare Marittimo** (Maritime Military Arsenal) built in 1860-1865, features diving suits dating from WWII, carved prows of 19th-century ships (including a huge green salamander), gargantuan iron anchors, and tiny replicas of Egyptian, Roman, and European vessels. (☎0187 78 30 16, fax 78 29 08. Open M-Sa 8:30am-1pm and 4:15-9:45pm, Su 8:30am-1:15pm. €1.55.) The **Museo Amadeo Lia,** V. Prione, 234, in the ancient church and convent of the Friars of St. Francis from Paola, houses a beautiful collection of 13th- through 17th-century paintings, including Raphael's *San Martino and the Beggar* in **Room 6.** In **Room 7** there is a small collection of works from the 16th century, including Titian's *Portrait of a Gentleman* and Bellini's *Portrait of an Attorney.* (☎0187 73 11 00, fax 72 14 08. Open Tu-Su 10am-6pm. €6, students €4.) The **Museo Civico Entografico,** V. Prione, 156 has an important collection of traditional costumes, furniture, jewelry, and pottery from the surrounding region. (☎/fax 0187 75 85 70. Open W-Su 9am-noon and 3-6pm, Tu 3-6pm. €3). The **Museo del Sigillo,** V. del Priore, 236, in the Palazzina delle Arti, displays one of the largest collections of seals in the world. Many of the pieces, once used for important legal enterprises, are tiny and carved with great skill. (☎0187 77 85 44; www.castagna.it/museodelsigillo. Open M-Su 10am-noon and 4-7pm, Tu 4-7pm. €3.)

RIVIERA DI PONENTE

SAVONA   ☎019

Behind the commercial facade of this Ligurian metropolis lies a rich history of culture and conquest. In politics as in tourism, Savona has long been overshadowed by its giant neighbor, Genoa: at war with the wealthy port since they took opposite sides in the Punic War, Savona fell to the state in 1528, and the *Genovesi* built a fortress on its Priamàr promontory. Rebuilt by Napoleon in the 18th century, Savona has again become a bustling port city. The clean, walkable city center blends 15th-century palaces, elegant clothing stores, and twisting medieval streets. Outside the center, the public gardens, medieval fort, and beaches beckon with opportunities for sport, exploration, and relaxation.

TRANSPORTATION

Trains depart to Genoa (45min., 1-3 per hr. 4:42am-10:12pm, €3.20) and Ventimiglia (2hr., 1-2 per hr. 8:15am-11pm, €7). **Luggage storage** is available at the station. (☎019 89 20 21. Ticket office open daily 6am-11pm.) From the train station, take bus #2 or any utilibus (€0.80) to the city center. ACTS runs **buses** to Finale Ligure (every 20min. 5:02am-10:22pm) from a stop outside the train station. Buses #4 and 5 go between P. Mamelli and the train station (every 15min. 5:15am-midnight, €0.80). Buy tickets at the train station, or on the bus for a €0.40 supplement. For a **taxi**, call ☎019 82 79 51. **Speed Wheel**, V. Veneto 17r (☎019 81 33 75), rents bikes for both kids and adults in the Public Gardens facing the sea. Take V. Dante until it ends at P. Eroe dei Due Mondi, and walk left over the bridge. (€3 per hr., €12 per day. Open M-F 10am-7pm, Sa-Su 10am-noon and 3-7pm.)

ORIENTATION AND PRACTICAL INFORMATION

The 16th-century fortress lies toward the water off **Piazza Priamàr**. The city's main parallel streets, **Corso Manzoni** and **Via Paleocapa**, bounded by the medieval *centro storico*, are filled with churches and palaces. **Via Calata Sbarbaro** or a pedestrian bridge from the *centro storico* leads across the harbor, where **Piazza Mancine** lies. **Via Baglietto,** site of Savona's summer social scene, runs along the harbor.

Tourist Office: C. Italia, 157r (☎019 840 23 21; www.inforiviera.it), 1 block south of P. Sisto IV. Provides **maps**, brochures, bus schedules, and free Internet (15min. limit). Open summer M-Sa 9:30am-1pm and 3-6:30pm, Su and holidays 9:30am-12:30pm; in winter M-Tu and Th 10am-12:30pm and 3-6pm, W and F-Sa 10am-12:30pm.

English-Language Bookstore: Libreria Assolibro, V. Pia, 88r (☎019 838 74 24). Small selection of classics and bestsellers. Open M-F 9:30am-7:30pm, Sa 9:30-11:30am and 3:30-7:30pm. MC/V.

Police: ☎112. **Ambulance** (☎118 or ☎019 827 27 27). **First Aid** (☎800 55 66 88).

Pharmacy: Farmacia della Ferrera, C. Italia, 13 (☎019 82 72 02), posts a list of pharmacies rotating 24hr. service. Open daily 8:30am-8pm.

Hospital: Ospedale San Paolo, V. Genova, 30 (☎019 840 41).

Post Office: P. Diaz, 9 (☎019 841 45 47). Phone cards and *fermoposta*. **Currency exchange** available 8:15am-5:30pm. Open M-Sa 8am-6:30pm. **Postal Code:** 17100.

ACCOMMODATIONS AND CAMPING

Hotel Riviera Suisse, V. Paleocapa, 24 (☎019 85 98 53; www.rivierasuissehotel.it). From the station, take V. Minzoni across the river and turn right into P. del Popolo. V. Paleocapa runs through the piazza to the left. Newly renovated hotel welcomes guests to comfortable rooms with TV, phone, and minibar. Some rooms with A/C. Singles €15-30, with bath €30-45; doubles €25-50/€55-95. MC/V. ❷

Hotel Savona, P. del Popolo, 53r (☎019 82 18 20, fax 82 18 21). From train station, take V. L. Pirandello and turn left at the roundabout onto C. Tardy and Benech, which becomes C. Mazzini across a bridge. Turn left on V. XX Settembre, and hotel is 2 blocks on the right. Conveniently located with bright rooms, all with bath, TV, phone, and balcony. Breakfast included. Singles €26-42; doubles €42-62. MC/V. ❸

Hotel Nazionale, V. Astengo, 55r (☎/fax 019 85 16 36), around the corner from Hotel Savona, where P. del Popolo meets V. Astengo. Spacious rooms have bath, TV, and phone. Friendly staff and comfortable common area with piano. Breakfast buffet €3. Reception 7am-midnight. Singles €45; doubles €65; triples €75. AmEx/MC/V. ❹

Ostello Villa de Franceschini, Villa alla Strà, 29, Conca Verde (☎019 26 32 22), 3km from the train station. No public transportation to hostel. Pick-ups can be arranged 9am-8pm for large groups only, otherwise a cab (€12) is the only option. Direct the driver to "Ostello Concaverde." The hostel is nestled in a thickly wooded hill overlooking Savona. Breakfast included. Reception 7am-10pm and 4pm-12:30am. Dorms €11; family rooms €13 per person. ❶

Camping Vittoria, V. Nizza, 111 (☎019 88 14 39). Catch the #6 bus (5am-11pm) on the V. Baselli side of P. Mamelli. Campgrounds are on the water with a small beach. Sites are small and close together. Reception 8am-11pm. €5 per person, €10 per tent, €3 per car, €2 per bike. Electricity €3. ❶

◖ FOOD

At ◧**Farinata e Vino** ❷, V. Pia, 15r, ancient cooking methods and fresh Savonese seafood keep this restaurant packed. Oven-baked swordfish (€8) and the unique specialty, *farinata bianca* (€3.80) appeal to the hungry or curious. *Farinata* is available for takeout all day. (☎393 29 58 11. *Primi* €4, *secondi* €7. Open daily noon-2pm and 7-9:30pm.) The port-side dining room of **Osteria Bacco** ❹, V. Quarda Superiore, 17-19r, sports distinctive decor: hanging boats, nautical maps, stolen treasure, and a patio strung with lights. The menu of hearty Ligurian cuisine changes daily. (☎019 83 35 35 05; www.osteriabacco.it. *Primi* from €10, *secondi* from €12. Open M-Sa 12:15-2:30pm and 7:30-10pm. AmEx/MC/V.) **Pizzeria Grotta Marina** ❷, P. del Popolo, 19r, prepares the flavors of Naples. Signature "Pizza Gigante," (€26) each quarter piled with different toppings, feeds an army. (☎019 82 96 28. Pizza €3-7. Open daily noon-3pm and 7pm-1am. MC/V.)

♫ ENTERTAINMENT

A **public beach** lies along the water in front of the public gardens. Take C. Italia to V. Dante and walk past the statue of a gallant Garibaldi to a small stretch of sand used for pick-up soccer matches. Many elegant bars line the water on the far side of the harbor, but most nightlife is in the nearby suburb of Albisola, only accessible by car. **Birrò,** V. Baglietto, 42r, is really the only option in Savona that caters to a younger crowd. Expect lots of reggae, as well as a live DJ every night at 11pm. (Beer €2.50, cocktails €4.50. Open nightly 9:30pm-1am.)

FINALE LIGURE ☎ 019

A plaque on the base of a statue along the promenade claims that Finale Ligure is the place for "*Il riposo del popolo,*" or "the people's rest." Whether *riposo* involves bodysurfing in the choppy waves, browsing chic boutiques, or scaling Finalborgo's looming 15th-century Castello di San Giovanni, there are countless ways to pass the time. Venture inward and uphill for respite from the bustling shores in historic medieval villages or along quiet mountain trails.

◰ TRANSPORTATION

The **train station** is in P. V. Veneto. Call ☎019 275 87 77 or 89 20 21 for timetables. Trains run to Genoa (1hr., every hr. 5:37am-3:31pm, €4) and Ventimiglia (30min., every hr. 6:40am-11:14pm; €4.90). Most trains to Genoa stop at Savona and most trains to Ventimiglia stop at San Remo. The ticket office is open daily 5:55am-

7:10pm. **ACTS buses** depart from the front of the train station to Finalborgo (5min., every 20min., €1) and Savona. Catch the **SAR bus** for Borgo Verezzi (10min., 8 per day, €1) across the street. Buy tickets at *tabacchi*. For a **bike rental,** check out **Oddonebici,** V. Colombo, 20. (☎019 69 42 15. Bikes €15 per day. Open Tu-Sa 8:30am-12:30pm and 3:30-8pm, Su 10am-12:30pm and 4-8pm. MC/V.)

✳ ⁊ ORIENTATION AND PRACTICAL INFORMATION

The city is divided into three sections: **Finalpia** to the east, **Finalmarina** in the center, and **Finalborgo,** the old city, inland to the northwest. The train station and most of the listings below are in Finalmarina. The main street winds through the town between the station and **Piazza Vittorio Emanuele II,** changing its name from **Via de Raimondi** to **Via Pertica** to **Via Garibaldi.** From P. V. Emanuele, **Via della Concezione** runs parallel to the shore. To reach the old city, turn left from the station, cross under the tracks, and keep walking left on **Via Domenico Bruneghi** for about 10min.

Tourist Office: IAT, V. S. Pietro, 14 (☎019 68 10 19; www.inforiviera.it). From the station, walk straight until the water, and then take the only right available. Office is on the main street overlooking the sea after a 5min. walk. Open M-Sa 9am-12:30pm and 3:30-6:30pm, Su 9am-noon; in winter closed Su.

Currency Exchange: Banca Carige, V. Garibaldi, 4, at the corner of P. V. Emanuele. €4.13 service charge. **ATM** outside. Open M-F 8:20am-1:20pm and 2:30-4pm. On Sa **post office** has lower rates (€3) and longer waits.

Bookstore: Cartolibreria Fae, V. Pertica, 39 (☎019 69 26 03). Open M-Sa 9am-12:30pm and 3:30-7:30pm, Su 9am-12:30pm and 4-7:30pm; in winter closed Su.

Emergency: Police, V. Brunenghi, 67 (☎112 or ☎019 69 26 66). **Ambulance** (☎118).

Pharmacy: Farmacia della Marina, V. Ghiglieri, 2 (☎019 69 26 70), at the intersection where V. Raimondi becomes V. Pertica. Open M-Sa 8:30am-12:30pm and 4-8pm. Ring bell for emergencies. List of 24hr. pharmacies posted.

Hospital: Ospedale Santa Corona, V. XXV Aprile, 128 (☎019 623 01), in Pietra Ligure.

Internet: Net Village Internet Cafe, V. di Raimondi, 21 (☎019 681 62 83), right across from the train station—cross 2 streets and it's on the left. 3 computers. €2 per 20min., €6 per 65min. Open daily 8am-10pm.

Post Office: V. della Concezione, 29 (☎019 69 04 79). Fax service. Open M-F 8am-6:30pm, Sa 8am-1:15pm. Currency exchange €2.58. **Postal Code:** 17024.

⌂ ⌂ ACCOMMODATIONS AND CAMPING

The youth hostel has the best prices—not to mention the best view. In July and August, it may be the only place that's not booked solid (they don't take reservations). For all other accommodations listed, reservations are strongly recommended. The tourist office can help find rooms for rent in private houses.

▨ **Castello Wuillerman (HI),** V. Generale Caviglia, 46 (☎/fax 019 69 05 15; www.hostelfinaleligure.com). From the train station, turn left on V. Raimondo Pertica, left on V. Rossi and left on V. Alonzo. Climb Gradinate delle Rose to the top. Small castle-turned-hostel has locking cabinets in rooms, a beautiful courtyard, Internet (€4.50 per hr.), and a restaurant. Breakfast and sheets included. Laundry €4 per load. Reception 7-10am and 5-10pm. Curfew 11:30pm. HI cardholders only. Dorms €12. MC/V. ❶

▨ **Pensione Enzo,** Gradinata delle Rose, 3 (☎019 69 13 83), has amiable owners and a fantastic view. Rooms are clean, sunny, and mostly spacious. All rooms have bath and TV, some have balcony. Hearty breakfast included. Reservations should be made far in advance in summer. Open mid-Mar. to Sept. Doubles €40-60. ❷

Albergo Carla, V. Colombo, 44 (☎019 69 22 85, fax 68 19 65). Conveniently located on a shady, cobblestoned street in the center of town. All rooms with bath and phone, some with sea view. Breakfast €4. Tastefully decorated restaurant downstairs also serves lunch and dinner. Singles €27-35; doubles €48-60. AmEx/MC/V. ❸

Albergo San Marco, V. della Concezione, 22 (☎019 69 25 33, fax 681 61 87). From the train station, walk down V. Saccone and turn left on V. della Concezione. Enter through restaurant. 14 spotless rooms have phone, bath, and shower; many have balcony with sea view. Across the street from the beach. Breakfast included. Open Easter-late Sept. Singles €35-48; doubles €52-61. Extra bed €12-15. AmEx/MC/V. ❹

Camping Tahiti, V. Varese (☎/fax 019 60 06 00). From P. V. Veneto take bus for Calvisio. Get off at Bar Paradiso and cross bridge at V. Rossini. Turn left and walk along river to V. Vanese. Hillside site features 8 terraces, 90 lots, and 360-person capacity. Reception 8am-8pm. Open Easter-Oct. 15. High season €6.50 per person, €5 per tent. Electricity €2.50. Hot showers €0.50. AmEx/MC/V. ❶

Del Mulino (☎019 60 16 69; www.campingmulino.it), on V. Castelli. From the train station, take the Calvisio bus to Boncardo Hotel, and follow brown, then yellow, signs. Popular, with sites along a terraced hillside. Only a 10min. walk from the center of town. Bar, pizzeria, and mini-market. Laundry €5. Reception 8am-8pm. Open Apr.-Sept. €4.50-6 per person, €5-7 per tent. Hot showers free. MC/V. ❶

◻ FOOD

Trattorias and pizzerias line the streets closest to the beach. Get basics like sunscreen or bottled water at the **Di per Di Express,** V. Alonzo, 10. (Open M-Sa 8:30am-1pm and 3:45-7:45pm, Su 9am-1pm. MC/V.)

▨ **Spaghetteria Il Post,** V. Porro, 21 (☎019 60 00 95). Follow V. Colombo from the beachfront past P. Cavour. Turn left onto V. Genova, which becomes V. Porro. Pasta is the specialty here: try *penne quattro stagioni* (with bacon, mushrooms, tomatoes, artichokes, and mozzarella; €6.50). Lots of vegetarian options. Bring a few friends, as each dish is made for 2. Cover €1. Open Tu-Su 7-10:30pm. Closed 1st 2 weeks of Mar. ❷

Il Dattero, on the fork where V. Pertica splits into V. Rossi and V. Garibaldi. Decadent flavors and acclaimed soft yogurt. Free toppings, too! Indulge on gelato-filled pastries (€2.20). 2 flavors €1.30. Yogurt €1.30. Open daily 11am-midnight. ❶

Farinata Vini, V. Roma, 25 (☎019 69 25 62). Small, popular, self-proclaimed *"trattoria alla vecchia maniera"* (old-school trattoria) serves up great seafood. Menu changes daily. *Primi* €5.50-8, *secondi* €7.50-15. Reservation recommended in summer. Open M and W-Su 12:30-2pm and 7:30-9:30pm. AmEx/MC/V. ❸

Sole Luna, V. Barrili, 31 (☎019 681 61 60). Grab food to go or stop in for a quick, fresh meal. Try the *farinata* (€1.50), a pie made from chickpeas and filled with meat and vegetables. Pizza slices €1.50-1.80. Grilled focaccia *panini* €1.50-3. Savory crepes €3. Open daily 10am-8pm. Cash only. ❶

Beigisela, V. Colombo, 2 (☎019 69 52 75), at the intersection of V. Alonzo and V. Colombo. Metallic furniture and a black-and-white color scheme give this restaurant a chic ambience. Delicious twists on local dishes, plus scrumptious homemade desserts (€5). *Primi* €5-8.80, *secondi* €7.30-10.30. Wine bar Th 7pm-12:30am. Open M-Tu and Th-F 7:30-10:30pm, Sa-Su 12:30-2pm and 7:30-10:30pm. ❸

◪ SIGHTS

Enclosed within ancient walls, **Finalborgo,** the historic quarter of Finale Ligure, is a 1km walk or bus ride up V. Bruneghi from the station. Past the **Porta Reale,** its main entrance, the Chiostro di Santa Caterina houses the **Museo Civico del Finale,** dedicated to Ligurian history. (☎019 69 00 20. Open in summer Tu-Su 9am-noon and 3:30-5pm; in winter Tu-Sa 9am-noon and 2:30-5pm, Su 9am-noon. Free.) Enjoy the town's medieval architecture and quiet ambience while sipping a caffè in one of many small piazzas. In P. Aycardi, the formerly illustrious **Teatro Aycardi,** now closed and vacant, stands as a reminder of Finalborgo's importance in days past; from the mid-1400s to the early 18th century, it was capital of the Marquisate of Del Carretto. Up a tough but fulfilling 1km bumpy cobblestone path, ◨**Castel Govone,** behind the larger ruins of San Giovanni, lends a spectacular view of Finale. The trail starts next to the post office in P. del Tribunale, at the opposite end of town from Pta. Reale. For further rock climbing in the area, the **Rock Store,** P. Garibaldi, 12, in Finalborgo, provides maps and necessary gear. (☎019 69 02 08. Open Tu-Su 9am-12:30pm and 4:30-7:30pm. MC/V.)

The towns surrounding Finale Ligure are picturesque and beckon with medieval mystery. SAR buses run to the medieval villages of **Borgio** and **Verezzi** (every 15min. 6:35am-1:41am, €1). Above the beaches of the new part of Borgio are the ancient churches and narrow roadways of its historic center. From Borgio, head up V. Nazario Sauro, turning left on the cobblestone path, V. Verezzi, that winds its way up the mountain, crossing several times over the roadway and finally rejoining it 100m from the top. The steep climb offers stunning views of the sea. At the end of the 1hr. hike, four small piazzas connected by winding footpaths are surrounded by medieval houses. It is possible to reach the lowest piazza by SAR bus, from the stop to the left around the corner from the **tourist office,** V. Matteoti, 158. (☎019 61 04 12. Open in summer daily 9am-6pm.) The lowest of the piazzas fill up on weekends in July and August, when the annual **Festival Teatrale** holds live theatrical performances by national touring companies. After dark in Verezzi, do not take a shortcut down the hillside—guard dogs run rampant off the main road. For a longer hike crossing Mt. Caprazoppa, take a 3km trail from Finalborgo to Verezzi, a gentle slope with panoramas along the way. Inquire at the Rock Store for info.

◨ ♫ BEACHES AND ENTERTAINMENT

Spray-painted on the inner wall of the tunnel that leads to the prime **free beach** in Finale Marina is *"Voglio il sole/Cerco nuova luce/nella konfusione"* (I want the sun/I look for new light/in the confusion). Those who empathize with the graffiti poet have come to the right place. Unfortunately, people tend to cram in like sardines on this narrow free strip. More adventurous souls should walk east along V. Aurelia and through the first tunnel to another beach, cradled by overhanging cliffs, a better spot to sunbathe away from the crowds.

Popular among locals and tourists, **Pilade,** V. Garibaldi, 67, features live music on some Friday nights, ranging from blues to soul. The wooden statue of the horn player on the sidewalk and live saxophonist inside draw people in like the Pied Piper—just be willing to do a little shouting above the music to order a drink (€5) or beer (€3 and up). The rest of the week, diners nod their heads in unison to rock and Italian techno, eyes glazed over from one too many Peronis. Pizza (€1.50-1.80 per slice), burgers, salads, crepes (dinner only; €2.60-6.20), and delicious *panini* (€2.60-3) are available for a sit-down meal or takeout. (☎019 69 22 20. Open daily 10am-2am. Closed Th in winter.) As the sun sets, it's easy to find more nightlife—just follow the crowds to the waterfront, where bathhouses turn into dance parties and bars fill up with dehydrated sunbathers along V. della Concezione.

LIGURIA

ALASSIO ☎0182

Sun-splashed Alassio has attracted high-class Italians and dedicated beachgoers to its sparkling seas for over a century. As a Riviera destination, the town lacks the stately history of Bordighera or the cocktail-society sex appeal of San Remo.

Instead, it maintains a cheery, unpretentious character that makes it both distinctly youth-friendly and very easy to love. Many vacationers come exclusively for its fine white-sand beaches. Others indulge in the excellent cuisine, surprisingly extensive nightlife, or a case of the town's signature *Baci* chocolate pastries.

▛ TRANSPORTATION

The **Stazione F. S. train station** is between V. Michelangelo and V. G. Mazzini. Call ☎89 20 21 for timetables. Trains run to: Finale Ligure (25min., every hr., €2.80); Genoa (1½hr., every hr., €5.70); Milan (3½hr., every 3hr., €12-20); and Ventimiglia (1½hr., every 15min., €4.20). **Luggage storage** is available daily 2-6pm to the left from the main exit. The ticket office is open daily 6am-7:15pm. **ACT buses** stop every 20min. along V. Aurelia. Buy tickets at *tabacchi*. For **bike rental,** stop by **Ricciardi,** C. Dante Alighieri, 144, to the left of the train station. (☎0182 64 05 55. Bikes €5 per hr., €15 per day. Open daily 9:30am-12:30pm and 3:30-7:30pm.)

✛ ❼ ORIENTATION AND PRACTICAL INFORMATION

Alassio is a small, navigable town with activity centering around the pedestrian walkways running along its seacoast. Head straight out of the **train station** and turn right on **Via G. Mazzini** in front of the park. V. G. Mazzini forms one part of the city's main street, collectively referred to as **Via Aurelia.** Three streets, V. Aurelia, **Corso Dante Alighieri,** and **Via Vittorio Veneto,** run parallel to the sea. Follow V. Aurelia from the train station to the second stoplight and turn left on **V. Diaz,** crossing over C. Dante Alighieri. Continue straight to arrive at the center of the seafront.

Tourist Office: APT, P. della Libertà, 1 (☎0182 64 70 27; www.inforiviera.it) near Viale Gibb, on V. Aurelia, by the train station. Offers useful **maps** and brochures, and books accommodations. Open M-Sa 9am-12:30pm and 3-6:30pm, Su 9am-12:30pm.

Currency Exchange: Unicredit Banca, V. Gibb, 14, 2 blocks left on V. Hanbury (V. Aurelia) from train station. 24hr. **ATM** available. Open M-F 8:20am-1:20pm and 2:35-4:05pm, Sa-Su 8:20-11:50am. AmEx/MC/V.

English-Language Bookstore: Libreria Marcello, V. Hanbury, 16, next to the bank. Open daily 9am-12:30pm, 4-7:30pm, and 9-11pm.

Emergency: Police, V. Hanbury, 19 (☎113). **Ambulance** (☎118).

Pharmacy: Farmacia Nazionale, V. V. Veneto, 3 (☎0182 64 06 06). Open daily 8:30am-12:30pm and 3:30-7:30pm.

Internet: Link, V. da Vinci, 153 (☎0182 64 80 82). Open M-F 10am-8pm. €5 per hr. **Bar Halloween,** V. Hanbury, 100 (☎0182 66 00 73). 2 computers. Open daily 9pm-2am (see **Entertainment**).

Post Office: V. Hanbury, 59 (☎0182 64 62 11). Open M-F 8am-1:15pm, Sa 8am-12:35pm. **Postal Code:** 17021.

⌂ ⌂ ACCOMMODATIONS AND CAMPING

Rooms disappear quickly in this tiny, lively resort town, so reserve early. Beachfront views come at hefty prices. The tourist office offers a free booking service.

Hotel La Balnearia, V. V. Veneto, 105 (☎0182 64 01 60, fax 64 62 55). From the train station, turn right on V. G. Mazzini and left on V. Torini. Follow to the sea, turning right on V. V. Veneto. Beachside charm, with marble interior, enormous rooms, and courteous staff. Buffet breakfast included. Singles €37-65; doubles €60-120. Cash only. ❸

Hotel Alfieri, V. Leonardo da Vinci, 146 (☎0182 64 02 39, fax 64 02 59). 2 blocks from the sea, spacious rooms and satellite TV, phone, and bath. Corner rooms have sweeping views. Singles €31-64; doubles €45-69, with balcony €48-72. ❹

Hotel Panama, V. Brennero, 27 (☎0182 640 03 95 or 64 59 16; www.panamava-canze.com). A private beach and cheery dining room enliven this hotel. All rooms have TV and phone, some have shower and bath. Breakfast included. Singles and doubles €20-70. Full pension €36-62. Prices peak July-Aug. AmEx/MC/V. ❸

Hotel Villa Claudia, C. Dante Alighieri, 83 (☎0182 64 04 94; www.hotelvillaclau-dia.com). Turn left on V. Volta from V. G. Mazzini and right on C. Dante. Quiet villa has airy rooms with balcony. Surrounded by private gardens. Breakfast included. Singles €35; doubles €70; triples €95; quads €115. Cash only. ❸

Camping La Vedetta Est, V. Giancardi, 11 (☎0182 64 24 07, fax 64 24 27), 1.5km from Alassio. From V. Mazzini across from the tourist office, take bus toward Albenga. Bus stops just in front, but still on the highway, so be extra careful. Spacious bungalows and tent sites on a hill overlooking the sea. (Open M and W-Su 8:30am-3pm and 6:30pm-midnight.) Free showers. Public phone. Open daily 8:30am-12:30pm and 3-10pm. €6-8 per person, bungalows €52-145, €24-32 for 2 people with a car and tent. Cash only. ❶

🔋 FOOD

Pizzerias and more gelaterias per capita than seem possible crowd Alassio's streets. Don't leave without sampling the famed *Baci di Alassio* (fudge pastry). Buy fresh produce at **K supermarket,** V. Hanbury, 39-45, a short walk from the town center. (Open M-Sa 8:30am-1pm and 4-7:50pm, Su 9am-12:45pm. AmEx/MC/V.)

🍴 **Gelateria Acuvea,** P. Matteotti, 3 (☎0182 66 00 60). After 25 years in business, these Sicilian wizards have the whole town in their power. While waiting for a chocolate *granita* (€1.50) or creamy gelato (2 scoops €1.50), watch flavors being hand-churned. Pay at the register and take your token to the counter. Open daily 8am-2am. Cash only. ❶

🍴 **Pizzeria Italia,** Passeggiata Toti, 19 (☎0182 64 40 95). Locals rave that these ultra-thin pizzas are the best in town. The *boscaiola* (grilled eggplant, *proscuitto,* and fresh moz-zarella; €7.50) packs a flavorful punch. Pizza €5.50-8. *Primi* €5-9, *secondi* €9-15.50. Cover €1. Open in summer daily 7pm-6am. Closed Sept.-Apr. AmEx/MC/V. ❷

Osteria Mezzaluna, V. Vico Berno, 6 (☎0182 64 03 87; www.mezzaluna.it), centrally located on the waterfront. Intimate *osteria* features Spanish-influenced atmosphere and Mediterranean cuisine. Wholesome fish, roasted vegetables, and creative use of spices. Try the *menù degustazione* (for 2 or more; €18 per person). Live music nightly. Main courses €6.50-8.50, salads €6.50-8.50. Open daily 7:30pm-2am. AmEx/MC/V. ❸

Pizza Al Sole, V. V. Veneto, 156/A (☎338 829 21 08, fax 0182 54 28 27). Great vari-ety of fresh pizza and focaccia near the beach. Pizza slices €1.50-1.80. Open M-W and F-Su 11am-2:30pm and 4-7:30pm. Cash only. ❶

Ristorante Sail Inn, V. Brennero, 30 (☎0182 64 02 32). A patio on the waterfront is perfect for a classy, fish-centered feast. High quality, generous portions, and hefty prices. *Primi* €9-14, *secondi* €10-20. Open Tu-Su for lunch and dinner. AmEx/MC/V. ❹

👁 📷 SIGHTS AND NIGHTLIFE

Alassio has kilometers of pristine, sandy **beaches** stretching in both directions down the coast, leaving little reason to venture inland. No beaches are free, but spending a few euros on a beach chair with an umbrella is worth it. Take a short stroll down the beach to the east to join the throng of local boys and older fisher-men at the **pier,** a favorite spot for loafing, line-casting, and relaxed sea-gazing, although jumping—once popular—is prohibited. Farther down the beach is the short, stout **Il Torrione,** a 16th-century Genovese tower. A 30min. walk or a short bus ride toward Andorra leads to **Laigueglia,** a peaceful fishing village. Combining Alas-sio's beachfront atmosphere with small-town charm, the pristine village is a maze of colorful houses, tiny piazzas, and twisting stone streets. A short walk uphill from

LIGURIA

THE FIRST KISS

Pasquale Balzola Jr. is the owner of Balzola Pasticceria. The store originated the Baci "kisses" di Alassio, patented in 1919.

On the beginnings: My grandfather invented [Baci di Alassio] in about 1900 when he came here from Turin. He thought Alassio was a place for tourism because we have the sea, and he thought that at the end of their holidays people would buy this type of cake, like a souvenir... Now they are a big business for us because those who come don't leave without buying the cakes.

On his father: My father worked 10 years after my grandfather as the baker for King Vittorio Emanuele III, the King of Italy. He was very famous in all of Europe.

On making a kiss: *Baci* are made with chocolate, sugar, honey, egg white, and hazelnut, the most important [ingredient]. The inside of the "kiss" is a bitter chocolate, not sweet. They are difficult to make... The problem is to cook them leaving the inside very soft. All the ingredients are natural—no preservatives—and they are only handmade, each one.

On acclaim: In Italy there is an important association of historical hotels and restaurants, and we are in it. There are only 125 or 130 places featured in all of Italy.

On the future: I have two boys and two girls; surely the name will stay in the family. It's tradition.

P. Matteotti, 26. ☎0182 64 02 09. Open daily 8am-4am.

the beach leads to the **Chiesa di Santa Maria** in P. San Pietro, a lovely cathedral with towering, frescoed domes and walls covered in soft paintings. (Open daily until 6pm. Mass Su 8, 9:30, 11am, and 5:30pm.

Alassio hops at night, stoked by tourists and an influx of youth from nearby towns. At ⚑**Zanzibar Cocktail and Disco Bar,** V. V. Veneto, 143, young crowds dance the night away on the tabletops and sometimes the bar itself. (☎0182 64 34 72; www.alassiovirtuale.com. Liquor and cocktails €3-5.50. Beer on tap €3. Open nightly 9pm-5am. Happy Hour 9-11pm. Entrance ticket free, but 1 drink mandatory. Cash only.) Decorated with red lanterns **Tokai Bar,** V. V. Veneto, 151, draws an international crowd for beach-front refreshments and loud tunes. (☎0182 64 00 25. Open M-Tu and Th-Su 11pm-3am. Cash only.) Local favorite **Bar Cabaret,** V. Hanbury, 58, has live music and raucous crowds singing along. This is a great spot to practice Italian over a pint (€3-6), as no other language can usually be heard here. (☎347 961 53 72. Open daily 9pm-3am. Cash only.) New and posh, **Bar Lume,** Pass. E. Toti, 2, is one of the busiest bars in town. (☎0182 64 57 15. Wine €12-18 per bottle. Liquor €4, cocktails €4.50-6. Live music nightly 9pm-closing.)

SAN REMO ☎0184

Once a glamorous retreat for Russian nobles, czars, *literati*, and artists, San Remo is now the largest casino resort town on the Italian Riviera. Recently it served as the backdrop for Matt Damon's murderous machinations in *The Talented Mr. Ripley*. San Remo upholds its glamorous profile with finely dressed couples and bikini-clad women gambling along the palm-lined promenade of Corso Imperatrice. Though it's a reputable destination for the wealthy, the winding alleys of La Pigna, the historic district, offer reasonable prices and a quieter ambience. Befitting its location on the Riviera dei Fiori (Riviera of Flowers), San Remo blooms with carnations year-round. Adding to the musical click of dice and chink of poker chips, the town explodes each summer with a symphony of fireworks, classic Italian song, and international jazz competitions.

▌▀ TRANSPORTATION

The **train station** faces C. F. Cavalotti. Trains run to: Genoa (2½hr., every hr. 4:46am-10:41pm, €7.35); Milan (4¼hr., every 2hr. 5:07am-7:17pm, €13.22); and Ventimiglia (15min., every 30min. 6:37am-12:31am, €1.45). Prices listed are the minimum and vary seasonally. (Ticket office open daily 7am-10pm.) For a **Radio Taxi**, call ☎0184 54 14 54.

⚓ 🔼 ORIENTATION AND PRACTICAL INFORMATION

The city is formed by three main streets that run east-west, parallel to the beach. The train station faces **Corso F. Cavalotti.** To get to the center of town, turn right on C. F. Cavalotti. Cross **Rondo Giuseppe Garibaldi** (a rotary) and veer left down **Corso Giuseppe Garibaldi.** At **Piazza Colombo,** either turn left down **Via Manzoni** to reach the intersection of **Via Roma** and **Via Nino Bixio,** or continue straight, veering left while crossing the piazza onto swanky **Corso G. Matteotti,** which leads to the *lungomare.* The tourist-free old town, La Pigna, is uphill from P. Colombo.

Tourist Office: APT, V. Nuvoloni, 1 (☎0184 590 59; www.sanremonet.com). Turn right out of the train station. From P. Colombo, veer left onto C. Matteotti and follow to the end. (15min.) Staff supplies **maps** and brochures. Open M-Sa 8am-7pm, Su 9am-1pm.

Bank: Banca Intesa, V. Roma, 62 (☎0184 59 23 11). Offers **currency exchange** and **ATM.** Open M-F 8:30am-1:30pm and 2:45-4:15pm, Sa 8:30am-1:30pm. There are a few other banks on V. Roma. **Banca di Genova San Giorgio** is right across the street.

Bookstore: Libreria Beraldi, V. Cavour, 8 (☎0184 54 11 11). Reasonable collection of best-sellers in English, French, German, and Spanish. Considerable travel section. Open daily 9am-noon and 3:30-7:30pm. MC/V.

Laundromat: Blu Acquazzura, V. A. Volta, 131 (☎338 818 02 22). Continue from Rondo Garibaldi along V. A. Volta for 50m. Self-service. Wash and dry €5 each for 7kg load, €7 for 16kg load. Open daily 6am-7:30pm.

Emergency: ☎118. **Police** (☎113).

Pharmacy: Farmacia Centrale, C. Matteotti, 190 (☎0184 50 90 65). Posts a lists of pharmacies rotating 24hr. service. Open M-Sa 8:30am-8:30pm.

Hospital: Ospedale Civile, V. G. Borea, 56 (☎0184 53 61).

Internet: Mailboxes, Etc., C. Cavallotti, 86 (☎0184 59 16 73). €4 for 30min., €7.50 per hr. **Photocopier** and **fax** also available. Open M-F 9am-6:30pm. AmEx/MC/V.

Post Office: V. Roma, 156. Open M-Sa 8am-6:30pm. **Postal Code:** 18038.

📍 ACCOMMODATIONS

San Remo enjoys a high standard of accommodation; even one-star hotels tend to be clean and comfortable.

Terminus Metropolis, V. Roma, 8 (☎0184 57 71 10). Head down C. Matteotti from P. Colombo. Turn left down onto V. Gaudio and right onto V. Roma. The hotel is 2 blocks from the sea. Old-world elegance down to the last detail—antique furniture and decorative fireplaces. Breakfast €5. Singles €30; doubles €45, with bath €50; triples €55. Prices €10-15 higher in Aug. Cash only. ❸

Albergo De Paoli, C. Raimondo, 53, 3rd fl. (☎0184 50 04 93). From the train station, turn right on C. F. Cavalotti and left on V. Fiume. Turn right on C. Orazio Raimondo; De Paoli is 50m on the right. Ring buzzer to enter. Directly across from the beach, this small hotel shares space with the more expensive Hotel Esperia. Large, tidy rooms and clean shared baths. Breakfast €5. Singles €20; doubles €35. Cash only. ❷

Hotel Mara, V. Roma, 93, 3rd fl. (☎0184 53 38 60). From the train station, turn right on C. F. Cavalotti, left on V. Fiume, and right on C. O. Raimondo until it becomes V. Roma. The hotel is on the right. Don't judge this place by its hallway—wallpapered rooms with dressers and closets are as nice as grandma's house. Clean shared baths. Singles €30; doubles €39; triples €54; quads €68. Cash only. ❸

Albergo Al Dom, C. Mombello, 13, 2nd fl. (☎0184 50 14 60). From the train station, turn left off C. Matteotti onto C. Mombello; on the left after V. Roma, in the city center. Rooms, all with bath and TV, furnished with care by friendly owners. Comfortable sitting room has TV, exercise equipment. Breakfast €5. Singles €25-30; doubles €50-60. ❸

LIGURIA

Hotel Graziella, Rondo Garibaldi, 2 (☎0184 571 031, fax 57 00 43). Two minutes from the train station. Turn right on C. F. Cavalotti, then right around Rondo Garibaldi. Hotel is set back from the road in a villa. Elegant rooms with high ceilings and private balconies. All with TV and phone, most with A/C. Breakfast €5. Singles €55; doubles €70. Prices €10-15 per person higher in Aug. AmEx/MC/V. ❹

⚫ FOOD

Amid San Remo's wealth of pizzerias and pricey restaurants are some unique, affordable dining options. Try *sardinara*, a local focaccia-like specialty topped with tomato sauce, herbs, and olives. Buy basics at Soft IF Discount **supermarket** in P. Eroi. (Open M-F 8:15am-1pm and 4:30-7:30pm, Sa 8:15am-7:45pm, Su 8:30am-1pm. MC/V.) The huge **indoor market,** the Mercato Ortofruitticolo, in neighboring P. Mercato, sells fresh produce, meat, and bread. (Open daily 6am-6:30pm.)

⬛ **Urbicia Vivas,** P. dei Dolori, 5/6 (☎0184 75 55 66; www.urbiciavivas.com), in a charming square in the old city. Join the locals for sumptuous fish dishes and delicious home-made pasta at this snug family-run trattoria. *Primi* €5-10, *secondi* €6-12. Open daily 8am-3pm and 7pm-midnight. AmEx/MC/V. ❷

Trattoria A Cuvèa, C. S. Garibaldi, 110 (☎0184 50 34 98). Follow C. Cavalotti away from the train station. Simple, fresh Ligurian cuisine, like *gnocchi* and ravioli, at an excellent value. *Primi* €5.70-8.25, *secondi* €7.60-8.60. Open daily noon-3:50pm and M-Sa 6pm-midnight. ❷

Dick Turpin's, C. N. Sauro, 15 (☎0184 50 34 99). Follow C. N. Sauro until it meets the beach. Something for everyone in a casual, pub-like atmosphere. Sweet or savory crepes €4.50, large variety of pizza €5-8, fresh seafood specials €16. Open daily noon-4pm and 7pm-1am. MC/V. ❸

Pizzeria Napoletana da Giovanni, V. C. Pesante, 7 (☎0184 50 49 54), off V. XX Settembre. A quiet side-street location and laid-back ambience make a nice change of pace from the crowded restaurants by the water. 41 kinds of pizza (€4.50-9). *Primi* and *secondi* €5.50-8. Four-course *menù* €15.50-23.50. Open M-W and F-Su noon-2:30pm and 7-10:45pm. AmEx/MC/V. ❷

Vin D'Italia, C. Mombello, 3 (☎0184 59 17 47). Casual, unpretentious, upscale atmosphere with stone walls and lots of wine. Best *sardinara* (€0.80) in town, hot from a grand wood-burning oven. *Primi* €7-12, *secondi* €13. Open M-Sa noon. MC/V. ❹

Polleria Gazera, V. Palazzo, 85, in the pedestrian zone. You'll smell it two blocks before you see it. There's nothing elegant about hot, juicy spit-roasted chickens (€6.25) and roast beef (€2.60 per 100g), but that doesn't stop the crowds. Take-out only. Open M-F 9am-7pm, Sa 9am-1pm. Cash only. ❶

⚫ SIGHTS

San Remo has a number of historical treasures. Across the street from the tourist office stands the Byzantine-style, onion-domed Russian Orthodox **Chiesa di Cristo Salvatore.** Though its frescoes were never completed, a picture of Christ painted onto the skylight watches the gallery of gleaming icons below. (Open Tu-Su 9:30am-12:30pm and 3-6pm. €1 suggested donation.) Leaving the church, follow C. Matteotti away from the sea, turning left onto the little V. Cappucini, which winds its way into P. San Siro. Here looms the 13th-century, Roman-Gothic **Basilica di San Siro,** regarded as the city's most sacred monument. (Open M-Sa 7:15am-noon and 3-5:45pm, Su 7:15am-noon and 3:30-7pm.) From here, steer through the vendors along the gelateria-lined V. Palazzo to **La Pigna,** San Remo's historic town, which most tourists miss entirely. Narrow, winding streets are crowded with tiny medieval churches that local lore holds are all connected by secret underground passageways. From La Pigna, follow the tree-lined road upward to reveal expansive views of the town and sea. Cobblestone mosaics from 1636 form the Genoese coat of arms. At the end of the road, in P. Assunta, is the stunning **Il Santuario della Madonna della Costa.** This 17th-century monument features a high dome covered in frescoes and a shimmering altar framed by rose windows. The *Madonna and Child* painting by Vilo of Voltiri dates to the late 14th century. (☎0184 50 30 00. Open daily 9am-noon and 3-5:30pm. Modest dress required.)

ENTERTAINMENT AND NIGHTLIFE

When nighttime hits in San Remo, so do the gamblers who frequent the enormous **Casino Municipale,** C. Inglesi, 18, at the end of V. Roma. The casino, built in 1905, is a dazzling example of Belle Epoque architecture. It's the oldest of Italy's three casinos and the only one purpose-built. No sandals or shorts are allowed upstairs; a coat and tie are required in winter. (☎0184 59 51; www.casinosanremo.it. Passport required. 18+. Cover F-Su €7.50 for upstairs rooms. Open M-F 2:30pm-2am, Sa-Su 2:30pm-4am.) Five hundred slot machines clang away on the lower floors, while the swank rooms upstairs host the Riviera's most dapper and well-endowed, all doing their best Bret Maverick. After dark, couples meander along the swanky **Corso Matteotti** for gelato or liqueurs. Between the casino at one end and a piazza at the other, cafes and bars line the street. Mellow **Sax Pub,** V. Roma, 160, sports jazz-inspired decor and outdoor seating to attract an all-ages crowd. Mixed drinks (€3, weekends €5) include appetizers. (☎0184 50 37 43. Open M-Tu and Th-Su 7pm-3am.) Directly across from the casino, young crowds huddle around the bar at **Il Teatrino di Mangiafuoco,** V. Roma, 26. Flashy music from the DJ and loud posters on the walls make heads swirl. Pasta and a staggering drink selection are available. (Open Tu-Su 7pm-2am. MC/V.) Five minutes from the casino is the town's only dance club on the beach, **Pico de Gallo,** Lungomare V. Emanuele, 11/13. Sip a Caribbean-inspired drink (€5) and dance the night away to live music on the sand. (☎0184 57 43 45; www.picosanremo.com. Open for dancing Th-Sa from 10:30pm. MC/V.) The sounds of the **Zoo Bizarre,** V. Gaudio, 10, emerge long before the bar does. It's on a little side street off C. Matteotti, left toward the casino. This trendy spot has electric green tables and chairs and a ceiling plastered with an overlapping hodge-podge of movie posters. The hip crowd kicks off its weekend evenings here around 9pm with drinks (€4-6.50) and trays of free tiny munchies. (☎0184 50 57 74. Open M-F 8am-2am, Sa-Su 8am-3am.)

Nighttime alternatives to dice and drinking are harder to come by. **Disco Ninfa Egeria,** C. Matteotti, 178, is the choice destination for those determined to dance. The cover is steep, though, and most of the younger crowd heads to other coastal towns. (☎0184 59 11 33. Cover €15. Open Sa from 11pm. Dancing begins well after midnight.) Italian speakers enjoy Italian and dubbed foreign-language films at **Teatro Cinema Ariston,** P. Borea D'Olmo, 33/35, at the upper end of C. Matteotti. (☎0184 50 60 60. Shows nightly from 4-10pm. €4-7.)

In the daytime, speedo- and bikini-clad crowds pack the beach and numerous *bagni* that line the water, so get down there early to snag a sand dune. Most commercial beaches are open 8am-7pm. Lounge chair and umbrella rental run around €3 each for the day. At the end of June, floats parade around for the annual festival **San Remo in Fiore.** Early July brings the week-long **Fiori di Fuoco** (www.fioridi-fuoco.it), a famed fireworks competition. The handiwork of masters from around the world fills the skies each night. The **Jazz and Blues Festival,** held in late July and early August, again draws international artists to soothe the sunburned crowds.

LIGURIA

BORDIGHERA ☎0184

When Italian writer Giovanni Ruffini crafted his 1855 melodrama, *Il Dottor Antonio*, he unwittingly laid the foundation for the development of both Bordighera and the Italian Riviera's tourism industry. English travelers were entranced by his story of an ailing English girl miraculously revived by Bordighera's Mediterranean charm. In the early 20th century, they turned the town into a summer vacation paradise, constructing glamorous seaside hotels and Italy's first tennis courts. Intellectuals and artists like Claude Monet and Louis Pasteur chose the town as their special retreat, and Italy's Queen Margaret took up permanent residence here. Bordighera's status as a summer haven endures today, as sun-seekers and Italian families revitalize themselves along its pebbly beaches and palm-lined promenade.

TRANSPORTATION. The **train station** is in P. Eroi Libertà. Trains run to: Genoa (3hr., 5:34am-10:32pm, €7.35); Milan (4hr., 4:57am-7:07pm, €25); San Remo (10min., every hr. 4:37am-9:56pm, €1.45); and Ventimiglia (10min, every 30min. 6:47am-12:40am, €0.95). The ticket office is open daily 6:15am-7:45pm. **Riviera Transporte buses** stop every 300m on V. V. Emanuele and run to San Remo and Ventimiglia (every 15min. M-Sa, every 30min. Su), on opposite ends of the #2 line. (20min. to both towns, 5:23am-1:18pm, €1.15.) Buy tickets at *tabacchi* on V. V. Emanuele or the post office.

ORIENTATION AND PRACTICAL INFORMATION. The bus from Ventimiglia stops on the main street, **Via Vittorio Emanuele,** which runs parallel to the **train station** one block in front of it. Behind the station, set apart from the rest of the town, the scenic **Lungomare Argentina,** a 2km beach promenade, runs parallel to the *città moderna* (new town), the site of most offices and shops. To get from town to the *lungomare*, use one of the many tunnels that go underneath the train tracks. To reach the old town, the *centro storico*, from the station, head through P. Ruffini to V. Libertà and continue uphill.

To reach the **tourist office,** V. V. Emanuele, 172, from the train station, walk along V. Roma and turn left on V. V. Emanuele; it's on the right near the park. (☎0184 26 23 22, fax 26 44 55. Open in summer M-Sa 9am-12:30pm and 3:30-7pm, Su 9am-noon; in winter M-Sa 9am-12:30pm and 3-6:30pm.) **Currency Exchange** is available at **Banca Intesa,** V. V. Emanuele, 153-155. There is also an **ATM** outside. (☎0184 26 67 77. Open M-F and Su 8:30am-1:30pm and 2:45-4:15pm.) In case of **emergency,** call ☎113, an **ambulance** (☎118), or the **police,** V. Primo Maggio, 49 (☎112 or 0184 26 26 26). **Farmacia Centrale,** V. V. Emanuele, 145, posts a list of rotating emergency service. (☎0184 26 12 46. Open M-F 8:30am-12:30pm and 3:30-7:30pm.) There is a **hospital** at V. Aurelia, 122 (☎0184 27 51). The **post office** is at P. Libertà, 5 (☎0184 26 91 51 or 26 91 31. Open M-F 8am-6:30pm, Sa 8am-12:30pm.) **Postal Code:** 18012.

ACCOMMODATIONS AND FOOD. In high season many hotels in Bordighera require that clients accept full or half pension. It is also standard practice to raise prices for guests staying under three days. Many large, expensive hotels in white fin-de-siècle architecture line the sea, but the town's few budget options are also pleasant. Walk straight out of the train station onto V. Roma, take a left on V. V. Emanuele, then turn right on V. Lagazzi to find the quiet **Villa Miki ❷,** V. Lagazzi, 14. Eighteen tiny, tidy rooms all have garden-view terraces; some have showers. (☎0184 26 18 44. Breakfast included. Singles €24-28; doubles €40-59. Half pension €36-48 per person; full pension €44-58.) Across from the train station on the left is **Albergo Nagos ❷,** P. Eroi della Libertà, 7, 3rd fl. Husband-and-wife managers create a homey feel. Ten small rooms all have sink, toilet, and seaview terrace; three have private shower. (☎0184 26 04 57. Singles €25; doubles €40. Half pension €33-35 per person; full pension €40-45.)

LIGURIA

To escape the crowds, head to a trattoria in the historic center for a traditional meal. *Rossesse*, a deliciously sweet but expensive red wine from Dolceacque and other nearby towns, is available year-round. An **outdoor market** on the *lungomare* sell produce and clothing every Thursday from early morning until 1pm. There is an IEFFE Discount **supermarket** at P. Garibaldi 32-35. (Open M-Sa 8:30am-1pm and 4:30-8pm, Su 8:45am-12:45pm. Reduced winter hours.) There is also a STANDA at V. Libertà, 32. (Open daily 8am-8pm. AmEx/MC/V.) **Ristorante la Piazzetta ❷**, P. del Popolo, 13 (☎0184 26 04 74), serves savory Ligurian fare in bountiful portions to a local crowd. Wood-fired pizza (€4.30-7) is the specialty. (*Primi* €6-8, *secondi* €8-15. *Tartufo bianco* and other beautifully-presented desserts €3.30. Open M-Tu and Th-Su noon-2pm and 7-11pm. Cover €1.20. AmEx/MC/V.) Local youths crowd the delicate marble tables of **Creperie-Caffè Giglio ❷**, V. V. Emanuele, 158 (☎0184 26 15 30). A dizzying selection of creative dinner crepes (€3.10-5.70) and *panini* (€2.85-3.35) is served alongside many vegetarian options. Dessert crepes (€4.70) get special attention; try one filled with seasonal fruit, sugar, and milk gelato. (Open Tu-Sa 7pm-3am, Su 3pm-3am.) Underneath all of the pirate-themed kitsch at **La Reserve ❹**, V. Aziglio, 20 (☎0184 26 13 22), at the eastern end of the *lungomare*, are traditional Italian dishes with a north-of-the-border twist. Try the monkfish *osso bucco* with bacon and red wine for €20. *(Primi €8.50-12.50, secondi €15.50-20. Open all day; meals served 8-10am, 12:30-2pm and 8-9:30pm.)* ❹

◉ ♫ SIGHTS AND ENTERTAINMENT. People come for one thing: the beach. Cross under the train tracks onto Lungomare Argentina, turn left, and stroll down the promenade to admire Bordighera's impressive turn-of-the-century hotels. Though there are jet-skis, windsurf boards, and motorboats for rent, all the vast majority of visitors want is an umbrella, a lounge chair, and a strip of beach to call their own. Sunbathers reach right up to the doorstep of the one-time home of the hermit Ampelio, the town's patron saint. His seaside grotto, on the eastern part of the *lungomare*, is now home to the tiny **Chiesa di Sant'Ampelio.** Before Easter each year, the elders and young fries of Bordighera prepare *palmureli* (palms) from local palm trees to sell to the Vatican for use during Holy Week; profits benefit the area's poor. Preferring *pesce* to prayers, town fisherman congregate on the rocks below the church. Continue past the church along V. Arziglia for 1km to the **Giardino Esotico Pallanca** or take a bus from V. V. Emanuele heading toward San Remo and ask the driver to stop at the Giardino. The exotic garden, once open only to scientists, contains over 3000 species of cacti and flora. The brochure's guided walking tour leads along meandering terraces carved out of the sandstone slopes. (☎0184 26 63 47. Open Tu-Su 9am-12:30pm and 2:30-6pm. €5.50.) Returning to town, the park rising above the Chiesa di Sant'Ampelio offers spectacular sea views and a glimpse of a statue of Queen Margherita Di Saviolo, one of Italy's first queens. The park leads to the town's *centro storico* (historic center), established in 1471, which is closed to cars.

Despite its small size, Bordighera loves revelry. In April each year, the city becomes **La Città dell'Umorismo,** when comedians and comic-strip artists descend upon the town for a famed competition. On May 14, the church hosts the **Festa di Sant'Ampelio,** when the whole town gathers in celebration with fireworks, a feast of gastronomic specialties, dancing, and music. Summer brings a host of outdoor festivities, including an international ethnic music festival at the end of July and a series of concerts and plays at the seaside gazebo **Chiosca della Musica.**

▨ NIGHTLIFE. A raucous crowd fills lounges and tables along the street at **Graffiti Pub/Risto House,** V. V. Emanuele, 122 (☎0184 26 15 90). Along with a wide choice of liquor (€3) and beer on tap (€2-4), they also serve cheap meals. (*Panini* €3-3.70. Open M-Sa 5pm-3am. 25+. MC/V.) The **Kursaal Club,** Lungomare Lutazio

Catulo, 7 (☎0184 26 46 85), has both live and recorded underground, house, and industrial music. (Open Sept.-July F-Su 11pm-5am, Aug. daily 11pm-5am. Younger crown on Sa, 25+ on F and Su. AmEx/MC/V.) Enjoy a plate of Spanish *paella* for 2 (€14-18), share *tapas* (€3-6), or sip one of many takes on the margarita (€6) at **Chica Loca** (☎0184 26 35 10), on Lungomare Argentina between the train station and Kursaal. (Occasional live music. Open daily July-Sept. noon-3pm and 7pm-6:30am.) **Il Barretto** (☎0184 26 25 66) is Bordighera's most renowned spot for beachside nightlife—you'll know it when you see it. Come for a cheap-eating, floor-packing, liquor-saturated good time. (Toast and hotdogs €2-4. Shots of Bacardi €3.50. Open daily noon-3pm and 7pm-6:30am.)

VENTIMIGLIA ☎0184

"Bonjour" is almost as common as "Buongiorno" in this petite, bustling commercial town. Ventimiglia is only a 10min. train ride from the French border, and until Napoleon's 1860 invasion established a border, the coastline between the town and Monaco were part of the same state. Better known for its rich history than for the seaside lounging offered by other Riviera destinations, Ventimiglia first entered the books when Augustus conquered it over 2000 years ago. The nearby Roman ruins, Romanesque churches, and winding streets of the 11th-century *città alta* bear witness to a vibrant past. French citizens commute for work and frequent the restaurants, but the town still feels distinctly Italian. Set out from Ventimiglia to explore Liguria and the Côte d'Azur—just don't forget your passport.

▐ TRANSPORTATION

The **train station** (☎0184 90 20 21) is in P. Cesare Battisti. **Trains** run to: Genoa (2hr., every 30min. 4:30am-10:25pm, €8.85) and Nice (40min., every hr. 8:50am-7:18pm, €9.40). **Buses** run to regional and local destinations, including San Remo (35min., 4 per hr. 5:30am-1:18am, €1.70) via Bordighera (15min., €1.15). Tickets are available in the *tabacchi* lining V. Cavour and at **Turismo Monte Carlo** (see below), which also provides schedules. The bus stops every 100m along V. Cavour. For **bike rental**, try **Eurocicli**, V. Cavour, 70/B. (☎0184 35 18 79. €1 per hr., €6 per day. Open M-Sa 8:15am-12:30pm and 3-7:30pm. MC/V.)

▚ ▟ ORIENTATION AND PRACTICAL INFORMATION

From the **train station,** walk straight down **Via della Stazione** to the *centro.* The second crossroad is **Via Cavour,** where V. della Stazione becomes **Corso Repubblica** as it continues toward the waterfront. Turn left onto **Lungo Roia Giolamo Rossi** to stroll along a restaurant-lined seaside promenade in the newer and commercial part of town. To visit France, hop on a train or a blue **Riviera Transporte** bus that leaves from stops along V. Cavour. Bring a passport.

> **Tourist Office:** V. Cavour, 61 (☎0184 35 11 83; infoventimiglia@rivieradefiori.org), 5min. from the train station. English- and French-speaking staff offers **maps** and information on local and nearby attractions. A stop here is particularly useful, as many interesting sights lie outside the city proper. Open M-Sa 9am-12:30pm and 3-7pm. The travel agency two doors down, **Turismo Monte Carlo,** V. Cavour, 57 (☎0184 35 75 77, fax 35 26 21), has **currency exchange** and bus and hotel info. Open M-Sa 9am-12:30pm and 2:30-7pm.

> **Bank: Banca Intesa,** V. Roma, 18/D. In central location with ATM outside. Open M-F 8:30am-1pm and 2:45-4:15pm AmEx/MC/V.

VENTIMIGLIA ■ 215

Bookstore: **Libreria Casella,** V. della Stazione, 1/D (☎0184 35 79 00). Books in Italian, French, German, and Dutch, with a small English selection. Open M-Sa 9am-12:30pm and 3-7:30pm. MC/V.

Emergency: ☎113. **Police,** V. Aprosio, 12 (☎112 or 0184 23 821). **Ambulance** (☎118). **Red Cross,** V. Dante Alighieri, 12 (☎0184 23 20 00). **Croce Verde,** P. XX Settembre 8 (☎0184 35 11 75). For emergencies at night, call ☎800 55 44 00.

Pharmacy: Farmacia Internazionale, V. Cavour, 28/A (☎0184 35 13 00). Open M-F 8:30am-1pm and 3:30-7:30pm, Sa 8:30am-12:30pm. Posts phone numbers for rotating after-hours service. AmEx/MC/V.

Hospital: Saint Charles (☎0184 27 51), just outside Bordighera.

Internet: Mail Boxes, Etc., V. V. Veneto, 4/B (☎0184 23 84 23), just past the Giardini Pubblici from C. Repubblica. Also a **Western Union.** €3 per 30min. Open M-F 8:30am-12:30pm and 3-6:30pm, Sa 8:30am-12:30pm.

Post Office: C. Repubblica, 8/C (☎0184 23 63 51), on the right after crossing V. Roma. Open M-F 8am-6:30pm, Sa 8am-7:30pm. **Postal Code:** 18039.

ACCOMMODATIONS AND CAMPING

Ventimiglia fills up quickly in July and August. Reservations are strongly recommended in summer; consider traveling to Bordighera or nearby Menton, France.

Calypso Hotel, V. Matteotti, 8/G (☎0184 35 15 88). Large rooms with handsome wooden floors and TV. Elegant decor and quiet central location. Garage €8 per day. Breakfast included. Reception 7am-midnight. Closed Jan. 15-Feb. 10. Singles €39; doubles €62, with bath €75; triples €85/100. AmEx/MC/V. ❹

Hotel XX Settembre, V. Roma, 16 (☎0184 35 12 22). Nine spacious rooms with smart tile floors, writing desks, and terraces, some with bath. Breakfast €4. Singles €30; doubles €45-50, with bath €65-70; triples €65-70. MC/V. ❸

Hotel Posta, V. Sottoconvento, 15 (☎0184 35 12 18 or 23 16 00; www.masterweb.it/hotelposta). From V. Cavour turn right on V. G. Mazzini before the tourist office, then left after 50m on V. Sottoconvento. Rooms have tasteful decorations, luxury carpeting, and balcony. Breakfast included. Parking €6. Singles €59; doubles €70; triples €95; quads €110; quints €120. ❺

Hotel Villa Franca, C. Repubblica, 12 (☎0184 35 18 71, fax 33 434). Great location next to the waterfront and public park. Utilitarian rooms, English-speaking management and a parrot in the lobby who says "ciao." Breakfast included. Singles €30; doubles €44, with bath €52; triples €72. AmEx/MC/V. ❸

Camping Roma, V. Freccero, 9 (☎0184 23 90 07; informazioni@campingroma.it). From the station, follow V. della Repubblica, turn right to V. Roma and cross the bridge, and make an immediate right to C. Francia. After 50m it becomes V. Freccero. Signs are posted along the way. Family friendly spot within the confines of the city has a well-maintained bungalow for every budget. Immaculate shared facilities. Open Nov.-Sept. €5-10 per person, €6-9 per tent, €7-9 for camper, €5 for car. Cabins for 2, 4, and 6 with kitchen €45-65, €65-100 with private bath. Showers free. MC/V. ❶

FOOD

The **covered market** (open M-Sa 8am-1:30pm), displays a staggering array of fruit and vegetable stands along V. della Repubblica, V. Libertà, V. Aprosio, and V. Roma. A **STANDA** is at the corner of V. Roma and V. Ruffini. (Open M-Sa 8am-8pm, Su 9am-8pm. AmEx/MC/V.) Along the beach on the Bassa side, there are five or six pizzerias offering similar fare for €8-12. Head to the Alta shore for more variety.

LIGURIA

La Vecchia Napoli, V. Trossarelli, 28 (☎0184 35 24 71), conveniently located just off the footbridge on the Alta side of town. Thin, crispy pizzas (€5-9), served by a cheerful Neapolitan family. Hearty, comfortable atmosphere. Try the ricotta-filled specialty pizza (€7) for a sumptuous twist. *Primi* €9.50-15, *secondi* €14.50-19. Open Tu-Su 10am-2:30pm and 6-11:30pm. MC/V. ❸

Ristorante Cuneo, V. Aprosio, 16/D. Turn right on V. Aprosio from C. Repubblica and follow for 75m. School-buddy owners bubble with enthusiasm. Delicious Ligurian cuisine includes homemade *gnocchi* (€7.50). *Primi* €5.50-9, *secondi* €11.50-18.50. 4-course *menù* €18.50. Open M-Sa noon-2:30pm and 6:30-10:30pm. MC/V. ❸

Pasta & Basta, Passeggiata Marconi, 20/A (☎0184 23 08 78). On the Alta side of the river, shortly before the Galleria Scoglietti. Mix and match 22 sauces (€5-9) with 9 freshly made pastas. If inventing *zuchinni al dente* (€7) over *gnocchi* (€2) isn't your style, try one of the house seafood specials instead. Elegant, air-conditioned, affordable. Open Tu-Th noon-midnight. ❷

Ristorante Nanni, V. Milite Ignoto, 3/D (☎0184 332 30). Across the street from the Giardini Comunali. Hearty portions and reasonable prices. Ligurian specialties like *tagliatte* with pesto (€5.16). *Primi* €5.16-9.30, *secondi* €9-15, 4-course *menù* €11.86-14.46. Open Tu-Su noon-2:30pm and 7:30-10:30pm. AmEx/MC/V. ❸

Ristorante Marco Polo, Lungomare F. Cavalotti, 2 (☎0184 35 26 78). Gorgeous candlelit terrace and mind-blowing flavors make this the place to splurge in Ventimiglia. Don't miss the *tagliatelle* with fresh basil and lobster (€20) or any special from the dessert cart. Service is poised and professional. *Primi* €10-20, *secondi* €11.50-25. Open Tu-Su noon-2:30pm and 7-10:30pm. Open daily July-Aug. AmEx/MC/V. ❺

👁 SIGHTS

While Ventimiglia is busy and commercial, it makes an excellent base for exploring stunning sights nearby. Pebbly **beaches** stretch along the waterfront—the quietest ones are across the river, along Passeggiata Marconi, but Ventimiglia is not known for its beach scene. For those set on sunbathing, a 15min. walk down a footpath from the end of Passegiata Marconi leads away from the city din and onto **Spiaggia Le Calandre,** the town's only stretch of sandy beach. A snack bar serves drinks and *panini* and rents essential beach equipment. (Two lounge-chairs plus umbrella €12 per half-day.) Head home before sundown—you don't want to negotiate the cliff-side path in the dark. (☎0347 431 53 93. Open daily 8am-9pm.)

Città Alta, Ventimiglia's medieval section, is a short walk from the town center. Cross the footbridge to Ventimiglia Alta and turn right on V. Trossarelli. Fifty meters ahead is Discesa Marina; climb to V. Galerina and then V. Falerina. Streets lead to P. Cattedrale, where the ancient **Cattedrale dell'Assunta,** a Romanesque cathedral, holds sentry over the town below. Nestled on the other side of the old town, off V. Garibaldi at P. Colleta, is the 11th-century church of **San Michele.** Its **crypt** was constructed using pilfered Roman columns. (Crypt open Su 10:30am-noon.) A 5min. ascent up V. Verdi from Ventimiglia Alta leads to the **Museo Archeologico,** V. Verdi, 41, also accessible by a nearby bus stop on the way to Ponte San Luigi. Roman artifacts found in the area are on display, including a dozen marble heads. The museum also holds rotating exhibitions by town artists. (☎0184 35 11 81. Open Tu-Sa 9am-12:30pm and 3-5pm, Su 10am-12:30pm. €3, under 18 €2.)

Blue Riviera Trasporti buses leave from the corner of V. Cavour and V. Martiri della Libertà (dir: Ponte San Luigi; 15min.; 12 per day, first bus leaves at 9:05am; €1.15), and stop at La Mortola, home of the ▨**Botanical Hanbury Gardens.** Begun in 1867 by English aristocrat Sir Thomas Hanbury, the stunning gardens hold exotic flora from three continents and cascade down the summit of Cape Mortola. Head down to the seaside cafe for *panini* (€3.10) or gelato (€1). The comprehensive course mapped out in the brochure takes about 2hr. (☎0184 22 95 07. Open in summer daily 9am-7pm, winter until 5pm. Last admission 1hr. before close. €6.50, ages 6-14 and groups €4.50.) For a brief but scenic hike, take the narrow footpath before the entrance to the Hanbury Gardens to a stretch of the ancient **Strada Romana.** Romans used the road, which traverses the hillsides and overlooks the sea, to travel to Provence. After 15min., the road reaches a street with a wide sidewalk, which continues for 550m under two tunnels to the **Balzi Rossi** (red cliffs). Alternatively, take the bus to Ponte San Luigi and walk 10min. Cro-Magnon man once lived in the enormous grottoes. Enter (free) to see a cave drawing of a horse painted thousands of years ago. The two small buildings of its **Museo Prehistorico** contain spectacular skeletons and fossils 1,500,000 years old. (☎0184 381 13. Open Tu-Su 8:30am-7:30pm. €3, €2.50 for groups.)

🎵 ENTERTAINMENT

Although nightlife in Ventimiglia is largely non-existent, the daytime hours are bustling enough. On Friday, the **Mercato Settimanale** wraps around the Giardini Pubblici and sprawls along the river. The humming *mercato*, the biggest market on the Riviera and the Côte d'Azur, is just the place to haggle over slinky French slips, suede coats, salami, and all manner of trinkets. Just look out for pickpockets. Mid- to late June brings the annual **Battaglia dei Fiori,** when floats decorated with flowers parade through town and locals compete in flower-flinging contests.

🔀 DAYTRIP FROM VENTIMIGLIA

🏛 DOLCEACQUA
Buses (20min.; 10 per day 6:10am-7:07pm, last return 7:32pm; €1.60) run from the corner of V. Cavour and C. Repubblica.

Dolceacqua's narrow, winding cobblestone streets, tiny low-ceilinged shops, and a towering castle usher travelers into another century. Though the city's origins are ancient—dating as far back as the 5th century BC—its landmark year came in 1270 when a Genoan captain constructed the famous Doria Castle. During the Middle Ages, Dolceacqua became the largest and strongest of a string of villages that rose up along the Roya River to accommodate traders between Ventimiglia and the rest of northern Italy. The castle endured years of military sieges before succumbing to mother nature in an 1887 earthquake, but the town has preserved its large medieval section, now filled with artist's workshops and galleries.

The bus stops at **Piazza Garibaldi,** the new town's central square. Visit the **IAT Tourist Office,** V. B. Colomba, 3, in the piazza for a comprehensive town brochure. (☎0184 20 66 66. Open daily 10am-1pm and 4-7pm.) The Roya divides the new city from the medieval town on the hill. Cross the stunning high-arched Roman footbridge, the *ponte vecchio* commemorated in an 1887 painting by Monet, into the older side of town. Follow the guided path through the narrow cobblestone streets uphill to the **Castello dei Doria,** where breezes swirl through the ruins and water trickles over rocks below. (☎0184 20 66 38. Open daily 10am-1pm and 2:30-6:30pm. Last entrance 30min. before close.) To the right of the castle, follow the well-marked footpath 10min. for a stunning panorama of the lush green valley. The hills around Dolceacqua are filled with olive trees, and many shops in town sell bottles of hand-pressed, extra-virgin olive oil at reasonable rates. Many of the ancient stone houses have been converted into artist's studios, containing everything from Monet-knock-offs of the town, to sculptures made from bathroom tiles. Admission to most galleries is free. At the bottom of the town, overlooking a piazza next to the river, stands the 15th-century parish church of **San Antonio Abate,** decorated with paintings and a frescoed ceiling. (Open M-Sa 11:30am-6pm. Mass Su 8am.)

LIGURIA

There are no hotels in Dolceacqua, but **Albergo Da Adolfo ❹** is a 5min. ride on the blue Riviera bus, on the outskirts of neighboring town Isolabona. (☎0184 20 81 11. Reception Tu-F 7am-9pm, Sa-Su 7am-1pm. Singles with bath €45; doubles with bath €50.) Step into **Vinoteca Re ❸**, V. P. Martiri, 26, for Ligurian delicacies like *tagliatelle* with pesto (€7) or a plate of *salumi* and local cheese (€5-7) with a glass of *Rossesse*, Dolceacqua's robust, fruity wine. (☎0184 20 61 37. Open M-W and F-Su 10:30am-3pm and 5:30-9:30pm. AmEx/MC/V.) Those in town for the night shouldn't miss a meal at **Pizzeria La Rampa ❷**, V. Barberis Colomba, 11, on the left side of P. Garibaldi. In 2002 the National Agency of Pizza Chefs named their pesto pizza with vegetables "Best 'Typically Regional' Pizza" in Italy, selected from 900 contenders. (☎0184 20 61 98. Open Tu-Su 7pm-midnight; all day every day during Aug. Pizza €4-7. *Primi* €4-6.50, *secondi* €4.50-7.50. Gluten-free pizza available. AmEx/MC/V.) Ask at the tourist office for info on August's **Ferragosto**, which fills the piazza with swirling regional *balletti*, traditional costumes, and mouth-watering *michetta*, a local pastry variant on the brioche.

LIGURIA

LOMBARDY

Ever since the Celts snatched this region from the Etruscans, the fertile land and strategic location of Lombardy have been under attack. The land has been coveted in turn by the Romans, Goths, French, Spaniards, Austrians, and Corsicans. Nevertheless, the disputing European powers failed to rob Lombardy of its prosperity, and the region remains the wealthiest in Italy. Economic preeminence has allowed the *Lombardesi* to cultivate an appreciation for the finer things. Historically, their luxury of choice has been opera—leading to the opening of theaters like Milan's La Scala (p. 232), as well as the cultivation of the first great operatic composer, Claudio Monteverdi. Financial wherewithal enticed such great artists as da Vinci and Bramante to design harmonious civic spaces and ornate private residences. In the surrounding foothills, majestic lakes attract affluent types from all over northern Italy and Central Europe. Critics contend that Lombard cultural sophistication is grounded in a desire for distance from the comparatively underdeveloped southern regions and the international immigrants that flock to its industrial cities. The strong presence of secessionist political party Lega Nord testifies to this tendency. Yet Lombardy's financial success also comes from a dedicated work ethic, and the region is generous with both its resources and its legacy, lending an aura of decorum to Italy's otherwise chaotic image.

HIGHLIGHTS OF LOMBARDY

EXPLORE Lombardy's Lake Country, where cultural greats from Longfellow to Liszt reposed by quietly murmuring waters and snow-capped mountains. (p. 259.)

DAYTRIP to Certosa di Pavia, where the monastery stands as a monument to the evolution of northern Italian art from early Gothic to Baroque. (p. 259.)

SPOT the *moda* of the minute as fashion-conscious *Milanesi* exhibit all that's in vogue. (p. 236.)

MILAN (MILANO)   ☎ 02

A steaming cappuccino sipped under a quaint shop window; a radiant smile from a passing stranger; a moment of solitary reflection stolen inside an ancient basilica: this snapshot could describe any European metropolis. But step deeper into the picture, and the cappuccino becomes a morning art form, the stranger a Gucci guru, and the basilica wall a da Vinci masterpiece. Packed with artistic gems and cultural treasures, Milan leaves little space for the traveler to comprehend all its offerings. Unlike Rome, Venice, or Florence, which wrap themselves in a veil of historic allure, Milan presents itself as it is: rushed, refined, and unabashedly cosmopolitan. Milan has its share of urban sores—thirsty mosquitos, traffic congestion, and the notoriety as one of the most expensive cities in Europe. But true *Milanesi* claim their city proudly. Once the capital of the Cisalpine Republic and the western half of the Roman Empire, Milan is now the center of Italian style, financial markets, and industry. Car tire giant Pirelli, fashion house Armani, and countless banks establish the city as Italy's economic powerhouse. Its artistic masterpieces include a superlatively ornate duomo, da Vinci's *Last Supper*, and La Scala's stunning operas. The city's pace quickens twice a year when local soc-

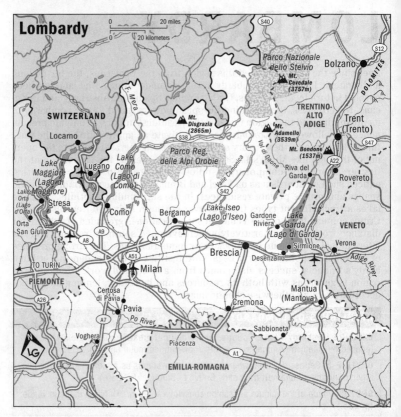

Lombardy

0 — 20 miles
0 — 20 kilometers

SWITZERLAND

Locarno

Lake
Maggiore
(Lago di
Maggiore)

Lake
Orta
(Lago
d'Orta)

Orta
San Giulio

Stresa

Lugano

Lago di Como)
Lake
Como

F. Mera

Mt.
Disgrazia
(2865m)

Parco Reg.
delle Alpi Orobie

Parco Nazionale
dello Stelvio

Mt.
Cevedale
(3757m)

Bolzano

DOLOMITES

TRENTINO-
ALTO
ADIGE

Mt.
Adamello
(3539m)

Val di Daone

Trent
(Trento)

Mt. Bondone
(1537m)

Riva del
Garda

Rovereto

Como

Bergamo

Lake Iseo
(Lago d'Iseo)

Valle Camonica

Gardone
Riviera

Lake
Garda
(Lago di Garda)

Sirmione

VENETO

Verona

Milan

Brescia

Desenzano

Adige River

TO TURIN

PIEMONTE

Certosa
di Pavia

Pavia

Po River

Mantua
(Mantova)

Cremona

Sabbioneta

Voghera

Piacenza

EMILIA-ROMAGNA

cer teams AC Milan and Inter Milan face off in matches with fanfare that rivals
many religious holidays. The *Milanesi* move fast and they do it with style, changing their fashions and those of the rest of the world twice a year.

✈ INTERCITY TRANSPORTATION

Flights: Malpensa Airport, 45km from the city. Intercontinental flights. **Luggage storage** and lost property services available (see **Local Services**). Express shuttle buses
run to and from Stazione Centrale (50min.; 2 per hr. to airport 4:30am-9:15pm, from
airport 6:35am-10:55pm; €4.50). Also, the **Malpensa Express** train departs from
Cadorna Metro station to airport (45min.; 5:50am-8pm, return 6:45am-9:45pm; €9,
onboard €11.50). **Linate Airport,** 7km from town, is logistically more convenient.
Domestic and European flights as well as intercontinental flights with European transfers. **STAM buses** (☎ 02 71 71 06) run from Linate to Stazione Centrale (20min.;
every 20min. to airport 5:40am-9:35pm, return 6:05am-11:35pm; €2.50). City bus
#73 also operates between Linate and Milan's San Babila Metro station (€1, but
more inconvenient and less secure). **General Flight Info** for both airports (☎ 02 748
52 200) is available 24hr. Nearby **Bergamo Airport** serves some budget airlines; a
shuttle runs to and from Stazione Centrale (1hr.; to airport 4:45am-9:15pm, to Milan
8:30am-12:30am; €6.70).

Trains: Stazione Centrale (☎01 478 88 088), in MM2: P. Duca d'Aosta. **Tourist office** opposite platform. Open M-Sa 9am-6pm, Su 9am-1pm and 2-5pm. **Luggage storage** and lost property services available (p. 225). To: **Bergamo** (1hr., 6:10am-11:40pm, €3.30); **Florence** (3½hr., 5:30am-10pm, €21.69); **Rome** (7hr., every hr. 5:30am-11:20, €38.17; Eurostar: 5hr., €46.48); **Turin** (2hr., every hr. 5:05am-12:20am, €7.90; Eurostar: 1¼hr., €15); **Venice** (3hr., 6:05am-8:55pm, €19.16; Eurostar: 1¾hr., €20.66). **Stazione Nord** is part of the local rail system which connects to **Como** and **Varese** (every 30min. 5:05am-10:46pm). **Porta Genova**, in P. Stazione di Pta. Genova, is on the western line to **Vigevano, Alessandria,** and **Asti. Porta Garibaldi**, P. Sigmund Freud, connects Milan to **Lecco** and **Valtellina.**

Buses: At Stazione Centrale. Signs for destinations, times, and prices posted outside. Tickets inside. **Intercity** buses depart from locations on the periphery of town. SAL, SIA, **Autostradale**, and many others depart from P. Castello (MM1: Cairoli) for **Bergamo, Certosa di Pavia,** the **Lake Country, Lugano (Switzerland), Rimini, Trieste,** and **Turin.**

ORIENTATION

Milan's layout is punctuated by a series of ancient concentric city walls. In the outer rings are suburbs built during the 50s and 60s to house southern immigrants. Within the inner circle are four central squares: **Piazza Duomo,** at the end of V. Mercanti; **Piazza Cairoli,** near Castello Sforzesco; **Piazza Cordusio,** connected to Largo Cairoli by V. Dante; and **Piazza San Babila,** the business and fashion district along C. V. Emanuele. The **duomo** and **Galleria Vittorio Emanuele** comprise the center of the circles. To the northeast and northwest lie two large parks, the **Giardini Pubblici** and **Parco Sempione. Stazione Centrale,** Milan's major transportation hub, lies northwest of the city center in a commercial district. To reach P. Duomo at the city's center, take Metro #3 to MM: Duomo. By foot from Stazione Centrale, walk straight ahead from the platforms through the station's main entrance into **Piazza Duca d'Aosta.** Follow **Via Pisani** through several name changes until reaching **Largo Cairoli,** off the Castello Sforzesco. A short walk down **Via Dante** leads to **Piazza Duomo.** From here, the Galleria Vittorio Emanuele opens into **Piazza della Scala,** home to Milan's renowned opera house. On the far side of the piazza are **Via Manzoni** and **Teatro Manzoni.** From V. Manzoni, turn left on **Via della Spiga** to reach the fashion district. To the south lies the hopping nightlife district, the **Navigli,** which can be reached directly from Stazione Centrale by taking Metro #2 to MM: Pta. Genova. **Via Vito Pisani** leads from the station to downtown through **Piazza della Repubblica,** continuing through such wealthy business districts as **Via Turati.** Most of Milan's budget accommodations are east of Stazione Centrale around **Piazza Loretto** and southeast of the station toward **Corso Buenos Aires.**

LOCAL TRANSPORTATION

The jumbled layout of Milan's streets makes them difficult to navigate. Pick up a map with a street index at the tourist office or any bookstore. The streets are generally safe at night, but, as in any metropolis, women are advised not to walk alone. An efficient public transportation system has a subway, trams, and buses.

Public Transportation: The **Metropolitana Milanese** ("MM") operates 6am-midnight and is by far the most useful branch of Milan's transportation network, despite occasional strikes. **Line #1** (red, "MM1") stretches east to west from the *pensioni* district east of Stazione Centrale, through the center of town, and west to the youth hostel (Molino Dorino fork). **Line #2** (green, "MM2") links Milan's 3 train stations and crosses MM1 at Cadorna and Loreto. **Line #3** (yellow, "MM3") runs from north of Stazione Cen-

LOMBARDY

Central Milan

♦ ACCOMMODATIONS
Camping Città di Milano, 23
La Cordata, 32
Hotel Aliseo, 29
Hotel Aurora, 16
Hotel Brasil, 19
Hotel Due Giardini, 10
Hotel Kennedy and
Hotel San Tomaso, 15
Hotel Italia and
Hotel Nazionale, 7
Hotel Porta Venezia, 13
Hotel Rallye, 9
Ostello Piero Rotta (HI), 20
Postello, 2

♦ FOOD
Big Pizza: Da Noi 2, 37
Boeucc, 22
Brek, 6
Caffè Vecchia Brera, 18
Don Lisander, 21
L'Osteria del Treno, 8
Osteria del Binari, 33
Osteria il Giardino dei
Segreti, 25

Il Panino Giusto, 17
Princi il Bread
& Breakfast, 26
Rinomata Gelateria, 34
Ristorante Asmara, 14
Ristorante
"La Colubrina," 12
Pizzeria/Ristorante
Casati 19, 11
Sapori di Romagna, 36
Savini, 24
Trattoria Milanese, 27

♪ NIGHTLIFE
Alcatraz, 1
Bar Magenta, 43
Le Biciclette, 30
Blueshouse, 3
C-Side, 40
Casablanca, 41
Exploit, 31
Hollywood, 4
Loolapaloosa, 5
Maya, 38
Old Fashion Café, 42
Pontell, 35
Scimmie, 39
Yguana Café Restaurant, 28

LOMBARDY

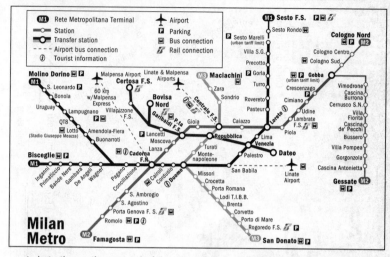

Milan Metro

trale to the southern sprawl of the city, crossing with MM2 at Stazione Centrale and MM1 at the duomo. Use the **bus** system for trips outside the city proper. **Trams #29** and **30** travel the city's outer road, while **buses #96** and **97** service the inner road. Tickets, €1, are good for 1¼hr. 24hr. bus/Metro pass €3, 48hr. €5.50. All available at *tabacchi* and ticket booths. Metro tickets can also be purchased at station machines (press the "Rete urbana di Milano" button). Always keep a few extra tickets, as *tabacchi* close at 8pm and ticket machines can be unreliable.

Taxis: White taxis are omnipresent. Or call **RadioTaxi** (☎02 85 85, 40 00, or 40 40). Meter starts at €3. Nighttime surcharge €3.10. Available 24hr.

Car Rental: All have offices built into Stazione Centrale facing P. Duca d'Aosta. A one-day economy car rental with insurance from **Avis** (☎02 669 02 80 or 670 16 54; open M-F 8am-8pm, Sa 8am-4pm) at €82 per day; from **Europcar** (☎02 669 81 589 or 80 001 44 10; open M-F 8am-1pm and 2-7pm, Sa 8:30am-3:30pm) starts at €57; and from **Hertz** (☎02 669 00 61; open M-F 8am-7pm, Sa 8am-2pm) at €60 per day.

🛈 PRACTICAL INFORMATION

TOURIST AND FINANCIAL SERVICES

Tourist Office: APT, V. Marconi, 1 (☎02 725 24 300; www.milanoinfotourist.com), in "Palazzo di Turismo" in P. Duomo, to the right facing the duomo. Local and regional info, including city **maps.** Accommodations booking available. Pick up *Milano è Milano* and *Milano Mese* for info on activities and clubs. Open M-Sa 9am-1pm and 2-6pm, Su 9am-1pm and 2-5pm. ■**Branch:** Stazione Centrale (☎02 725 24 370 or 725 24 360), off main hall on 2nd fl., through neon archway to left between 2 gift shops. Short lines, same outstanding service. Open M-Sa 9am-6pm, Su 9am-1pm and 2-5pm.

City Tours: A hop-on/hop-off sightseeing tram makes circuits of the city center from P. Garibaldi. Taped commentary in 8 languages. Buy tickets from the APT office or MM2: Garibaldi bus station. €20. 11am-4pm. Inquire at APT office about cheaper tours.

Consulates: Australia, V. Borgogna, 2 (☎02 77 70 41, fax 777 04 242). MM1: S. Babila. Open M-Th 9am-noon and 2-4pm, F 9am-noon. **Canada,** V. V. Pisani, 19 (☎02 675 83 420). MM2/3: Centrale F.S. Open M-F 9am-noon. **New Zealand,** V. G.

LOMBARDY

D'Arezzo 6 (☎02 480 12 544). MM1: Pagano. Open M-Sa 8:30am-noon and 1:30-5:30pm. **UK,** V. S. Paolo, 7 (☎02 72 30 01, emergency 03 358 10 68 57). MM1/3: Duomo. Open daily 9am-1pm and 2-5pm. **US,** V. P. Amedeo, 2/10 (☎02 29 03 51, emergency 29 03 52 98). MM3: Turati. Open M-F 8:30am-noon; info line open M-F 8:30am-12:30pm and 1:30-5:30pm.

Currency Exchange: Banks are everywhere and most are open M-F 8:30am-1:30pm and 2:30-4:30pm. **ATMs** also abound.

American Express: V. Larga, 4, (☎02 721 04 010). Near the Duomo, at the corner of V. Larga and S. Clemente. Holds mail free for 1 month for members. Moneygram international money transfer (fees vary; €500 wire costs €32). Also **exchanges currency.** Open M-F 9am-5:30pm.

LOCAL SERVICES

Luggage Storage: In the Malpensa Airport. €2 per bag per day. Open 24hr. In the Stazione Centrale. €3.50 for 5hr., €0.10-0.30 per additional hr. Open daily 6am-midnight.

Lost Property: Ufficio Oggetti Smarriti Comune, V. Friuli, 30 (☎02 884 53 900). Open M-F 8:30am-4pm. **Malpensa Airport** (☎02 585 80 069). **Linate Airport** (☎02 701 24 451). **Stazione Centrale** (☎02 637 12 667) at luggage storage. Open daily 6am-midnight.

English-Language Bookstore: The American Bookstore, V. Camperio, 16 (☎02 87 89 20, fax 720 20 030), at Largo Cairoli. Open M 1-7pm, Tu-Sa 10am-7pm. AmEx/MC/V. **Hoepli Libreria Internazionale,** V. Hoepli, 5 (☎02 86 48 71), off P. Media near P. Scala. Open in summer M 2-7pm, Tu-Sa 10am-7pm; in winter M-Sa 10am-7pm. AmEx/MC/V. **Rizzoli** (☎02 864 61 071), Galleria Vittorio Emanuele. Open summer Tu-Sa 10am-7:30pm; Oct.-May M 9am-8pm, Tu-Sa 9am-9pm, Su 10am-8pm. AmEx/MC/V. Also try **street vendors** along Largo Mattioli for cheaper options.

Gay and Lesbian Resource: ARCI-GAY "Centro D'iniziativa Gay," V. Bezzeca, 3 (☎02 541 22 225; www.arcigaymilano.org). Friendly staff. Open M-F 3:30-8pm.

Handicapped/Disabled Services: AIAS Milano Onlus, V. Taramelli 20 (☎02 676 54 740; www.milanopertutti.it).

Laundromat: Washland, V. Porpora, 14 (☎34 033 55 660). Wash €3, dry €3 for 18min. Open daily 8am-10pm, summer 8am-11pm. **Acqua Dolce,** V. B. Marcello, 32 (☎02 295 25 820). €3.10 wash, €3.10 dry. Open daily 8am-8pm.

Parking: Availability in the city center is limited and runs around €4-5 per hr. Many parking garages close for lunch. Outside the first ring, public parking runs €1-2 per hr.

EMERGENCY AND COMMUNICATIONS

Emergency: ☎118. **Police** (☎113). **Carabinieri** (☎112).

Tourist Police: SOS Turista, V. C. M. Maggi, 14 (☎02 622 61 or 336 030 60). Open daily in summer 9:30am-5pm, in winter 9:30am-6pm.

Medical Clinic: ☎02 345 67. **Red Cross** (☎02 38 83).

Pharmacy: ☎02 669 07 35 or 669 09 35. In Stazione Centrale's *galleria.* Open 24hr. Or try **Farmacia Carlo Erba,** P. Duomo, 21 (☎02 864 64 832). Open M 2-7pm, Tu-F 9:30am-1:45pm and 3-7pm. All pharmacy doors list late-night rotations.

Hospital: Ospedale Maggiore di Milano, V. Francesco Sforza, 35 (☎02 550 31), 5min. from the duomo on the inner ring road.

Internet:

Enjoy Internet, Viale Tunisia, 11 (☎02 365 55 805). Near MM1: Pta. Venezia. Speedy cable connection for €2 per hr. Open M-Sa 9am-1am, Su 2pm-midnight.

LOMBARDY

Gr@zia, P. Duca d'Aosta, 14 (☎02 670 05 43). To the left of Stazione Centrale's main door. Good connection and rates. €1 for 15min. Open daily 8am-2am.

Cafenet Dolphin Navigator, V. Padova, 2 (☎02 284 72 09). MM1/2: Loreto. Frappes and sandwiches €3. Fast connection. €1.30 for 15min. €5 per hr. Open M-F and Su 6:30am-7pm.

Internet Point, V. Padova, 38 (☎02 280 40 246). MM1/2: Loreto. 10 computers. Wire money, print, and fax. €3 per hr. Open daily 10am-10pm.

Post Office: V. Cordusio, 4 (☎02 724 82 223), near P. Duomo toward the *castello. Fermoposta* and **currency exchange.** Open M-F 8am-7pm, Sa 8:30am-noon. **Branches** in Stazione Centrale. Open M-F 8am-7pm, Sa 8:30am-7pm. **Postal Code:** 20100.

⌁ ACCOMMODATIONS

Milan has a remarkably high standard of living, and its accommodations are priced accordingly. Advanced booking is strongly advised. Prices vary considerably, as business conventions can turn any month of the year into high season.

EAST OF STAZIONE CENTRALE

Women should use caution when traveling alone at night in this area.

▨ **Hotel Sara,** V. Sacchini, 17 (☎02 20 17 73; www.hotelsara.it). MM1/2: Loreto. Take V. Porpora; V. Sacchini is the 2nd street on the right. Sleek rooms all with sparkling windows, bath, and TV. Free Internet. Reception 24hr. Singles €25-80, depending on A/C; doubles €45-113. AmEx/MC/V. ❹

Hotel Cà Grande, V. Porpora, 87 (☎/fax 02 261 44 001 or 261 45 295; www.hotelcagrande.it). MM1/2: Loreto. 6 blocks from P. Loreto in a yellow house. Or take tram #33 from Stazione Centrale and exit at V. Porpora (V. Ampere), 50m from hotel. Close the windows and crank up the A/C to make these the quietest rooms on V. Porpora. All have TV and phone. English spoken. Internet €2 per hr. Breakfast included. Reception 24hr. Singles €45, with bath €55; doubles €65/€75. AmEx/MC/V. ❹

Hotel Malta, V. Ricordi, 20 (☎02 204 96 15 or 295 21 210; www.hotelmalta.it). MM1/2: Loreto. Take V. Porpora and turn right on V. Ricordi. Or from the station, take tram #33 to V. Ampere, backtrack along V. Porpora. 15 rooms all have bath, TV, fan, and hair dryer, many with balcony overlooking a rose garden. Reception 24hr. Reserve ahead. Singles €36-60; doubles €50-80. MC/V. ❹

Hotel Ambra, V. Caccianino, 10 (☎02 266 54 65, fax 706 06 245). MM1/2: Loreto. V. Caccianino is about a block beyond Hotel Ca' Grande. Off a quiet side street, 19 simple, tidy rooms have bath, TV, telephone, and balcony. Breakfast €3. Reception 24hr. Reserve ahead. Singles €42; doubles €68; triples €91. Student discounts (up to €10) available July-Aug. AmEx/MC/V. ❹

Hotel Oriente, V. Porpora, 52 (☎02 236 12 98). From MM1: Loreto, take V. Porpora for about 10min.; the hotel is on the left. Floor-to-ceiling windows overlook neighborhood gardens. All rooms have bath, phone, TV, and fan. Reception 24hr. Singles €45-55; doubles €60-70; triples €85-100. MC/V. ❹

Albergo Villa Maria, V. Sacchini, 19 (☎02 295 25 618), next to Hotel Sara. 7 rooms at this family-run hotel have huge windows, strawberry-patterned sheets, and sorbet-colored walls. All have TV, fan, and phone. Shared bath. Singles €30; doubles €50. ❸

Hotel Soperga, V. Soperga, 24 (☎02 669 05 41; www.hotelsopergamilano.it). 300m from Stazione Centrale. Walk 10min. down V. F. Aporti, turn right on Viale Brianza, and make right on V. Soperga. Hotel is on the left. Luxurious 3-star lurks alongside train tracks. Soundproof walls enclose ample rooms with A/C, satellite TV, radio, phone, hair dryer, and sparkling tiles. Breakfast included. High season singles €80-160, low season €65; doubles €90/€90-212. AmEx/MC/V. ❺

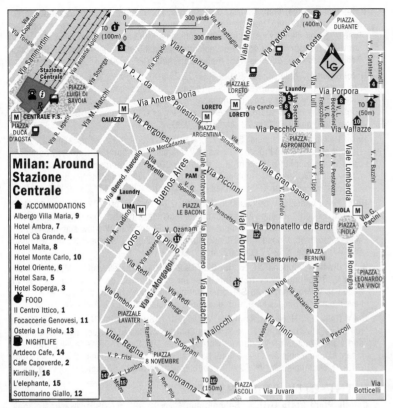

Milin: Around Stazione Centrale

♠ ACCOMMODATIONS
Albergo Villa Maria, 9
Hotel Ambra, 7
Hotel Cà Grande, 4
Hotel Malta, 8
Hotel Monte Carlo, 10
Hotel Oriente, 6
Hotel Sara, 5
Hotel Soperga, 3
🍴 FOOD
Il Centro Ittico, 1
Focaccerie Genovesi, 11
Osteria La Piola, 13
🎵 NIGHTLIFE
Artdeco Cafe, 14
Cafe Capoverde, 2
Kirribilly, 16
L'elephante, 15
Sottomarino Giallo, 12

Hotel Monte Carlo, V. Vallazze 39 (☎02 706 00 427, fax 02 706 39 189). MM1/2: Loreto. Take V. Porpora to Viale Lombardy and turn right. If you don't mind a few missing floor tiles, the price is right. All rooms with TV, phone, and fan. Reception 24hr. Singles €30, with bath €40; doubles €50/€62. MC/V. ❸

NEAR GIARDINI PUBBLICI

Hotel Aurora, C. Buenos Aires, 18 (☎02 204 79 60; www.hotelitaly.com/hotels/aurora/index.htm). MM1: Pta. Venezia. Just off hectic C. Buenos Aires, Aurora offers spotless, modern rooms with phone, TV, and serenity. Reception 24hr. Reserve ahead. Singles €41-46, with shower €46-54; doubles with bath €69-82. AmEx/MC/V. ❹

Hotel Aliseo, C. Italia, 6, 6th fl. (☎02 864 50 156, fax 80 45 35). MM3: Missori. On C. Italia on the right, near P. Missori; take the stairs on the left inside the courtyard. 5min. walk from the duomo. Large rooms, all with bath, balcony, TV, and fan. Movie and wildlife posters in the halls and a terrarium at reception. Breakfast included. Singles €45-55; doubles €68-78. MC/V. ❹

Hotel Due Giardini, V. B. Marcello, 47 (☎02 295 21 093 or 295 12 309; duegiardini-hotel@libero.it). MM1: Lima. Walk along V. Vitruvio 2 blocks to V. Marcello; turn left on far side of the street. Mint green decor spruces up 11 well-kept rooms, all with bath and TV. Internet. Breakfast €4. Singles €55; doubles €90-120. MC/V. ❹

LOMBARDY

Hotel San Tomaso, Viale Tunisia, 6, 3rd fl. (☎/fax 02 295 14 747; www.hotelsanto-maso.com). MM1: Pta. Venezia. From the C. Buenos Aires Metro exit, turn left on Viale Tunisia. Small rooms, most with shower and some with bath. Although there may be no hot water on your visit, it's still convenient to the MM2 line. English spoken. Reception 24hr. Singles €40; doubles €65; triples €85. AmEx/MC/V. ❸

Hotel Kennedy, Viale Tunisia, 6, 6th fl. (☎02 294 00 934; www.kennedyhotel.it). MM1: Pta. Venezia. 3 floors above Hotel San Tomaso. 13 rooms have TV, phone, and balcony. Nice enough to make a businessman happy, though street below can be noisy. Reception 24hr. Check-out 10am. Reserve ahead. Singles €40; doubles €55, with bath €75; triples €90; quads €100-120. AmEx/MC/V. ❸

Hotel Rallye, V. B. Marcello, 59 (☎/fax 02 295 31 209; h.rallye@tiscalinet.it). MM1: Lima. Walk along V. Vitruvio 2 blocks to V. Marcello and turn left. Homey, wooden fixtures and gleaming bathroom tiles decorate 20 simple rooms. All rooms have fan, phone, and TV. Spacious doubles and free breakfast under apricot tree in the garden. Singles €30, with bath €35; doubles €51/€70. AmEx/MC/V. ❸

Hotel Porta Venezia, V. P. Castaldi, 26 (☎02 294 14 227, fax 202 49 397). MM1: P. Venezia. Exit on C. Buenos Aires and, before reaching V. Tunisia, turn left on V. Castaldi. Turn right on V. B. Castaldi. Simple rooms have TV and fan. Window screens seal out Milan's formidable mosquitos. Friendly staff speaks English. Singles €31-42, with bath €36-47; doubles €52-77/€41-62. MC/V. ❹

Hotel Brasil, V. Modena, 20 (☎/fax 02 749 24 82; www.hotelbrasil.it). MM1: Palestro. Take V. Serbelloni away from the museum and turn left on V. Cappuccini, which becomes V. Modena. From Stazione Centrale, take bus #60 to V. Modena. Request keys if out late. Singles €39, with bath €57; doubles €52/€72. AmEx/MC/V. ❸

Hotel Italia and **Hotel Nazionale,** V. Vitruvio, 44/46 (☎02 669 38 26 or 670 59 11; nazionaleitalia@tiscali.it). From Stazione Centrale, walk into P. Duca d'Aosta, turn left and walk 3 blocks on V. Vitruvio. Hotels are on left. Run by same family, both have clean, simple rooms. Reserve ahead. Italia: singles €22-35; doubles €32-52, with bath €49-73. Nazionale: singles €22-35; doubles with bath €32-50. AmEx/MC/V. ❸

ON THE CITY PERIPHERY

Ostello Piero Rotta (HI), V. Salmoiraghi, 1 (☎02 392 67 095; www.hostelbook-ing.com), northwest of the city. MM1: QT8. Facing the white church with a cone-shaped roof, turn right on V. Salmoiraghi. 376-bed hostel is 300m on the right. Institutional building with helpful staff. Mostly 6-bed dorms; few triples and quads available. Phone card Internet. Breakfast and sheets included. Laundry €5.50. Reception 24hr. Check-out 9:30am. Lockout 9:30am-3:30pm. Reserve on website only. Closed Dec. 23-Jan. 13. Dorms €18.50; family rooms €22. Non-members add €3. MC/V. ❷

La Cordata, V. Burigozzo, 11 (☎02 583 14 675; www.lacordata.it). MM3: Missori. From P. Missori, take the tram 2 stops to Italia S. Lucia, walk same direction as tram for 1 block and turn right on V. Burigozzo. Entrance is around the corner from La Cordata camping store on V. Aurispa. With excellent proximity to the Navigli region, the hostel has become a crash pad for an older crowd. 16-bed bunkrooms each have communal bathrooms. Bath and kitchen available. Check-in 2-11pm. Check-out 11am. Doors locked 12:30am. Dorms €18. ❷

Postello, V. Pergola 5 (☎33 317 52 272). MM2: P. Garibaldi. Go through the train station to reach the V. Pepe exit, then turn left on V. Pepe and right on V. Carmagnola. V. Pergola is 3 blocks ahead. Milan's newest, cheapest hostel. Clean, no frills 4- and 8-bed dorms. Frequent movies, booktalks, and DJ performances in the garden courtyard, and communal dinners in the coffee shop next door. Convenient to clubs. English spoken. Free Internet (Linux or Windows) and wireless connection. Breakfast €2. Laundry with suggested donation. Sheets included. Reception 24hr. Dorms and singles €10.

Camping Città di Milano, V. G. Airaghi, 61 (☎02 482 02 999; www.parcoaquatica.com). MM1 to De Angeli, then bus #72 to S. Romanello Togni. Backtrack 10m and turn right onto V. Tongi. The campsite is a 10min. walk straight ahead. Enter at Aquatica waterpark. Large campground with modern facilities. Free volleyball and BBQ grills. Laundry €5. Closed Dec.-Jan. €7.50 per person, €6.50-8.50 per tent, €6.50 per car. 2 to 6-person cabins €37-88; deluxe bungalows with bath and A/C €80-120. MC/V. ●

☐ FOOD

Munch on focaccia with the lunch break crowd, clink champagne glasses over silver and satin, or take your palate on a world tour through the metropolis's ethnic neighborhoods. McDonald's gleams on practically every street corner but pales in comparison to **Brek** and **Ciao Ristorante,** two Italian self-serve chains for the health-conscious. Old-style trattorias still follow *Milanesi* culinary traditions with *risotto alla Milanese* (rice with saffron), *cotoletta alla Milanese* (breaded veal cutlet with lemon), and *osso buco* (shank of lamb, beef, or veal). Around Christmas, *panettone*, a traditional fruitcake, stacks up in every *pasticceria*.

Weary tourists near the duomo often succumb to the piazza's pricey but mediocre offerings, but those who venture out to V. Orefici can reap delicious rewards. **Peck ❷,** V. Cantu, 3, off V. Orefici near P. Duomo, is a deli-bakery wonderland, manned by no fewer than 16 butchers serving *foie gras*, black forest ham, and a thousand other delicacies since 1883. (☎02 869 30 17. Open M 3-7:30pm, Tu-Sa 8:45am-7:30pm.) **Pam supermarket,** V. Piccinni, 2, is off C. Buenos Aires. (MM1: Loreto. ☎02 295 12 715. Open M-Sa 8am-9pm.) The Free Shop SPA supermarket, in Stazione Centrale, has a hot deli and stocks traveler-friendly snacks. (Open daily 8am-11pm.) From P. Duomo, head past the tourist office down V. Marconi to **Viel ❶,** V. G. Marconi, 3, for fig and plum gelato, along with a slew of more exotic flavors. (☎02 869 25 61. 2 scoops €2. *Frappe* swirl €3.50. Open M-Sa 7:30am-7:30pm.) The **Fiera di Sinigallia,** a 400-year-old bargaining extravaganza, occurs on Saturdays on Darsena banks, a canal in Navigli around V. d'Annunzio.

IN THE CITY CENTER

Walking a few blocks outside of P. Duomo will save you a small fortune on lunch (or at least allow you to spend one on outstanding, rather than mediocre, food).

🍴 **Savini,** Galleria V. Emanuele II (☎02 720 03 433; www.thi.it). Opposite McDonald's—in every way. Italian writer Castellaneta once said, "Savini is as much a part of Milan as the Galleria and La Scala." Since its founding in 1867, this internationally renowned restaurant has maintained unvarying decor and clientele: extravagant and well-dressed. Pay dearly for exquisite food and superb service. *Primi* €14-20, *secondi* €21-29. Cover €7. Service 12%. Open M-Sa 12:30-2:30pm and 7:30-10:30pm. AmEx/MC/V. ❺

🍴 **Trattoria Milanese,** V. S. Marta, 11 (☎02 864 51 991). MM1/3: Duomo. From P. Duomo, take V. Torino; turn right on V. Maurilio and left on V. S. Marta. This trattoria cultivates *cucina milanese* under brick arches and sketches of old Milan. The *osso buco* (€18) and *costoletta alla milanese* (breaded rib; €14) are works of culinary genius. *Primi* €5-8, *secondi* €6-18. Cover €2. Service 11%. Open M and W-Su 12:30-3pm and 7pm-midnight. Closed last 2 weeks of July. AmEx/MC/V. ❸

Boeucc, P. Belgioso, 2 (☎02 760 20 224). MM3: Monte Napoleone. Take V. Manzoni toward the duomo; turn left on V. Morone until reaching P. Belgioso. Heavy doors guard an interior of statues and velvet drapes where banking gurus have taken their lunch breaks since 1696. *Primi* €11-13, *secondi* €19-24. Cover €5. Open M-F 12:40-2:30pm and 7:40-10:30pm, Su 7:40-10:30pm. AmEx. ❺

LOMBARDY

Caffè Vecchia Brera, V. Dell'Orso, 20 (☎02 864 61 695; www.vecchiabrera.it). MM1: Cairoli. Head straight up V. Broletto. Parisian chic with an Italian kick. Dreamy liqueur-soaked desserts make a favorite post-performance snack for the cast of La Scala. Crepes €4.50-7. *Primi* €6.50. Cover €1. Service 10%. Open daily 8am-2am. ❷

Don Lisander, V. Manzoni, 12/A (☎02 760 20 130). MM3: Monte Napoleone. Take V. Manzoni toward the duomo. Restaurant is on the left before Museo Poldi Pezzoli. Imaginative Italian fare with some French and Spanish surprises. Black-tie waitstaff serves a sophisticated clientele in the beautiful summer garden. *Primi* €10-14.50, *secondi* €19-22. Cover €3.10. Open M-Sa 12:30-2:30pm and 7:30-10:30pm. AmEx/MC/V. ❺

Osteria il Giardino dei Segreti, V. Sottocorno, 17 (☎02 760 08 376; www.ilgiardinodeisegreti.it). MM1: S. Babila. From P. S. Babila follow C. Monforte to P. del Tricolore, turn right on Viale Premuda, then left on V. Sottocorno. Far from tourist sights, this shady, intimate garden is an idyllic setting for savoring fresh mushroom dishes and fish. Excellent wine list. *Primi* €6-8, *secondi* €12-16. Open M-Sa noon-3pm and 6-11pm. ❸

Princi il Bread & Breakfast, V. Speronari, 6 (☎028 74 797), off P. Duomo. Busy bakery-deli with golden focaccia and luscious *strudel di miele* (strudel with honey). Huge crowd comes for fresh bread, *salumi*, and pasta salad. Open M-Sa 7am-8pm. ❶

NAVIGLI AND ENVIRONS

Boatloads of students mean cheap grub. Many bars also serve dinner; some have Happy Hour buffets.

☒ **Osteria del Binari,** V. Tortona, 1 (☎02 894 09 428). MM2: Pta. Genova. Head to the C. Colombo side of P. Stazione Porta Genova. Cross the train tracks by the overpass to V. Tortona. Walls woven from grapevines, an attentive and discreet staff, and exquisite regional cuisine make del Binari perfect for an intimate meal. Mortally chic patrons nibble daintily from the fine china. Unless explicitly refused, a platter of *antipasti* (€7) welcomes guests. *Primi* €10, *secondi* €12-17. Open M-Sa 8-11pm. MC/V. ❺

☒ **Big Pizza: Da Noi 2,** V. G. Borsi, 1 (☎02 83 96 77), takes its name seriously. Beer flows liberally while students wait for stone-oven pizzas of epic proportions. Serious eaters can get a bowl of pasta dumped over their pie for an extra €2. Pizza €5.50-8.50. Cover €1. Open M-F 11am-midnight, Sa-Su 6pm-midnight. Branches: Piazzale XXIV Maggio, 7 (MM2: Pta. Genova) and V. Buonarroti, 16 (MM1: Buonarroti). ❷

Sapori di Romagna, V. A. Sforza, 9 (☎33 964 62 402). Ham and cheese crepes are a meal in themselves, while *Nutella* and fruit makes dessert for two. Ravenous crowd means a worthwhile wait. *Piadine* €2-6. Open M-Sa noon-11:30pm. Cash only. ❶

Rinomata Gelateria, A. Naviglio Pavese, 2 (☎02 581 13 877), at the corner of Ripa di Porta Ticinese. There's no better way to end a night of bar hopping than with a scoop of watermelon gelato. 2 scoops €2. Open M-Sa 9am-midnight. Cash only. ❶

NEAR CORSO BUENOS AIRES

Osteria La Piola, Viale Abruzzi, 23 (☎02 295 31 271). MM1/2: Loreto. Feast on fresh, homemade pasta and local flavors where *Milanese* cuisine reaches its zenith with *tipica cotoletta con osso alla milanese* (breaded ox tail; €15). *Primi* €9-11, *secondi* €14-16. Open M-Sa 12:30-2:30pm and 7:30-11pm. AmEx/MC/V. ❸

Ristorante Asmara, V. L. Palazzi, 5 (☎02 295 22 453; www.ristoranteasmara.it). MM1: Pta. Venezia. Take C. Buenos Aires; V. L. Palazzi is the 3rd left. Cover €1.60. Vegetarian meals €10. Large *piatti* €10-11.50. Open M-Tu and Th-Su noon-2:30pm and 6pm-midnight. AmEx/MC/V. ❸

Il Panino Giusto, V. Malpighi, 3 (☎02 294 09 297). MM1: Pta. Venezia. From the piazza, head down Viale Piave and left on V. Malpighi. If you believe sandwiches are a gourmet item, that truffled olive oil, veal *patte*, or lard with honey and walnuts are reasonable fillings, and that lunch should cost under €10, welcome home. *Panini* €4.50-8. Open daily noon-12:30am. AmEx/MC/V. ❶

LOMBARDY

Focaccerie Genovesi, V. Plinio, 5. MM1: Lima. Take V. Plinio; eatery is on the left. *Focaccia formaggio* (€2.40): the nightmare of the Atkins diet, cardiologists, and businessmen in clean white shirts. For everyone else, a slice of oily, cheesy heaven. Locals fill this hole-in-the-wall par excellence. Open daily 10:30am-2pm and 4:30-8pm. ❶

Pizzeria/Ristorante Casati 19, V. F. Casati, 19 (☎02 204 72 92). MM1: Pta. Venezia. Go up C. Buenos Aires 4 blocks, then turn left on V. F. Casati. Near Hotels San Tomaso and Kennedy. Select fish from a trough of crushed ice, then kick back with a glass of *vino*. Lunch *menù* €7.50. Pizza €5.20-6.80. *Primi* €6.80-14, *secondi* €7.50-14. Open Tu-F and Su hoon-2:30pm and 7-11:30pm, Sa 7-11:30pm. AmEx/MC/V. ❷

Ristorante "La Colubrina," V. Felice Casati, 5 (☎02 295 18 427). MM1: Pta. Venezia. *Milanesi* classics like *scaloppine* and *risotto* run only €4 apiece at this neighborhood eatery. Lunch *menù* from €10. Large pizzas €3.50-7. *Primi* and *secondi* €4-10. Cover €1.30. Open daily 7pm-1am, also Sa-Su noon-3pm. MC/V, except July. ❷

NEAR STAZIONE CENTRALE

Il Centro Ittico, V. F. Aporti, 35 (☎02 261 43 774). MM2/3: Centrale F. S. 20min. walk down V. F. Aporti, which runs up the left-hand side of P. Duca d'Aosta. Once a fish market, now it serves the finest of the daily catch. Market prices: *primi* from €8, *secondi* from €12. Open M-Sa 12:30-2:30pm and 8pm-midnight. Cover €2.58. MC/V. ❸

L'Osteria del Treno, V. S. Gregorio, 46/48 (☎02 670 04 79). MM2/3: Centrale F. S. From P. Duca d'Aosta, take V. Pisani and turn left on V. S. Gregorio. A brassy, in-your-face attitude and daily menu scribbled in chalk appeal to the lunch crowd that tumbles in for heaping plates. Self-serve *primi* €3.10-4.13, *secondi* €4.65-6.20. Dinner prices rise a bit. Cover €1.30. Open Su-F noon-2:30pm and 7-10:30pm. Cash only. ❷

Brek, V. Lepetit, 20 (☎02 670 51 49), near Stazione Centrale. The shiniest, freshest, most edible chain of self-serve cafeterias in the world. Has A/C and non-smoking section. *Primi* €2.90-3.90, *secondi* €4-7. Open M-Sa 11:30am-3pm and 6:30-10:30pm. Branches: P. Cavour (☎02 65 36 19; off V. Manzoni; MM3: M. Napoleone) and Pta. Giordano (☎02 760 23 379; MM1: S. Babila). AmEx. ❶

◎ SIGHTS

NEAR THE DUOMO

▨**DUOMO.** The geographical and spiritual center of Milan and a good starting point for any walking tour of the city, the duomo is the third-largest church in the world. **Gian Galeazzo Visconti** began construction in 1386, hoping to coerce the Virgin to grant him a male heir. Building proceeded sporadically over the next four centuries and was finally completed at Napoleon's command in 1809. In the meantime, the structure accumulated a dense lacework of statues and bas reliefs, with more than 3400 statues, 135 spires, and 96 gargoyles. The fantastic facade juxtaposes Italian Gothic and Baroque elements and inside, 52 columns rise to canopied niches with statues as capitals. The church is a five-aisled cruciform shape, capable of seating 4000. The imposing 16th-century marble tomb of **Giacomo de' Medici** in the southern transept was inspired by the work of Michelangelo. Nearby, a gory statue of St. Bartholomew (1562) by **Marco d'Agrate,** depicts the saint wearing his own skin as a coat as a reminder that he was flayed alive. Climb (or ride) to the top of the cathedral from outside the northern transept, to enter the ▨**roof walkway,** which cuts through a forest of white marble statues and spires. A gilded statue of the "Madonnina" crowns the rooftop kingdom. Currently the entire facade is under wraps of restoration, as the same Veneranta Fabbrica that built it over hundreds of years restores it. *(MM1: Duomo. Cathedral open daily 7am-7pm, Nov.-Feb. 9am-4:15pm. Modest dress strictly* required. Roof open daily 9am-5pm. €3.50, with elevator €5.) The **Museo del Duomo** displays artifacts relating to the duomo's construction. (P. del Duomo, 14, to the right of the duomo. ☎ 02 86 03 58. Open daily 10am-1:15pm and 3-6pm. €6.)

■ **PINACOTECA AMBROSIANA.** The 23 palatial rooms of the Ambrosiana display exquisite works from the 14th- through 19th-centuries, including Botticelli's *Madonna of the Canopy*, da Vinci's *Portrait of a Musician*, Raphael's wall-sized sketch *School of Athens*, Caravaggio's *Basket of Fruit* (the first Italian still-life), Titian's *Adoration of the Magi*, and works by Brueghel and Bril. The courtyard's statues, fountains, and marble staircase are also enchanting. (P. Pio XI, 2. Follow V. Spadari off V. Torino and turn left on V. Cantù. ☎ 02 864 62 981. Open Tu-Su 10am-5:30pm. €7.50; under 18 or over 65 €4.50.)

■ **TEATRO ALLA SCALA.** Founded in 1778, La Scala has established Milan as the opera capital of the world. Its understated Neoclassical facade and lavish interior set the stage for premieres of works by Rossini, Puccini, Mascagni, and Verdi, performed by virtuosos like Maria Callas and Enrico Caruso. The theater is scheduled to reopen in December 2004 after a lengthy renovation project. (Through the Galleria Vittorio Emanuele from P. Duomo.) Visitors can soak up La Scala's history at the **Museo Teatrale alla Scala.** From poster art to a plaster cast of Toscanini's hand, the museum offers a glimpse into operatic past. (C. Magenta, 71. MM1: Conciliazione. Directly opposite the Chiesa S. Maria delle Grazie. From P. Conciliazione, take V. Ruffini for 2 blocks. ☎ 02 805 34 18. Open daily 9am-6pm, last entry 5:15pm. €5, students €4.)

■ **MUSEO POLDI PEZZOLI.** Poldi Pezzoli, an 18th-century nobleman and art collector, bequeathed his house and its art collection to the city "for the enjoyment of the people" in 1879. Today masterpieces hang in the Golden Room, overlooking a garden. Famous paintings include Andrea Mantegna's *Virgin and Child*, Botticelli's *Madonna and Child*, Bellini's *Ecce Homo*, Guardi's magical *Gray Lagoon*, and the signature piece, Pollaiuolo's *Portrait of a Young Woman*. Smaller collections fill Pezzoli's former private chambers. A tiny but sublime display of Italian military armaments fills one of the rooms. (V. Manzoni, 12, near La Scala. ☎ 02 79 48 89. Open Tu-Su 10am-6pm. €6, under 10 or over 60 €4. Free audioguide.)

GALLERIA VITTORIO EMANUELE II. An immense glass and steel cupola (48m) towers over a five-story arcade of overpriced cafes, shops, and offices. Intricate mosaics representing different continents sieged by the Romans adorn the floors and walls. Once considered the drawing room of Milan, the statue-bedecked Galleria exudes elegance. Spin on the mosaic bull clockwise three times for good luck. (On the left, facing the duomo. ☎ 06 46 02 72. Open M-Sa 10am-11pm, Su 10am-8pm. Free.)

PALAZZO REALE. This impressive structure served as the town hall in 1138 before becoming the residence of *Milanese* royalty until the 19th century. Giuseppe Piermarini, architect of La Scala, designed its facade with Neoclassical restraint. Today it houses temporary exhibits in the **Museo d'Arte Contemporanea.** (South of duomo. ☎ 02 620 83 219. Wheelchair accessible. Open Tu-Su 9:30am-7:30pm. Exhibits €6.20-9.30.)

MUSEO BAGATTI VALSECCHI. This beautifully preserved 19th-century aristocrat's house has antique ceramics, frescoes, mosaics, ivory, and Renaissance weapons. (V. Santo Spirito, 10. MM3: Monte Napoleone. From V. Monte Napoleone, V. Santo Spirito is the 2nd left. ☎ 02 760 06 132. Open Tu-Su 1-5:45pm. €6, students €3.)

NEAR CASTELLO SFORZESCO

■ **CASTELLO SFORZESCO.** Restored after heavy bomb damage in 1943, the Castello Sforzesco is one of Milan's best-known monuments. Its mighty towers and expansive courtyard have seen their share of history: originally constructed in

LOMBARDY

1368 as a defense against the Venetians, da Vinci also had his studio here before Spanish and Austrian invaders used the grounds as army barracks, horse stalls, and storage. Inside are the 12 **Musei Civici** (Civic Museums). The highlight is undoubtedly the **Museum of Antique Art,** which contains **Michelangelo's** unfinished **Pietà Rondanini** (1564), his last work. Da Vinci also painted the frescoes on the ceiling of the **Sala delle Asse;** his design was once considered so insignificant it was whitewashed over, actually protecting the original colors. The **Applied Arts Museum** showcases ornate household furnishings and the *Automa contesta di demonio.* Play puppeteer to the red-eyed wooden demon by cranking the lever below. *(MM1: Cairoli. ☎ 02 884 63 703. Open Tu-Su 9:30am-7:30pm. Combined admission €3.)*

CHIESA DI SANTA MARIA DELLE GRAZIE. The church's Gothic nave is dark and elaborately patterned with frescoes, contrasting the splendid, airy Renaissance tribune added by Bramante in 1492. *(P. di S. Maria delle Grazie, 2. From P. Conciliazione, take V. Ruffini for about 2 blocks. MM1: Conciliazione. Open M-Sa 7am-noon and 3-7pm, Su 7:15am-12:15pm and 3:30-9pm.)* Next to the church entrance is the *Cenacolo Vinciano* (Vinciano Refectory, or the convent dining hall), home to one of the best-known pieces of art in the world: **▥Leonardo da Vinci's Last Supper.** Following a 20-year restoration effort, it was re-opened to the public in 1999, though rumors persist that it may again be closed to the public; pieces have been flaking off almost since the day Leonardo finished it, and the roof of the building was blown off during World War II, leaving the interior exposed for several years. Advance booking is mandatory. Lone travelers with a flexible schedule should call at least one week in advance; groups and those with limited time should call several weeks ahead. Groups are allowed in the refractory for a maximum of 15min. *(Reservations ☎ 02 894 21 146 or 19 919 91 00. Wheelchair accessible. Refractory open Tu-Su 8:15am-7pm. €6.50, EU residents under 18 or over 65 €3.25. Reservation fee €1.50. Audioguide €2.50.)*

▥ PINACOTECA DI BRERA. The Brera Art Gallery presents a superb collection of 14th- to 20th-century paintings, with an emphasis on those from the Lombard School. Works include Bellini's *Pietà* (1460), Andrea Mantegna's brilliant *Dead Christ* (1480), Raphael's *Marriage of the Virgin* (1504), Caravaggio's *Supper at Emmaus* (1606), and Francesco Hayez's *The Kiss* (1859). A limited collection of works by modern masters includes pieces by Modigliani and Carlo Carrà, as well as Picasso's *Testa di Toro.* *(V. Brera, 280. Immediately after V. G. Verdi when approaching from La Scala. MM2: Lanza. ☎ 02 72 26 31. Wheelchair accessible. Open daily 8:30am-7:15pm. €5, EU citizens 18-25 €3, under 18 or over 65 free. Audioguide €3.50.)*

MUSEO NAZIONALE DELLA SCIENZA E DELLA TECNICA "DA VINCI". This family-friendly, hands-on museum traces the development of science and technology from the age of Leonardo to the present. The hall of computer technology features a piano converted into a typewriter by Edoardo Hughes of Turin in 1885. Don't miss the da Vinci room, which contains wooden mock-ups of his flying machines, cranes, and bridges. *(MM2: San Ambrogio. V. San Vittore, 21, off V. Carducci. ☎ 02 48 55 51. Open Tu-F 9:30am-4:50pm, Sa-Su 9:30am-6:20pm. €7, under 12 or over 60 €5.)*

BASILICA DI SANT'AMBROGIO. A prototype for Lombard-Romanesque churches throughout Italy, Sant'Ambrogio is the most influential medieval building in Milan. St. Ambrose presided over this building between AD 379 and 386 and his skeleton rests beside those of the martyrs Gervasius and Protasius, in a dim crypt below the altar. Ninth-century reliefs depict the life of Christ in gold on one side of the altar and the life of St. Ambrose, in silver, on the other. The 4th-century **Cappella di San Vittore in Ciel D'oro,** with exquisite 5th-century mosaics adorning its cupola, lies through the seventh chapel on the right. The asymmetrical **bell towers** are the result of an 8th-century feud between a group of Benedictine monks and the priests of the church, each of whom owned one tower. *(MM1: Sant'Ambrogio. Walk up V. G. Carducci; the church bulwark rises up to the right. Open M-Sa 7:30am-noon and 2:30-7pm, Su 3-7pm. Free. Chapel open Tu-Su 9:30am-11:45pm and 2:30-6pm. €2.)*

STADIO GIUSEPPE MEAZZA. In a country where *calcio* is taken as seriously as Catholicism, nothing compares to the rivalry between Milan's two soccer clubs, Inter and A.C. As passions roil, the city reaches a feverish pitch heightened by political overtones: Inter fans are often left-wing, while A.C. fans tend to be right-wing. The face-off takes place in their shared three-tiered stadium (capacity 85,700), architecturally distinct for its exterior spiralling ramps. *(V. Piccolomini, 5. MM2: Lotto. Take V. Fed. Caprilli. Entrance at Gate 21 on the south side. Tours on non-game days 10am-5pm. Buy A. C. tickets at V. Turati, 3. ☎02 622 85 660. MM3: Turati. Buy Inter tickets at V. Durini, 24. ☎02 771 51. MM1: S. Babila. Ticket One sells both: ☎02 39 22 61. €12.50, under 18 or over 65 €10. Includes admission to the soccer museum.)*

FROM NAVIGLI TO THE CORSO DI PORTA TICINESE

NAVIGLI DISTRICT. The Venice of Lombardy, the Navigli district boasts canals, footbridges, open-air markets, and trolleys. The Navigli are sections of a larger medieval canal system that transported thousands of tons of marble to build the duomo and linked Milan to northern cities and lakes. Da Vinci designed the original canal locks. *(Outside the MM2: Pta. Genova station, through the Arco di Porta Ticinese.)*

BASILICA DI SANT'EUSTORGIO. Founded in the 4th century to house the bones of the Magi, it lost its function when the dead sages were spirited off to Cologne in 1164. The present building, erected in 1278, sports a Lombard-Gothic interior of low vaults and substantial columns. The aesthetic pinnacle and one of the great masterpieces of early Renaissance art is the **▨Portinari Chapel** (1468), attributed to Michelozzo. It holds the tomb of St. Eustorgious (1339) in an ornate casket borne upon the marble shoulders of eight devotees. Look closer—one has three faces. Near the church is the squat 12th-century **Porta Ticinese.** *(P. S. Eustorgio, 3. Farther down C. Ticinese from San Lorenzo Maggiore. Tram #3. Open M and W-Su 9:30am-noon and 3:30-6pm. Capella entrance through adjoining museum. Open Tu-Su 10am-6pm. €5.)*

CHIESA DI SAN LORENZO MAGGIORE. The oldest church in Milan, San Lorenzo Maggiore testifies to the city's 4th-century greatness. Begun as an early Christian church according to an octagonal plan, it was later rebuilt to include a 12th-century *campanile* and a 16th-century dome. To the right of the church sits the 14th-century **Cappella di Sant'Aquilino,** which incorporates an old Roman door jamb. Inside, a 5th-century mosaic of a beardless Christ among his apostles looks over St. Aquilino's remains. *(MM2: Pta. Genova, then tram #3 from V. Torino. In P. Vetra. Open daily 7:30am-12:30pm and 2:30-6:45pm. Cappella €2, students €1.)*

PARCO DELL'ANFITEATRO ROMANO. This archaeological park opened in 2004 and is home to the paltry remains of Milan's once grand Roman ampitheater. Though Mediolaum, as it was known, boasted a 155m-long stadium for gladiatorial fights, it was disassembled in the 6th century out of fear the Longobards would overrun it and use it as a stronghold. Pieces of the structure were recycled into the town walls and St. Lorenzo Church. A small antiquarium holds artifacts from the digs. *(In the courtyard of V. De Amicis, 17. MM2: S. Ambrogio. ☎02 894 00 555. Park open Tu-Su 9:30am-5pm. Museum open M, W, F 9am-2pm. Both Free.)*

IN THE GIARDINI PUBBLICI

GALLERIA D'ARTE MODERNA. Napoleon and Josephine lived here when Milan was capital of Napoleonic Italy (1805-1814). Evocative of Versailles, the gallery displays modern Lombardian art as well as works from Impressionism onward. Of

LOMBARDY

special note are Modigliani's *Beatrice Hastings*, Picasso's *Testa*, Klee's *Wald Bau*, and Morandi's *Natura Morta con Bottiglia*, as well as pieces by Matisse, Mondrian, and Dufy. *(V. Palestro, 16, in the Villa Reale; do not confuse with Palazzo Reale. MM12: Palestro. ☎02 760 02 819. Currently undergoing restoration. Doors open to the public Tu-Su at 9 and 11am only; free tours Tu at 10am. Free.)* The adjacent **Padiglione D'Arte Contemporanea** is a rotating extravaganza of multimedia, photographs, and paintings. *(Open Tu-Th and Sa-Su 9:30am-5:30pm, F 9:30am-9pm. Free.)*

MUSEO CIVICO DI STORIA NATURALE. Milan's Museum of Natural History has amassed extensive geological and paleontological collections, including fossils of Italy's first dinosaur, the rat-sized Scipionyx, minerals, and geological and botanical specimens. *(C. Venezia, 55, in Giardini Pubblici. ☎02 78 13 02. Open M-F 9am-6pm, Sa-Su 9:30am-6:30pm. €3; free the last hr. before closing.)*

🎭 ENTERTAINMENT

The city sponsors free events to sustain its active cultural scene. Look for details in the monthly *Milano Mese* (free), distributed at the tourist office or *Milano è Milano*, a pamphlet published in English and Italian with entertainment and cultural venues (€3). *Milano Magazine* is a monthly publication of the Ufficio Informazione del Comune with info on bars, films, and seasonal events.

OPERA

Milan's famed tradition and unparalleled audience enthusiasm make it one of the best places in the world to see an opera. The city's beloved opera house will finally re-open for the 2004-05 season, beginning December 7, 2004. The theater's excellent acoustics enhance the art such that even those in the cheap seats appreciate a glorious sensory experience. During the interim, the La Scala troupe performs at **Teatro degli Arcimboldi.** A shuttle departs for Arcimboldi from P. Duomo in front of the McDonald's on performance nights (6:45-7:15pm, €1), as well as from MM1: Precotto. Tickets are available in La Scala's temporary ticket office, in the Metro station at the Duomo stop. Performances run year-round, with a break in August and September. *(☎02 720 23 339; www.teatroallascala.org. Tickets €12-114. At noon on performance day, left-over tickets are half-price. Open daily noon-6pm.)*

THEATER, MUSIC, AND FILM

Founded after WWII as a socialist theater, the **Piccolo Teatro**, V. Rovello, 2, near V. Dante, specializes in small-scale classics and off-beat productions. *(☎02 723 33 222. Performances Tu-Sa are usually 8:30pm, Su 4pm. €23-26, student rush tickets €12.50.)* The organization Teatri d'Italia sponsors **Milano Oltre** in June and July, a drama, dance, and music festival. Call the Ufficio Informazione del Comune *(☎02 864 64 094; www.comune.milano.it)*. Milan is known as the jazz capital of Italy, cementing its reputation with the **Brianza Open Jazz Festival** during the first two weeks of July. *(☎02 237 22 36; www.brianzaopen.com.)* Ask at the tourist office or see *Milano Mese* for details about free classical music concerts. Movie listings can be found in any major paper, particularly the Thursday editions. Many cinemas screen English-language films: Monday at **Anteo**, V. Milazzo, 9 (MM2: Moscova; ☎02 659 77 32; www.anteospaziocinema.com), Wednesday at **Arcobaleno**, Viale Tunisia, 11 (MM1: Pta. Venezia; ☎02 294 06 054), and Friday at **Mexico**, V. Savona, 57 (MM2: Pta. Genova; ☎02 489 51 802; www.cinemamexico.it).

FESTIVALS

Milan's increasingly popular **Carnevale** is the longest lasting in Italy. The masked mystique and medieval revelry radiates from the duomo and spreads throughout the city. *Carnevale* occurs annually during the days preceding Ash Wednesday.

⬛ SHOPPING

In a city where clothes really do make the man (or woman), fashion pilgrims arrive to watch the newest styles take their first sashaying steps down the runway. Spring and summer fashion shows are generally by invitation only, but once the music fades and designers take their bows, window displays and biannual *saldi* (sales) usher the new collections into the real world. With so many fashion disciples making idols of the illustrious Giorgio, Donatella, and Miuccia, the fashion district known as the Golden Triangle has become a sanctuary in its own right. Take the Metro to MM1: S. Babila and strut around **Via Monte Napoleone,** with its two **Prada** stores within 100m of each other. Head past V. Sant'Andrea and the **Versace** store, turning right on V. Gesù. Although distinctly less impressive, V. Gesù leads to the inner sanctum along V. Sant'Andrea. V. Sant'Andrea becomes V. Verri, home to the **Yves Saint Laurent** boutique. Toward the end of V. Gesù, the **Moschino** store, on V. della Spiga, is noted for its exquisite shoes. Turn right on V. della Spiga, pass the **Dolce e Gabbana, Cerruti 1881,** and **Armani** stores, and emerge on V. Sant'Andrea. This street is the high altar of the fashion world: **Fendi, Hermès, Chanel, Ferre,** another **Moschino, Armani, Prada,** and even **Armani Jr.**

Designer creations are available to mere mortals at the trendy boutiques around **Porta Ticinese** and **Porta Genova,** both near MM2: Pta. Genova. **Corso di Porta Ticinese,** which extends from **Piazza XXIV Maggio** toward the duomo, and its offshoot, **Via Molino delle Armi,** pack their displays with the latest looks. Trendsetters flock to shops along **Via Torino,** near the duomo, while the **Foro** in front of the Castle Sforzesco, near MM1:Cairoli offers a smaller and more sophisticated collection. Savvy shoppers unearth gems in the shops along **Corso Buenos Aires,** which becomes **Corso Venezia** after MM1: Pta. Venezia. The whole city goes on sale during the first week of January and July, and even though sales officially last for another two months, barbarian bargain hunters snatch up their finds early.

Fashionistas who can tolerate the stigma of being a season behind can buy top names at a discount from wholesale clothing outlets known as *blochisti* (stocks). *Milano è Milano* has a substantial list, as does the free "Shopping Map," available at the APT offices. The well-known **Il Salvagente,** V. Bronzetti, 16, is located off C. XXII Marzo. (Bus #60 from MM1: Lima or MM2/3: Stazione Centrale. Open M-Tu 3-7pm, W-Sa 10am-7pm.) For the die-hard discounter, **Gruppo Italia Grandi Firme,** V. Montegani #7/A, stocks Armani, Versace, and other big-name brands at 70% or more off. (MM2: Famagosta. Head 300m under the overpasses and across the river to V. Montegani and turn right. Open M 3:30-7pm, Tu-F 10am-1pm and 3:30-7:30pm, Sa 10:30am-7:30pm.) The guide *Milano è Milano* lists markets and second-hand stores. Shop around the area of C. di Porta Ticinese, the Navigli district, and C. Garibaldi for second-hand attire. **Eliogabalo,** P. Eustorgio, 2 (☎02 837 82 93), named after a Roman emperor renowned for his preoccupation with aesthetics, offers the latest styles. (Off of P. XXIV Maggio.) True Milanese bargain hunters attack the bazaars on **V. Fauché** (MM2: Garibaldi) Tuesday and Saturday, and **Viale Papinian** (MM2: Agostino) also on Saturday. The famous 400-year-old **Fiera di Sinigallia,** on V. d'Annunzio, is great for bargains (Sa only). Another fabulous option is the Italian department store **La Rinascente,** where Armani began his career. (In P. Duomo. www.rinascenteshopping.com. Open M-Sa 9am-10pm, Su 10am-10pm.)

⬛ NIGHTLIFE

Milan's nightlife resembles one of its sophisticated cocktails: the vibrant, the mellow, the chic, and the wild all intermixed in a concentrated space. The **Brera district,** once home to artists, exudes charm and whimsy in its plush, pricey bars. Its aperitifs have drifted to the nearby **Colonne di S. Lorenzo** and the **Porta Ticinese** (MM2: Pta. Genova, then tram #9 to Piazzale XXIV Maggio, and head onto C. di Porta Ticinese), where the young and beautiful sip fancy concoctions. A more down-to-earth crowd wallows the night away amid good music and down-to-earth fun at the **Navigli canal district** (MM2: Pta. Genova). *Milanesi* students descend upon the canal's endless stream of cafes, pizzerias, pubs, and bars, grooving to music or letting off steam among friends and tourists. The area's carnival-like atmosphere makes meeting new friends a breeze, while docked barges dot the canal and offer more intimate moments with wandering jazz tunes and wine. Before heading out, don't underestimate Navigli's sizeable mosquito population—insect repellent is the cologne of choice. The Metro closes around midnight and cabs are expensive, so stick near the hotel, or better yet, find a hotel near the clubs and bars. Milan is relatively safe at night, though suburbs and the areas around Stazione Centrale and C. Buenos Aires deserve an extra dose of caution.

Check any paper on Wednesday or Thursday for info on clubs and events. *Corriere Della Sera* publishes an insert called *Vivi Milano* on Wednesday, and *La Repubblica* produces *Tutto Milano* every Thursday. The best guide to nightlife is *Pass Milano*, published in Italian every two months and available in bookstores (€12.50). *Hello Milano*, published by the city's English-speaking community, contains the latest on hot nightspots and serves as an info exchange for expatriates.

CORSO DI PORTA TICINESE AND PIAZZA VETRA

Welcome to the land of the all-night Happy Hour buffet—one cocktail buys you dinner. Chill, well-dressed local crowds come to drink and socialize.

▨ **Le Biciclette,** V. Conca dei Naviglio, 10 (☎02 581 04 325). A *bici* dangling above the entrance recalls the bar's previous function as a bike shop. Relaxed on posh couches, or ponder the abstract canvases in this "art bar." No cocktail list, so describe what you want and cross your fingers. Beer and wine €4.50, cocktails €5.50. Happy Hour buffet 6-9:30pm. Open daily 6pm-2am, Su brunch 12:30-4:30pm. MC/V.

▨ **Yguana Café Restaurant,** V. P. Gregorio XIV, 16 (☎02 894 041 95), just off of P. Vetra. Beautiful people sipping huge fruit cocktails (€7-8) makes for a beautiful evening. Lounge on a couch upstairs or groove to the nightly DJs downstairs. Happy Hour daily 5:30-9pm. No cover. Sunday brunch 12:30-3pm. Open daily 5pm-2am.

Exploit, V. Piopette, 3 (☎02 894 08 675) on C. Porta Ticinese near Chiesa di S. Lorenzo Maggiore. Locals flock to this trendy bar and restaurant for its cheap beer (pint of Tennent's €3) and chatty atmosphere. No cover. Open daily noon-3pm and 6pm-2am.

THE NAVIGLI

From C. Porta Ticinese, walk south until the street ends. Veer right through the P. XXIV Maggio to V. Naviglio Pavese and V. A. Sforza, two streets bordering a canal. Alternatively, take the Metro to MM2: Pta. Genova. Walk along V. Vigevano until it ends and veer right onto V. Naviglio Pavese. Less refined and more diverse than its northern neighbor, the Navigli has a cafe, bar, or club for everyone.

▨ **Scimmie,** V. A. Sforza, 49 (☎02 894 02 874; www.scimmie.it). A legendary night club in three part harmony: the pizza pub on the river barge; the chill, polished ristorante; and the cool, blue bar itself, with nightly performances. Talented underground musicians play fusion, jazz, blues, Italian swing, and reggae. Concerts 10:30pm. Schedule online. Open daily 8pm-3am.

Maya, V. A. Sforza, 41 (☎02 581 05 168). Statues of the Mayan gods, and highly entertaining drinks, like the *cuccaracha de toro* (€5), make Maya a shrine to good times. Rowdy Happy Hour buffet 6-9pm. Open daily 6pm-2am.

LOMBARDY

Pontell, V. Naviglio Pavese, 2 (☎ 02 581 01 982). 1st bar on the right from V. Naviglio Pavese. Ahoy, matey—life preservers and rubber dinghies make this bar look like Gilligan's Island. Ask the buff waiters in muscle shirts for the *bierre a la pression* (€8). No cover. Open daily 6pm-2am.

C-Side, V. Castelbarco, 11 (☎ 02 583 10 682; www.c-side.it). From V. A. Sforza, head down V. Lagrange (next to Cafe Baraonda), which becomes V. Giovenale. At the 6-way intersection, take V. Castelbarco on the right. A well-dressed, youthful crowd revels in red lights and purple steam on some of Milan's biggest dance floors. Occasional live music. Cover for ladies €13, men €16. Free with student ID. Open W-Su 11pm-4am.

AROUND CORSO COMO

From MM2: Garibaldi, go south on C. Como. At the most glamorous clubbing scene in Milan (possibly the world), models mingle with movie stars over mojitos. All three close in August.

Hollywood, C. Como, 15 (☎ 02 659 89 96; www.discotecahollywood.com). Slip into something stunning and pout for the bouncer: this disco selects its revellers with the utmost discrimination. Hip-hop, house, and disco. Cover Tu-W €13 and Th-Su €16. Women with student ID free before 12:30am. Open Tu-Su 11pm-4am. MC/V.

Casablanca, C. Como, 14 (☎ 02 626 901 86; www.casablancacafe.it). An über-lounge for the the über-hot. Scads of mascara and a mojito complete the look. Cocktails €10. No cover. Open daily 10:30pm-3am.

Loolapaloosa, C. Como, 15 (☎ 02 655 56 93), next to Hollywood. Table-dancing is de rigeur at this vigorous alternative to the frosty hipper-than-thou scene nearby. Perfect place to toss back a pint and look gorgeous doing it. Reserve a table for Sa or risk standing by the bar all night. Cover €6. Open daily 6pm-3am.

AROUND LARGO CAIROLI

Old Fashion Cafe, Viale Alemagna, 6 (☎ 02 805 62 31; www.oldfashion.it). MM1/2: Cadorna F. N. A mainstay of the *Milanese* scene, with live music and theme nights. A well-dressed set gets artsy in this garden in the middle of the city. Cover €20. Restaurant opens daily 9pm; dancing midnight-4am.

Bar Magenta, V. Carducci, 13 (☎ 02 805 38 08). MM1/2: Cardona. A short walk down V. G. Carducci at the intersection with C. Magenta. More than a Guinness bar, this institution dates from 1807. Pints €5.50. No cover. Open daily 8am-4am.

EAST OF CORSO BUENOS AIRES

🏠 **Cafe Capoverde,** V. Leoncavallo, 16 (☎ 02 268 20 430). MM1/2: Loreto. Take V. Costa, for 10min., which becomes V. Leoncavallo. Greenhouse/bar/restaurant/plant store. Pick a cactus for mom; grab a fruit cocktail large enough to drown in yourself. Any closer to nature and you'd be in the jungle. Happy Hour buffet 6-8:30pm. Open 6pm-2am.

Artdeco Cafe, V. Lambro, 7 (☎ 02 295 24 760). MM1: Pta. Venezia. Walk 3 blocks up C. Buenos Aires and turn right on V. Melzo; it's 3 blocks down on the left. Interior and patrons trying really hard to be hip and artsy and mostly succeeding. House, hip-hop, and acid jazz. Happy Hour daily 6-9pm. No cover. Open daily 6pm-2am.

Kirribilly, V. Castelmorrone, 7 (☎ 02 701 20 151). MM1: Pta. Venezia. Take V. Regina Giovana from C. Buenos Aires. At P. Maria Adelaide di Savoia turn right on V. Castelmorrone. It's a cheery Australian pub with a giant shark's head on the wall, lads. When there's a football match on, they're open, period. No cover. Open M-F noon-3:30pm and 6pm-3am, Sa-Su 6pm-3am.

LOMBARDY

L'elephante, V. Melzo, 22 (☎02 295 18 768). MM2: Pta. Venezia. Take C. Buenos Aires 3 blocks; turn right on V. Melzo. Vaguely 60s interior with lava lamps and bizarre furniture exudes a sultry but easygoing atmosphere. Mostly lesbian, though the Happy Hour food draws all types. Mixed drinks €7-8. Happy Hour 6:35-9:30pm with drinks (€5) and sumptuous appetizers. No cover. Open Tu-Su 6:35pm-2am.

Sottomarino Giallo, V. Donatello de Bardi, 2 (☎33 954 54 127; www.sottomarino-giallo.it). MM1/2: Loreto. Take V. Abruzzi to V. Donatello de Bardi. The biggest lesbian club in town lives in a yellow submarine. Women only. Open Tu-Su 10:30pm-3:30am.

LIVE MUSIC

Alcatraz, V. Valtellina, 25 (☎02 690 16 352; www.alcatrazmilano.com). MM2: Pta. Garibaldi. Go through the train station, take the V. Pepe exit, and turn left. At V. Valtellina, turn right and walk 10min. Largest club and indoor concert venue in Milan, with different music playing on 3 floors. F dance music, Sa live music with local rock bands. Cover €14 or €39 with drinks. Open F-Sa 11pm-4am.

Blueshouse, V. S. Uguzzone, 26 (☎02 270 03 621; www.blueshouse.it). MM1: Villa S. Giovanni. Take V. Vipacco; turn right on V. A. Soffredini and left on V. S. Uguzzone. Jazz, blues, rock, and tribute bands. Concerts begin 11pm. Open W-Su 9pm-2:30am.

BERGAMO   ☎035

A trip to Bergamo is a visit to two different worlds. The *città bassa* (low city) is a modern, industrial burg whose Galleria dell'Accademia Carrara is packed with quintessential Renaissance art. On the bluff above, palaces, churches, and the huge stone fortifications used to defend Venice from Spanish-ruled Milan characterize the *città alta* (high city). When night falls in the summertime, hundreds of people roam the narrow, cobblestone streets of the medieval town, where shops stay open until midnight and the *enoteche* even later.

▆ TRANSPORTATION

The **train station** (☎035 24 76 24) is in P. Marconi, at the juncture of the Brembana and Seriana valleys. Trains run to: Brescia (1hr., every hr. 5:42am-11:03pm, €3.30); Cremona (1½hr., every hr. 6:30am-8:14pm, €5); Milan (1hr., every hr. 4:41am-10:25pm, €3.30); and Venice (2-4hr., 5:42am-11:03pm, €12.34). **Buses,** in the **Stazione Autolinee** to the left of the train station, run to Como (7 per day 6:25am-7:45pm, €4.15) and Milan (every 30min. 5:30am-11pm, €4.20). Buses from the neighboring SAB station serve suburbs and nearby towns. The **airport bus** runs between the station and Bergamo's **airport,** which has become a hub for RyanAir (15min., 5:30am-10:05pm, €1.05). For a **taxi,** call ☎035 451 90 90 or 24 45 05 from the station.

▆▆ ORIENTATION AND PRACTICAL INFORMATION

The train and bus stations and many budget hotels are in the *città bassa*. Tickets good on ATB city buses and funiculars are available from vending machines or *tabacchi* (€0.95 valid 1hr., day ticket €2.40). There are three ways to reach *città alta*: either take bus #1 to the *funicolare di città alta*, which ascends from **Via Vittorio Emanuele** to the Mercato delle Scarpe (8 per hr.); take bus #1a to the Colle Aperto, stopping at the top of the *città alta;* or climb the stairs on **Via Salita della Scaletta,** which starts to the left of the funicular on V. V. Emanuele, turn right at the top, and follow **Via San Giacomo** through **Porta San Giacomo** for 15min.

Tourist Offices: *Città alta* **APT**, Vco. Aquila Nera, 2 (☎035 24 22 26; www.apt.bergamo.it). Take bus #1 or 1a to the funicular, then follow V. Gombito to P. Vecchia, and turn right before P. Vecchia on Vco. Aquila Nera; office is 1st door on the right. Open daily 9am-12:30pm and 2-5:30pm. *Città bassa* **APT**, V. V. Emanuele, 20 (☎035 21 02 04 or 21 31 85). From the train station, head down V. Papa Giovanni 7 blocks and 2 name changes. Office is set off the road, behind a wrought-iron fence. Press buzzer to the left of the 1st gate for info and **maps.** Open M-F 9am-12:30pm and 2-5:30pm. After Oct. 2004, the *bassa* office may relocate to an as of yet undetermined location.

Currency Exchange: Banca Nazionale del Lavoro, V. Petrarca, 12 (☎035 23 80 16), off V. V. Emanuele, near P. della Libertà. Good rates. Open M-F 8:20am-1:20pm and 2:35-4:05pm, Sa 8:20-11:50am. Also at the **post office.** Open M-F 8:30am-5pm.

ATM: Throughout the *città bassa* and at the train station. In the *città alta*, P. Vecchia 1/A at **Credito Bergamasco.**

Western Union: World Center Agenti, V. Quarenghi, 37/D (☎035 31 31 24, fax 32 13 63), off V. P. Paleocapa. Offers cheap long-distance calls. Open daily 10:30am-8pm.

Luggage Storage: *Bassa* tourist office often allows free storage during business hours.

Emergency: ☎113. **Ambulance** (☎118). **Police,** V. Galgario, 17 (☎035 23 82 38).

Hospital: Ospedale Maggiore, Largo Barozzi, 1 (☎035 26 91 11).

Pharmacy: Farmacia Internazionale, V. Maj 2/A. Open M-F 9am-12:30pm and 3-7:30pm.

Internet: Chiocciol@, V. G. Camozzi, 32. €0.10 per min. or €5 per hr. Open Tu-Sa 10am-8pm.

Post Office: V. Locatelli, 11 (☎035 24 32 56). Take V. Zelasco from V. V. Emanuele. Open M-F 8:30am-7pm, Sa 8:30am-12:30pm. Packages are handled at V. Pascoli, 6 (☎035 23 86 98). Same hours. **Postal Code:** 24122.

▜ ACCOMMODATIONS

Prices rise with altitude; most affordable *alberghi* are in the *città bassa*. The tourist office has info on cheaper *agriturismi*.

▨ **Ostello della Gioventù di Bergamo (HI),** V. G. Ferraris, 1 (☎/fax 035 36 17 24; www.ostellodibergamo.it). From Pta. Nuova take bus #14 to Leonardo da Vinci, then backtrack 20m and climb the stairs to the right; hostel is on the right. Modern rooms all have bath and balcony. Expansive gardens and common room with TV, microwave, and fridge. Bike rental €10 per day. Phone card Internet €5.16 per hr. Breakfast buffet included. Check-in after 2pm. Lockout 10am-2pm. 4- to 6-bed dorms €15; singles €21; doubles €20; family rooms €18. Non-members add €3. MC/V. ❷

Albergo S. Giorgio, V. S. Giorgio, 10 (☎035 21 20 43; www.sangiorgioalbergo.it). Take bus #7, or walk from the train station down V. Giovanni XXIII. Turn left on V. P. Paleocapa, which becomes V. S. Giorgio. Modern rooms with fan, fridge, TV, and sink. English spoken. 68 beds. Wheelchair accessible. Reception 7:30am-midnight. Singles €30, with bath €45; doubles €45/€60. MC/V. ❸

Locanda Caironi, V. Torretta, 6B/8 (☎035 24 30 83). From the train station, take V. Papa Giovanni XXIII to V. Angelo Maj, turn right, and walk for several blocks. Turn left on V. Borgo Palazzo, then right at 2nd block. Accessible by bus #5 or 7 from V. Angelo Maj. The candle-lit garden trattoria burbles with conversation. Spartan rooms are graced by a large, shady courtyard. Shared bath. Singles €20; doubles €38. MC/V. ❷

Hotel Quarenghi, V. Quarenghi 33 (☎035 31 99 14). Take bus #6 or 14 from Pta. Nuova to Quarenghi. By foot, walk up V. Giovanni, turn left on V. P. Paleocapa, then right on V. Quarenghi. Large doubles and triples, many with modern bath. Convenient to the station. Singles €30; doubles €50, with bath €60; triples €70/€80. MC/V. ❸

Porta Sant'Alessandro
Colle Aperto
Viale delle Mura
Via Roccolino
Cittadella
PIAZZA MASCHERONI
Porta di San Lorenzo
Via Maironi da Ponte
Via del Paradiso
Via Vagine
Via della Boccola
Via Tre Armi
Via Delle Mura
V. della S. Grata
V. San Salvatore
Via Arena
Teatro Sociale
Torre Civica
Via Tassis
Via della Fara
V. Salvecchio Via B. Colleoni
Via Bartolomeo Via B. Colleoni
PIAZZA DUOMO
Biblioteca Civica
Battistero
Vco. Aquila Nera
Cappella Colleoni
PIAZZA VECCHIA
Santa Maria Maggiore
PIAZZA GIULIANI
Via S. Lorenzo
PIAZZA MERCATO D. FIENO
Duomo
Palazzo d. Ragione
Via Gombito
Via M. Lupo
Via G. Donizetti
Via Solata
CITTÀ ALTA
Parco delle Rimembranze
PIAZZA MERCATO D. SCARPE
Via San Giacomo
Via Rocca
La Rocca
Funicular Terminal
V. San Giacomo
Porta San Giacomo
Via Salita D. Scaletta
Via Porta Dipinta
Mura di S. Giacomo
San Agostio
Prato della Fara
Via Fara
Galleria Sant'Alessandro
Conca d'Oro
Il Fortino
Vic. San Carlo
Via Buttaro
Funicular Terminal
Sant'Andrea
San Michele al Pozzo Bianco
V. Porta Dipinta
Porta Sant'Agostino
Mura di S. Agostino
Viale Vittorio Emanuele II
Viale Vittorio Emanuele II
Via della Noca
Accademia Carrara
Via Zambelli
Via Brigata Lupi
Via Don C. Botta
Via S. Benedetto
Via Antonio Locatelli
Via Monte Ortigara
Via Comasello
Pelabrocco
Via Pignolo
Via San Tomaso
PIAZZALE REPUBLICA
Via M. Domigni
Via M. Zambianch
Via Zelasco
Via Masone
Via Albini
Via Pignolo
TO (1km)
Vic. delle Torri
Via F. Cuccchi
G. Garibaldi
PIAZZA DELLA LIBERTÀ
Pradello
San Bernardino
TO (3km)
ROTUNDA D. MILLE
Via Tasca
Via Petrarca
Via Giuseppe Verdi
Via Elisabetta
Via San Giovanni
Via C. Battisti
Via Roma
Via Dei Partigiani
PIAZZA SAN BARTOLOMEO
Giardini Caprotti
Via A. Pitentino
Via Borfuro
PIAZZA DANTE
LARGO BELOTTI
San Bartolomeo
CITTÀ BASSA
Via Pignolo
Parco Marenzi
LARGO DEL GALGARIO V. Suardi
Via XX Settembre
PIAZZA MATTEOTTI
Via Torquato Tasso
Santo Spirito
TO (100km)
TO (400m)
Via G. Tiraboschi
Teatro Gaettano Donizetti
Via Gabriele Camozzi
PORTA SAN ANTONIO
Via T. Frizzoni
V. A. Mazzi
Via D'Alzano
LARGO PORTA NUOVA
V. Galliccioli
Via S. Francis Assisi
V. Taramelli
Via Clara Maffei
Via del Casalino
V. Stezzano
Madonna della Neve
Via Borgo Palazzo
Fiume Morla
Via G. Ghislanzoni
Despar
Via Pietro Paleocapa
RX
Via Paseoli
Piazzale degli Alpini
V. Angelo Maj
Via Foro Boario
V. M. Ceralon
Via Div. Julia
Via dei Cappuccini
Via Torretta
TO (300m)
Viale Papa Giovanni XXIII
V. Tarchetti
Via G. Bonomelli
Stazione Autolinee
PIAZZALE MARCONI
Via Bartolomeo Bono
Stazione Autolinee SAB
PIAZZA S. ANNA
Laundromat ■

Bergamo
ACCOMMODATIONS
Albergo S. Giorgio, 13
Convitto Pensionato Caterina
   Cittadini, 8
Hotel Quarenghi, 14
Locanda Caironi, 15
Ostello della Gioventù di
   Bergamo(HI), 10
FOOD
Cooperativa Città Alta, 2
Taverna del Colleoni & Dell'Agnello, 5
Trattoria Casa Mia, 11
Trattoria da Ornella, 7
Trattoria del Teatro, 1
Trattoria Tre Torri, 6

NIGHTLIFE
Papageno Pub, 4
Pozzo Bianco, 9
Vineria Cozzi, 3

0   200 yards
0   200 meters

LOMBARDY

Convitto Pensionato Caterina Cittadini, V. Rocca, 10 (☎035 24 39 11), off P. Mercato delle Scarpe, in *città alta*. V. Rocca is the narrow street on the right after exiting the funicular. A courtyard and sun-lit rooftop terraces. Nuns in charge speak little English. Women only. Reception on 2nd floor. Curfew 10pm; if going out later, ask for a key. Reserve ahead. Singles €25, with bath €30; doubles €40. Cash only. ❸

🍴 FOOD

Meals conclude with a *formaggio* course—try the supple *branzi* and *taleggio* cheeses with the local *Valcalepio* red and white wines. Another traditional meal is *cavallo* (horse) or *asino* (donkey) with a side of polenta, a cornmeal paste. In the *città alta*, shops sell yellow *polentina* confections topped with chocolate blobs meant to resemble birds, but these treats are primarily pricey tourist bait. Pick up staples at Pellicano, a **supermarket** on the right side of V. V. Emanuele, past the *città bassa* tourist office at the bottom of the hill heading to the *città alta*. (Open M 8:30am-1:30pm, Tu-F 8:30am-1:30pm and 3:30-8pm, Sa 8:30am-8pm. MC/V.) A Despar supermarket, V. P. Giovanni, 23, is closer to the *città bassa's* center and boasts an eco-friendly label. (Open M 8am-1pm, Tu-Sa 8am-8pm.) Many of Bergamo's best restaurants are on the main tourist drag, V. Bartolomeo, and its continuations V. Colleoni and V. Gombito. In comparison to their grade-*alta* cousins, restaurants in the *città bassa* are often less traditionally *Bergamasco*, and the quality can be less than cloud-nine.

Trattoria del Teatro, P. Mascheroni, 3/A (☎035 23 88 62), at the start of V. Bartolomeo. Modest place serves exceptional local fare priced right. Cover €2.50. *Primi* €8-9, *secondi* €13-15. Open Tu-Su 12:30-3:30pm and 7:30-11:30pm. Cash only. ❸

Trattoria Tre Torri, P. Mercato del Fieno, 7/A (☎035 24 43 66). Heading away from P. Vecchia, turn left off V. Gombito onto V. S. Lorenzo. Unassuming *trattoria* offers authentically *Bergamasco* cuisine off the beaten path. *Antipasti* and *primi* €6.50, *secondi* €9. Cover €1.50. Open daily noon-3pm and 7:30-11pm. ❸

Trattoria da Ornella, V. Gombito, 15 (☎035 23 27 36). After exiting the funicular, walk up V. Gombito. Popular spot overlooking fountain and piazza specializes in rich *polenta taragna*, made with butter, local cheeses, and rabbit (€14). Cover €2. *Primi* €6-8, *secondi* €10-14. Open M-W and F-Su noon-3pm and 7-11pm. AmEx/MC/V. ❸

Cooperativa Città Alta, Vco. S. Agata, 19 (☎035 21 85 68, fax 413 00 56). Take V. Colleoni away from P. Vecchia, turn right on Vco. S. Agata. Unpretentious eatery hosts socializing students in a grape-arbored garden. *Bergamasco* fare (€4-7.50) and speedy service all night long. Cover €0.80. Sandwiches €2.10-3.10. Open daily noon-3am. ❶

Taverna del Colleoni & Dell'Agnello, P. Vecchia, 7 (☎035 23 25 96). Break out your dress or jacket and tie and head to this 300-year-old restaurant for a luxurious dining experience. Succulent cuisine is served at candle-lit tables in the shadow of the civic tower. *Primi* €13-15, *secondi* €13-24. Open Tu-Sa noon-2:30pm and 7:30-10:30pm, Su noon-2:30pm and 7:30-10pm. AmEx/MC/V. ❹

Trattoria Casa Mia, V. S. Bernardino, 20/A (☎035 22 06 76). From the train station walk straight to Pta. Nuova. Turn left on V. G. Tiraboschi, which becomes V. Zambonate. Then turn left on V. Bernadino. Locals pack in for the full home-style dinner *menù* (€11). Lunch *menù* €8.50. Open M-Sa noon-2pm and 7-10pm. ❷

👁 SIGHTS

CITTÀ ALTA

The compact *città alta* is a wonderfully preserved medieval town with panoramic views and archways around every corner. The town is accessible by funicular, bus, and on foot, but the narrow lanes make driving harrowing. From the Carrara gallery, the cobbled V. Noca ascends from the lower city to Pta. S. Agostino, a 16th-century gate built by the Venetians as a fortification. After passing through the gate, V. Porta Dipinta leads to V. Gombito, which ends in P. Vecchia.

■ **BASILICA DI SANTA MARIA MAGGIORE.** Despite a dim and crumbling Romanesque exterior, this 12th-century basilica, joined to the Cappella Colleoni, possesses a strikingly bright, ornate Baroque interior. No corner of the iridescent ceilings is left unfrescoed or unsculpted. Tapestries and oil paintings depicting biblical stories adorn the walls, surrounding the Victorian tomb of Bergamo's famous son, composer Gaetano Donizetti. *(Head through archway flanking P. Vecchia to reach P. del Duomo. ☎ 035 22 33 27. Open Apr.-Oct. M-Sa 9am-12:30pm and 2:30-6pm, Su 9am-1pm and 3-6pm; Nov.-Mar. M-Sa 9am-12:30pm and 2:30-5pm, Su 9am-noon and 3-6pm. Free.)*

CAPPELLA COLLEONI. Marble braids weave through the colorful facade, and 18th-century ceiling frescoes by Tiepolo illuminate the interior. A gruesome decapitation of John the Baptist shows visitors their way out. G. A. Amadeo, architect of the Certosa di Pavia, designed the *cappella* in 1476 as a funerary chapel for the celebrated *Bergamasco* mercenary Bartolomeo Colleoni. The elaborate exterior carvings combine biblical and classical allusions—the saints wear togas and Julius and Augustus Caeser are granted divine status. *(Right of the basilica. Open Apr.-Oct. daily 9am-12:30pm and 2-6:30pm, Nov.-Mar. Tu-Su 9am-12:30pm and 2:30-4:30pm. Free.)*

PIAZZA VECCHIA. This piazza houses a majestic ensemble of medieval and Renaissance buildings flanked by restaurants and cafes in the heart of the *città alta*. Splay out with locals on the steps of the white marble **Biblioteca Civica** (1594), the repository of Bergamo's rich collection of 16th-century manuscripts. Across the piazza is the massive Venetian Gothic **Palazzo della Ragione** (Court of Justice, 1199) and a 300-year-old sundial, on the ground beneath the portico. To the right, connected to the palazzo by a covered stairway, stands the 12th-century ■**Torre Civica** (Civic Tower). To commemorate the town's medieval curfew, the 15th-century bell rings 180 times nightly at 10pm. *(Tower open May to mid-Sept. M-Th and Su 10am-8pm, F-Sa 10am-10pm; mid-Sept. to Oct. M and F 9:30am-12:30pm and 2-7pm, Sa-Su 10am-7pm; Nov.-Feb. Sa 10:30am-12:30pm and 2-4pm, Su 10:30am-4pm; Mar.-Apr. Tu and Th-Sa 10:30am-12:30pm and 2-6pm, Su 10:30am-6pm. €3, under 18 or over 65 €2, includes admission to the historical museum inside.)* The **Teatro Sociale** frequently hosts all-night exhibitions of modern art. The interior itself, with four levels of now crumbling box seats made from weathered stone and wood beams, predates Shakespeare and often upstages the art. *(Just off the Piazza. Open Tu-Fr 3:30-11pm, Sa 10:30am-midnight. Free.)*

PARCO DELLE RIMEMBRANZE. Once a Roman military camp, this park's shady paths commemorate Italian battle casualties. In the middle, famed fortress **La Rocca** provides a view of the *città alta* and the Po Valley beyond. *(At the end of V. Solata. P. Brigate Legnano, 12. ☎ 035 24 71 16. La Rocca: ☎ 035 22 47 00. Open May-Sept. Sa-Su 10am-8pm; Sept. 16-Oct. Sa-Su 10am-6pm; Nov.-Feb. Sa-Su 10:30am-12:30pm and 2-4pm; Mar.-Apr. Sa-Su 10:30am-12:30pm and 2-6pm. €1, under 18 or over 60 €0.50. Park open daily Apr.-Sept. 9am-8pm; Oct. and Mar. 10am-6pm; Nov.-Feb. 10am-4pm. Free.)*

ABOVE THE CITTÀ ALTA. The **San Vigilio** funicular runs from the *città alta* to **Castello San Vigilio,** Bergamo's castle in the clouds. Some of the halls and staircases are open for exploration, and hiking trails run down to the historical center. *(Castle open daily Apr.-Sept. 9am-8pm, Mar. and Oct. 10am-6pm, Nov.-Feb. 10am-4pm. Free.)*

CITTÀ BASSA

The newer of the two parts of the city, situated at the base of the bluff, *città bassa* compensates for its generally lackluster appearance with the Galleria dell'Accademia Carrara, brimming with some of Italy's most notable works of art.

GALLERIA DELL'ACCADEMIA CARRARA. This art gallery, residing inside a Neoclassical villa, is one of the most important in Italy. The pieces displayed start from 13th-century Gothic, with an emphasis on Florentine humanism. Fifteen rooms exhibit canvases by the Dutch School and local greats like Fra' Galgario, Botticelli's not quite flattering *Ritratto di Giuliano de' Medici*, Lotto's *Ritratto di Giovinetto*, and works by Tiepolo, Titian, Rubens, Brueghel, Bellini, Mantegna, Goyen, van Dyck, and El Greco. There are several pieces by Rizzi in **Gallery VI**, including a diptych *Maddalena in Meditazione*, which finds Mary Magdalene looking down upon a crucified Christ. In *Maddalena Penitente*, still intent on the cross, she holds a Bible to her chest. The Rizzis are beside several Lottos, including *Nozze Mistiche di Santa Caterina. (P. dell'Accademia, 82/A. From Largo Porta Nuova, take V. Camozzi to V. Pignolo, turn right to V. San Tomaso. The gallery is in the white villa to the left. ☎035 39 96 43. Open Tu-Su Apr.-Sept. 10am-1pm and 3-6:45pm; Oct.-Mar. 9:30am-1pm and 2:30-5:45pm. €2.60, over 60 or under 18 €1.55.)*

OTHER SIGHTS. In the heart of *città bassa* is **Piazza Matteotti,** redesigned by the Fascists in 1924 and typically crawling with tourists and local youth. The **Chiesa di San Bartolomeo,** at the far right of the piazza, holds a superb altarpiece of the Madonna and Child by Lorenzo Lotto. *(Open daily 9am-4pm. Free.)* To the right of San Bartolomeo, V. Tasso leads to the **Chiesa del Santo Spirito,** marked by its mottled facade and modernist sculpture over the door. The stark gray Renaissance interior, completed in 1521, contrasts strongly with decorative paintings by Lotto, Borgognone, and Previtali. *(Open Sept.-June M-Sa 7-11:30am and 4-6:30pm, Su 8am-noon and 4-7pm; July-Aug. M-Sa 7-11am and 5-6:30pm, Su 8:30am-noon and 5-7pm.)* On the left, V. Pignolo connects the upper and lower cities, winding past handsome 16th- to 18th-century villas. Along the way is the tiny **Chiesa di San Bernardino,** covered with icons celebrating the town's agricultural and industrial heritage, as well as a splendid Lotto altar painting. *(Open daily 8am-noon and 3-6pm. Free.)*

🎵 🎭 ENTERTAINMENT AND NIGHTLIFE

The arts thrive in Bergamo. The opera season lasts from September to November, and the drama season follows in November through April at the **Donizetti Theater,** P. Cavour, 15 (☎035 416 06 02), in the *città bassa.* In May and June, the spotlight falls on the highly acclaimed **Festivale Pianistico Internazionale,** co-hosted by the city of Brescia. In September, Bergamo celebrates its premier native composer with a festival of Donizetti's lesser-known works. Contact the tourist office or the theater, P. Cavour, 14 (☎035 24 96 31), for info. During summer, the tourist office provides a program of free weekly events, *Viva la tua città.*

The *città alta* shape-shifts at night, as reams of people pack the eateries, pubs, and *vinerie.* Head down to **Pozzo Bianco,** V. Porta Dipinta, 30/B, by far the liveliest hangout, with a warm all-night kitchen. (☎035 24 76 94. Sandwich and drink €5. Open daily 7am-3pm and 6pm-3am. AmEx/MC/V.) A romantic Venetian alcove in the *città alta,* **Vineria Cozzi,** V. B. Colleoni, 22, stocks pastries and more than 330 Italian wines. (☎035 23 88 36; www.vineriacozzi.it. Cover €2.10. Open in summer M-Tu, Th, and Sa-Su 10:30am-2am, in winter M-Tu and Th-Su 10:30am-2am. MC/V.) The nearly 200 Belgian beers at **Papageno Pub,** V. B. Colleoni, 1/B, keep even the hardiest drinker busy. (☎035 23 66 24. Open M-W and F-Su 7am-2am.)

BRESCIA ☎030

Observed from afar, Brescia's glass highrises sparkle in the sun with a quintessentially Italian spectrum: the green of the duomo, the red terra-cotta roofs of the residential districts, and the white skeletons of the *centro storico's* Roman ruins. The city once owed its prosperity to the estates of wealthy aristocrats; currently its appliance-heavy export business is somewhat less than glamorous. The soul of this industrial town, however, is its thriving fashion district, where names like Ferragamo and Versace act as tantalizing *antipasti* to the glamour feast of Milan.

▐ TRANSPORTATION

Brescia lies between Milan and Verona on the Torino-Trieste line. **Trains** run to: Bergamo (1hr., 10 per day 5:10am-10:16pm, €3.30); Cremona (1¾hr., 11 per day 6:21am-9:32pm, €3.85); Milan (1hr., every hr. 5:06am-10:37pm, €5.10); Padua (1¾hr., every hr. 4:53am-10:46pm, €10.90); Venice (2¼hr., every hr. 4:13-9:13pm, €13.53); and Verona (45min., 10 per day 7:23am-1:34am, €3.36). The info office (☎147 88 80 88) is open from 7am to 9pm. To the left exiting the station SIA (☎030 449 15) **buses** run to destinations on the western shores of Lake Garda and to Milan (1¾hr., 4 per day 6:40am-9:20pm, €6). To the right exiting the train station, SAIA (☎030 377 42 37) buses run to Cremona (1¼hr., every hr. 6:30am-6:55pm, €4.25) and Mantua (1½hr., every hr. 5:45am-7:15pm, €4.95). The ticket office is open Monday to Friday 7am-12:30pm and 1:30-6:25pm and Saturday 7am-12:30pm and 1:30-3:10pm. **Taxis** (☎030 351 11) are available 24hr.

▄▐ ORIENTATION AND PRACTICAL INFORMATION

Women should be cautious in the area near the station at night.

The rectangular *centro storico* holds most of the city's architectural gems. To reach the center from the **train station**, take **Via Foppa** to **Via V. Emanuele II** and turn right, then eventually left onto **Via Gramsci.** Heading up V. Gramsci, a right onto **Via Moretto** leads to the Pinacoteca Civica Tosio Martinengo, while a right on **Corso Zanardelli** leads to the Teatro Grande, the tourist office, and some of the best shopping in the city. Less than a block after the Teatro Grande on the left is **Via Mazzini.** Up V. Mazzini are both of Brescia's duomos, as well as **Via dei Musei,** the Museo della Città, and Tempio Capitolino to the right; **Piazza della Loggia** is to the left. At the end of V. Mazzini, a short path leads to the **Via del Castello** and the castle itself.

Tourist Office: APT, C. Zanardelli, 34 (☎030 434 18). Helpful event fliers, **maps,** and walking guides for greater Brescia. Open M-F 9am-12:30pm and 3-6pm, Sa 9am-12:30pm. **City Tourist Office,** P. Loggia, 6 (☎030 240 03 57; www.comune.brescia.it). English-speaking with info on the city proper. Open Apr.-Sept. M-Sa 9am-6:30pm, Su 9am-1pm; Oct.-Mar. M-F 9:30am-12:30pm and 2-5pm, Sa 9:30am-1pm.

Car Rental: Avis, V. XX Settembre, 2/F (☎030 29 54 74). **Europcar Italia,** V. Stazione, 49 (☎030 28 04 87). **Hertz,** V. XXV Aprile, 4/C (☎030 45 32).

Emergency: ☎113. **Ambulance** (☎118). **Police** (☎112).

Hospital: Ospedale Civile, P. Spedali Civili (☎030 399 51).

Internet: Black Rose, V. Cattaneo, 22/A (☎030 280 77 04). 2 computers in a cozy cafe. €4.15 per hr. Open M-Sa 7am-midnight.

Bank: Banco di Brescia, C. Zanardelli, 54, to the right exiting the APT office. Open M-F 8:25am-1:25pm and 2:40-4:10pm. Has 2 24hr. **ATMs.**

Post Office: P. Vittoria, 1 (☎030 444 21). Open M-F 8:30am-7pm, Sa 8:30am-noon. **Postal Code:** 25100.

᚛ ACCOMMODATIONS

Albergo San Marco, V. Spalto, 15 (☎030 304 55 41). From the train station, take V. Foppa to its end, then turn right on V. V. Emanuele II, which turns into V. Spalto. Rooms are past their prime but generally clean. Location on a busy street means there's plenty of noise, but closing the windows should do the trick. Breakfast €1.65. Shared bath. Singles €24; doubles €41. AmEx/MC/V. ❷

Albergo Stazione, Vco. Stazione, 15-17 (☎030 377 46 14, fax 377 39 95). From the station, go left and take Viale Stazione; hotel is about 150m down Vco. Stazione. 36 clean and comfortable rooms have TV, phone, and A/C. Micro-bathrooms make showers an adventure. Singles €30, with bath €40; doubles €50/€60. MC/V. ❸

Hotel Solferino, V. Solferino, 1, 2nd fl. (☎030 463 00). Ring the buzzer. Simple rooms. Shared baths. No phone reservations. Singles €26; doubles €52. ❸

᚛ FOOD

Brescia's dishes include *manzo all'olio* (beef prepared in olive oil) and *tortelli di zucca* (zucchini tort). Food here, however, plays second fiddle to the wine. *Tocai di San Martino della Battaglia* (a dry white), *Groppello* (a medium red), and *Botticino* (a dry red of medium age) are all local favorites. Fast and cheap meals abound around the bus and train stations, while satin shirts and fancy dishes fill V. Beccari, a street winding through the pretty neighborhoods between P. Loggia and the duomos. Saturday morning brings the produce **market** to P. Loggia. For inexpensive staples, seek out the **open-air market** in P. Mercato. (Open M and Sa 8:30-11am, Tu-F 8:30am-6pm.) **PAM supermarket,** V. Porcellaga, 26, is on an extension of C. M. della Libertà. (Open M 1-8pm, Tu-Sa 8am-8pm.)

Trattoria Due Stelle, V. S. Faustino, 46 (☎030 423 70). Follow directions for Porteri to V. Solferino. It's 2 blocks on the right. At 150 years and counting, the oldest trattoria in Brescia is also among the most respectable. The tripe dishes, *casonsei* (meat-filled ravioli), and *zuppe di verdura* (vegetable soup) are culinary legends. *Primi* €8-9, *secondi* €8-12. Open Tu-Sa 11:30am-2pm and 7:30-10:30pm, Su noon-3pm. MC/V. ❷

Al Frate, V. Musei, 25 (☎030 377 05 50). Dressed-up patrons savor Brescian food with a twist, like *coniglio ai fichi e vino rosso* (rabbit with figs in red wine; €13). Candlelight, a quiet locale, and white tablecloths make it a picture of class. *Primi* €8-9, *secondi* €10-15. Cover €2.50. Open daily 12:30-2:30pm and 7:30-11:30pm. MC/V. ❸

Ristorante-Pizzeria Cavour, C. Cavour, 56 (☎030 240 09 00). Take V. Emanuele to C. Cavour; turn left. No gimmicks; the delicious pizza speaks for itself. Try the *cavour,* with tomatoes, mozzarella, and bacon. Steady stream of locals comes for takeout. Pizza €4-9. Pasta €6-8. Cover €1.50. Open M and W-Su 11am-3pm and 6:30pm-1am. V. ❶

Trattoria G. A. Porteri, V. Trento, 52 (☎030 38 09 47). Head through P. della Loggia and emerge on V. San Faustino, which becomes V. Trento. Ring buzzer for admission. Locals make the long walk to taste Brescian cuisine at its finest. *Primi* €8, *secondi* €10-12. Reservations are essential. Open Tu-Sa noon-2pm and 8-10pm. MC/V. ❸

᚛ SIGHTS

■**MUSEO DELLA CITTÀ DI SANTA GIULIA.** The former Benedictine nunnery of Santa Giulia served as the final retreat for Charlemagne's ex-wife, Ermengarda. Its structural roots, however, reach all the way back to Roman times—connected to the archaeological section of the museum are the remains of the two Roman villas, discovered underneath the abbey. The colorful mosaic floors and frescoed walls are beautifully preserved. Included in the collection are many rare cast bronze statues, including the second-century *Winged Victory*, Brescia's symbol. The museum's **Oratorio de S. Maria in Solario** displays the precious 8th-century *Cross of Desiderius*, encased in silver and 212 jewels, cameos, and a 4th-century ivory chest carved with biblical scenes. All captions are in English and Italian. *(Facing the Temple, turn right and go 250m to V. dei Musei, 14. ☎800 76 28 11; www.domusortaglia.it. Open Oct.-Mar. Tu-Su 9:30am-5:30pm, June-Sept. Tu-Sa 10am-6pm. €8, 14-18 or over 65 €4.)*

TEMPIO CAPITOLINO. Traces of Brescia's Classical past lie scattered on V. dei Musei. The Roman colony of Brixia lies buried 4m beneath the overgrown greenery in the **Piazza del Foro,** once the center of commercial, religious, and political life here. The ruins of Emperor Vespasian's vast Tempio Capitolino, built in AD 79, stand out as the obvious highlight. The white sections of its columns are from a 1930's restoration; the original pieces are the red terra-cotta brick. Adjoining the temple are the remains of a first century **teatro** that sat 15,000. *(From P. Paolo VI facing away from the duomo, take V. Mazzini to the left and turn right on V. dei Musei. Closed for restoration, but visible from behind the gates.)*

DUOMO NUOVO AND ROTONDA. Not content with just one cathedral, Brescia built the **Duomo Nuovo** in 1825, adjacent to the smaller **Rotonda** (old duomo, Santa Maria Assunta). The third-highest dome in Italy tops the courthouse-like Rococo structure and Corinthian columns of the newer church; sculptural details take the place of colors and paintings. A tiled roof, dark interior, and squat tower make up the 11th-century Romanesque rotonda. The building rests on top of the ancient 8th-century crypt of St. Filastrio. *(In P. Paolo IV, or P. del Duomo. From P. della Vittoria, take path through the archways and under clocktower. Rotonda open Apr.-Oct. Tu-Su 9am-noon and 3-7pm, Nov.-Mar. Sa-Su 9am-noon and 3-6pm. New duomo open M-Sa 7:30am-noon and 4-7:30pm, Su 8am-1pm and 4-7:30pm. Modest dress required.)*

PINACOTECA TOSIO-MARTINENGO. This 22-room palazzo displays a fine collection of paintings and frescoes by local masters. Moretto is particularly well-represented, as are Ferramola, Romanino, Foppa, and Lotto. Don't miss Raphael's *Cristo Benedicente* in **Room 7.** *(From P. Vittoria, take V. A. Gramsci to V. Moretto and turn left; museum is at the end of the street. Enter through center of the piazza, behind the statue. V. Martinengo da Barco, 1. ☎030 377 49 99; www.asm.brescia.it/musei. Open Tu-Su June-Sept. 10am-5pm, Oct.-Mar. 9:30am-1pm and 2:30-5pm. €3, ages 14-18 or over 65 €1.)*

CASTELLO. Like every proper hilltop fairy-tale castle, this castello is fitted with a drawbridge, underground tunnels, and ramparts. Though built continually from the 13th to the 16th centuries, the most striking features date from the time of the Viscontis, notably the fortified keep (c. 1343). During the Risorgimento, Austrian troops bombarded the town from within the castle walls to quell the Brescian rebellion, known as *dieci giorni*, or "ten days." The castle also contains the **Museo Civico del Risorgimento,** which details the town's role in the Risorgimento, and a **weapons museum,** displaying over 500 items of armor and weaponry crafted between 1300 and 1700. In summer, the castello is periodically converted to a restaurant featuring live music. *(On V. del Castello. Approaching the castle, keep to residential streets and the main road, as secluded paths on the hillside are frequented by drug users and dealers. Open daily 8am-8pm. Free. Civic Museum ☎030 441 76. Weapons museum ☎030 29 32 92. Both open Tu-Su June-Sept. 10am-5pm, Oct.-May 9:30am-1pm and 2:30-5pm. Each museum €3, ages 14-18 or over 65 €1. Inquire at tourist office for details about castle events.)*

⬛ ENTERTAINMENT

The **Mille Miglia** (thousand mile) car race, a round-trip between Brescia and Rome, complements Brescia's gamut of high-brow cultural events. Although the cut-throat version of the race ended with a fatal accident in 1957, a leisurely re-run of cars dating from 1927-1957 (the period when the original race ran) takes place each year in early May and ensures a fine showing of Ferraris, Maseratis, Alfa Romeos, Porsches, and Astin Martins. (See www.millemiglia.it for race info.) The annual **Stagione di Prosa,** a series of dramatic performances, runs from December to April. From April to June, the focus shifts to the **Festivale Pianistico Internazionale,** co-hosted by nearby Bergamo. The **Brescia Jazz Festival** is a three-day celebration at the end of July. (☎ 030 353 19 47; www.cipiesse-bs.it. Performances outdoors free, in castle €10.) From June to September, the city hosts an open-air cinema at the castle (€3), plus concerts, dance recitals, and opera. (Find schedules at the tourist office, or call ☎ 035 377 11 11 for more info.)

MANTUA (MANTOVA)　　　　☎ 0376

Mantua is full of subtle contrasts. Narrow alleys criss-cross the wide C. V. Emanuele, and flowers found in every window box ornament the subdued cream and peach stucco of Mantuan homes. In the historical center, stately stone churches and small *negozi* surround the spacious Piazze Sordello, Mantegna, and Marconi. The city's history is similarly rich in contrasts. Although Mantua owes its literary fame to its most renowned son, the poet Virgil, it was the Gonzaga family, ruling from 1328 to the mid-18th century, that transformed Mantua from a small village into a bustling cultural and literary haven. The legendary House of Rigoletto in P. Sordello stands as a monument to the town's role in inspiring Giuseppe Verdi's opera *Rigoletto*. Surrounding Mantua, small country towns like Castellaro, Cavriana, and Solferino offer historic architecture and scenic vineyards in what has become the third-largest wine producing province in Lombardy.

▐▐▌ TRANSPORTATION AND PRACTICAL INFORMATION

The **Train station** is in P. Don Leoni, at the end of V. Solferino (☎ 0376 89 29 21). The ticket office is open daily 5:40am-7:45pm. Trains run to Cremona (1hr., every hr. 5:50am-8:50pm, €4.15); Milan (2hr., 10 per day 5:25am-7:20pm, €8.05); and Verona (40min., 17 per day 6:05am-10:22pm, €2.30). The **bus station** is in P. Mondadori. Turn right and cross the street out of the train station. Cross C. V. Emanuele to V. Caduti. Buses run locally and to nearby towns. Check schedule outside bus terminal for individual destinations. Only buses listed in red run on Sunday. **Taxis** (☎ 0376 32 53 51) are available 5am-1am. **Mantua Bike,** V. Piave, 22/B, rents bikes depending upon the weather. Check the tourist office for bike itineraries around the city. (Open M-Sa 8am-12:30pm and 2-7:30pm. €1.60 per hr., €8 per day.)

From the train station in **Piazza Don E. Leoni,** head left on **Via Solferino,** then right on **Via Bonomi** to the main street, **Corso Vittorio Emanuele II.** Follow it into **Piazza Cavallotti** to pick up **Corso Umberto I. Piazza Marconi** is at the end and **Piazza Mantegna** is on the left. The tourist office and main attractions cluster around P. Mantegna. The helpful, English-speaking staff at the **tourist office,** P. Mantegna, 6, adjacent to Sant'Andrea's church, offers accommodations booking, free brochures, and maps. From the train station, turn left on V. Solferino, then right onto V. Bonomi. Turn left on C. V. Emanuele II, which turns into C. Umberto, until reaching P. Mantegna. (Open M-Sa 8:30am-12:30pm and 3-6pm, Su and holidays 9:30am-12:30pm.) In an emergency call ☎ 113 or the **police,** P. Sordello, 46 (☎ 0376 20 51). **Farmacia Dr. Silvestri,** V. Roma, 24, is one of many located all over the city. Hours change weekly; check any location to find rotating late-night service. (Open Tu-Sa 8:30am-12:30pm and 4-8pm.) **Bit and Phone,** V. Bertinelli, close to the train station, offers **Internet.** (☎ 0376 22 05 94; www.bitandphone.it. Open daily 10am-10pm. €3 per hr.) The **post office,** P. Martiri Belfiore, 15, up V. Roma from the tourist office, offers **currency exchange.** (☎ 0376 32 64 03. Open M-Sa 8:30am-7pm.) **Postal Code:** 46100.

Mantua

🏠 ACCOMMODATIONS
Albergo Bianchi, **1**
Albergo Giulia Gonzaga, **4**
Hotel ABC, **3**
Hotel Mantegna, **8**

🍎 FOOD
Antica Osteria ai Ranari, **9**
Masseria, **2**
Pizzeria/Ristorante
 Piedigrotta, **6**
Ristorante Corte
 Bondeno, **5**
Trattoria con Pizza
 da Chiara, **7**

ACCOMMODATIONS

Accommodations outside the city limits in smaller towns like Castellaro and Monzambano are less expensive. The tourist office has a pamphlet of *agriturismo* options that cost around €30.

Hotel ABC, P. Don Leoni, 25 (☎0376 32 33 47; www.hotelabcmantova.it), across from station. Patient staff speaks some English. Rooms are small, but include clean bath, fan, TV, and phone. Guests can relax on an outdoor patio. Buffet breakfast included. Luggage storage available. Prices vary according to payment method. Reserving online well in advance or paying in cash may get you a lower price. Singles and doubles €22-77; triples €77-110. ❹

LOMBARDY

Albergo Bianchi, P. Don Leoni, 24 (☎0376 32 64 65; www.hotelbianchi.mantova.com), across from train station. Pleasant staff and comfortable rooms with bath, TV, phone, and A/C. Some have balcony. Ivy-shaded courtyard provides a calming space. Reservation recommended. Singles €40-71; doubles €75-108; triples €130. AmEx/MC/V. ❺

Hotel Mantegna, V. Filzi, 10 (☎0376 32 80 19, fax 36 85 64), 2min. from P. Belfiore, in the heart of the historic district. 40 modern, carpeted rooms, all with TV and A/C. Breakfast and parking available. Hotel closes for 1 week in Aug.—check ahead. Singles €75; doubles €120; triples €140. AmEx/MC/V. ❺

Albergo Giulia Gonzaga, V. Vespasiano Gonzaga, 65 (☎0375 52 81 69), in Sabbioneta, 45min. from Mantua by bus. Well-kept hotel in quiet, walled city. Dark wooden ceilings lend a rustic feel, while hand-painted mosaics on room walls add charm. All 13 rooms have TV and bath. No curfew. Singles €35; doubles €50; triples €60. MC/V. ❹

FOOD

Mantuan cuisine is renowned for its *tortellini di zucca* (pumpkin-filled ravioli) and its heavy reliance on locally grown produce and livestock. Homegrown gastronomical delights include parmesan cheese, truffles, and risotto. Pigs outnumber people four to one in this area, so, not surprisingly, *risotto alla pilotta*, a specialty made with pork, is a Mantuan staple. The pig is so revered that every December, the people of Mantua celebrate **Festa dell'Osso** (see **Entertainment**), in which every part of the pig, including the less appetizing face, ears, tail, and feet, is consumed by a carnivorous, pork-mad crowd.

▓ **Ristorante Corte Bondeno** (☎348 775 90 07, fax 0376 43 62 66), on V. Mezzana Loria, in Sabbioneta. Exit the city north from P. Ducale via V. Pesente and follow the marked signs. V. Mezzana Loria becomes a dirt road as it approaches the restaurant, which is in a large, stone farmhouse. It is most easily accessible by car, but those who make the 40min. walk will forget their blisters when huge quantities of the freshest food in Mantua appear before them. Enjoy the owner Sanzio's favorite risotto and pasta hand-rolled by his 84 year-old grandmother. Complement a meal with a bottle of sparkling red *Lambrusco Mantovano* wine. 8 course set *menù* €33-36, including wine. Reservation required. Open Tu-Su at noon for lunch and 8:30pm until the last customer leaves. Live music F-Sa nights. AmEx/MC/V. ❹

Antica Osteria ai Ranari, V. Trieste, 11 (☎0376 32 84 31, fax 32 84 31), south of the town canal on V. Trieste. A friendly proprietor hustles around serving authentic regional dishes, including donkey meat and frog in this tavern-style trattoria. *Primi* €5-7, *secondi* €5-9. Cover €1.50. Open Tu-Su noon-2:30pm and 7:30-11:30pm; closed last 2 weeks of July and 1st week of Aug. AmEx/MC/V. ❷

Trattoria con Pizza da Chiara, V. Corridoni, 44/A/46 (☎0376 22 35 68). From P. Cavallotti, follow C. Libertà and turn left on V. Roma, then right on the narrow V. Corridoni. A winding staircase leads to 3 charming eating areas. House special is the delicious *risotto alla pescatore* (€6). Pizza, *primi*, and *secondi* all from €6. Cover €2. Open M and W-Su noon-3pm and 7pm-midnight. AmEx/MC/V. ❷

Masseria, P. Broletto, 8 (☎/fax 0376 36 53 03). The outdoor piazza of this romantic, candlelit restaurant is the perfect spot for people-watching on the busy Piazza Broletto. The diverse menu features authentic Mantuan concoctions from ingredients like pumpkin, tuna, and pickled apple. Cover €2. Delicious pizza from €5. Open Tu-Su 12:30-2:30pm and 7:30-11pm. AmEx/MC/V. ❷

Pizzeria/Ristorante Piedigrotta, C. Libertà, 15 (☎0376 32 70 14), just off of P. Cavallotti. 2nd location at V. Verde, 5 (☎0376 32 21 53), off of P. Mantegna. Boisterous staff serves a variety of pizzas and seafood dishes to locals and the occasional tourist.

Pizza €2.50-8.50. *Primi* €6, *secondi* from €6.50. Cover €1.50. Open daily noon-3pm and 6:30pm-12:30am. Libertà branch closed W; V. Verde closed M. MC/V. ❷

🧭 SIGHTS

■ **PALAZZO DUCALE.** The behemoth Palazzo Ducale, home of the Gonzaga family from the start of the 14th century, dominates the Mantuan skyline along its eastern shore. In medieval times, this was the largest palace in Europe, with 500 rooms and 15 courtyards constructed over a span of 300 years by the best architects and artists from the 14th through 17th centuries. Originally many separate buidings, the Palazzo grew as the Gonzagas continually annexed surrounding structures, the most prominent being the **Castello di San Georgio.** This four-towered castle once served as a fortress, and now boasts Andrea Mantegna's famed frescoes of the Gonzaga family (1474). Directly opposite **Piazza Sordello,** the original palazzo features more masterpieces. Begin a tour at the **Hall of Dukes,** where sections of Antonio Pisanello's frescoes (1439-44) were discovered under thick layers of plaster in 1969. In the **Zodiac Room** a continous fresco surrounds visitors with its vision of a pale Diana riding across an inky sky in her chariot. After passing through rooms draped with tapestries from Raphael's designs, the tour descends upon the Gonzagas' *sala dei fiumi* (room of rivers). Frescoed with vines and flowers, the room overlooks a garden bordered on three sides by a splendid portico. Audio tours available. *(P. Sordello, 40. ☎ 0376 22 48 32; www.mantovaducale.it. Open Tu-Su 8:45am-7:15pm. Ticket office under porticos facing the piazza. Open Tu-Su 8:45am-6:30pm. €6.50, students €3.25, EU citizens under 18 or over 65 free.)*

■ **TEATRO (BIBIENA).** The theater resembles a miniature fairy-tale castle and is one of the only ones in Northern Italy not modeled after Milan's La Scala. Upon entering, visitors are bathed in warm light from lanterns hung from each balcony illuminating the stage. Music lovers first filled the small, velvet couches in the rose and stone-gray balconies when Mozart inaugurated the building in 1769. Statues of Virgil and Pompanazzo peer out from niches in the back wall of the stage. *(V. Accademia, 4, at the corner of V. Accademia and V. Pomponazzo. ☎ 0376 32 76 53. Open Tu-Su 9:30am-12:30pm and 3-5pm. €2.10; students, under 18, or over 60 €1.10.)*

PALAZZO DEL TE. Built by Giulio Romano in 1534 as a suburban hideaway for Federico II Gonzaga and his mistress Isabella, this opulent palazzo constructed in

THE LOCAL STORY

BIRTH OF VIRGIL

Other than his grand monumen and his statue appearing promi nently in the Teatro Bibiena, Vir gil's marks on the city of Mantua are difficult to find. Instead, the countryside surrounding the city provides the proper venue for the continuing influence of this colos sus of classical literature.

Here in the farm fields and nature preserves, the spirit of Vir gil is maintained, consciously o not, by area farmers. Virgil con stantly espoused the value and importance of the agrarian life style. In fact he advises in the Georgics, one of his lesser knowr works, "plough naked, sow naked." While the Mantuan farm ers don't work the field in the buff they perpetuate Virgil's legacy.

It is in the countryside that the most enduring legend of Virgi occurs. Local folklore suggests that while Virgil was still in the womb, his mother dreamed she gave birth to an olive branch which grew into a robust adult tree when it touched the ground. The next day, she gave birth to Virgi and planted a real olive branch The tree became so fruitful and grew so quickly that local womer saw it as a symbol of fertility and often prayed by it. Subsequently in Mantua it became the tradition to plant a tree where a birth occurred. Virgil's tree no longe exists and the tradition has dimin ished. However, when in Mantua it's possible that the tree providing you shade was planted in honor o a birth long ago.

the Italian Mannerist style is a stunning testament to Federico's love, though not particularly discreet. The stately palazzo combines the layout of a Roman villa with flamboyant interior Renaissance frescoes. Racy murals of Psyche line Federico's banquet hall, and the **Room of Giants** is adorned with a continuous fresco depicting the demise of the Titans at the hands of Jupiter, as he punishes them with lightning bolts flung from the ceiling. Less monumental, though no less interesting, is the 16th-century graffiti that decorates the walls. Another wing of the palace features regular exhibitions of modern Italian works alongside a collection of Egyptian sculpture and Impressionist painting. *(At southern end of the city down V. P. Amedeo, which becomes V. Acerbi, through P. Veneto and down Largo Parri. ☎0376 32 32 66. Open M 1-6pm, Tu-Su 9am-6pm. Ticket office closes at 5:30pm. €8, over 60 €5.50, students and ages 12-18 €2.50, under 11 free, groups of 20 €4.50 per person.)*

ROTONDA DI SAN LORENZO AND CHIESA DI SANT'ANDREA. Bequeathed to the pope by Matilda di Canossa, a powerful and devout countess of Mantua, this 11th-century Romanesque church is dwarfed by the taller and brighter surrounding buildings. Nonetheless, the rotunda features an impressive collection of wooden sculptures and archways. An information sheet, available in English from guides at the door, directs visitors through the interior of the rotunda and its impressive 1000-year-old archways. *(In P. dell'Erbe, just south of P. Sordello. Open daily 10am-12:30pm and 2-6pm. Free.)* Opposite the rotunda rises Mantua's most important Renaissance creation, Leon Battista Alberti's **Chiesa di Sant'Andrea** (1472-1594). Its facade combines the classic arch design—a soaring barrel-vaulted portal and flanking pilasters—with a gigantic altarpiece and an imposing gilt organ at the front of the church. The gargantuan interior was the first monumental space constructed in the Classical style since the days of imperial Rome, and the plan served as a prototype for ecclesiastical architecture for the next 200 years. Giorgio Anselmi painted the dome's frescoes in muted colors. The painter Andrea Mantegna's tomb rests in the first chapel on the left after the entrance. The church's holy relic, a piece of earth supposedly soaked in Christ's blood, parades the streets in a religious procession every year on Good Friday. The rest of the year, the relic of the Precious Blood is kept in a crypt under the nave. *(Open daily 8am-noon and 3-7pm. Sunday services 8:30, 10, 11am, 6:30pm. Free.)*

PALAZZO D'ARCO. The former residence of the prominent D'Arco family since 1784. Each of 14 small rooms is furnished as it would have been in the 18th century. A separate wing houses a library and the kitchen, complete with pots, pans, and a dilapidated staircase. Navigate through the antique statues that dot the rose gardens to reach the palazzo's highlight: the extraordinary Giovan Maria Falconetto-designed zodiac chamber. The room is split into 12 sections, each decorated with frescoes dedicated to a specific astrological sign and its associated Italian town. *(Off V. Pitentino, near P. D'Arco. ☎0376 32 22 42. Open Mar.-Oct. Tu-Su 10am-12:30pm and 2:30-6pm; Nov.-Feb. Sa-Su 10am-12:30pm and 2-5pm. €3, students €1.)*

CASA DI RIGOLETTO. This supposed dwelling of Verdi's legendary opera hero now hosts temporary art exhibits and serves as the offices for Mantua's Tourguide Association. The small, pretty gardens in the front, featuring a balcony and statue honoring the composer's beloved joker Rigoletto, are open to the public. *(P. Sordello, 23. ☎0376 36 89 17. Gardens open daily 9:30am-12:30pm and 3:30-6:30pm.)*

🎵 🎭 ENTERTAINMENT AND FESTIVALS

The **Teatro Bibiena** (☎0376 32 76 53), on V. Accademia, hosts musical events, which are of no shortage in Mantua. Two classical concert seasons run from October to April and from April to June. Jazz performances also span from April to June. **Gra-**

zie, accessible by bus, holds its annual **Festa della Madonnari,** an international competition among street vendor painters on Ferragosto (Aug. 15). In early September, Italian speakers and scholars should check out **Festivaletteratura,** which attracts hordes of literary scholars from all over the world to meet and attend discussions and lectures. Every first weekend of December, the town of Castel D'Ario celebrates the pig at the **Festa dell'Osso.** Check out the comprehensive entertainment calendar on Mantua's website, www.comune.mantova.it.

🔁 DAYTRIP FROM MANTUA

SABBIONETA

Sabbioneta is 33km southwest of Mantua and easily accessible by bus #17 (45min., 4 per day 6:35am-7:50pm, €6.50). Get off in front of the city gates. Main tourist office: P. D'Armi, 1. Follow signs for office up V. V. Gonzaga. Office is at end of the brick piazza on the left. (☎0375 22 10 44; www.comune.sabbioneta.mn.it. Open Tu-Su 10am-1pm and 2-7pm. Sight hours change frequently, check the website for current times. It's easiest to buy tickets for monuments at the office, as they are not available for purchase in each location. €8 per person for entry to all monuments. €2 for single monument.

Sabbioneta's walls interrupt the flat green Mantuan countryside boldly, just as its founder, Vespasiano Gonzaga (1532-1591), a prince of the Holy Roman Empire, would have wanted. Built to rival his extended family's success in transforming Mantua into an artistic and cultural center, Gonzaga's efforts produced this bustling feudal town, which earned the title "Little Athens of the Gonzagas" for its importance as an artistic center in the late Renaissance. Now, town residents are just as proud of their slow, simple way of life and nature reserves. The tourist office's excellent guided tour of the *centro storico* begins at the **Palazzo del Giardino,** with its intricately decorated alcoves, one on the ceiling with the head of Medusa surrounded by rosettes in stucco relief. The long gallery is lined with windows and bright frescoes. The **Palazzo Ducale** has fewer surviving frescoes but is noteworthy for the **Sala delle Aquile,** which houses a collection of eerie, life-size wooden statues of Gonzaga family members on horseback. The tiny **Teatro Olimpico** has a colorful mural along the back wall of the balcony and a stage surrounded by columns imitating a Roman amphitheater. While meandering around Sabbioneta's quiet streets, note both the oldest gate in the town, the **Porta Vittoria,** and the more elaborate **Porta Imperiale** to the east. Tickets to the **Sinagoga** (Synagogue), an 1824 construction above 16th-century foundations, are available at Sabbioneta's other tourist office on V. Vespasiano Gonzago, 27. (☎0375 520 39. Open Tu-Sa 10am-12:30pm and 2:30-6pm. €2.50, groups €1.50 per person.) To see any of Sabbioneta's four churches, contact the priest 10 days ahead. (☎0375 520 35.) The Baroque interior of **Chiesa di Villa Pasquali** is open daily 10am-1pm and 2:30-5:30pm. A **map** at the tourist office outlines the scenic route to the parish church, past farmhouses and cornfields. On the second Sunday of the month, antique aficionados arrive for the exhaustive **Mercato dell'Antiquariato.** In September and October, traveling music, theater, and ballet groups also stop here.

CREMONA ☎0372

Climb to the top of the Torrazzo, and Cremona may resemble many other Italian cities: a sea of terra-cotta rooftops interrupted by piazzas and narrow alleys. At ground level, however, Cremona is a breathtaking encounter with melody, as music sounds from virtually every piazza. The city hosts several music festivals throughout the year, as well as an opera season at the renowned Teatro Ponchielli. Cremona's history attests the importance of musical arts, as Claudio Monteverdi was born here, and Andrea Amati created the first modern violin in 1530, establishing the Cremonese violin-making dynasty. Students now flock to the International School for Violin-Making to learn the craft.

�’🔃 TRANSPORTATION AND PRACTICAL INFORMATION. The **train station** is at V. Dante, 68 (☎89 20 21). The ticket office is open daily 6am-7:30pm. Trains run to: Brescia (45min., every hr. 5:24am-6:58pm, €3.85); Mantua (1hr., every hr. 6:24am-8:34pm, €4.70); Milan (1¼hr., 14 per day 5:02am-7:24pm, €5.10); and Pavia (2¼hr., 5:15am, €5). Trains also depart for Bergamo, Bologna, Brescia, Codogno, Fidenza, Parma, Piacenza, and Pisa. Check the newsstand in the station for schedules and prices, or ask at the ticket booth. The **bus station** (☎0372 292 12) is one block to the left of the train station. (Ticket office open M-F 7:40am-12:15pm and 2:30-6pm, Sa 7:40am-12:15pm.) Buses run to Brescia (every hr., Su less frequently; 6:10am-6:55pm; €4.15). Check at the station for scheduling information. Orange **local buses** run from the train station throughout the city. A **taxi** stand is in P. Roma (☎0372 213 00), and at the train station (☎0372 267 40).

Exiting the **train station,** walk straight ahead, to the left of the small stretch of grass. The road ahead is **Via Palestro,** which becomes **Corso Campi,** then **Via Verdi,** ending in **Piazza Stradivari.** Turn left at **Piazza Cavour** to **Piazza del Comune,** where the tourist office and duomo are located. The **APT Tourist Office,** P. del Comune, 5 (☎0372 232 33; info@aptcremona.it), has a brochure on hotels, museums, and restaurants, and offers the "City Card" for discounts around Cremona. (Open daily 9am-12:30pm and 2-6pm.) **Banco Nazionale del Lavoro,** C. Campi, 4-10 (☎0372 40 01), across the street and to the right of the main post office, has **currency exchange** and a 24hr. **ATM.** (Open M-F 8:20am-1:20pm and 2:30-4pm, Sa 8:20-11:50am.) In case of **emergency,** call ☎113, the **carabinieri** (☎112), **police,** V. Tribunali, 6 (☎0372 40 74 27), or an **ambulance** (☎118). The **hospital** (☎0372 40 51 11), is in Largo Priori. To get there, walk past P. IV Novembre to the east, take V. B. Dovara, and turn right on V. Giuseppina. The **post office,** V. Verdi, 1, has currency exchange. Bring a passport. (☎0372 59 35 63. Open M-Sa 8:30am-7pm.) **Postal Code:** 26100.

🖍🔃 ACCOMMODATIONS AND FOOD. From the train station, turn left onto V. Trento e Trieste, then right onto V. Poffacane. **La Locanda ❸,** V. Pallavicino, 4, is on the corner of C. G. Matteotti and V. Pallavicino. Friendly brothers rent clean, large rooms close to P. Roma. (☎0372 45 78 34. Singles €40; doubles €60. MC/V.) **Albergo Duomo ❸,** V. Gonfalonieri, 13, is in P. del Comune. Twenty-three well-kept rooms are small but have bath, TV, and A/C, as well as a tastefully decorated lobby. The hotel restaurant with outdoor seating is always full. (☎0372 352 42, fax 45 81 88. Breakfast €5. Parking garage free. Singles €45; doubles €60. AmEx/MC/V.) For **Esperia ❷,** V. Novati, 56, take bus #5 from the train station to V. F. Genala stop. Turn left onto V. Novati and cross the street to the hotel. Basic rooms have bath, TV, and small balcony overlooking a quiet backyard. P. del Comune is only a 10min. walk. (☎0372 45 29 93. Singles and doubles, €35. AmEx/MC/V.)

The *mostarda di Cremona,* first concocted in the 16th century, consists of cherries, figs, apricots, and melons preserved in a sweet mustard syrup. Most local restaurants prepare the *mostarda,* traditionally spread over boiled meats. Delicious *grana padano,* a sophisticated cousin of parmesan cheese, is available in any salumeria. Every sweet shop sells bars of *torrone* (an egg, honey, and nut nougat), another Cremonese specialty. At ◪**Pierot ❷,** Largo Boccaccino, 2 (☎0372 293 18), wait in line with everyone else in town for Cremona's best gelato (€1.50), or sit at one of their tables on the P. del Comunale and enjoy a *panino* (€3.50) and a drink. (Open M-Sa 9am-1am, Su noon-1am. AmEx/MC/V.) **Sperlari ❷,** at V. Solferino, 25 (☎0372 223 46), has been selling mounds of chocolate and licorice to Cremonese children since 1836. (Open daily 8:30am-12:30pm and 3:30-7:30pm. AmEx/MC/V.) Perpetually packed with locals, an open-air **market** in P. Stradivari sells fresh vegetables, fruits, and a variety of meats and cheeses on Wednesday and Saturday from 8am to 1pm. Vendors also sell clothing and household items. A GS **supermarket**, V. S. Tommaso, 9, is close to P. del Comune. (Open M-Sa 9am-8:15pm, Su 9am-1pm.) Locals crowd **Ristorante Pizzeria Marechiaro ❷**, C. Garibaldi, 85, for tasty pizzas starting at €4. Complimentary *bruschetta* starts each meal. (☎0372 262 89. *Primi* €5.50-9, *secondi* €7-12. Open daily 6:30pm-midnight. Cash only.)

◐ ⚜ SIGHTS AND FESTIVALS. The 250-year-old, lavishly decorated Baroque **Teatro Ponchielli**, C. V. Emanuele, 56, provided the testing ground for the Stradivari and Amati violins. One of the largest stages in Italy, it stands as one of the most beautiful opera houses worldwide. Visit the ticket office or website for an up-to-date schedule of performances. (☎0372 022 001/002; www.teatroponchielli.it. Ticket office open June-Sept. M-Sa 4:30-7:30pm, Oct.-May M-Sa 4-7pm.) A prime example of Cremonese Mannerism, the **Chiesa di San Sigismondo**, Largo B. Visconti, off V. Giuseppina, honors the union of the powerful Sforza and Visconti families in 1441, but it was redone in 1463 after a ravaging fire. Mannerist masters Boccaccino, Giulio, and Antonio and Bernardino Campi assert their talent in fresco on every pillar, arch, and vault in their typically ornate styles. Walk 30min. down V. Ghisleri from P. Libertà. Follow signs for the church. Or take bus #2 to San Sigimondo, the last stop. (☎0372 43 73 57. Open daily 8:30am-noon and 3-7pm. Free.)

MORE FOR YOUR MONEY. Those trying to see all Cremona has to offer should consider a *biglietto cumulativo*, which covers admission to the **Museo Civico** and **Stradivario** and the **Palazzo Comunale** (€10, students €5). Or purchase the City Card for discounts to all sights, some restaurants and festivals, and bus rides (€7.75). Both options are available at the tourist office.

The **Piazza del Comune** is the center of Cremonese life. Directly facing the **Palazzo Comunale**, the pink-marble 12th-century duomo **Santa Maria Assunta** is a fine example of the Lombard-Romanesque style. The interior displays a cycle of 16th-century frescoes. (Open M-Sa 7:30am-noon and 3:30-7pm, Su 7:30am-1pm.) To the left of the duomo rises the late 13th-century **▪Torrazzo**. Made completely of bricks and standing at 111m, it is the tallest *campanile* in Italy. Climb the 487 steps to the top for a close-up view of the world's oldest-known astrological clock. (Open from April 11 to the end of Oct. Tu-Su 10am-1pm.) The dome of the 1167 **baptistery** ascends in a perfect, unadorned octagonal pattern and shelters beautiful pieces of sculpture and painting within. (Cumulative ticket for Torazzo and Baptistery €5, single monument €4.) A grand marble staircase leads to the recently restored **Palazzo Affaitati**, V. Ugolani Dati, 4, which houses the **Museo Civico** and the **Museo Stradivario**. The Museo Civico has an extensive, diverse collection of paintings. Noteworthy pieces include Caravaggio's *San Francesco in Meditazione*, Genovesino's *Amore Dormiente* (featuring a nude cupid sitting atop a book, leaning on a skull with bow in hand), and a painting by Arcimboldi. Seen right side up, the painting is a remarkably detailed face made from vegetables, but upside down it looks like a pot of broccoli and carrots. In the same building, famous Stradivarian violins are displayed. Although the Museo Stradivario has no original Stradivarius violins, it does boast a room of his molds, models, drawings, and collection of other famous violins. A video tour in English explains the violins' production. (Palazzo Affaitati ☎0372 40 77 70. Museo Civico and Stradivario ☎0372 40 72 69. Open Tu-Sa 9am-6pm, Su 10am-6pm. €8, students and handicapped €4.)

In Cremona music and festivity is in the air year-round. The **Monteverdi Festival** (May-June), the city's most well-known celebration, honors the great *Cremonese* composer with music. The **Cremona Jazz Festival,** running from March to May, welcomes the summer with a series of concerts. The **La Danza Festival,** a celebration of dance, is held in June and July, and the **opera season** lasts during the winter months. Check with the tourist office for info on other festivals or events that spotlight antiquities, violin-making, cattle, and wedding gowns. (Teatro Ponchielli ticket booth at C. V. Emanuele, 52. ☎0372 407 27 30; www.teatroponchielli.it; Open June-Sept. M-Sa 4:30-7:30pm, Oct.-May 4-7pm. Tickets around €15.)

PAVIA   ☎0382

Down toward the southwestern tip of Lombardy, hills flatten into rice paddies and poplars lace the fertile terrain. In the heart of this region sits Pavia, where Romanesque churches share the limelight with a dense network of waterways designed by Leonardo da Vinci. An astounding achievement of engineering, these canals run all the way from the Navigli of Milan. In AD 452 Attila the Hun unsuccessfully tried to conquer the city. Those vying for entry today have had more success by brandishing Prada bags and a penchant for academics, as the prestigious Università di Pavia brings bustling student activity. A soothing retreat is only 10min. away at the Certosa di Pavia, one of Italy's premier monastic structures.

⌐ TRANSPORTATION

The **train station** is at the end of V. V. Emanuele. Trains run to Genoa (1½hr., every hr. 6:33am-10:45pm, €5.73) and Milan (30min., every hr. 5:08am-11:14pm, €2.80). Change at *Milan Rogar* for Cremona (2hr., every hr. 5:44am-9pm, €6.50). For the **bus station,** turn left from the train station and head to the brick building on V. Trieste. Tickets may be purchased at the green office under the terminal cover. SILA buses run to Milan (30min., 2 per hr., €2.60) via Certosa di Pavia (10min., €2.25). A **car rental** is at M.C.M. Auto, Viale Partigiani, 72, near Piazzale Porto Garibaldi. (☎0382 57 61 31. Cars from €35.80 per day, discounts for longer rentals.) For **taxis,** call ☎0382 57 65 76, 274 39 at the train station, or 291 90 in P. Vittoria.

✳🛈 ORIENTATION AND PRACTICAL INFORMATION

Pavia sits on the banks of the Ticino River not far from where it merges with the Po. The train station borders **Piazzale Stazione** in the western end of the modern town. To get from the station to the historic center, walk down **Viale Vittorio Emanuele II** to **Piazzale Minerva.** Continue on Pavia's main street, **Corso Cavour,** to the city's narrow central square, **Piazza della Vittoria,** a block away from **Piazza Duomo.** Past P. Vittoria, the main street changes to **Corso Mazzini.**

Tourist Office: V. Filzi, 2 (☎0382 221 56). From train station, turn left on V. Trieste and then right on V. Filzi. Open M-W 8:30am-12:30pm and 2-5pm, Th-F until 5:30pm, Sa 8:30am-12:30pm.

Currency Exchange: Banca Intesa, C. Cavour, 12. Also has 24hr. ATM. Open M-F 8:30am-12:30pm and 3:30-7:30pm.

English-Language Bookstore: Fox Books, C. Mazzini, 2/C (☎0382 30 39 16), off P. Vittoria. Open M-Sa 9am-1pm and 3-7:30pm, Su 10am-1pm and 3-7:30pm.

Emergency: ☎113. **Ambulance** (☎118 or 0382 52 76 00).

Pharmacy: Vippani, V. Bossolaro, 31 (☎0382 223 15), at corner of P. Duomo and V. Menocchio, has a list of pharmacies with late-night service. Open M-F 8:30am-12:30pm and 3:30-7:30pm.

Hospital: Proclinivo S. Matteo, P. Golgi, 2 (☎0382 50 11).

Internet: University Library. From P. Vittoria, turn left on C. Strada Nuova. Walk past the intersection with V. Mentana and take 1st right. Continue through courtyard toward a large, seated statue with a long sword. Behind the statue and on the right is a door with the words "Dipartimento di Scienza della Letteratura e dell'Arte Medievale e Moderna." Have a student ID ready. Open M-F 9am-noon and 2-8pm.

Post Office: P. della Posta, 2 (☎0382 39 22 81), off C. Mazzini. Open M-F 8:30am-7pm, Sa 8:30am-12:30pm. **Postal Code:** 27100.

ACCOMMODATIONS AND CAMPING

As accommodations in this student town aren't all student-priced, consider staying in Milan. Remote *agriturismi* are an option; ask at the tourist office. **Locanda della Stazione ❷**, V. V. Emanuele II, 14, straight across from the train station on the right, has a great location and a welcoming staff. Some rooms come with A/C. (☎0382 293 21. Singles €21; doubles €31. Cash only.) With white walls and Warhol-esque paintings, **Hotel Aurora ❹**, V. V. Emanuele, 25, straight ahead from the train station, resembles a trendy art gallery. All 19 rooms have shower, TV, and A/C. (☎0382 236 64. Internet €4 per hr. Reserve ahead. Singles €45; doubles €70. MC/V.) **Hotel Excelsior ❹**, P. Stazione, 25, lets traditionally decorated rooms, with bath, A/C, minibar, telephone, and TV. (☎0382 285 96, fax 260 30. Breakfast €6. Parking €8. Singles €50; doubles €73. AmEx/MC/V.) From the bus station, take bus #4 (dir: Sora) for 10min. to the Mascherpa stop (3 per hr. 5:39-8:26pm, €0.85), and follow the sign up the road to reach **Camping Ticino ❶**, V. Mascherpa, 10. The campsite has a swimming pool and clean, shared facilities. (☎0382 52 70 94. Laundry €3.50. Campgrounds open Mar.-Oct. €5.50 per person, over 65 €4.50, ages 5-12 €3. Tents €4. Cars €2.50. 2-person bungalows €30; 4-person €60.)

The *zuppa alla pavese*, a piping-hot broth served with a poached egg on top and sprinkled with grated *grana* cheese, is a *Pavese* favorite. *Coniglio* (rabbit) and *rana* (frog) are also local specialties; those who run from foods that hop can wander to the *tavole calde* on C. Cavour and C. Mazzini. Diehard gourmets should head to the taverns in Borgo Ticino, across the Ponte Coperto. Esselunga, next to the tourist office, is a huge **supermarket.** (☎0382 262 10. Open M-Sa 8am-9pm.) At **Antica Trattoria Ferrari ❹**, V. deil Mille, 111, the wood paneling suggests Swiss chalet, but the cuisine is strictly Italian. Fine *Pavese* selections and attentive service characterizes this inviting local

THE LOCAL STORY

UNREAL RELICS?

Dr. Luigi Garlaschelli is an organic chemist at the University of Pavia. In his spare time, he investigates the authenticity of religious blood relics.

LG: Why are relics everywhere in Italy?
A: In the Middle Ages, it was believed that they would protect the city from its enemies. [Relics include] the milk of the Virgin Mary and Christ's fingernails.

LG: What was your first project?
A: My first work was on the blood of St. Januarius, which is contained in a small vial kept in the duomo in Naples. St. Januarius was beheaded in AD 305. The relic appeared in the Middle Ages, 1000 years later, contemporary to the appearance of the Shroud of Turin. Normally blood taken from a living body will clot only once; the "miracle" of this blood is that it turns from solid to liquid and back again twice a year during religious ceremonies.

LG: How does that work?
A: Well, using only ferric chloride (an iron salt), which exists naturally near active volcanoes (like Vesuvius, active at the time of the discovery of the blood), calcium carbonate, kitchen salt, and techniques available in the Middle Ages, we created a substance of the same color and properties as the reputed blood of the saint. The matter would be closed were we to open the vial and take samples. But, of course, the vial is sealed.

eatery. (☎0382 53 90 25. *Primi* €6.50, *secondi* €9.50. Cover €3. Service 10%. Open Tu-Sa 12:30-2pm and 7:30-9:45pm. MC/V.) Enjoy gentle views and fine dining on the banks of the Ticino at **Ristorante Bardelli ❺**, V. Lungoticino Visconti, 2. The seasonal menu focuses on Lombard cuisine. (☎0382 274 41. *Primi* €10, *secondi* €13-16. Open M-Sa noon-2:30pm and 7:30-10:30pm. AmEx/MC/V.)

🔘 🔳 SIGHTS AND NIGHTLIFE

As the oldest building in town, the **⚑Basilica di San Michele** has witnessed many coronations, including that of Charlemagne in AD 774, Frederick Barbarossa in 1155, and various members of the Savoy family. In one legendary account, during Charlemagne's coronation light shone through one of the windows and onto his newly-crowned head. The Lombard Romanesque exterior was rebuilt in the 12th century after an earthquake; the decision to use all sandstone, rather than brick, as was popular at the time, means that most of the decorative sculptures are worn away. A 1491 fresco of the *Coronation of the Virgin* and 14th-century bas-relief decorate the chancel; an 8th-century crucifix of Teodote graces the *cappella*. (Take C. Strada Nuova to C. Garibaldi; turn right on V. S. Michele. Open M-Sa 7:30am-noon and 3-7pm, Su 8am-noon and 3-7:45pm.) Founded in 1361, the **Università di Pavia** counts Petrarch, Columbus, and Venetian playwright Goldoni among its alumni. The university's patron and renowned sadist, Galeazzo II of the Visconti family, earned notoriety for his research on human torture. Appropriately, the star of the modern-day university is the School of Medicine. Though Rabelais rendered its students as deviants and fops in his Renaissance narratives, the self-told story of the university unfolds at the **Museo per la Storia dell'Università di Pavia.** (C. Strada Nuova, 65, in the courtyard. Museum open M 3:30-5pm, F 9:30am-noon. Free.)

An all-star team of visionaries including Bramante, da Vinci, and Amadeo began work on the **Cattedrale Monumentale di Santo Stefano Martire** in the 15th century. One of Italy's earliest duomos built on a Greek-cross structure, it boasts the third highest dome in Italy, completed in the 19th century. To the cathedral's left are the remnants of the **Torre Civica.** The tower collapsed in 1989, killing four people and taking much of the left chapel with it; the duomo's brick interior was subsequently reinforced with concrete columns, and much of the interior has been closed. (In P. Duomo. Open daily 8am-noon and 3-6pm.) The **Castello Visconteo,** a colossal medieval castle dated to 1360, is set in a beautifully landscaped park. Richly colored windows and terra-cotta decorations border three sides of its vast courtyard; the fourth wall was destroyed in 1527 during the Franco-Spanish Wars. Pavia's Musei Civici reside here, with a formidable gallery of paintings and Lombard-Romanesque sculpture. (At the end of C. Strada Nuova. Castle ☎0382 338 53. Museum ☎0382 30 48 16. Open Tu-Su 10am-6pm. €6, students €4, courtyard €1.)

Across the street, the **Basilica di San Pietro in Ciel D'Oro** (St. Peter in the Golden Sky), a Lombard-Romanesque church built in 1132, holds the **remains of St. Augustine.** The saint rests on the high altar, in an intricately carved ark-shaped 14th-century Gothic marble sarcophagus. (From P. Castello, take V. Liutprando to P. S. Pietro in Ciel d'Oro. Open daily 7am-noon and 3-7pm.)

Pavia's student population stirs up a rocking nightlife. A taste of the islands awaits in the fresh fruit cocktails (€4.15) at **Morgan's Drink House,** C. Cavour, 30/C. (☎0382 268 80. Open M and W-Su 7pm-2am.) At **Malaika "Bar and Soul,"** V. Bossolaro, 21, off C. Cavour, tribal rhythms beat steadily as patrons enjoy *panini* and fruit desserts (from €2) on stools covered with leopard skin. Happy Hour (7-9pm) cocktails go for €4.50. (☎382 30 13 99. Open Tu-Su 6pm-2am.)

⚡ DAYTRIP FROM PAVIA

CERTOSA DI PAVIA

SILA buses from Milan-Famagosta (MM2) to Certosa (20min.; 2 per hr., first from Milan 6:15am, last from Certosa 8pm; €2.25), then to Pavia's train station on V. Trieste (10min., €1.20). Exiting the bus in Certosa, go to the traffic light and turn right; continue straight for a few blocks, then turn right up the long, tree-lined V. Certosa. The monastery lies at the end. (☎0382 92 56 13; www.apt.pavia.it. Open Tu-Su May-Sept. 9-11:30am and 2:30-6pm, Apr. 9-11:30am and 2:30-5:30pm, Oct. and Mar. 9-11:30am and 2:30-5pm, Nov. and Feb. 9-11:30am and 2:30-4:30pm. Free. Modest dress required.)

Eight kilometers north of Pavia stands the ▓**Certosa di Pavia** (Carthusian Monastery). Gian Galeazzo Visconti founded it in 1396 as a mausoleum for the Visconti clan, who ruled the area from the 12th through the 15th centuries. Started in 1396 by the Viscontis and finished by the Sforzas in 1497, the monastery is a monument to the evolution of Italian art, from early Gothic to Baroque. A profusion of inlaid marble, bas reliefs, and sculptures embellishes every available surface on the facade. The work required the efforts of over 250 craftsmen during the 15th-century Lombard Renaissance, and it shows. Statues of biblical figures, carvings of narratives, and 61 medallions adorn the base alone. The Old Sacristy houses a Florentine triptych carved in ivory; 99 sculptures and 66 bas-reliefs depict the lives of Mary and Jesus. The beautiful Great Cloister contains 24 houses, one for each Carthusian monk. In accordance with St. Benedict's motto *ora et labora* (pray and work), the monks are active in agriculture and distill excellent, potent liquors, sold on the premises. The monks lead **group tours** (usually in Italian).

THE LAKE COUNTRY

Travelers who need a respite from Italian bustle should follow the example of artistic visionaries like Liszt, Longfellow, and Wordsworth: retreat to the serene shores of the northern lakes, where clear waters lap at the foot of snowcapped

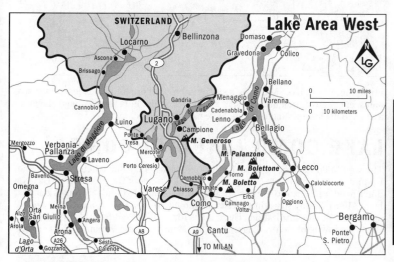

LOMBARDY

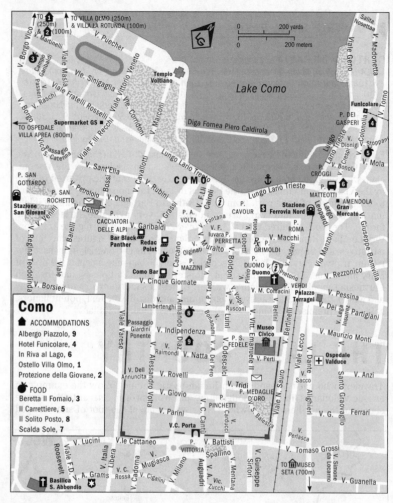

luxury hotels dot Lake Maggiore's sleepy shores, where tourism is least obtrusive and scenery most tranquil. Across the regional border in Piemonte, Lago Maggiore and Lago di Orta round out Italian Lake Country.

LAKE COMO (LAGO DI COMO)

The well-to-do have been using Lake Como as a refuge since before the Roman Empire, as the numerous luxury villas on the shores of the Lake attest. But you don't need a palazzo to appreciate the beauty that surrounds Europe's deepest lake (410m)—many struggling artists, including Rossini, Bellini, and Shelley relied upon this lake for inspiration. Three lakes form the forked Lake Como, joined at the three towns of Centro Lago: Bellagio, Menaggio, and Varenna. These towns make for a more relaxing stay than their more industrial neighbor Como, the largest city on the lake. Villages cover the dense green slopes—hop on a bus or ferry, and step off whenever a villa, castle, garden, vineyard, or small town beckons.

COMO   ☎031

Situated on the southwestern tip of the lake and closest to Milan, Como is the lake's token semi-industrial town, where physicist Alessandro Volta was born and Giuseppe Terragni immortalized his Fascist architectural designs. Though famous for silk manufacturing, the town serves mainly as a launch point for tourists arriving from Milan to explore the lakes. Mediocre beaches, impeccably dressed businessmen, and racing scooters don't inspire visitors to linger, but there are attractions enough to keep those passing through entertained. Como has quality hiking and fine restaurants within the old city walls.

⬛ TRANSPORTATION

Trains: Stazione San Giovanni (☎0147 88 80 88). Ticket window open daily 6:40am-8:25pm. To: **Chiasso** (20min., 2 per hr. 6:31am-1:31am, €0.95); **Milan Centrale** (1hr., every 30min. 6:28am-11:08pm, €4.85); **Venice S. Lucia** (4hr., every hr. 4:45am-7:55pm, €21.64) via **Milan. Ferrovia Nord** (**Como Nord;** ☎031 30 48 00), by P. Matteotti, runs only to Stazione Nord (Cadorna) in **Milan** (1hr., 2 per hr. 5:34am-10:35pm, €3.72), via **Saronno** (€1.96).

Buses: SPT (☎031 24 72 47), in P. Matteotti. Ticket office open daily 6am-10pm. Info booth open M-F 8am-noon and 2-6pm, Sa 8am-noon. **C30** to **Bellagio** (1hr., every hr. 6:27am-8:14pm, €2.50). **C46** to **Bergamo** (2hr., every hr. 6:50am-6:30pm, €4:25). **C10** to **Domaso** (2hr., every hr. 7:10am-6:40pm, €3.85); **Gravedona** (2hr., every hr. 7:10am-6:40pm, €3.85); **Menaggio** (1hr., every hr. 7:10am-8:30pm, €2.80).

Ferries: Navigazione Lago di Como (☎031 57 92 11). Ticket office open 8:30am-6:30pm. The most convenient way to travel the lake. Departs daily to all lake towns from piers along Lungo Lario Trieste in front of P. Cavour. Ferries run every 15min. One-way to Mennagio €6.10. Numerous day-passes covering various lake regions €4.60-17.10. Pick up the booklet *Orario* for a schedule, including summer night service.

Public Transportation: Buy bus tickets (€0.95) at *tabacchi,* bus station, or the hostel.

Taxis: RadioTaxi (☎031 26 15 15 or 26 27 72).

⬛ ⬛ ORIENTATION AND PRACTICAL INFORMATION

From Como's **Stazione San Giovanni,** head down the stairs, straight ahead through the park. Take **Via Fratelli Ricchi** on the left and then turn right on **Viale Fratelli Rosselli,** which turns into **Lungo Lario Trento,** then leads to **Piazza Cavour.** The **bus station** and **Stazione Ferrovia Nord** are in P. Matteoti, two minutes farther along the lake.

Tourist Office: P. Cavour, 16 (☎031 26 97 12; www.lakecomo.org), in the large lakeside piazza near the dock. **Maps** and extensive info. Ask the multilingual staff about hiking and hotels. Open M-Sa 9am-1pm and 2:30-6pm, Su 9:30am-12:30pm. Closed Su in winter. The staff at a small **Information Point,** in the building next to the Duomo, also has maps and general info. Open Tu-Su 10am-7pm.

Currency Exchange: Banca Nazionale del Lavoro, P. Cavour, 33 (☎031 31 31), across from the tourist office, has dependable rates and a 24hr. **ATM.** Open M-F 8:20am-1:20pm and 2:30-4pm. Currency exchange also available at the tourist office, train station, post office, and numerous other banks.

Luggage Storage: At train station cafe. Open daily 6:30am-10pm. €3.50 per piece.

Emergency: ☎113. **Ambulance** (☎118). **Police** (☎112).

Pharmacy: Farmacia Centrale, V. Plinio, 1, off P. Cavour. Open Tu-Su 8:30am-12:30pm and 3:30-7:30pm. List of late-night pharmacies posted.

Hospitals: Ospedale Valduce, V. Dante, 11 (☎031 32 41 11). **Ospedale Sant'Anna,** V. Napoleana, 60 (☎031 58 51 11). **Ospedale Villa Aprica,** V. Castel Carnasino, 10 (☎031 57 94 11).

Internet: Bar Black Panther, V. Garibaldi, 59 (☎031 26 65 35). €3 per hr., 30min. free with drink purchase. Open Tu-Su 7am-noon. **Como Bar,** V. Alessandro Volta, 51 (☎031 26 20 51). €1.70 for 30min. Open Tu-Su 7:30am-9:30pm. **Redac Point,** V. Alessandro Volta, 27 (☎031 275 35 17). Internet €3 per hr. Printing and CD burning. Open M-F 10am-11pm, Sa 3-11pm.

Post Office: V. V. Emanuele II, 99 (☎031 26 02 10), in the town center. Open M-F 8:30am-2pm, Sa 8:10am-12:30pm. **Postal Code:** 22100.

ACCOMMODATIONS

In Riva al Lago, P. Matteotti, 4 (☎031 30 23 33; www.inriva.info), behind the bus stop. Brand-new hotel rooms and multi-room tourist flats, all with bath, TV, and A/C. The pub downstairs is a popular student hangout. English spoken. Breakfast buffet €2-4. Reception 7:30am-11pm. Reserve ahead. Singles €30-40; doubles €50-60, with shared bath €40-45. Flats available for 2-11 people €20-25 per person. AmEx/MC/V. ❸

Ostello Villa Olmo (HI), V. Bellinzona, 2 (☎/fax 031 57 38 00; ostellocomo@tin.it), behind Villa Olmo. From Stazione S. Giovanni, walk down the steps and past the giant hands. Turn left and walk 20min. down V. Borgo Vico. Or take bus #1, 6, or 11 to Villa Olmo (€0.95). Lively, fun, and down-to-earth, run by a multilingual staff. Offers a bar and hefty 3-course dinner (€10.50). Breakfast included. Crowded rooms come with personal locker and sheets. Self-service laundry €3.50; ironing €1. Bicycle rental €12.50 per day. Reception daily Mar.-Nov. 7-10am and 4-11:30pm. Lockout 10am-4pm. Strict curfew 11:30pm. Reserve ahead. Dorms €13.50, non-members add €3. ❶

Hotel Funicolare, V. Coloniola, 8/10 (☎031 30 42 77; www.hotelfunicolare.com). Large, high quality rooms have TV, A/C, and bath. Friendly staff and excellent location. Parking €5. Singles €47; doubles €74. Extra person €24. AmEx/MC/V. ❹

Protezione della Giovane (ISJGIF), V. Borgovico, 182 (☎031 57 43 90 or 57 35 40), on the way to the youth hostel, on the right side. Take bus #1, 6, or 11. Nuns run 52 clean rooms with crucifixes everywhere. 18+; women only. Kitchen available. Laundry €3.60 per load. Curfew 10:30pm. Reservation required. Singles or doubles €13 per person for the first 3 nights, €11 thereafter. Cash only. ❶

Albergo Piazzolo, V. Indipendenza, 65 (☎031 27 21 86). From P. Cavour, take V. Bonta, which becomes V. Boldini and V. Luni. Pedestrian-only V. Indipendenza is on the right. Large, tastefully decorated rooms, some with fireplaces, all with modern bathroom and TV. Singles €40-45; doubles €52-60; triples €80; 1 quad €90. AmEx/MC/V. ❹

FOOD

Picnicking is the best way to experience regional specialties on the cheap; lakeside benches provide all the *al fresco* ambience one could ask for. *Resca* (sweet bread with dried fruit) and the harder, cake-like *mataloc* are great Como-specific treats sold at **Beretta II Fornaio,** Viale Fratelli Rosselli, 26/A. (Open M 7:30am-1:30pm, Tu-Sa 7:30am-1:30pm and 2-7:30pm.) Local cheeses *semuda* and *robiola* are available at most **supermarkets,** including GS, on the corner of V. Fratelli Recchi and V. Fratelli Roselli, across from the park (☎031 57 08 95; open M-F 8am-

LOMBARDY

8:30pm, Sa 8am-8pm, Su 9am-1pm), and Gran Mercato, P. Matteotti, 3 (open M-F 8am-noon and 2-6pm, Sa 8am-noon). An **open-air market** is held Tuesday and Thursday mornings and all day Saturday in P. Vittoria.

For the briny deep's finest flavors, try ▓**ll Carrettiere ❹**, V. Colonolia, 18, off P. A. De Gasperi, near P. Matteotti. Sure, it's a Sicilian outpost in the middle of Lombardy, but the boisterous crowds and *spaghetti allo scoglio*, a huge platter of mussels, crayfish, and other shelled things (€13) are reason enough to visit. (☎031 30 34 78. Cover €1.30. Pizza €4.20-7. *Primi* €5.50-13, *secondi* €7-15. Open Tu 7:30-11pm, W-Su noon-2:30pm and 7pm-12:30am. AmEx/MC/V.) Find a sea of collared shirts at **Scalda Sole ❺**, V. Alessandro Volta, 41, a lunch spot for local professionals. The seafood-heavy menu is as polished as the clientele. (☎031 26 38 89. *Primi* €8, *secondi* €13-14. Open Tu-Su 12:30-2pm and 7:30-10pm. AmEx/MC/V.) Locals crowd **Il Solito Posto ❹**, V. Lambertenghi, 9, for creative takes on classics, like *bresaola* (€9.30) with artichoke and noodles. (☎031 27 13 52. *Primi* €8.50-10.50, *secondi* €13.50-18. Open Tu-Su noon-2:30pm and 7-10:30pm. AmEx/MC/V.)

🖂 SIGHTS

Dating from 1396 and recently restored, Como's **duomo** harmoniously combines an octagonal dome and Romanesque, Gothic, Renaissance, and Baroque elements. The Rodari brothers' life-like sculptures of the Exodus from Egypt animate the exterior, while a collection of 16th-century tapestries brighten the huge interior. Statues of erstwhile Como residents Pliny the Elder and Pliny the Younger flank the door. (Near P. Cavour. Open daily 7am-noon and 3-7pm.) Just behind the duomo and across the railroad tracks, Giuseppe Terragni's Casa del Fascio—now called **Palazzo Terragni**—was built between 1934 and 1936 to house the local Fascist government. Uncharacteristically light designs have made it a world-famous piece of Modernist Italian architecture. The Neo-classical **Tempio Voltiano** was dedicated to Alessandro Volta, inventor of the battery. Displayed items include early attempts at wet-cell batteries the size of kitchen tables, as well as apparati for experimenting on frog muscles. (From P. Cavour, go left along the waterfront. ☎031 57 47 05. Open Tu-Su Apr.-Sept. 10am-noon and 3-6pm, Oct.-Mar. 10am-noon and 2-4pm. €1.50, groups and under 6 €1.) Volta's **tomb** is at **Camnago Volta.** (Take bus #4 from any stop or Stazione S. Giovanni; 15min., every 30min. 6:20am-8:20pm, €0.95.) The villas lining the lake include **Villa La Rotonda**, with Rococo *stuccato*, or plaster, and chandeliers, now home to the provincial government. (Open M-F 9am-noon and 3-5pm.) Farther north is the ambassadorial **Villa Olmo** in the statue-lined park of the same name. (Gardens open daily Apr.-Sept. 8am-11pm, Oct.-Mar. 9am-7pm.) **Museo della Seta** displays the worms and silk looms that put Como on the textile map. (V. Vallegio, 3. ☎031 30 31 80. Open Tu-F 9am-noon and 3-6pm. Call ahead to arrange group visits. €8, groups €5.50 per person, students €2.60.)

⬛ HIKING

To avoid a long uphill climb, take the ▓**funicolare** from P. dei Gasperi, 4, at the far end of Lungolago Trieste, to **Brunate** for an excellent hike back down to Como. (☎031 30 36 08. June-Sept. every 15min. 6am-midnight, Oct.-May every 30min. 6am-10:30pm. 1-way €2.30, return €4; students €2.05/€3.50. AmEx/MC/V.) For even better panoramas, hike up toward **Faro Voltiano** (906m), a lighthouse dedicated to Volta. It's easy to find; just keep heading up until reaching the summit. On the way, note **Santa Rita,** Europe's smallest sanctuary. On a clear day, views stretch from Milan to the Matterhorn, but even with cloudy skies, Como's majestic villas are visible. From Faro Voltiano, another 15min. of hiking leads to **San Maurizio,** and another 1hr. should be enough to reach **Monte Boletto** (1236m). There is a bus that runs from Brunate to approximately 1km past S. Maurizio and stops near Faro Voltiano (every 30min. 8:15am-6:45pm, €0.95). If the hike to M. Boletto isn't too exhausting, stroll for another hour to **Monte Bolettone** (1317m).

Another option is to head northwest between S. Maurizio and M. Boletto after the restaurant Baita Carla, on a path leading to lakeside **Torno,** 8km north of Como; this is a good place to catch a ferry home (every hr. 6:58am-8:14pm, €1.90). In Torno check out the opulent **Chiesa di San Giovanni** or the **Villa Pliniana,** 15min. north of the boat dock, closed to visitors but worth a look from afar.

For more extensive exploration of the mountains east of Como, take bus C40 from the Como bus station to **Erba** (30min.; every hr. 5:25am-10:20pm, last bus back to Como 10:56pm; €2.55). From Erba, make the beautiful hike to **Caslino D'Erba,** which leads to **Monte Palanzone** (1436m). Head to the cool recesses of Buco del Piombo for an encounter with prehistory: area caves formed furing the Jurassic Period over 150 million years ago. The **Museo Buco del Piombo,** V. Alpe Burati, 15, in Erba proper, displays materials from the caves and charts their history and development. (☎031 62 95 99; www.museobucodelpiombo.it. Open Apr.-Oct. Sa 2-6pm, Su 10am-6pm. Adults €5, children €4. Groups can visit with a booking.)

IL CENTRO LAGO

 Numerous towns line the beautiful central lake. Although they can all be reached by bus, the out-of-the-way trips often take more than 2hr. A more direct (and far more romantic) mode of travel is the ferry. **Navigazione del Lago** offers an all-day pass for €7.50 that covers travel to Bellagio, Varenna, Menaggio, Cadenabbia, Tremezzo, and Lenno. Most journeys last no more than 10min., with boats arriving daily roughly every 15min. 8:45am-7:45pm.

MENAGGIO   ☎0344

On Lake Como's Western shore, Menaggio is home to cobblestone streets, stunning hillside scenery, and a constant procession of motor tourists. Menaggio's central location and excellent ferry connections make it the perfect base for exploring any part of the lake, and its youth hostel allows travelers to do so at a fraction of the cost (and double the character) of any other establishment on the lake.

🖪🎦 TRANSPORTATION AND PRACTICAL INFORMATION. Buses and **ferries** link Menaggio to the other lake towns. In the *centro* at P. Garibaldi, 4, the **tourist office** has info on lake excursions and hiking as well as phone card Internet. (☎0344 329 24; infomenaggio@tiscali.it. Open M-Sa 9am-noon and 3-6pm.) **Ostello la Primula** (see **Accommodations**) has been known to offer short-term **work opportunities** (see **Alternatives to Tourism: Short-Term Work,** p. 86) in return for room, board, and a small stipend, but they require a face-to-face interview. In case of **emergency,** dial ☎113, or call the **police** (☎112) or an **ambulance** (☎118). P. Garibaldi also has a **pharmacy.** (☎0344 32 10 51. Open 8:30am-12:30pm and 3-7pm.) Menaggio's **hospital** (☎0344 331 11) is on V. Cazartelli. **Internet** is at **Video Mix,** across from the creperie. (☎0344 341 10. €1.50 for 15min. Open Tu-Sa 9:30am-12:30pm and 4:30-7:30pm.) The **post office,** V. Lusardi, 48, has **currency exchange.** (Open M-F 8:20am-6:30pm, Sa 8:20-11:30am.) **Postal Code:** 22017.

ACCOMMODATIONS AND FOOD. ◙Ostello La Primula (HI) ❶, V. IV Novembre, 106, offers the best budget value in the lake district, as well as a welcoming atmosphere. From the ferry dock, walk straight until reaching the road, turn left, and stick to the upward path that clings to the right side of the road. Expert staff recommends hiking and biking trips and provides free maps; they also set up climbing, horesback riding, and guided tours. The hostel provides guests with home-cooked local cuisine (3-course dinner €12), a washing machine (€3.50 per load), bike and kayak rental (€11 per day for guests), picnic lunch (€6.50), and free beach access. (☎034 43 23 56; www.menaggiohostel.com. Breakfast included. Reception 8-10am and 5-11:30pm. Lockout 10:30am-3pm; common rooms always open. Curfew 11:30pm. Call ahead to reserve. Open Mar.-Nov. Dorms €13.50; 4-6 bed family suites with private bath €14 per person. Cash only.) **Albergo il Vapore ❸**, P. T. Grossi, 3, just off P. Garibaldi, another inexpensive alternative, has small rooms, all with bath, and some with balcony facing the lake. (☎0344 322 29, fax 348 50. Breakfast €6.50. Reserve ahead. Singles €30; doubles €45-55. Cash only.) Lakeside **Camping Europa ❶**, a 15min. walk from the ferry docks, comes complete with a rocky swimming beach. (☎0344 311 87. €4.70 per person, €8.10 per tent; bungalows from €25 for 1 person to €60 for 6. Cash only.) Campers should consider taking the ferry to Domaso, which has more scenic sites.

The classy **Il Ristorante ❹**, Largo Cavour, 3, off P. Garibaldi, has over 300 wines and a lake view to write home about. Try the *carre de agnello seibacola* (€20) and tagliatelle (€8.50) with fresh lake fish. (☎0322 321 33. *Primi* €7.50-8, *secondi* €11-18. Open M-Su 12:30-10:30pm; closed Tu in winter. AmEx/MC/V.) Head uphill at the junction near Banca San Paolo for **Pizzeria Lugano ❸**, V. Como, 26, where a *quattro stagione* pizza is only €5.20. (☎0344 316 64. Pasta €4. Open M 6:30-11pm, Tu-Su noon-2:30pm and 6:30-11pm. AmEx/MC/V.) **Hotel du Lac's cafe ❶**, V. Mazzini, 21, has the best *tiramisù* (€3) in town. (☎0344 321 94. Open daily 6:30am-1am. Cash only.) A **grocery store** on the way to the Hotel du Lac provides picnic basics. (Open M 3:30-7pm, Tu-Sa 8am-12:30pm and 3:30-7pm.)

SIGHTS AND HIKING. The **Rifugio Menaggio ❷**, a mountain station, has three bunkrooms 1400m above the lake. Getting there requires a 30min. bus ride, followed by a 2hr. uphill hike. (☎034 43 72 82. Office open daily June-Sept., Oct.-May weekends only. €17 per person. AmEx/MC/V.) From the top, hikers can trek to **Monte Grona** and the **Chiesa di S. Amate** (1hr. each way). A number of shorter hikes start in Menaggio. The 2hr. hike (each way) winds through outlying villages and farms to the picturesque **Sass Corbee Gorge** and waterfall. Another low-commitment option is the 2hr. hike toward Lake Lugano to **Lago di Piano,** a small nature reserve in **Val Menaggio,** (from which **bus C12** heads back). The less hiking-happy can take the 30min. walk up to **La Crocetta.** Inquire at the tourist office or hostel for detailed directions, as some routes are complicated.

BELLAGIO ☎031

Favored by the upper-crust of Milanese society, Bellagio is one of the loveliest and most heavily visited central lake towns. Its name is a compound of *bello* (beautiful) and *agio* (comfort); fittingly, the town is filled with welcoming lakeside promenades, sidewalk cafes, and steep streets that lead to silk shops and the villas of Lombard aristocrats.

TRANSPORTATION AND PRACTICAL INFORMATION. To reach Bellagio from Milan, take a **ferry** from the train station in nearby Varenna. The C30 **bus** also runs from Como. The tourist office is at P. Mazzini next to ferry dock #1. The English-speaking staff has detailed daytrip info. (☎031 95 02 04; www.bellagiolake-como.com. Open M and W-Sa 9am-noon and 3-6pm, Tu and Su 10am-12:30pm and

LOMBARDY

3-5:30pm. In winter, closed Tu and Su.) In case of **emergency,** call the **police** (☎ 113), the **carabinieri** (☎ 112), or an **ambulance** (☎ 118). The **pharmacy,** V. Roma, 12, has late-night service. (☎ 031 95 01 86. Open June-Sept. M 3:30-7:30pm, Tu-Sa 8:30am-12:30pm and 3:30-7:30pm, Su 9am-12:30pm; Sept.-June M-Tu and Th-Sa 8:30am-12:30pm and 3:30-7:30pm.) **Banks** with **ATM** are on Lungo Lario Manzoni. The **post office,** Lungo Lario Manzoni, 4, offers **currency exchange.** (☎ 031 95 19 42. Open M-F 8:30am-2pm, Sa 8:30am-noon.) **Postal Code:** 22021.

▐▐ ▐▌ ACCOMMODATIONS AND FOOD. Expect higher rates in Bellagio than in other lake towns. **Albergo Giardinetto ❸,** V. Roncati, 12, off P. della Chiesa, is by far the best deal in town, with simple rooms overlooking quiet gardens and grape arbors. (☎ 031 95 01 68; tczgne@tiscali.it. Breakfast €6. Open Mar.-Nov. Singles €30; doubles €45, with bath €52; triples with bath €70.)

Mini-Market Negrini-Sancassani, V. Centrale, 3 (☎ 031 95 04 31) near P. della Chiesa, provides great *panini* and wine by the bottle (€3.50-115.50). **◪Ristorante Barchetta ❹,** S. Mella, 15, is in the heart of the old town and features creative Lombard cuisine. Try the *gnocchi* with shrimp and asparagus tips (€10.50). The *menù* (€20 per person for 2) is a gastronomic extravaganza. (☎ 031 95 13 89. Open noon-2:30pm and 7-10:30pm. AmEx/MC/V.) **Ristorante La Punta ❸,** V. Eugenie Vitali, 19 (from the dock walk straight to P. della Chiesa, and then turn left and walk about 400m), is situated on a small peninsula, near a park and beach. The vegetarian cheese and spinach ravioli in a cream walnut sauce (€8) is a dream. (☎ 031 95 18 88. Open daily noon-2:30pm and 7-10pm. AmEx/MC/V.)

◪ SIGHTS. The **Villa Serbelloni** (not to be confused with the stately five-star Grand Hotel Villa Serbelloni down the hill—€240 per night) offers spectacular views from the fortifications on the promontory and a lovely cyprus-lined garden. (☎/fax 031 95 15 51. 30min. tours Tu-Su 11am and 4pm. €6.50, children €3. Buy tickets in the tourist office 15min. before. Open Apr.-Oct. Tu-Su 9am-6pm.) The lakeside gardens of **Villa Melzi** blossom at the other end of town. Turn right at the ferry dock and follow the road that winds along the waterfront. The villa is still Duke Lodovico Galarati Scoti's private residence, but the **grounds,** including a chapel and museum with Roman and Napoleonic art, are open to the public. (Open daily Mar.-Oct. 9am-6pm. €5.) Only a 10min. ferry ride away lies **Lenno** (included in the Centro Lago all-day ferry pass), part of a lakefront stretch known as the "Riviera of the Azaleas" or Tremezzina, thanks to the vivid colors of its gardens in May and June. From Lenno, a motorboat leaves for the **◪Villa del Balbianello,** an 18th-century villa said to be the lake's most beautiful. The villa began as a Franciscan convent, but it recently gained infamy as the site of the wedding at the end of *Star Wars: Attack of the Clones*. (☎ 0344 561 10. Open Tu-F 10am-1pm and 2-6pm, Sa-Su 10am-6pm. Hours vary seasonally. €5, children 4-12 €2.50.)

VARENNA ☎ 0341

Only a ferry ride from Bellagio, Varenna is a decidedly less polished version of its more famous cousin. The low-key atmosphere warrants a daytrip; the prohibitively high prices require one. Varenna's gardens rival those anywhere on the lake in splendor, and its cobblestone streets are filled with local artists' galleries.

▐▀▐▌ TRANSPORTATION AND PRACTICAL INFORMATION. Varenna's **train station,** just uphill from the ferry docks, links the eastern side of the lake to Milan, making journeys into the central lake region easy. (☎ 0341 36 85 84. Trains depart Varenna for Milan every hr. 5:24am-10:30pm, €2.10.) Exiting the **ferry dock,** turn right and follow the promenade, then head uphill to reach the **tourist office,** in P. S.

Giorgio. A non-English-speaking staff is nonetheless accommodating, with an excellent selection of **maps**. (☎ 0341 83 03 67. Open May-Sept. M-Sa 9:30am-12:30pm and 2:30-5:30pm, Su 9:30am-12:30pm.) Also in P. S. Giorgio are a **bank** with **ATM** (open M-F 8:20am-1:20pm and 2:45-3:45pm); a **pharmacy** (open Th-Tu 9am-12:30pm and 3:30-7:30pm, W 9am-12:30pm); and a **post office** (on the water side; open M-F 8:30am-2pm and Sa 8:30am-12:30pm). In case of **emergency**, dial ☎ 113, or call the **carabinieri** (☎ 0341 82 11 21). **Postal Code:** 23829.

🏠🍴 ACCOMMODATIONS AND FOOD. **Albergo Olivedo ❺**, P. Martiri, 4, has large antique-filled rooms, with bath, TV, and A/C; many have great lake views. (☎ 0341 83 01 15; www.olivedo.it. Breakfast included. Closed mid-Nov. to mid-Dec. Doubles €90-125; triples and quads €150-200. Cash only.) Two **alimentari** grace P. S. Giorgio. (Open Tu-Sa 7:30am-12:30pm and 3:30-7:30pm, M and Su 7:30am-12:30pm.) The pizza (€5.70-7.30), crepes (€4.70-8.30), or *panini* (€4) at **Nilus Bar ❷**, Riva Garibaldi, 4, provide a filling lunch. (Open daily 10am-1am. AmEx/MC/V.) The superb **Vecchia Varenna ❹**, Cda. Scoscesa, 10, lies under the stone arches of a tranquil stetch of waterfront. The *robiola* cheese ravioli with pear and *grappa* sauce (€11) and pumpkin *gnocchi* (€11) artfully combine complex flavors. (☎ 0341 83 07 93. *Primi* €11, *secondi* €15-16. Cover €2. Open Tu-Su noon-3:30pm and 6:30-11pm. Closed Jan.)

🏛 SIGHTS. A passageway beside the water connects both sides of Varenna, offering lake vistas. Varenna's 13th-century **Chiesa di S. Giorgio,** looms above the main piazza. Its exceedingly simple late-Romanesque interior was restored in the 1950s, though it still contains a few traces of ornate frescoes. (Open daily 7am-noon and 2-7pm.) Varenna's most famous sights are the two lakeside **botanical gardens** of nearby 13th-century villas: **Villa Monastero,** 150m to the right of the church, is a former convent; its grounds contain 2km worth of paths past dark cyprus groves and otherwordly giant aloe plants. The smaller terraced gardens of the **Villa Cipressi,** former weekend home of Lombard aristocrats, can be entered through the Hotel Villa Cipressi, just beyond the church. (Gardens open daily Mar.-Oct. 9am-7pm. €2 for either, combined ticket €3.50.) Turn left at the ferry dock and head uphill to reach **La Sorgente del Fiumelatte.** At 250m, this river has the dubious distinction of being the shortest in Italy. A 20min. ascent past the piazza and uphill leads to the 12th-century **Castello di Vezio,** linked to its small tower by a drawbridge. Birds of prey swoop over the castle during daily 4-6pm falconing demonstrations. (V. del Castellano, 6. ☎ 335 46 51 86; www.castellodivezio.it. Open daily Apr.-Sept. 10am-sunset, in Aug. 10am-midnight. €4, students €3.)

DOMASO   ☎ 0344

The breezes in this tiny town on the north lake create perfect **windsurfing** conditions. Domaso lies 50km (2hr.) from Como or 90min. by hydrofoil. Surfers flock to the laid-back **Ostello della Gioventù: La Vespa (HI) ❶**, V. Case Sparse, 12. Exiting the ferry dock, turn right, follow the road across the river, then immediately turn right again. Murals to the sun gods and dismembered scooters decorate the rooms; the popular bar below pumps techno into the wee hours. (☎ 0344 974 49; www.ostellolavespadomaso.it. Wheelchair accessible. Breakfast included; dinner €12. Low windsurfing and mountain biking rates offered. Reception 10am-noon and 4-10pm. Curfew midnight. Open Mar.-Oct. Dorms €13. AmEx/MC/V.)

The tourist office is in the Villa Camilla, on the way to the hostel, and has **maps** and info on watersports. (☎ 0344 963 22. Open daily 10am-12:30pm, 5-7:45pm, and 8:15-10pm.) **Windsurfcenter,** at Camping Paradiso, on the lakefront past the hostel, outfits sailors and windsurfers for a day on the water and offers classes to neophytes. (☎ 380 700 00 10; www.windsurfcenter-domaso.com.

Board rental €17-21 per hr., €35-45 per day. Private lessons €68 per hr. Sailboats from €30 per hr., €50 per half-day.) If the wind isn't cooperating, **Canottieri Domaso**, V. Statale Regina, 30min. farther along the main road, takes out **wakeboarders**. (☎0344 974 62; www.canottieridomaso.it. Wakeboarding €1.80 per min., waterskiing €2 per min.)

ACROSS THE BORDER FROM LAGO DI COMO

LUGANO, SWITZERLAND ☎091

Lugano, Switzerland's third-largest banking center, rests on Lago di Lugano in a valley between the San Salvatore and Monte Brè peaks. Cobblestone streets widen into arcade-lined piazzas, where visitors can enjoy a seamless blend of religious beauty, artistic flair, and natural spectacle. There are two extraordinary youth hostels, both built from luxury villas, with swimming pools and magnificent gardens.

> **TIP** Remember to bring your passport for excursions into Switzerland.

 TRANSPORTATION AND PRACTICAL INFORMATION. Trains leave from P. della Stazione to Locarno (16.60SFr) via Bellinzona (30 min., every 30min. 5:36am-12:17am, 11.40SFr) and a direct train runs to Milan (45min., 7:14am-9:48pm, 21SFr). **Luggage Storage** is at the train station for 7SFr per piece or 4-7SFr per locker (open 9am-1pm and 2:30-6:45pm). **Public buses** run from neighboring towns to the center of Lugano and traverse the city. Schedules and ticket machines are at each stop. (1.10-1.90SFr per ride, 24hr. "Carta Giorno" day pass 5SFr.) For **taxis,** call ☎922 88 33, 971 21 21, or 922 02 22.

> Italy's **international dialing prefix** is 00. Switzerland's **country code** is 41, and the **city code** for Lugano is 091. Remember to drop the zero when calling internationally. Exchange rates for the **Swiss Franc (SFr)** are as follows: 1SFr=€0.65; €1=1.54SFr.

The 15min. downhill walk from the train station to the classically Italian **Piazza della Riforma**, the town's center, winds through Lugano's large pedestrian zone. For those who would rather avoid the walk, a funicular runs between the train station and the waterfront **Piazza Cioccaro** (1.10SFr, 5:20am-11:50pm). The **tourist office** is in the Palazzo Civico, Riva Albertolli, at the corner of P. Rezzonico. To reach it from the station, cross the footbridge labeled "Centro" and proceed down V. Cattedrale straight through P. Cioccaro as it becomes V. Pessina. Turn left on V. dei Pesci and left on Riva via Vela, which becomes Riva Giocondo Albertolli. The office is across from the ferry launch and offers free **maps** and guided city walks. (☎913 32 32; www.lugano-tourism.ch. Open Apr.-Oct. M-F 9am-7pm, Sa 9am-5pm, Su 10am-3pm; Nov.-Mar. M-F 9am-noon and 1-5pm.) **Internet** is available at Biblio-Café Tra, V. A. Vanoni, 3. (☎923 23 05. Open M-Th 9am-midnight, F 9am-1am, Sa 5pm-1am. 2SFr per 15min.) In case of **emergency,** call the **police** (☎117), **fire** (☎118), **ambulance** (☎144), or **medical services** (☎111). There are **pharmacies** in all major piazzas and along the waterfront. The **post office**, on V. della Posta, is two blocks up from the lake near V. al Forte. (Open M-F 7:30am-6:15pm, Sa 8am-noon. **Traveler's checks** cashed.) **Postal Code:** CH-6900.

Lugano

🔺🛖 ACCOMMODATIONS
Eurocampo, **8**
Hotel & Backpackers
  Montarina, **6**
La Palma, **9**
Ostello della Gioventù, **1**

🍴 FOOD
La Tinèra, **7**
Ristorante Manora, **3**
Taqueria El Chilicuil, **5**

🎵 NIGHTLIFE
Biblio-Café Tra, **2**
Mango Club, **4**

🔺🛖 **ACCOMMODATIONS AND FOOD.** Converted from a luxury villa, the palm-tree enveloped 🏠**Hotel & Backpackers Montarina ❷**, attracts students and young families with a swimming pool, reading room, kitchen, and terrace. From the station walk right 200m, cross the tracks, and then walk 50m uphill. (☎966 72 72; www.montarina.ch. Laundry 4SFr, soap 1.50SFr. Internet 10SFr per hr. Buffet breakfast 12SFr. Sheets 4SFr. Reception 8am-10:30pm. Open Mar.-Oct. Reserve ahead. Dorms 25SFr; singles 70SFR, with bath 80SFR; doubles 100SFr/120SFr. MC/V.) The sprawling, family-run **Ostello della Gioventù (HI) ❷**, V. Cantonale, 13, is in Lugano-Savosa. Note: there are 2 streets called V. Cantonale, one in downtown Lugano and one in Savosa, by the hostel. Take bus #5 (walk 350m left from the station, past the parking lot, and cross the street to the bus stop) to "Crocifisso," and then backtrack and turn left up V. Cantonale. Large gardens and pool complement comfortable rooms in several buildings. (☎966 27 28;

www.luganoyouthhostel.ch. Kitchen access 1SFr after 7pm. Internet 5SFr for 20min. Breakfast 8SFr. Sheets included. Towels 2SFr. Parking available. Laundry 5SFr. Reception 6:30am-noon and 3-10pm. Curfew 10pm; keys available with 20SFr deposit. Open mid-Mar. to Oct. Reserve ahead. Dorms 23SFr; singles 40SFr, with kitchenette 47SFr; doubles 60SFr/74SFr; family rooms for 2-6 people 90-120SFr. MC/V.) Lugano is near several campsites. Ask the tourist office for a complete list. For the lakeside **La Palma ❶** (☎605 25 61) and **Euro-campo ❶** (☎605 21 14, fax 605 31 87), take the Ferrovia-Lugano-Ponte-Tresa (FLP) tram to Agno (4.60SFr). From the station, turn left, then left again on V. Molinazzo. (La Palma 7SFr per person, plus 2SFr *Kurtax;* tents 8-10SFr. Euro-campo 87.9SFr per person, plus 2SFr *Kurtax;* tents 8SFr. Both have showers.)

Tasty fare is easy to find at the outdoor restaurants and cafes that pay homage to Lugano's Italian heritage, serving up convincing *penne* and *gnocchi* and freshly-spun pizzas. For some quick *al fresco* eats, the **market** in P. della Riforma sells seafood, produce, and veggie sandwiches for 4SFr (open Tu and F 7am-noon), or try the outdoor sandwich and fruit stands on V. Pessina, off P. della Riforma. The romantic **La Tinèra ❸,** V. dei Gorini, 2, is a low-lit, underground restaurant specializing in Lombard cuisine. Try the sausage with *risotto* (14SFr) or a 4SFr vegetarian goulash. (☎923 52 19. Daily *menù* 13-19SFr. Open M-Sa 8:30am-3pm and 5:30-11pm. AmEx/MC/V.) **Taqueria El Chilicuil ❶,** C. Pestalozzi, 12, down the C. Pestalozzi from P. Indipendenza, spices up Lugano's cuisine with tacos, quesadillas (5.50-8.50SFr), and margaritas (7SFr, pitcher 38SFr). During Happy Hour weeknights 5-7pm, drinks are 1-2SFr less. (☎922 82 26. Wheelchair accessible. Open May-Nov. M-Th 11:30am-11pm, F 11:30am-midnight, Sa-Su 7pm-midnight; Dec.-Apr. M-Th 11:30am-10pm, Sa-Su 5pm-midnight.) **Ristorante Manora ❷,** in the Manor Department Store in P. Dante, 3rd fl.; alternate entrance off Salita Mario e Antonio Chiattone. Hungry but tight-fisted travelers will love this gourmet spot's salad bar (4.50-10.20SFr), pasta (7.90-10.90SFr), hot daily specials (10-15SFr), and beer. (Wheelchair accessible. Open M-Sa 7:30am-10pm, Su 10am-10pm.)

◪ SIGHTS. The ornate frescoes of the 16th-century **Cattedrale San Lorenzo,** downhill from the train station, gleam with vivid colors. Marble female angels wielding bronze swords battle devils in one side altar. Bernardio Luini's gargantuan fresco, *Crucifixion,* painted in 1529, fills an entire wall in the **Chiesa Santa Maria degli Angioli,** 200m right from the tourist office. The small 14th-century **Chiesa San Rocco,** in P. Maghetti two blocks to the left of P. della Riforma, houses an ornate Madonna altarpiece and a series of 20 frescoes depicting the life of its patron saint. The **Museo Cantonale d'Arte,** V. Canova, 10, has a permanent collection of 19th- and 20th-century art, including works by Swiss artists Vela, Ciseri, Franzoni, and Klee, though the collection is frequently replaced by special exhibitions of contemporary art. (Across from the Chiesa San Rocco. ☎910 47 80. Wheelchair accessible. Open Tu 2-5pm, W-Su 10am-5pm. Permanent collection 7SFr, special exhibits 10SFr, students 7SFr. MC/V.) An elegant lakeside villa houses the **Museo delle Culture Extraeuropee,** V. Cortivo, 24. Six hundred and fifty wood-carved masks, statues, and shields from Africa, Oceania and Asia adorn the Neoclassical villa's marble staircases. On the footpath to Gandria in the Villa Heleneum. From the tourist office take bus #1, dir: Castagnola, to "San Domenica" and walk down to the street below. The Villa is 700m on the right. Or take the ferry to the Museo Helenum stop. (☎971 73 53. Open Apr.-Oct. W-Su 10am-5pm. 5SFr, students 3SFr.)

🏄 OUTDOOR ACTIVITIES. The dock for the **Società Navigazione del Lago di Lugano** is across the street from the tourist office. (☎923 17 79; www.lakel-ugano.ch.) Tours of Lake Lugano pass tiny, unspoiled towns along the shore, including Gandria (11.50SFr, round-trip 19.20SFr), Morcote (16.90SFr/

LOMBARDY

28.20SFr), and Paradiso (3SFr/5SFr). A "grand tour" of the lake in English (3½hr.) costs 32.60SFr, 19.60SFr with SwissPass; 62SFr/52SFr allows a week of unlimited lake travel. Walks along the lake to the east provide access to these beautiful villages. The tourist office and Ostello della Gioventù have topographical maps and trail guides (15SFr) into the Ticinese mountains. The most rewarding hike is to **Monte Boglio;** a 5hr. round-trip can be extended over two days by staying at the Pairolhütte (ask at hostels or tourist office). Reach the peaks of **Monte Brè** (933m) and **Monte San Salvatore** (912m) by funicular, 20min. down the river to the left of the tourist office, just off of V. Castagnole. (☎971 31 71. Open daily 9:10am-6:45pm, July-Aug. until 10:05pm. 13SFr, round-trip 19SFr; ages 6-16 6.50SFr/9.50SFr.) The San Salvatore funicular is 20min. from the tourist office in the other direction; from the lakefront, follow V. E. Bosio inland just after the Paradiso ferry dock. (☎985 28 28. Departures every 30min. Mar.-Nov. 8:30am-11pm. One-way 14-17SFr, round-trip 20-14SFr; ages 6-16 7-8.50SFr/10-15.80SFr.) The adventure opportunities provided by **ASBEST Adventure Company,** V. Basilea, 28, based in the Hotel Continental, include: snowshoeing and skiing (full-day 90SFr), tandem paragliding (165SFr), canyoning (from 90SFr), river-diving (90SFr with appropriate training), rock-climbing (90SFr), and mountain biking. Most require group interest; lone travelers should call ahead. (☎966 11 14; www.asbest.ch.)

🎭 🎵 **ENTERTAINMENT AND NIGHTLIFE.** During the first two weekends of July, Lugano's **Festival Jazz** fills P. della Riforma with free music. Past performers include Miles Davis and Bobby McFerrin. The looser **Blues to Bop Festival** celebrates R&B, blues, and gospel in late August with free performances by international singers and local amateurs. In mid-October, Lugano reaffirms its Italian associations by celebrating the country's *aqua vitae* at the **Wine Harvest Festival.** From late June to early August, **Cinema al Lago** shows international films on a large screen installed on the lake nightly at 9:45pm, after July 15 at 9:30pm. (☎913 32 32; www.open-air-kino.ch. 15SFr, under 17 12SFr.)

The Latin American **Mango Club,** P. Dante, 8, mixes live salsa and techno in one of the premier clubs of Lugano. (☎922 94 38.) For a change of pace, head down V. Pretorio from P. Dante and turn left on V. Vanoni for the **Biblio-Café Tra,** V. Vanoni, 3, which attracts laid-back students from the neighboring university. Have a beer (3.60SFr) and a book from the extensive collection at one of the battered wood tables. (Internet available; see **Practical Information.** Same hours as above.)

LAKE GARDA (LAGO DI GARDA)

Lake Garda, the most popular and largest of the lakes in northern Italy, draws tourists by the busload to its hazy mountains and country-style resorts. Stretching 52km into the regions of the Veneto, Lombardy, and Trent, Lake Garda's shores wash up exotic produce as well as historical bounty, including the world's oldest wooden plough (2000 BC) and the remains of a Bronze Age civilization. Milan and Venice once competed for the region's freshwater fish, olives, citrus fruit, and white and black truffles. In 1426 Venice won out, gaining economic prestige (the tides have since turned). Every summer, German, Dutch, and Italian tourists crowd its pebbly beaches to bask in the sun, windsurf, hang-glide, and kayak. They also zip through Garda's towns and mountain tunnels on rented scooters.

SIRMIONE ☎030

Isolated on a peninsula from the surrounding lakeside towns, little Sirmione retains the elegance and charm that moved Catullus to establish his home here and praise the town's beauty in his poetry. Among the town's chief attractions are

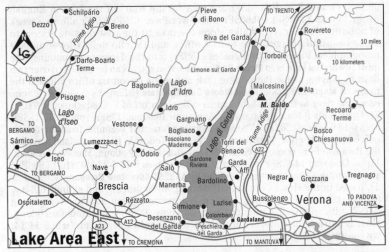

the healing powers of its spa waters, renowned since ancient times. Local authorities tried to maintain the town's peace and tranquility by cordoning off the historic center as a pedestrian-only zone, but the foot-traffic of summer tourists gives Sirmione the feel of a bustling resort. Trendy boutiques and sophisticated hotels now graciously share sidewalk space with pastel medieval architecture.

🚌 TRANSPORTATION AND PRACTICAL INFORMATION. Sirmione is a peninsula at the lake's southern end. **SAIA buses** run from Sirmione every hour west to Verona (1hr., €2.90) and east to Brescia (€2.75). Buses in both directions stop in Colombare (10min., €1). Three buses per day also run from Desenzano, the town with the closest train station (20min.; 7:40, 10:30am, 5:45pm; €2.45.) Ferries, though expensive, make better connections. **Navigazione Lago Garda** (☎800 55 18 01 or 030 914 95 11) runs boats to: Desenzano (20min., 10am-7:50pm, €2.60); Gardone (1¼-2hr., 8:25am-5:29pm, €5.50; speed service €8); and Riva (2-4hr., 8:53am-5:50pm; €8, speed service €11.30). For a **taxi,** dial ☎030 91 60 82 or 91 92 40.

The **tourist office,** V. Guglielmo Marconi, 2, is in the disc-shaped building. (☎030 91 61 14; www.comune.sirmione.bs.it. Open daily Apr.-Oct. 9am-9pm; Nov.-Mar. M-F 9am-12:30pm and 3-6pm, Sa 9am-12:30pm.) Sirmione's historic attractions are concentrated on the northern end of the peninsula. **Via Marconi** leads to **Via Vittorio Emanuele** and Sirmione's castle, **Rocca Scaligera.** The town of **Colombare,** 2km south of Sirmione's historical center, has additional services and a few slightly cheaper lodgings. The **Banca Popolare di Verona,** P. Castello, 3-4, has an **ATM.** (Open daily 8:25am-1:20pm and 2:40-6:10pm.) Rent **bikes** at **Adventure Sprint,** V. Brescia, 9, in the neighboring town of Colombare. (☎030 91 90 00. Bikes €8-19 per day.) In case of **emergency,** dial ☎113, or call the **Tourist Medical Clinic,** V. Alfieri, 6 (☎030 990 91 71; open June 15-Sept. 15), or the **police** (☎030 990 67 77). The **post office** is near the tourist office. (Open M-F 8:30am-2pm, Sa 8:30am-12:30pm.) **Postal Code:** 25019.

🛏🍴 ACCOMMODATIONS AND FOOD. A thorough exploration of Sirmione takes only an afternoon, but people looking for prolonged relaxation have several fairly pricey hotels to choose from. Reserve early for summer soujourns. In the historic center, the quiet **Hotel Marconi ❸,** V. Vittorio Emanuele II, 51, maintains

LOMBARDY

spacious rooms with thick mattresses, TV, A/C, and phone. Enjoy a sumptuous breakfast on a sunlit terrace or sunbathe on the private beach. For lower rates, ask for a room in the annex. (☎ 030 91 60 07; www.hotelmarconi.net. Breakfast included. Singles €35-58; doubles €62-95; triples and quads €120-150.) **Corte Regina ❹**, V. Anticha Mura, 11, keeps modern hotel rooms equipped with bath, A/C, and TV. (☎ 030 91 61 47; lorenzoronchi@libero.it. Breakfast included. Reserve 1 month ahead. Singles €50-70; doubles €75-90; triples €90-120. MC/V.) **Albergo Grifone ❸**, V. Bocchio, 4, off V. Dante, has country-style rooms with bath and lake views. (☎ 030 91 60 14, fax 91 65 48. Reservation required. Singles €36; doubles €55. Extra bed €20. Cash only.) There is also a campground, **Campeggio Sirmione ❶**, V. Sirmioncino, 9, in Colombare, a 30min. walk or 5min. bus ride from the post office. Bathers can choose between the swimming pool and beach. A small market and cafe are also onsite. (☎ 030 990 46 65, fax 91 90 45. Open Mar. 25-Oct. €6-9 per person. Tent sites €5.50-8. 2-person cabins €45-70; 4-person cabins €65-100.)

Ristorante Grifone ❸, at the hotel of the same name, serves pan-Italian on an outdoor terrace. (☎ 030 91 60 14. *Primi* €7, *secondi* €9. Cover €2.50. Open M-Tu and Th-Su noon-2:15pm and 7-10:15pm. AmEx/MC/V.) **Ristorante Pizzeria Valentino ❷**, P. Porto Valentino, 13, has delicious pizza (€4.50-10). Fish soup and *gnocchi* await those looking for more refined cuisine. (*Primi* €7-9, *secondi* €7.50-14. Open M-Th and Sa-Su 9am-3pm and 5:30pm-1am. AmEx/MC/V.) For more elegant and intimate dining, **Antica Trattoria La Speranzina ❺**, Viale Dante, 16, serves trout, seabass, and lobster inside or on a tiered terrace brightened with potted flowers. (☎ 030 990 62 92. Dinner reservation required. *Primi* €9.50-12, *secondi* €18. Seafood €9.50-21. Open Tu-Su noon-2:30pm and 7-10:30pm. AmEx/MC/V.) For a **supermarket**, head to **Catteli**, V. Colombare, 154, next to the Colombare bus stop. (Open M-F 8am-1pm and 3-7:30pm, Sa 8am-7:30pm; in Aug. daily 8am-8pm.) Also in Colombare is the **Ristorante-Pizzeria Roberto ❷**, on V. Garibaldi, which serves outstanding local fare for half the price of the tourist traps. House specialties include shrimp pizza (€8.70), *tagliolini* in cream sauce, and enormous salads (from €6). It's a 5min. walk toward Sirmione on V. Colombare away from the bus stop. (Pizza €3.50-8.70. *Primi* €4-8.90, *secondi* €7.30-10. Service 10%. Open Tu-Su 11:45am-2:30pm and 5:30-10:50pm.)

◪ SIGHTS. At the far end of the peninsula is the **Grotte di Catullo,** the best-preserved aristocratic Roman villa in northern Italy, spread over eight hectares of olive groves. Though Catullus wrote of his family's summer home in Sirmione, the ruins appear to be from the late first century BC, after the poet's death. Artifacts in the adjacent **archaeological museum** have English explanations. (☎ 031 91 61 57. Ruins and museum open Mar.-Oct. 8:30am-7pm, Nov-Feb. 8:30am-5pm. Free guided tours in Italian. Combined admission €4.) The 13th-century **Castello Scaligero** sits in the center of town as a testament to the power of the della Scala family, who controlled the Veronese region from 1260 to 1387. Completely surrounded by water, the commanding view from the turrets is the castle's main attraction. Save for some dirt and cannonballs, the interior is empty. (☎ 030 91 64 68. Same prices and times as Grotte.) Between the castle and the ruins are two public beaches and the **Chiesa di San Pietro in Mavino**, Sirmione's oldest church, dating to the eighth century. Sixteenth century frescoes decorate the interior of the simple church. Sirmione's **spa**, V. Punto Staffalo, 1 (☎ 030 990 49 23; www.termedisirmione.com), open year-round, attracts elderly customers looking to soothe afflictions from rheumatism to respiratory failure. Facilities include a thermal swimming pool, underwater massages (€25.50), beauty treatments, and mud baths (€14.70-28.20). See the tourist office for spa info. The town also has **summer events,** which generally include musical and dance performances, theater, art exhibitions, and trout tastings.

GARDONE RIVIERA ☎ 0365

Once a fashionable tourist destination of the European elite, the Gardone Riviera is now more quiet retreat than hot spot. Gracefully aging villas, lush gardens, and a tranquil lifestyle have replaced the boisterous likes of wealthy *Great Gatsby* types. Lacking the energy of Sirmione and Riva del Garda, Gardone Riviera is most characterized, it would seem, by steady self-indulgence.

⚟ 🛈 TRANSPORTATION AND PRACTICAL INFORMATION. Gardone's two main thoroughfares, **Gardone Sotto** and **Corso Zanardelli,** intersect near the bus stop. **Buses** (☎ 0365 210 61 or 800 41 25) run to: Brescia (1hr., 2 per hr., €2.75); Desenzano (30min., 6 per day, €2.25); and Milan (3hr., 2 per day, €8). Tickets are available at the **Molinari Viaggi Travel Agency,** P. Wimmer, 2, near the ferry stop. (☎ 0365 215 51. Open daily 8:30am-12:15pm and 3-6:30pm.) Speedier and more frequent service to major cities is available on the Milan-Verona **train** line; take the bus to Desenzano, then board at the train station next to the bus stop. The **ferry dock,** on Lungolago D'Annunzio, services Riva (1½hr.; 9:55am-6:39pm; €6.80, express €9.60) and Sirmione (2hr.; 10am-6:33pm; €5.50, express €8).

The **APT Tourist Office,** V. Repubblica, 8, in the center of Gardone Sotto, stocks schedules of Verona's opera season, info on the Garda region, and **maps** of Gardone, Brescia, and Venice. (☎/fax 0365 203 47. Open daily June-Sept. 9am-1pm and 3-7pm, Oct.-May 9am-12:30pm and 3:30-6:30pm.) For **currency exchange,** head to the **Banco di Brescia,** V. Roma, 6, across from the Grand Hotel. From the ferry dock, turn right and climb the stairs. (☎ 0365 200 81. Open M-F 8:25am-1:25pm and 2:40-3:40pm.) In case of **emergency,** dial ☎ 113, contact the **police** (☎ 112 or 0365 54 06 10), or call the **hospital** (☎ 0365 29 71). For after-hours **first aid,** dial ☎ 0365 29 71. The **post office,** V. Roma, 8, is next door to the bank. (☎ 0365 208 62. Open M-F 8:30am-2pm, Sa 8:30am-12:30pm.) **Postal Code:** 25083.

🛏 🍴 ACCOMMODATIONS AND FOOD. Budget travelers should consider exploring Gardone as a daytrip, as inexpensive accommodations are scarce. Located in a cobblestoned and flowered neighborhood en route to Il Vittoriale, **Locanda Trattoria Agli Angeli ❹,** P. Garibaldi, 2, has 16 rooms furnished with antiques, bath, A/C, and TV. Some suites have loft bedrooms with canopy beds. (☎ 0365 208 32; www.agliangeli.com. Open Mar.-Nov. Breakfast included. 1 single €50; doubles and suites €80-200. AmEx/MC/V.)

Pizzeria Ristorante Emiliano ❶, V. Repubblica, 57, by the ferry station, serves gigantic pizzas from €4.40. (☎ 0365 215 17. Cover €1. Open daily noon-2:30pm and 6-11pm.) Try **La Stalla ❷,** V. dei Colli, 14, off V. Roma, for romantic outdoor dining. The *trata alla griglia* (grilled fresh fish; €8) melts in your mouth. (☎ 0365 210 38. Open daily noon-2pm and 7pm-close. AmEx/MC/V.) **Taverna ❸,** V. Repubblica, 34, between the tourist office and the ferry station, grills gilled creatures to tasty perfection. If trout (€8-9) is just too freshwater, the seafood soup has cuttlefish and octopus. (*Antipasti* €7. *Primi* €7.50-8, fish *secondi* €7-13. Cover €1. Open M and W-Su noon-2pm and 6-11pm. AmEx/MC/V.)

🎟 🎭 SIGHTS AND ENTERTAINMENT. Off V. Roma and V. dei Colli lies ▨ Il Vittoriale, the sprawling estate of Gabriele D'Annunzio, the poet, novelist, occasional soldier, and latter-day Casanova. Following his retirement, D'Annunzio erected monuments to his victories and fallen comrades. Also on the grounds are **D'Annunzio's tomb** and shaded avenues lined with the urns of his wartime companions. (☎ 0365 29 65 11; www.vittoriale.it. Villa open Apr.-Sept. Tu-Su 8:30am-8pm. Gardens open Oct.-Mar. Tu-Su 9am-5pm. Obligatory guided tours of the villa in English, Spanish, and German leave about every 20-40min. House

€6, garden €6, house and gardens €11.) The **Giardino Botanico,** an oasis of criss-crossing brooks and intimate bridges at the corner of V. Roma and V. Disciplina, was planted in 1900 by Arturo Hruska, doctor to the Tsar. It squeezes more than 8000 varieties of plants and flowers into a 10,000-sq.-m space. Recent modifications by artist André Heller, like water-spitting statues and shrubs pruned in the shape of eyes, lend a wacky sense of humor. (☎0365 336 410 877. Open daily 9am-7pm. €7. €1 discount at Vittoriale with ticket to gardens.) The Riviera's Baroque-style **Chiesa di San Nicola** dates to 1391, though little of the original survived the church's early 18th-century reconstruction. Frescoes by Paolo Veronese's son Carlo Caliari adorn the walls and ceiling. The two caskets in the altar, unearthed from Roman catacombs, reputedly contain the bones and blood of Christian martyrs Feliciano and Zosimo. (Open daily 9am-noon and 3-7pm.)

The **Fondazione al Vittoriale,** next to San Nicola, sponsors summer arts programs in music, dance, theater, and opera in the outdoor **Teatro del Vittoriale.** (Ticket info ☎0365 29 65 06. Performances mid-July to early Aug. Tickets from €18.)

THE VENETO AND TRENTINO-ALTO ADIGE

HIGHLIGHTS OF THE VENETO AND TRENTINO-ALTO ADIGE

BEHOLD St. Mark's remains at Venice's Basilica di San Marco. (p. 293.)

HEARKEN the sweet sounds of fair Verona at the annual Opera Festival. (p. 318.)

FLIRT with Germanic culture in Trentino-Alto Adige, a northern region that rubs shoulders with Austria. (p. 327.)

SATISFY wanderlust with a ramble through the Dolomites. (p. 321.)

THE VENETO

From the rocky foothills of the Dolomites to the fertile valleys of the Po River, the Veneto's geography is as diverse as its history. Once loosely united under the Venetian Empire, the towns of the Veneto retained their cultural independence, and today visitors are more likely to hear regional dialects than standard Italian when neighbors gossip across geranium-cloaked windows. Thanks to the region's port supremacy and enviable location near the mid-section of the peninsula, heavy international and inter-provincial traffic ensured varied cuisines, dialects, and cultural traditions. This global history manifests itself in today's budding economies; Vicenza's booming technology sector hosts some of the most important conferences in Europe, while Venice's reluctant embrace of rampant tourism brings in billions of euros each year. International culinary influences marched in with the Austrians and continue to flavor cuisine. The tenacity of local culture may be a pleasant surprise for people who come expecting only mandolins and gondolas.

VENICE (VENEZIA)   ☎041

Venice is a city of contradictions, from its hedonistic, devil-may-care *Carnevale* to the penitent God-may-care-too services of its soaring marble cathedrals. While tourists are caught up in the fantasy of a waterside city, the *Veneziani* have a very different take—the same romantic arched bridges and waterways that lap at ancient doorways are but everyday sidewalks. Lavish palaces stand proudly upon wood supports that have been sinking since Attila the Hun roamed the area. Founded by Roman fishermen, the city supplemented its gondolas with sea-bound ships in the 11th century, soon gaining a monopoly on Eastern trade. The world depended on Venetian merchants for silks, spices, and coffee, and with the conquest of Constantinople in 1203, Venice gained control of parts of the Adriatic, modern Turkey, and mainland Italy, becoming the envy of the world. Over the next century, however, jealous European powers in the west and Turks in the east robbed Venice of its trade dominance and whittled away its wealthy empire.

Lately, Venice has abandoned naval prowess and a history of sea-based economics to embrace the booming tourism industry as a means of growth and preservation. People flock year-round to see seemingly infinite works by Titian, Tintoretto,

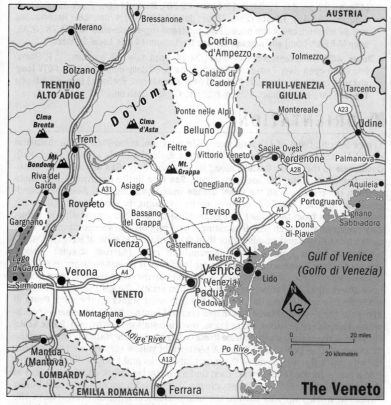

The Veneto

and Giorgione that fill churches and museums. While tourists rush through the labyrinthine streets with tilted map in hand, native Venetians watch them pass from the windows of quiet neighborhoods, bemused and a little protective of the small, less touristed canals and out-of-the-way cafes along the edges of the ever-evolving city they dearly love. In the end, Venice's wealth of architectural and cultural treasures proves that it is not *La Serenissima* (the Most Serene One) who surrenders to tourists, but rather they who succumb to her entrancing spectacle.

◼ INTERCITY TRANSPORTATION

Flights: Aeroporto Marco Polo (☎041 260 92 60; www.veniceairport.it), 10km north of the city. The ATVO shuttle bus (☎041 520 55 30) links the airport to P. Roma on the main island (30min., every hr. 5-9am and 10am-8:40pm, €3). Shuttle bus ticket office open daily 6:40am-7:30pm.

Trains: Stazione Santa Lucia, the main station (☎041 78 55 70), is in the northwestern corner. By train, disembark at S. Lucia, not Mestre on the mainland. Info office open daily 7am-9pm. Ticket windows open daily 6am-9pm. AmEx/MC/V. Wheelchair accessible. To: **Bologna** (2hr., 27 per day 12:04am-8:04pm, €8); **Florence** (3hr., 9 per day 6:32am-6:58pm, €19); **Milan** (3hr., 24 per day 5:17am-9:07pm, €20-30); **Padua**

(45min., 83 per day 12:04am-11:40pm, €2.50); **Rome** (4½hr., 7 per day 6:32am-6:32pm, €35-45); **Trieste** (2hr., 28 per day 12:10am-10:47pm, €8). Reservations may be required; check info booth. **Lost and found** (*oggetti rinvenuti;* ☎041 78 52 38; open M-F 8am-5pm) and **luggage storage** by Platform 14 (see **Local Services**).

Buses: ACTV (HelloVenezia hotline ☎041 24 24; open daily 7:30am-8pm), in P. Roma. Info office open daily 7am-8pm. Ticket window open daily 6am-11:30pm. **ACTV long-distance carrier** runs buses to **Padua** (1½hr., every 30min. 6:45am-11pm, €2.90) and **Treviso** (1hr., every 30min. 4:55am-8:55pm, €2.40). Cash only.

■ ORIENTATION

Venice is comprised of 118 land masses in a lagoon, connected to the mainland city of Mestre by a thin causeway. The city is divided into six *sestieri* (sections): **Cannaregio** to the north, **Castello** along the eastern shore, **San Marco** to the southeast, **Dorsoduro** along the southern shore, **San Polo** in the northwest, and **Santa Croce** in the middle, with the **Canal Grande** snaking throughout. *Sestiere* boundaries are vague but should be of some use in navigating the city's narrow alleys. It's best to accept from the outset that getting lost in Venice is practically inevitable. City navigation is much less frustrating if you rely on knowledge of major landmarks like bridges and canals rather than the confusing system of street signs.

Venice's layout consists of a labyrinth of *calli* (narrow streets), *campi* (squares), *lista* (large streets), and *ponti* (bridges). It is useless to try to follow a detailed map of the city. Many streets are too narrow to be plotted, most do not have street signs, and street numbers are often erratic. To get by, simply learn to navigate like a true Venetian. Locate the following sights on the map: **Ponte di Rialto** (in the center), **Piazza San Marco** (central south), **Ponte Accademia** (southwest), **Ferrovia** (or Stazione Santa Lucia, the train station, northwest), **Ponte Scalzi** (in front of the station), and **Piazzale Roma** (southwest of the station). These are the main orientation points for Venice. A plethora of yellow signs posted throughout the city point the way to all of the major landmarks and bridges. When trying to find a place, locate the *sestiere*, then find a nearby landmark and follow signs in that general direction. As you get closer, use the address numbers and busier streets to work your way toward the destination. As a general rule, follow the arrows on the yellow signs as precisely as possible. If a street suddenly leads into a *campo* and branches in five different directions, pick the street that follows the original direction of the arrow as closely as possible until reaching the next sign. Upon getting closer, locate the *campo* or main street nearest to the destination, and aim for that. Listings are indicated on the map with icons, making it easier to spot the orientation points. Also note that in Venice, addresses are not specific to a particular street, and every building in a *sestiere* is given a number ("3434, San Marco" is a typical address). Buildings are generally numbered consecutively, but there could be a large jump, with the next number one block behind or down a nearby alleyway. V #82 is the most direct way to get to **Piazza San Marco** or the **Rialto Bridge** from the train station or P. Rom; most lines take up to 30min. V #1 takes 10min. longer, but is often faster overall, as it runs more freuqnetly during the day. (Line #1 runs every 10min., while #82 runs every 20min.) On foot, follow signs to P. San Marco, starting left of the station on Lista di Spagna.

⊟ LOCAL TRANSPORTATION

The cheapest and often fastest way to see the city is to walk through it. Pedestrians can cross the Grand Canal at the *ponti* Scalzi, Rialto, and Accademia. ⬛**Traghetti** (gondola ferry boats) traverse the canal at seven locations, including Ferrovia, San Marcuola, Cà d'Oro, and Rialto (€0.40). *Vaporetti* (water buses) provide 24hr. ser-

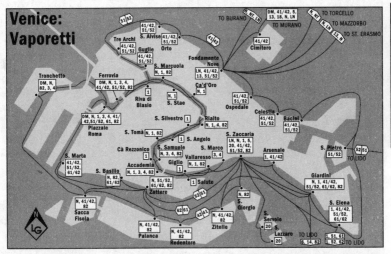

vice around the city, with reduced service after midnight. Tickets cost €3.50, or €5 for the Grand Canal. An extended pass is more economical for longer visits (24hr. pass €10.50, 3-day €22). Schedules, **route maps,** and tickets are available at tourist offices (see **Information Offices**). Stock up on tickets by asking for an unvalidated pass *(non timbrato)*, then validate before boarding by inserting tickets into one of the yellow boxes at each stop. Tickets are sold in front of stops and on *vaporetti* when boarding. Validate your tickets or risk a fine; the "confused foreigner" act won't work in a town where tourists often outnumber residents two to one.

MAIN VAPORETTO LINES

V #82: Runs from P. San Marco, up the Giudecca Canal, to the station, down the Grand Canal, back to P. San Marco, and then to Lido. Always crowded, with long lines.

V #1: Has a similar route to #82, but can be less crowded; offers a nice view of the canalside palaces. 10min. slower than #82, and with more stops.

V #41, 42, 51, 52: Circumnavigate Venice. #51 and 41 run from the station, through the Giudecca Canal to Lido, along the northern edge of the city, and back to the station; #52 and 42 follow the same route in the opposite direction.

V #LN: Runs from F. Nuove to Murano, Burano, and Lido with connections to Torcello.

DISABLED VISITORS

Informa Handicap offers an info hotline for physically disabled and deaf travelers in Italy. (☎041 534 17 00. Open Tu 9am-1pm and 3:30-6:30pm, Th 3:30-6:30pm, F 9am-1pm.) The **APT tourist office** provides a list of wheelchair accessible lodgings in Venice. Pick up a free **map** of the city outlining wheelchair-friendly routes in each *sestiere*. The APT provides keys for wheelchair lifts at the bridges, and V #1 and 82 are wheelchair accessible.

🛈 PRACTICAL INFORMATION

TOURIST AND FINANCIAL SERVICES
Information Offices:
   APT Tourist Offices are located all over the city. Avoid the **train station** office, as it is always mobbed. **Branches:** P. Roma (☎041 241 14 99; open daily 9:30am-6:30pm. AmEx/MC/V);

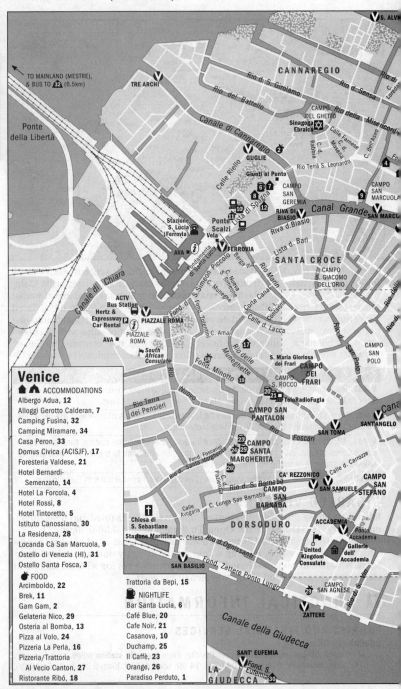

TO MAINLAND (MESTRE),
& BUS TO 32 (6.5km)

TRE ARCHI

Ponte
della Libertà

CANNAREGIO

Rio d. S. Girolamo

Rio d. Sensa

Rio del Battello

Canale di Cannaregio

CAMPO
DEL GHETTO

Sinagoga
Ebraica

Calle Farnese

C. d.
Rabbia

C. d.
Misena

C. dell'Asco

GUGLIE

2

Rio Terrà S. Leonardo

Calle Riello

Giunti al Punto

6 7

8

CAMPO
SAN
GEREMIA

9

CAMPO
SAN
MARCUOLA

Stazione
S. Lucia
(Ferrovia)

Ponte
Scalzi
Vela

10

11

12

Lista di Spagna

RIVA DI
BIASIO

Canal Grande

SAN MARCU

AVA

Riva d. Biasio

FERROVIA

Lista d. Bari

Fondamenta
di Santa Lucia

Berga ma

Rio Marin

SANTA CROCE

CAMPO
S. GIACOMO
DELL'ORIO

Canale di Chiara

Canale di Chiara

Canale di Chiara

ACTV
Bus Station

Hertz &
Expressway
Car Rental

PIAZZALE ROMA

PIAZZALE
ROMA

AVA

South
African
Consulate

Fond. Tolentini

C. Amai

C. Nueva
S. Simeone

C. Munegne

S. Simeon Piccolo

Corte Canal

C. l.
Contarini

Rio delle
Muneghette

Calle d. Lacca

17

S. Maria Gloriosa
dei Frari

CAMPO
DEI
FRARI

CAMPO
SAN
POLO

Rio del Gaffaro

Fond. Minotto

Nuovo

19

CAMPO
S. ROCCO

20

21

TeleRadioFugia

SANT'ANGELO

Rio Terra
dei Pensieri

CAMPO SAN
PANTALON

SAN TOMA

Foscari

Calle de Carrozze

Canal

Fond. Foscarini

Rio

23

CAMPO
SANTA
MARGHERITA

24 25

26

Rio di Ca' Foscari

CA' REZZONICO

SAN SAMUELE

CAMPO
SAN
STEFANO

Rio Terra
Santa Margherita

Rio d. S. Barnaba

CAMPO
SAN
BARNABA

C. Lunga San Barnaba

Calle
Avogaria

Chiesa di
S. Sebastiano

Stazione Marittima

C. Chiesa

Rio di Ognissanti

DORSODURO

ACCADEMIA

Ponte
Accademia

Gallerie
dell'
Accademia

United
Kingdom
Consulate

SAN BASILIO

Fond. Zattere Ponto Lungo

CAMPO
SAN AGNESE

29

Trattoria da Bepi, 15

ZATTERE

Canale della Giudecca

SANT' EUFEMIA

Fond. S.
Eufemia

30

LA
GIUDECCA

S. ALVI

Rio d.

C.
Loreta

Rio della Misericordi

C. dell'Asco

Fo

4

SAN MARCU

Rio delle

CAMPO
SAN
POLO

Venice

🏨🏠 ACCOMMODATIONS

Albergo Adua, **12**
Alloggi Gerotto Calderan, **7**
Camping Fusina, **32**
Camping Miramare, **34**
Casa Peron, **33**
Domus Civica (ACISJF), **17**
Foresteria Valdese, **21**
Hotel Bernardi-
  Semenzato, **14**
Hotel La Forcola, **4**
Hotel Rossi, **8**
Hotel Tintoretto, **5**
Istituto Canossiano, **30**
La Residenza, **28**
Locanda Cà San Marcuola, **9**
Ostello di Venezia (HI), **31**
Ostello Santa Fosca, **3**

🍴 FOOD

Arcimboldo, **22**
Brek, **11**
Gam Gam, **2**
Gelateria Nico, **29**
Osteria al Bomba, **13**
Pizza al Volo, **24**
Pizzeria La Perla, **16**
Pizzeria/Trattoria
  Al Vecio Canton, **27**
Ristorante Ribó, **18**

🍸 NIGHTLIFE

Bar Santa Lucia, **6**
Café Blue, **20**
Cafe Noir, **21**
Casanova, **10**
Duchamp, **25**
Il Caffè, **23**
Orange, **26**
Paradiso Perduto, **1**

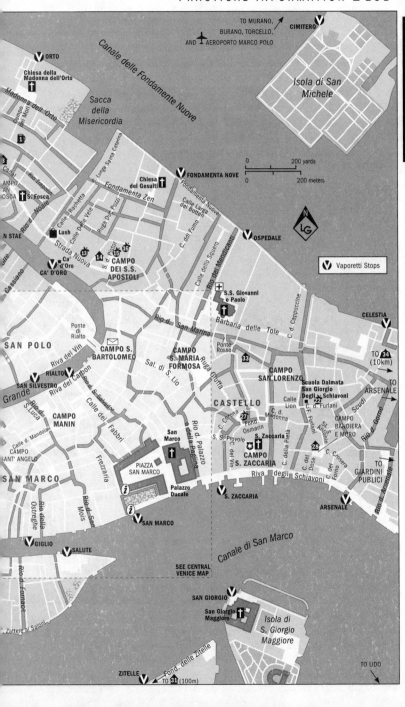

TO MURANO,
BURANO, TORCELLO,
AND ✈ AEROPORTO MARCO POLO

CIMITERO

Isola di San Michele

ORTO

Chiesa della Madonna dell'Orto

Sacca della Miseracordia

Canale delle Fondamente Nuove

Madonna dell'Orto

Campo dei Mori

S. Fosca

Lunga Santa Caterina

Chiesa dei Gesuiti

Fondamenta Zen

FONDAMENTA NOVE

Fondamenta Nuove

Calle Larga dei Botteri

0   200 yards
0   200 meters

N STAE

Lush

Strada Nuova

Ca' d'Oro
CA' D'ORO

CAMPO DEI S.S. APOSTOLI

Calle Racchetta

Calle Delle Vele

Ruga Due Pozzi

C. del Fumo

Calle dello Squero

Rio dei Mendicanti

OSPEDALE

Vaporetti Stops

CELESTIA

S.S. Giovanni e Paolo

Barbaria delle Tole

C. d. Cappuccine

SAN POLO

Ponte di Rialto

CAMPO S. BARTOLOMEO

Rio d. San Marina

CAMPO S. MARIA FORMOSA

Ruga Giuffa

Ponte Rosso

TO 34 (10km)

RIALTO

SAN SILVESTRO

Riva del Vin

Riva del Carbon

Sal. di S. Lio

CAMPO SAN LORENZO

Scuola Dalmata San Giorgio Degli Schiavoni

C. F. Furlani

TO ARSENALE

Grande

Calle dei Fabbri

CASTELLO

Calle Lion

CAMPO BANDIERA E MORO

CAMPO MANIN

Calle d. Mandola

CAMPO SANT' ANGELO

Calle d. Luca

Piera S. Luca

San Marco

Rio d. Palazzo o della Paglia

C. d. Corona

C. d. Madonna

33

Fond. Osmarin

S. Provolo

S. Zaccaria

CAMPO S. ZACCARIA

C. della Pietà

C. del Dose

C. del Forno

C. Crosera

TO GIARDINI PUBLICI

SAN MARCO

Frezzaria

PIAZZA SAN MARCO

Palazzo Ducale

Riva degli Schiavoni

ARSENALE

Rio della Ostreghe

Rio di San Moisè

S. ZACCARIA

SAN MARCO

GIGLIO

SALUTE

Canale di San Marco

Rio Fornace

SEE CENTRAL VENICE MAP

Zattere ai Saloni

SAN GIORGIO

San Giorgio Maggiore

Isola di S. Giorgio Maggiore

TO LIDO

ZITELLE

TO 31 (100m)

Fond. delle Zitelle

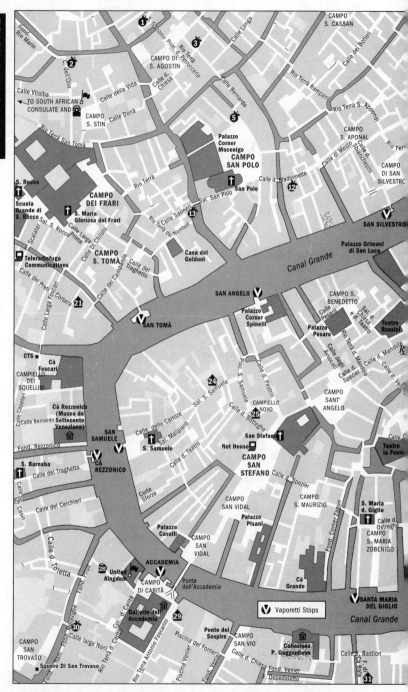

Vaporetti Stops

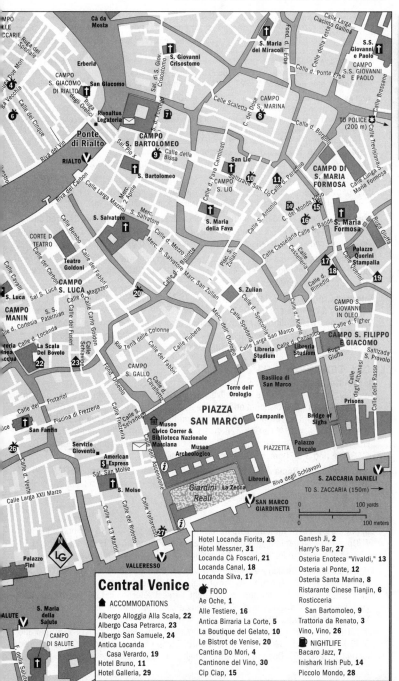

Central Venice

♦ ACCOMMODATIONS

Albergo Alloggia Alla Scala, **22**
Albergo Casa Petrarca, **23**
Albergo San Samuele, **24**
Antica Locanda
  Casa Verardo, **19**
Hotel Bruno, **11**
Hotel Galleria, **29**
Hotel Locanda Fiorita, **25**
Hotel Messner, **31**
Locanda Cà Foscari, **21**
Locanda Canal, **18**
Locanda Silva, **17**

🍴 FOOD

Ae Oche, **1**
Alle Testiere, **16**
Antica Birraria La Corte, **5**
La Boutique del Gelato, **10**
Le Bistrot de Venise, **20**
Cantina Do Mori, **4**
Cantinone del Vino, **30**
Cip Ciap, **15**

Ganesh Ji, **2**
Harry's Bar, **27**
Osteria Enoteca "Vivaldi," **13**
Osteria al Ponte, **12**
Osteria Santa Marina, **8**
Ristarante Cinese Tianjin, **6**
Rosticceria
  San Bartomoleo, **9**
Trattoria da Renato, **3**
Vino, Vino, **26**

🌙 NIGHTLIFE

Bacaro Jazz, **7**
Inishark Irish Pub, **14**
Piccolo Mondo, **28**

directly opposite the Basilica at P. S. Marco, 71/F (☎/fax 041 529 87 40; open daily 9am-3:30pm, AmEx/MC/V); Lido, Gran Viale, 6/A (☎041 526 57 21; open June-Sept. daily 9am-12:30pm and 3:30-6pm). Every location offers fairly pricey city tours and sells *vaporetto* tickets and schedules (€0.60), as well as the **Rolling Venice Card** (see below) and theater and concert tickets. **AVA** (☎041 171 52 88), in train station, to right of tourist office. Finds available hotel rooms and makes same-day reservations in Venice and Rome (€1). Open daily 8am-10pm. **Branches** at P. Roma (☎041 522 86 40) and at airport (☎041 541 51 33) book rooms for €2.

Rolling Venice Card: Provides discounts at over 200 restaurants, cafes, hotels, museums, and shops for people ages 14-29. Tourist offices provide lists of participating vendors. Card costs €3 and is valid 1 year from date of purchase. A 3-day *vaporetto* pass with card discount costs €15 instead of the undiscounted €22. Purchase it at the **ACTV VeLa** office (☎041 274 76 50; open daily 7am-8pm) in P. Roma, at all APT tourist offices, and at ACTV VeLa kiosks next to the **Ferrovia, Rialto, S. Marco,** and **Vallaresso** *vaporetto* stops.

Budget Travel: CTS, Fondamenta Tagliapietra, Dorsoduro, 3252 (☎041 520 56 60; www.cts.it). From Campo S. Barnaba, cross the bridge closest to the church and follow the road through the small piazza. Turn left at foot of large bridge. Sells ISICs and discounted plane tickets. Open M-F 9:30am-1:30pm and 2:30-6pm. MC.

Consulates: Cross Accademia Bridge from San Marco and turn right for **UK,** Dorsoduro, 1051 (☎041 522 72 07; open M-F 10am-noon and 2-3pm). **US** (☎02 29 03 51) and **Australian** consulates in Milan; **Canadian** consulate (☎049 878 11 47) in Padua.

Currency Exchange: Use banks whenever possible for best rates and inquire about additional fees beforehand. The streets around San Marco, San Polo, and the train station are full of banks and **ATMs.**

American Express: Cal. S. Moise, San Marco, 1471 (☎041 520 08 44 or 800 87 20 00 for lost or stolen checks, fax 041 522 99 37). Exit P. S. Marco facing away from the basilica and walk 2min. **Currency exchange** at average rates, but no commission for members or Rolling Venice card-holders. Office open for currency exchange M-F 9am-5:30pm, Sa 9am-12:30pm. Closed Sa in winter.

LOCAL TRANSPORT

Car Rental: Expressway, P. Roma, 496/N (☎041 522 30 00; www.expresswayautonoleggio.com). 18+. Free car delivery to and from airport. From €50 per day and €300 per week. 40% discount on full price rentals with *Let's Go* or student ID. Open M-F 8am-noon and 1:30-6pm and Sa-Su 8am-noon and 1:30-4:30pm. AmEx/MC/V. **Hertz,** P. Roma, 496/F (☎041 528 40 91, fax 520 06 14). 25+. Credit card required. From €55 per day. Open in summer M-F 8am-6pm, Sa-Su 8am-1pm; in winter M-F 8am-12:30pm and 3-5:30pm, Sa 8am-1pm. AmEx/MC/V.

24hr. Parking: P. Roma (☎041 272 73 01) and island of **Tronchetto** (☎041 520 75 55). Around €20 per day. Parking is considerably cheaper on the mainland. Consider parking in **Mestre** (1st train stop out of Venice).

LOCAL SERVICES

Luggage Storage: At the train station. €3.50 for the 1st 5hr., €0.30 per hr. for the next 7. Open daily 6am-midnight. Cash only. **Deposito Pullman Bar,** P. Roma, 497 (☎041 523 11 07), next to Pullman Bar. €3 per day. Open daily 6am-9pm. Cash only.

English-Language Bookstores: Libreria Studium, San Marco, 337/C (☎/fax 041 522 23 82). From P. S. Marco, head left on Cal. delle Canonico between the basilica and the clock tower; it's the last shop on the right. Largest selection in town, with novels and guidebooks. 10% discount with Rolling Venice card. Open M-Sa 9am-7:30pm. AmEx/MC/V. **Libreria Linea D'Acqua,** Cal. della Mandola, San Marco 3717/D (☎041 522 40 30). Follow Cal. Cortesia out of Campo Manin. Open M-Sa 10:30am-12:45pm and 3:30-7:15pm. AmEx/MC/V. **Giunti Al Punto,** Campo S. Geremia, 283/A, Cannaregio (☎041 275 01 52). Open M-Sa 9am-midnight, Su 10am-midnight. MC/V.

Laundromat: Lavanderie Self-Service, Cal. della Chioverette, Santa Croce, 665/B (☎348 301 74 57). From Ponte Scalzi, turn right on F. S. Piccolo and left on Cal. del Traghetto de S. Lucia. Wash €3 for 30min. Dry €2 for 20min. Open daily 7am-10pm.

Public Toilets: AMAV W.C. Under white and blue signs. €0.50. Open daily 9am-8pm.

EMERGENCY AND COMMUNICATIONS

Emergency: ☎113 or 112. **First Aid** (☎118). **Fire** (☎115).

Carabinieri: Campo S. Zaccaria, Castello, 4693/A (☎041 274 111). **Questura,** V. Nicolodi, 21, Marghera (☎041 271 57 67).

Pharmacy: Farmacia Italo-Inglese, Cal. della Mandola, San Marco, 3717 (☎041 522 48 37). Follow Cal. Cortesia out of Campo Manin. There are no 24hr. pharmacies in Venice, but late-night and weekend pharmacies rotate. Check the list posted in the window of any pharmacy. Open M-F 9am-12:30pm and 3:45-7:30pm, Sa 9am-12:45pm. MC/V.

Hospital: Ospedale Civile, Campo SS. Giovanni e Paolo, Castello (☎041 529 41 11).

Internet: The hip ◪**Casanova,** Lista di Spagna, Cannaregio, 158/A, keeps 5 computers with speedy connection. There may be a wait. (☎041 275 01 99. €4 for 30min. and €7 per hr., students €2.50/€4. Internet 9am-11:30pm. AmEx/MC/V for purchases of at least €10.) **Net House,** Campo S. Stefano, San Marco, 2967 and 2958, offers Internet and laptop connections. (☎041 227 11 90, fax 041 520 81 28. €7 per hr., with ISIC or Rolling Venice €5. Open daily 8am-3am. AmEx/MC/V.) **VeNice,** Lista di Spagna, Cannaregio, 149, has fax, webcams, and CD burning. Student discounts and international calling cards are available. (☎041 275 82 17. €4.50 for 30 min., €8 per hr. Open daily 9am-midnight. MC/V for purchases of at least €10.)

Post Office: Poste Venezia Centrale, Salizzada Fontego dei Tedeschi, San Marco, 5554 (☎041 271 71 11), off Campo S. Bartolomeo. Fermoposta at window #16. Open M-Sa 8:30am-6:30pm. Cash only. **Branch office** (☎041 528 59 49), through the arcades at the end of P. S. Marco and opposite the basilica, has ATM, pay phones, and a verbal/hearing-impaired phone. Open M-F 8:30am-2pm, Sa 8:30am-1pm. Cash only. **Postal Codes:** San Marco: 30124; Castello: 30122; San Polo: 30125; Santa Croce: 30135; Cannaregio: 30121; Dorsoduro: 30123.

▗▖ ACCOMMODATIONS AND CAMPING

The heavily touristed Venetian hotels are often more expensive than other areas of Italy, but savvy travelers can find cheap alternatives if they sniff out options early in the summer. Agree on a price before booking, and try to make reservations one month ahead. Dorm-style rooms are sometimes available without reservations even in summer. The **AVA** (see **Information Offices**) finds rooms with same-day availability, but they will not be cheap. If you're looking for a miracle, try religious institutions, which offer dorms and private rooms in the summer for €25-70. Options include: **Casa Murialdo,** Fondamenta Madonna dell'Orto, Cannaregio, 3512 (☎041 71 99 33); **Patronato Salesiano Leone XIII,** Cal. S. Domenico, Castello, 1281 (☎041 240 36 11); **Domus Cavanis,** Dorsoduro, 896 (☎041 528 73 74), near the Accademia Bridge; **Istituto Canossiano,** F. delle Romite, Dorsoduro, 1323 (☎041 240 97 11); and **Istituto Ciliota,** Cal. Muneghe S. Stefano, San Marco, 2976 (☎041 520 48 88).

CANNAREGIO AND SANTA CROCE

The station area, around the Lista di Spagna, has some of Venice's best budget accommodations. Although a 20min. *vaporetto* ride and a 15-25min. walk from most major sights, the neighborhood bustles at night with students and young travelers and offers easy island *vaporetti* (V:) access from Fondamente Nuove.

🏨 **Alloggi Gerotto Calderan,** Campo S. Geremia, 283 (☎041 71 55 62; www.casagerottocalderan.com). 34 bright rooms with squeaky-clean bath. Near the train and bus stations. Check-out 10am. Check-in 2pm. Curfew 12:30am. Reserve at least 15 days ahead. Dorms €21; singles €36, with bath €41; doubles €60/€93; triples €84/€93. 10% Rolling Venice discount; lower prices with extended stay. Cash only. ❷

🏨 **Locanda Cà San Marcuola,** Campo S. Marcuola, Cannaregio, 1763 (☎041 71 60 48; www.casanmarcuola.com). From the Lista di Spagna, follow signs for S. Marcuola. 2 stone lions flank the entrance next to V: San Marcuola. Large rooms have bath, A/C, and TV. Free Internet. Wheelchair accessible. Breakfast included. Reception 24hr. Singles €70-80; doubles €120-125; triples €150-160; quads €185-200. AmEx/MC/V. ❺

🏨 **Hotel Bernardi-Semenzato,** Cal. dell'Oca, Cannaregio, 4366 (☎041 522 72 57; mtpepoli@tin.it). From V: Cà d'Oro, turn right on Str. Nuova, left on Cal. del Duca, then right on Cal. dell'Oca. Staff is helpful. Check-out 10:30am. Curfew 1am; ask for key if returning later. Singles without bath €30; doubles €50-65, with bath €75-100; triples €90; quads €85/€110. 10% Rolling Venice discount on larger rooms. AmEx/MC/V. ❸

Hotel La Forcola, Cannaregio, 2353 (☎041 524 14 84; www.laforcolahotel.com). From the station, turn left on Lista di Spagna, then take a direct left after the 2nd bridge. Former Venetian palace with 23 rooms, many with canal views. All rooms have bath, A/C, TV, and minibar. Wheelchair accessible. Breakfast included. Reception 24hr. Singles €80-100; doubles €130-165; triples €180-215; quad €200-250. AmEx/MC/V. ❺

Hotel Tintoretto, Santa Fosca, 2316 (☎041 72 15 22; www.hoteltintoretto.com). Head down Lista di Spagna from the station and follow the signs. 3 floors of cheery, wide rooms, with carpet, bath, A/C, and TV; many have canal view. Amenities vary from hotel to annex. Breakfast included. Reception 24hr. Singles €41-120; doubles €74-175. Extra bed €37. Prices vary seasonally. AmEx/MC/V. ❹

Ostello Santa Fosca, Fondamenta Canal, Cannaregio, 2372 (☎/fax 041 71 57 75; www.santafosca.it). From Lista di Spagna, turn into Campo S. Fosca. Cross 1st bridge and turn left on Fondamenta Canal. Student-operated, church-affiliated, and quiet. Internet available. July-Sept. curfew 12:30am. Oct.-June no curfew. Dorms €18; singles €21; doubles €42. €2 discount with ISIC or Rolling Venice. MC/V. ❷

Hotel Rossi, Lista di Spagna, Cannaregio, 262 (☎041 71 51 64; rossihotel@interfree.it). Friendly staff keeps 14 spacious rooms with A/C in a small hotel at the end of a quiet alley. Small bookshelf with multilingual selection. Breakfast included. Reception 24hr. June-Sept. reserve at least 1 month ahead. Singles €53, with bath €69; doubles €77/€92; triples €112; quads €132. 10% Rolling Venice discount. MC/V. ❹

Albergo Adua, Lista di Spagna, Cannaregio, 233/A (☎041 71 61 84; www.aduahotel.com). Large rooms with A/C and TV, but stark white walls, furniture, and bedspread lack any memorable character. Breakfast €6. Singles €50, with bath €90; doubles €70/€120; triples €90/€180 depending on season. Hotel offers cheaper rooms at a different location; inquire at reception or call for more information. AmEx/MC/V. ❹

Ostello di Venezia (HI), Fondamenta Zitelle, Giudecca, 87 (☎041 523 82 11; www.hostelbooking.com). Take V #41, 42, or 82 to Zitelle. Turn right along canal. Efficiently managed with sparkling baths and sweeping view of the water. 250 beds on single-sex floors. Must book through website; do not call to reserve. Breakfast included. Dinner €8. Sheets included. Reception 7-9:30am and 1:30-11:30pm. Lock-out 9:30am-1:30pm. Curfew 11:30pm. HI members only; cards for sale. Dorms €16.50. MC/V. ❷

Istituto Canosiano, Ponte Piccolo, Giudecca, 428 (☎/fax 041 522 21 57). Take V #82 or 41 to Palanca, and cross the bridge on the left. Women-only. 35 beds in large dorms. Sheets included. Reception 3pm-curfew. Lockout noon-3pm. Strict curfew in summer 10:30pm; in winter 10pm. Dorms €15. ❷

SAN MARCO AND SAN POLO

Surrounded by designer boutiques, souvenir stands, scores of restaurants, near-domesticated pigeons, and many of Venice's most popular sights, these accommodations are pricey options for those in search of Venice's showy side.

▨ **Albergo Casa Petrarca,** Cal. Schiavine, San Marco, 4386 (☎041 520 04 30). From Campo S. Luca, follow Cal. Fuseri, take 2nd left and then a right. Cheerful proprietors run a tiny hotel with 7 bright rooms, most with bath. Most rooms A/C. Singles €45-48; doubles €90-110. Cash only. ❹

Albergo San Samuele, Salizzada San Samuele, San Marco, 3358 (☎/fax 041 522 80 45; www.albergosansamuele.it). Follow Cal. delle Botteghe from Campo S. Stefano and turn left on Salizzada S. Samuele. Large, clean rooms in an aging hotel with a dark interior courtyard. Location 2min. from V: San Samuele and 10min. from P. S. Marco is a bargain. Reception until midnight. Reserve 1-2 months ahead. Singles €26-45; doubles €36-75, with bath €46-105; triples €135. Cash only. ❸

Hotel Locanda Fiorita, Campiello Novo, San Marco, 3457/A (☎041 523 47 54; www.locandafiorita.com). From Campo S. Stefano, take Cal. del Pestrin, then climb onto the raised piazza. A sunny courtyard and terrace lead to large carpeted rooms, all with A/C and TV. 3-star annex nearby has satellite TV and Internet jacks. Breakfast included. Reception 24hr. Singles without bath €80; doubles €110-180, depending on location and whether shower is private. Extra bed 30%. AmEx/MC/V. ❺

Domus Civica (ACISJF), Campiello Chiovere Frari, San Polo, 3082 (☎041 72 11 03, fax 522 71 39). From station, cross Ponte Scalzi and turn right. Turn left on Fondamenta dei Tolentini and left through the courtyard onto Corte Amai. The hostel's rounded facade is to the right, after the bridge. 123 beds in spartan white, dorm-style rooms with window, table, chair, and cabinet. Shared coed bath, TV room, and piano. Reception 7:30am-11:30pm. Strict curfew 11:30pm. Open June-Sept. 25. Singles €28.50; doubles and triple €52. 15% Rolling Venice discount; 20% ISIC discount. Cash only. ❸

Casa Peron, Salizzada S. Pantalon, San Polo, 84 (☎041 71 00 21; www.casaperon.com). From station, cross Ponte Scalzi and turn right. Turn left just before the bridge and continue down Fond. Minotto until Casa Peron appears on the left. All rooms with A/C. Proximity to Campo Santa Margherita. Breakfast included. Reception until 1am. Singles €30, with bath €90; doubles €50/€95; triples €80/€120. V. ❸

Albergo Alloggia Alla Scala, Corte Contarini del Bovolo, San Marco, 4306 (☎041 521 06 29, fax 522 64 51). From Campo Manin facing the bridge, turn left on the alley and look for signs to La Scala del Bovolo; hotel is just beyond, in the alleyway. Superb location and simple rooms with bath, but aging furniture and decor give a dated feel. Breakfast €9. Reception 24hr. Singles €55; doubles €90; triples €117. AmEx/MC/V. ❹

CASTELLO

Castello, the *sestiere* where most Venetians live, is arguably the prettiest part of Venice. A second- or third-floor room with a view of the sculpted skyline is worth the inevitability of getting lost in the dead ends and barricaded alleys of some of the narrowest and most tightly clustered streets in the city.

▨ **Foresteria Valdese,** Castello, 5170 (☎041 528 67 97; www.diaconiavaldese.org/venezia). From Campo S. Maria Formosa, take Cal. Lunga S. Maria Formosa; it's over the 1st bridge. An 18th-century private guest house run by Venice's largest Protestant church, 2min. from major sights. 64 beds. Breakfast included. Lockout 10am-1pm. No curfew. No reservations except for groups. Internet €5 per hr. Dorm-style bed €21-22; doubles with TV €57, with bath and TV €75; quads with bath and TV €104; 5-person rooms with bath €126; apartments (no breakfast) €104-116. Rooms larger than singles require min. 2-night stay. Rolling Venice discount €1; discount for cash payment 2%. MC/V. ❷

▓ **La Residenza,** Campo Bandiera e Moro, Castello, 3608 (☎041 528 53 15; www.venicelaresidenza.com). From V: Arsenal, turn left on Riva degli Schiavoni and right on Cal. del Dose into the *campo*. In 15th-century palace. All rooms with bath, safe, A/C, TV, and minibar. Breakfast included. Reception 24hr. Singles €60-95; doubles €100-155. Extra bed and breakfast €30-35. MC/V. ❺

▓ **Antica Locanda Casa Verardo,** Castello, 4765 (☎041 528 61 27; www.casaverardo.it). From the Basilica, take Cal. Canonica, turn right before bridge and left over the bridge on Ruga Giuffa into Campo S. Filippo e Giacomo. Follow Cal. della Chiesa left out of the *campo* until reaching a bridge. 16th-century palace boasts 20 rooms with A/C and TV. Most have tub and shower. Terrace breakfast included. Singles €60-100; doubles €80-240. Discounts for web reservations or cash payment. AmEx/MC/V. ❺

Hotel Bruno, Salizzada S. Lio, Castello, 5726/A (☎041 523 04 52; www.hoteldabruno.com). From Campo S. Bartolomeo, take the Salizzada S. Lio, crossing the bridge. This elegant hotel's rooms have carved headboards, bath, TV, phone, and A/C. Breakfast included. Singles €60-160; doubles €80-215; triples €120-260. AmEx/MC/V. ❺

Locanda Silva, Fondamenta del Rimedio, Castello, 4423 (☎041 522 76 43 or 523 78 92; www.locandasilva.it). From P. S. Marco, walk under clock tower, turn right on Cal. Larga S. Marco, and left on Cal. d. Angelo before the bridge. Head right on Cal. d. Rimedio before next bridge and follow to the end. Breakfast included in sunny nook over canal. Reception 24hr. Open Feb.-Nov. Singles €40-45, with bath €65; doubles €70/€100; triples €120-135; quads €130-155. MC/V. ❹

Locanda Canal, Fondamenta del Rimedio, Castello, 4422/C (☎041 523 45 38, fax 241 91 38), next to Locanda Silva. 7 clean rooms in a converted 14th-century palazzo; some overlook the canal. Showers, toilets, and beds share the same area. Some rooms without shower. Breakfast included. Doubles €70-83; triples €90-105. ❺

DORSODURO

Spartan facades line the still canals that trace the quiet streets of Dorsoduro. Here, art museums draw visitors to canalfront real estate, while the interior remains a little visited residential quarter around Campo Santa Margherita, the city's most vibrant student social hub. Situated near the Grand Canal between Chiesa dei Frari and Ponte Accademia, most hotels here tend to be pricey.

▓ **Locanda Cà Foscari,** Cal. della Frescada, Dorsoduro, 3887/B (☎041 71 04 01; www.locandacafoscari.com), in a quiet neighborhood. From V: San Tomà, turn left at the dead end, cross the bridge, turn right, then turn left at the alley. *Carnevale* masks embellish this tidy hotel, run for 40 years by the Scarpa family. Breakfast included. Reception 24hr. Book 2-3 months ahead. Closed July 28-1st week in Aug. Singles €62; doubles €72, with bath €93; triples €90/€114; quads €112. MC/V. ❹

Hotel Galleria, Rio Terra Antonio Foscarini, Dorsoduro, 878/A (☎041 523 24 89; www.hotelgalleria.it), on the left facing the Accademia museum. 10 rooms on the small side, but hardwood floors lend an aura of elegance mere meters from the Grand Canal. Breakfast included. Reception 24hr. Singles €75; doubles €100, with bath €115, with view €180; triples €130/€190. Extra bed 30%. AmEx/MC/V. ❺

Hotel Messner, Madonna della Salute, Dorsoduro, 216/217 (☎041 522 74 43; messnerinfo@tin.it). From V: Salute, walk up F. della Salute and turn right over last bridge. Street ends at F. di Cà Bala. 31 rooms range from institutional singles to quads with bath and kitchenette. All rooms have bath, phone, and A/C on request. Cheaper one-star annex rooms do not have A/C or TV. Buffet breakfast included. Reception 24hr. Singles €80-100, doubles €120/€160; triples €140/180. Annex singles €70-90; doubles €90-115; triples €130-145; quads €140-160. AmEx/MC/V. ❺

CAMPING

Plan on at least a 20min. boat ride from Venice. In addition to these listings, the Litorale del Cavallino, on the Lido's Adriatic side, has multiple beach campsites.

Camping Miramare, Lungomare Dante Alighieri, 29 (☎041 96 61 50; www.camping-miramare.it). A 40min. ride on V #14 from P. S. Marco to Punta Sabbioni. Campground is 700m along the beach on the right. 3-night min. in high season. Open Apr. 1-Nov. 2. €4.30-6.40 per person, €8.90-13.70 per tent; bungalows €27-62 plus normal per person camping charge. Rolling Venice discount only on per person cost 15%. MC/V. ❶

Camping Fusina, V. Moranzani, 93 (☎041 547 00 55; www.camping-fusina.com), in Malcontenta. From Mestre, take bus #1. Restaurant, garden, laundromat, ATM, Internet, and TV onsite. Call ahead to reserve cabins. Free hot showers. €7 per person, €4 per tent, €14 per car with tent. Cabin singles €13; doubles €26. AmEx/MC/V. ❶

⬚ FOOD

In Venice, authentic, untouristed dining may require some exploration—beware the overpriced restaurants that line the canals around San Marco and shamelessly advertise their *menù turistico*. With few exceptions, the best restaurants lie along less traveled alleyways. Naturally, Venetian cuisine is dominated by fish. *Sarde in saor* (sardines in vinegar and onions) is available only in Venice and can be sampled cheaply at most bars with *cicchetti*. The Veneto and Friuli regions produce an abundance of excellent **wines.** Local whites include *Prosecco della Marca*, the dry *Tocai*, and *bianco di Custoza*. For reds, try a *Valpolicella*. The least expensive option is by no means inferior: a simple *vino della casa* (house wine) is usually a highly drinkable local merlot or chardonnay. For informal alternatives to traditional dining, visit an *osteria* or *bacaro* for filled pastries, seafood, rice, or *tramezzini* (soft white bread with any imaginable filling).

Venice's internationally renowned Rialto **markets,** once the center of trade for the Venetian Republic, spread between the Grand Canal and the San Polo foot of the Rialto every morning from Monday to Saturday. Smaller produce markets set up in Cannaregio, on Rio Terra S. Leonardo by Ponte delle Guglie, and in many of the city's *campi*. The BILLA **supermarket,** Str. Nuova, Cannaregio, 3660, offers standard grocery fare with small bakery and deli near *Campo San Fosca*. (Open M-Sa 8:30am-8pm, Su 9am-8pm. AmEx/MC/V.) Smaller FULL **Alimentari,** Cal. Carminati, 5989, Castello, is just north of P. S. Marco. (Open M-Th 9am-1pm and 3:45-7:30pm, F-Sa 9am-7:30pm. MC/V.)

CANNAREGIO

Trattoria da Bepi, Cannaregio, 4550 (☎/fax 041 528 50 31; dabepi@tin.it). From Campo SS. Apostoli, turn left on Salizzada del Pistor. Tourists and locals find attentive service and traditional Venetian cuisine at this warm trattoria. Enjoy the rich *frittura mista di pesce con polenta* (€14.50) and steady pedestrian parade past the popular tables outdoors. *Primi* €7-11, *secondi* from €10. Cover €1.50. Reservation suggested for outdoor seating. Open M-W and F-Su noon-2:30pm and 7-10pm. MC/V. ❸

Pizzeria La Perla, Rio Terra dei Franceschi, Cannaregio, 4615 (☎/fax 041 528 51 75). From Str. Nuova, turn left on Salizzada del Pistor in Campo SS. Apostoli. Follow to the end, then follow signs for the Fondamente Nuove. Friendly staff serves heaping portions of no fewer than 90 types of hearty pizza and pasta. Wheelchair accessible. Pizza €4.65-7.90. Pasta €6.10-8.20. Cover €1.10. Service 10%. Open M-Tu and Th-Su noon-3pm and 7-9:45pm, daily in Aug. AmEx/MC/V. ❷

Gam Gam, Canale di Cannaregio, Cannaregio, 1122 (☎041 71 52 84). From Campo S. Geremia, cross the bridge and turn left. Religious artwork adorns the interior of the only Jewish kosher restaurant in Venice. Join Shabbat service on F night and enjoy a free Shabbat dinner after; all are welcome. Falafel platter €8.75. Pasta €7.50-9. 10% discount with *Let's Go.* Open M-Th noon-10pm and Su noon-5pm. Cash only. ❸

Osteria al Bomba, Cannaregio 4297/98 (☎041 520 51 75; www.osteriaalbomba.it). From Hotel Bernardi-Semenzato, exit right onto Strada Nuova, then turn right into the next alleyway. Sidle up to the bar and order a glass of *prosecco* (€1) or nab a plate of Venetian *cicchetti* (€1 for a skewer, €14 for a large mixture) of almost any variety. Open W-Sa 6-10pm, Su 11am-2:30pm and 6-10pm. MC/V. ❶

Brek, Lista di Spagna, Cannaregio, 124/A (☎041 244 01 58; www.brek.com). From the station, turn left. Mix and match flavorful dishes at this bustling fast-food chain. Vegetarian options available. Menu and prices change daily. *Primi* €3.40-4.10 *secondi* €3-5.50. Rolling Venice discount 10%. Open daily 8-10:30am for breakfast; Mar.-Sept. 11:30am-10:30pm, Oct.-Feb. 11:30am-10pm for dinner. AmEx/MC/V. ❷

CASTELLO

🖾 **La Boutique del Gelato,** Salizzada S. Lio, Castello, 5727 (☎041 522 32 83). From Campo Bartolomeo, walk under Sottoportego de la Bissa, then go straight, crossing the bridge into Campo S. Lio. Follow Salizzada S. Lio; it's on the left. Popular stand doles out rich, heavy gelato to scores of passers-by. Single scoop €0.80, 2 scoops €1.50. Open July-Aug. daily 10am-midnight; Sept.-June 10am-8:30pm. Cash only. ❶

Alle Testiere, Cal. del Mondo Novo, Castello, 5801 (☎/fax 041 522 72 20). From Campo S. Maria Formosa, take Cal. Mondo Novo. Traditional cuisine meets modern restaurant design in this tiny trattoria. *Primi* €14, *secondi* €22-23. Reservation recommended. Open Tu-Sa noon-3pm and 7pm-midnight. Closed July 24-Aug. 24. MC/V. ❹

Pizzeria/Trattoria Al Vecio Canton, Castello, 4738/A (☎041 528 51 76). From Campo S. Maria Formosa, with church on right, cross the bridge and follow Ruga Giuffa. Turn right at the end. A bustling neighborhood favorite. Cover €2. Service 12%. *Primi* €6-10, *secondi* €8-20. Open M and W-Su noon-3pm and 7pm-midnight. MC/V. ❷

Arcimboldo, Cal. dei Furlani, Castello, 3219 (☎/fax 041 528 65 69). From Riva Schiavoni, take Cal. Dose to Campo Bandiera and follow Salizzada S. Antonin straight to Furlani. Turn right at Scuola S. Giorgio on Cal. dei Furlani. Try specialty *pesce al forno con verdure di stagione* (baked fish with seasonal vegetables; €26, serves 2). Reservation recommended in summer. Pasta €8-14. Open M and W-Su noon-3pm and 7pm-midnight. Closed 10 days in mid-Aug. AmEx/MC/V. ❹

Cip Ciap, Cal. Mondo Novo, 5799/A (☎041 523 66 21). From Campo S. Maria Formosa, follow Cal. Mondo Novo. Huge pizzas from €3.65 to €8 calzones are surprisingly filling. There's no seating, but box it up and nab a bench in the campo nearby. Open M and W-Su 9am-9pm. Cash only. ❶

Osteria Santa Marina, Campo S. Marina, Castello, 5911 (☎/fax 041 528 52 39; www.osteriadisantamarina.it). From Cal. Lio, take Cal. Carminati to the end, turn right, follow to the end and turn left. Restaurant specializes in fish and delicate dishes like *insalate di granceda con asparagi e uova di quaglia* (€14). *Primi* €12, *secondi* €19-25. Cover €3. Open Tu-Sa 12:30-2:30pm and 7:30-10pm, M 7:30-10pm. MC/V. ❹

SAN MARCO

🖾 **Le Bistrot de Venise,** Cal. dei Fabbri, San Marco, 4685 (☎041 523 66 51; www.bistrotdevenise.com). From P. S. Marco, head through 2nd Sottoportego dei Dai under the awning. Follow road around and over a bridge; turn right. Scrumptious Venetian pasta dishes listed with century of origin served under an outdoor awning or in the art-adorned dining room. The motto is "cucina e cultura," and Oct.-May afternoon exhibitions draw local artisans, poets, and musicians. *Primi* from €10, *secondi* from €22. Service 15%. Rolling Venice discount 10%. Open daily noon-1am. MC/V. ❹

Vino, Vino, Ponte delle Veste, San Marco, 2007/A (☎041 241 76 88). From Cal. Larga XXII Marzo, turn on Cal. delle Veste. No-frills wine bar serves over 350 kinds. *Primi* €5.50, *secondi* €9-10.50. Cover €1. Open M, W-F, and Su 10:30am-midnight, Sa 10:30am-1am. Rolling Venice discount 15%. Cash only. ❸

Rosticceria San Bartomoleo, Cal. della Bissa, San Marco, 5424/A (☎/fax 041 522 35 69). From Campo S. Bartolomeo, follow the Calle de la Bissa to the neon sign. Full-service restaurant upstairs serves lunch. *Panini* from €1.10. Entrees from €5.90. Cover for restaurant €1.30. Open M 9am-4pm, Tu-Su 9am-9:30pm. AmEx/MC/V. ❶

Harry's Bar, Cal. Vallaresso, San Marco, 1323 (☎041 528 57 77), around the corner from the Venice Pavilion. Founded in 1931 by a Bostonian dismayed at the Venice bar scene, this cafe's white-jacketed waiters have expertly mixed drinks for notables like Ernest Hemingway, Katharine Hepburn, Robert DeNiro, and Tom Cruise. €13 buys the signature *Bellini,* a frothy pink favorite. Table service 15%. Open daily 10:30am-10:55pm. AmEx/MC/V. ❹

DORSODURO

▨ **Cantinone del Vino,** Fondamenta Meraviglie, Dorsoduro, 992 (☎041 523 00 34). From the Frari, follow signs for the Accademia bridge. Just before Ponte Meraviglie, turn right toward the church of S. Trovaso. Cross the 1st bridge. Individually priced bottles of wine fill long wooden shelves—enjoy a glass (from €0.70) at the bar with some flavorful *cicchetti* (from €1). Bottles €3-200. Open M-Sa 8:30am-8:30pm. Cash only. ❶

Gelateria Nico, Fondamenta Zattere, Dorsoduro, 922 (☎041 522 52 93). Near V: Zattere, with a great view of the Giudecca Canal from outdoor seating. For a guilty pleasure, try the Venetian ▨ **gianduiotto al passagetto** (a chunk of dense chocolate-hazelnut ice cream dropped into a cup of whipped cream; €2.30). Gelato €1, 2 scoops €1.50, 3 scoops €2. Open M-W and F-Su 6:45am-11pm. Cash only. ❶

Pizza al Volo, Campo S. Margherita, Dorsoduro, 2944 (☎041 522 54 30). Students and locals come for delicious, cheap pizza, ready-made by a young, friendly staff. Takeout only. House specialty *al volo* is a sauceless pizza topped with mozzarella and eggplant. Thin, massive slices from €1.50. Pizza from €3.50. Oversized pizza for 2 from €7. Open daily 11:30am-4pm and 5pm-1:30am. Cash only. ❶

ON THE MENU

VENETIAN FLAIR

After centuries of trade, tourism, and international traffic, certain cultural influences are bound to worm their way into Venice's staunchest local tradition. Even the most omnipresent local cuisine possesses a certain international flavor. *Cicchetti,* the small finger foods served at nearly every bar, cafe, and *enoteca* on the island, are a type of cuisine you'd be hard pressed to find in such massive amounts in any other Italian city.

Venice reportedly fell in love with these bite-sized snacks after Spaniards and Arab merchants introduced *tapas,* small mix-and-match plates of meats, vegetables, and fish, to their Italian clientele in the seaside port.

Eventually, the tradition took on its own decidedly Venetian flavor with regional sausages, vegetables, hard-boiled eggs, miniature *bruschette* topped with wet sauces, and of course, the city's famous sardines. *Cicchetti* come in a range of sizes and prices, from the €1 skewers of fried green olives that nearly every bar offers to the heaping €11-14 plates that offer a smorgasbord of food for the ultra-hungry to share. For the true experience, order a glass of wine, stand at the bar, take a deep breath, and sample the celebrated Venetian sardines in miniature—though the roots are global, the tradition's rich flavor and flair are unmistakably Venetian.

SAN POLO AND SANTA CROCE

Ae Oche, Santa Croce, 1552A/B (☎041 524 11 61). From Campo S. Giacomo, take Cal. del Trentor. Unfinished wood walls lined with relics like typewriters and coffee cans house over 100 types of pizza (€3.50-7.80) and a bustling crowd that spills out onto canal-side tables. *Primi* €5.50-7, *secondi* €6.50-12.50. Restaurant cover €1.40. Open daily noon-3pm and 7pm-midnight. Service 12%. MC/V. ❷

Osteria Enoteca "Vivaldi," San Polo, 1457 (☎041 523 81 85). From the Campo. S. Polo, opposite the church, cross the bridge to Cal. della Madonnetta. Try traditional Venetian *sarde in saor* (€8-10). *Primi* €8-10, *secondi* from €10. Cover €1.50. Service 10%. Reservations recommended F-Sa nights. Open daily 10:30am-2:30pm and 5:30-10:30pm. Kitchen opens at noon. AmEx/MC/V. ❸

Osteria al Ponte, Cal. Saoneri, San Polo, 2741/A (☎041 523 72 38). From Campo S. Polo, follow signs to Accademia; it's immediately across the 1st bridge. Hungry Venetians fill polished tables at this popular trattoria. Cover €1.50. *Primi* €6.50-9, *secondi* €7-14. Open M-Sa 10am-2:30pm and 6-10pm. AmEx/MC/V. ❷

Ristorante Ribò, Fondamenta Minotto, Santa Croce, 158 (☎041 524 24 86; www.ristoranteribo.com). From the station, cross Ponte Scalzi, then turn right. Turn left on F. dei Tolentini just before the bridge, then left on F. Minotto. Canal-side restaurant features private garden and stylish dining room. Business lunch with *primo, secondo,* vegetable, and coffee, water, or wine just €12. *Primi* €10.50-14.50, *secondi* €14-25. Cover €3. Open M-Tu and Th-Su 12:15-3pm and 7:15-10:30pm. AmEx/MC/V. ❹

Ganesh Ji, Cal. dell'Olio, San Polo, 2426 (☎/fax 041 71 98 04). From the station, cross the Scalzi Bridge, continue straight, and turn left on Cal. della Bergama. Turn right on Fond. Rio Marin and right on Cal. dell'Olio. Indian food served on a canalfront terrace. Vegetarian lunch €12, regular €13.50. Cover €2.20. Open Tu-W and F-Su 12:30-2pm and 7pm-midnight, Th 7pm-midnight. Rolling Venice discount 10%. MC/V. ❹

Antica Birraria La Corte, Campo S. Polo, San Polo, 2168 (☎041 275 05 70; www.anticabirrarialacorte.com). The expansive interior of this former brewery houses a large restaurant and bar. Beer €1.50-4.30. Pizza €4.50-9. *Primi* €7-7.50, *secondi* €9.50-16.50. Cover €1.80. Open daily 10am-3pm and 6pm-midnight; mid-July to mid-Aug. Sa-Su open for lunch. AmEx/MC/V. ❷

Ristorante Cinese Tianjin, Ruga Rialto, San Polo, 649 (☎/fax 041 520 46 03). From V: San Silvestro, enter Campo San Silvestro and exit across the campo left onto Sal. Silvestro. Take the next right onto Rugo Rialto. Mix and match small plates (from €3.70-12) or add rice for a full meal. Open daily 10:30am-midnight. AmEx/MC/V.

Cantina Do Mori, Cal. dei Do Mori, San Polo, 429 (☎041 522 54 01). From the Rialto, follow signs to Campo S. Giacomo. Follow Orefici out straight; it turns into Ruga dei Spezier. Take 1st left, then the 1st right to find Venice's oldest wine bar. An elegant place to have a glass of local wine. No seating. Open M-Tu and Th-Sa 8:30am-2:30pm and 4:30-8:30pm, W 4:30-8:30pm, with sporadic closings summer afternoons. ❶

Trattoria da Renato, San Polo, 2245/A (☎041 524 19 22). Cross the bridge away from the Frari, turn left, and cross into Campo S. Stin; turn right on Cal. Donà and cross bridge. The decor is slightly offputting—neon orange plastic chairs and linoleum-patterned tile floors—and service can be rushed, but the €12 *menù* includes *primo, secondo,* salad, and fruit/cheese for one low price. Cover €1. *Primi* €5-8.50, *secondi* €6.50-14. Open M-W and F-Su 1-3:15pm and 7:15-10:30pm. Cash only. ❸

◎ SIGHTS

AROUND THE RIALTO BRIDGE

▨**THE GRAND CANAL.** Over 3km long, the Grand Canal loops through the city and passes under three bridges: **Ponte Scalzi, Rialto,** and **Ponte Accademia.** Coursing past the facades of the cheek-to-cheek palaces that crown its banks, the blue-green river is an undeniable reminder of Venice's history and immense wealth. Although each individual palazzo displays its own unique architectural blend of loggia, canal-side balconies, and marble sculptures; most share the same basic structural design. The most decorated floors, called *piani nobili* (noble floors, or second and third stories), housed luxurious salons and bedrooms. Rich merchant families stored their goods in the ground floor rooms, and servants slept in tiny chambers below the roof. The candy cane posts used for mooring boats on the canal are called *bricole* and are painted with the family colors of the adjoining palazzo. *(For great facade views, ride V #82 or the slower #1 from the train station to P. S. Marco. The facades are floodlit at night, producing a dazzling play of reflections.)*

■ RIVOALTUS LEGATORIA. Step into the tiny, book-lined Rivoaltus on any given day and hear Wanda Scarpa shouting greetings from the attic, where she has been sewing leather-bound journals for an international cadre of customers and faithful locals for three decades. The shop, run by arguably the nicest husband and wife tandem in Italy, overflows with Wanda's deep red portfolios, colorful leather journals, and heavy photo albums, all hand-crafted copies of 13th-century work made with vegetable dye leather and cotton paper from the Amalfi Coast. Giorgio Scarpa jokes that he chains her there to make her work. Though Venice is now littered with shops advertising handmade journals, Rivoaltus was the first, and sells products of such renowned quality that even movie stars have been known to send their agents specifically to this shop to buy portfolios—but unchanging prices mean that anyone can enjoy the books' love-laced quality craftsmanship. *(Ponte di Rialto 11, just over the hump of the bridge. ☎ 041 523 61 95. Basic notebooks €18-31, photo albums €31-78, Murano glass fountain pens with ink €5. Open daily 10am-7:30pm.)*

THE RIALTO BRIDGE. This impressive architectural structure was named after Rivo Alto, the first colony built in Venice. Originally built of wood, the bridge collapsed in the 1500s. Antonio da Ponte designed the current stone structure (1588-91), where strips of boutiques separate a wide central lane from two side passages with picture-perfect canal views. Pricey stores dominate the commercial space on the bridge, but unauthorized vendors manage to find their way to the heavily trafficked thoroughfare. Beware of overpriced, cheaply made goods that make the bridge's original wooden structure look positively invincible.

AROUND PIAZZA SAN MARCO

■ BASILICA DI SAN MARCO. Venice's crown jewel, San Marco is a spectacular fusion of gold mosaics on huge marble walls and rooftop balconies, gracing **Piazza San Marco** with symmetrical arches and incomparable mosaic portals. As the city's largest tourist attraction, the **Basilica di San Marco** also has the longest lines. Visit in the early morning for the shortest wait or in late afternoon for the best natural illumination. Construction of the basilica began in the 9th century, when two Venetian merchants stole St. Mark's remains from Alexandria and packed them in pork meat to smuggle them past Arab officials. After the first church dedicated to St. Mark burned down in the 11th century, Venice redesigned the church, snubbing the Roman Catholic Church's standard cross-shaped layout, opting for a Greek-cross plan with four short arms topped by five bulging domes. A cavernous interior sparkles with massive Byzantine and Renaissance mosaics. The blue-robed **Christ Pantocrator** (Ruler of All) sits above the high altar. Twelfth-century stone mosaics cover the floor in crisp geometric designs, though the church's foundation, which has been sinking for 900 years, has created uneven, wavy patches throughout. Behind the altar screen the large, rectangular **Pala D'Oro** relief frames a parade of saints in gem-encrusted gold; behind this masterpiece, the cement tomb of St. Mark himself rests within the altar, adorned only with a single gold-stemmed rose. Steep stairs in the atrium lead to the **Galleria della Basilica,** with an eye-level view of the tiny golden tiles that compose the Basilica's vast ceiling mosaics, a balcony overlooking the piazza below, and an intimate view of the bronze **Cavalli di San Marco** (Horses of St. Mark). Nearby, the **Cassine** displays mosaic heads (the most valuable and artistically challenging section of a masterpiece) removed during 1881 renovations. *(Basilica open M-Sa 9:30am-5pm and Su 2-4pm. Illuminated 11:30am-12:30pm. Free. Modest dress required. Baggage prohibited, follow signs to free baggage storage at the nearby Ateno San Basso on Calle San Basso, open daily 9:30am-5:30pm. Pala D'Oro open M-Sa 9:45am-5pm, Su 2-4pm. €1.50. Treasury open M-Sa 9:45am-5pm. €2. Galleria open M-F 9:45am-4:15pm, Sa-Su 9:45am-4:45pm. €3.)*

■ **PALAZZO DUCALE (DOGE'S PALACE).** Once the home of Venice's mayor, or Doge, the Palazzo Ducale museum contains spectacular artwork, including Veronese's *Rape of Europa.* When the city enlarged the palace in the 15th century, it maintained the original carved white marble design, despite opposition from Renaissance architects who claimed the building looked "upside-down." In the courtyard, Sansovino's enormous sculptures, *Mars* and *Neptune,* flank the Scala dei Giganti (Stairs of the Giants), upon which new Doges were crowned. On the balcony stands the Bocca di Leone (Lion's Mouth), into which the Council of Ten, the Doge's assistants, who acted as judges and administrators, would drop the names of those they suspected guilty of crimes. Climb the elaborate Scala d'Oro (Golden Staircase) to the Sala delle Quattro Porte (Room of the Four Doors), where the ceiling is covered in biblical judgements and masterful representations of mythological tales related to events in Venetian history. More doors lead through the courtrooms of the much-feared Council of Ten, the even-more-feared Council of Three, and the Sala del Maggior Consiglio (Great Council Room), dominated by *Tintoretto's Paradise,* the largest oil painting in the world. Near the end, thick stone lattices and uneven stones line the covered Ponte dei Sospiri (Bridge of Sighs) and continue into the prisons. Casanova was condemned by the Ten to walk across this bridge, which gets its name from 19th-century Romantic writers' references to the mournful groans of prisoners descending into the small, damp cells. *(☎041 520 90 70. Audioguides €5.50. Open Nov.-Mar. daily 9am-5pm, last entry 4pm; Apr.-Oct. 9am-7pm, last entry 6pm. Wheelchair accessible. €11, students €5.50, ages 6-14 €3. MC/V. Includes entrance to Museo Correr, Museo Archeologico, and Biblioteca Nazionale Marciana. Pass for above museums €15.50, students €10.)*

PIAZZA SAN MARCO. Unlike the labyrinthine streets that tangle through most of Venice, Piazza San Marco, Venice's only official piazza, is a magnificent expanse of light, space, architectural harmony, and pigeons. Enclosing the piazza are rows of cafes and expensive jewelry and glass shops along the ground floors of the Renaissance **Procuratie Vecchie** (Old Treasury Offices), the Baroque **Procuratie Nuove** (New Treasury Offices), and the Neoclassical **Ala Napoleonica** (more Treasury Offices). At the end of the piazza near the shoreline of the lagoon sits the **Basilica di San Marco,** where gold mosaics and marble horses overlook the chaos below. Between the basilica and the Procuratie Vecchie perches the **Torre dell'Orologio (Clock Tower),** constructed between 1496 and 1499, according to Coducci's design. The 24hr. clock indicates the hour, lunar phase, and ascending constellation. Unfortunately, this time-keeping treasure has been hidden from view for several years by restoration scaffolding. The 96m brick **campanile** (bell tower) provides one of the best elevated views of the city. Though it originally served as a watchtower and lighthouse, cruel and unusual Venice took advantage of its location to create a medieval tourist attraction by dangling state prisoners from its top in cages. The practice ceased in the 18th century, but public fascination with the tower did not. During a 1902 restoration project, it collapsed, but was reconstructed in 1912 with the enlightened addition of an elevator. On a clear day, Croatia and Slovenia are visible from the top, and panorama of the entire island of Venice and a lagoon full of trolling yachts is almost guaranteed. *(☎041 522 52 05. Audioguide €3. Campanile open daily 9am-9pm. €6.)*

PIAZZA SAN MARCO'S MUSEUMS. Beneath the arcade at the short end of P. San Marco lies the entrance to a trio of museums. The **Museo Civico Correr,** a Venetian history museum, fills most of the two-story complex with curiosities from the city's imperial past, including maps and models from naval planning, ornate Neo-classical artwork, weapons like a 16th-century key that fires poison darts, and ridiculously enormous platform shoes worn by sequestered noblewomen. The early rooms of the museum demonstrate the Neoclassical French influence on Venetian art, while others contain a medley of works by Bellini and Carpaccio. Near the end of the first floor, the **Museo Archeologico** houses a sizeable collection of ancient pieces, from first-century Egyptian funeral parchment to Greek and Roman sculpture. Also, a series of ceiling paintings by seven artists, including Veronese, adorn the dark, gilt-edged reading room of the **Biblioteca Nazionale Marciana,** built between 1537 and 1560. (☎041 522 49 51. Free guided tours in English for Museo Archeologico Sa-Su 11am; for Biblioteca Nazionale Marciana Sa-Su 10am, noon, 2, and 3pm. Museums open Apr.-Oct. daily 9am-7pm; Nov.-Mar. 9am-5pm. Ticket office closes 1hr. before museums. €11, students €5.50. Includes entrance to Palazzo Ducale. Passes that include the Museo Vetrario di Murano, and Museo del Merletto di Burano also available. Cash only.)

LA SCALA DEL BOVOLO. This brick and snow-white marble "staircase of the snails," as it translates into English, takes guests up five stories of tightly spiraling marble *loggia* to a circular portico at the top. Legend has it that the staircase was designed by Leonardo da Vinci and constructed by his assistants. It once led to the top floors of a now-destroyed palace. Today the top only affords views of the green courtyard below. (From the Campo Manin, facing the bridge, turn left down the alley and look for the signs. ☎041 271 90 12. Open Apr.-Oct. daily 10am-6pm; Nov.-Mar. Sa-Su 10am-4pm, daily in Carnevale. €3, groups of 10 or more €2.50. Cash only.)

 WHERE IT'S @. The "@" symbol reputedly originated in Venice. When Venetian merchants exported goods, they would write "@" in front of the package's address to distinguish the destination from the shipping point. La Scala del Bovolo was reportedly built in an "@"-like spiral shape because it was once attached to the palace of a wealthy merchant.

SAN POLO

SCUOLA GRANDE DI SAN ROCCO. The most illustrious of Venice's *scuole,* or guild halls, stands as a monument to Jacopo Tintoretto, who left Venice only once in his 76 years, and sought to combine "the color of Titian with the drawing of Michelangelo." To achieve the effect of depth, he often built dioramas and posed his models within so he could portray them with spatial accuracy. The school commissioned Tintoretto to complete all the paintings in the building, a task that took 23 years. The large room on the second floor provides hand mirrors to admire the delicate paintings mounted on the ceiling, but the wall-to-wall *Crucifixion* in the last room upstairs is the collection's crowning glory. Lined with intricately carved columns and colored marble, the *scuola* is a masterpiece in itself; step outside to admire it to the strains of classical music performed by street musicians outside. (Behind Basilica dei Frari in Campo S. Rocco. ☎041 523 48 64; www.scuolagrande-sanrocco.it. Audioguides free. Open daily Mar. 28-Nov. 2 9am-5:30pm; Nov. 3-Mar. 27 10am-4pm. €5.50, students and Rolling Venice cardholders €4, under 18 free. AmEx/MC/V.)

CAMPO SAN POLO. The second-largest *campo* (piazza) in Venice, **Campo San Polo** once hosted bull-baiting matches during the *Carnevale* where authorities would release a wild bull into the crowds, then set dogs on its tail. After the dogs began to tear the bull's flesh, the defeated animal would be decapitated before a cheering mob. A painting that depicts the ensuing chaos hangs in the Museo Correr in P. S. Marco. Today the paved *campo* is dotted with elderly women gossiping on benches, trees struggling through the cobblestones, and gelato-stained children, so modern visits generally involve less bloodshed. *(Between the Frari and Rialto Bridges. V: S. Silvestro. Straight back from the vaporetto. Or from in front of the Frari, cross bridge, then turn right, left on Rio Terà, right on Cal. Seconda d. Saoneri, and left at the end.)*

DORSODURO

■ **COLLEZIONE PEGGY GUGGENHEIM.** Guggenheim's elegant waterfront Palazzo Venier dei Leoni, once her home and a social haven for the world's artistic elite, now displays a private modern art collection maintained by the Solomon Guggenheim Foundation. The museum includes works by Duchamp, Klee, Kandinsky, Picasso, Magritte, Pollock, Dalí, and Guggenheim's confidante, Max Ernst. Look for the atypical *Sacrifice* by Rothko, which marks a departure from his usual abstract, color-focused technique. Guggenheim and her beloved pet Shih Tzus, from Sir Herbert to Peacock, are buried in the peaceful garden. The Marini sculpture *Angel in the City*, which sits (apparently aroused) on horseback on the terrace, was designed with a detachable penis so Ms. Guggenheim could make emergency alterations and not offend her more prudish guests. The ivy-lined marble terrace offers an unobstructed waterfront view of the Grand Canal. *(Fondamenta Venier dei Leoni, Dorsoduro, 710. V: Accademia. Turn left and follow the yellow signs. ☎ 041 240 54 11, fax 520 68 85. Audioguide €4. Open M and Th-Su 10am-6pm. Tickets close 5:45pm. €10, seniors €8, ISIC or Rolling Venice cardholders €5, under 12 free. AmEx/MC/V.)*

■ **GALLERIE DELL'ACCADEMIA.** This colossal gallery boasts the most extensive collection of Venetian art in the world. Among the enormous altarpieces in Room II, Giovanni Bellini's *Madonna Enthroned with Child, Saints, and Angels* stands out with its soothing serenity. Rooms IV and V display more Bellinis, including the magnificent *Madonna and Child with Magdalene and Saint Catherine*, and two works by Giorgione. Giorgione defied contemporary convention by creating works that apparently told no story. Attempts to find plot or moral in *The Tempest* have been fruitless. An X-ray of the pictures reveals that Giorgione originally painted a bathing woman where the young man now stands. In Room VI, three paintings by Tintoretto, *The Creation of the Animals*, *The Temptation of Adam and Eve*, and *Cain and Abel*, get progressively darker as one moves from the glowing God commanding flocks of animals to the graphic murder of Abel by Cain, who stands naked in darkness near a calf's severed head. Venetian Renaissance works line the rooms leading to Room X, home to Veronese's colossal *Supper in the House of Levi*. Originally painted as a Last Supper, the infuriated Inquisition council tried to force Veronese to modify his unorthodox interpretation of the memorable event, which depicts a Protestant German, a midget, dogs, and fat men. Instead, Veronese cleverly changed the title, saving his artistic license and his life. Several Tintorettos facing the entrance display the artist's virtuosity at painting figures in motion. On the opposite wall is Titian's last painting, a *Pietà* intended for his tomb, a request that was apparently ignored. In Room XX, works by Gentile Bellini and Carpaccio display Venetian cityscapes so accurately that scholars use them as "photos" of Venice's past. *(V: Accademia. ☎ 041 522 22 47, to pre-order tickets, call Teleart M-F ☎ 041 520 03 45. Audioguides €4. Guided tours in English, French, or Italian Tu-Su 11am-noon; €5.50. Open M 8:15am-2pm, Tu-Su 9:15am-7:15pm. €6.50, EU citizens under 18 or over 65 free. Cash only.)*

CÀ REZZONICO. Longhena's great 18th-century *palazzo* houses the newly restored **Museo del Settecento Veneziano** (Museum of 18th-Century Venice). Known as the "Temple of Venetian Settecento," this grand palace features a regal ballroom, complete with flowing curtains and Crosato's frescoed ceiling. Other rooms contain elaborate Venetian Rococo decor. Upstairs, two extensive portrait galleries display works by Tiepolo, Guardi, Longhi, and Tintoretto. *(V: Cà Rezzonico. Go straight into Campo S. Barnaba, cross 1st bridge on the right and turn right on Fondamenta Rezzonico. Reserve 24hr. ahead. ☎041 241 01 00. Audioguide €4. Open Apr.-Oct. M and W-Su 10am-6pm; Nov.-Mar. 10am-5pm. €5.50, students and Rolling Venice €4.50. Cash only.)*

CASTELLO

SCUOLA DALMATA SAN GIORGIO DEGLI SCHIAVONI. Some of Carpaccio's finest paintings, rendering episodes from the lives of St. George, Jerome, and Tryfon, decorate the ground floor of this modest, early 16th-century building. *(Castello, 3259/A. V: S. Zaccaria. From the Riva Schiavoni, take Cal. Dose to Campo Bandiera e Moro. Follow S. Antonin to Fondamenta Furlani. ☎041 522 88 28. Open Apr.-Oct. Tu-Sa 9:30am-12:30pm and 3:30-6:30pm, Su 9:30am-12:30pm; Nov.-Mar. Tu-Sa 10am-12:30pm and 3-6pm, Su 10am-12:30pm. Ticket office closes 30min. before Scuola. €3. Modest dress required.)*

GIARDINI PUBBLICI AND SANT'ELENA. Let's be honest, on a paved island surrounded by water, it's not easy being green. For a short commune with nature, walk through the shady gravel lanes of the bench-lined Public Gardens, installed by Napoleon, where children swarm over two playgrounds, trees and bushes sprout in droves, and the local geriatric elite gather to sit on benches and gossip. For a larger area to lounge, continue past the gardens and bring a picnic lunch to the shady lawns of Sant'Elena. *(V: Giardini or S. Elena. Free.)*

CANNAREGIO

JEWISH GHETTO. In 1516, the Doge forced Venice's Jewish population into the old cannon-foundry area, creating the first Jewish ghetto in Europe. *(Ghetto* is the Venetian word for foundry.) At its height, the ghetto housed 5000 people in buildings up to seven stories high, making them among the tallest tenements in Europe at the time; now, locals gather in this sequestered spot for the trees, cafes, and scattered marble benches of the **Campo del Ghetto Nuovo.** In the campo, the **Schola Grande Tedesca** (German Synagogue), the oldest area synagogue, now houses the **Museo Ebraica di Venezia** (Hebrew Museum of Venice). The opulent **Schola Levantina** (Levantine Synagogue) and **Schola Spagnola** (Spanish Synagogue), both designed at least in part by Longhena, stand in the adjacent Campiello d. Scuole. The Canton and Italian synagogues also occupy the area. *(Cannaregio, 2899/B. V: S. Marcuola. Follow signs straight, then turn left into Campo del Ghetto Nuovo. ☎041 71 53 59. Hebrew Museum open June-Sept. M-F and Su. 10am-7pm; Oct.-May 10am-4:30pm. €3, students €2. Entrance to synagogues by guided tour only. English tours leave from the museum June-Sept. every hr. 10:30am-5:30pm; Oct.-May 10:30am-3:30pm. Museum and tour €8, students €6.50. MC/V.)*

CÀ D'ORO. Built between 1425 and 1440, the intricate facade of this "Golden House" combines interlinked arches with delicate spires. Today it houses the **Galleria Giorgio Franchetti.** Highlights of the small museum include Andrea Mantegna's *Saint Sebastian,* Bonaccio's *Apollo Belvedere,* one of the most important bronzes of the 15th century, and two open balconies above the Grand Canal. For the best view of the balconies and adornments of Cà D'Oro's tiered "wedding cake" facade, take a *traghetto* across the canal to the Rialto Markets. *(V: Cà d'Oro. ☎041 52 23 49. Open M 8:15am-2pm, Tu-Su 8:15am-7:15pm. Audioguides €4. Tickets close a 30min. before galleria. €5, EU students and under 25 €2.50, art students free. Cash only.)*

CHURCHES

The Foundation for the Churches of Venice sells the **Chorus Pass** that covers admission to all of Venice's churches. A yearly pass (€8, students €5), which includes S. Maria dei Miracoli, S. Maria Gloriosa dei Frari, S. Polo, Madonna dell'Orto, Il Redentore, and S. Sebastiano, is available at most participating churches. (For information, call ☎ 041 275 04 62; www.chorusvenezia.org.)

◼ **CHIESA DI SAN ZACCARIA (SAN MARCO).** Dedicated to the father of John the Baptist and designed in the late 1400s by Coducci, among others, the Gothic-Renaissance church holds S. Zaccaria's incorruptible corpse in an elevated, glass-windowed sarcophagus along the right wall of the nave. Nearby, watch for Giovanni Bellini's *Virgin and Child Enthroned with Four Saints*, one of the masterpieces of Venetian Renaissance painting. Its rich tones and meticulous shading are a testament to the Venetian attention to detail. *(V: S. Zaccaria. From P. S. Marco, turn left along the water, cross the bridge, and turn left on Cal. Albanesi. Turn right, then go straight. ☎ 041 522 12 57. Open daily 10am-noon and 4-6pm. Free.)*

CHIESA DI SAN GIACOMO DI RIALTO (SAN POLO). Between the Rialto and surrounding markets stands Venice's first church, diminutively called "San Giacometto." An ornate clock-face adorns its *campanile.* Across the piazza, a statue called *il Gobbo* (the hunchback) supports the steps. Once a podium for public announcements, it was at the foot of this sculpture that convicted thieves, forced to run naked from P. S. Marco and lashed all the way by bystanders, could finally collapse. *(V: Rialto. Cross bridge and turn right. Church open daily 10am-5pm. Free.)*

BASILICA DI SANTA MARIA GLORIOSA DEI FRARI (SAN POLO). Franciscans began construction on the Gothic church, also known simply as *I Frari*, in 1340. Today, the cavernous gray interior boasts two paintings by Titian as well as the Renaissance master himself, who is entombed within the cathedral's cavernous terra-cotta walls. His ◼**Assumption** (1516-18), on the high altar, marks the height of the Venetian Renaissance. Titian's other work, *The Madonna and Child with Saints and Members of the Pesaro Family* (1547), is on the left from the entrance. Titian's elaborate tomb, a lion-topped triumphal arch with bas relief scenes of Paradise, stands directly across from the enormous pyramid in which the sculptor Canova (1757-1822) rests. Donatello's gaunt wooden sculpture *St. John the Baptist* (1438) stands framed in gold in the Florentine chapel to the right of the high altar. An amazingly life-like work by Bellini, *Virgin and Child with Saints Nicholas, Peter, Benedict, and Mark* (1488), hangs in the sacristy to the far right of the apse. Nearby, Cabianca and Brustolon's *Altar of Relics* holds shelves of chalices and holy memorabilia in a large, ornate glass case framed with thick gold leaf, three bas relief crucifixion scenes, and gilded, flitting cherubs. *(V: S. Tomà. Follow signs back to Campo dei Frari. www.basilicadeifrari.it. Open M-Sa 9am-6pm, Su 1-6pm. Ticket office closes 5:45pm. €2.50. Cash only.)*

CHIESA DI SANTA MARIA DELLA SALUTE (DORSODURO). The *Salute* (Italian for "health") is a hallmark of the Venetian skyline: from the church's perch on Dorsoduro's long peninsula just southwest of San Marco, its domes are visible from everywhere in the city. In 1631, the city commissioned Longhena to build the church for the Virgin, whom they believed would then give them a break and end the plague. These days, Venice celebrates the end of the plague on the third Sunday in November by building a wooden pontoon bridge across the Canal and lighting candles in the church (see **Entertainment: Festivals**). Next to the *Salute* stands the *Dogana*, the old customs house, where ships sailing into Venice were required to stop and pay appropriate duties. When nearby construction ends, walk along the *fondamenta* to the tip of Dorsoduro, where a superb ◼panorama of the city awaits. *(V: Salute. ☎ 041 522 55 58. Open daily 9am-noon and 3-5:30pm. Free. Entrance to sacristy with donation. The inside of the Dogana is closed to the public.)*

CHIESA DI SAN SEBASTIANO (DORSODURO). The Renaissance painter Veronese took refuge in this small white marble and brown stucco 16th-century church when he fled Verona in 1555 after allegedly killing a man. By 1565 he had filled the church with an amazing cycle of paintings and frescoes. His *Stories of Queen Esther* covers the ceiling, while the artist himself rests under the gravestone by the organ. Also displayed are works by Titian. *(V: S. Basilio. Continue straight ahead. Open M-Sa 10am-5pm, Su 1-5pm. Tickets close at 4:45pm. €2.50. Cash only.)*

CHIESA DI SANTISSIMI GIOVANNI E PAOLO (CASTELLO). This imposing terracotta and marble structure, also called San Zanipolo, is primarily built in the Gothic style, but has a Renaissance portal and an arch supported by columns of Greek marble. Inside, monumental ceilings enclose the tombs and monuments of the Doges. One fresco depicts the gory death of Marcantonio Bragadin, who valiantly defended Cyprus from the Turks in 1571, only to be skinned alive after surrendering. His remains rest in the urn above the monument. Next to Bragadin is an altarpiece by Giovanni Bellini depicting St. Christopher, St. Sebastian, and St. Vincent Ferrer. The bronze equestrian statue of local mercenary Bartolomeo Colleoni, stands on a marble pedestal outside. Colleoni left his inheritance to the city on the condition that a monument in his honor would be erected in front of S. Marco; the city, unwilling to honor anyone in such a grand space, decided to place the statue in front of the Scuola di S. Marco to satisfy the conditions of the will and claim his fortune. The statue was designed in 1479 by da Vinci's teacher Verrochio. *(V: Fondamenta Nuove. Turn left, then right on Fondamenta dei Mendicanti. ☎041 523 59 13. Open M-Sa 9:30am-7pm, Su 1-7pm. €2.50, students €1.25. Cash only.)*

CHIESA DI SANTA MARIA DEI MIRACOLI (CASTELLO). The Lombardi family designed this small Renaissance jewel in the late 1400s. Inside the tiny pink, white, and blue marble exterior sits a fully functional parish with a dark golden ceiling and pastel walls interrupted only by the vibrant blue and yellow window above the apse. *(From S. S. Giovanni e Paolo, cross Ponte Rosse and continue straight. At the dead end, follow the alley to your right. Open M-Sa 10am-5pm, Su 1-5pm. €2.50. Cash only.)*

CHIESA DELLA MADONNA DELL'ORTO (CANNAREGIO). Tintoretto's squat brick 14th-century parish church contains ten of his largest paintings, the final resting place of the painter and his children, and other works by Van den Dyck and Titian. Look for Tintoretto's *Last Judgment,* a spatially intense mass of souls, and *The Sacrifice of the Golden Calf* near the high altar. On the right apse is the brilliantly shaded *Presentation of the Virgin at the Temple.* There is a light switch for illuminating the works at each of the far corners. *(V: Madonna dell'Orto. For information, call the Associazione Chiese di Venezia, ☎041 275 04 62; www.chorusvenezia.org. Open M-Sa 10am-5pm. Ticket office closes 4:45pm. €2.50. Audioguides €0.50. Cash only.)*

CHIESA DEI GESUITI (CANNAREGIO). Founded in the 12th century and reconstructed in the 18th, Dei Geuiti features a dizzying ceiling with gilt-rimmed stucco around painted portals to Heaven. Thick, soaring exterior columns open onto a sea of green and white marble that stretches from the floor to the realistic stone curtain in the pulpit. Titian's dark *Martyrdom of Saint Lawrence* hangs in the altar to the left of the entrance to the church, while Tintoretto's lighter *Assumption of the Virgin* shows a blue-robed Mary taking off in flight. *(V: Fondamenta Nuove, 4885; turn right, then left on Sal. dei Specchieri. Open daily 10am-noon and 4-6pm. Free.)*

SAN GIORGIO MAGGIORE AND GIUDECCA

BASILICA DI SAN GIORGIO MAGGIORE. Standing on its own monastic island, S. Giorgio Maggiore contrasts sharply with most other Venetian churches. Palladio ignored the Venetian fondness for color and opted for an austere design. Light fills the enormous open interior, although unfortunately it does not hit Tintoretto's

Last Supper by the altar; a light switch illuminates the wraith-like angels hovering over Christ's table. The beautiful courtyard, to the right of the church, is closed to the public. Take the elevator to the top of the **campanile** for a marvelous view of the city. *(V: S. Giorgio Maggiore. ☎041 522 78 27. Open in summer M-Sa 9am-12:30pm and 2:30-6:30pm; in winter 2:30-5pm. Basilica free. Campanile €3. Pay the brother in the elevator.)*

TEMPIO DEL S. S. REDENTORE. Palladio's religious masterpiece, this narrow church, like the *Salute*, commemorates a deal that Venice struck with God to end a plague. Every year the city celebrates with fireworks in the **Festa del Redentore** (see **Entertainment: Festivals**). Paintings by Veronese and Bassano hang in the sacristy. *(V: Redentore. Ask to enter the sacristy. Open M-Sa 10am-5pm, Su 1-5pm. €2.)*

ISLANDS OF THE LAGOON

■ **LIDO.** The sunny, breezy resort island of Lido provided the tragic setting for *Death in Venice*, Thomas Mann's haunting novella of love and lust. Visonti's film version was also shot here at the famous **Hotel des Bains**, Lungomare Marconi, 17. Today, tree-lined streets, crashing blue waves, and the broad shoreline of the popular public beach offer a free, relaxing alternative to Venice's paved urban seafront, attracting an array of visitors from lithe sunbathers to local families. An impressive shipwreck looms at one end. The island also offers a casino, horseback riding, and one of Italy's finest golf courses. *(V #1 and 82: Lido. From the vaporetti stop, cross the street and continue until you reach the pink marble sidewalk, which traverses the island to the beach. Beach open daily 9am-8pm. Free. Services available for afternoon (from 2:30pm) or daily prices include lockable changing rooms for €13.50/€23.20, beach umbrella and chair €12/€15.40, long deck chair €9, and small safe €3. MC/V.)*

■ **MURANO.** Famous since 1292 for its glass (Venice's artisans were forced off Venice proper because their kilns started fires), the six-island cluster of Murano affords visitors the opportunity to witness free of charge resident artisans blowing and spinning crystalline creations. Quiet streets are lined with tiny shops and glass boutiques with jewelry, vases, and delicate figurines for a variety of prices; for demonstrations, look for signs directing to the *fornace*, concentrated around the Colona, Faro, and Navagero *vaporetto* stops. The speed and grace of these artisans are stunning, and some studios let visitors blow their own glass creations. The **Museo Vetrario** (Glass Museum) houses a collection that begins with funereal urns from the first century and ends with pieces like an ornate model garden made entirely of glass and a cartoonish, sea green octopus presumably designed by Carlo Scarpa in 1930. Farther down the street, a marble *loggia* lines the second story of the light brick, 12th-century **Basilica di Santa Maria e San Donato,** which features glass and marble mosaic floors, blue chandeliers in the side apses, and a holy water font with fused pieces of bright yellow, red, green, and blue glass. If you look carefully, the curved bones of the dragon slain by Saint Donatus hang behind the altar. *(V #DM, LN, 5, 13, 41, 42: Faro from either S. Zaccaria or Fondamenta Nuove. Museo Vetrario, Fondamenta Giustian, 8. ☎/fax 041 73 95 86. Open Apr.-Oct. M-Tu and Th-Su 10am-5pm; Nov.-Mar. M-Tu and Th-Su 10am-4pm. €4, students or Rolling Venice cardholders €2.50. MC/V. Included on combined Palazzo Ducale ticket or full museum pass. Basilica ☎041 73 90 56. Open daily 8am-noon and 4-7pm. Free.)*

■ **BURANO.** Curtains billow from the doorways of bright yellow and electric blue houses in this traditional fishing village, where carefully hand-tatted lace has become a community art. The small **Scuola di Merletti di Burano** (Lace Museum), once the home of the island's professional lace-making school, features strips from the 16th century and yellowing lace-maker diplomas. The pink stucco facade and violently canting *campanile* of the basilica, **Chiesa di S. Martino,** sit across from the museum. *(40min. by boat from Venice. V #LN: Burano from Fondamenta Nuove. Museum in P. Galuppi. ☎041 73 00 34. Open M and W-Su 10am-5pm. €4. Included on combined Palazzo Ducale ticket or full museum pass. Church open daily 8am-noon and 3-7pm. Free.)*

TORCELLO. Torcello, a safe haven for early fishermen fleeing barbarians on the mainland, was the most powerful island in the lagoon before Venice usurped its inhabitants and its glory. A cathedral, **Santa Maria Assunta,** contains 11th- and 12th-century mosaics depicting the Last Judgment and the Virgin Mary. The soaring *campanile* affords splendid views of Torcello, a distant Burano, and the outer lagoon, but watch your head—they've padded the iron supports, but steep ramps and forward momentum mean they still pack a punch. *(45min. by boat from Venice. V #T: Torcello from Burano. Cathedral ☎041 73 01 19. Open daily 10:30am-6pm. Ticket office closes 5:30pm. €3, audioguides €1. Combined church, campanile, and museum admission €8 with free audioguide included. Combination tickets close at 4:30pm. Cash only.)*

ISOLA DI SAN MICHELE. Venice's cemetery island, S. Michele, is home to Coducci's tiny Chiesa di S. Michele in Isola (1469), the first Renaissance church in Venice. Enter the cyprus-lined grounds through the church's right-hand portal, ornamented by a relief depicting St. Michael slaying a dragon. Beautiful, quiet grounds offer a much appreciated opportunity for peaceful reflection away from the hustle and bustle of Venice. Poet, Fascist sympathizer, and enemy of the state Ezra Pound is buried in the Protestant cemetery, while Russian composer Igor Stravinsky and choreographer Sergei Diaghilev are entombed in the Orthodox graveyard. *(V: Cimitero, from Fondamenta Nuove. Church and cemetery open Apr.-Sept. daily 7:30am-6pm; Oct.-Mar. 7:30am-4pm. Free.)*

🎵 ENTERTAINMENT

The weekly *A Guest in Venice,* free at hotels and tourist offices and online at www.unospitedivenezia.it, lists current festivals, concerts, and gallery exhibits.

GONDOLAS

Gondolas were once displays of multicolored brilliance. Legend has it that their lavish reds and purples turned to black when the Plague struck; to stop further contamination from spreading throughout the disease-infested canal waters, the wooden boats were supposedly coated with tar and pitch. The morbid color was also a sign of respect for Venice's dead and dying. A more likely story, however, is that a 17th-century city ordinance ordered that all boats be painted black to prevent noble families from waging gondola-decorating wars. Certain dignitaries, of course, were exempt. Now, the boats are mainly filled with tourists seeking the most gorgeous views of Venetian houses and palaces via their original canal pathways. Rides are most romantic about 50min. before sunset and most affordable if shared by six people. The rate that a gondolier quotes is negotiable and the most bargain-friendly gondoliers are those standing by themselves, rather than those in the groups as "taxi-stands" throughout the city. The "official" price starts at €62 for 50min., with a maximum of six people; prices rise at night.

ORCHESTRAL MUSIC

Venice swoons for **orchestral music,** from the outdoor chamber orchestras in P. S. Marco to costumed concerts. **Vivaldi,** the red-headed priest and one-time choirmaster of the Chiesa di S. Maria della Pietà (a few blocks along the waterfront from P. S. Marco), was forgotten for centuries after his death. Today, his compositions, particularly *The Four Seasons,* can be heard almost nightly in the summer and regularly during the winter. The **Chiesa di S. Vidal,** next to Campo S. Samuele in San Marco, hosts classical performances using 15th-century instruments. (Open daily 9am-5pm. Concerts Tu, Th, and Sa at 9pm. €22, students €17. Purchase tickets at the church or visit www.interpretiveneziani.com.)

THEATER, CINEMA, AND ART EXHIBITIONS

Teatro Goldoni, Cal. del Teatro, San Marco, 4650/B (☎041 240 20 11; teatrogoldini@libero.it), near the Rialto, showcases varying types of live productions, often with a seasonal theme. Check with the theater for upcoming listings. (Rolling Venice discount 10%, AmEx/MC/V.) The **Mostra Internazionale di Cinema** (Venice International Film Festival), held annually from late August to early September, is a worldwide affair, drawing both rising talents and more established names like Steven Spielberg. Movies are shown in their original languages. (☎041 521 88 78. Tickets €20, sold throughout city. Some late-night outdoor showings free.) Venice's main cinemas include: the **Accademia,** Cal. Gambara, Dorsoduro, 1019 (☎041 528 77 06), to the right of the museum, screening original language films; the **Giorgione,** Campo S. Apostoli, Cannaregio (☎041 522 62 98); and the **Rossini,** San Marco, 3988 (☎041 523 03 22), off Campo Manin, which generally shows films in Italian. The famed **Biennale di Venezia** (info ☎041 521 18 98; for tickets, HelloVenezia ☎041 24 24, open daily 7:30am-8pm; www.labiennale.org), an international contemporary art exhibition with musical and dance performances, takes over the Giardini Pubblici and the Arsenal with provocative art in odd-numbered years.

FESTIVALS

Banned by the church for several centuries, Venice's famous **Carnevale** was successfully reinstated in the early 1970s. During the 10 days preceding Ash Wednesday, masked figures jam the streets and street performances spring up throughout the city. On **Mardi Gras,** the population of the city doubles. Contact the tourist office in December or January for details and make lodging arrangements far ahead. Venice's second most colorful festival is the **Festa del Redentore** (3rd Su in July), originally held to celebrate the end of a 16th-century plague. It kicks off on Saturday night with a fireworks display at 11:30pm. On Sunday, maintenance craftsmen build a pontoon bridge, open to the public, across the Giudecca Canal, connecting **Il Redentore** to the **Zattere.** On the first Sunday in September, Venice stages its classic **regata storica,** a gondola race down the Grand Canal. During the religious **Festa della Salute** (3rd Su in Nov.), which also originated to mark the end of a plague, the city celebrates with the construction of another pontoon bridge, this time over the Grand Canal.

SHOPPING

Be wary of shopping in the heavily touristed P. S. Marco or around the Rialto (excluding Rivoaltus). Shops outside these areas often have better quality products and a greater selection for about half the price. Interesting clothing, glass, and mask boutiques line the streets leading from the Rialto to Campo S. Polo and Str. Nuova and from the Rialto toward the station. The map accompanying the Rolling Venice card lists many shops that offer discounts for card holders. The most concentrated and varied selections of Venetian glass and lace require trips to the nearby islands of Murano and Burano, respectively. For buying or just browsing, try **Lush,** Strada Nuova, Cannaregio, 3822 (☎041 241 12 00), one branch of a luxury soap store with small shops throughout Italy. Stacks of cheese-wheel sized soaps and cosmetics packed in a dairy case complete the grocery-store environment, where hygiene is sold by the kilogram but fragrance is free. If you spend a little too much on eternal youth ("Dorian Gray" bottles from €3.46), pick up some soul-redeeming soaps. (Open M-F and Su 10am-7:30pm, Sa 10am-8pm. MC/V.)

■ NIGHTLIFE

Though pubs and bars are not uncommon, most residents agree that a truly vibrant nightlife in Venice is virtually nonexistent. Most locals would rather spend an evening sipping wine or beer and listening to string quartets in P. S. Marco than bumping and/or grinding in a disco, but the island's fluctuating population means that new establishments spring up (and wither and die) with some regularity. Student nightlife is concentrated around **Campo Santa Margherita**, in Dorsoduro, and the areas around the **Lista di Spagna**, in Cannaregio.

■ **Paradiso Perduto,** Fond. della Misericordia, Cannaregio, 2540 (☎041 72 05 81). From Str. Nuova, cross Campo S. Fosca, cross bridge, and continue in same direction, crossing 2 more bridges. Students flood this unassuming bar, where waitstaff doles out large portions of *cicchetti* (mixed plate €11.36). Live jazz Su 9pm. Open Th-Su 7pm-2am.

■ **Piccolo Mondo,** Accademia, Dorsoduro, 1056/A (☎041 520 03 71). Facing away from the canal toward the Accademia, turn right and follow the street around. Disco, hip-hop, and vodka with Red Bull (€10) keep a full house at this small but popular *discoteca,* and 40 years in operation make it the most stable bet for a night on the town. Framed collages of the wide-ranging clientele include notables like Michael Jordan, Boy George, Shaquille O'Neal, Mick Jagger, and Prince Albert of Monaco. Ring bell to enter. Drinks from €7. Cover varies, free with *Let's Go.* Open nightly 10pm-4am. AmEx/MC/V.

■ **Café Blue,** Campo S. Pantalon, Dorsoduro, 3778 (☎041 71 02 27). From S. Maria Frari, take Cal. Scalater and turn right at the end. Grab some absinthe (€6) and a stool in the brick-walled back room and watch the daytime coffee crowd turn young and trendy as night falls. Free Internet. Live jazz F and Su evenings in winter. Happy Hour in winter 6-8pm. Open in summer noon-2am; in winter 8am-2am. Cash only.

Orange, Dorsoduro 3054/A (☎041 523 47 40; www.orangebar.it). Across from Duchamp in Campo S. Margherita. Modern art canvases and a TV playing music videos dot the bright walls of this hip new bar, where everything except the lush aquamarine garden is consistently and totally orange. To match the theme, try the tequila sunrise (€5). Beer from €1.20. Wine from €1. Open M-Sa 7am-2pm, Su nights. AmEx/MC/V.

Cafe Noir, Dorsoduro 3805 (☎041 71 09 25). Faded images of Marilyn Monroe and a saxophone player cover the walls of Cafe Noir, where dark brown lamps, a blue glass mosaic bar, and tightly packed wooden tables give off an artistic vibe. The back room has less of a view, but black leather booth and street-side windows in front are great for coffee or people-watching outside. Open M-Sa 7am-2am, Su 9am-2am. Cash only.

Duchamp, Campo S. Margherita, Dorsoduro 3019 (☎041 528 62 55). A student-heavy crowd keeps Duchamp packed, from the plentiful seating on the campo to the shrug-inducing interior (complete with brick walls and painted windows into space). Pint of beer €4.30. House wine €1.50. Open M-F and Su 9am-2am, Sa 5pm-2am. Cash only.

Casanova, Lista di Spagna, Cannaregio, 158/A (☎041 275 01 99). This stylish club claims to be the only real disco in Venice and draws a mixed crowd of tourists and students. Crowd is small, but there's room on the dance floor to enjoy the techno beats. F €13 cover includes free drink, Sa €10 cover. Open daily 10pm-4am. AmEx/MC/V.

Bacaro Jazz, Campo S. Bartolomeo, San Marco, 5546 (☎041 528 52 49; www.bacaro-jazz.com). From post office, follow the sounds of jazz across the street. Portraits of Billie Holliday and Duke Ellington dot colorful jazz murals as 20- and 30-somethings share large plates of *cicchetti* (€15) under jazz concerts on a plasma screen. Happy Hour 4-6:30pm. Open M-Tu and Th-Su 4pm-3am. AmEx/MC/V.

Inishark Irish Pub, Cal. del Mondo Novo, Castello, 5787 (☎041 523 53 00), off Campo S. Maria Formosa. A giant inflatable shark dangles over the noisy interior of this dark, mid-sized Irish pub. Guinness and Harp €4.50. Open Tu-Su 6pm-1:30am. Cash only.

THE VENETO AND TRENTINO-ALTO ADIGE

Bar Santa Lucia, Lista di Spagna, Cannaregio 282/B (☎041 524 28 80), near the train station. The foreign currency that lines the walls complements the tourist-heavy clientele. Bright interior and a handful of street-side tables. Good selection of Irish beers. Pint of Guinness €5. Wine €2.50. Open M-Sa 6am-2am. Cash only.

Il Caffè, Campo S. Margherita, Dorsoduro, 2963 (☎041 528 79 98). A low-key environment for drinks and lively conversation. Wine €0.80. Open M-Sa 7am-1am. Cash only.

PADUA (PADOVA)   ☎049

Padua's oldest institutions are the ones that still draw visitors—pilgrims flock to St. Anthony's tomb, athletes skate along the looping Prato della Valle, and even today, lecturers and academics frequent the hallowed university halls where Dante, Petrarch, Galileo, Copernicus, Mantegna, Giotto, Donatello, and other luminaries once fostered the city's long-standing reputation as a center of learning. Padua's university, founded in 1222 and second in seniority only to Bologna's, brings scores of students into the city's cluster of busy piazzas, where crowds of twenty-somethings stay to roam the brightly-lit streets late into the night.

⌐ TRANSPORTATION

Trains: In P. Stazione, at the northern end of C. del Popolo, the continuation of C. Garibaldi. Open 5am-midnight. Tickets open daily 6am-9pm. Info booth open daily 7am-9pm. **Luggage storage** available (see **Practical Information**). To: **Bologna** (1½hr., 34 per day 12:41am-10:43pm, €5.73); **Milan** (2½hr., 25 per day 5:50am-9:40pm, €11.21); **Venice** (30min., 82 per day 4:33am-11:08pm, €2.45); **Verona** (1hr., 44 per day 5:03am-11:28pm, €4.23).

Buses: SITA (☎049 820 68 11), in P. Boschetti. From the train station, walk down C. del Popolo, turn left on V. Trieste, and bear right at V. Vecchio. Ticket office open M-Sa 5:30am-8:30pm, Su 6:20am-8:40pm. To: **Montagnana** (1½hr., 19 per day 6:20am-8:30pm, €3.40); **Venice** (45min., 5:25am-10:25pm, €2.90); **Vicenza** (1hr., 30 per day 5:50am-8:15pm, €3.15). Reduced service Su. Cash only.

Local Buses: ACAP (☎049 824 11 11), at the train station. To reach downtown, take buses #8, 12, or 18 M-F and #8 and 32 Sa-Su. 1hr. pass €0.85. Ticket office open daily 6am-midnight.

Taxis: RadioTaxi (☎049 65 13 33). Available 24hr.

Car Rental: Europcar, P. Stazione, 6 (☎049 875 85 90), across parking lot from train station. 19+. Open M-F 8:30am-12:30pm and 3-7pm, Sa 8:30am-12:30pm. AmEx/MC/V. **Maggiore National,** P. Stazione, 15 (☎049 875 86 05, fax 049 875 62 23), after exiting train station, turn right. Must have had license for 1 year. Open M-F 8:30am-12:30pm and 2:30-6:30pm, Sa 9am-noon. MC/V.

✈⁊ ORIENTATION AND PRACTICAL INFORMATION

The **train station** is on the northern edge of town, outside the 16th-century walls. A ten minute walk down **Corso del Popolo,** which becomes **Corso Garibaldi,** leads to the heart of town and main area of the **Università degli Studi di Padova.**

Tourist Office: In the **train station** (☎049 875 20 77). Open M-Sa 9am-7pm, Su 8:30am-12:30pm. **Main office,** P. Pedrocchi, 11 (☎049 876 79 27; infopedrocchi@turismopadova.it), to the right of Caffè Pedrocchi, off P. Cavour. Helpful staff. Open M-Sa 9am-1:30pm and 3-7pm.

Budget Travel: CTS, Riviera Mugnai, 22 (☎049 876 16 39). Sells ISICs and train tickets. Open M-F 8:30-11:30am and 3-6:30pm, Sa 8:30-11:30am. Cash only.

English-Language Bookstore: Feltrinelli International, V. S. Francesco, 14 (☎049 875 07 92; padova.international@lafeltrinelli.it). From the train station, turn left off V. Cavour. Wide selection of magazines, novels, and travel guides. Open June-Aug. M-Sa 9am-1pm and 3-8pm; Sept.-May M-Sa 9am-1pm and 3:30-7:30pm. AmEx/MC/V.

Internet Access: Tempo Reale, V. Petrarca, 9 (☎049 65 84 84), across the bridge from the intersection of V. Dante and V. S. Fermo. Internet €6 for 1st hr., €3 each additional hr. Open M-F 10am-2am and Sa 4pm-2am. Cash only.

Laundromat: Fastclean, V. Ognissanti, 6, off V. del Portello. Take bus #9. Wash €3.70. Open M-F 9am-12:30pm and 3:15-7pm, Sa 9am-12:30pm.

Luggage Storage: At the train station. €3.87 per bag per day. Open daily 6am-10:30pm. Cash only.

Emergency: ☎112 or 113. **Ambulance** (☎118). **Carabinieri** (☎049 21 21 21), on Prato della Valle.

Hospital: Ospedale Civile, V. Giustiniani, 1 (☎049 821 11 11), off V. Ospedale.

Post Office: C. Garibaldi, 33 (☎049 875 54 75). Open M-Sa 8:30am-6:30pm. AmEx/MC/V for financial services only. Open M-Sa 8:30am-1:30pm. **Postal Code:** 35100.

ACCOMMODATIONS AND CAMPING

Padua's size and major attractions mean high hotel prices, though some relatively inexpensive options can be found in good locations.

Locanda la Perla, V. Cesarotti, 67 (☎049 875 89 39), near the Prato della Valle. From the *centro*, take V. S. Francesco to the end and turn right. The ever-affable Paolo rents 8 clean, bright rooms with stone floors and phone 5min. from the Basilica di Sant'Antonio. Shared bath. Open Sept.-July. Singles €30-32; doubles €40-42. Cash only. ❸

Ostello Città di Padova (HI), V. Aleardi, 30 (☎049 875 22 19; pdyhtl@tin.it), near Prato della Valle. From the train station, follow C. del Popolo through several name changes and turn right on V. Rogati. Go to V. Aleardi and turn left; walk 20min. to the end of the block. Coed hostel with TV room and location 10min. from *centro*. Laundry €5. Internet €5.16 per hr. Breakfast, shower, and sheets included. Reception 7-9:30am and 4-11pm. Lockout 9:30am-4pm. Curfew 11pm. Reserve 1 week in advance. 8-bed dorms €14.50; 4-person family rooms €58. Wheelchair accessible. HI members only; memberships available for €3. MC/V. ❶

Hotel Al Santo, V. del Santo, 147 (☎049 875 21 31, fax 878 80 76), near the basilica. Stone-inlay artwork graces the lobby of this well-kept hotel. Small but sunny rooms have bath, fan, and TV. Restaurant downstairs. Breakfast included. Lunch or dinner *menù* €15. Reception 24hr. Singles €52-55; doubles €90; triples €130. AmEx/MC/V. ❹

Hotel Sant'Antonio, V. S. Fermo, 118 (☎049 875 13 93; www.hotelsantantonio.it). Rooms have TV, A/C, and phone; some have river view. Breakfast €7. Single without bath €40, with bath €60-62; doubles €78-82; triples €102; quads €120. MC/V. ❹

Hotel Corso, C. del Popolo, 2 (☎049 875 08 22; htlcrs@virgilio.it), at the intersection of C. del Popolo and V. Trieste. Keycards open small carpeted rooms with high ceilings; all have bath, phone, A/C, TV, and views of the heavy traffic outside. Buffet breakfast included. Reception 24hr. Singles €78-85; doubles €103-124. AmEx/MC/V. ❺

Opera Casa Famiglia (ACISJF), V. Nino Bixio, 4 (☎049 875 15 54), off P. Stazione. From train station, walk to the right, and turn left on the street just before Hotel Monaco. Watch for the address—the buzzer is next to a blank brown door with no sign. Exercise caution in the area around the station. 30 beds in well-used but clean doubles, triples, and quads. Women under 30 only. Curfew 10:30pm. Beds €18. Cash only. ❷

Sporting Center, V. Roma, 123/125 (☎049 79 34 00), 15km from Padua; take train to Montegrotto. Campgrounds with tennis and beach volleyball. Restaurant discounts for guests. Electric connection and hot showers included, day pass for pool €5. Open Mar. 5-Nov. 15. €5.50-7.50 per person, €7.50-10.20 per car with tent. Cash only. ●

🍴 FOOD

Morning **markets** are held in P. delle Erbe and P. della Frutta from 8am to 2pm; sidewalk vendors also sell fresh produce, meats, and cheeses. A PAM **supermarket** is downtown in P. Cavour. (Open M-Tu and Th-Sa 8am-8pm and W 8am-2pm. Cash only.) For an inexpensive taste of the gourmet, visit **Franchin,** V. del Santo, 95, which sells fresh meats, cheeses, breads, and wine. (☎049 875 05 32. Open M-Tu and Th-Su 8:30am-1:30pm and 5-8pm, W 8:30am-1:30pm. MC/V.) Wine-lovers should sample a glass from the nearby Colli Euganei wine district. Visitors to the Basilica di Sant'Antonio can nibble on *dolci del santo* (saint's sweets), a flaky, powdered cake with creamy nut and fig filling, in nearby *pasticcerie*.

🍴 **Pizzeria Al Borgo,** V. Luca Belludi, 56 (☎/fax 049 875 88 57), near the Basilica di S. Antonio, just off P. del Santo, heading toward Prato della Valle. Satisfied diners devour thick, flavorful pizzas (from €3.70) in wooden booths. Enjoy the stunning basilica view from tables on the busy deck outdoors. Cover €2. Reservation recommended. Open M and W-Su noon-2:30pm and 7pm-midnight. MC/V. ●

🍴 **Patagonia Ice Cream,** P. dei Signori, 27 (☎049 875 10 45), on the side closest to V. Dante. Lactose-craving mobs flock to this tiny, wildly popular gelato stand for heaping scoops of thick gelato packed into sweet, crispy waffle cones. €0.90 per scoop. Open M-F 11am-midnight, Su 11am-1pm and 3pm-midnight. Cash only. ●

🍴 **Alexander Birreria Paninoteca,** V. S. Francesco, 38 (☎049 65 28 84). From the basilica, take V. del Santo to V. S. Francesco and turn left. Wide range of sandwiches €3-4. 20% student discount for lunch, 10% for dinner. Open M-F 10am-2am, Sa-Su noon-2am. ●

Trattoria Pizzeria Marechiaro, V. Manin, 37 (☎049 875 84 89). Friendly service and upbeat music make this narrow trattoria a cheery place to enjoy *marechiaro* (€6.20), a specialty pizza packed with seafood and oregano. Pizza from €4.20. Pasta from €4.65. Cover €1.55. Open Tu-Su noon-2:30pm and 6:30pm-midnight. Closed in Aug. MC/V. ●

Lunanuova, V. G. Barbarigo, 12 (☎049 875 89 07), heading off P. Duomo. Ring the bell for entrance. Mix and match vegetarian pasta and Middle Eastern dishes like *riso basmati con dhal di piselli* (€4.80) in the dining room or amid ivy-covered brick walls in the lamp-lit garden. Individual plates €4.10-4.80, 2 for €7.30, 3 for €8.80, 5 for €9.90. Open Tu-Sa 12:30-2:15pm and 7:30pm-midnight. Cash or traveler's checks only. ●

L'Azdora, V. del Santo, 7 (☎328 466 10 21), serves piping hot pitas full of rich cheeses and meats to students at the nearby University. *Nutella* €2, half-sized snack portions with 2 ingredients €2, 3 ingredients €2.20. Open in summer M-F 11:30am-3pm and 7-10pm, in winter 11:30am-9pm. Cash only. ●

Antica Trattoria Paccagnella, V. del Santo, 113 (☎/fax 049 875 05 49). A wall of wood-rimmed mirrors reflects murmuring diners enjoying plates of rich, authentic Paduan cuisine in this quiet neighborhood restaurant. *Primi* €5-9, *secondi* €6.80-15. Cover €2. Open daily noon-2:30pm and 7-10pm. AmEx/MC/V. ●

👁 SIGHTS

BASILICA DI SANT'ANTONIO (IL SANTO). An array of rounded gray domes and conic spires cap the facade of Padua's enormous brick basilica. Bronze sculptures by Donatello grace the high altar, which is surrounded by the artist's *Crucifixion* and several Gothic frescoes. Upon entering, look right for the **Tomba di**

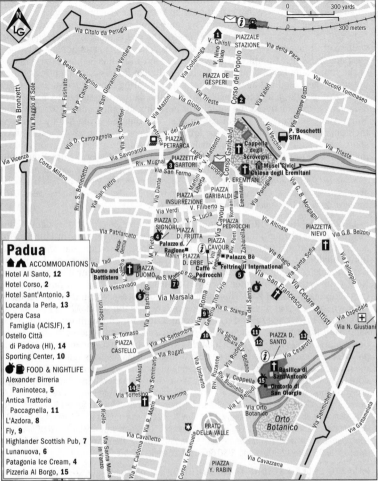

Padua

▲ ⌂ ACCOMMODATIONS
Hotel Al Santo, 12
Hotel Corso, 2
Hotel Sant'Antonio, 3
Locanda la Perla, 13
Opera Casa
  Famiglia (ACISJF), 1
Ostello Città
  di Padova (HI), 14
Sporting Center, 10

◖▯ FOOD & NIGHTLIFE
Alexander Birreria
  Paninoteca, 5
Antica Trattoria
  Paccagnella, 11
L'Azdora, 8
Fly, 9
Highlander Scottish Pub, 7
Lunanuova, 6
Patagonia Ice Cream, 4
Pizzeria Al Borgo, 15

Sant'Antonio, which sits elevated on a platform under a huge marble arch. Each year, thousands of pilgrims crowd the deep marble bas-reliefs to cover the dark black stone of the sepulchre with framed requests, thanks, and prayers. Behind the main altar in the apse sits the **Cappella delle Reliquie,** where shrines contain everything from Saint Anthony's tunic to his jawbone. A **multimedia show** in the courtyard (follow "Mostra" signs) details St. Anthony's life. Exit the basilica and turn right to reach the tiny **Oratorio di San Giorgio,** which displays vivid Giotto-school frescoes, and the **Scuola del Santo** includes three frescoes by the young Titian. *(P. del Santo. ☎ 049 878 97 22. Basilica open daily Apr.-Sept. 6:30am-7:45pm; Nov.-Mar. 6:30am-6:45pm. Modest dress strictly enforced. Free. Mostra open daily 9am-12:30pm and 2:30-6pm. Audio tour in English available at front desk. Free. Oratorio and Scuola ☎/fax 049 875 52 35. Open daily Apr.-Sept. 9am-12:30pm and 2:30-7pm; Oct.-Mar. 9am-12:30pm and 2:30-5pm. Wheelchair accessible. €2, students €1.50. Cash only.)*

■ **CAPPELLA DEGLI SCROVEGNI (ARENA CHAPEL).** Enrico Scrovegni dedicated this thin, tall brick chapel to the Virgin Mary in an attempt to save the soul of his father Reginald, a usurer famously lambasted in the 17th canto of Dante's *Inferno*. Pisano carved the three statues for the chapel, and Giotto covered the walls with frescoed scenes from the lives of Jesus, Mary, and her parents, Sts. Joachim and Anne. Completed between 1305 and 1306, this 38-panel cycle is one of the first examples of depth and realism in Italian Renaissance painting. Above the door, the Last Judgment depicts the halo-wearing blessed to the left of the cross; to the right, a less-fortunate crowd of the damned are eaten by hairy blue demons. Scrovegni sits in the middle, offering his tiny pink chapel to the Virgin Mary. Along the bottom, allegorical figures depicting the seven deadly sins face their opposites across the nave—the four cardinal and theological virtues. Down a short gravel path, the **Musei Civici Erimitani** has assembled an art collection including ancient Roman inscriptions and a beautiful crucifix by Giotto that once adorned the Scrovegni Chapel. *(P. Eremitani, 8. ☎ 049 820 45 51. Entrance to the chapel only through the museum. Open daily Feb.-Oct. 9am-7pm; Nov.-Jan. 9am-6pm. Tickets may be purchased at the Musei Civici ticket office or at www.cappelladegliscrovegni.it. Museum €10; combination ticket €12, students €5, handicapped €1. AmEx/MC/V.)*

PALAZZO BÒ AND ENVIRONS. The university campus is spread throughout the city, but centers around the two bustling interior stone courtyards of Palazzo Bò, adorned with students' coats of arms, a war memorial, and marble accents. The **Teatro Anatomico** (1594), a medical lecture hall that was the first of its kind in Europe, hosted medical pioneers like Vesalius and Englishman William Harvey. Nearly all Venetian noblemen received their mandatory law and public policy instruction in the **Great Hall.** The chair of Galileo is preserved in the **Sala dei Quaranta,** where the great physicist once lectured. Across the street, ■**Caffè Pedrocchi,** founded in 1772, once served as the headquarters for 19th-century liberals who supported Risorgimento leader Giuseppe Mazzini. A turning point in the revolution occurred here in 1848, when a battle exploded between students and Austrian police. The **Museo Risorgimento e dell'Eta Contemporanea** displays relics focusing on the human aspects of war, from propaganda posters to a powerful, shakily written note from World War II simply reading: "You saved two members of my family and my vanishing belief in the human race." *(Palazzo Bò, in P. delle Erbe. ☎ 049 827 30 47; www.unipd.it. Guided tours M, W, F 3:15, 4:15, and 5:15pm; Tu, Th, Sa 9:15, 10:15, and 11:15am. 45min. tours €3, students €1.50. Buy tickets 15min. before tour. Caffè Pedrocchi, V. VIII Febbraio, 15. ☎ 049 878 12 31; www.caffepedrocchi.it. Open daily from the end of June-mid Sept. 9am-1am; mid-Sept.-end of June 9am-9pm. AmEx/MC/V. Piano Nobile ☎ 049 878 12 31. Open Tu-Su 9:30am-12:30pm and 3:30-6pm. €4, students €2.50. Cash only.)*

PALAZZO DELLA RAGIONE (LAW COURTS). Astrological signs adorn the walls of this palazzo, whose lower loggia contains a busy row of fruit, bread, and clothing markets under a gray barrel vault roof. The original ceiling, once painted as a starry sky, survived a 1420 fire only to topple in a 1756 tornado. With typical Italian efficiency, workers are still repairing the damage. To the right of the entrance sits the **Stone of Shame.** Inspired by the exhortations of St. Anthony in 1231 to abolish debtors' prisons, Padua adopted the progressive practice of forcing half-clothed debtors onto the stone to repeat before a crowd of at least one hundred hecklers, "I renounce my property." *(Enter through city hall on V. Febbraio, 8. ☎ 049 820 45 01. Open M-W and F-Su 9am-7pm, Th 9am-11pm. €8, students and Padova Card €5.)*

PRATO DELLA VALLE. Originally a Roman theater, this verdant ellipse is now the second largest square in Europe, after Moscow's Red Square. On the paved outermost track, joggers and bikers orbit the dog walkers, teenagers, and families who cross the moat to find small green fields, pebbly paths, and a large fountain dotted with 78 statues of famous Paduan men.

DUOMO. Michelangelo supposedly participated in the design of this hulking church, erected between the 16th and 18th centuries. The duomo's simplicity makes the steps of the apse especially unusual—chunky, half-carved marble interpretations of Sts. Prosdocimo, Gregorio, and Giustina accompany a golden, praying figure whose flowing hair melds with a marble tree to create the church's lectern. Next door, the colorful 12th-century **Battistere** is dedicated to St. John the Baptist. The interior walls are covered in vivid frescoes of New Testament scenes, while a massive wide-eyed Christ and rings of painted saints look down from the hollow dome above. (*P. Duomo. Duomo ☎ 049 66 28 14, Battistero ☎ 049 65 69 14. Duomo open M-Sa 7:30am-noon and 3:45-7:45pm, Su 7:45am-1pm and 3:45-8:30pm. Free. Battistere open daily 10am-6pm. €2.50, students €1.50. Cash only.*)

ORTO BOTANICO. Leafy trees and high stone walls ring a circular grid of iron fences, gravel walkways, and low fountains in the oldest university botanical garden in Europe. Palm trees welcome guests to a quiet oasis of water lilies, cacti, medicinal herbs, and one palm tree planted in 1585 in the heart of this congested city. (*V. Orto Botanico, 15. Follow signs from basilica. ☎ 049 827 21 19. Open daily Apr.-Sept. 9am-1pm and 3-6pm; Oct.-Mar. M-F 9am-1pm. €4, 65 and over €3, students €1. Cash only.*)

🎵 ENTERTAINMENT

Restaurant terraces begin to fill around 9pm. The **Highlander Scottish Pub,** V. S. Martino e Solferino, 69, greets customers with a ceiling beam that reads "There's a guid time com'in"—and with lively patrons filling this cavernous two-story pub, they're usually right. (☎ 049 65 99 77. Pints from €4.50. Open daily 11am-3pm and 6pm-2am. AmEx/MC/V.) The bold interior and nearby pedestrian area at **Fly,** Galleria Tito Livio, 4/6, draws a laid-back crowd to the steel bar. The ingredients to the *ciupito alla panna* (€2.50-3) are a secret, but they involve a shot glass, liquor, a flurry of sparks, and a flaming bar. (☎ 049 875 28 92. Wine from €2. Open M-Sa 8am-2am. MC/V.) Nightlife rages in Padua, but a listing of clubs is nearly impossible to find. Try asking about specific discotheques like **Limbo, Extra Extra,** and **Banale.** Pilgrims pack the city on June 13, as Padua commemorates the death of its patron St. Anthony with a procession bearing the saint's statue and jawbone. An **antique market** assembles in the Prato della Valle on the third Sunday of the month. Every Saturday the area holds an **outdoor market** selling food and clothing.

VICENZA   ☎ 0444

Bustling Vicenza has one of the highest average incomes in Italy and is orbited by dozens of stately villas, the present-day legacies of a 15th-century real estate boom in which nobles moved from nearby Venice to the mainland. Inside the city, affordable accommodations dot tiny side alleys while majestic examples of native architect Andrea Palladio's finest works line a number of piazzas.

🚍 TRANSPORTATION

The **train station** is at P. Stazione, at the end of V. Roma, across from Campo Marzo. (Info office open daily 8:30am-7:30pm. Ticket office open daily 6am-8:30pm. AmEx/MC/V). **Luggage Storage** is available (see **Practical Information**). **Trains** run to: Milan (2½hr., 29 per day 6:13am-10:02pm, €14.36); Padua (30min., 56 per day 6:28am-11:19pm, €3.80); Verona (40min., 51 per day 5:20am-11:47pm, €5); Venice (1¼hr., 46 per day 7:36am-11:49pm, €5.50). **FTV,** V. Milano, 7 (☎ 0444 22 31 15), left after exiting the train station, runs **buses** to Montagnana (1¼hr., 5 per day 7am-5:30pm, €3.55) and Padua (30min., 30 per day 5:50am-8:20pm, €3.55). Reduced service Sa-Su. Info office open M-Th 7:30am-noon and 1-5pm, F 7:30am-12:30pm.

Ticket office open daily 7am-7:30pm. Cash only.) **RadioTaxi** (☎ 0444 92 06 00) is available at either end of C. Palladio 24 hr. **Maggiore** (☎ 0444 54 59 62) rents cars at the train station. (Open M-F 8:30am-12:30pm and 3-6:30pm, Sa 8:30am-noon. €50 and up. AmEx/MC/V.) **Hertz** is across the hall. (☎ 199 11 33 11. Open M-F 8:30am-12:30pm and 2:30-6:30pm, Sa 8:30am-noon. MC/V.)

■ ■ ORIENTATION AND PRACTICAL INFORMATION

The train station and adjacent intercity bus station occupy the southern part of the city. **Viale Roma** leads from the station into town. At the **Giardino Salvi**, turn right under the Roman archway on **Corso Palladio**. Walk straight several blocks to the old Roman wall that serves as a gate to the **Teatro Olimpico**. The tourist office is the door just to the right. **Piazza Matteotti** lies in front, at the end of C. Palladio.

Tourist Office: P. Matteotti, 12 (☎ 0444 32 08 54; www.vicenzae.org). Free city **map** and map of villa locations. **Branch** at P. dei Signori, 8 (☎ 0444 54 41 22; iat.signori@libero.it). Both open daily 9am-1pm and 2-6pm.

Budget Travel: AVIT, V. Roma, 17 (☎ 0444 32 08 12; info@avit.it), before supermarket PAM. BIJ and Transalpino tickets, budget travel planning services €20. Open M-F 9am-12:30pm and 3-7pm, Sa 9:30am-12:30pm. Cash only.

Currency Exchange: At train station and post office (see listing). **ATMs** in the train station, on Contrà del Monte, and throughout the downtown area.

Luggage Storage: ☎ 0444 32 08 28. In train station. €3.87 per 24hr. Deposit and pick-up 9am-noon and pick-up 3-7pm. Cash only.

Emergency: ☎ 113. **Ambulance** (☎ 118).

Internet: Galla 2000, at V. Roma, 14. Open Tu-Th and Sa 9am-12:30pm and 3:30-7:30pm, F 9am-12:30pm and 3:30-11pm. €2.50 per 30min. AmEx/MC/V.

Pharmacy: Farmacia Dott. Doria, P. dei Signori, 49 (☎ 0444 32 12 41). Open June-Aug. M-F 8:45am-12:30pm and 4-7:30pm, Sa 8:45am-12:30pm; Sept.-May M-F 8:45am-12:30pm and 3:30-7pm, Sa 8:45am-12:30pm. Closed Aug. 15-31. 24hr. rotation available. MC/V.

Post Office: Contrà Garibaldi, 1 (☎ 0444 33 20 77), between duomo and P. Signori. Open daily 8:30am-6:30pm. **Currency exchange** until 6pm. Cash only. **Postal Code:** 36100.

■ ■ ACCOMMODATIONS AND CAMPING

Accommodations in Vicenza are conveniently located right in the heart of town, but, with the exception of the hostel, can be fairly pricey.

Ostello Olimpico Vicenza (HI), V. Giuriolo, 9 (☎ 0444 54 02 22, fax 54 77 62). From the tourist office, walk up the street with Museo Civico on your right. The Ostello is the bright yellow building on the left. 84 beds available; largest room has 6 beds. HI members only; non-members can purchase a stamp card at the desk for €18. Wheelchair accessible. Lockers included. Breakfast €1.75 served in cafe across the street. Other meals €10. Reception 7:30-9:30am and 3:30-11:30pm. Curfew 11:30pm. Dorm beds €15; singles €16.50; doubles with bathroom €18. MC/V. ❷

Hotel Vicenza, Str. dei Nodari, 5 (☎/fax 0444 32 15 12), off P. Signori on the street across the piazza from Soraru Sergio. Aging hotel with quiet hallways and large windows. Rooms have rustic mosaic stone floors and bath. Reception 24hr. Singles €45; doubles €60. Prices vary seasonally. Cash only. ❹

Hotel Giardini, V. Giuriolo, 10 (☎/fax 0444 32 64 58; info@hotelgiardini.com), across the street from Ostello Olimpico Vicenza. 18 spotlessly elegant rooms with large beds. Amenities include satellite TV, A/C, bath, and minibar. Breakfast included. Reception 7am-1am. Singles €83; doubles €114; triples €119. AmEx/MC/V. ❺

Campeggio Vicenza, Str. Pelosa, 239 (☎0444 58 23 11; www.ascom.vi.it/camping). Only accessible by car: take SS11 toward Padua, turn left on Str. Pelosa, and follow signs. TV, bar, and mini-golf. Showers included. Laundry €5.50. Open Mar.-Sept. €7 per person, €13.60 per tent with car. AmEx/MC/V. ❶

🍴 FOOD

Vicenza's specialties include dried salted cod with polenta, asparagus with eggs, and *torresani* (pigeon). A daily **produce market** opens in P. delle Erbe behind the basilica. A larger **market** in P. Erbe, P. Signori, and V. Roma sells cheese, chicken, fish, produce, and clothing. (Open Th 7:30am-1pm.) Buy essentials at **PAM** supermarket at V. Roma, 1. (Open M-Tu and Th-Sa 8am-8pm, W 8am-1pm. AmEx/MC/V.)

Zi' Teresa, Contrà S. Antonio, 1 (☎0444 32 14 11), at the end of the street just left of the post office. Soft yellow decor and attentive staff make any meal here relaxing. The baked sea bass *menù* is excellent (includes *antipasto*; €35). Pizza from €4. 3-course *menù* €25. Cover €1.50 for pizza and €2 for restaurant. Open M-Tu and Th-Su 11:30am-3:30pm and 6:30pm-midnight. AmEx/MC/V. ❹

Nirvana Caffè Degli Artisti, P. Matteotti, 8 (☎0444 54 31 11), from C. Palladio, enter the piazza and turn left. Marble tables with beaded lamps dot the interior of this vegetarian cafe, where casually draped saris and lilting folk music accompany organic ingredients and meatless versions of Italian dishes. Warm up with rich cappuccino (€1.40) or cool down with a non-alcoholic signature drink like the creamy Siddhartha (€3.50). Primi from €4, secondi €3.50-7.50. Open daily 8am-2am. Cash only. ❷

Righetti, P. del Duomo, 3 (☎0444 54 31 35), with another entrance at Contrà Fontana, 6. Set your table with bread and silverware and pass through the meal line at this self-service trattoria. *Primi* from €3.10, *secondi* from €4.65. Cover €0.30. Open M-F noon-3pm and 6:30pm-1am; closed first 3 weeks of Aug. Cash only. ❶

Soraru Sergio, Pta. Palladio, 17 (☎0444 32 09 15), past the statue of Palladia to the right of the Loggia del Capitano. Mirrored shelves of bottled liqueurs and jars of candy are tempting, but the real draws are the pastries and creamy gelato (like the deliciously smooth *nocciola*) made fresh on-site. 2 scoops €1.60. Open M-Tu and Th-Su 8:30am-1pm and 3:30-8pm. Cash only. ❶

👁 SIGHTS

The 🏛**Piazza dei Signori** was Vicenza's showpiece when the town was under Venetian control. Andrea Palladio's revamping of the **Basilica Palladiana** brought the young architect his first taste of fame. In 1546, Palladio's patron, the wealthy Giovan Giorgio Trissino, agreed to fund his proposal to repair the collapsing Palazzo della Ragione, a project that had frustrated some of the best architects of the day. Palladio applied pilasters on twin *loggie* of the basilica to mask the Gothic structure beneath. The **Torre di Piazza,** a brown brick clock tower on the left of the building, reveals a glimpse of the basilica's pre-Palladio, Gothic architecture. The **Loggia del Capitano,** across from the Torre di Piazza, shows the aftermath of the reconstruction, with two stories of white marble arches and thick pillars masking the crumbling brick beneath. (☎0444 32 36 81. Basilica open Tu-Sa 10am-7pm. Entrance to basilica only during exhibitions. €3-5.) The 🏛**Teatro Olimpico,** in P. Matteotti, is the last structure planned by Palladio; he died before its completion. A garden of sculpted figures leads to the ticket office and short portrait gallery. Inside the Teatro, carved figures fill the walls under an oval fresco of cloudy blue sky overhead, while three doors on stage reveal narrow Vicenzian streets crafted in perspective with excruciating attention to detail. (☎0444 22 28 00; www.olimpico.vicenza.it. Open Tu-Su 9am-

5pm. Last admission 4:45pm. €7, students €4, includes entrance to Museo Civico. Cash only.) Each summer the city showcases local and imported talent in the Teatro Olimpico; check www.comune.vicenza.it for a list of productions. (☎0444 22 28 01. €11-20, students €8-15.50. Audioguides in English, Spanish, and German available. AmEx/MC/V.) Housed in Palladio's stately white **Palazzo Chiericati,** the **Museo Civico's** substantial collection includes Giovanni Battista's first signed and dated work, *The Madonna of the Pergola,* as well as Montagna's *Madonna Enthroned,* Tintoretto's *Miracle of St. Augustine,* and Van Dyck's *Le Quattro Eta Dell'Uomo.* (Across from tourist office. ☎0444 32 13 48. Open Tu-Su 9am-5pm. Last admission 4:45pm. Descriptions of major works in English. Purchase tickets at the Teatro Olimpico; entrance included with ticket for theater.) For an elevated view of Vicenza's rooftops and many of Palladio's works, exit the train station and turn right onto Viale Venezia for about 10min., then turn left and go uphill at V. X Giugno. A long white-arched *loggia* to the left contains a steep ramp leading up **Monte Berico** to the expansive plateau of **Piazzale Vittoria,** where a long railing and two stone balconies jut out over the hillside and provide a magnificent view of the city far below.

■ DAYTRIP FROM VICENZA: PALLADIAN VILLAS

Venetian expansion to the mainland began in the early 15th century as Venice's maritime supremacy faded and nobles turned their attention to the acquisition of real estate on the mainland. The Venetian senate decreed that nobles build villas rather than castles to preclude the possibility of petty fiefdoms. The rush to build these rural residential estates provided scores of opportunities for Palladio to display his talents. The Veneto now contains hundreds of the most splendid villas in Europe. Some offer classical music concerts during June and July; others can be rented for exorbitant rates—Neoclassical luxury doesn't come cheap. Check with local and regional tourist offices for details and contact info for dozens of regional villas. Many of the Palladian villas scattered throughout the Veneto are difficult to reach, but fortunately, some of the most famous lie within a scenic 30min. walk of Vicenza. One the most harmonious architectural achievements of the 16th century is the ◙**Villa Rotonda.** Begun in 1550, its geometrical precision and alignment with the cardinal points produced a majestic configuration. It became a model for buildings in France, England, and the US, most notably Thomas Jefferson's Monticello. *(From Mt. Berico's P. Vittoria, head straight, keeping the mountains on the right. Bear left and continue down Stradella Valmarana. Or from Viale Roma, take bus #8 (€1). ☎0444 32 17 93. Open Mar. 15-Oct. 15. Exterior grounds open Tu-Su 10am-noon and 3-6pm, €5; interior open W 10am-noon and 3-6pm, €10.)*

VERONA   ☎045

Verdant gardens and breathtakingly realistic sculptures fill Verona with enough artistic majesty and tragedy to overwhelm any hopeless romantics who haplessly wander into its walls. From dank tombs to dizzying towers, Verona offers all the perks of a large city with a healthy supply of rich wines, authentic local cuisine, and an internationally renowned opera with low student prices. The city's medley of monuments and natural splendor inspired Shakespeare to use it as the setting of his *Romeo and Juliet;* travelers who arrive in search of a tangible remnant of this tragic romance will find an authentic balcony but nary a Montague or monk.

▐ TRANSPORTATION

Flights: Aeroporto Valerio Catullo (☎045 809 56 66; www.aeroportoverona.it), 12km from city center. For shuttles from train station (5:40am, then every 20min. 6:10am-11:10pm; €4.20), buy tickets on bus. Cash only.

Trains: ☎045 89 20 21. In P. XXV Aprile. Ticket office open daily 5:50am-9:30pm. Info office open daily 7am-9pm. **Luggage storage** available (see **Practical Information**). To: **Bologna** (2hr., 27 per day 3:48am-11:01pm, €6); **Milan** (2hr., 37 per day 5:34am-10:42pm, €7); **Rome** (7hr., 8 per day 5:35am-11:01pm, €40); **Trent** (1hr., 25 per day 12:46am-10:48pm, €6); **Venice** (1½hr., 41 per day 5:52am-10:14pm, €6); **Vicenza** (45min., 48 per day 5:52am-10:42pm, €3.35).

Buses: APT in P. XXV Aprile, in the gray building in front of the train station. Station open M-Sa 6am-8pm, Su 6:30am-8pm. To: **Brescia** (2hr., every hr. 6:40am-6:10pm, €5.30); **Montagnana** (2hr., 3 per day 6:20am-6:10pm, €4); **Riva del Garda** (2hr., 17 per day 6:40am-6:45pm, €5); **Sirmione** (1hr., 17 per day 6:40am-8pm, €2.75). Reduced service Sa-Su.

Taxis: RadioTaxi (☎045 53 26 66). Available 24hr.

Car Rental: Hertz (☎045 800 08 32), **Avis** (☎045 800 06 63), **Maggiore** (☎045 800 48 08), and **Europcar** (☎045 59 27 59), at the train station. From €54 per day. All 21+. Discount for extended rentals. Hertz and Maggiore open M-F 8am-noon and 2:30-7pm, Sa 8am-noon; Avis open M-F 8am-12:30pm and 3-7pm, Sa-Su 8am-noon; Europcar open M-F 8:30am-noon and 2:30-7pm, Sa 8:30am-noon. AmEx/MC/V.

■✶🛈 ORIENTATION AND PRACTICAL INFORMATION

From the **train station** in P. XXV Aprile, walk 20min. up **Corso Porta Nuova,** or take bus #11, 12, 13, 72, or 73 (weekends take #91, 92, or 93; tickets €0.93, full-day €3.10) to Verona's center, the **Arena di Verona,** in **Piazza Brà.** Most sights lie between P. Brà and the **Fiume Adige. Via Mazzini** connects the Arena to the monuments of **Piazza delle Erbe** and **Piazza dei Signori.** The **Teatro Romano** and the **Giardino Giusti** lie across the bridges **Pietra, Navi,** and **Nuovo** on the Adige.

Tourist Office: At V. D. Alpini, 9 (☎045 806 86 80; iatverona@provincia.vr.it). From C. Pta. Nuova, enter P. Brà and stay left until you reach the office. Open M-Sa 9am-7pm, Su 9am-3pm. **Branches:** airport (☎/fax 045 861 91 63; iataeroporto@tiscalinet.it; open M-Sa 9am-6pm); train station (☎/fax 045 80 08 61; iatfs@tiscalinet.it; open M-Sa 9am-6pm and Su 9am-3pm).

HelpHandicap (☎045 59 62 49) provides information for those looking for hotels, sights, and transportation with disability assistance.

Luggage Storage: ☎045 802 38 27; info@grandistazioni.it. At train station. €3.50 for 1st 5hr., €0.30 for each of the next 7, and €0.10 for each of the next 12hr. 20kg limit for each piece of luggage. Open 6am-midnight. Cash only.

Lost and Found: V. del Pontiere, 32 (☎045 807 84 58). In police station.

English-Language Bookstore: The Book Shop, V. Interrato dell'Acqua Morta, 3/A (☎045 800 76 14), near Ponte Navi. Classic works and small French and German sections. Open M 3:30-7:30pm, Tu-F and Su 9:30am-12:30pm and 3:30-7:30pm. Cash only.

Work Opportunity: Youth Info Center (Informagiovani), C. Porto Borsari, 17 (☎045 801 07 96; www.informagiovani.comune.verona.it), helps travelers find employment or study opportunities in Verona. Open M, W, F 9am-1pm; M-Th 3-5pm.

Emergency: ☎113. **Ambulance** (☎118). **Police** (☎045 809 04 88).

Pharmacy: Farmacia Due Campane, V. Mazzini, 52 (☎045 800 66 60). Open M-F 9:10am-12:30pm and 3:30-7:30pm, Sa 9:10am-12:30pm. Check the *L'Arena* newspaper for 24hr. pharmacy listings. MC/V.

Hospital: Ospedale Civile Maggiore (☎045 807 11 11), on Borgo Trento in P. Stefani.

Internet: Internet Train, V. Roma, 17/A (☎045 801 33 94). From P. Brà, turn right on V. Roma. 2 blocks ahead on left. €2.50 for 30min. 1st-time users get a bonus hr. after paying €5 for 1st hr. Modern, high-speed computers. Open M-F 11am-10pm, Sa-Su 2-8pm.

Free for cardholders M-F 9-9:30pm. Card accepted at Bar Roma across the street. MC/V.
Realtà Virtuale, V. del Pontiere, 3/C (☎045 59 76 57, fax 59 31 33). From P. Brà, walk for about 5min. along the wall near the tourist office as it curves and turn right on V. Pontiere. €4 per hr. Open M-F 9am-1pm and 3-7pm, Sa 9am-noon. V.

Post Office: P. Viviani, 7 (☎045 805 93 11). Follow V. Cairoli from P. delle Erbe, the post office appears across a small parking lot on the right. Open M-F 8:30am-6:30pm and Sa 8:30am-1pm. Cash only. **Branch** office, V. C. Cattaneo, 23 (☎045 805 99 11). Open M-Sa 8:30am-6:30pm. **Postal Code:** 37100.

■ ACCOMMODATIONS

Budget hotels are sparse in Verona, and those that do exist fill quickly. Make reservations, especially during the opera season (June-Sept.). Prices are significantly lower in the low season.

Ostello della Gioventù Villa Francescatti (HI), Salita Fontana del Ferro, 15 (☎045 59 03 60, fax 800 91 27). Take bus #73 or night bus #90 to P. Isolo. By foot from the Arena, turn onto V. Anfiteatro and walk for 10min. until crossing Ponte Nuovo onto V. Carducci. Turn left and follow V. Giusti, then turn right on Vco. Borgo Tascherio and follow yellow signs for hostel, up the hill. Friendly staff and gorgeous gardens compensate for excessive lockout period. HI members only. Dinner €8. Internet €5.16 per hr., laundry €2.50 wash or dry. 5-night max. Check-in 5pm. Lockout 9am-5pm. Curfew 11:30pm, opera-goers allowed back until 1:30am. Lights out at midnight. Reservations accepted for family rooms. Dorms €13.50; family rooms €15 per person. Cash only. ❶

Locanda Catullo, Vco. Catullo, 1 (☎045 800 27 86, fax 59 69 87). At V. Mazzini, 40, turn on V. Catullo, then turn left on Vco. Catullo. Reception on the 2nd fl. Classic decor with hardwood floors and scattered painting and sculpture. Up-front payment required. Reception daily 9am-11pm. Advance reservations only for stays of 3 or more nights. Singles €40; doubles €55, with bath €65; triples €81/€96. Cash only. ❹

Casa della Giovane (ACISJF), V. Pigna, 7 (☎045 59 68 80; info@casadellagiovane.com). From P. delle Erbe, turn right at Palazzo Maffei onto C. S. Anastasia and take 1st left on V. Rosa; V. Pigna is 3rd street on the right. Bright rooms surround a cobblestone courtyard. Women only. Lockout 9am-1pm. Showers until 10pm. Laundry €1.55 for wash or dry; Internet €5.16 per hr. Curfew 11pm, except for opera-goers (must present a ticket upon return). Reserve ahead by email. Up-front payment required. Dorms €13; singles €18; doubles €28, with bath €34; triples €39/€42. Cash only. ❶

Hotel Mastino, C. Pta. Nuova, 16 (☎045 59 53 88; www.hotelmastino.it). Sleek furniture fills the lobby of this posh hotel. All rooms have bath, A/C, TV, and minibar; ask about bathtubs and balconies. Breakfast included. Wheelchair accessible. Prices vary by season. Singles €68-135; doubles €88-175; triples €160-220. AmEx/MC/V. ❺

Hotel Europa, V. Roma, 8 (☎045 59 47 44; www.veronahoteleuropa.com), minutes from P. Brà. Cool blue decor brightens clean rooms with bath, A/C, TV, minibar, and phone. Breakfast included. Singles €65, with bath €103; doubles €160; triples €185. Prices fall as much as 40% for winter and extended stays. AmEx/MC/V. ❺

■ FOOD

Verona is famous for its wines, among them the dry white *Soave* or the red *Valpolicella, Bardolino, Recioto,* and *Amarone*. For a large selection, try **Enoteca dal Zovo ❶** (see below), which supplies wine to many local trattorias. Local culinary specialties include *gnocchi*, pasta with beans, and asparagus from Rivoli. *Pan-*

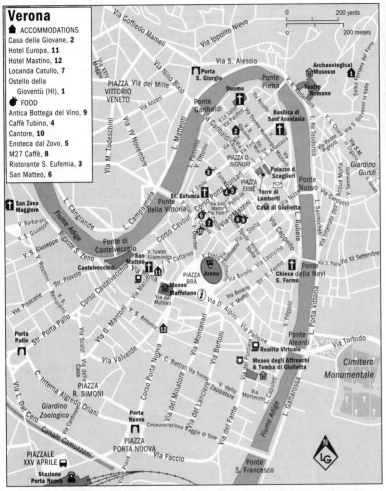

doro, a Christmas cake, is available year-round. **Pam** supermarket, V. dei Mutilati, 3, sells the essentials. (From P. Brà, pass through the arch onto C. Pta. Nuova and turn right onto V. Mutilati. Open M-Sa 8am-8pm, Su 9am-7pm. AmEx/MC/V.)

🦪 **Enoteca dal Zovo,** Vco. S. Marco in Foro, 7/5 (☎045 803 43 69; www.enotecadal-zovo.it), off C. Pta. Borsari. This tavern-like winery occupies a converted chapel—frescoes still adorn the ceiling just left of the entrance. Owners Oreste and Beverly dal Zovo serve impressive wines (from €0.90 a glass) while imparting insider knowledge about Verona. Open M-Th 8am-1pm and 2-8:30pm, F-Su 8am-1pm and 2-9pm. Cash only. ❶

🦪 **Ristorante S. Eufemia,** V. Emilei, 21/B (☎045 800 68 65; www.s.eufemia.it). Family-owned restaurant serves delicious dishes like onion bread and homemade pasta to up to 250 people in this refitted Roman palazzo, complete with shaded outdoor garden. *Primi* €6-15, *secondi* €11-16. Cover €2. Kitchen open June-Aug. daily noon-2:30pm and 6-10:30pm; Sept.-May M-Sa noon-2:30pm and 7:30-10:30pm. AmEx/MC/V. ❸

THE VENETO AND
TRENTINO-ALTO ADIGE

San Matteo, Vco. del Guasto, 4 (☎045 800 45 38; www.pizsmatteo@libero.it), from P. Erbe on C. P. Borsari, walk 5min. and turn left. An attentive staff serves flavorful pizzas (from €3.50) in a converted church building. Call ahead on Sa night to pre-order crepes suzette prepared by the chef who visits weekly. *Primi* €7.80-11, *secondi* €10-14. Open M-F noon-2:30pm and 7pm-12:30am, Sa-Su 6pm-12:30am. AmEx/MC/V. ❸

Antica Bottega del Vino, V. Scudo di Francia, 3 (☎045 800 45 35; www.bottegavini.it), off V. Mazzini. Turn left at Banco Nazionale Lavoro; it's the 1st door on the left. Light pours through stained glass windows, illuminating the frescoed yellow walls of this classy, century-old trattoria. *Primi* €6.50-16, *secondi* €8-21. Cover €3.70. Open M and W-Su 10:30am-3pm and 6pm-midnight. AmEx/MC/V. ❸

Cantore, V. A. Mario, 2 (☎045 803 18 30), near P. Brà. Fluffy crust and rich sauces make Cantore's pizza some of the heartiest in Verona. Enjoy the *spaghetti scoglio con frutti di mare* (with shellfish; €11.95) in a spacious interior or outside under a canopy. Pizza from €4.30. *Primi* €6.80, *secondi* €8. Cover €1.50. Open June-Aug. daily noon-3pm and 6-11pm; Sept.-May M-Tu and Th-Su noon-3pm and 6-11pm. AmEx/MC/V. ❸

M27 Caffè, V. Mazzini, 27 (☎329 134 19 78, fax 045 803 71 11), just down V. Mazzini from P. Brà. Take a colorful cocktail (from €3) and join the hip crowds exhausted from power-shopping in this hip new cafe. Stairs lead to a 2nd fl. with Internet access and couches. Open Tu-Su 9am-2am. Cash only. ❶

Caffè Tubino, C. Pta. Borsari, 15/D (☎045 800 95 02), near the intersection of Pta. Borsari and V. Fama. Housed in a 17th-century palazzo, this tiny cafe serves up healthy doses of coffee and kitsch with its rich brews and floor-to-ceiling wall of teacups. Seating is scarce, but the real draw is the popular ground coffee from €14.46 per kg. Espresso €0.83. Cappuccino €1.19. Open April 15-Oct. 15 M-W 6:45am-8:45pm, Th-Su 6:45am-11:45pm; Oct. 15-Apr. 15 daily 6:45am-11:45pm. Cash only. ❶

👁 SIGHTS

MY VERONA. Looking to save some cash while traveling? The **Verona Card** (day pass €8, 3 days €12) is an excellent money-saving option, covering entry to all museums, churches, and sights, excluding the Giardino Giusti and the Scavi Scaligeri. Purchase it at any participating museum or church. Churches also offer their own pass, permitting entrance to the basilica, duomo, San Fermo, S. Zeno, and S. Lorenzo. (€5, students and seniors €4.)

SHAKESPEAREAN HUBRIS. Verona's most prized attraction is the **Casa di Giulietta,** where tourists pose theatrically on the stone balcony or photographically assault the bronze Juliet below. Lovestruck tweens and modern day *amanti* crowd the courtyard, where graffitied professions of undying love cover the walls. The rooms inside the five-story palazzo are filled with paintings of the lovers, period dress, and a rather suggestive lone double bed. Contrary to popular belief, the del Cappello (Capulet) family never lived here. (*V. Cappello, 23.* ☎045 803 43 03. *Open M 1:30-7:30pm, Tu-Su 8:30am-7:30pm. Ticket office closes 6:45pm. €3.10, students €2.10. Cash only.*) A leafy canopy shades the walkway into the **Museo Degli Affreschi,** which houses an array of Veronese artwork. Native Torquato della Torre's marble *L'Orgia* and *Gaddo a*re on display; tributes to the city's patron saint include Louis Dorigny's huge *Saint Zeno Stops the Wagon Pulled by Demoniacal Oxen.* In the museum's garden is the **Tomba di Giulietta,** a subterranean cave with a single window illuminating the empty sepulchre. (*V. del Pontiere, 5.* ☎045 800 03 61. *Open M 1:30-7:30pm, Tu-Su 8:30am-7:30pm. Ticket office closes 6:45pm. €2.60, students €1.50.*) The **Casa di Romeo,** reportedly once the home of the Montecchi (Montague) family, sits around the corner from P. dei Signorì at V. Arche Scaligeri, 2. The villa is privately owned and closed to the public.

■ **PIAZZA DELLA ERBE AND PIAZZA DELLA SIGNORI.** Stunning architecture reminiscent of an earlier era surrounds a weekday fruit and shamelessly self-promoting souvenir market. At the far end, the green-shuttered windows of the Baroque **Palazzo Maffei** overlook the piazza and the winged lion perched atop the **Column of St. Mark,** a 1523 memorial to centuries of Venetian domination. In the center of the piazza, pigeons hop around both tiers of the **Madonna Verona's Fountain.** Ironically, fruit vendors' awnings nearly hide the pedestal of the squat four-columned **Berlina,** a platform on which medieval convicts were pelted with produce. P. delle Erbe lies near **Via Mazzini,** where pink marble leads local glitterati to Gucci and Louis Vuitton along the city's pedestrian-friendly fashion row. The **Arco della Costa** (Arch of the Rib) connects P. delle Erbe to **Piazza dei Signori.** A whale rib, prophesied to fall on the first passing person who has never told a lie, still dangles from the arch, and a statue of Dante Alighieri stands in the center of the piazza. The famous della Scala family, brutish warlords and avid patrons of the arts, lived here in the **Palazzo degli Scaligeri.** The 15th-century **Loggia del Consiglio** sits in the piazza just behind Dante's back. The view of Verona from the 83m-high ■**Torre dei Lamberti** (1172) is stunning; climb a whopping 368 stairs for panoramic views reaching from P. Erbe to misty hillsides miles away. *(Turn right after Arco della Costa right when P. dei Signori begins. ☎ 045 803 27 26. Open M 1:30-7:30pm, Tu-Su 8:30am-7:30pm. Ticket office closes 45min. before tower. Elevator €2.60, students €2.10; stairs €2.10. Cash only.)* Through the arch in P. dei Signori along V. Arche Scaligeri lie the medieval **Tombs of the Scaligeri,** visible only from the outside.

THE ARENA. A 12th-century earthquake toppled much of the outer wall of this first-century Roman amphitheater, but a lone marble slab still stands tall over 44 remaining seating tiers and interior tunnels. Each summer, the stadium gears up with sets and concession stands to become Verona's **opera house,** where the city stages the famed **Verona Opera Festival.** *(In P. Brà. ☎ 045 800 32 04. Wheelchair accessible. Open M 1:45-6:30pm, Tu-Su 8:30am-6:30pm. Tickets close 45min. before arena. Closes 4:30pm on opera nights. €3.10, students €2.10, children 7-14 €1 with accompanying adult.)*

BASILICA DI SANT'ANASTASIA. This Gothic church, the largest in Verona, hides artistic treasures behind crumbling brick, heavy steel-braced doors, and side towers capped with weeds. Inside, small rose windows illuminate a multicolored marble floor and fully 16 side altars and chapels. To the left of the main altar, the **Cappella del Rosario** boasts a dizzying three stories of marble cherubs, Palladian arches, and dark paintings of Passion scenes by Bernardi and Ridolfi; to the right, the **Cappella Pellegrini** depicts the life of Christ with Michele da Firenze's series of 24 terra-cotta reliefs. *(At the end of C. S. Anastasia. For information, call the Associazione "Chiese Vive" at ☎ 045 59 28 13. Open Mar.-Oct. M-Sa 9am-6pm, Su 1-6pm; Nov.-Feb. Tu-Su 10am-1pm and 1:30-4pm. €2. Ticket for 5 major local churches available for €5, students €4. Cash only.)*

DUOMO AND ENVIRONS. Thermal baths occupied the areas beneath and surrounding the duomo during the Roman period; the 12th-century church now rests on the remains of two previous basilicas. The excavated area, called the Church of St. Elena, is accessible through the duomo, just left of the apse. The duomo itself has been recently restored. Titian's *Assumption of the Virgin* is in the first chapel on the left. *(At the end of V. Duomo. From the basilica, turn on V. Massalongo, which becomes V. Duomo. ☎ 045 59 28 13. Audioguides inside in English; €1. Open Mar.-Oct. M-Sa 10am-5:30pm, Su 1:30-5:30pm; Nov.-Feb. Tu-Sa 10am-1pm and 1:30-4pm, Su 1:30-5pm. €2. Ticket for 5 major local churches available for €5, students €4. Cash only.)*

TEATRO ROMANO AND ENVIRONS. A crumbling **Roman theater** comes alive with productions of Shakespeare's works translated into Italian (see **Entertainment**). Behind the theater's seats, crumbling Roman stairs weave up a small hillside to the city's **archaeological museum.** Once a Jesuit monastery, the museum was built in 1480 and now displays Roman and Greek artifacts excavated from the area. In the center sits the **Grande Terrazza,** a quiet, leafy garden lined with Roman bas-relief and pedestals. *(V. R. Redentore, 2. Cross Ponte Pietra from the city center and turn right.* ☎ *045 800 03 60, fax 801 05 87. Open M 1:15-7:30pm, Tu-Su 8:30am-7:30pm. Ticket office closes 6:45pm. €2.60, students €1.50. Cash only.)* Behind a brown facade, the gates of the 16th-century **Giardino Giusti** open onto a spacious hillside dotted with gurgling moss-covered fountains and rows of meticulously trimmed hedges—including **Il Labirinto,** a thigh-high hedge maze. The cypress-lined avenue gradually winds upwards to a series of picturesque porticoes and curving balconies with breathtaking views of Verona. *(Down V. S. Chiara from Teatro Romano at V. Giusti, 2.* ☎ *045 803 40 29. Open daily 9am-8pm. €5, under 18 free. Cash only.)*

CASTELVECCHIO AND ENVIRONS. The castle was built in the 14th century by the della Scala family, whose coat of arms and frescoes still line the interior walls. The Veronese added "Vecchio" (old) to the castle's title to distinguish it from another later built by the Visconti. These days, the castle houses a **museum** of sculptures and paintings, among them Pisanello's celebration of natural paradise in *Madonna della Quaglia.* **Ponte Castelvecchio** to the left of the castle provides a lovely view of Verona along the swirling **Fiume Adige.** *(At the end of V. Roma from P. Brà on C. Castelvecchio, 2.* ☎ *045 59 29 85; www.comune.verona.it/castelvecchio/cvsito. Open M 1:30-7:30pm, Tu-Su 8:30am-7:30pm. Ticket office closes 6:45pm. €3.10, students €2.10. Cash only.)* Scipione Maffei's devotion to preserving stone inscriptions lives on in the nearby **Museo Maffeiano,** where much of the sizeable array of Greek, Roman, and Etruscan art is over 2000 years old. *(At the corner of V. Roma and C. Pta. Nuova.* ☎ *045 59 00 87. Open M 1:30-7:30pm, Tu-Su 8:30am-7:30pm. €2.10, students €1.50. Cash only.)*

SAN ZENO MAGGIORE. This massive brick church is one of Verona's finest examples of Italian Romanesque architecture, named for Verona's patron saint, who converted the city to Christianity in the 4th century. An urn in the crypt holds Zeno's remains, while the Porphyry Basin, which the saint famously commanded the Devil to move, rests near the base of the nave. *(From Castelvecchio, walk up Rigaste S. Zeno and turn left at the piazza on V. Barbarani, which leads to the church. For information, call the Associazione "Chiese Vive" at* ☎ *045 59 28 13. Open Mar.-Oct. M-Sa 8:30am-6pm, Su 9am-12:30pm and 1:30-6pm; Nov.-Feb. M-Sa 8:30am-1pm and 1:30-5pm, Su 9am-12:30pm and 1:30-5pm. €2. Ticket for 5 major local churches available for €5, students €4. Cash only.)*

SAN FERMO. This 11th-century church rests on the spot where Saints Fermo and Rustico were tortured to death in AD 304. The upper interior has a Gothic design; a staircase on the right leads to the Romanesque marble lower church's array of columns and the remains of the saints. *(Walk down V. Cappello toward P. Navi. Church is on the corner of Str. S. Fermo. For information, call the Associazione "Chiese Vive" at* ☎ *045 59 28 13. Open Mar.-Oct. M-Sa 10am-6pm, Su 1-6pm; Nov.-Feb. M-Sa 10am-1pm and 1:30-4pm, Su 1-5pm. €2. Ticket for 5 major local churches available for €5, students €4. Cash only.)*

🎵 ENTERTAINMENT

The Arena di Verona is the venue for the world-famous 🎭**Verona Opera Festival,** which attracts opera buffs in droves every year from June to September. Operas scheduled for 2005 include Puccini's *La Boheme* and *Turandot,* Ponchielli's *La Gioconda,* and Verdi's *Nabucco* and—of course—*Aida,* which is widely regarded as one of the festival's highlights. (Tickets and information at V. Dietro Anfiteatro 6/B, along the side of the Arena. ☎ 045 800 51 51; www.arena.it. Open M-F 9am-noon and 3:15-5:45pm, Su 9am-noon. During 2005 opera season (June 17-Aug. 31), open on performance days from 10am-9pm, non-performance days 10am-5:45pm. General admission on the Roman steps M-Th and Su €16.50-24.50, F-Sa €18.50-26.50. General admission ticket-holders should arrive 1hr. before showtime.

Reserved seats €73-157. AmEx/MC/V.) Also from June to September, the Teatro Romano stages dance performances and Shakespeare plays performed in Italian. June brings a jazz festival known as **Verona Jazz.** (Info ☎045 806 64 88 or 806 64 85; www.estateteatraleveronese.it. Ticket office, at Palazzo Barbieri, V. Leoncino, 61, open M-Sa 10:30am-1pm and 4-7pm. Tickets for both €10.33-20.66.) Those who aren't fans of opera (or its prices) can check out the **movie theater** at V. Poloni, 16 (☎045 800 67 77). Verona's nightclubs lie beyond walking distance of the city.

TREVISO
☎0422

Treviso, provincial capital of the Veneto, is known by two other names, *Città d'Acqua* (City of Water) and *Città Dipinta* (Painted City). Treviso's predominant aspect, however, is its wealth. In the birthplace of Benetton, local fashionistas find plenty of eye candy in the glitzy storefronts of ornate palaces. Also enjoyable are the wide cobblestone lanes and quiet canals that weave through the old city.

📧 TRANSPORTATION. Treviso is the main stop on the busy Venice-Udine train line. The **train station** is in P. Duca d'Aosta, south of the city center. For info, call Trenitalia. (☎89 20 21; www.trenitalia.it. Ticket counter open daily 6am-8pm. AmEx/MC/V.) Trains depart to: Trieste (2½hr., 15 per day 4:51am-10:25pm, €8.99); Udine (1½hr., 36 per day 12:04am-11:29pm, €5.73); and Venice (30min., 58 per day 5:06am-11:46am, €2). Trains to Milan or Padua connect in Venice. A variety of carriers operate from the **bus station** at Lungosile A. Mattei, 21 (☎0422 57 73 60), off C. del Popolo where it crosses the river. From the train station, turn left on V. Roma. **La Marca** (☎0422 57 73 11; www.lamarcabus.it) services the Veneto region and the **Palladian Villas,** sending buses to Padua (1½hr., 29 per day 6am-7:45pm, €3.60) and Vicenza (1½hr., 11 per day 6:15am-5:10pm, €4.20). The ticket window is open daily (6:25am-7:50pm). **ACTV** (☎041 528 78 86; informazioni@actv.it) runs buses to Venice (1hr., 40 per day 4:10am-8:10pm, €2.40). Check the ticket window (open daily 6:50am-1pm and 1:30-7:45pm). All buses run reduced service Saturday to Sunday.

📧📧 ORIENTATION AND PRACTICAL INFORMATION. Treviso lies 30km inland from Venice. Surrounded by the flowing waters of the Sile, the old city walls encompass Treviso's historic center and most points of interest. From the **train station,** the **ACTT** (intracity) bus hub is directly across from the busy **Piazza Duca d'Aosta.** Just left of the buses, **Via Roma** leads over the river and between the crumbling walls into the city center; it then becomes **Corso del Popolo,** crosses the river, and enters **Piazza della Borsa.** From there, a short walk up **Via XX Settembre** leads to **Piazza dei Signori,** Treviso's main square and near the **Palazzo dei Trecento.** Pedestrian-dominated **Via Calmaggiore** leads to the duomo.

The **APT tourist office,** P. Monte di Pietà, 8 (☎0422 54 76 32; www.provincia.treviso.it), on the side of Palazzo dei Trecento from P. dei Signori, has city **maps,** regional accommodations listings, and itineraries for walking tours along the Sile River. (Open M 9am-12:30pm, Tu-F 9am-12:30pm and 2-6pm, Sa-Su 9am-12:30pm and 3-6pm.) **Luggage storage** is available at the train station. (€3 for 1st 12hr., €2 each additional 12hr. Open M-F 7am-8pm and Sa-Su 8:30am-6pm. Cash only.) In case of **emergency, call** ☎113 or an **ambulance** (☎118). The **police** are located at V. Carlo Alberto, 37 (☎0422 57 71 11). **Ospedale Civile Ca' Foncello** is at P. Ospedale, 1 (☎0422 32 21). Find info on employment opportunities at **Informagiovani,** P. Duomo, 19 (☎0422 65 85 40; www.informagiovani.tv.it. Open Tu-Sa 9am-12:30pm and W-F 3-6pm) and **Internet** at **Attrazione Las Vegas,** V. Roma, 29 (☎0422 59 02 47; €5 for 50min. or €10 for 2hr.; open M-F and Su 10am-11pm, Sa 10am-12:30am. Cash only). The **post office,** P. Vittoria, 1 (☎0422 653 11), is at the end of V. Cadorna, off C. del Popolo (open M-Sa 8:30am-6:30pm). **Postal Code:** 31100.

⌐⌐ ACCOMMODATIONS AND FOOD. The four-star **Hotel Carlton ❺**, Largo Porta Altinia, 15, right off of V. Roma, 2min. from the train station, has rooms with A/C, satellite TV, phone, and minibar. Marble pillars, a sweeping staircase, and garden terrace are complemented by responsive, professional service. (☎0422 41 16 61; www.hotelcarlton.it. Impressive buffet breakfast included. Reception 24hr. Singles €95-118; doubles €160-190; triples €190. AmEx/MC/V.) **Albergo Campeol ❹**, P. Ancilotto, 4, is conveniently situated behind Palazzo dei Trecento. One of the better deals in town, it offers spacious rooms with bath, TV, phone, and cheery yellow decor. (☎/fax 0422 566 01. Breakfast €5. Reception 24hr. Reserve ahead. Singles €52; doubles €83. AmEx/MC/V.) To reach **Da Renzo ❹**, V. Terraglio, 108, exit the train station, turn right, mount the stairs to the overpass, and head right down Str. Terraglio for 10min. Or, take bus #7, 8, or 11 (€0.74) and ask the driver for Da Renzo or the Borgo Savoia stop. The 11 rooms of this tiny yellow villa share a marble staircase and a tiled breakfast nook. All rooms have bath, nighttime A/C, and phone. (☎0422 40 20 68; www.locandadarenzo.it. Breakfast included. Reception 7am-12:30am. Singles €48; doubles €68; triples €88. AmEx/MC/V.)

Treviso is famous for its cherries, which ripen in June; *radicchio*, which peaks in December; and *tiramisù*, a heavenly combination of espresso-and-rum-soaked cake layered with the delectable, mild *mascarpone* cheese, which is always in season. Its name means, literally, "pick me up," and it's the rumored dessert of choice among those with frustrated libidos. In summer, try a cool scoop of *tiramisù* gelato. To taste these delights, head to the Saturday and Tuesday morning produce **market** at the Stiore stop of the #2 or 11 bus. The fish and vegetable **market** is on tiny Isola dell'Pescheria, surrounded by the canals. (Open Tu-Sa 7:30am-12:30pm.) Head to the PAM **supermarket**, V. Zorzetto, 12, off C. del Popolo, for basics. (☎0422 58 39 13. Open M-Sa 8:30am-7:30pm. AmEx/MC/V.) ◤**La Vera Terra**, ❷ V. G. di Treviso, 5, across from Hotel Carlton, offers hearty vegetarian dishes in an elegant setting. Low prices and delicious plates like the *gazpacho adaluse al cumino* (€4.50) and *maccheroni al tofu e fiori di zucca* (€4.50) draw clientele ranging from hip locals to well-dressed businesspeople. (☎0422 41 02 03; laveraterra@libero.it. *Primi* from €4.50, *secondi* from €5. Cover €1. Open M-Sa 10am-2:30pm and 7:30-11pm. MC/V.) **All'Oca Bianca ❸**, V. della Torre, 7, is on a side street off V. Calmaggiore. This casual trattoria serves excellent fish dishes from a fresh seasonal menu. (☎0422 54 18 50. *Primi* €5-7, *secondi* and fish €9-13. Cover €2, includes mineral water. Open M-Tu and F-Su 12:30-2:15pm and 7:30-10:15pm, Th 7:30-10:15pm. AmEx/MC/V.) Fast food meets Italian style at **Brek ❶**, C. del Popolo, 25, where inexpensive buffet-style dining opens onto a streetside terrace and a second floor with a plant-filled garden. (☎0422 59 00 12. Pasta and salads €2.60-7. Open daily 11:30am-3pm and 6:30-10pm. AmEx/MC/V.) For local desserts, try **Nascimben ❶**, V. XX Settembre, 3, where plush red booths and tiny marble tables host a steady parade of indulgent diners. If *primi* seem a mere inconvenient delay, begin with a slice of ◤ *tiramisù* that perfectly tempers its rich rum and espresso with thin layers of mouthwatering *mascarpone*. (☎0422 59 12 91. Open M-Sa 7:30am-1:30am, Su 8am-1:30am. Cash only.)

◉ SIGHTS. From V. XX Settembre, skirt the right side of the busy, cafe-lined loggias of **Piazza dei Signori** to find the marble-staircase of the **Palazzo dei Trecento**, a *de facto* memorial to the 1944 Good Friday air raid that devastated the small town. A marble plaque under the stairs commemorates local citizens killed in German concentration camps. (☎0422 65 82 35. Closed to the public. Call to make a reservation or contact the tourist office about group tours.) To see and be seen, strut the busy and boutique-laden Calmaggiore, flowing from beneath the arcades of the P. dei Signori to the white and gray Palladian arch of the seven-domed **Neoclassical duomo.** In the stark moulded white and gray interior, its **Cappella Malchiostro** dates from 1519 and contains works by sworn enemies Titian and Pordenone. (Open M-Sa 7:30am-noon and 3:30-7pm, Su 7:30am-1pm and 3:30-8pm. Cappella illumination €0.30. Free.)

THE DOLOMITES (I DOLOMITI)

Somewhere between Trent and Innsbruck lies a land of shattered rocky peaks etched smooth with the passage of time. This surreal landscape takes its name from the hard magnesium-laced mineral of which it is largely composed. Its secluded heights have ensured the continued existence of groups such as the Ladins, who speak a 2000-year-old linguistic hybrid of Latin and Celtic. One glance at the lush conifers and snow-covered peaks of this panorama explains why back-packers and skiers still flock to the area Le Corbusier once called "the most beautiful natural architecture in the world." The Dolomites stretch from Trentino Alto-Adige, through the Veneto, into Friuli-Venezia Giulia. Public transportation can be

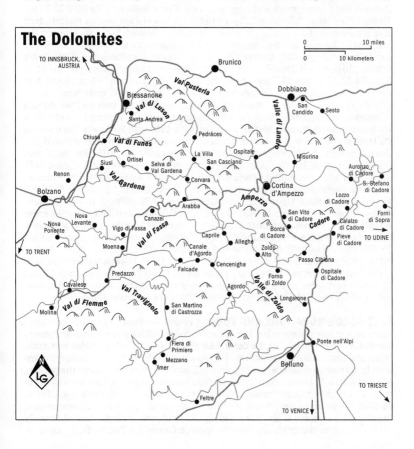

The Dolomites

a little spotty, but planning goes a long way in an area used to travelers and their needs. From mountain refuges to luxury hotels, the Dolomites offer customized adventure and beauty for any appreciative wayfarer.

BELLUNO ☎ 0437

On the southeastern border of the Dolomites, Belluno contains the best of both worlds for budget travelers: easy transportation to neighboring towns, but inexpensive dining and lodging just kilometers from gorgeous biking paths, hiking trails of every imaginable difficulty, and beautiful views. Belluno's welcoming charm ensures that visitors can usually find a knowledgeable helping hand in planning a hike—or an affordable hotel, hot shower, and comfy bed afterward.

🖥🔊 TRANSPORTATION AND PRACTICAL INFORMATION. Belluno runs trains to a wide number of cities, but some are much less frequent than others and it may be wise to plan in advance. **Trains** run to Belluno from Padua (2hr., 14 per day 6am-10:46pm, €5.73) via Conegliano (1hr., 9 per day 6:08am-7:31pm; €2.69), on the Venice-Udine line. From Conegliano, some scheduled trains run directly to Belluno, but many require a change in nearby Ponte nelle Alpi. (☎ 0437 72 77 91. Ticket office open daily 6am-7:25pm.) Belluno's bus station, across **Piazzale della Stazione** from the train station, is a regional hub for **Dolomiti Bus**, which serves the pre-Alps to the west and the eastern Dolomites. Buses run to: Calalzo (1hr., 12 per day 6:15am-8:05pm, €3); **Cortina** (2hr., 10 per day 6:25am-6:50pm, €3.70); **Feltre** (40min., 16 per day 6:20am-7:10pm, €2.50). For more information, call ☎ 0437 94 11 67 or 94 12 37. (Open M-F 8am-noon and 3-6pm, Sa 8am-noon. When closed, buy ticket from tourist office.) Orange **local buses** (€0.80) stop in P. della Stazione.

The city center, **Piazza dei Martiri**, is a 5min. walk from the **train** and **bus stations** in **Piazzale della Stazione**. From the train terminal, cross the parking lot and follow **Via Dante** through **Piazzale Battisti** and across **Via Caffi** onto **Via Loreto**. Turn left on **Via Matteotti** so that P. dei Martiri, overlooking several fountains and sculpted gardens, is in sight. **Banks** with similar exchange rates and 24hr. **ATMs** line the piazza. For maps, a list of Internet points, and hiking info, cross through the garden in P. dei Martiri and pass through **Porta Dante** onto **Via XXX Aprile**. After a two minute walk, the **tourist office** appears on the right at P. del Duomo, 2. (☎ 0437 94 00 83; www.infodolomiti.it. Open daily 9am-12:30pm and 3:30-5:30pm.) In case of **emergency**, call ☎ 113; the **police** (☎ 0437 94 55 08), on V. Volontari d. Libertà; or an **ambulance** (☎ 118). **Pharmacies** post the 24hr. rotation schedule in their windows; **Farmacia Dott. Perale**, P. V. Emanuele, 12, is centrally located and open late. (☎ 0437 25 271. Open M-Sa 8:45am-12:30pm and 4-7:30pm and Su 8:45am-12:30pm. AmEx/MC/V.) The **hospital** is at V. Loreto, 32 (☎ 0437 161 11). A **Telecom Italia** center at V. Caffi, 7, has **Internet** and rows of pay phones. (€5.16 per hr. Open daily 8am-11pm.) Belluno's **post office** offers fax and photocopy services at V. Roma, off P. Emanuele. (☎ 0437 95 32 11. Open M-Sa 8:30am-6:30pm.) **Postal Code:** 32100.

🏠🍴 ACCOMMODATIONS AND FOOD. Central locations and cliffside balconies come at low nightly rates. Inquire at the tourist office about cheap accommodations and *affittacamere*. **La Cerva B&B ❶**, V. Paoletti, 7/B, provides mountain bikes and home-cooked breakfast. Globetrotting students frequent homey rooms and the terrace overlooking the Dolomites. Exit the train station, cross the parking lot, and follow V. Dante. Turn left onto Viale Volantari Libertà, then cross V. Fantuzzi and turn left. After crossing wide street near V. Col di Lana, look for V. Paoletti on the right. (☎ 338 825 36 08; www.lacerva.it. Breakfast €2 per person. Singles €18; doubles €31. Extra bed €8.50. Cash only.) Elegance and friendly staff abound at the centrally located **Albergo Cappello e Cadore ❹**, V. Ricci, 8.

Rooms in the 1843 building come with minifridge, TV, Internet port, and phone; some have a jacuzzi and balcony. Take Viale Volontari Libertà from the station. Turn right on V. Fantuzzi, which changes to V. J. Tasso; V. Ricci branches off. (☎0437 94 02 46; www.albergocappello.com. Breakfast included. Singles €40-50; doubles €85-105; triples €110. AmEx/MC/V.) **Hotel Astor ❹**, P. dei Martiri, 26/E, features a terrace over a deep Dolomite valley, as well as spacious rooms. (☎0437 94 20 94; www.astorhotelbelluno.com. Buffet breakfast included. Reception 7:30am-11:30pm. Singles €47-57; doubles €70-€80; *superios* €70-€100. Prices rise about €5 in the summer. AmEx/MC/V.) **Albergo Centrale ❸**, V. Loreto, 2, offers 12 clean, affordable rooms. (☎0437 94 94 66. Breakfast included. Reserve ahead. Singles €31; doubles with bath €52.)

Dining options in the *centro* are plentiful and inexpensive. **Supermarket per Dolomiti,** P. dei Martiri, 9/10, has a hot deli as well as groceries. (☎0437 94 20 00. Open M-Tu and Th-Su 8am-1pm and 4:30-7:30pm, W 8am-1pm. V.) **La Trappola Birreria e Spaghetteria ❷**, P. le Cesare Battisti, 6, serves massive portions in a lively bar, including classic spaghetti *primo* (€6-8) with a salad served in a bowl the size of a small sink. (☎0437 274 17. Flavored regional *grappe* €2.50. Open M-F 11am-3pm and 5:50pm-2am, Sa 5pm-3am. AmEx/MC/V.) **Al Mirapiave ❷**, V. Matteotti, 29, has 60 types of pizza and vegetarian specials like *Belluna*, a salad with zucchini, potatoes, mushrooms, and cheese (€4). In warm weather, dine on the cliff-side balcony. (☎0437 94 18 13. Pizza €5.60-8. Pasta €4.80-10. Cover €1. Open M and W-Su 11:30am-3:30pm and 6pm-1am. MC/V.) Descend through the red-walled bar into **Ristorante Taverna ❸**, V. Cipro, 7, where local specialties like *galletti alla diavola* (devilish chicken) are served in the dining room. (☎0437 25 192. *Primi* €5.20-6, *secondi* €8-10. Cover €1. Open M-Sa noon-2:30pm and 7:30-10pm. AmEx/MC/V.) At **Ristorante delle Alpi ❷**, V.J. Tasso, 13, the specialty is fish of any variety, so ask about the freshest catches. (☎0437 94 03 02. *Primi* €5-8.50, fish *secondi* €7-13. Open M-Sa 12:30-2:30pm and 7:30-10:30pm. MC/V.) **La Buca ❷**, V. Carrera, 15/C, offers a menu of meats and pastas, but the real draw is the hearty marinara pizza, just €3.20. (☎0437 94 01 91. *Primi* €4.80-8.50, *secondi* €6.50-10.30. Cover €1. Open daily 11:30am-3:30pm and 6pm-2am.)

◪ SIGHTS. Changes in the city's government can be traced in the ornamental architecture of the **Piazza del Duomo.** On the gate of the **Palazzo Miari,** a residence of the Miari family, a second coat of arms appeared when Belluno switched branches of the

THE LOCAL STORY

NATURAL FLAVOR

Vittoria De Pian from La Cerva B&B in Belluno, takes plain grappa *and flavors it with natural products like fruit, mint, and honey for specific and vibrant tastes. Here she explains the techniques of this local process.*

LG: How do you flavor *grappa* with fruits and grasses?

A: The fruits used for flavoring must remain in the dark for different times. Raspberry needs three months, while cherry only needs one. Different grasses must remain one year. For cumin, one year is also best. Then you can add different spices, according to the type of *grappa* you are making.

LG: What's your favorite?

A: My favorite is blackberry, but this is a difficult one to make because you cannot buy the blackberries. You must go into the mountains and find them in August, as even the ones you buy in a shop aren't good enough quality.

LG: How long have you know how to flavor *grappa?*

A: I've been working on this for five or six years. I learned from older people, like my mother-in-law—but not my mother, because she comes from central Italy, and people who live here know the technique best. It's easier for them to make different kinds of *grappa.* Certain flowers and grasses grow only regionally and they make specific *grappas* with these, often specific to a town or even an individual mountain.

family tree from the 16th- to 17th-century. (Around the right corner of the post office. Privately owned, no entry.) In the mid-17th century, academics gathered in the nearby **Palazzo dei Giuristi,** whose benefactors' busts line the facade. Since 1876, the building has housed the **Museo Civico,** which exhibits preserved pottery, jewelry, and a wide collection of works by Caffi; the second floor's ornate metal flowers and Ridolfi's *Deposizione nel Sepolcro* are highly recommended. (☎0437 94 48 36; www.comune.belluno.it. Open Apr.-Sept. Tu-Sa 10am-noon and 4-7pm; Oct.-Apr. M-Sa 10am-noon and Tu-F 3-6pm. €2.30; students, over 60, or groups of 10+ €1.20, under 5 free. Ticket office closes 20min. before Museo.) Since 1838, the town government has rested next to the information office in the red **Palazzo Rettori,** which now houses the city's **Municipio.** Admittedly, Belluno's biggest attractions loom on its horizon: the vast **Parco Nazionale di Dolomiti Bellunese** (Bellunese Dolomites National Park) starts at the northern edge of Belluno. (☎0439 33 28; www.dolomitipark.it.) For a more aerial travel package, the **Botanical Garden of the Eastern Alps** rests at the top of a chairlift on the western slope of nearby **Monte Faverghera.** Buses from Belluno service the chairlift, which zooms 1500m up the mountain. (☎0437 94 48 30. Tourist office updates bus and chairlift schedules. Open June 9-Sept. 22 Tu-Su 9:30am-noon and 1-5:30pm. €1.50, 14 years and under €0.80.)

 HIKING. For Alpine info, visit the **CAI office,** P. S. Giovanni Bosco, 11. From the tourist office, cross the piazza and turn right into P. V. Emanuele. Continue straight ahead and down the stairs. Cross the river and take V. S. Antonio. When the road forks, take V. S. Giuseppe to P. S. Giovanni Bosco. The office is ahead, across the piazza. Buy membership for a reduced price at mountain *rifugi.* (☎/fax 0437 93 16 55; http://digilander.libero.it/caibelluno. Open Apr.-Oct. F 8:30am-10:30pm.) Belluno offers excellent hiking trails; one of the best is along the *altavia,* stretching north and south from Braies and Belluno, respectively. Hiking the entire *altavia* would take between eight and fifteen days, but the hike along the first stretch, from Belluno to **Rifugio #7,** can be done in a day. From Belluno's P. Martiri, take V. J. Tasso, which changes to V. Fantuzzi, and then V. Col di Lana. Follow this for about 1km until a sign points right, toward Bolzano; walk uphill about 9km. The paved road is easily cycled or walked in about 3hr., ending at Casa Bortot (707m). Stock up on food here—it's the last stop before Rifugio #7. Follow the small gravel path to the left, leading to the Parco Nazionale Dolomiti Bellunesi, or the start of **Altavia #1.** The route is well-marked and sticks close to the river gorge, with views of waterfalls and deep pools etched out of the dolomite rock. A 3-4hr. hike leads to a small meadow and Rifugio #7 at **Pils Pilon.** (☎0437 94 16 31, in winter 0445 66 11 28. Call ahead to confirm availability. Serves hot meals. Open June-Sept. Rooms €16, CAI members €8. Inquire about the more difficult surrounding hikes. Cash only.) For information on the *altevie,* visit www.dolomiti-altevie.it.

> **⭐TIP** **CLUB ALPINO ITALIANO (CAI).** Those intending to do a serious amount of hiking in Italy should consider purchasing a **Club Alpino Italiano membership.** CAI runs many mountain *rifugi,* and members pay half-price for lodgings. *Rifugi,* which generally operate from late June to early October, may also rent out *vie ferrate* hiking equipment essentials. Membership is €35, under 18 €11.50, with a €5.50 supplement for new members and €15.50 surcharge for non-Italians. It can be purchased at a CAI office; bring a passport photo.

CORTINA D'AMPEZZO ☎0436

As ski season heats up, the winding, brightly lit streets of Cortina d'Ampezzo suddenly fill with multinational glitterati (up to 40,000 during holidays) who find themselves drawn to the powdery snow, stylish boutiques, and a vast array of adventure sports offered by this mountain paradise. But trust-fund deficient travelers aren't left out in the cold, as prices of hotels and restaurants plummet in the low season to spread the area's (natural) wealth.

TRANSPORTATION AND PRACTICAL INFORMATION. Cortina's location high in the Dolomites also makes it difficult to reach without a car. The nearest **train station** is in Calalzo, but hourly buses run up a road from Calalzo to Cortina (1hr., 17 per day 7:33am-9:23pm, €2.41) and back (1 hr.; 17 per day 7:33am-9:23pm, last bus back 8:10pm; €2.41). Trains run to Calalzo from Belluno (1hr.; 9 per day 5:40am-8:43pm; €2.69); Milan (8hr.), and Venice. (3hr.) **Buses** run directly from Cortina to Belluno (2hr., 9 per day 5:35am-5:55pm, €3.70); Milan (7hr., June-Aug. F-Sa, €22.56); Venice (5hr.; June 23-Aug. daily, Sept.-June 22 Sa-Su only; €13.45). Train information available only from local public phones at ☎0436 89 20 21. The orange **urban buses** service Cortina and the Valle d'Ampezzo, and the nine lines are useful for reaching hotels, trails, and cable cars outside town. Buy tickets (€0.80) at newsstands, *tabacchi*, and bars near bus stops. For longer visits, buy urban bus passes in books of six (€4.20) or 12 (€8), or buy a Guest Card (€10.33) for a week of free transportation in the province on urban and Dolomite bus lines. For more info on all buses, call or stop by the **Dolomiti Bus information desk,** in the Cortina bus station. (☎0436 86 79 21. Open M-F 8:15am-12:30pm and 2:30-6pm and Sa 8:15am-12:30pm. MC/V.) For **RadioTaxi,** dial ☎0436 86 08 88. (Available 24hr.)

Pedestrian thoroughfare **Corso Italia,** lined with boutiques and anchored by the duomo's *campanile*, runs through the center of town. From the **bus station,** cross **Via Marconi,** head left, and take the long, sloping **Largo Poste** downhill to the *centro.* The **tourist office** is in Piazzetta S. Francesco, 8, off V. Mercato, on the opposite side of the duomo from the station and to the left. Ask for information on hiking, skiing, and local culture. (☎0436 32 31. Open M-F 9am-12:30pm and 3:30-6:30pm.) On weekends, try the **branch** at P. Roma, 1. (☎0436 27 11; www.infodolomiti.it. Open Sa-Su 9am-12:30pm and 3:30-6:30pm.) The **Banca di Trento e Bolzano,** C. Italia, 15, offers **currency exchange,** an **ATM,** and cashes **travelers checks.** (☎0436 86 62 48, fax 0436 86 64 08. Open M-F and Su 8:20am-1:20pm and 2:45-4:15pm.) In case of **emergency,** dial ☎113, or call the **police** (☎0436 86 62 00), on V. Marconi. **Ospedale Cortina** is at V. Roma, 121 (☎0436 88 51 11). **Farmacia Internazionale,** C. Italia, 151, offers long hours and posts a 24hr. rotation in its windows. (☎0436 22 23. Open

FROM THE ROAD

TIPS FOR BIKING THE DOLOMITES

#1. Bring water. You'd think that entrepreneurial types would supply sustenance for the steady procession of adventurers that regularly storm the mountain. Not only would you be wrong, you'd be really thirsty.

#2. Don't believe everything you're told. The woman in the tourist office who plotted my route said it only took her 50min. Clearly, she was speaking from her own mountain-hardened experience and didn't take my delicate constitution and aversion to sweat into account. Three hours later, I had heat stroke and a new vendetta.

#3. Check your brakes before you leave. Though it may take three hours of leg-pumping labor to inch up the side of a hill, it only takes about twenty minutes of 30-mile-per-hour curves and frantic brake pumping to fly back down again.

#4. Finally, listen to your body. After squeezing my handlebars for a white-knuckled flight down bone-jarring gravel, I noticed that I had blisters covering both of my hands. When I got off my bike to get water, my legs decided to stop working and I fell down. That should have been a sign to rest; instead I took it to mean that I should pedal from my calves. Now I can't use stairs. You live, you learn.

-Ryan Thoreson

M-Sa 8:45am-12:30pm and 4-7:30pm.) For those willing to spend some money, **Internet** is available at **Dolomiti Multimedia**, L. Poste, 59. (☎0436 86 80 90, fax 0436 86 67 04. €9.30 per hr., €4.65 per 30min. Open M-F 9am-12:30pm and 3-7:30pm. Cash only.) The **post office** and **ATM** are at L. Poste, 18. (☎0436 88 24 11, fax 0436 88 24 40. Open M-F 8:30am-2pm, Sa 8:30am-1pm.) **Postal Code:** 32043.

◖◗ ACCOMMODATIONS AND FOOD. Cortina is full of upscale hotels for the wealthy tourists who descend on the town in August and winter, but rates plummet in the low season. The cheapest in the *centro* is the four-story **Hotel Montana ❸**, C. Italia, 94, near the duomo. Clean rooms share a TV lounge with video games and movies. (☎0436 86 04 98; hmontana.cortina@dolomiti.org. Singles €34-50; doubles €62-90. AmEx/MC/V.) **Hotel Fiames ❹**, Località Fiames, 13, books rooms with bath and meals in Fiames, 5km north of town. Take bus #1 (10min., 14 per day 7:30am-7:34pm, €0.80) from the station to the last stop. (☎0436 23 66, fax 57 33. Breakfast included. Lunch or dinner €15.50. Singles €42-54; doubles €52-65.) **Hotel Oasi ❸**, V. Cantore, 2, offers soft bedding, TV, and hot showers for the hiker with a lust for luxury. Behind the bus station, turn left where Oasi sits on a small hill. (☎0436 86 20 91; www.hoteloasi.it. Breakfast included. Reception 8am-10pm. Singles €40-80; doubles €90-150; triples €90-180. MC/V.) **International Camping Olimpia ❶**, is in Località Fiames. Bus #1 stops at the access road just before Hotel Fiames; ask the driver for Olimpia. The grounds have a post office, sauna, bar, and restaurant. The list of rules may give pause—strict checkout at noon, cars are barred from entry, silence is enforced from 1-3pm and 11pm-7am, and visitors are charged the guest fee after one hour. (☎/fax 0436 50 57. Reception 9am-noon and 3-7pm. Adults €4.50-7.50, children under 10 €2.50-4, dogs €1.03; RVs and cars with tents or trailers €7-9; bunks €19-20 per day. Cash only.)

For a decadent end to a day of alpine sports, drop into **Mokarabia ❶**, C. Italia, 44, where patrons sample coffee, lavish desserts, and cocktails at chic backlit booths. Head barmaster and author Ettore Diana holds the Guinness World Record as creator of the world's largest cappuccino (1500L); digest a miniature version with his espresso. (☎0436 86 37 77. Espresso €1. Open M-W and F-Su 7:45am-10pm. AmEx/V.) At **Pizzeria Il Ponte ❶**, V. B. Franchetti, 8, enjoy German influence in the with the *Wurstel*, pizza covered in tomatoes, mozzarella, and frankfurt *wurstel* (€5.50). From the bus station, turn left onto V. Marconi and follow the road as it curves down the hill to reach V. B. Franchetti. (☎/fax 0436 86 76 24; www.ilpontez.supereva.it. Open Tu-Su 10am-3pm and 6:30pm-midnight. MC/V.) Hop across the street to the produce, packaged meats, and liquor arcade at Kanguro **supermarket**, V. B. Franchetti, 1. (☎0436 48 36. Open M-Sa 8:30am-12:30pm and 3:30-7:30pm. MC/V.) **Panificio Pasticceria ❶**, V. del Mercato, 10, offers fresh breads, a small dairy case, and pizza by the slice (margherita €9.40/kg) in a little bakery right in the *centro*. (Open M-Tu and Th-Su 6:30am-1pm and 3-7:10pm, W 6:30am-1pm. Cash only.)

◪ SIGHTS. Cortina's tourist office has a wealth of advice on local skiing, hiking, water sports, and nature walks. For those looking for a less strenuous mountain excursion, a flat 7km *passeggiata*, or pedestrian and bike path, traverses town from Cortina's famous ski-jump platform to the town of Fiames. V. Marconi (outside the train and bus stations) comprises the middle section of the *passeggiata*, so hikers can join halfway on either end of the street. One major plus is the magnificent view of **Croda del Pomogagnon**, a band of towering rock spires to the east. For more information and trail locations, contact the tourist office.

TRENTINO-ALTO ADIGE

The Mediterranean groove of the southern Italian regions gradually fades under Austrian influences in the rocky peaks of the Dolomites in Trentino-Alto Adige. At the onset of the 19th century, Napoleon conquered this integral part of the Holy Roman Empire, only to relinquish it to the Austro-Hungarians. A century after, Trentino and the Südtirol (South Tirol) came under Italian control at the end of World War I, and this relatively recent transition left linguistic patterns and cultural traditions scattered along a spectrum across Trentino. Though Germany cut short Mussolini's brutal efforts to Italianize the region, Benito managed to give

every German name an Italian equivalent—a practice still evident in the dual street and town names commonly used today. Mussolini found spicy *Wurst* carts, Austrian dolls, and shocks of blond hair slightly harder to control, and an aura of Germania bears witness to a deep-rooted Austrian culture that still thrives today.

BOLZANO (BOZEN)   ☎0471

The city's famous draw is the 5000-year-old Ice Man, a partially decayed body found frozen in 1991. The best sights in Bolzano, however, don't charge admission: snowy peaks beckon hikers in winter, while summer visitors head to the crystal-green Talvera River, catch an afternoon nap at Castel Roncolo, or gaze at the steep hills, resplendent with rows of grape vines. From the duomo's boxy Romanesque base and soaring Gothic spires to the two names—one German, one Italian—on every street sign, Bolzano weaves competing histories together to create a cultural atmosphere oblivious of national borders.

▐ TRANSPORTATION

Trains: ☎0471 97 42 92. In P. Stazione. Info office open M-Sa 8am-5:30pm, Su 9am-1pm and 2:30-5:30pm. **Luggage storage** available. To: **Bologna** (4hr., 21 per day 1:53am-1:07am); **Bressanone** (30min., 31 per day 4am-10:31pm, €3.25); **Munich** (4hr., 9 per day 2:25am-6:32pm); **Trento** (45min., 39 per day 1:53am-10:41pm); **Venice** (4hr., 2 per day 3:44am-3:30pm); **Verona** (1¾hr., 14 per day 8:15am-8:35pm).

Buses: SAD, V. Perathoner, 4 (☎0471 45 01 11), between train station and P. Walther. Bus station and tourist office distribute schedules detailing extensive service to the western Dolomites. Reduced service Su and after 6pm. MC/V.

Local Buses: SASA (☎0471 45 01 11 or 800 84 60 47). All lines stop in P. Walther or the station at V. Perathoner, 4. Buy tickets (€0.90) at *tabacchi* or from machines near some stops.

Cableways: 3 cableways, located at the edges of Bolzano, regularly carry visitors to nearby mountain towns. The tourist office gives advice about routes, publishes *Bolzano a Passeggio* (a guide to 14 walks in the surrounding hills), and distributes the *funivia* schedule in booklet form.

Funivia del Colle (☎0471 97 85 45), the world's oldest cableway, leads from V. Campiglio to **Colle** or **Kohlern** (9min.; 1-2 per hr. 7am-7pm; round-trip €2.60, bikes €2.10).

Funivia del Renon (☎0471 97 84 79), a 5min. walk from the train station, heads from V. Renon to **Renon** or **Ritten** atop **Monte Soprabolzano** (12min.; 3 per hr. 7:10am-8:20pm; one way €2.50, round-trip €3.50, bikes €1/2, luggage €1/2).

Funivia San Genesio (☎0471 97 84 36), on V. Sarentino, across the Talvera River near Ponte S. Antonio, connects Bolzano to **Salto's** high plateaus (9min.; 2-3 per hr. daily 10am-12:30pm and 2:30-7pm; round-trip €3.20, bikes €1).

Taxi: RadioTaxi, V. Perathoner, 4 (☎0471 98 11 11). Available 24hr.

Car Rental: Budget-National-Maggiore, V. Garibaldi, 34 (☎/fax 0471 97 15 31). From €70 per day. 21+. Open M-F 8am-12:30pm and 3-7pm, Sa 8am-12:30pm. AmEx/MC/V.

Bike Rental: Sportler Velo, V. Grappoli, 56 (☎0471 97 77 19), near P. Municipale. Mountain bikes €15 per day, €25 for 2 days, €77 per week. Wide selection of bikes and equipment. Open M-F 9am-12:30pm and 4:30-7pm, Sa 9am-12:30pm.

⊞⁊ ORIENTATION AND PRACTICAL INFORMATION

The *centro storico* lies between the **train station** and the **Talvera River** (Talfer Fluss). All major piazzas are within walking distance. Street and place names appear in Italian and German, and most maps mark both. A walk through the park on **Via Stazione** (Bahnhofshalle), from the train station, or **Via Alto Adige** (Südtirolerstrasse), from the bus stop, leads to **Piazza Walther** (Waltherplatz) and the duomo. Beyond, **Piazza del Grano** leads left to **Via Portici** (Laubenstrasse) and the swankiest district. Here, German and Italian merchants traditionally set up shop on opposite sides of the arcade. To reach **Ponte Talvera**, take V. Portici past **Piazza delle Erbe.**

Tourist Office: AST, P. Walther, 8 (☎0471 30 70 00; www.bolzano-bozen.it), has city maps and a list of lodgings and daily activities throughout the city. Organizes horseback riding expeditions in the hills. Open M-F 9am-6:30pm, Sa 9am-12:30pm.

Currency Exchange: Banca Nazionale del Lavoro, next to tourist office at P. Walther, 10. Good rates. Open M-F 8:20am-1:20pm and 2:30-4pm. An **ATM** is around the right corner of the bank and down the stairs, but plenty of others exist throughout the *centro*.

Alpine Information: Club Alpino Italiano, P. delle Erbe, 46, 2nd fl. (☎0471 97 81 72). Ring bell. Info on hiking, climbing, and tours. Open M-F 11am-1pm and 5-7pm.

Laundromat: Lava e Asciuga, V. Rosmini, 81, near Ponte Talvera. 35min. wash €3, 20min. dry €3, plastic bags €0.20, detergent tabs €1. Open daily 7:30am-10:30pm.

Emergency: ☎113. **Ambulance** (☎118). **Police** (☎112).

Pharmacy: Farmacia all'Aquila Nera, V. Portici, 46/B. Open M-F 8:30am-12:30pm and 3-7pm, Sa 8:30am-12:30pm. Pharmacies post late-night rotation on windows.

Hospital: Ospedale Regionale San Maurizio (☎0471 90 81 11), on V. Lorenz Böhler. Take bus #10 to last stop.

Internet: Telecom Italia, P. Parrocchia, 21, across from the duomo's main doors, offers three Internet terminals (€5.16 per hr.), a dozen phone booths, a fax station, and a library of regional phone books. Open M-Su 8am-11pm. **Caffè Meraner,** V. Bottai, 24. between Convento dei Francescani and Museo di Scienze Naturali, up the street from P. Municipio. Open M-F 7am-7:30pm, Sa 7am-1pm.

Post Office: V. della Posta, 1 (☎0471 97 94 52), by the duomo. Open M-F 8am-1:30pm, Sa 8am-12:30pm. **Postal Code:** 39100.

⌂⛺ ACCOMMODATIONS AND CAMPING

The tourist office lists affordable *agriturismi* options, but most require private transportation—find a bicycle and enjoy the countryside or call early for the inexpensive accommodations in the *centro* that fill up quickly in July and August.

Feighter Hotel, V. Grappoli, 15 (☎0471 97 87 68, fax 0471 97 48 03). From the train station, cross to the park and follow V. Laurin to V. Grappoli; Feighter is on the right. The decor is little more than brightly colored curtains and small steel lamps, but TV, phone, and proximity to the *centro* provide plenty to keep guests occupied. Breakfast included. Reserve ahead for mountain view. Singles €52; doubles €80. MC/V. ❹

Croce Bianca, P. del Grano, 3 (☎0471 97 75 52, fax 97 22 73). From the main doors of the duomo, cross the piazza past the tourist office to P. del Grano. Hotel is 50m to the right. Centrally located, with homey rooms and thick mattresses. Breakfast €4.13. Reserve ahead. Singles €28; doubles €47, with bath €55; triples with bath €72. MC/V. ❸

Schwarze Katz, Stazione Maddalena di Sotto, 2 (☎0471 97 54 17, fax 32 50 28), near V. Brennero, 15min. from the *centro*. From the train station, turn right at V. Renon; keep left along V. Renon as you pass the cable car station, and look for signs that lead 20m up an alley on the left. The aging linoleum and scratched doors feel slightly institutional, but the family who runs the nine rooms and popular garden restaurant are helpful and welcoming. Sinks, TV, some with bath. Breakfast included. Reception in restaurant is M-F 7am-midnight, Sa 7am-9pm. Reserve ahead. Singles €25; doubles €45. MC/V. ❷

Garni Thiulle, V. Thiulle, 5 (☎0471 26 28 77). A 15min. walk from train station. Cross Ponte Talvera, heading away from city center. Turn left on V. S. Quirino, take 1st right onto V. Peter Mayr, then turn left on V. Thiulle. Quiet, airy rooms, some with view of the building's gardens. Singles €25.82-41.32; doubles €51.65-67.14. Cash only. ❷

Moosbauer, V. S. Maurizio, 83 (☎0471 91 84 92; www.moosbauer.com). Take SAD bus (15 per day, 7am-10:20pm) toward Merano; ask driver to stop at Moosbauer. Though slightly off the beaten path, beautifully-tended campsite has pool, bar, Internet cafe (€0.10 per min.), market, playground, and laundry service (€1 for wash or dry). Reception open 8am-noon and 4-9pm. Shower included. Adults €5.50-6.50; children under 12 €4.50-5.50, dogs €3-4, tents €5-5.50, cars €5-5.50. MC/V after 1st night. ❶

🍴 FOOD

No trip to Bolzano would be complete without a sampling of the city's unique Austrian gastronomic culture. For a full smorgasbord, start with a bowl of *Rindgulasch*, a tasty beef stew; then munch on *Wurst*, a thick, spicy sausage, or *Speck*, a smoked bacon that has become ubiquitous on pizzas and breads across mainland Italy. Hearty *Knödel* (dumplings) come in dozens of rib-sticking varieties. For dessert, try three types of flaky Strudel, *Apfel* (apple), *Topfen* (soft cheese), and *Mohn* (poppyseed). Local vineyards bustle during the week-long *Südtiroler Törgelen* tasting spree each fall. An all-day **market** in P. delle Erbe and along V. della Roggia sells fine produce and cold meats (daily 7am-7pm). For a quick regional staple, try the market's **Wurst stand** at the intersection of V. Museo and P. delle Erbe. (Wurst, bread, and sauces €2.70; beer €1.55. Open M-Sa 8am-7pm. Cash only.) A Despar **supermarket** is downstairs in the indoor shopping center at V. della Rena, 40. (☎0471 97 45 37. Open M-F 8:30am-7:30pm, Sa 8:30am-6pm.)

Hopfen & Co., V. Argentieri, 36 (☎0471 30 07 88). Share a pitcher of *birra scura* (dark beer) or *chiara* (light) with friends (€13.80) in the wood-paneled bar, or savor traditional Bavarian specialties in the upper dining room. The *gulasch* (€11.50) is notable, and made with beer, of course. Open M-Sa 9:30am-1am, Su 5pm-1am. MC/V. ❸

Exil Lounge, P. del Grano, 2 (☎0471 97 18 14), next to Torre Bianca. Seek refuge from predominantly meaty Austrian cuisine among the white canvases and hardwood decor. Dishes like "Fit 4 Fun," a bowl of yogurt, granola, and seasonal fruits (€3.70) or the Exil Salad, piled high with *finocchi*, tomatoes, rucola, carrots, and Bufala cheese (€5) will delight vegetarians and *Wurst*-intolerant travelers. Open M-W 10am-midnight and Th-Su 10am-1am. Cash only. ❶

Hostaria Argentieri, V. Argentieri, 14 (☎0471 98 17 18). Specializes in fish and serene decor—shrubs around the patio hide quiet, candlelit interior under soft blue and yellow arches. *Primi* €7.50-15.50, *secondi* €8.50-19.30. Cover €1.50. Open M-Sa noon-2:30pm and 7-10:30pm. AmEx/MC/V. ❹

Blackout, V. Isarco, 11 (☎0471 30 02 56). Lives up to its name with ultra-low lighting and a young clientele that flits like moths around tiki torches outside. More bar than club, but with loud music, cheap drinks (beer or cola €1.80), and a late option for those unwilling to call it a night. Open daily 7:30pm-1am. Cash only. ❶

👁 🥾 SIGHTS AND HIKING

The tourist office in Bolzano offers a Museum Card (€2.50) for admission to five museums, a free guided city tour, and discounted entry to the Castel Roncolo. Nearby, the **duomo** is a veritable case study on the transition from Romanesque to Gothic religious architecture—dark, heavy doors are one of the only interruptions in an otherwise square and unadorned base; Gothic influences added the spined hollow spire of the bell tower and the ornate masonry around the eaves. (In P. Walther. Open M-F 9:45am-noon and 2-5pm, Sa 9:45am-noon. Free.) Outside of P. Walther, quiet, cobblestoned streets hide gems like the **Chiesa dei Francescani,** V. dei Francesca, 1, identifiable by the mosaic of St. Francis. From the main doors, the crucifix in the expansive apse seems to float in front of three tall stained-glass windows that fill the white-walled church with vibrant color. Another treasure is the altar crafted by Hans Klocker in 1500, where half-sized figures fill an ornate gilded Nativity scene. (Off P. delle Erbe. Open M-Sa 10am-noon and 2:30-6pm. Free.) The **South Tyrol Museum of Archaeology** extensively traces the region's history from the Mesolitic Era to the Copper Age, but most tourists come for a glimpse of the famous **Otzi,** a 5000-year-old body preserved in ice and discovered by hikers in the Alps. Other floors house domestic artifacts and detailed dioramas of early Tyrolean life. (V. Museo, 43, near Ponte Talvera. ☎0471 32 120; www.iceman.it. Wheelchair accessible. Open Tu-Su 10am-5pm, Th until 7pm. Audioguides €2; tour guides €2 for groups of 15+ people and must be booked 14 days in advance. €8, students and seniors €5.50, under 6 old free.) Perched on the vine-covered hills above town, **Castel Roncolo** is the most accessible of Bolzano's medieval fortresses. The winding path to the castle offers a spectacular view of the city. Inside, devil masks, demonic statues, and hollow-eyed mannequins are juxtaposed with lavish frescoes. (Up V. Weggerstein to V. S. Antonio. Take city bus #12 from P. Walther; every 30min. M-Sa 7:05am-7:15pm. €0.90. ☎0471 32 98 08; www.comune.bolzano.it/roncolo/ie. Open Tu-Su 10am-6pm. Gates for frescoes close 5pm. Adults €8, groups of 10+, students, and seniors €5.50.)

Bolzano is technically located in the pre-Alps, despite local allegiance to the Dolomites. The hiking available here pales in comparison to that in the Alps to the west or the Dolomites proper to the east. The **CAI office** (see **Alpine Information,** p. 328) is likely to be far more helpful than the tourist office for information on outdoor activities. The best hikes can be accessed by the three *funivie* that surround the town, which run straight to vista level. While **funivia del Renon** and **funivia del Colle** have limited marked trails, **funivia San Genesio** accesses extensive marked trails of moderate difficulty. On funivia del Renon, the ride itself is an attraction—get a bird's eye view of curving grape arbors from a cable car mere feet above the mountain treetops. All three *funivie* offer free **maps** that should suffice for the easier hikes. Drop by the San Genesio **tourist office** (☎0471 35 41 96; www.jenesien.net) before starting out. The gentle walk from the San Genesio funivia to the Edelweiss rest house, and then to the Tachaufenhaus and back to the *funivia* via the Locher rest house, makes for a pleasant 4½hr. hike. Even for the easiest hikes, take precautions against dehydration and exposure.

BRESSANONE (BRIXEN)   ☎0472

Northwest of the Dolomites and south of Austria, Bressanone's Alpine valley dazzles visitors with unimpeded views of green mountains, crystalline rivers, and rows of pastel houses. Its layout blends patches of urbanity with vast expanses of green space, where winding cobblestone roads coexist with swirling rivers and shady arbors. Modern touches like community theaters and tapas bars rub right against the walls of the *centro*—but inside, pedestrians pad through the arched walkways of the Altstadt, where public gardens and old buildings create a Brigadoon-like detachment from the bustle endemic to many other mountain towns.

🖉🏛 TRANSPORTATION AND PRACTICAL INFORMATION. Bressanone is an easy daytrip by train or bus from Bolzano or Trent. **Trains** run to: Bolzano (30min., every hr. 1:21am-12:24am, €2.27); Brennero (45min., every hr. 4:27am-11:04pm); Munich, Germany (5hr., 3-4 per day 8:33am-6:57pm, €42.53); Trent (1-1½hr., 17 per day 1:21am-12:34am, €4.65); and Verona (2hr., 23 per day 4:27-11:04, €8.99). Train info is available at ☎0472 89 20 21 or www.trenitalia.com. Baggage storage is available out the main doors and to the right. (€3.87 per day. Open Tu-Sa 8am-7pm.) To reach the *centro* in **Piazza del Duomo,** turn left from the bus and train stations onto **Viale Stazione,** walk 500m past the tourist office, on the right, and when Viale Stazione becomes **Via Bastioni Minore,** turn immediately right through the arch on the right to enter the courtyard of the **Palazzo Vescovile.** P. Duomo is to the left. The **tourist office,** Viale Stazione, 9, distributes town **maps** and info on suggested hikes; electronic hotel listings outside list up-to-date vacancies throughout town. (☎0472 83 64 01; www.brixen.info. Open M-F 8:30am-12:30pm and 2:30-6pm, Sa 9am-12:30pm.) In case of **emergency,** dial ☎113 or call an **ambulance** (☎118). A sign in the window of **Farmacia di Corte Principevescovile,** V. Portici Minori, 2/A, lists the weekly late-night rotation. (Open M-Tu and Th-Su 8am-12:30pm and 3-7pm, W 8am-12:30pm.) The **hospital** (☎0472 81 21 11) is on V. Dante, toward Brenner. **ATMs** line V. Bastioni Maggiore, at the end of Viale Stazione. **Green and Clean,** V. Dante, 13, offers self-service **laundry.** Enter through parking garage. Info ☎320 422 52 45. Wash €4 for 8kg or €7 for 18kg. Dry €4/30min. Open daily 7am-11pm. Cash only.) **Currency exchange** is available at Bressanone's **post office,** behind the tourist office at V. Cassiano 4/B. (☎0472 27 20 01, fax 0472 27 20 40. Open M-F 8am-6:30pm, Sa 8am-12:30pm.) **Postal Code:** 39042.

🏠🍴 ACCOMMODATIONS AND FOOD. Oddly, many of the more expensive hotels are near the river; the *centro* has three-star rooms in convenient locations for just €40-50. Head from P. del Duomo into P. Palazzo, then turn left onto V. Bruno to find **Ostello della Gioventù Kassianeum ❷,** V. Bruno, 2, where lightly finished pine furnishings blend well with the mountain setting. Rooms gleam thanks to assiduous cleaning, but the real dazzler is the view. (☎0472 27 99 99; jukas@jukas.net. Buffet breakfast and sheets included. Reception open M-Sa 8am-8pm, Su 8am-6pm. Dorms €19-27. MC/V.) From the train station, turn left and follow Viale Stazione until it connects with V. Bastioni in front of **Hotel Goldenes Kreuz (Croce d'Oro) ❹,** V. Bastioni Minori, 8. Myriad hallways of chandeliers and antique furniture give a positively palatial feel, but modern rooms come fully equipped with TV and bath. Pay extra for the sauna, hot tub, tanning bed, or solarium. (☎0472 83 61 55; www.goldeneskreuz.it. Breakfast included. Singles €45-70; doubles €70-120. Cash only.) From P. Stazione, walk down Viale Mozart for 15min. Turn left on the first street after the river or take a Skibus to the left of the train station and ask to be let off at the three-star **Hotel Senoner ❹,** V. Plose, 22/A. This 15th-century hotel hides age well behind deep colors and modern furnishings. Enjoy dinner in the restaurant or plasma TV in the breakfast nook. (☎0472 83 25 25, fax 83 24 36. Breakfast €7. Singles €45; doubles €76-86. AmEx/MC/V.)

Finsterwirt ❸, Vco. Duomo, 3, first served wine in the 12th century, but has since added classic Tyrolean fare to its menu. Grape arbors and stone fountains create a breezy setting for the *osteria* downstairs. Walk directly away from the duomo doors; Vco. Duomo is the alley to the left. (☎0472 83 23 44. *Primi* €6.20-9.30, *secondi* €14.50-18. Open Tu-Su 12:30-2:30pm and 6:30-10:30pm. MC/V.) Sit indoors or under canopy at **Torre Bianca ❶**, V. Torre Bianca, 6, which serves a wide variety of pizzas and traditional Tyrolean food on a quiet street in the *centro*. Walk past the left side of the cloister's *campanile* and pass through the arch. (☎0472 83 29 72. Open M and W-Su 9am-11:30pm. MC/V.) At the 100 year-old **Fink ❷**, Portici Minor, 4, waitresses in traditional garb serve dishes like *rösti*, a pizza-sized mat of fried potatoes and veggies, (€7) and Alto Adige wines (€3-5.20. ☎0472 83 48 83, fax 0472 83 52 68. Open M-Su 11am-11pm. AmEx/MC/V.) A Despar **supermarket**, V. B. Minori, 4, is near the *centro*. (☎0472 83 70 32. Open M-Sa 8am-7pm. MC/V.)

◪ ◪ **SIGHTS AND HIKING.** For a break from the boutiques and traffic of central Bressanone, follow Ponte Aquila behind the duomo and cross the bridge to the winding footpaths of the **Altstadt** (old town), where shops and pastel houses huddle along quiet streets. For more directed sightseeing, head to **Piazza del Duomo.** A few meters south of the piazza, look for a golden lamb-topped monument in P. Palazzo, where the pale yellow **Palazzo Vescovile**, completed in 1595, houses the **Museo Diocesano.** Its predominantly ecclesiastical collection traces the development of Western Christianity. Medieval and Renaissance portraits, including copies of works by Hans Klocker and Albrecht Dürer, round out the exhibits. Explanatory info is in Italian and German only. (☎0472 83 05 05. Open Mar. 15-Oct. 31. Tu-Su 10am-5pm, Dec. 1-Jan. 31 daily 2-5pm. €5.) The candy-colored **duomo** is as colorful inside as outside—Baroque and Neoclassical additions in 1595, 1754, and 1790 covered almost every inch with frescoes. To the right of the duomo, the squat gray **cloister** displays traditional Stations of the Cross, but the large gilded organ in the back reveals a touch of stunning ornamentation. The garden contains floral arrangements and a monument to local soldiers killed in both World Wars. (Both open M-Sa 6am-noon and 3-6pm, Su 3-6pm. Guided duomo tours meet M-Sa at 10:30am and 3pm just left of the main doors. Free.)

The **Plose Plateau,** towering over Bressanone to the east at heights of over 2000m, is a popular area for skiers, made accessible by the **Sant'Andrea Cable Car** (July 7 to October 3. 10min.; 2 per hr. 9am-6pm; round-trip €6.20, bikes €2.50), which operates from the nearby hillside town of **Sant'Andrea. SAD bus #126** makes round-trips between the Bressanone train station and S. Andrea (20min., 7 per day 7:54am-7:15pm) and Bressanone (7:15am-7:25pm, round-trip €2). Buy tickets on the bus. From the upper cable-car station, **trail 30** leads along the smooth terrain of the Plose's western slope, and **trail 17** follows the meadows on the Plose's southern slope. For a longer, more strenuous hike, **trail 7** traverses the three summits of the Plose massif, Monte Telegrafo, Monte Fana, and Monte Forca, reaching altitudes of 2600m. Before tackling this hike, check the weather and plan for possible overnights in *rifugi*. Two overnight *rifugi*, **Plose** and **Rossalm,** also offer hot meals. A tourist office brochure details three easy 3-6hr. hikes on the Plose. Verify bus and lift schedules and be prepared to face rough terrain and high altitudes.

TRENT (TRENTO, TRIENT)   ☎0461

Within the Alpine threshold but connected to the Veneto by a deep valley, Trent was the Romans' strategic gateway to the north. For centuries to follow, the region was the base for fortresses such as the Castello del Buonconsiglio. Political ownership of Trent, contested in the 19th-century, was finally settled in Italy's favor at the end of WWI, though Germanic influences are still highly evident. Trent was recently named Alpine City of the Year in 2004 for its local pride and carefully preserved culture, manifested in near year-round rotation of festivals, tours, and exhibits. From the meeting place of the Council of Trent to a yearly festival that transforms it into a garden, the central Piazza del Duomo epitomizes the historical riches and local enthusiasm of this busy foothill city.

⌐ TRANSPORTATION

Trains: ☎0461 98 36 27. On V. Dogana. Ticket office open daily 5:40am-8:30pm; info office M-F 8:30am-12:15pm and 1:15-4:30pm. To: **Bologna** (3hr., 9 per day 1:38am-9:41pm, €10.12); **Bolzano** (45min., 35 per day 1:40am-10:51pm, €2.89); **Venice** (3-4hr., 12 per day 4:15am-5:20pm, €10.12); **Verona** (1hr., 2 per hr. 2:26am-9:12pm, €4.65).

Buses: Atesina and **Trentino Transporti** (☎0461 82 10 00; www.ttspa.it), on V. Pozzo next to the train station. Info office in terminal open M-Sa 7am-7:30pm. To: **Riva del Garda** (1¾hr., every hr. 5:57am-7:50pm, €3.20) and **Rovereto** (50min., every hr. 5:57am-7:50pm, €3.20). Baggage storage available. (Daily 8:30am-12:15pm and 1:30-3:30pm. €2 for 2hr., €1 for next 3hr., €2 for additional hours up to 24.)

Local Buses: Atesina operates an extensive local network. Tickets on sale at dispenser in the bus station or *tabacchi* for €0.80 (valid for 1hr.) or €1 (valid for 100min.).

Cableways: Funivia Trento-Sardagna (☎0461 23 21 54), on Lung'Adige Monte Grappa. From bus station, turn right on V. Pozzo; take 1st right on Cavalcavia S. Lorenzo. Cross bridge over train tracks and head across the intersection to the building to the left of the river bridge. Open daily 7am-10:30pm. To **Sardagna** on Mt. Bondone (4min., every 15-30min. €0.80 for 60min. ticket, €1 for 100min. ticket. Cash only).

Bike Rental: Public Bike Rental is across the street from the train terminal. €5 key deposit at Ufficio Relazioni con il Pubblico, V. Belenzani, 3 (☎0461 88 44 53). Office open M-F 9am-6pm and Sa 9am-noon. Bicycles available 6am-8pm daily, late drop fee €5 plus €2 for each additional day. **Moser Cicli**, V. Calepina, 63 (☎0461 23 03 27), rents mountain bikes. €15 per day. Open M 3-7pm and Tu-Su 9am-noon and 3-7pm.

Taxi: RadioTaxi (☎0461 93 00 02).

◢◤ ⁷ ORIENTATION AND PRACTICAL INFORMATION

The **bus** and **train stations** are on the same street, between the **Adige River** and the gardens and circle-of-hell statue of **Piazza Dante**. The town center lies east of the Adige. From the stations, walk right to the intersection with **Via Torre Vanga**. Continue straight as **Via Pozzo** becomes **Via Orfane** and then the curving **Via Cavour** before reaching **Piazza del Duomo** in the town's center. **ATMs** are nearby. For **Castello del Buonconsiglio,** follow **Via Roma** eastward, away from the river as it becomes **Via Manci,** then **Via San Marco.**

Tourist Office: APT, V. Manci, 2 (☎0461 98 38 80; www.apt.trento.it). Turn right from the train station and left on V. Roma, which becomes V. Manci. Offers information on biking, theater, frequent festivals, free wine tasting, and local tours. (July-Aug., free wine tasting Sa 10am, visit to the *centro* Sa 3pm. Meet at the office, no reservation required; tours limited to groups of ten or less.) Open daily 9am-7pm.

English-Language Bookstore: Libreria Disertori, V. M. Diaz, 11 (☎0461 98 14 55; info@libreriadisertori@virgilo.it), near Piazzale C. Battisti. Classic literature and thrillers comprise a slim selection of English books in the back of this predominantly Italian bookstore—helpful with local, regional, and international **maps** aplenty. Open M 3:30-7:30pm, Tu-Su 9am-noon and 3:30-7:30pm. MC/V.

Emergency: ☎113. **Ambulance** (☎118). **Police,** P. Mostra, 3 (☎112).

Pharmacy: Farmacia dall'Armi, P. Duomo, 10 (☎0461 23 61 39). Serving the city since 1490. Late-night rotation posted in any pharmacy window. Open M-Sa 8:30am-12:30pm and 3:30-7pm. Cash only.

Hospital: Ospedale Santa Chiara, Largo Medaglie d'Oro, 9 (☎0461 90 31 11), up V. Orsi past the swimming pool.

Internet: Call Me, V. Belenzani, 58 (☎0461 98 33 02), off P. del Duomo. Internet (€4 per hr.), fax, Western Union, phone booths, and international phone cards available. Open daily 9am-9pm. Laptop users can find affordable wireless access at **Caffè Olimpia,** V. Belenzani, 33/1 (☎0461 98 24 45). €2.50 per hr. M-Sa 11am-11:30pm, bar open M and W 6am-9pm, Tu and Th-Sa 6am-midnight. Cash only.

Post Office: V. Calepina, 16 (☎0461 98 47 15), offers fax services just off P. Vittoria. Open M-F 8am-6:30pm, Sa 8am-12:30pm. **Branch** (☎0461 98 23 01) next to train station on V. Dogana. Open M-F 8am-6:30pm, Sa 8am-12:30pm. **Postal Code:** 38100.

ACCOMMODATIONS

■ **Ostello Giovane Europa (HI),** V. Torre Vanga, 11 (☎0461 26 34 84, fax 22 25 17). Exit train station and turn right; hostel is the white building on the corner, past the bus station. Turn right to enter a clean, well-run hostel with TV room, terraces, and small restaurant decorated with posters of Trentino. Simple breakfast, shower, phone, and sheets included. Internet €5.16. Buffet breakfast €3. Dinner of *primi, secondi,* and dessert €9. Wash €4, dry €2. Lockers €3. Reception 7:30am-11pm. Check-out 10am. Curfew 11:30pm (ask for door code to return later). Reserve ahead. 6-bed dorms €13; singles €25; doubles €40. AmEx/MC/V. ❶

Hotel Venezia, P. Duomo, 45 (☎/fax 0461 23 41 14). This hotel features two-star rooms overlooking the duomo and one-star rooms along the less majestic V. Belenzani. All share a duomo-side lobby with plush leather couches—and the morning bells that come along with it. Singles €43; doubles €63. MC/V. ❹

Hotel Paganella, V. Aeroporto, 27 (☎/fax 0461 99 03 55). From the station, cross the street and turn left to reach the bus stop. Take bus #14 to P. della Chiesa. From there, back-track and turn right on V. Aeroporto; it's 50m on the left. Out-of-the-way, but rooms are homey and share very clean baths. Singles €35; doubles €60. MC/V. ❸

Hotel Aquila d'Oro, V. Belenzani, 76 (☎0461 98 62 82; www.aquiladoro.it). About 20m from P. del Duomo, Aquila D'Oro's rooms set the gold standard, with floor-to-ceiling mirrors and polished wood furnishings, as well as TV (Italian channels free, additional options €10.50 for 12hr.), in-room Internet lines (€5.50 for 12hr.), and phone. Breakfast included. Singles €63; doubles €95; triples €115. AmEx/MC/V. ❺

FOOD

Trentino cuisine owes much to the local production of such sterling cheeses as Nostrano, Tosela, and the highly prized Vezzena. *Piatti del Malgaro* (Herdsman's plates) include cheeses, polenta, mushrooms, and sausage. Another favorite is the chewy *minestrone trippe* (tripe soup). A Germanic undercurrent shows itself in the exceptional local version of *Apfel Strudel.* The **open-air market** around P. del Duomo sells flowers and produce every Thursday. (Open 8am-1pm.) **Supermercati Trentini** lies across P. Pasi from the duomo at P. Lodron, 28. (☎0461 22 01 96. Open M 2:30-7:30pm, Tu-Su 8:30am-7:30pm. MC/V.) The Poli **supermarket** sits where V. Orfane meets V. Roma at V. Orfane, 2. (☎0461 98 50 63. Open M-Tu 8:30am-7:15pm, W 8:30am-1pm, and Th-Sa 8:30am-7:15pm. AmEx/MC/V.)

🍽 **Osteria Il Cappello,** P. Lunelli, 5 (☎0451 23 58 50). From the stations, turn right, then left on V. Roma. After 4 blocks, turn right onto V. S. Pietro, then take the tunnel by #27. A highly attentive staff and small shading trees set the tone for a delicious and relaxing Trentino-Tuscan meal, like the house specialty of *tagliolini di pasta fresca al pesce di lago* (€8). *Primi* €7-7.50, *secondi* €10-14.50. Cover €2. Open Tu-Sa noon-2pm and 7:30-10pm, Su noon-2pm. AmEx/MC/V. ❸

Ristorante Al Vo, Vco. del Vo, 11 (☎0461 98 53 74). From the stations, turn right and walk to V. Torre Vanga. Turn left; the restaurant is 200m on the right. Friendly staff serves classic Trentino dishes in quiet location complete with crisp table linens and airy atrium. Menu changes daily, but lunch with *primo, secondo,* and side dish costs €13. Open M-W and Sa-Su 11:30am-3pm, Th-F 11:30am-3pm and 7-9pm. AmEx/MC/V. ❸

La Cantinota, V. San Marco, 22/24 (☎0461 23 85 27). From the stations, turn right and then left on V. Roma. Take another left on V. San Marco. Cantinota offers everything from champagne in the elegant gold and ivory piano bar upstairs to horse pizza (€10) in the stone and wood trattoria on ground level. *Primi* €7.50-9, *secondi* €13-17, single plate meals for €10-12. Restaurant open M-W and F-Su noon-2:30pm and 7pm-midnight, piano bar open M-W and F-Su 10pm-2:30am. MC/V. ❸

Forst Birreria/Ristorante, V. Oss Mazzurana, 38 (☎0461 23 55 90). When heading up V. Roma from the stations, turn right onto V. O. Mazzurana. Light, flaky pizza (from €3.80) and quick service make the patio perfect for a short, affordable meal. A full menu and helpful staff keep the expansive bar and tables in the dining room full of faithful patrons. The *gnocchi verde,* a tangy *primo* of potatoes in salsa, is a great take on a classic regional dish (€5.29). Cover €1.09. Open daily 6-10pm. AmEx/MC/V. ❷

Antica Trattoria Due Mori, V. San Marco, 11 (☎0461 98 42 51, fax 0461 22 13 85), across from Cantinota. A heavy wooden ceiling, thick stone pillars, and low hanging lamps set the mood for locals enjoying the hearty lunch buffet (€3.60-7.20). *Primi* €4.10-8.50, *secondi* €7.20-23.80. Cover €1.60. Open M-W and F-Su noon-2:30pm and 7-10:30pm, Su noon-2:30pm and 7-10pm. AmEx/MC/V. ❷

🔆 SIGHTS

Trento's **Piazza del Duomo** offers everything from major religious history to modern shops and services. The **Fontana del Nettuno** at the center of the piazza is anchored by smug-looking Neptune waving a trident as mer-people spit feebly around his feet, and the Piazza steps provide a good view of the **Cazuffi houses** throughout the busy arena. Nearby stands the **Cattedrale di San Vigilio,** whose dark, somber interior housed the historic Council of Trent during the sacred public relations blitz of the Counterreformation. One notable relic near the altar is the small bone of Santa Paolina, a Brazilian saint who died in 1942. Dark, rich art fills the massive building, illuminated only by sunlight and clusters of red votive candles. (Open daily 6:40am-12:15pm and 2:30-8pm. Masses are mornings and evenings, open to tourists 10am-5pm. Free.) Underneath, the **Basilica Sotterranea di S. Vigilio** displays altars and statues uncovered in excavations around the duomo. (Open Tu-Sa 10am-noon and 2:30-6pm. €1, ages 12-18 €0.50.) Nearby, the dull white stone castle with the square tower houses the **Museo Diocesano,** officially reopened by Pope John Paul II in 1995 after renovations for elaborate tapestries, paintings, and illuminated manuscripts from various regional churches. (P. del Duomo, 18. ☎0461 23 44 19; www.museodiocesanotridentino.it. Free audioguides in English with ID deposit. Museum open June-Sept. M and W-Su 9:30am-12:30pm and 2:30-6pm, Oct.-May M and W-Su 9:30am-12:30pm and 2:30-5:30pm. Tickets close 15min. before museum. €3, ages 12-18 €0.50. Entrance includes access to the archaeological excavations beneath the church.) The **Castello del Buonconsiglio** contains a wealth of local history from the medieval period to World War I. In the **Loggia** at the end of the castle's rooftop garden, the ceiling features Diana depicted as the moon and Apollo as the sun with scenes from Greek, Roman, and Hebrew history and mythology in the lunettes. Stairs lead down from the *loggia* to the **Fossa dei Martiri**, the castle's old moat and execution site of famed martyrs Cesare Battisti, Damiano Chiesa, and Fabio Filzi in 1916. Photos of the executions, monuments at the three death sites, and gravestones dot the grounds. The castle is most famous, however, for the famed **Ciclo dei Mesi**, a series of International Gothic paintings. For access, ask about tours of the **Torre dell'Aquila.** Tours depart from the *loggia*. (10 per day from 10:30am-5:15pm. €1. Free audioguides in multiple languages.) Take V. Belenzani and turn right on V. Roma. (☎0461 23 37 70. Open Apr.-Sept. Tu-Su 9am-noon and 2-5:30pm, Oct.-Mar. Tu-Su 9am-noon and 2-5pm. €5, students and under 18 or over 60 €2.50. Torre d'Aquila an additional €1. Ticket price includes admission to museum and Tridentum, an excavation of Roman ruins under P. Battisti.)

ROVERETO ☎0464

Nestled in the Dolomites, the town of Rovereto is far from the attention of camera-toting tourists. Cobblestone alleys weave around elegantly frescoed buildings, decorative stone fountains dot the piazzas, and cool mountain breezes waft delicately through the streets. The *centro* feels decidedly urban, but the small shops along pedestrian side streets retain a more rural air. The surrounding country offers ample opportunities for biking, hiking, walking, and horseback-riding.

◆⊿ TRANSPORTATION AND PRACTICAL INFORMATION. The **train station** is at P. Orsi, 9. **Trains** run to: Bologna (3hr., 14 per day 5:25am-9:58pm, €10.15); Bolzano (1hr., 24 per day 2:59am-10:36pm, €4.30); Trent (15min., 32 per day 2:59pm-11:35pm, €2.40); Verona (1hr., 31 per day 2:42am-9:58pm, €3.36). Check schedules at ticket office. (☎0464 89 20 21; www.trenitalia.com. Ticket office open M-F 5:50am-7:30pm, Sa 9am-6:30pm. AmEx/MC/V.) The **bus station** is at C. Rosmini, 45. **Buses** run frequently to Riva (1hr., 24 per day 6:41am-10:30pm, €2.20) and Trento (50min., 24 per day 5:07am-6:56pm, €4.15). Check station for schedules. (Open M-F 9am-1pm and 3-7pm, Sa 9am-12:30pm. MC/V.) The **tourist office,** C. Rosmini, 6/A, provides a town **map,** lodgings guide, and info on festivals and outdoor activities in the area. (☎0464 43 03 63; www.apt.rovereto.tn.it. Open M-F 8:30am-12:15pm and 2:30-6pm.) On weekends, visit the **branch** at C. Bettini, 43. (☎0464 48 95 46. Open Tu-Su 10am-1pm and 2:30-6pm.) There is an **ATM** in the train station; others are located throughout town. **Internet** is available at C. A. Bettini, 59. (€3.50 per hr. Open Tu-Th 9:30am-noon, 3-7pm and 9-11:30pm; F-Sa 9:30am-noon and 3-7pm). To reach the **police station,** V. Sighele, 1, follow the signs across the street from the train station. A **pharmacy** lies between the bus and train stations at V. Dante, 3. (☎0464 42 10 30. Open M-F and Su 8:30am-12:15pm and 3-6pm, Sa 8:30am-12:15pm.) The **post office,** V. Largo Posta, 7, is up C. Rosmini from the bus station. (☎0464 40 22 18. Open M-F 8am-6:30pm, Sa 8am-12:30pm). **Postal Code:** 38068.

◪⊡ ACCOMMODATIONS AND FOOD. Low tourist traffic means that budget hotels are scarce in Rovereto. The tourist office offers a printed list of local lodgings, but affordable living may require a short hike. To reach **Lizzanella ❷,** C. Verona, 115, exit the *centro* along V. Dante, cross the bridge at the end, and turn right onto C. Verona at the fork with V. Santa Maria. After about 15min., the hotel appears on the right. The friendly Proserpio family maintains two stories of spacious rooms with shared baths, bright windows, and kitchens in a quiet area down the hill from the Campana della Pace. (☎0464 43 85 93. Call before arrival. Breakfast included. Singles €25; doubles €50; triples €75. Cash only.)

Savor traditional *gulasch nach trentino con polenta* (€10.50) or a bowl of tripe soup (€5) at **Vecchia Trattoria Birrara Scala della Torre ❸**, V. Scala della Torre, 7, a *Trentino* restaurant with an Austrian twist. (From P. della Erbe, ascend the staircase to the left of the fountain. ☎0464 43 71 00. *Primi* from €5.20, *secondi* from €6.70. Bread and cover €1. Open daily noon-2:30pm and 7:30-9:30pm. Cash only.) Trentini **supermarket**, at V. Mazzini, 65, stocks basics. (☎0464 42 11 97. Open M 8:30am-1:30pm, Tu-Sa 8:30am-12:30pm and 3:15-7:15pm. V.) Nightlife in Rovereto is fairly tame, but **Bacchus ❶**, V. G. Garibaldi, 29, manages to keep its patrons out late with trademark drinks like the decadent Shakerato (€3.50). The patrons at the barrel-shaped tables change noticeably as the day progresses, and quiet afternoons turn into nights of pulsing beats as the local crowd becomes a few decades younger and louder. (Open M and W-Su 11am-1:30pm and 5pm-close. Cash only.)

🄂 **SIGHTS.** The 🄺Museo d'Arte Moderna e Contemporanea (commonly known as "il Mart"), C. Bettini, 43, is the largest modern art museum in Italy. Banners unfurling on every street corner direct visitors to its gigantic glass-and-steel cupola. Inside, 5600 sq. m of sleek rooms house over 7000 pieces. Fortunato Depero's massive *Scenario Plastico per le Chant du Rossignol* anchors the extensive futurist wing, while 20th-century Italian pieces and American works like Warhol's *Four Marilyns*, Lichtenstein's *Hot Dog*, and Rosenquist's *Sliced Bologna* complete the collection. (☎0464 43 88 87; www.mart.trento.it. Open Tu-Th 10am-6pm, F 10am-9pm, Sa-Su 10am-6pm. €8, under 18 €5. Audioguides in Italian or English €3. AmEx/MC/V.) Looming ominously from its perch high above the city the dark gray **Castello di Rovereto**, V. Castelbarco, 7, has served mostly military purposes since its construction in the fourth century. From P. Podestà, follow V. Della Terra (near the cannon), turn right onto V. Castelbarco, and head up the stairs. The **Museo della Guerra** (Museum of War) now fills the castle with war materials ranging from medieval spears and chain mail to bombshells and trench newspapers from WWII. Above the museum, an observation deck affords a 360-degree view of Rovereto and the surrounding valley. (☎0464 43 81 00; www.museodellaguerra.it. Open Tu-Su 10am-6pm. €5.50, ages 6-18 €2. Cash only.) About a 20min. walk uphill from the *centro*, the **Campana della Pace** (Bell of Peace) on V. Miravalle commemorates war casualties. The largest ringing bell in the world, the massive *campana* was cast in 1924 from 226.39 tons of bronze recycled from the cannons of the 19 nations involved in WWI and later blessed by Pope Paul VI. Each night, it tolls 100 times for victims of war. (☎0464 43 44 12. Open Jan.-Feb. and Nov.-Dec. daily 9am-noon and 2-4pm; Mar. and Oct. daily 9am-noon and 2-6pm; Apr.-May M-F 9am-noon and 2-7pm, Sa-Su 9am-7pm; June-Sept. M-F 9am-noon and 2-7pm, Sa-Su 9am-7pm, and public bell-ringing 9-9:30pm. Cash only.) The **Civic Museum,** Borgo Santa Caterina, 41, provides guided tours to the astronomic observatory on Monte Zugna and to the **Dinosaur Tracks** in the southern part of Rovereto. Over 200 million years ago, 250 herbivores and carnivores paced along the steep slope of an ancient landslide. From various places along the mountain trail, their tracks are still clearly visible in the gray stone hillside (☎0464 43 90 55, fax 43 94 87. Call to arrange a tour.)

RIVA DEL GARDA
☎0464

With lake waters lapping at the foot of the Brenta Dolomites, Riva is a spot for those who love *belle viste* (beautiful views) but who are traveling on *pochi soldi* (a tight budget). Gentle mountain winds make Garda ideal for windsurfing, and Riva's aquatic sports schools are internationally renowned. The area is also a prime location for hiking, canoeing, whitewater rafting, kayaking, bicycling, and swimming—all made accessible and affordable by the attractive youth hostel.

▢ TRANSPORTATION

Buses: Viale Trento, 5 (☎0464 55 23 23). From: **Rovereto** (1hr., 18 per day 7:39am-10:04pm, €2.20); **Trent** (1½hr., 20 per day 7:39am-10:04pm, €3.20); **Verona** (2hr., 14 per day 6:15am-7:10pm, €5). Ticket office open M-Sa 6:30am-7:15pm, Su 9:05am-noon and 3:35-7:05pm. Urban tickets available at dispenser in station.

Ferries: Navigazione Lago di Garda (☎030 914 95 11, fax 030 914 95 20), in P. Catena. To **Gardone** (1½-3hr., 8:40am-5pm, €6.80-9.60) and **Sirmione** (2-4hr., 8:40am-5pm, €8-11.30). Also offers sightseeing tours 8am-6pm (from €10.60). Ticket office open M-Sa 9am-noon and 3-6:30pm, Su 10am-noon and 4-6:30pm.

Bike Rental: Fiori e Bike, Viale dei Tigli, 24 (☎/fax 0464 55 18 30). Mountain and city bikes €8-13 per day. Ask for multiple-day discounts and free guided tours. Open M-Sa 9am-noon and 3-7pm. AmEx/MC/V.

Scooter Rental: Santorum Autonoleggio, Viale Rovereto, 76 (☎0464 55 22 82). 1hr. €13, 5hr. €29, 1 day €44, 2 days €75, 1 week €160. Open Mar.-Nov. M-Sa 9am-12:30pm and 2:30-7pm, Su 9am-noon; Nov.-Mar. M-F 9am-12:30pm and 2:30-7pm, Sa 9am-12:30pm. AmEx/MC/V.

Taxi: ☎0464 55 22 00.

▣ ▢ ORIENTATION AND PRACTICAL INFORMATION

To reach the town center from the **train station,** walk straight on **Viale Trento,** then cross the traffic circle to take **Via Roma** to reach **Piazza Cavour.** The **tourist office,** Giardini di Porta Orientale, 8, is near the water's edge on V. della Liberazione. It lists hotel vacancies and offers a variety of cheap regional tours. Ask for a city **map** and hiking routes. (☎0464 55 44 44; www.gardatrentino.it. Free guided tour to the neighboring town of Arco Su 9:30am-noon. Free Riva tour Sa 9:30am-12:30pm. Electronic booking board outside. English spoken. Wheelchair accessible. Open M-Sa 9am-noon and 3-6:30pm, Su 10am-noon and 4-6:30pm.) In case of **emergency,** call ☎113, contact the **police** (☎112), or call an **ambulance** (☎118). There are **pharmacies** at V. Dante Alighieri, 12/C (☎0464 55 25 08; open M-F 8:45am-12:30pm and 3:30-7:30pm), and V. Maffei, 8 (☎0464 55 23 02; open M-Sa 8:45am-12:30pm and 3:30-7:30pm, Su 9am-12:30pm and 3:30-7pm), in P. delle Erbe. For speedy **Internet,** try **Caffè Italia,** P. Cavour, 8. (☎0464 55 25 00. €1 for 10min., €4 per hr. Open daily 7am-1am. MC/V.) The **post office** and **ATM** are at V. Disciplini, 32. (☎0464 57 87 43. Open M-F 8:10am-6:30pm, Sa 8:10am-12:30pm.) **Postal Code:** 38066.

▢ ▤ ACCOMMODATIONS AND CAMPING

Hotel Benini, V. S. Alessandro, 25 (☎0464 55 30 40, fax 52 10 62). 1km from the city center. Elegant hotel features a garden, pool, and bicycle rental for guests. Rooms have bath, A/C, phone, and TV. Buffet breakfast included. Reception 8am-11pm. Singles €42; doubles €72; triples €108. Wheelchair accessible. AmEx/MC/V. ❹

Ostello Benacus (HI), P. Cavour, 10. (☎0464 55 49 11; www.garda.com/ostelloriva), in the center of town. From bus station, walk down V. Trento, cross the traffic circle to V. Roma, turn left under the arch, and cross left through P. Cavour. Breakfast, sheets, and hot shower included. Reception 7-9am and 3pm-midnight. Silence at 11pm; ask for key to return after midnight. Reserve ahead. Dorms €13. AmEx/MC/V. ❶

Locanda La Montanara, V. Montanara, 20 (☎0464 55 48 57, fax 56 15 52.), off V. Florida. 9 bright and comfortable rooms with hardwood floors, some with bath. Breakfast €6. Reserve 1 month ahead in summer. Restaurant downstairs. Singles €17; doubles €32, with shower €36; triples €49. MC/V. ❷

THE VENETO AND
TRENTINO-ALTO ADIGE

Albergo Ancora, V. Montanara, 2 (☎0464 52 21 31; hotelancora@rivadelgarda.com). Light-hued furniture and embroidered curtains give the individually furnished rooms an antique vibe, but all have modern amenities like bath, telephone, and TV. Wheelchair accessible. Discount for extended stay and groups of 10 or more. Singles €56-59; doubles €88-94; triples €120; quads €170. AmEx/MC/V. ❹

Albergo Garni Rita, V. Brione, 19 (☎/fax 0464 55 17 98). Friendly owners run a spacious B&B with large private pool, stone terrace, and rooms with TV and bath in a quiet area 25min. outside of the city center. Call ahead for reservations. Breakfast included. Open March 10-Nov. 5. Singles €36; doubles €51. Cash only. ❸

Villa Maria, V. dei Tigli, 19 (☎0464 55 22 88; www.garnimaria.com). A 10min. walk from the city center, this pink villa features a sunny rooftop terrace with mountain view. Clean rooms all have bath, TV, Internet jacks, and A/C. Breakfast included. Reception 8am-10pm. Singles €35; doubles €60. MC/V. ❸

Camping Monte Brione, V. Brione, 32 (☎0464 52 08 85; www.campingbrione.com). Flowering trees shade a pool, bar, laundry services, and minimarket situated 500m from the lake, next to biking trails. Reception 8am-1pm and 3-5:30pm. Free hot showers. Reserve ahead. €6.50-7.50 per person, €7.50-8.70 per small site without electricity; €9.40-11 per large site at foot of hill with parking and electricity. MC/V. ❶

Bavaria, V. Rovereto, 100 (☎0464 55 25 24; www.bavarianet.it), on road toward Torbole. Pizzeria on premises. Behind the campground, **Surfsegnana** (☎464 50 54 98; www.surfsegnana.it) offers lessons in windsurfing, sailing, and canoeing. (Surfsegnana open daily 8:30-6pm. Camping reception daily 8am-1pm and 2:30-7pm. Hot shower €1.30. Silence 11pm-8am and 3-5pm. No entry by car 11pm-7am. Open Apr.-Oct. €6.80 per person, €9 per site. AmEx/MC/V for €60 or more. ❶

🄵 FOOD

An **open-air market** sells fruits and vegetables in P. delle Erbe. (Open M-Sa mornings.) A Despar **supermarket** sells standard grocery fare just outside the centro at V. Roma, 19. (Open M-Sa 8:30am-1pm and 3:30-7:15pm, Su 9am-12:30pm. Cash only.)

Ristorante Ancora, V. Montanara, 2 (☎0464 52 21 31). Ancora's sunny, wicker-furnished interior and lamp-lined terrace are accompanied by attentive service. Try *la trota del lago salmonata alla griglia,* juicy salmon with a crispy, flavorful exterior (€9.50). *Primi* from €8, *secondi* €9.50. 10% discount for patrons of attached hotel. Open daily noon-2:30pm and 7pm-midnight; June-Sept. closed afternoons. AmEx/MC/V. ❸

Leon d'Oro, V. Fiume, 28 (☎0464 55 23 41). Authentic dishes like *speck tirolese* (€6.50) draw local families and well-heeled diners of all stripes to bustling tables under wooden arches. *Primi* from €6.50, fish *secondi* from €8.50. Bread and cover €1.30. Open daily mid-March-mid-Nov. 11:30am-3pm and 5:40-11pm. AmEx/MC/V. ❸

Ristorante-Pizzeria La Leonessa, V. Maffei, 24 (☎0464 55 27 77), just off P. delle Erbe. Bright yellow tablecloths and colorful wall paintings spice up house specialties like the *sorpresa della casa* (pasta with capers, olives, and tomatoes wrapped inside pizza dough; €6). Open M-Tu and Th-Su noon-2:30pm and 6-10pm. AmEx/MC/V. ❷

Birreria Spaten, V. Maffei, 7 (☎0464 55 36 70), in P. delle Erbe. Caricatures of stodgy, vaguely disapproving nobles overlook checkered tables where patrons of all ages get rowdier as the night progresses. *Wurstel* €7.50. *Gulasch* from €8.50. Large beer €3.70. Open M-Tu and Th-Su 11am-3pm and 5:30pm-midnight. AmEx/MC/V. ❷

👁 🄽 SIGHTS AND OUTDOOR ACTIVITIES

For stunning lake views, freshwater swimming, or pebbly sunbathing, follow the lakeside path behind the tourist office and head away from the mountains. Three kilometers outside Riva, the 20,000-year-old **Cascata Varone** has chiseled a huge gorge in the mountain and cascades 87m over three tiers of mossy rock. Foliage arches softly over surrounding mountain paths, making them ideal for easy strolls. (Take bus #1 or 2 from V. Martiri. ☎ 0464 52 14 21. Open daily May-Aug. 9am-7pm; Mar. and Oct. 10am-12:30pm and 2-5pm; Apr. and Sept. 9am-6pm. €4. Cash only.) On the lake itself, find **Noleggio Rudderboat Rental** along *Lungalago Marinai d'Italia* for hourly paddle boat rentals and low key, high energy fun. (☎ 335 605 44 54. 2 people €7, 4 people €8, 5 people €9. Open daily 8:30am-7pm. Cash only.)

In the cliffs above the lake, historical hotspots draw hikers out of the city *centro*. Follow V. Dante to the mountains as it changes to V. Bastione, then take a left up the ramp and follow the winding cobblestone path for 20min. to the 15th-century **Bastione,** a circular fortress that survived Napoleon's onslaught in 1796 but lost its upper half as a result. Today hikers can explore the edges of the historical treasure or admire the aerial view of Riva in minature with tiny boats dotting the vibrant blue of Lake Garda. Farther up, a steep 1hr. hike leads to **Chiesetta Santa Barbara,** a tiny chapel poised over misty mountains and the valley below.

⬛ NIGHTLIFE

Lakeside clubs are popular weekend spots, while pubs are an early evening or weekday alternative. **Party boats** cruise across the lake to Latin techno beats. Ask at the tourist office for a listing of free musical concerts. (Cover €12.50 includes 1 drink. Reservation required. Cruises late July-Aug.) **Pub Barracuda**, V. dei Fabbri, 11, serves stylish cocktails to a young local crowd. The specialty is anything with a South or Central American twist, including drinks like the "Panamanian." (From P. Cavour, take V. Disciplini onto V. Diaz. V. dei Fabbri is at the intersection with V. Fiume. ☎ 0464 55 55 62. Open daily 8pm-2am. MC/V.) **Pub All'Oca**, V. S. Maria, 9, attracts the young and fashionable to an interior lined with old leather booths. Sip wine (€2.50) while listening to classy, eclectic tunes—music ranges from jazz to swing. (☎ 0464 55 34 57. Open daily 6pm-2am. Cash only.) A fun, young crowd converges at **Cafe Latino**, V. Giacomo Cis, 15, a swanky tri-level *discoteca* overlooking the lake. Pick out the bartenders by their glittery facial tattoos. (☎ 0464 55 57 85. Cover €8, includes 1 drink. Get a drink card to keep track of drink purchases—lose it and pay €70. Open F-Sa 11pm-4am. AmEx/MC/V.)

FRIULI-VENEZIA GIULIA

Bounded by the Veneto to the west and Slovenia to the east is the kaleidoscope Friuli-Venezia Giulia. It derives its formal name from several distinct provinces unified by the clergy between the 6th and 15th centuries and was claimed by the ruling Hapsburgs in the early 1700s as an important economic epicenter for Austria and Hungary. Since then, parts have circulated between countries for decades, resulting in a potpourri of cuisines, architecture, and styles unique to each town. James Joyce wrote the bulk of *Ulysses* in coffee houses that still dot the cityscape of Trieste; Ernest Hemingway found part of his plot for *A Farewell to Arms* in the region's white Carso cliffs; and Franz Liszt, Sigmund Freud, and Rainer Maria Rilke all worked around Friuli, inspired by its natural beauty. Though smaller towns retain their idyllic charm, its growing gothams prove Friuli-Venezia Giulia truly has something to offer everyone.

HIGHLIGHTS OF FRIULI-VENEZIA GIULIA

STOP OVER at Italy's gateway to the East, the border city Trieste. (p. 341.)

TREAT YOURSELF to the luxuries of Grado, the former official treatment resort of the Austro-Hungarian Empire. (p. 348.)

SOAK UP historical vibes at medieval Cividale del Friuli on the banks of the Natisone River. (p. 352.)

TRIESTE   ☎ 040

After volleying between Italian, Austrian, and Slavic allegiances for hundreds of years, Trieste (pop. 241,000) has finally settled down, celebrating its 50th anniversary as an Italian city in 2004. Nonetheless, subtle reminders of Trieste's Eastern European past are manifest in city architecture, the cuisine, and the Hapsburg rulers smirking from the portraits that line the walls of museums. While hip locals

strut along bustling quays, shielded by designer labels and their own allure, the sapphire waters of the Adriatic Sea frame Trieste's constant excitement and drama with breathtaking natural beauty.

⌐ TRANSPORTATION

Flights: Aeroporto Friuli-Venezia Giulia/Ronchi dei Legionari, V. Aquileia, 46 (☎0481 77 32 24 or 77 32 25), 20km from the city center. To get to the airport, take the SAF bus (1hr., M-Sa every hr., €3.50). Ticket counter open daily 7am-noon and 1-7pm.

Trains: P. della Libertà, 8 (☎040 41 26 95), down C. Cavour from the quay. Ticket counter (☎040 41 86 12) open daily 5:40am-9:30pm. Info office open daily 7am-9pm. To: **Budapest, Hungary** (12hr., 2 per day 10:52am-10:32pm, €73); **Ljubljana, Slovenia** (3hr., 3 per day 10:52am-10:32pm, €20); **Udine** (1½hr., 37 per day 5am-9:19pm, €4.23); **Venice** (2hr., 29 per day 4:30am-9:25pm, €7.90).

Buses: P. della Libertà, 11 (☎040 42 50 01), next to train station.

Ferries: Adriatica di Navigazione, P. Unità, 7 (☎040 36 37 37), off C. Cavour, sails to: **Albania, Croatia, Greece,** and **Slovenia. Anek Lines,** Molo Bersaglieri, 3 (☎0403 22 05 61), off Riva del Mandracchio, runs ferries to Greece. **Agemar Viaggi,** P. Duca degli Abruzzi 1/A (☎0403 63 32 22), off C. Cavour, has detailed departure schedules and sells tickets for both lines. Open M-F 9am-12:30pm and 3-6pm.

Public Transportation: A.C.T. orange buses travel city and provincial routes to **Carso, Miramare,** and **Opicina.** Tickets (€0.90) for sale at *tabacchi* and bars.

Tram: A **funicular** links P. Oberdan with Opicina, a city on the Carso Plateau above Trieste. From P. Oberdan (25min., every 20min. 7:11am-8:11pm, €0.90).

Taxis: RadioTaxi (☎040 30 77 30). Available 24hr.

Car Rental: Maggiore/Budget/Alamo (☎040 42 13 23), in the train station. €70 per day, €303 per week. Open M-F 8:30am-12:30pm and 3-7pm, Sa 8:30am-12:30pm.

▣ ⚑ ORIENTATION AND PRACTICAL INFORMATION

The center of Trieste is organized as a grid, bounded to the east by **Via Carducci,** which stretches south from **Piazza Oberdan** toward the historic **Capitoline Hill.** To the west, the bustling **Corso Italia** runs south from the spectacular **Piazza dell'Unità d'Italia,** a vast, uncluttered square beside the harbor. The two streets intersect at the busy **Piazza Goldoni.** Steps from P. Unità along C. Italia lies the **Piazza della Borsa,** where the *Triestini* come to strut their stuff.

Tourist Office: APT, P. dell'Unità d'Italia, 4/B (☎040 347 83 12, fax 347 83 20), has a wealth of info and lists of *manifestazioni* (artistic events). Open daily 9:30am-7pm.

Consular Services: UK, V. Dante Alighieri, 7 (☎040 347 83 03, fax 347 83 11, emergency 349 355 81 10). Open Apr.-Oct. Tu 10am-noon, F 2:30-4:30pm; Nov.-Mar. call for hours. **US,** V. Roma, 15 (☎040 66 01 77, fax 63 12 40). Open M-F 10am-noon.

Currency Exchange: Deutsche Bank, V. Roma, 7 (☎040 63 19 25). Cash advances on Visa. Open M-F 8:20am-1:20pm and 2:35-3:50pm.

Emergency: ☎113. **Ambulance** (☎118). **Police** (☎112).

Pharmacy: Farmacia alla Borsa, P. della Borsa, 12/A (☎040 36 79 67). Open M-F 8:30am-1pm and 4-7:30pm, Sa 8:30am-1pm. For 24hr. pharmacy rotation, check at the window or at the tourist office.

Internet: One Net, V. S. Francesco d'Assisi, 28/C (☎040 77 11 90). €6.50 per hr. Open M-Sa 10am-1pm and 4-9pm. **Interland,** V. Gallina, 1 (☎040 372 86 35, fax 372 54 13). €1.29 for 15min. Open M-F 10:30am-8:30pm, Sa 2:30-8:30pm.

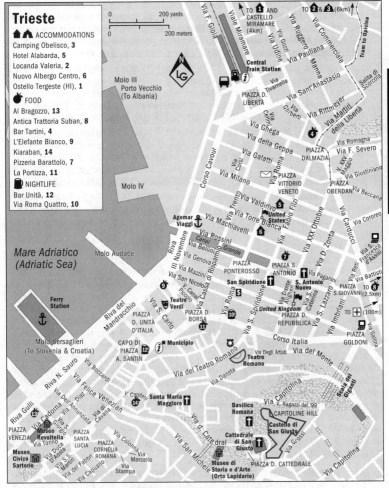

Trieste

♠ ⌂ ACCOMMODATIONS
Camping Obelisco, **3**
Hotel Alabarda, **5**
Locanda Valeria, **2**
Nuovo Albergo Centro, **6**
Ostello Tergeste (HI), **1**

● FOOD
Al Bragozzo, **13**
Antica Trattoria Suban, **8**
Bar Tartini, **4**
L'Elefante Bianco, **9**
Kiaraban, **14**
Pizzeria Barattolo, **7**
La Portizza, **11**

■ NIGHTLIFE
Bar Unità, **12**
Via Roma Quattro, **10**

Post Office: P. V. Veneto, 1 (☎040 676 41 11), along V. Roma. From the train station, take 3rd right off V. Ghega. Open M-Sa 8:15am-7pm. **Postal Code:** 34100.

🏠 🏕 ACCOMMODATIONS AND CAMPING

▨ **Hotel Alabarda,** V. Valdirivo, 22, 3rd fl. (☎040 63 02 69; www.hotelalabarda.it), in the city center. From the train or bus station, head south on C. Cavour and turn left onto V. Valdirivo. A cheerful staff complements 18 pleasant rooms. Internet €5.16 per hr. Satellite TV. Wheelchair accessible. Breakfast included. Singles €33, with bath €38; doubles €45/€68; triples €60/€91. 10% discount with *Let's Go.* AmEx/MC/V. ❸

Ostello Tergeste (HI), V. Miramare, 331 (☎040 22 41 02; ostellotrieste@hotmail.com), 4km from the city center. From train station, take bus #36 (€0.90) from V. Miramare. Ask for the Ostello stop. A friendly staff runs an efficient hostel in a beautiful villa. Bar and terrace share unfettered views of the Adriatic. Some rooms have private terrace. Internet €2 per hr. Breakfast included. Dinner €8.50. Reception daily 8am-11:30pm. Lockout 10am-1pm. Curfew midnight. Guests expected to do minimal cleaning chores. Reserve ahead. Must be an HI member. Permanent HI memberships are sold on-site for €18, temporary stamps available for €3 a night. €13. Cash only. ❶

Nuovo Albergo Centro, V. Roma, 13 (☎040 347 87 90; www.hotelcentrotrieste.it). Though the hotel's proximity to transportation and sights can get noisy, its thick bedspreads and muted tones give it a tranquil vibe. Internet €6 per hr. Satellite TV and phone. Breakfast included. Reception daily 8am-midnight. Singles €35, with bath €48; doubles €42/€60; triples €60/€80; quads €75/€100. AmEx/MC/V. ❸

Locanda Valeria, Str. per Vienna, 52 (☎040 21 12 04; info@trattoriavaleria.com), in Opicina, 7km east of Trieste. From P. Oberdan, take the tram to the last stop, or bus #39 from P. della Libertà to Str. per Vienna. Valeria is 3 blocks away. The multilingual staff makes guests at this 100-year-old hotel feel at home. Breakfast €3.50. Reservation recommended. Singles €25; doubles €45; triples €55. AmEx/MC/V. ❷

Camping Obelisco, Str. Nuova per Opicina, 37 (☎040 21 16 55, fax 21 27 44), in Opicina. Take tram from P. Oberdan, ask for Obelisco stop, and follow yellow signs. Showers, bar, and tents provided. €3.10-4 per person, €5.70-7.25 per tent. Cash only. ❶

🍴 FOOD

Trieste's cuisine has distinct Central European overtones, evident in the city's sauerkraut, strudel, and *iota* (sauerkraut, bean, and sausage stew). There's no shortage of quality restaurants along Riva N. Sauro and Riva Gulli that cater to seafood lovers. **Osmizze** are informal seasonal restaurants that sprouted in 1784, when a decree allowed peasants living on the Carso, a rural plateau outside Trieste, to sell local produce for eight days each year. Families in the Carso still celebrate the proclamation by serving regional vegetables and wine (such as *Terrano del Carso,* a dry red valued for its therapeutic properties) to the public for two weeks every year. Ask the tourist office for schedules and locations. The alimentari on V. Carducci provide an ideal place to wine with friends without worrying about your pocketbook; most cooking needs can be found at the well-stocked Euro Spesa **supermarket** at V. Valdirivo, 13/F, off C. Cavour. (☎040 76 39 38. Open M-Sa 8am-8pm.) At Trieste's **covered market,** V. Carducci, 36/D, dishware booths and magazine vendors surround tables piled high with fruits and cheeses. (On the corner of Viale della Majolica. Open M and W 8am-2pm, Tu and Th-Su 8am-6:30pm.)

🍽 **Antica Trattoria Suban,** V. Comici, 2 (☎040 543 68), serves Hungarian, Austrian, and Italian dishes (including honey strudel and veal croquettes with *parmigiano* and egg yolks) so heavenly that even Pope John Paul II has indulged. Cover €2.50. *Primi* €6-8, *secondi* €11-16. Open M 7:30-10:15pm, W-Su 12:30-2:30pm and 7:30-10pm. Closed first 2 weeks in Aug. Reservation recommended. AmEx/MC/V. ❷

Pizzeria Barattolo, P. S. Antonio, 2 (☎040 63 14 80; www.albarattolo.it), along the canal. A menu in Italian, English, and German describes favorites like *schiacciata* (€7), a pizza with grilled vegetables, cheese, basil, and garlic. Wide umbrellas on the piazza are perfect for leisurely lunches. Pizza €4.30-9.20. Cover €1. *Primi* €4.20-5.50, *secondi* €5.80-16. Service 15%. Open daily 8:30am-midnight. AmEx/MC/V. ❶

Bar Tartini, V. S. Martiri Libertà, 2 (☎040 63 61 03), has faux ivory tables and Christmas lights in a location below street level, creating a Trieste hotspot. In the spring, try the veggie strudel or pasta plate (€5). Open daily 8am-midnight. ❶

L'Elefante Bianco, Riva III Novembre, 3 (☎040 36 26 03; www.elefantebianco-trieste.com). Dine in the candlelit interior, but be warned—rooms may be reserved for Italian pop stars or politicos who come for the hand-selected ingredients and international wine list. 7-course tasting *menù* is €43; "fast business lunch" costs only €10-12. Open M-F 12:30-3pm and 7:15-11:45pm, Sa 7:15-11:45pm. AmEx. ❺

Kiaraban, V. Capitelli, 3, on the ground floor of the Scuola di Musica, 55. Turn right off of Largo Riccardo Pitteri onto V. Sebastiano and onto C. Capitelli. Music students drink here as they work—the backlit red bar is enough to rouse anyone's muse. Because it's part of the school, the bar is only open until 8pm, but ask about concert times, when music calls for extra hours. (Wine €1.50-4. Open 8am-8pm daily.) ❶

La Portizza, P. della Borsa, 5 (☎040 36 58 54). Take a break from marathon shopping and let one of the young, impeccably groomed and probably pierced staffers serve up one of Portizza's big salads (€4) or sandwiches (€1.60). Open daily in summer from 6:30am, in winter 6:30am-9pm. AmEx/MC/V. ❶

Al Bragozzo, Riva Nazario Sauro, 22 (☎040 30 30 01), makes the most of Trieste's proximity to the sea, with a sailboat full of chilled wine. All meals are dished up on carts in front of your table—exciting when the fish is still on fire and needs to drop a skeleton. Full meal €30. Open Tu-Su noon-3pm and 7-10pm. AmEx/MC/V. ❺

  SIGHTS

> 💡 **T FOR TWO.** The **Trieste for You** card, available free at Trieste's hotels to visitors of two nights or more, gives discounts at hotels, restaurants, sights, and stores. For more information, contact the tourist office.

CITY CENTER

MUSEO REVOLTELLA. The Revoltella, also known as the Galleria d'Arte Moderna, displays temporary modern art exhibits and an extensive permanent collection. Be sure to see Magni's *Fontana della Ninfa Aurisiana*, a marble fountain of a woman symbolizing the city Trieste. *(V. Diaz, 21. ☎040 31 13 61 or 30 09 38; revoltella@comune.trieste.it. Open M and W-Su 9am-2pm and 4-7pm. €5, students €3.)*

CITTÀ NUOVA. The oldest areas in the southern half of the Trieste sport a tangle of roads in no discernible pattern; in the 1700s, Empress Maria Theresa of Austria commissioned a *Città Nuova* plan which 19th-century Viennese urban planners implemented between the waterfront and the **Castello di San Giusto.** The resulting street grid, lined with Neoclassical palaces, centers around the Canale Grande. Facing the canal from the south is the Serbian Orthodox **Chiesa di San Spiridione,** a 9th-century neo-Byzantine church with blue domes and an array of Greek crosses frescoed throughout the interior. *(Open Tu-Sa 9am-noon and 5-8pm. Modest dress required.)* The vast **Piazza dell'Unità d'Italia,** Italy's largest square along the waterfront, provides a full view of the green crescent coastline of the Adriatic. On the eastern side of the piazza, the **Municipio** (Town Hall) faces the *Mazzoleni Fountain of the Four Continents*, representing the world as it was known upon the fountain's completion in 1750.

CASTELLO DI SAN GIUSTO. The 15th-century Venetian castle presides over the **Capitoline Hill,** the city's historic center. From P. della Cattedrale, the right side of the castle encloses a **museum** of Roman statuary and mosaics. Within the castle walls, a staircase leads to a bird's eye view of Trieste. To avoid the winding roads up Capitoline Hill, brace yourself for the flower-lined twin staircases of the 265-

step **Scala dei Giganti** just south of P. Goldoni. (*Take bus #24 from the station to the last stop. ☎040 30 93 62. Viewing subject to change due to electrical rewiring throughout the castle. Castle open daily Apr.-Sept. 9am-7pm, Oct.-Mar. 9am-5pm. Museum open Tu-Su 9am-1pm. Free.*)

PIAZZA DELLA CATTEDRALE. This hilltop piazza on the site of an ancient Roman basilica overlooks the Adriatic and downtown Trieste. The remains of the old Roman city center lie directly below, and the restored **Cattedrale di San Giusto** is across the street. San Giusto assumed a roughly square shape rather than the cross design traditional of cathedrals after a 14th-century renovation combined the original church with the basilica of S. Maria Assunta. The mosaics from both original apses still grace the chambers on either side of the main altar. (*☎040 30 93 62. Open Tu-Sa 8am-7:30pm, Su 8am-6:30pm; closed to tourists early Su mornings for mass. Free. Printed guides available for €1 in English, Italian, German, and French.*)

TEATRO ROMANO. In the first century AD, the Emperor Trajan supervised the building of this amphitheater, which staged both gladiatorial games and dramatic performances. Today, the crumbling structure is overtaken by weeds and a thriving community of stray cats, though still impressive when illuminated after dusk. (*On V. del Teatro Romano, off C. Italia. From Capitoline Hill, descend toward P. Ponterosso. Free.*)

MUSEO DI STORIA E D'ARTE. This art history museum provides an archaeological history of Trieste and the upper Adriatic from pre-Roman times. Inside, glass cases of Greek and Egyptian jewelry, glass, and pottery line walls surrounding a mummy and sarcophagus. Outside, the **Orto Lapidario** (Rock Garden) arranges pieces of Roman architecture in a garden of history, but heavy weeds and broken benches dampen the experience. (*P. Cattedrale, 1. ☎040 31 05 00 or 30 86 86. Open Tu and Th-Su 9am-1pm, W 9am-7pm. €2 adults, €1 with youth discount.*)

CITY ENVIRONS

■**CASTELLO MIRAMARE.** Archduke Maximilian of Austria commissioned this castle in the mid-19th century. Lavishly decorated apartments feature crystal chandeliers, rich tapestries, and Asian porcelain. Legend holds that visitors can still hear the wailing ghost of Carlotta, Maximilian's wife, whose player piano plucks notes in a particularly eerie upper room. Poised on a promontory over the gulf, Miramare's turrets are easily visible from the Capitoline Hill in Trieste and most points along the **Barcola,** a cafe-lined boardwalk extending 7km between the Castello and Trieste. On the second Sunday in October, Trieste stages the annual *Barcolana,* a regatta that blankets the harbor with thousands of billowing sails. (*To reach Miramare, take bus #36 (15min., €0.90) to the hostel and walk along the water for 15min. ☎040 224 70 13. Open M-Sa 9am-7pm and Su 8:30am-7pm, ticket office open daily 9am-6:30pm. €4, for EU citizens 18-25 €2, EU citizens under 18 or over 65 free. Guided English tours €3.50, audioguides €3.50 or 2 for €5. Gardens free.*)

MARINE PARK. Part of **Castelletto Miramare,** V. Miramare, 349, in the gardens of the Castello, this small World Wildlife Federation aquatic museum offers scuba tours of a pristine underwater landscape just off the Mediterranean shore. Call ahead to inquire about guided tours. (*☎040 22 41 47; www.riservamarinamiramare.it. Sea watching June-Sept. M-F, scuba diving Apr.-Oct. Sa-Su. Free. Scuba certification and reservation required. Snorkel, fins, and mask included. Must be in groups of 10; ask to be grouped with others if your group is less than 10. Scuba tours 9am and 2pm. Office open M-F 8:45am-6:45pm, Sa 10am-6pm. Entrance to Castelletto's Marina Museum €14.50, children €10.50.*)

KUGY PATH AND GROTTA GIGANTE. The tram to Opicina from P. Oberdan is one of the longest running funiculars in Europe. After a steep climb, the tram runs past vineyards and breathtaking views of the Adriatic coastline. Hop off at the Obelisk stop to meet up with the Kugy Path, a popular trail that cuts along the sides of the Carso cliffs. At the end of the tram route is the Grotta Gigante, claimed to be the world's largest touristed cave. Staircases wind in and around the 107m interior. *(V. Donota, 2. Bus #42 arrives in the small parking lot across V. Nazionale from the tram stop. Buy 2 tickets in town for the return. ☎ 040 32 73 12. Open Jan.-June and Sept.-Dec. Tu-Su 10am-6pm, July-Aug. daily 10am-6pm. Tours every 30min. €7.50, groups of 25 or more €5.50.)*

RISIERA DE SAN SABBA. Italy's only WWII concentration camp occupied this abandoned rice factory outside Trieste. The *risiera* now houses a museum detailing Trieste's role in the Slovenian-born resistance movement that confronted Nazi occupation. *(Ratto della Pileria, 43. Bus #8. ☎ 040 82 62 02. Open daily 9am-7pm. Free.)*

FARO DELLA VITTORIA. Built on the foundations of Fort Kressich, this lighthouse is a tribute to those who gave their lives at sea in WWI. Inaugurated in 1927 in the presence of Vittorio Emanuele III, the 70m tower incorporates the anchor of the first Italian ship to enter the harbor during the 1918 liberation. *(Str. del Friuli, 141. ☎ 040 41 04 61. Open Apr.-Sept. M-Sa 9-11am and 4-6pm, Oct.-Mar. Sa-Su 10am-3pm. Free.)*

🔊 🎵 NIGHTLIFE AND ENTERTAINMENT

The night heats up early at the new ▇ **Via Roma Quattro,** whose name is also its address. The orange walls and animal print seat cushions are barely visible in the sea of young trendsetters who stop here before a night of clubbing. (☎ 040 63 46 33. Open 7:30am-10:30pm. AmEx/MC/V.) Trieste's glitterati are out in full force along the bars of **Capo di Piazza A. Santin,** part of the pedestrian shopping district that connects P. della Borsa to P. dell'Unità. On summer evenings, the hip crowd gravitates toward fresh cocktails and Europop at **Bar Unità,** at Capo di P. A. Santin 1/B on the southwestern corner of P. dell'Unità. (☎ 040 36 80 33. Open M-Sa 6:30pm-1am.) The acclaimed **Teatro Verdi** opera house hosts operas from November to May and a six-week operetta season from July to mid-August. Buy tickets or make reservations at the **box office,** Riva III Novembre, 1. Enter on the other side of the building at P. Giuseppe Verdi. (☎ 040 672 22 98; www.teatroverdi-trieste.com. Open Tu-Sa 9am-noon and 4-7pm and Su 9am-noon. Tickets €8-40.)

ily Chronicle

IN RECENT NEWS

NEW TRIESTE

When Austro-Hungarian rulers redirected major routes through Trieste in 1719, the small fishing village exploded into the center of economic development for the empire. Two centuries later, the city's reputation rapidly decayed as it was shuffled among five ruling powers in 50 short years. When Italy gained permanent control of the region in 1954, the Iron Curtain had severed the trade route between Europe that had fueled Trieste's fiery growth. Trieste's economy ground to a halt and the port decayed.

After 50 years of stagnant port growth, many *Triestini* are cautiously optimistic about a new golden age for the city. On May 1, 2004, Hungary and Slovenia joined the European Union (EU) and effectively opened a consumer base of 75 million people to the region, but a number of factors still threaten Trieste's rebirth. Crumbling railways and port infrastructure are only slightly more developed now than at the beginning of the 1900s and could severely limit chances for immediate growth. Additionally, much of the new East/West trade that would conceivably pass through Trieste depends on stable trade policies between Europe and China, a relationship where future economic growth is not guaranteed. Still, most observers view the new trade routes as a symbolic beginning, one where old unions— and hopes—are restored.

DAYTRIP FROM TRIESTE

GRADO

This spa resort town is accessible by bus. Buses run to: Aquileia (15min., 31 per day 5:35am-11pm, €0.85); Trieste (1½hr., 6 per day 6:20am-7pm, €3.80); Udine (1¼hr., 20 per day 5:35am-11pm, €3.15). Buses arrive from Trieste (1½hr., 4 per day 9:07am-10:07pm) and Udine (1¼hr., 18 per day 8am-10:20pm).

Grado's connections with other cities in the region are few and far between—visitors come principally for spa treatments at the **terme,** a centralized set of spas along the lagoon on Grado's south side. As a result, they're willing to pay top dollar for proximity to the solariums and saunas that keep tourists flocking to the tiny island. For those reluctant to splurge on eternal youth, fees for the beach along the *terme* vary based on time of day and season, but tickets are usually available along V. Regina Elena for less than €10. **Santa Eufemia** (☎/fax 0431 801 46), a 7th-century basilica along P. Duca d'Aosta, still hosts visitors under its soaring wood-beamed ceiling, and nearby an unearthed mosaic is on display for public viewing via raised walkway. The basilica itself had a piece of floor removed to reveal a mosaic from the late 4th century hidden underneath.

City buses 37A and 37B stop at major points across the island and at the wide array of spas and hotels along the south side of the island. For a **map** of the island or listings of spa treatments and prices, visit the **tourist office.** From the bus station, take V. Roma, continue onto V. Venezia, then turn left onto V. Dante Alighieri and look for number 72. (☎ 0431 87 71 11; www.gradoturismo.info. Open daily 8am-5pm.) For a **pharmacy,** leave the bus station, walk toward the bay, and bear left on P. S. Marco into V. Orseolo. The **police** are directly across the street. Find **Internet** at **Tabacchi Tarallo,** V. A. Manzoni, 25. (☎/fax 0431 87 70 50. €6 per hr., €1. Open daily June-Aug. 8am-1pm and 4-10:30pm, Sept.-May 8am-1pm and 4-8pm.) A **hospital** is on V. Amalfi, 1. (☎/fax 0481 53 30 34. Open daily 8am-2pm.) A **post office** is at V. Caprin 34. (Open M-F 8:30am-2pm, Sa 8:30am-1pm.) **Postal Code:** 34073.

Though downtown hotels are pricey, a couple of options are within walking distance of the sea. Seafoam green and wicker aside, **Hotel Capri ❹,** Viale Vespucci, 1, offers amazing terrace views of the lagoon, A/C, phone, TV, bath, a lounge, and some in-room jacuzzis. (☎ 0431 800 91; hotelcapri@libero.it. Breakfast €5 extra. Reception open 7am-midnight. Open Easter-Nov. Singles €30; doubles €60. AmEx/MC/V.) Genial proprietors run **Meublé Al Sole ❷,** Viale Del Sole, 31, set back a few blocks from the lagoon with furnished balconies and a small patio. (☎ 0431 803 70; solemare@xnet.it. Breakfast included. Open Easter-Nov. Singles €25-30; doubles €50. MC/V.) **Alimentari Corbatto,** at V. Manzoni, 9, is an indoor market with cheese, meats, breads, and alcohol. (☎ 0431 801 27. Open M-Sa 8am-12:30pm and 4:30-7:30pm.) For true gastronomical indulgence, head to **Ristorante Al Canevon ❷,** Calle Corbatto, 11, the master of all fish on its menu. (☎/fax 0431 816 62. *Primi* €7-9.50, *secondi* €11-15. Cover €2.10. Open daily in summer noon-2pm and 7-10pm, in winter M-Tu and Th-Su noon-2pm and 7-10pm. AmEx/MC/V.) If a leisurely meal isn't in the cards, grab some rich, hearty pizza across from the post office on the corner of V. Morosini and V. Caprin at **Pizza Number One ❶,** V. Morosini, 21, a small pizzeria with enormous helpings. The location is perfect to nab a mouthful of the spicy salami pizza (€1.80) or crisp salad (€2) and head to the beach. (☎ 0431 804 77.) Head south on P. Duca d'Aosta and look to your right for **Agli Artisti ❹,** Campiello Porta Grande #2, where evidence of Roman walls is still visible in the floor. A typical plate of fish costs €27, but the real draw is the old and beautifully narrow neighborhood where Artisti is hidden. (☎/fax 0431 830 81. Open M and W-Su noon-2:30pm and 6-10pm. AmEx/MC/V.)

AQUILEIA
☎ 0431

After passing a series of small towns and hurtling through a handful of gateways, low vegetation is replaced by glimpses of Roman pillars still standing (more or less) along the roadside, marking the entrance to Aquileia. The former Roman city and gateway to the Adriatic for the Eastern Empire retains a sense of peaceful detachment from the major thoroughfare that cuts its quiet streets in half. Strolls along back roads reveal small canals and churches that don't appear on any major map.

FRIULI-VENEZIA GIULIA

🖪🔄 TRANSPORTATION AND PRACTICAL INFORMATION. Aquileia can be reached by **bus** from Udine (1hr., 16 per day 6:10am-9:40pm, €2.80). From Cervignano, a **train station** on the Trieste-Venice line, buses leave to Aquileia *centro* (15min., every 30min. 6am-8:30pm, €1.40). For a list of budget accommodations and nearby camping, including the island of Grado (15km south on V. Beligna, the main thoroughfare), consult the **APT Tourist Office**, P. Capitolo, 4. From the bus stop facing the basilica, head toward the church; the **tourist office** is on the right. (☎ 0431 910 87. Open daily Apr.-Oct. 9am-7pm, Nov.-Mar. 9am-noon.) In case of **emergency**, dial ☎ 113, or call the **police** (☎ 0431 91 03 34), on V. Semina. The largest local **pharmacy** is on C. Gramsci, two blocks from Albergo Aquila Nera. (☎ 0431 91 00 01. Open M-F 8:30am-12:30pm and 3:30-7:30pm, Sa 8:30am-12:30pm.) For **currency exchange** and **postal services** July through September, walk two blocks along V. Augusta (toward Cervignano) to the **Poste Italiane** kiosk. (Open M-F 9am-12:30pm and 3:30-5pm.) Otherwise, the central **post office** is in P. Cervi, off C. Gramsci. (☎ 0431 91 92 72. Open M-F 8:30am-2pm, Sa 8:30am-1pm.) **Postal Code:** 33051.

🖪🔄 ACCOMMODATIONS AND FOOD. While Aquileia has hotels aplenty around the basilica, the real gems are often hidden in quieter areas. **Domus Augusta (HI) ❶**, V. Roma, 25, has an animated clientele and enviable location just blocks from the basilica. (☎ 0431 910 24; www.ostelloaquileia.it. Internet €4. Breakfast and sheets included. Bike rental €2 per hr. Reception 2-11:30pm. Check-out 10am. Lockout 10am-2pm. Curfew 11:30pm. Dorms €15; singles with private bath €23. MC/V.) At **Albergo Aquila Nera ❸**, P. Garibaldi 5, a short walk up V. Roma from V. Augusta, all rooms feature phone, TV, safe, and bath. A restaurant and bar downstairs are popular in this central neighborhood. (☎/fax 0431 91 045. Breakfast included. Singles €35; doubles €70; triples €95. AmEx/MC/V.) Sleep near Roman ruins at **Camping Aquileia ❶**, V. Gemina 10, which features a swimming pool and a restaurant mere blocks from the ruins at the end of Porto Fluviale. (May 15-Sept. 15 ☎ 0431 910 42, Sept. 16-May 14 0431 91 95 83. Reception 7am-11pm. One electrical hookup per campsite. Open May 15-Sept. 20. Prices vary seasonally. May 15-Sept. 15 €5.25-€6.30 per person, Sept. 16-May 14 €4.20 per person. Tent sites €9, 3-person bungalow €36-45; 4-person bungalow €52-65. MC/V.)

Grab a pink table at **La Colombara ❺**, V. S. Zilli, 42, and sample the fresh *sardelle in savor* (sardines in onions; €5.50), or call ahead about "At Table with the Ancient Romans," a theme meal where even the helpful waiters don togas. From the bus stop across from the basilica, turn immediately left, turn right onto V. Gemina, and follow the road as it curves for about 20min. (☎ 0431 915 13; www.lacolombara.it. Dinner €20-40. Open Tu-Su noon-2:30pm and 7-10:30pm. AmEx/MC/V.) From the basilica, exit the piazza back to the main road to Cervignano. Turn left, onto V. G. Augusta and **La Pergola ❷**, V. Beligna, 4, is on the left after a short walk. Baked shin of pork with potatoes (€11.30) is the house specialty. (☎ 0431 913 06. *Primi* €4.70-6.50, *secondi* €6.40-11.30. Open Mar.-Dec. M and W-Su 10am-3pm and 5-10pm. AmEx/MC/V.)

◙ **SIGHTS.** Aquileia's **basilica** still functions as a religious site, but just barely. Plexiglass and steel walkways allow tourists to take flashless pictures of the interior and fading fresco in the apse. The church's floor, a remnant of the original building, is a massive mosaic of over 700 sq. m of geometric patterns and striking images of animals, cherubs, and field workers. Beneath the altar, the crypt's 12th-century frescoes illustrate the trials of Aquileia's early Christians in addition to scenes from the life of Christ. Damp catwalks guide visitors through the **Cripta degli Scavi** and its half-uncovered mosaics. The first-century Roman house is buried in other artifacts and variated stone. (☎0431 910 67. Basilica open daily 9am-7pm. Free. Crypt open daily 9am-6:30pm. €2.60, under 10 free.) The nearby **campanile** (bell tower) was constructed in 1031 using the remains of the Roman amphitheater. Today the structure enjoys unobstructed views of the Slovenian Alps to the north, Trieste to the east, and the Adriatic to the south. (Open daily 9:30am-1pm and 3-6:30pm. €1.10.) **Porto Fluviale,** the cypress-lined alley behind the basilica that spans the former dockyard of Aquileia's thriving Roman river harbor, is listed as one of UNESCO's most valuable world sites and conveniently emerges near the Roman ruins at the forum. From there, cross V. Gemina and follow the signs to head to the **Museo Paleocristiano** in P. Pirano to see mosaics that document the region's transition from Classical paganism to Christianity. (☎0431 911 31. Open daily 8:30am-1:45pm. Free.) The **Museo Archeologico,** at the corner of V. Augusta and V. Roma, displays ancient ruins featuring the preserved remains of a row boat used by Roman citizens. (☎0431 910 16. Open M 8:30am-2pm, Tu-Su 8:30am-7:30pm. €4, between 18 and 25 €2, under 18 or over 65 free.)

UDINE ☎0432

Udine's Piazza della Libertà blends arches, platforms, statues, and monuments in a firestorm of regional pride. The "City of Tiepolo" features the Renaissance painter's works in many of its major landmarks, from courtroom ceilings to small chapels. Once ruled by the Patriarch of Aquileia, Udine later changed hands among Venetian, French, and Austrian powers, and suffered severe bombing in WWII. The city is easily accessible for the day with trains running frequently from Aquileia, Trieste, Cividale, or Venice, but visitors wishing to settle down off the beaten path can easily find a comfy bed for a longer stay in Udine.

◪◩ **TRANSPORTATION AND PRACTICAL INFORMATION.** Udine is most easily accessible by **train.** The train station is on V. Europa Unità. The info office (☎1478 880 88) is open daily 7am-9pm, and the ticket and reservations counter is open 7am-8:30pm. Trains depart to: Milan (4½hr., 5:45am and 6:49pm, €24.79); Trieste (1½hr., 36 per day 5:20am-11:43pm, €4.23); Venice (2hr., 33 per day 4:39am-10:32pm, €6.82); and Vienna, Austria (7hr., 5 per day 9:52am-1:45am, €54.87). **Buses** run from V. Europa Unità. Cross the street from the train station and walk one block to the right. SAF (☎0432 60 81 53) runs buses to: Aquileia (every hr. 6:50am-9pm, €2.60); Cividale (every hr. 6:40am-7:15pm, €1.80); and Trieste (2 per hr. 5:10am-10:55pm, €4.27). For a **taxi,** call RadioTaxi (☎0432 50 58 58).

Udine's **train** and **regional bus stations** are both on **Via Europa Unità,** in the southern part of town. All local bus lines pass the train station, but only buses #1, 3, and 8 run from V. Europa Unità to the center, passing by **Piazza della Libertà** and **Castello Hill.** To walk from the station (15min.), go right to **Piazza D'Annunzio,** then turn left under the arches to **Via Aquileia.** Continue up **Via Veneto** to P. della Libertà. From the southern end of P. della Libertà, turn right on V. Manin to reach the **tourist office,** P. 1° Maggio, 7. They distribute **maps** and info for Udine, Trieste, and Aquileia. (☎0432 29 59 72; arpt_ud1@regione.fvg.it. Also accessible by bus #2, 7, or 10. Open M-Sa 9am-5pm.) **Currency Exchange** is available in the streets around P.

della Libertà, all with comparable rates. In case of **emergency**, call ☎ 113, an **ambulance** (☎ 118), or the **carabinieri**, V. D. Prefettura, 16 (☎ 112). A **pharmacy** is at P. della Libertà, 9. (☎ 0432 50 28 77. Open M-Sa 8:30am-12:30pm and 3:30-11pm. Ring bell 11pm-8am.) Check **Internet** at **InternetPlay**, V. Francesco, 33. (☎/fax 0432 215 84; www.internetplay.it. €4 per hr., €1 min. Open M-Sa 9am-1pm and 3:10-7:50pm.) The **post office**, V. Veneto, 42, has *fermoposta* and fax. (☎ 0432 22 33 54, fax 232 08. Open M-Sa 8:30am-7pm. **Postal Code:** 33100.)

▛ ACCOMMODATIONS. Most hotels in downtown Udine would send any budget traveler into sticker shock, but moderately priced hotel options do exist outside the city center. Take bus #4 from the station, get off at P. Oberdan, and walk down V. Pracchiuso on the far side of the piazza. **Al Bue ❹**, V. Pracchiuso, 75, has rooms with bath, TV, and phone, around a central terrace. A garden with a well-stocked bar provides a getaway even in this peaceful neighborhood. (☎ 0432 29 90 70; www.locandaalbue.it. Restaurant downstairs. Reception 7am-midnight. Singles €60; doubles €90; triples €110; 5-person suite €135. MC/V.) At **Hotel Quo Vadis ❸**, Piazzale Cella, 28, bath, TV, A/C, and access to a major automotive roadway make this hotel especially popular with university guests between May and September. Reserve ahead. (☎ 0432 210 91; hotelquovadis@libero.it. Reception 7am-midnight. Singles €37; doubles €60; triples €75. V.) Exiting the train station, cross the street, turn right, and walk two blocks to reach **Hotel Europa ❹**, V. L. Europa Unità, 47. The elegant rooms all have tiled bath, A/C, TV, and full mini-bar. For an aperitif, pack into the phone booth-sized elevator and hit up the expansive ground-level bar. (☎ 0432 50 87 31 or 29 44 46, fax 51 26 54. Breakfast included. Singles from €50; doubles €75. AmEx/MC/V.) The scarred wooden floors and parabolic mattresses of **Al Vecchio Tram ❷**, V. Brenari, 32, are managable for guests taking advantage of its proximity to piazzas. Be cautious in the neighborhood after dark. (☎ 0432 50 25 16. Reception 6am-10pm. Singles €21; doubles €35.)

▛ FOOD. *Udinese* cuisine blends Italian, Austrian, and Slovenian influences into such regional specialties as *brovada e museto*, a stew made with turnips and sausage. Shop for produce on weekday mornings in the **markets** on V. Redipuglia, in P. 1° Maggio, and in P. Matteotti near P. della Libertà. Dimeglio (☎ 0432 50 48 19), a well-stocked **supermarket**, is on Viale Cesare Battisti, 9, between P. XX Settembre and P. Garibaldi. (Open Tu-Sa 8:30am-7:30pm.) Sidle up to one of the wooden tables at **▛Trattoria al Chianti ❷**, V. Marinelli, 4, and try a *primo* of *cjersons* (ravioli sweetened with ricotta) and *secondo* of *frico* (a cheese and potato dish) for €5.20 each. One of over 40 wines will go well with any dish. (☎ 0432 50 11 05. *Primi* €4, *secondi* €5-9.30. Cover €1. Open M-Sa 8am-3pm and 6pm-midnight; kitchen closes at 10:30pm. MC/V.) **▛Ristorante Vitello d'Oro ❹**, Viale E. Valvason, 4, has been dishing out *Udinese* classics like *cotechino* since 1849. (☎ 0432 50 89 82. *Primi* €6.50-10.50, *secondi* €15.50-18. Cover €2.60. Open in summer M 7-11pm and Tu-Sa noon-3pm and 7-11pm, in winter M-Tu and Th-Su noon-3pm and 7-11pm. AmEx/MC/V.) **Al Vecchio Stallo ❷**, V. Viola, 7, is a local epicenter of Italian cuisine. The jovial proprietor rightfully insists that the rich *di frico* (potatoes, cheese, and chicken) and pastas are a must-have. (☎/fax 0432 212 96. Lunch *menù* with *primo*, *secondo*, and side €10. *Primi* €5-6, *secondi* €6-10. Cover €1. Open M-Sa 11am-3:30pm and 7pm-midnight.) Students populate the combination coffeehouse and cafeteria **Zenit ❶**, Piazza XX Settembre, 22. Enjoy a lunch of a *primo*, *secondo*, side dish, and dessert (under €10) within the colorful interior or out in the piazza. (☎ 0432 50 29 80. Open M-F 8:30am-3pm, Sa 11:30am-3pm. MC/V.) Grab a *menù* of regional favorites at the cozy, family-owned **Ristorante da Brando ❷**, Piazzale Cella, 16.

FRIULI-VENEZIA GIULIA

(☎ 0432 50 28 37. Fixed *menù* with *primo*, *secondo*, side, and a 0.25L bottle of wine for €10. *Primi* from €3.65, *secondi* from €4.65. Cover €1.55. Open M-Sa 8am-midnight. AmEx/MC/V.)

☉ ♫ SIGHTS AND ENTERTAINMENT. The multi-tiered **Piazza della Libertà** has morphed from the political center of old Udine to the city's social center today. Along one edge are the gothic arches of the narrow **Arcado di San Giovanni,** and atop the bell tower, two automated Moorish figures gong out the hours to the people below. Across from the arcade, the **Loggia del Lionello,** built in 1488, serves as a public gathering place. In the highest corner of the square, through the **Arco Bollani,** a castle is accessible by road, stone staircase, or arched promenade. Once home to Venetian governors, the castle now holds the **Civici Musei e Galleria di Storia ed Arte Antica,** which contains paintings like Bellunello's *La Crocifissionè*. (☎ 0432 50 18 24. Open Tu-Sa 9:30am-12:30pm and 3-6pm, Su 9:30am-12:30pm. €2.55, ages 6-18 or over 60 €1.78.) Upon exiting the museum, turn right until you reach stairs, then circle around back and stay on the path until you reach **Chiesa di Santa Maria di Castello,** Udine's oldest church. The mossy exterior attests to its almost 500 years atop the hill. Church hours vary, but visitors will find a relatively untouristed haven. The **duomo** was consecrated in 1335 as *Santa Maria Annunziatta* and renovated in 1909. Frescoes by Tiepolo appear on the first and second altars on the right side, across from the glass-encased body of Patriarch Bertrando, murdered in 1350. The squat brick **campanile** houses the small **Museo del Duomo** with 14th-century frescoes by Vitale da Bologna. (☎ 0432 50 68 30. Open Tu-Sa 9am-noon and 4-6pm, Su 4-6pm. Free.) Udine has been called the city of Tiepolo, and some of this Baroque painter's finest works adorn the **Oratorio della Purità.** The *Assumption* (1759) on the ceiling and the *Immaculate Conception* on the altarpiece demonstrate his love of light and air. (Across from duomo. Free.) The **Museo Dicesane e Galleria de Tiepolo** occupies a 16th-century palazzo and displays early Tiepolo frescoes, most notably, the chilling *Solomon's Judgement* in the Patriarch's red courtroom. (P. Patriarcato, 1, at the head of Viale Ungheria. Entrance beneath the ornate coat of arms. ☎ 0432 250 03. Open W-Su 10am-noon and 3:30-6:30pm. €5, under 10 €4. Arrange in advance for free guided tours.)

In summer, P. 1° Maggio becomes the fairgrounds for **Estate in Città,** a series of outdoor concerts and guided tours of the city. **Bar Americano,** P. della Libertà, 7, provides an outstanding vantage point to sip a cocktail and people-watch the piazza at night. (☎ 0432 24 80 18. Open daily in summer 6:30am-midnight, in winter 6:30am-9pm.) The **Black Stuff,** V. Gorghi, 3/A, gives its Irish theme an Italian twist with dishes like hamburger panini served in the requisite barroom full of Guinness ads and low stools. (☎ 0432 29 78 38. Open M and W-Su 6pm-3am. Cash only.)

CIVIDALE DEL FRIULI ☎ 0432

On the banks of the Natisone River, this tiny town is perhaps the most enchanting in Friuli. Founded by Julius Caesar as Forum Iulii, Cividale became the capital of the first Lombard duchy in AD 568 and flourished as a meeting point of artists and nobility in the Middle Ages. Now, the town is full of neighborhood pastry shops, though it has retained a fiercely independent character throughout the years.

☐ ↗ TRANSPORTATION AND PRACTICAL INFORMATION. Cividale is best reached from Udine by **train** (15min., 25 per day 6am-8:05pm, €1.80). **Buses** from Udine (€1.60) are less frequent. The **train station,** which opens onto Viale Libertà, is close to the center of town. (☎ 0432 73 10 32. Open M-Sa 5:45am-8pm, Su 7am-8pm.) From the train station, take V. G. Marconi and turn left through the stone gate, **Porta Arsenale Veneto,** when the street ends. Cross P. Dante and turn right onto V. S. Pellico, then left on Largo Boiani. The duomo is straight ahead. The **tourist office**, V. P. d'Aquileia, 4, is to the right of the duomo and offers free **maps** and listings of local accommodations. (☎0432 73 14 61; arpt_cividale1@regione.fvg.it. Open M-Th 9am-1pm and 3-5pm, F 9am-1pm, Sa-Su 10am-1pm and 4-6pm.) **Banca Antoniana Popolare Veneto**, Largo Boiani, 20, has an **ATM**. (Open M-Sa 8:20am-1:20pm and 2:35-3:35pm, Su 8:20am-11:20pm.) In case of **emergency**, dial ☎113, call the **police** (☎0432 70 61 11), on P. A. Diaz, off P. Dante, or contact the reference desk of **Ospedale Cividale** (☎0432 70 81), in P. dell'Ospedale. **Farmacia Minisini** is at Largo Boiani, 11. (Open M 3:30-7:30pm, Tu-F and Su 8:30am-12:30pm and 3:50-7:30pm, Sa 8:30am-12:30pm.) **Internet** is at Largo Boiani, 23. (€0.10 per min. Open M 9am-12:30pm, Tu 9am-12:30pm and 3-7:30pm.) The **post office**, Largo Boiani, 37-39, has an **ATM** and phone booths outside. (☎0432 70 57 11, fax 0432 70 57 40. Open M-F 8:30am-7pm, Sa 8:30am-1pm.) **Postal Code:** 33043.

ACCOMMODATIONS AND FOOD. Quiet Cividale lacks a wide variety of budget-conscious accommodations, but lists of *affittacamere* are available at the tourist office. Turn right from the tourist office and right on Str. Matteotti to reach the heavy green door of **Casa Il Gelsomino ❷**, Str. Matteotti, 11, a small white-walled villa with friendly proprietors. One single and one double room each have a shower. (☎0432 73 19 62. Breakfast included. Reserve ahead. €25 per person, €23 per night after the second day. Cash only.) At the centrally located **Al Pomo d'Oro ❹**, P. S. Giovanni, 20, ask for rooms with private balconies. (☎0432 73 14 89; www.alpomodoro.com. Wheelchair accessible. Breakfast included in attached restaurant. Rooms held until 6pm. Singles €50; doubles €70. AmEx/MC/V.)

Regional culinary specialties are *picolit* (a dessert wine), *frico* (a cheese and potato pancake), and *gubana* (a large fig-and prune-filled pastry laced with *grappa*). For a compact version, try the nutty, flaky *gubanetta* or sweet fruit tart (both €0.70) at ■ **Gubane Cividalese ❶**, V. P. D'Aquileia, 10, the self-proclaimed *"Dolci and Gubane"* of dessert production in the region. (☎0432 73 21 52. Open daily 7:30am-1:30pm and 3:30-8pm. Cash only.) Cividale's **open-air market** fills P. Diacono every Saturday from 8am to 1pm. **Coopca**, V. A. Ristori, 17, sells an array of groceries. (☎0432 73 11 05. Open M and W 8:30am-12:45pm, Tu and Th-Su 8:30am-12:45pm and 4-7:30pm. Cash only.) At **Antica Trattoria Dominissini ❷**, in the courtyard of Casa il Gelsomino on Str. Matteotti, 11, try the *gnocchi alla carniga* (stuffed with meat, €6.20) in a lively bar setting. (☎0432 73 37 63. *Primi* €5-6.20, *secondi* €5-10. Cover €1. Open Tu-Su 10:30am-3pm and 6-11pm. AmEx/MC/V.) **Alla Frasca ❸**, V. Stretta de Rubeis, 11, offers delicious mushroom dishes under a canopy of grapevines. (☎0432 73 12 70. *Primi* €6.20, *secondi* €10-15.50. Cover €1.80. Open in summer Tu-Su 12:30-2:30pm and 7-10pm, in winter Tu-Su 12:30-2:30pm and 7-9:30pm. MC/V.) Under dark frescoed ceilings, **Antica Osteria alla Speranza ❸**, Foro Giulio Cesare, 16, across from the post office on Largo Boiani, offers a rotating seasonal menu and bottles of Friulian wine. (☎0432 73 11 31. *Primi* €6.20-7, *secondi* €8-12. Cover €1. Open M and W-Su 8am-midnight. MC/V.)

SIGHTS. From the duomo, follow V. P. D'Aquileia to **Ponte del Diavolo**, a 15th-century stone bridge set between verdant cliffs 22m above the emerald green **Natisone River**. Cross the bridge, turn right, and descend through the bushes down stairs to the river to get a clear view of the stone Satan himself supposedly tossed under the bridge. Head behind the **Chiesa San Martino** to reach another intimate lookout point on the river and the private balconies that line the steep banks. Explore the silent, steep stone tunnels of **Ipogeo Celtico**, Monastero Maggiore, 10, an ancient Roman prison with open-jawed skulls engraved in the walls to indicate its former status as a graveyard. (Turn off of V. P. D'Aquileia onto Viale Monastero Maggiore right before the bridge. 10 people maximum. For the key to the door, visit Bar all'Ipogeo at Monastero Maggiore 2. ☎ 0432 70 12 11. Open Tu-Su 7am-8pm. On M, call the tourist office. Free.) In the town center, the 16th-century **duomo's** towering gray pillars are accented by a variety of dark wooden confessionals and heavy red marble fonts lining the walls. The Renaissance sarcophagus of Patriarch Nicolò Donato lies to the left of the entrance. Annexed to the duomo is the **Museo Cristiano,** where displays include the octagonal **Battisterio di Callisto,** commissioned by the first Aquileian patriarch in Cividale, and the **Altar of Ratchis,** a Lombard sculpture from AD 740. (☎ 0432 73 11 44. Duomo and museum open M-Sa 9:30am-noon and 3-6pm, Su 3-5:30pm. Free.) Upon exiting the duomo itself, circle around the right side to the back of the building and follow Riva Pozzo di Callisto to the bottom of the stairs where signs point to the **Tempietto Longobardo,** an 8th-century sanctuary built on the remains of Roman homes. Inside, a sextet of stucco figures, called *The Procession of Virgins and Martyrs,* stare down at the carved stalls from their high perch high. (☎ 0432 70 08 67. Open Apr.-Sept. M-F 9:30am-12:30pm and 3-6:30pm, Sa-Su 9:30am-1pm; Oct.-Mar. M-F 9:30am-12:30pm and 3-5pm, Sa-Su 9:30am-12:30pm and 2:30-6pm. €2, students €1.)

LIVING LA DOLCE VITA

When I accepted a teaching position at an international school in Italy, I imagined it would be a wonderful way to experience life in another country. I would be that "American living abroad" tasting *la dolce vita*. However, I soon understood it was not all glamour and adventure. I had no television, no telephone; I did not have a real bed, and felt disoriented in Trieste, the small, northern Italian city I was to call home. I felt disconnected.

At the international school I was a pre-nursery assistant, working with two-year-olds under the supervision of a permanent teacher. Most of the children were Italian; there were only three foreign students in the classroom. I thought it was slightly ironic that children could be called "foreign students" *(stranieri)* at an international school, but that's the way it was. Not knowing Italian, I only spoke to the children in English, although Italian was spoken in the classroom. Of course, I didn't think that was fair to the non-Italian speakers, but I wasn't in charge. Despite the language barrier, however, I began to adjust to the job. I would play with the children, sing songs with them, do activities like painting, coloring, and reading—basic nursery activities. I grew really close with the kids, and their parents were nice to me even if we couldn't communicate in a common language.

Adjusting to daily life in Trieste itself was harder. Located right on the Adriatic, the city used to be a major Hapsburg port, but its importance has since diminished. There are beautiful hills behind the city, with the sea in front, creating picturesque views from the coast. There are some beautiful buildings: the Castello Miramare, built as Maximillian's summer retreat outside the city, and the Castello San Giusto and the duomo, both of which celebrated their 700th anniversaries in 2003. There is also the Barcola, Trieste's paved beach area, that's great for sunning and swimming in warm weather. At first inspection, it seems like the makings for another lovely Italian city.

Trieste can in fact be lovely, but what you don't realize as a tourist is that bitter winters and the *bora*, a tremendous northern wind, can make it really unpleasant. Furthermore, when you're living there—though you might not notice if you were only visiting for a day—you can sense a sort of stagnation. People and things here are set in their

ways, with little progression. Most of the population is elderly, a growing problem throughout Italy as the average age of the population continues to rise due to plummeting birth rates. To find something fun to do on the weekends, young people usually have to drive out of the city. There are some bars and cafes, but if you want to go to a nice club you need a car or a friend who'll give you a ride.

I think that teaching in Italy, rather than just traveling as a tourist through the country, allowed me to see real Italian life, beyond the pasta eating and wine drinking I imagined it to be. It's easy to travel somewhere as a tourist and think how "cute" and "rustic" everything is, then go back to your hotel room and watch MTV like you're not far from home. Having to ride the bus everyday, I saw the fatigue of people who dragged themselves to low-paying jobs every day—I even began to recognize some regulars. I had to learn the unspoken rules of the daily bus commute in Trieste, sometimes the hard way: after being yelled at by three elderly women on a crowded bus for standing too close to the exit too soon before my stop, and at other times for not getting up there soon enough, I began to get the hang of things. From the frequent bus strikes to the lack of orderly lines, things were definitely different in Trieste, but you eventually discover that life goes on and things don't have to be the same as back at home. It was less convenient, but not unmanageable.

Ultimately, teaching in Italy was an experience that has changed the way I approach my life. For me, experiencing life abroad meant working toward assimilation. I wanted to be a part of those living around me. I learned the streets, shops, and restaurants of neighboring Venice and Florence without needing to consult a map. I learned how to enjoy a three hour meal and not ask for the check, and how not to take immediate offense if a salesperson didn't offer the service I'd been used to at home. I learned that florists are closed Monday and Wednesday afternoons for no reason I could discern and that you shouldn't take showers after 11pm, or your elderly neighbors might confront you in the hallway. While I may never feel quite Italian or entirely American again, living and teaching in Italy taught me to carve a new identity that just might belong anywhere.

Abby Garcia, from Goliad, Texas, graduated from Harvard University in 2003 with a degree in Psychology. This former collegiate cheerleader recently returned to her native Texas after 10 months living in Italy and traveling throughout Europe. She hopes to one day return to Europe to live and work for an extended period.

EMILIA-ROMAGNA

Italy's wealthiest wheat- and dairy-producing region, Emilia-Romagna spans the fertile plains of the Po River Valley and fosters some of the finest culinary traditions on the Italian peninsula. Gorge on Parma's famous cheese and *prosciutto*, Bologna's fresh pasta and *mortadella*, and Ferrara's *salama* and *grana* cheese. Complement these dishes with regional wines like the sparkling red *Lambrusco*, also from Parma. Although the Romans originally settled this region, most of the visible ruins are remnants of medieval structures. Here, travelers find bustling urban scenes that have escaped the heavy tourism of other major Italian cities, offering rich, authentic cuisine without the omnipresent *menù turistico*, well-preserved sights with low admissions fees, and enough quiet to contemplate the art and natural beauty of one of Italy's most impressive regions.

HIGHLIGHTS OF EMILIA-ROMAGNA

INDULGE in Bologna's delectable regional cuisine, some of Italy's finest. (p. 356.)

WANDER the timeless cobblestoned streets of San Leo. (p. 387.)

ESCAPE Italy proper for majestic views off San Marino's Rocca Guaita. (p. 389.)

BIKE Ferrara's 9km lamp-lined medieval wall. (p. 364.)

MAKE MERRY with students and backpackers at Rimini's superb clubs. (p. 382.)

BOLOGNA
☎051

Since antiquity, Bologna has been known as the *grassa* (fat) and *dotta* (learned) city. The fruits of the fertile Po Valley now line tables with hearty egg pasta and savory local wines. The city is also the site of Europe's oldest university, founded in 1088 as a law school by a group of scholars to settle disputes between the Holy Roman Empire and the papacy. Academic liberalism drives political activism: the city's history as a hotbed of the 19th-century socialist movement earned it the moniker "Red Bologna," which its citizens wear with pride—after all, the same

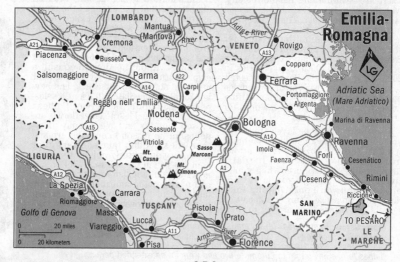

stoic individualism also yielded an impressive number of heroes who stood their ground against the looming spectre of fascism to save hospitality and the free exchange of ideas. All eyes, however, are on the city's art. Priceless treasures reside in museums and churches, whose 700-year-old porticos line the avenues.

TRANSPORTATION

Flights: Aeroporto G. Marconi (☎051 647 96 15), at Borgo Panigale, northwest of the city center. The **Aerobus** (☎051 29 02 90) runs to the airport from Track D outside the train station (every 15min. 5:30am-11:57pm, €4.50).

Trains: Info office open daily 7am-9pm. Information through TrenItalia (☎89 20 21). **Disability assistance** (☎199 30 30 60) at window #10 or assistance office; open daily 7am-midnight. To: **Florence** (1½hr., 53 per day 5:13am-10:46pm, €7.75); **Milan** (3hr., 63 per day 3:44am-10:15pm, €10.12); **Rome** (4hr., 39 per day 1:34am-9:36pm, €28.41); **Venice** (2hr., 25 per day 4:35am-9:42pm, €7.90).

Buses: ATC (☎051 29 02 90; www.atc.bo.it.), in P. XX Settembre, 6. To reach the piazza, turn left from the train station. To **Ferrara** (1hr., 15 per day 6:35am-8pm, €3.30). MC/V. **Terminal Bus** (☎051 24 21 50), next to ATC ticket counter, provides **Eurolines** bus service. Open M-F 9am-6:30pm, Sa 8:30am-6pm, Su 3-6:30pm. Cash only.

Public Transportation: ATC (☎051 29 02 90) runs efficient **buses** that get crowded in the early afternoon and evening. Intracity tickets (€1) are good 1hr. after validation onboard. Purchase at newsstands, self-service machines, or *tabacchi*. Buses #25 and 30 run up V. Marconi and across V. Ugo Bassi and V. Rizzoli from the train station.

Car Rental: Hertz, V. Amendola, 16/A (☎051 25 48 30). Turn right from the train station, then left on V. Amendola. Must be 25+ to rent. Cars start from €55 per day. Open M-F 8am-8pm, Sa 8am-1pm. AmEx/MC/V.

Taxis: C.A.T. (☎051 53 41 41). RadioTaxi (☎051 37 27 27). Available 24hr.

ORIENTATION AND PRACTICAL INFORMATION

From the **train station,** turn left on **Viale Pietro Pietramellara** and head to **Piazza XX Settembre.** From there, take **Via dell'Indipendenza,** which leads to **Piazza del Nettuno;** behind it is **Piazza Maggiore,** the city center. At P. del Nettuno, V. dell'Indipendenza intersects **Via Ugo Bassi,** which runs west, and **Via Rizzoli,** which runs east to **Piazza Porta Ravegnana. Via Zamboni** and **Strada Maggiore** lead out of this piazza.

> **NO BOLOGNA.** Treat Bologna like a big city—use caution and hold on to your wallet. At night, solo travelers may want to avoid the train station, northern V. dell'Indipendenza, and the areas surrounding the university.

Tourist Office: P. Maggiore, 1 (☎051 24 65 41), in Palazzo del Podestà. Offers **maps** and info on cultural events and lodgings. Open daily 9am-8pm. **CST** (☎051 648 7607; www.cst.bo.it) is an accommodations service. Open M-Sa 10am-2pm and 3-7pm, Su and holidays 10am-2pm.

Budget Travel: CTS, Largo Respighi, 2/F (☎051 26 18 02 or 23 48 62), across Largo Respighi from the Teatro Communale. Open M-F 9am-12:30pm and 2:30-6pm. Meets needs of the budget traveler: ISICs (€10), train tickets, tour packages, and discounts on air and sea travel. Posters concerning accommodations rentals are outside. MC/V.

Luggage Storage: At the train station. Max. bag weight 20kg. €3.50 for first 5hr. and €0.30 per hr. for the next 7hr. Open daily 6am-midnight. Cash only.

English-Language Bookstore: Feltrinelli International, V. Zamboni, 7/B (☎051 26 80 70). Classics, new novels, and travel guides. Open M-Sa 9am-7:30pm. AmEx/MC/V.

Gay and Lesbian Services: ARCI-GAY, V. Don Minzoni, 18 (☎051 649 44 16; www.arcigay.it). Sociopolitical organization with a reference and counseling center. Nightclub downstairs (see **Nightlife**). Open M-Sa 2:30-7:30pm.

Laundromat: Lavarapido, V. Petroni, 38/B, off P. Verdi, near V. Zamboni. €3.40 per 8kg, 25min. wash. Detergent €0.60. Open daily 9am-9pm. Cash only.

Emergency: ☎113. **Ambulance** (☎118). **Police,** P. Galileo, 7 (☎051 26 66 26).

Pharmacy: Farmacia Comunali AFM Bologna, P. Maggiore, 6 (☎051 23 85 09). Open daily 24hr. AmEx/MC/V.

Internet: Sportello Iperbole, P. Maggiore, 6 (☎051 20 31 84). Requires identification. Reserve a few days ahead. Limit 1hr. per week. Free. Open M-Sa 8:30am-7pm. **Intrage,** V. Amendola 2/G (☎/fax 051 25 66 54), has 12 fast computers. €6 per hr. Open M-F 10am-7pm. Cash only.

Post Office: ☎051 23 06 99. On P. Minghetti, southeast of P. Maggiore, off V. Farini. Open M-Sa 8am-1:30pm. **Currency exchange. Postal Code:** 40100.

▌ ACCOMMODATIONS

Bologna's hotels are rather pricey; reservations are recommended. The most affordable establishments are located around V. Ugo Bassi and V. Marconi.

Albergo Panorama, V. Livraghi, 1, 4th fl. (☎051 22 18 02; www.hotelpanoramabologna.it). Take V. Ugo Bassi from P. del Nettuno, then take the 3rd left. Small lobby that leads to enormous, sunny rooms with high ceilings, sink, and TV overlooking the nearby P. Maggiore. 3 huge shared baths with tubs. Reception 7am-3am. Curfew 3am. Singles €55; doubles €70; triples €85; quads €95; quints €105. AmEx/MC/V. ●

Ostello due Torre San Sisto (HI), V. Viadagola, 5 (☎/fax 051 50 18 10), off V. S. Donato, in Località di S. Sisto. Take bus #93 from V. Marconi, 69 (15min., M-Sa every 30min. 6:10am-8:20pm) or 301 from bus station (limited service). Exit at S. Sisto stop. Colorful rooms with laundry service (€2.60 per wash or dry), basketball court, Internet (€5.16 per hr.), and satellite TV. Wheelchair accessible. Reception 7:30-10am and 3:30-11:30pm. Lockout 10am-3:30pm. Curfew 11:30pm. Dorms €14.50, €3 extra for non-HI members; doubles €33; family rooms €14.50 per person. AmEx/MC/V. ●

Garisenda, Galleria Leone, 1, 3rd fl. (☎051 22 43 69, fax 22 10 07). Take V. Rizzoli and turn right into the gallery for a tiny hotel with small rooms full of wooden furniture. Breakfast included. Singles €45-50; doubles €65-70; triples €100. MC/V. ●

Hotel San Vitale, V. S. Vitale, 94 (☎051 22 59 66, fax 23 93 96). Follow V. Rizzoli past the towers onto V. S. Vitale. Ring bell to enter. Small hotel offers 17 quiet rooms with bath, TV, and a sunny interior courtyard. Wheelchair accessible. Reception until 2am. Curfew M-F and Su 1:30am. Singles €52-62, in July €42; doubles €72-86/€62; triples €90-110/€84; quads €110-128/€96. Cash only. ●

Albergo Centro, V. della Zecca, 2, 3rd fl. (☎051 22 51 14; werterg@tin.it). Take V. Ugo Bassi from P. del Nettuno, then 2nd left on V. della Zecca. Professional staff runs elegant hotel with hardwood floors and bright halls. All rooms with TV and A/C. Singles and triples have bath; some doubles do not. Breakfast €8. Singles €70; doubles €75, with bath €92; triples €118; quads €130. Extra beds €20-22. AmEx/MC/V. ●

Pensione Marconi, V. Marconi, 22 (☎051 26 28 32). Turn right from train station, then left on V. Amendola, which passes through P. dei Martiri to become V. Marconi. Colorful graffiti just outside the front door contrasts with clean, basic rooms with bath. Reception 24hr. Singles €48; doubles €75; triples €99. Cash only. ●

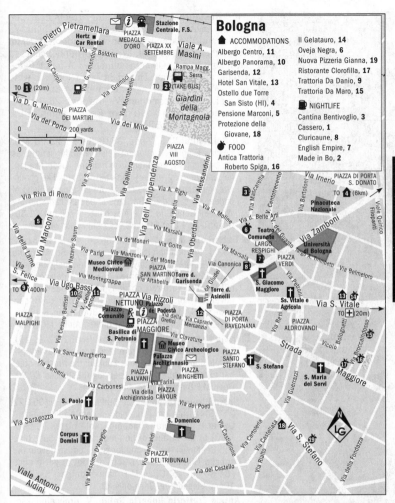

Bologna

🏠 **ACCOMMODATIONS**
Albergo Centro, **11**
Albergo Panorama, **10**
Garisenda, **12**
Hotel San Vitale, **13**
Ostello due Torre
   San Sisto (HI), **4**
Pensione Marconi, **5**
Protezione della
   Giovane, **18**

🍴 **FOOD**
Antica Trattoria
Roberto Spiga, **16**

Il Gelatauro, **14**
Oveja Negra, **6**
Nuova Pizzeria Gianna, **19**
Ristorante Clorofilla, **17**
Trattoria Da Danio, **9**
Trattoria Da Maro, **15**

🍷 **NIGHTLIFE**
Cantina Bentivoglio, **3**
Cassero, **1**
Cluricaune, **8**
English Empire, **7**
Made in Bo, **2**

EMILIA-ROMAGNA

Protezione della Giovane, V. S. Stefano, 45 (☎051 22 55 73). Past the church, on the right. Ring buzzer and climb the large staircase at the end of the long hallway. Lovely building with frescoed ceilings and French windows overlooking a garden filled with potted trees. 1 large dorm partitioned by wood furnishings. Breakfast included. Curfew 10:30pm. Call and reserve ahead. Dorm €15. Women only. Cash only. ❷

🍴 FOOD

Pasta comes in all shapes and sizes in Bologna. The best of the stuffed variety are *tortellini*, made with ground meat, and *tortelloni*, with ricotta and spinach. Bologna is also renowned for its large variety of salami and ham, including *mortadella*, a sausage-like creation that bears little resemblance to America's processed "bolo-

ALLA BOLOGNESE

For centuries, the fertile Po Valley has yielded rich, bold wines, pasta-perfect grains, and hearty local livestock. Generations have honed these flavors into a gastronomic culture so intense that other Italians joke that the opinionated *Bolognesi* only stop arguing when their mouths are full.

The most internationally recognized of Bologna's meats is *mortadella* (from the Latin word for mortar), a sausage named for the violent pounding its 2000-year-old preparation techniques advise. Omnivores worldwide know the final product as *bologna*. The thin, processed version bears little resemblance to the hearty, spiced original.

This fresh meat finds a wide number of uses in *ragù*, a thick pork and tomato sauce. The sauce manages to make its way into nearly every pasta recipe at some stage, including the layers of *ragù* and *besciamella* that fill thick slabs of lasagna. Also called *bolognese*, the sauce is only verboten on spaghetti plates—heavily-touristed restaurants insist that you try the regional specialty of *spaghetti alla bolognese*, but locals and true connoisseurs agree that spaghetti isn't the right type of pasta and won't touch the stuff. Instead they combine the savory topping with a slightly more solid dish like tortellini. All told, Bolognese cuisine is the pinnacle of the country's culinary expertise—and in Italy, that's saying a mouthful.

gna." Restaurants cluster on side streets near the *centro;* try the areas around V. Augusto Righi, V. Piella, and V. Saragozza. The vast, indoor **Mercato delle Erbe,** V. Ugo Bassi, 27, sells produce, cheese, meat, and bread. (Open in summer M-W and F 7am-1:15pm and 5-7:30pm, Th and Sa 7am-1:15pm; in winter M-W and F 4:30-7:30pm. Cash only.) Buy essentials at PAM **supermarket,** V. Marconi, 26, by the intersection with V. Riva di Reno. (Open M-Sa 7:45am-8pm. AmEx/MC/V.)

🌑 **Il Gelatauro,** V. S. Vitale, 98/B (☎051 23 00 49). Cosimo Filomene's gourmet gelato is widely touted as the best in Italy. Imported fresh fruit and flavors like fennel and zenzero (ginger) flank old favorites like chocolate with orange. Try the *crema del pastone,* a blend of coffee, eggs, and ricotta. Kids under 14 can spin the Wheel-of-Gelatauro for a free cone. 2 scoops €1.80. Open Tu-Su 11am-11pm. Closed Aug. Cash only. ❶

🌑 **Trattoria Da Maro,** V. Broccaindosso, 71/B (☎051 22 73 04; trattoriamaro@libero.it), between Str. Maggiore and V. S. Vitale. This tiny, wildly popular neighborhood trattoria dishes up favorites like pasta *con le sarde* (€6) amid cluttered bottles, hanging baskets, old advertisements, and neon paintings. *Primi* €5-6, *secondi* €5-8. Open Tu-Sa noon-2:30pm and 8-11pm. Cover €1.50 for lunch, €2 for dinner. AmEx/MC/V. ❷

🌑 **Oveja Negra,** V. Largo Respighi, 4 (☎051 22 46 79). Folk music, unmatched furniture, and original artwork fill this popular student cafe. Look for the brushed steel bar and signature black sheep logo. Espresso €0.90. Open M-F 8am-midnight. Cash only. ❶

Nuova Pizzeria Gianna, V. S. Stefano, 76/A (☎051 22 25 16). Locals know this hidden gem as "Mamma's." Owner Gianna crafts incomparable pizzas (€2.90-6.80) to the strains of pop-rock behind a busy blue bar. Seating in the tiny interior is limited, so devour the special Gianna (€6.80) from a stool or get a slice (€1.80) to go. Open M-F 7am-midnight, Sa 7am-10pm. Closed Aug. Cash only. ❶

Antica Trattoria Roberto Spiga, V. Broccaindosso, 21/A (☎051 23 00 63), between Str. Maggiore and V. S. Vitale. Black and white photos of old Bologna line the walls of this friendly, family-run restaurant. Menu changes daily. Bologna specialty €14 (W only). *Primi* €5.50-8.50, *secondi* €6-9. Cover €1.50. Open M 8-11pm, Tu-Sa noon-2:30pm and 8-11pm. Closed Aug. MC/V. ❷

Ristorante Clorofilla, Str. Maggiore, 64/C (☎051 23 53 43). Trendy, almost exclusively vegetarian. Try the couscous with tofu, vegetables, beans, and tomato sauce (€5.80) with organic wine (from €3.70 per ¼L). Cover €1. *Piatti caldi* from €4.50, salads from €5.40. Open M-Sa 12:15-2:45pm and 7:30-11pm. Closed Aug. AmEx/MC/V. ❷

Trattoria Da Danio, V. S. Felice, 50/A (☎/fax 051 55 52 02). This casual trattoria, open since 1937, offers huge portions of Bolognese cuisine. The 3-course meal with drinks (€11.50) and *menù turistico* (€7.50) are a good deal. *Primi* from €5.50, *secondi* from €4.50. Open daily noon-3pm and 7-11pm. AmEx/MC/V. ❷

�"eye" SIGHTS

The 40km of porticoed buildings lining Bologna's streets were the city's answer to a 14th-century housing crisis, but the several centuries that the building boom spanned produced a singular array of Gothic, Renaissance, and Baroque styles.

📷 PIAZZA MAGGIORE. Aristotle Fioravanti, designer of Moscow's Kremlin, remodeled the Romanesque **Palazzo del Podestà,** now the boxy brick home of various cafes, shops, and information centers lining its piazza-level *loggia*. The 15th-century building is considered a feat of architectural engineering: the weight of the palace rests on columns, not on the ground itself. Directly across the brick piazza sits the half-marble, half-brick **Basilica di San Petronio,** designed by Antonio da Vincenzo in 1390. The *Bolognesi* originally plotted to make their basilica larger than St. Peter's in Rome, but the jealous Church ordered that the funds be used to build the nearby Palazzo Archiginnasio. The basilica's cavernous Gothic interior hosted both the Council of Trent and the 1530 ceremony in which Pope Clement VII gave Italy to German Kaiser Karl V. Large golden panels and prim cherubs fill the **Cappella di S. Petronio** to the left of the entrance. From the base of the nave nearby, a marble track dotted with constellation symbols and a single golden line extends across the church's mosaic floor to create the largest **zodiac sundial** in the world. The tiny **museum** contains beautiful chalices and illuminated books. (*P. Maggiore, 3. ☎ 051 22 54 42. Basilica and museum open daily 7:30am-1pm and 2:30-6pm. Free.*)

📷 PALAZZO ARCHIGINNASIO. This palazzo, the first seat of the city's university, features thousands of names and coats of arms of professors and students who worked here—most of them reconstructed after an Allied air raid decimated the structure in 1944. The building now houses the **Biblioteca dell'Archiginnasio,** a city library with over 800,000 texts. Above the 30 arches of the central courtyard sits the **Teatro Anatomico,** a wooden lecture hall. A marble table marks where dissections were performed under the watchful Apollo and other star-adorned constellations on the ceiling. (*V. Archiginnasio, 1, next to the Museo Archeologico. Follow signs from P. Maggiore. ☎ 051 27 68 11. Palazzo open daily 9am-1pm. Closed 1st 2 weeks in Aug. Free.*)

PINACOTECA NAZIONALE. The Pinacoteca displays artwork spanning from the Roman era to Mannerism, with pieces by Giotto, Titian, and Giovanni Battista. For impressive works by Bologna's own Guido Reni, try **Gallery 24**'s triumphant *Sampson Victorious and the Pietà detta dei Mendicanti,* a floor-to-ceiling canvas. **Gallery 26** displays Francesco Albani's beautiful *Madonna e Bambino* and **Gallery 22** holds several large canvases, including Vasari's *Christ in Casa di Marta.* (*V. delle Belle Arti, 56, off V. Zamboni. ☎ 051 420 94 11; www.pinacotecabologna.it. Open Tu-Su 9am-7pm. Tickets close at 6:30pm. €4, EU students €2, under 18 or over 65 free. Cash only.*)

PIAZZA DEL NETTUNO. This piazza contains Giambologna's famous 16th-century stone and bronze fountain *Neptune and Attendants.* Affectionately called "The Giant," a nude Neptune, trident in hand, reigns over a collection of water-babies and sirens spraying water from every strangled fish and bodily orifice. Nearby, a wall of black and white portrait tiles commemorates members of the Bolognese resistance to Nazi occupation, while a Plexiglas plaque lists the names and ages of more recent victims of Fascist terrorism from the 1974, 1980, and 1984 bombings of the Bologna train station and two individual trains.

PALAZZO COMUNALE. Nicolò dell'Arca's terra-cotta *Madonna* and an Alessandro Menganti bronze statue of Pope Gregory XIV adorn the outskirts of this palazzo. The top floors house the **Collezioni Comunali d'Arte,** a collection of classic sculpture and stoic portraits displayed amid period furniture and frescoes. *(P. Maggiore, 6. Office ☎051 20 39 30; tickets ☎051 20 35 26. Open Tu-Sa 9am-6:30pm, Su 10am-6:30pm. €4, students €2. Cash only.)* The adjoining **Museo Morandi** displays numerous framed oil paintings, watercolors, and the reconstructed Via Fondazza studio of early 20th-century painter Giorgio Morandi, famous for his muted oil still-lifes of jugs, cups, and bottles. *(P. Maggiore, 6. ☎051 20 36 46; www.museomorandi.it. Wheelchair accessible. Open Tu-Su 10am-6pm. €4, students €2. Cash only.)*

MUSEO CIVICO MEDIOEVALE. Can't decide what type of museum to visit? Anything remotely associated with Bologna is featured here, including a seven statue collection of the patron saints of Bologna, wax seals of local nobility, violent weaponry, and an impressive collection of ancient sepulchre lids. Watch for a 17th-century dagger that splits apart once inside the body and the 17th-century Roman Sileno con Otre, a rare example of an obese marble statue. *(V. Manzoni, 4. Off V. dell'Indipendenza, near P. Maggiore. ☎051 20 39 30; www.comune.bologna.it/iperbole/MuseiCivici. Open Tu-Su 9am-6:30pm, Su 10am-6:30pm. €4, students €2. Cash only.)*

THE TWO TOWERS. After seismic shifts left Bologna's observational defense system with the unexpectedly angular **Torre degli Garisenda,** the determined city strove for height (and architectural accuracy) with 97.20m of brown brick in the soaring **Torre degli Asinelli.** Breathless climbers mount 498 narrow wooden steps past four landings to a breezy rooftop where a sea of red rooftops, Gothic church spires, bright yellow houses, and miles of uninterrupted horizon sit stories below. *(P. Porta Ravegana, at the end of V. Rizzoli. Open daily 9am-6pm. €3. Cash only.)*

MUSEO CIVICO ARCHEOLOGICO. This impressive museum of artifacts unearthed near Bologna features glass cases and shelves crammed with Roman inscriptions, red and black Greek pottery, and two dirt-swaddled, half-unearthed Etruscans. An Egyptian collection in the basement displays items from 2640 BC, including stone reliefs from the tomb of one-time Pharaoh Horemheb. *(V. Archiginnasio, 2. Follow signs from P. Maggiore. ☎051 275 72 11; www.comune.bologna.it/Musei/Archeologico. Open Tu-Sa 9am-6:30pm, Su 10am-6:30pm. €4, students €2. Cash only.)*

CHURCHES

◪CHIESA SANTO STEFANO. This cluster of squat buildings and open courtyards assumed its present shape from foundational remains of a group of seven temples used by ancient Egyptian monks—a stone tablet marks it as the former shrine to the goddess Isis. Four of the seven brick churches of the original **Romanesque basilica** remain. Originally built to hold the relics of Saints Vitalis and Agricola, the **Cripta** now contains the tomb of Martin the Abbot. In the small, circular **Chiesa di San Sepolcro,** another of Bologna's patron saints, San Petronio, is entombed in the towering stone **Edicola del Santo Sepolcro,** supposedly modeled from Christ's sepulchre in Jerusalem. In the rear courtyard is the **Cortile di Pilato** (Basin of Pilate), where the governor reportedly absolved himself of responsibility for Christ's death. *(In P. Santo Stefano. Follow V. S. Stefano from V. Rizzoli. ☎051 22 32 56. Open M-Sa 9am-noon and 3:30-6pm, Su 9am-12:45pm and 3:30-6:30pm. Modest dress required. Free.)*

CHIESA DI SANTA MARI DEI SERVI. A long yellow-walled walkway with dark, badly marred lunettes and faded patches of fresco hides the bottom half of this soaring brick basilica from street-level view. Inside the well-preserved Gothic structure, octagonal red-brick columns support an unusual blend of arches and ribbed vaulting covering shallow, fenced altars flanking the nave. Cimabue's *Maestà* hangs in a chapel on the left behind an exquisite altar sculpted by Giovanni Antonio Montorsoli, a pupil of Michelangelo. *(Take Str. Maggiore to P. Aldrovandi. ☎ 051 22 68 07. Open daily 7am-1pm and 3:30-8pm. Free.)*

CHIESA DI SAN DOMENICO. Tall marble columns line the clean interior of San Domenico, but its signature minimalism stops at the two transept chapels. In the **Cappella di San Domenico,** the body of St. Dominic lies in a marble tomb with religious figures sculpted by Nicolò Pisano and Michelangelo. Across the nave in the **Cappella del Rosario,** 15 small paintings by Fontana, Carracci, and others depict the mysteries of the Rosary and frame a statue of the Virgin. The chapel is especially notable here, since St. Dominic is largely credited with the institution of the Rosary as a conventional form of Christian prayer. *(From P. Maggiore, follow V. Archiginnasio to V. Farini and turn right on V. Garibaldi. ☎ 051 640 04 11. English tours daily at 3pm; ask for Tarcisio. Open daily 7:30am-1pm and 2:30-8pm. Free.)*

CHIESA DELLE SANTISSIME VITALE E AGRICOLA. The church's facade incorporates shards of capitals and columns from Roman temples into its brick and stone face, while the orange painted walls of local homes on the sides bar all but the polygonal capped brick spire from street view. Underneath the building, an 11th-century crypt holds paintings by Francia and Sano di Pietro. Look for a sculpture of Christ based on the Shroud of Turin's (p. 143) anatomical clues. *(V. S. Vitale, 48. ☎ 051 22 05 70. Open daily 7:45am-noon and 3:45-7:30pm.)*

CHIESA DI SAN GIACOMO MAGGIORE. The church's exterior combines Romanesque and Gothic styles. Despite the peeling paint on the walls and ceiling, the artwork inside is impressive. The aging structure sits next to the **Oratorio di Santa Cecilia,** which contains a crisp, colorful fresco cycle depicting St. Cecilia's marriage and martyrdom at the stake. *(Follow V. Zamboni to P. Rossini. ☎ 051 22 59 70. Open daily 7am-noon and 3:30-6pm. Enter the oratorio from V. Zamboni, 15. Open daily in summer 10am-1pm and 3-7pm, in winter 10am-1pm and 2-6pm. Free.)*

ENTERTAINMENT

Every year from June to September, the city sponsors an **entertainment festival** of dance, music, cinema, and art. Many events are free, but some cost €5. Summer visitors should contact the tourist office for a program. The **Teatro Comunale,** Largo Respighi, 1, hosts world-class operas, symphonies, and ballets. To order tickets ahead, call or sign up outside the ticket office two days before performances. (☎ 051 52 99 99; www.comunalebologna.it. 10% surcharge for pre-order. Tickets €8-999. Box office open M-F 3:30-7pm, Sa 9:30am-12:30pm and 3:30-7pm. AmEx/MC/V.) See the pride of Bologna play *calcio* (soccer) at the **Stadio Comunale,** V. Andrea Costa, 174. Take bus #21 from the train station or 14 from Pta. Isaia. The season runs from September to June, with matches on Saturday or Sunday afternoons. Tickets for matches against Juventus or AC Milan go fast. The Bologna Football Club (☎ 051 57 74 51; www.bolognafc.it) provides info and tickets.

NIGHTLIFE

Bologna's student population accounts for the city's large number of bars, pubs, and clubs. Call ahead for hours and cover, as info changes frequently. In June and July, nightclubs shut down and the party scene moves outdoors. The tourist office has a list of outdoor music venues. But don't expect much activity in August—even the outdoor *discoteche* shut down, and locals head to the beach.

Cluricaune, V. Zamboni, 18/B (☎051 26 34 19). Students fill this dim Irish pub's low stools and bicycle, wedged up in the rafters. Pints €3.10-4.20. Happy Hour W 7:30-10:30pm with €2.50 pints. Open M-F and Su 11am-3am, Sa 4pm-3am. AmEx/MC/V.

Cassero, V. Don Minzoni, 18 (☎051 649 44 16). Take V. Marconi to P. dei Martiri and turn left on V. Don Minzoni. This popular gay club draws chatty crowds of men and women down a steel catwalk to the basement and breezy wooden terrace of a former 17th-century salt warehouse. Drinks €3-6. ARCI-GAY card required; notify bouncer if you're not an Italian resident. Open M-F 10pm-2am, Sa-Su 10pm-3am. Cash only.

English Empire, V. Zamboni, 24, near the University. British pubs draw crowds of loyal patrons throughout Italy, and cultural imperialism has never felt so good. Orange lights, pumping music, and throngs of students fill the bar. Enjoy wine (from €3 per glass), light meals (burger, drink, and coffee for €4.50), and the buzz of conversation. Open M-F noon-3am, Sa-Su 6pm-3am. Cash only.

Cantina Bentivoglio, V. Mascarella, 4/B (☎051 26 54 16), near Largo Respighi and the Teatro Comunale. Wine bottles line the walls of this upscale bar, which also serves food. Live jazz relaxes the atmosphere on the umbrella-covered patio. Wine from €4.50 per glass. Open daily 8pm-2am, in summer M-Sa. MC/V.

Made in Bo, V. del Fonditore, 16 (☎051 53 38 80; www.madeinbo.it), in Parco Nord, accessible by bus #25. There's no return bus, so take a cab (€10-20). Outdoor concerts and events throughout the summer. Cover varies: some events free, some up to €30. Check tourist office for details and programs. Open early June to mid-July.

FERRARA ☎0532

Rome has its mopeds, Venice its boats, and Ferrara its *biciclette*. In a city with a ratio of 160,000 bicycles to 135,000 residents, bikers are a far more common sight than pedestrians. Businessmen with cell phones, elderly ladies, and girls in stilettos dodge the tiny cars that brave the low arches and narrow streets of the area outside the *centro*. Between 1208 and 1598, the d'Este family ruled the city, creating a legacy of art and beautiful architecture throughout the easily navigable 16th-century street grid. On the city's outskirts, racing aficionados can spend a day cycling a gorgeous 9km bike path atop the crumbling brick city walls, while old palaces full of period furniture, art museums, and an ominous *castello* offer eye-candy and adventure to the exertion-phobic crowd.

▐ TRANSPORTATION

Trains from Ferrara run to: Bologna (30min., 52 per day 1:41am-11:47pm, €2.80); Padua (1hr., 39 per day 3:52am-11:48pm, €4.25); Ravenna (1hr., 22 per day 6:33am-8:15pm, €4.15); Rome (3-4hr., 11 per day 4:40am-7:50pm, €30.73); and Venice (1½hr., 26 per day 5:02am-10:10pm, €6). The ticket office is open daily 6:15am-9:10pm. (AmEx/MC/V.) ACFT (☎0532 59 94 92), GGFP, and most other **buses** leave from the train station. Buses run to: local beaches (1½hr., 12 per day 7:30am-6:50pm, €4.23); Bologna (1½hr., 15 per day 5:20am-7:50pm, €3.31); and Modena (2hr., 13 per day 5am-7:32pm, €4.65). From the bus #2 stop, turn on V. S. Paolo for the *biglietteria* (ticket office), open daily 6:15am-8pm. (Reduced service Su. Cash only.) **RadioTaxi** (☎0532 90 09 00) is available 24hr. Head to Pirani e Bagni, P. Stazione, 2, for **bike rental.** (☎0532 77 21 90. €2 per hr., €7 per day. Open M-F 5:30am-8pm, Sa 6:30am-1pm. Cash only.)

▧ ▐ ORIENTATION AND PRACTICAL INFORMATION

To get to the *centro storico*, turn left from the **train station** on **Viale Costituzione,** which becomes **Viale Cavour** and runs to the **Castello Estense.** Alternatively, take bus #2 to the Castello stop or bus #1 or 9 to the post office (every 15-20min.

Ferrara

🏠 ACCOMMODATIONS

Albergo Nazionale, **6**
Campground Estense, **2**
Hotel de Prati, **3**
Ostello della Gioventù
 Estense (HI), **1**
Pensione Artisti, **9**

🍴 FOOD

Il Ciclone, **7**
Osteria Al Brindisi, **5**
Osteria degli Angeli, **8**
Ristorante Italia Big Night da
 Giovanni, **4**
Ristorantino Viaragnotrentino, **10**

5:42am-8:30pm, €0.83). Turn right after the *castello* on **Corso Martiri della Libertà.** The **tourist office** is located in Castello Estense, near P. Castello. (☎0532 20 93 70; www.ferrarainfo.com. Open M-Sa 9am-1pm and 2-6pm, Su 9:30am-1pm and 2-5:30pm.) **Currency Exchange** is available at Banca Nazionale de Lavoro, C. Pta. Reno, 19. (☎0532 78 16 11. Open M-F 8:20am-1:20pm and 2:35-4:05pm, Su 8:50-11:50am.) In case of **emergency** call ☎113, an **ambulance** (☎118), or the **police,** C. Ercole I d'Este, 26 (☎0532 29 43 11), off Largo Castello. Fides **pharmacy,** C. Giovecca, 125, is open daily 8am-11pm. (☎0532 20 25 24; AmEx/MC/V.) **Internet** is available at **Speedy Internet Club,** C. Pta. Po, 37. From the youth hostel, cross the street and turn right. (☎0532 24 80 92. €4 per hr. Also offers printing, photocopy, and fax. Open M-Sa 9am-9pm. Cash only.) The **post office,** V. Cavour, 29, is a block toward the train station from the *castello.* (☎0532 29 73 11. Offers *fermoposta.* Windows #11, 12, and 13 provide currency exchange. Open M-F 8am-6:30pm, Sa 8am-12:30pm. Mail services cash only.) **Postal Code:** 44100.

📷 📷 ACCOMMODATIONS AND CAMPING

The friendly staff at 🏠**Hotel de Prati ❹**, V. Padiglioni, 5, lets 16 rooms with spacious bath, A/C, TV, refrigerator, and 18th-century wood furnishings. Take C. Ercole I d'Este from Viale Cavour and turn right. (☎0532 24 19 05; www.hoteldeprati.com. Wheelchair accessible. Buffet breakfast included. Singles €47-70; doubles €70-105; suites €110-140. Extra bed €16. AmEx/MC/V.) From C. Martiri d. Libertà, turn left at the cathedral, right on V. S. Romano, left on V. Ragno, and then immediately left to reach 🏠**Pensione Artisti ❷**, V. Vittoria, 66. Spacious rooms have salt-and-pepper stone floors and in-bedroom sink. Guests share access to an ivy-covered garden, minibar, and gas burners. (☎0532 76 10 38. Lockout 12:30am. Singles €22; doubles €40, with bath €57. Cash only.) Just minutes from the *centro*, 🏠 **Ostello della Gioventù Estense (HI) ❶**, C. B. Rossetti, 24, boasts a social atmosphere and large, clean rooms. From the *castello*, Walk up C. Ercole I d'Este, then turn left on C. Rossetti. (☎/fax 0532 20 42 27. Internet €5.16 per hr. Breakfast included. Reception 7-10am and 3:30-11:30pm. Lockout 10am-3:30pm. Curfew 11:30pm. Dorms €15; private rooms for 2-5 people €16 per person. AmEx/MC/V.) Low prices, proximity to the *centro*, and rooms with TV and bath alleviate the lack of aesthetic charm in the aging 20-room **Albergo Nazionale ❹**, C. Pta. Reno, 32. (☎/fax 0532 20 96 04. Singles €40, with bath €50; doubles with bath €60-65; triples €75-85. Cash only.) Take bus #1 to P. S. Giovanni (€0.83) then take V. Gramicia for 15min., through the traffic circle to **Estense ❶**, V. Gramicia, 76, a campsite 1km from the city center. If driving from the *castello*, take C. Ercole I d'Este, turn right on C. Pta. Mare and left on V. Gramicia. Campgrounds are past V. Pannonio. (☎/fax 0532 75 23 96. Open daily 8am-10pm. Closed mid-Jan. to late Feb. Bike rental €5 per day and €3 per half-day. €5 per person, under 8 free, €6.50 per car and tent space, RVs for rent €26 per night. Electricity €2. Free hot showers. MC/V over €50.)

📷 FOOD

Ferrara's specialties include *salama da sugo* (a 15th-century dish of pork, spices, and wine) and *Pasticcio alla ferrarese* (sweet bread stuffed with macaroni and meat sauce). Eel, clams, scallops, sea bass, and mullet are integral to the seafood-heavy regional diet. Corpus Domini nuns invented Ferrara's famous *pampepato* (chocolate cake with almonds, candied fruit, and chocolate icing). For wine, try the slightly sparkling *Uva D'Oro* (Golden Grape). A Conrad **supermarket** is at V. Garibaldi, 53. (Open daily 8:30am-8pm. MC/V.) Ferrara Frutta, a local fruit and vegetable **cooperative**, is in P. Castello, 24-26. (☎0532 20 31 36. Open M-W, F, Su 8am-1pm and 5-7:30pm; Th and Sa 5-7:30pm. Cash only.) Open the huge riveted doors at 🏠**Osteria degli Angeli ❸**, V. delle Volte, 4, where friendly staff serves the mysterious beef *Segreto degli Angeli* (Secret of the Angels; €12) in a 16th-century dining room. From the basilica, take C. Pta. Reno and turn left under the arch. (☎0532 76 43 76. *Primi* €7, *secondi* €8-11. Open Tu-Su noon-2pm and 7-10pm. MC/V.) Through the arch to the left of the duomo, 🏠**Osteria Al Brindisi ❸**, V. G. degli Adelardi, 11, has wined and dined such luminaries as Copernicus, Cellini, and Pope John Paul II since 1435. (☎0532 20 91 42. Cover €2. Open Tu-Su 9am-1am. MC/V.) Though the menu is limited, swanky **Ristorantino Viaragnotrentino ❸**, V. Ragno, 31/A, features eclectic dishes like whole-wheat *tagliatelli*. (☎0532 76 90 70. *Primi* from €8, *secondi* €13. Open M and W-Su 12:30-2:30pm and 7:30-10:30pm. AmEx/MC/V.) At **Il Ciclone ❸**, V. Vignatagliata, 11, 2nd fl., the specialty is *Pizza Ciclone* (€7), a whirlwind of pepperoni, ricotta, and mozzarella.

IT'S AS EASY AS

one, two, three

uno, dos, tres

un, deux, trois

один, два, три

일 , 이 , 삼

Immerse yourself in a language.

Rosetta Stone® software is hands-down the fastest, easiest way to learn a new language — and that goes for any of the 27 we offer. The reason is our award-winning Dynamic Immersion™ method. Thousands of real-life images and the voices of native speakers teach you faster than you ever thought possible. And you'll amaze yourself at how effortlessly you learn.

Don't force-feed yourself endless grammar exercises and agonizing memory drills. Learn your next language the way you learned your first — the natural way. Order the language of your choice and get free overnight shipping in the United States!

Available for learning:
Arabic • Chinese • Danish • Dutch • English
French • German • Hebrew • Hindi • Indonesian
Italian • Japanese • Korean • Latin • Pashto
Polish • Portuguese • Russian • Swahili • Swedish
Spanish • Thai • Turkish • Vietnamese • Welsh

The guaranteed way to learn.

Rosetta Stone will teach you a language faster and easier than other language-learning methods. We guarantee it. If you are not satisfied for any reason, simply return the program within six months for a full refund!

Learn what NASA, the Peace Corps, thousands of schools, and millions around the world already know: Rosetta Stone is the most effective way to learn a new language!

FREE OVERNIGHT SHIPPING
In the United States
(Use promotion code lge005s)
1-800-788-0822
www.RosettaStone.com/lge005s

Personal Edition. Solutions for Organizations also available.

hostelbookers.com

Great Hostels. Free Booking. No Worries.

Guaranteed lowest cost internet hostel booking

No booking fees

Genuine hostels featured

Fast and easy to use

Book Worldwide hostels online at

www.hostelbookers.com

(☎0532 21 02 62, fax 21 23 22. Cover €1.50. Fixed-p[...]
13.50, *secondi* €8-16. Open Tu-Su noon-3pm a[...]
Inspired by the struggling Italian brothers of the [...]
Night, **Ristorante Italia Big Night da Giovanni ❹**, V. [...]
gant dishes like ravioli with potatoes and *taleggio* [...]
red turnip sauce. (☎0532 24 23 67. *Primi* €10-20, [...]
Open M-Sa 12:30-2:15pm and 8:15-10:15pm. AmEx/M[...]

EMILIA-RO[...]
Pta. Mare, 9. [...]
n-1pm and 3-6[...]
Ottocento/Bold[...]
8 ■ **SINAGO[...]
ghetto[...]

EMILIA-ROMAGNA

🅖 SIGHTS

Leonello d'Este, ruler and patron of the arts, molded Ferrara in[...]
artistic center with its own school of painting, the *Officina Ferrarese*. w[...]
Pisanello, Alberti, Piero della Francesca, and Titian grace the city's palaces and
monuments. Those yearning for arboreal beauty can ride or walk down the tree
and lamp-lined 9km concourse that runs along—and atop—the city's medieval
wall, stopping only for the panoramic view from one of its stone outcroppings.

■ **CASTELLO ESTENSE.** This castle and its murky green moat debuted as a small
fortress in the 14th century. Other rulers added the red-tiled **Garden and Loggia of
the Oranges,** where Eleonora of Aragon filled her terrace with orange trees. Less
heartwarming are the narrow tunnels of the dank **prigioni** (prisons), where Nicolo
III's son, Ugo, and second wife, Parisina, literally lost their heads after the king got
wind of their illicit affair. (☎0532 29 92 33. *Open Tu-Su 9:30am-5pm. Audioguides €3 for
adults, €2.50 for minors. €6, students and 65 and over €5. Supplement for tower €1. Cash only.*)

■ **DUOMO SAN ROMANO.** Dedicated to the city's patron saints, the cathedral is a
stunning masterpiece of *loggia*, rose windows, and bas-reliefs. Rosetti designed
the arches and terra-cotta apse, and Alberti fashioned the pink *campanile*. A dim
interior houses the beautiful Santuario Beata Vergine delle Grazie. Across the
street, the **Museo della Cattedrale** displays the church's precious works, including
the *Officina Ferrarese* statues by Jacopo della Quercia. (*Museum across the street
from the duomo, through the courtyard on V. S. Romano. Duomo open M-Sa 7:30am-noon and 3-
6:30pm, Su 7:30am-12:30pm and 3:30-7:30pm. Museum ☎0532 76 12 99. Open Tu-Su 9am-
1pm and 3-6pm. Tickets close 30min. before museum. €4.50, students €2. Cash only.*)

PALAZZO DIAMANTI. Built in 1493 by Biagio Rossetti, the palace is easily recognizable by the rough white points that cover its facade. Inside is the **Pinacoteca
Nazionale,** a collection of art including Carpaccio's *Passing of the Virgin* and
Garofalo's *Massacre of the Innocents*. (*C. Ercole I d'Este, 1. ☎0532 20 58 44. Just
before the intersection with C. Rossetti. Open Tu-W and F-Sa 9am-2pm, Th 9am-7pm, Su 9am-
1pm. Tickets close 30min. before museum. Cash only.*)

MUSEO MICHELANGELO ANTONIONI. This small museum contains a handful of
posters for the Ferrarese director's internationally acclaimed films as well as
Antonioni's own Enchanted Mountain paintings, a craggy, muted series created in
the 1970's and 80's. Upstairs find his other notable experiments, including watercolors and oil paintings, some smaller than a thumbnail. (*C. Ercole I d'Este, 17, near
Palazzo Diamanti. ☎0532 20 99 88. Open Tu-Su 9am-1pm and 3-6pm. Tickets close 30min.
before museum. €2, EU students €1.50, under 18 free. Cash only.*)

PALAZZO MASSARI. Once a 16th-century residence, the palazzo now houses
museums. The **Padiglione d'Arte Contemporanea** has temporary modern art exhibitions. The **Museo d'Arte Moderna e Contemporanea Filippo de Pisis** displays a large
collection by Ferrarese masters. Upstairs, tapestry-covered walls accent Giovanni
Boldoni's famous works in the **Museo Ferrarese dell'Ottocento/Museo Giovanni Bold-**

...urn right off C. Ercole I d'Este. ☎0532 20 99 88. Museums open Tu-Su ...pm. Ticket office closes 5:30pm. Filippo de Pisis €2, students €1.50. ...i €4.50/€2. Combination ticket €6.50/€4.50. Cash only.)

...HE E MUSEO EBRAICO. The city's Jewish museum is in the heart of the ...and contains art and documents chronicling the history of the Jews of Fer-...a. Inquire here for info and directions to the **Cimitero Ebraico** (Jewish Cemetery), ...where most of Ferrara's 19th- and 20th-century Jewish community is buried. The tourist office also provides a map of Jewish itineraries throughout the city. *(V. Mazzini, 95. From the duomo, the museum is on the left side of the street. ☎0532 21 02 28. Guided tours M-Th, Su 10, 11am, and noon. €4, students €2. For the cemetery, head down C. Giovecca from the castello. Turn left on V. Montebello and continue to end. Open F-Sa.)*

PALAZZO SCHIFANOIA. Glazed pottery, delicate ivory sculptures, and intricate statues like Fanelli's *San Giorgio che uccide il drago* fill the ground floor. The faded **Hall of the Months,** an exquisite Renaissance fresco series representing each month, its astrological sign, and its corresponding Greek deity, is the palazzo's main attraction. The final room houses the *Corale Olivetano A-R*, a collection of choral manuscripts. *(V. Scandiana, 23. From P. Cattedrale, follow V. Adelardi to V. Savonarola. Turn right on V. Madama and left on V. Scandiana. ☎0532 641 78. Open Tu-Su 9am-6pm. €4.20, students €2. Combination with Palazzina Marfisa €6.70/€4.20. Cash only.)*

CASA ROMEI. After a legal tug of war, this 15th-century Renaissance showpiece, halfway house, and one-time candidate for demolition opened as a museum in 1952. Giovanni Romei, an ambitious merchant, constructed the immense brick palazzo to bolster his reputation. Rooms are filled with ceiling frescoes, artwork from destroyed churches, and one of Ferrara's oldest thermals. *(V. Savonarola, 30. Take V. Adelardi left of the duomo and follow it straight until it becomes V. Savonarola. ☎0532 24 03 41. Open Tu-Su 8:30am-7:30pm. €2, EU students €1, under 18 free. Cash only.)*

PALAZZINA MARFISA D'ESTE. The well-preserved frescoes and furniture in this brick dwelling are positioned as if the palazzina were still in use. Note the walnut benches that C. Rava called "one of the most perfect creations of Tuscan furniture of the 1500s." *(C. Giovecca, 170. Follow C. Giovecca from Largo Castello, or take bus #9. ☎0532 20 74 50. Open Tu-Su 9am-1pm and 3-6pm. €2, over 65 €1.50, under 18 free. Combination with Palazzo Schifanoia and Museo della Cattedrale €6.50, students €4.50. Cash only.)*

MUSEO ARCHEOLOGICO NAZIONALE. Two walls of a neighboring low brick building and two stories of marble *loggia* compose the courtyard of the Palazzo di Ludovico il Moro, built in 1495 for an official of the d'Este court. Glass cases display artifacts from Spina, the Greek-Etruscan city that disappeared in the Adriatic 2000 years ago, and painted maps of Etruscan territories. *(V. XX Settembre, 122. A short walk down V. Pta. d'Amore from Palazzo Schifanoia. From P. Trento Trieste, follow V. Mazzini, which becomes V. Saraceno, to the end; turn left on V. Mayr, then right on V. Borgovado. ☎0532 662 99; mnafe@tiscalinet.it. Open Tu-Su 9am-2pm. €4, students €2. Cash only.)*

🎵 ENTERTAINMENT

On the last Sunday of May, Ferrara revives the ancient **Palio di San Giorgio.** Dating from the 13th century, this event begins with a lively procession of delegates from the city's eight *contrade* (districts), followed by a series of four races held in P. Ariostea: the boys' race, the girls' race, the donkey race, and the great horse race. During the last full week of August, street performers display their talents at the **Busker's Festival.** (☎0532 24 93 37; www.ferrarabuskers.com.) Even the finicky will appreciate the countless methods of eel-preparation at the annual **Eel Festival,** celebrated at the beginning of October in the province of Comacchio.

MODENA

On a Sunday evening, the side streets of Modena a[re]
bustling. Mass has just ended and locals gather in fr[ont of]
the priest and each other. While the rhythm of life he[re]
beat, don't be fooled. Modena is a small town that [is home to]
Luciano Pavarotti, the Ferrari and Maserati fac[tories, and its]
renowned balsamic vinegar, a flavorful marvel. Th[e]
ancient structures to make it a traditional sightseein[g]
tures, tantalizing flavors, and cultural history make it

TRANSPORATION AND PRACTICAL INFORMA[TION]

The **train station** is in P. Dante Alighieri. (☎ 1478 88 088. Info office open daily 8am-7pm.) Trains run to: Bologna (30min., every hr., €2.40); Milan (2hr., every hr., €9); and Parma (30min., 2 per hr., €3.15). ATCM **buses** (☎ 199 11 11 01) leave from V. Fabriani, off V. Monte Kosica to the right of the train station, for Maranello (every 1-2hr., €2.42). Call a **taxi** (☎ 059 37 42 42) for 24hr. service.

From the **train station**, take bus #7 or 11 (€1) to **Piazza Grande** and the town center. On foot, take **Via Galvani** from the station and turn right on **Via Monte Kosica.** Turn left on **Via Ganaceto**, which leads to **Via Emilia.** Turn left on V. Emilia and continue through **Piazza Matteotti** to **Piazza Torre**, which opens into P. Grande on the left. V. Emilia changes names from **Via Emilia Ovest** on the west side, to **Via Emilia Centro** in the center, to **Via Emilia Est** on the east. From P. Grande, take V. Castellaro and then the first left to reach the **tourist office**, V. Scudari, 12. (☎ 059 20 66 60. M 3-6pm, Tu-Sa 9am-1pm and 3-6pm, Su 9am-1pm.) **Modenatur**, V. Scudari, 8 (☎ 059 22 00 22; www.modenatur.it), offers a variety of tours through the city. **Informagiovani**, P. Grande, 17, geared toward younger travelers, provides travel info, job listings, and **Internet.** (☎ 059 20 65 83. Open M-Sa 9am-1pm and 3-7pm.) **Currency exchange** is available at Credito Italiano, V. Emilia Centro, 102, across from V. Scudari. (☎ 059 21 80 86. Open M-F 8:20am-1:20pm and 2:45-4:45pm, Sa 8:20am-12:45pm.) **ATMs** are in the Rolo Banca 1473 building in P. Grande. In case of **emergency** call ☎ 118, the **police** (☎ 113), an **ambulance** (☎ 059 34 31 56), or **first aid** (☎ 059 422 23 37). **Farmacia del Pozzo**, V. Emilia Est, 416 (☎ 058 36 00 91), is open 8am-8pm. Look for the green sign outside any pharmacy to see which has late-night service. **Internet** is available at Space Net, P. Grande, 34. (☎/fax 059 21 20 96. €1 for 15min. Open daily 10am-8pm.) The **post office**, V. Emilia Centro, 86 (☎ 059 205 32 11), is open Monday to Saturday 8am-6:30pm. **Postal Code:** 41100.

ACCOMMODATIONS

To reach **Ostello San Filippo Neri (HI) ❶**, V. S. Orsola, 48-52, walk straight down V. Galvani, then right along V. Monte Kosica, a left on V. Ganaceto, and another onto V.S. Orsola. A pleasant staff tends this multi-level hostel with full amenities: clean bathrooms, sturdy closets with locks, Internet, public phone, TV, VCR, large patios, and an elevator. (☎/fax 059 23 45 98. Lockout 10am-2pm. Curfew midnight. Dorms €14.50. AmEx/MC/V.) **Albergo Bonci ❸**, V. Ramazzini, 59, has dimly-lit but clean, spacious rooms with TV and phone. From the station, turn left down V. Ganaceto, right on V. Cerca, and keep straight. (☎ 059 22 36 34. Reception 7am-1am. Shared bath. Singles €36; doubles €50; triples €65. AmEx/MC/V.) From V. Ganaceto, turn right on V. Emilia, then left, to reach **Locanda Sole ❸**, V. Malatesta, 45, with its central but quiet location. Some rooms have TV. (☎ 059 21 42 45. Shared bath. A/C €15-20. Closed 1st 3 weeks in Aug. Singles €30; doubles €50. Cash only.) To reach **International Camping Modena ❶**, V. Cave Ramo, 111, in Località Bruciata,

...ubiera, 6:20am-8:30pm) and ask the driver to stop in front of ... . Walk to the right around the factory for 800m. Out of the way ...elatively expensive camping facilities. (☎059 33 22 52. Open Mar.- ...r 1 person and tent, €6 for each additional person.)

FOOD

Though Modena specializes in *prosciutto crudo* and the sparkling *Lambrusco* red wine, its most prominent product is fragrant balsamic vinegar, poured over salads in liberal quantities. The social ◪**Mercato Albinelli,** down V. Albinelli from P. XX Settembre, sells produce and squid. (Open June-Aug. M-Sa 6:30am-2pm; Sept.-May daily 6:30am-2pm, Sa also 4:30-7pm.) Feast on elaborate salads (€7-8) at candlelit tables outside or in the elegant interior of ◪**Ristorante Uva' d'Oro ❹**, P. Mazzini, 38. Modenese specialties are prepared to perfection—the pumpkin *tortelloni* with pistachio cream (€11) will bring tears to you eyes. (☎059 23 91 71. Vegetarian options €9-12. *Primi* €9-10, *secondi* €12-16. Open M-F noon-2:30pm and 7:30-10:30pm, Sa-Su 7:30-10:30pm. AmEx/MC/V.) Classic pizzeria ◪**Ristorante/Pizzeria Al Grottino ❷**, V. del Taglio, 26, has outdoor seating on a wide but isolated street. Follow V. Rismonodo one block from V. Emilia. (☎059 22 39 85. Pizza from €3.50. *Primi* from €5. Cover €2. Open M-Tu and Th-Su noon-2:30pm and 7pm-midnight. AmEx/MC/V.) At **K2 ❶**, C. Canal Grande, 67, off V. Emilia, each cone is sculpted into a flower-shaped treat. (☎059 21 91 81. Cones from €1.60. Open M-Tu and Th-Su 9am-midnight. Cash only.) Grandma's kitchen goes gourmet at **Trattoria da Omer ❸**, V. Torre, 33, off V. Emilia, across from P. Torre. Try the *tortelloni fiocchi di neve* (with fresh ricotta, butter, and sage; €7.50), or garnish a salad from the *insalata mista* buffet (€4) with as much balsamic vinegar as your tastebuds can handle. (☎059 21 80 50. Reservation recommended for weekend nights. *Primi* €8, *secondi* €7.50. Open M-Sa 1-2pm and 8-10:30pm. Cash only.) Cross V. Emilia from P. Mazzini to hit **Caffè dell'Orologio ❷**, Piazzetta delle Ova, 4. Relax with espresso inside or indulge in an evening cocktail at one of the swanky outdoor tables. (☎338 925 66 08. Live music. Cocktails from €6. Open M and W-Su in summer 7am-midnight, in winter 7am-9pm. Cash only.)

🅖 SIGHTS

◪ **DUOMO.** From the 12th century, Modena's Romanesque duomo is built over the grave of its patron saint, San Geminiano. The church houses a relic of Geminiano: his encased arm takes to the streets in a religious procession in January. Legend holds that Geminiano prevented Attila the Hun from destroying Modena by enshrouding the city in mist. Sculptor Wiligelmo and his students decorated most of the duomo with carvings of local, Roman, biblical, and Celtic themes; scenes from the Old Testament and Geminiano's travels frame the door. *(P. Grande. ☎059 21 60 78; www.duomodimodena.it. Open daily 6:30am-12:30pm and 3:30-7pm.)*

◪**PALAZZO DEI MUSEI.** Inside the palazzo, the **Biblioteca Estense** holds a collection of exquisitely illuminated books, including a 1501 Portuguese world map. The library's **Sala Campori** houses the **Biblia di Borso d'Este,** a 1200-page Bible partially illustrated by *Emiliano* painter Taddeo Crivelli. Large glass cases contain musical instruments, 19th-century scientific instruments, and artifacts from the Americas, Asia, and Africa. *(In Largo S. Agostino at the western side of V. Emilia. Biblioteca ☎059 22 22 48; www.cedoc.mo.it/estense. Exhibits open daily 9am-1pm. Call the library in advance for an appointment to see the Sala Campori and Biblia di Borso d'Este. €2.60, under 19 or over 65*

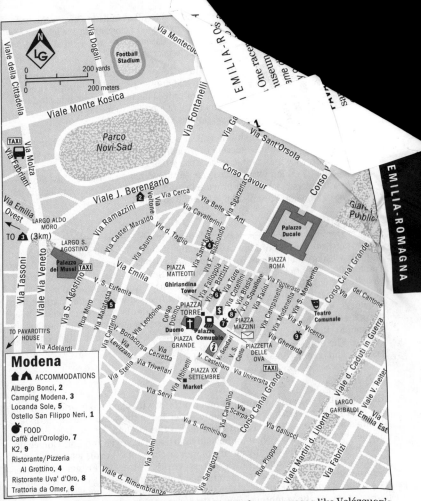

Via Montecu...

Via Fontanelli

Via Ga...

Via Sant'Orsola

Corso Cavour

Corso

One race...
museum...
me...

EMILIA-ROS...

EMILIA-ROMAGNA

Football
Stadium

200 yards

200 meters

Viale Monte Kosica

Viale della Cittadella

Via Dogali

Parco
Novi-Sad

Via Molza

Via Fabriani

TAXI

Viale J. Berengario

Via Cerca

Via Belle

Arti

Via Voltone

Via Cavallerini

Via Emilia
Ovest

LARGO ALDO
MORO

TO 3 (3km)

LARGO S.
AGOSTINO

Via Ramazzini

Via Castel Maraldo

Via Sauro

Via d. Taglio

Via Sant'Agata

Via F. Rismondo

Palazzo
Ducale

PIAZZA
ROMA

Palazzo
del Musei

TAXI

Via Emilia

V. S. Eufemia

PIAZZA
MATTEOTTI

Ghirlandina
Tower

Via Battisti

Via Falloppia

Via Torre

Via Cotelini

Via Blasia

Via lo Squallore

Via Farini

Via Fonteraso

Via Campanelia

Via Modenella

Via S. Margherita

Via S. Vicenzo

Corso C.nal Grande

Corso Via

del Cantone

Via Tassoni

Viale Via Veneto

Via S. Agostino

Rua Muro

Via Malatesta

Corso Duomo

Via Leodoino

PIAZZA
TORRE

Duomo

Palazzo
Comunale

PIAZZA
MAZZINI

Teatro
Comunale

TO PAVAROTTI'S
HOUSE

Via Adelardi

Via Canfera

Via Bonacorsa Cervetta

Via Levizzani

Via Cervetta

PIAZZA
GRANDE

V. S.
Carlo

Via Seudani

PIAZZETTA
DELLE
OVA

Via Gherarda

9

Via Stella

Via Trivellari

V. Castellaro

PIAZZA XX
SETTEMBRE

Market

Via Albinelli

Via Universita

TAXI

Viale d. Caduti in Guerra

Viale V. Reiter

Via Servi

Via Canalino

Via Scarpa Canal Grande

Corso Canal Grande

LARGO
GARIBALDI

Via
Emilia Est

Via Selmi

Via S. Geminiano

Via Gallucci

Viale Martiri d. Liberta

Rua Pioppa

Via Fabrizi

Viale d. Rimembranze

Viale d. Saragozza

Modena

ACCOMMODATIONS

Albergo Bonci, **2**
Camping Modena, **3**
Locanda Sole, **5**
Ostello San Filippo Neri, **1**

FOOD

Caffè dell'Orologio, **7**
K2, **9**
Ristorante/Pizzeria
Al Grottino, **4**
Ristorante Uva' d'Oro, **8**
Trattoria da Omer, **6**

free.) Above the library, the **Galleria Estense** displays huge canvases like Velázquez's *Portrait of Francesco d'Este* and Bernini's bust of the same subject. (☎ 059 439 57 11; www.galleriaestense.it. Open Tu-Su 8:30am-7:30pm. €4, students €2.)

GHIRLANDINA TOWER. This 95m tower, built in the 13th century, incorporates both Gothic and Romanesque elements. Climb to the top for a spectacular view of Modena's stucco rooftops. A memorial to those who died fighting the Nazis and Fascists during WWII stands at the base. (*P. Torre. Open Apr.-July and Sept-Oct. Su and holidays only 9:30am-12:30pm and 3-7pm and with a reservation through the tourist office. €2.)*

FERRARI FACTORY. Modena's flashiest claim to fame is the Ferrari. The factory is southwest of Modena in **Maranello.** Visitors are allowed to sneak a peek into this top-secret complex only if they own a Ferrari, but antique and modern Ferraris,

re displayed to all at **Galleria Ferrari,** the com-
errari, 43. From Ferrari factory bus stop, continue along
8m; turn right at Galleria Ferrari sign. ☎ 0536 94 32 04.
(G for seniors and students under 18.)

:30am fans of the Three Tenors, Pavarotti's house is a neces-
OTTI'S hoping to hear Luciano belt out *"La donna è mobile"*
y stop, al be disappointed. Not only is his house far outside Modena's
rom his ba known to be something of a recluse. *(The big villa hidden at the
city center hiesa and V. Giardini. Not open to the public.)*

corner of S Modenese cuisine is full of legends and lore. For the hungry or
FOOD T tours reveal the secrets of *prosciutto* and balsamic vinegar. Others
curio picking or wine-tasting. *(general info ☎ 059 20 66 60. Modenatur offers specific
go ch ☎ 059 22 00 22; www.modenatur.it. Most tours require a minimum of 4-5 people;
foo at least 2 weeks in advance.)* For wine-tasting, contact the Consorzio Tutela del
co rusco di Modena, V. Schedoni, 41 (☎ 059 23 50 05).

FESTIVALS

Every year near the end of May or beginning of June, Modena's main park *Novi
Sad* fills with aria enthusiasts for **Pavarotti and Friends,** a benefit concert with the
Three Tenors. For tickets, contact the tourist office in May and check Pavarotti's
website for details (www.lucianopavarotti.com). From late June to early July,
Modena stages the **Serate Estensi,** a week-long festival with jousting, art shows,
fireworks, and a costumed bonanza in which residents parade in Renaissance
dress. Perhaps the most important event is **Balsamica** (www.comune.modena.it/
balsamica), the festival that reflects the *Modenesi*'s dedication to their balsamic
vinegar. The event runs for three weeks from mid-May and features exhibitions,
tastings, and cooking classes. For info call ☎ 059 22 00 22.

PARMA   ☎ 0521

Although a trip to Parma, where platters overflow with aged *parmigiano* cheese
and rosy-pink *prosciutto*, will certainly never leave the taste buds unsatisfied,
Parma's artistic excellence is not confined to the kitchen. In the 16th century,
Mannerist painting flourished under native artists Parmigianino and Correggio.
The city was also the birthplace of composer Giuseppe Verdi, who resided in
Parma while writing some of his greatest works. Pervasive French influences
inspired Stendhal to choose the picturesque town as the setting of his 1839 novel
The Charterhouse of Parma. Today the city combines the mannered elegance of
its heritage with the youthful energy of the nearby Università degli Studi di Parma.

TRANSPORTATION

Flights depart from **G. Verdi Airport,** V. dell'Aeroporto, 44/A (☎ 0521 95 15). Parma
lies northwest of Bologna, on the Bologna-Milan train line. **Trains** leave the station
in P. Carlo Alberto della Chiesa (☎ 89 20 21; ticket office open 6am-midnight) for:
Bologna (1hr., every 30min., €4.30); Florence (3hr., 4 per day, €14.85); and Milan
(1½hr., every hr., €7.20). **Buses** stop at P. C. A. della Chiesa, 7/B, at a small stand in
front of a building with purple "Infobus" awning to the right from the train station.
(☎ 0521 28 27 56.) Buses run to: Bardi (M-Sa 6:15am, 12:40, 5:30pm; Su 8am; €3.70);
Busseto (M-Sa 12 per day 6:40am-7:15pm; Su 9am, 6:50pm; €3.15); and Colorno
(M-Sa 7:15am-7:15pm, €1.50). Call a **taxi** (☎ 0521 25 25 62) for 24hr. service.

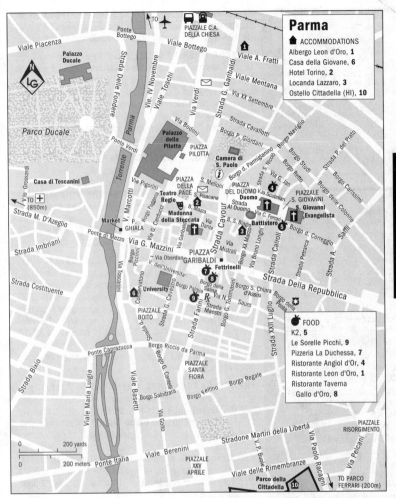

E M I L I A - R O M A G N A

including Leonardo da Vinci's *Testa d'una Fanciulla* (Head of a Young Girl), as well as a gallery devoted to Parmigianino and Correggio. *(From Str. Cavour, turn left on Str. Pisacane and cut across P. della Pace to P. Pilotta. ☎0521 23 33 09. Open Tu-Su 8:30am-2pm, ticket office closes 1pm. Theater €2, students €1. Gallery and theater €6, students €3.)* Downstairs, the **Museo Archeologico Nazionale** displays bronzes, and sculptures of ancient origin. *(☎0521 23 37 18. Open Tu-Su 8:30am-2pm. €2, students €1.)*

DUOMO AND BATTISTERO. Parma's 11th-century, Romanesque duomo balances vibrant paintings of *putti* with more austere masterpieces such as the Episcopal throne and Benedetto Antelami's bas-relief *Descent from the Cross* (1178). The stunning dome features Correggio's *Virgin* ascending to heaven in a spiral of white robes, pink *putti*, and blue sky. The pink- and white-marble baptistery displays well-preserved medieval wall frescoes. *(In P. del Duomo. From P. Garibaldi, follow*

THE LOCAL STORY

MEDIEVAL MEDICINE

Sick and tired of that pesky cough? Try some treacle, a potion made with roasted skin of viper. Want that toothache to disappear? Hold a candle to the tooth, and heat will cause the worms rotting it to fall from your mouth.

Though perhaps less effective than modern medicine, these more colorful prescriptions were found at the Antica Spezieria di San Giovanni Evangelista, Parma's 700-year-old pharmacy. Tucked behind the duomo, it served the community until 1896. Historical sources indicate that pharmacy foundations date to as early as the 10th century, when it was developed by Benedictine monks to serve their brothers and the Parman community. It was not until the 13th century that it became fully operational, and by the 16th century sported over 100 syrups, salves, and gums.

While they don't fill prescriptions anymore, the four chambers can still be explored. Massive granite mortar and pestles the size of a small child dominate the Room of Mortars, delicate glass distillers span the height of the Room of Alembics, and porcelain urns used to store dangerous plants and minerals adorn the Room of Sirens. Along each room's ceiling, frescoes offer words of wisdom. One compelling inscription reads, "This is the place to preserve poison so that what is skillfully produced as curative does not become dangerous through an inexperienced hand."

Directly behind the duomo. Open M-F 8:30am-1:45pm. Tickets €2, under 18 or over 60 €1.

Str. Cavour and turn right on Str. al Duomo. ☎ 0521 23 58 86. Duomo open daily 9am-12:30pm and 3-7pm. Baptistery open daily 9am-12:30pm and 3-6pm. €3, students €1.50.)

CAMERA DI SAN PAOLO. This aged monastery boasts several rooms with detailed ceiling frescoes, but the most impressive is the central vault, depicting the coat of arms of the Abbess, under whose direction the monastery prospered. *(From P. Garibaldi, head up Str. Cavour, turn left on Str. Melloni, and follow the signs. Open Tu-Su 8:30am-2pm, ticket office closes at 1pm. €2, ages 18-25 €1, under 18 or over 65 free.)*

CHIESA DI SAN GIOVANNI EVANGELISTA. This 10th-century church is a longstanding Italian classic. The interior dome was frescoed by Correggio; frescoes by Parmigianino run along the left nave, over the first, second, and fourth chapels. The bell tower was constructed in 1613. *(In P. S. Giovanni, behind the duomo. ☎ 0521 23 55 92. Open M-F 9-11:45am and 3-6:45pm, Su 8am-12:45pm and 3-7:45pm.)*

PARMIGIANO AND PROSCIUTTO FACTORIES. *Parmigiano* cheese fans should contact the Consorzio del Parmigiano-Reggiano to arrange a 2hr. tour of the factory, with free samples. *(V. Sonnino, 35/A. ☎ 0521 29 27 00; www.parmigiano-reggiano.it.)* To arrange a visit to a *prosciutto* factory, contact the Consorzio del Prosciutto di Parma. *(V. M. dell'Arpa, 8/B. ☎ 0521 24 39 87, fax 24 39 83. Factories lie in the Province of Parma, outside the city walls. At least 10 people required for tour. Call tourist office for more info.)*

FRENCH GARDENS AND COMPOSERS. Although many of the French palaces were destroyed during WWII, Marie-Louise's tailored gardens still thrive by the Baroque palace in **Parco Ducale.** *(West of Palazzo della Pilotta over Ponte Verdi. Open May-Sept. daily 7am-midnight, Oct.-Apr. 7am-8pm.)* Toscanini enthusiasts can visit **Casa Natale e Museo di Arturo Toscanini,** to see *maestro* memorabilia. *(Borgo Rodolfo Tanzi, 13. ☎ 0521 28 54 99. Tours in English. Open Tu-Su 9am-1pm and 2-6pm. €2, students €1.)*

🎭 ENTERTAINMENT

The **Teatro Regio** (Str. Garibaldi, 16, next to P. della Pace; ☎ 0521 21 86 78) is one of Italy's premiere opera houses. Check with the tourist office for the price of standing-room tickets. The opera season runs from November to April. **E' grande Estate** brings classical music, opera, jazz, and tango concerts to P. della Pilotta in July. *(☎ 0521 21 86 78. Tickets from €10-15.)* The popular **Verdi Festival,** honoring the native-born composer, takes place each year from late April to late June.

PIACENZA ☎ 0523

Piacenza was one of the first Roman colonies in northern Italy and the long-time headquarters of Julius Caesar. Today, C. V. Emanuele and V. XX Settembre are filled with shoppers for the latest fashions, P. dei Cavalli gets packed during concerts, and Galleria Ricci Oddi is a shrine for modern art. Reluctant to encourage a tourist economy, Piacenza was nevertheless recently voted one of Italy's most hospitable cities. It is an ideal stopover on the way to Parma, Bologna, or Milan.

TRANSPORTATION AND PRACTICAL INFORMATION

Trains leave from P. Marconi. Luggage storage and self-service lockers are available 24hr. Trains head to: Bologna (1½hr., every hr. 6:01am-10:04pm, €7.50); Milan (1hr., every hr. 4:34am-11:30pm, €4.80); and Turin (2½hr., 9 per day 3:59am-10:05pm, €10). For a **taxi**, call ☎ 0523 59 19 19.

From the **train station**, walk along the left side of the park on **Via dei Mille** and turn right on **Via Giulio Alberoni**, which turns into **Via Tibini**. Follow it onto **Via Roma**, and then turn left on **Via Daveri**, which leads to **Piazza Duomo**. From there, a right onto **Via XX Settembre** leads straight to **Piazza dei Cavalli**. The **IAT Tourist Office**, P. dei Cavalli, 7, is in the large building behind the horse statues. (☎/fax 0523 32 93 24; iat@comune.piacenza.it. Open Tu-Sa 9am-1pm and 3-6pm.) In case of **emergency**, call ☎ 113, an **ambulance**, ☎ 118, or the **police**, Viale Malta, 10 (☎ 0523 39 71 11). A **hospital, Ospedale Civile da Piacenza,** is on V. G. Taverna, 49 (☎ 0523 30 11 11). The **post office,** V. Sant'Antonino, 38-40, **exchanges currency.** (☎ 0523 31 64 68. Open M-F 8am-6pm, Sa 8am-12:30pm.) **Postal Code:** 29100.

ACCOMMODATIONS AND FOOD

To reach **Hotel Astra ❸**, V. Boselli, 19, take bus #8 from the station (€0.85) to the intersection of V. Boselli and V. G. M. Damiani (near the supermarket). The hotel is on the right, at the corner of V. Boselli. Ten rooms, situated above a street cafe, with lounge and garden patio, are simple and spotless. (☎ 0523 45 70 31. Curfew 11pm. Reserve ahead. Singles €25.85; doubles €33.60. Cash only.) From C. V. Emanuele, turn right on V. Tempio for **Protezione della Giovane ❷**, V. Tempio, 26. Immaculate rooms are well-tended by nuns. (☎ 0523 32 38 12. Women only. Curfew Su-Th 10:30pm, F-Sa midnight. Singles and doubles €28, with breakfast €30. Monthly stays available from €330. Cash only.)

An **open-air market** is held every Wednesday and Saturday in P. Duomo and P. dei Cavalli. Enjoy dinner outdoors under a lattice covered in bogonias and vines at **Osteria del Trentino ❷**, V. del Castello, 71, off P. Borgo. Options include seasonal meat and fish menus. (☎ 0523 32 42 60. *Primi* from €7, *secondi* from €10. Open M-Sa noon-3pm and 8pm-midnight. AmEx/MC/V.) **Trattoria/Pizzeria dell'Orologio ❸**, P. Duomo, 38, serves delicious pizza (from €4.50) and traditional cuisine in the shadow of the duomo. (☎ 0523 32 46 69. *Primi* €6.50-8, *secondi* €10.50-13. Open M-W and F-Su noon-2:30pm and 6:30pm-12:30am. AmEx/MC/V.)

SIGHTS

PIAZZA DEI CAVALLI. This central square is named for the two 17th-century equestrian statues that grace the piazza in tribute to Duke Rannucio I and his father, Duke Alessandro Farnese, but the masterpiece is the Gothic **Palazzo del Comune,** or **Il Gotico,** constructed in 1280, when Piacenza led the Lombard League, one of Italy's most powerful trade groups. A monument to war veterans also sits

EMILIA-ROMAGNA

under the palazzo. From P. dei Cavalli, follow V. XX Settembre to the **duomo,** constructed between 1122 and 1233. Its **crypt,** a maze of thin columns, is one of Italy's spookiest. A vigil is kept over the bones of Santa Giustina at its center. *(Duomo open daily 7:30am-noon and 4-7pm. Modest dress required.)*

MUSEUMS. The commanding **Palazzo Farnese** houses the **Museo Civico,** the **Pinacoteca,** and the **Museo delle Carrozze.** The most notable work in the Pinacoteca is a Botticelli fresco depicting Christ's birth. *(P. Cittadella, 29, at the end of V. Cavour opposite P. dei Cavalli. Take V. Cavour from P. dei Cavalli and turn left on V. Bacchiochi. ☎ 0523 32 69 81. Open Tu-Th 8:45am-1pm, F-Sa 8:30am-1pm and 3-6pm, Su 9:30am-1pm and 3-6pm. Museo Civico and Pinacoteca €4.20, students €3.15; Museo delle Carrozze €2.10, students €1.60. All the museums €5.25, students €4.20.)* The ▊**Galleria Ricci Oddi** displays modern art from the early 1800s to present day. *(V. S. Siro, 13. Take C. V. Emanuele from P. dei Cavalli and turn left on V. S. Siro. ☎ 0523 32 07 42. Open Tu-Sa 10am-noon and 3-6pm. €4.)*

RAVENNA ☎ 0544

After the decline of the Roman empire, Ravenna rose from the ashes as a bejeweled pillar of strength. Justinian and Theodora, rulers of the Byzantine Empire, selected the city as the central administrative point for restoring order to the anarchic West and created a thriving artistic culture still visible in its churches and baptisteries. Today, streets paved with colored stones are almost entirely car-free, and travelers walk past monuments like Dante's tomb (to the ire of Florentines, who maintain an empty sepulchre for their exiled son).

▐▀ TRANSPORTATION

The **train station** is in P. Farini. Trains run to Bologna (1hr., 19 per day 5:07am-8:35pm, €4.60) Ferrara (1hr., 22 per day 6:20am-9:33pm, €4.15), with connections to Florence and Venice; and Rimini (1hr., 30 per day 12:05am-9:35pm, €2.80). AmEx/MC/V. The ticket counter is open daily 6:05am-8:35pm. The station is open daily 4:45am-11:30pm. Call Trenitalia (☎ 89 20 21). ATR (regional) and ATM (municipal) **buses** leave outside the train station for Lido Adriano (20min., every 30min. 5:40am-8:10pm, €1) and Marina di Ravenna (20-30min., every 30min. 5:40am-7:55pm, €1). Tickets (3-day pass €3) are sold at the booth marked "PUNTO" across from the station. Return tickets are hard to get outside Ravenna but can be bought onboard for a surcharge. (☎ 0544 68 99 00. Office open M-Sa 6:30am-8:30pm, Su 7am-8:30pm; in school year M-Sa 6:30am-7:30pm, Su 7:30am-7:30pm. MC/V.) **RadioTaxi** (☎ 0544 338 88), in P. Farini, is available 24hr.

✦▓ ORIENTATION AND PRACTICAL INFORMATION

The **train station** is in **Piazza Farini** at the eastern end of town. **Viale Farini** leads from the station to **Via Diaz,** which runs to **Piazza del Popolo,** the center of town. Ask about city **maps** and accommodations listings at the **tourist office** at V. Salara, 8. From P. Garibaldi, turn left into P. del Popolo, walk to the end, turn right onto V. Matteotti and follow the signs. (☎ 0544 354 04; www.turismo.ravenna.it. Open Apr.-June M-Sa 8:30am-7pm, Su 10am-4pm; July-Sept. M-Tu, Th, and Sa 8:30am-7pm, W and F 8:30am-7pm and 8:30-11pm, Su 10am-4pm; Oct.-Mar. M-Sa 8:30am-6pm, Su 10am-4pm.) In case of **emergency,** call ☎ 113, **first aid** (☎ 118), or the **police,** V. Berlinguer, 20 (☎ 0544 29 91 11). The **hospital, Santa Maria delle Croci,** is at Viale Randi, 5 (☎ 0544 28 51 11). To get there, take minibus #2 or 4 from the station. **Internet** is available with photo ID at **Biblioteca Classense,** V. Baccarini, 3. From P. del Popolo, turn left on V. Cairoli, bear right into P. Caduti, and head straight on V. Baccarini. (☎ 0544

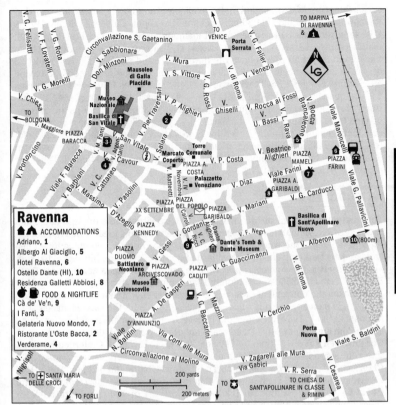

Ravenna

▲▲ ACCOMMODATIONS

Adriano, **1**
Albergo Al Giaciglio, **5**
Hotel Ravenna, **6**
Ostello Dante (HI), **10**
Residenza Galletti Abbiosi, **8**

✪ 🍴 FOOD & NIGHTLIFE

Cà de' Ve'n, **9**
I Fanti, **3**
Gelateria Nuovo Mondo, **7**
Ristorante L'Oste Bacca, **2**
Verderame, **4**

48 21 14. €2.07 per hr. Open M-F 8:30am-7pm, Sa 8:30am-1:30pm; closed Aug. 9-21. Cash only.) The **post office**, P. Garibaldi, 1, is off V. Diaz before P. del Popolo. (☎0544 24 33 04, fax 0544 384 85. Open M-F 8am-6:30pm, Sa 8am-12:30pm. Cash only.) **Currency exchange** is also available. **Postal Code:** 48100.

🏠 ACCOMMODATIONS

Take V. Farini and turn right across P. Maneli to reach **Albergo Al Giaciglio ❷**, V. Rocca Brancaleone, 42, just outside the *centro*, where the 18 rooms with TV, fan, and sink are the best deal in town. (☎/fax 0544 394 03; mmambo@racine.ra.it. Breakfast €5. Restaurant downstairs open M-F. Reserve ahead. Singles €25-38, with bath €30-43; doubles €42-55/€60-65. Extra bed €10. MC/V.) A former orphanage has aged gracefully into the **Residenza Galletti Abbiosi ❹**, V. Roma, 140, now offering A/C, TV, and bath in brightly lit rooms. (☎0544 21 51 27; residenza@ravennamosaici.it. Breakfast included. Reception M-F 8am-6:30pm, Sa-Su 8am-6pm. Singles €47; doubles €89; triples €112-129; quads €135-164. AmEx/ MC/V.) To reach **Ostello Dante (HI) ❶**, V. Nicolodi, 12, take bus #1 or 70 from V. Pallavicini, across from the station (every 10-20min. 5:40am-8:10pm, every 30-40min. 8:30-11:30pm). A cheery staff offers book exchange, Internet (€5.16 per hr.), and foosball. (☎0544 42 11 64; hostelravenna@hotmail.com. Wheelchair accessible. Breakfast included. Safes available. Laundry €2.50 per wash or dry. Reception 7-10am and 5-11:30pm. Lockout 10am-5pm. Curfew 11:30pm. Dorms €13; family rooms €14 per person. HI members only, one-night stamps €3, full memberships €18. MC/V.) At **Hotel Ravenna ❹**, V. Maroncelli, 12, a right turn from the station, 26 small rooms have tile floors, fans, and satellite TV. (☎0544 21 22 04, fax 21 20 77. Wheelchair accessible. Reception 7am-midnight; notify if leaving after hours. Singles €35-40, with shower €40-48; doubles €40-55/€45-70; triples €90-94; quads €110-119. AmEx/MC/V.) Bus #1 departs across from the train station (every 30min. 6:30am-8pm, every hr. 8:30-11:30pm) and stops at camping **Adriano ❶**, V. di Campeggio, 7, in Marina di Ravenna, 8km from the *centro*. Four-star facilities near a public beach have pool, *bocce* courts, and a soccer field. (☎0544 43 72 30; info@campingparkadriano.com. Bungalows require reservation. Reception daily 8:30am-1pm and 3-8pm. Open mid-Apr. to mid-Sept. €3.80-9 per person, €7-15 per tent. MC/V.)

☕ FOOD

The distinctive flavors of *Ravennese* salt, extra virgin olive oil, and chestnuts characterize Ravenna's hearty cuisine. Accompany a filling meal with a full-bodied *Albana* or *Trebbiano* wine. For dessert, try *zuppa inglese*, a combination of biscuits and custard enlivened with a splash of cordial. A red and blue speckled spin on the dessert is the creamy *zuppa inglese gelato* at **Gelateria Nuovo Mondo ❶**, V. Farini, 60. (☎0544 355 38. Open daily 10am-midnight. Cash only.) Hostel guests benefit from the convenient **Coop,** across the street at V. Aquileia, 110. (Open M 3-8pm, Tu-Sa 8am-8pm.) Fruit, meat, and cheese stands fill the **covered market** at P. A. Costa, 2, up V. IV Novembre from P. del Popolo. (Open M-Th and Sa 7am-2pm, F 7am-2pm and 5-8pm. Most stands cash only.) From P. Garibaldi, turn right on V. Gordini, then left on V. Ricci for 🔳**Cà de' Ve'n ❷**, V. Ricci, 24. Underneath Byzantine ceilings, patrons enjoy fresh pastas and efficient service. (☎0544 301 63. *Primi* and *secondi* from €6. Open Tu-Su 11am-4:15pm and 6-10pm. AmEx/MC/V.) An attentive staff serves heavy, delicious regional specialties at **Ristorante L'Oste Bacca ❷**, V. Salara, 20. Try the *tortellaci di ortica* (pasta stuffed with cheese and served with fish and tomatoes), *piadine* (hot, triangular pieces of flatbread) dipped in melted *squaquerone*, a mild local cheese, or the *mortadella*, a round sausage, covered with cheese and served on a bed of lettuce (☎0544 353 63. *Primi* €5.50-7, *secondi* €7-14. Cover €1.60. Open M and W-Su 12:15-2:30pm and 7:15-10:30pm. AmEx/MC/V.) For a blast of local color, try **Verderame ❶**, V. Cavour, 82. *Ravennese* artists designed everything from the Middle Eastern sconces to the bathrooms, but the real draw is the famous hot chocolate. (☎/fax 0544 322 48. Open in summer M 8:30am-8:30pm, Tu-W and F-Sa 8:30am-midnight, Th 8:30am-2pm; in winter M-Th and Su 8:30am-8pm and F-Sa 8:30am-midnight. Cash only.)

◎ SIGHTS

🖼**BASILICA DI SAN VITALE.** Light from thin windows illuminates the octagonal **Basilica di San Vitale,** lending a sparkling glow to the interior mosaics. Above the apse, Christ Pantocrator sits on a sky-blue globe with the *Book of Seven Seals*. On either side, Byzantine mosaics depict Empress Theodora offering a golden chalice, while Emperor Justinian brings a gilded plate. *(V. S. Vitale, 17. From the tourist office turn right on V. Cavour, then again on V. Argentario. ☎0544 21 62 92. Open daily Apr.-Sept. 9am-7pm, Mar. and Oct. 9am-5:30pm, Nov.-Feb. 9am-4:30pm. Cash only.)* Across the courtyard, mosaics cover the interior of the tiny brick **Mausoleo di Galla Placidia,** where a sin-

RAVENNOUS FOR ART. The **Ravenna Card** provides admission to six museums and monuments: the Museo Arcivescovile, Battistero Neoniano, Basilica di Spirito Santo, Basilica di Sant'Apollinare Nuovo, Basilica di San Vitale, and the Mausoleo di Galla Placidia. Individual tickets to the sites are not available. From June 16 through February, the card costs €6.50, students €5.50; March 1 to June 15 €8.50, students €7.50. Purchase it at any participating site. For information on the card or any of the churches, contact the Ufficio Informazioni e Prenotazioni dell'Opera di Religione della Diocesi di Ravenna, V. Canneti, 3 (☎ 0544 54 16 80, fax 0544 54 16 80), open M-F 9am-12:30pm and 3:30-6pm.

gle, dim lamp reveals three stone sarcophagi said to contain the remains of Costanzo III, Empress Galla Placida, and Valentiniano III. Above the door, a pastoral mosaic depicts Christ caring for his flock. *(Behind S. Vitale. Same hours as basilica.)*

■ BASILICA DI SANT'APOLLINARE IN CLASSE. This spacious, 6th-century brick church is lined with little more than unlabeled marble sepulchers—the real draw is the massive mosaic above the apse, where St. Apollinare and flocks of sheep fill the enormous half-dome. *(In Classe, south of the city. Take bus #4 or 44; both stop across from the train station. ☎ 0544 344 24. Open M-Sa 8:30am-7:30pm, Su 9am-7pm. Tickets close 30min. before basilica. €2, €1 for EU students 18-25, under 18 or over 65 free. Combo with Museo Nazionale €6.50/€3; Su 9am-1pm free. Cash only.)*

DANTE'S TOMB AND THE DANTE MUSEUM. Ravenna's most popular monument is the green-domed tomb of Dante Alighieri, who was exiled from Florence in 1301 and died in Ravenna in 1321. A suspended lamp has burned with Florentine oil since 1908 and illuminates a relief of Dante leafing through his books. The nearby Dante Museum contains Wostry Carlo's illustrations of Dante's works, the fir chest that held the poet's bones, 18,000 scholarly volumes on his works, and the trowel and hammer that laid the cornerstone of Rio de Janeiro's Dante Monument. *(V. D. Alighieri. From P. del Popolo, cut through P. Garibaldi to V. D. Alighieri. Museum ☎ 0544 336 67. Tomb open daily 9am-7pm. Free. Museum open Apr.-Sept. Tu-Su 9am-noon and 3:30-6pm, Oct.-Mar. 9am-noon. €2, under 18 free. Cash only.)*

MUSEO NAZIONALE. This former Benedictine monastery features Roman, early Christian, Byzantine, and medieval works like the 6th-century bronze cross from the roof of the S. Vitale cupola and the original apse vault of St. Apollinare in Classe, where the original design reveals birds and the Tree of Life originally situated where sheep and St. Apollinare now stand. *(On V. Fiandrini. Ticket booth to the right of entrance to Basilica di San Vitale. Museum is through courtyard. Info ☎ 0544 340 57 or 344 24. Tickets ☎ 06 32 81 01. Open Tu-Su 8:30am-7:30pm. Tickets close 30min. before museum. €4, EU students €2, under 18 or over 65 free. Cash only.)*

BASILICA DI SANT'APOLLINARE NUOVO. The 6th-century basilica, which passed into Christian hands a mere 40 years after its construction, features arched windows, white tile floors, and mortar made from crushed seashells. Long mosaics of saints line the central aisle, and frescoes in the central apse recount miracles performed by Jesus. Outside, a tall circular brick *campanile* spirals up six stories over the church's sloping red tile roof. *(On V. di Roma. ☎ 0544 21 99 38. Open daily Apr.-Sept. 9am-7pm, Mar. and Oct. 9:30am-5:30pm, Nov.-Feb. 9:30am-4:30pm.)*

BATTISTERO NEONIANO. The central dome of the baptistery next door to the duomo features Jesus in the Jordan River with John the Baptist and a representation of the river as a nude old man, just one of the mosaics ordered by Bishop Neon in 452 that earned the baptistery its name. The baptismal font is at the center of the room, 3m above the now-covered Roman bath that Bishop Ursus built upon

EMILIA-ROMAGNA

in the early 5th century. *(From P. del Popolo, follow V. Cairoli, turn right on V. Gessi, then head toward P. Arcivescovado. Open daily Apr.-Sept. 9am-7pm; Mar. and Oct. 9:30am-5:30pm; Nov.-Feb. 9:30am-4:30pm. Duomo open daily 7:30am-noon and 3:30-6:30pm. Free.)*

MUSEO ARCIVESCOVILE. This one-room museum displays tattered priestly garments, a flower-shaped marble Easter calendar from 532-626, and detailed mosaics of the Virgin Mary and four saints from the now-destroyed Ursian Basilica. The real showpiece is the *See of Maximilian*, an ivory throne trimmed with ornate vines, tiny fowl, and relief panels of the life of Christ, which sits illuminated in the center. *(To the right of the Battistero Neoniano. ☎0544 21 99 38. Open daily Apr.-Sept. 9am-7pm, Mar. and Oct. 9:30am-5:30pm, Nov.-Feb. 9:30am-4:30pm.)*

ENTERTAINMENT AND FESTIVALS

A host of fairly similar bars and cafes stay open late around P. del Popolo, but one notable night spot is **I Fanti**, at V. M. Fanti, 9/A, off V. Cavour. A hip bar with low tables and a red leather booth hosts films, poetry readings, and original art throughout the summer; year-round, expect friendly service and wine from €4 to €6. (☎0544 351 35. Open M-Sa 8am-11pm. AmEx/MC/V.) If the mosaics of the basilica left you breathless, channel your slack-jawed awe at **Fuschini Colori-Belle Arti,** P. Mameli, 16, off Viale Farini, which sells *tesserae* so people can make their own. (☎0544 373 87. Open M-W, F, and Su 9am-12:30pm and 4:30-7:30pm; Th and Sa 9am-12:30pm. AmEx/MC/V.) From late June to early September, the city streets fill with spectators for the **Bella di Sera.** Every Friday in July and August, shops and monuments stay open until around midnight. Watch for the **Organ Music Festival,** held annually in late July in the Basilica di San Vitale. Since 1990, some of the world's most famous performers have come together each June and July for the renowned **Ravenna Festival.** (Info office at V. D. Alighieri, 1. ☎0544 24 92 11; info@ravennafestival.org. Ticket office at V. Mariani, 2. ☎0544 24 92 44; www.ravennafestival.org. Open M-W and F-Sa 10am-1pm, Th 4-6pm. During festival, open M-Sa 10am-1pm and 4-6pm, Su 10am-1pm. Reserve ahead for popular events. Tickets from €10-15.) In the second week of September, Dante's legacy comes to life with the exhibits and theatricals of the **Dante Festival** (☎0544 302 52).

RIMINI ☎0541

From the hundreds of multi-storied pastel hotels that crowd the shoreline of the Adriatic to the bemused look on your doorman's face when he lets you in disheveled and mojito-stained at three in the morning, Rimini is clearly a city that's used to playing fast and loose. Inland, the historic center preserves its Roman heritage with an alluring jumble of streets overshadowed by the Malatesta Temple and the Augustan Arch. Get used to buses crammed with sleeveless teens singing drinking songs and colorful explosions of impromptu fireworks as you shuffle home well past midnight. Beaches and wide boardwalks filled with small boutiques, fortune tellers, and caricature artists all contribute to a society where it's perfectly acceptable—and admirable—to collapse into bed and wish the rising sun goodnight.

TRANSPORTATION

Flights: Miramare Civil Airport (☎0541 71 57 11), on V. Flaminia. Mostly charter flights. Serves many European cities. Bus #9, across from the train station, goes to the airport (daily every 20min. 5:37am-10:52pm and 1:02am, €1).

Trains: in P. C. Battisti and V. Dante (☎89 20 21). Station open daily 5am-12:30am. Info office open M, Th, and Sa 8:30am-7:30pm, Tu-W, F, and Su 8am-7:30pm. Tickets open daily 5:15am-10:15pm. To: **Ancona** (1¼hr., 51 per day 12:14am-10:35pm,

€4.65); **Bologna** (1½hr., 58 per day 2:28am-11:02pm, €6.35); **Milan** (3hr., 25 per day 2:28am-8:05pm, €15.44); **Ravenna** (1hr., 34 per day 5:20am-10:53pm, €2.80); **Riccione** (10min., 45 per day 4:13am-9:53pm, €1). Cash only.

Buses: TRAM intercity bus station (☎0541 30 05 33; www.tram.rimini.it), at V. Roma in P. Clementini, near the station. From the train station, follow V. Dante Alighieri and take 1st left. Urban bus tickets available (valid for 90min.; €1, €1.50 if purchased onboard). 24hr. service to many inland towns (1hr., €1.03-€3.36). Ticket booth open daily 6:10am-12:20am. **Fratelli Benedettini** (☎0549 90 38 54) and **Bonelli Bus** (☎0541 37 24 32) run the most convenient buses to **San Marino** (50min., 11 per day 7:40am-7:10pm, €3.10). Buy tickets at kiosk to the right of the train station. Buses depart from the train station and fill quickly, so arrive 15min. before departure.

Taxis: RadioTaxi (☎0541 500 20). Available 24hr.

Car Rental: Hertz, Viale Trieste, 16/A (☎0541 531 10, fax 532 14), near the beach, off V. Vespucci. Bus #11: stop 12. 23+. €10 surcharge if under 25. Small cars from €69. Open M-Sa 8:30am-12:30pm and 3-7pm. AmEx/MC/V.

Bike Rental: On Viale Fiume off V. Vespucci (☎0541 39 10 72). Bus #11: stop 12. Open daily Apr.-Oct. 9am-midnight. €3 per hr. Cash only.

Scooter Rental: P. Kennedy, 6 (☎0541 270 16). Rentals start at €13 per hr. Also rents *ciclocarrozzelle* (pedal-powered cars). Open daily Apr.-Oct. 9am-midnight. Cash only.

◼✚ 🛈 ORIENTATION AND PRACTICAL INFORMATION

To reach the beach from the **train station** in **Piazzale Cesare Battisti**, turn right from the station, right into the tunnel at the yellow arrow indicating *al mare*, and follow **Viale Principe Amedeo**. To the right, **Viale Vespucci**, the hub of Rimini activity, runs one block inland along the beach. Bus #11 (every 15min. 5:30am-2am) runs to the beach from the train station and continues along V. Vespucci and V. R. Elena. Bus stops are numbered. Buy tickets (90min. €1, 24hr. €3) at the kiosk in front of the station or at *tabacchi*. To reach the historic center, take **Via Dante Alighieri** from the station and continue to **Piazza Tre Martiri**. The center of Rimini is **Marina Centro**. **Rimini Sud** (south) branches out from the main city along the coast and comprises the neighborhoods of Bellariva, Marebello, Rivazzurra, and Miramare. **Rimini Nord** (north) goes toward the less-visited Rivabella, Viserba, and Viserbella.

Tourist Offices: IAT, P. Fellini, 3 (☎0541 569 02, fax 565 98), at the beginning of V. Vespucci. Bus #11: stop 10. Open daily in summer 8:30am-7pm, in winter 9:30am-12:30pm and 3:30-6:30pm. **Branch,** P. C. Battisti, 1 (☎0541 513 31; www.riminiturismo.it), to the left after the train station. Open in summer M-Sa 8:30am-7pm, Su 9:30am-12:30pm; in winter M-Sa 10am-4pm. **Hotel Reservations Adria** (☎0541 69 36 28; www.iperhotel.com), in train station, books rooms for free. Phone open daily 8am-8pm; office open daily 8:15am-8pm, phone and office closed winter.

Budget Travel: CTS/Grantour Viaggi, V. Matteucci, 4 (☎0541 510 01 or 555 25), off V. Principe Amedeo. Sells tickets and ISICs (€10). Open M-W and F 9am-noon and 3:30-6:30pm, Th 9am-4pm, Sa 9:30am-noon. MC/V.

Luggage Storage: In train station. €2.10-3.70 for 24hr. Coin-operated.

Laundromat: Lavanderia Trieste Express, Viale Trieste, 16 (☎0541 267 64). Wash €5, dry €5. No self-service. Open M-F 8:30am-12:30pm and 4-7pm, Sa 2-6pm.

Pharmacy: Farmacia del Kursaal, V. Vespucci 12/E (☎0541 217 11). Open daily 8:30am-1pm and 4-10pm. Cash only.

Emergency: ☎113. **Ambulance** (☎118). **Police,** C. d'Augusto, 192 (☎0541 510 00, dial ☎112 for emergencies).

Hospital: Ospedale Infermi, V. Settembrini, 2 (☎0541 70 51 11). In case of **emergency,** call ☎0541 70 57 57.

Internet: Central Park, Viale Vespucci, 21 (☎0541 37 44 50). 9 coin-operated computers. €1 for 10min., €2 for 30min., €5 for 80min. Open daily in summer 9am-2am, in winter 10am-2pm. Cash only.

Post Office: C. d'Augusto, 8 (☎0541 78 16 73), off P. Tre Martiri, near the Arch of Augustus. Open M-F 8am-6:30pm, Sa 8am-12:30pm. **Currency exchange** available. **Postal Code:** 47900.

▌ ACCOMMODATIONS

The smaller streets off Viale Vespucci and Viale R. Elena between stops 12 and 20 of bus #11 are filled with more hotels than homes. Prices peak in August and reservations are necessary far in advance. If plans fall through, the tourist office provides a complete list of hotels and campgrounds.

▧ Hotel Cirene, Viale Cirene, 50 (☎0541 39 09 04; www.hotelcirene.com). Bus #11: stop 13. Pleasant owners offer rooms with high ceiling, richly colored drapes and bedspreads, porcelain bathroom, phone, and TV. Some rooms have balcony. Breakfast included. Half and full pension available. Open May-Sept. Singles €25-52; doubles €30-57; triples €50-62; quads €62-67. AmEx/MC/V. ❸

Hotel Italia, V. Misurata, 13 (☎0541 39 09 94; hotelitaliarimini@virgilio.it). Bus #11: stop 13. A friendly staff maintains 23 clean, white rooms with bath. Buffet breakfast included. Reception 24hr. Half or full pension required Aug. 9-22 (€41/€45). Rooms €20-28. Surcharge for single room €7. MC/V. ❸

Saxon, Viale Cirene, 36 (☎/fax 0541 39 14 00). Bus #11: stop 13. Exit bus to the left, turn right on V. Misurata, then left on V. Cirene. This hotel has 30 rooms with TV, phone, and minibar above a small, street-side terrace and lobby with plaster statuary and sea green trim. Breakfast included. Singles €45; doubles €60. AmEx/MC/V. ❸

Albergo Filadelfia, Viale Pola, 25 (☎0541 236 79, fax 273 38). Bus #11: stop 12. From V. Trento, turn left on V. Sauro. An affable couple runs this clean 3-story hotel, but rooms vary—many doubles have balcony, some rooms have bath, and the sloped ceilings in the handful of third-floor rooms make them notably small. Breakfast buffet €4. Open Apr. 15-late Sept. Prices vary seasonally and according to occupancy. Singles €20-30; doubles €36-54; triples €51-78. AmEx/MC/V. ❷

Milord, Viale Ariosto, 19 (☎0541 38 17 66, fax 38 57 62). Bus #11: stop 16. Exit the bus to the right and head left on V. Ariosto; just off V. R. Elena. Large rooms with bath, TV, and phone, many with balcony. Call ahead for A/C. Beach cabins and a restaurant downstairs. Breakfast included. Half pension available. Rooms €20-35. AmEx/MC/V. ❷

Camping Maximum, Viale Principe di Piemonte, 57 (☎0541 37 26 02, fax 37 02 71). Bus #11: stop 33. This campground sits a bus ride south of Rimini's main drags. Reception daily 9am-10pm. Open June-Sept. €4-9 per person, €4-5 per child, €9-16 per tent. Bungalows from €41. MC/V. ❶

▐ FOOD

Rimini's **covered market** between V. Castelfidardo and the Tempio provides an array of foods. (Open M, W, and F-Sa 7:15am-1pm and 5-7:30pm, Tu and Th 7:15am-1pm.) The **STANDA supermarket,** V. Vespucci, 133, is between P. Kennedy and P. Tripoli. (Open daily 8am-10:30pm. AmEx/MC/V.)

Osteria Pizzeria Le Logge, Viale Trieste, 5 (☎0541 559 78). Crowds gather under the raffia awning and patio for fresh air, friendly service, and the specialty *Nino,* a huge pizza with mozzarella, gorgonzola, spicy salami, and crisp red onions (€6.20). Pizza €3.40-9. Cover €1. Open daily 7pm-1:30am. AmEx/MC/V. ❷

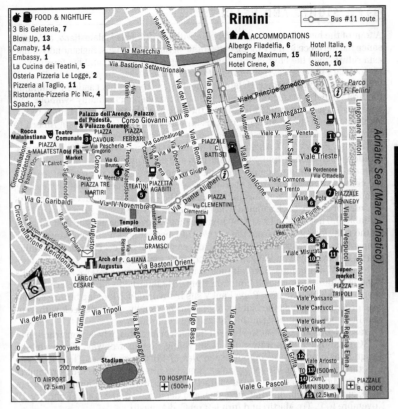

FOOD & NIGHTLIFE
3 Bis Gelateria, 7
Blow Up, 13
Carnaby, 14
Embassy, 1
La Cucina dei Teatini, 5
Osteria Pizzeria Le Logge, 2
Pizzeria al Taglio, 11
Ristorante-Pizzeria Pic Nic, 4
Spazio, 3

Rimini

Bus #11 route

ACCOMMODATIONS
Albergo Filadelfia, 6   Hotel Italia, 9
Camping Maximum, 15   Milord, 12
Hotel Cirene, 8   Saxon, 10

EMILIA-ROMAGNA

Ristorante-Pizzeria Pic Nic, V. Tempio Malatestiano, 30 (☎0541 219 16). From V. IV Novembre heading toward P. Tre Martiri, turn right at the sign. An attentive staff serves specialties like the pizza *Pic Nic* (with prosciutto, wurstel, peppers, and artichokes) in a photo-adorned interior, expansive garden, and glass-windowed patio. *Primi* €6.50-8, *secondi* €7-13. Cover €1.50. Open daily noon-3pm and 7pm-1am. AmEx/MC/V. ❷

La Cucina dei Teatini, P. Teatini, 3 (info ☎0541 280 08, reservations 339 238 76 95), just off V. IV Novembre, close to the temple. A young staff serves artistically crafted dishes in an interior filled with modern art. For a more serene environment, try seating at the tree-shaded wooden deck across the street. *Primi* €8-10, *secondi* €10-16. Open M-F 12:30-2:30pm and 7:30-10:30pm, Sa 7:30-10:30pm. AmEx/MC/V. ❸

3 Bis Gelateria, Viale Vespucci, 73 (☎328 261 89 79). Flat screen TVs dot the sleek walls of this combination gelateria-*creperia,* where cups of creamy gelato are heaped high with cookies and fresh berries. Try the *pan di stelle,* a divinely sweet concoction of cookies-and-cream (€1.50 for a scoop). Hot crepes (€2.50-3.50) are stuffed with fresh fruit, *Nutella,* cream, or gelato. Open daily Mar.-Sept. noon-1am. Cash only. ❶

Pizzeria al Taglio, Viale Misurata, 5 (☎0541 39 28 78), off V. Vespucci, close to P. Kennedy. Thick pizzas like the *caprese* (cheese, basil, and tomato; €4.80) or the *diavoli* (mozzarella, tomato, and salami; €4.70) and teens crowd into the bright interior. Take-out available. Pizza €3-6. Open daily noon-3pm and 5:30pm-2am. Cash only. ❶

◉ 🏖 SIGHTS AND BEACHES

A tour of the historic center should begin with the ■**Tempio Malatestiano,** a Renaissance masterpiece in the Franciscan-Gothic style. In the 1440s, Sigismondo Malatesta refurbished the church with funereal chapels for himself and his fourth wife. Piero della Francesca's *Sigismondo Pandolfo Malatesta in preghiera davanti a San Sigismondo* shows Malatesta kneeling in front of his castle in Rimini; in the first chapel, a statue of the ruler sits atop two elephants, family symbols. The apse holds a painted crucifix by Giotto, the only work by the artist in Rimini today. On the exterior, the small brick protrusion was added by Leon Battista Alberti to resemble the Arch of Augustus (see below) as per Malatesta's orders. (On V. IV Novembre. Follow V. D. Alighieri from the train station. ☎0541 511 30. During restoration, open Sa 3:30-7pm, Su 8:30am-1pm and 3:30-7pm. Free.)

Piazza Cavour, Rimini's center, contains a varied assortment of architecture from the centuries. Shops and bars surround the 18th-century **pescheria** (fish market), located under the brick arches in the piazza. The four stone fish in each corner of the interior arcade once spouted water for cleaning (visible under the rows of market tables). The stone pillars of the Renaissance **Palazzo Garampi**—the first building on the right facing away from the *pescheria*—bear almost no resemblance to the connected brick **Palazzo dell'Arengo** and the smaller **Palazzo del Podestà.** Perpendicular to the municipal building lies the modern **Teatro Comunale,** which lost its auditorium to WWII bombs. Two statues stand in the piazza center—**Fontana della Pigna** is a four-tiered marble fountain from 1543, adorned with an inscription by Leonardo da Vinci. Nearby, Pope Paul V sits by two vicious looking bronze eagles, little protection against the blanket of pigeons he usually wears. (Check with tourist office about exhibitions at the Palazzo del Podestà.)

Grassy debris are piled at the base of the **Arch of Augustus,** whose construction in 27 BC establishes it as Italy's oldest surviving Roman archway. The arch was designed as a peace offering after decades of Roman civil war. The top of the structure, probably destroyed by an earthquake, is refinished with brick ramparts from the Middle Ages, and the arch itself still features original marble pillars in relief, an inscription honoring Augustus, and depictions of the gods. (Follow V. IV Novembre to P. Tre Martiri and turn left on C. d'Augusto.)

Most of the shoreline is privately owned by hotels, which offer guests a strip of beach for a minimum charge of about €3 for a lounge chair and use of whirlpools, volleyball courts, lockers, Internet, and other facilities. The fun continues at night with bars and live music. Vendors along the beach offer equipment for kayaking, jet-skiing, parasailing, and deep-sea diving. A public beach, located at the top of the shore, is slightly less picturesque and offers no storage or lounge amenities; however, the beach is free and the waves are huge.

🎭 🎆 NIGHTLIFE AND FESTIVALS

Rimini is notorious for its non-stop partying, with clubs near the *lungomare* in Rimini Sud. ■**Bus #11** is an institution in and of itself—by 11pm, expect a crowd of strangers singing drinking songs, comparing outfits, and cheering (on the rare occasion a group waiting at the stop can successfully fit inside). The route runs from Rimini to the bus station in Riccione, where Bus #46 allows easy access to seven more nightclubs grouped together in a valley. Clubs change their hours and prices frequently, and many close in winter. Prices are steep, so hang on to the **discount passes** that promoters distribute along V. Vespucci and V. R. Elena. Many clubs offer free bus services (check at the travel agency in P. Tripoli for schedules; open M-Sa 8:30am-7pm, Su 9am-noon), but there is also a **Blue Line bus** (mid-July to

Aug., every 10-20min, €3) for disco-goers. It departs from the station and travels the bus #11 route to the nearby beach towns. Buy tickets onboard. The last bus leaves around 5:30am, after which bus #11 resumes service.

A bustling nightlife scene lights up the historic center by the old fish market. From P. Cavour, follow **Via Pescheria,** where pubs and bars stay open until 3am. ■**Embassy,** Viale Vespucci, 22, a 5min. walk from P. Kennedy, is the only nightclub within walking distance of Rimini *centro.* Crowds spill from a steamy main floor to a smaller room playing top-40 hits. The garden is complete with plentiful seating and a bustling bar. (☎0541 239 34. Cover €10-16; discount cards often handed out at the door. Drinks €6. Open daily midnight-4am.) The friendly staff at **Spazio,** P. Cavour, 5, mans a strikingly trendy bar with an outdoor terrace perfect for people-watching. (☎054 12 34 39. Wine from €4 a glass. Open M-Sa 5pm-2am. MC/V.) At **Blow Up**, Viale Regina Elena, 209, globetrotters groove to hip-hop and disco down a marble staircase lined with neon. Take bus #11 to stop 21. (☎0541 38 60 60; www.blowupdisco.it. Cover €8-15, drinks €3-7. Open daily 9:30am-4am. AmEx/MC/V.) In Bellariva, **Life,** V. R. Margherita, 11, hosts two floors of party-goers, from the teenage glitterati to a mixed crowd later in the night. The top level has a laid-back bar, while the bottom kicks it up a notch with a fog machine and an elevated stage. Take bus #11 to stop 22; the club also offers a free bus service. (☎0541 37 34 73. Free drink at 2:30am. Cover €9 with discount pass, available near the door. Open daily 10pm-4am. Cash only.) Past the yellow VW bug wedged above the door at **Carnaby,** V. Brindisi, 20, in Rivazzurra, a teenage crowd packs a third-floor bar, a second-floor discotheque, and "the Cave," an underground dance floor that positively reeks of neon trim and puberty. Take bus #11 to stop 26, turn right, then turn left down V. Brindisi or use the free bus service. (☎0541 37 32 04; www.carnaby.it. Cover €12-25, with discount pass €10. Open daily 10pm-4am. Cash only.)

In September of even-numbered years, Rimini hosts a wild **beach festival.** Classical concerts and parties erupt beneath fireworks displays.

▷ DAYTRIP FROM RIMINI

SAN LEO

San Leo is accessible by buses operated by Ferrovie Emilia Romagna. Buses depart across from the Rimini train station at 8:40am, 12:10, 1:10, and 5:30pm; all but the 12:10pm departure require a brief connection via van at Pietrascuta. Buses leave San Leo at 6:38, 7:13, 8am, 1, and 6pm; all but the 7:13am departure need a connection. Direct trips cost €2.53. Connecting trips €1.96 for the 1st leg, €1 for the 2nd. Buy Ferrovie Emilia-Romagna tickets at the kiosk outside the Rimini train station. Buy tickets for the connection on the van. Ask the Rimini tourist office about schedule changes.

Perched atop the Apennine mountains and surrounded by sheer craggy cliffs, San Leo once served as the papacy's maximum security prison. Today, the tiny hamlet is noticeably more hospitable and offers a quiet, largely untouristed alternative to the swarming streets of nearby San Marino. It takes only 2hr. to explore the entire area, but plan to linger and indulge in San Leo's timeless charm. Staircases off the main piazza lead to a treasure trove of cliff top balconies with views of the hillsides below. Across from the tourist office sits **La Pieve,** a tiny church made of sandstone blocks that contains one row of pews and a simple brick apse; in the basement, the 18th-century statue *Madonna del Rosario col Bambino* houses a relic of patron St. Leo. On either side sit 17th-century painted wood depictions of St. Leo and St. Marino. (Open daily 9am-12:45pm and 3-7:15pm. Free.) Just before P. D. Alighieri, signs point up a rocky path that zig-zags steeply to the **fortress.** Inside, glass cases contain fortress relics, but the view of the sweeping hillsides from the cliffside is worth more than the steep entry fee. (☎0541 91 63 02. Open daily 9am-7pm. €8, over 65 €5, between 6 and 14 free. Cash only.)

EMILIA-ROMAGNA

The **tourist office** at the far end of P. D. Alighieri provides **maps** and brochures. (☎0541 91 63 06 or 800 55 38 00, fax 0541 92 69 73. Open daily 9am-7pm.) Though an ideal daytrip from Rimini, San Leo has a few good lodging options. **Albergo Castello ❹,** in the main piazza, has 16 rooms with TV, phone, and bath. (☎0541 91 62 14; albergo-castello@libero.it. Singles €35; doubles €55. AmEx/MC/V.) **Albergo Rocca ❹** has seven basic rooms with bath, large terrace, and restaurant downstairs two blocks from the piazza. (☎0541 91 62 41. Reception 8am-10:30pm, notify desk if arriving later. Breakfast €5. Doubles €50-65; triples €70-91; quads €90-117. AmEx/MC/V.) For info on less expensive *affittacamere*, call ☎0541 91 62 84. At **Il Bettolino ❷,** V. Montefeltro, 4, a friendly staff serves piles of pasta in the quiet interior or at canopied tables along the street. (☎0541 91 62 65; federico.calcagnini@libero.it. Pizza €2.10-6.70. *Primi* €5.20-7.20, *secondi* €5.70-10.30. Cover €1. Open M-Tu and Th-Su noon-3pm and 7-10pm. AmEx/MC/V.) After exiting the tourist office, turn left for **La Corte ❷,** V. Michele Rosa, 74, which offers traditional dishes (like the meaty *salsiccia di San Leo*, €6.20) on a wooden deck or booths inside. The attached **gelateria** has the most flavors in San Leo, from €1.50 a scoop. For lighter eaters, the *conini* (tiny cones of gelato dipped in chocolate) are just €0.50. (☎0541 91 61 45; osterialacorte@libero.it. *Primi* €6.20-7.30, *secondi* €6.20-9.50. Cover €1.50. Open M-F 12:15-2pm and 7:15-9pm, Sa 15:2-2:30pm and 7:15-10pm, Su 12:15-2:30pm and 7:15-9pm. Closed Tu in winter. MC/V.)

RICCIONE ☎0541

In Riccione, a tangible rift exists between the quiet, shady streets where residents make their homes and the steamy streets by the beach, where bewildered vacationers wander through wide boardwalks lined with brightly lit video arcades, risqué sex shops, and a constant stream of busy disco-bars and hotels. The city itself is humming with electricity and neon until early in the morning, but die-hard divas will swoon over a hillside of world-renowned *discoteche* just a bus ride away.

🖅🔀 TRANSPORTATION AND PRACTICAL INFORMATION. The **train station** (☎89 20 21), between Piazzale della Stazione and Piazzale Vittorio Veneto, is open 5:40am-8:30pm; binario #1 is open all night (tickets 5:45am-8:17pm). There's no luggage storage, so leave bags behind if clubbing in town overnight. Trains run to: Bologna (1¾hr., 25 per day 5:55am-10:35pm; €6.35); Pesaro (20min., 52 per day 12:42am-10:05pm, €1.90); and Rimini (10 min., 39 per day 5:08am-11:30pm, €1). **Local bus #11** (€1, €1.50 if purchased onboard) runs along the waterfront from the southern edge of Riccione and travels north to Rimini.

To get to the beach, exit the train station toward P. V. Veneto and walk down **Viale Martinelli** and turn left on **Via Gramsci;** then head right on V. Ceccarini for two blocks to **Piazzale Roma.** The public beach is on the other side of the piazzale. The *lungomare* runs along the sea. An **IAT Tourist Office,** Piazzale Ceccarini, 10, offers accommodations booking and a free **map.** (☎0541 69 33 02; iat@comune.riccione.rn.it. Open daily June-Aug. 8am-10pm, Sept. 8am-8pm, Oct.-May 8am-7pm.) In case of **emergency,** call ☎113, an **ambulance** (☎118), or the **police,** V. Cortemaggio, 6/A (☎0541 69 94 44). **Ospedale G. Ceccarini** is at V. Cervi, 48 (☎0541 60 85 11). **Internet** is available at Phone Center and Internet Point, V. Amendola 17/C. (☎/fax 0541 69 76 66; phoneserv@interfree.it. €1 for 15min., €4 per hr. Open daily 9am-midnight. Cash only.) **Currency exchange** is available at the **post office,** V. Corrodoni, 13. (☎0541 47 39 01. Open M-F 8am-6:30pm, Sa 8am-12:30pm.) **Postal Code:** 47838.

🏠🏳 ACCOMMODATIONS AND FOOD. Although there are 500 hotels in Riccione, reservations are essential for prime vacation season. During the rest of the year, bargains abound. The tall **Hotel Nizza ❹,** Lungomare D'Annunzio, 165, features a spacious TV room, rooftop terrace, and large rooms with TV, bath, and balcony. Walk to the waterfront and take bus #11 to stop 40. (☎0541 64 14 93; www.hotelnizza.it. Reception 24hr. Open May-Sept. Full pension doubles €34-€58. Singles supplement €5. Prices vary seasonally. V.) **Hotel La Nidiola ❹**, V. Bixio, 30, is by the beach. Exit the train station at P. Veneto and turn right on V. Trento e Trieste. Walk straight for 10min.; the hotel is on the left. The hotel offers free bikes to guests on the go, but rooms with TV, bath, and balcony comfort those who stay in. (☎0541 60 15 58; www.lanidiola.com. Reception 24hr. Half pension singles €34-57; doubles €60-102; full pension singles €37-60; doubles €66-108. AmEx/MC/V.) Take bus #11 one stop past Hotel Nizza and walk two blocks inland to reach **Hotel Maris Stella ❸**, V. Oriani, 7. Inside, rooms with large, colorful beds and thick towels feature TV, phone, and blessedly cool fans; half have balcony. (☎0541 64 23 75; www.marisstella.it. Half pension €27-52; full pension €30-€55. Singles supplement €5. Prices vary seasonally. AmEx/MC/V.)

In a town with so many tourists, conformity reigns in countless cookie-cutter cafes and pizzerias. A little way from the *centro* sits **Supermarket Abissinia**, V. Trento Trieste, 64, which stocks basic fare. (☎0541 60 25 02. Open M-Sa 7:30am-8pm and Su 7:30am-1pm. MC/V.) One of the most unique places (and a reprieve from the stiflingly humid summer air) is ☒**Campi di Fragole ❶**, V. Dante, 180, a gelateria named for the Beatles's "Strawberry Fields Forever." After sampling the freshly made gelato, add your tag to the graffitied mirrors with neon gel pens from the counter. (1 scoop €1.50, 1 scoops €2. Open daily Apr.-Sept. 10am-2am. Cash only.) One of the biggest of the standard pizzerias near the *centro* is **Frankly ❷**, V. Ceccarini, 113, where pizzas like the Frankly (with cheese, cherry tomatoes, prosciutto, and arugola; €8.50) are served in an open-walled interior. (☎/fax 0541 69 33 27. Pizza €4.10-8.50. Pasta and seafood €6.15-19. Open daily noon-3pm and 6pm-2am. AmEx/MC/V.) On one of the main pedestrian malls, **Meza Café ❸**, V. Dante, 170/A, offers a well-priced daily pasta *menù*. (Just off V. Dante. ☎0541 64 63 28. Pasta dishes about €3.50-4.50. Open daily 7am-3am. AmEx/MC/V.)

🎵 **NIGHTLIFE.** The real action is in the clubs, conveniently nestled together in a valley accessible by bus. From the bus station near the waterfront, take bus #46 to the Discoteche stop—from there, signs point to **Peter Pan** (Viale Abruzzi, 147; ☎0541 64 13 35), Byblos (see below), **Prince** (☎0541 69 48 39), and **Villa delle Rose** (V. Camilluccia, 33; www.villadellerose.net), and down another street to Cocorico (see below), **Peschio** (V. Sardegna, 1; ☎0541 60 42 07), and **Acquafan** (V. Pistoia, 13; ☎0541 60 30 50). **Cocorico**, V. Chietti, 44, looks like a suburban house with a white picket fence, but the four-floor parties here are far from the Tupperware variety. (☎0541 60 51 83. Cover €20, including 1 drink. Open F-Sa. Call for schedule.) In Miramare, **L'Altro Mondo Studio's**, V. Flaminia, 328, is off the beaten path but worth the effort. Strobes illuminate a huge floor lined with portals, sliding doors, and various steel platforms. A stylish, international crowd of all ages grooves to house and techno, pausing only for the laser show around midnight. (☎0541 37 31 51; www.altromondo.com. Cover about €25, €10 with discount. Open daily 11pm-4am, though closing time depends on the size of the crowd. Cash only.) Sophisticated **Byblo's Disco Dinner Club**, V. P. Castello, 24, in Misano, lures chic 20-somethings to its outdoor floor with a siren's song of house and Latin. (☎0541 69 02 52; www.byblosclub.com. Cover about €10. Open W and F-Su 9:30pm-6am.)

SAN MARINO ☎0549

The Most Serene Republic of San Marino was founded in AD 301 by Marinus, a pious stone-cutter, when a woman's unwanted attentions drove him to seek refuge on Mt. Titano. When the pagan son of the noblewoman who owned the mountain

EMILIA-ROMAGNA

tried to attack Marinus, God paralyzed him. His mother swore to convert to Christianity and to give Marinus and his followers her mountain if God restored her son. God agreed, and Marinus's mountain now hums with life as a heavily touristed independent republic—in proportion to its population, the 26-square-km country is the most visited in the world. Tax-free shopping, friendly locals, and monuments ranging from the seat of the Republic's modern Parliament to three towering castles composing its defensive structure keep visitors streaming in by the busload.

COUNTRY CODE	San Marino's country code is ☎378. It is only necessary to dial when calling from outside Italy. Within Italy and San Marino, just dial the city code, ☎0549.

TRANSPORTATION

The closest train station is in Rimini. **Fratelli Benedettini** (☎0549 90 38 54) and **Bonelli Bus** (☎0541 37 24 32) run from San Marino's center to Rimini's train station (50min., 12 per day 6:30am-7pm, €3.10). Arrive 15min. before departure. In town, a **funivia** (cableway) connects Borgo Maggiore to the *centro storico*. (☎0549 88 35 90. Every 15min. in summer 7:50am-8:30pm, in winter 7:50am-6:30pm; from July 26-Sept. 3, special hours from 7:50am-1am. €2.10, round-trip €3.10). **Taxis** (☎0549 99 14 41) are in P. Lo Stradone.

ORIENTATION AND PRACTICAL INFORMATION

To get from one monument to another, directional signs are easily the best bet—the city is difficult to navigate without wandering off once or twice. San Marino's streets wind around **Monte Titano.** From the bus, exit to the left, climb the staircase, and pass through the **Porta San Francesco** into P. P. Feretrano to begin the ascent. From the piazza, **Via Basilicus** leads to **Piazza Titano.** From there, hang a sharp right along the street to **Piazza Garibaldi.** From there, follow **Contrada del Collegio** to **Piazza della Libertà.** The **tourist office,** Contrada del Collegio, 40, stamps passports for €2.50. (☎0549 88 29 14; www.sanmarino2000.sm. Open M-F 8:30am-6:30pm and Sa-Su 9am-1:30pm and 2-6:30pm. Cash only.) San Marino mints coins interchangeable with the euro, though they're more collector's items than anything else. Pick them up, along with stamps and phone cards, at the **Coin and Stamp Office,** P. Garibaldi, 5. (☎0549 88 23 70. Open M 8:30am-1pm, Tu-Th 8:30am-5:30pm, F 8:30am-2pm, Sa-Su 9am-1pm and 2-6pm. MC/V.) In case of **emergency,** call ☎113, an **ambulance** (☎118), or the **police** (☎0549 88 88 88). The **post office** is at Viale Onofri, 87. (☎0549 88 29 09. Open M-F 8:30am-6pm, Sa 8:30am-noon. Cash only.)

ACCOMMODATIONS AND FOOD

Most of San Marino's affordable hotels are small, family-run affairs above adjoining restaurants—otherwise, the options are mostly ritzier four-star hotels, so book ahead to ensure a room. The **Diamond Hotel ❸,** Contrada del Collegio, 48, across from the Basilica di San Marino, offers six large rooms with bath, high ceiling, and ornate wooden furniture (and one with pink polka-dotted floors and a tub). The attached **restaurant ❹** serves large portions of pizzas and entrees. (☎/fax 0549 99 10 03. Open daily Mar.-Oct. 8:30am-10pm. Pizza €4.50-8. *Primi* €7-9, *secondi* €9-12. Breakfast included. Singles €35; doubles €55; triples €78. AmEx/MC/V.) At **Hotel La Rocca ❸,** Salita alla Rocca, 33, down the street from the castle, the hallways are a bit dim, but the ten rooms with TV and bath are spotless, and the staff is friendly. There's also a **restaurant ❸** downstairs. (☎0549 99 11 66, fax 99 24 30.

Pizza €3-9. *Primi* €5-8.50, *secondi* €5.50-15. Breakfast included. Singles €51; doubles €70; triples €92; quads €116. AmEx/MC/V.) The streets are overrun with bars and small restaurants offering *prix fixe menùs* for throngs of visitors.

Fresh produce is available at the small **market,** Contra Omereli, 2, just off P. Titano. (☎0549 99 16 13. Open June-Sept. M-Sa 8am-8pm, Su 9am-noon; Oct.-May M-Sa 8am-1pm and 3-7pm and Su 9am-noon. Cash only.) Find **supermarket** fare at Alimentari Chiaruzzi, Contra del Collegio, 13, between P. Titano and P. Garibaldi. (☎0549 99 12 22; daniloc@omniway.sm. Open daily Aug. 7am-midnight, Sept.-July 8am-7:30pm. Cash, traveler's checks, or US dollars only.) For a sizable sampler of regional pastas, try **Buca San Francesco ❷,** Francesco Piazzetta Placido Feretrano, 3, past the Pta. S. where the specialty is *Tris della Buca* (€7), a plate of ravioli, *tagliatelle,* and cheesy lasagna in a light ragu. (☎0549 99 14 62. *Primi* €4.50-7, *secondi* €6-7.50. *Piatto unico* with drinks and side dish €7.50-10. Bar open daily 9:30am-6:30pm, restaurant open daily noon-3pm. AmEx/MC/V.) To escape the packed streets, slip into the serene **Caffè del Titano ❶,** Piazzetta del Titano, 4. The gooey *brioche cioccolato* (€1.20) and rich cappuccino (€1.70) are without equal. (☎0549 99 24 73. Open daily 7:30am-10:30pm. Cash only.)

🔵 🎵 SIGHTS AND ENTERTAINMENT

The late 19th-century ◪**Palazzo Pubblico,** built atop the ruins of the *Domus Comunis Magna,* is the seat of San Marino's parliament. The marble interior features the *Sala del Consiglio* (Hall of the Council), where the city is still run amid allegorical lunettes of Justice (holding a broadsword) and Peace (whose single olive branch puts him at a slight disadvantage). The changing of the guard takes place in front of the palace from April to September at half past the hour from 8:30am to 6:30pm. Arrive 10min. early to secure a spot. (P. della Libertà. ☎0549 88 51 52. Open daily Apr.-Sept. 8am-8pm, Oct.-Mar. 9am-6pm. Tickets close 30min. before Palazzo. €3, €4.50 includes Museo San Francesco. Cash only.) Three points along San Marino's defensive network are open to the public, but poking along their in-between paths offers many of the same views and crumbling remnants without the fee. The first tower is the **Castello della Guaita,** an 11th-century structure carved out of the mountain. The tower once served as the principal defense bulwark of Mt. Titano and San Marino. (Follow signs from P. Libertà. ☎0549 99 13 69. Open daily Apr.-Sept. 8am-8pm, Oct.-Mar. 9am-5pm. Tickets close 30min. before castle. €3, combined with Castello della Cesta €4.50. MC/V.) Farther along the trail, the **Castello della Cesta** houses the **Museo delle Armi Antiche,** an arms museum with a rare telescoping sword that could be used on horseback and extended for foot battles. Die-hard castle lovers can follow the rustic trail outside to the third tower, **Torre del Montale,** a squat, mossy turret closed to the public. Nearby, stone outcroppings offer quiet views of the fields below, but little else. (☎0549 99 12 95. Open daily Apr.-Sept. 8am-8pm, Oct.-Mar. 9am-5pm. Tickets close 30min. before castle. €3, combined with Castello della Guaita €4.50. MC/V.) In the Museo della Tortura, browse over 100 torture toys, from the gruesome *schiacciatesta,* which screws down until the victim's brain squeezes out of a cracked skull, to the humiliating "Good for Nothing's Necklace," a chain laden with wooden cards and dice, worn by addicts through the streets. (Near P. S. Francesco, to the right after the main gate. ☎0549 99 12 15; www.museodellatortura.com. Open daily July-Aug. 9am-midnight, Sept.-May 10am-7pm. €6, students €4, groups of 10 or more €3. Family discount available. Cash only.)

In August and September, a **medieval festival** brings parades, food, musicians, and jugglers. The **Palio delle Balestre,** or crossbowman's show, also in early September, commemorates the establishment of the republic; increased bus service makes dropping in for the day easy. (For dates and info, call ☎0549 88 29 98.)

TUSCANY (TOSCANA)

Recently, Tuscany has been spotlighted in popular culture as a sun-soaked sanctuary of art, nature, and Italian culture. For once, popular culture has gotten it right. In Tuscany, every medieval town is home to a Renaissance master, every modern highway provides vistas of ancient hills, and each year, locals celebrate their illustrious culture with costumed parades, festivals, and galas. The region's concentration of art, architecture, and world-renowned wine and cuisine lures millions of tourists every summer. Tour groups shuffle from duomo to museum, clogging narrow medieval streets. As a result booking accommodations in advance is essential in high season. While it's nearly impossible to get completely off the beaten path, a little effort can still yield memorable personal moments. You don't need an art history degree to stroll through the silent sanctuary of a hidden 15th-century Romanesque church, to bike leisurely through the mesmerizing clay hills of the town of La Crete, or to take a shaded walk atop Lucca's *baluardi* (city walls). So go ahead and pose against the tower in Pisa, gaze open-mouthed at the Botticellis in the Uffizi, and loiter in Siena's Il Campo. Just remember that patience, good timing, and a bit of wanderlust can ensure an even richer experience.

HIGHLIGHTS OF TUSCANY

TRAIPSE the grounds of the original Etruscan settlement at Fiesole. (p. 424.)

DROWN in a wealth of high art at Florence's Uffizi Galleries. (p. 412.)

ROOT for your favorite *contrada* as horse and jockey teams race through Il Campo during **Siena's** famed Palio. (p. 432.)

TOUR the tallest towers in Tuscany, topped off by Pisa's Leaning Tower. (p. 464.)

FLORENCE (FIRENZE)

Florence is a wonder not just for its art, but for its mere existence. Ravaged by the Black Death, floods, famine, and war, it's perhaps surprising that this city, complete with a river contaminated by tannery chemicals and streets filled with animal carcasses, became so pivotal in the formation of the Western World. Nonetheless, Florence was already one of the largest cities in Europe by the 14th century. The imposing Palazzo Vecchio, still Florence's town hall, had been built; and Florentines Cimabue, Giotto, Boccaccio, and Dante had created the works that laid the foundation for the Renaissance. The city flourished in the 15th century, when, under the leadership of the brilliant and shrewd Cosimo de' Medici (or Cosimo the Elder), it became the most important center of artistic and intellectual achievement since the Classical era. The Medicis, who rose from middle-class origins to produce popes, queens, and powerful dukes, oversaw Florence's most prominent periods. With money to spare, the family supported the arts, amassing grand collections while nurturing the masters. Cosimo was patron to Donatello, Ghiberti, and Brunelleschi. His grandson, the charismatic Lorenzo the Magnificent, supported Botticelli and the young Michelangelo; Lorenzo's son, Pope Leo X, is known both for commissioning Raphael and excommunicating Martin Luther. Florence yielded "Renaissance men" in the arena of political thought as well. Machiavelli's *The Prince*, penned in an attempt to regain favor with the Medici clan when he was charged with conspiracy, praised their cold brutality and willingness to torture; his masterpiece is the source of the hardball political philosophy that the "ends justify the means."

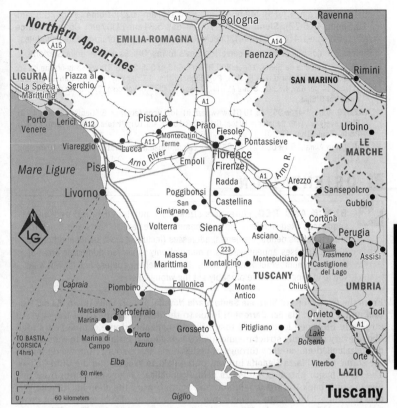

Tuscany

When the 1966 flooding of the Arno swamped Santa Croce and the Uffizi, Florentines and foreigners braved 6m of water to rescue the paintings, sculptures, and books yielded by this golden age. Today it is tourists who flood the city to wallow in its splendid art and perpetually fascinating history. Although the *centro storico* is surprisingly compact, Florence contains many days worth of sightseeing and learning.

✈ INTERCITY TRANSPORTATION

Flights: ☎055 306 15; www.aeroporto.firenze.it. In the suburb of Peretola. Mostly domestic and charter flights. The orange ATAF bus **#62** connects the train station to the airport (€1). Buy tickets from *tabacchi* on the upper level of the airport, departure side. **SITA,** V. S. Caterina da Siena, 157 (☎800 373 76 046 or 055 28 46 61), runs buses (€4) between the station and the airport. **Galileo Galilei Airport** (☎050 50 07 07), in **Pisa.** Take airport express from Florence train station (1¼hr., 10 per day, €4.85). In Florence, ask for info at the "air terminal" (☎055 21 60 73) halfway down platform **#5** in the train station. Open daily 7:30am-5pm.

Trains: Stazione Santa Maria Novella, just north of S. Maria Novella church. Info office open daily 7am-9pm; after hours call national train info ☎848 88 80 88. **Luggage storage** and lost property services available. Trains depart every hour to: **Bologna** (1hr.,

5:48am-1:47am, €7.75); **Milan** (3½hr., 6am-1:47am, €22); **Rome** (3½hr., 5:55am-10:55pm, €15-22); **Siena** (1½hr., 10 per day 5:31am-11:07pm, €5.30); **Venice** (3hr., 5:18am-1:47am, €15.94). Check out www.trenitalia.it for up-to-date schedules.

Buses: 3 major bus companies serve Tuscany's towns. Offices near P. della Stazione.

    SITA, V. S. Caterina da Siena, 15r (☎800 373 76 046 or 055 28 46 61; www.sita-on-line.it). To: **Arezzo** (2½hr., 3 per day, €64.10); **Poggibonsi** (1hr., 11 per day, €6.10); **San Gimignano** (1½hr., 14 per day, €7.60); **Siena** (1½hr., 2 per day, €5.90); **Volterra** (2hr., 6 per day, €14) via **Colle Val D'Elsa**.

    LAZZI, P. Adua, 1-4r (☎055 35 10 61; www.lazzi.it). To: **Lucca** (every hr. 6:50am-8:15pm, €4.70); **Pisa** (every hr., with transfer in Lucca; 6:10am-8:15pm, €6.10); **Pistoia** (6:50am-6pm, €2.70); **Prato** (6am-11pm, €2.20).

    CAP, Largo Alinari, 9 (☎055 21 46 37; www.capautolinee.it). To **Prato** (50min., 6:40am-8pm, €2.20).

ORIENTATION

> **BLACK AND RED.** Florence's streets are numbered in red and black sequences. Red numbers indicate commercial establishments and black (or blue) numbers denote residential addresses (including most sights and hotels). Black addresses appear here as a numeral only, while red addresses are indicated by a number followed by an "r." If you reach an address and it's not what you're looking for, you've probably got the wrong color.

From the front steps of **Stazione Santa Maria Novella**, a short walk down **Via dei Panzani** and a left on **Via dei Cerrentari** leads to the **duomo**, the heart of the city. All streets in Florence lead to this instantly recognizable dome, which soars high above every other city structure and makes being lost a little easier to remedy. **Via dei Calzaiuoli**, dominated by throngs of pedestrians, leads south from the duomo to the statue-filled **Piazza Signoria** in front of the **Palazzo Vecchio** and the **Uffizi Gallery**. The other major piazza is the **Piazza della Repubblica**. Major streets run from this piazza north back toward the duomo and south toward the shop-lined **Ponte Vecchio** (literally, "Old Bridge"). The Ponte Vecchio is one of five bridges that cross from central Florence to the **Oltrarno**, the district south of the **Arno River**. When navigating Florence, note that most streets change names unpredictably, often every few blocks. For guidance, grab a **free map** (one with a street index) from the tourist office across from the train station (see **Practical Information**).

LOCAL TRANSPORTATION

Public Transportation: Orange **ATAF** buses cover most of the city 6am to 1am. Buy tickets at any newsstand, *tabacchi*, or coin-operated ticket dispenser. €3.90 for 4 tickets; €1 per 1hr., €1.80 per 3hr., €4 per 24hr., €7.20 per 3 days, €12 per week. Validate ticket onboard using orange machine or risk €50 fine. Once validated, ticket allows unlimited bus travel for the allotted time. Tickets sold on bus 9am-6pm (€1.55). From the train station, ATAF info and ticket office (☎800 42 45 00; www.ataf.net) is on the left. Open M-F 7:15am-1:15pm and 1:45-7:45pm, Sa 7:15am-1:15pm. Free bus map. Bus **#7** to **Fiesole**, **#10** to **Settignano**, **#17** to **Villa Camerate** (€1).

Car Rental: Hertz, V. Finiguerra, 33 (☎055 239 82 05; www.hertz.com). 25+. Open M-F 8am-8pm, Sa 8am-7pm, Su 8am-1pm. **Maggiore** (☎055 31 12 56; www.maggiore.it), at airport. 19+. Open daily 8:30am-10:30pm. Also at V. Finiguerra, 11r (☎055 29 45 78). Open daily 8:30am-10:30pm. **Avis** (☎055 31 55 88; www.avis.com), at airport. 25+. Open 8am-7pm. Branch: also at Borgo Ognissanti, 128r (☎055 21 36 29). Open M-F 8am-7pm, Sa 8am-1pm.

Bike and Scooter Rental: Alinari Noleggi, V. Guelfa, 85r (☎055 28 05 00, fax 271 78 71), rents scooters for €30-60 per day; bikes €15-20 per day. Open M-Sa 9:30am-1pm and 3-7:30pm, Su and holidays 10am-1pm and 3-7pm. AmEx/MC/V. **Florence by Bike,** V. S. Zanobi, 120/122r (☎055 48 89 92; www.florencebybike.it), rents bikes (€3.70 per hr., €19-28 per day) and **scooters** (50-650cc, €30-95 per day). Bike rental includes helmet, water bottles, locks, spare tubes, pump, insurance, maps, and suggested itineraries. Reserve ahead. Open daily Mar.-Oct. 9am-7:30pm. AmEx/MC/V.

Parking: Most city center hotels don't offer parking. Small garages dot the city but keep unpredictable hours; look for a blue sign with a white 'P.' Lots at the train station and beneath P. della Libertà. Open 24hr.

Towed-Car Retrieval: Depositeria Comunale, V. dell'Arcovata, 6 (☎055 30 82 49). ATAF buses **#23** and **33** stop nearby.

Taxis: ☎055 43 90 or 47 98 or 42 42. Outside the train station.

▋ PRACTICAL INFORMATION

TOURIST AND FINANCIAL SERVICES

Tourist Offices: Informazione Turistica, P. della Stazione, 4 (☎055 21 22 45 or 238 12 26; turismo3@comune.fi.it), directly across the piazza from station's main exit. Info on cultural events, walking tour brochures, listings of hours for all sights in the city, and free **maps.** Ask for a map with street index. Open M-Sa 8:30am-7pm, Su and holidays 8:30am-2pm. **Branches:** V. Cavour, 1r (☎055 29 08 32 or 29 08 33); Borgo Santa Croce, 29r (☎055 234 04 44); V. Manzoni, 16 (☎055 233 20); airport (☎055 31 58 74). **Consorzio ITA** (☎055 28 28 93 and 21 95 37), in train station by track #16 next to pharmacy, offers help with finding accommodations. Lines can be long. €3-8.50 commission depending on the star rating of the hotel; not always the best value. Maps €0.50. Open M-Sa 8:30am-7:30pm, in winter M-Sa 8:30am-6:30pm.

Biking Tours: Florence by Bike, V. S. Zanobi, 120/122r (☎055 48 89 92; www.florencebybike.it), leads tours of historic Florence, the Chianti region, and Florentine hills (€23.24-60.43). Reserve ahead. Open daily 9am-7:30pm. **I Bike Italy** (☎055 234 23 71; www.ibikeitaly.com) offers 1- and 2-day bike tours and hikes of varying difficulty through Fiesole, Chianti, and Tuscan vineyards. Reserve ahead.

Budget Travel: CTS, V. dei Ginori, 25r (☎055 28 95 70), provides Transalpino tickets, discount airfares, car rentals, organized trips, and ISICs. Get there early and take a number. Open M-F 9:30am-1:30pm and 2:30-6pm, Sa 9:30am-12:30pm.

Consulates: UK, Lungarno Corsini, 2 (☎055 28 41 33). Open M-F 9:30am-12:30pm and 2:30-4:30pm. Can be reached by phone M-F 9am-1pm and 2-5pm. **US,** Lungarno Amerigo Vespucci, 38 (☎055 239 82 76), at V. Palestro, near the station. Open M-F 9am-12:30pm. For any consulate not listed, consult www.corpoconsolarefirenze.it.

Currency Exchange: Local banks offer the best exchange rates. Most open M-F 8:20am-1:20pm and 2:45-3:45pm. 24hr. **ATMs** all over the city.

American Express, V. Dante Alighieri, 22r (☎055 509 82 20; fes.florence@aexp.com). From duomo, walk down V. dei Calzaiuoli, turn left on V. dei Tavolini, and continue to the small piazza. Cashes personal checks for cardholders. Mail for cardholders and traveler's check customers at no cost; all others €1.55 per inquiry. €1.55 to leave messages. Open M-F 9am-5:30pm. Open only for financial services Sa 9am-12:30pm.

LOCAL SERVICES

Luggage Storage: In train station at track #16. €3 for 12hr. €2 each additional 12hr. for up to 90 days. Open daily 6am-midnight.

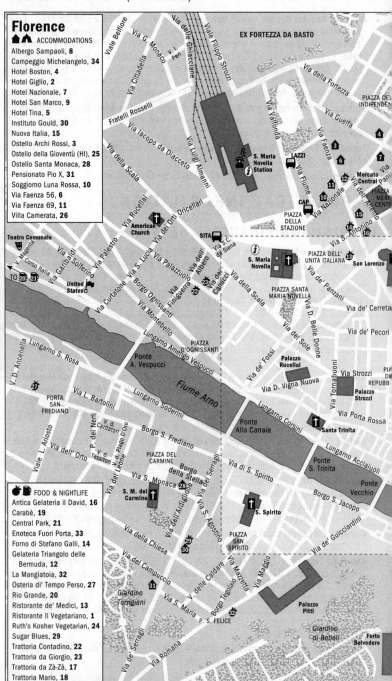

Florence

🏠🏠 ACCOMMODATIONS

Albergo Sampaoli, **8**
Campeggio Michelangelo, **34**
Hotel Boston, **4**
Hotel Giglio, **2**
Hotel Nazionale, **7**
Hotel San Marco, **9**
Hotel Tina, **5**
Instituto Gould, **30**
Nuova Italia, **15**
Ostello Archi Rossi, **3**
Ostello della Gioventù (HI), **25**
Ostello Santa Monaca, **28**
Pensionato Pio X, **31**
Soggiorno Luna Rossa, **10**
Via Faenza 56, **6**
Via Faenza 69, **11**
Villa Camerata, **26**

🍎🍸 FOOD & NIGHTLIFE

Antica Gelateria il David, **16**
Carabè, **19**
Central Park, **21**
Enoteca Fuori Porta, **33**
Forno di Stefano Galli, **14**
Gelateria Triangolo delle Bermuda, **12**
La Mangiatoia, **32**
Osteria di' Tempo Perso, **27**
Rio Grande, **20**
Ristorante de' Medici, **13**
Ristorante Il Vegetariano, **1**
Ruth's Kosher Vegetarian, **24**
Sugar Blues, **29**
Trattoria Contadino, **22**
Trattoria da Giorgio, **23**
Trattoria da Zà-Zà, **17**
Trattoria Mario, **18**

TUSCANY

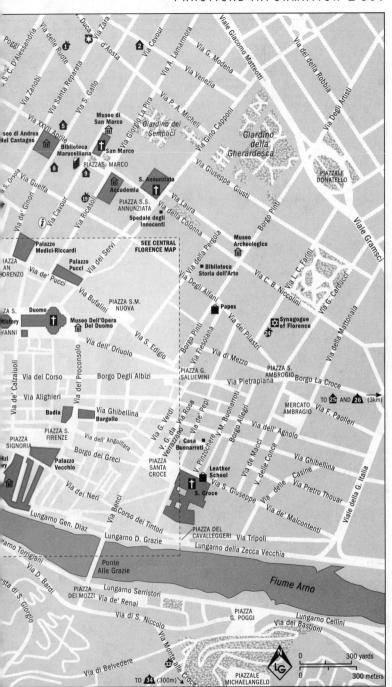

TUSCANY

TUSCANY

A   B   C

PIAZZA DELLA STAZIONE

Via del Canto

Via S. Antonio

Via Faenza

Via Amorino

PIAZZA
DELL' UNITA
ITALIA

PIAZZA MADONNA
ALDOBRANDINI

Basilica di
San Lorenzo

Via del Melarancio

Santa Maria
Novella

Via della Scala

V. Benedetta

Capello
dei Medici

Via de Panzani

Via del Giglio

Via de' Conti

Via F. Zannetti

Chiasso
del Armati

Via dell'Alloro

Via Palazzuolo

PIAZZA
S. MARIA
NOVELLA

Via dei Banchi

Via dei Cerretani

P. d. Olio

Via del
Trebbio

Via dei Rodinelli

V. Teatina

Via de' Vecchietti

V. Antinori

Via Degli Agli

Via de' Pecori

Via del Porcellana

Via delle Belle Donne

Via del Sole

PIAZZA
ANTINORI

V. d. Giacomini

Via dei Corsi

Via Campidoglio

Via

PIAZZA
OTTAVIANI

Via della Spada

Via de' Pescioni

Via Brunelleschi

0   100 yards
0   100 meters

Via dei Fossi

Via del Moro

V. d. Palchetti

Via de' Federighi

Via Strozzi

PIAZZA
DELL
REPUBE

Borgo Ognissanti

Lungarno Amerigo
Vespucci

BM Bookstore

PIAZZA
CARLO
GOLDINI

Via della Vigna Nuova

Palazzo Rucellai

Via del
Purgatorio

Via dell'Inferno

Palazzo
Strozzi

PIAZZA
STROZZI

Via de' Sassetti

Via d. Anselmi

Via d.

Via Pellicceria

Via

TO U.S.
EMBASSY

Via del Parione

Via dei Tornabuoni

PIAZZA
DAVANZATI

Via Pariontcino

Lungarno Corsini

Santa Trinità

PIAZZA SANTA
TRINITA

Via Porta Rossa

Palazzo
Davanzati

UNITED KINGDOM

Ponte Alla Carraia

Lungarno Guicciardini

Via Geppi

Via di San Spirito

Via delle Terme

Borgo S. S. Apostoli

Chiasso
Cornino

Nol

Via Maffia

PIAZZA
FRESCOBARDI

Lungarno Acciaiuoli

Gastronomia
Tassini

Via Por S. M.

Ponte S. Trinita

Fiume Arno

Via di Coverelli

Santo Spirito

PIAZZA
ANGOLIERI

Vaggi

Ponte Vecchio

Volta

Via del Presto di San Martino

Via del Vellutini

Via Toscanella

Via dello Sprone

Via de' Rumagliumi

Borgo San Jacopo

Via Barbadori

Via de' Bardi

Via Maggio

Via del Vellutti

Via Squazza

Via de' Guicciardini

T-Show

PIAZZA
D' FELICITA

Costa di San Giorgio

PIAZZA
SANTO SPIRITO

Michelozzi

TO PALAZZO PITTI (200m)

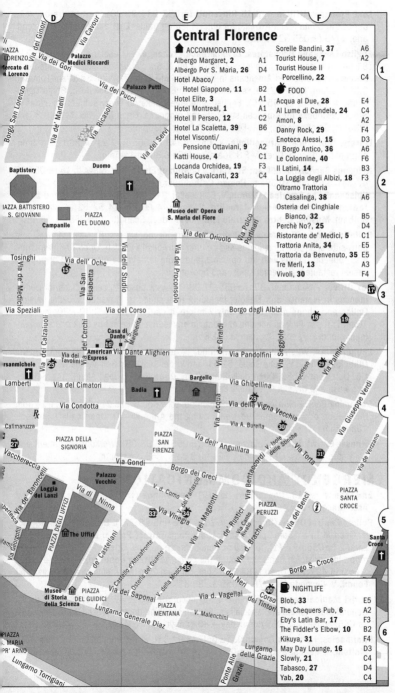

Central Florence

🏠 ACCOMMODATIONS

Albergo Margaret, **2**	A1	
Albergo Por S. Maria, **26**	D4	
Hotel Abaco/		
Hotel Giappone, **11**	B2	
Hotel Elite, **3**	A1	
Hotel Montreal, **1**	A1	
Hotel Il Perseo, **12**	C2	
Hotel La Scaletta, **39**	B6	
Hotel Visconti/		
Pensione Ottaviani, **9**	A2	
Katti House, **4**	C1	
Locanda Orchidea, **19**	F3	
Relais Cavalcanti, **23**	C4	

Sorelle Bandini, **37**	A6
Tourist House, **7**	A2
Tourist House II	
Porcellino, **22**	C4

🍴 FOOD

Acqua al Due, **28**	E4
Al Lume di Candela, **24**	C4
Amon, **8**	A2
Danny Rock, **29**	F4
Enoteca Alessi, **15**	D3
Il Borgo Antico, **36**	A6
Le Colonnine, **40**	F6
Il Latini, **14**	B3
La Loggia degli Albizi, **18**	F3
Oltrarno Trattoria	
Casalinga, **38**	A6
Osteria del Cinghiale	
Bianco, **32**	B5
Perchè No?, **25**	D4
Ristorante de' Medici, **5**	C1
Trattoria Anita, **34**	E5
Trattoria da Benvenuto, **35**	E5
Tre Merli, **13**	A3
Vivoli, **30**	F4

🌙 NIGHTLIFE

Blob, **33**	E5
The Chequers Pub, **6**	A2
Eby's Latin Bar, **17**	F3
The Fiddler's Elbow, **10**	B2
Kikuya, **31**	F4
May Day Lounge, **16**	D3
Slowly, **21**	C4
Tabasco, **27**	D4
Yab, **20**	C4

TUSCANY

TUSCANY

Lost Property: Ufficio Oggetti Rinvenuti (☎055 235 21 90), next to the baggage deposit in Santa Maria Novella, for objects left on trains. **Lost and Found,** V. Circondaria, 17/B (☎055 32 83 33).

English-Language Bookstores: ■**Paperback Exchange,** V. Fiesolana, 31r (☎055 247 81 54; www.papex.it). Take a book, leave a book. Special *Italianistica* section features novels about Brits and Americans in Italy. Open M-F 9am-7:30pm, Sa 10am-1pm and 3:30-7:30pm. Closed 2 weeks in mid-Aug. AmEx/MC/V. **BM Bookstore,** Borgo Ognissanti, 4r (☎055 29 45 75). English-language books on every subject imaginable. Stocks textbooks for American study-abroad programs. Open Mar.-Oct. M-Sa 9:30am-7:30pm, Su afternoons; Nov.-Feb. M-Sa 9:30am-7:30pm.

Library: Biblioteca Marucelliana, V. Cavour, 43 (☎055 272 21 or 260 62), 2min. north of the duomo. Open M-F 8:30am-7pm, Sa 8:30am-1:45pm.

Religious Services: Anglican: St. Mark's Church of England, V. Maggio, 16 (☎055 29 47 64). Su 9 and 10:30am. **Roman Catholic:** English service at the duomo Sa 5pm. **Episcopal: The American Church,** V. B. Rucellai, 9 (☎055 29 44 17). Su 9 and 11am. **Jewish (Orthodox): Tempio Israelito,** V. Farini, 4 (☎055 24 52 52). F sunset, Sa 8:45am. **Muslim: Centro Culturale Islamico,** P. degli Scarlatti, 1 (☎055 71 16 48).

Bulletin Boards: The American Church lists ads for roommates, English teachers, and baby-sitters, as well as religious and cultural activities in English. Open Tu-F 9am-1pm. Also, bulletin boards with job openings and room rentals are often found at popular casual restaurants, Internet cafes, and bookstores.

Box Office: V. Alamanni, 39r (☎055 21 08 04; www.boxol.it), sells tickets for performances in Florence and Fiesole, including rock concerts. Advance booking service. Online and phone reservations only with credit cards. Open M 3:30-7:30pm, Tu-Sa 10am-7:30pm. Pick up a listing of events in any tourist office or buy the city's entertainment monthly, *Firenze Spettacolo* (€1.85).

Laundromats: Wash and Dry Lavarapido, V. dei Servi, 105r, 2 blocks from duomo. Other locations at V. della Scala, 52-54r and V. del Sole, 29r. Self-service wash and dry €6. Detergent €0.80. Open daily 8am-10pm. **Onda Blu,** V. degli Alfani, 24r. Self-service wash and dry €6. Open daily 8am-10pm.

Swimming Pool: Bellariva, Lungarno Colombo, 6 (☎055 67 75 21). Take Bus **#14** from the station or walk 15min. upstream along the Arno. €6.50. Open daily June-Sept. 10am-6pm.

Fitness: Everfit SRL, V. Palazzuolo, 49r (☎055 29 33 08). Workout equipment and daily step aerobics. €11 per day, €24 for 3 days, €68 per month.

EMERGENCY AND COMMUNICATIONS

Emergency: ☎113. **Carabinieri** (☎112). **Ambulance** (☎118). **Fire** (☎115). **Road Assistance** (☎116).

Police: Central Office (Questura), V. Zara, 2 (☎055 49 771). **Branch:** P. del Duomo, 5. Open M-Th 8:15am-6pm, F-Sa 8:15am-2pm. **Tourist Police: Ufficio Stranieri,** V. Zara, 2 (☎055 497 71), for visa or work-permit problems. Open M-F 8:30am-noon. To report lost or stolen items, go around the corner to **Ufficio Denunce,** V. Duca d'Aosta, 3 (☎055 497 71). Open M-Sa 8am-8pm, Su 8am-2pm. Also, check out the **Lost and Found,** V. Circondaria, 17/B (☎055 32 83 33).

Tourist Medical Service: V. Lorenzo il Magnifico, 59 (☎055 47 54 11; medserv@tin.it). General practitioners and specialists. English-speaking doctors on-call 24hr. Office visits €45; house calls €65 during day, €80 at night. AmEx/MC/V.

Pharmacies: Farmacia Comunale (☎055 28 94 35), at the train station by track #16. **Molteni,** V. dei Calzaiuoli, 7r (☎055 28 94 90). Late-night rotation posted on window.

Internet: Walk down any busy street and an Internet cafe is sure to pop up. **Internet Train** has 15 locations in the city, all listed on www.internettrain.it. Offers telnet, email, and web-cruising. €4 per hr., students €3. Hours vary slightly depending on location. Most open M-F 9am-midnight, Sa 10am-8pm, Su noon-9pm. AmEx/MC/V. **Libreria Edison,** P. Repubblica, 27r, has a great atmosphere amid books and coffee upstairs. €3 per hr. Open daily 10am-8pm.

Post Office: ☎055 273 64 80. On V. Pellicceria, off P. della Repubblica. To send packages, go behind the building to V. dei Sassetti, 4. Open M-F 8:15am-7pm, Sa 8:15am-12:30pm. Telegram office in front open 24hr. **Postal Code:** 50100.

🗲 ACCOMMODATIONS

Because of the constant stream of tourists, it is best to reserve a room at least 10 days ahead, especially for visits during Easter or summer. Most *pensioni* prefer reservations in writing with at least one night's deposit in the form of a money order; others simply ask for a phone confirmation. Yet Florence has such a large number of budget accommodations that it is possible to find a room even without a reservation. The **Consorzio ITA** in the train station (see **Tourist and Financial Services**) provides info on available rooms and going rates on the one-star *pensioni* and private *affittacamere* that flood the city. Hotel owners are often willing to suggest alternatives if their establishments are full, so don't hesitate to ask. Complaints should be lodged with the **Ufficio Controllo Alberghi,** V. Cavour, 37 (☎055 276 01). The municipal government strictly regulates hotel prices, so proprietors must charge within the approved range for their category and must also post these rates in a place visible to guests. Rates uniformly increase around 10% every year, and new rates take effect in March or April. For **long-term housing** in Florence, check **bulletin boards** (p. 400), classified ads in *La Pulce,* published three times weekly (€2), or *Grillo Fiorentino,* a free monthly paper, for apartment, sublet, and roommate listings. Reasonable prices range €200-600 per month.

TUSCANY

TIP   **BOOSTER SHOT.** Each day at Stazione Santa Maria Novella, boosters assail unwitting travelers with offers of rooms at ridiculously cheap prices. These fly-by-night operations are illegal and best avoided. The police routinely evacuate illegal *pensioni* during the night, leaving bleary-eyed backpackers to fend for themselves in the wee hours of the morning. As they are unregulated by the government, they may also be dangerous. All legitimate hotels, hostels, campsites, and *affittacamere* in Tuscany are subject to annual government inspections and must post their official rating outside their establishment (from one to five stars). Look for the stars when securing accommodations. Better yet, just stick with us.

HOSTELS

 Ostello Archi Rossi, V. Faenza, 94r (☎055 29 08 04; ostelloarchirossi@hotmail.com), 2 blocks from the train station. Exit left from station on V. Nazionale. Take 2nd left onto V. Faenza. Look for *ostello* sign. Basic, busy place in easy location. Floor-to-ceiling murals, ceramic tiles, and brick archways. Courtyard patio and dining/TV room brimming with travelers. Home-cooked breakfast included; dinner €3.60-4.20. Laundry €5.20. Free Internet. Luggage storage. June-Sept. arrive before 8am, or earlier if in a large group to secure a bed because no reservations are accepted. Check-out 9:30am. Room lockout 9:30am-2:30pm; hostel lockout 11am-2:30pm. Curfew 2am. 9-bed dorms €18; 6-bed dorms €22; 3-5-bed dorms €23.50; private room for families €23.50. Single-night stay €20. Wheelchair accessible rooms €26. Slight discounts with cash payments. ❷

Instituto Gould, V. dei Serragli, 49 (☎055 21 25 76; gould.reception@dada.it), in Oltrarno. Take bus #36 or 37 from the station to the 2nd stop across the river. Beware—building is not well marked. Look for the signs of the larger Instituto Gould complex, then ring correct buzzer for the hostel. Spotless rooms, 88 beds, and a large colonnaded courtyard in a busy residential area. Reception M-F 9am-1pm and 3-7pm, Sa 9am-1pm. All rooms with multiple beds may be rented out dorm-style. Singles €30, with bath €35; doubles €44/€50; triples €56/€63; quads €72/€80. MC/V. ❸

Pensionato Pio X, V. dei Serragli, 106 (☎/fax 055 22 50 44), a few blocks beyond Instituto Gould. It's on the right—don't be fazed by construction in the courtyard. Rooms are nothing fancy but very clean and larger than average. 54 beds with 3-5 beds per room. Dark, co-ed shared bath; bring flip-flops. Check-out 9am. Curfew 12:30am. Reserve ahead in summer. Dorms €16, with bath €18. Cash only. ❷

Ostello della Gioventù Europa Villa Camerata (HI), V. Augusto Righi, 2-4 (☎055 60 14 51, fax 61 03 00), northeast of town. Take bus #17 outside train station (near track #5), or from P. dell'Unità across from station; ask for Salviatino stop. Walk 10min. up driveway, passing a vineyard. Tidy and popular, in a beautiful (if remote) villa with 322 beds and a *loggia* (roofed open-air arcade), bar, and TV room with English-language movies every night 9pm. 4, 6, or 8 beds per room. Breakfast and sheets included. Dinner €8.50. Self-service laundry €5.20. 3-night max. stay. Reception daily 7am-12:30pm and 1pm-midnight. Check-out 7-10am. Lockout 10am-2pm. Strict midnight curfew. Make reservation in writing. Dorms €16.50. €2.58 extra without HI card. ❷

Ostello Santa Monaca, V. S. Monaca, 6 (☎055 26 83 38; www.ostello.it). Follow directions to Instituto Gould, but turn right off V. dei Serragli on V. S. Monaca. 114 beds stacked into high-ceilinged rooms. Friendly management. Few kitchen facilities, so bring utensils. Sheets included. Self-service laundry €6.50 per 5kg. Internet €4 per hr. June-Sept. arrive before 9am. 7-night max. stay. Reception 6am-1pm and 2pm-1am. Lockout 9:30am-2pm. Curfew 1am. Hot water for showers 7-9am and 2-11pm. Reserve by email or fax 3 days ahead. 10-bed dorms €16. AmEx/MC/V. ❷

HOTELS

PIAZZA SANTA MARIA NOVELLA AND ENVIRONS

The budget accommodations that cluster around this piazza in front of the train station offer convenient access to the duomo and town center. What could be nicer than stepping out of a *pensione* to witness Alberti's masterful facade on Santa Maria Novella church? Ask for a room overlooking the train station piazza.

Hotel Abaco, V. dei Banchi, 1 (☎055 238 19 19; www.abaco-hotel.it). From train station, cross behind Santa Maria Novella. Walk past church into P. S. Maria Novella and turn left on V. dei Banchi. 7 beautiful rooms named after Renaissance greats, with reproduced 17th-century headboards, noise-proof windows, and prints of famous works. All rooms have phone and TV. Breakfast free when bill is paid in cash, €5 otherwise. Free Internet. A/C €5 extra. Laundry €7 per load. Parking €24/day. Singles €70; doubles €75, with bath €90. Extra bed €25. Discount with *Let's Go.* MC/V. ❺

Hotel Elite, V. della Scala, 12 (☎055 21 38 32, fax 21 53 95). Exit train station right on V. D. Orti Oricellari, which leads to V. della Scala; turn left. Friendly owner Nadia makes Uffizi and other reservations for guests. Cozy breakfast and sitting areas enhance these well-maintained rooms, all with TV, phone, and A/C. Quieter rooms in the back. Breakfast €6. Singles with shower €70, with toilet €80; doubles with bath €90; triples €110; quads €120. AmEx/MC/V. ❺

Soggiorno Luna Rossa, V. Nazionale, 7 (☎055 26 86 75). Exit train station left on V. Nazionale. Airy rooms with trim furnishings, TV, and fan, and colorful stained-glass windows. Small shared baths. Breakfast included. Singles €40; doubles €60; triples €75, with shower €90; quads with shower €100. AmEx/MC/V. ❸

Hotel Montreal, V. della Scala, 43 (☎055 238 23 31; www.hotelmontreal.com). Follow directions to Hotel Elite. 22 tasteful, wood-furnished rooms with phone, TV, and A/C. Breakfast €5. Flexible curfew 1:30am. Singles €55, with bath €70; doubles €65/€75; triples €85/€105; quads €120. Cash only. ❸

Hotel Giappone, V. dei Banchi, 1 (☎055 21 00 90; www.hotelgiappone.com). Follow directions to Hotel Abaco. 10 refined rooms sport large beds, phone, TV, A/C, and Internet jacks. Immaculate shared bath. Singles €50, with shower €55, with full bath €60; doubles €72/€85. Extra bed €26. MC/V. ❹

Albergo Margaret, V. della Scala, 25 (☎055 21 01 38; www.dormireintoscana.it/margaret). Follow directions to Hotel Elite. 7 rooms decked in red linens and puffy orange quilts. Rooms have TV and A/C. Curfew midnight. June-Aug. singles €60; doubles with shower €70, with full bath €90. Discounts Sept.-May and for longer stays. Cash only. ❺

Tourist House, V. della Scala, 1 (☎055 26 86 75; www.touristhouse.com), very near P. S. Maria Novella; see directions to Hotel Elite. Extremely friendly proprietors also run Hotel Giappone. Enormous, comfortable rooms with bath, TV, and fan, some with A/C. Breakfast included. Singles €67; doubles €85; quads €125. AmEx/MC/V. ❻

Pensione Ottaviani, P. Ottaviani, 1 (☎055 23 962, fax 29 33 55), above Hotel Visconti. Simple rooms, sunny dining area, and amiable reception. No A/C, but ceiling fans in most rooms. Internet €3 per hr. Breakfast included. Singles €40, with bath €50; doubles with shower €60, with bath €70. Extra bed €25. Cash only. ❸

Hotel Visconti, P. Ottaviani, 1 (☎/fax 055 21 38 77). Exit train station and cross straight to the back of Santa Maria Novella. Walk around church into P. S. Maria Novella, then across the left side of the piazza until reaching the tiny P. Ottaviani. 10 rooms, polished shared baths, bar, and TV lounge. Breakfast included. Miniscule singles €40; doubles €60, with bath €90; triples €80/€100; quads €90. Cash or traveler's checks. ❸

OLD CITY (NEAR THE DUOMO)

Closest to Florence's premiere monuments, this area is also the most expensive. Follow V. dei Panzani from the train station and turn left on V. dei Cerretani to reach the duomo.

▩ Hotel Il Perseo, V. dei Cerretani, 1 (☎055 21 25 04; www.hotelperseo.com). Exit the train station and take V. dei Panzani, which becomes V. dei Cerretani. Aussie-Italian couple and English-speaking staff welcome travelers to 19 bright rooms and large, gleaming baths. All have fans; some have breathtaking views of the duomo and the city center. Cozy bar and TV lounge decorated with proprietor's art. Breakfast included. Internet €1.50 for 15min. Parking €15.50 per day. Singles €55; doubles €75, with bath €95; triples €100/€125; quads €120/€145. MC/V. ❹

Tourist House Il Porcellino, P. del Mercato Nuovo, 4 (055 21 85 72; www.hotelporcellino.com), on the western side of Mercato Nuovo. In one of oldest buildings in Florence, this recently renovated hotel boasts 2 singles and 6 doubles full of character. All rooms with wrought-iron beds, handpainted furniture, bath, TV and phone. 3 rooms with A/C. Pay for portion of stay in advance. Singles €52-68; doubles €78-93. AmEx/MC/V. ❹

Relais Cavalcanti, V. Pellicceria, 2 (☎055 21 09 62; www.relaiscavalcanti.com), steps from P. della Repubblica. Warm mother-daughter owners Anna and Francesca welcome guests to gold-trimmed rooms with antique wardrobes. Look for the cookie jar in the shared kitchen. All rooms have bath, A/C, phone, satellite TV, and fridge. Free luggage storage. Check-out 11am. Singles range from €70-100; doubles from €95-125, with view €120; triples from €120-155. Ask for *Let's Go* discount. MC/V. ❺

Albergo Por S. Maria, V. Calimaruzza, 3 (☎055 21 63 70), between the Uffizi and P. della Repubblica. Bubbly proprietor's airy rooms come with A/C, phone, shower, and vistas of the Ponte Vecchio or P. Signoria. Small shared baths. Singles €55; doubles €85, with bath €95. Cash only. ❹

Locanda Orchidea, Borgo degli Albizi, 11 (☎055 248 03 46; hotelorchidea@yahoo.it). Turn left off V. Proconsolo from the duomo. Dante's wife was born in this 12th-century palazzo, built around a still-intact tower. 7 graceful rooms with marble floors, some opening onto a garden. Friendly and helpful English-speaking management. Book exchange. Shared baths, some rooms with shower. Singles €55; doubles €75; triples with shower €100; quads €120. Cash only. ❹

VIA NAZIONALE AND ENVIRONS

From P. della Stazione, V. Nazionale leads to budget hotels that are a short walk from both the duomo and the train station. The buildings on V. Nazionale, V. Faenza, V. Fiume, and V. Guelfa are filled with inexpensive establishments, but rooms facing the street may be noisy due to throngs of pedestrians.

▨ **Katti House,** V. Faenza, 21 (☎/fax 055 21 34 10; www.kattihouse.com). From the train station, take V. Nazionale for 1 block and turn right on V. Faenza. A jewel among Florentine travel lodgings, it's been lovingly renovated to feature hand-made drapes and 400-year-old antiques. Attentive staff. Large rooms have A/C, TV, and bath. Singles €60; doubles €80; triples and quads €105. Prices drop significantly Nov.-Mar. MC/V. ❺

Hotel Nazionale, V. Nazionale, 22 (☎055 238 22 03; www.nazionalehotel.it). From train station, turn left on V. Nazionale. 9 sunny and spacious rooms, newly renovated in the winter of 2004, all with comfy bed, bath, and A/C. Breakfast served in bed 8-9:30am for €6. Singles €47, with bath €57; doubles €72/€88; triples €97/€110. MC/V. ❹

Via Faenza, 56. These 5 *pensioni*, all with the same amenities, are among the best deals in the city. Same directions as Katti House.

Pensione Azzi (☎055 21 38 06; www.hotelazzi.com), styles itself as a *locanda degli artisti* (an artists' inn) with stylish prints on the walls. But all travelers, not just bohemians, will appreciate the friendly management, 12 large rooms, and relaxing terrace. Wheelchair accessible. Breakfast included. Singles €60, with bath €80; doubles €80/€90. Extra bed €25. AmEx/MC/V. ❺

Locanda Paola (☎055 21 36 82). 7 minimalist rooms, some with views of Fiesole and surrounding hills. Breakfast included. Flexible 2am curfew. Doubles €65, with bathroom €110. Extra bed €25. Cash only. ❹

Albergo Merlini (☎055 21 28 48; www.hotelmerlini.it). Murals and red geraniums freshen the solarium. Some rooms have views of the duomo. Breakfast €5. Internet €5 per hr. Flexible 1am curfew. Doubles €75, with bath €90; triples €105; quads €115. MC/V. ❺

Albergo Marini (☎055 28 48 24). Welcoming and liveable, with a wood corridor leading to 10 inviting rooms. The #7 double has a large terrace. Breakfast €5.16. Flexible 1am curfew. Singles €48, with bath €75; doubles €65/€96; triples €86/€117. Extra bed €21. Payment required in advance. MC/V. ❹

Albergo Armonia (☎055 21 11 46). Posters of American films adorn 7 basic rooms with high ceilings and wooden beds. Shared baths. Singles €42; doubles €66; triples €90; quads €100. Prices drop 25% in winter. ❹

Via Faenza, 69. 2 comfortable, no-frills accommodations under the same roof:

Hotel Nella/Pina, 1st and 2nd fl. (☎055 265 43 46; www.hotelnella.net). 14 basic rooms with wood paneling and comfy blue bedspreads at good prices, with free Internet. Nella rooms have A/C, phone, and satellite TV. Nella: singles €55, with bath €60; doubles €85. Extra bed €20. Pina: singles €47; doubles €62. Ask for Let's Go discount (10%). AmEx/MC/V. ❹

Locanda Giovanna (☎/fax 055 238 13 53). 7 fair-sized, well-kept rooms, some with garden views, top floor of building. Singles €40; doubles €60, with bath €70; triples €80/€85. ❸

Hotel Boston, V. Guelfa, 68 (☎055 47 03 84, fax 47 09 34). Exposed wood-beam ceilings and intricate tiled floors spruce up 14 comfortable rooms, all with A/C, TV, and phone. Enjoy breakfast in the beautiful Old World dining room or on the patio garden. Singles €60, with bath €100; doubles €150. ❺

Nuova Italia, V. Faenza, 26 (☎055 26 84 30). Prints and posters crowd the lobby. 2-star rooms have lots of light from large windows and beds, A/C, phone, and TV. Breakfast included. Singles €99; doubles €133; triples €153; quads €173. AmEx/MC/V. ❺

NEAR PIAZZA SAN MARCO AND THE UNIVERSITY

This area is calmer than its proximity to the center and university suggests. All accommodations listed are within a few blocks of the delicate beauty of the infrequently touristed Chiesa di San Marco. To reach this neighborhood, exit the train station and turn left on V. Nazionale. Then turn right on V. Guelfa, which intersects V. S. Gallo and V. Cavour.

Hotel Giglio, V. Cavour, 85 (☎055 48 66 21; www.hotelgiglio.it). With a fantastic staff and veritable overflow of luxuries—hard-wood floors, embroidered drapes, ornate furnishings, fluffy towels—Giglio doesn't miss a beat. All rooms have bath, A/C, TV, and phone. Internet available for €3 per hr. Breakfast included. Singles €65-90; doubles €85-130; triples €105-150; quads €120-170. Discount with Let's Go. AmEx/MC/V. ❺

Albergo Sampaoli, V. S. Gallo, 14 (☎055 28 48 34; www.hotelsampaoli.it). The large common area has handsome wooden furniture, and all rooms have fan and hair dryers; some have balcony. Refrigerator available. Free Internet (30min.). Singles €48, with bath €60; doubles €65/€84; triples €110; quads €140. AmEx/MC/V. ❹

Hotel Tina, V. S. Gallo, 31 (☎055 48 35 19, fax 48 35 93). Small pensione with blue carpets, decorated walls, and bright, voluminous bedspreads. Cozy sitting room stocks the Herald Tribune and other international magazines. 18 rooms with A/C and phone. Larger shared baths upstairs. Singles €44; doubles with shower €65, with bath €75; triples €83/€95; quads with shower €103. MC/V, but cash preferred. ❹

Hotel San Marco, V. Cavour, 50 (☎055 28 18 51; san_marco@inwind.it). 2 floors hold airy basic rooms. Call ahead to reserve the spacious double with balcony on the top floor. Prices vary seasonally; get a confirmation in writing. Singles €45, with bath €55; doubles €60/€75; triples €105. MC/V. ❹

IN THE OLTRARNO

Across the Arno and only 10min. from the duomo, this area offers a respite from the bustling centro. From Chiesa di San Spirito to Palazzo Pitti to the Boboli gardens, there are enough sites nearby to make this an attractive location.

Hotel La Scaletta, V. Guicciardini, 13/B (☎055 28 30 28; www.lascaletta.com). Cross the Ponte Vecchio and continue on V. Guicciardini. 13 gorgeous rooms filled with antique furniture and connected by stairways and alcoves. Most rooms have A/C. Rooftop terrace with spectacular view of Boboli Gardens. Breakfast included. Singles €51, with bath €100; doubles €120, with bath €140, with garden view €130. Extra bed €25-30. 10% Let's Go discount with cash payment. MC/V. ❹

Sorelle Bandini, P. Santo Spirito, 9 (☎055 21 53 08, fax 28 27 61; pensionebandini@tiscali.it). From Ponte S. Trinità, continue down V. Maggio and take 3rd right into P. S. Spirito. 12 rooms on top 2 floors of a 500-year-old palazzo. Wrap-around loggia overlooks the Oltrarno. Heavy wooden furniture fills spacious rooms that show their age. Breakfast €8. Singles €96; doubles €112, with bath €130; triples €148/€178. ❺

CAMPING

Campeggio Michelangelo, V. Michelangelo, 80 (☎055 681 19 77; www.ecvacanze.it), beyond Piazzale Michelangelo. Take bus #13 from the station (15min., last bus 11:25pm). Very crowded, but it offers a distant vista of the city and a chance to doze under olive trees. Alimentari, Internet (€7.50 per hr.), laundry (€8), towels (€1), bedsheets (€3), and bar available for use. Reception daily 6am-midnight. Apr.-Nov. tent rental €10.50. €9.50 per person, €6 per tent, €5 per car, €4.40 per motorcycle. MC/V accepted with €100 min. ❶

Villa Camerata, V. A. Righi, 2-4 (☎055 60 03 15, fax 61 03 00). Take bus #17 outside train station (near track #5), or from P. dell'Unità across from station; ask driver for Salviatino stop. Walk 10min. down driveway from street, passing a vineyard. Same

TUSCANY

reception and same entrance as HI hostel (p. 402). Breakfast at hostel €2. Reception daily 7am-12:30pm and 1pm-midnight; if closed, stake out a site and return during open hours to register and pay. 6-night max. stay. Check-out 7-10am. €6 per person, €4.80 with camping card; €5-€10.50 per tent. Bungalows €50. €10.50 per car. ●

◼ FOOD

Florentine cuisine developed from the peasant fare of the surrounding country-side. Characterized by rustic dishes created with fresh ingredients and simple preparations, Tuscan food ranks among Italy's best. White beans and olive oil are two staple ingredients. A famous specialty is *bruschetta*, toasted bread doused with olive oil and garlic, usually topped with tomatoes, basil, and anchovy or liver paste. For *primi*, Florentines favor the Tuscan classics *minestra di fagioli* (a delicious white bean and garlic soup) and *ribollita* (a hearty bean, bread, and black cabbage stew). Florence's classic *secondo* is *bistecca alla Fiorentina* (thick sirloin steak); locals order it *al sangue* (very rare; literally "bloody"), though it's also available *al puntito* (medium) or *ben cotto* (well-done). The best local cheese is *pecorino*, made from sheep's milk. A liter of house wine costs €3.50-6 in a trattoria; stores sell bottles for as little as €2.50. Avoid ordering sodas at restaurants; they usually more than €3 for a can, though often prices are not marked on menus. The local dessert is *cantuccini di prato* (hard almond cookies with many egg yolks) dipped in *vinsanto* (a rich dessert wine made from raisins).

Quick and satisfying meals are everywhere—visit a *rosticceria*, *gastronomia*, or pizzeria, or stop by the students' **Mensa ❷**, V. dei Servi, 52, where a filling meal costs €8.50. (Open M-Sa noon-2:15pm and 6:45-9pm. Closed mid-July to Aug.) Buy fresh produce or stock up on tripe at the **Mercato Centrale,** between V. Nazionale and S. Lorenzo. (Open June-Sept. M-Sa 7:30am-2pm; Oct.-May Sa 7am-2pm and 4-8pm.) For basics, head to the **STANDA,** V. Pietrapiana, 1r. Turn right on V. del Proconsolo and the first left on Borgo degli Albizi. Continue straight through P. G. Salvemini; the supermarket is on the left. (Open M-Sa 8am-9pm, Su 9:30am-1:30pm and 3:30-6:30pm.) From behind the duomo, turn right on V. del Proconsolo and left on Borgo degli Albizi. Head two blocks down and look right to find **La Loggia degli Albizi ❶,** Borgo degli Albizi, 39r. A hidden treasure, this bakery and *caffè* offers an escape from the tourist throng. (☎055 247 95 74. Pastries from €0.80. Coffee from €0.80. Open M-Sa 7am-8pm.) Several health-food markets cater to vegetarians. The two best are named after the American book **Sugar Blues.** One is a 5min. walk from the duomo up V. de Martelli (which turns into V. Cavour) at V. XXVII Aprile, 46r. (☎055 48 36 66. Open M-F 9am-1:30pm and 5-7:30pm, Sa 9am-1:30pm.) The other is next to the Instituto Gould (see **Accommodations: Hostels**), in the Oltrarno at V. dei Serragli, 57r. (☎055 26 83 78. Open M-Tu, Th-F, and Su 9am-1:30pm and 5-8pm, W and Sa 9am-1:30pm.) Also try **La Raccolta,** V. Leopardi, 2r. (☎055 247 90 68. Open daily 8:30am-7:30pm.) **Ruth's Kosher Vegetarian ❷,** V. Farini, 2, serves kosher fare on the second floor of the building that is to the right of the synagogue. (☎055 248 08 88; kosherruth@katamail.com. Open M-Th and Su 12:30-2:30pm and 8-10:30pm.) The **Centro Culturale Islamico** (p. 400) provides info on halal vendors.

OLD CITY (NEAR THE DUOMO)

▧ **Acqua al Due,** V. della Vigna Vecchia, 40r (☎055 28 41 70), behind the Bargello. Florentine specialties in a snug, air-conditioned place popular with young Italians and foreigners. The *assaggio* (a selection of 5 pastas; €8) and *filetto al mirtillo* (steak in a blueberry sauce, €11.03) demand a taste. Excellent salads from €5. *Primi* around €7, *secondi* €7-19. Cover €1.03. Service 10%. Reservation strongly recommended. Open daily 7pm-1am. AmEx/MC/V. ❸

Al Lume di Candela, V. delle Terme, 23r (☎055 265 65 61), halfway between P. S. Trinità and P. della Signoria. Candlelit meals showcasing unique interpretations of Tuscan and Venetian favorites, served on golden platters. Try the fabulous *anatra ai frutti di bosco* (duck in wild berry sauce; €11.90). Service might be too slow for those on the go, but this is food to be savored. *Primi* €6.90-9.20, *secondi* with *contorni* €7.60-13.20. Open M-Sa noon-2:30pm and 6:30-11pm. AmEx/MC/V. ❸

Trattoria Anita, V. del Parlascio, 2r (☎055 21 86 98), behind the Bargello. Traditionally Tuscan, both in design—wooden shelves, aged wines near the ceiling—and cuisine. Fare includes filling pastas and an array of meat dishes from roast chicken to bistecca alla Fiorentina. Clientele is frequently young and American, but don't worry, you can puzzle out the menu together. *Primi* €4.70-5.20, *secondi* from €5.20. Fantastic lunch menù €5.50. Cover €1. Open M-Sa noon-2:30pm and 7-10pm. AmEx/MC/V. ❷

Danny Rock, V. dei Pandolfini, 13r (☎055 234 03 07), 3 blocks northwest of the Bargello. Casual pizzeria favored by locals with outdoor patio and large dining room. Check the specials, as they often feature toppings from different Italian regions. Pizzas from €4. Open daily 12:30-3pm and 7:30pm-1am. MC/V. ❷

Le Colonnine, V. dei Benci, 6r (☎055 23 46 47), near Ponte alle Grazie. The lighter fare and casual ambiance are pleasant, but for a real treat, conquer a skillet of *paella* (serves 2; €18) with a friend on the outdoor patio. Pizza from €4.70. *Primi* €6, *secondi* from €7. Pizza from €5. Open daily noon-3:30pm and 6:30pm-midnight. MC/V. ❷

Trattoria da Benvenuto, V. della Mosca, 16r (☎055 21 48 33). Pastel decor in a cool and quiet setting make for comfortable dining and a reprieve from the bustle. *Ribollita* only €5. *Primi* €4.50-8.50, *secondi* €6-13. Set dinner *menù* €12.50. Cover €1.50. Service 10%. Open M-Sa noon-2:30pm and 7-10:30pm. AmEx/MC/V. ❸

SANTA MARIA NOVELLA AND ENVIRONS

Trattoria Contadino, V. Palazzuolo, 71r (☎055 238 26 73). Casual, home-style meals. Only offers a fixed *menù* (€9.50); this is no *menù turistico*, though, but the real deal, including *primo, secondo*, bread, and 0.25L of house wine served to an almost exclusively Italian crowd. Airy dining room has classy black and white decor. Open M-Sa 11am-2:30pm and 7-9:30pm. Closed June-July Sa. AmEx/MC/V. ❷

Tre Merli, V. del Moro, 11r (☎055 28 70 62). Another entrance on V. de' Fossi, 12r. In a dining room with cushioned banquettes, matching ceramic tableware, and soft red light, settle down for a sumptuous meal. Talented young chef prepares tender, delicious dishes like *spaghettino all'Imperiale* (with mussels, clams, and shrimp; €13.50). Delightful owner Massimo welcomes *Let's Go* readers with a free glass of wine and 10% discount. *Primi* €7.50-13.50, *secondi* €12-18.50. Lunch *menù* €12. Cover €2. Open daily 11am-11pm. AmEx/MC/V. ❸

Il Latini, V. dei Palchetti, 6r (☎055 21 09 16; www.illatini.com). From Ponte alla Carraia, walk up V. del Moro; V. dei Palchetti is on the right. Convivial spirit pervades at this old favorite, with long wooden tables and solid Tuscan classics. *Bistecca alla Fiorentina* (€16) is a crowd-pleaser. Waiters keep the house wine flowing. *Primi* €6-8, *secondi* €10-18. Open Tu-Su 12:30-2:30pm and 7:30-10:30pm. AmEx/MC/V. ❸

Amon, V. Palazzuolo, 28r (☎055 29 31 46), look for the blue and white sign. Cheerful Egyptian owner cooks his own bread and serves scrumptious Middle Eastern food. Try *mousaka* (baked eggplant-filled pita) or *foul* (seasoned beans). The falafel is spicy and tasty. Stand-up or takeout. Falafel €2.60-3.20. Shish kebab €3.10. Open Tu-Su noon-3pm and 6-11pm. Cash only. ❶

Trattoria da Giorgio, V. Palazzuolo, 100r (☎055 28 43 02). Dark and cool dining room is always crowded for lunch and dinner. *Primo, secondo*, bread, water, and house wine included in fixed *menù* for lunch and dinner, both €9.50. Expect a wait. Open M-Sa noon-3:30pm and 7pm-12:30am. AmEx/MC/V. ❷

TUSCANY

THE STATION AND UNIVERSITY QUARTER

■ **Trattoria da Zà-Zà,** P. del Mercato Centrale, 26r (☎055 21 54 11). Wooden ceilings, brick arches, and wine racks cover host Italians and foreigners. Try the *tris* (bean and vegetable soup; €6) or the *tagliata di manzo* (cut of beef; €12-15.50). Cover €1.55. Reservation recommended. Open M-Sa noon-3pm and 7-11pm. AmEx/MC/V. ❹

■ **Trattoria Mario,** V. Rosina, 2r (☎055 21 85 50), around the corner from P. del Mercato Centrale. Informal lunch establishment with incredible pasta, cheap eats, and rabid following of Florentines and foreigners in the know. *Primi* menu offers a variety of traditional Tuscan soups from €3.10-3.40, *secondi* €3.10-10.50. Cover €0.50. Open M-Sa noon-3:30pm. Closed most of Aug. Cash only. ❷

Ristorante Il Vegetariano, V. delle Ruote, 30r (☎055 47 50 30), off V. S. Gallo. True to its name, this self-service restaurant nimbly fills the vegetarian niche, offering fresh dishes like *risotto al pesto* (€4.65) in a peaceful bamboo garden or indoor dining rooms. Smoke-free room available. Salads €4-5. *Primi* from €5, *secondi* from €6. Open Sept.-July Tu-F 12:30-3pm and 7:30pm-midnight, Sa-Su 7pm-midnight. Cash only. ❷

Ristorante de' Medici, V. del Melarancio, 10r (☎055 29 52 92), 1 block off P. dell'Unità Italia. Pink tablecloths and Medici portraits. Foreigners are the norm instead of the once almost exclusively Italian clientele. Good calzoni (€7) and pizza (€4-8). *Primi* €4-6, *secondi* €5-21. Cover €2. Open daily 12:30-11pm. AmEx/MC/V. ❷

Forno di Stefano Galli, V. Faenza, 39r (☎055 21 53 14). Wide variety of fresh breads and attractive pastries. Adorable small tarts (€.40) topped with fruits and custard. Pastries €80-2.50. Loaves of bread from €1. Open 7:30am-4:30am. Cash only. **Branches:** V. delle Panche, 91, and V. Bufalini, 31-35r. ❶

THE OLTRARNO

■ **Il Borgo Antico,** P. S. Spirito, 6r (☎055 21 04 37). Memorable pastas and fantastic salads (€6) come with ingredients like shrimp, avocado, and fresh mozzarella. *Primi* €7, *secondi* €10-20. Pizzas €7. Cover €2. Reservation recommended. Open June-Sept. daily 1pm-12:30am; Oct.-May 12:45-2:30pm and 7:45pm-1am. AmEx/MC/V. ❹

■ **La Mangiatoia,** P. S. Felice, 8r (☎055 22 40 60). Cross Ponte Vecchio, continue on V. Guicciardini, and pass Palazzo Pitti. Grab a table in the back dining room, or sit at the stone counter to watch the cooks baking pizza in a brick oven. Satisfying pasta and quality local fare. Pizza €4-6.50. *Primi* €3.50-5.50, *secondi* €4-7.50. Cover €1.50. Open Tu-Su 11am-3pm and 6:30-10pm. AmEx/MC/V. ❷

Osteria di' Tempo Perso, V. Pisana, 16r (☎055 22 31 45). Cross Ponte Alla Carraia; turn right on Borgo S. Frediano and exit through Pta. S. Frediano. Enthusiastic owner of this grapevine-canopied garden knows his seafood. Great deals on rotating daily *menù* for €9.50. *Primi* €6.50-7, *secondi* €7.50-15. Cover €1.50. AmEx/MC/V. ❸

Oltrarno Trattoria Casalinga, V. Michelozzi, 9r (☎055 21 86 24), near P. S. Spirito. Basic Tuscan dishes and specialties. Popular with families. Good quality for the price. Try the *ravioli al sugo a coniglio* (ravioli with ham, sausage, and sauce; €11.50.) *Primi* €4-6, *secondi* €5-9. Cover €1.50. Open M-Sa noon-2:30pm and 7-10pm. MC/V. ❸

Osteria del Cinghiale Bianco, Borgo Jacopo, 43r (☎055 21 57 06; www.cinghialebianco.it). Candles, wooden lofts, mounted boars. Impressively fresh game-heavy menu in hunting season Sept.-Apr. *Primi* €7-9, *secondi* €9-15. Reservation recommended. Open M-Tu and Th-F 6:30-11:30pm, Sa-Su noon-3pm and 6:30-11:30pm. MC/V. ❹

GELATERIE

■ **Vivoli,** V. Isole delle Stinche, 7 (☎055 29 23 34), behind the Bargello. The household name of Florentine gelaterias, Vivoli is a long-standing contender for the best ice cream in Italy. Pint-sized interior with huge selection, including unusual fruit flavors and heavenly chocolate mousse. Pay first and order with receipt. Cups from €1.50. Open Tu-Sa 7:30am-1am, Su 9:30am-1am. AmEx/MC/V. ❶

Gelateria Triangolo delle Bermuda, V. Nazionale, 61r (☎055 28 74 90). Gelato so good, you'll never want to escape. *Crema venusiana*, a blend of hazelnut, caramel, and merengue, is absolute bliss; so are strawberry and rose sorbets. Plus, the sweet, wafery cones are well above average. Outdoor seating area on busy V. Nazionale is a great spot for people-watching, but watch out for the extra charge for sitting at the table. Cones from €1.60. Open daily 11am-midnight. ●

Antica Gelateria il David, V. San Antonino, 28r (☎055 21 86 45), off V. Faenza. This hidden gem is short on variety but long on quality. Hand-crafted, pure flavors and large scoops at low prices. Cones from €1.60. Open M-Sa 11am-midnight. ●

Perchè No?, V. Tavolini, 19r (☎055 239 89 69), off V. dei Calzaiuoli. Why not, indeed! This centrally located parlor keeps 2 counters filled with excellent flavors: coffee crunch, mouth-watering chocolate, and chunky *nocciolosa*. Pay first, then order. Cones €2. Open Apr.-Oct. daily 11am-12:30am, Nov.-Mar. M and W-Su 10am-8pm. ●

Carabè, V. Ricasoli, 60r (☎055 28 94 76; www.gelatocarabe.com). Enjoy pistachio, *nocciola*, and the unusual *susine* (plum). Owners Antonio and Loredana get the lemons for their lemon gelato from Sicily every week. *Granite* (from €2.10) are outstanding, particularly *mandorle* (almond) and *more* (blackberry). Cups from €1.55. Open daily May-Sept. 10am-midnight, Oct. and Mar.-Apr. noon-midnight. ●

 THE REAL DEAL. Gelato is said to have been invented in Florence centuries ago by the Buontalenti family. Before shelling out €1.50 for a *piccolo cono*, assess the quality of an establishment by looking at the banana flavor: if it's bright yellow, it's from a mix—keep walking. If it's slightly gray, real bananas were used. Metal bins also signify homemade, whereas plastic tubs indicate mass-production. Most *gelaterie* serve *granite*, flavored fruit, and coffee ices that are easier on the waistline.

ENOTECHE (WINE BARS)

Check out an *enoteca* to sample some of Italy's finest wines. A meal can often be made out of free side-dishes (cheeses, olives, toast-and-spreads, and salami).

Enoteca Alessi, V. dell' Oche, 27/29r (☎055 21 49 66, fax 239 69 87), 1 block from the duomo. Among Florence's finest, stocking over 1000 wines. Doubling as a chocolate and candy store, it offers nibbles between sips. Cool, spacious, and high-ceilinged. Open M-F 9am-1pm and 4-8pm. AmEx/MC/V. ●

Enoteca Fuori Porta, V. Monte alle Croce, 10r (☎055 234 24 83; www.fuoriporta.it), in the shadows of S. Miniato. This more casual and withdrawn *enoteca* serves reasonable meals of traditional Tuscan pasta, with an extensive *bruschetta* and *crostino* menu. On the way down from Piazzale Michelangelo, it's a great alternative to the expensive hilltop cafes. Open M-Sa 10am-2pm and 5-10pm. ●

⊙ SIGHTS

With the views from Brunelleschi's dome, the perfection of San Spirito's nave and the overwhelming array of art in the Uffizi Galleries, it's hard to take a wrong turn in Florence. For comprehensive listings on museum openings, check out www.firenzeturismo.it. To make phone reservations, call **Firenze Musei**. (☎055 29 48 83; www.firenzemusei.it. Open M-F 8:30am-6:30pm, Sa 8:30am-12:30pm.)

PIAZZA DEL DUOMO AND ENVIRONS

THE DUOMO (CATTEDRALE DI SANTA MARIA DEL FIORE). In 1296 the city fathers commissioned Arnolfo di Cambio to erect a cathedral so magnificent that it would be "impossible to make it either better or more beautiful with the

VENI, VIDI, MEDICI. Florentine museums charge up to €8.50, so breezing in and out of attractions on a whim starts to add up fast. Sadly, capital letters at most museum entrances remind visitors that there are **NO STUDENT DISCOUNTS.** The price of a ticket should not, however, keep any visitor from seeing the best collections of Renaissance art in the world. Choose carefully and plan to spend a few hours at each landmark. Also consider investing in cheap audio tours, as their descriptions provide a valuable context for understanding the works. Additionally, many of Florence's churches are free treasuries of great art. In the summer, inquire at the tourist office about **Sere al Museo,** evenings when certain museums are free 8:30-11pm. Note that most museums stop selling tickets 30min.-1hr. before closing. Reserve tickets for the Uffizi, Accademia, Medici Chapels, Galleria Palatina, Museum of San Marco, Bargello, and Encounter with Giorgio Vasari on the Internet at **www.florenceart.it.**

industry and power of man." Arnolfo succeeded, completing the massive but domeless nave by 1418. Finally, Filippo Brunelleschi, after studying Classical methods of sculpture, devised the ingenious techniques needed to construct a dome large enough for the nave. For the duomo's sublime crown, now known simply as **Brunelleschi's Dome,** the architect designed a revolutionary double-shelled structure that incorporated self-supporting, interlocking bricks. During construction, Brunelleschi, an obsessive task-master, built kitchens, sleeping rooms, and lavatories between the two walls of the cupola so the masons would never have to descend. The **Museo dell'Opera del Duomo** (p. 411) chronicles Brunelleschi's engineering feats in an in-depth exhibit. A 16th-century Medici rebuilding campaign removed the duomo's incomplete Gothic-Renaissance facade. The walls remained naked until 1871, when Florentine architect Emilio de Fabris won the commission to create a facade in neo-Gothic style. Especially when viewed from the southern side, his beautiful green, white, and red marble walls are impressively grand.

Today the duomo claims the world's third-longest nave after St. Peter's in Rome and St. Paul's in London. It rises 100m into the air, making it as high as the hills surrounding Florence and visible from nearly every corner of the city. Though ornately decorated on the outside, the church's interior is rather chilly and stark, with unadorned dark stone left mostly bare, and aimed at encouraging devotion through modesty. An exception is the visions of the apocalypse painted on the dome's ceiling. Notice, too, Paolo Uccello's celebrated *trompe l'oeil* monument to the mercenary captain Sir John Hawkwood on the cathedral's left wall, and his *orologio* (clock) on the back wall. The clock doesn't give the time of day, however; this 24hr. timepiece runs backward, starting its cycle at sunset, when the *Ave Maria* is traditionally sung. (*Duomo open M-Sa 10am-4:45pm, Su 1:30-4:45pm; 1st Sa of the month 10am-3:30pm. Shortest wait at 10am. Mass daily 7am-12:30pm and 5-7pm. Ask inside the entrance, to the left, about free guided tours in English.*) Climb the 463 steps inside the dome to Michelangelo's ■lantern for an unparalleled view of the city from the 100m-high external gallery. Halfway up, visitors can enjoy a great view of the dome's frescoed interior. (*Entrance on southern side of duomo.* ☎055 230 28 85. *Open M-F 8:30am-7pm, Sa 8:30am-5:40pm. €6.*)

■**ORSANMICHELE.** Built in 1337 as a granary, the Orsanmichele was converted into a church after a great fire convinced city officials to move grain operations outside the city walls. The *loggia* structure and ancient grain chutes are still visible from the outside. Secular and spiritual concerns mingle in the statues along the facade. Within these niches, look for Ghiberti's *St. John the Baptist* and *St. Stephen,* Donatello's *St. Peter* and *St. Mark,* and Giambologna's *St. Luke.* Inside,

TUSCANY

a Gothic tabernacle designed by Andrea Orcagna encases Bernardo Daddi's miraculous *Virgin*, an intricately wrought, expressive marble statue of Mary at her most beatific. The top floor occasionally hosts special exhibits. Across the street, the Museo di Orsanmichele exhibits numerous paintings and sculptures from the original church. (*V. Arte della Lana, between duomo and P. della Signoria. ☎ 055 28 49 44 for church and museum. Church open daily 9am-noon and 4-6pm. Museum open daily 9am-noon. Both closed 1st and last M of the month. Free.*)

BATTISTERO. Though built between the 5th and 9th centuries, in Dante's time the octagonal baptistery was believed to have originally been a Roman temple. The building's exterior has the same green and white marble patterning as the duomo, and the interior contains magnificent 13th-century Byzantine-style mosaics. Dante was christened here and later found inspiration for *The Inferno* in the murals of the devil devouring sinners. Florentine artists competed fiercely for the commission to execute the famous **bronze doors**, which depict scenes from the Bible in exquisite detail. In 1330 Andrea Pisano left Pisa to cast the first set of doors, which now guard the southern entrance (toward the river). In 1401 the cloth guild announced a competition to choose an artist for the remaining two sets. Two young artists vied for this honor: Brunelleschi (then 23 years old) and Ghiberti (then 20). They were asked to work in partnership, but the uncompromising Brunelleschi left in an arrogant huff, leaving Ghiberti to complete the project. The competition panels are displayed side by side in the Bargello. Ghiberti's project, completed in 1425, was so admired that he immediately received the commission to forge the final set of doors. The **🖾Gates of Paradise**, as Michelangelo reportedly called them, are nothing like the two earlier portals. Originally intended for the northern side, they so impressed the Florentines that they were placed in their current honored position facing the cathedral. (*Opposite the duomo. Audioguide €2. Open M-Sa noon-7pm, Su 8:30am-2pm. Mass M-F 10:30am and 11:30am. €3.*)

CAMPANILE. Also called "Giotto's Tower," the 82m-high bell tower next to the duomo has a pink, green, and white marble exterior that matches the duomo and baptistery. The construction of the landmark required decades and the leadership of three great Renaissance minds: Giotto drew the design and laid the foundation in 1334, but died soon after. Andrea Pisano added two stories to the tower, and Francesco Talenti completed the ensemble in 1359. The original exterior decoration is now in the Museo dell'Opera del Duomo. The 414 steps to the top, somewhat steeper than the climb up the duomo's cupola, reveal successive beautiful views of the duomo, the baptistery, and the rest of the city. The best time to make the trek up the stairs is in the early morning, when there is no smog to obscure the view. (*Open daily 8:30am-7:30pm. €6.*)

MUSEO DELL'OPERA DEL DUOMO. Most of the duomo's art resides in this modern-looking museum, including a late *Pietà* by Michelangelo, up the first flight of stairs. He started working on it in his early 70s, and the soft curves and flowing lines of the marble and limpness of Christ's body are said to reflect the artist's conception of his own mortality. Allegedly, Michelangelo severed Christ's left arm with a hammer in a fit of frustration. An over-eager apprentice touched up the work soon after, leaving visible scars on Mary Magdalene's head. Also in the collection are Donatello's wooden **🖾St. Mary Magdalene** (1455), Donatello and Luca della Robbia's **cantorie** (choir balconies with bas-reliefs of cavorting children), and four frames from the baptistery's **Gates of Paradise**. A huge wall displays all of the paintings submitted by architects in the 1870 competition for the duomo's facade. (*P. del Duomo, 9, behind the duomo. ☎ 055 230 28 85. Audioguide €4. Open M-Sa 9am-7:30pm, Su 9am-1:40pm. €6.*)

PIAZZA DELLA SIGNORIA AND ENVIRONS

From P. del Duomo, **V. dei Calzaiuoli,** one of the city's oldest streets, leads to P. della Signoria. Built by the Romans, V. dei Calzaiuoli now bustles with crowds, chic shops, street vendors, and gelato shops.

■**THE UFFIZI.** From P. B. S. Giovanni, go down V. Roma past P. della Repubblica, where the street turns into V. Calimala. Continue until V. Vacchereccia and turn left. The Uffizi is straight ahead. Giorgio Vasari designed this palace in 1554 for Duke Cosimo and called it the Uffizi because it housed the offices (uffizi) of the Medici administration. An impressive walkway between the two main branches of the building, full of vendors hawking trinkets and prints, leads grimly from P. della Signoria to the Arno River. Beautiful statues hold sway over the walkway from niches in the columns; play spot-the-Renaissance-man and try to find Leonardo, Vespucci, Machiavelli, and Petrarch. To avoid disappointment at the museum, note that a few rooms are usually closed each day and famous works often go on temporary loan, so not all works are available for viewing. A sign outside the ticket office lists the rooms that are closed for the day; ask if they will reopen the next day.

Before visiting the main gallery on the second floor, stop to see the exhibits of the Cabinet of Drawings and Prints on the first floor to the left. These include rare sketches by Botticelli, Leonardo, Raphael, del Sarto, and Michelangelo. Upstairs, in a U-shaped corridor, is a collection of Hellenistic and Roman marble statues. Arranged chronologically in rooms off the corridor, the collection promises a thorough education on the Florentine Renaissance, as well as a choice sampling of German and Venetian art. Framing the entrance to Room 2 are three gold *Madonne* by the great Renaissance forefathers Cimabue, Duccio di Buoninsegna, and Giotto. Room 3 features art from 14th-century Siena, including works by the Lorenzetti brothers and Simone Martini's Annunciation. Rooms 5 and 6 hold examples of International Gothic art, popular in European royal courts. Check out the rounded war-horses in the The Battle of San Romano, Paolo Uccello's noble effort to conquer the problem of perspective.

Room 7 houses two paintings by Fra Angelico (also called Beato Angelico) and a *Madonna and Child* by Masaccio. Domenico Veneziano's *Sacra Conversazione (Madonna with Child and Saints)* is one of the first paintings of Mary surrounded by the saints. Piero della Francesca's double portrait of Duke Federico and his wife Battista Sforza stands out for its translucent color and honest detail. (A jousting accident gave the Duke's nose its, er, unusual shape.) Room 8 has Filippo Lippi's touching *Madonna and Child with Two Angels.* Works by the Pollaiolo brothers and Botticelli's *Return of Judith* occupy Room 9.

Rooms 10-14 are a shrine to Florence's cherished Botticelli—the resplendent *Primavera, Birth of Venus, Madonna della Melagrana,* and *Pallas and the Centaur* glow from recent restorations. Room 15 moves into the High Renaissance with Leonardo da Vinci's *Annunciation* and the more remarkable unfinished *Adoration of the Magi.* Room 18, the tribune designed by Buontalenti to hold the Medici treasures, has a mother-of-pearl dome and a collection of portraits, most notably Bronzino's *Bia de' Medici,* Vasari's *Lorenzo il Magnifico,* and del Sarto's *Woman with the Petrarchino.* Also note Rosso Fiorentino's often-duplicated *Musician Angel.* Room 19 features Piero della Francesca's students Perugino and Signorelli. Rooms 20 and 22 detour into Northern European art. Note the contrast between Albrecht Dürer's life-like *Adam and Eve* and Lucas Cranach's haunting treatment of the same subject, as well as his portrait of Martin Luther. Room 21 contains 15th-century Venetian artwork. Bellini's *Sacred Allegory* and Mantegna's *Adoration of the Magi* highlight Room 23.

Room 25 showcases Florentine works, including Michelangelo's only oil painting in Florence, *Doni Tondo*. Raphael's *Madonna of the Goldfinch* and Andrea del Sarto's *Madonna of the Harpies* rest in Room 26. Room 28 displays Titian's erotic and inviting *Venus of Urbino*. Parmigianino's eerily lovely and regal *Madonna of the Long Neck*, now in Room 29, was discovered unfinished in the artist's studio following his death. Works by Paolo Veronese and Tintoretto dominate Rooms 31 and 32. Room 33, in fact a corridor, holds Vasari's *Vulcan's Forge* and an El Greco. The staircase vestibule (Rooms 36-40) contains a Roman marble boar, inspiration for the brass Porcellino in Florence's New Market. Rooms 41 and 43-45 house many works by Rembrandt, Goya, Rubens, and Caravaggio, currently on display after lengthy restorations.

Vasari's designs included a secret corridor running between the Palazzo Vecchio and the Medici's Palazzo Pitti. The corridor runs through the Uffizi and over the Ponte Vecchio, housing more art, including a special collection of artists' self-portraits. The corridor is opened sporadically and requires both separate entrance fee and advance booking. (☎ *055 238 86 51. Audioguide €4.65. Open Tu-Su 8:15am-6:50pm. €8.50; save hours of waiting by purchasing advance tickets for €3 extra.*)

■ **PALAZZO VECCHIO.** Arnolfo del Cambio designed this fortress-like palazzo, built between 1299 and 1304 as the seat of the *comune*'s government. The massive brown stone facade has a square tower rising from its center and turrets along the top. Its apartments once served as living quarters for members of the *signoria* (city council) during their two-month terms, during which they prayed, ate, and lived together in complete isolation from the outside world. The building later became the Medici family home, and in 1470, Michelozzo decorated the courtyard. He filled it with religious frescoes and placed ornate stone pediments over every door and window. The courtyard also has stone lions and a copy of Verrocchio's 15th-century *Putto* fountain. There are numerous tour offerings at the Palazzo Vecchio. The worthwhile Activities Tour ticket includes the Secret Routes and Invitation to Court tours. Secret Routes fulfills Clue®-fans' fantasies of hidden passages with visits to stairwells tucked in walls behind beautiful oil paintings, an area between the ornate ceiling and the roof of the Salone, and the private chambers of Duke Cosimo I de' Medici. Invitation to Court, conducted by a guide playing Cosimo's wife, Eleonora di Toledo, includes re-enactments of Medici court life. The Encounter with Giorgio Vasari tours through the Monumental Apartments with a guide playing the part of Vasari, Duke Cosimo I de' Medici's court painter and architect and a biographer of Renaissance artists. The Monumental Apartments, which house the palazzo's extensive art collections, are accessible as a museum, not just on a tour. The rooms contain 12 interactive terminals with virtual tours of the building's history and detailed computer animations. (☎ *055 276 82 24 or 276 85 58; www.museoragazzi.it. Office open daily 9am-7pm. Tours daily in English and French. 20-person group max. Reservation recommended. Monumental apartments tour €6, ages 18-25 €4.50; Activities Tour €2 extra, ages 18-25 €1.*)

The city commissioned Michelangelo and Leonardo da Vinci to paint opposite walls of the Salone del Cinquecento, the meeting room of the Grand Council of the Republic. Although they never completed the frescoes, their preliminary sketches for the *Battle of Cascina* and the *Battle of Anghiari*, both powerful depictions of humans and horses in strenuous motion, were studied by Florentine artists for years. The Salone's ceiling is so elaborately decorated with mouldings and frescoes that the walls can hardly support its weight; an intricate network of beams between the ceiling and roof suspend each wall painting. The tiny Studio di Francesco I, built by Vasari, is a treasure trove of Mannerist art, with paintings by Bronzino and Vasari as well as bronze statuettes by Giambologna and Ammannati. The Mezzanino houses some of the palazzo's best art, including Bronzino's portrait

TUSCANY

of the poet Laura Battiferi and Giambologna's *Hercules and the Hydra.* (☎055 276 84 65. *Open June 15-Sept. 15 M and F 9am-11pm, Tu-W and Sa 9am-7pm, Th and Su 9am-2pm; Sept.-May M-W and F-Sa 9am-7pm, Th and Su 9am-2pm. Palazzo €6, ages 18-25 €4.50; courtyard free. Cumulative ticket with Cappella Brancacci and Palazzo Veccoi €8/€6.)*

PIAZZA DELLA SIGNORIA. The blank-walled, turreted Palazzo Vecchio on the western side and the corner of the Uffizi Gallery to the south dominate this 13th-century piazza. The space is filled with crowds, drawn here by day by its central location and at night by the street performers and the upscale cafes that line the eastern and northern boundaries of the piazza, serving elaborate desserts until early morning. The piazza indirectly came into existence because of the struggle between Guelph and Ghibelline factions, when the Guelphs destroyed many Ghibelline homes in the 13th century and created this open space. With the construction of the Palazzo Vecchio, the square blossomed into Florence's civic and political center. In 1497 religious zealot Girolamo Savonarola convinced Florentines to light the Bonfire of the Vanities in the piazza. This grand roast of luxury items consumed some of Florence's best art, including, legend has it, all of Botticelli's secular works held in public collections. A year later, disillusioned citizens sent Savonarola up in smoke on the same spot, marked today by a comparatively discreet commemorative disc. Monumental sculptures cluster around the Palazzo Vecchio, including Donatello's *Judith and Holofernes*, a copy of Michelangelo's *David*, Giambologna's equestrian *Cosimo I*, and Bandinelli's *Hercules*. The awkward *Neptune*, to the left of the Palazzo Vecchio, so revolted Michelangelo that he decried the artist: "Oh, Ammannato, Ammannato, what lovely marble you have ruined!" Apparently, most *Fiorentini* share his opinion. Called *Il Biancone* (the Big White One) in derision, *Neptune* is regularly subject to attacks of vandalism by angry aesthetes. The graceful 14th-century stone Loggia dei Lanzi adjacent to the Palazzo was built as a stage for civic orators. Now, it is one of the best places in Florence to see world-class sculpture for free.

THE PONTE VECCHIO. Built in 1345, this is indeed the oldest bridge in Florence. In the 1500s, butchers and tanners lined the bridge and dumped pig's blood and intestines in the river, creating an odor that, not surprisingly, offended the powerful bankers as they crossed the Arno on their way to their offices. In an effort to improve the area, the Medici clan kicked out the lower-class shopkeepers, and the more decorous goldsmiths and diamond-carvers moved in; their descendants now line the bridge selling their wares from medieval-looking boutiques. The shops are so numerous and dense that it appears as if they are dragging the bridge down into the Arno, all the while clinging on to the sturdy stone walkways for dear life. While technically open to vehicles, it is chiefly tourists and street musicians who swamp the bridge. The Ponte Vecchio was the only Florentine bridge to escape German bombs during WWII. A German commander who led his retreating army across the river in 1944 couldn't bear to destroy it, choosing instead to make it impassable by toppling nearby buildings. From the neighboring ■**Ponte alle Grazie,** the view of the Ponte Vecchio melting in the setting sun is nothing less than heart-stopping. *(Toward P. Santa Croce. From the Uffizi, turn left on V. Georgofili and right at the river.)*

THE BARGELLO AND ENVIRONS

■ **BARGELLO.** In the heart of medieval Florence, this dour 13th-century brick fortress was once the residence of Florence's chief magistrate. Later it became a brutal prison with public executions held in its courtyard. In the 19th century, the Bargello's one-time elegance was restored, and it now gracefully hosts the **Museo Nazionale,** a treasury of Florentine sculpture. From the outside, the Bargello looks like a three-story fortress, but the arched windows of the inner courtyard offer glimpses of refined, sculpture-lined colonnades. On the second floor and to the right is the spacious, high-ceilinged **Salone di Donatello,** which contains Donatello's bronze *David*, the first free-standing nude since antiquity. David's coy eyes, placid face, and playful posture provide quite the contrast to Michelangelo's determined, furrow-browed figure in the Accademia. (Donatello's earlier marble *David*, fully clothed and somewhat generic, stands near the left wall.) On the right are two beautiful bronze panels of the *Sacrifice of Isaac* submitted by Ghiberti and Brunelleschi to the baptistery door competition (p. 411). The next floor contains some dramatic works by Andrea del Verrochio, teacher of Leonardo da Vinci, as well as a vast collection of small bronzes and coins. Dominating the ground floor are some of Michelangelo's early works, including a debauched *Bacchus*, an intense bust of *Brutus*, and an unfinished *Apollo*. Cellini's models for *Perseus* and *Bust of Cosimo I* occupy the same room, as does Giambologna's deftly balanced *Mercury* and Ammannati's downright disturbing *Leda and the Swan*. The spacious courtyard is filled with plaques of dozens of noble Florentine families' coats of arms. *(V. del Proconsolo, 4, between duomo and P. della Signoria. ☎ 055 238 86 06. Audioguide €3.80. Open daily 8:15am-1:50pm; closed 2nd and 4th M of the month. Hours and closing days vary by month. €4.)*

BADIA. This was the site of medieval Florence's richest monastery. Buried in the interior of a residential block, the treasures inside this church prove the adage "Don't judge a museum by its facade." Filippino Lippi's stunning *Apparition of the Virgin to St. Bernard*, one of the most appreciated paintings of the late-15th century, hangs in eerie gloom to the left of the entrance to the church. Note the beautiful frescoes and Corinthian pilasters. Visitors are asked to walk silently among the prostrate, white-robed worshippers. *(Entrance on V. Dante Alighieri, off V. Proconsolo. ☎ 055 26 44 02. Open to tourists M 3-6pm.)*

CASA DI DANTE. This residence is reputedly identical to the house Dante inhabited. Anyone who can read Italian and has an abiding fascination with Dante will enjoy the displays, which trace the poet's life from youth to exile and pays homage to the artistic creation that immortalized him. Check out Giotto's early but representative portrait of Dante on the third floor. Nearby is a facsimile of the abandoned and melancholy little church where Beatrice, Dante's unrequited love and spiritual guide in *Paradiso*, attended mass. *(Corner of V. Dante Alighieri and V. S. Margherita within 1 block of the Bargello. Under construction summer 2004. ☎ 055 21 94 16. Open M and W-Sa 10am-5pm, Su 10am-2pm. €3, groups over 15 €2 per person.)*

MUSEO DI STORIA DELLA SCIENZA. This impressive and unique collection is well worth a visit between jolts of Botticelli. It boasts scientific instruments from the Renaissance, including telescopes, astrological models, clock workings, and wax models of anatomy and childbirth. The stellar **Room 4** displays a number of Galileo's tools, including his embalmed middle finger and the objective lens through which he first observed the satellites of Jupiter in 1610. Detailed English guides are available at the ticket office. *(P. dei Giudici, 1, behind Palazzo Vecchio and the Uffizi. ☎ 055 26 53 11. Open M and W-F 9:30am-5pm, Tu and Sa 9:30am-1pm; Oct.-May also open 2nd Su of each month 10am-1pm. €6.50.)*

PIAZZA DELLA REPUBBLICA AND FARTHER WEST

After hours of contemplating great Florentine art, visit the area that financed it all. In the early 1420s, 72 banks operated in Florence, most in the area around the Mercato Nuovo and V. Tornabuoni. With a lower concentration of tourist sights, this area is quieter and more residential. Surrounding cafes are often overpriced.

■ **CHIESA DI SANTA MARIA NOVELLA.** The wealthiest merchants built their chapels in this church. Constructed between 1279 and 1360, the Dominican *chiesa* boasts a Romanesque-Gothic facade considered one of the greatest masterpieces of early Renaissance architecture. The facade is geometrically pure and balanced, a precursor to the Classical revival of the high Renaissance. The church was originally a home to Dominican friars, or *Domini canes* (Hounds of the Lord), who took a bite out of sin and corruption. Thirteenth-century frescoes covered the interior until the Medici commissioned Vasari to paint new ones. Fortunately, Vasari spared Masaccio's powerful ■**Trinity,** the first painting to use geometric perspective. This fresco, on the left side of the nave, creates the illusion of a tabernacle. The **Cappella di Filippo Strozzi,** to the right of the high altar, contains cartoon-like frescoes by Filippo Lippi, including a rather green Adam, a woolly Abraham, and an excruciating *Torture of St. John the Evangelist.* Brunelleschi's *Crucifix* stands in the Gondi Chapel as a response to Donatello's *Crucifix* in Santa Croce, which Brunelleschi found to be too full of "vigorous naturalism." Supposedly, Donatello had just finished grocery shopping when Brunelleschi unveiled his work; upon the unveiling, Donatello, in admiration and awe, dropped his bag of eggs on Brunelleschi's kitchen floor. A cycle of Ghirlandaio frescoes covers the **Tournabuoni Chapel** behind the main altar. (☎ 055 21 59 18. Open M-Th and Sa 9:30am-5pm, F and Su 1-5pm. €2.50, ages 13-18 €1.50.) The adjoining **Cappella Spagnola** (Spanish Chapel) displays 14th-century frescoes by Andrea di Bonaiuto. (☎ 055 21 59 18. Open M-Th and Sa 9:30am-5pm, Su 9am-2pm. €2.60.)

PIAZZA DELLA REPUBBLICA. The largest open space in Florence, this piazza teems with crowds and street performers in the evenings. An enormous arch filling in the gap over V. Strozzi marks the western edge of the square. The rest of the piazza is lined with overpriced cafes, restaurants, and gelaterias. In 1890 the piazza replaced the Mercato Vecchio as the site of the city market. The inscription *"Antico centro della città, da secolare squalore, a vita nuova restituito"*—the "ancient center of the city, squalid for centuries, restored to new life"— makes a derogatory reference to the fact that the piazza is the site of the old Jewish ghetto. When the "liberation of the Jews" of Italy in the 1860s allowed Jews to live elsewhere, the ghetto slowly diminished. An ill-advised plan to demolish the city center's historic buildings and remodel Florence sought the destruction of the Old Market, but an international campaign successfully thwarted the razing.

CHIESA DI SANTA TRINITÀ. Hoping to spend eternity as they had lived—in elite company—the most fashionable palazzo owners commissioned family chapels in this church. The facade, designed by Bernardo Buontalenti in the 16th century, is an exquisite example of late-Renaissance architecture that verges on Baroque in its ornamentation. Scenes from Ghirlandaio's *Life of St. Francis* decorate the **Sassetti chapel** in the right arm of the transept. The famous altarpiece, Ghirlandaio's *Adoration of the Shepherds*, resides in the Uffizi. This one is a convincing copy. (In P. S. Trinità. ☎ 055 21 69 12. Open M-Sa 8am-noon and 4-6pm, Su 4-6pm.)

MERCATO NUOVO. Under their Corinthian-columned splendor, the *loggie* of the New Market have housed gold and silk traders since 1547. Today vendors sell purses, belts, clothes, and produce, as well as gold and silk. Pietro Tacca's pleasantly plump statue, *Il Porcellino* (The Little Pig; actually a wild boar) appeared some 50 years after the market opened. Reputed to bring good luck, its snout shines from tourists' rubbing. (Off V. Calimala, between P. della Repubblica and the Ponte Vecchio. Sellers hawk wares from dawn-dusk.)

PALAZZO DAVANZATI. As Florence's 15th-century economy expanded, its bankers and merchants flaunted their new wealth by erecting grand edifices. The great *quattrocento* boom began with construction of the Palazzo Davanzati. Today the cavern-like palazzo finds life as the Museo della Casa Fiorentina Antica. With reproductions and original furniture, restored frescoes, and wooden doors and ornaments, this museum recreates the 15th-century merchants' life of luxury. *(V. Porta Rossa, 13. ☎055 238 86 10. Open daily 8:30am-1:50pm. Closed 1st, 3rd, and 5th M and 2nd and 4th Su of the month. Video screenings 10, 11am, and noon, on 4th fl. Free.)*

PALAZZO STROZZI. The modesty of the Palazzo Davanzati's stone facade gave way to ever more extravagant constructions. The Palazzo Strozzi, begun in 1489, may be the grandest of its kind, occupying an entire block. Its regal proportions and three-tiered facade, made of bulging blocks of brown stone, embody the Florentine style and boldly challenge the rules of aesthetic visual balance. Closed to the public, the palazzo shelters several cultural institutes and occasionally hosts public art exhibits. The courtyard is open to everybody and worth a look. *(On V. Tornabuoni at V. Strozzi. Enter from P. della Strozzi. ☎055 28 53 95. Art exhibit tickets around €10.)*

SAN LORENZO AND FARTHER NORTH

ACCADEMIA. Michelangelo's triumphant ▨David stands in self-assured perfection under the rotunda designed just for him. Yes, of course you have seen pictures, but from 5ft. away, Michelangelo's painstaking attention to details, like the veins in David's hands and at the back of his knees, will awe you, and the sheer size of the sculpture will take your breath away. In a series of unfortunate events, the statue's base was struck by lightning in 1512, damaged by anti-Medici riots in 1527, and was finally moved here from P. della Signoria in 1873 after a stone hurled during a riot broke David's left wrist in two places. If this real *David* seems a bit different from the copy in front of the Palazzo Vecchio, there's a reason: Michelangelo exaggerated his head and torso to correct for distortion from viewing far below, and the statue here stands on a higher pedestal, thus appearing a bit less top-heavy. In the hallway leading up to the *David* are Michelangelo's four ▨Slaves and a *Pietà*. The master left these intriguing statues intentionally unfinished—remaining true to his theories of living stone, he chipped away only enough to show their figure emerging from the marble. In addition to these commanding sculptures, check out Botticelli's Madonna paintings as well as works by Uccello. Two panel paintings, Lippi's *Deposition* and Perugino's *Assumption*, sit in the room just before the rotunda. The Serviti who commissioned the two-sided panel disliked Perugino's depiction so much that they only displayed Lippi's portion in their church. An impressive collection of Gothic triptychs lurks on the second floor in Room 2. *(V. Ricasoli, 60, between the churches of San Marco and S. S. Annunziata. ☎055 29 48 83. Most areas wheelchair accessible. Open Tu-Su 8:15am-6:50pm. €6.50.)*

BASILICA DI SAN LORENZO. In 1419 Brunelleschi designed this spacious basilica, another Florentine example of early-Renaissance simple lines and proportion. Because the Medicis lent the funds to build the church, they retained artistic control over its construction. Their coat of arms, featuring five red balls, appears all over the nave, and their tombs occupy the two sacristies and the Cappella dei Principi (see below) behind the altar. The family cunningly placed Cosimo dei Medici's grave in front of the high altar, making the entire church his personal mausoleum. Donatello created two ornate **pulpits**, one for each aisle; his *Martelli Sarcophagus* (in the left transept) takes the form of a wicker basket woven in marble. Michelangelo designed the church's exterior, but disgusted by the murkiness of Florentine politics, he abandoned the project to study architecture in Rome. The basilica still stands unadorned. *(Open M-Sa 10am-5pm. €2.50.)*

The ▨Cappelle dei Medici (Medici Chapels) consist of dual design contributions by Matteo Nigetti and Michelangelo. Intended as a grand mausoleum, Nigetti's **Cappella dei Principi** (Princes' Chapel) emulates the baptistery in P. del Duomo. Except for the gilded portraits of the Medici dukes, the decor is a rare glimpse of the Baroque in Florence. Michelangelo created and sculpted the entire **New Sacristy**—architecture, tombs, and statues—in a mature, considered style that reflects his study of Brunelleschi. Designed to house the bodies of four of the Medici family, the room contains two impressive tombs for Medici dukes Lorenzo and Giuliano. Lounging on the tomb of the military-minded Lorenzo are the smooth, minutely rendered female *Night* and the muscle-bound male *Day*, both left provocatively "unfinished." Michelangelo rendered the hazier Dawn and Dusk with more androgynous figures for the milder-mannered Giuliano's tomb, which is closer to the entrance. Some of the artist's sketches are in the basement. (☎ *055 238 86 02. Walk around to the back entrance in P. Madonna degli Aldobrandini. Open daily 8:15am-5pm; closed 1st, 3rd, and 5th M of the month and 2nd and 4th Su €6.*) The adjacent **Laurentian Library** houses one of the world's most valuable manuscript collections. Michelangelo's famous entrance portico confirms his virtuosity; the *pietra serena* sandstone staircase is one of his most innovative architectural designs. (☎ *055 21 07 60. Open daily 8:30am-1:30pm. Free with entrance to San Lorenzo.*)

MUSEO DELLA CHIESA DI SAN MARCO. Remarkable works by Fra Angelico adorn the Museo della Chiesa di San Marco, one of the most peaceful and spiritual places in Florence. A large room to the right of the lovely courtyard contains some of the painter's major works, including the church's altarpiece. The second floor houses Angelico's most famous *Annunciation*, across from the top of the stairwell, as well as the monks' quarters. Every cell in the convent contains its own Fra Angelico fresco, each painted in flat colors and with sparse detail to facilitate the monks' somber meditation. To the right of the stairwell Michelozzo's library, based on Michelangelo's work in S. Lorenzo, is a fine example of purity and vigor in structural modeling. In cells 17 and 22, underground artwork peeks through a glass floor, excavated from the medieval period. Look also for Savonarola's cell, which displays some of his relics. On the way out, the **Museo di Firenze Antica** is worth a quick visit of Florence's ancient roots. These two rooms showcase numerous archaeological fragments, mostly pieces of stone work from Etruscan and Roman buildings in the area. (*Enter at P. di San Marco, 3.* ☎ *055 238 86 08 or 238 87 04. Open daily 8:15am-6:50pm. Closed 2nd and 4th M and 1st, 3rd, and 5th Su of the month. €4, EU citizens 18-25 €2, over 65 or under 18 free.*)

PALAZZO MEDICI RICCARDI. The palace's facade is the work of Michelozzo. This stands as the archetype for all Renaissance palaces. The private chapel inside features Benozzo Gozzoli's beautiful, wrap-around fresco of the ◾**Three Magi** and several Medici family portraits. The palazzo hosts rotating exhibits ranging from Renaissance architectural sketches to Fellini memorabilia. (*V. Cavour, 3.* ☎ *055 276 03 40. Open daily 10am-7pm. €4, children €2.50.*)

MUSEO ARCHEOLOGICO. Unassuming behind its bland plaster facade, the archaeological museum has a surprisingly diverse collection. Its rooms teem with collections of statues and other monuments of the ancient Greeks, Etruscans, and Egyptians. A long, two-story gallery devoted to Etruscan jewelry runs the length of the plant-filled courtyard. In almost any other city in the world, this museum would be a major cultural highlight, but in Florence, it's possible to enjoy it without large crowds. Don't miss the *Chimera d'Arezzo* in **Room 14**. (*V. della Colonna, 38.* ☎ *055 235 75. Open M 2-7pm, Tu and Th 8:30am-7pm, W and F-Su 8:30am-2pm. €4.*)

PIAZZA SANTA CROCE AND ENVIRONS

◾**CHIESA DI SANTA CROCE.** The Franciscans built this church as far as possible from their Dominican rivals at S. Maria Novella. Started in 1210 as a small oratory, the ascetic Franciscans ironically produced what is arguably the most splendid church in the city, with a unique Egyptian cross layout. Breathtaking marble sculptures adorn the grand tombs of the luminaries of Florence past on both sides of the main aisle, frozen in expressions of grief and mourning. The Renaissance greats buried here include Michelangelo, who rests near the beginning of the right aisle (his tomb is by Vasari, but his body is actually buried in the floor slightly to the left); Galileo, directly opposite in the left aisle; and Machiavelli, further down and on the right. Donatello's *Crucifix*, which so agitated Brunelleschi, is in the Vernio Chapel of the left transept under heavy scaffolding; the artist's gilded *Annunciation* is to the right of humanist Leonardo Bruni's tomb. The Florentines, who banished Dante, eventually prepared a tomb for him here. Dante died in Ravenna, however, and the literary necrophiles there have never sent him back. To the right of the altar, the frescoes of the **Cappella Peruzzi** vie with those of the **Cappella Bardi.** Giotto and his school painted both, but unfortunately, the works are badly faded. While wandering through the church, note the high water mark about 8ft. up on the walls and pillars, an enduring reminder of the flood of 1966. (☎ *055 24 46 19. Open Mar. 15-Nov. 15 M-Sa 9:30am-5:30pm, Su and holidays 3-5:30pm; Nov. 16-Mar. 14 M-Sa 9am-5:30pm, Su and holidays 3-5:30pm. €4, under 18 €2.)*

The **Museo dell'Opera di Santa Croce,** which forms three sides of a peaceful courtyard, is accessible through a door from the right aisle of the church. At the end of the cloister next to the church is Brunelleschi's small ⬛**Cappella Pazzi,** a humble marvel of perfect proportions. Its decorations include Luca della Robbia's *tondi* of the apostles and Brunelleschi's moldings of the evangelists. Across the courtyard down a gravel path, a former dining hall contains Taddeo Gaddi's imaginative fresco *The Tree of the Cross,* and beneath it, his *Last Supper.* Also in the room is Cimabue's *Crucifixion,* left in a tragic state by the 1966 flood. *(Enter through the loggia in front of Cappella Pazzi. Open M-Tu and Th-Su 10am-7pm. Free with entrance to church.)*

SYNAGOGUE OF FLORENCE. This synagogue, also known as the **Museo del Tempio Israelitico,** is hidden behind gates and walls and contains Sephardic domes and horseshoe arches. David Levi, a wealthy Florentine Jewish businessman, donated his fortune in 1870 for the construction of "a monumental temple worthy of Florence," in recognition of the fact that Jews were newly allowed to live and worship outside the old Jewish ghetto. Architects Micheli, Falchi, and Treves created one of Europe's most beautiful synagogues. *(V. Farini, 4, at V. Pilastri. The museum includes free, informative tours every hr.; book in advance. ☎ 055 24 52 52 or 24 52 53. Open M-Th and Su 10am-6pm, F 10am-2pm. €4.)*

CASA BUONARROTI. This unassuming little museum houses Michelangelo memorabilia and two of his most important early works, *The Madonna of the Steps* and *The Battle of the Centaurs.* Both pieces are to the left of the second-floor landing. He completed these panels, which illustrate his growth from bas-relief to sculpture, when he was only 16. A selection of his rare sketches is on rotating display. *(V. Ghibellina, 70. ☎ 055 25 17 52. From P. S. Croce, follow V. dei Pepi and turn right on V. Ghibellina. Open M and W-Su 9:30am-2pm. €6.50, students €4.)*

IN THE OLTRARNO

The far side of the Arno is a lively, unpretentious quarter. Though you'll likely cross over the Ponte Vecchio on the way to the Oltrarno, consider coming back along V. Maggio, a street lined with Renaissance palaces, many of which have markers with historical descriptions. Head over the Ponte S. Trinità, which affords excellent views of the Ponte Vecchio, or dally a bit in P. San Spirito, which thrives with markets in the day and street artists at night.

TUSCANY

TUSCANY

■**PALAZZO PITTI.** Luca Pitti, a 15th-century banker, built his palazzo east of S. Spirito against the Boboli hill. The Medici family acquired the palazzo and the hill in 1550 and enlarged everything they could. During Italy's brief experiment with monarchy, the structure served as a royal residence. Today the **Palazzo Pitti** is fronted with a vast uninhabited piazza and houses a gallery and four museums. *(Ticket office is on the right before the palazzo.* ☎ *055 29 48 83. Cumulative 3-day ticket €12.50.)* The ■**Galleria Palatina** was one of only a few public galleries when it opened in 1833. Today it houses Florence's second-most important collection (after the Uffizi). Its artistic smorgasbord includes magnificent works by Botticelli, Tintoretto, Veronese, Velasquez, Titian, Perugino, del Sarto, Raphael, Vasari, Canova, Caravaggio, and Rubens. Frames hang so close together and plaques are so small that visiting is like a grand game of hide-and-seek. Artemisia Gentileschi's *Judith* hangs in the corner of Iliad Room. The **Appartamenti Reali** (Royal Apartments), at the end of the galleria house, are lavish reminders of the time when the palazzo served as a royal House of Savoy's living quarters and hold a few Renaissance and Baroque greats. *(Open Tu-Su 8:15am-6:50pm. Palatine Gallery €8.50, Royal Apartments €4.25.)* In the **Galleria d'Arte Moderna** lies one of Italian art history's big surprises, the early 19th-century proto-Impressionist works of the Macchiaioli group. The collection also includes Neoclassical and Romantic pieces, like Giovanni Dupré's sculptural group *Cain and Abel.* Find out if the clothes make the Medici in the **Galleria del Costume,** a decadent display of the family's finery. *(Open daily 8:15am-1:50pm; closed 1st, 3rd, 5th M and 2nd and 4th Su of the month. Modern Art Gallery €5, Costume Gallery €2.50.)* The **Museo degli Argenti** on the ground floor exhibits the Medici family treasures, including cases of precious gems, ivories, silver pieces, and Lorenzo the Magnificent's famous collection of vases. The Salone depicts a floor-to-ceiling fresco of a blind Homer and the nine muses leaving Mount Parnassus, alluding to scholars who fled to Tuscany from Greece after the Turkish invasion of 1453. *(Open 8:15am-1:50pm. €2.)* An elaborately landscaped park, the ■**Boboli Gardens** is an exquisite example of a stylized Renaissance garden and provides teasing glimpses of Florence and wonderful views of the surrounding countryside. A large oval lawn sits just up the hill from the back of the palace, marked by an Egyptian obelisk and lined with a hedge dotted by marble statues. Labyrinthine avenues of cypress trees lead eager meanderers to bubbling fountains with nudes and shaded picnic areas. Be sure to see the fountain of a portly Bacchus, sitting astride a very strained turtle. The **Museo della Porcellana,** hidden in back of the gardens, exhibits fine ceramics from the Medici collection. *(Gardens open in summer daily 8:15am-7:30pm, in winter 8:15am-4:30pm. Porcellana Museum open daily 9am-1:30pm except the 2nd and 4th M and 1st, 3rd, and 5th Su of the month. Gardens €6, Porcellana Museum €3.)*

CHIESA DI SANTA MARIA DEL CARMINE. Inside this church, the ■**Brancacci Chapel** holds Masaccio's stunning 15th-century frescoes, declared masterpieces in their own time. Fifty years later, a respectful Filippino Lippi completed the cycle. Masolino's *Adam and Eve* and Masaccio's pain-filled *Expulsion from Eden* stand face to face, demonstrating the latter's innovative depiction of human forms. With such monumental works as the *Tribute Money*, this chapel became a school for artists including Michelangelo. *(Church open daily 9am-noon. Free. Chapel open M and W-Sa 10am-5pm, Su 1-5pm. €4, included with cumulative Palazzo Vecchio ticket €8.)*

CHIESA DI SANTO SPIRITO. Brunelleschi envisioned a barrel-vaulted, four-aisled nave surrounded by round chapels, which would have created a softly undulating outer wall. Unfortunately for the original design, Brunelleschi died when the project was only partially completed, and the revised plans betrayed his vision of a conventional flat-roofed, three-aisled nave. Tall, thin columns make the church feel airy and light, while the unusually high clerestory admits illuminating shafts of sunlight onto each distinctive family chapel. (☎055 21 00 30. Open M-Tu and Th-F 8:30am-noon and 4-6pm, W 8:30am-noon, Su 8am-noon and 4-7pm.)

SAN MINIATO AL MONTE AND ENVIRONS

▧**SAN MINIATO AL MONTE.** One of Florence's oldest churches, San Miniato gloriously surveys all of Florence. Its inlaid marble facade and 13th-century mosaics provide a prelude to the incredible pavement inside, patterned with lions, doves, and astrological signs. Inside, the **Chapel of the Cardinal of Portugal** holds a collection of superlative della Robbia terra-cottas. The cemetery is an overwhelming profusion of tombs and mausoleums. (Take bus #13 from the station or climb stairs from Piazzale Michelangelo. ☎ 055 234 27 31. Open daily 8am-7:30pm. Free.)

PIAZZALE MICHELANGELO. With its copy of Michelangelo's *David*, Piazzale Michelangelo is the best place for a romantic moment in all of Florence. The spectacular lighting of sunset casts a warm glow over the city's stunning panorama. The large piazza doubles as a parking lot, home to hordes of tour buses on summer days, and occasionally hosts concerts as well. (Cross Ponte Vecchio and turn left, walk through the piazza, and turn right on V. de' Bardi. Follow it uphill as it becomes V. del Monte alle Croci, where a staircase to the left heads to the Piazzale.)

🎜 🌿 ENTERTAINMENT AND FESTIVALS

Florence disagrees with England over who invented modern soccer, but every June, the various *quartieri* turn out in costume to play their own medieval version of the sport, known as **calcio storico.** Two teams face off over a wooden ball in piazzas around the city; unsurprisingly, matches often blur the boundary between athletic contest and riot. A makeshift stadium in P. Santa Croce hosts three nights of matches in June. Check newspapers or the tourist office for the exact dates and locations of historic or modern *calcio*, and always book tickets ahead. The **stadio,** north of the city center, is home to modern soccer matches. Tickets (from €10 in the bleachers to €40 in the smaller, less crowded stands along the sidelines) are sold at the **Box Office** and at **Marisa,** the bar across the street from the stadium.

The most important of Florence's traditional festivals celebrates the patron saint, **San Giovanni Battista** on June 24. A tremendous fireworks display in Piazzale Michelangelo starts around 10pm—grab a spot anywhere along the Arno for a fine view. Watch for the specially coordinated combinations of red, purple and white fireworks in honor of Florence's newly Series-A soccer team. The summer also swings with music festivals, starting in late April with the classical **Maggio Musicale.** Take in an evening of opera or ballet with locals in the **Teatro Comunale;** ticket prices range €15-150, with opening-night tickets generally more expensive. To avoid an obstructed view, always ask to see a seating chart before springing for the cheapest seats. The **Estate Fiesolana** (June-Aug.) fills the Roman theater in Fiesole with concerts, opera, theater, and film.

In summer, the **Europa dei Sensi** program hosts **Rime Rampanti,** nightly cultural shows with music, poetry, and food from a chosen European country. Call the information office (☎348 580 48 12; www.rimerampanti.it) to make reservations. The same company also hosts the more modern and lively **Le Pavoniere,** with live music, pool, bar, and pizzeria, in the Ippodromo delle Cascine (along the river and past the train station). Call the office (☎055 321 75 41) for information and reservations. In September, the **Festa dell'Unità** brings music to the Campi Bisenzia (bus #30). The **Festa del Grillo** (Festival of the Cricket) is held the first Sunday after Ascension Day, which is 40 days after Easter. Crickets in wooden cages are sold in the Cascine park to be released into the grass.

TUSCANY

◻ SHOPPING

It's hard to grow up or live in Florence without developing an eye for beauty. As a result, the Florentines design their window displays (and their wares) with flair. For the budget shopper seeking a special gift and the big spender who's looking to make the splurge of a lifetime, Florence offers ample options and even more temptations to drop some cash. Watch for store windows to flood with "Saldi" signs in January and July, which mark the end-of-season sales. In July and August, Florentine families rush to the beach for the weekend and nearly all stores close early on Saturday. Some close for the entire month of August. For more comprehensive information about shopping in Florence, email italyinfo1@yahoo.com.

V. Tornabuoni's swanky boutiques and the well-stocked goldsmiths on the Ponte Vecchio serve a sophisticated clientele. To join this crowd, try **Vaggi,** Ponte Vecchio 2/6r and 20r. Charms start at €25, and 18k gold earrings cost €40 or more. (☎ 055 21 55 02. Open M-Sa 9am-7:30pm.) Florence makes its contribution to *alta moda* with a number of fashion shows, including the biannual Pitti Uomo show in January and June, Europe's most important exhibition of menswear.

The city's artisan traditions thrive at the open markets. **San Lorenzo,** the largest, cheapest, and most touristed, sprawls for several blocks around P. S. Lorenzo. In front of the leather-shop storefronts, stands stock all kinds of goods—bags, clothes, food, toys, and flags. High prices are rare, but so are quality and honesty. (Open M-Sa 9am-twilight.) Stands throughout the city stock the same small selection of generic, oversized t-shirts; skip these and try **T-Show,** V. Guicciardini, 15r, with two stories' worth of *Italia-* and *Firenze*-printed merchandise. Most t-shirts cost €8-15; bags are €10. (☎ 055 28 47 38. Open M-Sa 9:30am-7:30pm, Su 10am-7pm. MC/V.) For everything from potholders to parakeets, visit the market at **Parco delle Cascine** on Tuesday morning, which begins four bridges west of the Ponte Vecchio at P. V. Veneto and stretches along the Arno River. For a flea market specializing in old furniture and postcards, visit **Piazza Ciompi,** off V. Pietrapiana from Borgo degli Albizi. (Open Tu-Sa.) Even when prices are marked, don't hesitate to bargain. As a general guideline, start with half of the price offered or at least show disinterest to get the price lowered; but never ask for a price you're not willing to pay. Don't bargain if paying by credit card.

Books, paper goods, and **art reproductions** make great souvenirs. **Alinari,** L. Alinari, 15, stocks the world's largest selection of art prints and high-quality photographs from €25. (☎ 055 239 51. Open M-F 9am-1pm and 2:30-6:30pm, Sa 9am-1pm. AmEx/MC/V.) **Abacus,** V. dei Ginori, 30r, sells beautiful photo albums, journals, and address books, all made of fine leather and *carta fiorentina*, paper covered in intricate floral designs. (☎ 055 21 97 19. Open M-Sa 9:30am-1:30pm and 3-7:30pm.)

Epicures shouldn't miss a visit to **Gastronomia Tassini,** V. Apostoli, 24r, which offers authentic and affordable tastes of Italy. Jars of hit pasta sauces—pesto, olive, *cinghiale* (boar), and *tartufo* (truffle)—start at €2. *Let's Go* readers get a discount, plus cooking tips and recipes offered by friendly owner Giorgio and staff. All products are bubble-wrapped and vacuum-packed to travel. (☎ 055 28 26 96. Open M-Sa 8:30am-2pm and 4:30-7:30pm. MC/V.)

Florentine **leatherwork** is affordable and known worldwide for its high quality. Some of the best leather artisans in the city work around P. S. Croce and V. Porta S. Maria. The **Santa Croce Leather School,** in Chiesa di Santa Croce, offers first-rate products at reasonable prices. (On Su, enter through V. S. Giuseppe, 5r. ☎ 055 24 45 33 and 247 99 13; www.leatherschool.it. Open Mar. 15-Nov. 15 M-Sa 9am-6:30pm, Su 10:30am-12:30pm and 3-6pm; Nov. 16-Mar. 14 M-Sa 9am-12:30pm and 3-6pm.) **NOI,** at V. delle Terme, 8, produces leather apparel of superb quality

for hotshot clientele but also carries more affordable goods for the not-so-rich and famous. (10% discount with *Let's Go*. Wallets from €25; bags €60-
200; jackets from €250.)

NIGHTLIFE

For reliable info, consult the city's entertainment
monthly, *Firenze Spettacolo* (€2), or entertainment
website, www.informacittafirenze.it. Street performers draw crowds to the steps of the duomo, the
arcades of the Mercato Nuovo, and P. della Signoria.
Piazza Santo Spirito in Oltrarno has regular live music
in the summer. Take the #25 bus from the station to
the **Giardini del Drago** (Gardens of the Dragon) for a
pick-up game of soccer. For clubs or bars that run
late and are far from the centro, keep in mind that the
last bus may leave before the fun winds down, and
taxis are rare in the area of Central Park and Rio
Grande, so plan ahead and make sure you have the
number of a taxi company.

BARS

May Day Lounge, V. Dante Alighieri, 16r (www.mayday-
club.it). This eclectic lounge is lit by all manner of
lamps and light installations. Play pong on the 80s
gaming system or sip mixed drinks (€4.50-6.50) to a
funk beat. Try the "banana cow" shot (rum, creme of
banana, panna, granatina; €3). Draft beer €4.50.
Happy Hour 8-10pm. Th is watermelon night. Open
daily 8pm-2am. AmEx/MC/V.

Kikuya, V. Benci, 43r (☎055 234 48 79). An international blender—a Japanese name for a neighborhood
Irish pub cherished by local Florentines and foreigners
of all ages. Dimly-lit bar room and comfortable red-
cushioned bench make for lively conversations over a
pint (€4.50) and a burger (€5). Open daily 7:30pm-
2am. MC/V.

Slowly, V. Porta Rossa, 63r (☎055 264 53 54). Sleek
room with jazzy pop sets a suave tone. The place for
trendy Italian 20-somethings to see and be seen. Cocktails and long drinks worthy of applause; don't miss the
popular mojito (€8). Good food, too—not that you
came to eat. *Primi* €10-12. Cocktails €7-10. Open
daily 7pm-2:30am. MC/V.

Eby's Latin Bar, V. dell' Oriuolo, 5r (☎338 650 89 59).
Shake it to the blaring Latin music while waiting in line
for tasty fresh-fruit cocktails blended with seasonal
ingredients. Fantastic burritos and the best nachos in
Florence. Beer €3, cocktails €5.50. Happy Hour 6-
9pm, M and Tu until midnight. Open M-Sa noon-3pm
and 6pm-3am.

THE HIDDEN DEAL

THE ART OF SAVING

Looking to save on those Gucci
wrap-arounds? In Italy, even discount shopping is done with
style, and some of the best
designer outlets are right outside
Florence. With savings of over
50%, it may be worth a break
from the Uffizi.

The Mall (☎055 86 577
750), includes Gucci, Yves St.
Laurent, Bottega Veneta, Loro
Piana, Giorgio Armani, and Sergio
Rossi outlets. From Santa Maria
Novella in Florence, take the train
to Rignano Sull'Arno and a taxi
(☎055 865 71 63 or 347 886
27 31) to Leccio. Open M-F 9am-
7pm, Su 3-7pm.

Dolce & Gabbana (☎055
833 13 00). From Florence, take
the train to Montevarchi (about a
40min. ride on the local train on
the way to Arezzo). A cab from
the station to the outlet costs
about €11. Open M-F 9am-7pm,
Su 3-7pm.

Prada (☎055 919 05 80).
Same directions as Dolce & Gabbana above. Open M-F 9:30am-
7pm, Su 2-7pm.

Another popular option is the
€25 round-trip shuttle bus that
leaves from Florence M-Sa
9:30am (return 1:30pm) and
2:30pm (return 6:30pm), Su
2:30pm (return 6:30pm). Call
☎055 865 77 75 to reserve.
Additional information at www.out-
let-firenze.com.

The Chequers Pub, V. della Scala, 7/9r (☎ 055 28 75 88). Attracts the liveliest crowd of all, especially on soccer match evenings. Wide range of beers (pints €4.50). Happy Hour daily 6:30-8pm (pints €2.50). Open Apr.-Oct. M-Th and Su 12:30pm-1:30am, F-Sa until 2:30am; Nov.-Mar. 6pm-1:30am, F-Sa until 2:30am. AmEx/MC/V.

The Fiddler's Elbow, P. S. Maria Novella, 7r (☎ 055 21 50 56). Ex-pat bartenders serve cider and beer (€4.50 per pint) to crowds of convivial foreigners. Patio overlooks P. Santa Maria Novella. Open daily M-Th and Su 3pm-1am, F-Sa 2pm-2am. AmEx/MC/V.

DISCOS

Central Park, in Parco delle Cascinè. Open-air dance floors pulse with hip-hop, reggae, and Italian "dance rock." Favored by Florentine and foreign teens and college students. No cover for foreign students before 12:30am, after that, the regular €11 cover is charged. Mixed drinks €8. Open M-Tu and Th-Sa 11pm-late, W 9pm-late. AmEx/MC/V.

Rio Grande, V. degli Olmi, 1 (☎ 055 33 13 71; www.rio-grande.it), near Parco delle Cascinè. This and Central Park are the most popular of Florence's discos, with Rio Grande catering to a slightly older crowd. Open-air dance floors make for wild summer nights. €16 cover includes 1 drink; each subsequent drink €7. Special nights include soul, hip-hop, house, and reggae. Call for schedule. Open Tu-Sa 11pm-4am. AmEx/MC/V.

Yab, V. Sassetti, 5 (☎ 055 21 51 60; www.yab.it), seethes with American students and the occasional pack of locals with cash to burn. Huge dance floor, mercifully free of strobe light, is jammed by midnight. Cocktails €5-6. Classic R&B and reggae on M. Open in summer for M night dance parties. Open in winter daily 9pm-1am.

Blob, V. Vinegia, 21r (☎ 055 21 12 09), behind Palazzo Vecchio. Laid-back bar becomes a dance club when the mood strikes. From mellow evenings to boisterous early mornings, Blob offers plenty: DJs, an open mic, movies, and foosball. Cocktails €5.50-6.50. 2-for-1 Happy Hour 6-10pm. Open daily until 4am. Closed June-Aug. AmEx/MC/V.

Tabasco Gay Club, P.S. Cecilia, 3r (☎ 055 21 30 00), in tiny alley across P. della Signoria from Palazzo Vecchio. This dark basement club features smoke machines, strobe lights, and low-vaulted ceilings. Caters to gay men. 18+. Cover €10 before 1am, €13 after 1am, includes 1st drink. Open Tu-Su 10pm-4am. AmEx/MC/V.

◪ DAYTRIP FROM FLORENCE

FIESOLE

A 25min. bus ride from the city. Catch the ATAF city bus #7 from the train station exit near track #16 or P. S. Marco; it stops at P. Mino da Fiesole in the town center. The tourist office, V. Portigiani, 3 (☎ 055 59 87 20, fax 59 88 22; www.comune.fiesole.fi.it), is next to the Teatro Romano, half a block off P. Mino da Fiesole, directly across the piazza from the bus stop. Office provides a free map with museum and sights listings. Open M-Sa 9am-6pm, Su 10am-1pm and 2-6pm.

Older than Florence itself, Fiesole is the site of the original Etruscan settlement. Florence was colonized and settled as an off-shoot. Fiesole has long been a welcome escape from the sweltering summer heat of the Arno Valley and a source of inspiration for famous figures: Alexander Dumas, Anatole France, Paul Klee, Marcel Proust, Gertrude Stein, and Frank Lloyd Wright all had productive sojourns here. Leonardo da Vinci even used the town as a testing ground for his famed flying machine. For the more passive visitor, Fiesole's location provides incomparable views of Florence and the rolling countryside to the north.

Facing away from the bus stop, walk half a block off P. Mino da Fiesole to the entrance of the **Museo Civico,** V. Portigiani, 1 (☎ 055 594 77). One ticket gains admission to three constituent museums. The **Teatro Romano** includes the perfectly rectangular foundations of Etruscan thermal baths and the toppled

TUSCANY

columns and sturdy archways of temple ruins. The well-preserved structure of the amphitheater is gussied up in modern sound equipment and spotlights for concerts in summer. The amphitheater grounds lead into the **Museo Civico Archeologico**, housing an extensive collection of Etruscan artifacts, well-preserved Grecian urns, a reconstructed tomb complete with skeleton, and vases from *Magna Graecia* (present-day Southern Italy under the Greek Empire). Hop across the street to breeze through the **Museo Bandini**, V. Dupre, 1, holding a collection of 15th-century Italian paintings. (☎055 594 77. Ruins and museums open Apr.-Oct. daily 9:30am-7pm, Sept.-Mar. M and W-Su 9:30am-6pm. €6.50, students or over 65 €4.50. Combined bus and museum entrance ticket available at Firenze Santa Maria Novella station. €7, students €5.50.) Additionally, a walk uphill from the bus stop and to the left leads to the **Convento Francesco** and **public gardens.** The climb is dauntingly steep but mercifully short, and the breathtaking panorama is well worth the effort. The monastery contains a frescoed chapel and a tiny museum of precious Chinese pottery, jade figurines, and Egyptian artifacts (including a mummy) brought back by Franciscan missionaries. (☎055 591 75. Open June-Sept. M-F 9am-noon and 3-7pm, Sa-Su 9-11am and 3-6pm; Oct.-Mar. M-F 9am-noon and 3-6pm, Sa-Su 9-11am and 3-5pm.)

Accommodations in Fiesole are expensive, but the town is a great place to sit down for lunch. Grab a bite at **Pizzeria Etrusca ❷**, in P. Mina da Fiesole, near the bus stop. (☎055 59 94 84. *Primi* from €5.50, *secondi* from €9. Pizza €5-10. Cover €1.30. Open M-W and F-Su noon-3:30pm and 6pm-1am. AmEx/MC/V.) Take in the fantastic view of the Arno Valley over coffee (from €0.80) or gelato (€1.55-2.60) at **Blu Bar ❷**, P. Mino, 10. The table charge can be expensive. (Crepes €6. Pizza €5-6. Cocktails €10. Open Apr.-Oct. daily 8am-1am, Nov.-Mar. M and W-Su 8-1am.)

SIENA   ☎0577

Much smaller than the swamped hubs of Florence and Rome but conveniently situated in the middle of Tuscany, Siena combines an elegant historical center with a distinctive savvy and fierce pride in its origins. After all, it wasn't always the more sedate peer to these major cosmopolitan centers. In the 13th century, Sienese tradesmen, bankers, and politicians crafted a sophisticated metropolis. The city's vehement rivalry with Florence gave rise to its grandiose Gothic architecture, though the preeminence and innovation came to a halt with the Black Death. These days, the Sienese celebrate their heritage with events like the semiannual Palio, an intoxicating display of pageantry in which jockeys from the city's 17 *contrade* (districts) race bareback horses around Il Campo, the central square. Siena's manageable size and vast art collection make it an optimal base for exploration and a favorite with connoisseurs.

▐ TRANSPORTATION

Trains: In P. Rosselli, 15min. by bus from city center. Ticket office open daily 5:50am-12:30pm and 1-7:30pm. From Rome and points south, change at Chiusi; from points north, change at Florence. **Luggage storage** available (see **Practical Information**). Departures to **Florence** (1¾hr., 19 per day 5am-9:22pm, €5.50) and **Rome** (3hr., 12 per day 5:57am-8:18pm, €16.30) via **Chiusi.**

Buses: TRA-IN/SITA (☎0577 20 42 46). Ticket office is in the underground terminal in P. Gramsci. Open daily 5:45am-8:15pm. Some intercity buses leave from P. Gramsci and others from its location at the train station (☎0577 20 24 28). To: **Arezzo** (8 per day, €4.60); **Florence** (express bus every hr., €6.50); **Montalcino** (8 per day, €2.50); **Montepulciano** via Buonconvento or Torrenieri (20 per day, €4.30); **San Gimignano**

via Poggibonsi (31 per day, €5); **Volterra** (M-F 4 per day, €2.50; get off at Colle Val d'Elsa and buy tickets at newsstand for a **CPT** bus to Volterra). **TRA-IN** also runs buses within Siena. Buy tickets (valid for 1hr., €0.90) at the office in P. Gramsci or from any vendor that displays a TRA-IN sign. All buses have reduced service Su.

Taxis: RadioTaxi (☎0577 492 22) is open daily 7am-9pm.

Car, Bike, and Moped: Perozzi Noleggi, V. dei Gazzani, 16-18 (☎0577 23 73 85). Cars €72 per day; vans €115 per day; bikes €10 per day; 50cc scooters €26 per day, 100cc €52 per day. Insurance included. Open M-Sa 8:30am-12:30pm. AmEx/MC/V.

ORIENTATION AND PRACTICAL INFORMATION

From the train station, cross the street and take bus #3, 4, 7, 8, 9, 10, 14, 17, or 77 to the town center. These buses stop in either **Piazza del Sale** or **Piazza Gramsci.** Some buses stop just before P. Gramsci, making it difficult to know when to get off; ask the bus driver. From either piazza, follow the numerous signs to **Piazza del Campo** (a.k.a. Il Campo), Siena's historic center. Buy local bus tickets from vending machines by the station entrance or at the *biglietteria* window for bus tickets (€0.90). From the **bus station** in P. S. Domenico, follow the signs to P. del Campo. **Piazza del Duomo** lies 100m west of Il Campo.

Tourist Office: APT, Il Campo, 56 (☎0577 28 05 51; infoaptsiena@terresiena.it). Knowledgeable staff provides snappy brochures on sights in and around Siena, but are generally swamped with inquiries and unable to grant much personal attention. Open Mar. 16-Nov. 14 daily 9:30am-1pm and 2:30-6pm; Nov. 15-Mar. 15 M-Sa 8:30am-1pm and 3-7pm, Su 9am-1pm. **Prenotazioni Alberghiere** (☎0577 28 80 84, fax 28 02 90), in P. S. Domenico, finds lodgings for a €2 commission. Also books reservations for **walking tours** of Siena (2hr. tour M-F 4:30pm, book by 1pm, €20) and San Gimignano. Open Apr.-Oct. M-Sa 9am-8pm; Nov.-Mar. M-Sa 9am-7pm.

Budget Travel: CTS, V. Sallustio Bandini, 21 (☎0577 28 58 08). Student travel services. Open M-F 9am-12:30pm and 3:30-7pm.

English-Language Bookstore: Libreria Ticci, V. delle Terme, 5/7 (☎0577 28 00 10). Extensive selection. Open M-F 9am-7:45pm, Sa 9am-2:30pm. **Feltrinelli,** V. Banchi di Sopra, 64 (☎0577 27 11 04; www.lafeltrinelli.it). Classic and popular fiction; some English-language magazines. Open M-Sa 9am-9:30pm, Su 11am-7:30pm. MC/V.

Laundromat: Lavorapido, V. di Pantaneto, 38. Wash €3 per 8kg. Dry €3. Open daily 8am-9pm. **Onda Blu,** Casato di Sotto, 33 (☎0800 86 13 46). Wash €3 per 6½kg. Dry €3. Open daily 8am-10pm.

Luggage Storage: At TRA-IN ticket office beneath P. Gramsci. €2-3.50. No overnight storage. Open daily 7am-7:45pm.

Emergency: ☎113. **Police,** (☎112). On V. del Castoro near the duomo.

First Aid: ☎118. **Ambulance:** V. del Porrione, 49 (☎0577 431 11).

Pharmacy: Farmacia del Campo, P. del Campo, 26. Open in summer daily 9am-noon and 4-8pm; in winter 9am-noon and 3:30-7:30pm. Pharmacies rotate late-night shifts.

Hospital: V. Le Scotte, 14 (☎0577 58 51 11). Take bus #77 from P. Gramsci.

Internet: Cafe Internet/International Call Center, Galleria Cecco Angiolieri, 16. €0.03 per min., €0.99 for 20min. Open M and Su 11am-10:30pm, Tu-Sa 9:30am-10:30pm. **Internet Train,** V. di Città, 121 (☎0577 22 63 66). €5.16 per hr. Wireless connections available for laptops. Open M-Sa 10am-8pm, Su noon-8pm. V. Pantaneto, 54 (☎0577 24 74 68). Open M-F 10am-9pm, Su 4-9pm.

Post Office: P. Matteotti, 36, offers **currency exchange.** €2.58 fee for amounts over €5.16. Open M-Sa 8:15am-7pm. **Postal Code:** 53100.

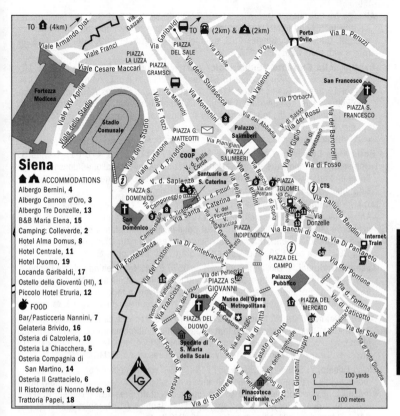

Siena

▲ ♠ ACCOMMODATIONS
Albergo Bernini, 4
Albergo Cannon d'Oro, 3
Albergo Tre Donzelle, 13
B&B Maria Elena, 15
Camping: Colleverde, 2
Hotel Alma Domus, 8
Hotel Centrale, 11
Hotel Duomo, 19
Locanda Garibaldi, 17
Ostello della Gioventù (HI), 1
Piccolo Hotel Etruria, 12

🍎 FOOD
Bar/Pasticceria Nannini, 7
Gelateria Brivido, 16
Osteria di Calzoleria, 10
Osteria La Chiacchera, 5
Osteria Compagnia di
  San Martino, 14
Osteria Il Grattacielo, 6
Il Ristorante di Nonno Mede, 9
Trattoria Papei, 18

TUSCANY

🏠🏠 ACCOMMODATIONS AND CAMPING

Finding a room in Siena can be difficult and expensive in summer. Book far ahead for Palio (see **Entertainment**). For visits over a week, *affittacamere* are an attractive option. The APT and Prenotazioni Alberghiere tourist offices can provide a list of these private rooms.

Piccolo Hotel Etruria, V. Donzelle, 3 (☎0577 28 80 88; www.hoteletruria.com). Family-run establishment maintains immaculate, modern rooms with floral bedspread, phone, TV, and hair dryer at some of the best prices in Siena, and only a stone's throw from Il Campo. Breakfast €5. Curfew 12:30am. Singles €45, with bath €50; doubles €80; triples €105. Extra bed €25. AmEx/MC/V. ❹

B&B Maria Elena, Vco. di Vallepiatta, 12 (☎0577 28 33 50). 3 rooms overlook Chiesa di San Domenica from a pleasant private garden. Queen-size bed/futon, clean bath with fluffy towels, TV, and laundry machine. Extensive breakfast included. 3-night min. stay. Reserve ahead. €50 per person. ❹

Hotel Centrale, V. C. Angiolieri, 26 (☎0577 28 03 79; hotelcentrale.siena@libero.it). Don't be deceived the dark staircase—this hotel is a well-kept gem. Rooms with wood-beam ceilings, hair dryer, phone, satellite TV, ceiling fan and great views of La Torre and the duomo. Breakfast €6. Singles €50-55; doubles €75. Cash only. ❹

Albergo Tre Donzelle, V. Donzelle, 5 (☎0577 28 03 58, fax 22 39 33). The basic rooms have tasteful wood furnishings and lots of space. Close to Il Campo, but often noisy as a result. Curfew 1am. Singles €33; doubles €46, with bath €60. Extra bed €18, in rooms with bath €19. AmEx/MC/V. ❸

Ostello della Gioventù "Guidoriccio" (HI), V. Fiorentina, 89 (☎0577 522 12; www.a.franchostel.it), in Località Lo Stellino, a 20min. bus ride from town. Take bus #10 or 15 from P. Gramsci. Bus #15 stops at front door. For bus #10, continue from stop in bus's direction and take 1st right on winding uphill road. Look for small sign on right side pointing to the left. The hostel is a good value and has a young, friendly atmosphere. Key deposit €2. Breakfast €1.60; dinner €9. Lockout 9:30am-3pm. Curfew midnight. Reservation recommended. Dorms €14.46. ❶

Hotel Alma Domus, V. Camporeggio, 37 (☎0577 441 77, fax 476 01), behind S. Domenico. The rooms are somewhat cramped, but all have handsome, polished stone floors and refreshing A/C. All rooms with bath. Breakfast €6. Curfew 11:30pm. Singles €42; doubles €55; triples €60; quads €85. Cash only. ❹

Albergo Bernini, V. della Sapienza, 15 (☎0577 28 90 47; www.albergobernini.com). Antique-laden rooms have picture-perfect views of the duomo and San Domenico soaring above red rooftops. Outdoor breakfast patio is lined with plants. Breakfast €7. Curfew midnight. Check-out 10:30am. July-Sept. singles with bath €78; doubles €62, with bath €82. Extra bed €25. Sept.-July prices drop 20%. Cash only. ❹

Locanda Garibaldi, V. Giovanni Dupré, 18 (☎0577 28 42 04), behind Palazzo Pubblico and P. del Campo. Wood-trussed ceilings and low-vaulted sitting area. Most rooms with bath. Restaurant downstairs. Curfew midnight. Reservation recommended, constantly booked in summer. Doubles €75, with bath €82; triples €90; quads €115. ❸

Albergo Cannon d'Oro, V. Montanini, 28 (☎0577 443 21; www.cannondoro.com), near P. Matteotti. Classy simplicity with trim wood furniture. All rooms with bath, TV, fan, and phone. Wheelchair accessible. Breakfast €6. Singles €74; doubles €90; triples €101; quads €119. Prices drop precipitously during low season. AmEx/MC/V. ❺

Hotel Duomo, V. Stalloreggi, 38 (☎0577 28 90 88; www.hotelduomo.it). The luxurious rooms in this 17th-century mansion all have bath, satellite TV, and A/C, and many have magnificent views of the duomo. Warm, courteous staff. Breakfast included. Reserve ahead in summer. Early Mar.-Nov. singles €104; doubles €130; triples €171; quads €184. Prices drop 30% Nov.-early Mar. AmEx/MC/V. ❻

Colleverde, Strada di Scacciapensieri, 47 (☎0577 28 00 44; www.terresiena.it). Take bus #3 or 8 from P. del Sale. Confirm destination with driver. Buses run every 30min.; late #8 buses (10:37 and 11:57pm) run from P. del Sale. Campsite is well-kept, with grocery store, restaurant, and bar nearby. Open late Mar. to mid-Nov. Pool €1.55, children €1.03. €7.75 per person, €7.75 per tent, ages 3-11 €4.13. MC/V. ❶

▐ FOOD

Siena specializes in rich pastries. The most famous is *panforte*, a dense concoction of honey, almonds, and citron, first baked as trail mix for the Crusaders. For a lighter snack, try *ricciarelli*, soft almond cookies with powdered vanilla on top. Sample either (€1.90 per 100g) at the **Bar/Pasticceria Nannini ❶**, the oldest *pasticceria* in Siena, with branches at V. Banchi di Sopra, 22-24, and throughout town. **Enoteca Italiana ❶**, in the Fortezza Medicea near the entrance off V. Cesare Maccari, sells fine wines (from €1.60 per glass), including *Vernaccia*. (☎0577 28 84 97. Open M noon-10pm, Tu-Sa noon-1am. MC/V.) Siena's **open-air market** fills P. La Lizza each Wednesday 8am-1pm. For **groceries,** head to the COOP, in P. Matteoti, or the one a few blocks from the train station. Turn left from the station, then left again one block down at the overpass; it is in the shopping complex immediately to the right. (Open M-Sa 8am-7:30pm.)

Osteria di Calzoleria, V. Calzoleria, 12 (☎0577 28 90 10), behind the curve of Il Campo off V. Banchi di Sotto. Delicious aromas waft up from the intimate dining area downstairs. The patient, friendly waitstaff emerges bearing hearty Tuscan classics like *tagliatelle al ragu di coniglio* (with rabbit sauce; €6.50). *Primi* €5-7.50, *secondi* €6-13. Cover €1, service 10%. Open daily 12:30-2:30pm and 7-10pm. MC/V. ❸

Trattoria Papei, P. del Mercato, 6 (☎0577 28 08 94), on the far side of Palazzo Pubblico from Il Campo. Shady outdoor tables and a stone-arched dining room. Vast range of homemade pasta dishes, including scrumptious *tagliolini al sugo d'anatra* (with duck sauce; €6.20), and traditional *secondi,* such as savory *coniglio all'arrabbiata* (rabbit with sage and rosemary; €7). Wines come by the bottle (1L €7) but you're charged only what you drink. Cover €1.60. Open Tu-Su 12:30-3pm and 7-10:30pm. AmEx/MC/V. ❸

Osteria La Chiacchera, Costa di S. Antonio, 4 (☎0577 28 06 31), next to Santuario di S. Caterina. Frequented by young Italians, the restaurant offers hearty portions of Tuscan dishes at affordable prices. Enjoy the *spaghetti al ragu* (€4.50). *Primi* €4.20-5.50, *secondi* €4.80-7. Open M and W-Su noon-3:30pm and 7pm-midnight. AmEx/MC/V. ❷

Il Ristorante di Nonno Mede, V. Camporeggio, 21 (☎0577 24 79 66), down the hill to the left of San Domenico. Although indoor seating is cramped, choose from an extensive menu of "white pizzas" (minus the sauce) and enjoy in the expansive outdoor seating area that has great views of the duomo. Delicious *antipasto* buffet €8. Pizza €5-6.20. Open M, W-Su 12-2:30pm, 7-10pm. MC/V. ❷

Osteria Il Grattacielo, V. dei Pontani, 8 (☎0577 28 93 26), on a tiny street between V. dei Termini and V. Banchi di Sopra. Culinary delights abound here, including stewed baby artichokes, sun-dried tomatoes in oil, olives, and hunks of salami and pecorino. Just point at the jars and order. A full meal with wine runs less than €10. Open May-Sept. M-Sa 8am-3pm and 6:30-8pm; Oct.-Apr. 8am-2:30pm and 5-10pm. ❷

Osteria Compagnia di San Martino, V. Porrione, 25 (☎0577 493 06), off Il Campo. Tuscan food, like *tagliatelle al cinghiale* (flat noodles with wild boar; €6), served in no-frills outdoor area or dining room with A/C. *Primi* €5-6, *secondi* €6-16. Cover €1.50. Open M-Sa noon-3pm and 7-10:30pm. AmEx/MC/V. ❸

Gelateria Brivido, V. d. Pellegrini, 1-3 (☎0577 28 00 58). Quality gelato in intriguing flavors like kiwi and watermelon from the small, standing-room only store. Also serves some of the best *stracciatella* around. Cones from €1.50. Open daily 10am-9pm. ❶

 SIGHTS

 SIEN-ANY SIGHTS? Siena offers two *biglietti cumulativi* (cumulative tickets). The first allows five days of entry into the Museo dell'Opera Metropolitana, the baptistery, and the Piccolomini Library (€7.50). The second covers those three plus four others, including the Museo Civico, and is valid for seven days (€16). Both tickets can be bought at any of the included sights.

IL CAMPO. Siena radiates from the **Piazza del Campo,** the shell-shaped brick square designed for civic events. The piazza's brick paving is divided into nine sections, representing the city's medieval Council of Nine. Dante referred to the square in his account of the real-life drama of Provenzan Salvani, the heroic Sienese merchant who panhandled in Il Campo to pay for a friend's ransom. Later Sienese mystics such as San Bernadino used the piazza as a public auditorium. Now it has the dubious honor of entertaining local teenagers and wide-eyed tourists by day; in the evening, the elegant cafes pull back their awnings and the Sienese strut in a ritual *passeggiata.* For €1-2, buy a *caffè* or pastry and claim a table, or better yet, grab a bottle of wine and stake out a seat on the

TUSCANY

cobblestone piazza itself. Twice each summer, the **Palio** morphs the mellow Campo to mayhem as horses race around its edge (see **Entertainment**). At the top of the slope is the **Fonte Gaia,** a rectangular marble fountain nestled into the slanted piazza, surrounded by reproductions of Siena-native Jacopo della Quercia's famous carvings (1408-1419). The originals are in the **Spedale di S. Maria della Scala** (p. 431). The water here emerges from the same 25km aqueduct that has refreshed Siena since the 14th century. Closing the bottom of the shell-shaped piazza is the graceful **Palazzo Pubblico,** with its looming bell tower, the **Torre del Mangia.** In front of the palazzo is the **Cappella di Piazza,** which was started in 1348 but took 100 years to complete, due to the untimely interruption of the Black Death. The transition from Gothic to Renaissance architecture is evinced in the movement from pointed arches to graceful rounded ones.

▨ **PALAZZO PUBBLICO.** This impressive medieval building was home to Siena's Council of Nine in the Middle Ages. It still houses city government offices, but the main tourist draw is the **Museo Civico.** Although the Sienese art pieces here range from medieval triptychs to 18th-century landscapes, the greatest treasure is the collection of late medieval to early Renaissance painting in the distinctive Sienese style. The large and airy **Sala del Mappamondo,** named for a lost series of astronomical frescoes, displays Simone Martini's *Maestà,* which combines an overt religious quality with civic and literary awareness: the parchment the Christ Child holds is inscribed with the city motto of upholding justice, and the steps of the canopied throne are engraved with two stanzas from Dante's *Divine Comedy.* In the next room, the **Sala dei Nove** exhibits Pietro and Ambrogio Lorenzetti's famous frescoes, the *Allegories of Good and Bad Government and their Effects on Town and Country.* The fresco on the right shows the utopia of good government. The flaking fresco on the left depicts thieves, devils, and lost souls in the land of bad government. *(Open daily Nov.-Feb. 10am-5:30pm, Mar.-Oct. 10am-7pm. €6.50, students €4, under 11 free.)* The Palazzo Pubblico's other star attraction is the **Torre del Mangia,** named for gluttonous bell-ringer Giovanni di Duccio, or "Mangiaguadagni" (Eat the profits). At 102m, the tower is Italy's tallest secular medieval monument. Persistence pays off when over 500 winding, narrowing stairs conclude just underneath the highest bell of the tower. Siena's tile rooftops, farmlands, and vineyard hills form an enchanting mosaic. Tourists crowd it in the afternoon, so arrive early. *(Open daily Nov.-Mar. 15 10am-4pm, Mar. 16-Oct. 10am-7pm. €6 or €10 combined ticket with Museo Civico.)*

▨ **DUOMO.** Atop one of the city's seven hills, the duomo is one of few full Gothic cathedrals south of the Alps. To prevent the massive apse from hanging over the side of the hill, the **baptistery** was built below. A huge arch, part of a striped wall facing the front of the cathedral, is the sole remnant of Siena's 1339 plan to construct a new nave, which would have made this duomo the largest church in all Christendom. The grandiose effort ended when the Black Plague decimated the working populace. One of the duomo's side aisles has been enclosed and turned into the **Museo dell'Opera Metropolitana** (p. 411). Statues of philosophers, sibyls, and prophets, all by Giovanni Pisano, hold sway beneath impressive spires.

The bronze sun symbol on the facade of the duomo was the brainchild of St. Bernadino of Siena, who wanted the feuding Sienese to relinquish their loyalty to emblems of nobility and unite under this symbol of the risen Christ. Alas, his efforts were in vain—the Sienese continue to identify with the animal symbols of their *contrade* (districts). The inlaid marble floor, like the rest of the duomo, is richly ornate, depicting such widely varying and often violent themes as alchemy and the Slaughter of the Innocents. A series on the left showing multi-ethnic sibyls represents the spread of Christianity. Most of the pieces are covered for preservation purposes, except in September when visitors can look for the works by Machese d'Adamo, perhaps the most spectacular in the entire building. Halfway up the left aisle is the **Piccolomini altar,** designed by Andrea Bregno in 1503. The altar contains niches that house four small life-like statues; St. Paul, on the lower right with the most elaborate drapery, was sculpted by Michelangelo early in his career. In the neighboring chapel is Donatello's bronze statue of St. John the Baptist, graceful even in his emaciation. The statue was honorably built to host a very special holy relic—St. John's right arm. The lavish **Libreria Piccolomini,** commissioned by Pope Pius III, houses the elaborately illustrated books of his uncle Pius II. *(Duomo open M-Sa Mar. 15-Oct. 7:30am-7:30pm, Nov.-Mar. 14 7:30am-5pm; Su 2-5pm. €3, €4-5.50 when floor is uncovered in Sept. Library open Mar. 15-Oct. 9am-7:30pm, Nov.-Mar. 14 M-Sa 10am-1pm and 2-5pm; Su 2-4:45pm. €1.50. Modest dress required.)*

MUSEO DELL'OPERA METROPOLITANA. The cathedral museum holds all the art that won't fit in the church. The first floor contains some of the foremost Gothic statuary in Italy, all by Giovanni Pisano. Upstairs the magnificent 700-year-old *Maestà,* by Duccio di Buoninsegna, originally served as a screen of the cathedral's altar. Other noteworthy works are the Byzantine *Madonna degli Occhi Coressi,* paintings by Lorenzetti, and two altarpieces by Matteo di Giovanni. Climb the **Scala del Facciatore,** in Room 4 on the upper floor, to a balcony over the nave. A very narrow spiral staircase leads to a tiny tower for a breathtaking view of the duomo, Il Campo and the entire city. *(Museum entrance outside of duomo, exit portals and turn left. Open daily Mar. 15-Sept. 9am-7:30pm; Oct. 9am-6pm; Nov.-Mar. 14 9am-1:30pm. €6.)*

SPEDALE DI S. MARIA DELLA SCALA. Built as a hospital in the 13th century, the Spedale is now a museum, displaying its original frescoes, chapels, and vaults, as well as beautiful paintings and statues. The Sala del Pellegrinaio, or the "Pilgrims' Hall," used as a ward until the late 20th century, contains an expressive fresco cycle by Vecchietta. In the first panel, the pregnant mother of the legendary founder of the hospital, Beato Sorore, dreams of the future good deeds of her son. The narrative of the history of the hospital continues from there up until its role during the Renaissance, when the frescoes were painted. The Sagrestia Vecchia or Cappello del Sacro Chiodo houses masterful 15th-century Sienese frescoes. On the way downstairs, duck into the dim underground chapels and vaults, sites of rituals and "acts of piety for the dead" performed by various *contrada* fraternities. One level down is the entrance to the Museo Archeologico, included in admission to the Spedale. Established in 1933 to collect and preserve Etruscan artifacts from the Siena area, the museum is now almost entirely in the eerie medieval underground water works of the city. Signs point the way through dank, labyrinthine passageways before emerging into rooms containing well-lit glass cases of Etruscan pottery and coins. *(Opposite the duomo. Open daily Mar.-Nov. 10:30am-6:30pm; Dec.-Feb. 10:30am-4:30pm. Ticket office closes 30min. before museum. €6 without advanced booking, €5.50 with booking, students €3.50.)*

PINACOTECA NAZIONALE. Siena's superb art gallery displays works by every major artist of the highly stylized Sienese school. The masters represented include the seven followers of Onccio—Simone Martini, the Lorenzetti brothers, Bartolo di Fredi, Da Domenico, Sano di Pietro, and Il Sodoma—as well as many others. The museum is refreshingly free of the tourist hordes that can make it difficult to appreciate many of Siena's prime collections. *(V. S. Pietro, 29, in the Palazzo Buonsignori down V. del Capitano from the duomo. Open M 8:30am-1:30pm, Tu-Sa 8:15am-7:15pm, Su 8:15am-1:15pm. €4, EU citizens 18-26 €2, EU citizens under 18 or over 65 free.)*

SANTUARIO DI SANTA CATERINA. This sanctuary honors the *Sienese* Caterina, a simple girl who had a grand vision—herself as Christ's bride. Her eloquence persuaded pope Gregory XI to return to Rome from Avignon; in 1939 she was proclaimed the patron saint of Italy. The simple brick building, converted into a Renaissance *loggia,* opens onto many Baroque chapels. The **Chiesa del Crocefisso**

on the right is impressive, but don't overlook the beautiful, smaller **Oratorio della Cucina** on the left. *(Entrance at the intersection of Costa di S. Antonio and V. dei Pittori, down from P. S. Domenico on V. Sappienza. Open daily 9am-12:30pm and 3-6pm. Free.)*

BAPTISTERY. Lavish and intricate frescoes depicting the lives of Christ and St. Anthony decorate the baptistery. On the left is Vasari's *Morte del Generale Collignon.* The centerpiece, however, is the hexagonal Renaissance **baptismal font** (1417-30). Panels include Ghiberti's *Baptism of Christ* and *John in Prison,* as well as Donatello's *Herod's Feast. (Behind the duomo. Open daily Mar. 15-Sept. 9am-7:30pm, Oct. 9am-6pm, Nov.-Mar. 14 10am-1pm and 2:30-5pm. €3.)*

OTHER SIGHTS. As in many Italian towns, Siena's Franciscan and Dominican basilicas rival each other from opposite ends of town. The **Chiesa di San Domenico** contains Andrea Vanni's portrait of S. Caterina and several other dramatic frescoes illustrating her miraculous acts. The exquisite *cappella* inside, dedicated to S. Caterina, was built in 1460 to store her preserved head and half of one of her fingers. *(In P. S. Domenico. Open daily Nov.-Apr. 9am-1pm and 3-6pm, May-Oct. 7am-1pm and 3-7pm.)* The **Chiesa di San Francesco** houses two frescoes by Pietro and Ambrogio Lorenzetti, moved to the church after a fire. *(Open daily 7:30am-noon and 3:30-7pm.)* Those interested in the Palio may enjoy one of Siena's 17 **contrada museums.** Each neighborhood organization maintains its own collection of costumes, banners, and icons. *(Most require an appointment—ask at the tourist office. Schedule visits at least 1 week in advance.)* Take time out from sightseeing for a stroll within the brick walls of the **Fortezza Medicea,** filled with fountains and towers. *(Free.)*

🎭 ENTERTAINMENT

Siena's 🏇**Palio** overtakes the city twice each year, on July 2 and August 16. As the bare-backed horse races approach, Siena's emotional temperature rises and Il Campo undergoes a frenzied transformation from lounge to racetrack. Five trial races take place during the three days preceding the race, and the evening before, revelry carries into the late hours. Young partisans from 10 of 17 participating *contrade* chant in packs on the street, singing often obscene lyrics to the tune of "Twinkle, Twinkle, Little Star." At 2:30pm on the day of the race, the horses are led into the churches of their respective *contrade* and blessed. A 2hr. parade of heralds and flag-bearers prefaces the anarchy to come with regal pomp. The last piece in the procession is the *Palio* itself, a banner depicting the Madonna and Child, drawn in a cart by white oxen (the race is called *Il Palio* because the banner is bestowed upon the winner). At the beginning of the race, riders battle for position behind the starting-line until the announcer is satisfied that all is in order and drops the rope without warning. The race begins at 7:30pm, and it takes the jockeys about 90 seconds to tear around Il Campo three times. During the race, they have free rein, according to the age-old, barbaric set of rules that guide the event, to whip their opponents. The straps they use are no ordinary pieces of leather: they are made from the skin of a bull's penis, especially durable and said to leave deep welts and psychological scars.

So many people flock to witness this spectacle that it is nearly impossible to stay in Siena during this period without booking a room at least four months in advance. Budget accommodations are especially scarce. Contact the APT in March or April for a list of *affittacamere.* Also inquire about reserving seats in the grandstands for the best view of the race. (Starting at €200, tickets can be prohibitively expensive; ask around at Il Campo cafes in addition to the APT.) Otherwise, spectators may stand on tip-toe in the "infield" of the piazza for free if they stake out a spot early enough, although the only view may be of the surrounding sea of frenzied fans. For information on the Palio, ask at the tourist office and pick up the excellent program (available in English).

In late July, the **Accademia Chigiana** (☎0577 220 91; www.chigiani.it) sponsors a music festival, the **Settimana Musicale Sienese**. Siena hosts a **jazz festival** in July, featuring internationally known musicians. For information, call ☎0577 27 14 01.

⚑ DAYTRIPS FROM SIENA

THE CHIANTI REGION

Buses connect Siena to Radda in Chianti (1hr., 4 per day, €2.70), a major base for exploring vineyards. Buses also connect Radda to Florence (1½hr.; 3 per day; last bus to Florence 6:10pm, last bus to Siena 6:40pm).

Siena lies within easy reach of the Chianti region, a harmonious landscape of green hills, ancient castles, tiny villages, and of course, uninterrupted expanses of vineyard. In the Middle Ages, the small countryside towns of Castellina, Radda, and Gaiole formed a military alliance against invading French and Spanish invaders, adopting the black rooster as their symbol. Today the rooster adorns the bottles of Chianti wines, which are famous throughout the world.

Peaceful **Radda in Chianti** is just 9km away on bus #125 from Siena. Radda's **tourist office,** in P. del Castello, has a knowledgeable, multilingual staff willing to help find accommodations. Ask here about the few wineries within walking distance of the town center. To reach the tourist office, walk from the bus stop down V. XX Settembre with the city walls on the left. Turn left at the public gardens on V. Roma, the main street in town, and right on Sdrucciolo del Castello. (☎0577 73 84 94; proradda@chiantinet.it. Open Mar.-Oct. M-Sa 10am-1pm and 3-7pm, Su 10:30am-12:45pm.) For more information on touring the nearby wineries, vacation rentals, and excursions to the countryside, inquire at **A Bit of Tuscany,** V. Roma, 39. (☎0577 73 86 37; www.divinetours.com. Open M-F 10am-1pm and 3-6pm.) Since many wineries give free tastings or offer tours, consider getting a map of the local wineries and exploring them on your own. **Internet** is available at **Snappy Bar,** V. XI Febbraio, 2, for €3 per 30 min. (☎0577 73 87 11. Open Tu-Su 7am-10:30pm.)

Radda has very few budget accommodations, so it's hard to beat **Le Camere di Giovannino ❹,** V. Roma, 6-8, where the rooms are comfortable and full of country character, with wood-trussed ceilings and vases of dried flowers on every bureau. All come with bath and TV. (☎/fax 0577 73 56 01. Rooms €55, €65 with breakfast.) Like Castellina, Radda is home to numerous *enoteche.* Inside the atmospheric vault of the reputable **Porciatti Alimentari ❷,** P. IV Novembre, 1-3, master butchers sell aged, hand-made salami, pork sausages, and cheese. Wine bottles start at €7. (☎0577 73 80 55; www.casaporciatti.it. Open May-Oct. M-Sa 7:45am-1pm and 5-8pm, Su 7:45am-1pm, Nov.-Apr. M-Sa 8am-1pm and 4:30-7:30pm. MC/V.) The cheapest place to pick up wine is the COOP **supermarket,** V. Roma, 26, which stocks bottles from €3.10. (Open M-Tu and Th-Sa 8am-1pm and 4:30-8pm, W 8am-1pm.) The casual **Pizzeria da Michele ❸,** P. IV Novembre, down a flight of steps from the piazza, has fine valley views and interesting dishes, such as boar with olives for €12, or *tagliatelle ai porcini e panna* (with porcini mushrooms and cream) for €7.50. (☎0577 73 84 91. *Primi* €6.50-8, *secondi* €11-14. Cover €2.07. Pizza only at dinner. Open Tu-Su noon-2:30pm and 7pm-midnight.) Another option is the cheap, delicious **Enoteca Dante Alighieri ❶,** P. Dante Alighieri, 1, across from the bus stop. It specializes in *bruschette* and *crostini* (from €2.25) and has an extensive wine list (from €2 a glass). Takeout is also available. (☎0577 73 88 15. Open M-F and Su 7am-10pm.) After a rigorous day of wine tasting, relax in the shaded **public gardens** outside the city walls.

SAN GALGANO

While most easily reached by car, one FMF bus connects Siena to San Galgano M-F at 8:55am. Tickets are €3.10 each way and can be purchased from the ticket office at P. Gramsci. The bus itself departs from the train station at box 10, which is across the street. The return bus to Siena picks up at Bar Piazellotta, a 2.5km walk from San Galgano, at 5:25pm. Take a left from the road that leads to the church onto the main highway and remain on the road until the bar is reached.

The 13th-century **Abbazia di San Galgano** looms majestically on a remote plain surrounded by the green hills of the Upper Merse Valley. In ruins now, without a roof and with grass as a floor, the abbey was built to honor the colorful and fantastic life of Saint Galgano. According to legend, the knight Galgano Guidotti had a vision of Jesus and the Apostles that commanded him to renounce his worldly possessions and take up the life of holy contemplation as a hermit. To this, Galgano replied that while doing so would be noble, it would serve no purpose in bettering the world—in fact, it would be like trying to slice the stone on which he stood with his sword like butter. As he said this, his sword cut through the stone easily. There it remains to this day, literally frozen in stone, up the hill from the abbey and housed by the **Cappella di San Galgano a Montesiepi,** which surveys the ruins of the church and the woodland hills. The cappella is a cylindrical structure with a striped dome, consecrated in 1185, just four years after San Galgano's death in 1181. The side chapel contains frescoes by Ambrogio Lorenzetti, depicting scenes from the life of the saint, a maesta, and an Annunciation. The Annunciation was censored because it originally depicted Mary clinging to a column in fear of the Angel Gabriel. This was soon covered by the painting of a more serene Mary. Also in the side chapel is an arm that belonged to one of the "three envious men" who attempted to extract the sword from the stone while San Galgano was away. Their arms were soon after torn off by a wolf who was a friend of San Galgano.

The **tourist office** is found to the right of the abby, under the second archway. (☎0577 75 67 38; www.prolocochiusdino.it. Open daily 10:30am-6pm.) For sustenance, **Wine Bar Salendo**, found downhill from the chapel, makes refreshing cocktails and *panini*, and has a large selection of wines. Try the mimosas (€3) or prosciutto and melon plate (€3.50). Outdoor seating on expansive lawn in comfortable wicker chairs. (www.salendo.net. Open daily 11:30am-8:30pm.) To stay overnight, the **Coop Agricola San Galgano Piccola ❸**, at the entrance of the drive leading to the Abbazia, rents rooms with bath, frescoes, and rustic stone floors. (☎ 0577 75 62 92; www.sangalgano.it. Singles €35; doubles €42; triples €63. MC/V.)

AREZZO ☎0575

Arezzo and its neighboring valleys were once home to Renaissance titans Piero della Francesca and Michelangelo, the poet Petrarch, the humanist Bruni, and the artist and historian Giorgio Vasari. It's also the hometown of Roberto Benigni, director and star of the Oscar-winning *La Vita è Bella (Life is Beautiful)*, who shot many of the film's key scenes here. The delightful historical district preserves many vestiges of past genius, from Vasari's stunning architecture in Piazza Grande to Francesco's unparalleled *Legend of the True Cross* in the Basilica di San Francesco. In addition, a stroll outside the eastern portion of the medieval city walls yields striking views of the countryside, and glimpses into private backyards full of olive trees, flowerbeds, and vegetable gardens.

▐ TRANSPORTATION

Arezzo lies on the Florence-Rome train line. In Piazza della Repubblica, **trains** run to Florence (1½hr.; 2 per hr. 4:30am-9:50pm; €5.10, InterCity €8) and Rome (2hr., every 1-2hr. 6:30am-10:11pm, €11.50/€18). The info booth is open Monday to Friday 8am-noon and 3-6pm, Saturday 9am-noon. To the left of the train station, **TRAIN**, **SITA**, and **LFI buses** run to: Cortona (1hr., every hr., €2.50); Sansepolcro (1hr., SITA every hr., €3.10); Siena (1½hr., 7 per day, €4.60). Call ☎0575 38 26 51 for more info. Buy tickets at ATAM ticket office, ahead and left from train station exit. (☎800 38 17 30. Open daily 6am-noon and 1:30-7:45pm.) For **taxis**, contact **Radio-Taxi**. (☎0575 38 26 26; open 24hr.) **Car rental** is available at **Autonoleggi Ermini**, V. Perrenio, 21. (☎0575 35 35 70. €55-105 per day. 21+. Open M-F 8:30am-12:30pm and 3:30-7:30pm, Sa 8:30am-12:30pm.)

ORIENTATION AND PRACTICAL INFORMATION

Via Guido Monaco, which begins directly across from the **train station** at **Piazza della Repubblica**, parallels **Corso Italia**; together they form the backbone of the commercial district. To get to the historic center, follow V. Guido Monaco from the station to the traffic circle at **Piazza Guido Monaco**. Turn right on **Via Roma** and then left on the pedestrian walkway, C. Italia, which leads to the old city. **Piazza Grande** lies to the right, 250m up C. Italia. **Via Veneto** begins a block to the right of the train station, going under the train tracks and continuing to the back of the station.

Tourist Office: APT, P. della Repubblica, 28 (☎0575 208 39; www.apt.arezzo.it). Turn right leaving station. English spoken. Free **maps**. Info on surrounding valleys. Open Apr.-Sept. M-Sa 9am-1pm and 3-7pm, Su 9am-1pm; Oct.-Mar. M-Sa 9am-1pm and 3-6:30pm.

Budget Travel: CTS, V. V. Veneto, 25 (☎0575 90 78 09 or 90 78 08), sells Eurail passes and plane tickets. Open M-F 9am-1pm and 3-7:30pm, Sa 9am-1pm.

Currency Exchange: Banca Nazionale del Lavoro, V. G. Monaco, 74. 24hr. **ATM.** Open M-F 8:20am-1:35pm and 2:45-7:05pm.

Emergency: ☎113. **Carabinieri** (☎112). **Ambulance:** (☎118).

Police: V. Dardano, 9 (☎113 or 0575 90 66 67), off V. Fra Guittone by the train station.

Pharmacy: Farmacia Comunale, Campo di Marte, 1 (☎0575 90 24 66), next to CONAD supermarket on V. Veneto. Open 24hr.

Hospital: Ospedale Civivo, on V. Fonte Veneziana (☎0575 25 51). **Misericordia** (☎0575 242 42).

Internet: InformaGiovani, P. G. Monaco, 2 (☎0575 37 78; informagiovani@comune.arezzo.it). 30min. free. Open M-Sa 9:30am-7:30pm.

Post Office: V. G. Monaco, 34 (☎0575 33 24 11). **Currency exchange** (€0.50 commission) at booth #1 (same hours). Open M-F 8:15am-7pm, Sa 8:15am-12:30pm. **Postal Code:** 52100.

ACCOMMODATIONS

Hotels fill to capacity during the **Fiera Antiquaria** (Antique Fair) the first weekend of every month. Otherwise, finding a room should be a cinch. **Ostello Villa Severi ❶**, V. Redi, 13, is a bit of a hike from town: take bus #4 (€0.80) from P. G. Monaco to two stops after Ospedale Vecchio (7min.). Disembark when the town park is on the left; the hostel is surrounded by the park. The tall, yellow villa is a spacious budget option with high ceilings and wood-beam detail. (☎0575 29 90 47; www.peterpan.it/ostello.htm. Breakfast €3. Lunch or dinner, including several courses and wine, €11. Reserve ahead for meals. Reception daily 9am-1pm and 6-11:30pm. Lockout 1-6pm. Dorms €15.) To get to **Albergo Cecco ❸**, C. Italia, 215, follow V. G. Monaco from the train station, turn right on V. Roma and another right on C. Italia. Do not follow signs for Hotel Cecco; they are misleading. The rooms are basic but spacious and clean, and all come with TV, phone, and large windows. (☎0575 209 86, fax 35 67 30. Breakfast €3. Singles €30, with bath €40; doubles

TUSCANY

€50; triples €70; quads with bath €88. AmEx/MC/V.) The higher-end **Hotel Continentale ❺**, P. G. Monaco, 7, features tasteful, modern rooms with bath, A/C, and TV. The reception staff is personable and knowledgeable, offering sightseeing and dining suggestions. The roof terrace boasts a panorama of the sloping historical quarter. (☎0575 202 51; www.hotelcontinentale.com. Buffet breakfast €8. Singles €67; doubles €98; triples €132; quads €165. AmEx/MC/V.)

◘ FOOD

A well stocked **CONAD** is on the corner of V. V. Veneto and V. L. B. Alberti, behind the train station. (Open M-Tu and Th-Sa 8am-8:30pm, W 8am-1:30pm.) An **open-air market** takes place in P. Sant'Agostino on weekdays. Head to **La Mozzarella**, V. Spinello, 25, for a great variety of cheeses. (Open M-Sa 8am-1pm and 4-8pm.)

> **Le Taste Vin**, V. de' Cenci, 9 (☎0575 283 04). Walking up V. G. Monaco, take 2nd right after P. G. Monaco to V. di Tolletta. Continue walking to V. de' Cenci. The French name seems to allude to the chic, antique-style interior rather than to the traditional Tuscan tastes, like *ribollita* (€5) and 3 different types of *carpaccio*. *Primi* €5-7, *secondi* €8-10. Open Tu-Su 12:30-3pm and 7-11:30pm. Closed Aug. 5-20. AmEx/MC/V. ❸

> **Trattoria Il Saraceno**, V. Mazzini, 6 (☎0575 276 44), off C. Italia. Boasts Arezzo specialties like duck and pecorino cheese in honey. Sardine-like seating. Pizza €6-8 (evening only), *primi* €6-8, *secondi* €6-12. Cover €2. Open M-Tu and Th-Su noon-3:30pm and 7:30-11pm. AmEx/MC/V. ❸

> **Ristorante Chicco di Riso**, P. San Gemignano, 1 (☎0575 30 24 20). From C. Italia, go right on V. Garibaldi, then left uphill to the piazza. Mainly-veggie, all-organic, macrobiotic meals, like brown rice *risotto* and simple salads. Offer student special: €3.50 for soup and entree sampler. Cover €1. Open M-Sa 12:30-2:30pm and 7:30-9:30pm. ❷

> **Paradiso di Stelle**, V. G. Monaco, 58 (☎0575 274 48). Come for first-rate homemade gelato—the *nocciola* and *tiramisù* are superb (from €2)—or try a toasty *nutella*-filled crepe (€2.10). Open Tu-Su Mar.-Sept. 10:30am-midnight, Oct.-Feb. 10:30am-9pm. ❶

◉ SIGHTS

BASILICA DI SAN FRANCESCO. This extraordinary 11th-century basilica houses gorgeous frescoes, among them Piero della Francesca's ▧*Leggenda della Vera Croce* (Legend of the True Cross), which portrays the story of the crucifix and its role in early Christianity. The narrative begins with the death of Adam and proceeds to major events such as the conversion of Emperor Constantine. St. Francis is the figure kneeling at the foot of the cross. (*Up V. G. Monaco from train station, right into P. San Francesco. Basilica open daily 8:30am-noon and 2-7pm. Free. Chapel containing della Francesca's frescoes open M-F 9am-7pm, Sa 9am-6pm, Su 1-6pm. Visitors admitted in groups of 25 every 30min.; last visit begins 30min. before chapel closes. Reservation required. Call ☎0575 206 30 or visit the office to the right of the church. €5.03, students 18-25 €3.03, art students or under 18 €1.03. Upper portion of the fresco cycle free.*)

PIAZZA GRANDE. This piazza contains the **Chiesa di Santa Maria della Pieve**, Arezzo's most important monument, a spectacular Romanesque church that dates from the 12th century. Elegant columns and rounded arches frame Benedetto da Maiano's 15th-century portico. On the elevated presbytery sits Pietro Lorenzetti's brilliantly restored polyptych, depicting the *Annunciation* and *Madonna and Child*. Below lies the ninth-century church upon which the Pieve was built. The adjoining tower is known as the "Tower of a Hundred Holes." (*Open M-Sa 8am-noon and 3-7pm, Su 8:30am-noon and 4-7pm.*) Surrounding the church is Arezzo's best architecture: the 14th-century Romanesque **Palazzo della Fraternità dei Laici** and the hulking 16th-century Baroque **Loggiato dei Vasari.** The piazza also hosts the monthly **antique fair** and the semiannual **Giostra del Saraceno** (see **Festivals**) each summer.

THE DUOMO. The massive 13th-century cathedral, built in Tuscan Gothic, houses Arezzo native Piero di Francesca's *Maddalena* and Bishop Guido Tarlati's tomb, on the left side of the nave near the altar. Carved reliefs relate stories about the iconoclast's unconventional life. The six circular teal and purple stained-glass windows were designed by Guglielmo de Marcillat. The *Capella della Madonna del Conforto*, off the severe nave, holds a terra-cotta *Crucifixion* by Andrea della Robbia. *(Up V. Andrea Cesalpino from P. S. Francesco. Modest dress required. ☎0575 239 91. Duomo open daily 7am-12:30pm and 3-7pm.)*

CHIESA DI SAN DOMENICO. As was often the case, the Dominicans built their church on the end of town opposite the Franciscan establishment. The church contains a superb Cimabue crucifix (1265), Spinello Aretino's *Annunciation*, and a Marcillat rose window depicting St. Augustine. *(Take V. Andrea Celaspino from P. S. Francesco, turn left at P. Libertà on V. Ricasorli, then right on V. di Sassoverde, leading to the Chiesa. Open daily 8am-noon and 2:30-7:30pm. Hours may vary. Closed during mass.)* Near the church lies the **Logge Vasari,** which the historian and artist built for himself and decorated with impressive portrait-frescoes of Michelangelo and del Sarto. In the adjacent room, Vasari crowns the ceiling with depictions of the muses, one in the likeness of his fiancee, Niccolosa. He even painted himself contemplating the lovely view from one of the windows. *(V. XX Settembre, 55. Just off V. San Domenico. ☎0575 229 06 . Open M and W-Sa 8:30am-1pm and 3:30-7:30pm, Su 8:30am-1:30pm. Ticket office open M and W-Sa 8:30am-7pm, Su 8:30am-1pm. €2, students €1. Ring bell to enter.)*

FESTIVALS

Arezzo's **antique fairs** take place in and around P. Grande on the first Sunday and preceding Saturday of every month. Beautiful antique furniture and religious paraphernalia would be tough to lug home through customs, though sundry bric-a-bracs can make nice souvenirs. The **Giostra del Saraceno,** a medieval joust, happens on the third Sunday of June and the first Sunday of September. In a ritual recalling the Crusades and fostering intercultural tolerance, "knights" representing the four quarters of the town charge a wooden effigy of a Turk with lances drawn.

DAYTRIP FROM AREZZO

SANSEPOLCRO

Sansepolcro is most easily accessible by the hourly SITA bus from Arezzo (1hr., 15 per day, €3.10). Some routes require a change in Le Villel; ask the driver. The bus arrives just outside the walls of the old city. From the bus stop, enter the old city on V. N. Aggiunti. Follow the street 5 blocks, until passing the Museo Civico on the right. Turn right under an arch on V. G. Matteotti, and turn immediately left into P. Garibaldi. Sansepolcro's tourist office, P. Garibaldi, 2 (☎/fax 0575 74 05 36), is 1 block ahead on the left. Open daily 9:30am-1pm and 3:30-6:30pm.

Nestled in the valley of the Tiber at the foot of the densely forested Apennines, Sansepolcro's claim to fame is as the birthplace of painter Piero della Francesca. The **Museo Civico,** V. Aggiunti, 65, displays some of della Francesca's finest works. *The Resurrection* features a triumphant Jesus towering above the sleeping guards. An exultant Christ rests one foot on his coffin and meets the viewer's eyes with an intense, disconcerting gaze. The polyptych

Madonna della Misericordia depicts a stern Madonna. (☎ 0575 73 22 18. Open daily June-Sept. 9am-1:30pm and 2:30-7:30pm, Oct.-May 9:30am-1pm and 2:30-6pm. €6, over 65 €4.50, ages 10-16 €3. Groups €4.50 per person. Audioguides €2.) The left chapel of the Romanesque-styled **duomo** that began construction in 1002 shelters the town's other cherished sight, the mysterious **Volto Santo,** a large wooden crucifix depicting a blue-robed Jesus (Holy Face), V. Matteotti, just off P. Torre di Berta. Believed by some to be much older than its 12th-century attribution, the Holy Face's Assyrian features suggest Oriental origins. Scholars speculate that the same artist produced the much-celebrated Volto Santo in Lucca. (Open 8am-noon and 3-6pm.)

CORTONA ☎ 0575

The ancient town of Cortona regally surveys Tuscany and Umbria from its vine-ringed mountain peak. Watch from Piazza Garibaldi while the distant hills across the valley fade to dusky blue in the haze of sunset. Though currently peaceful, the city once rivaled Perugia, Arezzo, and even Florence in power and belligerence. In 1411 Cortona lost its autonomy and was appropriated by the king of Naples, who soon sold it to the rival Florentines. For all its grumbling, Cortona enjoyed peace and prosperity under Florentine rule. Impressive art collections and architecture from this period of grandeur linger within the small city's walls, including two altarpieces by Fra Angelico and the paintings of Luca Signorelli, the great precursor to Michelangelo. Today, Cortona is a desireable and popular destination for art lovers, families, and hill town romantics of all ages.

▐ TRANSPORTATION

Trains depart **Camucia-Cortona station** to Florence (every hr., €6.40) and Rome (every 1-2hr., €9.10). **LFI buses** (☎ 0575 30 07 48) run to Cortona's P. Garibaldi from this station (15min., €1) and from **Terontola train station** (30min., every hr., €1.50; buy ticket on bus). Buses also arrive in P. Garibaldi from Arezzo (1hr., 12 per day, €2.50). Buy LFI bus tickets from the tourist office, a bar, or *tabacchi.* For **taxis,** call ☎ 335 819 63 13.

▣ ▐ ORIENTATION AND PRACTICAL INFORMATION

Buses from neighboring cities stop at **Piazza Garibaldi** just outside the city wall. Enter the city by turning left uphill, following **Via Nazionale,** which leads into **Piazza della Repubblica,** the center of town. Diagonally across the piazza is **Piazza Signorelli,** Cortona's main square. The **tourist office,** on V. Nazionale, 42, provides **maps,** bus schedules, and tickets for buses, trains, and tours. (☎ 0575 63 03 52; www.apt.arezzo.it. Open June-Sept. M-Sa 9am-1pm and 3-7pm, Su 9am-1pm; Oct.-May M-Tu and Th-F 9am-1pm and 3-5pm, W and Sa 9am-1pm. Train tickets are not sold Sa-Su.) **Currency exchange** and a 24 hr. **ATM** are available at **Banca Popolare,** V. S. Margherita, 2/3. (Open M-F 8:20am-1:20pm and 2:35-3:35pm.) In case of **emergency,** dial ☎ 113, call an **ambulance** (☎ 118), or reach the **police** at V. Dardano, 9 (☎ 0575 60 30 06). **Farmacia Centrale** is at V. Nazionale, 38. (☎ 0575 60 32 06. Open M-Sa 9am-1pm and 4:30-8pm.) The **hospital,** Ospedale Civico, is on V. Maffei (☎ 0575 63 91). Use the **Internet** at **Agenzia Viaggi e Turismo,** V. Guelfa, 26. At the end of V. Nazionale, turn left onto V. Guelfa and walk halfway down hill. (☎ 0575 60 52 35. €3 per hr., need an ISIC card for use. Open M-F 9am-1pm and 4-8pm, Sa 9am-1pm.) **Telenet,** V. Roma, 20, also offers **Internet,** a phone center, Western Union, cell phone rental and shipping services; English spoken. (☎0575 63 17 35. €5 per hr. Open M-Sa 9:30am-1pm and 4-8pm, Su 4-8pm.) The **post office** is uphill from P. della Repubblica at V. Santucci, 1. (☎0575 60 30 21. Open M-F 8:15am-1:30pm, Sa 8:15am-12:30pm.) **Postal Code:** 52044.

ACCOMMODATIONS

Ostello San Marco (HI), V. Maffei, 57 (☎0575 60 17 65; www.cortonahostel.com). From bus stop, walk 5min. uphill on V. S. Margherita and follow signs curving left to the hostel. Clean and bright rooms make for an enjoyable overnight, although hallway bathrooms are small. Breakfast, showers, and sheets included. Complete dinner €8.50. Reception 7-9am and 5pm-midnight. Lockout 9:30am-5pm. Open to individuals mid-Mar.-Nov., year-round for groups. Dorms €11.50. Cash only. ❶

Casa Betania, V. G. Severini, 50 (☎0575 628 29, fax 60 42 99), downhill on V. Severini from P. Garibaldi. Cross street and take an immediate right into the gates. Rooms are simply furnished with sturdy furniture and small sinks, and have large, sunny windows. Singles €25, with bath €30; doubles €36/€41. Cash only. ❷

Istituto Santa Margherita, V. Cesare Battisti, 15 (☎0575 63 03 36, fax 63 05 49). Downhill on V. Severini from P. Garibaldi. Istituto on corner of V. Battisti, on the left. Get thee to this nunnery (actually a former college). All rooms with large, tiled baths, though showers occasionally run cold. Breakfast €3. Flexible midnight curfew. Singles €32; doubles (no unmarried couples) €46; triples €56; quads €66. Cash only. ❸

Hotel San Luca, P. Garibaldi, 1 (☎0575 63 04 60; www.sanlucacortona.com). Wide hallways lead to refined rooms, some with balcony and sweeping vistas of the Val di Chiena valley. Comfortable common areas. All rooms have bath, satellite TV, A/C, phone, and minibar. Singles €65, with breakfast €70; doubles €90/€100; triples €134; quads €170; quints €201. AmEx/MC/V. ❺

Albergo Italia, V. Ghibellina, 5 (☎0575 630 25; www.planhotel.com), off P. della Repubblica. New management has transformed rooms at this centrally located hotel into stylish sanctuaries. All sport antique furniture, funky new light fixtures, TV, bath, and A/C unit. Homecooked buffet breakfast included. Singles €70; doubles €97; triples €115; quads €138. AmEx/MC/V. ❺

FOOD

Cortona's restaurants serve home-style Tuscan dishes for reasonable prices. The best beef in Tuscany is raised in the surrounding valleys, so consider making the modest splurge on *bistecca alla Fiorentina*, a massive hunk of red meat served *au sang* (still bleeding). Steak is so popular that restaurants sell it per 100g. Complement dinner with the fine local wine, *bianco vergine di Valdichiana*. Pennypinchers can pick up a €2.50 bottle at **Despar**, P. della Repubblica, 23, which also makes *panini* with fresh ingredients for €3. (☎0575 63 06 66. Open Apr.-Oct. M-Sa 7:30am-1:30pm and 4-8pm, Su 7:30am-1:30pm; Nov.-Mar. M-Tu and Th-Sa 7am-1:30pm and 4:30-8pm, W 7am-1:30pm. AmEx/MC/V.) On Saturday P. Signorelli hosts an **open-air market.** (Open 8am-1pm).

Trattoria La Grotta, P. Baldelli, 3 (☎0575 67 80 67), turn left into courtyard at the P. della Repubblica end of V. Nazionale. The *gnocchi di ricotta e spinaci* (€6.50) bring tears of gastronomic joy to the eye. Follow up with the *carpaccio con rucola e parmiggiano* (€8). Indoor seating in converted wine cellar; outdoor seating in a secluded courtyard. *Primi* €5-9, *secondi* €6-16. Open M and W-Su 12-2:20pm, 7:30-11pm. MC/V. ❸

TUSCANY

Pizzeria Fufluns, V. Ghibellina, 3 (☎0575 76 41 40; www.fufluns.net.), off P. della Repubblica. Basic pizzas and good pasta have won this tiny, stone-walled restaurant many fans. 2 outdoor tables and the indoor tavern fill during lunch and dinner hours with adoring Cortonesi. Pizza €4-6. *Primi* €5-7.50, *secondi* priced to order. Open M and W-Su 12:30-2:30pm and 7:30pm-12:30am. MC/V. ❷

Trattoria Dardano, V. Dardano, 24 (☎0575 60 19 44). 2 dining rooms filled with tourists in the know and parties of Cortonese families, offer simple, filling dishes, with notably ample *secondi* portions. Succulent meat dishes, including a very reasonable steak (€2.50 per 100g). *Primi* €5-6, *secondi* €5-8. Cover €1. Open M-Tu and Th-Su noon-4pm and 7pm-midnight. Cash only. ❷

Ristorante Preludio, V. Guelfa, 11 (☎0575 63 01 04). Dress up a bit for Tuscan meals with a twist. Gray stone portals, high ceilings, and flowers on every table add a classy touch. *Primi* €7-9, *secondi* €7-15. Roasted meats €4-5 per 100g. Cover €2. Open daily 12:30-3pm and 7:30-10:30pm. MC/V. ❸

Il Cacciatore, V. Roma, 13 (☎0575 63 05 52), downhill from the main piazza and mercifully free of traffic noises. Good home-style cooking, with basic, well-prepared pasta and traditional Tuscan meat served in a dining room with A/C. *Primi* €3-8, *secondi* €9-14. Open M-Tu and Th-Su noon-2:30pm and 7:30-10pm. ❸

◉ SIGHTS

▨ **MUSEO DELL'ACCADEMIA ETRUSCA.** Perfectly preserved Egyptian sarcophagi and mummies, Roman coins, and golden altarpieces mingle to fantastic effect in this extravagant collection. Also check out oil paintings by old masters and native sons Luca Signorelli and Pietro Berrettini (called Pietro da Cortona), as well as by the futurist Gino Severini. In the main hall on the first floor is an unusual 5th century BC Etruscan chandelier, decorated with intricate allegorical carvings. In the Medici Room, lined with coats of arms, are two 1714 globes by Silvestro Moroncelli; one depicts the "Isola di California" floating in the Pacific, the other sports vivid illustrations of all the constellations. *(Inside the courtyard of Palazzo Casli, to the right of P. della Repubblica in P. Signorelli. ☎057 63 72 35; www.accademia-etrusca.org. Guided visits daily at 10:30am for €1, 6 person max. Open Apr.-Sept. daily 10am-7pm; Nov.-Mar. Tu-Su 10am-5pm. €4.20, groups of 15+ €2.50 per person.)*

▨ **MUSEO DIOCESANO.** The upstairs gallery of this small Renaissance art museum houses the stunning *Annunciation* (c. 1432-4) by Fra Angelico in Room 3 as well as Luca Signorelli's masterpiece, *The Deposition* (1502), a vivid portrayal of the removal of Christ's dead body from the cross. Christ's agonized face looks down from Pietro Lorenzetti's fresco of *The Way to Calvary.* Severini's modern interpretations of traditional Biblical scenes line the stairwell. *(From P. della Repubblica, pass through P. Signorelli and follow the signs. ☎0575 628 30. Open daily Apr.-Oct. 10am-7pm, Nov.-Mar. 10am-5pm. €5, 14 and under €3. Audioguides available for €3.)*

FORTEZZA MEDICEA. Views of the Val di Chiana and Lake Trasimeno beyond are more breathtaking at this fortress than from P. Garibaldi. The courtyards and turrets contain temporary art installations, and shrines decorated with mosaics, based on Severini's series in the Museo Diocesano, line the uphill path. On the way is the **Basilica di Santa Margherita,** whose white marble facade belies the bold combinations of primary colors within—blue ceilings are fancifully dotted with gold stars. The body of Santa Margherita rests eternally in a glass coffin at the center of the altarpiece. *(A thigh-burning 15min. walk up V. S. Margh-*

erita from P. Garibaldi. To reach the fortress, take a right out of the church and climb the small uphill road. ☎ 0575 60 37 93. Fortress open May-Sept. Tu-Su 10am-6pm. €3, under 18 €1.50. Basilica free. Modest dress required.)

PALAZZI AND PIAZZAS. In P. della Repubblica, the 13th-century **Palazzo Comunale** overlooks the surrounding shops and cafes. At night, tourists cluster on the steps to enjoy their gelato and watch the locals make their *passeggiate*. **Palazzo Casali,** to the right and behind the Palazzo del Comune, dominates P. Signorelli. Only the courtyard walls, lined with coats of arms, remain from the original structure; the facade and interlocking staircase are 17th-century additions. **Piazza del Duomo** lies to the right and downhill from the Palazzo Casali. Inside the towering cathedral are paintings by Signorelli and del Sarto, as well as an impressive Baroque-canopied high altar. *(Duomo open 8am-12:30pm and 3-5:30pm.)*

FESTIVALS

When August 14-15 rolls around, Italian cows start trembling. Yes, it's time for the **Sagra della Bistecca** (Steakfest), the most important town festival, when the populace converges upon piles of superb steak in the public gardens behind the church of S. Domenico. The next culinary extravaganza follows in the third weekend in August with the **Festa dei Porcini,** which fills the gardens with mushroom-lovers. Tickets are sold at the garden entrance. In early June, neighborhoods commemorate a nobleman's 1397 marriage with religious ceremonies, processions, period dress, and the **Giostra Dell'Archidado,** a crossbow challenge in which participants compete for the *verretta d'oro* (golden dart). Musical and theatrical events cluster July, when Cortona absorbs the spillover from the Umbria Jazz Festival (p. 485). Relax in the gardens or join in the *passeggiata* in the park, which screens movies, played in the original language (usually English), weekly from mid-June through early September. (Films start 9:45pm in the gardens, in Teatro Signorelli in bad weather. Tickets €5.)

MONTEPULCIANO ☎ 0578

Stretched along the crest of a narrow limestone ridge, this small medieval hamlet is Tuscany's highest hill town. Montepulciano was built in four phases, first to protect against belligerent neighbors and later to ward off disease-ridden pilgrims. Dozens of 16th-century palaces, charming squares, and dignified churches lie within its walls. The town, neglected for some centuries following the Renaissance, is wealthy and heavily-touristed today, thanks largely to its famous red wine industry. At many local wineries, the traveling epicure can savor the garnet-colored *Vino Nobile* that put the town on the map.

▐ TRANSPORTATION

Montepulciano lies on the Siena-Chiusi line. The train station (☎ 0578 200 74), is 10km from town center. **Trains** run to Chiusi (20min., every hr., €2.50). **LFI buses** (☎ 0578 311 74) run to the town from the train station (Sept.-May 6am-9pm, €1), but service is infrequent in summer and the alternative is a €13-16 cab ride. From June through August, take the train to Chiusi and a bus to the town center. **TRA-IN buses** (☎ 0578 20 41 11) run to Florence (2hr., €7.70) and Siena (1½hr., M-Sa 5 per day, €4.50), some via Buonconvento. **LFI** buses run to Chiusi (1hr., every hr. 7am-9:50pm, €2). Tickets are available at agencies displaying LFI Biglietti and TRA-IN signs. Check at tourist office for schedule. For a **taxi,** call ☎ 0578 639 89. For **24hr. taxi** and **car rental,** call ☎ 0578 71 60 81.

✦ 🛈 ORIENTATION AND PRACTICAL INFORMATION

Buses to Montepulciano make a midway stop in the *centro storico* but end at the bottom of the hill outside of town. To avoid an uphill trek, ask the driver to stop at **Porta delle Farine** and disembark before the bus descends to the **bus station.** A short, steep climb leads to the **Corso,** the main street. Divided nominally into four parts (V. di Gracciano nel Corso, V. di Voltaia nel Corso, V. dell'Opio nel Corso, and V. del Poliziano), the Corso winds laboriously up a precipitous hill. At the end, the street starts to level off; from here, on **Via del Teatro,** an incline on the right leads to **Piazza Grande,** the main square. Orange **ATAF buses** ease the journey (€0.90). Regional buses leave frequently from the bus station; from Porta delle Farina, follow V. di Oriolo to V. delle Lettere (15min.) to the station on the right.

The **tourist office,** P. Grande, 7, provides **maps** and bus schedules, makes free arrangements for hotels and *affittacamere* in the town and countryside, and sells tickets for town wine and oil tours (light dinner provided, 5 person min., €31 per person), offered Wednesday 5:30pm and Friday 3pm. (☎0578 71 74 84; www.stradavinonobile.it. Open M-Sa 10am-1pm and 3-6pm.) **Banca Toscana,** P. Michelozzo, 2, offers **currency exchange** and has an **ATM** outside. (Open M-F 8:20am-1:20pm and 2:45-3:45pm.) Currency exchange is also available at the post office and the 24hr. exchange machines in P. Savonarola. In case of **emergency,** dial ☎113. For an **ambulance,** dial ☎118. The **police** (☎112) are at P. Savonarola, 16. **Farmacia Franceschi** is at V. di Voltaia nel Corso, 47. (☎0578 71 63 92. Open M-Sa Apr.-Sept. 9am-1pm and 4:30-7:30pm, Oct.-May 9am-1pm and 4-7pm.) **Farmacia Sorbini** (☎0578 75 73 52), on V. Calamandrei, fills urgent prescriptions. **Internet** and **phone center** can be found at **Internet Train,** V. Gracciano nel Corso, 26. (☎0578 71 72 53. Open M-F 9am-1pm and 3-8pm.) The **post office,** V. delle Erbe, 12, uphill from P. delle Erbe and the Corso, offers currency exchange for a €0.50 commission. (Open M-F 8:15am-7pm, Sa 8:15am-12:30pm.) **Postal Code:** 53045.

🛈 ACCOMMODATIONS

Most lodgings in Montepulciano cost as much as three- or four-star hotels elsewhere. *Affittacamere* (rooms for rent) are the best option.

Affittacamere Bellavista, V. Ricci, 25 (☎347 823 23 14 or 338 229 19 64), downhill from the tourist office. Basic but comfortable rooms for rent, some with fantastic views of the countryside. Reserve ahead, then call upon arrival from the pay phone outside; key will be delivered in 20min. Singles €35; doubles with bath €46-48. ④

Albergo La Terrazza, V. Piè al Sasso, 16 (☎/fax 0578 75 74 40). From P. Grande, take V. del Teatro downhill, left of the duomo. In Piazzeta del Teatro, turn left on V. di Cagnano and walk 4 blocks to hotel. Climb 2 flights of stairs to an outdoor terrace and garden with a well-stocked bar. All rooms have private bath, A/C, TV, and phone. Breakfast included. Singles €60; doubles €85; triples €108.50; quads €124. MC/V. ④

Meuble Il Riccio, V. Talosa, 21 (☎/fax 0578 75 77 13; www.ilriccio.net), just off P. Grande. Art, columns, and stairwells allude to the distinguished past of the building as a former seminary. Stunning views from the rooftop terrace survey the Val di Chiana and its shimmering lakes. Reservation recommended. Breakfast €8. All rooms €85 year-round. AmEx/MC/V. ⑤

Ristorante Cittino, V. della Nuova, 2 (☎0578 75 73 35), off V. di Voltaia del Corso. The 3 family-run rooms are spacious and comfortable, and delicious smells drift up from the restaurant below. Shared bath sometimes lacks hot water. Call to reserve when restaurant is open (M-Tu and Th-Su 9am-11pm). Singles €30-35; doubles €55. ❸

🍴 FOOD

Minimarkets line the Corso. A CONAD **supermarket** is near P. Savonarola, outside the city walls. (Open M-Tu and Th-Sa 8:30am-7pm, W 8:30am-noon.) Thursday brings the **open-air market** to the lot behind the bus station. (Open 8am-1pm.)

Il Cantuccio, V. delle Cantine, 1-2 (☎0578 75 78 70), off V. di Gracciano nel Corso. Tuxedo-clad waiters with ESP—your glass will never be empty—serve Tuscan fare with an Etruscan twist in the low-ceilinged restaurant. Try *pollo e coniglio all'Etrusca* (Etruscan-style chicken and rabbit; €11.40). *Primi* €6.20-9.30, *secondi* €7-16. Service 12%. Open Tu-Su 12:30-2:30pm and 7:30-11pm. Closed 1st 2 weeks of July. MC/V. ❸

Trattoria Diva e Maceo, V. Gracciano nel Corso, 92 (☎0578 71 69 51). Homestyle Tuscan meals served by jovial staff to tourists and locals. Dine on *cannelloni* (stuffed with ricotta and spinach; €7) and *ossobuco* (beef stew; €7.50). *Primi* €5.50-7.50, *secondi* €7-13. Cover €2. Open M and W-Su 12:30-2:30pm and 7:30-9:30pm. AmEx/MC/V. ❷

Osteria dell'Acquacheta, V. del Teatro, 22 (☎0578 75 84 43 or 71 70 86), off the Corso. Very small but delicious selection of typical Tuscan food. Get a platter of *pecorino di pienza al tartufo* (aged cheese with truffles; €5.20) for a classic taste. *Primi* €5.20, *secondi* by weight from €2.10-2.80 per 100g. Open M and W-Su 12:30-3pm and 7:30-10:30pm. MC/V. ❸

Caffè Poliziano, V. del Voltaio nel Corso, 27 (☎0578 75 86 15). Marble tabletops and a brass-accented bar complete this classy cafe and its delectable pastries (from €0.70). 2 tiny terraces offer a splendid view. Open daily 7am-1am. AmEx/MC/V. ❶

TUSCANY

🅖 SIGHTS

CHIESA DI SAN BIAGIO. Built with the Greek-cross shape, this Sangallo master-piece is a stunning example of high Renaissance symmetry. Majestically rooted on a wide grass-covered plateau, the church looks out onto hills of tall grass. The cavernous interior was redone in the 17th century in overwrought Baroque, but the simple skeleton still peeks through. The walk offers great views of the countryside, and in the summer, lots of blooming lilacs. *(From P. Grande, follow V. Ricci to V. della Mercenzia. Turn left down staircase before Piazzetta di S. Francesco. Follow signs on switchbacks, through the city walls, and along V. di San Biagio. Open daily 9am-1pm and 3:30-7pm.)*

PIAZZA GRANDE. The piazza is surrounded by the unfinished duomo on the north, the 14th-century Palazzo Comunale on the east, the Palazzo Tarugi on the south and the Palazzo Contucci on the west. The construction of the **duomo** began in the 16th century; after several years of commissioning and firing architects, the town council settled on Ippolito Scalza, a native of Orvieto. He produced the stark duomo, whose incomplete, bulky and crumbling stone facade is overshadowed by the surrounding structures. The church's interior is equally sparse, its simplicity emphasized by several great oil paintings dotting its bare walls. In particular note the Sienese master Taddeo di Bartolo's poignant *Assumption of the Virgin* hanging in a triptych above the high altar. *(In P. Grande, at the top of the hill. Open daily 9am-12:30pm and 3:15-7pm.)* The elegant facade of **Palazzo de'Nobili-Tarugi** faces the duomo. A ground-level archway visually elongated by pilasters gives the building a structured yet vibrant feel. The nearby **Palazzo Contucci** is a graceful, if eccentric, hybrid of architectural styles. The Contucci family has made fine wine here for well over a century and today runs a charming *enoteca* (wine store) on the ground floor. In the mid-1400s Michelozzo completed **Palazzo Comunale,** a smaller version of the Palazzo Vecchio in Florence, complete with tower and turrets; it took nearly a century to build and now serves as Montepulciano's municipal center. Its tower offers views of Siena to the north and of Gran Sasso Massif to the south. *(Tower open M-Sa 10am-6pm. €1.55.)* Down V. Ricci, the **Palazzo Neri-Orselli** houses the **Museo Civico,** one of Montepulciano's foremost attractions, containing a collection of enameled terracotta by Andrea della Robbia, Etruscan funerary urns, and over 200 paintings. *(V. Ricci, 10. Open Tu-Su 10am-1pm and 3-7pm. €4.13, under 18 or over 65 €2.58.)*

🎵 ENTERTAINMENT

Tourists to Montepulciano keep themselves plenty busy browsing the wine stores and tasting free samples. Try the store at Porta di Bacco, on the left immediately inside the city gates. (Open daily 9am-8pm.) In the first half of August, the town fills with musicians who perform at **Cantiere Internazionale d'Arte.** Around August 15, the **Bruscello** (a series of amateur concerts and theatrical productions) occurs on the steps of the duomo. Visit on the last Sunday in August to see the **Bravio delle Botti,** a raucous barrel race through the streets between teams from each of the town's eight neighborhood militias that fended off the Florentines and Sienese.

MONTALCINO ☎ 0577

Perched atop a hill overlooking vineyards and stately clusters of cyprus, Montalcino is yet another town with a view. What makes it distinct from its neighbors are the narrow alleys and steep stairways that have changed little since medieval times when it was a Sienese stronghold, and its relatively low influx of tourists. Its heavy walls are enduring evidence of prior belligerence, but the tiny town has long since traded warmongering for wine making. Its foremost industry today is the production of the heavenly *Brunello di Montalcino*, a wine acknowledged as Italy's finest red. Sample the *Brunello* in the numerous wine shops or leave the city walls for a winery tour and a free taste.

🖃🛈 TRANSPORTATION AND PRACTICAL INFORMATION. To reach Montalcino, take one of the daily **TRA-IN buses** from Siena (1¼hr., 7 per day, €3.10). The last bus to Montalcino departs at 10:15pm, and the last bus back to Siena departs at 8:30pm from Montalcino's P. Cavour. In Siena, The buses leave from the **train station,** not P. Gramsci, but the TRA-IN ticket window in both places sells tickets (see **Siena: Transportation,** p. 425) Coming from Montepulciano (1¼hr., €3.50), change buses at Torrenieri. There is no actual bus stop, so flag the bus down as it approaches. Contact the **Pro-Loco** tourist office, Costa del Municipio, 8, for information about tours of the local vineyards, free **maps,** hotel booking, and **currency exchange.** From P. Cavour, where the bus stops, walk up V. Mazzini into P. del Popolo. The tourist office is under the clock tower. (☎0577 84 93 31; www.prolocomontalcino.it. Open Apr.-Oct. daily 10am-1pm and 2-5:50pm; Nov.-Mar. Tu-Su 10am-1pm and 2-5:40pm.) Rent a **mountain bike** (€13 per day) or **scooter** (from €26 per day) at **Minocci Lorenzo Noleggio,** V. P. Strozzi, 31, in the gas station. (☎0577 84 82 82; montalcinolmnoleggio@libero.it. Open by appointment only from 9am, so call first.)

🖩🛈 ACCOMMODATIONS AND FOOD. Hotel rooms are expensive and scarce in Montalcino; *affittacamere* are generally well-kept and run €42-52 for a double with bath. The tourist office provides a list of all hotels and *affittacamere* in the area. **◪Anna Affittacamera** provides luxury for a small price. Rooms have ceiling frescoes, comfortable beds, TV, and bath. Reception is in Albergo Giglio; rooms are located on a nearby side street. (☎0577 84 86 66, fax 0577 84 81 67. Singles €42; doubles €64.) Closest to the bus stop is the friendly **Albergo Il Giardino ❹,** P. Cavour, 4. Its large, tasteful rooms all have bath. The rooms in back have smaller baths but are free from the din of piazza activity. (☎0577 84 82 57. Singles €45; doubles €53; triples €72.) **Il Barlanzone Affittacamere ❹,** V. Ricasoli, 33, rents four rooms and an apartment with TVs, large baths, and an unobstructed view of the fortress. (☎0577 84 61 20. Singles €45; doubles €55; apartment €75. Weekly rentals receive 10% discount. MC/V.) **Affittacamere Mariuccia ❹,** P. del Popolo, 28, offers three rooms with immaculate bath and TV. Reception is across the street in Enoteca Pierangioli. (☎0577 84 91 13. Singles €38; doubles €46-48. Cash only.) The oldest hotel in town, **Albergo Il Giglio ❹,** V. S. Saloni, 5, has rooms with fantastic views, all with bath, phone, TV. (☎0577 84 81 67; hotelgiglio@tin.it. Singles €53; doubles €75; triples €85. Breakfast €6.50. AmEx/MC/V.)

Montalcino's wine menus are generally twice as thick as the food menus. The best deals on *Brunello* (€16-27) are at the **COOP,** on the corner of V. Sant'Agostino and V. della Libertà. (Open M-Tu and Th-Sa 8am-1pm and 4-8pm, W 8am-1pm.) *Enoteche* line V. Mazzini, the town's main street, all offering huge selections of *Brunello* and tasty snacks like *bruschette* (€4-7) and cheese and meat plates (€3-7). In the brightly painted **Taverna Il Grappolo Blu ❸,** Scale di V. Moglio, 1, down a small staircase off of V. Mazzini, a memorable ravioli with pecorino cheese and ragu (€6.50) is just one of a slew of superior options. (☎0577 84 71 50. Cover €1.50. Open M-Th and Sa-Su noon-3pm and 7-10pm. AmEx/MC/V.) Complement a meal at Maria Pia's **Re di Macchia ❹,** V. S. Saloni, 21, with Il Consiglio di Antonio (€14), four of Montalcino's premier wines. (☎0577 84 61 16. Cover €2.50. *Primi* €8, *secondi* €10-12. Open W and F-Su 12:30-2pm and 7:30-9:30pm. AmEx/MC/V.)

TUSCANY

◙ SIGHTS. Montalcino's most inspiring sight, the ◙**Abbazia di Sant'Antimo,** is in Castelnuovo, a town 10km from Montalcino on the same La Peschiera route as the Fattoria dei Barbi; return times at 7:45am, 2:25, and 4:55pm (€1.10 one way). The walk from Castelnuovo to the abbey takes about 8min. and passes the sloping hills and cypress trees characteristic of the Tuscan countryside. Lore holds that Charlemagne founded the abbey in 780 as thanksgiving for the miraculous curing of the plague that was scourging his army. The actual structure standing was built in the early 12th century, with a rounded apse and carved alabaster capitals, and is one of Tuscany's most beautiful Romanesque structures. Inside, monks perform mass in **Gregorian chant** seven times each day (during which time the church is closed to the public). Chants float through speakers throughout the rest of the day. (☎0577 83 56 69; www.antimo.it. Open M-Sa 10:30am-12:30pm and 3-6:30pm, Su 9-10:30am and 3-6pm.) Back in town stands Montalcino's 14th-century **fortezza,** which sheltered a band of republicans escaping the Florentine siege of Siena in 1555. The fortress is almost perfectly preserved, with five towers and part of the town walls incorporated into the structure. Two interior courtyards, one shaded by foliage, the other sunny and cheered by geraniums, make nice picnic spots. Many visitors bypass the fortress itself in favor of the sophisticated **Enoteca La Fortezza,** which offers cheese plates (€8) and local wines (€3-9 per glass; *Brunello* €6-12). A climb up the stairs, through the turret, and onto the panoramic walls is €3.50. (Fort and Enoteca open Apr.-Oct. daily 9am-8pm; Nov.-Mar. Tu-Su 9am-6pm.)

To appreciate the area vineyards, use the local shuttle service, **La Peschiera,** (☎0564 95 31 34) to visit **Fattoria dei Barbi.** Shuttles depart daily from P. Cavour at 7:10am, 1:45, 2:45, and 7pm; return 7:45am, 2:25, and 4:55pm. Tours of the extensive cellars are followed by a tasting of three delicious wines (one *Brunello,* one blend, and one dessert wine). Tastings are available any time during open hours; ring the bell for service. The winery also includes a restaurant, which is open for lunch and dinner. (☎0577 84 11 11; www.fattoriadeibarbi.it. Open M-F 10am-1pm and 2:30-6pm, Sa 2:30-6pm. Free tours given M-F every hr. 11am-noon and 3-5pm.) The **Palazzo Comunale,** in the P. del Popolo, hosts wine exhibitions.

VOLTERRA ☎0588

Atop a huge bluff known as *Le Balze,* Volterra stands alone in a surrounding checkerboard of green and yellow farmland. Once an important Etruscan settlement, the town shrunk to its current size during the Middle Ages, when outlying parts fell from the eroding hillside. Etruscan-era alabaster statues and medieval architecture draw tourists, while the semolina fields and distant mountains outside the city gates lend Volterra a natural beauty.

▛ TRANSPORTATION

The **train station** that services Volterra is in the nearby town of Cecina. To get there, take the CPT bus to Saline (6 per day, Su and Aug. 2 per day; €1.50). From Saline, transfer to another CPT bus to Cecina for trains to Pisa (€6.50) and the coast. Service to Cecina via Saline runs five times a day during the week (last bus at 6:20pm), and only two times on Sunday. For other schedules and information, consult the tourist office or call ☎0588 861 50. **Buses** (☎0588 861 50) are in P. Martiri della Libertà, with daily departures to Florence (1½hr., €6.56). **TRA-IN** connects to San Gimignano (1½hr., €4.25), Siena (1½hr., €4.40), and other points in Tuscany. Some destinations require a change at Colle Val d'Elsa; be sure to anticipate plenty of time for connections. **CPT** runs buses between Volterra and Colle Val d'Elsa, and also runs to Pisa (2hr., 10 per day, €4.91) via Pontederra. Buy tickets at **Associazione Pro Volterra**, at *tabacchi*, or at vending machines near the bus stop. **TRA-SITA** runs buses from Colle Val D'Elsa to other points in Tuscany. Buy tickets at travel agencies or ticket offices in towns. For **taxis,** call ☎ 0588 872 57.

■✱ 🔲 ORIENTATION AND PRACTICAL INFORMATION

To get from the bus stop in **Piazza Martiri della Libertà** to the town center in **Piazza dei Priori,** walk into town and turn left on **Via Ricciarelli.** Most of Volterra's main streets radiate from P. dei Priori.

Tourist Office: Consorzio Turistico, P. dei Priori, 20 (☎ 0588 860 99; www.volterratur.it). Provides **maps,** brochures, and audio walking tours (€7 per person, €10 for 2). Also makes hotel and taxi reservations for free. Open daily Apr.-Oct. 10am-1pm and 2-7pm, Nov.-Mar. 10am-1pm and 2-6pm. **Associazione Pro Volterra,** V. Turazza (☎ 0588 861 50; www.provolterra.it), just off P. dei Priori, sells CPT bus tickets and provides schedule and fare information on trains to Pisa and buses to Florence, Pisa, Saline di Volterra, San Gimignano, and Siena.

Currency Exchange: Cassa di Risparmio di Volterra, V. Matteotti, 1, has a 24hr. exchange machine and an **ATM** outside. Also in P. Martiri della Libertà.

Internet: 🔲 **Web and Wine,** V. Porte all'Arco, 11/13 (☎ 0588 815 31; www.webandwine.com). After surfing the web, kick back with a glass of chianti and cast an eye over Etruscan ruins visible through the glass floor. €5 per hr. Open Tu-Su 7am-1am. **SESHA,** P. XX Settembre, 10. €6 per hr. Open daily 9am-1pm and 4-8pm. MC/V.

Emergency: ☎ 113. **Ambulance** (☎ 118).

Pharmacy: Farmacia Amidei, V. Ricciarelli, 2 (☎ 0588 860 60). Open M-Sa 9am-1pm and 4-8pm; open Su for emergencies.

Hospital: ☎ 0588 91 911. On Borgo S. Lazzaro.

Post Office: P. dei Priori, 14 (☎ 0588 869 69). Open M-F 8:15am-7pm, Sa 8:15am-12:30pm. **Postal Code:** 56048.

🛏🏕 ACCOMMODATIONS AND CAMPING

Hotels can get expensive, so ask the tourist office for a list of *affittacamere*. Singles start at €30, doubles at €40.

🔲 **La Torre,** V. Guarnacci, 47 (☎ 0588 800 36 or 348 724 76 93). From bus stop, turn left on V. Marchesi, right on V. delle Prigioni, right on V. dei Sarti, and left on V. Guarnacci. Great *affittacamere* in the historic center. Rooms sport matching wood furniture, comfy beds, large bath, and TV. Owner supplies city maps and generously stocks free drinks. Call ahead or book through tourist office. Singles €33; doubles €42. Cash only. ❸

🔲 **Seminario Vescovile,** V. V. Veneto, 2 (☎ 0588 860 28, fax 907 91), in P. S. Andrea, next to the church. From P. M. della Libertà, turn left, then immediate right on V. Matteotti. Turn right on V. Gramsci, walk through P. XX Settembre, then turn left. Exit city through Pta. Marcoli and follow the road, bearing left until seeing Sant'Andrea. High, arched ceilings, frescoed doorways, and views of the walled city and Tuscan countryside. 2-4-person rooms, no unmarried couples. Breakfast €3. Reception 8am-midnight. Curfew midnight. Reservation required. Rooms €14, with bath €18. AmEx/MC/V. ❷

Albergo Etruria, V. Matteotti, 32 (☎ 0588 873 77). Exit P. M. della Libertà to the left and make the 1st right on V. Matteotti; the Etruria is a few blocks down. Tidy rooms with TV and phone, a private garden, and a classy lounge make this a congenial place. Breakfast €6. Singles €42, with bath €46; doubles €67. Extra bed €30. MC/V. ❹

Hotel La Locanda, V. Guarnacci 24/28 (☎0588 815 47; www.hotel-lalocanda.com). A former convent turned 4-star hotel. Rooms adorned with matching bedspreads, curtains, and upholstered furniture are hung with artwork from a local gallery. All have bath, satellite TV, fridge, and safe. Buffet breakfast included. Singles €92; doubles €115, wheelchair accessible double €115; triples €155; quads €207. AmEx/MC/V. ❺

Le Balze, V. Mandringa, 15 (☎0588 878 80). Exit through Pta. S. Francesco and bear right on Strada Provincial Pisana. Turn left on V. Mandringa after 20 min. Campground has pool and bar, and most sites are partially shaded by small trees. Store sells tickets for bus into town (every hr. 8:18am-9:21pm). Showers included. Reception 8-10am and 3:30-10pm. Cars must be parked by 11pm. Open Apr.-Oct. €6 per person, €4 per tent, €7 per camper. AmEx/MC/V. ❶

⬛ FOOD

Excellent local cheeses and game dishes are available at any of the *alimentari* along V. Guarnacci and V. Gramsci. Sample *salsiccia di cinghiale* (wild boar sausage) and *pecorino* (sheep's milk cheese). For a sweet snack, try *ossi di morto* (bones of the dead man), a rock-hard local confection made of egg whites, sugar, hazelnuts, and a hint of lemon, or *pane di pescatore* (fisherman's bread), a dense and delicious sweet bread full of nuts and raisins. Pick up groceries at **Despar,** V. Gramsci, 12. (Open M-F 7:30am-1pm and 5-8pm, Sa 7:30am-1pm.)

L'Ombra della Sera, V. Gramsci, 70 (☎0588 866 63), off P. XX Settembre. A local favorite whose outdoor patio on the busy V. Gramsci during a summer evening makes for great people watching. Rich Volterran classics, such as *tagliolini al tartufo* (€7.80) are stellar choices. *Primi* €6-7.80, *secondi* €9-13.90. Cover €1.30. Service 10%. Open Tu-Su noon-3pm and 7-10pm. AmEx/MC/V. ❸

Trattoria Il Poggio, V. Porte all'Arco, 9 (☎0588 852 57). Pasta dishes with meat sauces and a "medieval" *menù* featuring local cheeses are the highlights at this casual restaurant, accompanied by medieval paraphernalia, photos, and maps of Volterra hanging from the walls. Pizza €4.50-6.50. *Primi* €6-7.50, *secondi* €6.50-13. MC/V. ❷

Pizzeria/Birreria Ombra della Sera, V. Guarnacci, 16 (☎0588 852 74). Frantic cooks toss delicious pizzas with thin, crispy crusts, while diners relax on wooden benches under the warm glow of red lanterns and sleek cross-vaulted ceilings. Popular for take-out pizza. Pizza €4.20-7.20; salad €5.70; pasta €5.50-7. Cover €0.90. Service 10%. Open Tu-Su noon-3pm and 7-10pm. MC/V. ❶

Ristorante Etruria, P. dei Priori, 6/8 (☎0588 860 66). Shaded outdoor seating amid towers and palaces on Volterra's main piazza. Rich soups and local game. *Primi* €4-10, *secondi* €4.50-14. *Menù* €12.50. Service 10%. Open M-Tu Th-Su noon-3pm and 7-10pm. AmEx/MC/V. ❷

⬛ SIGHTS

PINACOTECA COMUNALE. This graceful building contains Volterra's best art, held in understated, dimly-lit rooms with few labels. The first floor showcases two dramatic works: Rosso Fiorentino's spectacular *Deposizione della croce*, in which Christ's body has a greenish tinge (most likely the result of aging and poor restoration); and Luca Signorelli's far richer *Annunciazione*, filled with finely-realized details of architecture and cloth. Fiorentino's painting spills from the canvas onto the frame, creating the mesmerizing illusion that his subjects are not confined to the flat surface. *(V. dei Sartiri, 1. Up V. Buonparenti from P. dei Priori. ☎0588 875 80. Open daily 9am-7pm. A combo ticket including Pinacoteca, Museo Etrusco, and Museo dell' Opera del Duomo di Arte Sacra is available at any sight. €7, students €5.)*

PIAZZA DEI PRIORI AND FORTEZZA MEDICEA. Life in Volterra revolves around Piazza dei Priori, which is surrounded by sober, dignified palaces. The **Palazzo dei Priori,** the oldest governmental palace in Tuscany (1208-1254), presides over the square. Regal coats of arms line the walls of the first floor. Inside, the council hall and antechamber are open to the public. Jacopo di Cione Orcagna's damaged *Annunciation with Four Saints* occupies the right wall. The *sinopia,* the fresco's preliminary drawing, is in the adjoining antechamber. *(Open daily 10am-1pm and 2-6pm. €1.)* Across the piazza, **Palazzo Pretorio's** 13th-century buildings and towers house municipal offices. Volterra's most prominent structure is the elegant **Fortezza Medicea,** now a state prison. The neighboring **public park** is a great picnic spot with views. *(From bus stop, walk into town and take 1st right. Road turns uphill; follow it to park entrance. Park open daily 8am-8pm.)*

DUOMO. Construction began on Volterra's pre-Romanesque cathedral in the 12th century and continued for three centuries. By the time the choir at the end of the nave was completed, architects had already switched to a Gothic design, indicated by the transition from rounded arches to pointed ones. Inside and on the left, the oratory houses a series of wooden statues depicting the life of Jesus. The chapel off the left transept holds frescoes by Rosselli, including the luminous *Missione per Damasco.* Also note the spectacular use of perspective in the *Annunciation* by M. Albertinelli and Fra Bartolomeo on the left wall. *(Down V. Turazza from P. dei Priori to P. S. Giovanni. Open daily 8am-12:30pm and 3-7pm.)*

MUSEO ETRUSCO GUARNACCI. The Etruscan museum displays over 600 finely carved funeral urns from the 4th to the 1st centuries BC. The pieces are not well displayed and lack explanatory signs, but an audio tour (€4.50) covers a few rooms. The first floor (Room XIV) holds the museum's most famous piece, the elongated bronze figure dubbed *l'Ombra della Sera* (Shadow of the Evening). The farmer who unearthed it used it for years as a fireplace poker until a visitor recognized it as an Etruscan votive figure. In Room XIX, the famous urn *Urna degli Sposi* depicts an obviously embittered married couple. *(V. Minzoni, 15. From P. dei Priori, head down to V. Matteotti, turn right on V. Gramsci, and follow it to V. Minzoni. ☎0588 863 47. Gallery and museum open daily mid-Mar. to Oct. 9am-7pm, Nov. to mid-Mar. 9am-2pm.)*

ROMAN AMPHITHEATER. These impressive ruins include partly grass-covered stone seating and Corinthian columns salvaged from the stage. Walk at the edge of the ruins behind metal rails, or admire them from a bird's-eye view for free on V. Lungo le Mura. *(Just outside the city walls next to Pta. Fiorentina. From P. dei Priori, follow V. delle Prigioni, turn right at the T-junction and left on V. Guarnacci. Proceed out the porta and through the parking lot to the left. Open daily 10am-1pm and 2-6pm. €2.)*

SAN GIMIGNANO ☎0577

The hilltop village of San Gimignano looks like an illustration from a medieval manuscript. Prototypical towers, churches, and palaces loom above the city's walls as if from a fairy-tale. San Gimignano's 14 famous towers, all that remain of the original 72, date from a period when prosperous families battled, using their towers to store grain for sieges. They were also conveniently used for dumping boiling oil on attacking enemies. After WWII, the skyline began to lure tourists, whose tastes and wallets resuscitated production of the golden *Vernaccia* wine. With hordes of daytrippers, an infestation of souvenir shops, and innumerable eateries, San Gimignano now has something of the feel of a medieval Disneyland. But the fortress-top sunsets, nighttime gelato strolls, and ample spots for lounging on piazza steps make an overnight stay worthwhile.

⊏ TRANSPORTATION

The nearest **train station** is in Poggibonsi; buses connect the station to town (20min; M-F every 30min. 6:10am-8:35pm; Sa-Su every hr. 7:40am-8pm; €1.35). **TRAIN buses** (☎0577 20 41 11 or 93 72 07) leave from P. Montemaggio, outside Pta. S. Giovanni. Schedules and tickets are at Caffè Combattente, V. S. Giovanni, 124, on the left after entering the city gates. Tickets are also available from *tabacchi* or at the tourist office. Change at Poggibonsi for Siena (1hr., every 1-2hr., €5.20) and Florence (1½hr., every hr., €6). Also try **Bruno Bellini**, V. Roma, 41, 200m down the hill from Pta. S. Giovanni. (☎0577 94 02 01; www.bellinibruno.com. Bikes €5-10 per hr., €11-21 per day. Scooters from €35 per day. Cars from €60 per day. Open daily 9am-1pm and 3-8pm. AmEx/MC/V.)

⬛🖈 ORIENTATION AND PRACTICAL INFORMATION

Buses to San Gimignano stop in **Piazzale Martini Montemaggio,** just outside the city walls. To reach the center, pass through **Porta San Matteo** and climb the hill, following **Via San Giovanni** to **Piazza della Cisterna,** which merges with **Piazza del Duomo** on the left. Addresses in San Gimignano are marked in both faded black stencil and etched clay tiles; since most establishments go by the black, these are listed.

Tourist Office: Pro Loco, P. del Duomo, 1 (☎0577 94 00 08; prolocsg@tin.it), has lists of hotels and rooms for rent, as well as bus and train schedules and bus tickets. Excellent free **maps.** Offers 2½hr. tours of wineries Tu 11am and Th 5pm. Includes multiple tastings (all with food) and transportation by bus for €26 (€18 with own transportation). Reserve by noon the day before. Also makes private room reservations in person. Open Mar.-Oct. daily 9am-1pm and 3-7pm; Nov.-Feb. 9am-1pm and 2-6pm.

Accommodations Services: Siena Hotels Promotion, V. S. Giovanni, 125 (☎0577 94 08 09, fax 94 01 13), on the right entering the city gates; look for *"Cooperativa Alberghi e Ristoranti"* sign. Reserves hotel rooms in San Gimignano and Siena for 5% commission. Open M-Sa 9:30am-7pm. **Associazione Strutture Extralberghiere,** P. della Cisterna, 6 (☎/fax 0577 94 31 90). Patient staff makes free reservations for *affittacamere,* or private rooms. Doubles with bath €50-60. Call a week ahead to stay in the countryside; the city center is easier to book. Open Mar.-Nov. daily 9:30am-7:30pm.

Currency Exchange: Pro Loco tourist office and post office offer best rates. Rip-offs elsewhere. **ATMs** scattered along V. S. Giovanni, V. degli Innocenti, and P. della Cisterna.

Police: ☎112. **Ambulance:** ☎118. **Carabinieri:** ☎0577 94 03 13, on P. Martiri.

Pharmacy: P. Cisterna, 8 (☎0577 94 03 69). Fills urgent prescriptions all night; call ☎0368 713 66 75. Open M-Sa 9am-1pm and 4:30-8pm.

Internet: Edicola La Tuscia, right at the gates at the beginning of V. S. Matteoti. Open 7am-1pm and 2:30-8pm, except W and Su afternoons.

Post Office: P. delle Erbe, 8, behind the duomo. Open M-F 8:15am-7pm, Sa 8:15am-12:30pm. **Currency exchange** available. **Postal Code:** 53037.

🚪 ACCOMMODATIONS

San Gimignano caters to wealthy tourists, and most accommodations are well beyond budget range. *Affittacamere* provide an alternative to overpriced hotels, with most doubles with bath from €50-60. Look for the signs for "Camere/Rooms/Zimmer" that hang in souvenir shops, restaurants, and other storefront windows along main streets. The tourist office and the **Associazione Strutture Extralberghiere** (see **Practical Information**) have lists of budget rooms.

🏨 **Camere Cennini Gianni,** V. S. Giovanni, 21 (☎347 074 81 88; www.sangiapart-ments.com). From the bus stop, enter through Pta. S. Giovanni. Reception is at the *pasticceria* at V. S. Giovanni, 88. Each room is homey yet astonishingly luxurious, with large bath, heated towel-rack, and skylight. Use of kitchens for groups of 4, €15 extra. Reserve ahead. Singles €45; doubles €55; triples €65; quads €75. Cash only. ❹

Albergo Il Pino, V. Cellolese, 6 (☎/fax 0577 94 04 15), just off V. S. Matteo before exiting Pta. S. Matteo. Quilted comforters and dark wood furnishings fill rustic and spacious rooms with bath, comfy sofa chairs, and TV. Reservation recommended. Dogs allowed. Singles €45; doubles €55. AmEx/MC/V. ❹

Hotel La Cisterna, P. della Cisterna, 24 (☎0577 94 03 28; www.hotelcisterna.it). Large rooms with flowing curtains and floral designs complement the balcony's pastoral panorama. All rooms have bath, A/C, and satellite TV. Buffet breakfast included. Singles €70; doubles €90-95, with view €103-115. Extra bed €30. AmEx/MC/V. ❺

Il Boschetto di Piemma (☎0577 94 03 52; www.boschettodipiemma.it), at Santa Lucia, 2.5km downhill from Pta. S. Giovanni. Buses (€0.90) run from P. dei Martiri. Confirm destination with driver before boarding. Small, wooded sites close together, but near community pool. Bungalows available for €20. Bar and market on premises. Hot showers free. Reception daily 8am-1pm and 3-10pm. Open year-round. €6.40 per person, €4.50 per child, €6 per small tent. ❶

🍴 FOOD

If the sad glass eyes of stuffed tuskers around town aren't hint enough, San Gimignano specializes in boar and other wild game. It also caters to less daring palates with mainstream Tuscan dishes at higher prices. A weekly **open-air market** is in P. del Duomo. (Open Th 8am-noon.) Purchase the famous *Vernaccia di San Gimignano*, a lightly sweet white wine, from **La Buca,** V. S. Giovanni, 16, for around €4.50. This cooperative also offers terrific sausages and meats produced on its own farm. The boar sausage *al pignoli* (with pine nuts; €2.07 per 100g) and the oddly satisfying *salame con mirto* (with blueberry) are delicious. (☎0577 94 04 07. Open Apr.-Oct. daily 9am-8pm; Nov.-Mar. 9am-7pm. AmEx/MC/V.)

🍴 **Trattoria Chiribiri,** P. della Madonna, 1 (☎0577 94 19 48). From the bus stop, take the 1st left off V. S. Giovanni and climb a short staircase. Tiny restaurant serves amazing local fare at unusually affordable prices. The dining room can get overheated, but service is pitch-perfect. *Primi* €5-7, *secondi* from €7.50. Open Mar.-Oct. M-Tu and Th-Su 11am-11pm; Nov.-Feb. M-Tu and Th-Su noon-2pm and 7-10pm. Cash only. ❷

🍴 **Pluripremiata Gelateria,** P. della Cisterna, 4 (☎0577 94 22 44). 3 counters hold gelato flavors never seen before. Try the *limoncello* or refreshing *tuttobosco*. Cups start at €1.50. 3 flavors in a chocolate-lined cone €2.20. Open 11:30am-9pm. ❶

La Stella, V. San Matteo, 77 (☎0577 94 04 44). Food made with produce from the restaurant's own farm and served in long narrow restaurant with an alleyway of tables. Sample homemade pasta with wild boar sauce (€7.80) or try an assorted *primi* platter (€8.75). Extensive wine list includes the crisp *Vernaccia*. *Primi* €4.95-8.75, *secondi* €7.75-11.95. *Menù turistico* €15. Cover €1.85. Open Apr.-Oct M-Tu and Th-Su noon-2:30pm and 7-9:30pm; Nov.-Mar. noon-2pm and 7-9pm. AmEx/MC/V. ❸

Ristorante Perucà, V. Capassi, 16 (☎0577 94 31 36). Behind V. San Matteo. Quieter, somewhat more casual spot, hidden away from the tourist bustle. *Primi* €7-11, *secondi* €10-16. Cover €2. Open M-W and F-Su noon-2:30pm and 7-10:30pm. AmEx/MC/V. ❸

Ricca Pizza, V. S. Matteo, 5 (☎0577 94 22 73). Prime location just left off of P. Duomo. Delicious pizza available by the slice or whole, with traditional toppings like mushroom or ham. Take slices to the steps of the basilica with the other happy lunchers. Slices €2.50. Small pizza €5, large €10. Open 11am-9:30pm. ❶

TUSCANY

SIGHTS

Famous as the *Città delle Belle Torri* (City of the Beautiful Towers), San Gimignano has always appealed to artists. During the Renaissance, they came in droves, and the collection of their works complement San Gimignano's cityscape. Now the narrow, car-less streets cater to throngs of sightseers and souvenir-hunters.

> **TICKET FOR *TUTTO*.** Cumulative tickets for the town's museums are available at varying rates. *Biglietti interi* (€7.50) are full-priced adult tickets; *biglietti ridotti* (€5.50) are discounted tickets available to students under 18 and children between the ages of 8 and 18. Children under 7 are allowed *ingresso gratuito* (free entrance). One ticket allows entry into nearly all of San Gimignano's sights. Tickets are available at participating tourist sights.

PIAZZA DELLA CISTERNA AND PIAZZA DEL DUOMO. As in any other proper hill town, the central Piazza della Cisterna (1237) is surrounded by towers and palaces. It adjoins Piazza del Duomo, site of the impressive tower of the **Palazzo del Podestà.** To its left, tunnels and intricate *loggie* riddle the Palazzo del Popolo (see below). To the right of the palazzo rises its **Torre Grossa,** the town's highest tower and the only one people can climb. Also in the piazza stand the twin towers of the Ardinghelli, truncated due to a medieval zoning ordinance that regulated tower envy by prohibiting structures higher than the Torre Grossa.

MUSEO DELLA TORTURA. This disturbing museum (a sign near the entrance to the first room actually forbids the entrance of "sensitive people") displays over 50 torture devices put to use from the Middle Ages to the present. The nine rooms are filled with axes, swords, chastity belts, spiked collars, guillotines, the rack, an Iron Maiden, and even a primitive electric chair. Morbidly fascinating captions in multiple languages explain the history and mechanics of the devices. If that wasn't enough, diagrams accompany each display, depicting the torture device in use—particularly instructive in the case of the rectal pear. *(V. del Castello, 1, off P. Cisterna. Open daily mid-July to mid-Sept. 10am-midnight, Apr. to mid-July and mid-Sept. to Oct. 10am-8pm, Nov.-Mar. 10am-6pm. €8, students €5.50.)*

PALAZZO DEL POPOLO. A frescoed medieval courtyard leads to the entrance to the **Museo Civico** on the second floor. The first room of the museum is the **Sala di Dante,** where the bard spoke on May 8, 1300 in an attempt to convince San Gimignano to side with the Florentines in their ongoing wars with Siena. On the walls, Lippo Memmi's sparkling *Maestà* blesses the accompanying 14th-century scenes of hunting and tournament pageantry. Up the stairs, Taddeo di Bartolo's altarpiece, *The Story of San Gimignano,* tells the tale of the city's namesake saint, originally a bishop of Modena. Within the museum lies the entrance to the 218-step climb up **Torre Grossa.** While the final steps are precarious, they are well worth it, as the tower offers views of a half dozen of San Gimignano's towers, the ancient fortress, several piazzas and the Tuscan landscape stretching to the horizon in all directions. The tower's bell rings daily at noon. *(Palazzo del Popolo, Museo Civico, and Tower open daily Mar.-Oct. 9:30am-7pm, Nov.-Feb. 10am-7pm. €5, students €4.)*

BASILICA DI SANTA MARIA ASSUNTA. The bare facade of this 12th-century church seems unfit to shelter such an exceptionally frescoed interior. Off the right aisle, the **Cappella di Santa Fina** is covered in Ghirlandaio's splendid frescoes on the life of Santa Fina, the town's ascetic local saint: a virgin who was stricken with a fatal disease at the age of 10, she spent her final five years lying on an oak plank on the ground. In the main church, Bartolo di Fredi painted beautiful frescoes of Old

Testament scenes along the north aisle, while Barna da Siena provided the extremely impressive New Testament counterparts along the south aisle. *(In P. del Duomo. Church and chapel open Apr.-Oct. M-F 9:30am-7:30pm, Sa 9:30am-5pm, Su 1-5pm; Nov.-Mar. M-Sa 9:30am-5pm, Su 1-5pm. Closed Feb. €3.50, students €1.50.)*

FORTEZZA. Follow the signs past the Basilica di Collegiata from P. del Duomo to this tiny, crumbling fortress. The courtyard is often full of street artists and musicians, and the turret offers a beautiful view of the countryside. Park benches protected by trees make for a great picnic or lounge spot when visitors clear out in the evening. There are weekly screenings of movies in the courtyard at night in July and August. *(Schedule and info at the tourist office. Movies €6.20.)*

PISTOIA ☎ 0573

Many travelers recognize Pistoia only as a stop on the train between Florence and Lucca. In fact it's the quintessential small Tuscan city, complete with solid stone houses and palm-lined streets. The black and white checkered duomo, baptistery, and *campanile* dominate the perfectly flat Piazza del Duomo. And Pistoia's history is as checkered as its buildings. In 1177 the town joined several other Italian city-states in declaring its independence, but was soon surpassed by its neighbors in military, political, and economic strength. Thereafter, Pistoia became a murderous backwater, whose inhabitants Michelangelo maligned as "enemies of heaven." Lending its name to the pistol and *pistole* dagger, the town's bloody reputation spawned a debauched and enduring mythology. The more peaceful residents of today prefer to pick their battles, haggling over produce prices in the open-air markets of Piazza della Sala or rooting for the closest soccer team.

⌐ TRANSPORTATION

Pistoia is accessible by train or bus. The **train station** is in P. Dante Alighieri. Trains run to: Florence (40min., every hr. 4:40am-11pm, €2.60); Pisa (1hr., every 2hr. 6:50am-11:30pm, €4); Rome (4hr., every hr., €25-32) via Florence; and Viareggio (1 hr., every 2hr. 6:15am-10:30pm, €4). **COPIT buses** run from the train station to Empoli (1¼hr., 6:20am-8pm, €3.10) and Florence (1hr., 5am-10:20pm, €3.10). Buy tickets at COPIT vendors or across from the train station at V. XX Settembre, 71. **Cooperative Pistoia Taxi** (☎ 0573 21 237 or 24 291) is in P. Garibaldi, P. San Francesco, and the train station. Night service is available until 1am. **Cicli Bencini,** C. Gramsci, 98, rents mountain bikes for €15 per day. (☎ 0573 251 44. Open M-Sa 8:30am-1pm and 2:30-7:30pm. AmEx/MC/V.)

⊁ 🔋 ORIENTATION AND PRACTICAL INFORMATION

To reach the *centro* from the **train station,** walk up **Via XX Settembre** and continue straight as it changes names to **Via Vanucci,** and then to **Via Cino.** When the street becomes **Via Buozzi** and bears slightly left, proceed one block and turn right on the narrow **Via degli Orafi,** which leads to **Piazza del Duomo,** the heart of the town. Local buses #1 and 3 (€0.60) stop at **Piazza Gavinana.** From there, turn right on **Via Cavour** and left on **Via Roma,** which runs in P. del Duomo. An **APT Tourist Office,** P. del Duomo, 4, is in Palazzo dei Vescovi. The English-speaking staff distributes free **maps** and brochures and helps find accommodations. (☎ 0573 216 22, fax 343 27. Open daily 9am-1pm and 3-6pm.) **Currency exchange** (traveler's checks and cash) is available at **Cassa di Risparmio di Pistoia e Pescia,** V. S. Matteo, 3. (☎ 0573 36 91. Open M-F 8:20am-1:20pm and 2:50-3:50pm.) In case of **emergency,** call the **police** at ☎ 112 or an **ambulance** at ☎ 118. A **pharmacy** is at V. Cino, 33. (☎ 0573 36 81 80. Open

T U S C A N Y

daily 8:30am-1pm and 3:30-8pm.) For the **hospital,** call ☎ 0573 35 21. **Internet** is available at the tourist office (€5 per hr.) and at **Telnet Internet Point,** V. G. Carducci, 7. (☎ 0573 99 35 71. €3 per hr. Open M-F 9:30am-1pm and 3:30pm-midnight; Sa, 2nd and 4th Su of the month 3:30-8pm.) The **post office,** V. Roma, 5 (☎ 0573 99 53 03), is near the bank. It exchanges currency and American Express traveler's cheques. (Open M-Sa 8:15am-7pm.) **Postal Code:** 51100.

ACCOMMODATIONS AND FOOD

As Pistoia is rather small, most rooms are centrally located and consequently somewhat expensive. *Affittacamere* listings are available from the tourist office, but most of the cheaper rooms are in localities far from town. As one happy guest wrote in their guest book, staying at ▧**Bed & Breakfast Canto alla Porta Vecchia** ❸, V. Curtatone e Montanara, 2, is living like a real Pistoian. Take V. XX Settembre from the train station; the road changes names several times before becoming V. Curtatone e Montanara. There is no sign, so watch for the address in front. In front of the large wooden doors, walk up the steps to buzz the owners. Carved dark wooden beds, red satin couches, antique furniture, and original sketches furnish the four frescoed rooms. Friendly owners Anna and Giovanni serve complimentary drinks and guests gather on the terrace to chat. (☎/fax 0573 276 92. Singles €30; doubles €60, with bath €70. Cash only.) Up the street to the left, **Albergo Firenze** ❸, V. Curtatone e Montanara, 42, offers comfort and relative value. All rooms have A/C, satellite TV, high ceilings, and lace decor. (☎ 0573 231 41; www.hotel-firenze.it. Breakfast and Internet included. Singles €45, with bath €65; doubles €75/€85. Extra bed €25. AmEx/MC/V.)

Grocery stores and specialty shops line the side streets. Bargain hunters browse the **open-air market** in and around P. del Duomo for deals on items from shower curtains to silver jewelry. (Open W and Sa 7:30am-2pm.) P. della Sala has been the site of a fruit and vegetable **market** since medieval times. (Open daily 8am-7pm.) A **Dimeglio** is on V. Veneto, across from the train station and to the right. (Open M-Tu and Th-Su 8am-10pm, W 8am-1:30pm.) **Trattoria dell'Abbondanza** ❸, V. dell'Abbondanza, 10, serves an excellent *panzanella di Farro*, a summer salad of oil-soaked bread, basil, tomatoes, parsley, and garlic. (☎ 0573 36 80 37. *Primi* €6-8, *secondi* €6-13. Open daily 12:15-2:15pm and 7-10:30pm, no lunch hours Tu and Th. MC/V.) Sample from the lengthy wine list at **La Botte Gaia** ❷, V. Lastrone, 17/19, or try gourmet cheeses, salads, and other delectables at swanky black tables with stylish residents of Pistoia. The *bruschette* (€4.70) with sun-dried tomato and *pecorino* (sheep's milk cheese) are small but heavenly. (☎ 0573 36 56 02. *Antipasti* from €4.20. *Primi* and *secondi* €5-10. Cover €1.50. Reservation recommended. Open Tu-Sa 10:30am-3pm and 6:30pm-1am, Su 6:30pm-1am. AmEx/MC/V.) Menus in multiple languages present the ample choices at **Ristorante San Jacopo** ❸, V. Crispi, 15. The emphasis is on meaty Tuscan dishes, like *coniglio con olive* (rabbit with olives; €7.50), and the dining room is airy, with cream table cloths to match the color of the vaulted walls. (☎ 0573 231 41. *Primi* €5.50-8, *secondi* €6.50-12. Open Tu 7-10:30pm, W-Su 12:15-2:30pm and 7-10pm. AmEx/MC/V.)

SIGHTS

CATTEDRALE DI SAN ZENO. Activity in Pistoia converges on the perfectly flat cobblestones of the vast P. del Duomo. The green-and-white marble **Cattedrale di San Zeno** houses an impressive store of early Renaissance art, as well as San Zeno's greatest treasure, the ▧**Dossale di San Jacopo.** Between 1287 and 1456, nearly every significant Tuscan silversmith (including the young Brunelleschi) lent a hand to this altarpiece, a tremendously ornate affair with relief work detailing biblical scenes and a procession of saints in a plain chapel off the right aisle. *(☎ 0573 250 95. Open daily 8:30am-12:30pm and 3:30-7pm. Altar open 11:20am-noon and 4-5:30pm. Free; altar €2. Modest dress required.)* Across from the duomo is the octagonal **baptistery,** designed by Andrea Pisano in the 14th century. Nino and Tommaso Pisano's sculpture *Virgin and Child* enlivens a modest bricked-line interior. *(Open Tu-Sa 9:30am-12:30pm and 3-6pm, Su 9:30am-12:30pm.)* The **campanile,** adjacent to the duomo, has sounded the hour since the 12th century. With its pyramid-shaped spire rising 66m high, on clear days vistas from the small arched windows span to Florence. *(☎ 0573 216 22. Open M and F-Su 9am-1pm and 3-6pm. Visits must be booked beforehand at the tourist office. €5.)*

PALAZZO COMUNALE. A 13th-century structure next to the duomo facing the piazza. Left of the central balcony on the dark brick facade, about halfway up, an arm reaches out of the wall, brandishing a club above the black marble head below—a tribute to the 1115 Pistoian victory over the Moorish king Musetto. Inside, the **Museo Civico** houses artwork dating to the 13th century. With its Gothic windows and archways, the courtyard is also well worth a peek. *(☎ 0573 37 12 96. Open Tu-Sa 10am-6pm, Su 9am-12:30pm. Museum €3.50, under 18 or with ISIC card free. Cumulative ticket for museum, the Centro Marini, and other museums €6.50, students €5.20.)*

CENTRO MARINO MARINI. Celebrates one of Italy's most renowned 20th-century artists, native Marino Marini. The collection's pieces are connected by a maze of stairs and include sculptures (many of the sensuous Pomono, ancient Roman fertility goddess), studies, and paintings. *(C. Silvano Fedi, 30, in the Palazzo del Tau. ☎ 0573 302 85; www.museomarinomarini.it. Open May-Sept. Tu-Sa 10am-1pm and 4-7pm, Su 9am-12:30pm; Oct.-Apr. Tu-Sa 10am-1pm and 3-6pm, Su 9am-12:30pm. €3.50.)*

CHIESA DI GIOVANNI FUORCIVITAS. The single-naved interior of the 12th-century construction is a vast space with vibrant stained-glass windows. The church contains Luca della Robbia's terra-cotta *Visitation* (1445) on the left and a Romanesque relief of *The Last Supper* on the lintel. Giovanni Pisano's font and Guglielmo de Pisa's pulpit are both among the finest of 13th-century carving. *(At the intersection of V. Cavour and V. Crispi. Open daily 9am-noon and 5-6:30pm.)*

CHIESA DI SANT'ANDREA. This typically Pisan-Romanesque church was founded in the 8th century. In 1298 Giovanni Pisano carved the pulpit, now considered his masterpiece. Supported by seven red marble columns, the pulpit's five white marble panels have delicately carved figures illustrating the *Nativity, Adoration of the Magi, Massacre of the Innocents, Crucifixion,* and *Last Judgment.* *(Exit P. del Duomo by V. del Duca, from the corner opposite the duomo, and continue as it changes to V. dei Rossi and then V. Sant'Andrea. ☎ 0573 96 41 30. Open daily in summer 8:30am-12:30pm and 3:30-7pm, in winter 8:30am-12:30pm and 3:30-6pm.)*

📷 🌸 NIGHTLIFE AND FESTIVALS

With Staropramen, Hopf Weizen, and Bass on tap (€4 per pint), **Vecchia Praga,** P. della Sala, 6, at the end of V. del Lastrone, is a beer-lover's haven in a sea of *vino.* Cocktails, liquor, wine, and light food are also available. *(☎ 0573 311 55.* Open M-Sa 10am-1am, Su 6pm-1am. In Aug. daily 6pm-1am. MC/V.) Europe's remaining flower children converge each July in P. del Duomo for the **Pistoia Blues** concert series. The past two summers featured Santana, Jethro Tull, and Ike Turner. *(☎ 0573 35 86; www.pistoiablues.com.)* During the festival, the city allows free camping in designated sites near the stadium. On July 25, Pistoia holds the **Giostra dell'Orso**

(Joust of the Bear). In accordance with 13th-century custom, 12 contemporary knights from four competing districts joust a defenseless bear-shaped target, earning points for the accuracy of their lunges.

🔼 DAYTRIP FROM PISTOIA

MONTECATINI TERME

Despite its fairly small size, Montecatini Terme has two train stations 2min. apart. Most trains stop at both. Get off at the second Montecatini stop, Stazione Centrale. From Stazione Centrale, walk straight ahead up V. Manzoni or through P. XX Settembre until arriving at P. del Popolo. Walk through to Viale Verdi. Pick up a map and a list of spa locations at the tourist office, Viale Verdi, 66-68. (☎0572 77 22 44; apt@montecatini.turismo.toscana.it). Open M-Sa 9am-12:30pm and 3-6pm, Su 9am-noon. Free Internet.

Just 10min. by train from Pistoia, Montecatini Terme offers a taste of the affluent life without draining the pocketbook. Famous for its thermal baths, Montecatini is the classic spa town where upper-crust Italians and European tourists pass their days shopping at glamorous boutiques and relaxing under palm trees. Time moves slowly in Montecatini, and so do its older residents, usually seen strolling down the well-manicured and pedestrian-friendly streets. The town's most famous bath is the Neoclassical ▓**Tettuccio,** at the end of Viale Verdi, filled with rotundas, gardens, and bubbling fountains. The spa is famous for the supposed healing waters that spring from the fountains, allegedly soothing for liver and digestive problems. Visitors can pay €0.50 for a plastic cup or bring an empty bottle to drink and see for themselves. (☎0572 77 85 01. Open May-Oct. 7:30am-noon and 5-7pm. €12.50, 11am-noon and 5-7pm €5.) For winter visitors, the **Excelsior** offers spa services year-round. (☎0572 77 85 11. Treatments available M-F 7:30am-noon and 4-7pm, Sa 7:30am-noon. Thermal wellness available M-Sa 8:30am-7pm, Su 8am-1pm.)

Montecatini has several fine hotels and restaurants. For a lavish dining experience at a reasonable price, eat at the patio restaurant of ▓**Grand Hotel Tettuccio ❹,** V. Verdi, 74. Servers decked in black ties and vests weave elegantly between tables serving guests on satin-cushioned chairs. Try the fabulous *maccheroni all'Astice* (€12), flat noodles topped with a half-lobster. (☎0572 780 51. *Primi* €10-12, *secondi* €14-20. Cover €4. Open daily noon-2pm and 7-10pm. AmEx/MC/V.) **Hotel Corona D'Italia ❸,** V. Verdi, 5, is open year-round. All rooms have antique furnishings, marble floors, TV, phone, and bath. Reserve ahead for a double with balcony at no extra cost. (☎0572 792 17; hcorona@italway.it. Breakfast €6. Singles €36; doubles €47. Additional bed 10% extra. AmEx/MC/V.) Near the station, family-run **Corsaro Verde ❸,** P. XX Settembre, 11, serves a large selection of good Tuscan fare, like *giganti alle erbe* (€6), ravioli stuffed with curd cheese and spinach. (☎0572 91 16 50. *Primi* €5-7, *secondi* €7-15. Tourist *menù* €18.50. Open daily 11:30am-3pm and 7-11pm, Nov.-Apr. closed M. AmEx/MC/V.)

LUCCA   ☎0583

Comfortably settled behind a ring of Renaissance walls, the handsome provincial capital of Lucca manages visitors with a grace and composure all its own. The town began as a Roman colony and during the Middle Ages rivaled Florence and Siena in military and political might. Its impressive 4km stone walls have maintained the historic center's neat, balanced appearance, and the scenic, tree-lined promenade running along the wall's top draws cycling *Luccese* daily. With flowering industries in textiles and olive oil production and a calm but steady tourist flow, Lucca quietly maintains a tradition of eminence and commercial prosperity. It offers many fine Romanesque churches, medieval storefronts, and for opera enthusiasts, the childhood home of Giacomo Puccini.

TRANSPORTATION

Trains: ☎0583 470 13. In P. Ricasoli, just outside the city walls. Trains provide the most convenient transport to Lucca. Info booth open daily 8am-noon and 3-8:30pm. To: **Florence** (1½hr., every hr. 5:10am-10:19pm, €4.75); **Pisa** (30min., every hr. 6:40-12:17am, €2.95); **Viareggio** (20min., every hr. 6:22am-11:11pm, €2.95).

Buses: Lazzi (☎0583 58 40 76), in P. Verdi, next to tourist office. To **Florence** (1½hr., every hr. 6:25am-7:45pm, €5) and **Pisa** (50min., every hr. 5:55am-8pm, €3).

Taxis: ☎0583 58 13 05, in P. Verdi; ☎0583 49 49 89, in P. Stazione; ☎0583 49 26 91, in P. Napoleone; ☎0583 49 41 90, in P. S. Maria.

Bike Rental: Cicli Bizzari, P. S. Maria, 31 (☎348 380 01 26), 2 doors down from the regional tourist office, offers a large selection of bikes and multi-day rentals. Basic bikes €2.10 per hr., €9.30 per day; mountain and racing bikes €3.15/€19.90; tandem bikes €5.15 per hr. Open daily 9am-8pm. **Antonio Poli,** P. S. Maria, 42 (☎0583 49 37 87; www.biciclettepoli.com), on the other side of the regional tourist info office, offers virtually identical services and prices. Open daily 8:30am-8pm.

ORIENTATION AND PRACTICAL INFORMATION

To reach the city's historic center from the **train station,** cross the roadway and turn left. Enter the city with the cars at **Porta San Pietro** to the right, then head left on **Corso Garibaldi.** Turn right on **Via Vittorio Veneto** and follow it one block to **Piazza Napoleone** (P. Grande), the hub of the city. Arriving by bus, follow **Via San Paolino** toward the center of town and turn on V. Veneto to reach P. Napoleone.

Tourist Office: Centro Accoglienza Turistica (☎0583 44 29 44), in Piazzale Verdi. Walk into the city through Pta. S. Pietro, turn left on V. Carrara, right on V. V. Veneto, left on V. S. Paolino, and continue to P. Verdi. Office is on the right. English-speaking staff provides free **maps,** train and bus info. Self-guided audio tours (€9 for 1 unit, €12 for 2) and bike rental. (€2.50 per hr.) Free room reservation service, but not for the cheaper hotels. Open daily 9am-7pm.

Agenzia per il Turismo, P. S. Maria, 35 (☎0583 91 99 21). From V. Roma, turn left on V. Fillungo. Follow V. Fillungo until it ends, turn left on V. S. Gemma Galgani and left into P. S. Maria. Office is on the left between the bike shops. Detailed brochures and free hotel and *affittacamere* reservation service. Open daily 9am-8pm.

Currency Exchange: UniCredit Banca, P. S. Michele, 47 (☎0583 475 46) is open 24hr. **ATM** in front. Open M-F 8:20am-1:20pm and 2:45-4:15pm, Sa 8:20-12:45pm.

Luggage Storage: At tourist office. €2 per hr.

Emergency: ☎113. **Carabinieri** (☎112). **First Aid** (☎118).

Pharmacy: Farmacia Comunale, in P. Curtatone, heading right from the exit of the train station. Open 24hr.

Hospital: Campo di Marte (☎0583 97 01).

Laundry: Lavanderia Niagara, V. Michele Rosi (☎335 629 20 55). Open daily 8am-10pm.

Internet: Mondo Chiocciola Internet Point, V. Gonfalone, 12 (☎0583 44 05 10). €4.50 per hr. Open M-F 9:30am-8pm.

TUSCANY

Post Office: ☎0583 433 51. On V. Vallisneri, off P. del Duomo. Open M-Sa 8:15am-7pm. **Postal Code:** 55100.

⚑ ACCOMMODATIONS

▨ **Ostello per la Gioventù San Frediano (HI),** V. della Cavallerizza, 12 (☎0583 46 99 57; www.ostellolucca.it). From P. Napoleone, walk 2 blocks on V. Beccheria. Turn right on V. Roma and left on V. Fillungo. After 6 blocks, turn left into P. S. Frediano and right on V. della Cavallerizza. The hostel is on the left. (15min.) Good-sized rooms and immaculate bathrooms. Breakfast €1.55; dinner €8. Towels €1.50. Sheets included. Laundry facilities available. Reception daily 7:30am-10am and 3:30-10pm. Checkout 9:30am. Lockout 10am-3:30pm. Curfew 1am. Dorms €16, with bath €18; family rooms (2-6 people) with bath €23 per person. HI card required, sold on-site for €2.58. ❷

Piccolo Hotel Puccini, V. di Poggio, 9 (☎0583 554 21; www.hotelpuccini.com), around the corner from Puccini's birthplace. Each room is decorated with framed playbills from his operas. Attentive owner speaks English, Spanish, and French. Cozy, comfortable rooms have bath, TV, phone, and safe. Singles €58; doubles €83. AmEx/MC/V. ❹

Affittacamere San Frediano, V. degli Angeli, 19 (☎0583 46 96 30; www.sanfrediano.com). Follow directions to hostel, but turn left on V. degli Angeli 2 blocks before P. S. Frediano. Collages of thank-you cards line the stairway leading to rooms with TV, big windows, and antique furniture. Matching color schemes and fluffy quilts make these rooms a perky delight. Large, clean shared baths. Breakfast included. AmEx/MC/V. ❸

Zimmer La Colonna, V. dell'Angelo Custode, 16 (☎/fax 0583 44 01 70 or 339 460 71 52), off P. Maria Foris Portam. Spacious rooms with TV and quaint antique decor; windows open onto a courtyard. Clean shared baths. Doubles €50, with bath €75. ❹

🍴 FOOD

The central **market** occupies the large building on the east side of P. del Carmine. (Open M-Sa 7am-1pm and 4-7:30pm.) An **open-air market** overruns V. dei Bacchettoni. (Open W and Sa 8am-1pm.) The closest **supermarket** is Pam, V. Diaz, 124. Turn right from Pta. Elisa, and turn left on V. Diaz. It's at the end of the block. (☎0583 49 05 96. Open M-Tu and Th-Su 8am-8pm, W 8am-1:30pm.)

▨ **Ristorante da Francesco,** Corte Portici, 13 (☎0583 41 80 49), off V. Calderia between P. S. Salvatore and P. S. Michele. Ample patio seating and well-prepared dishes in sometimes skimpy *secondi* portions. The delicious *raviole lucchese* (meat ravioli with ragu; €5.70) could be a meal on its own. *Primi* €4.70-5.70, *secondi* €8-12. Wine €7.20 per L. Cover €1.50. Open Tu-Su noon-2:30pm and 8-10:30pm. Cash only. ❷

▨ **Trattoria Rusticanella,** V. S. Paolino, 32 (☎0583 553 83). Tavern setting caters to regulars returning home from work. Jovial atmosphere, warm peppered bread, and delicious eats. Seafood pizza has clams, mussels, and calamari (€5.16). Pizza from €4.50. *Primi* and *secondi* from €5. Cover €1. Open M-Sa 11am-3pm and 6-10pm. MC/V. ❷

Pizzeria Centro Storico, V. S. Paolino (☎0583 534 09), at the intersection with V. Galli Tassi. English- and German-speaking owner Michele has many fans. Pizza slice €1.70. *Primi* €5, *secondi* €4.95. Takeout available and is cheaper than sitting at their outdoor tables. Open daily 9am-midnight. AmEx/MC/V. ❶

Ristorante del Teatro, P. Napoleone, 25 (☎0583 49 37 40). Tuxedo-clad waiters, leather booths, and outdoor piazza-watching of stylish *Luccese*. Seafood-heavy *primi* €10, *secondi* from €10. Cover €3. Open M and W-Su noon-3pm and 7-11pm. AmEx/MC/V. ❹

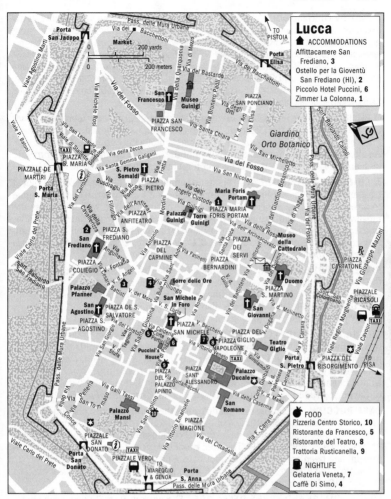

Lucca

⌂ ACCOMMODATIONS
Affittacamere San
  Frediano, **3**
Ostello per la Gioventù
  San Frediano (HI), **2**
Piccolo Hotel Puccini, **6**
Zimmer La Colonna, **1**

🍎 FOOD
Pizzeria Centro Storico, **10**
Ristorante da Francesco, **5**
Ristorante del Teatro, **8**
Trattoria Rusticanella, **9**

🍸 NIGHTLIFE
Gelateria Veneta, **7**
Caffè Di Simo, **4**

TUSCANY

🔵 SIGHTS

▨ **DUOMO DI SAN MARTINO.** Architects designed the multi-layered and arched facade of this ornate, asymmetrical duomo around its bell tower, constructed two centuries earlier. The 13th-century reliefs that decorate the exterior include Nicola Pisano's *Journey of the Magi* and *Deposition*. Matteo Civitali, Lucca's famous sculptor, designed the floor and contributed the statue of St. Martin to the right of the door. His prized *Tempietto*, halfway up the left aisle, houses the 11th-century **Volto Santo** (Holy Face). Reputedly carved by Nicodemus at Calvary, this wooden crucifix is said to depict the true image of Christ. Other highlights include Tintoretto's *Last Supper* (1593), in the third chapel on the right, and *Madonna and*

Saints by Ghirlandaio, in the sacristy off the right aisle. The **Museo della Catte-drale,** left of the duomo, holds religious objects from the duomo. An enlightening guided audio tour costs €1. *(P. S. Marino, between bell tower and post office. From P. Napoleone, take V. del Duomo. Duomo open M-F 9:45am-6pm, Sa 9am-7pm, Su between masses 9-9:50am, 11:30-11:50am, and 1-5:45pm. Sacristy open M-F 9:30am-5:45pm, Sa 9:30am-6:45pm, Su 9-9:50am, 11:30-11:50am, and 1-5:45pm. €2. Museo della Cattedrale open Apr.-Oct. daily 10am-6pm; Nov.-Mar. M-F 10am-2pm, Sa-Su 10am-5pm. €3.50. Combination ticket for Sacristy, Museo della Cattedrale, and Chiesa di S. Giovanni €5.50.)*

■ **BALUARDI.** No tour of Lucca is complete without seeing the perfectly intact city walls known as the Baluardi. The shaded 4km path, closed to cars, passes grassy parks and cool fountains as it progresses along the *baluardi* (battlements). An excellent way to appreciate the layout of the city and the beautiful countryside high above the moat, the path is perfect for a breezy afternoon picnic and *siesta*.

■ **CHIESA DI SAN GIOVANNI.** This unassuming church hides an archaeological treasure trove. The simple plaster dome off the left transept crowns the entrance to a recently excavated second-century AD Roman complex, which includes the mosaic pavement and ruins of a private house and bath (the church's foundations), a Longobard burial site, and a Paleochristian chapel, as well as 12th-century crypt. *(Walk past San Giovanni from P. S. Martino and around the corner to the right. Open Apr.-Oct. daily 10am-6pm; Nov.-Mar. M-F 10am-2pm, Sa-Su 10am-5pm. €2.50.)*

PIAZZA NAPOLEONE. Also called "Piazza Grande" by locals, this central piazza is the town's administrative center. The 16th-century **Palazzo Ducale** now houses government offices. In the evening, prime *passeggiata* time, *Luccese* young and old pack the piazza. **Piazza Anfiteatro** is also quite popular with locals and tourists, its closely packed buildings creating a nearly seamless oval wall.

CHIESA DI SAN MICHELE. Construction on this church began in the eighth century on the site of a Roman forum. The church's large interior holds beautiful and dramatic oil paintings. Lippi's bold *Saints Helen, Roch, Sebastian, Jerome* hangs toward the end of the right aisle; Robbia's *Madonna and Child* is near the front. Original religious statues were replaced in the 19th century with likenesses of Cavour, Garibaldi, and Napoleon III. *(Open 7:40am-noon and 3-6pm. Free.)*

CASA PUCCINI. Music lovers shouldn't miss the birthplace and childhood home of Giacomo Puccini (1858-1924), composer of La Bohème and Madama Butterfly. The fourth-floor apartment displays original compositions and scribbled revisions, letters, and assorted playbills. The final room holds the Steinway piano on which Puccini had been composing Turandot before he succumbed to throat cancer. *(C. S. Lorenzo, 9, off V. Poggi. ☎ 0583 58 40 28. Open June-Sept. daily 10am-6pm, Mar.-May and Oct.-Dec. Tu-Su 10am-1pm and 3-6pm. €3.)*

TORRE GUINIGI AND TORRE DELLA ORE. The narrow **Torre Guinigi** rises above Lucca from the mute stone mass of Palazzo Guinigi, which is not open to the public. At the top of 230 stairs, a grove of trees provides a shaded view of the city and hills beyond. *(V. S. Andrea, 41. From P. S. Michele, follow V. Roma for 1 block, turn left on V. Fillungo and right on V. S. Andrea. ☎ 0583 31 68 46. Open daily June-Sept. 9am-11pm, Oct.-Jan. 9am-4pm, Feb.-May 9am-6pm. €3.50.)* For more exercise, climb the 207 steps of the **Torre della Ore** (clock towers), two of the 15 towers remaining of medieval Lucca's original 250. *(V. Fillungo, 22. On the way to Torre Guinigi. Open daily in summer 10am-7pm, in winter 10am-5:30pm. €3.50.)*

■ ■ **NIGHTLIFE AND ENTERTAINMENT**

For evidence that Lucca is a sleepy Tuscan town at heart, look no further than **Gelateria Veneta,** V. Vittorio Veneto, 74, the epicenter of activity for the throngs on V. Vittorio Veneto. *The* place to see and be seen on late Saturday nights, Veneta offers interesting flavors and swank seating. (☎0583 46 70 37. Cones €1.70-3.50. *Granita* €2.20. Open M-F and Su 10am-1am, Sa 10am-2am.) **Caffè Di Simo,** V. Fillungo, 58, gleams with chandeliers and a zinc bar. In the 19th century, the marble tables hosted writers, Risorgimento-plotters, and musicians like Puccini. (☎0583 49 62 34. Coffee €0.90, at table €2.10. Open Tu-Sa 8am-10pm.)

Lucca's calendar bulges with artistic performances, especially in the summer. The **Summer Festival** (☎0584 464 77; www.summer-festival.com) takes place throughout July and has featured performances by pop stars such as Jamiroquai, Paul Simon, James Taylor, Dido, and Oasis. Sample **Teatro Comunale del Giglio's** opera season, starting at the end of September, or their ballet season, starting in January. The king of Lucca's festivals is the **Settembre Lucchese** (Sept. 13-22), a lively jumble of artistic, athletic, and folkloric presentations. The annual **Pallo della Balestra,** a crossbow competition dating from 1443 and revived for tourists in the early 1970s, takes place here. Participants wear traditional costume on July 12 and September 14 for the competition.

PISA   ☎050

Each year in the *Campo dei Miracoli*, millions of tourists arrive to marvel at the famous Leaning Tower, forming a gelato-slurping, photo-snapping mire. But Pisa is far more than a *torre pendente*, commanding a beautiful stretch of the Arno River and sheltering enough monumental architecture to trump any souvenir stand. In the Middle Ages, the city earned its living as a port and had a trade empire extending to Corsica, Sardinia, and the Balearics; with time, though, silt began to fill the Arno, stopping its flow and drying up Pisa's fortunes. Luckily, the impressive tower brought enough tourist revenues to revive the cathedral, baptistery, and cemetery that cluster in the same piazza. Pisa has also thrived as a university town. So after that hackneyed Kodak moment, take some time to wander the sprawling university neighborhood through Piazzas Cavalieri and Dante Alighieri, along alleys lined with elegant buildings and impassioned political graffiti.

TUSCANY

◪ TRANSPORTATION

Flights: Galileo Galilei Airport (☎050 50 07 07; www.pisa-airport.com). Trains that make the 5min. trip (€1) between train station and airport coincide with flight departures and arrivals. Bus #3 runs between the airport, train station, and other points in Pisa and environs (every 20min., €0.85). Charter, domestic, and international flights. To: **Barcelona** (3½hr., 2 per day); **London** (2¼hr., 11 per day); **Paris** (2hr., 3 per day).

Trains: ☎147 80 888. In P. della Stazione, at southern end of town. Info office open daily 7am-9pm. Ticket booth open 6am-9:30pm; self-service ticket machines available 24hr. To: **Florence** (1hr., every hr. 4:12am-12:49am, €5.05); **Genoa** (2½hr., 6am-10:40pm, €7.90); **Livorno** (20min., every hr., €1.50); **Rome** (3hr., 12 per day, €15.40-23.50). Regional trains to **Lucca** (20min., every 30min. 6:24am-9:40pm, €1.95) stop at Pisa's **San Rossore,** closer to the duomo and the youth hostel. If leaving Pisa from S. Rossore, buy tickets at *tabacchi,* as there is no ticket office in the station.

Buses: Lazzi, P. V. Emanuele, 11 (☎050 462 88; www.lazzi.it). To: **Florence** (change at Lucca; 2½hr., every hr., €7.40); **La Spezia** (3hr., 4 per day, €7.40); **Lucca** (40min., every hr., €2.20). **CPT** (☎800 01 27 73; www.cpt.pisa.it), in P. S. Antonio, near train station. To **Livorno** (45min., 5am-7:30pm, €2.37) and **Volterra** (1½hr., 7 per day, €5.11) via **Pontederra.**

Taxis: RadioTaxi (☎050 54 16 00 or 412 52), in P. Stazione; (☎050 56 18 78), in P. del Duomo; (☎050 285 42), at the airport.

Car Rental: Avis (☎050 420 28; 25+), **Hertz** (☎050 432 20; 23+), and **Maggiore** (☎050 425 74; 21+) have offices at the airport. From €61 per day.

■ ⚡ ? ORIENTATION AND PRACTICAL INFORMATION

Pisa lies near the mouth of the Arno River, which splits the town. Most sights lie to the north of the Arno; the main **train station** is to the south. To reach the **Campo dei Miracoli (Piazza del Duomo)** from the station, take bus #3 (€0.85). Alternatively, walk straight up **Viale Gramsci,** through **Piazza Vittorio Emanuele,** and stroll along the busy **Corso Italia.** Cross **Ponte di Mezzo** and follow the river left, turn right on V. Santa Maria which hits the duomo and Leaning Tower after 30min.

Tourist Office: ☎050 422 91; www.turismo.toscana.it. In P.V. Emanuele. Walk straight from station exit and take left at large piazza. English-speaking, knowledgeable staff provides detailed **maps.** Detailed list of local hotels and campsites, including prices and locations, is available. Open Apr.-Oct. M-Sa 9am-7pm, Su 9:30am-3:30pm; Nov.-Mar. M-Sa 9am-6pm, Su 9:30am-3:30pm. Another **branch** (☎050 56 04 64) is behind the Leaning Tower. Open M-Sa 9am-7pm, Su 10:30am-4:30pm.

Budget Travel: CTS, V. S. Maria, 12 (☎050 483 00 or 292 21, fax 454 31), by the Hotel Galileo. International tickets and boats to nearby islands. English spoken. Open M-F 9am-1pm and 4-7:30pm, Sa 9:30am-12:30pm.

Luggage Storage: At the airport. Drop-off available 10am-6pm, pick-up 8am-8pm. €6 per bag per day.

English-Language Bookstore: The Bookshop, V. Rigattieri, 33/39 (☎050 57 34 34). Best selection in town. Classics, guide books, and some contemporary titles. Open Aug.-June M-F and Su 9am-8pm; July 9am-1pm and 4-8pm.

Gay and Lesbian Resources: ARCI-GAY Pride! V. S. Lorenzo, 38 (☎050 55 56 18; www.gay.it/pride). Open M-F 1:30-7:30pm.

Laundromats: Bucato Point, V. Corridoni, 50m from train station (☎800 08 04 03). Wash €3. Dry €3. Soap €0.50. Open daily 8am-10pm.

Emergency: ☎113. **Ambulance** (☎118). **Police** (☎050 58 35 11).

Pharmacy: Farmacia, V. Lugarno Medaceo, 51 (☎050 54 40 02). Open 24hr.

Hospital: ☎050 99 21 11. On V. Bonanno near P. del Duomo.

Internet: Internet Point 77, V. Corridoni, 77, 2 blocks from the train station. €3 per hr. Open M-Sa 11am-10pm. **Internet Planet,** P. Cavolloti (☎050 83 97 92; info@internet-planet.it). From P. del Duomo, follow V. S. Maria and take 2nd left into P. Cavolloti. €2 for 30min., €3.10 per hr. Open M-Sa 10am-midnight, Su 3pm-midnight.

Post Office: P. V. Emanuele, 8 (☎050 18 69), near the station, left of the large traffic circle. Open M-Sa 8:30am-7pm. **Postal Code:** 56100.

■ 🏠 ⚡ ACCOMMODATIONS AND CAMPING

Albergo Helvetia, V. Don G. Boschi, 31 (☎050 55 30 84), off P. Arcivescovado, near duomo. Bright, well-kept rooms—fluffy quilts, TV, ceiling fan, and phone. Small shared baths. Welcoming bar downstairs. Breakfast €5 (order night before). Reception 8am-midnight. Singles €35, with bath €52; doubles €45/€62. Extra bed €15. ❸

Centro Turistico Madonna dell'Acqua, V. Pietrasantina, 15 (☎050 89 06 22), behind old Catholic sanctuary 2km from the Tower. Bus #3 from station (4 per hr., last 9:45pm); ask to stop at *ostello*. Board bus across the street from 1st departure point in piazza, outside Hotel Cavalieri. Located by a creek, which attracts mosquitoes and chirping crickets. Kitchen available. Sheets €1. Reception daily 6am-midnight. Check-out 9:30am. Dorms €15; doubles €42; triples €54; quads €64. MC/V. ❶

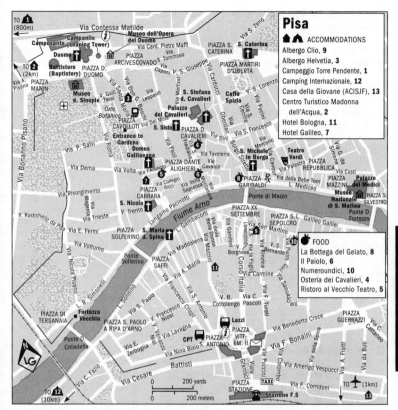

Pisa

▲ ⛺ ACCOMMODATIONS

Albergo Clio, **9**
Albergo Helvetia, **3**
Campeggio Torre Pendente, **1**
Camping Internazionale, **12**
Casa della Giovane (ACISJF), **13**
Centro Turistico Madonna dell'Acqua, **2**
Hotel Bologna, **11**
Hotel Galileo, **7**

🍴 FOOD
La Bottega del Gelato, **8**
Il Paiolo, **6**
Numeroundici, **10**
Osteria dei Cavalieri, **4**
Ristoro al Vecchio Teatro, **5**

Casa della Giovane (ACISJF), V. F. Corridoni, 29 (☎050 430 61), 15min. right of station, in a neighborhood that shuts down by 10pm. Large abode with basic furnishings, large baths, and breakfast included. Sheets provided, but no towels or daily cleaning service. Women only. Reception daily 7am-11pm. Check-out 9am. Curfew 11pm. Singles €26, with bath €30; doubles €36/€40. Cash only. ❸

Hotel Galileo, V. S. Maria, 12 (☎050 406 21; hotelgalileo@pisaonline.it). Don't be put off by the dark entryway: a solar system of stellar rooms lies ahead, all with frescoed ceilings, TVs, and antique tiling and furniture. Narrow baths. Singles with bath €45; doubles €48, with bath €66. Extra bed €15. ❹

Hotel Bologna, V. Mazzini, 57 (☎050 50 21 20; www.albergobologna.com). Great management, elevators, and wood floors make this place luxurious. Rooms have bath, TV, minibar, A/C, and cherubic paintings. Internet €1 per hr. Breakfast included. Check-out 11am. Singles €85; doubles €105; triples €125; quads €145. AmEx/MC/V. ❺

Albergo Clio, V. S. Lorenzino, 3 (☎050 284 46), off C. Italia, 1 block from the Ponte Mezzo. Vintage Hollywood dream of a lobby: pink chairs, black-and-white tiled floor, and mirrored moldings. Tiled hallways lead to bare rooms and small bathrooms. Singles €30; doubles €45, with bath €55; triples with bath €65. Cash only. ❸

Campeggio Torre Pendente, V. delle Cascine, 86 (☎050 56 17 04), 1km from tower. Bus #3 to P. Manin. With city wall on right, walk 2 blocks and turn left on V. delle Cascine, following camping signs. Walk through long concrete underpass, emerge, and walk past industrial-looking buildings; campground is on the right, in a convenient location. Swimming pool and decent bathrooms; some sites not shaded. Open Mar.-Oct. €7.50 per person, €3.50 per child; €6.30 per tent. Bungalows €32-82. ❶

Camping Internazionale (☎050 352 11; www.pisacamping.com), 10km away on V. Litoranea in Marina di Pisa, across from its private beach. Take CPT bus (intercity bus) from P. S. Antonio to Marina di Pisa (buy ticket in CPT office entering P. S. Antonio from P. V. Emanuele; €1.50). Sites are small but partially shaded. Bar and market on premises. Open May-Sept. €5 per person, €4 per child; €6 per small tent, €7.50 per large tent. July-Aug. prices increase by €1-2. AmEx/MC/V. ❶

🍴 FOOD

Steer clear of the tower and head for the river; the restaurants here offer a more authentic ambiance and consistent high quality, and many prominently feature seafood. Cheap meals are plentiful in the university area. In P. Vettovaglie, an **open-air market** spills into nearby streets. Bakeries and salumerias fill Pisa's residential quarter. For conveniently pre-packaged yummies, try Pam, V. Pascoli, 8, just off C. Italia. (Open M-Sa 8am-8pm.)

Il Paiolo, V. Curtatone Montanara, 9 (☎050 425 28), near the university. Lively pub atmosphere, with bench seating and great music. Order the hearty *bistecca* for €2.70 per 100g (make sure to get a weight or price quote), or try some heavenly *risotto* with mussels, tiny calamari, and chunks of salmon (€5.20) with the light, sweet house white wine (0.25L for €2.10). *Primi* and *secondi* from €4.15-7.75. Cover €1. Open M-F 12:30-3pm and 7:30pm-2am, Sa-Su 7:30pm-2am. Cash only. ❷

La Bottega del Gelato, P. Garibaldi, 11. Overwhelming range of flavors, plus specials of the day. Grape, whiskey cream, Nutella, *limoncello*... Decide before reaching the counter, or end up swallowed in the crowd. Busiest after sundown. 2 generous scoops in a small cup or cone €1.30. Open M-Tu and Th-Su 11am-1am. ❶

Numeroundici, V. S. Martino, 47. Munch on generously-sized sandwiches (€2.50) and superb vegetable torte (€2.30) on wooden benches in this casual establishment. Cavernous dining room filled with Tibetan lanterns. Self-service. *Primi* €4, *secondi* €6. Open M-F noon-10pm, in summer closes 11:30pm. MC/V ❶

Ristoro al Vecchio Teatro, P. Dante, 2 (☎050 202 10). Delicious, traditional Pisan cuisine built around fresh vegetables and seafood. Try the *risotto mare* (with seafood; €7) or the buttery *sfogliata di zucchine* (zucchini torte; €7). *Primi* and *secondi* €7. Dessert €3. Cover €1.50. Open M-Sa noon-3pm and 8-10pm. Closed Aug. AmEx/MC/V. ❷

Osteria dei Cavalieri, V. San Frediano, 16 (☎050 58 08 58). Wine-laden dining room with slick jazz posters hops with tourists and locals. Quality place to sneak in some traditional *trippa, coniglio,* or *cinghiale* before parting for the sea. *Primi* €6-8, *secondi* €8-13. Open M-F 12:30-2pm and 7:45-10pm, Sa 7:45-10pm. MC/V. ❷

👁 SIGHTS

LEANING TOWER. *Campo dei Miracoli* (Field of Miracles) is an appropriate nickname for the piazza that houses the Leaning Tower, duomo, baptistery, and Camposanto. But look closely—*all* of the buildings are leaning at different angles, thanks to the mischievous, shifty soil. Of course, none lean quite so dramatically as the famous *campanile* of the duomo, which tilts 5½ degrees to the south. Bonanno Pisano began building it in 1173, and the tower had reached a height of 10m

TOWER POWER. The city offers a joint ticket to the duomo, baptistery, Camposanto, Museo delle Sinopie, and Museo del Duomo (€10.50), to 1 of the above monuments (€5), 2 of the above monuments (€6), to 4 monuments (€6) and to everything but the duomo (€8.50). Tickets for just the duomo are €2.Tickets for the Leaning Tower are sold separately (€15). Combination tickets can be bought at the two *biglietteria* on the *Campo dei Miracoli* (at the Museo del Duomo and next to the tourist office behind the tower).

when the soil beneath shifted unexpectedly. The tilt intensified after WWII, and thanks to those tourists who climb its 294 steps, it continues to slip 1-2mm every year. In June of 2001, the steel safety cables and iron girdles that had imprisoned the Tower during a several-year stabilization effort were finally removed. One year later, the Tower reopened, albeit on a tightly regulated schedule: once every 30min., guided groups of 30 visitors are permitted to ascend. *(Make reservations at the ticket offices in the Museo del Duomo or next to the tourist information office. Tours depart daily June-Aug. 8:30am-10:30pm, Sept.-May 8:30am-7:30pm. Assemble next to information office 10min. before scheduled time. Childen under 8 not permitted, under 18 must be accompanied by an adult. Free baggage storage. €15. Cash only.)*

■ **DUOMO.** The dark green and white facade of the duomo is the archetype of the Pisan-Romanesque style; indeed, this is one of the most important Romanesque cathedrals in the world. Begun in 1063 by Boschetto (who had himself entombed in the wall), the cathedral is the Campo's oldest structure. Enter the five-aisled nave through Bonanno Pisano's bronze doors (1180). Although 1595 fire destroyed most of the interior, paintings by Ghirlandaio still hang along the right wall, Cimabue's spectacular gilded mosaic *Christ Pantocrator* graces the apse, and bits of the intricately patterned marble Cosmati pavement remain. The cathedral's elaborate chandelier is falsely rumored to have inspired Galileo's theories of gravity. Giovanni Pisano's last and greatest pulpit, designed to outdo his father's in the baptistery, sits majestically in the center. Relief panels depict classical and biblical subjects, including the Nativity, the Last Judgment, and the Massacre of the Innocents. Always up for a good allegory, Pisano carved the pulpit's supports into figures symbolizing the arts and virtues. *(Open M-Sa 10am-8pm, Su 1-8pm. €2. Free during Su mass, but the roped-off area at the end of the nave provides only a partial view.)*

■ **BATTISTERO.** The baptistery, an enormous barrel of a building, was begun in 1152 by a man known as Diotisalvi ("God save you"). It measures 107m in girth and is 55m tall. Blending architectural styles, it incorporates Tuscan-Romanesque stripes with a multi-tiered Gothic ensemble of gables, pinnacles, and statues. Guido Bigarelli's fountain (1246) dominates the center of the ground floor. Nicola Pisano's pulpit (1260) recaptures the sobriety and dignity of classical antiquity and is one of the harbingers of Renaissance art in Italy. The dome's acoustics are astounding: a choir singing in the baptistery can be heard 2km away. A staircase embedded in the wall leads to a balcony level just below the dome; farther up, a space between the interior and exterior of the dome yields teasing views of the surrounding piazza. *(Open daily late Apr.-late Sept. 8am-8pm, Oct.-Mar. 9am-6pm. €6, includes entrance to 1 other museum or monument on the combination ticket list.)*

■ **CAMPOSANTO.** This cloistered courtyard cemetery, covered with earth that Crusaders brought back from Golgotha, holds the Roman sarcophagi whose reliefs inspired Nicola Pisano's pulpit in the baptistery. Fragments of frescoes shattered by Allied bombs during WWII line the galleries. The **Cappella Ammannati** contains haunting frescoes of Florence succumbing to the plague; its unidentified 14th-century creator is known as the "Master of the Triumph of Death." *(Open daily*

TUSCANY

TOP TEN LIST

TOWERS OF TUSCANY

10. **Clock Tower of Palazzo Comunale, Cortona:** A good choice not for height or climbing, but for sitting under. Popular with gelato-laden hoards.

9. **Tower of the Museo dell'Opera Metropolitana, Siena:** Up the precarious Scala del Facciatore from Room 4. Has the best views in the city of the duomo and baptistery.

8. **Campanile, Pistoia:** Sweeping views to Florence on clear days from its 66m pyramid-shaped spire.

7. **Palazzo Comunale, Montepulciano:** Views of regal Siena and Gran Sasso Massif.

6. **Campanile, Florence:** Hands down the most beautiful facade. But ticket prices might not be worth the smog-obscured view.

5. **Torre dei Guinigi, Lucca:** Trees provide shade to relax and enjoy views of Lucca's dark hills.

4. **Torre delle Ore, Lucca:** A similarly spectacular view minus the trees at the top.

3. **Torre de Mangia, Siena:** The 102m tower casts a menacing shadow over Piazza del Campo. Italy's tallest secular monument.

2. **Leaning Tower, Pisa:** Beautiful and quirkily slanted. And pretty photogenic—but worth the €15 entrance fee?

1. **Torre Grossa, San Gimignano:** The tower overlooks the most breathtaking countryside in the region, and looms large on the city's horizon.

late Apr.-late Sept. 8am-8pm, Mar. and Oct. 9am-5:40pm, Nov.-Feb. 9am-4:40pm. €6, includes entrance to 1 other museum or monument on the combination ticket list.)

MUSEO NAZIONALE DI SAN MATTEO. Thirty rooms showcase spectacular panels by Masaccio, Fra Angelico, and Simone Martini. Sculptures by the Pisano clan and a bust by Donatello also grace this converted convent. (Off P. Mazzini on Lugamo Mediceo. Open Tu-Su 9am-7pm. €4, ages 18-26 €2, under 18 or over 65 free.)

MUSEO DELL'OPERA DEL DUOMO AND MUSEO DELLE SINOPIE. The Museo dell'Opera del Duomo displays artwork from the three buildings of P. del Duomo. The *Madonna del Colloquio* (Madonna of the Conversation) by Giovanni Pisano was named for the expressive gazes exchanged between mother and child. The display also includes a small collection of Egyptian art, works by Tino Camaino and Nino Pisano, and an assortment of Roman and Etruscan pieces tucked into the church in the Middle Ages. (Behind the Leaning Tower. Open daily Apr.-late Sept. 8am-7:20pm, Mar. and Oct. 9am-5:20pm, Nov.-Feb. 9am-4:20pm. €6, includes entrance to 1 other museum or monument on the combination ticket list.) Across the square from the Camposanto, the **Museo delle Sinopie** displays fresco sketches by Traini, Veneziano, and Gaddi, as well as other sketches discovered during the post-WWII restoration. (Same hours and admission cost and conditions as Museo dell'Opera del Duomo.)

PIAZZA DEI CAVALIERI. Designed by Vasari and built on the site of the Roman forum, this piazza once held the town hall. Now it is the seat of the **Scuola Normale Superiore,** one of Italy's premier universities. Though not open to the public, a walk around the exterior is worth it. The wrought-iron baskets on either end of the **Palazzo dell'Orologio** (Palace of the Clock) were once receptacles for the heads of delinquent Pisans. In the palazzo's **tower,** Ugolino della Gherardesca was starved to death in 1208 along with his sons and grandsons, as punishment for treachery. This murky episode in Tuscan politics is commemorated in Shelley's *Tower of Famine,* as well as in Dante's *Inferno* with gruesome cannibalistic innuendo.

OTHER SIGHTS. Of Pisa's many churches, three merit special attention. The **Chiesa di Santa Maria della Spina** (Church of Saint Mary of the Thorn), which faces Gambacorti near the river, is quintessentially Gothic. It was built to house a thorn taken from Christ's Crown of Thorns. Visitors can view the interior only during Italy's annual Culture Week. (From the Campo, walk down V. S. Maria and over *the bridge. Ask the tourist office for info.)* The **Chiesa di San Michele in Borgo** is notable for Latin scribblings concerning a 14th-century electoral campaign for University Rector, found on its stone facade. *(From Santa Maria della Spina, walk with the river on the left, cross the 1st bridge, and continue straight 1 block.)* At **Chiesa di San Nicola**, off P. del Duomo, the famous altarpiece in the fourth chapel on the right shows St. Nicholas deflecting the arrows that God aims at Pisa. The bell tower of the church inclines, not unlike its more famous cousin. *(Between V. S. Maria and P. Carrara. Open daily 7:45-11:30am and 5-6:30pm.)* If all the gray stone becomes monotonous, go to the **Orto Botanico** public garden for palm trees and fresh air. *(Entrance at V. L. Ghini, 5, between V. Roma and V. S. Maria. Open M-F 8am-5:30pm, Sa 8am-1pm. Last entrance 30min. before closing.)*

🎵 🍷 ENTERTAINMENT AND NIGHTLIFE

Occasional concerts take place in the duomo. Call **Opera della Primaziale** (☎ 050 56 05 47). The annual **Gioco del Ponte** revives the city's tradition of medieval pageantry. Pisans divide, pledging their allegiance to one side of the Arno or another. The opposing sides converge on a bridge to see which side's cart can claim the largest portion of the bridge. (☎ 050 92 91 11; last Su in June.) The night before the holiday of the patron saint Nicholas in mid-June, the **Luminara di San Ranieri** brings the illumination of Pisa (including the tower) with 70,000 lights. The main street of the University District, which runs up from P. Garibaldi on the river, changing names from Borgo Stretto to V. Oberdan to V. Carducci, is lined with places to drink beer, sip coffee, or enjoy gelato—as is C. Italia, toward the station.

VIAREGGIO ☎ 0584

The resort town of Viareggio sits at the foot of the Riviera, tucked between the colorful beach umbrellas of the Versilian coast and the olive and chestnut groves cloaking the foothills of the Apuan Mountains. Young Italians arrive each morning to slather on oil and soak up the sun; by night, European tourists stroll along the shore's promenade, taking in grandiose 1920s architecture and glitzy boutiques.

🚆 **TRANSPORTATION.** Viareggio lies on the Rome-Genoa and Viareggio-Florence train lines. **Trains** service Florence (2hr., 5:45am-10pm, €5.90); Genoa (2½hr., 3:02am-12:30am, €11.50); La Spezia (1hr., 5:52am-3:02am, €5.30); Livorno (30min., 5:39am-2:32am, €4.85) via Pisa; Rome (3hr., every hr., 5:39am-2:32am, €26). **Lazzi buses** (☎ 0584 462 33) connect Viareggio to: Florence (2¼hr., every hr., €5.70); La Spezia (2hr., 4 per day, €3.50); Lucca (45min., every hr., €2.50); Pisa (20min., 20 per day, €2.50). All buses stop in P. Mazzini, the town's main square near the waterfront. **Taxis** (☎ 0584 454 54) are available at the train station.

🖥 🛈 **ORIENTATION AND PRACTICAL INFORMATION.** A **tourist office** at the train station has good **maps,** local bus schedules, and information on hotels. (Open May-Sept. W-Sa 9:30am-12:30pm and 3-5:30pm, Su 9:30am-noon; reduced hours Oct.-Apr.) To get to the main **tourist office,** V. Carducci, 10, from the main exit of the train station walk directly across the piazza, then head right. Take the first left and walk 20min. down V. XX Settembre to P. Mazzini. At the other end of the piazza, turn right on V. Carducci and walk two and a half blocks. The personable staff supplies decent maps, brochures, and information on hikes and car tours. Train schedules are posted outside. (☎ 0584 96 22 33; www.versilia.turismo.toscana.it. Open M-Sa 9am-2pm and 3:30-7pm, Su 9:30am-1pm and 4-7pm.) Several of their recommended itineraries require a car. Rent one at **EuropCar,** right at the train station. (☎0584 43 05 06. Open M-F 9am-12:30pm and 3:30-6:30pm, Sa 9am-12:30pm.) Adjacent to the tourist office, the **booking office** has hotel information and can reserve rooms for a 5% commission. (☎0584 317 81. Open May-Sept. W-Sa 9:30am-12:30pm and 3-5:30pm, Su 9:30am-noon; reduced hours Oct.-Apr.) **Luggage storage** is available at the train station, left before the exit and after the bar. (€3 for 12hr. Open daily 8am-8pm.) **Currency exchange** is available at the post office or at any of the banks along V. Garibaldi. In case of **emergency,** dial ☎113; for **first aid,** call ☎118. An all-night **pharmacy** is at V. Mazzini, 14. The **post office** is at the corner of V. Garibaldi and V. Puccini. (☎0584 303 45. Open M-F 8:15am-7pm, Sa 8:15am-12:30pm.) **Postal Code:** 55049.

⏏ ▢ ACCOMMODATIONS AND FOOD. Amid the splendor and pretense of four-stardom hide budget accommodations. Many, however, turn into *pensioni* in the summer, catering to Italians on extended holidays and making it difficult to find short-term accommodations in July and August. Call several weeks ahead. **Hotel Rex ❸,** V. S. Martino, 48, has small and refined rooms with bath, TV, phone, and A/C. (☎0584 96 11 40; hotelrex.vg@libero.it. Breakfast included. Late June-Aug. singles €35-40; doubles €60-100; triples €120. Low-season prices drop €20. AmEx/MC/V.) **Albergo Sara ❹,** V. S. Martino, 59, only two blocks from the beach, has tidy rooms, all with TV, bathroom, and fan. The €45 per person half pension deal also includes breakfast and dinner, both served in their outdoor covered patio. (☎/fax 0584 460 42. Doubles with breakfast €50. MC/V.) Close to the beach, **Hotel Albachiara ❹,** V. Zanardelli, 81, offers modest rooms with bath. (☎0584 445 41. Breakfast included. Sept.-June doubles €65; full pension €44. July-Aug. doubles €70; full pension €47-49. AmEx/MC/V.)

Accustomed to catering to a wealthy clientele, Viareggio's restaurants are none too cheap. To avoid high cover charges, head away from the waterfront to **Ristorante da Giorgio ❹,**V. Zanardelli, 71, to savor fresh seafood in a cool dining room. (*Primi* €9, *secondi* €25. ☎0584 444 93. Open Tu-Su noon-2pm and 7:30-10pm. AmEx/MC/V.) For an affordable splurge, drop €4.50 on coffee and dessert at the ritzy terrace of the **Gran Caffè Margherita ❷,** overlooking the sea. From P. Mazzini facing the sea, turn left on the main drag; the restaurant is ahead on the right.

◪ ▤ BEACHES AND ENTERTAINMENT. Most of the shoreline has been roped off by the owners of Viareggio's private beaches. This doesn't mean visitors can't walk through these areas to the water; they just can't park beach towels there. Walking to the left facing the water across the canal along Viale Europa, 30min. from P. Mazzini, leads to the **free beach,** at the southern edge of town. Or, take city bus #9 (tickets €0.80, €1.50 if bought onboard) from the train station and save some precious tanning time. Bus #10 returns from the beach to the station. The crowd here is younger, hipper, and noticeably less pretentious than the private beach set.

LIVORNO   ☎0586

Dwarfed by monstrous ocean liners awaiting departure for destinations like Sardinia, Corsica, Greece, and Spain, Livorno is a rough-and-ready port town with a convenient ferry system. Henry James's assertion that Livorno "may claim the distinction, unique in Italy, of being the city of no pictures" is true enough; nevertheless, visitors usually find the town perfectly serviceable for an evening stay and early morning departure. Those awaiting ferries will find fresh and affordable seafood, views of the surrounding countryside, and inexpensive accommodations.

TRANSPORTATION

Trains: Frequent service connects Livorno to: **Florence** (1½hr., €5.95); **Piombino** (1½hr., €5); **Pisa** (15min., €1.85); **Rome** (3½hr., €14.80).

Buses: ATL (☎0586 88 42 62; www.atl.livorno.it) sends buses from P. Grande to **Piombino** (8 per day, €6.46) and **Pisa** (16 per day, €2.17).

Ferries: At Stazione Marittima. From the train station, take bus #1 to P. Grande (buy ticket from *tabacchi;* €0.85). Ticket offices open before and after arrivals and departures. From P. Grande, take PB 1, 2, or 3 bus, or take V. Cogorano, cross P. Municipio, and take V. Porticciolo, which becomes V. Venezia and leads to the port and Stazione Marittima. (10min.) Stazione Marittima has **currency exchange, luggage storage,** and a **restaurant.** Schedules and docks vary by season. Prices increase in summer and on weekends. Port taxes (€3-8) may apply. **Corsica Marittima** (☎0586 21 05 07; www.forti.it/sncm/Inglese/homeing.html) runs quick service to **Bastia, Corsica** (2hr., Apr.-Sept. 2-4 per day, €16-30) and **Porto Vecchio, Corsica** (10hr., June-Sept. 1-2 per week). **Moby Lines** (☎0586 82 68 25; www.moby.it) runs to **Bastia** (3hr., June-Sept. daily, €15-28) and **Olbia, Sardinia** (8-10hr., Mar.-Sept. daily, €20-46). **Corsica** and **Sardinia Ferries** (☎0586 88 13 80; www.corsicaferries.com) runs to **Bastia** (4hr., daily May-Sept., €16-28) and **Golfo Aranci, Sardinia** (6-8hr.; June-Aug. Tu-Su 2 per day, greatly reduced service in low season; €21-47).

Taxi: Radio Taxi (☎0586 88 20 20).

ORIENTATION AND PRACTICAL INFORMATION

From the **train station,** take bus **#1** to reach **Piazza Grande,** the town center. Buses **#2** and **8** also stop at P. Grande, but only after trips to the suburbs. Buy tickets (€0.85) at the booth outside the station, at *tabacchi,* or at one of the orange vending machines. The **tourist office** is at P. Cavour, 6, 3rd fl. (☎0586 89 81 11; www.costadeglietruschi.it), up V. Cairoli from P. Grande. (Open M-F 9am-1pm and 3-5pm, Sa 9am-1pm; reduced hours Sept.-May.) Near P. Grande, a right on V. Corogano leads to a tourist kiosk in P. Municipio that supplies well-detailed street **maps.** (☎0586 82 01 11. Open daily 9:30am-7pm.) There is also a **branch** office in Stazione Marittima. (☎0586 89 53 20. Open June-Sept. M 8am-1pm and 4-8pm, Tu and Th-Su 8am-1pm and 2-8pm, W 8:30am-2pm and 3-8pm.) **Currency exchange** is available at the train station (open daily 8-11:45am and 3-5:45pm), Stazione Marittima, the post office, and the banks on V. Cairoli. Self-service **luggage storage** lockers are in the train station. (€2-4 per 24hr. No large bags.) In case of **emergency,** dial ☎113, call an **ambulance** (☎118), or contact the **hospital** (☎0586 22 31 11). **Farmacia Comunale,** P. Grande, 8 (☎0586 89 44 90), is open 24hr. The **post office** is at V. Cairoli, 12/16. (☎0586 276 41. Open M-F 8:30am-7pm, Sa 8:30am-12:30pm.) **Postal Code:** 57100.

ACCOMMODATIONS

Hotel Cavour, V. Adua, 10 (☎/fax 0586 89 96 04). From the main tourist office, cross P. Cavour and follow V. Michon to V. Adua. Simple rooms with big bright windows and clean baths. Satellite TV in the comfortable lounge. Singles €24, with bath €29; doubles €40/€52 triples €55/€70; quads with bath €80. Cash only. ❷

Hotel Marina, C. Mazzini, 24 (☎0586 83 42 78). From main tourist office, continue through P. Cavour, follow V. Ricasoli 1 block, and turn right on V. Mazzini. Handsome stone tiles, soft beds, and immaculate baths in rooms with TV and A/C. Common room has TV, pool table, and board games. Singles €47; doubles €62; triples €72. MC/V. ❹

Hotel Boston, P. Mazzini, 40 (☎0586 88 23 33; www.bostonh.it). From P. Grande, follow V. Grande to the harbor, go left on S. C. Cialdini, which becomes S. C. Novi Lena, and cross the park when P. Mazzini appears on the left. Luxurious 3-star hotel has tastefully furnished, green-accented rooms with phone, TV, and large bath. A/C €10 extra. Singles €67-72.50; doubles €85-96. AmEx/MC/V. ❺

Ostello/Albergo Villa Morazzana, V. Collinet, 40 (☎0586 50 00 76), just within city limits. Bus #1 to P. Grande (€0.85) and transfer to bus #3. (20min., M-F every hr.) #3 buses run different routes, so ask at info booth in P. Grande which goes to hostel, or call hostel for exact directions. Some rooms in this 17th-century villa have views of the countryside and sea. Minutes from a quiet beach. Breakfast included. Lockout 9:30am-5pm. Curfew 11:30pm. Wheelchair accessible. Dorms €18; singles €36, with bath €42; doubles with bath €62. AmEx/MC/V. ❷

🍴 FOOD

Livorno owes its culinary specialties to the sea. The city has its own variation of bouillabaise: a fiery, tomato-based seafood stew they call *cacciucco*. Fill up at the **Central Market** in P. Cavallotti (open M-F 5am-3pm, Sa 5am-8pm), or **STANDA,** V. Grande, 174, off P. Grande. (Open Mar.-Oct. M-Sa 8:30am-12:30pm and 4-8pm, Su 9am-1pm and 4-8pm; Nov.-Feb. M-Sa 8:30am-12:30pm and 3:30-7pm.) Head to **Osteria del Mare ❸,** Borgo dei Cappuccini, 5, for understated elegance and affordable meals. The *risotto mare* (€6.20) is a specialty. From P. Mazzini, near Hotel Boston, take V. Navi to Borgo dei Cappuccini. (☎0586 88 10 27. *Primi* €6.20-6.70, *secondi* €8-13. Open M-W and F-Su noon-3pm and 7:30-10:30pm. AmEx/MC/V.) **Ristorante Vecchia Livorno ❸,** Scali delle Cantine, 32, across from Fortezza Nuova, is a popular spot among locals, serving *tagliatelle vongole* (€7.25) and other classic *Livornese* fare. (☎0586 88 40 48. *Primi* €5.50-10, *secondi* from €13 or €5-6/100g. Cover €1.55. Open M and W-Su noon-2:30pm and 7-10pm. Cash only.) Two blocks from Hotel Marina is **Luna Rossa ❷,** C. Mazzini, 222, which serves cheaper food in a relaxed interior. The takeout pizza *menù* (€13-22) is extensive and popular. (☎0586 88 14 42. *Primi* €4-6.50, *secondi* €5-11. Cover €1.29. Service 10%. Open Tu-Su noon-3pm and 7:30-10pm. MC/V.)

📷 🎭 SIGHTS AND ENTERTAINMENT

The **Fortezza Nuova,** circled by a large moat, is in the heart of **Piccola Venezia,** where canals course through the city. **Fortezza Vecchia** sprawls out on the water. Down the waterfront in P. Micheli is the **Monumento del Quattro Mori,** Bandini's marble figure of Duke Ferdinand I (1595), joined by Tacca's manacled bronze slaves (1626).

In mid-July, rowers in the **Palio Marinaro** race traditional crafts toward the old port. At the end of the month, **Effeto Venezia** transforms Livorno's Piccola Venezia into an open-air theater with 10 days of concerts and exhibitions.

ELBA   ☎0565

According to legend, the enchanting island of Elba grew from a precious stone that slipped from Venus's neck into the Tyrrhenian Sea. Since then, Elba has seen its share of notable visitors, its 150km of coastline drawing the likes of Jason and the Argonauts and eminent Roman patricians. Elba, nicknamed Aethalia, or "Sparks," by the Greeks and renowned since Hellenic times for its mineral wealth, also derived considerable fame from its association with Napoleon. The Little Emperor was sent into his first exile here in 1814, creating both a temporarily warfree Europe and the famous palindrome: "Able was I ere I saw Elba." All vanquished conquerors of Europe should be so lucky. Elba's turquoise waters, dra-

TUSCANY

matic peaks, velvety beaches, and diverse attractions can accommodate almost any interest. Each zone of the island attracts a distinct variety of visitor—families lounge in Marina di Campo and Marciana Marina, beach bums and club kids waste away in Capoliveri, yacht-clubbers gallivant in Porto Azzurro, and nature lovers gravitate to the island's mountainous northeastern tip.

TRANSPORTATION TO ELBA. Elba's **airport** (☎0565 97 60 11, fax 97 60 08), in Marina di Campo, sends flights to Milan, Munich, Parma, Rome, Vienna, and Zurich. The best way to reach Elba is to take a **ferry** from Piombino Marittima (or Piombino Porto), on the mainland, to Portoferraio, Elba's largest city. Ferries also dock at Porto Azzuro, on the opposite side of the island. **Trains** on the Genoa-Rome line travel straight to Piombino Marittima but usually stop at Campiglia Marittima (from Florence, change at Pisa). From Campiglia Marittima, a connecting **intercity bus** (30min., €1.20), timed to meet incoming trains, connects to Piombino Marittima. Tickets to Piombino purchased at a train station include the bus ticket. Meet the bus when exiting the station. Both **Toremar** (ferry 1hr., €5.70-7.51; hydrofoil in summer 30min., €6.74-9.84) and **Moby Lines** (1hr., €6.50-9.50) run about 20 trips to Elba per day, 6:40am-10:30pm. The ticket offices of Toremar (☎0565 311 00; www.toremar.it) and Moby Lines (☎0565 22 52 11; www.moby.it) are in the **Stazione Marittima** at the ferry docks in Piombino; buy tickets for the next departing ferry at these offices or at the **FS booth** in the Campiglia Marittima train station. Remember to allow 10min. to descend from the ticket office to the dock.

PORTOFERRAIO
☎0565

Portoferraio has split personalities: to the west of the Medici Fortress is a modern, rather unattractive port, while to the east lies a picturesque Tuscan beach town. As the island's main port, it is probably the Elba's liveliest city and contains most of its essential services. Though frequent boats make Portoferraio the easiest area to access from the mainland, the imposing sealiners keep at a comfortable distance from centuries-old sights and gorgeous stretches of white, pebbly beaches.

TUSCANY

☞ TRANSPORTATION

Portoferraio can be accessed by bus. **ATL,** V. Elba, 20, across from the Toremar landing, runs hourly buses to Capoliveri, Cavo, Lacona Marciana, Marciana Marina, Marina di Campo, Pomonte, Porto Azzuro, and Rio Elba. (☎0565 91 43 92. Tickets €1.20-3.10. Day pass €6.50, 6-day pass €18. Open daily June-Sept. 8am-8pm; Oct.-May M-Sa 8am-1:20pm and 4-6:30pm, Su 9am-12:30pm and 2-6:30pm.) **Ferry** service is available at **Toremar,** Calata Italia, 22 (☎0565 91 80 80), and **Moby Lines,** V. Elba, 4 (☎0565 91 41 33, fax 0565 91 67 58). For **taxis,** call ☎0565 91 51 22. **Rent Chaippi,** Calata Italia, 38 (☎0565 91 41 33, fax 0565 91 67 58), rents **cars** (€42-62 per day), **mopeds** (€18-40), and **mountain bikes** (€10).

◼◼◼ ORIENTATION AND PRACTICAL INFORMATION

Though it's Elba's largest city, Portoferraio *centro* is still tiny. From the harbor, a left leads to **Calata Italia** and a right to **Via Emanuele II; Via Manzoni** cuts between them. From Calata Italia, turn on **Via Elba,** which goes further inland toward services like banks and grocery stores. V. Emanuele II turns into **Calata Mazzini,** which curves with the borders of the harbor; follow street signs and turn left through a brick arch, **Porta Medicea,** to **Piazza Cavour.** Cut through this piazza to reach **Piazza della Repubblica,** the center of town.

Tourist Offices: APT, Calata Italia, 44 (☎0565 91 46 71; www.aptelba.it). From the docks facing away from the water, proceed left. Walk past a series of private tourist companies and cafes and cross V. Elba. Office is 5min. ahead on the right. Accommodations info for all of Elba, bus schedules, and restaurant listings. Open in summer daily 8am-8pm; in winter 8am-1pm and 4-8pm.

Boat Excursions: Linee di Navigazione Archipelago Toscano (☎0565 91 47 97; www.elbacrociere.com) offers tours of Elba's coast as well as excursions to nearby islands (€25.80-36.20). Less expensive but more crowded, **Visione Sottomarina** (☎328 709 54 70) runs trips along the coast (€15) in glass-bottomed boats for prime underwater views. Arrive 20min. early for decent seats. Also departs from Marciana Marina.

Currency Exchange: The waterfront is full of rip-offs, even in private agencies. Walk to V. Manganaro, near Hotel Nobel, for a **Banca di Roma** (☎0565 91 90 07), which also has an **ATM.** Open M-F 8:30am-1:30pm and 3:10-4pm.

Emergency: ☎113. **Ambulance** (☎0565 91 40 09).

Internet: Internet Train, V. Cairoli, 47 (☎0565 91 64 08), across from Albergo Le Ghiaie. €5 per hr. Open M-Sa 9:30am-12:30pm and 3:30-7:30pm.

Post Office: In P. Pietro Gori (☎0565 91 40 52), off P. della Repubblica. Open M-F 8:15am-7:30pm, Sa 8:15am-noon. **Branch** on V. Carducci, closer to the port. Open M-F 8:30am-1:30pm, Sa 8:15am-12:30pm. **Postal Code:** 57037.

☞ ACCOMMODATIONS

Nestled in a heavenly beach, ◼**Albergo Le Ghiaie ❹,** V. A. de Gasperi, has comfortable rooms with bath and towels in abundance. Mornings start with coffee on the wooden terrace. From the harbor, take V. Manzoni and bear left on V. Cairoli for 10min. (☎0565 91 51 78. Breakfast included. Private parking. Singles €45-50; doubles €75-82; triples €90-97; quads €95-110. AmEx/MC/V.) Family owners welcome visitors to the cheery **Ape Elbana ❹,** Salita Cosimo de' Medici, 2, in a great location overlooking P. della Repubblica. All rooms come with bath, and some have TV and A/C. (☎0565 91 42 45, fax 0565 94 59 85. Breakfast included. Singles €55; doubles

€67. Half pension €85; full pension €95. About €15 cheaper in winter. MC/V.) **Hotel Massimo ❹**, Calata Italia, 23, on the port, lets large rooms, all with bath, TV, A/C, and phone. Its high neon-yellow sign can be seen on the left when pulling into the harbor. (☎0565 91 47 66, fax 0565 93 01 17. Buffet breakfast included. Singles €34-76; doubles €99; triples €106; quads €119. Prices drop 20% in low season. MC/V.) The basic rooms and shabby bath at **Hotel Nobel ❸**, V. Manganaro, 72, are a decent option for tight budget in high season. Follow V. Elba from the port for 10min. until it merges with V. Manganaro; the hotel is on the right. (☎0565 91 52 17, fax 0565 91 54 15. Singles €20-30, with bath €25-35; doubles €40/62; triples with bath €80. AmEx/MC/V.) **Acquaviva ❶**, Loc. Acquaviva, has good camping about 4km west of the *centro*. Located right on the beach, this campsite features its own bar, restaurant, grocery store, and playground. (☎0565 93 06 74; www.campingacquaviva.it. €11 per person, €12 per tent, €2.50 per car. Cash only.)

🔆 FOOD

Two Elban specialties to note are *schiaccia*, a bread cooked in olive oil and studded with either onions or black olives, and *aleatico*, a sweet liqueur. Elba as a whole suffers from an infestation of overpriced, tourist-snaring restaurants, but Portoferraio has several options for value-conscious diners. For groceries, head to the centrally located **CONAD**, P. Pietri, 2-4, off V. Elba, next to the Banca di Roma. (Open M-Sa 7:30am-9pm, Su 7:30am-1pm and 4-8pm.) At **Ristorante Frescantico ❸**, V. Carducci, 132, the charming wine bar prepares meals that are reliably worth each euro. Homemade pastas (€7-8) are seasoned to suit every taste, from *cinghiale* (boar) to *gamberetti* (shrimp). Expensive entrees (about €18) make Frescantico a better bet for lunch. (☎0565 91 89 89. Cover and service 10%. Open daily May-Nov. 12:30-3pm and 7-11pm, Dec.-Apr. M-Sa 12:30-2:30pm and 7:30-11pm. MC/V.) Dwarfed by ships, **Ristorante Stella Marina ❸**, on Banchina Alto Fondale, across from the Toremar dock, offers courteous service and small, fabulous seafood dishes in place of seaside views. Try some *tagliolini ai frutti di mare* (with mussels, clams, shrimp, octopus; €10) or splurge on Elban lobster. (☎0565 91 59 83. *Primi* €6-11, *secondi* by weight. Open May to mid-Nov. or Dec. Tu-Su noon-2pm and 7:30-11pm. AmEx/MC/V.) **Trattoria-Pizzeria Napoletana da Zucchetta ❷**, P. della Repubblica, 40, is a lively, family oriented spot in the historic center with popular outdoor seating. (☎0565 91 53 31. Neapolitan pizza €4.60-8.20. *Primi* €7-9, *secondi* €8-23. Open daily 11:30am-3pm and 6-11:30pm. AmEx/MC/V.) More cafe than ristorante, **Residence Bar ❶**, on the corner of Calata Italia and V. Elba, offers affordable pizza slices and ready-made pastas (€2-7). Grab a harbor-facing table or take food to go. (☎0565 91 68 15. Bar open daily May-Oct. 6:30am-11pm, Nov.-Apr. M-W and F-Su 6:30am-11pm. Self-service 11:30am-3:30pm. AmEx/MC/V.)

👁🔆 SIGHTS AND BEACHES

Inside Napoleon's one-time residence, the **Villa dei Mulini,** find his personal library, a number of letters, some silk chairs once graced by his imperial derriere, and the sovereign Elban flag that he designed. (☎0565 91 58 46. Ticket office open M and W-Sa 9am-7pm, Su 9am-1pm. €3; cumulative ticket good for 3 days also allows entry to the Villa Napoleonica, €5.) Monogrammatic 'N's emblazon the **Villa Napoleonica di San Martino,** placed there after Napoleon's death. Note especially the Sala Egizia, with friezes depicting his Egyptian campaign. (Take bus #1 6km out of Portoferraio. ☎0565 91 46 88. Ticket office open M and W-Sa 9am-7pm, Su 9am-1pm.) The **Museo Archeologico della Linguella** exhibits finds from ancient trading boat wrecks dating back to the fifth century. (Fortezza del Lingrella. ☎0565 91 73 38. Open daily Sept.-June 9am-1:30pm and 3-7pm, July-Aug. 9:30am-2pm and 6pm-midnight. €2, children and individuals in large groups €1.) The **Medici Fortress** overlooking the port is worth a quick peek. Cosimo de' Medici, Grand Duke of Tuscany, founded the complex in 1548. So imposing was its structure that in 1553 the dread Turkish pirate Dracut declared the building impenetrable, calling off his planned attack on Portoferraio. (Open daily 9am-7pm. €2, children €1.)

Many large signs from the harbor point to **Spiaggia delle Ghiaie,** so unsurprisingly, its shores crowd early with copious visitors. But even the thickest of umbrella-wielding swarms can't mar the beauty of this rocky shoreline. Bring a towel and claim a spot to avoid the roped-off areas and their corresponding fees. Farther east, down a long flight of stairs from the **Villa dei Mulini,** is the more secluded **Spiaggia delle Viste,** less than 400m long. Appropriately named for its views, this beach is quaintly shaded between cliffs.

PORTO AZZURRO   ☎ 0565

A favorite sunspot of the ultra-rich and ultra-thin, Porto Azzurro shelters some of the island's finest beaches. All this beauty doesn't come cheaply, though, so those intending to stay in Porto Azzurro should brace for a major financial outlay.

Campgrounds are in Località Barbarossa, near a beach of the same name. To reach the beach while enjoying breathtaking views, skirt the port and take the narrow set of steps leading to a dirt trail that climbs the hill and overlooks the water. (15min.) From the beach, a 2min. walk down a dirt path will bring you to **Il Gabbiano ❶,** with shaded grounds near the road. (☎0565 950 87. €9 per person, €8.50-10.50 per tent, €2 per car. Cash only.) Also near the beach is the comfortable **Arrighi ❶,** which has a supermarket and air-conditioned common area. (☎0565 955 68; www.campingarrighi.it. €11.50 per person, €9.40 per tent, €2.50 per car in early July-late Aug. Open Easter-Oct.) To reach **Albergo Barbarossa ❹,** take the bus headed toward Marina di Campo (be sure to ask the driver if it stops at Barbarossa). To walk, follow the signs for the *carabinieri* from the main square bordering the sea, pass the *carabinieri* office, continue walking until the main road, then turn right. Look for the camping signs along the 15min., partially uphill walk. The rooms are charmingly old-fashioned and the garden is beautiful. (☎0565 950 87. Singles €40; doubles €52, with bath €62; triples €70.) For comfortable digs back in town, check out **Hotel Belmare ❹,** Banchina IV Novembre, 21, across from the ferry dock. Seaside rooms all have balcony and bath. (☎0565 950 12; www.elba-hotelbelmare.it. Singles €52 in low season; €60 in Aug.; doubles €72/€94. Closed Dec.-Feb. AmEx/MC/V.)

La Creperia ❷, V. Marconi, 2, just off the main square, is just right for a quick bite. The Nutella and mascarpone crepe (€3.10) is a sweet sensation. (Open Apr.-Oct. daily 11am-midnight. Cash only.) **Ristorante Bella H'Briana ❸,** V. D'Alarcon, 29, serves more elegant meals. (*Primi* €5.50-8, *secondi* €7-14. Cover €2. Open noon-3pm and 6-11pm.) Wind down the evening with the mellow late-night crowd at **Bar Tamata,** V. Cesare Battisti, 3. (☎0347 381 39 86. Open M-Tu and Th-Su 10am-2pm and 5pm-2am.) **Morumbi,** 2km down the road to Capoliveri, is one of the island's hottest discos, with dance floors, a pizzeria, and a pagoda. (☎0565 92 01 91. Weekend cover €13. Women free. Open June 30-Sept. 15.) Escape the hedonism by busing to **Portoferraio** (30min., 7am-8:55pm) for the night. In **emergencies,** call the **carabinieri** (☎112) or an **ambulance** (☎118).

MARCIANA MARINA   ☎ 0565

The pebbly border of Marciana Marina's waterfront is just one of countless beaches hiding in isolated coves along the island. Explore the lopsided rocks, stake out a sunny niche, and bring along goggles to watch schools of fish swim in the still waters. Numerous stretches of shoreline are accessible only by boat: the nicest ones lie between Sant'Andrea and Fetovaia, the western border of Elba, an area reputed to contain the island's clearest waters. At night, the harbor hosts sizeable crowds of vacationers savoring gelato and browsing the jewelry stands.

⚠ PRACTICAL INFORMATION. Reach Marciana Marina from Portoferraio by **car, boat,** or **bus** (30 min., €1.80). The **tourist office** stands in a small wooden gazebo near the shore in P. Vittoria. (☎0565 90 42 44. Open Tu-Su 5-11pm.) In case of **emergency,** call the **carabinieri** (☎112) or an **ambulance** (☎118). The **post office** is on V. Lloyd. (Open M-F 8:15am-1:30pm, Sa 8:15am-12:30pm.) **Postal Code:** 57033.

⌂☐ ACCOMMODATIONS AND FOOD. The tourist office offers info on cheap *affittacamere,* though these fill up as quickly as the hotels in the summer; call ahead to reserve. Follow V. Amedeo away from the harbor on a slight incline and turn right and take Loc. Ontanelli for 15min. to reach **Casa Lupi ❸,** Loc. Ontanelli, 15. The immaculate, green-shuttered rooms all have bath, and the terrace looks out toward mountains and the sea. (☎/fax 0565 991 43. July-Sept. singles €36; doubles €67. Aug. singles €41; doubles €67. Cash only.) **Hotel Imperia ❹,** V. Amedeo, 12, is steps from the sea. The staff is personable and knowledgable, and breakfast is served in a fragrant garden alive with songbirds. Book ahead for a room with balcony at no extra cost. (☎0565 990 82; imperia@elbalink.it. Buffet breakfast included. Singles €45; doubles €70. Cash only.) Located on the harborfront, **Hotel Marinella ❹,** V. Margherita, 38, provides large rooms in warm hues, all with bath, TV, and great views. (☎0565 990 18 or 99 68 75, fax 998 95. Prices per person for high season: June €46-56; July €61; Aug. €75. Half pension €49-83. AmEx/MC/V.)

Across from Hotel Imperia, **CONAD,** V. Cerboni 4, supplies cheap cold cuts, salads, fruit, and drinks. (☎0565 99 67 95. Open daily 8am-8pm.) For a filling snack head to **Ultima Spiaggia ❶,** V. A. Saffi, 9 (☎0565 992 62; www.ultimaspiaggia.info). This perfect alternative to a formal restaurant serves crepes for breakfast, lunch, and dinner. Every confection has a suggested beer and wine to complement the rich flavor. Simple crepes start at €4, and prices increase depending on your taste. With a limited but very tasty selection of dishes, diners should fall for **First Love ❶,** V. G. Dussol, 9/13, at first bite. (☎0565 993 55. *Primi* €7-8, *secondi* €7.50-17. Open daily 7pm-2am. MC/V.) Follow a growling stomach to P. Vittoria for a slew of good restaurants. **Ristorante Zorba ❷,** P. Vittoria, 14, offers filling food in ample portions. The *antipasti di mare* (warm plate of calamari, mussels, clams, and shrimp; €8) doubles as a great entree. (☎0565 992 25. Open 12:15-2:30pm and 7:15-11pm. AmEx/MC/V.)

◧ SIGHTS. A visit to **Monte Capanne** (1019m), Elba's highest peak, provides an uplifting excursion from Marciana Marina. The mountaintop offers views of the entire island, with sea and sky blending in a periwinkle haze. On clear days, the view extends all the way to Corsica; otherwise, the far-off island appears to float in a mist of passing clouds. The strenuous uphill trek takes 2hr., but a **cable car** can shorten the trip. (☎0565 90 10 20. Cable car open for ascent 10am-12:15pm and 2:30-6pm, for descent 10am-12:45pm and 2:45-6:30pm. Round-trip €12.) To reach Monte Capanne, take the bus (15min., €1.20) from Marciana Marina toward **Marciana,** a medieval town clinging to the mountainside. Ask the driver to stop at Monte Capanne; look for a parking lot and the "Cabinovia" signs that points to the lifts. Be sure to buy a round-trip ticket, as there are no *tabacchi* near the mountain.

TUSCANY

MONTE ARGENTARIO

Originally an island, Monte Argentario is now anchored to the mainland by three isthmuses. The promontory is a popular holiday destination for native Italians and home to a nature reserve, many pebbly beaches, and ports Ercole and Santo Stefano. It's also a good base for visiting the nearby Isola di Giglio.

Monte Argentario is best reached through Orbetello, on the promontory's middle isthmus. The Orbetello-Monte Argentario train station lies on the Roma Termini-Torino line. **Trains** depart to: Civitavecchia (45min., 15 per day 4:43am-10pm, €3.35); Florence (3½hr., 5 per day 5:58am-7:25pm, €19.20); Livorno (2hr., 10 per day 12:43am-10:03pm, €8.60); Pisa (2¼hr., 9 per day 12:42am-10:03pm, €14.40); and Rome (2hr., 10 per day 5:15am-7:56pm, €6.80). Rama (☎0564 85 00 00; www.griforama.it) runs **buses** from the train station to P. S. Stefano (22min., 1-2 per hr. 4:58am-11:15pm, €1.55) and P. Ercole (27 min.; M-Sa 11 per day, Su 6 per day, 6:50am-10pm; €1.34). Buses also go to the beaches of Feniglia and Giannella. Purchase tickets at the *tabacchi* in the train station.

PORTO SANTO STEFANO ☎0564

The more developed of the two ports, P. S. Stefano was once a tranquil fishing town; these days it reels in more tourist activity than marine life.

⁊ PRACTICAL INFORMATION. Taxis are available through Colonnelli Alessandro (☎0564 81 26 25 or 337 70 43 61). The **tourist office,** C. Umberto 55/A, is up the stairs next to the post office entrance. (☎0564 81 42 08. Open M-Sa 9am-1pm and 5-6pm.) Pick up a map of the region and info on the archipelago. Continue up the same flight of stairs and make a right onto **Corso Umberto,** which runs parallel to **Lungomare dei Navigatori.** Further down the street on the left is a **pharmacy,** Farmacia Toschi (☎0564 81 25 36). In case of **emergency,** call the carabinieri (☎112) or an ambulance (☎118). The last **Rama** bus stop is just outside the **post office** on Lungomare dei Navigatori, 31/32 (☎0564 81 71 04. Open M-F 8:15am-5pm, Sa 8:15am-12:30pm.) **Postal Code:** 58019.

⁊⌂ ACCOMMODATIONS AND FOOD. The tourist office has information on good restaurants and hotels; note that accommodations on Monte Argentario tend to be expensive. **Pensione Weekend ❹,** V. Martiri D'Ungheria, 3, 50m from Lungomare dei Navigatori. Clean, spacious rooms often have balcony and sea views. Ask the English-speaking owner for the 15% discount at nearby restaurant Lo Sfizio. (☎0564 81 25 80; www.pensioneweekend.it. All rooms with bath. Breakfast included. Doubles €55, in Aug. €65; triples €75/€90. Cash only).Well-located near the ferries and a small **open-air market, Hotel Alfiero ❹,** V. Cuniberti, 12, offers small rooms with TV, bath, breakfast, and great sea views. (☎0564 81 40 67; www.hotelalfiero.com. Doubles €80, in Aug. €90; triples €90/€100. AmEx/MC/V.) Also near the ferry dock, **La Terrazza del Cafe ❶,** on V. Barelai, 40, offers many *panini* in large portions (€3.50-4.50). The specialties are fresh fish sandwiches and salads. (☎0564 81 27 67. Salads €4. Open M and W-Su 8am-10pm. Cash only.) If you can get over the tacky fish decor, **Lo Sfizio ❸,** V. Lunogrmare dei Navigatori, 26, is a great choice. The friendly staff serves tasty fresh fish and seafood dishes, as well crepes, *bruschette,* and over 40 types of pizza. (☎0564 81 25 92; www.trattorialosfizio.com. Pizza €5.50. *Menùs* €22-30. Open T-Su noon-2pm and 7-11pm. AmEx/MC/V.) The happening **La Strega del Mare** (☎0564 82 41 91), on V. Panoramica, spins hip-hop and house music with two DJs and piano bar live music. (Open daily 11pm-6am.)

◙ **SIGHTS.** The 17th-century Fortezza Spagnola (☎ 0564 81 06 81), in P. del Governato, dominates the city scenery. This one-time military fort now holds the **Museo dei Maestri D'Ascia** (Museum of the Masters of the Axe) and the **Memorie Sommerse** (Submerged Memories), which display archaeological findings from the sea of Monte Argentario. (Open daily June-Sept. 6am-midnight, Oct.-May 10:30am-12:30pm and 3:30-7:30pm. €4, groups and students €2.) The **Aquario Mediterraneo della Costa D'Argento,** Lungomare dei Navigatori, 44/48, hosts an impressive exhibit of the region's marine life. (☎ 0564 81 59 33. Open M-F 10:30am-12:30pm and 4-8pm, Sa-Su 10:30am-12:30pm and 4pm-midnight. €4.50.)

PORTO ERCOLE   ☎ 0564

Less of a tourist base than P. S. Stefano, Porto Ercole feels much more like the fishing town that it is. Two Spanish fortresses frame the harbor not far from where painter Caravaggio died of sunstroke in 1610 and is now buried. Rama **buses** make trips to the train station in Orbetello (19min., 10 per day 7:10am-7:30pm) and to the Feniglia beach (8min., 23 per day 8:27am-6:53pm). In case of **emergency,** call the carabinieri (☎ 112) or an ambulance (☎ 118). The **post office** is at V. Campagnatico, 1 (☎ 0564 83 39 09). **Postal Code:** 58018.

Reasonably priced accommodations in Porto Ercole are even harder to find than in P. S. Stefano. The three-star **Hotel Marina ❺,** Lungomare A. Doria, 30, has small but elegant rooms and clean bathrooms. (☎ 0564 83 31 23; www.hotelmarina.it. Singles €67.14; doubles €103.29. AmEx/MC/V.) A much cheaper option is **Camping Feniglia ❶,** about 1.5km north of Porto Ercole. Though most of the campground is occupied by trailer homes, what's left is only 50m from the sea. (☎ 0564 83 10 90. Open Apr.-Oct. €8 per person, €7 per tent. Cash only.) For a meal, the best value for its price is **La Lampara ❸,** (☎ 0564 83 30 24), Lungomare A. Doria, 67. Enjoy excellent Neapolitan pizza (€5-12) and regional dishes. (*Primi* €7-9, *secondi* €8-15. Open daily noon-2:20pm and 7-10:30pm; Cash only.)

TUSCANY

UMBRIA AND LE MARCHE

HIGHLIGHTS OF UMBRIA AND LE MARCHE

JOURNEY to one of Italy's most revered pilgrimage sites, the Basilica di San Francesco in Assisi, an elaborate monument to the ascetic St. Francis. (p. 494.)

SAMPLE world-famous Perugina chocolate in Perugia. (p. 482.)

HIKE to the Eremo delle Carceri, St. Francis's favorite place for relaxation. (p. 496.)

UMBRIA

Umbria is known as the "green heart of Italy." This landlocked region is rich in wild woods and fertile plains, craggy gorges and gentle hills, tiny cobblestoned villages and lively international universities. Three thousand years ago, Etruscans settled this regional crossroads between the Adriatic and Tyrrhenian coasts, leav-

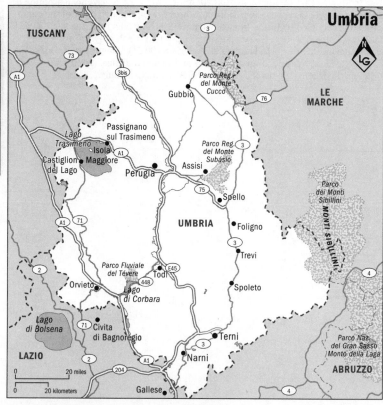

ing *necropoli*, tombs, and ruins. Another conqueror, Christianity, transformed Umbria's architecture and regional identity. St. Francis shamed the extravagant church with his legacy of humility, pacifism, and charity that persists in Assisi to this day. The region holds Giotto's greatest masterpieces and produced medieval masters Perugino and Pinturicchio, and Umbria's artistic spirit gives life today to the internationally acclaimed Spoleto Festival and Umbria Jazz Festival.

PERUGIA   ☎ 075

One of the earliest seats of Etruscan power, Perugia rose to political prominence after chasing the ancient *Umbri* tribe into surrounding valleys. Obscure wars with neighboring cities dominate the town's history. Periods of prosperity during peacetime, however, gave rise to the stunning artistic and architectural achievements for which Perugia is known today. The town served as a meeting ground for 13th- through 15th-century Tuscan and Umbrian masters, and the Galleria Nazionale dell'Umbria, one of Italy's most important art museums, preserves that legacy. Pietro Vannucci, mentor to Raphael, is known as "Perugino" because of his long association with the town, and many of his frescoes survive here. Other attractions include a summer jazz festival, Italy's best chocolate, an Italian university, and the University for Foreigners, which draws students from around the world.

▐█ TRANSPORTATION

Trains: Perugia FS, in P. V. Veneto, Fontiveggio lies on the Foligno-Terontola line. Info office open M-Sa 8:10am-7:45pm. Ticket window open daily 6am-8:40pm. To: **Arezzo** (1½hr., 1 per hr., €3.82); **Assisi** (25min., every hr., €1.60); **Florence** (2½hr., 18 per day, from €7.90); **Foligno** (40min., every hr., €2.20); **Orvieto** (2hr., 9 per day, €6) via **Terontola; Passignano sul Trasimeno** (30min., every hr., €2); **Rome** (2½hr., 6 per day 4:55am-6:10pm, from €10.12) via **Terontola** or **Foligno; Spoleto** (1½hr., every hr., €3.50) via **Foligno**. A secondary station is **Perugia Sant'Anna**, in P. Bellucci Giuseppe. The commuter rail runs to **Sansepolcro** (1½hr., 14 per day 6:18am-8:31pm, €3.90) and **Terni** (1½hr., 19 per day 7:31am-12:30am, €4.30) via **Todi** (1hr., 5 per day 6:53am-8:39pm, €2.70).

Buses: City buses in P. dei Partigiani, down the escalator from P. Italia. Bus #6 (€0.80) connects with the train station. **APM** (☎075 573 17 07), in P. dei Partigiani. To: **Assisi** (1hr., 8 per day 6:25am-8:05pm, €2.80); **Chiusi** (1½hr., 7 per day 6:20am-6:35pm, €4.80); **Gubbio** (1¼hr., 11 per day 6:40am-8pm, €4); **Todi** (1½hr., 8 per day 6:30am-7:30pm, €4.80). Reduced service Su. Additional buses leave from **Stazione Fontiveggio,** next to Perugia FS train station. Tickets at RadioTaxi Perugia, to the right of the train station. To **Siena** (every 2hr., €9).

Taxis: RadioTaxi Perugia (☎075 500 48 88). In P. Italia (☎075 573 60 92), on C. Vannucci (☎075 572 19 79).

Car Rental: Hertz, P.V. Veneto, 2 (☎337 65 08 37), near the train station. Cars from €85 per day. Open M-F 8:30am-12:30pm and 3-7pm, Sa 8:30am-1pm.

▄█ ▐▌ ORIENTATION AND PRACTICAL INFORMATION

From **Perugia FS train station** in **Piazza Vittorio Veneto,** Fontiveggio, buses #6, 7, 9, 13d, and 15 go to **Piazza Italia** (€0.80). Otherwise, it's a 2km trek uphill. To get to P. Italia from the **bus station** in **Piazza dei Partigiani** or from the nearby **Perugia Sant'Anna train station** at **Piazza Giuseppe,** follow the signs to the **escalator** that goes underneath the old city into P. Italia (6:15am-1:45am; free). From P. Italia, **Corso**

Vannucci, the main shopping thoroughfare, leads to **Piazza IV Novembre** and the duomo. Behind the duomo lies the university district. One block off C. Vannucci is **Via Baglioni,** which leads to **Piazza Matteotti,** the municipal center.

Tourist Office: P. IV Novembre, 3 (☎075 572 33 27 or 573 64 58, fax 573 93 86). The knowledgeable staff provides **maps** and info on accommodations, restaurants, and cultural events. Open M-Sa 8:30am-1:30pm and 3:30-6:30pm, Su 9am-1pm. **Info Umbria,** L. Cacciatori delle Alpi, 3/B (☎075 573 29 33; www.guideinumbria.com), next to the bus station. Private office provides maps, sells tickets to concerts, shows, and sporting events, and provides free booking for many hotels and farmhouses. **Internet** €3 per hr. **Luggage storage** €1.30 for 1st hr., €0.80 each additional hr. Open M-Sa 9am-2pm and 2:30-6:30pm.

Budget Travel: CTS, V. del Roscetto, 21 (☎075 572 02 84), off V. Pinturicchio toward the bottom of the street, offers vacation deals to ISIC holders. Open M-F 10am-1pm and 3-6pm. **SESTANTE Travel,** C. Vannucci, 2 (☎075 572 60 61), books flights, sells train tickets, and rents cars. Open M-F 9am-1pm and 3:30-7pm, Sa 10am-1pm.

Currency Exchange: Banks have the best rates; those in P. Italia have 24hr. **ATMs.** The Perugia FS train station charges no commission for exchanges of less than €40.

Luggage Storage: FS train station €3.87 per 24hr. Open daily 6am-9pm. Also available at **Info Umbria** (see above).

English-Language Bookstore: Libreria, V. Rocchi, 3 (☎075 753 61 04). Small selection of classics, a few recent best-sellers, and travel guides. Open M-Sa 10am-1pm and 3:30-8pm, Su 10:30am-1pm.

Laundromat: 67 Laundry, V. Fabretti, 7/A. Wash €3 per 7kg, dry €1. Open daily 8am-10pm. **Bolle Blu,** C. Garibaldi, 43. Wash €3 per 8kg, dry €3. Open daily 8am-10pm.

Emergency: Ambulance (☎118). **Police,** V. Cortonese, 157 (☎112 or 075 506 21).

Pharmacy: Farmacia S. Martino, P. Matteotti, 26 (☎075 572 23 35). Open 24hr.

Hospital: Central line (☎075 57 81). **Ospedale Silvestrini** (☎075 578 22 96).

Internet: Service Economy, C. Garibaldi, 30 (☎075 572 07 30). From P. IV Novembre, walk past the duomo on the right and left through P. Danti; follow V. Rocchi to P. Braccio Fortebraccio. Cross the piazza and bear left on C. Garibaldi. The street is lined with Internet points, but Service Economy charges only €1 per hr. with no time restrictions.

Post Office: In P. Matteotti. Open M-Sa 8:10am-7:30pm, Su 8:30am-5:30pm. Offers **currency exchange** M-F 8:10am-5:30pm, Sa 8:10am-1pm, Su 8:30am-5:30pm. **Postal Code:** 06100.

ACCOMMODATIONS AND CAMPING

Make reservations well in advance for July during the Umbria Jazz Festival.

Ostello della Gioventù/Centro Internazionale di Accoglienza per la Gioventù, V. Bontempi, 13 (☎/fax 075 572 28 80; www.ostello.perugia.it). From P. IV Novembre, walk right, passing duomo and P. Danti, into P. Piccinino, then turn right on V. Bontempi; hostel is nearby on the right. Palpable good cheer and great views of the city dominate the space beneath 300-year-old frescoed ceilings. Kitchen, lockers, spacious showers, towels, lobby phone, Internet, and TV room. Sheets €1.50. 2-week max. stay. Lockout 9:30am-4pm. Curfew midnight, 1am during Jazz Festival. Open Jan. 16-Dec. 14. Dorms €12. Groups can request 8-person room with bath at no extra charge. AmEx/MC/V. ❶

Hotel Umbria, V. Boncambi, 37 (☎075 572 12 03), on the left off P. della Repubblica. Narrow rooms with TV and large sparkling baths. Singles €38-48; doubles €55-70. Prices are negotiable; haggling is worth it. AmEx/MC/V. ❸

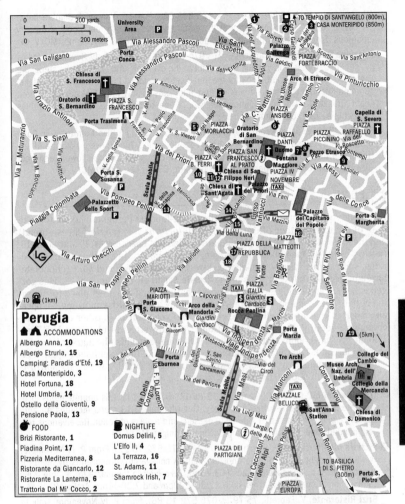

Perugia

♠ ⛺ ACCOMMODATIONS

Albergo Anna, **10**
Albergo Etruria, **15**
Camping: Paradis d'Eté, **19**
Casa Monteripido, **3**
Hotel Fortuna, **18**
Hotel Umbria, **14**
Ostello della Gioventù, **9**
Pensione Paola, **13**

🍴 FOOD

Brizi Ristorante, **1**
Piadina Point, **17**
Pizzeria Mediterranea, **8**
Ristorante da Giancarlo, **12**
Ristorante La Lanterna, **6**
Trattoria Dal Mi' Cocco, **2**

🍸 NIGHTLIFE

Domus Delirii, **5**
L'Elfo II, **4**
La Terrazza, **16**
St. Adams, **11**
Shamrock Irish, **7**

UMBRIA AND LE MARCHE

Hotel Fortuna, V. L. Bonazzi, 19 (☎075 572 28 45; www.umbriahotels.com), off P. della Repubblica. This converted 13th-century palazzo has fluffy towels and free Internet midnight-8am. All rooms have bath, A/C, telephone, TV, minibar, and hair dryer. Buffet breakfast included. Singles €67, with bath €80; doubles €97/€115. AmEx/MC/V. ❺

Casa Monteripido, V. Monteripido, 8 (☎075 422 10). From C. Garibaldi out of Pta. S. Angelo, take the straight road onto V. Monteripido. Although a 20min. walk from the *centro*, these rooms are a superior value. The establishment keeps a garden out back. Singles €16, with bath €20; doubles €30/€35. Cash only. ❶

Albergo Etruria, V. della Luna, 21 (☎075 572 37 30), off C. Vannucci. Well located, with antique furnishings and an immense 13th-century sitting room with English magazines. Buzzing in at each return can be a hassle. Shower €3. Curfew 12:30am. Singles €27; doubles €40, with bath €54; triples with bath €75. Cash only. ❸

Albergo Anna, V. dei Priori, 48 (☎/fax 075 573 63 04), off C. Vannucci. Climb 3 floors to cozy 17th-century rooms, some with ceramic fireplaces and great views of the city roof-tops. Singles €30, with bath €40; doubles €48/58; triples €75. AmEx/MC/V. ❹

Pensione Paola, V. della Canapina, 5 (☎075 572 38 16). From P. IV Novembre, follow V. dei Priori, turn left on V. della Cupa, right at the overlook, and go down the steps; the hotel is ahead on the left. Look for the small set of stairs as there are no visible signs. Comfortable rooms, a solicitous staff, and many cats to play with. ATM nearby. Shared bath. Breakfast included. Common area with TV and kitchen use. Singles €33; doubles €52; triples €72. Cash only. ❸

Paradis d'Eté, V. del Mercato, 29/A (☎/fax 075 517 31 21), 8km from town, in Colle della Trinità. Take a city bus from P. Italia (dir: Colle della Trinità; every 1-2hr.) and ask the driver to stop at the campgrounds. Attractive camping with hot showers and pool use included. €6.20 per person, €4.80 per tent, €3 per car. AmEx/MC/V. ❶

 FOOD

Although you'd be insane to bypass the world-famous Perugian chocolate, take note of the town's other offerings too. Both *torta di formaggio* (cheese bread) and the *mele al cartoccio* (apple pie) are available at **Ceccarani ❶**, P. Matteotti, 16. (☎075 572 19 60. Open M-Sa 7:30am-8pm, Su 9am-1:30pm.) For other local confections, such as *torciglione* (eel-shaped sweet almond bread) and *baci* (chocolate-hazelnut kisses), follow aromas to **Pasticceria Sandri ❸**, C. Vannucci, 32. This gorgeous bakery and candy shop doubles as a bar/cafe and is a great place for morning coffee. (Open Tu-Su 8am-10pm.) On Tuesday and Saturday morning, an **open-air market** in P. Europa sells meat, cheese, and vegetables. On other days try the **covered market** in P. Matteotti; the entrance is below street level. (Open M-F 7am-1:30pm, Sa 7am-1:30pm and 4:30-7:30pm.) On summer nights, the market becomes an outdoor cafe. The **COOP**, P. Matteotti, 15, stocks all the essentials. (Open M-Sa 9am-8pm.) Complement meals with one of the region's native wines: try *sagrantino secco*, a full-bodied, dry red, or *grechetto*, a light, dry white.

🏆 **Trattoria Dal Mi' Cocco,** C. Garibaldi, 12 (☎075 573 25 11). This unpretentious local favorite leaves diners stuffed and giddy. Overwhelming €13 *menù* includes an *antipasto*, 2 *primi*, 2 *secondi*, a side dish, dessert, and a glass of liquor. Reservations recommended. Open Tu-Su 1-3pm and 8:30pm-midnight. MC/V. ❸

🏆 **Pizzeria Mediterranea,** P. Piccinino, 11/12 (☎075 572 13 22). From P. IV Novembre, walk to the right of the duomo and turn right. A college crowd descends by night for upscale pizza at downscale prices (€3.70-5). Take food to the piazza for a more lively atmosphere. Cover €1.10. Open daily 12:30-2:30pm and 7:30-11pm. AmEx/MC/V. ❶

Brizi Ristorante, V. Fabretti, 75-79 (☎075 572 13 86). From P. IV Novembre, walk to the right of the duomo, go left through P. Danti, and right down V. Rocchi to P. Fortebraccio. On far side of piazza, turn left on V. Fabretti. Mixed grill with lamb, sausage, and chicken €6.20. *Primi* €3.62-4.65, *secondi* from €4.13. Complete *menù* €10.50. Cover €1.30. Open M and W-Su noon-2:30pm and 7-10:30pm. MC/V. ❷

Ristorante da Giancarlo, V. dei Priori, 36 (☎075 572 43 14), 2 blocks off C. Vannucci. Fresh and tasty meals in a sedate, sheltered dining room. *Primi* €5-13, *secondi* €6-17. Cover €2. Open M-Th and Sa-Su noon-3pm and 6-10pm. MC/V. ❸

Ristorante La Lanterna, V. Rocchi, 6, near the duomo. Enjoy *gnocchi lanterna* (ricotta and spinach dumplings with mushrooms, truffles, and cheese (€7.50) in brick-vaulted rooms or outside by the teeming piazza. Waiters in formal dress hover attentively. *Primi* €7.50-10, *secondi* €10-14.50. Cover €2. Open daily May-Aug. noon-3:30pm and 7:30-10:30pm, Sept.-Apr. closed Th. AmEx/MC/V. ❹

Piadina Point, V. Bonazzi, 7 (☎0267 352 05 46). For a cheap and healthy lunch, head toward P. Italia on C. Vannucci and turn right at the outdoor seating. Regional specialty *piadinas,* which look like tortillas but thicker and crunchier, made with your choice of cheeses, meats, and veggies (€2 with prosciutto, €2.50 with 2 ingredients, €0.30 for each extra ingredient). Take food to the outdoor seating for a lively atmosphere. Open daily 11:30am-3pm and 5pm-midnight. Cash only. ❶

◎ SIGHTS

PIAZZA IV NOVEMBRE

Perugia's most visited sights frame P. IV Novembre on the northern end of the city, and most other monuments lie no more than a 15min. walk away. The **Fontana Maggiore,** designed by Fra' Bevignate and decorated by Nicola and Giovanni Pisano, sits in the center of the piazza. Bas-reliefs depicting both religious and Roman history cover the double-basin fountain.

PALAZZO DEI PRIORI AND GALLERIA NAZIONALE DELL'UMBRIA. The 13th-century windows and sawtooth turrets of this palazzo are remnants of an embattled era. This building, one of the finest examples of Gothic communal architecture, shelters the impressive **Galleria Nazionale dell'Umbria.** The collection contains magnificent 13th- and 14th-century religious works by Duccio, Fra Angelico, Taddeo di Bartolo, Guido da Siena, and Piero della Francesca. Among these early masterpieces, Duccio's skillful rendering of the transparent garments in his *Virgin and Child and Six Angels* in **Room 2** is worth a closer look. Another highlight is della Francesca's awe-inspiring *Polyptych of Saint Anthony* in **Room 11.** Native sons Pinturicchio and Perugino share **Room 15.** The former's *Miracles of San Bernardino of Siena* uses sumptuous colors and rich tones that contrast with Perugino's characteristic soft pastels. Upstairs three rooms display Baroque and Neoclassical works. *(In P. IV Novembre at C. Vannucci, 19. ☎075 572 10 09; www.gallerianazionaledellumbria.it. Open daily 8:30am-7:30pm. Closed Jan. 1, Dec. 25, and 1st M of the month. €6.50, EU citizens ages 18-25 €3.25, EU citizens under 18 or over 65 free.)* To the right of the Galleria sits the **Sala dei Notari,** once the citizens' assembly chamber. Thirteenth-century frescoes adorning the eight Romanesque arches that support the vault portray scenes from the Bible and Aesop's fables. *(Up the steps across from the fountain and across from the duomo. Open daily June-Sept. 9am-1pm and 3-7pm; closed M Oct.-May. Free admission. Sometimes closed for public performances.)*

CATTEDRALE DI SAN LORENZO. Perugia's imposing Gothic duomo was begun in the 14th century, but builders never completed the facade. Though not as ornate as other cathedrals in Tuscany and Umbria, its 15th- to 18th-century embellishments create a sense of harmony within the church, enhanced by occasional organ music at night. The church preserves the Virgin Mary's wedding ring, snagged from Chiusi in the Middle Ages, though it is kept out of public view and under lock and key. *(P. IV Novembre. Open M-Sa 9am-12:45pm and 4-5:15pm, Su 4-5:45pm.)*

COLLEGIO DELLA MERCANZIA (MERCHANTS' GUILD). The walls of this audience chamber are covered in magnificent wood panelling, most likely the work of a northern craftsman. The elegant carved bench was created by a Perugian artist, Costanzo di Mattiolo and the illuminated lists of members of the merchant's guild are preserved in the archives. *(C. Vannucci, 15, next door to Galleria Nazionale dell'Umbria. ☎075 573 03 66. Open Mar.-Oct. and Dec. 20-Jan. 6 M-Sa 9am-1pm and 2:30-5:30pm, Su and holidays 9am-1pm; Nov.-Dec. 19 and Jan. 7-Feb. 28 Tu and Th-F 8am-2pm, W and Sa 8am-4:30pm, Su 9am-1pm. €1.03, €0.52 groups of 10 or more, combination ticket including Collegio del Cambio €3.10, groups or over 65 €2.60.)*

UMBRIA AND
LE MARCHE

COLLEGIO DEL CAMBIO (EXCHANGE GUILD). The 88 members of Perugia's merchant guild have met in this richly paneled structure to debate tax laws and local commerce since 1390. The books in the annexed archive record the guild's members dating back to the Middle Ages. On the walls of the **Sala dell'Udienza** (Audience Chamber), Perugino's frescoes portray heroes, prophets, and even the artist himself, alongside grotesque depictions of Roman gods and a decapitation of John the Baptist. *(Next to the Galleria Nazionale and Merchant's Guild at C. Vannucci, 25. ☎ 075 572 85 99. Open Mar.-Oct. and Dec. 20-Jan. 6 M-Sa 9am-12:30pm and 2:30-5:30pm, Su and holidays 9am-1pm; Nov.-Dec. 19 and Jan. 7-Feb. Tu-Su 9am-12:30pm. €2.60, combination ticket including Collegio della Mercanzia €3.10, groups or over 65 €2.60)*

VIA DEI PRIORI. Don't be misled by its present-day calm and *pietra serena* (gray stone-like serenity). V. dei Priori, which begins under the arch at Palazzo dei Priori, was one of the goriest streets of medieval Perugia: the spikes on the lower walls of the street were once used to impale the rotting heads of executed criminals. The attractive **Chiesa di San Filippo Neri** has several fading 14th-century frescoes. *(1 block off C. Vannucci, hidden in a plain brick building left on V. S. Agata. Open daily 8am-12:30pm and 3:30-6:30pm.)* The Baroque **Chiesa di Sant'Agata** resides solemnly in P. Ferri; Santa Maria di Vallicella's heart is kept here, along with many large, bright paintings. *(2 blocks farther from Chiesa di San Filippo Neri. Open daily in summer 7am-noon and 4:30-7:30pm; in winter 8am-noon and 4-6pm.)* **Piazza San Francesco al Prato** is a rare grassy square that invites leisurely lounging and strolling. At its edge is the colorful **Oratorio di San Bernardino.** Finely carved reliefs and sculptures embellish its Renaissance facade, built between 1457 and 1461. *(A few blocks farther from Chiesa di San Filippo Neri, to the right down V. San Francesco. Open daily 8am-12:30pm and 3:30-6pm.)*

THE NORTHEAST

VIA ROCCHI. From behind the duomo, medieval V. Ulisse Rocchi, the city's oldest street, winds through the northern city gate to the **Arco di Etrusco,** a perfectly preserved Roman arch built on Etruscan pedestals. Walk straight through P. Braccio Fortebraccio and follow C. Guiseppe Garibaldi toward the jewel-like **Tempio di Sant'Angelo** (also known as Chiesa di San Michele Arcangelo), a 5th-century circular church constructed with stone and wood taken from ancient pagan buildings. *(Past Palazzo Gallenga, to the right near the end of C. Garibaldi. ☎ 075 572 26 24. Open Tu-Su 9:30am-noon and 3:30pm-sunset.)* The **Porta Sant'Angelo,** an arch and tower that welcomes visitors to the city, stands next door.

CAPPELLA DI SAN SEVERO. The chapel housing the *oratorio* is also home to *The Holy Trinity and Saints,* one of many collaborations by Perugia's favorite mentor-student tag-team: a fresco painted in two parts, the upper section is by Raphael, the lower by his master, Perugino. *(On the way back from Tempio di Sant'Angelo, veer to the left of P. B. Fortebraccio to a stairwell that winds up the hillside. Continue straight for 1 block from the top of the stairs, and then head right into P. Michelotti. Take V. Aquila on the left of the piazza and then take the 1st right into P. Raffaello. ☎ 075 573 38 64. Open daily Apr.-Oct. 10am-1:30pm and 2:30-6:30pm; Nov.-Mar. 10:30am-1:30pm and 2:30-5pm. €2.50, including Pozzo Etrusco and Casero di Porta Sant'Angelo.)*

POZZO ETRUSCO. With its impressive depth of 36m, the Pozzo Etrusco (Etruscan Well) dates to the 3rd century BC and was once Perugia's main water source. Descend stairs to the footbridge that spans the well just meters above the chilly water. *(P. Danti, 18, across from duomo. Follow V. Raffaello, turn left, then right on V. Bontempi. ☎ 075 573 36 69. Open M and W-Su 10am-1:30pm and 2:30-6:30pm; daily in Aug.)*

THE EAST SIDE

BASILICA DI SAN PIETRO. Now shared with students at the university, this 10th-century church consists of a double arcade of closely spaced columns that lead to a choir. Its art-filled interior contains solemn, majestic paintings and frescoes depicting saints and soldiers, all in brilliant color on a dramatic scale. Look for Perugino's *Pietà* along the northern aisle. At the far end is a neat medieval garden; its lower section offers a must-see view of the surrounding countryside. Downstairs a perfectly preserved ancient Etruscan crypt is also on display. *(At the end of town on V. Borgo XX Giugno, past Pta. S. Pietro. Open daily 8am-noon and 3-6:30pm.)*

CHIESA DI SAN DOMENICO. This grandiose cathedral is the largest church in Umbria. The huge Gothic rose window brightens an otherwise simple white interior, rebuilt in 1632. The magnificently carved **Tomb of Pope Benedict XI** (1325), by Lorenzo Maitani, rests in the Capella del Santissimo Sacramento to the right of the high altar. The church is under renovation, so expect scaffolding. *(In P. Giordano Bruno, on C. Cavour. Open daily 8am-noon and 4pm-sunset.)*

MUSEO ARCHEOLOGICO NAZIONALE DELL'UMBRIA. Housed in the vast cloisters attached to the Chiesa di San Domenico, this museum houses an extensive collection of Roman and Etruscan artifacts, including the *Cippo Perugino*, a memorial stone with one of the longest inscriptions in the Etruscan language. An extensive collection of funerary urns from as early as 2 BC spans the outdoor corridor. The excavated Etruscan tomb of *Cai Cutu* lies near the entrance. A tunnel passes around the tiny cross-shaped chamber with windows looking over 50 stone burial urns. *(Piazza G. Bruno, 10. ☎075 572 71 41. Entrance in courtyard to left of entrance to Chiesa di San Domenico. Open M 2:30-7:30pm, Tu-Su 8:30am-7:30pm. €2.)*

GIARDINI CARDUCCI. These well-maintained public gardens are named after the 19th-century poet Giosuè Carducci. From the garden wall, enjoy the splendid panorama of the Umbrian countryside; a castle or an ancient church crowns every hill. *(At the far end of C. Vannucci, the main street leading from P. IV Novembre.)*

ROCCA PAOLINA. The rock is all that is left of the grandiose fortress built by the architect Antonio Sangallo il Giovane at the behest of Pope Paolo III Farnese in the 1500s. The escalator that goes through it connects the upper and lower parts of the city. *(On V. Marzia. Open daily 8am-7pm. Free.)*

FESTIVALS AND NIGHTLIFE

Every July the 10-day **Umbria Jazz Festival** draws world-class performers like B.B. King and Alicia Keys. (For info call ☎800 46 23 11 or go to the ticket office V. Mazzini, 9, off C. Vannucci, open M-Sa 10am-1pm and 3:30-7:30pm. www.umbriajazz.com. €12-50, some events free.) Summer brings **Teatro è la Notte,** a series of musical, cinematic, and dance performances. In September, the **Sagra Musicale Umbra,** which began in 1937, brings together many Umbrian cities and fills local churches with religious and classical music. Check Palazzo Gallenga for film and event listings or www.sagramusicaleumbra.com. Contact the tourist office or www.eurochocolate.perugia.it about the **Eurochocolate Festival** which takes place at the end of October. This extravaganza draws crowds from both Perugia and neighboring towns, and tourists from all over, for its one week duration. On the streets of the *centro*, chocolate becomes the focus of fanciful creations and throngs of chocolate devotees wait for their free samples.

Perugia has more nightlife options than any other Umbrian city, and its large university population keeps clubs packed nearly every night of the week from September to May. During the academic year, join the nightly bandwagon at **P.**

UMBRIA AND LE MARCHE

Fortebraccio, where free buses depart for several nearby clubs (starting at 11pm). Once there, cover charges between €13-26 land patrons in the thick of deafening electronic music and scantily-clad clubbers. Within the city, Perugia's two hottest discos are **Domus Delirii,** V. del Naspo, 3, just off P. Morlacchi, and **St. Adams,** V. della Cupa, 6, left off V. dei Priori from C. Vannucci. (Both open nightly midnight-5am.) **Shamrock Irish,** P. Danti, 18, on the way to the Pozzo Etrusco, is home to the best Guinness in town, and each pint (€4.50) includes a free shot of whiskey. The atmosphere is laid-back, and the staff and patrons are indistinguishable. (☎ 075 573 66 25. Happy Hour 6-9pm. Open nightly 6pm-2:30am.) Head to the student hangout **La Terrazza,** in P. Matteotti, on the rooftop terrace behind the Mercato Coperto, for cheap drinks (walk through the arch and go right). It often hosts open-air movies and book readings. (Open daily 6pm-3am, weather pending.) **L'Elfo II,** V. del Verzaro, 39, off P. Morlacchi near the university, features a lively crowd of local students. (Beer €3.50-3.80, cocktails €5.50. Open daily 9pm-2am.) Late-night cafes lining V. Mazzini and P. Matteotti are a popular alternative to bar-hopping.

◨ DAYTRIP FROM PERUGIA: LAKE TRASIMENO

Expansive Lake Trasimeno, 30km west of Perugia, is a refreshing oasis away from the hot and tourist-packed metropolitan center. Though a pleasant daytrip destination today, Lake Trasimeno was once wracked with violence. After advancing down the Alps in 217 BC during the Second Punic War, Hannibal's elephant-riding army routed the Romans just north of the lake. The names of the lakeside villages, Ossaia (place of bones) and Sanguineto (bloody), recall the brutal slaughter of 16,000 Roman soldiers. The mass graves of these dead have recently been discovered under the battlefields of Tuero, between the two main towns on the lake: Passignano sul Trasimeno and Castiglion del Lago. A system of ferries connects Passignano sul Trasimeno, Castiglion del Lago, Tuero, San Feliciano, and Lake Trasimeno's two largest islands—Isola Maggiore and Isola Palvese.

CASTIGLION DEL LAGO

Castiglion del Lago lies on the Florence-Rome train line. From Perugia, change at Terontola to a train headed for Rome or Chiusi (1hr., 15 per day, €3.05). From the train station, turn left on V. Longo, left on V. Cairoli, and right on V. Buozzi (follow the "centro" signs). Follow V. B. Buozzi to its end, take the broad flight of stairs straight ahead, then the smaller stairs. To the right through the city walls is V. V. Emanuele, the main street of the tiny centro storico. The tourist office, P. Mazzini, 10, in the main square, provides boat schedules, exchanges money, and helps find rooms in hotels or in private residences. ☎ 075 965 24 84. Open M-F 8:30am-1pm and 3:30-7pm, Sa 9am-1pm and 3:30-7pm, Su and holidays 9am-1pm and 4-7pm. To reach the ferry dock, swing right before entering Pta. Senese, turn left on V. Belvedere, and then take an immediate right down the stone steps. Turn left, then right on V. Pescatori to a public beach and dock.

The largest resort on Trasimeno, Castiglion del Lago nevertheless remains a much quieter town than in past centuries, when it was conquered by Byzantium, Arezzo, Cortona, and finally Perugia in 1184. Clinging to a limestone promontory covered in olive groves, its medieval walls enclose two main streets and a single square. At the end of V. V. Emanuele, next to the hospital, stand the **Palazzo della Corgna** and the medieval **Rocca del leone.** The 16th-century palazzo is notable for its frescoes by Niccolò Circignani, or "Il Pomarancio." The courtyard of the imposing, crumbling Rocca is free and open to the public, and its sloping grass lawn sometimes serves as a venue for open-air concerts. Visitors can walk around the entire courtyard atop the high fortress walls. (☎ 075 965 82 10. Open daily Apr. 9:30am-1pm and 3:30-7pm, May-June 10am-1:30pm and 4-7:30pm, July-Aug. 10am-1:30pm and 4:30-8pm, Sept.-Oct. 10am-1:30pm and 3:30-7pm, Nov.-Mar. 9:30am-4:30pm. Walls €3.)

Budget lodgings are scarce in the immediate vicinity of Castiglion del Lago, but **La Torre ❹**, V. V. Emanuele, 50, offers rooms with bath in the heart of the old town. (☎/fax 075 95 16 66; www.trasinet.com/latorre. Breakfast €5. Singles €50; doubles €65; triples €85. AmEx/MC/V.) Also worth a try is **Il Torrione ❹**, V. delle Mura, 4, right on V. Battisti just inside the gates. Suites have bath and many have picturesque views of the lake. (☎ 075 95 32 36. Singles €55; doubles €62.) Gourmet food shops line the busier streets, while cheap pizzerias crowd V. V. Emanuele. Prices average €4-6 per person. For a fancier dining experience, **La Cantina ❸**, V. V. Emanuele, 93, is a certified Umbrian cuisine restaurant with beautiful views and attentive service. (*Primi* €4.50-7.50, *secondi* €8.50-17. Cover €1.60. Open June-Sept. M and W-Su 12:30-3pm and 7-10:30pm, Oct.-May W-Su 12:30-3pm and 7-10:30 pm. AmEx/MC/V.) **Ristorante L'Acquario ❸**, V. V. Emanuele, 69, offers a variety of lunch *menù* options (€12.50-16.40) incorporating fresh lake fish. (*Primi* €6-8.50, *secondi* €8-30. Cover €1.80. Open Mar.-Oct. M-Tu and Th-Su noon-2:30pm and 7-10:30pm, Nov.-Feb. Tu and Th-Su noon-2:30pm and 7-10:30pm. AmEx/MC/V.)

ISOLA MAGGIORE

Passignano sul Trasimeno is the most convenient ferry point to Isola Maggiore from Perugia. It lies on the Foligno-Terontola line, where trains from Perugia (30min., 19 per day, €2.05). A ferry system connects the island to Passignano sul Trasimeno (25min.; every hr. 6:40am-7:45pm; €3.30, round-trip €5.40) and Castiglion del Lago (30min.; every 1½hr. 8:35am-7:05pm; €3.30, round-trip €5.90). Buy tickets onboard when coming from the island or at the docks in the towns. A tourist information booth is by the dock. Open daily 10am-6pm. Glossy guides to the island €3.

Follow in St. Francis's footsteps and spend a delightful day on Isola Maggiore, Lake Trasimeno's only inhabited island. Turn right from the dock and follow the path to the tip of the island and the ruined **Castello Guglielmi.** The decaying Baroque chapel, with peeling plaster and fading frescoes, is the only part that is accessible to the public (9am-5pm). From the castle, turn left down the dirt-and-tree-root stairs to check out the windmill. To the right, walk up Str. S. M. Arcangelo to the 12th-century **Chiesa di San Michele Arcangelo** for 14th-century Umbrian frescoes and a 12th-century wooden crucifix. (Open daily 10:30am-1pm and 3-6pm. Tour €3.) The **Chiesa di San Salvatore,** dating from 1155, has Frederick I's effigy set in the facade. (☎ 075 825 42 33. Call ahead to arrange a visit. All inclusive tickets to enter the sites €2.60, €1.60 for students and seniors.) On the coast opposite the castle, some headstrong tourists have been known to sneak a dip in the island's small private beach, but *Let's Go* does not recommend trespassing. For a public beach, complete with playground and cafe, take a ferry to Castiglion del Lago.

GUBBIO   ☎ 075

With its picturesque medieval streets and rugged mountain-locked setting, Gubbio preserves its past, manifested in numerous local festivals and a thriving ceramics trade. The town's famous Eugubine Tablets—the only existing record of the ancient Umbrian language—offer a glimpse even farther back into Umbria's history and provide important evidence of an Umbrian and Roman alliance against the invading Etruscans. The ruins of an amphitheater attest to the past grip of the Roman emperors, and splendid palaces recall years of subjugation under the powerful Dukes of Urbino. Gubbio's greatest distinction may lie in its school of painting or its favorite son Bosone Novello Raffaelli, Italy's first novelist.

▣ ⁈ TRANSPORTATION AND PRACTICAL INFORMATION

The nearest **train station** is in **Fossato di Vico**, 19km away on the Rome-Ancona line. Trains run to: Ancona (1½hr., 15 per day, from €4.23); Rome (2½hr., 10 per day, €10.12); Spoleto (1¼hr., 10 per day, €3.36). **APM buses** (☎075 50 67 81) run to and from Perugia (1hr.; M-F 11 per day, Sa-Su 4 per day; €4) and are much more convenient than the train. The **bus** is the easiest way to reach Gubbio from Fossato (M-Sa 12 per day, Su 6 per day; €2). Tickets sold at the newsstand in P. Quaranta Martiri, at the Perugia bus stop, and at the newsstand in Fossato's train station. If stranded in Fossato without bus service, call a taxi at ☎075 91 92 02 or 033 53 37 48 71. In Gubbio, **taxis** (☎075 927 38 00) are available in P. Quaranta Martiri.

Gubbio is a tangle of twisting streets and alleys opening into piazzas. Buses stop in **Piazza Quaranta Martiri**. A short uphill walk on **Via della Repubblica** from the **bus station** leads to **Corso Garibaldi**. Signs point uphill to **Piazza Grande**, the civic headquarters on the hilltop. Some of the best ceramics are sold on **Via dei Consoli** and in P. Grande. An **IAT Tourist Office**, P. Oderisi, 6, off C. Garibaldi, offers bus schedules and **maps**. (☎075 922 06 93; www.umbria2000.it. Open M-F 8:30am-1:45pm and 3-6pm, Sa 9am-1pm and 3-6pm, Su 9:30am-12:30pm and 3-6pm.) A 24hr. **ATM** is at P. Quaranta Martiri, 48. In case of **emergency**, dial ☎113, call an **ambulance** (☎118) or the **hospital** (☎075 23 94 67 or 23 94 69), or contact the **police** (☎075 22 15 42), on V. Leonardo da Vinci. Four pharmacies rotate 24hr. service. **Farmacia Luconi** is at C. Garibaldi, 12. (☎075 927 37 83. Open Apr.-Sept. M-Sa 9am-1pm and 4:30-8pm, Oct.-Mar. 9am-1pm and 4-7:30pm.) The **post office** is at V. Cairoli, 11. (☎075 927 39 25. Open M-F 8am-6:30pm, Sa 8am-12:30pm.) **Postal Code:** 06024.

▣ ◖ ACCOMMODATIONS AND FOOD

A private garden and conscientious staff make ▣**Residence di Via Piccardi** ❸, V. Piccardi, 12, an ideal place to relax. Six large, comfortable rooms all have bath and TV. (☎075 927 61 08; e.biagiotti@tiscali.it. Breakfast included. Check-in before 8pm. Singles €35; doubles €50; triples €60. Cash only.) Walk up from P. Quaranta Martiri on V. Della Repubblica, and turn right on V. Gioia to reach **Hotel Grotta dell'Angelo** ❸, V. Gioia, 47. Spacious rooms all have bright linens, TV, phone, and bath. (☎075 927 17 47; www.grottadellangelo.it. Breakfast €5. Singles €38; doubles €55; triples €65. AmEx/MC/V.) Rooms at **Locanda del Duca** ❹, V. Piccardi, 3, are large and squeaky-clean, all with bath and TV. From P. Quaranta Martiri, turn right on V. Piccardi. (☎075 927 77 53. Restaurant below. Singles €45; doubles €60. AmEx/MC/V.) **Residenza Le Logge** ❹, V. Piccardi, 7/9, is on the same street as Locanda. Big, clean rooms are the standard here as well. Looking for a splurge? Ask for the massive double suite with a whirlpool tub. (☎075 927 75 74; www.paginegialle.it/residenzalelogge. Singles €47; doubles €57; suite €80.)

For a quick bite, grab a sandwich (€2.20) from the **alimentari**, P. Quaranta Martiri, 36, across from the bus station. (Open daily 8am-1pm and 4:30-8pm.) Every Tuesday brings a bustling **market** under P. Quaranta Martiri's *loggie*. Local delicacies await at **Prodotti Tipici e Tartufati Eugubini** ❶, V. Piccardi, 17, like *salumi di cinghiale o cervo* (boar or deer sausage) and the region's prized white-truffle oil. (Open daily 10am-1pm and 2:30-8pm.) **Taverna del Buchetto** ❷, V. Dante, 30, near Pta. Romana off C. Garibaldi, prepares hearty, homemade meals with care inside a converted granary. (☎075 927 70 34. Pizza €3.62-7. *Primi* €4.13-7.75, *secondi* €7-11. Cover €1.29. Open Tu-Su noon-3pm and 7-11pm. AmEx/MC/V.) *Funghi porcini e tartufi* (mushrooms and truffles) are the specialties at **La Cantina Ristorante/Pizzeria** ❷, V. Francesco Piccotti, 3, off V. della Repubblica. (☎075 922 05 83. Pizza €4.50-7. *Primi* €6.50-10.50, *secondi* €6.50-13. Cover €1. Open Tu-Su noon-2:30pm and 7-10pm; open for pizza noon-3pm. MC/V.) The quaint stone dining room of **San Francesco e il Lupo ❷**, at V. Cairoli and C. Garibaldi, pumps out tasty servings to hungry crowds. (☎075 927 23 44. Pizza €4-7.50. *Primi* €5-10, *secondi* €6-25. Cover €2. Open M and W-Su noon-2pm and 7-10pm. MC/V.) Locals and tourists come to the two elegant dining rooms of **Ristorante La Lanterna ❷**, V. Gioia, 23, for staples of *Eugubine* fare. (☎075 927 66 94. *Primi* €5-10, *secondi* €9-11. Open M-W and F-Su noon-3pm and 7:30-10:30pm. MC/V.)

🎯 SIGHTS

PIAZZA QUARANTA MARTIRI. In the middle of the piazza stretches the **Giardino dei Quaranta Martiri** (Garden of the 40 Martyrs), a memorial to those slain by the Nazis in reprisal for the assassination of two German officials. With a gorgeous moss-covered fountain and well-kept red flowers, it's a great place to relax while enjoying an afternoon snack. **Chiesa di San Francesco,** one of multiple places claiming to be the site where St. Francis experienced his powerful conversion, stands on one side of the square. The central apse holds the *Vita della Madonna* (Life of the Madonna), a partially destroyed 15th-century fresco series by Ottaviano Nelli, Gubbio's most famous painter. Across the piazza from the church is **Loggia dei Tiratoi,** where 14th-century weavers (*tiratoi*) stretched their cloth so it would shrink evenly. V. Matteotti runs from P. Quaranta Martiri outside the city walls to the **Teatro Romano,** which still stages productions. The nearby **Antiquarium,** built on an archaeological excavation, displays impressive mosaics found in this and other areas of the city. *(Church open daily 7:15am-noon and 3:30-7:30pm.)*

PALAZZO DEI CONSOLI. This white stone palace was built in 1332 for the high magistrate of Gubbio. Inside, the **Museo Civico** displays a collection of *Eugubine* and Roman artifacts. Statues, pieces of marble friezes, and tablets are arranged along the walls. In a room upstairs, to the left beyond the staircase, are the 🎯**Tavole Eugubine** (Eugubine Tablets), comparable to the Rosetta Stone for their linguistic significance. Five of these seven bronze tablets, dating from 300 to 100 BC, form one of the few remaining documents of the ancient Umbrian language. The last two tablets are in Latin. An illiterate farmer discovered them in 1444 in an underground chamber of the Roman theater just outside the city walls; he was subsequently tricked into swapping them for a worthless piece of land. The ritual texts spell out the social, religious, and political organization of early Umbria and describe how to read religious omens from animal livers. Through the opposite door, stroll around the **Archaeological Museum's** exhibits of Egyptian statues and Roman tools. *(In P. Grande. ☎075 927 42 98. Open daily Apr. to Oct. 10am-1pm and 3-6pm, Nov. to mid-Mar. 10am-1pm and 2-5pm. €5, ages 7-25 €2.50, under 7 free.)*

PALAZZO DUCALE AND DUOMO. Federico da Montefeltro commissioned Luciano Laurana, architect of his Urbino palace, to build the 15th-century Palazzo Ducale. To the right of the entrance, stairs descend to the excavation beneath the castle. Facing the palazzo, the unassuming pink Gothic duomo displays 12th-century stained-glass windows, art by Perugino's student Dono Doni, and Pinturicchio's *Adoration of the Shepherds. (Follow the signs from P. Grande. Museum open M-Sa 9am-1pm and 2:30-6:30pm, Su 9am-12:30pm. Palazzo entrance €2, ages 18-25 €1, under 18 or over 60 free. Duomo open daily Apr.-Sept. 9am-7pm, Oct.-Mar. 10am-5pm.)*

MONTE INGINO. When the museums close for lunch, the rather shaky 🎯**funivia** (cablecar chairlift, 6min.) climbs to the peak of Monte Ingino, location of splendid views and perfect picnic spots. Work up an appetite with a visit to the **Basilica and Monastery of Sant'Ubaldo,** Gubbio's patron saint, which houses the saint's sinewy pickled body in a glass case above the altar. The stained glass at the entrance tells

UMBRIA AND LE MARCHE

the story of his life, and the three *ceri*, large wooden candles carried in the **Corsa dei Ceri** procession each May, are also on display. Each December, lights transform the entire hill into the world's largest Christmas tree. Follow the steep dirt trail behind the Basilica up to the scaffolding where the star is placed atop the 'tree' and then continue up to an ancient but well-preserved tower for spectacular panoramas. *(To reach the funivia, turn left out of Pta. Romana. From the uphill entrance to the basilica, bear left and continue upward on a dirt path to the top of the mountain. Chairlift open June M-Sa 9:30am-1:15pm and 2:30-7pm, Su 9am-7:30pm; July-Aug. M-Sa 8:30am-7:30pm, Su 8:30am-8pm; Sept. M-Sa 9:30am-1:15pm and 2:30-7pm, Su 9:30am-1:15pm and 2:30-7:30pm; Mar. M-Sa 10am-1:15pm and 2:30-5:30pm, Su 9:30am-1:15pm and 2:30-6pm; Apr.-May M-Sa 10am-1:15pm and 2:30-6:30pm, Su 9:30am-1:15pm and 2:30-7pm; daily Oct. 10am-1:15pm and 2:30-6pm; daily Nov.-Feb. 10am-1:15pm and 2:30-5pm. €4, round-trip €5.)*

■ ENTERTAINMENT

The annual **Corsa dei Ceri,** 900 years old and going strong, takes place every May 15, the day of patron saint's Ubaldo's death. Intended to represent candles, the three *ceri* are huge wooden blocks carved like hourglasses and topped with little saints. Each one corresponds to a distinct section of the populace: the masons (S. Ubaldo), the farmers (S. Antonio Abate), and the artisans (S. Giorgio). After 12 hours of furious preparation and frenetic flag-twirling, squads of runners (*ceraioli*) clad in Renaissance-style tights heave the heavy objects onto their shoulders and run a wild relay race up Monte Ingino. This raucous festival turns Gubbio's quiet medieval streets into a chaotic stomping ground bristling with intense ritual fervor. Visitors will likely be entranced; locals will almost certainly be drunk. During the **Palio della Balestra,** held in P. Grande on the last Sunday in May, archers from Gubbio and nearby Sansepolcro have been gathering for a fierce crossbow contest since 1461. The contest provides an excellent excuse for Gubbio to throw itself a huge party every year and maintain a healthy industry in medieval-weaponry toys.

ASSISI   ☎ 075

Assisi's serene atmosphere and renowned spirituality are owed to the legacy of St. Francis, patron saint of Italy and the town's favorite son. The 12th-century monk founded the Franciscan order and sparked a religious revolution with his audacious asceticism. Young Franciscan monks and nuns dressed in their brown *cappucci* robes still fill Assisi, resembling the tiny votive statues that overflow souvenir stands. The town is an important pilgrimage site, especially among Italian youth, who converge here for religious conferences and festivals. Of course, fervent religiosity is hardly a prerequisite for a visit to Assisi. Many people come simply for the beautiful architecture of so many of the city's buildings. The Basilica di San Francesco is perhaps the most frequented sight in Umbria, housing the saint's relics and Giotto's renowned fresco series of St. Francis's life. Local ruins attest to Assisi's Etruscan and Roman roots, while grand palaces and majestic *rocce* (castles) from a later era tower above tile roofs. Renovations have repaired most of the damage caused by 1997's devastating earthquakes.

▢ TRANSPORTATION

Trains: Near Basilica di Santa Maria degli Angeli. On F. S. Foligno-Terontola line (☎ 075 80 40 272*).* Office open 6am-8pm. **Luggage storage** available (see **Practical Information**). To: **Ancona** (8 per day, from €6.82); **Florence** (2-3hr., 13 per day 5:13am-7:32pm, €8.99); **Perugia** (30min., 1-2 per hr. 5:13am-10:45pm, €1.65); **Rome** (2½hr., 14 per day 5:15am-8:38pm, €8.99).

Assisi

♦ ACCOMMODATIONS

Albergo Anfiteatro Romano, **11**
Camere Annalisa Martini, **2**
Hotel Grotta Antica, **4**
Hotel Lieto Soggiorno, **5**
Hotel Roma, **10**
Hotel La Rocca, **8**
Ostello Fontemaggio, **12**
Ostello della Pace (HI), **1**

♠ FOOD

Pizzeria Il Lupo, **13**
Pizzeria Otello, **6**
Ristorante Anfiteatro Romano, **7**
Trattoria da Erminio, **9**
Trattoria Pallotta, **3**

UMBRIA AND
LE MARCHE

Buses: Buses leave from P. Unità d'Italia, near Basilica di San Francesco. Buy **SULGA** (☎075 500 96 41, www.sulga.it) tickets onboard. To: **Florence** (2½hr., 7am, €6.40) and **Rome** (3¼hr.; 1:45, 4:30pm; €8.26). Buy **APM** (☎80 05 12 141) tickets at newsstands. To: **Foligno** (1hr., M-Sa 10 per day 6:50am-7:20pm, €3.36) via **Spello** and **Perugia** (1½hr., 12 per day 6:30am-6:25pm, €2.70). Buy **SENA** (☎075 728 32 08) tickets onboard. Bus to: **Siena** (2¼hr.; 10:20am, 5:45, 8:45pm; €7) leaves from S. Maria degli Angeli near train station. Bus schedules available at tourist office.

Public Transportation: Local buses (2 per hr., €0.80) run from the train station to bus stops at P. Unità d'Italia (near basilica), Largo Properzio (through Pta. Nuova), and P. Matteotti. Buy tickets onboard or at *tabacchi* in the train station.

Taxis: ☎075 81 31 93 in P. del Comune; 075 81 26 00 in P. San Chiara; 075 81 23 78 in P. Unità d'Italia; 075 804 02 75 at the train station.

Car Rental: Agenzia Assisiorganizza, V. S. Gabriele dell'Addolorata, 25 (☎075 81 23 27). Cars from €75 per day, €347 per week. 21+. Open M-Sa 11am-10pm, Su 4-10pm. Credit card required. AmEx/MC/V.

◈ 🛈 ORIENTATION AND PRACTICAL INFORMATION

Towering above the city to the north, the **Rocca Maggiore** can help orient those lost among Assisi's winding streets. The bus from the train station stops first at **Piazza Unità d'Italia;** get off here for direct access to the Basilica di San Francesco. Stay on the bus until **Piazza Matteotti** to access the bulk of the town. To reach the *centro* at **Piazza del Comune**, from P. Matteotti take **Via del Torrione** to **Piazza San Rufino**, take the downhill left in the piazza, and then walk down **Via San Rufino**. **Via Portica** becomes V. Fortini, V. Seminario, and V. San Francesco and connects P. del Comune to the Basilica di San Francesco. Heading in the opposite direction, **Corso Mazzini** leads to the Chiesa di Santa Chiara.

Tourist Office: ☎075 81 25 34; www.assisi.umbria2000.it; in P. del Comune. Walking into P. del Comune on V. S. Rufino, office is at far end of the piazza. Provides brochures, bus info, train timetable, and a decent **map.** Open M-Sa 8am-2pm and 3-6pm, Su and holidays 9am-1pm.

Currency Exchange: The post office exchanges traveler's checks for €1-2.60. For other options, try **Banca Toscana**, in P. S. Pietro, or **Banca dell'Umbria**, in P. del Comune. Banks open M-F 8:20am-1:20pm and 2:35-3:35pm. **ATMs** outside.

Luggage Storage: In train station. €3 for 12hr. Open daily 6:30am-7:30pm.

Emergency: ☎113. **Ambulance** (☎118). **Carabinieri**, P. Matteotti, 3 (☎075 81 22 39).

Hospital: Ospedale d'Assisi (☎075 81 391), on the outskirts of town. Take the "Linea A" bus from P. del Comune.

Internet: Agenzia Casciarri, V. Borgo Aretino, 39 (☎075 81 28 15). €4.20 per hr. Open M-F 9am-12:30pm and 4-7pm, Sa 9am-12:30pm. **Internet World**, V. S. Gabriele dell'Addolorata, 25 (☎075 81 23 27; internetworld@tiscali.it). DSL line €3.20 per hr. Open M-Sa 11am-1pm, Su 4-9pm.

Post Office: Largo Properzio, 4, up the stairs to the left just outside of Pta. Nuova. Open M-Sa 8:35am-1:25pm. Branch at P. S. Pietro, 41. Open M-F 8:10am-7pm, Sa 8:10am-1:25pm. **Postal Code:** 06081.

🏠 ⛺ ACCOMMODATIONS AND CAMPING

Assisi sees lots of tourists and passers-through, so it's full of competing hotels. Still, reservations are crucial around Easter and Christmas and strongly recommended for the **Festa di Calendimaggio** in early May. If you don't mind turning in around 11pm, ask the tourist office for a list of **religious institutions.** The tourist office also provides a list of *affittacamere*, rooms for rent in private residences.

■ **Camere Annalisa Martini**, V. S. Gregorio, 6 (☎/fax 075 81 35 36; cameremartini@libero.it). Follow V. Portico from P. del Comune and turn left on V. S. Gregorio. Centrally located *affittacamere* at excellent prices boast soft chairs and spacious bath. If there's no space left, Annalisa can refer you to her friends. Laundry €5. Singles €24, with bath €26; doubles €38; triples €52; quads €62. Cash only. ❸

Ostello/Hotel/Camping Fontemaggio, V. per l'Eremo delle Carceri, 8 (☎075 81 36 36, fax 81 37 49). V. Eremo begins in P. Matteotti and leads through Pta. Cappuccini; follow 1km up the road and then bear right at the sign. Hostel, hotel, bungalows, campgrounds, and market available for those who don't mind the trek. Check-out 10am. Curfew 11pm. Dorms €20; singles €36; doubles €52; triples €72; quads €80; 4- to 8-person bungalows €50-130. Camping at Ostello Fontemaggio also available. €5.50 per person, €4.50 per tent, €2.50 per car. Cash only. Hotel ❷/Camp ❶

Hotel Roma, P. S. Chiara, 13 (☎075 81 23 90, fax 81 67 43). Nice rooms with pleasant decor, but beware the shoebox-sized elevator. Many rooms have views of the beautiful piazza. Request rooms without breakfast for a lower price. All rooms have bath, TV, and phone. Singles €40, with breakfast €45; doubles €62/€72. MC/V. ❹

Albergo Anfiteatro Romano, V. Anfiteatro Romano, 4 (☎075 81 30 25, fax 81 51 10), off P. Matteotti. Modest rooms with views of the Rocca are a good departure point for a daytrip to Eremo. Hotel check-in is at the restaurant (see **Food**). Singles, all without bath, €22; doubles €34, with bath €44. AmEx/MC/V. ❷

Ostello della Pace (HI), V. di Valecchi, 177 (☎/fax 075 81 67 67; www.assisihostel.com). From P. Unità d'Italia, walk downhill on V. Marconi, then turn left at sign. From the train station, go left on V. Carducci, then right on main road for 500m; follow signs. Rooms with 2-3 bunk beds and shared baths. Breakfast included. Dinner €8. Laundry €3.50. Internet €5 per hr. Reception 7-10am and 3:30-11:30pm. Check-out 9:30am. Lockout 9:30am-3:30pm. Common areas locked 11:30pm. Reserve ahead. HI card required; on sale at hostel. Dorms €14, with bath €16. MC/V. ❶

Hotel La Rocca, V. di Pta. Perlici, 27 (☎/fax 075 81 22 84). From P. del Comune, follow V. S. Rufino uphill and cross the piazza. Go up V. di Pta. Perlici until hitting the old arches. All rooms have bath; many have great views of the Rocca. Restaurant downstairs. Open Feb. 5-Jan. 15. Singles €38; doubles €45; triples €63. AmEx/MC/V. ❸

Hotel Lieto Soggiorno, V. Portica, 26 (☎075 81 61 91). Follow V. San Francesco until it becomes V. Portica. The hotel is on the left before the Foro Romano. This antique home has been remodeled to offer spacious rooms with bath, TV, phone, and A/C. The best price for such a central location—only a few minutes from major sights. Singles €26; doubles €50 with breakfast. AmEx/MC/V. ❷

Hotel Grotta Antica, Vco. dei Macelli Vecchi, 1 (☎075 81 34 67). From P. del Comune, walk downhill on V. dell'Arco dei Priori (under the arch); turn right on Vco. dei Macelli Vecchi. Well located hotel has simple rooms, all with bath and TV. Singles €30; doubles €38; triples €49; quads €56. Cash only. ❸

FOOD

Assisi's luring array of nut breads and sweets includes the mouth-watering *torrone* (a sweet nougat of almonds and egg whites; €2.90 per kg) and the divine *brustengolo* (packed with raisins, apples, and walnuts; €21 per kg). **Pasticceria Santa Monica**, V. Portica, 4, right off P. del Comune, sells these and other treats. (Open daily 9:30am-8pm.) On Saturday morning, an **open-air market** takes over P. Matteotti. For fresh fruits and vegetables on weekdays, head to V. S. Gabriele.

Pizzeria Otello, V. S. Antonio, 1 (☎075 81 24 15). Head downhill on V. dell'Arco dei Priori (under arch) and take 1st left. Pizza at excellent value and in many varieties, sized for 1 (€5-7). Or try the deliciously creamy *strangozzi al tartufo* (pasta with truffles; €6.80). Open daily noon-3pm and 7-10:30pm. AmEx/MC/V. ❷

UMBRIA AND LE MARCHE

Trattoria da Erminio, V. Monte Cavallo, 19 (☎075 81 25 06). From P. del Comune, follow V. S. Rufino and onto V. Pta. Perlici, then take the 1st right. Real men don't eat *tartufi*—here's *the* place for carnivores. The savory aroma of crackling, roasting meat wafts down the street. *Primi* €4.70-8.30, *secondi* €5.20-10.90. Cover €1.30. Open M-W and F-Su noon-2:30pm and 7-9pm. AmEx/MC/V. ❷

Trattoria Pallotta, Vco. della Volta Pinta, 13 (☎075 81 26 49), off P. del Comune, tucked under the arch opposite Tempio di Minerva. Succulent Umbrian classics served beneath stone arcades. Excellent veggie options. *Primi* €6-10, *secondi* €8-12. Cover €2.50 with water. Open M and W-Su noon-2:30pm and 7:15-9:30pm. AmEx/MC/V. ❸

Pizzeria Il Lupo, V. S. Rufino, 1 (☎075 81 23 51). From P. del Comune, take V. S. Rufino. Pizza slices for cheap (€2), *panini* for cheaper (€1.50). Divine pepperoni sandwich. Very few seats, so eat by the nearby fountain and shady benches. Cash only. ❶

Ristorante Anfiteatro Romano, V. Anfiteatro Romano, 4 (☎075 81 30 25), off P. Matteotti. Downstairs from the hotel. Hearty portions of Umbrian cuisine. Vine-rimmed patio smells of honeysuckle and a beautiful Roman fresco lines the back wall. *Primi* €4-8, *secondi* €5-9. Cover €1.60. Open daily noon-2:30pm and 7-9pm. AmEx/MC/V. ❷

◔ SIGHTS

At age 19, St. Francis (1182-1226) abandoned military and social ambitions, rejected his father's wealth, and embraced asceticism. His love of nature, devoted humility, and renunciation of the church's worldliness earned him a huge European following and posed an unprecedented challenge to the decadent papacy and corrupt monastic orders. St. Francis continued to preach chastity and poverty until his death, when the order he founded was gradually subsumed into the hierarchy that it had criticized. Ironically, the Church has glorified the modest saint in countless opulent churches constructed to draw people to the places where he grew up, went to school, and immersed himself in prayer.

▦ BASILICA DI SAN FRANCESCO. A major pilgrimage site covered with frescoes by the all-stars, **Basilica di San Francesco** is one of the greatest spiritual and artistic attractions in Italy. When construction began on the building in the mid-13th century, the Franciscan order protested, complaining that the elaborate church was an impious monument to the conspicuous consumption that St. Francis had scorned. Brother Elia, the vicar of the order, insisted that a double church be erected, the lower level built around the saint's crypt, the upper level used as a church for services. The subdued art in the lower church commemorates Francis's modest life, while the upper church pays tribute to his sainthood and consecration. The basilica suffered during the 1997 earthquake, but after vigorous restoration efforts, very few traces of damage remain. The walls of the upper church are covered with Giotto's renowned *Life of St. Francis* fresco cycle, while Cimabue's magnificent *Madonna and Child, Angels,* and *St. Francis* grace the right transept. Visitors who have been to Arezzo will recognize one of the images as an almost exact copy of his famous crucifix in the Chiesa di S. Domenico (p. 485). Tragically, some of Cimabue's frescoes in the transepts and apse have so deteriorated that they now look like photographic negatives. Pietro Lorenzetti decorated the left transept with his outstanding *Crucifixion, Last Supper,* and *Madonna and Saints.* Also stunning are Simone Martini's frescoes in the first chapel off the left wall, depicting the life of St. Martin. Descend through a door on the right side of the apse to enter the room housing St. Francis's tunic and sandals. **St. Francis's tomb,** the inspiration for the entire edifice, lies below the lower church. The coffin itself was hidden in the 15th century for fear that the war-mongering *Perugini* would desecrate it. The rediscovery of the Neoclassical tomb was met with disdain from friars in 1818; a simplified version came in 1935. The stone coffin sits above the altar in the crypt, surrounded by the sarcophagi of four of the saint's dearest friends. (☎075 819 00 84. *Tours given by monks begin outside lower basilica daily 9am-noon and 2-5:30pm. Arrange in advance; call or visit info window across from entrance to lower basilica. €1. Info window open daily 9am-noon and 2-5pm. Lower basilica and tomb open daily 6am-6:45pm. Upper basilica open daily 8:30am-6:45pm. Modest dress required.*)

ROCCA MAGGIORE. The dramatic Rocca Maggiore looms uphill from the duomo. Check out the view of the town and the Basilica di San Francesco from the sun-baked gravel lot outside the Rocca, or better yet, pay a nominal fee to enter the fortress and crawl through a 50m tunnel to Torre Poligonale. The ◼view is breathtaking with miles of countryside stretching in all directions but the trip through the tunnel is not recommended for claustrophobes. (☎075 81 52 92. *From P. del Comune, follow V. S. Rufino to P. S. Rufino. Continue up V. Pta. Perlici and take 1st left up a narrow staircase. Open daily 10am-sunset. Closed in bad weather. €1.70, students €1. All-inclusive ticket for Pinacoteca, Foro Romano, and Rocca €5.20; students €4.*)

BASILICA DI SANTA CHIARA. While the exterior shimmers with pale stone, the interior of the Basilica di Santa Chiara is a beautifully subdued example of early Gothic architecture. It stands at the opposite end of Assisi from the Basilica di San Francesco, on the site where St. Francis attended school. The church shelters the tomb and relics of St. Claire, as well as the painted crucifix that supposedly spoke to St. Francis, instigating his conversion. The nuns in the convent are sworn to seclusion. (☎075 81 22 82. *Open daily 6:30am-noon and 2-7pm. Free.*)

DUOMO (CHIESA) DI SAN RUFINO. V. S. Rufino climbs steeply from P. del Comune between closely packed houses, opening onto P. S. Rufino to reveal the squat duomo and its massive bell tower. San Rufino's tomb is not particularly exciting; a glimpse through the church's glass-tiled floor should suffice. (☎075 81 27 12. *Open daily 7am-1pm and 3-6:30pm. €3, students €2.50; includes museum and crypt.*)

OTHER SIGHTS. From Basilica di San Francesco, V. S. Francesco snakes between medieval buildings and their 16th-century additions. Not far along, the pink facade of the **Palazzo Vallemani** shelters the **Pinacoteca.** The museum contains works by important Umbrian artists such as Dodo Dodi and a collection of Renaissance frescoes lifted from city gates and various shrines. Up the street, the colorfully frescoed **Oratorio dei Pellegrini** (Pilgrim's Oratory) is worth a brief peek. Built in 1457, this oratory was used to care for the health of poor pilgrims who came to visit the tomb of St. Francis. At the end of the street, P. del Comune sits on the **Foro Romano.** Enter from the crypt of St. Nicholas on V. Portica and walk among the columns and statues of the old Roman forum, which stretches the length of P. del Comune. (*Forum* ☎075 81 30 53; *Pinacoteca 075 81 20 33. Both open daily Mar. 16-Oct. 15 10am-1pm and 2-6pm, Oct. 16-Mar. 15 10am-1pm and 2-5pm. €2.50 for each sight, students €2.*) Above ground sits the **Tempio di Minerva,** a majestic Roman temple turned into a Christian church that is still guarded by six crumbling Corinthian columns. (*Open daily 7am-7pm.*) Finally, just off the square, don't miss the beautiful and silent **Chiesa Nuova,** which features high domes, a rounded central apse, and heavily frescoed interior. (☎075 81 23 39. *Open daily 6:30am-noon and 2:30-5pm.*)

⬛ ENTERTAINMENT

All of Assisi's religious festivals involve feasts and processions. An especially long, dramatic performance marks **Easter Week.** A mystery play reenacts the Deposition from the Cross on Holy Thursday, and traditional processions trail through town on Good Friday and Easter Sunday. Assisi welcomes spring with the **Festa di Calendimaggio** (first Th, F, and Sa of May) with an invocation of the

UMBRIA AND
LE MARCHE

medieval spirit. A queen is chosen and dubbed *Primavera* (Spring), while the upper and lower quarters of the city compete in a clamorous musical tournament. Ladies and knights overtake the streets in celebration of the young St. Francis, who wandered the streets of Assisi singing serenades at night. Legend has it that it was on one such night that he encountered a vision of the *Madonna della Povertà* (Lady of Poverty). Classical music concerts and organ recitals occur once or twice each week from April to October in the various churches. October 4 marks the **Festa di San Francesco**, which kicks off in **Chiesa di Santa Maria degli Angeli**, the site of St. Francis's death. Aside from various religious ceremonies, the highlight of this celebration is the offering of oil for the cathedrals' votive lamp. Each year a different region of Italy offers the oil, and traditional dances and songs.

▶ DAYTRIPS FROM ASSISI

EREMO DELLE CARCERI AND MONTE SUBASIO

From P. Matteotti, exit the city through Pta. Cappuccini and turn immediately left up the dirt road, parallel to the city wall. At the Rocca Minore, follow the trail uphill to the right. A little over halfway up, the trail flattens and follows the flank of the mountain, giving spectacular views of the fertile valley below. Follow the paved road to the right, instead of crossing and taking the trail uphill. Loose rocks can make the descent difficult. For an easier walk (or drive) from Pta. Cappuccini, follow the dirt trail next to the paved road uphill and take shortcuts via dirt roads on the right to bypass long, winding turns for cars. ☎ 075 81 23 01. Open 6:30am-5pm. Taxis make the climb for €6 from the centro.

An intense but gorgeous 1hr. hike up Monte Subasio reveals the inspiring sanctuary ◪**Eremo delle Carceri** where St. Francis often retired in prayer. Though cars crowd the front gates, once inside visitors can relax among shady trees. The central courtyard gives access to the **Grotta di San Francesco**, a series of tiny cells and chapels where St. Francis slept and prayed. (Modest dress required, so bring a scarf or other appropriate attire in addition to hiking clothes.) The trails that run through the natural beauty of Monte Subasio, where St. Francis so often retreated, can be easily navigated with a Kompass map (€6.20) or the less-detailed Club Alpino Italiano map (€4.65), available from any bookshop or newsstand in Assisi.

Several churches associated with St. Francis and St. Claire stand in the immediate vicinity of Assisi. A 15min. stroll down the steep road outside Pta. Nuova leads to the **Convent of San Damiano**, where St. Francis heard his calling and later wrote the *Canticle of the Creatures*. (☎ 075 81 22 73. Open daily 6:30am-noon and 2-7pm.) The train to Assisi passes **Basilica di Santa Maria degli Angeli**, a church inside a church. From Assisi, take the frequent bus marked S. M. degli Angeli from P. Matteotti, Largo Properzio, or P. Unità d'Italia and get off one stop after the train station. From the train station, exit left and take the first left, over the tracks, on Viale Patrono d'Italia. The basilica is 10min. ahead on the left. This structure, with a Renaissance facade and Baroque interior, encompasses two buildings that used to sit quietly in the woods until the basilica was constructed in the 15th century. St. Francis built the small **Porziuncola** chapel and instituted the annual **Festa del Perdono** here on August 2. The **Cappella del Transito**, the small Benedictine cell in the right transept, is the site of St. Francis's death. In order to overcome temptation, St. Francis supposedly flung himself on the thorny rosebushes in the garden just outside the basilica, staining the leaves eternally red. Through the rose garden lies the **Museo di Santa Maria degli Angeli**, which houses relics from the Porziuncola chapel. (☎ 075 805 14 32. Basilica open daily 6:15am-8pm, July-Sept. until 9pm. Museum open daily 9am-noon and 3:30-6:30pm. Free.)

SPELLO
☎ **0742**

Nestled on the slopes of Monte Subasio, medieval Spello's urban planning began before the time of Augustus and was completed by 1 BC. Today, travelers wander the narrow streets of this beautiful hill town amid centuries-old wine cellars, Roman ruins, and churches brimming with art. The main gate to the city, **Porta Consolare,** dates from the Augustan age and attests to Spello's Roman roots. The **Chiesa di Santa Maria Maggiore** in P. Matteotti, built on the ruins of a Roman temple, displays flowing stone sculptures. Floor-to-ceiling frescoes done by Pinturicchio in 1501 adorn the Baglioni chapel. (Open daily 8:30am-noon and 2:30-7pm.) Farther up is the **Chiesa di Sant'Andrea,** currently being remodeled, which holds a medieval oil painting of a crucifix by a follower of Giotto. Between the two churches, the **Pinacoteca Civica,** P. G. Matteotti, 10, displays Renaissance gold-leaf pieces and a rare Christ with moveable arms. The **Arco di Augusto** stands solidly on V. Giulia, a testament to Emperor Augustus's declaration that this city was his "most splendid colony." Both **Via Torri di Properzio** and **Via Torre Santa Margherita** were named for the former guard towers still standing on these roads. Every February the **Festival of the Olive and Bruschetta** is held with the intent of improving olive picking and pressing techniques as well as spreading word of the town's high quality product. During the **Infiorate,** a June festival which takes place the night before the feast of Corpus Domini, flower petals are used to create 80 beautiful pictures and designs throughout Spello's charming streets. The town wakes up to this delightful sight on the morning of the feast.

By **bus,** Spello *centro* can be reached from Foligno (30min., 15 per day); Spello *borgo* can be reached from Assisi (15min., 7 per day) and Perugia (45min., 5 per day). By **train,** Spello lies on the Perugia-Foligno line, which runs from Perugia (45min., 1-3 per hr., €2.05). From the **train station,** follow V. Marconi uphill, turn right at the T-intersection, right on V. Centrale Umbra, then left on V. Roma to reach the city gates. Bear right after the arch on V. Sant'Anna and follow signs to *centro*. The **tourist office,** P. Matteotti, 3, has a helpful **map** that includes a city guide. (☎0742 30 10 09; prospello@libero.it. Open daily 9:30am-12:30pm and 3:30-5:30pm.) Town services include a **pharmacy** in P. della Repubblica (☎0742 30 14 88), **bike rental,** V. Centrale Umbra (☎0742 65 11 01), and the **police** (☎0742 65 11 15). A **bank** (☎0742 65 14 86; Open M-F 8:20am-1:20pm and 2:30-3:30pm), **ATM,** and **post office** (☎0742 80 08 40; open M-F 8am-6:30pm, Sa 8am-12:30pm) are located in P. della Repubblica, just past the tourist office on V. Garibaldi.

With tourism on the rise, Spello is outgrowing its limited hotels and restaurants. For magnificent views and good lodgings in the *centro*, try **Il Cacciatore ❸,** V. Giulia, 42. Follow V. Cavour as it turns into V. Garibaldi, then turn right on V. Giulia. Large bedrooms with refined stone floors and matching wood furniture, all with bath and TV, are steeped in mouth-watering aromas from the restaurant downstairs. (☎0742 65 11 41, fax 30 16 03. Singles €45; doubles €75; triples €85. MC/V.) Just outside the city walls, a manageable walk from the *centro*, sits the modern **Hotel Il Portonaccio ❸,** V. Centrale Umbra, 46, at the intersection of V. Centrale Umbra and V. Roma. Rooms are cheaper but smaller than those at Il Cacciatore. (☎0742 65 13 13. Singles €42; doubles €62. AmEx/MC/V.) From the train station, keep to V. Centrale Umbra to reach the campgrounds of **Campeggio Subasio/Rifugio La Spella ❶.** (☎3336 62 96 80. Open Apr.-Sept. €6 per person, €6 per tent.) Alimentari and cafes filled with cheap snacks and drinks line V. Cavour, but for a more substantial meal, **Ristorante La Cantina ❷,** V. Cavour, 2, serves delicious, simple food. Service is so good, the waitstaff might be mind-readers. (☎/fax 0742 65 17 75. *Primi* €5-8, *secondi* €5-12. Open M-Tu and Th-Su 12:30-2:30pm and 7:30-10pm. MC/V.) From V. Guilia, turn right on Vco. del Fontanello to reach **Il Trombone ❸,** V. Fontanello, 1. Though the food isn't remarkable, the view from the shaded patio far surpasses that of any other eatery in town. (☎ 0742 30 10 06. *Primi* €6-11, *secondi* €8-14.) Just past S.M. Maggiore, **Ristorante Il Molino ❸** provides shaded outdoor seating and local favorites such as *Tagliatelle alla Molino* (€7.50).

SPOLETO   ☎ 0743

A magnificent gorge and thick walls surround Spoleto, sheltering a town comprised of narrow, winding streets, and fine medieval and Roman monuments. Though Spoleto is one of Umbria's picture-perfect hill town stops, until a mere 43 years ago, it was only the gorge—spanned by the 14th-century Ponte delle Torri—that attracted significant tourist attention. In 1958 composer Giancarlo Menotti selected Spoleto as the trial site for a summer arts festival, and his *Festival dei Due Mondi* (Festival of Two Worlds) hasn't left since.

🖪🔃 TRANSPORTATION AND PRACTICAL INFORMATION

The **train station** (☎ 0743 485 16) is in P. Polvani. Its ticket window is open daily 6am-8pm. **Luggage storage** is available (see **Practical Information**). Trains run to: Ancona (2hr., 10 per day, €7.90); Assisi (40min., 5 per day, €2.40); Orte (1hr., 6 per day, €8.26); Perugia (1½hr., 7 per day, €3.50); and Rome (1½hr., every 1-2hr., €6.82). Trains also run to Assisi and Perugia via Foligno. **SSIT buses** (☎ 0743 21 22 09; www.spoletina.com) depart from P. della Vittoria to Foligno (45min., M-F 6 per day, €2.60) and Perugia (2hr., 2 per day, €5.40). **Taxis** are in P. della Libertà (☎ 0743 445 48), in P. Garibaldi (☎ 0743 499 90), and at the train station (☎ 0743 22 04 89).

Have patience with Spoleto's narrow, cobblestone streets; a map, available from the tourist office in **Piazza della Libertà,** makes them more navigable. To get there from the train station, take an ATAF bus (direct to *centro*, €0.80). Buy tickets at the newsstand in the station. From **Corso Mazzini,** turn left up **Via del Mercato** to **Piazza del Mercato,** the bustling center. Many streets radiate from P. del Mercato. **Via del Municipio** runs to **Piazza del Municipio** and **Piazza Campello,** while **Via Saffi** leads to **Piazza del Duomo.** Most of the city's sights are in these three squares.

The **tourist office,** P. della Libertà, 7, offers detailed info about tours and lodgings and English and German maps of the city and nearby trails. (☎ 0743 23 89 20 or 23 89 21; info@iat.spoleto.pg.it. Open Apr.-Oct. M-F 9am-1pm and 4-7pm, Sa-Su 10am-1pm and 4-7pm; Nov.-Mar. M-F 9am-1pm and 3:30-6:30pm, Sa 10am-1pm and 3:30-6:30pm, Su 10am-1pm.) The **bank, Cassa di Risparmio di Spoleto,** P. Mentana, 3, just off C. Mazzini, has a 24hr. **ATM.** (Open M-F 8:20am-1:20pm and 2:50-3:50pm, Sa 8:20-11:50am.) In case of **emergency,** call ☎ 113; or an **ambulance** at ☎ 118. The **police** (☎ 0743 22 38 87) are located at V. dei Filosofi, 57. To reach the **Farmacia Scoccianti,** on V. L. Marconi (☎ 0743 22 32 42), head straight from the train station and then take the first right. **Internet** is available at **Zeppelin Pizza, Internet Point,** in P. della Libertà (see **Food**). There is a **post office** at V. L. G. Matteotti, 2. (☎ 0743 40 373. Open M-F 8:10am-6pm, Sa 8am-12:30pm.) **Postal Code:** 06049.

🛏🍴 ACCOMMODATIONS AND FOOD

Finding accommodations is almost impossible during the summer music festival (the last week of June and the first week of July). Contact **Consploeto,** P. della Libertà, 7, for help in finding a room. (☎ 0743 22 07 73; www.consploeto.com. Open M-Sa 9am-1pm and 3-7pm). Prices are higher during the festival. 🏆**Hotel Panciolle ❹**, V. del Duomo, 3, has hallways filled with beautiful wooden furnishings. (☎/fax 0743 456 77. Breakfast €5. Singles €40; doubles €55; triples €65.) **Albergo Due Porte ❹**, P. della Vittoria, 5, is a 10min. walk from the train station; follow Viale Trento e Trieste and bear right into P. della Vittoria. The hotel is just before the

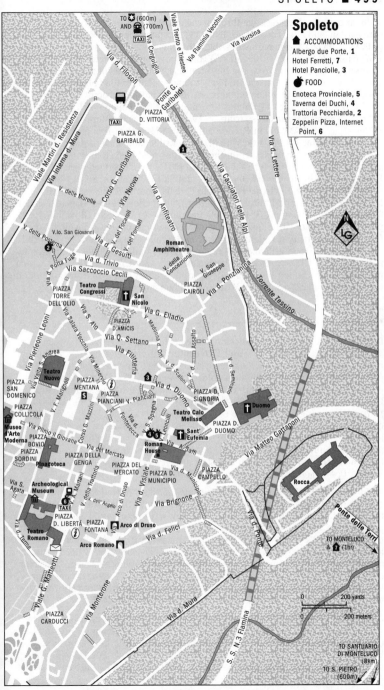

Spoleto

🏠 ACCOMMODATIONS
Albergo due Porte, 1
Hotel Ferretti, 7
Hotel Panciolle, 3

🍎 FOOD
Enoteca Provinciale, 5
Taverna dei Duchi, 4
Trattoria Pecchiarda, 2
Zeppelin Pizza, Internet Point, 6

walls to the left of the passage through the city gates. Friendly management, private garden, and large rooms with bath, TV, and phone make this a pleasant stop. (☎ 0743 22 36 66. Wheelchair accessible. Breakfast included. Singles €40; doubles €57; triples €75; quads €100. MC/V.) High above Spoleto, **Hotel Ferretti ❸**, Loc. Monteluco, 20, is 5min. from the bus stop that runs uphill roughly every hr. (or walk 30min. on trail #1). It's more likely to have openings than places downtown, plus, there's a piano in the common room. Rooms have bathroom, TV, and phone. (☎ 0743 498 49, fax 22 23 44. Singles €45; doubles €59. Required half pension.)

An **open-air market** sells fresh fruits and vegetables in P. del Mercato. (Open M-Sa 8:30am-1pm.) A **STANDA** is in P. Garibaldi. (Open M-Sa 9am-1pm and 4-8pm.) The pleasant ▧**Taverna dei Duchi ❷**, V. Saffi, 1, cooks its handmade pastas perfectly *al dente*. Don't fill up completely on the superior bread basket, and try the simple *spaghetti alla bolognese* for €5.50. (☎ 0743 403 23. Tender grilled meats €5-11.50. Pizza from €6, evening only. Open M-Th and Sa 12:15-7:30pm. MC/V.) Locals frequent ▧**Zeppelin Pizza, Internet Point ❶**, in P. della Libertà, for pizza (from €1), filling *panini* (€2-4), and Internet (€3 per hr.), all at cheap prices. (Open 10:30am-3:30pm and 5-9:30pm. MC/V.) **Trattoria Pecchiarda ❸**, Vco. San Giovanni, 1, is a pretty place to eat, with a spacious, plant-filled patio. From P. Garibaldi, follow C. Garibaldi, turn right on V. della Posterna, and turn left up the stairs. (☎ 0743 22 10 09. *Primi* and wood-grilled *secondi* €7-12. Open daily 1-3:30pm and 8pm-midnight. AmEx/MC/V.) At **Enoteca Provinciale ❸**, V. Saffi, 7, near the Pinacoteca museum, torch lamps burn outside as diners enjoy food on sturdy wooden benches. (☎ 0743 22 04 84. Open M and W-Su 11am-3pm and 7-11pm. AmEx/MC/V.)

ⓖ SIGHTS

DUOMO. Spoleto's Romanesque cathedral was built in the 12th century and later augmented by a portico (1491) and 17th-century interior redecoration. Eight rose windows, the largest one bearing the symbols of the four evangelists, animate the elegant facade. Inside, brilliantly-colored scenes by Fra Filippo Lippi fill the domed apse. Check out the 15th-century Cappella dell'Assunta covered in eroding frescoes and the more lavish 17th-century Cappella dell'Icone. ▧*The Annunciation* in the lower left of the fresco cycle is particularly stirring. Lorenzo de' Medici commissioned Lippi's tomb, which was decorated by the artist's son, Filippino, and is now in the right transept. The soaring bell tower is a mixture of styles and materials: stone blocks, fragments of inscriptions, friezes, and other remnants of the Roman era combine to form this structure. *(Down shallow flight of steps from Casa Romana. Open daily 8:30am-12:30pm and 3:30-7pm.)*

ROCCA AND PONTE DELLE TORRI. The **papal fortress,** named **Rocca,** up V. Saffi from P. del Duomo, sits on the hillside above Spoleto. This fortress served as a high-security prison until 1982, used during WWII to confine Slavic and Italian prisoners. In 1943 the prisoners staged a dramatic escape to join the partisans in the Umbrian hills. The Rocca is under perpetual renovation (one day it will house a museum), but thin scaffolds do not detract from its solid stone walls. On the far side of the Rocca is the massive ▧**Ponte delle Torri,** a stunning achievement of 14th-century engineering built on an ancient Roman aqueduct. Ten 80m arches support the bridge, and the view across the Tessino gorge is riveting. *(Open M-F 10am-1pm and 3-7pm, Sa-Su 10am-7pm. Guided tours every hr. ☎ 0743 437 07. €4.65.)*

CHIESA DI SANT'EUFEMIA. Situated on the grounds of the former bishop's residence, this church was constructed in the 12th century. Sweeping arches and concentric decorations on the heavy portals attest to the heavy influence of Romanesque architecture on Spoleto's artists. *(Left from P. del Duomo, in P. Archi Vescovile. Enter off V. Saffi. Open M and W-Sa 10am-1pm and 4-7pm, Su 10:30am-6pm. €2.50.)*

THE MUSEUM OF MODERN ART. The fairly impressive permanent collection here includes early works by Moore, Consacra, Pomodoro, Leoncillo, and Calder. *(Follow V. Mercato as it turns into V. Giovane and go down a flight of stairs. The museum lies straight ahead. ☎0743 464 34. Open daily Mar. 16-Oct. 14 10:30am-1pm and 3:30-7pm; Oct. 15-Mar. 15 10:30am-1pm and 3-5:30pm. €4, 15 to 25 or over 65 €3, 7-14 €1.50. Ticket including Pinacoteca and Casa Romana €6, €4, and €1.50.)*

ROMAN RUINS. Spoleto's classical ruins, a testament to the city's prominence in Roman times, are found mainly in P. della Libertà. The well-preserved **theater** stands just beyond the Roman walls. Take V. S. Agata from the piazza to reach the entrance of the adjacent **Museo Archeologico,** which houses ceramic and statuary artifacts from the area. *(☎0743 22 32 77. Open daily 8:30am-7:30pm. €2. EU citizens 18-25 €1, EU citizens under 18 or over 65 free.)* The **Arco Romano,** at the top of V. Monterone, once marked the town's entrance. Farther along, the **Arco di Druso** celebrated Emperor Druscu's military triumphs and led to the forum (now P. del Mercato).

CASA ROMANA. Duck into the first-century "Roman house," ancient home to Vespasia Polla, Emperor Vespasian's mother. *(Beneath city hall, entrance at V. di Visiale, 9. From P. del Duomo, take right on V. del Duomo, then 1st left. ☎0743 22 46 56. Open daily Mar.16-Oct.14 10am-8pm; Oct.15-Mar.15 8am-6pm. €2.50, 5 to 25 or over 65 €2, 7-14 €1. Ticket including Museum of Modern Art and Pinacoteca €6, €4, and €1.50 available; see above.)*

PINACOTECA. A small museum with half a dozen rooms houses works by Umbrian artists from the middle ages and on. The museum has made a permanent move to Palazzo Spada in P. Sordini, so ignore the outdated street signs pointing to the city hall. *(☎0743 459 40. Open daily Mar.16-Oct.14 10:30am-1pm and 3:30-7pm; Oct.15-Mar.15 10:30am-1pm and 3-5:30pm. €3, 5 to 25 or over 65 €2.50, 7-14 €1.50. Ticket including Museum of Modern Art and Casa Romana available; see above.)*

MONTELUCO. The climb along Spoleto's "mountain of the sacred grove" crosses over Ponte delle Torri and through the shade of a canopied forest. Then, the zigzag footpath passes tiny mountain shrines and a few spots with downhill views. At the crest of the mountain are hotel-restaurants, a flat grass clearing perfect for picnics, and the tiny 13th-century **Santuario di Monteluco**—once the refuge of St. Francis of Assisi and St. Bernadino of Siena. *(Open 9am-noon and 3-6pm.)* The path back passes the churches of **San Giuliano** and **San Pietro.** Rain renders the return path a rocky, impassable stream, so it's best to travel on a sunny day or when buses are running. *(Buses leave P. della Libertà for Monteluco every 1½hr., mid-June to early Sept. Cross the Ponte delle Torri and follow the stairs up to trail #1, which leads to the sanctuary.)*

🎵 ENTERTAINMENT

The 🖼**Spoleto Festival** (known as the **Festival dei Due Mondi,** or Festival of Two Worlds) has become one of the world's most prestigious international arts events. Each June and July it features concerts, operas, and ballets, and also brings film screenings, modern art shows, and local craft displays. Purchase tickets beginning in late April from the ticket office at P. della Libertà, 12. (☎0743 05 19; boxoffice@spoleto.festival.it. Open daily 9am-1pm and 3-7pm.) During the festival, box offices at **Piazza del Duomo, Teatro Nuovo,** and **Rocca Albornoziana** open 1hr. before the start of most performances in addition to regular hours (Tu-Su 10:30am-1pm and 4-7pm). Advance bookings are recommended. For more details write to the **Associazione Festival dei Due Mondi,** Biglietteria Festival dei Due Mondi, 06049 Spoleto, Italia. The renowned **Stagione del Teatro Lirico Sperimentale di Spoleto,** an experimental opera season, runs from late August to September. The **Istituzione Teatro Lirico Sperimentale di Spoleto,** P. G. Bovio, 1, provides info (☎0743 22 16 45).

UMBRIA AND LE MARCHE

▶ DAYTRIP FROM SPOLETO

TREVI

Take a SSIT bus from Foligno, the branching point for the Rome-Florence line (30min.; M-Sa 8 per day; last bus to Trevi 7pm, last bus to Foligno 6:30pm). Foligno train schedule is posted outside the Trevi tourist office and at the tabacchi next to P. Garibaldi in Trevi.

Removed and unhurried in comparison to more trafficked Umbrian hill towns, Trevi lies along near-vertical slopes striped with olive groves. The **Pinacoteca Rascolta d'Arte di San Francesco** houses a collection of religious Renaissance art, including some dramatic large-scale works. The unique **Museo della Civilta Dell'Ulivo** offers a history of the city's staple industry as well as free olive oil samples and Italian recipes. Follow V. S. Francesco from P. Mazzini to reach the museum. (☎0742 38 16 28; www.sistemamuseo.it. Open June-July Tu-Su 10:30am-1pm and 3:30-7pm, Aug. daily 10:30am-1pm and 3-6:30pm, Oct.-Mar. F-Su 10:30am-1pm and 2:30-5pm, Apr.-May and Sept. Tu-Su 10:30am-1pm and 2:30-6pm. €3, students €2.) The **Flash Art Museum,** V. P. Riccardi, 4, showcases avant-garde art in a 15th-century palazzo. The museum is associated with the trendy contemporary Italian art magazine *Flash* and hosts rotating exhibits of modern art. (☎0742 38 18 18; www.flashartonline.com. Open Tu-Su 3-7pm.) The **Illumination Procession,** one of Umbria's oldest religious festivals, takes place January 28.

Contact the **Pro Loco Tourist Office,** P. del Comune, 5, in the shadows of a large bell tower, for great free **maps** but otherwise out-of-date info. (☎0742 78 11 50; www.protrevi.com. Open daily 9am-1pm and 4-8pm.) Hotels in Trevi are expensive, but try **Il Terziere ❹,** V. Salerno, 1, left and uphill from P. Garibaldi, a pleasant hotel with an elegant, moderately priced restaurant. (☎0742 783 59. Singles €50; doubles €75; triples €87. Restaurant open M-Tu and Th-Su. AmEx/MC/V.)

TODI ☎075

According to legend, the ancient founders of Todi built their city at the site where an eagle dropped a tablecloth it had stolen from their dinner feast—high on an Umbrian cliff. The eagle is now the official symbol of this stately hill town, whose central yet insular location has made it an established retreat for Romans with class. Notable for its beautifully preserved medieval architecture, Todi also bears traces of its ancient past under Etruscan and Roman rule. Its three concentric protective walls reveal an early ground-swell as the city outgrew its boundaries. Shops selling postcards and film sit next to centuries-old edifices, and afternoon daytrippers stream from buses into the piazza honoring Jacopone di Todi, the town's patron saint, who once preached the renunciation of worldly possessions.

⛶ TRANSPORTATION AND PRACTICAL INFORMATION. Todi can be reached by bus from Perugia. The **bus station** is in P. Consolazione, a short ride on city bus A or a 1km walk uphill from the *centro.* **APM** (☎075 894 29 39 or 800 51 21 41) runs **buses** to and from Perugia (1¼hr.; M-Sa 8 per day; last bus from Todi 5pm, last bus from Perugia 7:30pm; €4.80) and to Orvieto (1½hr., M-Sa 5:50am-6:20pm, €4). Todi is also accessible by **train** on the Perugia-Terni line from Ponte Rio (45min., 13 per day, €2.70). The last train leaves from Terni at 8:10pm and from Perugia at 8:50pm; city bus C runs to P. Jacopone until 7:45pm. **Taxis** are available in P. Garibaldi (☎075 894 23 75), P. Jacopone (☎075 894 25 25), or by calling ☎0347 774 83 21. The **IAT Tourist Office,** P. Umberto I, has free **maps,** transportation schedules, and info on restaurants and lodgings. (☎075 894 25 26. Open daily 9:30am-

1pm and 3-6:30pm.) In case of **emergency,** call the **police** (☎112 or 075 895 62 43), an **ambulance** (☎118), or the **hospital** (☎075 88 581). **Farmacia Pirrami** (☎075 894 23 20) is at P. del Popolo, 46. (Open 9am-1pm and 4:30-8pm.) **Postal Code:** 06059.

⛏️🍴 ACCOMMODATIONS AND FOOD. Todi's accommodations force a trade-off between price and distance, with high-priced luxury hotels located inside the city walls and less expensive options a 20min. downhill walk from the center. The best budget option, however, is the **Casa per Ferie L. Crispolti ❸,** near P. del Popolo. Walking down V. del Duomo, turn right on V. di S. Prasse and left on V. Cesia, 96. Although religiously affiliated, there's a bar, the 8pm curfew is not strict, and men and women can share a room—28 are available, all spacious, each with four to five beds and bath. After sunset, darkness floods the windowless halls—pay attention to the location of the light switch outside your room! (☎075 894 53 37; www.crispoltiferie.it. Breakfast €2.50. Dorms €18-22; singles €30-37; doubles €46-58. AmEx/MC/V.) Hotels with comparable amenities and pricier rooms are 20min. downhill from the city center. From Pta. Romana, head down V. Cortesi, turn left on V. del Crocefisso, then right on V. Maesta dei Lombardi to find the three-star **Tuder ❹,** V. Maesta dei Lombardi, 13. The road lacks sidewalks and is full of curves and blind spots, making the trek potentially perilous after dusk, so traveling by day is preferable. The comfortable lounge and spacious rooms make up for the hike. (☎075 894 21 84; www.hoteltuder.com. All rooms with bath and TV. Breakfast included. Singles €40-60; doubles €60-95. AmEx/MC/V.)

Pick up provisions at **COOP,** at the intersection of V. Cortesi and V. del Crocefisso, 5min. outside Pta. Romana. A small €0.50 bottle of water from here can run up to €2 in the town center. (Open M-Sa 9am-8pm.) Grab a quick bite or stop for a full meal and good people-watching on the covered patio of **Pizzeria Italo ❶,** P. Bartolomeo d'Alviano, 1. (Pizza slices from €1. Lasagna from €4. Open Tu-Su 8am-3pm and 5:30pm-midnight. MC/V.) **Antica Hosteria de la Valle ❷,** V. Ciuffelli, 19, serves pleasant meals (*primi* €7-12, *secondi* €7-9, full course dinner €18-25) in a stately room of brick and wood. (☎075 894 48 48. Open Tu-Su noon-2:30pm and 7-10pm. MC/V.) Just down the street is a sitting area with park benches and a lovely view of the city and surrounding countryside.

◪ SIGHTS. At the foot of Todi's hills lies the Renaissance **Tempio di Santa Maria della Consolazione,** whose elegant green domes and detailed reliefs are thought to have been based on architectural genius Bramante's early draft for St. Peter's in Rome. Equally impressive are the magnificent baroque altarpiece and 12 enormous statues of the region's saints. (Open daily 9am-12:30pm and 2:30-7pm.) Follow a sinuous dirt path from P. della Consolazione—appropriately named Viale della Serpentina—or the less curvy V. della Consolazione to reach **La Rocca,** a ruined 14th-century castle that fronts a quaint public park. From the park, follow V. della Rocca directly to the towering **Tempio di San Fortunato.** Built by the Franciscans between the 13th and 15th centuries, the church features a high vaulted ceiling with decorative medallions, intricate sculptures and reliefs, and beautifully aged frescoes such as *The Madonna* and *Jesus With Angels* by Masolino da Panciale. The musky tomb of San Jacopone sits in its basement crypt, together with the tomb of the city's saints. (Open M 3-7pm, Tu-Su 9am-1pm and 3-7pm.)

An impressive staircase descends upon V. Mazzini and finally into the main square. **Piazza del Popolo** has become a link between modern and historical Todi, ringed by three palaces-turned-municipal-centers, half a dozen souvenir shops, two gelaterias, and a 900-year-old church. The 12th-century **duomo** is at the far end of P. del Popolo atop a flight of broad stone steps. The sumptuous rose window cuts through a huge interior fresco of the Last Judgement, and both attract attention with their intricate decoration. (Open daily 8:30am-12:30pm and 2:30-6:30pm.)

Across the piazza, the **Palazzo dei Priori**, built in the late 12th century, dominates the vista with its irregular trapezoidal tower and medieval facade. The long-standing seat of Todi's various rulers, the palace still serves as the town hall, with an appropriately mundane interior. The piazza remains the focal point of the town, just as it was in medieval times. The top floor of the **Palazzo del Capitano** and the 13th century **Palazzo del Popolo** (joined in the early 1900s for practical reasons) contain the **Museo Pinacoteca**, with excellent religious art from the fourth through eighth centuries and ancient Roman and Etruscan artifacts. Worthy of notice is the **Sala del Consiglio dei Priori**, frescoed with scenes of the legend of Todi's origin and a map of the diocese completed in 1613 which shows all the castles of the area. (☎ 075 894 41 48. Open Tu-Su 10:30am-1pm and 2:30-6:30pm. €3.50, under 15 €2, ages 15-25 or over 60 €2.50. AmEx/MC/V. An all-inclusive ticket allows you to see the bell tower of San Fortunato and the Roman cisterns. €6, reduced €5.)

ORVIETO ☎ 0763

A city upon a city, Orvieto was built in layers. Medieval structures stand over ancient subterranean remains: in the 7th century BC, Etruscans burrowed for *tufo* (a volcanic stone out of which most of the medieval quarter is built), creating a companion city beneath Orvieto's ground surface. Five centuries later Romans sacked and reoccupied the plateau, calling their "new" city, strangely enough, *urbus ventus* (old city), from which the name Orvieto is derived. Here fervent Christians planned their crusades, Thomas Aquinas lectured in local academies, and countless churches sprang up along the winding streets. Today the town is a tourist destination made popular by its spectacular duomo, brooding underground chambers, and delightful *Orvieto Classico* wine.

▐ TRANSPORTATION

Orvieto lies midway along the Rome-Florence train line. **Trains** depart to Arezzo (1hr., every hr. 7:30am-11:57pm., €5.80); Florence (2½hr., every hr. 7:30am-8:44pm, €9.90) via Cortona (45min.); Rome (1½hr., every hr. 4:27am-11:28pm, €6.82). **Luggage storage** is available (see **Practical Information**). **Buses** leave from P. Cahen or the train station. **COTRAL** (☎ 0763 73 48 14) runs buses to Viterbo (8 per day 6:20am-5:45pm, €2.80). Purchase tickets at the *tabacchi* in the train station. **ATC** (☎ 0763 30 12 24) runs buses to Perugia (1½hr., 5:55am, €6) and Todi (1hr., 1:40pm, €4.80). Purchase tickets at the funicular ticket office, at *tabacchi* on C. Cavour, or on the bus with a surcharge. **Taxis** are in P. Matteotti and Orvieto Scalo, or call ☎ 0763 30 19 03.

▐▌▐ ORIENTATION AND PRACTICAL INFORMATION

Across from the **train station**, the **funicular** (every 10min.; €0.80, with shuttle €0.90) travels up the hill to **Piazza Cahen**, where **ATC buses** stop. A shuttle connects P. Cahen and **Piazza del Duomo**. On foot, follow **Corso Cavour** for 10min. slightly uphill to its intersection with **Via Duomo**. The left branch leads to the duomo and surrounding museums; the right, to **Piazza del Popolo**. Sprinkled between V. Duomo and the **Piazza della Repubblica** along C. Cavour are most of the city's restaurants, hotels, and shops. The medieval and oldest surface-level district is past P. della Repubblica. The **tourist office**, P. del Duomo, 24, supplies great free **maps** and info on hotels, restaurants, and sights. The office also offers deals on underground tours of Orvieto and sells the **Orvieto Unica card** (€12.50, students €10.50), which includes an underground tour, round-trip ticket for funicular-minibus or five hours of parking, and entrance to Museo Faina, the

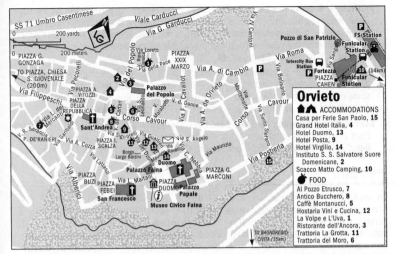

Orvieto

▲⌂ ACCOMMODATIONS
Casa per Ferie San Paolo, **15**
Grand Hotel Italia, **4**
Hotel Duomo, **13**
Hotel Posta, **9**
Hotel Virgilio, **14**
Instituto S. S. Salvatore Suore
    Domenicane, **2**
Scacco Matto Camping, **10**

🍎 **FOOD**
Al Pozzo Etrusco, **7**
Antico Bucchero, **8**
Caffè Montanucci, **5**
Hostaria Vini e Cucina, **12**
La Volpe e L'Uva, **1**
Ristorante dell'Ancora, **3**
Trattoria La Grotta, **11**
Trattoria del Moro, **6**

Torre del Moro, and the Cappella della Madonna di San Brizio, as well as discounts at participating businesses. (☎ 0763 34 17 72, fax 34 44 33. Open M-F 8:15am-1:50pm and 4-7pm, Sa-Su and holidays 10am-1pm and 3-6pm.) The **Tourist Information Point**, Borgo Largo Barzini, 7, just off V. Duomo, helps find accommodations and offers **traveler's check** and **currency exchange** for 5% commission. (☎ 0763 34 22 97. Open M-Sa 9am-1pm and 4-7pm.) **Luggage storage** is available at the train station ticket office. (€2.58 per 24hr. Open daily 5:55am-9pm.) In an **emergency**, call ☎ 113, an **ambulance** (☎ 118), or the **police** (☎ 112 or 0763 34 00 88), in P. della Repubblica. The **hospital** (☎ 0763 30 71) is across the tracks from the train station in Loc. Ciconia. A **post office** (☎ 0763 34 09 14) is on V. Ravelli. (Open M-Sa 8:10am-4:45pm.) **Postal Code:** 05018.

🏨 ACCOMMODATIONS

Hotel Virgilio, P. Duomo, 5 (☎ 0763 34 18 82; www.hotelvirgilio.com). Great prices for a hotel located just a few meters from the duomo. Many rooms have a view over the piazza, and all have TV, fan, and bath. Breakfast included. Singles €42-62; doubles €52-85; triples €110. AmEx/MC/V. ❸

Hotel Duomo, V. Maurizio, 7 (☎ 0763 34 18 87; www.orvietohotelduomo.com), 1st right from P. del Duomo, steps from the duomo. Beautiful but expensive rooms feature classy furniture and modern sculpture, A/C, satellite TV, modem jacks, and minibar. Breakfast included. English-speaking staff. Singles €60-70; doubles €85-105. AmEx/MC/V. ❺

Grand Hotel Italia, V. del Popolo, 13 (☎ 0763 34 20 65; www.bellaumbria.net/Grand-Hotel-Italia). Lounge in the comfortable lobby or on the 3rd-fl. terrace. Bright, well-maintained rooms with bath, satellite TV, minibar, and telephone. Breakfast included. Singles €50-67; doubles €85; suite €100, with private terrace €110. AmEx/MC/V. ❹

Casa per Ferie San Paolo, V. Postierla, 20 (☎ 0763 34 05 79 or 3496 93 21 21; cscorvieto@tiscalinet.it). Face the duomo and follow the street which runs to the right of Palazzo Papale for 10min. Enter gate on right; reception is in building on the left. A trek to P. del Duomo, but close to the station and simple rooms a great value. Phone in reception for common use. Curfew 8pm. Reserve 4-5 days ahead. Singles €20.65, with bath €25.85; doubles €46.50. Cash only. ❷

Instituto S. S. Salvatore Suore Domenicane, V. del Popolo, 1 (☎/fax 0763 34 29 10). Safely enclosed behind thick doors and overseen by kindly nuns. Decently priced rooms fill up quickly during high season and religious holidays, so reserve ahead. Breakfast €3. 2-night min. stay. Curfew 10:30pm, in winter 9:30pm. Closed July. Singles €45-50; doubles with bath €52. Cash only. ❹

Hotel Posta, V. Luca Signorelli, 18 (☎0763 34 19 09). Old building constructed on grand scale, somewhat past its heyday. Quirky mix of chipped paint and old furniture, some of it antique and some merely scuffed. Breakfast €6. Reserve 20 days ahead July-Aug. Singles €31, with bath €37; doubles €43/€56. Cash only. ❸

Scacco Matto Camping (☎0744 95 01 63, fax 95 03 73), on Lago Corbara, 14km from town. From station take local, infrequent Orvieto-Baschi bus at campgrounds. Beach and hot showers. €5.50 per person, €5.50 per tent, €3 per car. Cash only. ❶

🛒 FOOD

In antiquity, Orvieto was known as *Oinarea*, or "city where wine flows." The stream is still steady, with prices for bottles starting as low as €2.50. Pair a hearty wine with local treats like baked *lumachelle* (snail-shaped buns with ham and cheese), *tortucce* (fried bread dough), *mazzafegate* (sweet or salty sausages), and other foodstuffs with double consonants. The sociable, family-run **Panini Imbottiti,** V. del Duomo, 36, sells bottles of *Orvieto Classico* from €3.30. (Open M-Tu and Th-Sa 7:30am-noon and 5:15-9pm, W 7:45am-2pm.) To sample before investing in a whole bottle, stop by **Cantina Freddano,** C. Cavour, 5, which offers free wine-tasting. Bottles start at €4. (☎0763 30 82 48. Open daily 9:30am-7:30pm.)

🍴 **Hostaria Vini e Cucina,** V. del Duomo, 25 (☎0763 34 24 02), to the right of the duomo. Inventive, eclectic decorations, pillow-lined couches, and inexpensive food earn this *hostaria* a devoted clientele that fills seats quickly in the evening. Try the simple but satisfying *spaghetti pachino e basilico* (with cherry tomatoes and basil; €6). Pizza €3.50-7.50. *Primi* €5-7, *secondi* €7-13. Open daily 7-11pm. Cash only. ❷

🍴 **Trattoria La Grotta,** V. L. Signorelli, 5 (☎/fax 0763 34 13 48), to the right of the duomo. Feast on *pappardelle al cinghiale* (pasta with boar sauce; €8) and *tiramisù* (€4) and bask in the attentive service. *Primi* and *secondi* €4-13. Open Tu-Su noon-3pm and 7-10pm. AmEx/MC/V. ❷

Ristorante dell'Ancora, V. di Piazza del Popolo 7/11 (☎0763 34 27 66), offers a peaceful retreat from the busy main streets. Eat in intimate indoor rooms or opt to sit in the large, sheltered garden, which offers much-needed shade and cool breezes. *Primi* €8-10, *secondi* €6-13. Open daily noon-4pm and 6:30-10pm. AmEx/MC/V. ❸

La Volpe e L'Uva, V. Ripa Corsica, 2/A (☎/fax 0763 21 72 99), at the corner of V. della Pace, behind Palazzo del Popolo. Snug and neat interior, with excellent vegetarian fare as well as a variety of meat dishes, all €6-10. Open W-Su 1-11pm. MC/V. ❷

Trattoria del Moro, V. S. Leonardo, 7 (☎0763 34 27 63). From Piazza del Popolo facing C. Cavour, the trattoria is on the right. Good-sized portions for the price; try the *agnello* (lamb) *alla bracia* (€8.50). Small dining rooms have an intimate feel. *Primi* €4-5, *secondi* €6-8. Open M-Th and Sa-Su noon-3:30pm and 7-11pm. AmEx/MC/V. ❷

Al Pozzo Etrusco Ristorante, P. de' Ranieri, 1/A (☎0763 34 44 56). Follow V. Garibaldi from P. della Repubblica to P. de' Ranieri. Basic, hearty food, in a semi-sheltered dining space with an actual Etruscan well. *Primi* €4.50-7.50, *secondi* €5.50-11.50. Open M and W-Su noon-3pm and 7-10pm. AmEx/MC/V accepted for over €26. ❷

Ristorante Antico Bucchero, V. de' Cartari, 4 (☎0763 34 17 25). Escape C. Cavour to this car-free alley. *Orvietano* fare served in the dining room or outside under umbrellas. *Primi* and *secondi* €6-11. Open daily noon-3pm and 7-10pm. AmEx/MC/V. ❸

Caffè Montanucci, C. Cavour, 21 (☎0763 34 12 61). Eye-pleasing pastries—tarts, pie slices, and decadent chocolate concoctions—starting at just €0.50. Internet €3.10 for 30min. Open daily 7am-midnight; closed W Nov.-Apr. MC/V. ●

🔘 SIGHTS

📖 DUOMO. Designed in the late 13th century by Sienese architect Lorenzo Maitani, the facade of Orvieto's pride and joy is an example of the transitional Romanesque-Gothic style. With carved marble pillars, spires, sculptures, and mosaics, the duomo dazzles admirers with scrupulous details and brilliant use of color. Initially envisioned as a smaller chapel, it was later enlarged with a transept and nave. The bottom level features carved bas-reliefs of the Creation and Old Testament prophecies as well as the final panel of Maitani's *Last Judgment*. Set in niches surrounding the rose window by Andrea Orcagna (1325-1364), bronze and marble sculptures emphasize the Christian canon. Thirty-three architects, 90 mosaic artisans, 152 sculptors, and 68 painters worked for over 600 years to bring the duomo to this point, and the work continues—the bronze doors were only installed in 1970. The facade has been obscured behind scaffolding but is expected to be fully restored soon. *(For information call ☎0763 34 11 67. Duomo open M-Sa 7:30am-12:45pm and 2:30-7pm, Su and holidays 2:30-6:45pm. Crypt open weekdays 10am-noon. Free. Modest dress required.)*

📖Cappella della Madonna di San Brizio, also called the Cappella Nuova, off the right transept, includes Luca Signorelli's wall-to-wall, floor-to-ceiling frescoes of the Apocalypse. His vigorous craftsmanship, mastery of human anatomy, and dramatic compositions inspired Michelangelo in his work on the Sistine Chapel. Skeletons and muscular humans pull themselves out of the earth while apparitions of the damned swarm about in the unsettling *Resurrection of the Dead.* Beside it hangs the *Inferno,* depicting Signorelli as a blue devil embracing his mistress. Signorelli modeled the "Whore of Babylon," carried on his back above the pictured masses, after a woman who rejected his advances. The chapel also holds the gold-encrusted **Reliquario del Corporale** (chalice-cloth) from the miracle of Bolsena, said to have been soaked with the blood of Christ. *(Cappella open Apr.-Sept. M-Sa 10am-12:45pm and 2:30-7:15pm, Su 2:30-6pm; Mar. and Oct. M-Sa 10am-12:45pm and 2:30-6:15pm, Su 2:30-5:45pm; Nov. 1-Feb. 28 M-Sa 10am-12:45pm and 2:30-5:15pm, Su 2:30-5:15pm. Tickets and information at tourist office. €3, before 10am free.)*

UNDERGROUND CITY. The city's official tour of Etruscan Orvieto, Underground City Excursions, is the most complete and accessible tour available through the dark, twisted bowels of the city. The ancient Etruscan town Velzna was burrowed into the soft *tufa* of the cliff below modern Orvieto. Although Velzna was sacked by the Romans, its cisterns, mills, pottery workshops, quarries, wine cellars, and burial sites lie preserved beneath the earth. *(☎0763 34 48 91; speleotecnica@libero.it. 1hr. tours leave from the tourist office daily 11am, 12:15, and 5:15pm. €5.50, students €3.50.)*

PALAZZO PAPALE. From this austere, 13th-century "Palace of the Popes," Pope Clement VII rejected King Henry VIII's petition to annul his marriage with Catherine of Aragon, condemning both Catherine and English Catholicism to excommunication. Set back in the palazzo is the **Museo Archeologico Nazionale,** where visitors can examine Etruscan art from the area and walk into a restored tomb decorated with faded 4th-century frescoes. *(To the right of the duomo. Open daily 8:30am-7:30pm. €2, with tomb entrance €3; EU citizens under 18 or over 60 free.)* Above the archaeological museum is the **Museo dell'Opera del Duomo,** which displays art and cultural artifacts from the 13th through 17th. Featured pieces include Simone Martini's *Politico di S. Domenico,* Andrea Pisano's *Madonna and Child,* and Francesco Mochi's marble

Annunciation. Entrance requires guided tours. *(For reservations call ☎0763 34 35 92 or check out www.opsm.it. Open Tu and Th 10am-noon, Sa 11am-1pm and 3-6pm, and Su 10am-1pm and 3-6pm. €5. Ask for special rates when combined with duomo and Cappella di S. Brizio.)*

CHIESA DI SAN GIOVENALE. Built at the beginning of 1000, the city's oldest church was dedicated to the city's first bishop, represented in a fresco near the entry. Directly next to the doors on the left is a 14th-century "Tree of Life"—a family tree of the church's founders. Just inside the old city walls, the church offers stunning views of the countryside below. Graves of victims of the Black Death of 1348 fill the slope below P. San Giovanni. *(From P. della Repubblica, walk uphill along V. Filippeschi, which turns into V. Malabranca. The church is at the end of the street on the right.)*

CHIESA DI SANT'ANDREA. The church and its surrounding piazza mark the beginning of Orvieto's medieval quarter. Built upon the ruins of an Etruscan temple, the Romanesque Gothic church served as a community meeting place. The **crypt** on the right contains recently excavated remains from an underground Etruscan temple. *(In P. della Repubblica. Free. Modest dress required.)*

MUSEO CIVICO AND MUSEO FAINA. Ensconced in the Palazzo Faina directly oppos.te the duomo, the museums hold an extensive collection of Etruscan artifacts. Exhibits include collections of over 3000 coins, bronze urns, Roman ornaments, and red and black figure vases attributed to Athenian artists from the 6th century BC—all collected by Claudio Faina during hazardous excavations of local necropoli. *(Piazza del Duomo, 29. ☎ 0763 34 15 11. Open daily Apr.-Sept. 9:30am-6pm; Oct.-Mar. Tu-Su 10am-5pm. €4.50, students and seniors €3.)*

🎵 ENTERTAINMENT

Orvieto has no shortage of festivals. No matter when you come, locals are always celebrating: look for craft fairs, food and wine tasting events, and theater and music festivals. Spring brings the **Palio dell'Oca,** which has tested dexterity on horseback since medieval times. On Pentecost, 50 days after Easter, Orvieto celebrates the **Festa della Palombella:** at the stroke of noon, Campo della Fiera lights up with fireworks when a white dove descends across a wire to ignite the explosives. For two days the streets are lined with antiques and crafts. In June the **Procession of Corpus Domini** celebrates the Miracle of Bolsena, when a communion wafer is transformed into flesh and blood. A week of medieval banquets precedes the procession, when ladies and flag-wavers dance in the streets to period music. Also in June is the **Festa della Repubblica,** during which entertainers blast trumpets and make balloon animals for throngs of kids and tourists. From December 29 through January 5, **Umbria Jazz Winter** swings in theaters, churches and palaces, with the grand finale in the duomo. For details contact **Servizio Turistico Territoriale IAT dell'Orvietano,** P. Duomo, 24 (☎0763 34 19 11 or 34 36 58), or **Informazioni Turistiche** (☎0763 34 17 72, fax 34 44 33), at the same address.

🢂 DAYTRIP FROM ORVIETO

CIVITA DI BAGNOREGIO

Take the COTRAL bus from Piazza Cahen or from the funicular station to Bagnoregio P. Albana (50min.; M-Sa 9 per day, last bus leaves Bagnoregio at 4:40pm; €1). In the piazza, an EPF city bus goes to Civita di Bagnoregio, stopping at the base of the footbridge (or "Mercatello"). Walking, take C. Manzini to the right of the station, which turns into Viale Agosti. Follow to V. Tecchi for 15min. and turn right. Climb the sturdy uphill bridge to the city and enter through Pta. S. Maria. For bus schedules and information about the town, go to www.civitadibagnoregio.it.

Clinging to an outcrop of volcanic stone, Civita presents itself without warning, an island surrounded by a vast, eroded valley. A footbridge connects the tiny, fragile village to Bagnoregio, keeping it free of cars and undiscovered even by hill town connoisseurs. This millennia-old Etruscan town was once a prosperous city-state. It controlled the surrounding territories throughout the Middle Ages and stood on a paved road—a straight path to Rome and the Tiber Valley. Since then economic decline and the accelerating erosion of the clay beneath the stone have left Civita high and all but uninhabited, and it has long been known as *il paese che muore,* or the "dying town." Bicycles and tractors bring food and provisions to the town's 20-odd residents and the swank Italians, students, and tourists who sustain them.

Civita's social life centers around the **Piazza S. Donato,** in front of the commanding 8th-century **Chiesa S. Donato.** The church harbors a lovely altar and delicate frescoes from the school of Giotto. The road left of the piazza leads to a 16th-century **olive oil mill.** (Open daily 10am-10pm. Free, but donations encouraged.) Next door, the **Antico Frantoio** (open 8am-7pm) serves dozens of different *bruschette* (€2) with glasses of wine (€2-4). Around a right curve, the path leads to the grotto of **Madonna del Carcere,** a tomb buried inside an Etruscan cave once used as a Romans prison. Medieval houses line Civita's streets, ground-level doorways lead to subterranean wine cellars, and stone walls and stairways support clotheslines and flower pots. The ancient street grid is evident in the town's main thoroughfare, with narrow sidestreets that branch toward the cliff face before abruptly ending.

Those planning to spend the night should head to **Civita B&B ❹,** V. della Fraticella, 4. At Pta. S. Maria, take the first left, then turn right on V. del Cassero, and go up the stairs. Three bright, comfortable rooms overlook the main square. Half pension (€15) includes breakfast and full course dinner with the house wine. (☎0761 76 00 16 or 347 611 54 26; www.civitadibagnoregio.it. English, Spanish, and French spoken. Singles €40, with bath €42; doubles €62/€68; triples €73.) Downstairs from Civita B&B, **Trattoria Antico Forno ❷** offers simple but well-prepared dishes and outdoor seating in the summer. (☎0761 79 23 54. *Primi* €5-7, *secondi* €6-10. Open daily noon-3pm and 7-10pm.) At the bottom of the footbridge near the bus stop, tuck into filling regional staples like *cinghiale* (boar) and truffle pasta in the homey dining room of **Hostaria del Ponte ❸,** Loc. Mercatello, 11. (☎0761 79 35 65. *Primi* €5-6, *secondi* €8-11. Closed M. AmEx/MC/V.)

LE MARCHE

Green foothills separate the umbrella-laden beaches along the Adriatic Sea from the craggy Apennines. Remains of the Gauls, Picenes, and Romans fill the rural towns dotting these hills. The Renaissance geniuses Raphael and Donato Bramante left their legacy in Urbino, which, along with the palm-lined boardwalk of San Benedetto del Tronto, the untainted windy streets of Ascoli Piceno, and the hidden beauty of Ancona, form the highlights of unassuming Le Marche.

UMBRIA AND
LE MARCHE

PESARO
☎ 0721

Pesaro strikes a balance between hip Rimini and laid-back Fano, offering a blend of culture, couture, and sea-side serenity. Its historic center is appealing, its beaches relatively uncrowded, and though overpriced boutiques dominate the larger piazzas, Pesaro also has many back-alley bookshops and street concerts.

◼ TRANSPORTATION

The **train station** is at the end of V. Risorgimento and Viale della Liberazione. The ticket counter is open daily 6:10am-8:30pm. AmEx/MC/V. **Luggage storage** is available (see **Practical Information**). Trains depart to: Ancona (1hr., 55 per day 12:35am-11:51pm, €2.94); Bologna (2hr., 29 per day 5:35am-10:13pm, €7.40); Fano (15min., 44 per day 4:55am-10:56pm, €1.24); and Rimini (30min., 43 per day 4:48am-11:11pm, €2.40.) The **bus depot** (☎ 0721 324 01; cash only) is at Piazzale Gonzaga, 15. From the train station, turn right. Buses #10, 11, 14, 20, 30, 40, 50, 60, 70, 130, and C/S also stop at P. Matteotti, and run to Fano (15min., every 30min. 6:30am-9pm, €1) and Gradara. (20min., every hr. 6:08am-7:08pm, €1.25. Cash only.) **SOGET** (☎ 0721 54 96 20) runs buses ιο Urbino from the train station (55min.; M-Sa 11 per day 6:50am-8:05pm, Su 6 per day 8:30am and 2:20-8:20pm; €2.05). **Bucci** runs a bus to Tiburtina station in Rome from Piazzale Matteotti (4½hr., 6am, €20.75). Buy tickets on the bus. **Taxis** run outside the train station (☎ 0721 311 11; available 24hr.), P. del Popolo (☎ 0721 314 30), and P. Matteotti (☎ 0721 340 53). **Bicycle rental** (☎ 347 752 96 34) is available in Piazzale d'Annunzio, at the intersection of Viale Trieste and V. Verdi. (€2 per hr. Open 9am-midnight late Apr.-Sept. Cash only.)

◼ ◼ ORIENTATION AND PRACTICAL INFORMATION

From the **train station**, take **Via Risorgimento** and walk straight to reach **Piazza del Popolo**, the old city center. **Corso XI Settembre** runs west toward Chiesa di Sant'Agostino, while **Via San Francesco** runs east to **Piazzale Matteotti** and the bus station. **Via Rossini** runs straight toward **Largo Aldo Moro**, which leads to **Viale Repubblica, Piazzale Libertà**, and the sea. **Viale Trieste** runs along the beach. The **IAT Tourist Office** (☎ 0721 693 41; iat.pesaro@regione.marche.it), in P. della Libertà, to the right of the giant bronze globe, organizes guided tours of town sights. (Open daily in summer 8:30am-1:30pm and 3-7pm, in winter M-Sa 9am-1pm and 3:30-6:30pm.) For more guided tours, call ☎ 0721 38 77 14. The **Regional Tourist Office**, V. Rossini, 41 (☎ 800 56 38 00; www.turismo.pesarourbino.it), is past P. del Popolo on the left, off Largo Aldo Moro. It has info on the region, including tours and recommended sights. (Open M-Sa 9:30am-1pm and 4-7pm, Su and holidays 9:30am-12:30pm.) **Luggage storage** is near the "Taxis" sign outside the train station. (€3 for 1st 12hr., €2 for each additional 12hr. Open daily 6am-11pm. Cash only.) In case of **emergency**, call ☎ 113 or 0721 12 23 44, an **ambulance** (☎ 118), or **police** (☎ 0721 38 61 11). Speedy **Internet** is available at **Max3D**, V. Passeri, 177. (☎ 0721 351 22. Open M-Sa 9:30am-1pm and 3:30-10pm. €4 per hr. in the morning, €5 per hr. in the afternoon. Cash only.) The **post office** is at P. del Popolo, 28. (☎ 0721 43 22 85. Open M-F 8:30am-6:30pm, Sa 8:30am-12:30pm.) **Postal Code:** 61100.

◼ ◼ ACCOMMODATIONS AND FOOD

With many reasonably priced lodgings, Pesaro is a real low-season deal. High season runs mid-June to August, but even then bargains are available for the persistent. **Hotel Athena ❸**, Viale Pola, 18, is a 20min. walk from the train station. Follow Viale della Liberazione to Viale Mameli, then turn right; after the street

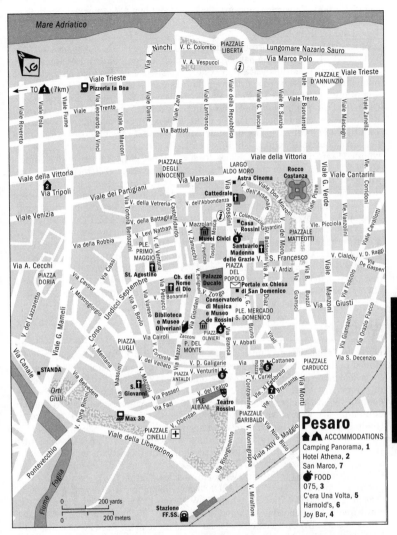

UMBRIA AND LE MARCHE

Pesaro

⛺▲ ACCOMMODATIONS

Camping Panorama, 1
Hotel Athena, 2
San Marco, 7

🍎 FOOD

075, 3
C'era Una Volta, 5
Harnold's, 6
Joy Bar, 4

changes to V. Fiume, turn left on V. Tripoli and walk one block; it's on the right. Rooms are sunny, with bath, phone, and TV. Best of all, they're 5min. from the beach. (☎0721 30 114, fax 338 78. Singles €35; doubles €50; triples €60. AmEx/MC/V.) To get to **San Marco ❹**, Viale XI Febbraio, 32, follow V. Risorgimento from the train station and bear right into Piazzale Garibaldi. Turn right on the busy Viale XI Febbraio. A friendly staff runs forty spacious rooms with squeaky-clean bath, phone, and TV. (☎/fax 0721 313 96; sanmarco@abanet.it. Breakfast included. Wheelchair accessible. Reception 24hr. Singles €40; doubles €65; triples €80. AmEx/MC/V.) **Camping Panorama ❶**, has free hot showers, electricity, and a pool. (7km north of Pesaro on Str. Panoramica toward Gabicce Mare. ☎/

fax 0721 20 81 45; www.panoramavillage.it. Take bus #14, 4 per day, from Piazzale Matteotti and stop at Fiorenzuola. Open May-Sept. €5.60-7.25 per person, €7-10 per tent. AmEx/MC/V.)

Most establishments surround Piazzale Lazzarini. A STANDA **supermarket** is at V. Canale, 41. (Open M-Sa 8am-8pm, Su 7am-2pm. AmEx/MC/V.) At the tavern-style trattoria **C'era Una Volta ❶**, V. Cattaneo, 26, just off Piazzale Lazzarini, the main attraction is the pizza, massive in both diameter and variety—there are over 75 options. (☎0721 309 11. Pizza €2.50-7.50. *Primi* €4.70-7.50, *secondi* €5-24. Open Tu-Su noon-2:30pm and 7pm-1am. AmEx/MC/V.) For authentic regional *vini*, cheeses, canned fish, salami, and oils, look no further than **075 ❶**, V. Rossini, 18. Enjoy the local art inside this chic *enoteca* or opt for outdoor seating in the palazzo's courtyard. (☎0721 649 16. Open M-Tu and Th-Su, in summer 6-11pm, in winter 11am-2pm and 5-9pm. Wines from €2.50 per glass, €9 per bottle. AmEx/MC/V.) Three doors down from Teatro Rossini snag some of **Harnold's ❶**, P. Lazzarini, 34, heavy, affordable fare. You may have to wait for service at the busy outdoor tables, but the filling food, ranging from fresh *panini* and salads to the "Big Ben" double-decker cheeseburger (€4.20) is well worth it. (☎0721 651 55. From P. del Popolo, follow V. Branca away from the sea. *Panini* €2-4.20. Open daily 8am-3am. Closed Su in winter. AmEx/MC/V.) Celebrate Pesaro's proximity to the Adriatic at **Trattoria da Sante ❸**, V. Bovio, 27, with delicious seafood pasta. (☎0721 336 76. Follow C. XI Settembre north from P. del Popolo and turn left on V. Bovio. *Primi* €6-8, *secondi* €8-10. Daily special €8. Cover €1. Reserve for weekend dinner. Open daily noon-2:30pm and 7-10:30pm. Cash only.) Try **Joy Bar ❶**, V. Pedrocchi, 11, for sweet cappuccino (€1) or a scoop of gelato with a variety of toppings (€1.50) and quirky decorating. (☎0721 338 95. Open daily 7am-8pm. Cash only.)

◎ SIGHTS

Piazza del Popolo, Pesaro's main square, holds the massive **Palazzo Ducale,** commissioned in the 15th century by Alessandro Sforza. (Open to visitors only for exhibitions held in the interior. Ask the tourist office about scheduled events.) The crafting of ceramics is a long-standing tradition in Pesaro, and the **Musei Civici** showcase centuries-worth of pieces from regional kilns, from prehistoric artifacts to colorful contemporary works. Nearby, a gallery holds the fiery *Fall of the Giants* by Guido Reni, four still-life paintings by Benedetto Sartori, and Bellini's remarkable *Incoronazione della Vergine,* an image surrounded by 15 panels depicting scenes ranging from Christ's Nativity to St. George (somewhat unimpressively) slaying an iguana-sized dragon. (V. Toschi Mosca, 29. From P. del Popolo, head down C. XI Settembre and turn right on V. Toschi Mosca. ☎0721 38 75 41; www.museicivicipesaro.it. Open July-Aug. Tu and Th 9:30am-12:30pm and 4-10:30pm, W and F-Su 9:30am-12:30pm and 4-7pm; Sept.-June Tu-W 9:30am-12:30pm, Th-Su 9:30am-12:30pm and 4-7pm. €4, combined ticket with Casa Rossini €7, 15-25 or over 65 €2/€3, under 14 free. Cash only.) Opera enthusiasts can spend hours in the **Casa Rossini.** The 1792 birthplace of Gioachino Rossini now houses a museum displaying photographs, theatrical memorabilia, letters, signed opera scores, and even Rossini's piano. Extend a visit with opera screenings in the brick cellar. (V. Rossini, 34. ☎0721 38 73 57. Open July-Aug. Tu and Th 9:30am-12:30pm and 4-10:30pm, W and F-Su 9:30am-12:30pm and 4-7pm; Sept.-June Tu-W 9:30am-12:30pm, Th-Su 9:30am-12:30pm and 4-7pm. €4, with Musei Civici €7; 15-25 or over 65 €2/€3, under 14 free. Cash only.) In the **Orto Giuli,** cobblestone streets wind up a tree-shaded hillside dotted with bases of old pillars, inscriptions, and weather-worn benches—a welcome change from the urban *centro,* but shabby in places. Call ahead to schedule a guided tour. (☎0721 319 90. Open daily 8am-4pm. Free.)

🎵 ENTERTAINMENT

Pesaro hosts the **Mostra Internazionale del Nuovo Cinema,** or the International Festival of New Films (☎ 0644 566 43), during the second and third weeks of June. Live theater and movie screenings are held in buildings along V. Rossini and at the **Teatro Comunale Sperimentale** (☎ 0721 38 75 48), an experimental theater on V. Rossini, just off P. del Popolo. Native composer Rossini founded the **Conservatorio di Musica G. Rossini,** P. Olivieri, 5, which sponsors events year-round. Contact **Teatro Rossini,** P. Lazzarini, 29 (☎ 0721 38 76 26), off V. Branca, for show times and prices. The annual **Rossini Opera Festival** begins in early August, with performances and concerts continuing through September. Reserve tickets at the box office of Teatro Rossini. (☎ 0721 380 02 94, fax 0721 380 02 21. Info line open M-F 10am-1pm and 3-6pm. Teatro Rossini box office open daily in Aug. 10am-noon and 4-6:30pm and at the theater 1hr. before the performance.) At **Astra Cinema** (☎ 0721 341 39), V. Rossini, 82, international blockbusters play soon after their initial release. (Showings nightly at 8:30 and 10:30pm. Tickets €7, reduced prices on W. Cash only.)

◪ DAYTRIP FROM PESARO

FANO

Fano is accessible from Pesaro by train (10min., 33 per day 4:30am-11:02pm, €1.24) and from Bucci by bus (€2). Buy bus tickets on the bus or in any tabacchi. For the beach, exit the train station right on V. Cavallotti and turn right on V. C. Battisti. To reach P. XX Settembre, the town center, turn left on V. Garibaldi from V. Cavallotti and then right on C. Giacomo Matteotti.

Fano is a sleepy town stretching 12km along the coast from Pesaro to some of the quietest seaside retreats. Even in summer, vacationers are scarce on the beaches to the north; further inland, a quiet *centro* offers relatively untouristed churches and many restaurants serving savory regional specialties. The town's oldest highlight is the **Arco d'Augusto,** a tall Roman arch from AD 2 squeezed between two buildings. Though hotels reserve most of the shoreline for their customers, the first entrance to the public **beach** sits across from Viale Adriatico, 150. (Open daily 5am-11pm. Free.) The **tourist office,** Viale Battisti, 10, provides a city **map** and a list of local events. (☎ 0721 80 35 34; www.turismofano.com. Open M-F 9am-1pm and 3:30-6:30pm, Sa and bank holidays 9am-1pm.) Although Fano makes a nice daytrip, overnighters can contact **Associazione Albergatori,** Viale Adriatico, 132, an organization that offers travelers free help with finding lodgings. (☎ 0721 82 73 76, fax 82 57 10. Open Oct.-May M-F 9am-12:30pm and 4-7pm; June-Sept. M-Sa 9am-12:30pm and 4-7pm, Su 9:30am-12:30pm.) A PuntoSMA **supermarket** is at V. Garibaldi, 53. (Open M-W and F-Su 8am-12:45pm and 5-8pm, Th 8am-12:45pm. MC/V.) **Trattoria Quinta ❸,** V. d'Adriatico, 42, at the northern edge of town, provides inexpensive, home-style meals. (☎ 0721 80 80 43. *Primi* €5.60-6, *secondi* €9. Cover €1.10. Open M-Sa noon-3pm and 7-11pm. MC/V.) Inland, **La Vecchia Fano ❸,** V. Vecchia, 8, serves authentic *Fanese* plates like *tagliolini al farro* (€6.50). Turn right off V. Cavour away from P. XX Settembre. (☎/fax 0721 80 34 93. *Primi* €6.50-7.50, *secondi* €6.50-18. Open Tu-Su noon-2:30pm and 7:30-10:30pm. AmEx/MC/V.)

URBINO ☎ 0722

With picturesque stone dwellings scattered along steep city streets and a turreted palace ornamenting its skyline, Urbino encompasses all that is classic Italy. The fairy-tale city is home to many art treasures and Renaissance monuments, including Piero della Francesca's *Ideal City* and Raphael's ornate house. The cultural beauty within the city walls is rivaled only by the magnificence of the region's surrounding mountains and valleys. Urbino's youthful vitality endures owing to its university population and stream of international visitors.

☞ TRANSPORTATION

Buses stop in Borgo Mercatale. Urbino's bus timetables are posted at the beginning of C. Garibaldi, in P. della Repubblica, under the portico at the corner bar. Blue **SOGET** (☎ 0722 223 33) **buses** run to P. Matteotti and the depot outside the train station in **Pesaro** (55min.; M-Sa 11 per day 6:40am-6:45pm, Su 6 per day 7:30am-8:05pm; €2.05). Buy a ticket on the bus. **Bucci** (☎ 0721 324 01) runs buses to **Rome** (5hr., 4pm, €22). **Luggage storage** is available (see **Practical Information**). **Taxis** are in P. della Repubblica (☎ 0722 25 50) and near the bus stop (☎ 0722 32 79 49).

◪ ⁊ ORIENTATION AND PRACTICAL INFORMATION

After winding up steep hills, the bus stops at **Borgo Mercatale,** below the city center. A short walk up **Via Mazzini** leads to **Piazza della Repubblica,** the city's hub, from which **Via Raffaello, Via Cesare Battisti, Via Vittorio Veneto,** and **Corso Garibaldi** branch out. Another short walk uphill on V. Veneto leads to **Piazza Rinascimento.**

Tourist Office: V. Puccinotti, 35 (☎ 0722 26 13; iat.urbino@regione.marche.it), across from Palazzo Ducale. Open M-F 9am-1pm and 3-6pm, Sa-Su 9am-1pm. **Info booth** in Borgo Mercatale. Open M-Sa 9am-6pm, Su 9am-1pm.

Budget Travel: CTS, V. Mazzini, 60 (☎ 0722 32 92 84), sells train or plane tickets and offers student tour info. Open M-F and Su 9am-1pm and 3:30-7:30pm, Sa 9am-1pm.

Luggage Storage: At the car parking office in Borgo Mercatale. €1 for 24hr. per bag. Open daily 8am-8pm. Cash only.

Laundromat: Powders, V. Battisti, 35. €3.75 per wash, €1.75 per dry. Open M-Sa 9am-10pm. Cash only.

Emergency: ☎ 113. **Ambulance** (☎ 118). **Police** (☎ 112).

Hospital (☎ 0722 301 11), on V. B. da Montefeltro, off V. Comandino. Bus #1 and 3 from Borgo Mercatale stop in front.

Internet: Tourist office allows free 10min. **The Netgate,** V. Mazzini, 17 (☎/fax 0722 24 62), has more than 20 computers. €4.98 per hr., students €3.98. Open M-F 10am-midnight, Sa noon-midnight, Su noon-11pm. Cash only.

Post Office: V. Bramante, 28 (☎ 0722 37 79 17), off V. Raffaello. **Currency exchange** and **ATM** available. Open M-F 8am-6:30pm, Sa 8am-12:30pm. **Postal Code:** 61029.

☗ ☖ ACCOMMODATIONS AND CAMPING

Cheap lodgings are relatively rare in Urbino, and reservations are a good idea. One alternative is to stay in Pesaro and make Urbino a daytrip.

Pensione Fosca, V. Raffaello, 67 (☎ 0722 32 96 22 or 0722 32 25 42), on top floor. 5 doors down from Casa di Raffaello (see **Sights**). Pleasant owner keeps 9 clean, plain rooms with soft pillows; some overlook a courtyard. Shared bath. Call ahead and arrange a check-in time. Singles €21; doubles €35; triples €45. Cash only. ❷

Hotel San Giovanni, V. Barocci, 13 (☎ 0722 28 27 or 32 90 55). From P. della Repubblica, head toward V. Mazzini and turn right, following the signs. Modern hotel in medieval building has simple rooms and small bathrooms. Restaurant downstairs. Closed last three weeks of July. Singles €24, with bath €34; doubles €35/€52. Cash only. ❸

Piero della Francesca, V. Comandino, 53 (☎0722 32 84 28, fax 32 84 27), in front of hospital. Bus #1 from Borgo Mercatale. A 15min. walk from P. della Repubblica. Follow signs for hospital. Modern rooms have balcony, bath, TV, and phone. Reception 24hr. Singles €31; doubles €52; triples €68. AmEx/MC/V. ❹

Hotel Italia, C. Garibaldi, 32 (☎0722 27 01; www.albergo-italia-urbino.it), just off P. della Repubblica. Just across the street from the towering Palazzo Ducale, rooms have A/C, TV, phone, minibar, and sparkling bath. Breakfast €8. Reception 24hr. Singles €41-67; doubles €62-114; triples €108-139. AmEx/MC/V. ❺

Camping Pineta (☎0722 47 10), on Loc. Monti delle Cesane, 2km from Urbino. Take bus #7 from Borgo Mercatale; ask to be let off at camping. Secluded sites have a great view of the city. Open 1 week before Easter-Sept. Office daily 9am-10pm. Free showers and electricity. €5 per person, €10.60 per tent; July-Aug. prices rise 10%. Cash only. ❶

FOOD

Urbino's cuisine is simple but delicious. *Caciotta* is a delicate cheese that pairs well with a glass of sparkling *Bianchello del Metauro*. **Supermarket Margherita,** at V. Raffaello, 37, has meats, cheeses, and packaged food but no fruits or veggies. (☎0722 32 97 71. Open M-Sa 7:30am-1:55pm and 4:30-8pm. Cash only.) For something a little greener, try **Frutta e Verdura,** 18/A V. Bramante. (Open M-W and F-Su 7am-1pm and 5-8pm, Th 7am-1pm. Cash only.) The university **Mensa** on V. Budassi, offers a huge dinner for around €4 with student ID. (Closed June-Aug.) At **Bar del Teatro ❶,** C. Garibaldi, 88, enjoy the best view in town: a theater next door, the Palazzo Ducale on one side, the valley on the other. (☎0722 29 11. Espresso €0.80; cappuccino €1.10. Open M-Sa 7am-2am. Cash only.)

Pizzeria Le Tre Piante, V. Voltaccia della Vecchia, 1 (☎0722 48 63). From P. della Repubblica, take V. Veneto, turn left on V. Nazario Sauro, right on V. Budassi, and left and down the stairs on V. Foro Posterula. Packed with locals, this gem serves sizeable pizzas (€2.30-6). Watch the sun set over the rolling green Apennines from the terrace. *Primi* €5.50-6.20, *secondi* €8-13. Open Tu-Su noon-3pm and 7-11pm. Cash only. ❸

La Trattoria del Leone, V. Battisti, 5 (☎0722 32 98 94). Fine dining at affordable prices. Try regional specialties like the *galletto al coccio* (a whole young rooster; €7.50). *Primi* €6-7.50, *secondi* €5-12. Cover €1.70. Open daily 12:30-2:30pm and 7:30-10:30pm. AmEx/MC/V. ❷

Ristorante Ragno d'Oro, Viale Don Minzoni, 2/4 (☎0722 32 77 05). Follow V. Rafaello to the statue at the top of the hill. Turn right on Viale Don Minzoni. At noon, a stream of students make the hike to this trattoria. Try the signature pizza, the *Ragno d'Oro,* topped with mozzarella, spinach, ricotta, and speck (€5.70). Pizza €2.50-7.50. *Primi* €5-7.50, *secondi* €6-14. Cover €1.30. Open daily noon-3pm and 7-10:30pm. AmEx/MC/V. ❸

Ristorante La Vecchia Fornarina, V. Mazzini, 14 (☎0722 32 00 07). Cozy and quiet, this quaint restaurant serves traditional *Urbinese* cuisine in a small brick building. *Primi* €7-10, *secondi* €10-20. Open daily noon-2:30pm and 7-10:30pm. AmEx/MC/V. ❹

Un Punto Macrobiotico, V. Pozzo Nuovo, 4 (☎0722 32 97 90). From P. della Repubblica, take C. Battisti and 1st right. Eager waitstaff and long benches promote a community feel, though prices at this sunny organic eatery can be steep. The first meal requires a €10 membership and €10 surcharge (students €10/€7); each subsequent buffet is €5 (students €2). Open M-Sa 12:30-2:30pm and 7:30-9pm. Cash only. ❸

Caffè del Sole, V. Mazzini, 34 (☎0722 26 19). Popular student hangout serves *panini,* drinks, and hearty helpings of local personality. Jazz concerts Sept.-May W-Th nights. Open M 7am-1am, Tu-Sa 7am-2am. AmEx/MC/V. ❶

👁 SIGHTS

The turreted silhouette of the Renaissance ⊠**Palazzo Ducale** dominates the Urbino skyline. A stairway inside and to the **Galleria Nazionale delle Marche,** in the former residence of Duke Frederico da Montefeltro. The gallery contains the most important art collection in Urbino, including works like the *Ideal City* by Piero della Francesca. In the last rooms, Berruguete's *Portrait of Duke Federico with a Young Guidubaldo,* Raphael's *Portrait of a Lady,* and Paolo Uccello's narrative panel *The Profanation of the Host* are also on display. Ambrogio Barocchi designed the palazzo's facade of two slender brick towers flanking three stacked marble balconies. The building also contains the **Museo Archeologico's** varied collection of Roman art and artifacts. Free art exhibits are on display in the **Sale del Castellare;** the entrance is next to the duomo. (In P. Rinascimento. ☎ 0722 32 26 25. Open M 8:30am-2pm, Tu-Su 8:30am-7:15pm. €8, EU students 18-25 €4, Italian citizens under 18 or over 65 free. Ticket office closes M 1pm, Tu-Su 6:15pm. Cash only.) The site of Raphael's birth in 1483, **Casa Natale di Raffaello,** is now a delightful museum filled with period furnishings and paintings. The only decoration in the museum attributed to the artist himself is a fresco of the Virgin and Child, in the room to the left when facing the *Annunciation,* a work by Raphael's father Giovanni Santi. (V. Raffaello, 57. ☎ 0722 32 01 05, fax 0722 32 96 95. Open Mar.-Oct. M-Sa 9am-1pm and 3-7pm, Su 10am-1pm; Nov.-Feb. M-Sa 9am-2pm, Su 10am-1pm. Ticket office closes 20min. before museum. €3. Cash only.) Next to Palazzo Ducale sits the stark facade of the **duomo.** Inside hang notable paintings like Veronese's fantastic *Traslazione della Santa Casa e Sant'Andrea.* (Open daily 7:30am-1pm and 2-7pm. Free.) The Gothic frescoes by L. J. Salimbeni (1416) decorating the 14th-century **Oratorio di San Giovanni Battista** represent events from the life of St. John; its painters are said to have drawn their sketches with lamb's blood. (At the end of V. Barocci. From P. della Repubblica, take V. Mazzini and turn right up the small path on the right, following the sign. ☎ 347 671 11 81. Open M-Sa 10am-12:30pm and 3-5:30pm, Su 10am-12:30pm. €2. Cash only.)

🎭 🎵 NIGHTLIFE AND ENTERTAINMENT

The main piazzas stay lit well into the night, when people spill into the spaces outside local cafes for one last shot of espresso (and/or tequila, as the case may be). Nightclubs are scarce, but the **The Bosom Pub,** V. Budassi, 14, is packed with dancers by midnight during the school year and flooded with international students in summer. Watch for occasional festival parties, such as the costume party **Festa di Bacco** in mid-July. (☎ 0722 47 83. Bottled beer €3-4; cocktails €4. No cover. Open Aug.-May daily 4:30pm-3am, June-July 10:30pm-3am. Cash only.) In July the town resounds with Renaissance music during the **Antique Music Festival.** Saturdays are amateur nights—if you brought your 3rd-century lute, feel free to rock and roll. The third Sunday in August brings the **Ceremony of the Revocation** of the Duke's Court, and the night before the festival, jousting matches erupt. The **Festa dell'Aquilone,** held on the first Sunday in September, is a fierce kite-flying competition between different cities (weather permitting; otherwise, second Sunday of September).

ANCONA   ☎ 071

Midway down the boot, Ancona is northern Italy's major transportation hub for boats bound for Croatia, Slovenia, and Greece. Though industry and transportation are the main interests of this busy city, the old town and seacoast provide pleasant escapes from the cranes and ships crowding the harbor. For either a long or short stay, a gorgeous duomo and the beautiful Passetto beach are must-sees.

☐ TRANSPORTATION

Trains: In P. Rosselli. Ticket office open daily 5:55am-8:45pm. To: **Bologna** (2½hr., 43 per day 1:25am-9:31pm, €10.12); **Milan** (5hr., 24 per day 1:32am-7:13pm, €19.37); **Pesaro** (1hr., 41 per day 3:50am-10:22pm, €2.89); **Rimini** (1½hr., 50 per day 1:32am-10:22pm, €4.65); **Rome** (3-4hr., 10 per day 3:37am-7:07pm, €13.22); **Venice** (5hr., 4 per day 2:25am-6:14pm, €25.20). AmEx/MC/V.

Ferries: Ancona offers ferry service to **Croatia, Greece,** and **Northern Italy.** Schedules available at **Stazione Marittima** (☎071 20 11 83), on the waterfront. Call the day before departure to confirm, as cancellations can occur. Reserve July-Aug. **Luggage storage** available (see **Practical Information**).

Adriatica (☎071 502 11 621; www.adriatica.it). To: **Bar, Yugoslavia** (16hr.; €46/€51); **Durazzo, Albania** (15hr.; €64, July-Aug. €85); **Spalato, Croatia** (8hr.; €38/€46). AmEx/MC/V.

ANEK (☎071 207 22 75; www.anekitalia.com). Offers 20% discount for those 26 and under and 10% discount for families and seniors. To **Igoumenitsa, Greece** (15hr.) and **Patras, Greece** (20hr.; €54, July-Aug. €73). Round-trips discounted 30%. AmEx/MC/V.

Jadrolinija (☎071 20 43 05; www.jadrolinija.tel.hr/jadrolinija) runs to **Split, Croatia** (9hr.; €36.50 one-way, €47 late June-Aug.; 20% discount on round-trip). AmEx/MC/V.

SEM Maritime Co (SMC; ☎071 20 40 41; www.marittimamauro.it). To **Split, Croatia** (9hr.; €38, round-trip €68; prices increase 20% from late July-late Aug.) and **Hvar Island.** AmEx/MC/V.

☀☐ ORIENTATION AND PRACTICAL INFORMATION

The **train station** is a 25min. walk from **Stazione Marittima.** From the island directly in front of the entrance to the train station, buses #1, 1/3, and 1/4 head along the port toward Stazione Marittima and up **Corso Stamira** to **Piazza Cavour,** the city center. Buy tickets (€0.80) at *tabacchi* in the train station. For Stazione Marittima, disembark at **Piazza Repubblica** (the first stop after turning inland), walk back toward the water and turn right on the waterfront. To get to the tourist office from the train station, take bus #1/4 from platform 2 under the canopy outside the train station and stay on it until **Piazza IV Novembre.** The **tourist office** is at V. Thaon de Revel, 4, across from a parking lot. (☎071 35 89 91; iat.ancona@regione.marche.it. Open in summer M-F 9am-2pm and 3:30-6:30pm, Sa 9am-1pm and 3:30-6:30pm; Su 9am-1pm; in winter M-Sa 9am-1pm and 3-6pm.) There's a **branch** in Stazione Marittima that has ferry info. (☎071 20 11 83. Open July-Aug. daily 9am-7pm.) Info on long-term housing, employment, and cultural opportunities is at **InformaGiovani,** V. Palestro, 6/A, which also offers 30min. free **Internet.** (☎071 549 54 ext. 8; www.comune.ancona.it. Open M and Sa 10am-1pm, Tu and Th 10am-1pm and 4:30-7pm, F 4:30-7pm.) **Luggage storage** is available in Stazione Marittima. (Open daily 8am-9pm. €1 per bag per day for 1st 2 days, thereafter €2 per bag per day. Cash only.) In case of **emergency,** call ☎112 or 113, the **police** (☎071 228 81), an **ambulance** (☎118), or **first aid** (☎071 596 40 12). The hospital, **Ospedale Regionale Umberto I** (☎071 59 61) is on V. Conca-Torrette. **Internet** is available in the *centro* at **Rocket Jump,** P. Cavour, 29. (☎071 20 728 32. Open M-F 9am-1:30pm and 4-11pm, Sa 9am-1:30pm and 4pm-midnight, Su 4:30pm-midnight. €3 per half hour or €5 per hour. Cash only.) The **post office** is at P. XXIV Maggio, 2, off P. Cavour (☎071 501 21 77. Open M-F 8am-6:30pm and Sa 8am-12:30pm.) **Postal Code:** 60100.

☐ ACCOMMODATIONS

Ostello della Gioventù (HI) ❶, V. Lamaticci, 7, keeps clean rooms and equally spotless bathrooms. From the train station, cross the piazza, turn left, then take the first right and make a sharp right behind the newsstand. (☎/fax 071 422 57. Sheets included. Reception 6:30-11am and 4:30pm-midnight. Check-out 9:30am.

UMBRIA AND LE MARCHE

Lockout 11am-4:30pm. Curfew midnight. Dorms €14. HI members only. AmEx/
MC/V.) The clean rooms at **Hotel City ❹**, V. Matteotti, 112/114, all have bath, A/C,
TV, and minibar. From P. Cavour, facing away from the port, turn left down the
street just before Largo XXIV Maggio, and turn left at the end on V. Matteotti.
(☎071 207 09 49; www.hotelcityancona.it. Buffet breakfast included. M-Th sin-
gles €60; doubles €96; triples €98. F-Su singles €56; doubles €92; triples €98.
AmEx/MC/V.) Stairs just off a main drag past P. Cavour lead to **Hotel Viale ❹**,
Viale della Vittoria, 23, which has a garden terrace and compact rooms with bath,
A/C, TV, and phone. (☎071 20 18 61; www.hotelviale.it. Singles €47; doubles €72;
triples €80. AmEx/MC/V.) Sparsely furnished rooms offer little more than an
inexpensive place to sleep at **Pensione Euro ❷**, C. Mazzini, 142, 2nd fl., off P.
Cavour. Bring earplugs, as foot traffic on C. Mazzini is audible well past midnight. (☎338 588 21 36. Singles €30; doubles €35; triples €50. Cash only.) Facing
away from the port, walk to the far end of P. Cavour, turn right on V. Vecchini,
walk straight and go up staircase to **Pensione Milano ❷**, V. Montebello 1/A. 14
clean, non-descript rooms come with basic furnishings and shared baths. (☎071
20 11 47. Reception 7am-11:30pm. Singles €21; doubles €31. Cash only.)

◨ FOOD

The best **grocery** deals are at CONAD, V. Matteotti, 115. (Open M-W and F 8:15am-
1:30pm and 5-7:35pm, Th 8:15am-1:30pm, Sa 8:15am-12:45pm and 5-7:40pm. Cash
only.) From P. Roma, head toward the horse fountain and turn right on V.
Mazzini. Then, turn left into P. delle Erbe for **Mercato Pubblico**, P. delle Erbe, 130.
Pack a meal for the ferry ride at this old-fashioned indoor market. (Open in summer M-Sa 7:30am-12:45pm and 5-8pm, in winter M-Sa 7:30am-12:45pm and 4:30-
7:30pm. Most vendors cash only.) At **◪La Cantineta ❷**, V. Gramsci, 1, find a trattoria teeming with locals at tightly packed tables. Don't be deceived by the
cracked tile floor—a genial, welcoming staff offers huge bread baskets, heavy portions of regional cuisine like *stoccafisso* (€12.91), and amazing prices. At least
locally, this secret is out—come early or be prepared to wait. (☎071 20 11 07. Open
Tu-Su noon-2:45pm and 7:15-10:45pm. *Primi* €2.58-7.50, *secondi* €4.13-12.91.
Cover €1.55. AmEx/MC/V.) From P. Roma, head toward the horse fountain and
turn left to find **Bontà delle Marche ❸**, C. Mazzini, 96, an indoor specialty deli and
lunch restaurant. Trays of gourmet meats and cheeses from Le Marche tempt from
the display cases, while crisp white tables dot the pedestrian thoroughfare outside. (☎071 539 85; www.bontadellemarche.it. Market open M-Sa 8am-8pm. Restaurant open M-Sa 12:30-3:30pm. AmEx/MC/V.) For low-key dining, head to **Osteria
Brillo ❷**, C. Mazzini, 109. This small, pub-style eatery serves hearty Italian fare at
outstanding prices. *Primi* specials change daily. From P. Roma, head toward the
horse fountain and turn right on C. Mazzini. (☎071 207 26 29. Pizza €2.60-6.50. *Secondi* €5.50-13.50. Open M-Sa 12:30-3pm and 7:30-11pm. AmEx/MC/V.)

◔ SIGHTS

Far from the port's industrial clutter, **◪Pasetto Beach** offers a taste of natural
beauty. Families flock here for the sapphire-blue waves, and sunbathers spread
out on the wide railing. Above the beach, marble vistas and hundreds of stairs lead
to the snow-white **Monumento ai Caduti**, a tribute to the soldiers who perished in
World War II. (In P. IV Novembre. Take bus #1/4 from the station or P. Cavour
along Viale della Vittoria to the shoreline. Free.) In the **old city**, the **Piazzale del
Duomo** atop Monte Guasco offers a beautiful view of the town below. In the piazzale stands the **Cattedrale di San Ciriaco**, a Romanesque church built above the
remains of an early Christian basilica and an even earlier Roman temple to Venus.

Look in the basement on the left for the tomb of St. Ciriaco and a photograph of the body. From P. Cavour, follow C. Mazzini to the port and turn right on V. Gramsci at P. Repubblica. Continue to P. Del Senato and climb 246 steps to the duomo. (☎071 222 50 45. Open in summer M-Sa 8am-noon and 3-7pm, in winter M-Sa 8am-noon and 3-6 pm. Free.) Ancona's painting gallery, the **Pinacoteca Comunale Francesco Podesti,** housed in the 16th-century **Palazzo Bosdari,** V. Pizzecolli, 17, has amassed a collection of work by the Camerte school. Carlo Crivelli's *Madonna con Bambino* and Titian's *Apparition of the Virgin* are the highlights of the museum. From P. Roma, head down C. Garibaldi toward the port. Turn right at P. Repubblica on V. Gramsci and go straight. (☎071 22 25 045. Open M 9am-1pm, Tu-F 9am-7pm, Sa 8:30am-6:30pm, Su 3-7pm. €4.20, ages 16-25 €3.20. Cash only.) The enormous 16th-century **Palazzo Ferretti** houses Le Marche's foremost archaeological museum, the **Museo Archeologico Nazionale delle Marche,** an impressive collection including the Ionian Dinos of Amandola, Greek pottery, and jewelry unearthed by regional tomb excavations in the 1900s. Atop the museum are two life-size bronzes of unknown Roman emperors. (V. Ferretti, 6. From Palazzo Bosdari, continue toward the duomo. ☎071 20 26 02; museo.ancona@archeomarche.it. Open Tu-Su 8:30am-7:30pm. €4, ages 18-25 €2, under 18 or over 65 free. Cash only.)

ASCOLI PICENO ☎0736

According to legend Ascoli was founded by Sabines guided westward by a *picchio* (woodpecker). The bird gave the city its name and Le Marche a feathered mascot. By other accounts, Ascoli was the metropolis of the Piceno, a Latin tribe that controlled much of the coastal marches and had the woodpecker as its totem. Whatever the origins of its name, the city is one of Le Marche's most interesting, offering travelers a variety of sights, spirited local festivals, and an urban landscape awash with ancient towers made from travertine, a mineral consistently included in local architectural projects for the past 2000 years.

▐ TRANSPORTATION

The **train station** is in Piazzale della Stazione, at the end of V. Marconi. (Ticket counter open M-Sa 8am-noon and 3-6pm.) **Trains** depart to San Benedetto (30min., M-Sa 16 per day 6:24am-9:05pm, €2.22), but require a transfer at the P. d'Ascoli station from July-early Sept. **Buses** to San Benedetto are more crowded than trains and take twice as long, but run much more consistently. Buses leave from Viale Gasperi, behind the duomo. **Start** sells bus tickets from **Agenzia Cameli,** V. Dino Angelini, 129 (☎800 44 30 40; www.startspa.it), off P. Roma, and runs buses to San Benedetto (50min.-1hr.; M-Sa 34 per day 5:10am-11:30pm, Su 15 per day 7am-10:40pm; €1.70) and Acquasanta Terme (1¼hr., 13 per day 5am-7:15pm, €3.45). Buy tickets at the newsstand near the bus stop. Buses to Rome (3hr.; M-Sa 4 per day 3:20am-4:30pm, Su 4 per day 3:20am-5:30pm; €11.90) depart from P. Orlini. (Ticket office open M-Sa 9am-12:45pm and 4-7pm, Su 9-9:30am and 4-5:30pm.)

▐ ▐ ORIENTATION AND PRACTICAL INFORMATION

From the **train station,** walk one block to **Viale Indipendenza,** turn right, and continue straight to **Piazza Matteotti.** Turn right on **Corso Mazzini;** follow it into **Piazza del Popolo** (10min.). The main bus stop is on **Viale Gasperi,** behind the duomo. Walk around the duomo to **Piazza Arringo,** then to **Via XX Settembre** and **Piazza Roma.** From there, **Via del Trivio** leads to C. Mazzini and P. del Popolo. Two tourist offices serve Ascoli: **Centro Visitatori,** P. Arringo, 7 (☎0736 29 82 04 or 29

UMBRIA AND LE MARCHE

82 12; www.comune.ascolipiceno.it; open daily 9:30am-12:30pm and 4-7pm), and **Ufficio Informazioni,** P. del Popolo, 17 (☎0736 25 30 45; open M-F 8:30am-1:30pm and 3-7pm, Sa-Su and holidays 9am-1pm). Head to **Banca Nazionale del Lavoro,** C. Trento e Trieste, 10/C, for **currency exchange.** (☎0736 29 61. Open M-F 8:20am-1:20pm and 3-4:30pm, Sa 8:20am-11:50pm.) In case of **emergency,** dial ☎113, or call the **police** (☎112), or an **ambulance** (☎118). There is a **pharmacy** at P. Roma, 1. (☎0736 25 91 83. Open daily 9am-1pm and 4:30-8pm. After-hours rotation posted outside.) **Edinternet,** C. Mazzini, 97, near P. S. Agostino, has five computers with **Internet.** (☎0736 24 72 95. €1.50 for 30min., €3 per hr. Open M 4-8pm, Tu-Su 8:30am-1pm and 4-8pm. Cash only.) Ascoli's **post office,** on V. Crispi, offers currency exchange. (☎0736 24 22 83. Open M-F 8am-6:30pm, Sa 8am-12:30pm.) **Postal Code:** 63100.

🛏️🍴 ACCOMMODATIONS AND FOOD

Accommodations in Ascoli Piceno are cheap and often rustic, but not run-down. The best deal in town is the pleasant ⬛**Ostello dei Longobardi ❶,** R. dei Longobardi, 12. An 11th-century building with 20th-century plumbing, this quiet hostel offers 16 beds separated into single-sex dorms. From P. del Popolo, take C. Mazzini to P. S. Agostino and turn right on V. delle Torri, then left on V. Soderini. (☎0736 26 18 62. Reception open daily 6pm-midnight. Dorms €13. Cash only.) In the heart of town, **Cantina dell'Arte ❸,** V. della Lupa, 8, is a quaint little hotel decorated with family photos. Rooms have marble floors, high ceilings, bath, TV, and phone. Follow C. Trento e Trieste to P. S. Maria Inter Vineas and turn right on V. delle Canterine, then right on V. della Lupa. (☎0736 25 57 44 or 25 56 20, fax 25 51 91. Reserve ahead. Singles €35; doubles €40-50; 5-person apartments €100. AmEx/MC/V.)

Ascoli's cuisine relies heavily upon local produce—including wild fungi (especially truffles), onions, capers, garlic, fennel, and anise. Olives have grown in this province since Roman times; today, Ascolian chefs specialize in *olive all'ascolana,* stuffed with minced meat and fried. Fried sweet cream ravioli and savory anise-flavored cakes topped with powdered sugar are holiday favorites. The region's wines include *Rosso Piceno* and *Falerio dei Colli Ascolani;* the local liqueur of choice is *Anisetta Meletti.* An **open-air market** is in P. S. Francesco, behind P. del Popolo. (Open M-Sa 8am-1pm.) Tigre **supermarket** is at P. S. Maria Inter Vineas, 1, at the end of C. Trento e Trieste. (Open M-W and F 8:30am-1:30pm and 5-8pm, Th 8:30am-1:30pm, Sa 8:30am-1:30pm and 4:30-8pm. MC/V.)

Take C. Mazzini from P. del Popolo and turn left, following signs for ⬛**Ristorante dal Vagabondo ❷,** V. D'Argillano, 29. Admire tasteful modern art on the walls while Gennaro serves up tasty Ascoli-Picenian fare to Italian tourists and local residents. (☎0736 26 21 68. *Primi* €5-7, *secondi* €10. Open daily noon-3pm and 7-11pm. AmEx/MC/V.) There's no better place to try local *anisetta meletti* (€5 per glass, €12.40 per bottle) than **Caffè Meletti ❶,** P. del Popolo, 20, the same spacious, hundred-year-old cafe where Silvio Meletti first pushed his now-famous liqueur, still a local favorite. (☎0736 25 96 26. Open in summer daily 7am-midnight, in winter Tu-Su 7am-midnight. AmEx/MC/V.) Quell a ravenous appetite at **Cantina dell'Arte ❷,** V. della Lupa, 5, across from the hotel of the same name (see **Accommodations**). The stone interior renders the generously portioned *menù* (€8.75) even more delectable. (☎0736 25 56 90. *Primi* €4-5, *secondi* €5-6. Open M-Sa noon-1:30pm and 7-10:30pm. MC/V.) At the cafe-style **Trattoria Laliva ❷,** P. della Viola, 13, try the specialty *sibille* (lasagna with sheep cheese, *Parmese* ham, and chilis; €5.50). Take V. Giudea from P. del Popolo. (☎0736 25 93 58. *Primi* €5-7.50, *secondi* €5-7.50. Open M and Th-Su noon-5:30pm and 7:30-11:30pm, Tu noon-5:30pm. AmEx/MC/V.)

UMBRIA AND LE MARCHE

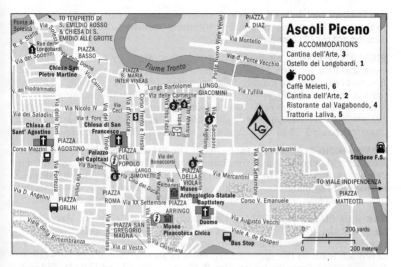

Ascoli Piceno

▲ ACCOMMODATIONS
Cantina dell'Arte, **3**
Ostello dei Longobardi, **1**

🍴 FOOD
Caffè Meletti, **6**
Cantina dell'Arte, **2**
Ristorante dal Vagabondo, **4**
Trattoria Laliva, **5**

👁 SIGHTS

PIAZZA DEL POPOLO. This vast piazza was once the Roman forum, and still buzzes with political and consumer activity along *logge* filled with cafes, boutiques, and city offices. The gleaming pavement is made of travertine, an off-white mineral that's been used to construct the city's major buildings and piazzas for over two millennia. An effort at 16th-century urban renewal left porticoes and columns around two sides of the rectangular square, while the third side houses the 13th-century **Palazzo dei Capitani,** the city's former town hall. Visitors can stroll under its central portal and elegant archways to a paved open-air courtyard. During a Christmas Day squabble in 1535, an angered papal commissioner ordered that the building be burned when a group of rebels barricaded themselves inside; a decade later, the contrite arsonist dedicated the refurbished palace to Pope John III and erected a statue in his honor. The palazzo stood without controversy until 1938, when it served as a seat of the Fascist Party. (☎ 0736 24 49 75. Open daily 9am-1pm and 3-7pm. Free.) The eastern end of the Romanesque-Gothic **Chiesa di San Francesco** borders the fourth side of P. del Popolo, and contains a 14th-century wooden crucifix, the only art saved from the 1535 fire. The church's "singing columns," two sets of low columns flanking the outer door on the V. del Trivio side, sound a dull pop if you draw your hand quickly across them. *(Open daily 8am-noon and 3:30-7:30pm. Call ☎ 0736 25 94 46 for all of Ascoli's church-viewing times. Free.)* The **Loggia dei Mercanti** (Merchants's Gallery), abutting the church on the side facing V. del Trivio, was built between 1509 and 1513 and has wood carvings.

PIAZZA ARRINGO. On the other side of town is Piazza Arringo (Oration Square), which derives its name from its role as a local podium. On one end, the massive travertine **duomo** combines Classical, Romanesque, and Baroque styles and features work from the 5th- through 18th-centuries. A Roman basilica serves as the transept, topped by an 8th-century octagonal dome. The two towers were built in the 11th and 12th centuries, while the lateral naves and central apse were constructed in the 1400s. Inside, freshly restored frescoes decorate the ceiling, while stairs on the right lead down into the dim **Cripta di**

UMBRIA AND
LE MARCHE

San Emidio, which holds the tomb of Ascoli's first bishop and patron saint. Next to the cathedral stands the squat 12th-century **baptistery.** *(Duomo open daily 7am-12:30pm and 5:30-7:45pm. Free.)*

PINACOTECA CIVICA. Medieval and Renaissance works by Crivelli, Titian, van Dyck, and Reni line the walls of the art museum, housed amid period furniture and frescoed ceilings in the massive Palazzo Arringo. Check out the sunny courtyard garden and the life-like sculptures scattered throughout the building—Ascoli native Romolo del Gobbo's ▨**Paolo e Francesca** is especially striking. *(To the left after exiting the duomo in P. Arringo. Enter the garden courtyard, turn immediately left, then another left up the staircase.* ☎ *0736 29 82 13. Open daily 9am-1pm and 3:30-7:30pm. €5. Cash only.)*

MUSEO ARCHEOLOGICO STATALE. Inside the **Palazzo Panichi** is a three-floor museum with a collection of Greek and Roman artifacts, some excavated from nearby San Benedetto. The most impressive piece is a mosaic floor that depicts the face of a boy in the center; when viewed from the opposite side, it becomes the face of an old man. *(P. Arringo, 28. Open Tu-Su 8:30am-7:30pm. €2, students €1.)*

NORTH OF PIAZZA DEL POPOLO. From the piazza, turn left on C. Mazzini and right on V. del Trivio. Bear left on V. Cairoli, which becomes V. delle Donne, then pass the church on the left and follow tiny V. di Solestà as it curves to the right. V. di Solestà leads to the single-arched **Ponte di Solestà,** one of Europe's tallest Roman bridges. From the bridge, take V. Rigante, turn right on Viale M. Federici, turn left on V. Carso and follow it under the roadway to reach **Chiesa di Sant'Emidio alle Grotte,** whose Baroque facade is crafted from the natural rock wall. Inside, **catacombs** contain the remains of the first Ascoli Christians.

▓ FESTIVALS

Ascoli's **Carnevale** is one of Italy's liveliest; insanity reigns on the days preceding Ash Wednesday. On the first Sunday in August, the colorful medieval pageant of **Tournament of Quintana** honors the city's patron Saint Emidio, with 1500 enthusiasts in medieval garb, man-on-dummy jousting and a torch-lit procession, ultimately culminating in a fierce competition where all six neighborhoods of the town bandy for the coveted winner's banner, the *Palio*. On the third Sunday of each month (except July), an **Antique Market** unfolds in the *centro*.

SAN BENEDETTO DEL TRONTO ☎ 0735

With over 7000 palm trees and nearly as many children playing under their waving fronds, San Benedetto draws summering Italian families and a smattering of foreign tourists. Don't come expecting to compromise beach time with high culture—the height of the local art scene is the stretch of sand castles along the miles of beach. Rest, relaxation, and an entertaining nightlife are this town's priorities.

▐ TRANSPORTATION. The **train station** is at Viale Gramsci, 20/A. The ticket counter is open daily (6:40am-8:35pm; AmEx/MC/V). Trains run to: Ancona (1hr., 28 per hr. 12:28am-9:13pm, €4.13); Bologna (2½-3½hr., 12 per day 12:28am-8:31pm, €13.22); and Milan (5hr., 6 per day 12:38am-4:14pm, €23.50). **Start** runs **buses** from the train station to Ascoli Piceno (1hr.; M-Sa 34 per day 6am-12:10am, Su 15 per day 7am-midnight; €1.70). Buy tickets at the train station or at Caffè Blue Express (open 3am-8pm) across from the station. **Local buses** stop in front of the train station. Bus #2 departs across the street from the station (every 10-20min. 5:57am-12:45am, €0.75). **Taxis** (☎ 0735 58 41 27) run from F. S. Stazione.

⊞ 🛈 ORIENTATION AND PRACTICAL INFORMATION. From the **train station,** cross the street and take bus #2 to the **seaside,** or turn left on **Via Gramsci** and left again on **Via Monfalcone** toward the beach. **Viale Trieste,** the *lungomare,* intersects V. Monfalcone and runs along the shore, changing from **Viale Marconi** to **Viale Europa/Scipioni,** and then to **Viale Rinascimento. Via Trento,** which becomes **Via Volta,** runs parallel to the *lungomare.* To reach the **tourist office,** Viale delle Tamerici, 5, turn left from the train station on V. Gramsci, then left on V. Fiscaletti; follow it to the sea and turn right on Viale dei Tigli. (☎ 0735 59 50 88; www.rivieradellepalme.it. Open June-Sept. M-Sa 9am-1pm and 4-7pm, Su 9am-1pm.) In case of **emergency,** call ☎ 113, an **ambulance** (☎ 118), or the **police** (☎ 112). The **Ospedale Civile** (☎ 0735 79 31) is on V. Silvio Pellico. From the train station, turn left on V. Gramsci and right on V. Montello, then left on V. Silvio Pellico. **Farmacia Mercuri,** Viale de Gasperi, 61/63 (☎ 0735 78 01 51), posts a 24hr. rotation outside. **Pub Adams,** V. Crispi, 133 (☎ 0735 59 23 99), has **Internet** access (open daily 7:30pm-2am). **Currency exchange** is available at the **post office,** V. Roma, 125, in the parking lot outside the train station. (Open M-F 8am-1:30pm and Sa 8am-12:30pm.) **Postal Code:** 63039.

🛏 ACCOMMODATIONS. V. Volta has a number of budget lodgings. Most hotels include private beach access in their fee, though public beaches dot the waterfront. Look for areas marked *"spiaggia libera."* Numerous shacks rent storage cabins from €5.20 and umbrellas from €6.20. To get to **La Playa ❷,** V. Cola di Rienzo, 25/A, at the end of the beach, take bus #2 to the rotunda stop at V. del Mare. Continue straight on V. dei Laureati and turn right on V. F. Ferrucci. Walk 1 block and turn left on V. Cola di Rienzo. The accommodating staff and oversized rooms with polished tile floors, bath, TV, minibar, and balcony make this budget locale feel like a splurge. (☎/fax 0735 65 99 57. Open June-Oct. No singles in Aug. Singles €26-32; doubles €36-60. Prices rise in July and Aug. Cash only.) For elegance at reasonable prices, try **Hotel Fortuna ❷,** V. Virgilio, 5, a large hotel with private beach access and A/C, TV, phone, and bath. (☎/fax 0735 848 72. Reception 24hr. Singles €28-30; doubles €48-52. Half pension €37-56; full pension €43-63. AmEx/MC/V.) The **Albergo Patrizia ❹,** V. A. Volta, 170, has a private beach and offers guests a free chair, umbrella, and shiny bicycles for the bike promenade. All 33 rooms have high ceilings, bath, TV, and phone; some have balcony. From the station, take bus #2 to stop 6. (☎ 0735 817 62; www.albergopatrizia.it. Breakfast included. Open June-Sept. Prices peak in Aug. Singles €53; doubles €60; triples €70. Full pension €33.50-64 per person. Cash only.) Campers can appreciate **Seaside ❷,** V. dei Mille, 125, for its pool, market, restaurant, electricity, and hot showers, all located in a spacious grove walled off from the *centro* traffic outside. Take bus #2 to stop 11, or on foot from Viale Rinascimento, turn right on V. A. Negri and bear left on V. dei Mille. (☎ 0735 65 95 05; seaside@libero.it. Open June-Sept. €12 per site, €6.50 per half-site, €7 per adult, €3 per child age 3-7, €2.50 per car. Prices rise July 31-Aug. 18. Cash only.)

🍴 FOOD. San Benedetto's specialty is *brodetto alla sambenedettese,* a stew of fish, tomatoes, peppers, and vinegar. On Tuesday and Friday morning, head to the **open-air market,** on V. Montebello. The Tigre **supermarket** is at V. Ugo Bassi, 10. (Open in summer M-Sa 8:30am-1pm and 5-8:30pm, Su 9am-1pm; in winter M-Tu and Th-Sa 8:30am-1pm and 4:30-8:30pm, W 8:30am-1pm, Su 9am-1pm. AmEx/MC/V.) Dine by candlelight at the chic **⧉Bagni Andrea ❸,** Viale Trieste, on the left heading away from the train station between beaches #8 and 9. The all-white, beachside restaurant specializes in fish, but the *menù* changes daily (€8-18). Reservations are recommended for dinner on the weekends. (☎ 0735 838 34. F-Sa piano bar 10pm. Open daily 1-3pm and 8:30-11pm, but late-night Latin/swing disco closes

3am (free entrance). AmEx/MC/V.) At **Trattoria Molo Sud ❹**, on Porto Molo Sud., hungry locals wolf down fish specialties on the busy palm-lined patio and breezy, open-windowed interior. Fantastic seafood *gnocchi* are available Thursdays (€7.75). From Viale Trieste heading to the station, turn right on Viale delle Tamerici—Molo Sud is on the water, right before the bend in the road. (☎0735 58 73 25. *Primi* €7.75, *secondi* from €10.35. Cover €1.05. Reservations recommended. Open Tu-Su 12:30-4pm and 8-10:30pm. AmEx/MC/V.) From the train station, turn left on V. Gramsci, and left on V. Francesco Fiscaletti to reach **Marina Al Centro Ristorante ❸**, V. Colombo, 7. Stylish outdoor seating on the raised street-side terrace compensates for a slightly limited menu. Smooth jazz accompanies small, flavorful dishes. (☎0735 58 37 20. *Primi* €6, *secondi* €8-13. Open Tu-Su 7:30pm-midnight. MC/V.) Dim globe lights illuminate a crowd of patrons enjoying hearty Italian fare in the comfortable, pub-like interior of **Bar San Michele ❷**, V. Piemonte, 111. From the train station, turn left on Viale Gramsci, which becomes V. Ugo Bassi and then V. Piemonte. (☎0735 824 29. Pizza €2.10-6.50. *Panini* €4-6. *Primi* €4-6, *secondi* €4-8. Cover €0.60. Open daily noon-3pm and 7:15pm-2:30am. AmEx/MC/V.)

ABRUZZO AND MOLISE

The foothills of the secluded Apennine mountains are home to clusters of thatched orange roofs, the occasional medieval castle, and a sprawling, varied wilderness. Visitors to Abruzzo and Molise unfailingly sense the area's deeply rural character; a serene, even otherworldly quality pervades the landscape. About two hours from Rome and a far cry from its frenzied tourism, these highlands offer a natural beauty and a unique retreat. While youths nod to their Discmans, shirtless men lead donkeys, and women tote copper pots of well-water. A single region until 1963, Abruzzo and Molise lie at the juncture of northern and southern Italy. Abruzzo, the wealthier of the two, offers beach and ski resorts, mountain lakes, lush pines, and stunning wildlife in the Abruzzo National Park. The smaller Molise, dubbed a religious center by the Samnite religious order, is home to phenomenal ruins, medieval festivals, and flavorful food.

HIGHLIGHTS OF ABRUZZO AND MOLISE

GLIMPSE herds of wild horses on the Gran Sasso d'Italia. (p. 528.)

FIND OUT why L'Aquila is 99 times better than any other town in the region. (p. 525.)

SPEND time, not money, exploring each of Tremiti's verdant isles. (p. 537.)

HUDDLE in your tent in Abruzzo National Park, populated chiefly by animals of uncommon stature. (p. 531.)

L'AQUILA ☎0862

In 1254, 99 lords from 99 castles banded together to build L'Aquila (The Eagle), Abruzzo's majestic capital. The lords honored the founding of the city by constructing a 99-spout fountain—a stately structure that flows today just as steadily as it did some 700 years ago. Local legend claims that the town has 99 medieval streets, 99 piazzas, and 99 churches, one of which tolls its bells 99 times at 9:09 every evening. Local legend also claims that the "fresh mountain air" renders hotel air conditioning unnecessary—a myth that remains unsubstantiated.

▐ TRANSPORTATION. The **train station** (☎0862 41 92 90) is on the outskirts of town. Take bus **#M11, 5,** or **8** to the center, or follow signs to the Fontana delle 99 Cannelle and hike 2km uphill. Trains head to Sulmona (1hr., 13 per day 6:27am-8:25 pm, €4.50) and Terni (2hr., 10 per day 6:27am-7:57pm, €5.89). L'Aquila has two bus systems: municipal buses and ARPA regional buses. The yellow **municipal buses** (one-way €0.80, for 1½ hr. €1, for a whole day €1.90) stop at **AMA** markers and serve surrounding towns and sights. Tickets are available at *tabacchi*, newsstands, bars, and at the **City Bus Station,** just past P. del Collemaggio on V. G. Caldora. A handy subterranean tramway connects the station with P. del Duomo. Monday through Saturday, blue **ARPA buses** connect L'Aquila to: Avezzano (50min., 26 per day 5:55am-8:30pm, €4.50); Pescara (1½hr., 7 per day 6am-9:10pm, €7.23); Rome (1¾hr., 17 per day 4:40am-8pm, €8.73); and Sulmona (1hr., 7 per day 6:20am-7:20pm, €5.06). The **station ticket office** (☎0862 41 28 08) is open Monday through Saturday 5:30am-8:30pm and Sunday 7:30am-1:15pm and 2:30-8pm.

▐▐ ORIENTATION AND PRACTICAL INFORMATION. Corso Vittorio Emanuele II, the main street, stretches between the **Castello Cinquecentesco** in the north and **Piazza del Duomo,** the heart of L'Aquila's historic district, in the south. Beyond P. del Duomo, away from the castle, the street continues as **Corso Federico II** until

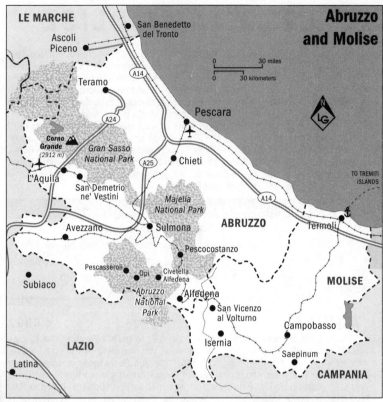

reaching the lush gardens of the **Villa Comunale** and **Via XX Settembre.** Picking up a map at the tourist office is an absolute must, as L'Aquila's small and often unlabeled streets are difficult to navigate.

The **APT branch office,** P. Maria Paganica, 5, has info on hotels, sites, and transportation. Visitors planning to explore the park should pick up a Sasso information booklet. Walking toward the castle, turn left off C. V. Emanuele on V. Leosini. (☎0862 41 08 08 or 41 03 40. Open M-Sa 9am-1pm and 4-7pm, Su 9:30am-1pm). The main **APT Tourist Office,** V. XX Settembre, 8, stocks that indispensable free **map.** (☎0862 223 06. Open M-Sa 9am-1pm and 4-7pm, Su 9:30am-1pm.) **Club Alpino Italiano,** V. Sassa, 34, offers **hiking information,** including maps and guide references. (☎0862 243 42. Open M-Sa 7-8:15pm.) The **Centro Turistico Gran Sasso,** C. V. Emanuele, 49, has bus and train schedules and info on the Gran Sasso park. (☎0862 221 46. Open M-F 9am-1pm and 4-7pm, Sa 9am-1pm.) The **police** (☎112 or 113) are at V. del Beato Cesidio. An **Internet** point, complete with bar and computers, is at C. P. Umberto, 20. (☎086 22 73 64. €4 per hr. Open daily 9am-1am.) Take C. V. Emanuele from the duomo, turn left on C. P. Umberto and it's at the end of the colonnade on the left. The **post office,** in P. del Duomo, **exchanges currency.** (Open M-Sa 8am-6:30pm.) **Postal Code:** 67100.

ACCOMMODATIONS AND FOOD. There are no true budget accommodations in L'Aquila. The rooms in **Hotel Duomo ❹,** V. Dragonetti, 6, just across from P. del Duomo, are on the smaller side, but many have splendid duomo views, and all have a bath, TV, and phone. As do most of L'Aquila's hotels, Duomo lacks A/C; still, these comfortable rooms are the best values for this part of town. (☎ 0862 41 07 69, fax 41 30 58. Singles €52-57; doubles €78-88. AmEx/MC/V.) **Albergo Orazi ❷**, V. Roma, 175, is a lone, cheap option—a long walk from sights, but relatively close to the train station. From P. Duomo on C. V. Emanuele, turn left on C. Umberto, which turns into V. Roma. (☎ 0862 41 28 89. Shared baths for some rooms. Singles €30; doubles €45. Apartments also available upon request.)

Torrone, a honey and almond nougat, is L'Aquila's specialty. Some of the more popular kinds are available at **Caffè Europa ❶**, C. Emanuele, 38, for €8 per box. Though on the touristy side, Europa still attracts locals who linger at the counter over *caffè macchiati*. (Open daily 6:30am-8:30pm.) **Ristorante Tre Marie ❹**, V. Tre Marie, 3, prides itself on its first-rate regional fare. From P. Duomo, head left on C. V. Emanuele, then left again on V. Tre Marie; the restaurant is on the right. Throw on some snappy threads and savor the *prosciutto di Monfagna antipasto* (€10.33) amid antique urns, stained glass, and a tranquil atmosphere. (☎ 0862 41 31 91. *Primi* €11, *secondi* €14. Open Tu-Sa 9am-3pm and 7-10:30pm, Su 9am-3pm. AmEx/MC/V.) **Trattoria Da Lincosta ❸**, P. S. Pietro a Coppito, 19, off V. Roma, offers substantial servings of their specialty, *funghi al formaggio* (mushrooms in cheese sauce, €15) and pleasant outdoor seating in the piazza. (☎ 0862 286 62. Open M-Th and Sa-Su noon-3:30pm and 7:30-10:30pm.) Find everything from fresh fruit and cured meats to clothes at the busy **market** in P. Duomo. (Open M-Sa 8am-noon.) A small STANDA **supermarket**, C. Federico II, is two blocks up from V. XX Settembre. Enter on the corner of V. Monteguelfi and V. S. Agostino. (☎ 0862 264 82. Open M-Sa 8am-8pm. AmEx/MC/V.)

◪ SIGHTS. Chiesa di San Bernardino, built in the 15th century and restored in 1703 after an earthquake, peers over the mountains south of L'Aquila. Though bereft of its original rose windows, the towering church remains a stunning sight. The interior boasts the beautifully sculpted tomb of San Bernardino. Each year on May 22 school-children from Sienna make a pilgrimage to L'Aquila to bring oil that will light the lamp in front of the church's mausoleum for the rest of the year. Across from the church, a stairway frames a breathtaking mountain view; to reach it, walk down V. S. Bernar-dino from C. V. Emanuele. (Open daily 7:30-10am and 6-8pm. Modest dress required.)

Built in 1292, the **Fontana delle 99 Cannelle** (Fountain of 99 Spouts) is L'Aquila's oldest monument. Take V. Sallustio from C. V. Emanuele and bear left onto V. XX Settembre. Follow the small roads down the hill, staying to the left at the bottom. The fountain's source remains a mystery, and the water's quality is similarly murky. Rule of ▨thumb: don't drink from the fountain. L'Aquila's **Castello Cinque-centesco** dominates the park at the end of C. V. Emanuele. The Spanish viceroy Don Pedro da Toledo built this fort in the 16th century to defend himself against the rebelling *Aquilesi*. Naturally, they were forced to pay for its construction. The moat's outer wall drops 12m to the courtyard below. Within the walls of the fort, the **Museo Nazionale di Abruzzo** showcases local art and artifacts: sacred paintings, Roman sarcophagi, Renaissance tapestries, a million-year-old mammoth skeleton, and some local modern art. (☎ 0862 63 31. Open Tu-Su 9am-8pm. €4, free for uni-versity students and those under 18 or over 65.) To find the ▨**Basilica di Santa Maria di Collemaggio,** take C. Federico I past V. XX Settembre and turn left on V. di Collemaggio, after the Villa Comunale. At the request of Pietro da Marrone (later Pope Celestine V), L'Aquila's citizens began constructing this church in 1287. The pink-and-white-checkered facade belies an austere interior, as Baroque embellish-ments were stripped away in 1972 to restore the striking medieval design. (Open in summer daily 9am-1pm and 3-8pm; winter hours vary. Modest dress required.)

Outside L'Aquila, in the forested terrain which conceals isolated medieval towns, abandoned fortresses, ancient churches, and monasteries, find well-pre-served ruins at historian Sallust's birthplace, **Amiternum,** an ancient Sabine town conquered by the Romans in 293 BC. The remains of a theater, amphitheater, and aqueduct survive from the Roman era, and may be explored daily between 9:30am and 1pm (free). **ARPA buses** service this sight from both L'Aquila and Sulmona (1-2hr., 2-3 per day, €2.65-4.33.)

NEAR L'AQUILA

GROTTOES OF STIFFE

Take the Paoli bus from Pta. Paganica (25min., 5 per day, €2.65). For more info, contact the APT office in L'Aquila.

The **Grottoes of Stiffe** at San Demetrio ne' Vestini, 21km southeast of L'Aquila, were formed in prehistoric times when an underground river carved the caverns and rock formations that now form waterfalls and small lakes. The beautiful caves are famous for both the visual and sound effects created by the water. A recent cavern collapse has restricted access to parts of the grottoes, but what remains open is breathtaking. (☎0862 861 42; www.grottestiffe.it. Open year-round. Tours 10am, 1, 3, and 6pm.) For tour reservations, call or write the **Gruppo Speleologico Aquilano** at Svolte della Misericordia, 2, 67100 L'Aquila. (☎/fax 0862 41 42 73.)

SASSO D'ITALIA (GREAT ROCK OF ITALY)

The snow-capped Gran Sasso d'Italia, the highest mountain ridge contained entirely within Italy's borders, looms 12km north of L'Aquila. Midway up the Sasso (and above the tree line), a flat plain called **Campo Imperatore** is home to herds of wild horses, shepherds, and landscapes that seem to stretch on forever. On a clear day, you can see both of Italy's coasts from the **Corno Grande**, the range's highest peak (2912m). The **trail map** (€7.40), available at the **Club Alpino Italiano** near P. Duomo in town or at the base of the mountain, is useful for planning hikes. *Sentieri* (paths) are marked by difficulty, and only the more taxing routes reach the top. The peaks are snowed in from September to July and only experienced mountaineers should venture to hike near the summit during this period. A **funivia** (☎0862 60 61 43; every 30min. 8:30am-5pm, round-trip €13) ascends the 1008m to Campo Imperatore, making the Sasso an easy afternoon excursion from L'Aquila.

In winter Gran Sasso teems with **skiers.** The trails around the funicular are among the most difficult, offering one 4000m and several 1000m drops. In total, 10 trails descend from the funicular and the two lifts. Purchase a weekly pass at the *biglietteria* at the base of the funicular. **Campo Felice** (☎0862 40 00 12), at nearby Monte Rotondo, has 16 lifts, numerous trails of varying difficulty, and a ski school. From **L'Aquila,** take the yellow **bus #76** (30min., 12 per day, €1) from the bus station. Buy tickets at newsstands, *tabacchi*, or the station. The *funivia* is closed in parts of June and October. Trails start at the upper *funivia* station. Call **Club Alpino Italiano** (☎0862 243 42) for current Apennine conditions. For info on mountain guides, inquire at the tourist office or Club Alpino Italiano, or write to Collegio Regionale Guide Alpine, V. Serafino, 2, 66100 Chieti (☎0871 693 38).

The map and the info booklet from L'Aquila's APT list overnight *rifugi* (hiker's huts), which run €8-14 (☎0862 40 00 11). Another option is the hostel **Campo Imperatore ❶**, which offers bunkbeds and shared bathrooms. Call from the lower ropeway station to get picked up. (☎0862 40 00 11. Dorms €11 per person.) **Camping Funivia del Gran Sasso ❶** is an inviting patch of grass downhill from the lower cableway where people pitch tents. (☎0862 60 61 63. €4-5 per person, €6-8 per large tent.) Call these lodgings before setting out, and bring food and warm clothing, as it's windy and cool at Campo Imperatore year round.

SULMONA   ☎ 0864

Hidden deep within Abruzzo's Gizo River Valley, Sulmona is surrounded on all sides by extensive national parks. Small and often overlooked by tourists, the town has pleasant public gardens, factories tossing out its famous *confetti* candy (sold in bouquets, bags, and handfuls), and great pride in its most famous son, Roman poet Ovid. The letters "SMPE," adorning Sulmona's streets and inscribed on buildings, are shorthand for the poet's famous proclamation, *"Sulmo mihi patria est"* ("Sulmona is my homeland"). The mountains around Sulmona tempt many travelers with leisurely walks and hikes, although a day spent simply meandering the friendly city streets can be equally enjoyable.

▐ TRANSPORTATION. Two kilometers outside the city, the **train station** (☎ 0864 21 10 41) joins the Rome-Pescara and Carpione-L'Aquila-Terni lines. The way into town is long and hilly, so it's best to take **Bus A** (5:30am-8pm, €0.70) from the train station to the *centro;* ask to stop at P. XX Settembre. Catch the bus back to the train station from the stop next to the public gardens. **Trains** run to: Avezzano (1½hr., 11 per day 4:47am-7:49pm, €3.36); L'Aquila (1hr., 9 per day 6:34am-8:30pm, €3.36); Naples (4hr., 4 per day 6:29am-3:26pm, €12.34); Pescara (1-1¼hr., 21 per day 5:10am-9:18pm, €3.36); and Rome (1½-2½hr., 5 per day 5:47am-5:23pm, €7-12). **ARPA** runs a **bus** to Castle di Sangro in Abruzzo National Park (1hr., 3 per day 8:10am-6:10pm, €6.55; reduced service Su). For a **taxi**, call ☎ 0864 317 47.

▐▌ ORIENTATION AND PRACTICAL INFORMATION. Viale Stazione runs from the train station into Sulmona; upon reaching town, it becomes **Viale Roosevelt** and continues past the public gardens, becoming **Corso Ovidio**, Sulmona's main street; this runs past **Piazza XX Settembre** and **Piazza Garibaldi**, then exits the *centro storico* through **Porta Napoli**. The **IAT Tourist Office**, C. Ovidio, 208, provides free city **maps**, as well as hotel and restaurant listings. It also sells **Club Italiano Alpino** maps for €7.40. (☎/fax 0864 532 76. M and W 9am-1pm and 4-6pm, Tu and F 9am-1pm.) A cheery crew mans the **UST Tourist Office**, across the street in P. dell'Annunziata, providing detailed hiking information, train and bus schedules, Club Italiano Alpino maps, free city maps, and references for local mountain guides. (☎ 0864 21 02 16, fax 20 73 48. Open daily 9am-1:30pm and 4-8pm.) In case of **emergency**, reach the **police** at ☎ 113. For an **ambulance**, call ☎ 118. Access the **Internet** at **Totoricevitora**, P. Garibaldi, 25. **Western Union** service is also available. (☎ 0864 21 27 14. Open M-Sa 9am-1pm and 3:30-8:30pm. €6 per hr., students €5.) The **post office** is in P. Brigata Maiella, behind P. del Carmine. (☎ 0864 24 711. Open M-F 8am-6:30pm, Sa 9:15am-1pm.) **Postal Code:** 67039.

▐▐ ACCOMMODATIONS AND FOOD. Make reservations in summer, since this region is popular with mountain bikers and hikers. The recently renovated **Albergo Stella ❸**, V. Panfilo Mazara, 18/20, off C. Ovidio, near the aqueduct, features spacious, beautifully decorated rooms with wooden furniture. All rooms have bath, phone, TV, hair dryers, and electric card entry. The management speaks no English but strives to accommodate all needs. (☎ 0864 526 53; www.hasr.it. Breakfast included at the bar and restaurant. Singles €35-40; doubles €55-65. MC/V.) **Hotel Italia ❷**, P. S. Tommasi, 3, to the right off P. XX Settembre, has clean rooms with high ceilings, some with balconies and views of mountains and the dome of S. Annunziata. Bring flip-flops for the shared showers. (☎ 0864 523 08. Singles €24, with bath €32; doubles €41/€53.) A stone wall shelters the quiet **Hotel Armando ❹**, V. Montenero, 15, which offers spacious rooms and a serene garden. All rooms have bath, TV, and balcony. Exit the old city though Pta. Napoli onto V. Mazzini; take the fourth left onto V. Diaz until reaching V. Montenero. (☎ 0864 21 07 83.

ABRUZZO AND MOLISE

Breakfast included. Singles €42-45; doubles €72-75. AmEx/MC/V.) The UST tourist office rents three **apartments ❶** in the center of town, two of which hold up to four people (€39 per night) and one that holds up to seven (€52-72 per night). Rooms include beds, microwave, sink, stove, fridge, TV, and bath. Call for info and booking. (☎0864 21 02 16.)

⬛Cesidio ❷, V. Solimo, 25, has been preparing local fare at reasonable prices for 50 years. The house specialty, spicy *spaghetti al Cesidio* (€4.13), is pasta perfection. (☎0864 34 940. *Menù* €13. Open Tu-Su noon-3:30pm and 7-10:30pm. AmEx/MC/V.) The chic and colorful **Osteria Del Tempo Perso ❷**, Vco. del Vecchi, 7, serves splendid pizzas (€4-5) to a packed house; an impressive selection of vegetarian toppings is available. Heaping plates of *antipasti* (from €6.50) are accompanied by freshly baked focaccia. (☎0864 525 45. Open M-Tu, Th-Su 12:30-3pm and 7:30pm-2am. AmEx/MC/V.) Dine *al fresco* at **Ristorante Frangiò ❷**, V. Ercole Ciofano, 51, where trellises and arbors on the peaceful outdoor terrace complement fresh, fragrant meals. (☎0864 21 27 73. *Primi* and *secondi* from €5.50.)

◩ 🏛 SIGHTS AND ENTERTAINMENT. The Romanesque-Gothic **Cattedrale di San Panfilo** is at the end C. Ovidio, near the public gardens. Its center was built 1000 years ago on the ruins of a temple to Apollo and Vesta. From the gardens near P. XX Settembre, follow C. Ovidio to the **Chiesa di Santissima Annunziata,** on the left, with carved cherubs in high relief staring down from the facade. The 15th-century Gothic palazzo adjacent to the church has a very small **museum** presenting rare Sulmonese Renaissance goldwork and its characteristic patterns of sublime intricacy. There is also a collection of wooden statues from local churches. (☎0864 21 02 16. Open Tu-F 9am-1pm, Sa-Su 10am-1pm and 4-7pm. €1.) Behind, one block off C. Ovidio, the **Museo in Situ** features intact ruins of an ancient Roman house. (Open Tu-Su 10am-1pm. Free.) The colossal **Piazza Garibaldi** surrounds the Renaissance **Fontana del Vecchio,** which flows with mountain water channeled from the nearby **medieval aqueduct.** With its backdrop of towering Apennines, P. Garibaldi is a lovely sight, particularly in the early evening.

Sulmona's *confetti* candy is made at the **Pelino factory,** V. Stazione Introdaqua, 55. Turn right after the arch at the end of C. Ovidio onto V. Trieste, continue 1km down the hill as it becomes V. Stazione Introdaqua, and enter the Pelino building. The Pelino family has been making *confetti* since 1783 with traditional machinery, some of which is displayed in the free **museum.** Check out the somewhat sacrilegious pictures of prior popes and Padre Pio munching on candied religious instruments. (☎0864 21 00 47. Open M-Sa 8am-12:30pm and 3-6:30pm.)

The last weekend of July heralds the Giostra Cavalleresca di Sulmona, a festival in which mounted, beacon-bearing knights ride figure-eights around P. Garibaldi. Each knight's crest represents one of the seven borghi (neighborhoods) of medieval Sulmona. Purchase a seated ticket from the Giostra (☎0864 21 09 69) or the UST, or stand on tip-toe in the crowd to watch for free. In preparation for the big event, the borghi host public festivals on June weekends and hang crest-flags from windows. The first weekend of July brings another joust, the Giostra Cavalleresca di Europa, this time featuring international knights. In October Sulmona hosts international film and opera festivals.

🥾 HIKING. The mountains of **Majella National Park** (also spelled "Maiella") tower over Sulmona. Several trails are easily accessible by foot or **ARPA bus** from the town center; the UST tourist office has information on the capricious bus schedule. High up on the cliffs, one can visit the cave retreat of the saintly hermit who became Pope Celestine V. It's a fairly easy hike (1½hr. round-trip) from the town of **Badia,** which is accessible by bus (20min., 11 per day 7:35am-7:40pm, €1, reduced service on weekends) from Sulmona's public gardens on C. Ovidio; purchase tickets from *tabacchi*. Several longer routes can be reached from **Campo di Giove,** accessible by bus (25min., 4 per day 6:30am-6pm, €2.20, reduced service on weekends) from Sulmona. For information on hiking trails and available guides, consult the UST tourist office and the helpful **Club Alpino Italiano** map (€7.40), available from the tourist offices. Each hike is designated by a series of colored blazes placed along the trails at regular intervals. The difficulty levels in the Club Alpino Italiano guide refer to mountaineering experience, not hiking experience— so hikes of "moderate difficulty" may be challenging for those not used to mountain climbing. The beginning sections of almost all trails are manageable. **Hike 7a** is 45min. from the village of Fonte D'Amore to the ruins of a sanctuary dedicated to Hercules (or, according to old Sulmonese lore, a villa belonging to Ovid). Take the 5km hike through forested hills to Morrone to find the sacred site. These trailheads, 4km from Sulmona, are served by local buses. Schedules are available from the tourist office; when planning a hike, keep mid-afternoon service gaps in mind.

ABRUZZO NATIONAL PARK

The Abruzzo National Park (Parco Nazionale d'Abruzzo) is central Italy's fourth-largest park. Its peaks, the highest in the Apennines, provide spectacular views of lush woodlands and crystal-clear lakes as frigid as they are pristine. Within the park, 44,000 hectares of mountainous wilderness bristle with fascinating wildlife. The park is a healthy habitat for local fauna; lynx have been reintroduced near Civitella Alfedena, joining Marsican brown bears, Apennine wolves, and Abruzzo chamois antelopes. Cowbells clang in the park's sprawling pastures, and lizards dart in the brush. Despite reported glimpses of the park's more formidable wildlife, incidents of confrontation with visitors are rare: leave the animals alone and they'll leave you alone. Avezzano is the gateway into the park, while Pescasseroli, the park's administrative center, provides the best base for exploration. Many exciting trails wind through the outward expanses. The ARPA bus falls short of many of these marvelous sites and quaint villages, so renting a car is certainly worth it. Those with cars can request the free *Guide to Abruzzo's Hidden Wonders* at the park's tourist office. For serious bikers, the *Abruzzo Guide to Mountain Biking*, also available at the tourist office, lists many trails.

■✚ 🛈 TRANSPORTATION AND PRACTICAL INFORMATION

Trains run from Avezzano to: Pescara (2hr., 6 per day 6:13am-8:10pm, €9.65); Rome (2hr., 13 per day 4:30am-8:50pm, €9.11); and Sulmona (1¼hr., 11 per day 6:13am-8:10pm, €5.52). An **ARPA bus** (☎0863 265 61 or 229 21) runs from Avezzano through the park to Castel di Sangro (2¾hr., M-Sa 5 per day 6:40am-4:15pm, €5.21), making five stops en route: Barrea (2¼hr., €4.41); Civitella Alfedena (2hr., €4.21); Opi (1¾hr., €4.21); Pescasseroli (1½hr., €3.90); and Villetta Barrea (2hr., €4.26). Buses run to Pescasseroli from Rome's Tiburtina station (3hr., 7:45am, one-way €13.21).

In Pescasseroli, check out the **Ufficio di Zona,** V. Piave, 7, and pick up the essential park **map** (€6). From the bus stop in P. Antonio, walk along the right side of the school; the office is on the right. (☎0863 91 27 60. Open daily 9am-1pm and 3:30-7pm.) The **IAT Information Office,** V. Piave, 2, off P. Antonio, provides info on lodgings and restaurants. Most of the info is printed in French and German. (☎0863 91 04 61; www.pescasseroli.net. Open daily 9am-1pm and 4-7pm.) For **carabinieri,** call ☎0863 91 07 16. The **Farmacia del Parco,** P. V. Emanuele, 12, stocks everything from medication for sunburn to moleskin for blistered feet. (☎0863 91 07 53. Open M-W and F-Su 9am-1pm and 4-8pm.) The **post office** is at V. Piave, 1/A. (☎0863 91 07 31. Open M-F 8am-1:30pm, Sa 8am-noon.) **Postal Code:** 67032.

🅰🅱 ACCOMMODATIONS AND FOOD

AVEZZANO. If there is one thing to be said about Avezzano, it's that it used to be beautiful. In 1915, however, a violent earthquake shook the town to pieces, and today its primary aesthetic features are the *telespazio* (a satellite transmission system) and several unbelievably ghastly fountains (the most offensive is directly in front of the train station). However, the town is unquestionably the most convenient gateway to Abruzzo National Park. Buses to the park depart from the **bus station,** directly behind the **train station;** a *sottopassaggio* (underground passageway), connects the two. **Hotel Velino ❹,** V. Montello, 9, is quiet and close to the train station. Rooms, though small, have satellite TV, phone, and clean bath. A bar and comfortable piano lounge compensate for the building's somewhat dreary, modern architecture. (☎0863 41 26 96, fax 34 26 31. Singles €45-52; doubles €65-72. AmEx/MC/V). COAL **supermarket,** 304 V. XX Settembre, stocks water, fruit, bread, and deli meats. (☎0863 41 09 09. Open M-Sa 8am-1pm and 4:30-8pm. AmEx/MC/V.) Stop by **Pizzeria Il Golosone ❶,** P. M. Banoli 10, to enjoy focaccia or a generous slice of pizza *margherita* (€1, with olives €1.30) with a young crowd.

PESCASSEROLI. Set in the middle of the park, this is a popular place to stay. Solo travelers may have a hard time finding a single room, since most establishments offer only doubles. **Hotel Dafne ❹,** on V. Rovereto, opens into a lovely rose garden. The management is polite, and rooms have smart decor and plush quilts, in addition to bath, TV, and phone. (☎0863 91 28 38; hoteldafne@interfree.it. Reserve ahead for July-Aug. Doubles €52. Required half pension; in Aug. required full pension €65. AmEx/MC/V.) Near Pensione Dafne, **Pensione Claudia ❷,** V. Tagliamento, 35, 200m across the gravel lot on the main street leading out of town, has 10 quiet rooms, all with bath. Small and rustic, this lovely hotel has mountain-lodge charm and friendly management. Its sign is partially hidden behind a tree, so be on the lookout. (☎0863 918 37; m.finamore@ermes.it. July-Aug. rooms €32 with required half pension; Sept.-June rooms €15. Cash only.) **Pensione al Castello ❹,** V. Gabriele d'Annunzio, 1, has seven pleasant rooms, all with bath and TV. (☎0863 91 07 57. Breakfast €3. Doubles €42; triples €53; quads €64. MC/V.) Five campgrounds are within 21km of town. The best is **Campeggio dell'Orso ❶.** Conveniently situated 1km from Pescasseroli on the main road to Opi, these quiet grounds are a choice spot. Call ahead to reserve. (☎0863 919 55. €3.50 per person, €3.50 per tent.)

For picnic supplies, head to Delfina A&O **supermarket** on V. S. Lucia, the main highway, past the zoo and the park office. (☎0863 919 34. Open daily 9am-1pm and 4-8pm. AmEx/MC/V.) **Pasticceria Alpina ❶,** Traversa Sangro, 6, serves an array of award-winning sweets. (☎0863 91 05 61. Open Tu-Su 7am-10pm.) Pescasseroli's restaurants close early, so expect to make it an early evening. For traditional fare, head to **Trattoria Da Pitone ❷,** at 17 V. Colli dell'Oro, behind the *Municipo*. Succulent dishes (tender lamb €7) are served on pink checkered tablecloths. (☎0863 91 27 69. *Primi* €6.50, *secondi* €7. Cover €1.50. AmEx/MC/V.) For a thick, delicious slice of pizza (from €1.10) in a simpler and more sequestered spot, **La Rotonda ❶,** Viale Colli del Oro, 3, is a good bet. Service is zealously efficient. Heading toward Opi, bear left onto V. Seggiovia; it's on the left. (☎3603 642 11. Open daily 11am-3pm and 7-10pm. Cash only.)

OPI. ARPA buses follow the park road to the village of Opi, named for the pagan goddess of abundance whose temple rested here in ancient times. **La Sosta ❷,** V. Nazionale, 17, is a spotless six-room B&B half a kilometer past Opi on the park's bus route. Rooms are simple, comfortable, and affordable. A fan-

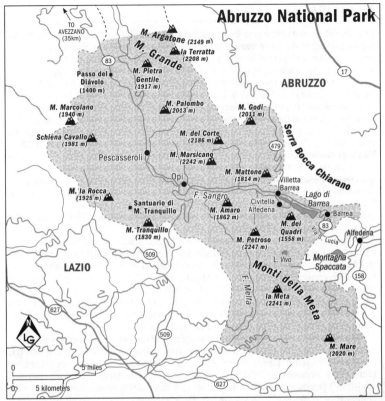

Abruzzo National Park

TO AVEZZANO (35km)

M. Argatone (2149 m)

M. Grande

la Terratta (2208 m)

Passo del Diávolo (1400 m)

M. Pietra Gentile (1917 m)

ABRUZZO

M. Marcolano (1940 m)

M. Palombo (2013 m)

M. Godi (2011 m)

Schiéna Cavallo (1981 m)

M. del Corte (2186 m)

Serra Bocca Chiarano

Pescasseroli

M. Marsicano (2242 m)

Opi

M. Mattone (1814 m)

Villetta Barrea

Lago di Barrea

M. 'la Rocca (1925 m)

F. Sangro

Civitella Alfedena

Barrea

Santuario di M. Tranquillo

M. Amaro (1862 m)

M. dei Quadri (1558 m)

Via S. Lucia

Alfedena

M. Tranquillo (1830 m)

M. Petroso (2247 m)

LAZIO

L. Vivo

L. Montagna Spaccata

F. Melfa

Monti della Meta

la Meta (2241 m)

M. Mare (2020 m)

N LG

0   5 miles

0   5 kilometers

ABRUZZO AND MOLISE

tastic backyard terrace provides peace and quiet, while the balconies off of every room offer serene mountain views. (☎ 0863 91 60 57. All rooms with bath. €18-23.) **Vecchio Mulino ❶** occupies a peaceful spot 2km past the village on the bus route. This campground has a restaurant, bar, and efficient management. (☎ 0863 91 22 32; ilvecchiomulino@tiscalinet.it. €5.50-6 per person, €5.50 per tent. AmEx/MC/V.)

CIVITELLA ALFEDENA. Ten kilometers past Opi, the ARPA bus reaches the village of **Villetta Barrea**. The turn-off to Civitella Alfedena, 200m farther down the road, leads to the clean, no-frills **Camping Le Quite ❶**, bordered by the River Sangro. (☎ 0864 891 41. €2.58-3.10 per person, €3.10-3.62 per large tent.) In Civitella Alfedena, **Alberghetto La Torre ❹** and **Albergo Autico Borgo ❹**, V. Castello, 3, under the same management, offer rooms with beautiful views of the Sentiero delle Valdirose mountains, bath, TV, and phone. (☎ 0864 89 01 21. Doubles €39; triples €49.) The **Museo del Lupo,** on the left when entering town, documents the history of the Apennine wolf and lynx. Though not as thrilling as an actual wildlife encounter, it's likely the only opportunity to see the creatures at all. (☎ 0864 89 01 41. Open daily 10am-1pm and 3-7pm. Closed M in July. €3.) Frigid **Barrea Lake** cuts into the mountains, stretching 7km between Villetta Barrea and the town of **Barrea.**

🏔 HIKING

The ascent from Avezzano to Pescasseroli is breathtaking; this trail, which marks the beginning of the park, passes by fields of poppies, dazzling valleys, and rocky outcrops. The indispensable trail map (€5.60) from the **Pescasseroli Ufficio di Zona** indicates prime viewing spots for brown bears, deer, wolves, and eagles. If the park's creatures still prove elusive, there's always Pescasseroli's **Centro di Visita**, Viale Colle dell'Orso, 2, off V. S. Lucia heading toward Opi, which has a museum and a small zoo. (Open daily 10am-1pm and 3-7pm. €5.16.) The trails are arranged such that all paths beginning with the same letter start from the same point. For a short hike, take **trail B1** to the castle ruins at Monte Ceraso (50min. round-trip). To really stretch those legs, tackle the beautiful 5hr. round-trip hike on **trail C3** to **Vicolo di Monte Tranquillo** (Tranquil Mountain Pass, 1673m). The trail starts at the southern end of town and leads up through the green Valle Mancina, past the Rifugio Della Difesa station. The climb to the pass is lined by forests of graceful birch trees and boasts mighty views of the mountain peaks to the north. **Trail C5,** which intersects trail **C3,** more comprehensively examines the ridges. True adventurers can take on one of the park's highest peaks, **Monte Marsicano** (2245m), with the steep and arduous **trail E6** from Opi (7-8hr. round-trip).

Clever coordination of hikes with the ARPA bus schedule can enable travelers to venture farther afield. From Civitella Alfedena (15km from Pescasseroli), take **trail I1** to **K6** through the sublimely beautiful **Valle di Rose** to see the park's largest herd of chamois. From mid-July to early September, this area can only be explored with a guide (€7 per person). Go to an *ufficio di zona* the day before a planned excursion for more information about the trails or to obtain a permit and reserve a guide. From Barrea, 20km from Pescasseroli, **trail K5** runs to the **Lago Vivo** (3½hr. round-trip), which dries up between June and October.

Mountain bikes are available from the agency in the center of Pescasseroli at V. Sorgenti, 1. (€10 per day. Open daily 9am-7pm.) Several paths, including **trail C3,** are great for biking. **Ecotur,** V. Piave, 7, 2nd fl., in Pescasseroli, offers organized hikes and excursions. (☎ 0863 91 27 60; www.ecotur.org. Open daily 9am-1pm and 3:30-7pm.) During winter, this area offers excellent skiing across three peaks, with challenging slopes and heavy snowfall. Package deals called *settimane bianche* (white weeks) provide accommodations, lift tickets, and half pension. For ticket info, call ☎0863 91 22 16. For the regional snow bulletin, call ☎0862 66 510.

PESCARA ☎085

The central transportation hub for Abruzzo and Molise, Pescara holds little in the way of aesthetic appeal but offers exciting nightlife in the summer and great shopping year-round. Italian vacationers swarm over its 20km shoreline in July and August and leave its architecturally lackluster buildings deserted during the rest of the year. Even so, travelers waiting for a train or boat to Croatia can manage to find something worthwhile besides the beach. In the old city, several museums and traditional restaurants deftly showcase the best of local culture. Mid-July brings the city's celebrated jazz festival, which attracts internationally famous musicians—recent years have included Chic Corea and Bobby McFerrin.

📠 ✈ TRANSPORTATION AND PRACTICAL INFORMATION. Flights leave from Aeroporto d'Abruzzo connecting to major Italian cities and cities in Europe. Bus #38 (€0.70) runs between the train station and the airport. **Trains** run from Stazione Centrale on C. V. Emanuele, in the center of the new city, to: Bari (3½-4hr., 17 per day 1am-8:08pm, €13.22-25.73); Lecce (6hr., 12 per day 3am-8:08pm, €19.37-

34.29); Milan (6½hr., 11 per day 12:44am-11:59pm, €39.88-42.25); Naples (5hr., 11 per day 3:32am-8:08pm, €14.31-34.54); Rome (4hr., 11 per day 6:15am-10:12pm, €11.21); Sulmona (1hr., 18 per day 5:13am-10:12pm, €3.50); and Termoli (1½hr., 23 per day 3am-9pm, €4.30-6.15). ARPA **buses** run from the front of the train station. Buses to l'Aquila, Avezzano, Rome, and Sulmona run on varying schedules. Consult the info booth in front of train station for departure times. **Ferries** depart from beyond the harbor in the old city, across the river from the beach. **SNAV** (☎085 451 08 73; www.snavoli.com) runs ferries June-September to the Croatian islands of Hvar, Brac, Korcula, and Spalato. Call for times (one-way €88.65-114). Jetline (☎085 451 62 41) runs ferries to the Tremiti Islands (2½hr., 8am, €20.50).

Buses and trains stop at **Stazione Centrale** in the center of the new city, on the main street, **Corso Vittorio Emanuele.** To the right, C. V. Emanuele extends toward the **River Pescara.** Across the bridge to the right is the **old city,** and a short walk to the left leads to the **tourist harbor.** Straight across the bridge is Pescara's extensive public park. The main stretch of beach runs parallel to C. V. Emanuele, a few blocks straight out of the train station. To reach the **APT Tourist Office,** make a right directly in front of the train station on C. V. Emanuele; it will be the first establishment on the right. (☎085 42 90 01; www.abruzzoturismo.it. Open M-F and Su 10am-2pm, Sa 8-4pm.) The helpful, English-speaking staff provides a good **map** and advice on accommodations, museums, hiking, and restaurants. The **post office** is on C. V. Emanuele between the station and the river. (☎085 42 791. Open M-Sa 8am-6:30pm.) For **police,** dial ☎113; the station is at P. Duca d'Aosta. **Sport Net Centre,** V. Venezia, 14, off C. V. Emanuele, offers **Internet.** (☎085 421 93 68. €4 per hr. Open M-Sa 9:30am-1pm and 4:30-8pm.) **Postal Code:** 65100.

📍🖥 **ACCOMMODATIONS AND FOOD.** The best budget lodgings are off C. V. Emanuele, across from the train station. Beachfront hotels aren't worth the prices—the only views are of Pescara's sprawling beach-umbrella forest, and the train station isn't that far from the beach. **Hotel Adria ❸,** V. Firenze, 141, is a pleasant option on a street running parallel to C. V. Emanuele, one block toward the waterfront. Thirty modestly sized rooms come with fridge, bath, and TV. (☎085 422 42 46, fax 422 24 27. Singles €40; doubles €70. MC/V.) **Hotel Alba ❹,** V. M. Forti, 14, has more spacious rooms, some of which are equipped with A/C, TV, phone, and bath. (☎085 38 91 45; www.hotelalba.pescara.it. Breakfast included. Singles €49-65; doubles €72-100. AmEx/MC/V.) From the train station, walk down C. V. Emanuele away from the river and turn right on V. Piave to get to **Albergo Planet ❷,** V. Piave, 142. Rooms in this recently renovated hotel aren't very attractive—done up in sickly pink shades and tacky linoleum—but are clean and spacious. Odd Kandinsky prints cover the walls. (☎/fax 085 421 16 57. Singles €25, with bath €30; doubles €50. AmEx/MC/V.)

Foods of choice in Pescara fall into two categories: seafood and traditional *Abruzzese* cuisine. The local wines, including the white *Trebbiano* and red *Montepulciano,* satisfy broad tastes. The best seafood options are along the water, and on summer weekends, reservations are essential. **Le Terrazze Esplanade ❹,** P. I. Maggio, 46, Hotel Esplanade's rooftop terrace restaurant, is a haven from noisy beachfront nightlife. The gorgeous waterfront views make the meal more special. (☎085 29 21 41, fax 421 75 40. *Primi* from €16, *secondi* from €22. Open daily 8pm-midnight. MC/V.) **Jambo ❸,** Viale Rivera, 38, features elegant patio dining, a colorful bar, and an excellent waitstaff. The *gnocchi agli scampi* (€9) has seafood fans rejoicing. (☎085 421 27 949. Open daily 8am-3am. AmEx/MC/V.) At **Alcyone ❸,** along the beach at Viale Rivera, 24, a lively, casually dressed crowd downs fresh local seafood and superior pizza. *Tagliatelle all'Umberto* (pasta, fish, and eggs; €10) is a house specialty. (☎/fax 085 421 68 30. Pizza €3.50-10.50. Cover €2. Open daily 9am-1am. MC/V.) The popular **La Cantina di Jozz ❷,** V. delle Caserme, 63,

ABRUZZO AND MOLISE

offers scenic outdoor seating across from the museum in the old city. Patrons linger over plates of *pesce fritto* (€4.50) late into the evening. (☎ 085 451 88 00. Open Tu-Sa noon-3pm and 8pm-midnight, Su noon-3pm. AmEx/MC/V.) For picnic supplies, head to **Marcellerie Ianetti ❶** at V. Leopoldo Muzii, 108, where fresh meats, great sandwiches, and a range of local foodstuffs are available on the cheap. Facing the water, head left on Lungomare Matteotti until hitting V. Leopoldo Muzii on the left. (☎ 085 421 68 96. Open M-F 7am-1pm and 4-6:30pm, Sa 7am-1pm.)

◐ ♫ SIGHTS AND ENTERTAINMENT. All the attractions of a seaside sports resort crowd Pescara's vibrant **beach:** basketball, soccer, volleyball, music, windsurfing, and miles of sunbathing. Almost all of the sea-front space is private; admission costs €5-7 depending on location. A paltry public stretch lies a 5min. walk to the left of P. I. Maggio, when facing the sea. Pescara's cultural area resides on the other side of the river, with a couple of decent museums and a pleasant harbor. Cross the bridge and take the first right to reach the **Museo delle Genti d'Abruzzo,** V. delle Caserme, 24, which celebrates 4000 years of Abruzzo's history. Chronological galleries show the development of local crafts like pottery and furniture-making from paleolithic times to the present. (☎ 085 451 00 26. Open M-F 9:30am-1pm and 3:30-6pm, Su 10am-1pm. €5, EU students and citizens under 18 or over 65 €2.) Straight ahead across the bridge, the **Museo Civico,** V. Marconi, 45, celebrates the remarkable 20th-century artwork of six members of the influential Cascella family. (☎ 085 428 35 15. Open Tu-Su 9am-1pm. €2.50, EU students 18-24 €1.50, EU citizens under 18 or over 65 free.)

Pescara hosts a world-renown annual **jazz festival** in mid-July, attracting renowned Italian and international acts for performances in P. della Rinascità. (☎ 085 29 220; www.pescarajazz.com. Tickets €10-18.) The popular annual **film festival,** also in July, screens both Italian and international films in several of Pescara's cinemas. Contact the APT tourist office for more information. (☎ 085 42 90 01; www.abruzzoturismo.it. Tickets €10 and up.)

TERMOLI
☎ 0875

Despite its pristine coastline and quaint old city streets, Termoli is surprisingly small and untouristed. Most travelers come to catch ferries or stay the night while daytripping to the Tremiti Islands (p. 537). The **FS train station** lies at the western end of town. Trains run to Bari (17 per day 4:01am-9:04pm, €9.80-21.28); Milan (9 per day 2:27am-11:40pm, €37.37); Naples (1 per day 11:27am, €12.34); Pescara (28 per day 12:06am-11:55pm, €4.30-9.15); and Rome (2 per day 6:54am-5:45pm, €17.40-34.23). From the station, **Corso M. Milano** extends left to **Lungomare Colombo,** a waterfront strip lined with hotels. Restaurants and shops line **Corso Umberto,** which runs from the station to the old town. To get to the **port,** walk down C. Milano and turn left on Lungomare Colombo. The ferry docks and ticket offices are past the fishing boats on the long breakwater. The **tourist office** is on the *lungomare,* a block to the right of the intersection with C. M. Milano. The staff doesn't speak English, but a free **map** has info on hotels and restaurants. (☎ 0875 70 83 42. Open M-Sa 9am-1pm and 5-7pm.) For **Internet,** take C.M. Milano and turn right one block before the *lungomare* onto V. Ruffini. **@dria 2000** is on the right. (☎ 0875 71 44 36. Open daily 9:40am-1pm and 5pm-1:30am. €3 per hr.)

Travelers passing through have several options for accommodations and food. The best is **Pensione Villa Ida ❸,** C. M. Milano, 27, between the station and the beach. Its 23 generously sized rooms have A/C, bath, TV, and phone. (☎ 0875 70 66 66; www.pensionevillaida.it. Breakfast included. Singles from €37 in April to €42 in Aug.; doubles €52-62. AmEx/MC/V.) **Hotel Rosary ❹,** Lungomare Colombo, 24, at the intersection with C. M. Milano, is a short walk from the station and a stone's throw from the beach. All rooms have bath and TV. (☎ 0875 84 944. Open Apr.-Oct. Doubles €57; triples €75; quads €95. AmEx/MC/V.) From the train station, turn right from C. Nazionale on V. Alfano and then right on V. Ruffino for **La Sacrestia** ❶, V. Ruffini, 48. Divine pizzas (€3-5.16) served steaming from the oven. (☎ 0875 70 56 03. Open daily noon-2pm and 7:30-11pm. MC/V.) **Lineapane** ❶, V.M. Milano, 18, is the perfect place to pick up quality baked goods for the ride. The locally famous *cancellate* (€0.50), flat iron-cooked cookies, are a sure bet. (Open M-Sa 7am-1:15pm and 4:30-9pm; also open July-Aug. Su 7am-1pm.)

TREMITI ISLANDS ☎ 0882

Covered with lush vegetation and rich in natural resources, the Tremiti Islands are a relatively well-kept secret. San Domino, the largest in the archipelago, is dubbed the Green Pearl of the Adriatic because of its complex flora. Its neighbor San Nicola, the only island populated year-round, was most famously home to Emperor Augustus's daughter Julia, there exiled for her naughty behavior. When summer hits, the four islands swell with Italian daytrippers, but after the evening ferries depart they become peaceful and relaxing retreats. Just 35km from the Gargano Peninsula on the mainland, *i Tremiti* make a fun daytrip—each can be crossed on foot in less than 2hr.—or a base for more prolonged exploration.

E TRANSPORTATION. Ferry service from Termoli only operates June-Sept. **Hydrofoils** make the trip in 1hr., ferries in 1½hr. Several companies serve the islands: the popular **M/N Venere** (☎ 0875 70 51 98; daily 8:50am, return 5:45pm; €7.50-8.50); **Navigazione Libera** (☎ 0875 70 48 59; www.navlib.it; daily June 1-Sept. 15 8:40am, 9:15, 10:55am, 5:20pm; return 9:45am, 4:10, 5:30, 6:40pm); and **Adriatica** ferries (M-Th 9:45am, return 4pm; F, Sa, and Su 9:35am, return 4pm, 7pm.)

◼◪ ORIENTATION AND PRACTICAL INFORMATION. There are four Tremiti islands: **San Domino, San Nicola, Capraia,** and **Pianosa.** San Domino is the largest, with the archipelago's only hotels, while San Nicola is home to an 11th-century abbey. The last two are small and desolate, hospitable to seagulls but not much else. **Motorboats** (€3) run throughout the day between San Nicola and San Domino. For **carabinieri** on both islands, call ☎ 112. A 24hr. **first aid station** (☎ 0882 46 32 34) is at the port in San Domino, a good hike up the hill. A **pharmacy** is in the village on San Nicola, (☎ 0882 46 33 27. Open daily June-Sept. 9am-1pm and 5-9pm; Oct.-May 9:30am-12:30pm and 5-7:30pm.) **Post offices** are on San Domino (☎ 0882 46 32 59) and San Nicola (☎ 0882 46 30 21). Postal service is spotty at best.

◪◻ ACCOMMODATIONS AND FOOD. San Domino hosts the islands' only hotels, most of which offer doubles and require half or full pension. Reservations are a good idea in summer, as the few rooms fill up quickly. **Hotel La Vela** ❺, on V. Federico II, 4, offers half pension rooms a short walk up from the boat harbor on San Domino. Call to be picked up from the port. Though average in size, the rooms are bright and pleasant, and have bath and phone. (☎ 0882 46 32 54; www.hotel-lavela.it. Reservation required. Rooms with seafront view €52-80 per person; garden view €47-75; prices vary seasonally.) **Albergo Rossana** ❷, conveniently located near the port on San Domino, has six simple but spacious rooms, all with double bed, bath, and A/C. (☎ 0882 46 32 98. Breakfast included. €25-34 per person. Prices peak at €57 in Aug. MC/V.) **Villagio International** ❹, on Punta del Diamante, is an economic choice in a quiet area near the shore. There are two housing options: bungalows and prefabricated hut/tent hybrids. (☎ 0882 46 34 05. www.puntadeldiamante.it. Prefab units €30-49 per person, required half pension in Aug. €54; bungalows €44-52 per person, required half pension in Aug. €76. MC/V.) **Ristorante**

Diomeda ❷, V. Della Torreta, 8, on San Nicola, is a good spot to refuel after the hike up to the monastery. Outdoor tables offer an amazing view of the archipelago. (☎/fax 0882 46 30 25. Open daily 9am-6pm, €15 all inclusive.) At **Ristorante Bel Mare ❷,** San Domino Marina, 1, the only restaurant right on the beach of San Domino, customers choose their favorite seafood dishes from a large self-service table. (☎3396 87 44 57. Open daily in summer 9am-6pm; €15 for self-service bar.)

◪◙ OUTDOOR ACTIVITIES AND SIGHTS. Paths snake through the thick **pine forest** on San Domino, alive with the sound of cicadas and the smell of dried pine needles. Many lead down to the small rocky coves along the coast, where vacationers swim in sapphire waters—in secluded spots, sans suits. Some Italians take to the seas with **spear guns** for fishing adventures, while others are content to contemplate its marine life more peacefully while **snorkeling.** The **Marlin Club,** up the hill and to the left from Hotel La Vela (☎0882 46 37 65; www.marlintremiti.it), affiliated with Hotel Eden, offers **scuba diving instruction** at many experience levels in Italian and English, for €50 with equipment and guide. **M.G.M.,** in the colorful kiosk farthest to the left on the port, offers two tours of the archipelago's natural caves, both in a glass-bottomed boat; the long tour (€13) includes all of the islands while the shorter tour (€9) covers only San Nicola and San Domino (☎368 70 00 341 or 333 58 32 718.) The fortified **Abbazia e Chiesa di Santa Maria** (Abbey of Santa Maria) has crowned the cliffs of neighboring island San Nicola since the 11th century. The dreary structure might be more interesting for its historical value than its architecture. A tradition of exile began when Emperor Augustus's adulterous daughter Julia was banished here in the 1st century and continued in the early 20th century with victims of the Fascist regime's purges. Portions of the original mosaic floor that have survived numerous renovations are blocked off to prevent further damage. The monastery is accessible by a short path from the harbor. **Alidaunia's** 15min. helicopter tours are a quick way to see the islands, though they miss much of the beautiful scenery found in local caves. (☎088 16 17 961 or 16 10 267. Depart from Termoli 8:45am and 4pm, €22.) One of the islands' only clubs, **Discoteca Diomede,** P. Sandro Pertini, 1, San Domino, has a huge dance floor and attractive green and white decor. Though entrance is free, there is an obligatory drink; try Cuba Libera for €4.50. (☎0882 46 34 03. Open daily 8am-3am.)

CAMPANIA

Sprung from the shadow of Mt. Vesuvius, Campania thrives in defiance of natural disasters. The submerged city at Baia, lava-smothered Pompeii, and ruins of Benevento attest to a land resigned to harsh natural outbursts. Although rich in historical importance and natural beauty, the region's true treasure is its people. The human element asserts itself most tenaciously in the bustle of Neapolitan nightlife, the splendor of the region's churches and museums, and the static eternity of its ancient cities, reminders of both human achievement and mortality. When the city streets get too hot and the complexities of history too overwhelming, head to the Amalfi Coast, the unrivaled titan of the southern Italian coast.

HIGHLIGHTS OF CAMPANIA

PAY HOMAGE at the tomb of epic author Virgil, narrator of the celebrated *Aeneid*, a chronicle of Rome's foundations. (p. 555.)

PEEK into the past at Herculaneum, where impressively intact ruins reveal conditions of everyday life 2000 years ago, before Mt. Vesuvius devastated the town. (p. 565.)

REPOSE on the incomparable Amalfi Coast. (p. 581.)

DRIFT through the shadows of Paestum's mortarless Doric Temples, some of the best preserved in the world. (p. 596.)

NAPLES (NAPOLI)   ☎081

From the zipping Vespas to the bustling throngs, Naples moves a million miles per minute. Neapolitans spend every waking moment out on the town, eating, drinking, shouting, laughing, and enjoying themselves. Italy's third largest city is Southern Italy at its best. Surrounded by the ancient ruins of Pompeii and the gorgeous Amalfi Coast, it is the anchor of Campania, full of excitement and energy. Over the years, Naples has acquired a bad reputation as a city of crime and grime. But to skip out on Naples is to miss one of Europe's greatest cities: recently, UNESCO declared Naples's historic center the most architecturally varied in the world; the city's streets are world renowned as a treasure trove of piazzas, palaces, and exquisite churches. With police officers working to ensure safety in the streets and the advent of the "Napoli 99," a citizens' group determined to preserve art and public monuments, Naples is beginning to outgrow its shady reputation. The birthplace of pizza and the modern-day home of tantalizing seafood and pasta, Naples will please even the pickiest of gourmands. But its best offering is its people, who will never shy away from sharing an espresso and some conversation. Once you get used to the heartbeat of Naples, every other place seems just a little bit boring in comparison.

◪ INTERCITY TRANSPORTATION

Flights: Aeroporto Capodichino, V. Umberto Maddalena (☎081 789 61 11), northeast of the city. The convenient **Alibus** leaves from P. Municipio and P. Garibaldi (Stazione Centrale) for the airport (15-20min., 6am-10:30pm, €3). The **3S** city bus also runs from P. Municipio and P. Garibaldi (Stazione Centrale) to the airport (€1). Although cheaper than the Alibus, the city bus makes many more stops. A **taxi** from P. Municipio costs €16. All taxis to and from the airport have set prices, depending on the neighborhood from which you depart or to which you are going. The taxi driver should not turn on the meter, and there should be no supplementary fees or charges. **Alitalia,** V. Medina, 41/

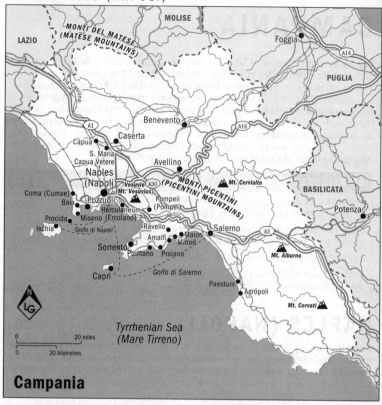

Campania

42 (☎848 86 56 43), off P. Municipio. Open M-F 9am-4:30pm. **British Airways** (☎848 81 22 66). Open M-F 8am-8pm, Sa 9am-5pm. **Lufthansa** (☎06 656 840 04). Buy tickets for the 3S bus at any *tabacchi*.

Trains: Naples is served by 3 train companies from **Stazione Centrale** in P. Garibaldi.

FS: ☎081 89 20 21. Frequent connections to: **Brindisi** (5hr., 5 per day 11am-8pm, €9.25); **Milan** (8hr., 13 per day 7:30am-10:30pm, €50-60); **Rome** (2hr., 34 per day 4:30am-10:06pm, €10.19); **Salerno** (45min., 8 per day 8am-9pm, €2.74); **Syracuse** (10hr., 6 per day 10am-9:30pm, €28.41).

Circumvesuviana: ☎081 772 24 44. From Stazione Centrale to: **Herculaneum** (€1.70); **Pompeii** (€2.30); **Sorrento** (€3.10). Trains depart every 30min., 5:09am-10:39pm.

Ferrovia Cumana and **Ferrovia Circumflegrea:** (☎800 00 16 16). Luggage storage available (see **Practical Information**). Both run trains from Montesanto station to **Pozzuoli** and **Cumae**. Trains depart every 20min. Info booth in Stazione Centrale open daily 7am-9pm.

Ferries: The daily newspaper *Il Mattino* (€0.80) carries current ferry schedules. Port taxes may apply. Hydrofoils depart from **Molo Beverello** and **Mergellina,** and ferries from **Molo Beverello, Molo Angioino** (next to Stazione Marittima), and **Pozzuoli.** Molo Angioino is for longer trips to **Sicily** and **Sardinia.** Molo Beverello is at the base of P. Municipio. Take the R2 bus from P. Garibaldi to P. Municipio.

Caremar: ☎081 551 38 82. Ticket office on Molo Beverello. Open daily 6am-10pm. Ferries and hydrofoils depart for: **Capri** (ferry: 1½hr., 7 per day 5:40am-9:10pm, €4.80; hydrofoil: 1hr., 4 per day 7:55am-6:30pm, €9.60); **Ischia** (ferry: 1½hr., 8 per day 6:25am-9:55pm, €4.80; hydrofoil: 1hr., 6 per day 7:50am-6:15pm, €9.60); **Procida** (ferry: 1hr., 7 per day 6:25am-9:55pm, €4.80; hydrofoil: 40min., 5 per day 7:40am-5:55pm, €9.60).

SNAV: ☎081 428 55 55. Open daily 9am-7pm. Runs hydrofoils Apr.-Oct. to: **Capri** (1hr., 7 per day 7:10am-6:10pm, €10); **Ischia-Casamicciola Terme** (1hr., 4 per day 8:20am-6:40pm, €10); **Procida** (40min., 4 per day 8:20am-6:40pm, €10); and ferries to **Palermo** (5hr., 7:30pm, €27).

Siremar: ☎081 580 03 40. Ticket office at Molo Angioino. Open daily 9am-7pm. Depart from Stazione Marittima. Ferries run in summer 2 per week; in winter 3 per week. To: **Lipari** (12hr.); **Stromboli** (8hr.); **Vulcano** (13hr.); points along these routes. Prices vary.

Tirrenia: ☎199 12 31 99. Ticket office at Molo Angioino. Open daily 8:30am-1:15pm and 2:30-5:30pm. Ferries to **Cagliari** (16hr., depart weekly, biweekly in summer) and **Palermo** (11hr., depart daily). Required supplemental port tax. Schedules and prices vary.

Alilauro: ☎081 551 33 52 or 552 28 38. Ticket office at Molo Angioino. Depart from Molo Beverello. Open daily 9am-7pm. Ferries to **Ischia** (8 per day 7:35am-8pm, €10-20).

ORIENTATION

Think of Naples as divided into four areas: **Stazione Centrale, waterfront** (from P. del Mercato to Mergellina), **centro storico (Spaccanapoli),** and **Plebiscito** (including V. Toldeo and the Spanish Quarter). **Stazione Centrale** sits prominently at the head of **Piazza Garibaldi,** directly opposite the statue of Garibaldi. Although sometimes a grid-locked mess of buses and *motorini*, the Stazione Centrale district is worth exploring to check out the ethnic food markets and to hone your bargaining skills with the street vendors. Several budget lodgings await nearby, but the area is fairly seedy, so exercise caution. P. Garibaldi is also the central hub for the many bus lines that service Naples. The **waterfront** district spans the entire length of Naples from P. del Mercato in the east to Mergellina in the west. From P. Garibaldi, take a left onto C. Garibaldi and walk until it ends at the water in P. G. Pepe. With the water on your left, **V. Nuova Marina** stretches all the way to P. Plebiscito, passing through P. del Mercato, and near P. Bovio and P. Municipio (the end of the R2 bus line) along the way. The waterfront district is full of little restaurants and shops tucked away on tiny side streets. Mergellina is accessible by Metro line #2. **Via Toledo,** a chic pedestrian shopping street, links the waterfront to the **Plebiscito** district and the Spanish Quarter. The well-to-do hang around P. Plebiscito and shop at the **Galleria Umberto,** and the narrow streets of the **Spanish Quarter** are a prime place to see loud neighbors shouting to each other from their balconies. **Piazza Dante** and **Piazza Carità,** along V. Toledo, lie on the western extreme of the **centro storico (Spaccanapoli).** Walking away from the waterfront, a right at any of these will lead to the winding roads of the lively, beautiful historical district. A right off V. Toledo onto V. Maddaloni leads through the central piazzas of the historical district, **Piazza Gesù Nuovo** and **Piazza San Domenico Maggiore;** shortly after, the street intersects **Via Duomo,** after which a right and then a left leads to **Piazza Garibaldi.**

 DON'T TAKE CANDY FROM STRANGERS. Though violent crime is rare in Naples, theft is common. Be smart. Don't carry money in wallets or purses. Don't wear flashy jewelry or flaunt a camera. Women should travel in groups when possible and avoid eye contact with strangers. Also, when choosing accommodations, *always* ask to see a room before committing, and never stay anywhere that feels even a little unsafe. The city has many excellent hostels and hotels, but many awful ones too, and that can make the difference between a nice visit or a lousy one.

LOCAL TRANSPORTATION

One "*UnicoNapoli*" ticket is valid for all modes of transport in Naples: **bus, Metro, train,** and **funicular.** Tickets are available at *tabacchi* in three types: 1½hr. (€1), full-day (€3), and weekend (good for Sa or Su, €2.50). Weekly tickets are available (€9), as are monthly tickets (€30). The buses and Metro stop running around midnight, and the *notturno* (nighttime) buses are unreliable and unsafe. Transportation around the environs of Naples includes the Circumvesuviana train to Pompeii and the Metro to Pozzuoli. All transportation in Campania is on one ticketing system and ticket costs depend upon the *fascia* (zone) of your destination.

Bus: Look for the internal orange buses. All stops have signs indicating their routes and destinations. **R1** travels from P. Bovio to Vomero (P. M. Oro) and **R2** runs from P. Garibaldi to P. Municipio. **3S** connects the 3 stations: the airport, the Stazione Centrale in P. Garibaldi, and Molo Beverello, where boats leave for the islands in the Bay of Naples and more distant destinations.

Metropolitana: To cover long distances (e.g., from the train station to P. Cavour, Montesanto, P. Amedeo, or Mergellina), use the efficient Metro that runs west to Pozzuoli from P. Garibaldi. Go to platform #4, 1 floor underground at Stazione Centrale. Line #1 stops at **P. Cavour** (Museo Nazionale), **Montesanto** (Cumana, Circumflegrea, funicular to Vomero), **P. Amedeo** (funicular to Vomero), **Mergellina,** and **Pozzuoli.** Transfer at P. Cavour for line #2. For Procida or Ischia, take the Metro to Pozzuoli.

Funiculars: Info: ☎800 56 88 66. 3 connect the lower city to Vomero: **Centrale,** most frequently used, runs from V. Toledo to P. Fuga; **Montesanto** from P. Montesanto to V. Morghen; **Chiaia** from V. del Parco Margherita to C. Cimarosa. Centrale and Chiaia have intermittent stops at C. V. Emanuele. A 4th, **Mergellina,** connects Posillipo to Mergellina. Available M-Sa 4 per hr., 7am-10pm; Su reduced service, 8am-7pm.

Taxis: Napoli (☎081 556 44 44), **Free** (☎081 551 51 51), **Partenope** (☎081 556 02 02), **Consortaxi** (☎081 552 52 52). Only take taxis with meters, and inquire about prices up front; even well-known companies have been known to charge dubiously high rates. For all taxis, the meter starts at €2.60; and an additional €0.05 is charged for every 70m. Expect to pay a min. €4.15, and a €2.10 surcharge 10pm-7am. Service to and from the airport is at a set rate. *Qui Napoli* lists the prices for airport service, or inquire at the tourist office.

Car Rental: Avis (☎081 554 30 20), C. A. Lucci, 203, just off P. Garibaldi near the train station. Cars from €165.20 for 2 days, €355.82 per week. Open M-F 8am-7:30pm, Sa 8:30am-1pm and 4-6pm, Su 9am-1pm. Branch in the airport (☎081 780 57 90). Additional 12% tax on cars rented at the airport. Offices open daily 7am-midnight. AmEx/MC/V. **Hertz,** P. Garibaldi, 91 (☎081 20 62 28). From €57.80 per day, €300-350 per week. Another office near the airport at V. Scarfoglio, 1 (☎081 780 29 71). Additional 12% tax applies. Open M-F 8am-1pm and 2-7pm, Sa 8:30am-1:30pm. AmEx/MC/V. **Maggiore** (☎081 28 78 58), in Stazione Centrale. From €78 per day, €312 per week. Open M-F 8am-1pm and 3-7pm, Sa 8:30am-1:30pm. AmEx/MC/V.

◪ PRACTICAL INFORMATION

TOURIST, FINANCIAL, AND LOCAL SERVICES

Tourist Office: EPT (☎081 26 87 79, fax 20 66 66), at Stazione Centrale. Calls hotels and ferry companies. Grab a free **map** and the indispensable ◪ *Qui Napoli,* a monthly tourist publication full of schedules, events, and listings (newest editions found at the airport). English spoken. Open M-Sa 8:30am-8pm, Su 8am-2pm. **Main office,** P. dei Martiri, 58 (☎081 410 72 11). Open M-Sa 9am-8pm. **Branch** at Stazione Mergellina (☎081 761 21 02). Open M-Sa 8:30am-8pm, Su 8am-2pm. **OTC** (☎081 252 57 11, fax 41 86 19), at Palazzo Reale in P. Plebiscito, offers friendly information on accommodations and sights. Open M-F 9am-6:30pm.

Budget Travel: CTS, V. Mezzocannone, 25 (☎081 552 79 60), off C. Umberto on the R2 line. Student travel info, ISIC and FIYTO cards, and booking services. Open M-F 9:30am-1:30pm and 2:30-6:30pm, Sa 10am-1pm. **Branch:** V. Cinthia, 36 (☎081 767 78 77; open M-F 9:30am-1pm and 4-7pm, Sa 9:30am-1pm). **CIT,** P. Municipio, 70 (☎081

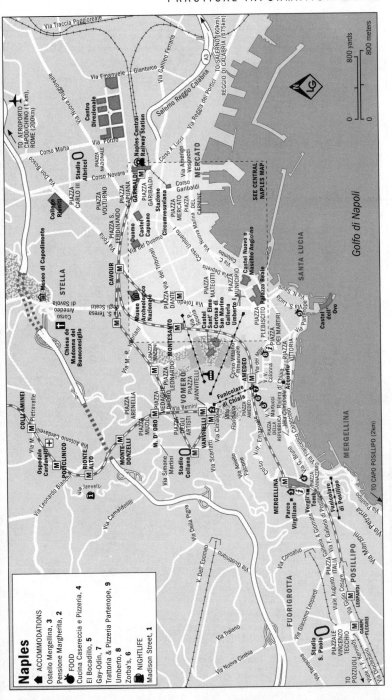

Naples

CAMPANIA

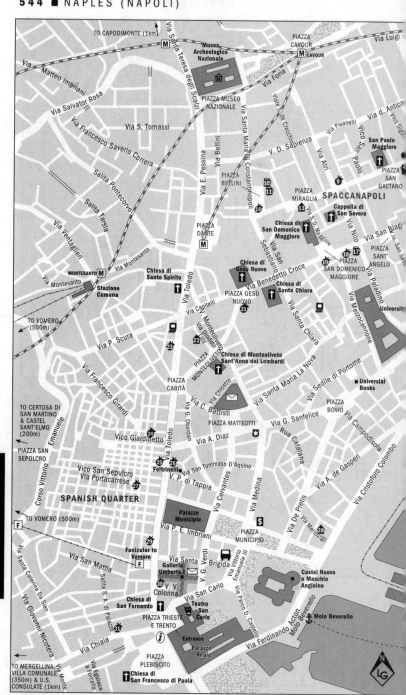

TO CAPODIMONTE (1km)

Museo Archeologico Nazionale

PIAZZA CAVOUR

Via Luigi

CAVOUR

Via Santa Teresa degli Scalzi

Via Matteo Imbriani

Via Salvator Rosa

Via Francesco Saverio Correra

Via S. Tomassi

Via Foria

PIAZZA MUSEO NAZIONALE

Via d. Antica

Via Pisanelli

Via San Paolo

San Paolo Maggiore

PIAZZA SAN GAETANO

Salita Pontecorvo

Salita Tarsia

Via Ventaglieri

Via Santa Maria di Constantinopoli

Via Bellini

Via E. Pessina

PIAZZA BELLINI

V. D. Sapienza

Viale de Crecchio

Via Atri

PIAZZA MIRAGLIA

SPACCANAPOLI

Cappella di San Severo

PIAZZA SANT' ANGELO

Via S. D. Maggiore

Chiesa di San Domenico Maggiore

PIAZZA SAN DOMENICO MAGGIORE

Via Nilo

Via San Biagio

Vo. San Se

MONTESANTO

Chiesa di Santo Spirito

PIAZZA DANTE

Chiesa di Gesù Nuovo

Via San Sebastiano

Via Benedetto Croce

Chiesa di Santa Chiara

Via Paladino

University

Via Montesanto

Stazione Cumana

Via Toledo

PIAZZA GESÙ NUOVO

Via Santa Chiara

Via Mezzocannone

TO VOMERO (500m)

Via P. Scura

Via Capitelli

Via Monteoliveto

Chiesa di Monteoliveto Sant'Anna dei Lombardi

PIAZZA MONTEOLIVETO

Via Santa Maria La Nova

Via Sedile di Portome

Universial Books

Via Francesco Girardi

PIAZZA CARITÀ

Via C. Battisti

Via Chiostro

PIAZZA MATTEOTTI

Via G. Sanfelice

PIAZZA BOVIO

Via Campodisola

TO CERTOSA DI SAN MARTINO & CASTEL SANT'ELMO (200m)

Corso Vittorio Emanuele

PIAZZA SAN SEPOLCRO

Vico Giardinetto

Via Toledo

Via G. Oberdan

Via A. Diaz

Rua Catalana

Via A. de Gasperi

Via Cristoforo Colombo

Vico San Sepulcro

Via Portacarrese

Feltrinelli

SPANISH QUARTER

V. P. di Tappia

Via San Tommaso D'Aquino

Via Cervantes

Via Medina

Via De Pretis

TO VOMERO (500m)

Funicular to Vomero

Via San Mattia

Salita S. A. di Palazzo

Palazzo Municipio

Via P. E. Imbriani

PIAZZA MUNICIPIO

Castel Nuovo o Maschio Angioino

Via Santa Catarina Da Sien

Via Giovanni Nicotera

Chiesa di San Fernando

Galleria Umberto I

V. V. Colonna

Via Santa Brigida

V. G. Verdi

Via San Carlo

Teatro San Carlo

PIAZZA TRIESTE E TRENTO

Via Vittorio Emanuele III

Via Parco D. Castello

Molo Beverello

Via Ferdinando Acton

Via Chiaia

Via Egiziaca a Forcella

PIAZZA PLEBISCITO

Entrance

Palazzo Reale

TO MERGELLINA, VILLA COMUNALE (350m) & U.S. CONSULATE (1km)

Chiesa di San Francesco di Paola

CAMPANIA

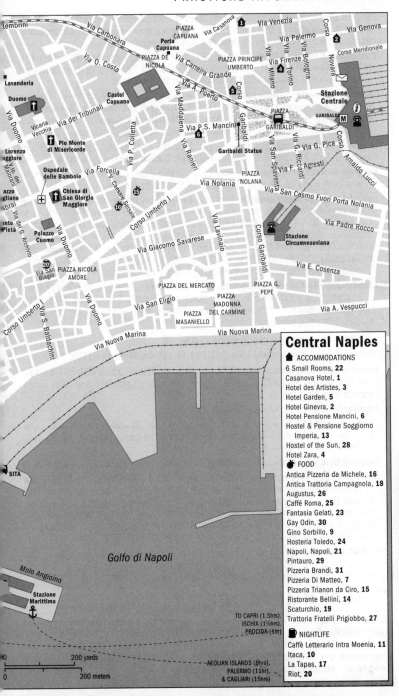

Central Naples

🏠 ACCOMMODATIONS
6 Small Rooms, **22**
Casanova Hotel, **1**
Hotel des Artistes, **3**
Hotel Garden, **5**
Hotel Ginevra, **2**
Hotel Pensione Mancini, **6**
Hostel & Pensione Soggiorno
 Imperia, **13**
Hostel of the Sun, **28**
Hotel Zara, **4**
🍴 FOOD
Antica Pizzeria da Michele, **16**
Antica Trattoria Campagnola, **18**
Augustus, **26**
Caffé Roma, **25**
Fantasia Gelati, **23**
Gay Odin, **30**
Gino Sorbillo, **9**
Hosteria Toledo, **24**
Napoli, Napoli, **21**
Pintauro, **29**
Pizzeria Brandi, **31**
Pizzeria Di Matteo, **7**
Pizzeria Trianon da Ciro, **15**
Ristorante Bellini, **14**
Scaturchio, **19**
Trattoria Fratelli Prigiobbo, **27**

🌙 NIGHTLIFE
Caffé Letterario Intra Moenia, **11**
Itaca, **10**
La Tapas, **17**
Riot, **20**

CAMPANIA

552 54 26), is a general travel agency. Open M-F 9am-1pm and 3-6pm. **Italian Youth Hostel Organization** (☎081 761 23 46), at the Mergellina hostel (see **Accommodations**), supplies HI cards (€15). Open M-F 9am-1pm and 3-6pm.

Consulates: Canada, V. Carducci, 29 (☎081 40 13 38). **UK,** V. dei Mille, 40 (☎081 423 89 11). **US** (☎081 583 81 11; 24hr. emergency ☎033 794 50 83), P. della Repubblica at the western end of Villa Comunale. Open M-F 8am-5pm.

Currency Exchange: Several banks operate in P. Municipio and P. Garibaldi. **Thomas Cook** at airport has decent rates. Open M-F 9:30am-1pm and 3-6:30pm. **Branches:** P. Municipio, 70 (☎081 551 83 99). **Stazione Centrale** has expensive 24hr. currency exchange. Smaller offices along **C. Umberto** charge more reasonable fees.

American Express: Every Tour, P. Municipio, 5 (☎081 551 85 64). Open 9am-1:30pm and 3:30-7pm. Also provides currency exchange. **Branch** in Stazione Centrale.

Luggage Storage: In Stazione Centrale near the info desk. Also near Ferrovia Circumflegrea in Montesanto. Depending on size, €4-8 per 12hr. Open 8am-8pm.

English-Language Bookstores: The area near the university teems with bookstores selling books in English and many other languages. Near the Spanish Quarter, **Feltrinelli,** V. S. T. d'Aquino, 70/76 (☎081 552 14 36), just north of the *Municipio*. Turn right off V. Toledo and onto V. P. di Tappia. It's 20m ahead on the left. Extensive selection awaits upstairs. Open M-F 9am-8pm, Sa 9am-2pm and 4-8:30pm. AmEx/MC/V. **Libreria Universal Books,** C. Umberto, 22 (☎081 252 00 69; unibooks@tin.it), in a palazzo off C. Umberto by P. Bovio. Open daily 9am-3:30pm and 4-7pm. MC/V.

Laundromats: Self Service Lavenderia, Largo Donnaregina, 5 (☎328 619 63 41). From C. Umberto, take a right onto V. Duomo, toward the duomo. 1 block past the duomo, Largo Donnaregina will be on the right. Free detergent. Wash and dry €7-10. Open M-Sa 8:45am-7:30pm. Cash only.

EMERGENCY AND COMMUNICATION

Emergency: ☎113. **Police** (☎113 or 081 794 11 11). **Carabinieri** (☎112).

Tourist Police: Ufficio Stranieri, at the **Questura,** V. Medina, 75 (☎081 794 11 11), near P. Municipio on the R2 bus line. Assists with passport problems and helps travelers who have been victims of crime.

Ambulance: ☎081 752 82 82.

Pharmacy: ☎081 26 88 81, at Stazione Centrale by FS ticket windows. Open 24hr., with a few exceptions on Su and holidays. When closed, the **Basic Chemist,** nearby in P. Garibaldi, is always open. *Il Mattino* lists the schedule.

Hospital: Cardarelli (☎081 747 28 59 or 747 28 48), north of town on R4 bus line.

Internet Access: Internet Point, V. Toledo, 59/A (☎081 497 60 90). Cheap rates, fast connections, and convenient location. €2 per hr. Printing €0.15 per page. Open daily 9:30am-8:30pm. **Internet Cafe Multimedia,** V. Pignatelli, 34 (☎081 551 47 08). From P. Municipio walk away from the water on V. Toldeo. Turn right at V. Capitelli. V. Pignatelli is the 2nd right after P. Gesù Nuovo. Over 20 computers, all with fast connections. Printing available. €1.50 per hr. Open daily 9:30am-9:30pm.

Post Office: ☎081 552 42 33. In P. Matteotti, at V. Diaz. Take the R2 line. Also in Galleria Umberto I (☎081 552 34 67) and outside Stazione Centrale. Notoriously unreliable *Fermoposta*. Open M-F 8:15am-6pm, Sa 8:15am-noon. **Postal Code:** 80100.

ACCOMMODATIONS

Hotels litter the hectic and seedy-by-night area around **Stazione Centrale,** some of which solicit customers at the station. Don't trust anyone who approaches you in the station—people working on commission are happy to lead naïve foreigners to unlicensed, overpriced hotels. Stazione Centrale has several comfortable and inexpensive options, that are quiet despite their bustling surroundings. The **water-**

front and **centro storico** areas are more expensive. **Vomero,** albeit a 15min. commute to the sights, provides views and tranquility. Although Naples has some great bargain lodgings, be cautious. Don't surrender documents or passports before seeing a room. Always agree on the price in writing *before* unpacking. When selecting a place to stay look for an intercom system or night attendants. For camping, check out **Pozzuoli** (p. 558) and other small towns on the Bay of Naples.

STAZIONE CENTRALE

Hostel Pensione Mancini, V. Mancini, 33 (☎081 553 67 31; www.hostelpensionemancini.com), off far end of P. Garibaldi from station. Friendly owners often share their encyclopedic knowledge of Naples. Simple, roomy, and renovated. Breakfast included. Check-in and check-out noon. Reservations suggested 1 week in advance. Dorms €18; singles €35, with bath €45; doubles €50, with bath €60; triples €70, with bath €80; quads €90, with bath €100. 10% discount with *Let's Go.* Cash only. ❷

Hotel Zara, V. Firenze, 81 (☎081 28 71 25; www.hotelzara.it). Quiet, spacious, renovated rooms, all with TV, A/C, and bath; some with LAN hookup and radio. Internet €4 for 1hr. Breakfast €4. Reservations recommended. Singles €35; doubles €62; triples €87; quad €112. AmEx/MC/V. ❸

Hotel Garden, C. Garibaldi, 92 (☎081 28 43 31, fax 553 60 69), off P. Garibaldi. Luxury value, with a lovely rooftop terrace. Spacious rooms all have TV, phone, balcony, A/C, and bath with hair dryer. Some rooms have wireless Internet. Reservations recommended May-Sept. With *Let's Go,* singles €57; doubles €80. AmEx/MC/V. ❹

Casanova Hotel, C. Garibaldi, 333 or V. Venezia, 2 (☎081 26 82 87; www.hotelcasanova.com). From P. Garibaldi, go down C. Garibaldi. This clean hotel features 18 airy rooms and a rooftop terrace bar. All rooms with A/C, some with TV, minibar, and phone. Some may find the location on a shadowy corner of an unlit street scary; use caution at night. Breakfast €4. Luggage deposit. Check-out noon. Reserve ahead. Singles €30; doubles €50, with bath €60; AmEx/MC/V. ❸

Hotel Ginevra, V. Genova, 116, 2nd fl. (☎/fax 081 28 32 10; www.hotelginevra.it). Exit P. Garibaldi on C. Novara, turn right on V. Genova. A short walk from the train station, good for late-night arrivals. Clean and family-run. English and French spoken. Reserve 1 week ahead. Singles €30, with bath €55; doubles €50, with bath €60; triples €65, with bath €80; quads €75, with bath, €85. A/C €15 extra. AmEx/MC/V. ❸

WATERFRONT

Ostello Mergellina (HI), V. Salita della Grotta, 23 (☎081 761 23 46, fax 761 23 91). M: Mergellina. From Metro station, make 2 sharp rights on V. Piedigrotta and right on V. Salita della Grotta. Turn right on long driveway after overpass. 200 beds vary in quality but are generally well maintained. Internet and free storage downstairs. Breakfast, shower, and sheets included, but no towels. Laundry €5.20. Lockout 9am-3pm. Strict curfew 12:30am. Reservations recommended July-Aug. Dorms €14; doubles from €50; family rooms €16 per person, €13 with more than 2 beds squeezed in. Cash only. ❶

Hostel of the Sun, V. Melisurgo, 15 (☎/fax 081 420 63 93; www.hostelnapoli.com), across from Bella Capri. Buzz #51. Young owners make this a happening spot, with large dorms and private rooms. Kitchen available. Fast Internet €3 per hr. Breakfast included. Laundry €3. Dorms €18; singles €40; doubles €50, with bath €70; triples €75/€90; quads €90/€100. 10% discount with *Let's Go.* Cash only. ❷

CENTRO STORICO (SPACCANAPOLI)

6 Small Rooms, V. Diodato Lioy, 18 (☎081 790 13 78; www.at6smallrooms.com). From Stazione Centrale take the Metro to P. Dante; change line at P. Cavour. From P. Dante, turn left on V. Toledo, make a left onto V. Senise, and right onto V. Lioy. There is

CAMPANIA

no sign; look for the name on the call button. Small, cozy, with a great vibe. Chill with the hip Australian owner. Big rooms. Kitchen and English video collection available. Key (€5 deposit) available for after midnight curfew. Reservations not accepted for dorm beds more than 24hr. in advance. Dorms €18; doubles €54. Cash only. ❷

🏠 **Hostel and Pensione Soggiorno Imperia,** P. Miraglia, 386, 6th fl. (☎/fax 081 45 93 47). From train station, take R2, exit at the University, take V. Mezzocannone through P. S. Domenico Maggiore. Buzz 1st green doors to left on P. Miraglia. Climb 6 flights to reach this 16th-century palazzo and its 9 bright, clean rooms. Kitchen facilities available. Reserve ahead. Dorms €18; singles €35; doubles €50, with bath €70; triples €75/€90; quad €90/€100. Cash only. ❷

Hotel des Artistes, V. Duomo, 61 (☎081 44 61 55; www.hoteldesartistesnaples.it). Intimate and inviting, all 11 rooms have balcony and luxurious bedspreads. Bath, A/C, phone, and TV. Chandeliers and fancy mirror trimmings blend well with decor. Singles €70-80; doubles €80-115; triples €95-120; quads €115-130. 10% discount with *Let's Go.* AmEx/MC/V. ❺

VOMERO

Pensione Margherita, V. Cimarosa, 29, 5th fl. (☎081 578 28 52, fax 556 70 44), take the funicular from near P. Plebiscito, exit the station, and go around the corner to the right and buzz to enter (in the same building as the Centrale funicular station). 19 cavernous rooms share 6 spotless baths. A little out of the way, but leaving the bustle of Naples behind as you head to the quiet hills of Vomero is well worth the trek. Check-out 11am. Curfew 1am. Singles €32; doubles €58; triples €82. Closed Aug. 1-15. AmEx/MC/V. ❸

🍴 FOOD

PIZZERIE

If you ever doubted that Neapolitans invented pizza, Naples's pizzerias will take that doubt, beat it into a ball, throw it in the air, spin it on their collective finger, punch it down, cover it with sauce and mozzarella, and serve it *alla margherita.*

🍕 **Gino Sorbillo,** V. dei Tribunali, 32 (☎081 44 66 43; www.accademiadellapizza.it), in the historic center near Vco. S. Paolo. The only pizzeria with 21 pizza-making children in this generation. Peer inside the kitchen to watch the frenzied action and original, flame-spewing oven. No reservations, so expect long waits. *Marinara* €2.10, *margherita* €3. Open daily noon-3:30pm and 7-11:30pm. MC/V. ❶

🍕 **Pizzeria Di Matteo,** V. dei Tribunali, 94 (☎081 45 52 62), near V. Duomo. A brick oven churns out the best *marinara* around (€2). Extremely popular with Neapolitans. Pizzas burst with flavor and the building bursts with aficionados—sign up on the list, and try some of the fried zucchini while you wait. Open M-Sa 9am-midnight. Cash only. ❶

Antica Pizzeria da Michele, V. Caesare Sersale, 1/3 (☎081 553 92 04). From P. Garibaldi, take C. Umberto I and turn right. Huge line outside says "Quality!" more loudly than a legion of reviews. Only serves *marinara* (tomato, garlic, oregano, oil) and *margherita* (tomato, mozzarella cheese, basil). Watch sweltering chefs toss pies from pizza-board to flame-licked oven, and then onto plates—all with superhuman grace and dexterity. Pizza €3.10-4.15. Drinks from €1.50. Open M-Sa 10am-11pm. Cash only. ❶

Pizzeria Brandi, Salita S. Anna di Palazzo, 1 (☎081 41 69 28, fax 400 29 14), off V. Chiaia. In 1889, Raffaele Esposito invented the *margherita* in Brandi's ancient oven to symbolize Italy's flag with the green of basil, red of tomato sauce, and white of mozzarella. Famous customers include Luciano Pavarotti, Isabella Rossellini, and Gerard Depardieu. *Margherita* €4. Cover €1.50. Service 12%. Weekend reservations recommended. Open Tu-Su 12:30-3pm and 7pm-midnight. AmEx/MC/V. ❷

Napoli, Napoli, V. T. de Amicis, 12 (☎081 545 58 80), right in P. Gesù Nuovo. Solid, cheap pizza that is great for taking out and eating in one of the many piazzas. The spicy *diavolo* (€4) is a favorite. Chat with the chefs as they make your pizza, and learn all you need to know about Naples. Pizza €4-7. Open daily 11am-midnight. MC/V.

Pizzeria Trianon da Ciro, V. Pietro Colletta, 42/44/46 (☎081 553 94 26), 1 block off C. Umberto I. Spacious interior boasts elusive A/C and amicable service. House speciality is the filling *"Gran Trianon"* pizza (€6.50), with 8 distinct sections of top-notch toppings. Pizza €3-7. Beer €1-3. Service 15%. Open M-Sa 10am-3:30pm and 7-11pm. ❷

RESTAURANTS AND TRATTORIE

Locally caught fish and shellfish enjoy an exalted place on the city's tables. Devour plentiful *cozze* (mussels) with lemon or as a soup. Savor *vongole* (clams) in all their glory, and don't miss their more expensive cousin, the *ostrica* (oyster). Try not to gawk as true Neapolitans suck the most elusive juices from the heads of *aragosta* (lobster) or devour *polipo* (octopus) whole or in pieces. For fresh fruits and seafood, explore the bustling **market** on V. Soprammuro, off P. Garibaldi. (Open M-Sa 8am-1:30pm.) Fruit stands, groceries, and pastry shops line V. Tribunali in Spaccanapoli. Fruit stands are often closed on Monday afternoons, and fishmongers are often closed on Thursday afternoons. The **waterfront** offers a combination of traditional Neapolitan fare and a change of culinary pace. Take the Metro or C25 bus to P. Amedeo, on the waterfront in Mergellina, for informal, hearty seafood. In the *centro storico* (Spaccanapoli), small shops cling to side streets, away from the louder, more expensive trattorias. Some of the cheapest, most authentic options lie along V. dei Tribunali in Spaccanapoli.

CENTRO STORICO (SPACCANAPOLI)

▨ **Hosteria Toledo,** Vco. Giardinetto, 78/A (☎081 42 12 57), in the Spanish Quarter. Prepare yourself for a long meal full of Neapolitan comfort food. The *gnocchi* (€6) is hearty enough to be its own meal and the *pasta fagioli* (€8) is creamy and delightful. If you are feeling adventurous, try the chef's surprise. *Primi* €6-12, *secondi* €5-10. Open daily 8pm-midnight. AmEx/MC/V. ❸

Trattoria Fratelli Prigiobbo, V. Portacarrese, 96 (☎081 40 76 92). From V. Toledo walking from waterfront, turn left on V. Portacarrese. Intimate, friendly restaurant; great for a quiet lunch break from the V. Toledo

PIZZA FIT FOR A QUEEN

Neapolitans don't agree on which pizzeria is the best in town. Everyone has their own opinion. Many, however, agree that **Brandi** is one of the most prestigious. Founded by Enrico Brandi, this pizzeria has been churning out pizzas in the same location (with supposedly the same oven) since 1780. Over time, the restaurant passed to Raffaele Esposito, who in 1889 made the pizzeria famous.

Umberto and Margherita, the king and queen of the House of Savoy, made their way through Naples in 1889 while traveling through their kingdom. To mark the occasion, Esposito made a special pizza that celebrated the Italian flag, with the red of tomato sauce, the white of mozzarella, and the green of basil. Queen Margherita loved it so much that she sent a letter to Esposito thanking him, a letter that is still in the restaurant today. Esposito named the pizza after her, and the rest is history.

The margherita pizza is not the only thing on the menu at Brandi. Special pizzas have been named after the celebrities who have enjoyed them. The Pavarotti pizza, only for the brave, has 20 toppings and is meant for four people, but Pavarotti is rumored to have eaten it all by himself.

Pizzeria Brandi, Salita S. Anna di Palazzo, 1 (☎081 41 69 28). Open Tu-Su 12:30-3pm and 7pm-midnight. AmEx/MC/V. ❷ mob. Lovely *primi* including *gnocchi alla mozzarella* (€3) and seafood including roasted calamari (€4), though servings are small. Pizza from €2.50. House wine €2.50 per bottle. Open M-Sa 8am-midnight. ❶

Ristorante Bellini, V. Santa Maria di Constantinopoli, 79-80 (☎/fax 081 45 97 74), just off P. Bellini. Come for obliging service and an evening *al fresco,* surrounded by screens and fragrant flowers. Try the *linguine al cartoccio* (€11) or anything from the *pesce* menu. Open daily 9am-4pm and 7pm-late. Closed Su in summer. MC/V. ❸

Antica Trattoria Campagnola, Piazzetta Nilo, 22 (☎339 207 31 49). Heaping portions of regional cuisine at this outstanding trattoria, including excellent *fritto di aliei.* Simple outdoor seating offers a calm alternative to the bustling pizzerias nearby. Efficient service and wide selection of wines. *Menù* €12. Open daily 10am-11pm. AmEx/MC/V. ❸

WATERFRONT

Zorba's, V. Martucci, 5 (☎081 66 75 72). M: Mergellina. 2 blocks off P. Amedeo, to the right exiting the station; turn left at the sign, and it's 3 doors down. This delightful change from the relentless pasta parade serves Greek cuisine. *Satanas* (devilishly spicy mini-sausages; €7) are sure to spark strong reactions. Fresh baklava €3. Open M-F and Su 8pm-1am, Sa 8pm-3am. Cash only. ❷

El Bocadillo, V. Martucci, 50 (☎081 66 90 30). M: Mergellina. Real, honest Brazilian-style barbecue, i.e., juicy slabs of name-your-animal. The campy decor may not be inspiring, but the delicious cuisine truly is. Entrees €4.50-10. *Paella* €8.50. 1L *sangría* from €5. Open daily 7pm-3am. Cash only. ❷

Cucina Casereccia e Pizzeria, P. Sanazzaro, 69 (☎081 66 65 64). Welcoming staff and platefuls of seafood make this an excellent splurge. Specializes in *cozze* (mussels), found in the crowd-pleasing *zuppa di cozze* (€6.71); those seeking serious substance should spring for *zuppa di cozze super* (€9.45). Open daily noon-late. MC/V. ❸

Umberto, V. Alabardieri, 30/31 (☎081 41 85 55; www.umberto.it). M: Mergellina. V. Alabardieri leads out of P. dei Martiri; restaurant on the left. Accented with tea lights and bamboo, this waterfront locale serves local fare with flare. House specials is *tubettoni d' 'o treddeta* (tube pasta stuffed with seafood; €9.50). *Primi* €4.50-9.50, *secondi* €5-9. Reservations recommended. Open Tu-Su noon-3pm and 7:30pm-midnight. Closed 2 weeks in Aug. AmEx/MC/V. ❸

Trattoria and Pizzeria Partenope, V. Partenope, 12/H (☎081 764 23 17). M: Mergellina. Linger over fantastic *calamari* (€7.50) at outdoor tables. Evening brings lovely views of the city. Pizza €4-13. Open daily 12:30-4pm and 7:30pm-2am. MC/V. ❷

GELATERIE AND PASTICCERIE

Naples's most beloved pastry is *sfogliatella,* filled with sweetened ricotta cheese, orange rind, and candied fruit. It comes in two forms: the popular *riccia,* a flaky-crust variety, and a softer, crumblier *frolla.* Walking the streets, an abundance of cheap gelato calls out to be devoured. Many vendors sell atrocious concoctions laden with unnatural dyes and carrying a mass produced label. Avoid these and look for creamy textures and muted colors instead.

▨ **Fantasia Gelati,** V. Toledo, 381 (☎081 551 12 12), comes close to gelato perfection. The shop's fruit flavors, including heavenly *arancia* (orange) and tangy papaya, are made with real juices, yielding tart, refreshing results. Very generous scoops. Cones €1.30-2. Open daily 7am-11pm. Cash only. ❶

▨ **Gay-Odin,** V. V. Colonna, 15/B (☎081 41 82 82; www.gay-odin.it), off P. Amedeo; V. Toledo, 214 (☎081 40 00 63). No Norse gods, just delicious chocolate treats. Try the *foresta,* a sweet and crumbly chocolate stalk (from €2.20 for a small twig to €8.40 for a branch best devoured with friends). Open M-Sa 9:30am-1:30pm and 4:30-8pm, Su 10am-2pm. AmEx/MC/V. ❶

Augustus, V. Toledo, 147 (☎081 551 35 40, fax 551 62 19). Though there's often a long wait at the counter, the time will be useful for important deliberations—gelato (from €1.40) or sumptuous fruit tarts *(*€1.50)? Aromatic cappuccino (€1.05) or pungent espresso (€0.85)? Toward the back, a well-stocked counter has fresh cheese and prime cuts of meat, perfect for a *panino* to go. Open daily 7am-9pm. Cash only. ❶

Scaturchio, P. S. Domenico Maggiore, 19 (☎081 551 69 44). With divine desserts and a quiet spot in the piazza, sit here and pass the afternoon watching Neapolitans go by. Specialty is *ministeriale,* a chocolate and rum pastry (€2.50), and excellent gelato (cones from €1.30). Open M-Sa 7:20am-8:40pm. Cash only. ❶

Pintauro, V. Toledo, 275 (☎081 41 73 39). This tiny bakery invented *sfogliatella* in 1785. Try it piping hot from €1.30. *Meringues* €1.30. Open M-Sa 9:15am-8:15pm. Cash only. ❶

Caffè Roma, V. Toledo, 325 (☎081 40 68 32). Huge variety of *panini* and pastries (try the *profiterolles;* €1.50). For a quick snack, go for focaccia (from €0.80) or a *granita* (€1.80) instead. Open M-Sa 9am-9pm. Cash only. ❶

◎ SIGHTS

The exquisite architecture that forms a backdrop to daily life in Naples is a narrative of successive conquests, featuring Greek, Roman, and Spanish styles. Excavations *in sito* can be found at the Museo Archeologico Nazionale or Museo and Gallerie di Capidomonte. The Palazzo Reale's apartments and the city's castles give a taste of 18th-century royal Neapolitan life. The **Campania Artecard** is a worthwhile investment for those taking a few days to tour regional sights, granting free admission to two of 48 museums and sites in and around the city (including Pompeii), and half-price admission to the rest, as well as free public transportation, special transportation on weekends, and discounts on audio guides. (☎800 60 06 01; www.campaniartecard.it. €13, ages 18-25 €8.) All museums allow entrance until 1hr. before closing, and all religious sights require modest dress.

CENTRO STORICO (SPACCANAPOLI)

Naples's most renowned neighborhood is replete with brilliant architecture. The main sights get lost among ornate banks, *pensioni*, and *pasticcerie*, so watch for the shoebox-sized signs on buildings. To get to the historic center from P. Dante, walk through Pta. Alba and past P. Bellini before turning down V. dei Tribunali, the former route of a Roman road that now contains some of Naples's best pizzerias.

▓ **MUSEO ARCHEOLOGICO NAZIONALE.** Situated in a 16th-century palazzo and former barracks, one of the world's most important archaeological museums houses treasures from Pompeii and Herculaneum. Unreliable labeling makes the color guidebooks or a tour a helpful investment. The ground floor's Farnese Collection displays sculptures snatched from Pompeii and Herculaneum, as well as imperial portraits and colossal statues from Rome's Baths of Caracalla. The massive Farnese Hercules depicts the exhausted hero after his last labor, though which labor that is remains unclear; a diverging mythic account extends the traditional 12 labors to include a 13th, bedding 100 women in one night. Check out the Farnese Bull, the largest extant ancient statue. Sculpted from a single slab of marble, the bull was further freed from the stone by a benevolent Michelangelo. The mezzanine contains a room filled with exquisite mosaics from Pompeii, most noticeably some delicious-looking fruits and the Alexander Mosaic, which shows a young and fearless Alexander the Great routing a Persian army. Though most people have heard of the lovely Aphrodite, the *Gabinetto Segreto* (or

C
A
M
P
A
N
I
A

Secret Cabinet) will introduce the curious to her lesser-known counterpart Hermaphrodite, blessed with a curvy feminine form and handy masculine member. The collection, specializing in erotic paintings and objects from Pompeii, includes everything from images of (intimate) godly love to phallic good luck charms replete with hanging bells. Check in at the ticket desk to gain entrance. *(M: P. Cavour. Turn right from the station and walk 2 blocks. A short walk from the historic center.* ☎ *081 44 01 66. Open M and W-Su 9am-7:30pm. Entrance €6.50, EU students €3.25, under 18 or over 65 free. Included under Campania Artecard.)*

DUOMO. Naples's duomo lies quietly in a small piazza, its modest 19th-century facade belying an ornate interior. Inaugurated in 1315 by Robert of Anjou, the duomo has been subject to countless additions and renovations. Inside on the right, the main attraction is the **Cappella del Tesoro di San Gennaro,** decorated with Baroque paintings. A beautiful 17th-century bronze grille protects the high altar, which possesses a reliquary containing the saint's head and two vials of his coagulated blood. According to legend, disaster will strike the city if the blood does not liquefy on the celebration of his **festa.** Behind the main altar of the church lies the saint's **crypt,** decorated with Renaissance carvings in white marble. Visitors can also view the newly opened underground **excavation site,** an intimate tangle of Greek and Roman roads constructed over several centuries. The entrance is halfway up the right side of the church. *(Walk 3 blocks up V. Duomo from C. Umberto I or take the #42 bus from P. Garibaldi.* ☎ *081 44 90 97. Open M-Sa 9am-noon and 4:30-7pm, Su 9am-noon. Free, excavation site €3.)*

CHIESA DI SANTA CHIARA. One of the most important Angevin monuments in Naples, Santa Chiara was built in the 1300s by the rulers of the house of Anjou. Since then, it has been renovated several times, most recently after a WWII bombing. Narrow stained-glass windows stretch up the wide walls, casting a golden glow over the interior. The church is littered with sarcophagi and tombs from the Middle Ages, including the 14th-century tomb of Robert of Anjou behind the main altar. Spend some time in the adjoining garden, archaeological site, and monastery, adorned with Gothic frescoes and majolica tiles. *(From P. Dante, take V. Toledo and turn left on V. B. Croce. The church is in P. Gesù Nuovo.* ☎ *081 552 62 80. €4, EU students €2.50. Open M-F 9:30am-1pm and 2:30-5:30pm, Sa-Su and holidays 9:30am-1pm.)*

GESÙ NUOVO. Originally built for the Prince of Salerno, the church's 15th-century Jesuit facade suggests simplicity, but the interior is awash in opulent Baroque, from inlaid marble floors to colorful ceiling frescoes. The magnificent main altar, featuring a triumvirate of marble statues and a towering golden sun, is overwhelming. Outside the church is a spectacular Baroque spire glorifying the lives of Jesuit saints. *(Across from the Chiesa di Santa Chiara, in P. Gesù Nuovo.* ☎ *081 551 86 13. Open daily 9am-12:15pm and 4:15-7pm. Modest dress required.)*

PIO MONTE DELLA MISERICORDIA. This small chapel was built by a group of nobles dedicated to helping the needy and sick, housing pilgrims, and ransoming Christian slaves held prisoner by infidels. The church has seven arches, each with its own altar and painting, and the main archway holds Caravaggio's *Our Lady of Mercy,* the central attraction. In an archway to the left is the creepy *Resurrection of Tabatha;* teeming with vivid characters, it merits more than a passing glance. In the piazza outside, a spire reaches to the sky; it's dedicated to S. Gennaro for having saved the city from the 1656 plague. *(V. Tribunali, 253, 1 block after V. Duomo, in a small piazza.* ☎ *081 44 69 44. Call in the morning to book a tour, Tu, Th, and Sa only.)*

PLEBISCITO

PALAZZO REALE AND BIBLIOTECA NAZIONALE. Huge statues of the various rulers of Naples decorate the palazzo in P. Plebiscito. Vomero, towering majestically in the distance, provides a picturesque backdrop for the square's superb architecture. Inside the 17th-century palazzo is the **Museo di Palazzo Reale,** comprised of opulent royal apartments maintaining original Bourbon furnishings, paintings, statues, and porcelains. Its immense chambers reveal lavish royal life, including the king's ornate throne and walls lined with mirrors and paintings. The palazzo is an intellectual mecca, housing the 1,500,000-volume **Biblioteca Nazionale.** The library contains the carbonized scrolls from the Villa dei Papiri in Herculaneum. *(Take the R2 bus from P. Garibaldi to P. Trieste e Trento and walk around the palazzo to the entrance on P. Plebiscito; or, make the short walk from anywhere in the historical center.* ☎ *848 80 02 88. Open M-Tu and Th-Su 9am-8pm. Included under Campania Artecard. Library* ☎ *081 781 91 11. Public access varies, so call for details.)* Also in the palazzo is the famous **Teatro San Carlo,** built in 1737 and reputed to have better acoustics than the revered La Scala in Milan (p. 232). So be careful what you whisper. For more information on performances, see **Entertainment.** *(Theater entrance on P. Trieste e Trento.* ☎ *081 797 21 11. Tours July M-Tu, Th, and Sa-Su 10am; Sept.-June Sa-Su 2pm. €3.)*

CATACOMBS. The catacombs of San Gennaro, San Gaudioso, and San Severo all date back to the early centuries AD, and provide a glimpse of the ancient Neapolis. Tours of the city's subterranean alleys are fascinating, but not for the claustrophobic: guides set people crawling through narrow underground passageways, grottoes, and catacombs, spotting Mussolini-era graffiti, and exploring Roman aqueducts. *Napoli e la Città* explores the area underneath Castel Nuovo and downtown, and *Napoli Sotterranea* drags the intrepid underneath the historic center. *(Napoli e La Città Sotterranea office at Vco. S. Anna di Palazzo.* ☎ *081 40 02 56. Tours Th 9pm; Sa 10am and 6pm; Su 10, 11am, and 6pm. €5. Tours leave from Bar Gambiunes in P. Trieste e Trento, but call first. Napoli Sotterranea, P. S. Gaetano, 68. Take V. Tribunali and turn left right before San Paolo Maggiore.* ☎ *081 29 69 44; www.napolisotterranea.com. Tours every 2hr. M-F noon-4pm; Sa, Su, and holidays 10am-6pm. €5.)*

MASCHIO ANGIONO. It's impossible to miss this five-turreted landmark towering mightily over the Bay of Naples. The fortress was built in 1286 by Charles II of Anjou as his royal residence in Naples. Its most stunning feature is the triumphal entrance, with reliefs commemorating the arrival of Alphonse I of Aragon in 1443. The magnificent Hall of the Barons, where King Ferdinand once trapped rebellious barons and where Naples's city council holds spirited meetings today, is inside. The splendid Cappella Palatina, also called the Chapel of St. Barbara, is a cool retreat from the castle's open churchyard. *(P. Municipio.* ☎ *081 795 58 77. Take the R2 bus from P. Garibaldi or walk from anywhere in the historic center. Open M-Sa 9am-7pm. €5.)*

GALLERIA UMBERTO. Although now a shopping mall, complete with street vendors selling designer knock-offs, the building itself is one of the most beautiful in Naples. In the shape of a cross, the atrium has a high, arched ceiling covered in glass panes. It seems a bit out of place in Naples, and is more architecturally akin to buildings in Milan, but it is a unique treat to shop in this 17th-century wonder. *(P. Trieste e Trento. Stores open daily 10am-1pm and 4-8pm, but the building is open all day.)*

CAPPELLA SAN SEVERO. The chapel, founded in 1590, is now a private museum. Several remarkable 18th-century statues inhabit its lovely corridors, including the *Veiled Christ* by Giuseppe Sanmartino. Don't forget to look up at the breathtaking fresco on the ceiling, with its luminous figures and delicate scrollwork. Legend claims that the chapel's builder, alchemist prince Raimondo of the S. Severi, mur-

C A M P A N I A

A PIAZZA PRIMER

Neapolitans keep to the streets. Come summer evenings, club kids pack piazzas by the hundreds, bouncing the streets with slices and *Peronis* in hand. To maximize your enjoyment of Naples's bustling nocturnal scene, check out *Let's Go*'s crash course in Piazza personalities.

Piazza Gesù Nuovo: At night, university students break from their relentless bongo-playing but not from their firm convictions in the "healing powers" of certain botanicals. Plentiful fast food keeps them contentedly munching.

Piazza San Domenico Maggiore: Always stuffed to bursting, and frequented by all ages. A busy cafeteria serves late-night snacks, and several indoor bars satisfy liquor demands. Sociable Neapolitans embrace zestfully and plant kisses on each others' cheeks; shrill squeals of glee are common.

Piazza Bellini: Quieter, and replete with outdoor seating and hanging plants. The bars here, hosting a mix of locals and tourists, are on the expensive side. But the low-key ambience might well provide the respite you crave after a hard day of sightseeing.

Piazza Vanvitelli: Chic, young, happening, and just a short funicular ride up V. Toledo. Don't bother showing up unless you pass for under 28 and don't mind seeing amorous couples...do their thing. (Beware: buses and funiculars may not run past 11pm.)

dered his wife and her lover by injecting them with a poison that preserved their veins, arteries, and vital organs. Sadly, even though the rumor lingers, these aren't on display. *(V. De Sanctis, 19. Near P. S. Domenico Maggiore. ☎ 081 551 84 70; www.ic-napoli.com/sansevero. Open M and W-Sa 10am-6pm, holidays 10am-1:30pm.)*

CHIESA DI SAN DOMENICO MAGGIORE. This 13th-century church, founded when Naples was a center of learning in Europe, has been restructured several times over the years, finally settling on a 19th-century, spiked Gothic interior. To the right of the altar in the Chapel of the Crucifix hangs the 13th-century painting that allegedly spoke to St. Thomas Aquinas, when he lived in the adjoining monastery. Fine Renaissance sculptures decorate the side chapels, but many have been moved to the Capodimonte museum. *(P. S. Domenico Maggiore. ☎ 081 45 91 88. Open M-F 8:30am-noon and 5-8pm, Sa-Su 9:30am-1pm and 5-7pm.)*

CAPODIMONTE

■ MUSEO AND GALLERIE DI CAPODIMONTE. Housed in a royal palazzo, the museum sits inside a pastoral park where youngsters play soccer and lovers, well, play. In addition to its plush royal apartments, the palace houses the Italian National Picture Gallery. The **Farnese Collection** on the first floor is full of masterpieces, many of them removed from Neapolitan churches for safety's sake. Among these incomparable works are Bellini's *Transfiguration*, Masaccio's *Crucifixion*, and Titian's *Danae*. The second floor traces the development of the Neapolitan realist style, from Caravaggio's visit to Naples (his *Flagellation* is on display) to Ribera and Luca Giordano's adaptations. *(Take the #16 bus from the Archaeological Museum and exit at the gate to the park, on the right. The park has 2 entrances, Pta. Piccola and Pta. Grande. ☎ 081 749 91 11. Open Tu-Su 8:30am-7:30pm. €7.50, after 2pm €6.50.)*

VOMERO

MUSEO NAZIONALE DI SAN MARTINO. Once the monastery of St. Martin, it is now home to an excellent museum of Neapolitan history and culture. In addition to extensive galleries, the monastery sports a lavish chapel, festooned with Baroque marbles and statuary. Collection highlights include Riberia's *Deposition of Christ*, held to be one of his finest works, and a *Nativity* by Guido Renis. Numerous balconies and a multilevel garden allow superb views of the city below, but beware of amorous couples, who monopolize all available benches for their scandalous purposes. *(From V. Toledo, take the funicular to Vomero and turn right on V. Cimarosa. Continue straight up 2 flights of stairs, along V. Scarlatti, and then veer left, walking for about 10min., keeping left; Castel Sant'Elmo and Piazzale S. Martino emerge on the right. ☎081 578 17 69. Open Tu-Sa 8:30am-7:30pm. €6, EU students €3. Included under Campania Artecard.)* The massive **Castel Sant'Elmo** next door was built to deter rebellion and hold political prisoners. Nowadays, however, it's more concerned with tourism and glamor. There are grand panoramic views from the battlements. *(☎081 578 40 30. Open Tu-Su 8:30am-7:30pm. €2.)*

MUSEO DUCA DI MARTINA. Ceramics fans should visit this crafts gallery inside the lush gardens of the **Villa Floridiana** for 18th-century Italian and Asian porcelain. Though on the smaller side, this collection is thoughtfully presented and full of treasures. *(V. Cimarosa, 77. To get to the entrance, take the funicular to Vomero from V. Toledo, turn right out of the station, then turn left on V. Cimarosa. Enter the gardens and keep walking downhill. ☎081 578 84 18. Open Tu-F 8:30am-2pm, Sa-Su 9am-2pm. €2.50, EU students €1.50, EU citizens under 18 or over 65 free.)*

WATERFRONT

▨ VIRGIL'S TOMB. *Mirabile dictu!* Anyone who studied Latin in high school may have at least a passing interest in seeing the poet's resting place at Salita della Frotta. Below the tomb is the entrance to the closed *Crypta Neapolitana*, a tunnel built during the reign of Augustus; the Metro line of antiquity, it connected ancient Neapolis to Pozzuoli and Baia. Nearby lies the tomb of Leopardi, moved from the church of S. Vitale in Fuorigrotta in 1939. Call ahead and arrange a translator to describe and explain the inscriptions, or just come for the amazing view. *(M: Mergellina, take 2 quick rights. Entrance between overpass and tunnel. Guided tours upon request. ☎081 66 93 90. Open daily 9am-1hr. before sunset. Free.)*

CASTEL DELL'UOVO (EGG CASTLE). This massive Norman castle of yellow brick and odd angles sits on a rock that was later connected to the mainland, dividing the bay in half. Legend has it that Virgil hid an egg within the castle walls and that with the collapse of the egg would come the collapse of the castle. It offers beautiful views of the water and Naples. *(Take bus #1 from P. Garibaldi or P. Municipio to S. Lucia and walk across the jetty. ☎081 240 00 55. Only open for special events; call ahead.)*

AQUARIUM. On the waterfront, in Villa Comunale, this world-class aquarium is a proud reminder of Naples's attachment to the sea. Founded in the late 19th century, it's Europe's oldest, displaying 30 tanks with 200 local species. *(Easily accessible by bus #1 from P. Garibaldi or P. Municipio. ☎081 583 32 63. Open in summer Tu-Sa 9am-6pm, Su 9:30am-7pm; in winter M-Sa 9am-5pm, Su 9am-2pm. €1.50, children €1.)*

♫ ▨ ENTERTAINMENT AND FESTIVALS

Once famous occasions for revelry, Naples's religious festivals are now excuses for sales and shopping sprees. On September 19 and the first Saturday in May, the city celebrates the **Festa di San Gennaro.** Join the crowd to watch the procession by the duomo in May and see the patron saint's blood miraculously liquefy in a vial. The **Festa di Madonna del Carmine** (July 16) features a mock burning of Fra' Nuvolo's *campanile* and culminates in fireworks. In July, P. S. Domenico Maggiore holds concerts, while summers are full of neighborhood celebrations, sporting events, music, and shows. The Neapolis Festival, every year in July, hosts pop concerts at Arena Flegrea in Campi Flegrei. The **Cinema Teatro Amedeo,** V. Marcucci, 69 (☎081 68 02 66), four blocks off P. Amedeo, shows films in English during the summer. **Teatro S. Carlo** (☎081 797 21 11) at Palazzo Reale hosts opera performances (Oct.-June) and the symphony (Oct.-May). Gallery tickets start at €12 and

CAMPANIA

should be purchased in advance. Consult the ticket office and *Il Mattino* for schedules. Catch a soccer match at **Stadio S. Paolo** (☎ 081 239 56 23), in Fourigrotta, for a truly accurate portrait of Neapolitan life. Take the Metro to Campi Flegrei. **Napoli**, in Serie B, the second division, is still a powerhouse, packing spectators for matches from August through June. Tickets start at €20.

Two weekends of every month (1 per month in June and July) **Fiera Antiquaria Napoletana** hosts flea markets filled with ancient and expensive artifacts. Though such items come with hefty price tags, hundreds wander through the stands along V. F. Caracciolo on the waterfront to browse stamps, books, coins, and art. (☎ 081 62 19 51. Open 8am-2pm.) From early December to early January, Neapolitan artisans gather along the Spaccanapoli and surrounding streets to hand-work fine porcelain Nativity scenes renowned throughout Europe for their delicate beauty. This spectacle draws a huge international crowd.

▢ SHOPPING

A thriving black market and low prices make Naples an enticing place for shopping. Just keep this in mind: street vendors are craftier than you are. That's why they're in the business and you're a dazed shopper. If a transaction seems too good to be true, it is. Clothing is usually a good deal, though that new shirt may come apart in the washing machine, or turn everything a ghastly shade of purple. *Never* buy electronic products from street vendors. Even sealed, brand-name boxes have been known to be filled with newspaper, water bottles, or rocks. Vendors hawk defunct cell phones and digi-cams in P. Garibaldi, hoping to ensnare naïve buyers. Cases of music and computer CDs and DVDs often contain old copies of Microsoft DOS or simply are blank, so try them out if possible. And do *not* fall for those Mickey Mouse dolls that "dance" to a boombox—they're ingenious deceptions. With that said, designer knock-off belts, purses, and sunglasses are plentiful, and none of your friends will know the difference, so go all out. Finally, a word about bargaining: do it. In the dog-eat-dog world of unregulated transactions, bargaining is the law and the most aloof is king. The moment a vendor notices a happy person (also known as a tourist) carrying a backpack and admiring the indigenous goods with reverent awe, he doubles the prices and lays on the compliments. So offer less than half, and be damned if you're going to budge.

V. S. Maria di Constantinopoli, south of the Archaeological Museum, has old books and antique shops. **Spaccanapoli** and its side streets near the Conservatorio house small music shops with inexpensive manuscripts; used copies of pricey European editions are available for cheap. **Via Toledo** provides high-class shopping for a lower budget, and the streets south of **San Lorenzo Maggiore** house craftsmen of Neapolitan *creches*. For formal shopping, **Piazza Martiri** houses a roll call of Italian designers, including Gucci, Valentino, Versace, Ferragamo, Armani, and Prada, and **Galleria Umberto** has plenty of higher-end stores. The most modern and expensive shopping district is in the hills of **Vomero** along the perpendicular **Via Scarlatti** and **Via Luca Giordano.** Many smaller artisans' workshops inhabit the winding streets nearby, hawking everything from wrought iron to delicate cameos. For jeans, head to the market off **Porta Capuana.** (Most markets open M-Sa 9am-5pm, but many close at 2pm.)

▧ NIGHTLIFE

Content to groove at the city's small clubs and discos during winter, Neapolitans instinctively return to the streets and piazzas in warmer weather. Each piazza hosts a slightly different nighttime crowd and takes on a distinct demeanor and rhythm. In winter, clubs and pubs open at around 11pm and remain open until everyone goes home at around 4 or 5am. In summer, the Sunday evening *passeggiata* fills the Villa Comunale along the bay (bus #1), and young couples flood picturesque V. Petrarca and V. Posillipo. As night goes on, piazzas fill with laughing Neapolitans, beer and wine in hand, who just hang out, tell stories, and disturb the neighbors. For obvious reasons, most take their cars. According to eager Italian men, a kiss here means seven years good luck. *Il Mattino* and *Qui Napoli* print decent club listings. **ARCI-GAY/Lesbica** (☎ 081 552 88 15, open W-F 5-8pm) has information on gay and lesbian nights at different clubs.

CAFES, BARS, AND PUBS

Caffè Letterario Intra Moenia, P. Bellini, 70 (☎ 081 29 07 20; www.intramoenia.it). Appealing to the intellectual crowd by keeping books out for skimming, you can easily spend a night here in deep conversation. Top off the sumptuous setting with a cocktail (€6-7), beer (€3.50-6), or the delightful *dolce, Delizia Caprese* (€8). Open daily 10am-2am. AmEx/MC/V.

Itaca, P. Bellini, 71 (☎ 081 822 66 132). Black decor and eerie trance music beckon to the dark side and to the mod hipsters. Lip rings don't hinder patrons from guzzling candy-coated cocktails (€6-7). Beer €3-4. Open daily 10am-3am. AmEx/MC/V.

La Tapas, V. Paladino, 56 (☎ 347 847 44 75). A low-key favorite of university students, close to the bustling nightlife of P. San Domenico Maggiore. Outdoor seating in an alcove just down V. Nilo from V. dei Tribunali. Enjoy *sangria* (glass €2, 1L €9). Service 10%. Open daily 7pm-2:30am.

NIGHTCLUBS AND DISCOTHECHE

Riot, V. S. Biagio, 39 (☎ 081 767 50 54), off C. Umberto I. Hear local artists play jazz and sing the blues at this smoky den frequented by a crowd from college and beyond. Though usually low-key, fans vocalize their support of live performers. Cocktails from €4. Open Th-Su 10:30pm-3am. AmEx/MC/V.

Madison Street, V. Sgambati, 47 (☎ 081 546 65 66), in Vomero. Dance until the sun comes up to the latest europop hits. Ample room and an older crowd. Cover €10. Open Sept.-May F-Su 10pm-4am.

▶ DAYTRIPS FROM NAPLES

CAMPI FLEGREI

To Baia, take the SEPSA bus from M: Pozzuoli (30min.). Don't be confused by the outdated signs on the Ferrovia Cumana; this rail line no longer goes through Baia. In Baia itself, buy an Unico Fascia 1 ticket (€1.70) and ride all modes of transportation all day. To Cumae, take the SEPSA bus marked Miseno-Cuma from the train station at Baia to the last stop in Cumae (15min., €0.60), and walk to the end of the V. Cumae. The "Cuma" stop on the Ferrovia Circumflegrea is in the modern town, several kilometers away from the archaeological sites. Reach Miseno using the Miseno-Cuma SPESA bus from either Baia or Cumae, and Pozzuoli using either the Ferrovia Cumana, Ferrovia Circumflegria, or Naples Metro. Ask any of the tourist offices in Naples for info and maps for Campi Flegrei.

The Campi Flegrei (Phlegraean Fields) are a group of tiny coastal towns west of Naples nestled among a chain of lakes and inactive volcanoes. Ancient Greeks colonized this area and associated the thermal nature of the land with Hades, god of the Underworld. The Greek legacy lives on in the ruins at **Cumae,** also immortalized in Virgil's *Aeneid* as Aeneas's landing point in Italy. Later, the Roman elite used the region's hot springs for the intricate bath houses that still stand on the hill over **Baia,** and built an impressive amphitheater near their believed gate to hell in **Pozzuoli.** Modern Italians dot the scorching yet breezy coast of **Miseno** with their own culture, fishing boats, relaxing beaches, pizzerias, and restaurants. The sights are too far apart to walk from one to another, so use the omnipresent orange and blue SEPSA buses. Frequent bus stops are on the side of the road; the front of the bus will list the towns that its route stretches between, and you can always tell your driver your intended destination and ask him to tell you when to get off.

Perched on a hill overlooking the bustling port center of **Baia,** where SESPA buses drop passengers off, is Baia's central attraction: the luxurious **Roman Baths.** Climb up the stairs and stroll through the well-preserved ruins, remarkable for their multiple stories, beautiful mosaics, and detailed ceilings. At the base of the hill sits the gem of the bath houses, known misleadingly as the ◼**Tempio di Mercurio** or the Temple of Echoes. Light shines through the oldest domed ceiling in the world, bounces off the water, and reflects onto the wall. Faint of heart be warned: lizards and snakes abound in the ancient stone walls. (☎081 868 75 92; www.ulixes.it. Open daily 9am-7pm. 2-day pass grants admission to the Baths, the Archaeological Museum in Baia, the *scavi* in Cumae, and the Amphitheater in Pozzuoli. €4, with student pass €2.) A short bus ride from the center of Baia accesses the **Castello Aragonese** and the **Museo Archeologico dei Campi Flegrei** with a small collection of ancient artifacts and a beautiful view of Baia's harbor. (☎081 868 75 92. Open Tu-Su 10am-6pm. Entrance with archaeological pass.) For a less conventional view of ruins, try the glass-bottomed boat *Cymba* out of Baia's port to see the **Submerged Roman City.** The boat runs from March 18th to November 3 and can hold 48 people. (☎081 526 57 80. Launches Sa noon, 4pm; Su 10:30am, noon, and 4pm. €7.75, children 6-12 €6.20, under 5 free.)

Cumae (Cuma), founded in the 8th century BC, was the earliest Greek colony on the Italian mainland. Mythologically, it was the place where Aeneas, father of Rome, first washed up after being shipwrecked in Virgil's *Aeneid.* The highlight of Cumae's *scavi* (excavations) is the ◼**Antro della Sibilla,** a man-made cave gallery that was used as a pizza oven until 1932, when archaeologists realized what it actually was. Stroll through the cave and see where the mythical Sibyl, the most famous oracle this side of Delphi, gave her prophecies. Then gape at the **Augustan Tunnel,** a deep and intricate shaft used for transportation inland from the Cumaean coast. Remnants of Cumae's Greek past are found in the **Tempio di Apollo,** located one flight of stairs above Sibyl's cave, and the **Tempio di Jupiter,** a short hike up the hill from the Temple of Apollo. Though little remains of the original temples, the spectacular view of Ischia and the coastline make the hike worthwhile.

Pozzuoli, the Campi Flegrei town most accessible from Naples, is a busy port to Ischia and Procida. Be sure not to miss the famous volcanic crater **Solfatara,** accessed either by hiking from the center of Pozzuoli (follow the frequent signs) or by riding bus #152. Solfatara was believed by the ancients to be a portal to Hades—not an unwarranted superstition, considering its eerie glowing yellow rocks, jets of sulfuric gas, rank odor, and unnatural warmth. (☎081 15 26 23 41; www.solfatara.it. Open daily Apr.-Sept. 8:30am-7pm; Oct.-Mar. 8:30am-1hr. before sunset. €5.50, children 5-10 €3.) Beneath the Solfatara crater, a short walk from both the waterfront and the train station, is the ◼**Flavian Amphitheater,** built in the first century AD. Wander around the beautiful remains and pretend you're a gladiator. (☎081 526 60 07. Open daily in summer 9am-8pm; in winter 9am-7pm. Entrance with the archaeological pass.)

Although Baia and Cumae are ideal daytrips from Naples, take advantage of the pleasant beachfront hotels in **Miseno.** Take the **SEPSA** bus from Baia or Cumae to Miseno. The **Villa Palma Hotel ❹,** V. Misena, 30, is at the last Miseno bus stop. This modern and comfortable choice is steps from the beach. (☎081 523 39 44. 15 rooms all with bath. Breakfast included. Doubles €38-62. AmEx/MC/V.) On the high promontory at the tip of the Campi Flegrei is the **Cala Moresca ❺**, V. Faro, 44, with an amazing view that extends from Miseno's beach all the way to Naples. (☎ 081 523 55 95. 28 with A/C and bath. Breakfast included. Singles €62-67; doubles €93-108. Reservations suggested. AmEx/MC/V.) On the other side of the Miseno Port, there is the **Hotel Miseno ❹**, V. Miseno, 30, with breezy, small rooms overlooking fishing boats. (☎ 081 523 50 00. 17 rooms with bath. Breakfast included. Singles €40-50; doubles €45-55. AmEx/MC/V.)

CASERTA   ☎ 0823

Caserta is easily accessible by train. Trains to and from Naples (40min., 35 per day 4:50am-9:20pm, €2.80) and Rome (2½-3½hr., €9.30-16.10). The Caserta train station is a major stop for local buses (€0.77-0.88). The Reggia is directly opposite the train station. (☎ 0823 32 14 00. Open Tu-Su 9am-7:30pm; park open 9am-6:30pm. €6.50 for entrance to both.) EPT tourist offices operate inside the Reggia and at C. Trieste, 43, at the corner of P. Dante. (☎ 0823 32 11 37. Both offices open M-F 9am-3:45pm.) Mediaservice, at P. Amico, 8, provides Internet for €3 per hr. (Open M-F 9am-1pm, 3:30-8:30pm, Sa 9am-1:30pm.) For Capua, take the train to "Santa Maria Capua Vètere" (€1.25), walk straight 1 block, and make the 1st left. Take the next left onto V. Achille, walk 150m, and turn right on V. E. Ricciardi, which becomes V. Amfiteatro. Or take the blue bus from the Caserta train station (€0.88) to P. Adriano near the ruins. Buses leave for Naples from the intersection 1 block north of the Capua train station.

Few palaces, no matter how opulent, can hold a candle to Caserta's glorious ⏹**Reggia,** often referred to as "The Versailles of Naples." A world apart from the brunt brutality of Pompeii and markedly more vivacious than Naples's quiet churches, the palace and grounds resonate with a love of art and a human passion for beauty. When Bourbon King Charles III commissioned the palace in 1751, he intended it to rival that of Louis XIV, outshining the Sun King's famously spectacular abode. The vision endures; the grounds are lovely and serene, and the palace's interior is capable of leaving anyone tripping over their own jaws. Completed in 1775, the expansive lawns, fountains, sculptures, and carefully pruned trees culminate in a 75m man-made waterfall—setting for the final scene of *Star Wars* (1977). On the 3km walk through the park, visitors can peer into the gently rippling pools, where fish dart and disappear among a trove of aquatic plants. At the base of the waterfall are many exquisite sculptures, notably a grouping showing Diana transforming the hunter Octane into a deer, his hounds poised to pounce on him. To the right are the **English Gardens,** complete with fake ruins inspired by Pompeii and Paestum (inquire at the Reggia ticket desk for info on guided tours). Instead of making the lovely walk to the waterfall, another option is to take a romantic horse-and-buggy ride from the entrance to the gardens (or a less-romantic sojourn on one of the park's rattling orange minibuses). The **palazzo** itself boasts 1200 rooms, 1742 windows, 34 staircases, and a preposterously ornate bassinet: it's overseen by an angel, suspended over a bed of sculpted bronze fruit, and held aloft by a fluttering cherub. Mechanical clocks and an intriguing collection of 18th-century children's toys also inhabit the halls. The main entrance stairway, guarded by a pair of sculpted lions, is a highlight of the palace's architecture. Frescoes and intricate marble floors adorn the grandiose royal apartments, some boasting beds guarded by sculptures of fearsome mythical beasts. One train stop from Caserta lies **Capua** and an impressive **Roman amphitheater,** much smaller but as fully intact as the Colosseum in Rome. The *hypogeum*, an elaborate basement with tunnels, brought gladiators and beasts into the arena. One of the world's best preserved, it was the site of many bloody *munera* (gladiatorial contests) and *venationes* (spectacularly staged beast hunts) in antiquity. (Open daily 9am-7:30pm. €2.50.)

CAMPANIA

BENEVENTO   ☎0824

Benevento is accessible by train from Caserta (1hr., 7 per day 8:03am-10:42pm, €3.68), Naples (1½hr., 14 per day 7:18am-10:39pm, €4.20), and Rome (3hr., 9 per day 3:25am-8:57pm, €9.86). Local buses (☎0824 210 15) leave from the train station, including bus #1 (€0.70) to C. Garibaldi and P. Roma, the center of town. Buses to Naples and local towns leave from the Terminal Autobus Extraurbani, several blocks north of the castle on C. Garibaldi. For taxis, call ☎0824 200 00. The EPT Tourist Office, in P. Roma (off C. Garibaldi, follow the information signs), has maps and information. (☎0824 31 99 38. Open M-F 8am-1:45pm and 3-5:45pm.) Postal Code: 82100.

Legend has it that this town's original name was *maleventum* (bad wind) until the Romans defeated Pyrrhus here in 275 BC and decided it was a *benevento* (good wind) after all. *Calmaventum* might have been a better name, as Italian vacationers and leisurely local shopkeepers lend Benevento the character of an idle, playful breeze. In addition to well-coiffed Italians and their fashionably pint-size dogs, Benevento has several fantastic historical sites. **Museo del Sannio** in P. Matteotti, once the monastery of the adjacent **Chiesa di Santa Sofia**, dating from 762, now exhibits Samnite artifacts, headless Roman statues, and contemporary works by local artists. (☎0824 218 18. Open Tu-Su 9am-1pm. €3, students €1.) South of the museum at P. IV Novembre sits the **Roca Dei Rettori** museum, where visitors may peer through plexiglass at an excavated Roman aqueduct below or ponder works by sculptor Mino Palladino in the adjoining garden. (☎0824 77 45 45. Open Tu-Su 10am-1pm and 4-8pm. €3.50, students €2.25. Garden free.) North of P. Roma is the ■**Arco Traiano** (Trajan's Arch, 114-117 BC), a stately Classical structure that illustrates the ruling tactics of the Emperor Trajan. The detailed sculptures that encircle the arch are superbly preserved and almost entirely intact. At the opposite end of town rests a well-preserved second-century **Roman theater**. (☎0824 472 13. Open 9am-1hr. before dusk. €2, students €1.) Today this structure hosts public concerts and a theater festival every September. Contact the tourist office for details.

The **Albergo della Corte ❸** occupies the left side of an alley at P. Piano di Corte, 11. Follow the narrow V. Bartolomeo Camerario off C. Garibaldi. Housed in a renovated palazzo, this hotel maintains 11 tidy rooms, all with bath and TV. (☎0824 548 19. Singles €32; doubles €47. MC/V.) The **Hotel President ❹**, V. Perraso, 1, has attentive, professional management. All rooms are clean, spacious, and equipped with phone, TV, A/C, and comfortable beds. (☎/fax 0824 31 67 16. Singles €46; doubles €67. AmEx/MC/V.) A short distance uphill from Trajan's Arch, **Ristorante e Pizzeria Traiano ❷**, V. Manciotti, 48, serves simple but delectable meals. (☎0824 250 13. *Primi* and *secondi* from €4. Open M and W-Su noon-4pm and 7pm-midnight.) Travelers on the go can grab a hearty sandwich or snack at **Salumeria Borai ❶**, C. Garibaldi, 158, a deli that offers a welcome alternative to C. Garibaldi's indistinguishable trattorias. (Open M-F 7am-2pm and 5-8:30pm, Sa 7am-2pm.) When dining out, look for the rich *mozzarella di buffala*, a regional specialty. The only thing more sumptuous is Benevento's bewitching ■*Strega* liqueur, named after the town's legendary hags— *strega* means witch. If swigging it straight will have you falling off your broom, at least try the bright yellow *Strega*-flavored gelato. To stock up on produce, water, and other essentials, visit the conveniently located Margherita **market,** at the corner of V. S. Fillipo and V. S. Gaetano, two streets behind the duomo. (Open M-Sa 9am-2pm and 4-8pm.)

The long bus ride back to Naples winds through the rugged backcountry and pauses at the small village of Montesarchio, easily explored in 2hr. Splayed out atop a steep hill, its serpentine streets lead to an ■**Aragonese tower** and fabulous views. The Benevento tourist office can provide a bus schedule.

AVELLINO ☎ 0825

Avellino is best accessed from Naples by bus. Take the bus from Stazione Centrale (1hr., every 30min. 5:40am-11:30pm, €4.50) or from Rome (daily 4, 5, and 8pm). Buses stop in P. Kennedy. To reach the center of town, follow C. Garibaldi out of the piazza, turn left onto V. Nappi, which becomes V. Casale and takes you into P. Duomo. The tourist office is at V. Due Principati, 32/A, and provides free maps and info. (☎0825 74 73 21. open daily 9am-7pm, call for directions from P. Kennedy.) For emergency medical service call ☎118; carabinieri can be reached at ☎112. Taxis (☎0825 243 44) are available from P. Kennedy to anywhere in the surrounding areas.

Originally called Abellinum, Avellino was once world-famous as the medieval capital of the Lombards. Today this small town is a quiet escape from Naples. Nestled in the hills of Campania, it is home to the Monte Vergine, a hilltop shrine to the Virgin Mary that has been the destination of many pilgrims for the past 800 years. The shrine was originally constructed by San Guglielmo, and today his remains lie on the site in the **Abbazia San Guglielmo.** Take the 7min. *funiculare* from the town to get to the summit, or attempt the long, steep hike. Visitors are rewarded with an ornate shrine, a glorious view of the surrounding countryside, and the steaming sulphur mines below (open daily dawn-dusk; free). The 12th-century **duomo,** Madonna dell'Assunta, lies in the center of town and is smaller and less exquisite than most other duomos in the area. Earthquakes have ravaged the region and destroyed the duomo many times, but the locals have always rebuilt it.

Accommodations in Avellino are few and far between. It is best visited as a day-trip. For a solid meal, however, head to **La Maschera ❷,** Rampa San Modestino, 1, near P. Kennedy. The courtyard seating provides great ambiance to complement the many pastas, like fusilli and tagliatelle, available with all sorts of sauces. (☎0825 376 03. *Primi* €3-8, *secondi* €4-10. Open daily 7pm-midnight. AmEx/MC/V.) On your way out of town, be sure to try one of the many delightful chocolates, called *torrones*, at the candy stores in the center. Available in both hard and soft varieties, these treats are a local specialty.

POMPEII (POMPEI) ☎ 081

On the morning of August 24, AD 79, a deadly cloud of volcanic ash from the eruption of nearby Mt. Vesuvius overtook the Roman city of Pompeii, engulfing the city in black clouds and catching the prosperous residents by surprise. Mere hours after the eruption, stately buildings, works of art, and—ghastliest of all—human bodies were sealed in hardened casts of ash, natural tombs that would remain undisturbed for centuries. Visitors to the site today bear witness to an intimate record of the town's demise. Since excavation efforts began in 1748, archaeologists continually turn up new discoveries in their ongoing mission to understand daily life in the Roman era. Most of the interesting artifacts from Pompeii are in the Museo Archeologico Nazionale in Naples. What remains at the site are the homes and streets and public buildings. If you are looking to learn about how people lived around the time of 79 AD when Vesuvius erupted, start your day at the museum at Naples looking at the extensive Pompeii collection.

HEAT EXHAUSTION. The sites afford visitors few water fountains and little shade. Bring lots of water and a parasol to avoid heat stroke. Around 15 people per year die from heat-related illnesses at Pompeii. If you need medical attention, flag down a guide or call ☎113.

CAMPANIA

▢ ▨ TRANSPORTATION AND PRACTICAL INFORMATION

The quickest route to Pompeii (25km south of Naples) is the **Circumvesuviana train** (☎081 772 24 44). Board at **Naples's** Stazione Centrale (dir: Sorrento, 40min., 2 per hr. 5:39am-10:42pm, €2.30), or from Sorrento's station. Get off at the Pompei Scavi stop, ignoring Pompeii. Eurail passes are not valid. The Porta Marina entrance to the ruins is downhill to the left. Less frequent FS trains also leave from the Naples station, stopping at modern Pompeii en route to **Salerno** (30min., every hr., €2.20). The FS train station is a 10min. walk from the excavation's eastern entrance; to reach this entrance, walk to the end of V. Sacra and turn left on V. Roma.

The excavations stretch along an east-west axis, and the modern town (with hotels and restaurants) is clustered at the eastern end. Stop by the central **tourist office,** V. Sacra, 1 (☎081 850 72 55), or the info booth at the site, for a free **map.** From the "Pompei Scavi" stop, take a right; follow the road down the hill to the **branch office** at P. Porta Marina Inferiore, 12. (☎800 01 33 50. Both offices open M-F 8am-3:30pm, Sa 8am-2pm.) Free **luggage storage** is available at the entrance to the ruins. There is a **police station** and **post office** at the site entrance, at P. Schettini, 1 (☎081 850 61 64), and another police station at P. B. Longo, where V. Roma ends.

Food at the site cafeteria is horribly expensive and barely digestible, so bring a pre-packed lunch or stock up at **GS**, on V. Statale, the main road between the entrances to the archaeological site. (Open M-Sa 9:30am-1pm and 4:30-8:30pm, Su 9:30am-1pm.) A few restaurants and fruit stands cluster outside the excavation entrances, beckoning insidiously to strollers on V. Pilino. The best alternative to the nearby McDonald's is **La Vinicola ❸**, V. Roma, 29, which provides mild comforts like an outdoor courtyard, a decent *menù* (€13, excluding drinks), and a bubbly waitstaff. (☎081 863 12 44. Cover €1. Open daily 9am-midnight. AmEx/MC/V.)

◉ SIGHTS

Pompeii entrances are open daily 8:30am to 7:30pm, with last entrance at 6:30pm. A comprehensive exploration takes all day. (Tickets €10, EU students €5, EU citizens under 18 or over 65 free.) Budget-conscious Classicists looking for an engaging tour should consider the excellent **audioguides,** available at the site's entrance. Consult the free **map** and punch in the sight's audio code to hear an informative, accessible description (€6, children's guide €4.50). Call **GATA Tours** (☎081 861 56 61) or **Assotouring** (☎081 862 25 60) for information on **guided tours,** which are more expensive than the audio guides and usually available only to groups. However, guides also gather solo travelers by the ticket office to form tour groups. A tour is a worthwhile investment: otherwise, endure hefty admission fees and a poor labeling system to get a peek at the 2000-year-old ruins.

NEAR FORUM. The **basilica** walls, to the right upon entering the ruins, are decorated with faux-marble stucco. Before the eruption, lawyers and prominent citizens fought legal battles on this floor. Walk farther down V. D. Marina to reach the **forum,** ringed by a marble colonnade. Once dotted with statues of emperors and gods, this site was the commercial, civic, and religious heart of the city. Glass display cases house gruesome body casts of Vesuvius's victims, contorted in surprise and agony. The wasted **Tempio di Giove**—largely destroyed by an earthquake that struck 17 years before the eruption—stands at the upper end of the forum. To the left, the **Tempio di Apollo** contains statues of Apollo and Diana (originals displayed in the **Museo Archeologico Nazionale,** p. 551) and a column topped by a sundial. On the opposite side of the forum, the **Tempio di Vespasian** retains a delicate frieze depicting the elaborate preparation for a sacrifice. To the right, the **Building of Eumachia** has a door frame carved with animals and insects in acanthus scrolls.

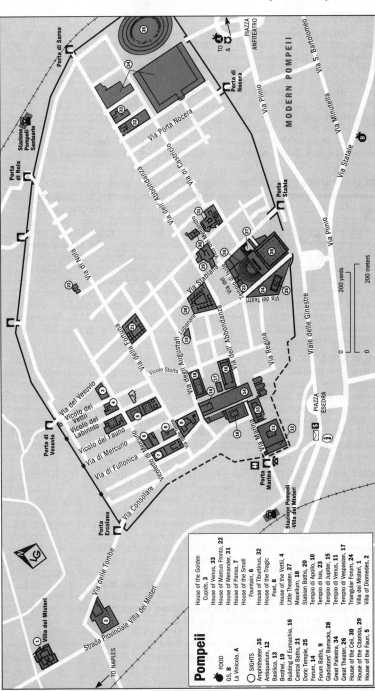

Pompeii

● FOOD

GS, B

La Vinicola, A

○ SIGHTS

Amphitheater, 35

Antiquarium, 12

Basilica, 13

Brothel, 19

Building of Eumachia, 16

Central Baths, 21

Doric Temple, 25

Forum, 14

Forum Baths, 9

Gladiators' Barracks, 28

Great Palestra, 34

Great Theater, 26

House of the Ceii, 30

House of the Citarista, 29

House of the Faun, 5

House of the Golden Cupids, 3

House of Venus, 33

House of Marcus Fronto, 22

House of Menander, 31

House of Pansa, 7

House of the Small Fountain, 6

House of Tiburtinus, 32

House of the Tragic Poet, 8

House of the Vettii, 4

Little Theater, 27

Macellum, 18

Stabian Baths, 20

Tempio di Apollo, 10

Tempio di Isis, 23

Tempio di Jupiter, 15

Tempio di Venus, 11

Tempio di Vespasian, 17

Triangular Forum, 24

Villa dei Misteri, 1

Villa of Diomedes, 2

NEAR HOUSE OF THE FAUN. At the **Forum Baths,** archaeologists have chipped away parts of body casts to reveal teeth and bones beneath. Over the course of the excavations, the **House of the Faun** has yielded stunning treasures, among them a dancing bronze faun and the spectacular Alexander Mosaic (originals now in the **Museo Archeologico Nazionale,** p. 551). The building's opulence leads archaeologists to believe that it was the dwelling of one of the richest men in town. The **House of the Vettii,** adorned with vivid frescoes, was the home of two brothers whose rivalry is apparent on every wall. A famous painting of the fertility god Priapus, flaunting his more than ample endowment, is in the vestibule. Phalli were believed to scare off evil spirits in ancient times. *(Exit Forum through the upper end, by the cafeteria; Forum Baths are on the left. A right on V. della Fortuna leads to the House of the Faun. Continuing on V. della Fortuna, turn left on V. dei Vettii to reach the House of the Vettii on the left.)*

NEAR BROTHEL. A quick right off V. degli Augustali, a well-worn road frozen in a perpetual state of reconstruction leads to the small brothel, the **Lupanare** (literally, dwelling of she-wolves). Above each bedstall, a pornographic painting advertises the specialty of its occupant with unabashed precision. Even 2000 years later, this is still the most popular spot in town. Expect a wait. The street continues down to the main avenue, V. dell' Abbondanza. The **Stabian Baths,** to the left, were privately owned and therefore fancier than the Forum Baths. More body casts—some of the site's most affectingly macabre—rest in dusty glass cases. The separate men's and women's sides both include a dressing room, cold baths (*frigidarie*), warm baths (*tepidarie*), and hot steam baths (*caldarie*); on the women's side there is an impressive marine-creature mosaic. Look down to see the remnants of the *hypocaust,* an intricate system used to channel hot steam underneath the floor. *(From V. dei Vettii, cross V. della Fortuna over to V. Storto, and turn left on V. degli Augustali.)*

NEAR GREAT THEATER. The **Great Theater** was built during the 2nd century BC. Many stone-walled cells, once home to gladiators during their training, line the edges of the field in front. Music and dance concerts were held in the **Little Theater,** built slightly later. North of the theaters stands the **Tempio di Isis,** Pompeii's monument to the Egyptian fertility goddess. Through the exit on the right, the road passes the fine **House of the Ceii** and the **House of Menander.** At the end of the street, take a left to re-connect to the main road. The altar here was built to ward off evil spirits, which Romans believed gathered at crossroads. *(Across the street, V. dei Teatri leads to the Great Theater and the Little Theater.)*

NEAR AMPHITHEATER. Red graffiti crowds the walls along V. dell'Abbondanza, expressing everything from political slogans to insults to declarations of love. Popular favorites include "Albanus is a bugger," "Restitutus has deceived many girls many times," and the lyrical "Lovers, like bees, lead a honey-sweet life." At the end of the street await the **House of Tiburtinus** and **House of Venus,** where gardens have been replanted according to modern knowledge of ancient horticulture. Nearby is the oldest standing **amphitheater** in the world (80 BC), which once held crowds of 12,000. The disenchanted spectators determined whether a gladiator would live or die during battle with a casual thumbs down or ▨thumbs up. The **Villa dei Misteri** is the best preserved Pompeiian villa. The *Dionysiac Frieze* depicts a bride's initiation into the cult of Dionysus. Nearby, the famed **Cave Canem mosaic** still guards the entry to its master's villa, though now it only aims to protect the home from the myriad flashbulbs of tourists. Head through the *porta* for a great view of the entire city. *(For the Villa of the Mysteries go to the far western end of V. della Fortuna, turn right on V. Consolare, and walk all the way up Pta. Ercolano.)*

▶ DAYTRIPS FROM POMPEII

MOUNT VESUVIUS

Trasporti Vesuviani buses run from Ercolano up to the crater of Vesuvius (round-trip €3.80, buy tickets on the bus; schedule at the tourist office or on the bus). Buses leave from outside the Ercolano Circumvesuviana station. Vesuvius stop is part way up the crater; it's a 20-30min. walk to the top. Admission to the area around the crater €6.

Peer into the only active volcano on mainland Europe, and watch steam ominously rise from the depth. In the good old days (around 1700) visitors could clamber about in the crater to their hearts' content. Now they have to settle for a front row seat on Vesuvius's steep lip. Every eruption (a total of 28 since AD 79) has helped widen and deepen the aperture, each fiery belch expanding the cavernous yawn. Scientists believe that, on average, volcanoes should erupt every 30 years—and Vesuvius hasn't blown its top since March 31, 1944. A geological station monitors tectonic rumblings, and local governments are always at the ready with a comprehensive evacuation plan. In the summer of 2003, a geological station near the site detected significant subterranean activity, prompting much speculation and concern. Experts agree that the next eruption will likely be the most violent since the particularly vehement blast of 1631—which boasted almost as much sheer destructive force as the AD 79 blast that buried Pompeii.

▨ HERCULANEUM (ERCOLANO)

To reach Ercolano, take a Circumvesuviana train from Naples's Stazione Centrale to the "Ercolano Scavi" stop (dir: Sorrento, 20 minutes). Walk 500m downhill to the ticket office. The Municipal Tourist Office, V. IV Novembre, 84, is on the way (☎081 788 12 43; open M-Sa 9am-3pm). The archaeological site is open daily 8:30am-7:30pm. €10, EU students €5, EU citizens under 18 or over 65 free. The guided tours are especially enlightening; inquire at the tourist office. Grab an illustrated guidebook (€4-6) at the shops that flank the entrance, or pick up the free Brief Guide to Herculaneum and map at the entrance.

Neatly excavated and impressively intact, the remains of the prosperous Roman town of Ercolano hardly deserve the term "ruins." Indeed, exploring the 2000-year-old houses, complete with frescoes, furniture, mosaics, small sculptures, and even wooden doors, can make even the most respectful visitor feel like a *voyeur*. Ercolano is much more intact and better preserved than Pompeii and displays artifacts in context, which lends to a very rewarding and informative experience.

Though archaeologists long held the opinion that most of Herculaneum's residents escaped the eruption that destroyed Pompeii, recent discoveries of tangled remains suggest that much of the fleeing population was buried in avalanches of volcanic mud. Only a small part of the southeastern quarter, about 45% of the city, has been excavated; between 15 and 20 of these excavated houses are open to the public. One of the more alluring is the **House of Deer,** named for the gristly statues of deer being mauled by packs of ghoulish creatures. Here, archaeologists also found the statues *Satyr with a Wineskin* and *Drunken Hercules*, a majestic marble representation of the hero struggling to relieve himself. The **palestra,** a gym and exercise complex, still holds wooden shelves once laden with massage oils and the *strigiles* used to scrape the skin clean after a rubdown. The large vaulted swimming pool, *caldarium* (warm bath), and *frigidarium* (cold bath) in the **baths** are still largely intact. Towering columns in the atrium and bits of delicate stone carving attest to ancient opulence. The **House of the Mosaic of Neptune and Anfitrite** is famous for the breathtaking **mosaic** that gives the structure its name. Two textured, shimmering figures stand beneath a vivid fan of blues and greens, and to the left, bizarre masks cast indelible expressions over some exquisite hanging flower garlands. In front of the house is a remarkably well-preserved **wine shop.** A mock stucco colonnade distinguishes the **Samnise House.** Down the street, the **House of the Wooden Partition** still has a door in its elegant courtyard, and an ancient clothes press around the corner. Outside the site, 250m to the left on the main road, lies the theater, perfectly preserved, though buried underground. (☎081 739 09 63. Occasionally open for visits; call to check.) The **Villa dei Papiri,** 500m west of Herculaneum, was recently the site of quite a stir when a trove of ancient scrolls from the library appeared to include works by Cicero, Virgil, and Horace. (Rarely open to the public; Campania Artecard holders can view the site by special arrangement. Contact the municipal tourist office at ☎081 788 12 43.)

BAY OF NAPLES

SORRENTO   ☎081

Built high on the cliffs above the glittering Bay of Naples, Sorrento's magic lies in its tiny alleys and quiet sidestreets. The piazzas and main roads are overrun with tourists and the 13,000 hotel beds in the city are often full during summer. However, Sorrento's old city and Marina Grande offer serviceable areas to window shop or stroll. More significantly, Sorrento makes a convenient stopover, thanks to cheap accommodations, swift connections, and proximity to the Amalfi Coast.

▐ TRANSPORTATION

Circumvesuviana railway (☎081 772 24 44), just off P. Lauro, runs 39 **trains** per day, from 6:17am-11:55pm, to: Herculaneum (45min., €1.80); Naples (1hr., €3.20); and Pompeii (30min., €1.80). Ferries and hydrofoils depart to the Bay of Naples islands. The port is accessible from P. Tasso by bus (€1). **Linee Marittime Partenopee** (☎081 807 18 12) runs **ferries** (40min., 5 per day 8:35am-4:55pm, €7) and **hydrofoils** (20min., 10 per day 7:20am-5:40pm, €11:10) to Capri. It also runs hydrofoils to Ischia (45min., 9:30am, €12.50) and Naples (35min., 6 per day 7:20am-6:35pm, €7). **Caremar** (☎081 807 30 77) runs ferries to Capri (50min., 4 per day 7:45am-7pm, €5). Ticket offices open as boats depart. **SITA buses** leave from Circumvesuviana station for the Amalfi Coast and are the best way to connect to locations south of the city. Twenty-one buses per day 6:30am-9:30pm, head to Amalfi (1¼hr., €2.30) and Positano (40min., €1.20). The city runs orange **internal buses** (€1) every 20min. Buy tickets for SITA and local lines at a bar, *tabacchi*, or at the hotel in P. Lauro. The Sorrento tourist office has ferry, bus, and train schedules.

✻❷ ORIENTATION AND PRACTICAL INFORMATION

Most of Sorrento rests atop a flat shelf that descends steeply to the Bay of Naples. **Piazza Tasso** is at the town's center; steep stairways and roads connect it to **Marina Piccola. Corso Italia** runs through P. Tasso; facing the sea, the **train** and **bus stations** are in **Piazza Lauro** to the right, and the old city is to the left. **Corso S. Caesaro** runs parallel to C. Italia on the old city side of P. Tasso.

> **Tourist Office:** Lungomare de Maio, 35 (☎081 807 40 33). From P. Tasso, take Lungomare de Maio to the far end of P. S. Antonio and continue toward the port. The office is to the right in the Circolo dei Forestieri compound. Good free **maps**. Open Apr.-Sept. M-Sa 8:45am-7:45pm; Oct.-Mar. M-Sa 8:30am-2pm and 4-6:15pm.

> **Currency Exchange:** No-commission currency exchange is everywhere and easy to find.

> **Car and Scooter Rental: Rent A Car,** C. Italia, 210/A (☎081 878 20 01). Scooters from €35 per day. Insurance included. Driver's license and credit card required. 18+. Cars with chauffeurs available. Open daily 8am-1pm and 4-8:30pm. AmEx/MC/V.

English-Language Bookstore: Libreria Tasso, V. S. Cesareo, 96 (☎081 807 16 39; www.libreriatasso.com), stocks thrillers, including the incomparable 📖*Let's Go.* Classics and new fiction also available. Open M-Sa 9:30am-1:30pm and 5-10:45pm, Su 11am-1:30pm and 7-10:45pm. MC/V.

Laundromat: Wash and Dry, V. Fuoro, 3, just off C. Italia. 6 washers and 6 dryers. 1hr. per load. (€8). Open daily 8am-10pm.

Emergency: ☎113. **Police** (☎081 807 30 88), on Vco. 3° Rota. From the station, go right on C. Italia and turn left after V. Nizza.

Hospital: Ospedale Civile di Sorrento, C. Italia, 129 (☎081 533 11 11).

Internet Access: Blublu.it, V. Fuorimura, 20/D (☎/fax 081 807 48 54; www.bublu.it). Take V. Fuorimura from P. Tasso. Friendly English-speaking staff and fast connection. Pick up floppy disks, CDRs, and other gadgets. Photocopying and printing available. €3 for 30min. Open M-F 10am-1pm and 5-10pm, Sa 3:30-10pm.

Western Union: V. S. Cesareo, 86 (☎081 877 85 52). Open daily in summer 10am-10pm, closed in winter.

Post Office: C. Italia, 210 (☎081 807 28 28), near P. Lauro. Open M-F 8am-6:30pm, Sa 8am-12:30pm. **Postal Code:** 80067.

🏠 🏕 ACCOMMODATIONS AND CAMPING

Reasonably priced accommodations and a well-run transportation network make Sorrento a convenient gateway to the Amalfi Coast or more southern destinations. Many visitors head to nearby beaches and towns in the day and return to Sorrento's hotels at night. Reserve ahead in summer. To avoid being overcharged, ask hotel managers to see an official price list. Prices below are for high season.

Hotel Elios, V. Capo, 33 (☎081 878 18 12), halfway to the Punta del Capo. Take bus A from P. Tasso. The 14 rooms are not impressive, but 2 large terraces and a hilltop location make for great views. A hike from Sorrento's bus and train stations, but quiet as a result. Open Apr.-Oct. Singles €30-40; doubles €50-60. Cash only. ❸

Hotel Savoia, V. Fuorimura, 46 (☎/fax 081 878 25 11; www.hotel-savoia.com), 200m from P. Tasso. Tranquil hotel has 15 spacious rooms with tiled floors and leather armchairs, all with TV, bath, and ceiling fan. Friendly management works to ensure a comfortable stay. Breakfast included. Singles €65-70; doubles €80-100. AmEx/MC/V. ❺

Hotel City, C. Italia, 221 (☎081 877 22 10; hotelcity@libero.it), left on C. Italia from the station. Though dusty and plain, it's in the heart of the city. Offers currency exchange, bus tickets, maps, and English newspapers. Internet €6 per hr. Reserve 1 month ahead for summer. Singles €39-52; doubles €53-90. AmEx/MC/V. ❹

📷 **Nube d'Argento,** V. del Capo, 21 (☎081 878 13 44; www.nubedargento.com). Bus A from P. Tasso. Manicured grounds and a professional staff make Nube d'Argento a pleasant and convenient place. Camping complex is near the sea, with a pool, hot showers, market, and restaurant. Laundry €7. Reservations needed for bungalows; in Aug. reserve 2 months ahead. €6-9 per person, €10-14 per tent, 2-person bungalows €45-80. 10% discount with *Magic Europe* camping brochure (available at any campsite) or International Camping Card. AmEx/MC/V. ❶

🍴 FOOD

Forgo the crowded central tourist haunts, skip the unappetizing British cuisine, and seek out Sorrento's trattorias and restaurants for decent Italian fare. Many places offer good prices and substantial portions. Local favorites include *gnocchi alla Sorrentina* (potato dumplings smothered in tomato sauce, mozzarella, and basil) and *cannelloni* (pasta stuffed with meat or cheese). **Fabbrica Liquori,** V. S.

C
A
M
P
A
N
I
A

Cesareo, 51, provides free samples of *nocillo*, a mysterious dark walnut liqueur, and *limoncello*, its omnipresent lemon cousin. Follow V. S. Cesareo from P. Tasso for a **market** where sweet, ripe fruit awaits.

▨ **Ristorante e Pizzeria Giardiniello,** V. Accademia, 7 (☎081 878 46 16; ristorantegiardi-niello@libero.it). Take 2nd left off V. Giuliani, which runs off C. Italia at the cathedral. Mamma Luisa does the cooking in this family-run nook. Try her delightfully starchy *gnocchi* (€5) or *linguini al cartoccio* (with mixed seafood, €7). Secluded seating in a bamboo enclosure. Cover €1.50. Open June-Sept. daily 11am-2am, Oct.-May M-W and F-Su 11am-2am. AmEx/MC/V. ❷

La Pasteria Di Corso, V. Pietà, 3/5 (☎081 877 34 32), in the alley behind the Tasso statue in P. Tasso. Dine by candlelight on old-style *cucina Sorrentina*. Close to the main piazza but quietly secluded around a corner. Enjoy *antipasti* with fresh cucumber and eggplant (€10-13) and a delectable fruit brandy after dinner. *Primi* €7-9, *secondi* €9-12. Cover €2. Open W-Su 7pm-midnight. AmEx/MC/V. ❸

Davide, V. Giuliani, 39 (☎081 878 13 37), right off C. Italia, 2 blocks from P. Tasso. Enjoy Sorrento's best gelato from a seat on the bar's garishly postmodern furniture. With refined "Peach Delicate," "Fig Heavenly," and the mysterious "Perfume of Sorrento" alongside traditional offerings, choosing from over 50 flavors is nearly impossible. 2 scoops €3. Open daily 10am-midnight. Cash only. ❶

The Red Lion, V. Marziale, 25 (☎081 807 30 89; www.theredlion.it), a right off of C. Italia going to the train station from P. Tasso (follow the signs). Popular among the tourists for its roaring atmosphere (especially during soccer games), decent food, and very low prices, it's packed every night—expect lines in summer. Full meal €10. AmEx/MC/V. ❷

Pizza a Metro, V. Nicotera, 15 (☎081 879 83 09), in Vico Equense, 10min. away by train. Take the Circumvesuviana to V. Equense, walk straight from the station, and follow the winding road uphill to P. Umberto. Turn left on V. Roma and left on V. Nicotera. This 2-story, 3000-seat super-restaurant has wood-burning ovens that cook 1m long pizzas (€18-30). Service tries valiantly to keep up with demand, but lag-time can be long when it's crowded, which it usually is. Smaller pizzas €5.50-8. Cover €1.50. Service 13%. Open daily noon-1am. AmEx/MC/V. ❷

◉ ♫ SIGHTS AND ENTERTAINMENT

Sorrento's popularity among tourists, compared to the more beautiful and serene towns nearby on the Amalfi Coast, is remarkable. The **Marina Grande,** far from the crowds swarming around P. Tasso, provides a pleasant setting for relaxing on a bench after a long day of walking, beaching, or daytripping, if you're willing to conquer the stairs. A walk to **Punta del Capo** is another fine option, as the ruins of **Villa di Pollio Felice** are clustered around a beautiful cove. Take bus A from P. Tasso to the end of the route, then take the footpath to the right of the stop. Bring a suit and a towel for a memorable swim among the ruins.

The **old city** and the area around **Piazza Tasso** heat up after dark. Hands-down the most stylish bar in Sorrento, **Gatto Nero,** V. Correale, 21, has a garden and creative interior: each wall is painted in the style of a different artist, among them Picasso and Matisse. Jazz and blues fuel the crowd, which gathers by 11pm in summer. (☎081 877 36 86. Open Tu-Su noon-3pm and 7pm-midnight.) At the rooftop lemon grove of **The English Inn,** C. Italia, 56, a fun-loving crowd comes after 10:30pm on summer evenings to dance to blasting music. (☎081 807 43 57. Open daily 9am-1am, much later on weekends.)

BAY OF NAPLES ISLANDS

The pleasure islands of Capri, Ischia, and Procida lure innumerable visitors with their Siren songs of tranquility, comfort, and beauty. Each island offers unique amenities to the weary traveler. Capri's expensive shops and pristine waters are the playground of the rich and the envy of everyone else. Ischia's hot springs and curative waters beckon those seeking health of mind and body. Procida, the quietest island, retains winding streets and empty shores that call to the independent voyager. July and August are busy, but a low-season jaunt ensures a break from crowds and intense sunshine. Veer fearlessly from main avenues and take narrow sidestreets to glimpse town life. Merge with crowds at the famous villas and grottoes, but come back later to take a private dip. Above all, just take it easy.

Ferries (*traghetti*) or faster, more expensive **hydrofoils** (*aliscafi*) depart from Naples and Sorrento, and connect a few islands to each other. For trips to Ischia and Procida from the mainland, going through Pozzuoli (easily reached on the Naples Metro, line #1) is shortest and cheapest; for Capri, Sorrento makes an efficient base. The most frequented routes to Capri and Ischia are through Naples's Mergellina and Molo Beverello ports. To reach Molo Beverello from Stazione Centrale, take bus R2 from P. Garibaldi to P. Municipio on the waterfront. For Mergellina, take the Naples Metro, line #1 to the "Mergellina" stop (accessible from Stazione Centrale in P. Garibaldi). Ferries and hydrofoils also run between the islands, but with less frequency than between the major ports.

CAPRI AND ANACAPRI   ☎ 081

Gem-like in both size and sparkle, glittering Capri has been a destination of the rich and famous for thousands of years. Augustus fell in love with Capri in 29 BC but traded its rocky cliffs for the fertile, volcanic Ischia. His successor Tiberius passed his last decade here, however, leaving scattered villas and a legacy of idyllic retirement homes. In the late 19th century, writer Axel Munthe was bewitched by Anacapri, building his final abode amid sunlit walkways and flowering vines. In Capri today, the truly glamorous (and those who can merely afford to pretend) flit like hummingbirds between ritzy boutiques and top notch restaurants. Perched on the hills above Capri, the quaint Anacapri is an oasis of budget hotels, lovely villas, and deserted mountain paths. Both share access to the island's beautiful attractions, including the aqua waters of the Blue Grotto and the majestic views of the Faraglioni peaks. There are more Ferragamo stores than affordable eateries, and crowds and prices still soar in summer, making late spring or early fall ideal to visit. But a languid stroll along Capri's cobblestone paths, admiring the friendly—and beautiful—sunbathed faces, reveals that any season here is splendid.

▐ TRANSPORTATION

Ferries and Hydrofoils: Capri's main port is **Marina Grande.** Naples and Sorrento are the main gateways to Capri; several different companies service these cities. Check ticket offices at Marina Grande for details.

> **Caremar** (☎ 081 837 07 00) runs to **Naples** (ferries: 1¼hr., 3 per day 5:45am-2:50pm, €5.60; hydrofoils: 40-50min., 8 per day 6:50am-10:20pm, €10.50) and **Sorrento** (hydrofoils: 25min., 4 per day 7am-6:15pm, €5.80).

CAMPANIA

SNAV (☎081 837 75 77) runs hydrofoils to **Naples** Mergellina (40-50min., 6 per day 9:10am-8:10pm, €10.30). Ticket office opens around time of first departure.

Linea Jet (☎081 837 08 19) runs hydrofoils to **Naples** (40-50min., 11 per day 8:30am-6:25pm, €12) and **Sorrento** (25min., €9.50). Ticket office opens around time of first departure.

Local Transportation: SIPPIC buses (☎081 837 04 20) depart from V. Roma in Capri for Anacapri (every 15min., 6am-1:40am), Marina Piccola, and points in between. In Anacapri, buses depart from P. Barile, off V. Orlandi, for the *Grotta Azzurra* (Blue Grotto), the *faro* (lighthouse), and more. Direct line between Marina Grande and P. Vittoria in Anacapri (every hr.; 5:45am-10:10pm; €1.30, day pass €6.70). Visitors rarely use the all-day pass enough to make it worthwhile, so buy individual tickets as needed. A **funicular** runs from Marina Grande to Capri (every 10min., 6:30am-1:30am, €1.60).

Taxis: Ride in style in a convertible cab. Available at main bus stop in Marina Grande (☎081 837 05 43), at bus stop in Capri (☎081 837 05 43), or in P. Vittoria, in Anacapri (☎081 837 11 75). To avoid being overcharged, tell the driver to start the meter.

■ 🛈 ORIENTATION AND PRACTICAL INFORMATION

There are two towns on the isle of Capri: **Capri** proper, near the ports, and **Anacapri**, higher up the mountain. Ferries dock at **Marina Grande**, below the town of Capri. The alternative to taking the funicular from the marina to Capri town is a steep and winding 1hr. hike past people's back yards and up a narrow stairway. Expensive boutiques and bakeries line the narrow streets that radiate from P. Umberto. **Via Roma**, to the right exiting the funicular, leads to Anacapri. The bus to Anacapri ends at **Piazza Vittoria;** Villa San Michele and the Monte Solaro chairlift are nearby. **Via Giuseppe Orlandi,** running from P. Vittoria, leads to the best budget accommodations, running past several decent restaurants on the way.

Tourist Office: AAST (☎081 837 06 34, www.capritourism.com) in Capri, at the end of the dock at Marina Grande. **Branches:** Capri in P. Umberto (☎081 837 06 86), under the clock; Anacapri at V. Orlandi, 59 (☎081 837 15 24), right from bus stop. All provide detailed **maps** (€2), ferry and bus info, and the publication *Capri è...*, a magazine with detailed information about the island's accommodations and restaurants. Open June-Sept. M-Sa 9am-7pm; Oct.-May M-Sa 9am-1pm and 3:30-7pm.

Currency Exchange: V. Roma, 31 (☎081 837 47 68), across from the main bus stop, and in P. Umberto. Another agency in the center of Anacapri at P. Vittoria, 2 (☎081 837 31 46). No commission. Open in summer daily 8:30am-6pm, winter hours vary.

Luggage Storage: Outside Capri's funicular. €2.85 per bag, for 2 hr. Open daily in summer 8am-8pm; in winter 8:15am-6pm.

Public Toilets: On Marina Grande, at the funicular in Capri, and at P. Vittoria, 5, in Anacapri. While Capri's toilets are reasonably well maintained, Anacapri's are less pristine. Open daily 8am-9pm, €0.50.

Emergency: ☎113 or 081 838 12 05. **Police,** V. Roma, 70 (☎081 837 42 11). **Ambulance** (☎081 838 12 05).

Hospital: Ospedale Capilupi, V. Provinciale Anacapri, 5 (☎081 838 11 11), a few blocks down V. Roma from P. Umberto.

Tourist Medical Clinic: V. Caprile, 30 (☎081 838 12 40), in Anacapri.

Internet: Capri Internet Point (☎081 837 32 83), in P. Vittoria, in Anacapri, has 4 fast computers. €4 per hr. Open daily 9am-9pm. **Capri Graphic,** V. Listrieri, 17 (☎081 837 52 12) is slower and costs more. From P. Umberto take V. Longano and turn right on V. Listrieri. €2.50 for 15min. Open M-Sa 9:30am-1pm and 4-9pm.

English-Language Bookstore: Librerie Studio La Conchiglia, V. le Botteghe, 12 (☎081 837 65 77), in Capri, off P. Umberto I. Open daily in summer 9:15am-1:15pm and 4:30pm-9pm; in winter 9am-1:30pm and 3-9pm. Decent pickings on

CAMPANIA

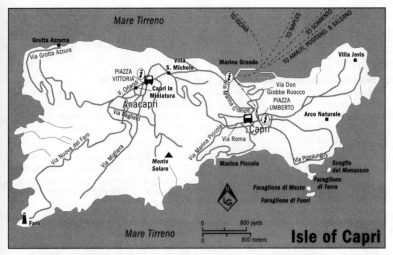

Isle of Capri

classics, new fiction, and beach trash. Smaller location in Anacapri, V. G. Orlandi, 205 (☎081 837 26 46). Open daily in summer 9:15am-1:15pm and 4:30-9pm; in winter 9am-1pm and 4-8pm.

Post Office: Anacapri, V. de Tommaso, 8 (☎081 837 10 15). Open M-F 8:30am-1:30pm, Sa 8:30am-noon. **Capri,** V. Roma, 50 (☎081 978 52 11). Open M-F 8:30am-7pm, Sa 8:30am-1pm. **Postal Codes:** Anacapri 80071; Capri 80073.

ACCOMMODATIONS

Lodgings in Capri proper are pricey year-round and become even more expensive in the summer. Anacapri offers serenity and economy, and Capri proximity and liveliness. The lower prices listed usually apply from October to May. Call ahead to confirm reservations and prices. **Makeshift camping is illegal and heavily fined.**

ANACAPRI

Bussola di Hermes, V. Traversa La Vigna, 14 (☎081 838 20 10; bus.hermes@libero.it). Call from P. Vittoria in Anacapri for pick-up rather than navigate Anacapri's tangled streets. By far the best budget lodgings on the island. Chat with the friendly proprietor Rita, who knows everything about Capri and loves hosting young travelers. Reserve early. Dorms €20-24; doubles with bath and breakfast €50-65. AmEx/MC/V. ❷

Il Girasole, V. Linciano, 47 (☎081 837 23 51; www.ilgirasole.com). Call from Marina Grande for pick-up or walk from the last bus stop, following signs. All 23 rooms have phone, fridge, TV, and shuttered doorways around a gorgeous terrace. Remote but picturesque, it's a great option for large groups. With *Let's Go*, singles €35-100; doubles €80-170; groups of 8 or more €15 per person. AmEx/MC/V. ❷

Villa Eva, V. La Fabbrica, 8 (☎081 837 15 49; www.villaeva.com). Call for a ride from Marina Grande. 28 bungalows with sparsely decorated rooms share a pool and bar. Most rooms have bath. Internet €5 per hr. Reserve early. Singles €25-30; doubles €70; triples €75; quads from €100. AmEx/MC/V. ❸

Il Mulino, V. La Fabbrica, 9 (☎081 838 20 84; www.mulino-capri.com). This converted country farmhouse boasts 7 beautiful rooms with sunny, plant-strewn terraces. Lush gardens are a nice place to relax and enjoy the *Caprese* atmosphere. All rooms have bath, A/C, TV, phone, and radio. Breakfast included. Reserve 1 month ahead in summer. Doubles €80-200; €10-20 for extra bed. €13 for A/C. AmEx/MC/V. ❺

CAMPANIA

Hotel Loreley, V. G. Orlandi, 16 (☎081 837 14 40), steps toward Capri on the edge of P. Vittoria, on the left. Easily accessible rooms are plain but spacious, with high ceiling and sizeable bath. Phone, TV, and safe in all rooms. Open Apr.-Oct. With *Let's Go*, singles €60, doubles €90; triples €110; quads €130. AmEx/MC/V. ❺

CAPRI

Bed and Breakfast Tirrenia Roberts, V. Mulo, 27 (☎081 837 61 19; bbtirreniaroberts@iol.it). Out of the way but worth the walk. From the center of Capri, walk 500m to the gas station; Tirrenia is below the station. Perched over Marina Piccola, these 3 rooms have incredible views. Tranquil atmosphere offers respite from the *centro*. Pool, sauna, and beach access. Call the friendly English-, German-, and French- speaking staff for directions. Reserve ahead. Doubles €90-110. Cash only. ❺

Hotel Gatto Bianco, V. V. Emanuele, 32 (☎081 837 02 03; www.gattobianco-capri.com). Easy access to beaches, buses, boutiques, and beauty salons. Rooms are nicely furnished with tiled floors, tasteful wall sconces, and stained wood. Terraces give an antique flavor, while large bath, TV, phone, safe, and minibar deliver modern convenience. Reserve ahead. Singles €100-155; doubles €155-215. AmEx/MC/V. ❺

Pensione 4 Stagioni, V. Marina Piccola, 1 (☎081 837 00 41; www.hotel4stagionicapri.com). From P. Umberto, walk 5min. down V. Roma. Turn left at the 3-pronged fork in the road and look for green gate on the left. Rooms are small and plain, but pristine. Avoid the cheaper rooms, which can be stuffy and bland. Pricier doubles enjoy garden access and sea views. Breakfast included. Singles €40-70; doubles €70-130, extra bed €20. Open Apr.-Nov. AmEx/MC/V. ❹

◖ FOOD

Capri's food is glorious. Savor creamy white, local mozzarella served with sweet red tomatoes, glistening yellow olive oil, and deep green basil in an *insalata caprese*—many consider it the *sine qua non* of summer dining. *Ravioli alla caprese* are hand-stuffed with a blend of local cheeses. Conclude with the indulgent *torta di mandorle* (chocolate almond cake), also known as *torta caprese*. Local wines bear *Tiberio* or *Caprense* labels. A step up (particularly price-wise) is the *Capri Blù*. Restaurants often serve *Capri DOC*, a light white. But beware: it's easy to pay a lot and receive very little. Be discerning around P. Umberto, where restaurants can serve €3 sodas and equally overpriced, stale pastries. Fruit stands around the island sell delectable cherries and ripe tomatoes at low prices. In Anacapri, try the well-stocked **supermarket,** V. G. Orlandi, 299. (☎081 837 11 19. Open M-Sa 8:30am-1:30pm and 5-8:30pm, Su 8:30am-noon.)

ANACAPRI

▨ **Ristorante Il Cucciolo,** V. La Fabbrica, 52 (☎081 837 19 17). Follow the signs for Villa Damecuta from bus stop or call for free ride from P. Vittoria. Fresh food at low prices, served on a seaside terrace. Considerable *Let's Go* discount: *primi* and *secondi* €6-9. *Bruschette pomodori antipasto* (€3.50) is unsurpassed. *Ravioli caprese* €5. Cover €1.50. Service 6%. F-Su reservations recommended. Open daily Mar.-Oct. noon-2:30pm and 7:30-11pm. AmEx/MC/V. ❸

La Rondinello, V. G. Orlandi, 295 (☎081 837 12 23), near P. Vittoria, on the left. Enjoy a romantic, candlelit feast with fresh *antipasti* and extensive seafood offerings. The *gamberoni* (shrimp; from €15) are particularly succulent. *Primi* €8-12, *secondi* €8-15. Cover €2. Open daily noon-3pm and 7-11:30pm. AmEx/MC/V. ❸

Ristorante Materita Bar-Pizzeria V. Orlandi, 140 (☎081 837 33 75, fax 837 38 81). Endure cramped outdoor seating to enjoy delicious pizza (from €4.50). After *primi* and *secondi* (€6-8.50), sip on a cooling *limoncello* (€3.50). Cover €1.50. Open noon-3:30pm and 7pm-midnight. AmEx/MC/V. ❷

Trattoria Il Solitario, V. Orlandi, 96 (☎081 837 13 82). A vine-covered path leads to a serene outdoor dining area. Treat taste buds to an aromatic *pizza rossa* (€4-6) or delightful *pizza bianca* (€5-8). Cover €1.50. Open M and W-Su noon-3:30pm and 7:30pm-midnight. AmEx/MC/V. ❷

La Giara, V. Orlandi, 67 (☎081 837 38 60). Delicious local fare in an informal outdoor setting. €16 fixed menu provides *primi, secondi,* and dessert. Expertly cooked pizza €4.40-7.70. Open M-Tu and Th-Su 10:30am-3:30pm, lunch only. AmEx/MC/V. ❷

CAPRI

▨ **Villa Verde,** Vico Sella Orta, 6/A (☎081 837 70 24, www.villaverde-capri.com). Follow the signs from V. V. Emanuele, off P. Umberto. Reserve ahead to eat as few have eaten before. Large portions of fresh fish, lobster, and vegetables. Prices are a bit VIP, as are the walls (plastered with pictures of sweaty celebrity visitors), but top-notch quality and quantity are worth the extra dough. House specialties are *linguini fra diavolo* (with lobster; €30) and rich desserts in beautiful presentations (€5-7). Daily specials €10-20. Service 12%. Open daily noon-4pm and 7pm-1am. AmEx/MC/V. ❹

▨ **Longano da Tarantino,** V. Longano, 9 (☎081 837 01 87), just off P. Umberto. Possibly the best deal in town, featuring a sea view and a €15 *menù* (with *primo, secondo,* coffee, dessert, and a shot of *limoncello* to finish it off). Seating is cramped, but service is friendly and efficient. Pizza from €4. Reservations recommended. Open Mar.-Nov. M-Tu and Th-Su noon-3:30pm and 7pm-midnight. AmEx/MC/V. ❸

Aurora Pizzeria, V. Fuorlovado, 20 (☎081 837 01 81). Just off P. Umberto. Celebrity pictures plaster the wall of this cozy establishment, which serves some of the best pizza on the island. The *pizza aurora* (with eggplant) is tasty and has the perfect crust. Pizza (€5.50-8). €2 cover. AmEx/MC/V. ❷

Buca di Bacco, V. Longano, 35 (☎081 837 07 23), off P. Umberto I, on the left when coming from the piazza, down a short alley. A simpler, less exclusive spot to savor superior cuisine. While enjoying the sea view, try pizza (€4-8, served for dinner only) or one of many savory pastas (€6-12). Open Sept.-July M-Tu and Th-Su noon-3pm and 7pm-midnight, Aug. daily noon-2:30pm and 7pm-midnight. AmEx/MC/V. ❷

Salumeria Simeoli, V. Botteghe, 12/A (☎081 837 55 43), off P. Umberto I. Tiny deli boasts fine *panini* (from €1.50), fresh *prosciutto* and *mortadella,* and a wide selection of cheeses, including creamy mozzarella. Cold beverages and *limoncello* (€10 and up) available at what might be the least exorbitant prices in town. Grab cold cuts to go for a tasty picnic lunch. Open daily 7am-9pm. AmEx/MC/V. ❶

⊙ ⚠ SIGHTS AND OUTDOOR ACTIVITIES

COAST. Daily **boat tours** (€8) reveal the ins and outs of the gorgeous coast, including the **Blue Grotto** (though it costs extra to enter; see listing). Departures from Marina Grande are at 9:30, 10:30, and 11:30am. *(Tickets and info at Grotta Azzurra Travel Office, V. Roma, 53, across from the bus stop. ☎081 837 07 02; g.azzurra@capri.it. Open M-Sa 9am-1pm and 3-8pm, Su 9am-12:30pm.)* Cavort in the clear water amid immense lava rocks, or rent a **motor boat** (€80 for 2hr.) from **Banana Sport,** in Marina Grande. *(☎081 837 51 88. Open daily 9am-6pm.)* Many pebbly **beaches** surround the island. Take a boat (€5) from the port or descend between leafy vineyards to **Bagni di Tiberio,** a bathing area set within ruins of an imperial villa. *(Take an internal bus. On foot, take V. Roma from P. Umberto I to the 3-pronged fork in the road; take the fork farthest to the left and head down the path to the left. A gorgeous stretch of Marina Piccola awaits at the bottom.)*

VILLA SAN MICHELE. Henry James once declared this Anacapri enclave a clustering of "the most fantastic beauty, poetry, and inutility." Built in the early 20th century by Swedish author-physician Axel Munthe, this magnificent building dis-

CAMPANIA

plays 17th-century furniture and Roman sculpture on the site of a former Tiberian villa. Glorious gardens, complete with flowering arbors, miniature streams, and a panoramic view of the Capri marina and coast, host Friday night concerts from June through August. (*Upstairs from P. Vittoria and to the left, past Capri's Beauty Farm. Open daily 9am-6pm. €5. Concert information available at ticket desk and Capri tourist offices.*)

THE BLUE GROTTO. The walls of La Grotta Azzurra, a water-filled cave carved into the cliffside, shimmer vivid blue when sunlight radiates from beneath the water's surface. Some who visit find the water amazing; others think it's pretty, but not pretty enough to justify €8 for a 6min. boat ride. Despite the narrowness of the cave opening and the sign warning that swimming is "strictly forbidden," many choose to take dips in the grotto during the organized tour or after boats stop at 5pm. Check with the tourist office to make sure that the grotto is not closed due to choppy water. (*Take the bus marked Grotta Azzurra from the intersection of V. De Tomaso and V. Catena. The grotto opening is accessible with the island boat tour as well.*)

CLIFFS. An exploration of the island's natural beauty can be a much-needed break from crowded piazzas and commercial streets. For those who prefer land to sea, trails lead to stunning panoramas. Hike a steep uphill path 1½hrs. to check out the ruins of Emperor Tiberius's magnificent **Villa Jovis.** Tiberius lived here during his more eccentric final years, in the largest of his 12 Capri villas. Ever the gracious host, the emperor was prone to tossing those who displeased him over the precipice; he also kept a school of young boys (whom he referred to as "minnows") on hand for purposes unprintable. The view from the **Cappella di Santa Maria del Soccorso,** built onto the villa, is unrivaled. (*V. Longano from P. Umberto. Don't miss the left on V. Tiberio. Open daily 9am-6pm. Free.*) At the island's eastern edge, a 1hr. walk connects the **Arco Naturale,** a majestic stone arch, and the **Faraglioni,** the three massive rocks featured on countless postcards. Parts of the path are unpaved dirt, so wear proper footwear. (*V. Tragara goes from Capri Centro to the Faraglioni, while the path to the Arco Naturale connects to the route to Villa Jovis through V. Matermania.*) The scenic overlook from **Punta Cannone** perfectly frames the cliffs of the southern coast. The tourist office map details several walking itineraries that lead through less-populated areas.

OTHER SIGHTS. Capri's location off the western coast of the mainland makes it ideal for surveying Italy's topography. Viewed from the peak of **Monte Solaro,** the Apennines loom ahead to the east; the mountains of Alabria are to the south on the right. A 12min. chairlift from P. Vittorio to the summit dangles from precipitous heights. (*Chairlift open Mar.-Oct. daily 9:30am-4:45pm. €5.50 round-trip.*) A difficult path also leads up the mountain, starting from the base near the Villa San Michele. A bus from P. Vittoria leads to the **Punta Carena Faro,** Italy's second-tallest lighthouse. The pedestrian stretch of V. G. Orlandi, off P. Vittoria in Anacapri, leads to the least expensive (yet still pricey) **tourist shopping** on Capri.

██ ██ NIGHTLIFE AND ENTERTAINMENT

Nocturnal action carries a hefty price tag, though Anacapri's prices are slightly lower. In typical Italian fashion, no one bothers heading out until around midnight. **Underground,** V. Orlandi, 259, is one of the town's most popular nightspots, although the atmosphere is less than chic. No cover and €5 cocktails make it popular among squealing study-abroad students and Italian locals. **Zeus,** V. Orlandi, 103, a few blocks from P. Vittoria, is a cinema most of the week; on Saturdays year-round and Thursdays in July and August, it becomes a packed disco with smoke machines, international DJs, and an over-the-top Greek theme—in other words, *the* place to be. (☎081 83 79 16. Cover €12. Open weekends midnight-4am.) The

Capri scene is classier and much more expensive. Covers are high and gatherings exclusive at the lounges and clubs near P. Umberto. Squeeze into the sweaty, frenzied **Number Two,** V. Camerelle, 1 (☎081 837 70 78), the hotspot for an older and wealthier crowd, including celebrities. Also in Capri is **Bara Onda,** V. Roma, 8 (☎ 081 837 71 47), which enjoys theme nights on many weekends. Both clubs are open all night. Those sufficiently self-assured to hang with dressed-to-kill Italians should recall that **buses** stop running at 1:40am.

ISCHIA ☎081

Ischia's combination of sea, sand, and sky presents a rich, earthy beauty so perfect, it's almost eerie. The island was once an active volcano, and hot springs, ruins, and lemon groves create an atmosphere that is downright Eden-like. Travelers have sought out Ischia since ancient times (gaining it mention in the *Iliad* and *Aeneid*), and the appeal has scarcely abated. The island is immensely popular with German tourists, so prepare to step off the ferry in summer to German signs, newspapers, and voices. The Italians keep to the therapeutic hot springs and thermal spas that, according to locals, bring relief from any ailment. Bargains and breathing room are hard to find, but *la dolce vita* is ever-present.

◰ TRANSPORTATION

Ferries: From Ischia, ferries and hydrofoils run to **Pozzuoli, Naples, Procida, Capri,** and **Sorrento.** Most ferries arrive and leave from **Ischia Porto,** where the main ticket offices are located. Some ferries arrive and depart from **Casamicciola,** on the northern side of the island. Take the #1, 2, or CS bus from Ischia Porto. Schedules and prices are subject to change. Call individual ferry lines for details.

Caremar (☎081 98 48 18) runs to: **Naples** (hydrofoils: 1hr., 6 per day 6:50am-7:10pm, €10.50; ferries: 1½hr., 8 per day 6:45am-8:10pm, €5.66); and **Pozzuoli** (ferries: 1hr., 3 per day 8:25am-5:35pm, €3.60); **Procida** (hydrofoils: 20min., 3 per day noon-4:15pm, €3.10; ferries: 35min., 8 per day 6:45am-7:30pm, €2.30). Most Caremar ferries leave from Ischia Porto. Ticket offices open approximately 30min. before departure of first boat.

Traghetti Pozzuoli (☎081 333 44 11; www.traghettipozzuoli.it) runs to **Naples** (1½hr., 6 per day 6:40am-6:50pm, €7) and **Pozzuoli** (1hr., 17 per day 2:30am-7pm, €7). Ticket offices open approximately 30min. before departure of first boat.

Alilauro (☎081 99 18 88; www.alilauro.it) runs hydrofoils to: **Capri** from Ischia Porto (40min., 10:40am, €12); **Naples,** Mergellina (45min.; from Ischia Porto 14 per day 8am-9pm,

THE LOCAL STORY

SOLE OF CAPRI

Everyday, shoemaker Antonio Viva sits on a stool outside his shop in Anacapri. His hands are always moving as he makes shoes and talks to passersby. There are many shoemakers on Capri, but signor Viva is the only one with a personality big enough to make him, and not just his shoes, a tourist attraction. With his two sons, Giancarlo and Antonio, signor Viva does the same thing day after day as the world around him changes.

On Capri: My family has been on Capri for four generations, and I've been making shoes here for 50 years. There are so many people here now, I don't know what will happen to Capri. It's hard in Italy now. Not many jobs. People are working very hard.

On himself: People come here for me. The shoes are good, but they come to talk to me. It's like a museum when I'm here. People come and look. I am here, there, everywhere. Posters, billboards, TV. People take pictures with me. Viva is like Julia Roberts.

On selling shoes: If a poor man comes to me, I try to give him shoes cheaper. I can see he is not rich. I can see he is not a bad man. I work for everyone. Workers, presidents, everyone in the middle. Everyone needs shoes. I want people to be happy. If you are nice and sit and talk, I'll help you and make a deal.

To visit Viva, go to L'Arte del Sandalo Caprese, V. Orlandi, 75 (☎081 837 35 83) in Anacapri.

€12.70; from Forio 4 per day 1-8:30pm, €12.70); **Naples,** Molo Beverello (45 min.; from Ischia Porto 11 per day 6:35am-7pm, €12.70; from Forio 8 per day 7am-6:30pm, €12.70); **Sorrento** from Ischia Porto (daily, 5:20pm, €13).

Buses: Orange **SEPSA buses** depart from the intersection on V. Iasolino and V. B. Cossa. Take a left from the ferry and walk along the port, following the road as it curves away from the port. The main lines are **CS, CD,** and **#1. CS** circles the island counter-clockwise, hitting Ischia Porto, Casamicciola Terme, Lacco Ameno, Forio, Panza Cava Grado (Sant'Angelo), Serrara, Fontana, Buonopane, and Barano. **CD** follows the same route in a clockwise direction (both every 15-30min., 4:20am-1am). **Bus #1** follows the CS route as far as Cava Grado (Sant'Angelo) and then comes back (every 15-30min., 5:05am-4:15am). Other routes are shorter, run less frequently, and stop running earlier; use these for reaching specific sites or more remote locations (€1.20, full-day pass €4, two-day pass €6). Don't expect breathing space; island buses are notoriously packed with passengers until the bitter, early-morning end.

Taxis: The pricey **Microtaxi** fleet (☎081 99 25 50) and **taxis** (☎081 333 10 93) wait at a taxi stand in front of the ticket offices on V. Iasolino. They take on many customers who would rather not go for a crowded bus ride inside someone else's armpit.

ORIENTATION AND PRACTICAL INFORMATION

Ischia's towns and points of interest lie largely on the coast; the main road (S.S. 270) wraps around the island and connects most of these places. In **Ischia Porto,** the main harbor town, C. V. Colonna runs parallel to V. de Luca from the port, one block from the waterfront. Counterclockwise, **Casamicciola, Lacco Ameno,** and **Forio** continue along the coast. And in the south, **Fontana,** reached by the CS and CD lines, is a good departure point for **Monte Epomeo.** An **AAST Tourist Office** (☎081 98 20 61) is on V. Iasolino, turn right off the boat and follow the port to the information sign. The staff provides local tour listings, a shoddy free **map,** a much better map for €2.60, and accommodations info. Baggage storage is €3 for 2 hr. (Open daily 9am-8pm.) The **police** are at V. delle Terme, 78 (☎081 99 13 36), two blocks from V. de Luca in Ischia Porto. They offer help with passport problems. (Open M, W, F 9am-noon, Tu and Th 9am-11am.) Call an **ambulance** at ☎081 507 92 67 or 507 91 11. **Ospedale Anna Rizzoli,** V. Fundera in Lacco Ameno, is accessible by bus #1, CS, or CD.

ACCOMMODATIONS

Despite the island's immense popularity, Ischia has several budget options, located principally in Forio. Hotels in Ischia Porto, Casamicciola Terme, and Lacco Ameno tend to be very expensive, since many hotels have pools fed (allegedly) by hot springs. Ischia's many tourists ensure the presence of hotels everywhere, and among these, some are truly appealing to the budget-minded traveler.

FORIO

Ostello Il Gabbiano (HI), Str. Statale Forio-Panza, 162 (☎081 90 94 22), on the road between Forio and Panza. CS, CD, and #1 bus stop outside. Provides bar, pool, and easy beach access. Friendly English-speaking staff and welcoming atmosphere. 100 beds. 4-, 6-, and 8-bed rooms. Breakfast, shower, and sheets included. Lockout 10am-2pm. Curfew 2am. Open Apr.-Sept. All beds €16 per person. V. ❷

Pensione di Lustro, V. Filippo di Lustro, 9 (☎081 99 71 63). Take the CS, CD, or #1 bus to Forio, exit at the seaside stop on V. Colombo, and make a slight left. Truman Capote slept here in 1968; will you in 2005? This family-run hotel has 10 comfortable rooms with bath, A/C, and TV. High domed ceilings and painted tiles provide beautiful accents. Breakfast included. In summer €40 per person per night; in winter €30, €5 discount in winter with *Let's Go.* AmEx/MC/V. ❸

CAMPANIA

Apartments in Ischia, V. Catello, 4 (☎081 98 25 94 or 347 056 42 03; EDP1@inter-free.it). Call English-speaking management for directions. 4 well maintained apartments with terrace and easy beach access. Call or email for reservations and directions. Apartments hold up to 6 people. With *Let's Go,* €20 per person. ❷

Hotel Green Flash, V. Genovino, 2 (☎081 333 21 33). From the bus stop, walk along V. Colombo (with the water on your right) until it becomes V. Genovino. Offers spacious rooms with seafront balconies. Sunbathe on the gleaming patio or just head to the nearby beach. Close to restaurants, bars, and Internet access. All rooms have bath, TV, A/C, and phone. Reserve 3 weeks ahead in summer. With half pension, singles €65-90; doubles €110-160. A/C €5. AmEx/MC/V. ❺

Hotel Villa Franca and **Baia Verde,** S.S. 270, #183 (☎081 98 74 20, fax 98 70 81). From Ischia Porto, take bus CS, CD, or #1. Exit at the stop after S. Francesco stop (ask bus driver) between Forio and Lacco Ameno. Continue walking in the same direction; the hotel will be on the left. 2 hotels near the beach share 35 rooms and same management. Relax in beautiful garden or heat things up in the solarium. 3 pools (2 cold mineral baths and 1 thermal bath). Breakfast included. Half pension required in July and Aug. Singles €30-65; doubles €50-120. AmEx/MC/V. ❹

ISCHIA PORTO

Pensione Crostolo, V. Cossa, 48 (☎081 99 10 94, fax 98 48 88). From Porto Ischia bus station, ascend the main street and turn right. Offers lovely terraces overlooking the sea. 15 rooms have bath, TV, fridge, and safe. Rooms €30-65 per person. AmEx/MC/V. ❸

Albergo Macri, V. Iasolino, 96 (☎081 99 26 03), along the docks, near where buses board. A quiet, family-run hotel away from the noise and bustle of V. Porto; follow signs. Though somewhat plain, the 22 rooms have comfortable beds and spotless bath. With *Let's Go,* singles €22-27; doubles €51-64; triples €70-83. AmEx/MC/V. ❷

Camping Internazionale, V. Foschini, 8 (☎081 99 14 49, fax 99 14 72), a 20min. walk from the port. Take V. Alfredo de Luca from V. del Porto and bear right onto V. Michele Mazzella at P. degli Eroi. Clean grounds and friendly staff; busy street nearby, but bushes and fences ensure privacy. Check-out at 11am. Open Apr. 1-Sept. 30. €6-9 per person, €3-6 per tent, 2-person bungalows with bath €20-60. Cash only. ❶

CASAMICCIOLA

Albergo Quisisana, P. Bagni, 35 (☎/fax 081 99 45 20). Take bus #3 from Ischia Porto. Homey establishment in the hills with nice, simple rooms. After a long day of strenuous beaching, stretch out in the rooftop garden. Easy access to ferries to Procida. Open May-Oct. €48-56 per person, per night. Full pension required in Aug. Extra bed €15. ❹

🍴 FOOD

While *cucina Ischitana* is a treat, it is difficult to find an eatery that is not tourist-oriented. Explore side streets to escape the omnipresent €4 *margherita*. Seafood and fruit are excellent, but the local delicacy is *coniglio* (rabbit).

Emiddio, V. Porto, 30 (☎081 99 24 32), at the docks in Porto. This family-run restaurant bustles with locals and tourists. Enjoy large portions and excellent desserts. Choose your fish from the many varieties just pulled from the water and on display. *Primi* €5-8, *secondi* €10-16. Cover €1. Open daily noon-3pm and 7pm-midnight. AmEx/MC/V. ❷

Scogli Innamorati, V. G Mazzella, 17 (☎081 99 70 44), between Forio and Citara; take the #1 or 2 buses. Sports a menu full of Ischian delights. Splurge on island specialty *zuppa di pesce* (€18) or go for the simple and tasty *margherita* (€5). The restaurant converts to piano bar at night (€5 cover). *Primi* €6-13. AmEx/MC/V. ❷

La Tinaia, V. Matteo Verde, 39 (☎ 081 99 84 48), in Forio, is a standout for its creamy, tasty gelato. Try the espresso in a chocolate dipped cone (€4), or simply sip espresso and watch the people go by. Open daily 8:30am-midnight. AmEx/MC/V. ❶

Mastu Peppe, V. Iasolino, 10 (☎081 98 19 12), on the water near the ferry docks of Porto. With your back to the noise and bustle of V. Porto, enjoy the pleasant seaside seating and lively waitstaff. Fare is hearty and simple, and a good meal runs cheap. *Antipasti* €4-8. *Primi* €4-10, *secondi* from €6. Cover €1.50. Cash only. ❷

👁 🏃 SIGHTS AND OUTDOOR ACTIVITIES

▨ MORTELLA GARDENS. Lady Suzanna Walton, wife of British composer Sir William Walton (1902-1983), planned and cultivated the fantastically exotic gardens, with over 800 rare and exotic plants. Stately buildings, including a monolithic, modern sun temple and an exquisitely incongruous Thai shrine, nestle among creeping vines, vivid blooms, and lily-covered pools. Allow at least an hour to fully absorb the site's beauty; a map given out at the entrance can help. Victoria's House has tropical plants and a gigantic Amazonian waterlily, one of the rarest flowers in the world. A fantastic panorama of Ischia's coast crowns the landscape just above the garden tea house. (*Take the CD or CS bus to the stop before S. Franceso; ask driver for V. Calise. Walk downhill, following signs for "spiaggia" (beach). Garden entrance is on the right, V. Calise, 39. Concerts in the summer €15, call for schedule and information.* ☎ 081 98 62 20; www.ischia.it/mortella. Open Tu, Th, Sa- Su, 9am-7pm. €10.)

CASTELLO ARAGONESE. Perched atop its own tiny island called Ischia Ponte, the Castello broods in lofty isolation. Connected to the rest of civilization by a 15th-century footbridge, this former stronghold hosts both the holy and the macabre. The castle cathedral, largely destroyed by WWII bombing, revels in a heady mix of Roman and Baroque styles. Below, the crypt houses colorful 14th-century frescoes by craftsmen from the school of Giotto. The nuns' cemetery has a ghastly history: whenever a nun died, the order would prop her decomposing body up on a stone as a fragrant reminder to the other nuns of their own mortality. For more family fun, visit the castle's Museum of Arms and Instruments of Torture, 200m past the main ticket booth. Here misbehaving visitors can be introduced to some tools that make even the strongest stomachs turn. (*Bus #7 runs to Ischia Ponte from Porto Ischia.* ☎ 081 99 28 34. Open daily 9am-7:30pm. €8.)

BEACHES AND HOT SPRINGS. Nestled on an inlet and surrounded on three sides by tall rock, the stunning Citara beach boasts coarse white sands against azure waters. Leave your frisbee at home; there won't be room for it on the crowded shore. (*Take bus #2 from Ischia Porto.*) Martoni, on the island's southern side, has calm water and a great view. (*Take bus #5 from Ischia Porto*). For a steamier experience, the hot springs at Sorgeto on the far side of the island range from tepid to boiling. The beach is the perfect spot to lounge and soak aching feet. Locals say that the cleansing lather formed by rubbing the light-green porous rocks together is fantastic for the skin. The springs are occasionally closed due to falling rocks, so ask the tourist office before setting out. (*Reach the beach from Panza by a 20min. hike. Lacco Ameno and Casamicciola Terme are densely packed with the thermal baths that originally attracted visitors to Ischia. Hikers should take the CS or CD bus to Fontana, a good departure point for a trek to the 788m peak of Monte Epomeo. On clear days, the summit overlooks Capri and Terracina.*)

🎵 NIGHTLIFE

Ischia's liveliest nocturnal scene is in Ischia Porto, along V. Porto and C. V. Colonna. The best of the bunch is the *discoteca* **New Valentino,** C. V. Colonna, 97, where young Italians grab each others' sweat-soaked bodies to blaring music.

(☎ 081 99 26 53. Open F-Su 11pm-6am, adjoining **Ecstacy** piano bar.) **Blue Jane,** on V. Iasolino, at Pagoda Beach near the port, features a packed disco and a smooth, floor-side hangout. Energetic bum-shakers vie for the coveted central spot on the dance floor. (☎ 081 99 32 96. Open July-Aug. daily 11:30pm-4am; June and Sept. F-Su 11:30pm-4am. Cover €10-20.)

PROCIDA ☎ 081

Calmly rippling waters and netted fishing boats bobbing in the port create a scene so exquisite that Procida has been used as a setting for such films as *Il Postino* and *The Talented Mr. Ripley.* Sun-baked buildings quietly crowd a port awash in cheery pastels. From the fresh seafood to the citrusy sweetness of the many lemon groves, Procida awakens the senses. The florid tones of the local dialect drift from open windows, and family-owned stores shelve only essentials. You've stumbled upon the most authentic, untouristed island in the Bay of Naples; cross your fingers and hope that others don't do the same.

⊟ TRANSPORTATION

Ferries and hydrofoils: To **Naples, Pozzuoli,** and **Ischia.** All boats dock at Marina Grande, near the ticket offices.

Caremar (☎ 081 896 72 80) runs to: **Ischia** (hydrofoils: 20min., 3 per day 10:35am-3:45pm, €3.10; ferries: 35min., 10 per day 7:30am-11pm, around €2.30); **Naples** (hydrofoils: 40min., 6 per day 6:50am-6:50pm, €7.60; ferries: 1hr., 5 per day 7:15am-8pm, €4.50); **Pozzuoli** (hydrofoils: 30min., 8:25am, €3.10; ferries: 50min., 3 per day 8:55-6:05pm, €2.60).

Procida Lines (☎ 081 896 03 28). Hydrofoils to **Pozzuoli** (30min., 8 per day 4am-7:15pm, €6).

SNAV (☎ 081 896 99 75) runs hydrofoils to **Naples** (40min., 8 per day 7:35am-8:05pm, €8.36) and **Ischia** (Casamicciola); (40 min., 8 per day 7:50am-9:10pm, €3.56). Confirm times and prices at port ticket offices.

Buses: SESPA buses (€0.80 at *tabacchi,* €1.10 onboard) depart from the port and serve entire island. Frequency and times vary seasonally; see schedules available at the tourist office or posted at many *tabacchi* and hotels.

L1 covers the middle section of the island, running past most of the hotels and campgrounds before stopping at the port of **Chiaiolella,** the site of the liveliest restaurants and beaches. (Every 20min. 6:10am-11pm.)

C1 follows much the same route, but also covers the less populated northwestern part of the island. (Every 40min. 6:50am-8:25pm.)

C2 runs to the northeastern part of the island. (Every 40min., 6:55am-8:25pm.)

L2 serves the southeastern part (Every hr. 6:25am-8:25pm.) Bus drivers rarely call out stops, tell your driver where you want to get off and ask him to remind you when the stop approaches.

Taxis and **microtaxis:** ☎ 081 896 87 85. Taxi-stand near the docks. However, walking around Procida can be an adventure, as cars, trucks, and *motorini* don't like to share the narrow streets with pedestrians. Flatten up against the nearest wall when they come speeding by. Street names and numbers are more like suggestions than cold, hard facts, so be prepared to get lost, which is half the fun of Procida.

🛈 PRACTICAL INFORMATION

The **AAST Tourist Office,** V. Roma, 92, is to the right from the dock on the main port, in the same building as the ferry ticket offices. Free **maps** are available with street names and site locations. (☎ 081 810 19 68. Open daily 9am-1pm and 3-6pm.) In case of **emergency,** call an **ambulance** (☎ 118) or the **carabinieri,** V. G. da Procida, 22 (☎ 112 or 081 896 71 60). A 24hr. **emergency clinic,** V. V. Emanuele, 191 (☎ 081 896 90 58), is accessible by bus L1, L2, or C1. **Internet** is available at **Bar Capriccio,** V.

C
A
M
P
A
N
I
A

Roma, 99, to the left of the ferry ticket office when facing away from the water. (☎081 896 48 06. €2 for 30min. Open daily 6:30am-2am.) There is an **ATM** is by the port, at V. Roma, 103. **Western Union** is available at **Navigator**, V. P. Umberto, 33, on the way to Terra Murata (open daily 10am-1pm, 5-8pm). The **post office**, at the corner of V. V. Emanuele and V. Liberta, also has an ATM. (☎081 896 07 01. Open M-F 8am-1:30pm, Sa 8am-12:30pm.) **Postal Code:** 80070.

ACCOMMODATIONS

Spending an inexpensive night on Procida is difficult, so budget travelers may want to make the island a daytrip from Naples. For those able or willing, however, Procida offers gorgeous options.

La Casa sul Mare, V. Salita Castello, 13 (☎081 896 87 99; www.lacasasulmare.it). Take bus C2. Arched doorways and clean white walls give this pristine hotel an authentic Mediterranean feel. 10 bright rooms all have A/C, TV, bath, phone, and terrace with views of the pastel-washed fishing village of Marina Corricella. Reserve ahead. Doubles €95-160, including breakfast. AmEx/MC/V. ❺

Hotel Celeste, V. Rivoli, 6 (☎081 896 74 88; www.hotelceleste.it). From Marina Chiaiolella, walk 1 block up V. Giovanni da Procida, taking the first right onto V. Rivoli. 35 spacious rooms share interior courtyard and have bath, TV, phone, and A/C. Terraces open onto vineyard views. Attentive staff. Easy access to beaches. Reserve ahead in summer. Mandatory half pension in Aug. Singles €50-60, half pension €90; doubles €60-92, half pension €140. AmEx/MC/V. ❹

La Rosa dei Venti, V. Vincenzo Rinaldi, 32 (☎081 896 83 85, www.vacanzeaprocida.it). Take a taxi from the port to this ideal space for secluded relaxation, located on the northwestern part of the island. The location is difficult to reach on foot. 20 *cassette* ("boxes" with kitchenette and dining area) offer a break from banal hotel living. Internet and breakfast €2.50. 2-6 person *cassetta* €25-37 per person, per night. Mandatory €100 refundable security deposit. AmEx/MC/V. ❸

Hotel Riviera, V. Giovanni da Procida, 36 (☎081 810 18 12; www.hotelrivieraprocida.it). Take bus L1 or L2, then ascend the winding drive. 25 comfortable rooms have bath, A/C, TV, and phone. Convenient access to beaches at Ciraccio and Ciracciello. Reserve ahead. Breakfast included. Open Apr.-Sept. Singles €42-60; doubles €60-90. 10% discount with *Let's Go,* excluding July-Aug. AmEx/MC/V. ❹

Pensione Savoia, V. Lavadera, 32 (☎081 896 76 16). Take bus L2. Decent accommodations are old but well maintained. Snug rooms share bath and roof terrace. Hotel has friendly management and a pleasant atmosphere. Breakfast €4. Singles €26; doubles €47. Extra bed €13. Cash only. ❸

Campeggio Caravella (☎081 810 18 38), on V. IV Novembre. Take bus L1 or C1. Clean, pleasant grounds with snack bar and flowers. 15min. from beach at Ciraccio. Open June 15-Sept. 15. Reserve in June for Aug. €6 per person, €6 per tent. Cash only. ❶

FOOD

Like accommodations, Procida's dining options are not typically for the budget-minded. For snacks on the go try the **Supermerc SAS,** V. Libertà, 72 (☎081 896 82 46), across the street from the **post office.** For those willing to pay, many excellent restaurants are located in both the **Porto** and **Chiaiolella** parts of town. Family-run **Il Galleone** ❸, V. Marina Chiaiolella, 35, distinguishes itself from the more touristy restaurants along the marina with open-air seating and very attentive service. Settle down for great seafood *antipasti* (€5-8), and watch the boats come and go. (☎081 896 96 22. *Primi* €7-8, *secondi* €8-13. Daily *menù* €15. Open daily 12:30-

2:30pm and 7:30-11pm. AmEx/MC/V.) Come to **Da Michele ❷**, V. Marina Chiaiolella, 29, for Procidan fare just above the fishing harbor. Try the succulent rabbit (€7), a highlight of island cuisine. (☎ 081 896 74 22. Pizza €2.50-6.50. *Primi* €4-9, *secondi* around €10. Cash only.) One of the many Porto restaurants is **Ristorante Sent'Cò**, V. Roma, 167 (open daily 6pm-2am). Enjoy the fresh seafood, just pulled from the harbor, as you watch people stroll down V. Roma. (*Primi* €7-10, *secondi* €6-10, pizza €3.10-6.50. MC/V.) After dinner, ask at any bar for the syrupy *limoncello*, made from Procidan lemons.

🧭 SIGHTS

Take bus C2 to the **Abbazia San Michele Arcangelo** (Abbey of St. Michael the Archangel), or make the steep uphill trek to Procida's easternmost and highest hilltop. From the left side of the port (facing away from the water), walk up V. V. Emanuele, taking the first left on V. P. Umberto. A plain yellow facade guards splendid 15th-century gold frescoes and eerie bleeding Christ figures within. The abbey's opulent scroll work and stately archways prove a jarring contrast to the quaint, unornamented island outdoors. Take a moment to admire the deeds of St. Michael, emblazoned on the domes. (☎081 896 76 12. Open daily 9:45am-12:45pm and 3pm-5:30pm. Free.) En route to the abbey, the medieval walls of **Terra Murata** are downhill from the monastery, on V. S. Michele. Procida's oldest settlement, this area has winding streets, squat stone buildings, and islanders roaring around on *motorini*. The **lookout point** before the old city walls opens onto the idyllic marina of **Corricella**; pack a picnic and enjoy the breeze. The night view is especially nice.

Procida has several **beaches**, most of which remain pleasantly uncrowded. The dark sand and calm water of **Ciraccio** stretches across the western shore, and is sprinkled with snack bars and drink stands. Its western end, near Chiaiolella, is at the end of the L1 line. Another popular beach is **Chiaia**, on the southeastern cove, accessible by L1, L2, and C1. Perhaps the prettiest of them all, **Pozzo Vecchia** (a.k.a. Il Postino Beach, after the movie was filmed here) rests amidst striking layered cliffs. Don't forget to pay homage to Sophia Loren, whose pictures adorn the entrance. **Procida Diving Center** runs scuba diving tours that introduce participants to a host of interesting sites and sea life. One dive and full equipment rental for €28. Kids, beginners, and advanced divers are all welcome. The offices are at Marina di Chiaiolella. (☎339 435 84 93; www.procidadiving.it. Open M-Sa 9am-1pm and 3:30pm-7pm.) Lemons are ubiquitous in Procida and honored for their place in Procidan culture in the **Festa del Limone**. Besides food tastings featuring lemons, highlights include a fashion show and a debate on—what else—the lemon.

AMALFI COAST

It happens almost imperceptibly: after the exhausting tumult of Naples and the compact grit of Sorrento, the highway narrows to a two-lane road that zigzags down the coastline. Then, the hazy horizon becomes illuminated with lemon orchards and bright village pastels, and after turning a curve—it's different for every person—it happens: the Amalfi Coast hits the bloodstream, and euphoria kicks in. Positano, Amalfi, and the nearby isles of Capri and Ischia combine simplicity and sophistication, earning the favor of Emperor Augustus, Ernest Hemingway, and Jacqueline Kennedy Onassis. But the region's ultimate appeal rests in the tenuous balance it strikes between man and nature. Whitewashed homes cling defiantly to rock, and scooters brazenly hug cliffside bends. But for all human enterprise, no attraction outdoes the coast's unassuming grandeur.

CAMPANIA

POSITANO
☎ 089

When John Steinbeck visited Positano in the 1950s, the town was a posh haven for artists and literati. Jack Kerouac and Tennessee Williams sought solitude in this bohemian retreat, where the fashion avant-garde invented the bikini and creativity ran wild like the bougainvillea. But this classy reputation soon drew ordinary millionaires in addition to the writers, painters, actors, and filmmakers who made it famous. Today its beachfront teems with vacationers from all walks of life and from all over the world. Steinbeck had estimated that Positano's cliffs could stack no more than 500 visitors at a time. He clearly underestimated local ingenuity: the *Positanesi* have managed to squeeze in over 2000 hotel beds, and crowds now overrun the tiny footpaths and narrow stairways. Though the nature of tourism here has changed considerably since Steinbeck's time, Positano remains the most fashionable of Amalfi's coastal towns—for better or worse.

■ TRANSPORTATION

Approaching by land, Positano is best reached by **bus**. Blue **SITA buses** run to Amalfi and Sorrento (7am-9pm, 25 per day, €1.30). There are two stops in Positano along the main coastal road, V. Marconi (see **Orientation**). Walk downhill from either stop to reach the *centro*. Tickets are sold at the friendly Bar Internazionale, by the Chiesa Nuova stop on V. Marconi, or at *tabacchi*. **Ferries** and **hydrofoils** run between the coast and islands. **Linee Marittime Salernitane** (☎089 81 11 64) runs ferries (50min., 9:10am, €10) and hydrofoils (30min., 10am, €14.50) to Capri. **Travelmar** (☎089 87 29 50) runs ferries to Amalfi (25min., 6 per day 10am-6:30pm, €5); Minori (30min., 4 per day noon-5:20pm, €5.50); and Salerno (1¼hr., 6 per day 10am-6:30pm, €6). Confirm times and prices in person.

■ ORIENTATION AND PRACTICAL INFORMATION

Positano clings to two huge cliffs overlooking the Tyrrhenian Sea. Coming from Sorrento, **Chiesa Nuova** is the first SITA stop in town on V. Marconi, in front of Bar Internazionale. From here, if you don't mind the steep downhill walk, take **Viale Pasitea**, or wait for one of Positano's frequent **internal buses** marked "Positano Interno" (every 15-30min. 7:15am-midnight, €0.80); the bus route ends downtown in **Piazza dei Mulini**. The second SITA stop at the intersection of V. Marconi and **Via Cristoforo Colombo**; internal buses don't run here, so walk 10min. downhill on V. C. Colombo to reach P. dei Mulini, the beginning of the *centro*. At P. dei Mulini, V. C. Colombo becomes Viale Pasitea. Also from P. dei Mulini, **Via dei Mulini** winds through town, past the church of Santa Maria, and to **Spiaggia Grande**, the main beach. Take the footpath from Spiaggia Grande to get to the cozier **Fornillo** Beach.

Tourist Office: V. del Saraceno, 4 (☎089 87 50 67), in a big red building near the church, provides good **maps,** hotel listings, and ferry and bus schedules. Open M-Sa 8am-2pm and 3-8pm; in winter M-Sa 9am-3pm, Sa 8:30am-noon.

Emergency: ☎113. **Carabinieri** (☎112 or 089 87 50 11), near the top of the cliffs down the steps opposite Chiesa Nuova. The nearest **hospital** is in Sorrento; a **tourist medical clinic** is in Amalfi.

Pharmacy: Viale Pasitea, 22. Open in summer daily 9am-1pm and 5-9pm.

Internet: Conwinum, V. Rampa Teglia, 12 (☎089 81 20 76; www.positano.conwinum.it), below Buca di Bacco, provides fast Internet with printing. €6 per hr. Drinks are available while you surf. Open daily from 9am until late.

English Language Bookstore: La Libreria, V. C. Colombo, 165 (☎089 81 10 77). Selection of classics, new fiction, and Italian cookbooks in a basement with A/C. Internet available (€8 per hr.). Open daily 10am-1am.

Currency Exchange: P. dei Mulini, 6 (☎089 87 58 64), on the V. Mulini side of the piazza. Open in summer 9:30am-1:30pm and 4-9:30pm, in winter 9:30am-1pm and 3:30-7:50pm. Decent rates, but commission on traveler's checks. (€1 per check, €3 per min.)

ACCOMMODATIONS

Staying in Positano can be rough on the wallet, so budget travelers might consider making Positano a day-trip from Sorrento or Salerno. For those looking to stay in the village, however, there are a few very good budget options. Contact the tourist office for help in arranging *affittacamere* for longer stays.

Ostello Brikette, V. Marconi, 358 (☎089 87 58 57; www.brikette.com). Accessible by orange Interno bus or SITA bus; exit both at Chiesa Nuova stop and walk 100m to the left of Bar Internazionale; hostel is on the right. If walking, take Viale Pasitea and then a left onto V. Marconi. Squeaky clean rooms and sublime views from 2 large terraces. Owner Cristianna loves to give her guests advice on sights and restaurants. Shower, sheets, and breakfast included in price. Lockout 10am-4pm. Lights-out curfew varies from midnight-2am with nightlife. Internet available. Reserve early. Open late Mar.-Nov. Dorms €24, €22 for longer stays; doubles €70. MC/V. ❷

Pensione Maria Luisa, V. Fornillo, 42 (☎/fax 089 87 50 23; www.pensionemarialuisa.com). Take the Interno bus down Viale Pasitea to V. Fornillo. 14 bright rooms with views from seaside terraces and private baths. Simple, quiet, and lovely, this pension promises comfort. Breakfast included. Doubles €65-70. ❸

Casa Guadagno, V. Fornillo, 36 (☎089 87 50 42, fax 089 81 14 07). Take the Interno bus down Viale Pasitea to V. Fornillo. Tiled floors, incredible views of the coast, and winter heating. Friendly husband and wife management team. Enjoy breakfast (included) on the hotel's idyllic covered terrace. All rooms have bath and private terrace overlooking the sea. Reserve ahead. Doubles €85; triples €95; quads €105. MC/V. ❸

Hotel Pupetto, V. Fornillo, 37 (☎089 87 50 87; www.hotelpupetto.it). Located just above Fornillo Beach. Relaxed atmosphere includes bath, A/C, balcony, phone, safe, and TV in each room. Reserve ahead in July-Aug. Call for directions. Singles €80-90; doubles €130-160. Half pension €18 per person per day. AmEx/MC/V. ❺

Hotel Il Gabbiano, Viale Pasitea, 310 (☎089 87 53 06; www.ilgabbianopositano.com). Gorgeous rooms all have harbor views, bath, and TV. Antiques provide tasteful accents. Breakfast included. Doubles €110; triples €145; quads €180. MC/V. ❹

FOOD

The *granita al limone* is a slushy Amalfitan specialty. The best kind boasts pieces of frozen lemon rind. Don't bother with the commercial machines that whirl their contents showily: they simply can't compare to the homemade, sun-ripened variety. Look no further than the ■granita stand in P. dei Mulini, near the Interno bus stop, and wait in what may be a long line for lemony ice piled over the brim of a cup. (*Granita* €1.50. Open in summer daily 8am-10pm.) As for the rest of food in Positano, generally speaking, high prices reflect high quality.

Da Gabrisa, Viale Pasitea, 219 (☎089 81 11 70, fax 81 16 07). Bright, cheery atmosphere and great service. Savor the tender pumpkin in the grilled vegetable antipasto (€5). The simple *pasta alla norma* (pasta in tomato sauce with eggplant; €8) is a treat. Primi €6-10, secondi €8-15. Open daily 7-11pm. AmEx/MC/V. ❸

Da Constantino, V. Corvo, 95 (☎089 87 57 38). From V. Marconi, with your back to Viale Pasitea, walk left until you reach the stairs just past Ostello Brikette; walk up the stairs. The elevated sea view overshadows even the most succulent meal. Sea breezes and inviting atmosphere make this the spot to cap off a long day. Try the specialty *cre-*

spolini al formaggio (crepes filled with cheese; €5.50). Pizza from €4.50. *Primi* €6-9, *secondi* €8-13. Open in summer daily noon-3:30pm and 7pm-midnight, in winter Tu-Th noon-3:30pm and 7pm-midnight. AmEx/MC/V. ❷

Mediterraneo Ristorante, Viale Pasitea, 236-238 (☎089 812 28 28). Enjoy the variety of offerings, outdoor seating, and attentive family-run service. Try the fried zucchini flowers or *calamarato con polipetti e pomodorini* (squid-shaped pasta with octopus and tomato). *Primi* €8-17.50, *secondi* €6-20. Open daily 9:30am-12:30am. MC/V. ❹

Il Grottino Azzurro, V. G. Marconi, 158 (☎089 87 54 66), next to Bar Internazionale. Excellent fish priced right. Guests linger for hours in a simple but inviting interior. Homemade pasta and fresh seafood from €5.50. Cover €1.50. Open M-Tu and Th-Su 1-3pm and 8-11pm. Closed Dec. to mid-Feb. Cash only. ❷

Vini e Panini, V. del Saraceno, 29-31 (☎089 87 51 75), near the tourist office. This well-stocked shop sells fresh sandwiches and plenty of cheeses. Wander the aisles for all manner of scrumptious Italian foodstuffs. *Panino* with mozzarella and tomato €3. Bottle of *limoncello* €10. Open Mar.-Dec. M-Sa 8am-2pm and 4:30-9pm. Cash only. ❶

Il Saraceno D'Oro, Viale Pasitea, 254 (☎089 81 20 50). If you are looking to avoid a traditionally lengthy Italian dinner, enjoy delicious pizza-to-go (dinner only) from €4.50. The incredible *gnocchi alla sorrentina* (€7) comes covered in perfectly baked mozzarella. Cover €1. Open in summer daily 1-3pm and 7-11pm, in winter M-Tu and Th-Su 1-3pm and 7-11pm. Cash only. ❶

La Zagara, V. dei Mulini, 6 (☎089 87 59 64). For a snack after trekking up and down Positano's innumerable stairs, or just for an after-dinner dessert, join the crowds and try the invitingly named *torta afrodisia* (€3). Prices are higher for patio, which becomes a piano bar in the evening. Open daily 8am-midnight. Cash only. ❶

⬛👁 BEACHES AND SIGHTS

For most, Positano's beaches are its main attraction. The biggest, busiest, and priciest is **Spiaggia Grande,** in the main stretch by the docks. At the less crowded, private **Lido L'incanto** (☎089 81 11 77), guests revel in the fact that they are surrounded only by the other people who shelled out €10 for a *lettino* (beach chair), umbrella, shower, and changing room. Outside the entrance, **Noleggio Barche Lucibello** (☎089 87 50 32, fax 089 87 53 26) rents motorboats from €33 per hour and rowboats from €12.50 per hour, and provides boat tours of the Blue Grotto and Emerald Grotto; call for prices and information. The serene and secluded **Fornillo Beach** is hidden from the docks and downtown blitz by a shady, rocky walkway. Take V. Positanese d'America, a footpath that starts from the left side of the port facing away from the water and winds past **Torre Trasita.** Three private beaches on this end offer amenities for a small fee. **Marinella** (€5) features a little sand underneath a time-worn boardwalk. Sit among chattering teenagers while flipping through this summer's beach-book or trashy magazine of choice. **Fratelli Grassi** (€12) and the slightly crowded **Puppetto** (€5-7) offer boat excursions to those with cash to burn.

The three **Isole dei Galli,** peeking out of the waters off Positano's coast, were allegedly home to Homer's mythical Sirens, who lured unsuspecting victims with their spellbinding songs. In 1925 the quartet of Stravinsky, Picasso, Hindemith, and Massine bought one of the *isole,* perhaps in honor of this legend. While swimming around these beautiful islands is permitted, setting foot on them is not.

Positano offers tremendous **hikes** for people with quads of steel. **Montepertuso,** a high mountain pierced by a large *pertusione* (hole), is one of three perforated mountains in the world (the other two are in India). Hike the 45min. trail up the hillside or take the bus, which leaves from P. dei Mulini near the port.

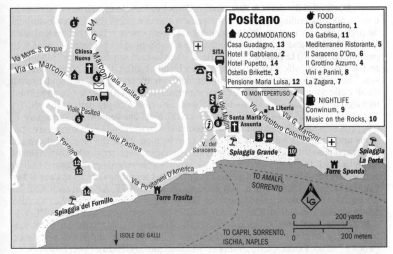

Positiano

🍴 FOOD
Da Constantino, **1**

🏠 ACCOMMODATIONS
Casa Guadagno, **13**
Hotel Il Gabbiano, **2**
Hotel Pupetto, **14**
Ostello Brikette, **3**
Pensione Maria Luisa, **12**

Da Gabrisa, **11**
Mediterraneo Ristorante, **5**
Il Saraceno D'Oro, **6**
Il Grottino Azzurro, **4**
Vini e Panini, **8**
La Zagara, **7**

🍷 NIGHTLIFE
Conwinum, **9**
Music on the Rocks, **10**

People looking to lighten their pocketbooks find ample opportunities in Positano. The tragically chic spend entire days, or at least unbearably hot afternoons, in exorbitant boutiques. Others take boat excursions along the coast and to neighboring islands. Frequent cruises embark to the **Emerald** (p. 586) and **Blue Grottoes** (p. 573), beautiful water-filled caves nearby. As numerous boating companies compete for these excursions, prices can sometimes be reasonable for shorter trips; check the tourist office and booths lining the port.

🎷 ENTERTAINMENT

The swank piano bar and disco **Music on the Rocks,** on the far left side of the beach facing the water, packs well-dressed thirty-somethings into a large cave with one side open to the water. Celebrities including Sharon Stone and Luciano Pavarotti have been known to drop in, but be forewarned that star status and a steep cover aren't the only prerequisites: so are classy threads. (☎089 87 58 74. Cover €20.) For less exclusive revelry, and to meet young locals, head to **Conwinum** (☎089 81 20 76). No cover and cocktails for €5 make this spot popular also among the backpacking crowd; the low lighting and red interior set the right mood. (Open daily from 9am as an Internet cafe during the day). People looking to quench their thirst begin to arrive around 10pm.

PRAIANO   ☎089

Praiano's vast coastline is just as beautiful as Positano's, but far less crowded. Towers that once stood watch over the sea are now crumbling, picturesque ruins punctuating landscape. Whether you choose the 25min. bus ride (€1.30) or the hour-long walk from Positano, the quiet of Praiano is a welcome change from the hordes of tourists on the rest of the Amalfi Coast.

🏠🍴 ACCOMMODATIONS AND FOOD. Enjoy the panorama from the campground **Villaggio La Tranquillità** ❶ and the **Hotel Continental** ❹, V. Roma, 21, housed within the same complex on the road leading to Amalfi (ask the driver to stop at Ristorante Continental). All rooms include bath and breakfast; most have exquisite ter-

C
A
M
P
A
N
I
A

races. Don't miss the domed, decorated ceilings inside. A long stairway descends to a stone dock extending out onto shimmering waters. (☎ 089 87 40 84; www.continental-praiano.it.) Parking available. Camping €14 per person, €12.50 per tent. Singles €60-68; doubles and two-person bungalows €68-88. Simpler accommodations €45 per person. MC/V.) **La Perla ❸**, V. Miglina, 2, 100m toward Amalfi from La Tranquillità on the main road, offers large rooms with bath and a rooftop terrace overlooking the sea. The bright lounge has streaming sunlight, comfy chairs, TV, bar, and a small book collection. (☎ 089 87 40 52, www.perlahotel.it. With *Let's Go*, breakfast included and singles €40-60; doubles €74-84. Sea view €20 per day. AmEx/MC/V.) Just down the road from La Perla toward Amalfi, **Hotel Ona Verde ❸**, V. Terramare, 3, has professional management and a welcoming atmosphere. All 20 rooms are spacious and equipped with bath and small tiled terrace. Take the elevator down six floors and pass through a stone hallway to reach the reception; climb down 200m of stairs to reach the beach. (☎ 089 87 41 43; www.hotelonaverde.com. Rooms €65-90 per person, breakfast included.) Find decent budget accommodations at **Casa di San Gennaro ❸**, on V. Capo Vettica. Ten spotless rooms have TV, A/C, and bath. Call for directions. (Walk toward Positano from Trattoria San Gennaro. ☎ 089 87 42 93. Also offers scooter rental from €25 per day. €40-70 per person per night. AmEx/MC/V.)

Ristorante Continental ❹, below Villagio La Tranquillità, specializes in local seafood. Enjoy local wine (from €5), the bright white interior, and lovely sea views. (☎ 089 87 42 93. Cover €1.70. *Primi* (€8-11), *secondi* (€11-15). Open Easter-Nov., daily noon-3pm and 8pm-midnight. MC/V.) On the road from Positano, next to the Chiesa di San Gennaro (with blue and gold domes), **Trattoria San Gennaro ❷**, V. S. Gennaro, 99, offers terrace and garden seating. Enjoy a big serving of *sciaiatielli San Gennaro* (€7), with mushrooms and clams. (☎ 089 87 42 93. Cover €1.50. Pizza from €4. Open daily noon-5pm and 7pm-midnight. AmEx/MC/V.)

🎥 🎬 **SIGHTS AND ENTERTAINMENT.** Praiano's openness and natural beauty make it the coast's best spot for a scenic **scooter** ride. **Praia Costa**, V. Marconi, 45 (☎/fax 089 81 30 82; www.praiacosta.com), offers rentals starting at €30 for 3hr. Casa di San Gennaro (see above) also rents scooters. From **Torre a Mare**, a well-preserved tower that serves as an art gallery for the works of sculptor and painter Paolo Sandulli, and heading around the bend from Praiano toward Amalfi, a ramp leads down **Via Terramare** to **Marina di Praia**. This 400-year-old fishing village, tucked in a tiny ravine, is home to the Amalfi Coast's most popular club since the early 1960s, **⊠Africana**. Fish swim through the grotto under the glass dance floor while music echoes off the dimly lit cave roof above, and boats dock at the stairwell right outside. If you meet a cute Italian, drop a flower in the well and make a wish; if the flower floats out of the grotto below, your wish will come true. If it doesn't, drown your sorrows in a *cocktail africana* for €5. (☎ 089 87 40 42. Cover €15-20, includes 1 drink. Open daily mid-June to Sept. 10pm-3am.)

A bit farther down V. Terramare heading toward Amalfi, the **Grotta Smeralda** (Emerald Grotto) lures tourists with the promise of luminous green water. SITA buses stop at the grotto's above-ground elevator, which leads to the cave. This 22m high cavern is just the thing for people who missed Capri's Blue Grotto or haven't had their fill of watery caves. The green-tinted water gives off a slight glow, and the cave's walls drip with stalactites. Multilingual guides reveal an underwater nativity scene, as well as a rock formation that is said to resemble Garibaldi. No swimming is allowed in the grotto. (Tour €7. Open daily 9am-4pm.)

AMALFI ☎ 089

It is almost impossible to decide on Amalfi's greatest attraction. It may be its location between the jagged rocks of the Sorrentine peninsula and the azure waters of the Tyrrhenian. Perhaps it is the lemon groves that bask under a brilliant sun, or the plump lemons themselves, which seem to give everything from icy *granita* to the afternoon breeze an unparalleled citrus zing. Monuments like the fanciful Arab-Norman duomo and medieval paper mills also give the city character. Amalfi was furthermore the seat of Italy's first sea republic and the preeminent maritime powerhouse of the southern Mediterranean, thanks in part to the compass, invented here by Flavio Gioia. Yet these achievements have never upstaged the effortless splendor of the coast's natural beauty.

⌨ TRANSPORTATION

The **bus terminal** is in P. F. Gioia, on the waterfront. **SITA buses** (☎089 87 10 16) go to: Positano (40min., 25 per day 6:30am-11pm, €1.30); Salerno (1¼hr., 20 per day 6am-10pm, €1.65); and Sorrento (1¼hr., 29 per day 5:15am-11pm, €1.85). Buy tickets in *tabacchis*. **Ferry** and **hydrofoil** tickets and departures are at the dock off P. F. Gioia. **Travelmar** (☎089 87 29 50) runs hydrofoils to: Minori (5min., 4 per day 12:45-6:20pm, €1.50); Positano (25min., 7 per day 9:20am-6pm, €5); and Salerno (35min., 6 per day 10:40am-7:10pm, €4). Rent **scooters** at **Financial Tour Travel** (see **Practical Information**). Call **taxis** ☎089 87 22 39.

✈ ⓘ ORIENTATION AND PRACTICAL INFORMATION

Think of Amalfi as a T-shape, with the top running along the shore and the stem, **Via Lorenzo di Amalfi,** running from the shore into the town's main square, **Piazza Duomo.** To reach P. Duomo, take V. di Amalfi from P. Flavio Gioia away from the sea and through the white arch. **Piazza Municipio** is a 100m walk along the coast in the direction of Atrani, up **Corso Repubblica Marinara** (on the left when facing the sea). Ferries and buses stop in **Piazza Flavio Gioia,** the intersection of the two roads. Facing the water, Atrani lies east and to the left, and Praiano is west to the right. Go through the tunnel on C. Repubblica Marinara to reach Atrani, 750m down the coast, or follow the public path through the restaurant just next to the tunnel, on the side facing the sea. The walk takes 10min.

The **AAST Tourist Office,** C. Repubblica Marinara, 27, is through a gate on the left heading up the road toward Atrani. Grab a free **map**, along with hotel and restaurant listings. Ferry and bus timetables are also available. (☎089 87 11 07. Open May-Oct. daily 8am-2pm and 3-8pm, Nov.-Apr. M-Sa 8am-2pm.) The **police,** V. Casamare, 19 (☎089 87 10 22), are on the left, up V. di Amalfi. For **medical assistance** dial ☎118 or contact **American Diagnostics Pharmaceutics** (☎033 545 58 74), with English-speaking doctors on-call 24hr. The facilities are clean and modern, and doctors perform blood tests and lab procedures. For **Internet,** head to **Financial Tour Travel,** V. di Amalfi, 29, which has three computers. It also offers **Western Union** services and rents **scooters** from €32 per day. (☎089 87 10 46. Internet €4 per hr. Open daily 9am-8pm.) The **post office,** C. Repubblica Marinara, 35, next to the tourist office, offers **currency exchange** with good rates. (☎089 87 29 96. Commission €0.52, €2.58 on checks over €51.65. Open M-F 8am-6:30pm, Su 8am-12:30pm). **Postal Code:** 84011.

⌂ ACCOMMODATIONS

Lodgings fill up in August, so reserve far ahead. Beware of illegal or unlicensed hostels that solicit patrons on buses or near transport stops.

🏨 **Hotel Lidomare,** V. Piccolomini, 9 (☎089 87 13 32; www.lidomare.it), through the alley across from the duomo, left up the stairs, then across the *piazzetta*. 15 cavernous rooms have terrace, TV, phone, fridge, A/C, and fantastic bath (most with jacuzzi). Locally made antiques adorn the halls. Small library available for perusal. Breakfast included. Singles €47-50; doubles €99-110. AmEx/MC/V. ❸

C A M P A N I A

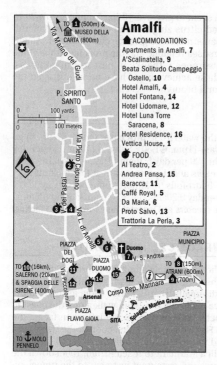

Amalfi

🏠 **ACCOMMODATIONS**
Apartments in Amalfi, **7**
A'Scalinatella, **9**
Beata Solitudo Campeggio
Ostello, **10**
Hotel Amalfi, **4**
Hotel Fontana, **14**
Hotel Lidomare, **12**
Hotel Luna Torre
Saracena, **8**
Hotel Residence, **16**
Vettica House, **1**

🍅 **FOOD**
Al Teatro, **2**
Andrea Pansa, **15**
Baracca, **11**
Caffé Royal, **5**
Da Maria, **6**
Proto Salvo, **13**
Trattoria La Perla, **3**

A'Scalinatella, P. Umberto, 6 (☎089 87 19 30 or 87 14 92; www.hostelscalinatella.com), up V. dei Dogi in Atrani, 10min. from Amalfi. Take C. Repubblica Marinara through the tunnel, and then take the stairs on your right. Follow the road to P. Umberto. Hostel is a 100m walk from Atrani's beach and a perfect starting point for hikes. Welcoming brothers also rent rooms in Atrani, plus campsites and scenic rooms above Amalfi. Laundry €5.50. Dorms €10-21; doubles €30-60, with bath €50-83; camping €5 per person. Prices vary seasonally; highest in Aug. Cash only. ❶

Hotel Amalfi, V. dei Pastai, 3 (☎089 87 24 40; www.starnet.it/hamalfi). From V. Lorenzo, turn left uphill on Salita Truglio. 3-star establishment has attentive management and a restaurant overlooking citrus gardens. Rooms include minibar, phone, safe, and TV. Call ahead for A/C (€10 extra) and reserve early for sea view. Breakfast included. Singles €60-100; doubles €80-130. Half pension add €10. AmEx/MC/V. ❹

Beata Solitudo Campeggio Ostello, P. Generale Avitabile, 4 (☎/fax 081 702 50 48; www.beatasolitudo.it), in Agerola. 30min. from Amalfi by bus. Amenities include kitchen, TV, laundry facilities, and Internet €4 per hr. Views and isolation make up for the long ride. 16 beds in 3 tidy rooms. Dorms €9.30; 4-person bungalows with bath and kitchen €51.65-62; camping €3.65-4.13 per person. MC/V. ❶

Vettica House, V. Maestra dei Villaggi, 96 (☎089 87 18 14; www.hostelscalinatella.com), shares management with A'Scalinatella. Call Gabriele for directions. A haven of tranquility amid natural beauty, 10 bright rooms with bath sit above lemon groves. Quick access to great hiking trails (not including the 270 stairs up from the road). Kitchen available. Doubles €52; quads €60, dorms from €12.50 with *Let's Go.* Call ahead to confirm prices. Cash only. ❹

Apartments in Amalfi, V. S. Andrea (☎089 87 28 04; www.amalfiapartments.com), next to the duomo, rents 2 small apartments with views of the sea and the piazza. The double apartment can fit 4 while the studio apartment is perfect for a couple; the 2 share a fantastic terrace. Friendly proprietors serve home-brewed *limoncello.* Reserve 1 month ahead and call for directions to navigate the winding maze of stairs. €50-65 for 2 people; €90-110 for 4 people. Cash only. ❷

Hotel Fontana (☎089 87 15 30), in P. Duomo, has comfortable rooms in an optimal, if noisy, location. High ceilings and gigantic mirrors lend a distinctive atmosphere. Breakfast included. Singles €55; doubles €85; triples €114; quads €143. AmEx/MC/V. ❹

Hotel Residence, C. Repubblica Marinara, 9 (☎089 87 11 83, fax 87 30 70), near P. Flavio Gioia. Decked with relics of a bygone era—rotary phones, brass chandeliers, and marble staircases. Lavish rooms have bath, TV, phone, and balcony. Buffet breakfast included. Doubles €114-124; triples €144-155; quads €155-180. AmEx/MC/V. ❺

Hotel Luna Torre Saracena, V. P. Comite, 33 (☎089 87 10 02; www.lunahotel.it). Built in 1200 by St. Francis of Assisi as a cloister, Luna looks like a medieval castle perched on the cliffs. The interior courtyard, teeming with citrus plants and comfy chairs, is perfect for leisurely reading. Past guests include Henrik Ibsen (he worked on *A Doll's House* here) and Richard Wagner. Enormous rooms have high ceiling, TV, phone, and views. Restaurant, across the street in a stone tower (erected in 1500), has amazing cuisine. Buffet breakfast included. Doubles €170-270; suites from €290-520. Singles discount €15. Extra beds €50. AmEx/MC/V. ❺

🍴 FOOD

Food in Amalfi is good but expensive. Indulge in fish, *scialatelli* (a coarsely cut local pasta), and the omnipresent pungent liqueur *limoncello* made from local lemons. The town's many *paninoteche* are perfect for a tight budget.

🦐 **Da Maria** (☎089 87 18 80), in P. Duomo. A 1st stop in quest for quality. Friendly owners provide daily seafood specials, as well as tried-and-true favorites like *scialatelli* and delectable seafood *risotto* (€11). Fast service despite the crowds. Pizza from €4.50. *Primi* from €10, *secondi* from €12. Fixed menu €20. Reservations recommended. Open Tu-Su 11am-3pm and 7pm-midnight. AmEx/MC/V. ❹

🦐 **Caffé Royal,** V. Lorenzo di Amalfi, 10 (☎089 87 19 82), near the duomo. The fantastic gelato made here (a labor of love) is the best on the Amalfi Coast. The biggest cones and over 30 flavors at the best prices (€2-3). Profiteroles covered in lemon cream (€3) are a specialty. Open 7am-3am daily; closed F Jan.-Feb. AmEx/MC/V. ❶

🦐 **Trattoria La Perla,** V. dei Pastai, 5 (☎089 87 14 40), around corner from Hotel Amalfi. Decent food in a quiet piazza. Try the *baccala fritto* (fried fish; €13) or the *delizia al limone* (lemon delight; €4). *Menù* with dessert €17. Cover €2. Open Mar.-Nov. daily noon-3pm and 7pm-midnight; Apr.-Oct. M and W-Su noon-3pm and 7-11:30pm. AmEx/MC/V. ❸

Al Teatro, V. E. Marini, 19 (☎089 87 24 73). From V. di Amalfi, turn left up Salita degli Orafi with a sign immediately after a shoe store, then follow the signs. A cozy place that caters to locals with inexpensive food and a lively atmosphere. Try the *scialatelli al Teatro* (with tomato and eggplant; €7). *Primi* and *secondi* from €4. Open M-Tu and Th-Su 11:30am-3:15pm and 7-11:30pm. Closed early Jan. to mid-Feb. AmEx/MC/V. ❷

Baracca, P. Dogi, 16 (☎089 87 12 85). Follow the signs away from P. Duomo. Fresh seafood in a perfect place to people watch. Excellent *spaghetti alla pescatore* (with seafood; €9). *Primi* €7-10. Lunch *menù* €16. Open M and W-Su noon-3pm and 6-11pm, daily in Aug. AmEx/MC/V. ❸

Proto Salvo (☎338 188 18 00), in P. Duomo. This is *the* place for great take-out snacks of pizza and sandwiches (€3). Thick focaccia with toppings from €1. Lunch and early evening bring large crowds, so plan to wait. Mixed salads and vegetarian *panini* available. Open daily 8:30am-midnight. Cash only. ❶

Andrea Pansa, P. Duomo, 40 (☎089 87 10 65). Opened in 1830, Amalfi's oldest pastry shop bears a bounty of outstanding confections, some made seasonally. In winter try the *sprocollati* (fig with ground almond); year-round, the *baba au limon* (€2) and *baba con crema* (€1.50) are delicious. Open daily 7am-midnight. AmEx/MC/V. ❶

🏛 SIGHTS

The 9th-century **Duomo di Sant'Andrea** is the dominant feature of P. Duomo, and perhaps the most dominant feature of Amalfi. Its facade has intricate geometric designs of vividly contrasting colors, typical of the Arab-Norman style. The **bronze doors,** crafted in Constantinople in 1066, are so handsomely wrought that they

C A M P A N I A

started a bronze door craze throughout Italy. (☎089 87 13 24. Open daily 9am-9pm. Modest dress required.) To its left, the **Chiostro del Paradiso** (Cloister of Paradise), a 13th-century cemetery for Amalfitan nobles, has 120 striking marble columns and an intricate fresco of the crucifixion. The elegant interlaced arches of both the cloister and the church, like the bell tower in the square, show a Moorish influence. The church **museum** houses mosaics, sculptures, and the church's treasury. Underneath, the crypt contains the body of the church's namesake, St. Andrew the Apostle, whose remains were brought to Amalfi during the Crusades. (Open daily in summer 9am-9pm, in winter 10am-5pm. Free multilingual guides available. Cloister, museum, and crypt €2.) In the center of the piazza, the **Fontana di Sant'Andrea** does its best to counteract the church's stately influence, featuring a marble female nude with water trickling from her nipples. Those who can put their Freudian complexes aside might venture a drink from the fountain, which was rebuilt in the 19th century according to an original medieval plan.

The 9th-century waterfront **arsenal** majestically guards the entrance to the city center and contains relics of Amalfi's former maritime glory, including examples of Amalfitan currency (the *Tari*), and early compasses by Flavio Gioia. To inject an ailing diet with a fiber-packed kick, head to the **Museo della Carta** (Paper Museum). From the arsenal, take V. di Amalfi; the road changes to **Via delle Cartiere**. The museum, in a 13th-century paper mill, exhibits the history of paper production, including paper samples made from pressed flowers and the water-powered machines that made Amalfi a paper-producing powerhouse. (☎328 318 86 26; www.museodellacarta.it. Open Tu-Su 10am-6pm. €2.) Shops in town sell hand-bound reproductions of traditional Amalfitan books made from local paper.

BEACHES AND HIKING

There are two small **beaches** in Amalfi; one is sandy, and the other is rocky. Bronzed Italians and pink tourists nap and read on the shores as children splash in the water. The sandy beach, though not stunning, is a stretch near the marina. Better (and free) options are at nearby **Atrani**, a 15-20min. walk away. Just around the bend from Amalfi, the village of Atrani used to be home to the Amalfi Republic's leaders; with about 1000 inhabitants today, it's a quiet place to escape Amalfi's crowds by day and enjoy lively bars and music at night. Try **La Risacca**, P. Umberto, 1 (☎089 87 10 87; open daily 7am-1pm; AmEx/MC/V), with super-friendly bartenders and a fun-filled atmosphere, or **Bar Directo**, P. Umberto, 2 (☎089 87 42 31; open daily 7am-1pm; AmEx/MC/V), with plentiful outdoor seating, to watch a soccer match. After the tunnel from Amalfi, descend a small winding staircase to the beach and P. Umberto. Atrani's only cobbled road, V. dei Dogi, leads from the beach and past P. Umberto; here a white stairway leads to **Chiesa di San Salvatore de Bireto,** with beautiful 11th-century **bronze doors** from Constantinople. The church's name refers to the ceremonial hat placed on the Republic's *doge*, or ruler, when he was inaugurated.

Hikers often tackle paths from Amalfi and Atrani into the imposing **Monti Lattari**, winding through lemon groves and mountain streams. From Amalfi, the **Antiche Scale** lead to the charming village of **Pogerola.** Trek through the **Valley of the Dragons,** named for the torrent of water and mist which plumes like smoke from a dragon and explodes out to sea every winter. Another favorite is the 4hr. **Path of the Gods,** leading from Bomerano to **Positano,** with great views along the way. The beautiful hike from Atrani to **Ravello** (1½-2hr.) runs through gently bending lemon groves, up secluded stairways, and down into green cliff valleys. From Ravello, it's only about 1hr. downhill to **Minori's** beautiful beaches, past quaint village churches and bountiful grapevines. SITA runs frequent bus service from both Minori and Ravello to Amalfi. Hike past the old paper mills in **Valle delle Ferriere,** which begins

Going abroad?

save now!

Wireless has never been cheaper!

GSM phones starting at

$99

To order, call (858)274-2686
or visit our website

Order with affiliate code: go2004

❋ FREE incoming calls

❋ No roaming charges

❋ Discount international
  calling rates

International
Cell Phones

Get the benefits of a cell phone
at the cost of a calling card.
Say goodbye to payphones and
exorbitant rental fees!

www.telestial.com

Telestial®
Wireless Solutions for Travelers™

Visit us at http://www.letsgo.com

LET'S GO
Travel Guides

Be sure to check out our new
website, beyondtourism.com,
for a searchable database of
international volunteer, work
and study opportunities, a
blog from fellow travelers
and feature articles
highlighting a variety of
destination-specific
opportunities.

Purchase one of our 48 guides
online or at your local bookstore

Alaska - Amsterdam - Australia - Austria & Switzerland - Barcelona - Brita
& Ireland - Brazil - California - Central America - China - Chile - Costa Ri
Ecuador - Eastern Europe - Egypt - Europe - France - Germany - Greece
Hawaii - India & Nepal - Ireland - Israel & the Palestinian Territories - Ita
Japan - London - Mexico - Middle East - New York City - New Zealand &
Fiji - Paris - Peru - Pacific Northwest - Puerto Rico - Roadtrip USA - Ro
San Francisco - South Africa - Southeast Asia - Southwest USA - Spa
Portugal & Morocco - Thailand - Turkey - Vietnam - USA - Washingto
D.C. - Western Europe

http://www.letsgo.cor

at the paper museum (see **Sights**). Naturally, the hikes can get steep, and a good map is essential (available at the tourist office in Amalfi). For a shorter walk, head from Amalfi's center to its terraced cliffs to reach the cliff where famous rebel Masaneillo hid from Spanish police. Although the cave is sporadically closed, the astounding views are a nice payoff along the way.

◪ DAYTRIPS FROM AMALFI

MINORI

SITA buses from Amalfi stop on V. G. Capone, which becomes V. G. Amendola as it heads 1km northwest to Amalfi. The Roman villa (☎089 85 28 43) is open daily 9am-7pm. Free.

With a decidedly low-key character and many pleasant seafront cafes, Minori is serene and inviting. Smaller and less touristed than Amalfi or Positano, the town is home to large stretches of beautiful **free beaches.** Sunbathers seeking the perfect day at the beach and hikers in search of the optimal trail-end spot can find peace and relaxation here. Hotels are more expensive than the ones in neighboring Maiori, so it's best to stay there and dodge the tourist buses on the 1km walk along the coastal road. The difficult 1hr. hike from Atrani (via Ravello) is enjoyable for its cliff vistas and shady lemon groves. Those seeking a break from the gleaming sun can take respite in the remains of Minori's Roman villa, which bears monochrome mosaics of a traditional Roman *venatio* (hunt), as well as preserved arcades. The small **villa museum** displays many artifacts excavated in and around the area. The site is several blocks from the beach, on V. S. Lucia. For a lunchtime *panino* (€3-6) or tasty gelato (€2), try **Suzy Beach ❶.** With plenty of breezy outdoor seating, this is the perfect place to reward tired feet after a long day's hike— or to further cultivate sloth-like tendencies after a long day of sunning.

MAIORI

The pedestrian-only C. Regina intersects V. G. Capone a few blocks down from the SITA bus stop, with the water on your right. The tourist office, C. Regina, 73, is several blocks up C. Regina, inside a garden on the left. (☎089 87 74 52, fax 85 36 72. Open M-Sa 8:30am-1:30pm and 3-6pm.) The nearest medical facilities are in Amalfi. Carabinieri may be reached at ☎089 87 72 07.

Only a few kilometers from well-known Amalfi, this beachfront town draws few foreign visitors. Though it lacks both the chic of Positano and the history of Amalfi, Maiori has low-priced hotels, excellent beaches, and several noteworthy sights. Much of Maiori was damaged during WWII, and what was left was ruined in a flood several decades ago. Thus the architecture is noticeably more modern than in the other towns along the coast, with squat, square buildings and metal balconies. Most visitors come to Maiori to lounge on the beaches or stroll up and down C. Regina. Although much of the beach is privately owned (€5-10 fee for access with chair and umbrella) there is a small public section near the SITA bus stop. For sights rather than sun, the town's main attraction is **Chiesa di S. Maria a Mare,** up a flight of stairs on the left side of a mini piazza three blocks up C. Regina from the beach. It has a beautiful 15th-century alabaster altar in front of the crypt.

Maiori has several inexpensive hotels near the beach. **Albergo De Rosa ❸,** V. Orti, 24, a left two blocks up C. Regina from the beach, has English-speaking management and clean rooms with bath and breakfast included. (☎/fax 089 87 70 31. Singles €35-40; doubles €50-60.) An inexpensive restaurant is **Dedalo ❸,** on V. Cerasuoli just off C. Regina, one block up from the beach. They serve a €15 *menù* and €3-6 pizzas in a vaguely mod interior with A/C. (☎089 87 70 84. Open daily noon-3pm and 6pm-2am.) For a bit more expensive fare at a beautiful spot along Maiori's beach, try **Ristorante La Vela ❹,** Lungomare G. Amendola, 7, to pick from their huge selection of local fish, including the house specialty *scialatelli* with seafood and vegetables for €10. (☎089 85 28 74. *Primi* €7-10, *secondi* €11-22. Open daily noon-1pm and 6pm-midnight. AmEx/MC/V.)

RAVELLO ☎089

Far from the beach on its cliff-top perch, Ravello presides over a patchwork of villages and ravines that tumble into the sea. Romans founded the town in AD 500, and Barbarians and Saracens later invaded, but artists and intellectuals have ultimately claimed the natural beauty and romantic decay of this once-formidable settlement. The exquisite gardens of Villa Rufolo inspired part of Boccaccio's *Decameron* and Wagner's opera *Parsifal;* to this day, Ravello is known as *la Città della Musica*, thanks to the concerts and performances it hosts all year.

📧🌐 TRANSPORTATION AND PRACTICAL INFORMATION. Take the blue **SITA bus** from Amalfi (20min., 30 per day 6:30am-midnight, €1) marked Ravello-Scala. For a gorgeous walk, hike along hills and lemon groves from Minori (1hr.), Atrani (2hr., via Scala), or Amalfi (2½hr., via Pontone). Ask at the tourist office in Amalfi for details. For a **taxi,** call ☎089 85 79 17. The **AAST Tourist Office** is at P. Duomo, 10 (☎089 85 70 96). The English-speaking staff provides brochures, event and hotel listings, and a **map.** The **carabinieri** (☎089 85 71 50) are on V. Roma, near the piazza. A **pharmacy,** P. Duomo, 14, is on the left side of the piazza facing the duomo. (☎089 85 71 89. Open in summer daily 9am-1pm and 5-8:30pm, in winter 9am-1pm and 4:30-8pm. Closed Dec.) Clean **public toilets** are located next to Cafe Calce (see **Accommodations and Food**). **Currency exchange** is at V. Roma, 15. (☎089 85 80 86. Open M-Sa 9:30am-1pm and 5-8pm.) Across the street is an **ATM;** another is at P. del Duomo, 5. Look for a faded bronze sign to the left of the kiosk. The **post office** is at P. Duomo, 15. (Open M-F 8am-1:30pm, Sa 8am-12:30pm.) **Postal Code:** 84010.

🏠🍴 ACCOMMODATIONS AND FOOD. Ravello offers many opulent options and several affordable ones. To get to **Hotel Villa Amore ❹,** V. dei Fusco, 4, follow V. San Francesco out of P. Duomo toward Villa Cimbrone, and take a left onto V. dei Fusco. Twelve clean, white-washed rooms share a garden overlooking cliffs and the sea. As its welcome sign says, "A stay at Villa Amore gives peace to the soul and joy to the heart." All rooms have terrace and view; some have bath. (☎/fax 089 85 71 35. Breakfast included. Reserve 1 month ahead. Singles €48-60; doubles €74-85. MC/V.) **Albergo Garden ❺,** V. G. Boccaccio, 4, before the tunnel into Ravello, by the SITA bus stop, lacks the intimacy of a smaller hotel, but compensates with great views. All 10 rooms have bath and balcony. (☎089 85 72 26; www.starnet.it/garden. Breakfast included. Reserve 1 month ahead for Aug. Doubles €88-95. Extra bed €15. Closed Nov. 15-Feb. 15.) On the other side of the piazza, **Hotel Parsifal ❹,** V. G. d'Anna, 5, hosts guests in a former Augustinian convent. Lush gardens overlook the dazzling cliffs, and creeping vines prompt the feeling that you have been transported onto the set of an opera. Rooms are bright, with big windows and beautiful furnishings. (☎089 85 71 44. Breakfast included. Singles €50-70; doubles €85-95.)

Wines with Ravello labels are revered around the globe, and as you stroll down V. Roma, step into one of the many wine shops and have a taste or even buy a bottle. **Cumpà Cosimo ❸,** at V. Roma, 44, has a large menu and a staff willing to chat about Ravello. The restaurant's atmosphere is informal and laid-back, perfect for casual meals. The *mista di pasta fatta in casa* (€14) mixes five delectable homemade pastas. (☎089 85 71 56. Cover €2. Open noon-4pm and 6:30pm-midnight. AmEx/MC/V.) **Cafe Calce ❶,** V. Roma, 2, serves excellent pastries and coffee. *Limoncello* costs €11 per bottle. (☎089 85 71 52. Cappuccino €2. Gelato €2. Open M-Tu and Th-Su 8am-1am. MC/V.)

◙ ♫ SIGHTS AND ENTERTAINMENT. The beautiful churches, ivy-covered walls, and meandering paths of the 13th-century **Villa Rufolo** inspired Wagner's magic garden, seen in the second act of his opera *Parsifal*. In summer, the villa puts on a concert series with performances in some of its most picturesque spaces (for details, see below). A medieval tower with Norman-Saracen vaulting and statues representing the four seasons serves as the entry to the famous **Moorish cloister.** Enter through the arch off P. Duomo near the tunnel. The main hall frequently hosts big-name art exhibitions. (☎089 85 76 57. Open daily 9am-8pm. €5, under 12 or over 65 €2.50) The Amalfi Coast's third set of famous **bronze doors,** cast by Barisano of Trani in 1179, is in the portal of Ravello's **duomo.** The doors have 54 panels depicting detailed scenes from the Passion of Christ. Inside, antique columns set off two pulpits with elaborate mosaics. An image of the town's patron saint stands in the **Cappella di S. Pantaleone.** Behind the painting, his blood is preserved in a cracked vessel. St. Pantaleone was beheaded on July 27, AD 290, at Nicomedia. Every year on this day the city holds a **religious festival,** during which the saint's blood is mysteriously liquefied. The **museum** within depicts the duomo's history through pagan and Christian eras with beautiful ancient mosaics and sculptures. (Duomo open Mar.-Nov. daily 9:30am-1pm and 3-7pm; Dec.-Feb. Sa-Su 9am-1pm and 2-5pm. Museum €2. Modest dress required.) Follow V. San Francesco out of P. Duomo to **Villa Cimbrone.** Renovated by Lord Greenthorpe in the 19th century, the villa sports floral walkways and majestic gardens, including the panoramic **Terrace of the Infinite.** The **Temple of Bacco** and the **Grotto of Eva** lie along the twisting paths, as well as some of the most magnificent views on the Amalfi Coast. A procession of notables has made the villa a famous retreat, including Greta Garbo, Leopold Stokowski, and Jacqueline Kennedy, a resident in 1962. (Open daily 9:30am-7:30pm. €4.50, children under 12 €3.)

During the year, internationally renowned musicians perform at **classical music festivals,** held around New Year's, Easter, and all summer. In warm weather, concerts are held in the gardens of Villa Rufolo; in winter they move inside the villa or duomo. Each season's festival is unified by a Wagnerian *leitmotiv,* and includes screenings of films and panel discussions on a range of musical and scientific topics. Tickets, usually €10-20, are sold at the Ravello Festival Box Office, V. Roma 10-12 (☎089 85 84 22; www.ravellofestival.com. Open daily 9am-2pm and 3-8pm).

SALERNO ☎089

As the capital of the Norman Empire from 1077 to 1127 and home to Europe's first medical school, Salerno played host to a proud, powerful culture. During WWII, however, the city was blasted by Allied bombs and much of its medieval past turned to rubble. Unlike the dreamy villages of the Amalfi Coast, Salerno is an urban reality, with a large population and an industrial core. The city gives travelers a wonderful taste of modern Italy, and though it serves well as a cheap base for visiting the Amalfi Coast and the ruins at Paestum, Salerno itself is a worthwhile destination. The snaking alleyways of the old city are charming, and you can find a treasure trove of excellent restaurants and cafes if you take the time to look.

▛ TRANSPORTATION

Trains: In P. Veneto. To: **Naples** (45min., 40 per day 3:41am-10:32pm, €4.77-10.35); **Paestum** (40min., 16 per day 5:52am-9:52pm, €3.11); **Reggio Calabria** (3½-5hr., 16 per day, €16.64-35.45); **Rome** (2½-3hr., 22 per day, €21.33-33); **Venice** (9hr., 11 per day 2:54am-8:50pm, €35.88-43.15).

CAMPANIA

Buses: SITA buses leave from the train station for **Amalfi** (1¼hr., 24 per day 5:15am-10pm, €3) and **Naples** (1hr., 38 per day 5:05am-10:10pm, €3). Buy tickets from a bar or *tabacchi* and ask where your bus leaves (either P. Veneto or P. della Concordia). **CSTP** runs buses from P. della Concordia to **Paestum** (1½hr., 12 per day 6:30am-7:30pm, €3.20) and from P. Veneto to **Pompeii** (1hr., 14 per day 6:10am-9pm, €3).

Ferries and Hydrofoils: Most ferries leave from P. della Concordia, 2 blocks from the train station. Others leave from Molo Manfredi, up the waterfront. **Linee Marittime Salernitane** (☎089 23 48 92) runs hydrofoils to **Capri** (2½ hr., 2 per day 8:10 and 8:40am, €11, from Molo Manfredi). **Travelmar** (☎089 87 29 50) runs to many destinations on the Amalfi Coast: **Amalfi** (35min., 6 per day 8:40am-3:30pm, €4); **Minori** (30min., 4 per day 7:50am-2:10pm, €4); and **Positano** (1¼hr., 6 per day, 8:40am-3:30pm, €6).

Local Transportation: The orange and blue **CSTP buses** connect the train station to the rest of the city. For routes and schedules, check the ticket booth in P. Veneto. Tickets €0.80 valid 1hr., full-day pass €1.40.

Taxis: ☎089 22 99 63 or 22 99 47.

■ 🛈 ORIENTATION AND PRACTICAL INFORMATION

Salerno's **train station** is in **Piazza Vittorio Veneto**. The pedestrian **Corso Vittorio Emanuele** veers right out of the piazza, becoming **Via dei Mercanti** upon reaching the old quarter, the liveliest and most historically interesting area of Salerno. **Via Roma,** home to many of the city's best restaurants, runs parallel to C. V. Emanuele, one block toward the waterfront. Along the waterfront in front of the train station is **Piazza della Concordia,** from which many intercity buses depart, and **Lungomare Trieste,** which runs to Salerno's port, **Molo Manfredi.**

Tourist Office: EPT (☎089 22 47 44), in P. Veneto, to the right when leaving the train station. The friendly staff here provides free **maps** and info on hotels and restaurants, as well as comprehensive bus and train info. Open M-Sa 9am-2pm and 3:30-7pm.

Car Rental: Travel Car, P. Veneto, 33 (☎089 22 77 22). Cars from €35 per day. Open daily 7:30am-1:30pm and 2:30-8:30pm. AmEx/MC/V. **Hertz** and **Avis** also have offices to the right as you exit the train station.

English-Language Bookstore: Libreria Leone, V. Settimo Mobile, 38 (☎089 40 51 59). Take a left out of the train station and another left under the train tracks. Decent selection of classics and new fiction. Open M-Sa 9am-1pm and 4:30-8:30pm. MC/V.

Work Opportunity: Ask the P. Veneto tourist office about short-term work options (see **Alternatives to Tourism: Short-Term Work** p. 86).

Emergency: ☎113. **Carabinieri** (☎112). **Ambulance** (☎089 24 12 33).

Hospital: S. Leonardo (☎089 67 11 11).

Internet: Attendere Prego..., V. Roma, 26, has 6 fast computers and printing capabilities. €3.50 per hr. Open daily 9am-9pm.

Post Office: C. Garibaldi, 203 (☎089 22 99 70). Open M-Sa 8:15am-6:15pm. Branch (☎089 22 99 98) at P. Veneto. Open M-Sa 8:15am-1:30pm. **Currency exchange** at main office only. **Postal Code:** 84100.

🛏 ACCOMMODATIONS

Ostello Ave Gratia Plena, V. Canali (☎089 23 47 76; www.ostellionline.org). Take C. V. Emanuele into the old district, where it becomes V. dei Mercanti, then turn right on V. Canali. The hostel is past the church, on the right. Good location, with proximity to restaurants and nightlife. Clean, comfortable rooms and a great indoor courtyard. Internet

€3.50 for 1hr. Sheets and hot shower included. Lockout 10:30am-3pm. Curfew 12:30am. Single-sex and coed dorms available. Dorms €14; singles €20; doubles €16.50 per person; triples €15.50 per person. Towels €2.50. Cash only. ❷

Hotel Salerno, V. Vicinanza, 42, 5th fl. (☎089 22 42 11, fax 22 44 32), 1st left off C. V. Emanuele. Choose between a long and steep staircase ascent or a 5-story elevator ride. Bright and clean with a comfortable TV lounge. Remarkably quiet considering its location by the train tracks. Some rooms have phone and TV. Singles €30, with bath €60; doubles €39/€65. AmEx/MC/V. ❸

Albergo Italia, C. V. Emanuele, 84 (☎/fax 089 22 66 53), in the heart of the shopping district. Rooms are clean, shiny, and polished. High ceilings and tasteful art on the walls. All rooms with A/C and bath. Singles €60; doubles €75. AmEx/MC/V. ❺

Hotel Montestella, C. V. Emanuele, 156 (☎089 22 51 22, fax 22 91 67) is a 10min. walk from the train station, on the right. Though the lounge is bizarre and minimalist, the rooms are elegant and generously sized. Staff is helpful but speaks limited English. All rooms have TV, phone, and A/C; some with balcony. Breakfast included. Singles €60; doubles €94; triples €104; quads €114. AmEx/MC/V. ❹

Albergo Santa Rosa, C. V. Emanuele, 14, 2nd fl. (☎/fax 089 22 53 46), 1 block from the train station on the right. 12 clean, comfortable rooms. Somewhat removed from most of Salerno's restaurants and bars, but within walking distance and still an excellent value. Ask to see a room before agreeing to stay, as quality varies. Singles €25, with bath €35; doubles €35-55. ❷

🍴 FOOD

While Salerno serves regional cuisine like *pasta e fagioli* (pasta and bean soup), it also has some unusual specials of its own—including *milza* (spleen).

🍴 **Il Caminetto,** V. Roma, 232 (☎089 22 96 14). Enjoy delicious seafood in an outdoor seating area protected from the noise and fumes of the busy V. Roma. Try the heaping dish of *zuppa di cozze* (mussels in marinara sauce; €4) or the slightly tangy *pasta fagioli* (€4). The prices are the lowest in town and the food some of the best. Cover €1.50. *Primi* €4-8, *secondi* €4-10. Open M-Tu and Th-Su 8pm-midnight. MC/V. ❷

🍴 **Hosteria Il Brigante,** V. F. Linguiti, 4 (☎089 22 65 92). From P. Duomo, head up the stairs and look for the sign on the left. As authentic as it gets: there's 1 menu, handwritten on brown laminated paper, and just 1 waiter/manager visible. Try the *pasta alla sangiovannara* (€3), a hodge-podge of pasta, tomato, cheese, and sausage. Open daily 1:15-3pm and 8:45pm-2am. ❸

🍴 **Gerry,** V. G. Da Procida, 33 (☎089 23 78 21). Packs of locals vie nightly to be next in line for Salerno's best gelato. Homemade and perfectly creamy, this is a treat worth the wait. Traditional (*fragola*) and more ambitious (*golosone*) flavors. Cones from €1.50 (generous) to €2 (semi-insurmountable). Open daily 10am-1pm and 5pm-1am. ❶

Panineria Sant Andrea, P. Sedile del Campo, 13 (☎089 75 04 18). Every kind of sandwich you could imagine from seafood, like the *polipo* (octopus; €6.50), to the simple mozzarella with various meats (from €2). Takeout window and popular outdoor seating in summer. Open Tu-Su noon-3pm and 9pm-1am. AmEx/MC/V. ❶

👁 🎵 SIGHTS AND ENTERTAINMENT

To take in the evening air, stroll down C. V. Emanuele or sit for a while in the lush gardens of the Villa Comunale off V. Roma. For a bit of historical flavor, the old city is a pleasing tangle of serpentine alleys and wonderful little shops. A particularly nice walk starts from C. V. Emanuele, turns right off V. Mercanti or V. Roma

C A M P A N I A

onto V. Duomo, then runs uphill to **Duomo San Matteo.** First constructed in AD 845, the duomo was destroyed and rebuilt 200 years later by the Norman leader Robert Guiscard. When Pope Gregory VII fled to Salerno in 1084, he consecrated the duomo. Its cosmopolitan design stands out among the city's other buildings, and the arches of the portico, the floor of the apse, and the two pulpits in the nave bear beautiful geometric mosaics, evocative of Islamic decorative motifs. The duomo also harbors many relics: a tooth from Evangelist Matthew, a hair from the Virgin Mary, and a splinter from the True Cross. (Open M-F 9am-6pm, Sa-Su 1-6pm.) To soak up some rays, take the bus along Lungomare Trieste and head to the sandy **beach** beyond the sailboat harbor.

Through July, the **Salerno Summerfestival,** at the Arena del Mare, near the Molo Manfredi, includes a concert series with jazz and blues. (☎ 089 66 51 76. Concerts usually start 10pm. Prices vary. Contact tourist office for info.) At night, younger crowds gather near the fountain at **Bar/Gelateria Nettuno,** V. Lungomare Trieste, 136-138 (☎ 089 22 83 75), or drink and lounge at **Cueva del Sol,** V. Roma, 218-220, serving exotic drinks. The house cocktail, *agave spinosa* (tequila, papaya juice, and lime; €5) has a refreshing tropical twist. (Open daily 9pm-4am. MC/V.) At P. Sedile del Campo, 6, the **Alcool Cafe** is another favored hangout, mostly for American students. Funky decor, including an anthropomorphic beer-can alien, and low drink prices keep blood alcohol levels elevated. (Beer €2. Open M-Sa 9pm-late.) The many bars along V. Roma are perfect spots to hang with locals or watch a soccer match. Nearby **Vietri sul Mare** is home to hundreds of artisans and a pleasant beach. Bus #4 and 9 run from the station. (10min., €0.80.)

▶ DAYTRIP FROM SALERNO

PAESTUM

CSTP buses from Salerno, P. della Concordia (1½hr., 12 per day 6:30am-7:30pm, €3.20), stop at V. Magna Graecia, the main modern road. Buy tickets from tabacchis. The tourist office in Salerno provides a list of return buses and trains from Paestum. The AAST Tourist Office, V. Magna Graecia, 887, is next to the museum. (☎ 0828 81 10 16. Open June-Sept. 15 M-Sa 9am-1pm and 2-7pm, Sept. 16-June 9am-1pm and 2-5pm.) Restoration work occasionally leaves temples fenced off or obscured. (Temples open in summer daily 9am-7:30pm, in winter 9am-4pm. Closed 1st and 3rd M of the month for restoration. Ruins and museum €6.50, EU students €3.25, EU citizens under 18 or over 60 free.)

Not far from the Roman ruins of Pompeii and Herculaneum, Paestum's three **Doric temples** rank among the best-preserved and most complete in the world, rivaling those of Sicily and Athens. Amazingly, these masterfully constructed structures were built without any mortar or cement, yet remained standing after the great earthquake of AD 69 reduced Pompeii's Temple of Jupiter to a pile of rubble. The town began as a prosperous Greek colony dedicated to sea god Poseidon, and then was conquered by the Romans, who expanded the settlement. Because Paestum is not urbanized, it may seem like you missed your bus stop. Fear not the dearth of modern urban squalor, gentle traveler: *ruins* are the point here. The ancient Greeks built Paestum on a north-south axis, marked by the paved **Via Sacra**; in some places tracks are still visible, worn into the stone by cart wheels. Farther south on V. Sacra is the **Roman forum,** larger than the one at Pompeii though more dilapidated. The Romans leveled most of the older structures in the city's center to build this proto-piazza, the commercial and political arena of Paestum. To the left, a shallow pit marks the pool of an ancient **gymnasium.** East of the gymnasium lies the Roman **amphitheater,** built during the reign of Julius Caesar.

When excavators first uncovered the three temples in the 18th century, they misidentified (and misnamed) them. Although recent scholarship has provided new info about the temples's dedications, the old names have stuck. There are three entrances. The northernmost (closest to the bus stop) leads to the **Tempio di Cere.** Built around 500 BC, this temple was used as a church in the early Middle Ages but was abandoned in the 9th century. South of the forum lies the 5th-century BC **Tempio di Poseidon** (actually dedicated to Apollo). More sophisticated than the temple of Ceres, and much more complete, this temple incorporates many of the optical refinements found in Athens's Parthenon. Small lions' heads (now on display in the museum) served as gargoyles on the temple roof. The southernmost temple, known as the **basilica,** is also the oldest, dating from the 6th century BC. Its unusual plan, with a main interior section split by a row of columns down the middle, has inspired the theory that the temple was dedicated to two gods, Zeus and Hera, rather than one. A ◪**museum,** on the other side of V. Magna Graecia, houses extraordinary pottery, paintings, and artifacts taken primarily from Paestum's tombs. The presentation is outstanding, with descriptive essays translated into several languages. Don't fail to look up at the dramatic friezes that encircle the first floor, which depict Hercules struggling mightily against his foes. The museum also holds samples of 2500-year-old honey and paintings from the famous **Tomb of the Diver,** dating from 475 BC. The second floor of the museum houses an exhibit of the artist Bartolomeo Gatto. (Museum open daily 9am-6:30pm. Ticket office open daily 9am-5:30pm. Closed 1st and 3rd Monday of the month. €4, EU students €2, EU citizens under 18 or over 60 free.) If visiting the temples inspires the mood to worship, bow to the sun-god on the golden **beach,** 2km to the west. Unfortunately, much of the beach property is private. For a free dip in the Mediterranean, head to a *spiaggia pubblica* (public beach)—ask for directions.

There is really no reason to stay in Paestum when hotels and restaurants are overpriced and the site can easily be visited as a daytrip. There are several campsites nearby, and the beachside **Ostello "La Lanterna" (HI) ❶,** V. Lanterna, 8, in nearby Agropoli, is the nearest budget option. (☎/fax 0974 83 83 64; lanterna@cilento.peoples.it. Sheets and shower included. 56 beds. Dorms €14; quads €48.) To get to **Agropoli,** take the **CSTP buses** from Paestum (10min., every hr. 7:30am-9:15pm, €1.10) or from Salerno (1hr., 23 per day 6:30am-8:15pm, €2.75). Agropoli is connected to Paestum by train (10min., 9 per day 6:10am-10:22pm, €1.15), but the Paestum train station is an expensive 20min. taxi ride from the site, while buses, a much better option, stop directly at the temples.

PUGLIA, BASILICATA, AND CALABRIA

HIGHLIGHTS OF PUGLIA, BASILICATA, AND CALABRIA

JOURNEY to the end of the Appian Way, the oldest and most famous Roman road, marked by one remaining column in Brindisi. (p. 615.)

VENTURE to the Gargano Massif, once among the most popular pilgrimage destinations in Europe. (p. 604.)

EXPLORE *trulli sassi* ancient lodgings in Alberobello (p. 605) and Matera (p. 620.)

REPOSE in the shelter of cliffside Tropea as azure waves lap sandy shores. (p. 636.)

DISCOVER buried treasures at Reggio di Calabria's Museo Nazionale. (p. 629.)

PUGLIA

Admirers through the centuries have paid homage to Puglia, the "heel" of Italy's boot. The ports of Brindisi, Bari, and Otranto are as bustling and international today as they were when the Greeks and Romans coveted them as trade routes to the East. Yet tourism has only recently begun to materialize in this rustic, sun-baked region, and Puglia remains a refreshing pause from Italy's more frequented destinations. The area, located in the middle of the Mediterranean, also maintains great cultural wealth, laying claim to remote medieval villages, cone-roofed *trulli* houses, and ports with a distinct Middle Eastern flavor. Its arresting castles and cathedrals eloquently recall the Middle Ages, when an onslaught of invaders shaped local culture. Travelers to Puglia will welcome its passionate and unique cultural heritage and distinctly Southern zest for life.

BARI   ☎ 080

A port launching ferries to Greece, tasty Puglian cuisine, and nightlife fueled by the university population add to Bari's complexity. Clothing shops and gelaterias tempt on every street, and the sea is never more than a few blocks away. Amid the constant commotion, reckless drivers zoom about and pickpockets dart down alleys. Although this city does not figure prominently on most itineraries, its bustling lifestyle is sure to excite, if only for a few days.

▣ TRANSPORTATION

ARRIVEDERCI, ITALIA. Bari is an important port for ferries to **Greece, Turkey, Albania, Israel, Bosnia-Herzegovina,** and **Serbia and Montenegro.** Many lines offer special student rates and discounts on round-trip tickets.

Flights: Bari Palese Airport (☎ 080 583 52 00), 8km west of the city. **Alitalia, Air France, British Airways,** and **Lufthansa** fly to major European cities. A shuttle bus leaves from P. Aldo Moro (12 per day 5:15am-6:30pm).

ABRUZZO
TO TREMITI ISLANDS (1½hrs)
Termoli
Gargano Massif
Monte Sant' Angelo
Manfredonia
TO ALBANIA (8hrs)
MOLISE
Santa Maria di Siponto
Barletta Trani
Bari
TO GREECE (10hrs)
LAZIO
Iserrua
Campobasso
Foggia
A14
Ruvo
Bitonto
Castellana Grotte
Monopoli
CAMPANIA
A16
Castel del Monte
Altamura
PUGLIA
Alberobello
Ostuni
Brindisi
TO TURKEY (30hrs)
TO ROME
A1
Formia
Caserta
Benevento
Gravina
Potenza
Matera
Lecce
Naples (Napoli)
Procida
Pompeii
Salerno
Taranto
Otranto
Ischia
Amalfi
BASILICATA
Metaponto
Gallipoli
Capri
Golfo di Salerno
A3
Golfo di Taranto
Sorrento
Positano
Maratea
Mare Tirreno
Golfo di Policastro
Praia a Mare
Sibari
Rossano
Mare Ionio
Castiglione
Camigliatello
Paola
Cosenza
(11hrs)
CALABRIA
Crotone
Lamezia Terme
Catanzaro
Golfo di Eufémia
Golfo di Squillace
AEOLIAN ISLANDS (ISOLE EOLIE)
Stromboli
Tropea
Soverato
Pizzo
0   50 miles
Ustica
Salina Panarea
Lipari
Villa San Giovanni
A3
Gerace
Roccella
0   50 kilometers
Alicudi
Filicudi
Vulcano
Scilla
Locri
Bovalino Marina Bianco
Puglia,
Basilicata,
and Calabria
Messina
Reggio di Calabria
Palermo
Cefalù
SICILY (SICILIA)
Brancaleone
TO MALTA (15hrs)

Trains: Bari is connected to 4 railways, all of which leave **Bari Centrale** (☎080 524 01 48) in P. Aldo Moro: **Ferrovie Dello Stato** (FS) (on the main tracks), **Ferrovie Sud Est** (FSE) (behind the FS tracks). To the right (you must exit and reenter the station) run **Ferrotramviaria Bari Nord** and **Ferrovie Appulo Lucana** (FAL).

FS, which serves large cities, runs trains to: **Brindisi** (1½-1¾hr., 14 per day 4:50am-12:30am, €5.73-10.33); **Foggia** (1½-2hr., 52 per day 12:03am-11:55pm, €6.70-13.94); **Lecce** (2hr., 24 per day 4:50am-10:55pm, €7.50-12.19); **Milan** (9½-10hr., 13 per day 12:03am-11:55am, €37.70-61.93); **Naples** (4½hr., 6 per day 12:13am-11:59pm, €19.17-27.47); **Reggio di Calabria** (7½-8hr., 6 per day 3:52am-10:04pm, €27.13-32.95); **Rome** (5-7hr., 7 per day 12:13am-6:42pm, €26.12-36); **Termoli** (2-3hr., 15 per day 12:03am-9:39pm, €10.12-21.28).

FSE (☎080 546 24 44) runs trains from track 11 to **Alberobello** (1½hr., 13 per day 5:40am-8:25pm, €3.60) and **Castellana Grotte** (1hr., 17 per day 5:40am-8:25pm, €2.43).

Ferrotramviaria Bari Nord (☎080 521 35 77), to the left of Bari Centrale. Departs for: **Andria** (1¼hr., €2.63); **Barletta** (1¼hr., 19 per day 5:30am-10:20pm, €3.05) via **Bitonto** (30min., €1.55); **Ruvo** (45min., €2.01). On Su the Ruvo route is served by bus from P. Aldo Moro.

FAL (☎080 524 48 81), next door to the Bari Nord station in P. Aldo Moro. Trains depart for **Matera** (1½hr., 8 per day 6:25am-7:05pm, €3.62) via **Altamura**.

Buses: SITA (☎080 556 24 46) buses leave from V. Capruzzi, 226, behind the train station. Call ahead for fares and schedules, or visit www.sita-on-line.it.

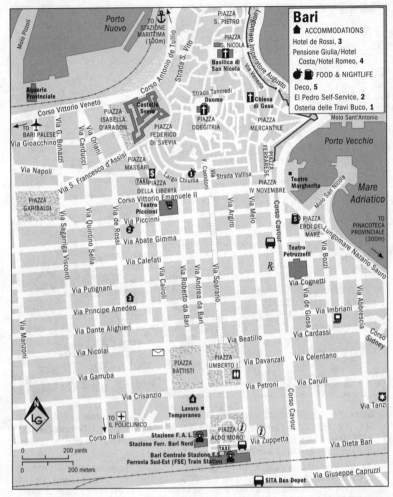

Bari

⚓ ACCOMMODATIONS
Hotel de Rossi, **3**
Pensione Giulia/Hotel
Costa/Hotel Romeo, **4**
🍎 🍴 FOOD & NIGHTLIFE
Deco, **5**
El Pedro Self-Service, **2**
Osteria delle Travi Buco, **1**

Ferries: Some reliable companies are listed below, but call ahead: schedules and prices vary, especially on weekends. Obtain tickets and info at the Stazione Marittima or at the below offices. **Check in at least 2hr. before departure.** Try to avoid walking through the desolate area surrounding the Stazione Marittima and port (see **Orientation**).

Marlines (☎080 523 18 24 or 527 54 09, fax 523 02 87; reservations 521 02 06). To **Durres** (schedules vary weekly July-Sept.; €62-130 in the high season, €45-105 in the low season).

Minoan Lines (☎080 521 02 66; www.minoan.gr) sails to Greece. To **Corfu** (7½hr., 3 per week June 14-Aug. 20) and **Igoumenitsa** (11hr., daily June 14-Aug. 20).

Superfast Ferries (☎080 528 28 28; www.superfast.com) sails overnight to Greece. To **Igoumenitsa** (8½hr., M-Sa 1 per day 10pm) and **Patrasso** (14½hr., M-Th and Sa 10pm). High season €95-430, low season €83-393 depending on the preferred type of seating.

Ventouris Ferries, V. Piccinni, 133, c/o P. Lorusso & Co. (☎080 521 76 99; www.ventouris.gr). Windows #18-20 in Stazione Marittima. To **Corfu-Igoumenitsa** (10hr.; 2 per week Feb. 2-Apr. 29, 5 per week May 2-Dec. 29) and **Durazzo** (13hr., at least 4 per week 11pm). Call for prices.

Public Transportation: Local buses leave from P. Aldo Moro, in front of the train station. Tickets sold at *tabacchi* (€0.77) or on the bus (€1). **Bus #20** makes hourly trips between Stazione Marittima and the train stations.

Taxis: ☎ 080 554 33 33 (for radio taxies) and 521 06 00 (for the taxi station).

🔁 🚹 ORIENTATION AND PRACTICAL INFORMATION

Via Sparano runs from the train station to **Piazza Umberto I**, Bari's main square. The end of V. Sparano intersects **Corso Vittorio Emanuele II** and the edge of the old city. To walk to the **port**, skirt the old city's winding streets by turning left on C. V. Emanuele II and right at **Piazza della Libertà**, onto **Via Giuseppe Massari**. Circle the castle, head right, and follow the coast. Otherwise, take the bus from the station (every hr.). For a calmer route to the sea (not the port), turn right off V. Sparano onto C. V. Emanuele II, continuing past **Corso Cavour** to **Piazza Eroi del Mare**.

Head right from the train station to reach the **APT Tourist Office**, P. Aldo Moro, 33/A, 2nd fl. (☎ 080 524 23 61, fax 524 23 29). The office supplies free **maps** of Puglia and Bari. (Open M-F 9am-noon.) **Lavoro Temporaneo**, in P. Maro Cesare, 59, near the FAL station, helps travelers find **short-term jobs** (see **Alternatives to Tourism: Short-term work**, p. 86). To sign up bring a Curriculum Vitae and recent photograph (☎ 080 524 98 25; bari@obiettivolavoro.it). There is a **laundromat** at V. Toma, 35. Take the pass over the train tracks onto C. Cavour and continue until turning left. (☎ 080 556 70 56. Open M-Sa 9am-1pm and 4-6pm. Wash €3, dry €2.) In case of **emergency**, dial ☎ 113; reach the **carabinieri** at ☎ 112 or at the station located on V. Tanzi, 5. Walk east on V. Carulli and turn right 2 blocks after the highway onto V. Abbrescia to find the station straight ahead. The local **hospital** is called the **Poli Clinino** and is located at P. Giulio Cesare, 11 (☎ 080 559 11 11). Take V. Carulli heading west and turn left after two lights on V. Quintino Sella; walk under the underpass; the hospital will be on your left. A **pharmacy**, **Lojacono di Berrino**, C. Cavour, 47, is across from the Teatro Petruzzelli. (☎ 080 521 26 15. Open M-F 4:30-11pm, Sa-Su 4:30-8pm.) Check the **Internet** on one of four computers at **Nuovo Caffè Cervino**, V. Imbriani, 57 (☎ 080 553 67 76. Open M-Su 6-8:30pm. €5 per 1½hr.). The **post office** is in P. Battisti, behind the university. From P. Umberto, turn left on V. Crisanzio, then immediately right on V. Cairoli. (☎ 080 575 71 87, fax 575 70 53. Open M-F 8am-6:30pm, Sa 8am-12:30pm.) **Postal Code:** 70100.

🛏 🍽 ACCOMMODATIONS AND FOOD

Though located in the heart of downtown, **Hotel de Rossi ❸**, V. de Rossi, 186, is reasonably quiet, and the management is friendly and organized. Its attractively decorated rooms have bath, A/C, and TV. (☎ 080 524 53 55; fax 080 524 55 02. Singles €35; doubles €55. AmEx/MC/V.) Three hotels occupy the same building, V. Crisanzio, 12, across the street from the university. ✒**Hotel Pensione Romeo ❸** has spacious rooms on the second floor all with TV and phone. (☎ 080 523 72 53, fax 521 63 52. Singles €26 with shared bath; €37 with bath; doubles €56. AmEx/MC/V.) **Pensione Giulia ❸** has large, basic rooms with A/C and clean sheets. (☎ 080 521 66 30; www.pagineitaliahotelgiulia.it. Breakfast included. Singles €42, with bath €52; doubles €52/€65; triples €70; quads €88. AmEx/MC/V.) Another alternative is the **Hotel Costa ❸**, which has narrow rooms, each with phone. (☎ 080 521 90 15, fax 21 00 06. Singles €40, with bath €62; doubles €88. AmEx/MC/V.)

Eating in the old city can feel like a time warp; often, restaurants provide neither menus nor itemized checks. However, outside the old city's walls, restaurants are a bit more up-to-date. Stock up for the ferry ride at **Super CRAI**, V. de Giosa, 97, four streets to the right of P. Umberto I facing away from the station (☎ 080 524 74 85;

PUGLIA, BASILICATA, CALABRIA

open M-Sa 8:30am-2pm and 5-9pm), or at **Supermercato Di per Di,** which has an ATM inside and is near the three hotels on V. Crisanzio. (Open daily 8am-2pm and 6:30-8:15pm, except Wednesday evenings.) Heading north on Lungomare Imperatore Augusto, turn left through the large arches at the entrance to the old city to find the simple **Osteria delle Travi Buco ❹,** Largo Chiurlia, 12, at the end of V. Sparano (two blocks into the old city), serving fresh food in large portions. Try the pasta with arugula or the *orecchiette con cavallo* (ear-shaped pasta with horse), a local specialty. (☎339 157 88 48. *Menù* with drink €16-19. Open Tu-Su 1-3:30pm and 8-11pm.) **El Pedro Self-Service ❷,** V. Piccinni, 152, off V. Sparano, is not a Mexican restaurant, but a busy cafeteria serving authentic Puglian fare. Lines may be long, but persevere—the food is certainly worth it. (☎/fax 080 521 12 94. Complete meal with drink €9-9.50. Open M-Sa 11am-3:30pm and 6:30-9:30pm. MC/V.)

🔘 SIGHTS

> **❗ SAFE SAILING.** A strategic port on the Italian coast, Bari has long been a prime target for invaders. To keep them at bay, citizens built the old city as a labyrinth in which they could hide or take attackers by surprise. Today it is mostly thieves who benefit from the maze of streets, and careless tourists are their favorite prey. **Do not venture into the old city at night.** Use maps discreetly, avoid wearing jewelry or flashy watches, and hold tightly to purses, bags, and cameras. At the same time, don't skip the sights solely for fear of petty crime; the old city is historically interesting and well worth exploring.

Looks like mom and dad were wrong—there really is a Santa Claus, and the **Basilica di San Nicola** proves it. In 1087 60 *Baresi* sailors stole St. Nicholas's remains from Turkey; the sailors initially refused to cede the body to local clergy, but ultimately gave it up when the Church built this rather spartan basilica as Santa's final resting place. Inside, 17th-century paintings enliven the gaudily trimmed ceiling. St. Nick himself occupies the crypt in the underground chapel, ready to receive homage or Christmas wish lists. On the back wall, several paintings commemorate the jolly saint's good deeds, including his resurrection of three children who were sliced to bits and plunged into a brine barrel by a nasty butcher. (Open daily 7am-noon and 4-7:30pm, except during mass.) Just outside the old city, off C. V. Veneto near the water, is the colossal **Castello Svevo,** built in the 13th century by Frederick II on Norman and Byzantine foundations. Isabel of Aragon and Sona Sforza added bulwarks in the 16th century. Visitors can't climb the ramparts, but the medieval cellar displays art from the region's cathedrals and castles. (☎080 528 61 11, tickets 62 25. Open daily except W and major holidays 9am-7pm; ages 18-25 €1, 25 or older €2.) Down Lungomare N. Sauro past P. A. Diaz is the **Pinacoteca Provinciale,** occupying the fourth floor. The gallery displays Puglian landscapes and works by Veronese, Tintoretto, Bellini, De Nittis, and Impressionist Francesco Netti, Bari's acclaimed hometown artist, as well as a vast collection of Greek art from the 1800s. (☎080 541 24 22. Open Tu-Sa 9am-1pm and 4-7pm, Su 9am-1pm. €2.58, students €0.52.)

🎵 🎭 ENTERTAINMENT AND NIGHTLIFE

Bari is the cultural nucleus of Puglia. On C. V. Emanuele, **Teatro Piccinni** offers a spring concert season and opera year-round. Purchase tickets at the theater (☎080 521 08 78; open daily 10:30am-12:30pm and 5-8pm except Sa and Su afternoons). Consult the ticket office or the *Bari Sera* section of *La Gazzetta del Mezzo-*

giorno (the local newspaper) for the latest information. From September through June, sports fans can catch **soccer matches** on any Sunday and often on other days of the week. (Tickets start at €15 and are available at the stadium or in bars.) On May 7-9, *Baresi* celebrate their stolen saint in the **Festival of San Nicola,** featuring a parade of costumed children and loads of traditional foods.

Most of Bari's clubs are open nightly from 8pm until 1 or 2am (3am on Sa), but they generally close in August, when the town university is on holiday. V. Sparano and P. Umberto are packed by night, and on weekends, students cram into P. Ferrarese and other piazzas along the breezy waterfront east of the old city, strolling about and stopping leisurely at pubs. A young crowd makes the trip from all over Southern Italy to visit one of Bari's hottest clubs, **Deco,** P. Eroi del Mare, 18 (☎ 080 524 60 70), which serves American food amid live music.

📍 DAYTRIPS FROM BARI

CASTEL DEL MONTE

In summer, take a train from Ferrotramviaria Bari Nord (☎ 0883 59 26 84) to Andria (1¼hr., 19 per day 5:30am-10:20pm, €2.63) and then a bus from the station to the castle 17km away (30min.; 8:30am, 1:45, 4:30pm; returns 10:15am, 2:15, 7pm; €1.30). Call ☎ 0883 29 03 29 or contact the Pro Loco Tourist Office (☎ 0883 59 22 83) to confirm schedule. Castel del Monte (☎ 0883 56 98 48) is open daily 8am-1:30pm and 2:30-8pm; ticket office open daily 8am-1:30pm and 2:30-7:30pm. €3, EU students 18-25 €1.50, EU citizens under 18 or over 65 free.

Castel del Monte towers mightily over Andria's countryside, halfway between the High Murge and the sea. Built in the 13th century by anonymous artists for Frederick II, the Swabian king who ruled Southern Italy, it remains the most striking and the best preserved of all his castles. According to legend, the imposing stone bastion housed the Holy Grail, though in reality it served in the less romantic role of a hunting lodge. Today the castle hosts exhibits of local art and ceramic work. The building's octagonal layout is aligned astronomically, leading scholars to hypothesize that the castle functioned as an observatory as well as a military structure.

CASTELLANA GROTTE

FSE trains depart from Bari for "Grotte di Castellana Grotte" (1hr., 17 per day 5:40am-8:25pm, €2.43). Do not disembark at "Castellana Grotte." This stop is for the city, 2km away from the grotte. The next, unmarked stop is for the grottoes. Not all trains stop here, so inquire before boarding. Caves are across the parking lot and to the left. Short tours (50min.; daily every hr. in summer 8:30am-7pm, in winter 8:30am-1pm; €8), longer tours (2hr.; daily every hr. in summer 9am-6pm except 1 and 2pm, in winter 9am-noon; €13), and English tours available (long tour 11am and 4pm, short tour 1 and 6:30pm).

Superstitious locals once feared that these breathtaking natural caverns were an entrance to hell. The Castellana Grotte, discovered in 1938, are famed for their impressive size, age, and eerie beauty. Over time, stalactites and stalagmites have developed into all sorts of whimsical shapes, including a Virgin Mary, a camel, a wolf, an owl, and an ice-cream cone. Even if the resemblances don't seem obvious, the various formations invite the imagination to run wild. Those with time to kill can even watch them grow—at the rate of 3cm per century. Visitors must take one of two **guided tours** (☎ 080 021 39 76 or 080 499 82 11; www.grottedicastellano.it. €8 and up). A short 1km jaunt and a longer 3km trek both start at La Grave, the enormous pit that was considered the opening to hell. The longer tour culminates in the stunning *Grotta Bianca* (White Cave), a giant cavern filled with white stalactites. Regardless of which tour, paid admission includes access to the observatory, the dinosaur park (for children), and the museum.

PUGLIA, BASILICATA, CALABRIA

THE GARGANO MASSIF

For Siponto, take the train to Foggia from Bari (1½-2hr., 52 per day 12:03am-11:55pm, €6.70-13.94) or Termoli (2-3hr., 15 per day 12:03am-9:39pm, €10.12-21.28). From there, another train goes to Siponto (20min., 27 per day 5am-10:30pm, €1.80). To get to the church, take the path that starts across the tracks next to the small amusement park. For Monte Sant'Angelo, take the SITA bus from the train station in Foggia (40min., 10 per day 5:45am-6:45pm, €3.62). Ferrovie del Gargano buses also run to Vieste (2hr., 5 per day 6:45am-5:45pm, €4.65) via Pugnochiuso (1¾hr., €4.65). SITA buses also run from Foggia to San Giovanni Rotondo, home of the famous Padre Pio—his tomb and the church built in his honor draw droves of pilgrims. (1hr., 9 per day 7:05am-10:05pm, €2.58.) Crypt open daily 9:30am-1:30pm and 4-7pm. For the beaches, the Foresta Umbra, and the Gargano Park, remain on the train one stop after Foggia (San Severo). There you can switch to the Ferrovie del Gargano (for schedules check www.ferroviedelgargano.com).

The Gargano Massif was once among the most popular pilgrimage destinations in Europe. Since then, it has gradually succumbed to beach-umbrella blight and myriad camping sites. Legend has it that the Archangel Michael appeared in a cave in **Monte Sant'Angelo** in the 5th century, the same cave a revered oracle reputedly occupied in ancient times. Today the peninsula is famed for the long stretches of sand on its northern and eastern coasts, with **Vieste, San Menaio, Peschici,** and **Pugnochiuso** among the most sought-after beach destinations. Inland from the shore is the cool **Foresta Umbra,** which abruptly gives way to capricious Mediterranean terrain in the south.

RUVO DI PUGLIA

For Ruvo, take the Ferrotramviaria Bari Nord train line from Bari's main FS station in P. Aldo Moro (40min., 19 per day 6am-10pm, €1.65). Ruvo is only serviced by bus on Su.

An easy half-day trip from Bari, **Ruvo** is home to one of the most beautiful 12th century Romanesque cathedrals in Puglia. Exit the station, turn right on V. Scarlatti, then turn left down the road on V. Fornaci, which turns into C. Cavour; the **cathedral** is to the left, near the public gardens. On the front, three doorways bear a fantastical assortment of motifs, derived from the Saracen, German, and French conquerors who ruled Puglia. Higher up on the facade, an intricate border winds its way around the eaves. Recently, the building's crypt has proven a fertile excavation ground, yielding bits of pots, mosaics, and coins. (Open daily 7am-6pm. For information call the Comune/Polizia Municipale ☎080 361 1014.)

TRANI   ☎0883

Hidden away on a stretch of coast between Bari and Foggia, Trani is a great half-day destination. It beckons quietly with its friendly streets, a beautiful sea port, and cool sea breezes. Refreshingly free of tourists—despite its gorgeous seaside Norman Cathedral—Trani is a magnificent place to relax and rejuvenate. Trani's **old city** is charming, but navigation around the 18th-century palazzo is close to impossible; streets fork, converge, and disappear on all sides. Allow extra time for meandering. To reach the stunning **Norman cathedral,** keep close to the water when skirting the harbor. This dramatic seaside structure unites three individual churches and many layers of history: Roman columns on the ground combine with 6th-century Christian architecture in the crypt and a plain Norman style in the main church. Remains of 12th-century mosaics decorate the altar. (Open M-Sa 8:30am-12:30pm and 3:30-7pm; Su and holidays 9am-12:45pm and 4-7pm.) Within sight is the town's **castle,** now open to the public after years of use as a prison. (☎0883 50 66 03. Open daily mid-Sept. to mid-June 8:30am-7:30pm; mid-June to mid-Sept. M-F and Su 8:30am-7:30pm, Sa 8:30am-10:30pm, €2.)

Trani is on the FS line between **Foggia** and **Bari.** (45min., 52 per day 12:03am-11:55pm, €2.58.) Trains also run to **Barletta.** (29 per day 4:36am-11:06pm, €1.) On Sundays, only 5 trains run from Trani to Bari; ask for departure times upon arrival. The train station lies in a less-than-appealing area in **Piazza XX Settembre.** From here, walk straight to **Via Cavour,** the main street, which leads through **Piazza della Repubblica** and **Piazza Plebiscito.** On the walk down V. Cavour, you will find two ATM machines. The disorienting but beautiful old city can be reached by turning left at P. della Repubblica. The **harbor** is to the left at P. Plebiscito and the public gardens are ahead.

Trani offers excellent accommodations for a range of prices. **Hotel Regia ❺,** next to the cathedral, is a stunning 18th-century palazzo with spectacular views of the harbor. Ten luxurious rooms all have bath, A/C, and TV. (☎/fax 0883 58 44 44. English spoken. Breakfast included. Singles, all with double beds, €110, doubles €120-140. AmEx/MC/V.) Unassuming **Albergo Lucy ❸,** P. Plebiscito, 11, crouches on the left side of the piazza. Its 12 rooms are clean, comfortable, and have bath. (☎0883 48 10 22. English spoken. Doubles €45; triples €60. AmEx/MC/V.)

The old city's serpentine streets wind around many small pizzerias, always a good bet for predictable, filling fare. The area near the public gardens on the other side of the harbor is a great place to sample local seafood dishes. **Il Melograno ❸,** V. G. Bovio, 189, near P. della Repubblica, has shellfish favorites like *spaghetti alle vongole* (€8-11). The hefty fried fish *secondo* is delicious, despite the scales and bones. (☎0883 48 69 66. Reserve ahead. Open M-Tu and Th-Su noon-3pm and 8pm-midnight. Cover €2. AmEx/MC/V.) The outdoor seating at **Ristorante La Locanda di Luigi Parlati ❸,** V. Zanardli, 10/12, is quieter and more intimate than at many other harborside restaurants. Before P. Plebiscito, turn left on V. Statuti Marittimi, then left on V. Zanardelli. (☎0883 48 02 18. *Menù* €15. Open M-Sa 7pm-midnight.)

ALBEROBELLO
☎0804

Alberobello's *trulli* are associated in Italian lore with magic and mystery, as very little is known about their use or origin. These peculiar limestone huts have existed in the Valley of Itria, between Bari and Taranto, since the 8th century or earlier. The typical *trullo* contains a central shared space with several offshooting bedrooms, each with its own conical roof. Ancient inhabitants inscribed symbols into the roofs, reputedly to ward off evil spirits or bring good luck. The more recent, mortarless form of the *trulli* did not appear until 1654, when a local court required that the squalid peasant inhabitations be built in a less permanent fashion so that they could be dismantled for royal visits. While some remain occupied, the more than 1000 *trulli* of Alberobello are primarily a tourist attraction and a UNESCO World Heritage site. The mere sight of the town's *trulli*-covered hills is well worth the trek out to Alberobello, though finding accommodations among these simple huts may prove less enjoyable.

◧❼ TRANSPORTATION AND PRACTICAL INFORMATION. Alberobello is just south of Bari. Take the **FSE train** from Bari (1½hr., 14 per day 5:30am-7:15pm, €3.60). To reach the *trulli* from the train station, bear left and take V. Mazzini (which becomes V. Garibaldi) to P. del Popolo. Though not English-speaking, the staff at the **tourist office,** in P. Fernando IV, off P. del Popolo, provides helpful **maps** of hotels, restaurants, and sights. (☎080 432 51 71. Open M-F 9am-1pm; three days of the week, it is also open from 2:30-5:30pm.) The **Pro Loco Tourist Office,** at V. Monte Nero, 1, in the *trulli* district, is extremely helpful and can provide information on sights, directions, and guided tours. (☎080 432 28 22. Open M-Sa 9am-1pm

THE LOCAL STORY

TRULLI A MYSTERY

The cone-roofed *trulli*, white and stout, emerge unassumingly from the hillsides of Alberobello. Clustered over the earth, these former peasant dwellings quietly harbor centuries of history. Though the precise origins of the *trulli* are unknown, historians suspect that their form arose from both Italian and Arabic influences. The square stone bases are strikingly similar to 12th- and 13th-century peasant huts found in Basilicata and Molise; and the stone roofs hearken convincingly to Moorish temples and minarets. As this area of Italy was continually besieged by Turkish pirates, this "East-West" composite is a sound hypothesis.

Written records concerning the *trulli*'s inhabitants, dating as far back as the 17th century, attest to a harsh, somewhat helpless existence. Unable to pay taxes to King Ferdinando IV, the Spanish king who then controlled the area, the *trulli* dwellers were seen as squatters and had few official rights. A compromise came in 1654, when the local Count of Conversano decreed that all *trulli* be made without mortar, so they could be dismantled for imperial visits.

In 1996 UNESCO declared the *trulli* at Alberobello a World Heritage site. A rule bans the building of new *trulli* in order to preserve the town's historical integrity. As locals say, "the *trulli* belong to history now"—rich in heritage, and unique in the world.

and 3:30-7:30pm.) For **police,** P. del Popolo, 32, call ☎0804 32 52 40. In case of **emergency,** call the **carabinieri** at ☎112 or **first aid** (☎0804 32 19 60).

⌐⌐ ACCOMMODATIONS AND FOOD. Eating and sleeping in Alberobello can be expensive; it's less costly to visit as a daytrip. But if you decide to spend the night, ▣**Trullidea ❹,** V. Monte Nero, 18, rents *trulli* by the night. Facing the *trulli*, V. Monte Nero goes left uphill. The price includes a spacious suite with simple furnishings, kitchen, bathroom, and breakfast at a nearby restaurant. Hot summers are not a problem as *trulli* remain cool. (☎/fax 080 432 38 60; www.trullidea.com. Singles €39-46; doubles €78-92; triples €77-114. Prices vary seasonally. AmEx/MC/V.) To reach **Didi Hotel ❸,** V. Piave, 30, take C.V. Emanuele from P. del Popolo, turning left on C. Trieste and left again on V. Piave. The hotel is notable for its great value: its 30 rooms each have A/C, TV, phone, bath, and fridge; many sport a balcony with great *trulli* views. (☎080 432 34 32, fax 432 34 33. Singles €40-55, all with bath.) For camping info call **Camping dei Trulli** (☎080 432 36 99). **Ristorante Terminal ❷,** V. Indipendenza, 4, provides a cool escape from the scorching Alberobello sun and makes for a perfect, low-key lunch break. Partake in hearty meals with fresh bread and Puglian olive oil. (☎080 432 41 03, fax 432 75 18. Open Tu-Su noon-3pm and 6:40pm-midnight.) **L'Olmo Bello ❷,** V. Indipendenza, 33, to the left before entering the *trulli* district, serves local specialties in a century-old *trullo*. Try the *orechiette alla buongustaio,* ear-shaped pasta in a tomato-basil sauce. (☎080 432 36 07. Cover €1.60. Open M and W-Su noon-2:30pm and 8-11pm.)

◪ SIGHTS. V. Monte S. Michele goes up a hill to the **Chiesa di Sant'Antonio.** To reach the **Trullo Sovrano,** the largest in Alberobello, take C. V. Emanuele from P. del Popolo and continue past the church at the end. Built as a seminary in the 16th century, this two-story structure is decorated to show how *trulli* were originally used. (Open daily 10am-7:30pm. €1.50.) To get to the **Museo del Territorio** from P. del Popolo, turn left by the Eritrea store to P. XXVII Maggio. Composed of 23 *trulli* linked together, the museum has various temporary exhibits and a permanent display explaining the history and structure of these abodes. (Open daily 10am-8pm. €3.10.) For a nominal fee, taste several locally-made olive oils on rustic bread at the fabulous **Oil Museum.** Inquire at the Pro Loco office (see **Practical Information**) for access. (Open by request M-Sa 9am-1pm and 3:30-6pm. €0.25.)

SALENTO PENINSULA

Foreign tourists often overlook Italy's sun-baked heel, home to hidden grottoes, medieval fortresses, and the beaches of two seas. With cultural roots stretching back to Ancient Greek times, the Salento modestly bears the laurels of centuries. Its art and architecture are some of the best preserved in Italy and its vistas pristine and unrivaled. Transportation within the peninsula can sometimes be complicated, but with some planning a sojourn along the varied coastline or inland in olive and wine country is both possible and worth the effort.

BRINDISI   ☎0831

As Italy's gateway to the East, Brindisi has always been more a departure point than a destination. Pompey made his escape from Julius Caesar's army here in the first century BC, and Crusaders used its port to sail for the Holy Land. The city's streets are crowded with travelers who only stay long enough to pick up their ferry tickets. But Brindisi is worth more than just a cursory stop. As the one-time terminus of the Appian Way and a present-day port of industry and travel, Brindisi has a striking mix of historical sights and modern Italian flavor. And as neighboring Lecce and Ostuni attest, this region amply repays travelers who stop to explore.

 ARRIVEDERCI, ITALIA. Brindisi is Italy's central port for passenger boats to **Greece.** To get to Athens, take the ferry from Brindisi to Patras (see **Ferries**) and then a train or bus from Patras to Athens (2½hr.); you can buy these tickets at Brindisi's Stazione Marittima. Ferries also run from Brindisi to Çesme, **Turkey** (30hr.) and Durres, **Albania** (9hr.). Brindisi is the only Adriatic-side port that accepts Eurail and Interrail passes, and only **Hellenic Mediterranean Lines** and **Italian Ferries** (see **Ferries**) do so officially; however, almost all companies provide unofficial discounts. No Eurail and Interrail passes are accepted on ferries to Çesme, Turkey or Durres, Albania.

⌐ TRANSPORTATION

Trains: In P. Crispi. Ticket office open daily 8am-8pm. **Luggage storage** available (see **Practical Information**). **FS** to: **Bari** (1¼-1¾hr., 26 per day 4am-10:44pm, €6-13); **Lecce** (20-35min., 27 per day 6:01am-10:47pm, €2.32); **Milan** (9-12hr., 10 per day 7:48am-11:24pm, €54-85); **Rome** (6-9hr., 9 per day 6:23am-10:45pm, €27-45); **Taranto** (1¼hr., 20 per day 4:45am-10:44pm, €3.62).

Buses: FSE, at the train station, handles buses throughout Puglia. **Marozzi buses** travel to **Rome** (7½-8½hr., 3 per day 11am-10pm, €35.65). **Miccolis** runs to **Naples** (5hr., 3 per day 6:35am-6:35pm, €23.60). Be sure to ask where you can meet the bus, since neither Marozzi nor Miccolis buses leave from the town center. Buy tickets for both companies at the helpful and efficient **Grecian Travel,** C. Garibaldi, 79 (☎0831 56 83 33, fax 56 39 67). Open M-F 9am-1pm and 4-8pm, Sa 9am-1pm.

Ferries: Ferries leave for **Corfu** (8hr.); **Igoumenitsa** (10hr.); **Kephalonia** (16½hr.); **Patras** (17hr.); **Paxi.** (13hr.) Catamarans operated by **Italian Ferries** (C. Garibaldi, 96/98; ☎0831 59 08 40), sail to **Corfu** (4hr.) and are only slightly pricier than ferries. The catamarans leave from the Stazione Marittima, not the Costa Morena. Prices for each ferry line are fixed by the transport authority, and all agencies charge the same amount for tickets. Unfortunately, some agencies are more than happy to book passage for a full or nonexistent ferry, so exercise caution—use a reputable agency and always ask for other options to avoid scams. Well-established ferry lines include **Med Link**

Lines, C. Garibaldi, 49 (☎ 0831 52 76 67), and **Fragline,** V. Spalato, 31 (☎ 0831 54 85 34). Port tax (€6) and the deck reservation fee (€3) are not included in ticket price. Most lines provide a **free shuttle** that runs 1km from Stazione Marittima to Costa Morena, where ferries depart. **Check in 2hr. before departure.** Bring your own food to avoid the overpriced seagull fodder found in the snack bars onboard.

Public Transportation: City buses (☎ 0831 54 92 45) run between the train station and port and to destinations around the city. **Local ferries** depart from the tourist office on V. Margherita every 10min., crossing the Seno di Ponente and landing near the Chiesa Maria del Casale. Purchase bus and ferry tickets at bars and *tabacchi* for €0.70.

Taxis: ☎ 0831 59 79 01. Make sure to take a licensed taxi, as unofficial taxi services tend to overcharge. Always agree on a price before taking off. Taxis from Stazione Marittima to Costa Morena cost €17.

ⓘ PRACTICAL INFORMATION

Corso Umberto runs from the train station through **Piazza Cairoli** and continues through **Piazza del Popolo** and **Piazza di Vittorio.** At P. di Vittorio, it becomes **Corso Garibaldi** and ends at the port on the water's edge. The **Stazione Marittima** is on **Via Regina Margherita,** to the right. Taking a left at the end of C. Garibaldi, V. Regina Margherita curves around the waterfront past the column that once marked the end of the Appian Way, becoming **Via Flacco** and then **Via Thaon de Revel;** these streets are full of bars, restaurants, food stands, and, in the summer, carnival rides.

The **APT Information Office,** V. Regina Margherita, 5, though useless for ferry info, provides a free **map** and advice about hotels, local services, and sights. From C. Garibaldi, turn left on V. Margherita. (☎ 0831 52 30 72. Open daily 8am-2pm and 3-8pm.) **Luggage storage** is available at the train station. (€5-10 per 24hr., depending on bag size. Open daily 6:30am-10:30pm.) In case of **emergency,** call ☎ 113, the **police** (☎ 0831 22 95 22), or the **carabinieri** (☎ 112 or 0831 15 29 11). **Ospedale Di Summa** (☎ 0831 53 71 11) offers emergency care (☎ 0831 51 98 22). **Internet** is available at **Internet Service Point,** C. Roma, 54 (☎ 0831 52 64 28; €5 per hr.; open daily 3:30-9pm), near P. del Popolo. Many ticket offices run Internet points on the side. The **post office** is at P. Vittoria, 10. (☎ 0831 47 11 11. Open M-F 8am-6:30pm, Sa 8am-12:30pm.) **Branch** in the Stazione Marittima. **Postal Code:** 72100.

ⓝ ACCOMMODATIONS

Hotel Altair, V. Giudea, 4 (☎/fax 0831 56 22 89), is close to the port and center. From Stazione Marittima, walk up C. Garibaldi and take the 3rd left. 15 rooms have high ceilings, TV, and fridge. No A/C. Reserve 1 week ahead. Singles €20, with bath €30; doubles €35-€50; triples with shower €60. MC/V. ❷

Hotel Venezia, V. Pisanelli, 4 (☎ 0831 52 75 11), is equidistant from train and Stazione Marittima. Straight out of the train station, pass the fountain and take the 2nd left off C. Umberto onto V. S. Lorenzo da Brindisi, following the signs pointing right onto V. Pisanelli. 12 comfortable rooms have high ceilings and shared baths. No A/C. Reserve 4 days ahead. Singles €15; doubles €25. Cash only. ❷

Hotel Regina, V. Cavour, 5 (☎ 0831 56 20 01; www.hotelreginaweb.com), off P. Cairoli. This American-style hotel offers a modern alternative to the smaller accommodations in town. All 43 rooms have A/C, fridge, and TV. Buffet breakfast included. Laundry service available. Singles €44-70; doubles €55-90. AmEx/MC/V. ❹

Hotel Torino, Largo Pietro Palumbo, 6 (☎ 0831 59 75 87; www.brindisiweb.com/torino). 14 plain but spacious rooms, all with private bath, A/C, and satellite TV. Garage parking available. Singles from €52; doubles from €60. AmEx/MC/V. ❸

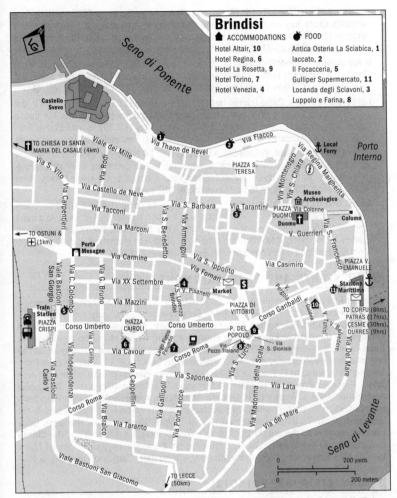

Brindisi

♠ ACCOMMODATIONS   🍴 FOOD

Hotel Altair, **10**
Hotel Regina, **6**
Hotel La Rosetta, **9**
Hotel Torino, **7**
Hotel Venezia, **4**

Antica Osteria La Sciabica, **1**
Iaccato, **2**
Il Focacceria, **5**
Gulliper Supermercato, **11**
Locanda degli Sciavoni, **3**
Luppolo e Farina, **8**

Hotel La Rosetta, V. S. Dionisio, 2 (☎/fax 0831 56 13 10), off C. Garibaldi. Enjoy sleek, modern decor as well as A/C, phone, and minibar in every room. Lobby area includes a well-stocked bar, lounge, and reading room with leather armchairs. English, German, and French spoken. Singles from €55-67; doubles €75-100. ❹

🍴 FOOD

Avoid the restaurants and cafes on C. Garibaldi near the port, where the ubiquitous "tourist *menù*" yields smaller portions, steep drink prices, and more insipid dishes. Better options lie on nearby side streets. An **open-air market**, off P. Vittoria on V. Fornari, sells fresh fruit. (Open M-Sa 7am-1pm.) Pick up supplies for your ferry ride at Gulliper, C. Garibaldi, 106, a **supermarket** one block from the port. (☎0831 56 25 66. Open M-Sa 8am-1:30pm and 4:30-8:30pm, Su 9am-1pm.)

PUGLIA, BASILICATA, CALABRIA

Iaccato, V. Flacco, (☎0831 56 70 45), directly on the water. Since 1950 this little fishermen's shack has been serving some of the town's top seafood. Watch the staff expertly fillet the salmon with green peppers right in front of you (€6.70). *Primi* €5.16-15.49, *secondi* €6.20-31. Open daily noon-3pm and 7-11pm. MC/V. ❷

Il Focacceria, V. Cristoforo Colombo, 5 (☎0831 56 09 30), offers more than its name implies. A favorite of sailors on leave in the port, this simply-styled restaurant dishes out tasty lasagna (€3) and takeout pizza (€3-5). Open daily 8am-11pm. Cash only. ❶

Luppolo e Farina, V. Pozzo Traiano (☎0831 59 04 96), just off C. Garibaldi near P. del Popolo. Wood-fueled oven masters have pizza tossing down to a science. The house pizza, with mozzarella and fresh and sun-dried tomatoes (€5.30), is unrivaled in Brindisi. *Primi* €4-8, *secondi* €4-10. Pizza €4-9. Open daily 7pm-midnight. AmEx/MC/V. ❷

Locanda degli Sciavoni, V. Tarantini, 43 (☎0831 52 20 50), a short walk from the front of the duomo. Favored by locals and tourists, the simple decor and lively atmosphere are fine accents to the tasty cuisine. The *spaghetti alle scampi* is a winning ticket. *Primi* €3-8, *secondi* €5-8. Open M-Sa 7pm-midnight. MC/V. ❸

Antica Osteria La Sciabica, V. Thaon de Revel, 29/33 (☎0831 56 28 70), from Stazione Marittima walk on the waterfront road with the port on your right. Located in a quiet spot on the harbor, with seating on a candlelit patio. Seafood is the house specialty, in particular the *maltagliata alle cozze nere* (local pasta with mussels; €7). *Primi* and *secondi* €7-10. Open daily noon-3pm and 8pm-midnight. AmEx/MC/V. ❸

👁 🎵 SIGHTS AND ENTERTAINMENT

Turning left at the seaside end of C. Garibaldi, V. Regina Margherita passes a stately set of marble steps. The huge ▨**column** here, recently restored, once marked the end of the **Appian Way.** Figures of Jove, Neptune, Mars, and eight tritons grace the marble capital. The column's twin, which stood on the adjacent base, now resides in Lecce. The towering **Monumento al Marinaio d'Italia** across the bay watches over Brindisi's seamen with solemn beatitude. V. Colonne runs from behind the column to P. Duomo. In the 11th-century **duomo** (rebuilt in the 18th century), Emperor Frederick II, married Jerusalem's Yolande. (Open daily 7am-noon and 4:30-7:30pm.) Nearby in P. Duomo, the **Museo Archeologico** traces Brindisi's rich history with pottery and other artifacts. (☎0831 56 55 01. Open M and W-Su 9:30am-1:30pm, Tu 9:30am-1:30pm and 3:30-6:30pm. Free.) Follow the signs from the train station to the outskirts of town to see Brindisi's pride and joy, the **Chiesa di Santa Maria del Casale.** Lovely 13th-century frescoes, including one of Mary blessing the Crusaders, enliven the interior. (Open daily 7am-noon and 4-7pm.)

▶ DAYTRIP FROM BRINDISI

OSTUNI

Ostuni is on the train line between Brindisi (30min., 16 per day 4am-10:44pm, €2.32) and Bari (1-1¼hr., 15 per day 6am-10:55pm, €4.10). From train station (☎0831 30 12 68), take the orange city bus to P. della Libertà, at the center of town (15min.; M-Sa every 30min., Su every hr. 7am-9:30pm; €0.70). Buy tickets at the train station bar. Buses are not numbered, so tell the driver your intended destination before boarding. In case of emergency, call the carabinieri at ☎112.

Rising from a landscape of sea, dark-red earth, and olive trees, Ostuni's *città bianca* (white city) appears ethereal. The *centro storico*'s white walls protect the city from the elements and lend a fairy-tale touch to the serpentine streets. The terrace at the top of C. V. Emanuele boasts a beautiful view of the old city. Just off P. della Libertà, the small church of **Santo Spirito** features a doorway with well-preserved reliefs from the late medieval period. From the piazza, V. Cattedrale runs through the old town center, leading to the **Convento delle Monacelle** (Convent of Little Nuns), V. Cattedrale, 15, an architecture student's dream, with an intricate Baroque facade and a white-tiled dome. Inside, a 24,500-year-old human skeleton resides at the **archaeological museum**. (☎0831 33 63 83. Open daily 9:30am-1pm and 3:30-7:30pm. €1.50; students, seniors, and children €0.75.) Crowning Ostuni's hill, the **duomo**, built in 1437, was the last Byzantine building to be erected in southern Italy. The remarkable facade, in the Spanish-Gothic style, contrasts sharply with the more austere Norman styles common in Puglia. (Open daily 7:30am-12:30pm and 4-7pm.) On August 26, Ostuni celebrates Sant'Oronzo with the **Cavalcata**, a parade of costumed horses and riders. Many praise Ostuni's nearby **beach**, accessible from P. della Libertà by bus.

Ostuni's **AAST Tourist Office**, C. Mazzini, 6, just off P. della Libertà, provides assistance with accommodations, **maps** of the *centro storico*, and a booklet of town historical information. (☎0831 30 12 68. Open M-F June-Aug. 8:30am-1:30pm and 3:30-6:30pm, Sept.-May 8:30am-noon and 4-7pm.) Unfortunately, there are few affordable options for those planning on staying the night; accommodations in Ostuni tend to be overpriced and poorly located. **Hotel Tre Torri ❸**, C. V. Emanuele, 294, is a 30min. walk from P. della Libertà. Its 20 rooms are plush and comfortable, but lack A/C. (☎0831 33 11 14. Singles €36-42; doubles €51-68.) Consult the tourist office for *agriturismo* options.

Small taverns and *osterie* abound in the old city. The streets can be tricky to navigate, but signs everywhere point to restaurants. **Porta Nova ❹**, V. Gaspare Petrolo, 38, is a little pricey but has fresh seafood and a pastoral view. (☎0831 33 89 83. *Primi* €8-15, *secondi* from €15. Cover €2. Open in summer daily noon-4pm and 7:30-midnight. Closed in winter.) Head to **Locanda dei Sette Peccati ❷**, for pizza or for a picnic lunch to go, taking a right off V. Cathedral onto V. Franc Ant Arc. Zaccania, then left on V. Francesco Campani. (☎0831 33 95 95. Pizza and *panini*, both from €3.50. Open Tu-Su 11am-4:30pm and 7pm-2am. AmEx/MC/V.) Nearby on Largo Lanza, **Ristorante Vecchia Ostuni ❸** has quiet outdoor seating and a menu specializing in all types of meat and fish (from €6). Call 30min. ahead to have special fish prepared. (☎0831 30 33 08. Open M and W-Su noon-3pm and 7pm-midnight. AmEx/MC/V.) Outside the old city near Hotel Tre Torri, **Panificio Grecio ❶** overflows with baked goods—breads, pastries, and excellent muffins. (Open M-F 8am-2pm and 4:30-10pm, Sa 8am-2pm.)

LECCE ☎0832

One of Italy's hidden pearls, Lecce is where Italians go when foreign tourists invade their country. Although a succession of conquerors—Cretans, Romans, Saracens, Swabians, and more—passed through here, the Spanish Hapsburgs wielded enduring influence in the 16th and 17th centuries, resulting in the beautiful buildings seen today. The city's famed Baroque architecture, a never ending pageant of graceful curls, sweeping arcs, floral carvings, and ornate facades is awe-inspiring. Most of the city's churches and palaces are sculpted from *tufigna*, the soft, locally quarried "Lecce stone" that hardens when exposed to air. At night, the lighted buildings make for a memorable *passeggiata* for posh and pampered vacationers. The university engenders a vibrant nightlife, centered chiefly around Irish pubs. Lecce, the "Florence of the South," is a great starting point for a tour of the Salento Peninsula, in the heel of Italy's boot.

▐▀ TRANSPORTATION

Trains: Lecce is the southeastern terminus of the state railway. The **FS Station** is in P. Massari, a short walk down V. Oronzo Quarta from the town center. **FS trains** (☎0832 30 10 16) to: **Bari** (1½-2hr., 11 per day 4:58am-9:23pm, €6-13); **Brindisi** (20-

40min., 16 per day 6:12am-11:04pm, €2.32-8.26); **Rome** (6-9½hr., 5 per day 6am-11pm, €30-44). **FSE** trains (☎0832 66 81 11) criss-cross the Salento Peninsula. Trains run M-Sa to **Gallipoli** (1hr., 11 per day 5:43am-9:24pm, €4.20) and **Otranto** (1¼hr.; 9:32am, 12:20, 5:43pm; €2.80) via **Maglie**. Buses **#24** and **28** (€0.62) run from in front of the station on V. Quarta to the center of town.

Buses: The **FSE Station** (☎0832 34 76 34), on V. Boito, is easily accessible by bus #4 (€0.62) from the train station. FSE buses depart from the **FSE Garage,** across from the train station on the left, and stop at the FSE station on their way out of town. Tickets are available in the train station bar. To **Gallipoli** (1hr., 6 per day, €2.84); **Taranto** (2hr., 5 per day 7am-4pm, €4.58). **STP** (☎0832 30 28 73), on V. Adua, heads to smaller towns of the Salento Peninsula. Pick up a schedule at the tourist office. In July and Aug., **Salento in Bus** is the most convenient way of traversing the peninsula, with buses running to **Gallipoli** (1¼-1¾hr., 10 per day 7:14am-1:14am, €3.50) and **Otranto** (1hr., 7:50am-12:23am, €3.50), as well as to other towns on the peninsula. Buses stop on V. Quarta, close to the FS station.

Taxis: ☎0832 24 79 78, at the train station. ☎0832 30 60 45, in P. S. Oronzo.

■✶🛈 ORIENTATION AND PRACTICAL INFORMATION

Lecce lies 35km south and inland from Brindisi. From the **train station,** take **Viale Oronzo Quarta** straight into **Via Cairoli** to get to the winding streets of the old city. Turn left on **Via Paladini** and wind around behind the duomo, stopping at **Via Vittorio Emanuele.** To the left, **Via Libertini** passes **Piazza Duomo** and Chiesa di San Giovanni Battista and exits the old city walls through **Porta Rudiae.** To the right lies **Piazza Sant'Oronzo,** Lecce's main square, with the Roman amphitheater to the left and the *castello* beyond.

Tourist Office: Information desk, in the entrance to Castello Carlo V, on V. XXV Luglio (☎329 460 35 33). Provides a great map for €1, help with accommodations, and restaurants. Open daily 9am-9pm.

Budget Travel: CTS, V. Palmieri, 91 (☎0832 30 18 62). From P. S. Oronzo, take V. Emanuele and turn right on V. Palmieri. Provides flight and train info and sells tickets. Open M-F 9am-1pm and 4-7:30pm.

Laundromat: Lavanderia Self-Service, V. dell'Università, 47 (☎339 683 63 96), halfway between Pta. Rudiae and Pta. Napoli. Wash €1.50 (moderately sized load) to €6.50 (industrial-sized stainless-steel washer). Dryers €1.50 per 20min. Open M-F 8:30am-8:30pm, Sa 9am-1pm.

Public Bathroom: In P. S. Oronzo, at the corner with V. Imperatore Augusto.

Police: Carabinieri are at V. Lupiae, 6 (☎112 or 0832 31 10 11).

Hospital: Ospedale Vito Fazzi (☎0832 66 11 11), on V. S. Cesario. In case of emergency, call ☎0832 66 14 03.

Medical Clinic: ☎0832 34 34 60.

Internet: Chatwin Internet Cafe & Traveller Point, V. Castriota 8/B (☎0832 27 78 59; www.chatwin-netcafe.it). Follow V. Rubichi out of P. S. Oronzo and turn right on V. Castriota. Friendly, English-speaking staff, bar, and lounge with international newspapers. Fast connection. €3 per hr. Open M-Sa 10am-1:30pm and 5-10pm.

Post Office: ☎0832 27 40 64. In P. Libertini, across from the *castello.* Open M-F 8am-6:30pm, Sa 8:30am-noon. **Postal Code:** 73100.

🏠 ACCOMMODATIONS

Lecce lacks ultra-cheap accommodations. B&Bs are an alternative to impersonal hotels, and the tourist office lists affordable *affittacamere,* or private rooms.

PUGLIA, BASILICATA, CALABRIA

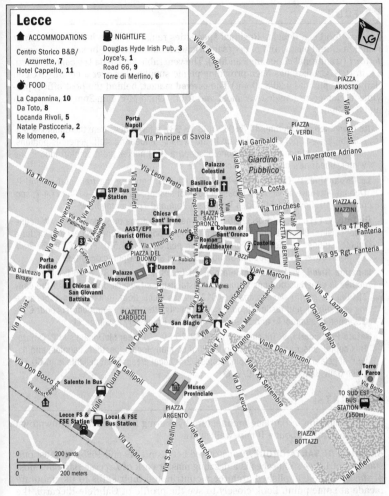

Lecce

⌂ ACCOMMODATIONS

Centro Storico B&B/
Azzurrette, **7**
Hotel Cappello, **11**

☕ FOOD

La Capannina, **10**
Da Toto, **8**
Locanda Rivoli, **5**
Natale Pasticceria, **2**
Re Idomeneo, **4**

🍸 NIGHTLIFE

Douglas Hyde Irish Pub, **3**
Joyce's, **1**
Road 66, **9**
Torre di Merlino, **6**

Centro Storico, V. A. Vignes, 2/B (☎0832 24 28 28; www.bedandbreakfast.lecce.it). From P. S. Oronzo, take V. Augusto Imperatore until it becomes V. Federico D'Aragona. V. Vignes is on the left. Small, well-tended B&B close to the historic center has 5 large rooms with A/C, TV, cooking facilities, and balcony. Reserve 1-2 weeks ahead. Singles €40; doubles €60; quads €120. MC/V. ❸

Azzurrette, V. A. Vignes, 3/B, shares management and building with Centro Storico. The 4 suites available are spacious and have big, sunny, windows. All have A/C, TV, kitchen, and balcony. Reserve 1-2 weeks ahead. Singles €40; doubles €60. MC/V. ❸

Hotel Cappello, V. Montegrappa, 4 (☎0832 30 88 81; www.hotelcappello.it). From the station, take the 1st left off V. Quarta onto V. Don Bosco and follow the signs. This modern hotel has 35 rooms, all with A/C, TV, and fridge. Bar in the lobby. Singles €30; doubles €44; triples €57. AmEx/MC/V. ❸

🍴 FOOD

Leccese food is a delight. Regional specialties range from the hearty *cicerietria* (chickpeas and pasta) and *pucce* (sandwiches made with olive-bread rolls) to *confettoni* (traditional chocolate candies). The venerable **Salumeria Loiacono,** V. Fazzi, 11, in P. S. Oronzo, has been providing picnic supplies for over a century. (Open daily 7am-2pm and 4:30-8:30pm.) The **covered market,** behind the post office, provides a chance to haggle over meat and fruit. (Open M-F 4am-2pm, Sa 4am-2pm and 3:30-9pm.)

Re Idomeneo, V. Libertini, 44 (☎0832 38 18 93), a few blocks from the duomo. A reasonably priced spot that crowds up in the evening. Endearing staff, generous portions, and a breezy atmosphere. Traditional *cicerietria* (€6) makes great comfort food in the winter. Under new management in 2005. ❷

La Capannina, V. Cairoli, 13 (☎0832 30 41 59), between the train station and P. Duomo. Attentive service and pleasant outdoor seating. Pizza €3.50-6. *Primi* €4-7, *secondi* €5-10. Cover €1.50. Open Tu-Su 9am-2pm and 7pm-midnight. ❶

Da Toto, V. F. Lo Re, 9 (☎0832 30 10 00), near the cinema on Viale Marconi. With fine local cuisine, this restaurant and pizzeria is quite popular among *Leccesi* looking for a quieter setting. Try the robust *orecchiette al pomodoro* (€4.50). Pizza €2.50-5. *Primi* €4.50-8. Cover €1.50. Open M-Sa noon-3:30pm and 7:30pm-midnight. ❷

Locanda Rivoli, V. Augusto Imperatore, 19 (☎0832 33 16 78). Food is hearty and comes in generous portions at this older establishment, which dates back to the early 1900s. The *risotto allo champagne* (€12) makes a chic treat. Indoor and outdoor seating is laid-back and rustic but buzzes with activity after 10pm. *Primi* and *secondi* €12-25. Open in summer M and W-Su 7pm-midnight. Hours vary in winter. ❸

Natale Pasticceria, V. Trinchese, 7 (☎0832 25 60 60), near McDonald's in P. Oronzo. This copper-ensconced pastry shop is full of so many locals, pastries, candies, and flavors of gelato, your head will spin. Cones €2-4. Local cream-filled delights from €0.70. Open daily 8am-midnight. MC/V. ❶

👁 SIGHTS

Get an education in Baroque architecture by touring the churches of downtown Lecce. They're all about a 10min. walk apart.

BASILICA DI SANTA CROCE. Constructed between 1549 and 1695, the most outstanding of Lecce's churches is a dazzling masterwork of *Leccese* Baroque. Most of the area's accomplished architects contributed their skills to its elaborate facade at some point. Look closely to see the profile of Gabriele Riccardi, the basilica's original designer, hidden between the upper window and the column to its left. Two rows of massive Corinthian columns tower inside, their acanthus leaves dancing majestically. F. A. Zantimbalo's 1614 altar adorns the chapel to the left of the apse. *(From P. S. Oronzo, head down V. Templari. Open daily 8am-1pm and 4:30-8:30pm. Modest dress required.)*

PALAZZO CELESTINI. The lower half of this palazzo's facade was designed by Giuseppe Zimbalo, nicknamed "Lo Zingarello" (the gypsy) for his tendency to wander from one project to another. The upper half is by Giuseppe Cino, Zimbalo's pupil, to whom he characteristically passed his unfinished projects. Though now an office space, visitors can view its inner courtyard, which hosts rock and classical music concerts in the summer. Keep an eye out for posters or ask at the AAST office for more information. *(Next to Basilica d. S. Croce.)*

DUOMO. Constructed in 1114, the duomo was "Zingarelloed" between 1659 and 1670. Except for two *Leccese* altars, the interior dates from the 18th century. At night, misty streams of light pour out of the **campanile** that rises from the left side of the cathedral. Opposite, the **Palazzo Vescovile** (Bishop's Palace) has been remodeled several times since its construction in 1632. On the right, with a Baroque well in its center, stands the **seminary,** designed by Giuseppe Cino in 1709. *(From P. S. Oronzo, take V. Emanuele. Duomo open daily 6:30am-noon and 5-7:30pm.)*

ANCIENT RUINS. The **Column of Sant'Oronzo,** one of two that marked the termination of the Appian Way in Brindisi (p. 610), towers melodramatically over P. S. Oronzo. A flowing-robed statue of the saint now tops the column. Nearby, the ruins of a 2nd-century amphitheater recede into the ground. In its prime, it held 20,000 spectators; these days, at least that many young people seem to gather there to flirt on summer nights. Near the station, the **Museo Provinciale** contains Apulian ceramics from the 5th century BC. *(V. Gallipoli, 28. ☎ 0832 24 70 25. Open M-Sa 9am-1pm and 2:30-7:30pm, Su 9am-1pm. Wheelchair accessible. Free.)*

OTHER SIGHTS. The wildly intricate **Chiesa di San Giovanni Battista** was Lo Zingarello's last work. The artist, who used Baroque norms as a basis for innovation, decorated the columns with unfettered glee. Fifteen altars within, surrounding a Roman Cross design, testify to his disdain for moderation. *(From P. del Duomo, take V. Libertini.)* The ornate **Porta Napoli** once stood on the road from Naples. The arch was erected in 1548 in honor of Holy Roman Emperor Charles V, whose coat of arms adorns the front. *(From P. del Duomo, take V. Palmieri.)*

🎭🎵 NIGHTLIFE AND ENTERTAINMENT

Every night, crowds gather outside the many bars, Irish pubs, and pizzerias along V. V. Emanuele and P. Oronzo. **Torre di Merlino,** V. G. Battista del Tufoi, 10 (☎ 0832 24 18 74), near the Roman theater, is a favorite among university students. (Open M-Tu and Th-Su 8pm-3am. Draft beer €3. MC/V.) **Joyce's,** V. Matteo da Lecce, 5, is another hot spot, with walls covered in creeping vines and U2 album covers, and glass cases containing texts of *Ulysses*. (Walk out of P. S. Oronzo toward the basilica and turn left on V. Matteo da Lecce. ☎ 0832 27 94 43. Open daily 8pm-2am.) **Road 66,** at V. dei Perroni, 8 (☎ 0832 24 65 68), near Pta. San Biagio, and **Douglas Hyde Irish Pub,** on V. B. Ravenna, are also good bets for nocturnal action. Most night-

THE LOCAL STORY

FOLK ON BAROQUE

How did rustic Lecce come to possess so much High Baroque architecture? Let's Go seeks the answers, one *Leccese* at a time.

1:05pm. Well-dressed woman walking tiny dog in P. Duomo. "Zingarello... forse... Zingarello?" she shrugs meekly.

She's correct! Zingarello, Lecce's Baroque mastermind, constructed some of the most breathtaking facades. He often worked—and gave up—on several projects at once.

1:32pm. Man in shirt with innumerable zippers, lolling by Chiesa di S. Croce. "Extra-terrestrials," he asserts, rolling his eyes.

No evidence is readily available to substantiate his claim. Though it's possible that Lecce's 16th century aristocracy fell under otherworldly inspiration, history suggests more earthly ambitions: newly wealthy from trade, they tried to outdo each other in public, commissioning increasingly ornate buildings.

1:53pm. Young woman in colorful shirt adorned generously with English phrases. "It sprang from the ground, right here," she says, bracelets jangling.

And surprisingly, she's not far from the truth. Natural forms—flora, fauna, fruit—were favorite Italian artistic subjects in the 16th century, intended to glorify God by exalting earthly gifts.

Conclusion: Equal parts celebration and vaingloriousness. Typically artistic, typically Italian.

clubs, especially during the summer, are on the coast and only accessible by car. For up-to-date information on the hottest nightlife options, chat with locals in the bustling piazza or consult the monthly publication *Salento in Tasca*, available at local bars. The yearly **MedFest** brings classical music to the Castello Carlo V with a series of concerts throughout the summer. Call ☎ 082 24 23 68 for info.

Lecce's soccer team has bounced between Serie A and Serie B in recent years, and its fans have rallied behind it 100% at every step. Those who visit during a match are likely to get caught up in the infectious cheering, parading, and flag-waving in the piazza. (Matches held Sept.-June. Buy tickets at *tabacchi* and lottery agencies, or contact the stadium at ☎ 0832 45 38 86. Tickets from €15.) The AAST office distributes the *Calendario Manifestazioni*, which describes Lecce's annual summer festivals and lists seasonal events in the province.

OTRANTO ☎ 0836

Although throngs of Italian tourists descend upon Otranto in July and August, its winding streets, crystal-clear waters, and medieval sights make it worth visiting year-round. Earlier visitors included a band of Turkish pirates who converted to Christianity after conquering the city. Unable to force Otranto's devoted Christian inhabitants to renounce their god by threatening them with gruesome deaths, the Turkish invaders instead gave up Islam—so convinced were they by the piety of these people. The bones of the *Martiri d'Otranto* (Martyrs of Otranto) attract some visitors but most are content to wade in the clear, warm waters.

⌨ **TRANSPORTATION AND PRACTICAL INFORMATION.** Otranto is 40km southeast of Lecce on the Adriatic coast, and it can be downright hard to reach by public transportation. Rustic **FSE trains** run from Lecce (1¼hr., 9 per day 6:45am-7:30pm, €2.58) to Maglie. Get off in Maglie and take the awaiting bus to Otranto. The FSE ticket to Lecce covers both. In July and August, **Salento in Bus** runs straight to Otranto's castle (30min., €2.50). Pick it up in Lecce on the right side of the V. Quarta, directly in front of the train station. The town's main strip of beach is along the **Lungomare d'Otranto,** ending at the **public gardens.** On the left after the gardens, V. V. Emanuele leads to **Piazza de Donno** and the entrance to the *centro storico*. Enter through the city gate and turn right on **Via Basilica** to reach the **duomo.** Left of the duomo entrance a few yards from the door, is a narrow passage leading to the piazza in front of the castle; here, the **APT Tourist Office** offers advice on lodgings and transportation to towns on the peninsula. (☎ 0836 80 14 36. Open daily 9am-1pm and 3-9pm.) For the **carabinieri,** call ☎ 0836 80 10 10. A **medical clinic,** V. Pantaleone, 4 (☎ 0836 80 16 76), is down the hill from the APT office. **Farmacia Ricciardi** is at V. Lungomare, 101. (☎ 0836 80 10 36. Open daily 8:30am-1pm and 4:30-8pm.) Check email at **Internet Cafe,** V. V. Emanuele, 11. (☎ 338 648 81 00. €5 per hr. Open Tu-Su 7am-2pm and 5pm-midnight.) The **post office** is by the stoplight on V. Pantaleone. (☎ 0836 80 10 02. Open M-Sa 8:15am-6pm.) **Postal Code:** 73028.

⌨ **ACCOMMODATIONS AND FOOD.** Lodgings in Otranto are very expensive from mid-July to August, when most hotels require half pension and all require reservations. The tourist office can help find *affittacamere*. **Hotel Miramare ❹,** V. Lungomare, 55, is right on the beach, with nicely furnished rooms, all with balcony and TV. Call in March to reserve a room in July or August. (☎ 0836 80 10 23. Singles €45-75; doubles €65-125. Prices vary seasonally. AmEx/MC/V.) The **Bellavista Hotel ❺,** V. V. Emanuele, 19, directly across from the public gardens and beach, has 22 rooms with bath, TV, and A/C. (☎ 0836 80 10 58. Singles €48-89; doubles €68-119.) A 10min. walk from the beach and near the FSE train station, the more rustic **B&B**

Hotel Pietra Verde ❺, V. P. Presbitero, has rooms with phone, TV, A/C, bath, and balcony. A low-key lounge with TV is also available to guests. (☎0836 80 19 01; www.hotelpietraverde.it. Singles €40-93; doubles €60-104.)

For water and other seaside essentials, visit the Gulliper **supermarket,** V. Vecchia, 10. Take V. Presbitero uphill, bearing right, and walk 10min. away from the shore. (☎0836 80 27 16. Open M-Sa 7:30am-1pm and 5-8:30pm, Su 8am-1pm.) The **market** by P. de Donno sells fruit, meat, and fish. (Open daily 8am-1pm.) Across from the public gardens, **Boomerang Self-Service ❶**, V. V. Emanuele, 14, serves basic but tasty dishes cafeteria-style. (☎/fax 0836 80 26 19. Pizza €3.10-5.50. *Primi* €4.50, *secondi* €4.50-7. Open Mar.-Sept. daily noon-12:30am.) The friendly **Acmet Pascià ❹**, at the end of V. V. Emanuele, provides outdoor dining with a gorgeous view. (☎0836 80 12 82. *Primi* €6-18, fish *secondi* €11-18. Open Tu-Su 10am-3:30pm and 7pm-1:30am. AmEx/MC/V.)

◘ SIGHTS. The *centro storico*, ensconced in stout ramparts, guards many of Otranto's proudest historical sites. Dante stayed here while writing parts of the *Divine Comedy*. The majestic ◙**duomo** is paved with a phenomenal 11th-century floor mosaic of the Tree of Life. The mosaic extends the entire length of the nave and depicts religious, mythological, and historical figures from Adam to Alexander the Great to King Arthur—and that's just the A's. Another section depicts the 12 zodiac signs and seasonal agriculture work. Equally impressive is the ceiling, a brilliantly colored and gilded affair well worth the pain in the neck. In the **Cappella dei Martiri,** a small chapel in the duomo's crypt, lie the skulls and bones of all 800 *Otrantini* who died for their faith. (Duomo open daily 8am-noon and 3-6:30pm, excluding mass. Modest dress required.) Red, pink, and blue frescoes of the Garden of Eden brighten the somewhat musty interior of the 8th-century Byzantine **Chiesa di San Pietro.** Take C. Garibaldi to P. del Popolo and follow the signs up the stairs on the left. (Open daily on request 9:30am-1pm and 3:30-7:30pm.) The 16th-century **Aragonese castle,** with its imposing walls and newly excavated moat, still looks ready for a siege. A gate in the ramparts leads to the quiet refuge of Otranto's small, picturesque sailboat harbor. (Open daily 10:30am-12:30pm and 6-11:30pm.) Every Wednesday a **market** surrounds the castle. (Open 9am-1pm.)

◪◫ BEACHES AND ENTERTAINMENT. In August Otranto's **beaches** show less sand than skin as Italian vacationers stake claims to every available patch of land. For those seeking fewer crowds, the fine sand and cerulean waters are just as enjoyable in early summer. The free public strips along the *lungomare* and further along on V. degli Haethey are the most popular and accessible. For €5, the beach closest to V. Pantaleone provides bathroom and changing facilities, but umbrella and chairs cost another €10. The beach one block down the road heading away from V. Presbitero is free, although the proximity of rusty old freighters, which belch smoke as they dock at the port, can make for a less than idyllic setting. In the evening, vendors arrive in droves to feed the crowds—try the delicious *noccioline zuccherate* (candy-coated peanuts; €1). If exploring the depths of the salty brine sounds more appealing than sunning on the sand, **scuba diving** is available by appointment at V. S. Francesco di Paola, 42. (☎/fax 0836 80 27 40.)

After dark Otranto's *lungomare* fills with people walking along the waterfront and hitting up the pubs, while those with cars head to the discos 5-6km away. The public gardens sport numerous food-stands with nuts and snacks (from €1.50) and, in summer, carnival-style rides for children. For a relaxing stroll, grab a friend and trek off to the beautiful **Chiesa S. M. dei Martiri,** walking straight out of the old city on V. Ottocento Martiri. This complex, with stately stone steps and a beautiful view, provides a delightful respite from all the beach buzz. On August 13, 14, and 15, Otranto welcomes tourists to the **Festa dei Martiri d'Otranto,** a festival in honor of the martyrs. On the first Sunday in September, the town celebrates the **Festa della Madonna dell'Altomare** (Festival of the Virgin of the High Seas).

TARANTO ☎ 0994

Mythology claims that Taranto was founded over 2500 years ago when Poseidon saved the sailor Taras from a ghastly Ionian shipwreck. Dolphins, summoned from the depths by the notoriously temperamental sea god, escorted Taras through the sea to these lovely shores, where he established the colony that became known as Taranto. Today the image of the dolphin is omnipresent, a reminder of ancient prosperity as the city attempts to refashion itself after a blighted period. High unemployment rates, government corruption, welfare dependency, and Mafia control have cast a shadow over the city, obscuring its seaside charm. However, young professionals are working to spark urban renewal. Reasonably priced accommodations abound, and a world-famous archaeological museum, delicious and inexpensive seafood, and sailboat-packed beaches give Taranto, home to Italy's naval fleet, some hefty appeal.

▐▀ TRANSPORTATION

The **train station** (☎ 147 88 80 88) is in P. Libertà, across from the old city over Ponte Porta Napoli. **FS** runs trains to: Bari (1¾hr., 22 per day 4:40am-10:22pm, €6.70); Brindisi (1¼hr., 21 per day 4:53am-10pm, €3.62); Naples (4hr., 6 per day 6:15am-midnight, €22.41-40.31); and Rome (6-7hr., 7 per day 6:15am-midnight, €23.50-36.96). A number of companies run **buses** from P. Castello. **Marozzi,** C. Umberto I, 67 (☎ 0994 59 40 89), a block from P. Garibaldi, has information on many of them. Daily services run to Bari (1¾hr.) and Lecce. (1¾hr.) **SITA buses** run to Matera (1¾hr., 4 per day 6:20am-7:20pm, €4.81). Local **AMAT buses** sell tickets (€0.70, 90min. ticket €0.95, 1-day ticket €1.65). Buy tickets at any *tabacchi* or bar.

▟✚ ⁊ ORIENTATION AND PRACTICAL INFORMATION

The buildings of Taranto's old city crowd atop a small island between two promontories. Bridges join the old city to the new **port** area and the **train station.** Be wary of pickpockets during the day, and avoid the old city at night. From the station, buses to the new city stop near **Piazza Garibaldi,** the main square. On foot, take **Via Duca d'Aosta** over Ponte Porta Napoli and bear left to reach **Piazza Fontana** in the old city. Walk for 20min. along the shore to **Piazza Castello** and cross the swinging bridge into the new city. P. Garibaldi is one block ahead. The **APT Tourist Office,** C. Umberto I, 113, offers free **maps.** Walk out of P. Garibaldi, heading away from the old city. (☎ 0994 53 23 92; apttaranto@pugliaturismo.com. Open M-F 9am-1pm and 4:30-6:30pm, Sa 9am-noon.) There's also a booth in Piazza Garibaldi that offers good **maps.** There are **public restrooms** in the public gardens. Facing away from the old city, take V. Cavour out of P. Garibaldi and turn right on V. Pitagora; restrooms are on the right. In case of **emergency,** call ☎ 113 or the **police** (☎ 112). **Internet** is available at **Chiocciolin@it,** C. Umberto I, 85, next to P. Garibaldi. (☎/fax 0994 53 80 51. €4 per hr. Open M 4:30-9pm, Tu-Su 9am-1pm and 4:30-9pm.) The **post office** is on Lungomare V. Emanuele. (☎ 0994 359 51. Open M-F 8am-6:30pm, Sa 8am-12:30pm.) **Postal Code:** 74100.

👤🍴 ACCOMMODATIONS AND FOOD

Albergo Pisani ❷, V. Cavour, 43, off P. Garibaldi, is conveniently located, reasonably priced, and comfortable. (☎ 0994 53 40 87, fax 70 75 93. Breakfast included. Singles with bath €25; doubles €44, with bath €46.) Continue down P. Cavour and turn left onto the *lungomare;* 500m down find the **New Astor Hotel ❸**, Viale Virgilio, 4, with rooms that are fairly small but dressed to the nines in plush upholstery. In the lounge, sprawling leather chairs overlook the glimmering Ionian sea. All rooms have TV, A/C, and bath. (☎/fax 0994 59 59 10. Singles €35; doubles €45.) **Hotel Plaza ❺**, in P. Garibaldi at V. d'Aquino, 46, spices up bland rooms with full amenities—all have bath, A/C, and TV. (☎ 0994 59 07 75. Breakfast included. Singles €55; doubles €78. AmEx/MC/V.) From the train station, walk left after the bridge into the old city to reach **Albergo Sorrentino ❷**, P. Fontana, 7. Most of its lackluster rooms overlook the sea. Some solo travelers might feel uncomfortable in the untouristed fishing harbor, but an 11pm curfew curtails late-night outings. (☎ 0994 70 74 56. Singles €20, with bath €28; doubles €26/€38. Cash only.)

Taranto's prosperous fishing industry fuels a seafood-heavy local cuisine; fish dishes here are plentiful and inexpensive. Try *cozze* (mussels) in basil and olive oil or spaghetti with *vongole* (clams). **🔊Queen ❷**, V. di Cesare, 20-22, offers delectable seafood, local specialties, and impeccable service. The €12 *menù* is offered the entire day and includes wine. Though the selection changes daily, the ace is the Queen pizza (€5) with everything on it. (☎ 0994 59 10 11. Beer from €1. *Primi* €2.50, *secondi* €3.60-6.70. Evening cover €1.30. Open M-Sa 7:30am-midnight.) At **🔊Nautilus ❷**, V. Virgilio, 2, find a feast for the senses: savor subtly flavored seafood dishes inside a gleaming white dining room with expansive seaside views. (☎ 0994 53 55 38. *Primi* €8-10.50, *secondi* €9.50-13. Open noon-2pm and 8pm-1am. AmEx/MC/V.) **Panificio due Mari,** between P. Garibaldi and the swinging bridge at V. Matteotti, 16, is the place to chow on sandwiches, pizza, and fresh bread baked daily. (Open daily 7am-1:30am.) Another option for quick eats is the **market** in P. Castello, which sells fish and fruit. (Open daily 7am-1:30pm.)

👁 SIGHTS

The **🔊Museo Nazionale Archeologico,** currently at Palazzo Pantaleo, Lungomare V. Emanuele II, houses the world's largest terra-cotta figurine collection, in addition to ancient pots, sculptures, mosaics, jewelry, and coins. (☎ 0994 71 84 92. Permanent address C. Umberto I, 41, in P. Garibaldi. Open M-F 8:30am-1:30pm and 2:30-7:30pm, Sa 9am-midnight. €2, under 18 or over 65 free.) From P. Garibaldi, a swinging **bridge,** built in 1887, hangs over the shipping canal. The first of its kind, it opens sideways to let ships through. The bridge still swings, and it's fun to watch—check the daily schedule of opening times posted on either side.

🎵 ENTERTAINMENT

V. d'Aquino pulses every night between 6pm and midnight; from throngs of trendy kids to bands of promenading grandmothers, people of all types stroll its walkways. **Caffè Italiano,** on V. d'Aquino, is livelier than most establishments, thanks largely to its (unofficially) public bathrooms. (Open 6pm-midnight.) The **Pizzeria & Birreria,** at the corner of P. Garibaldi and V. d'Aquino, is packed until 1am with customers wolfing down gigantic hot sandwiches. A quieter atmosphere can be found on the **Lungomare Vittorio,** where people cluster on benches to chat or munch cones of gelato. In P. Garibaldi, the Italian Navy band, in peak form, accompanies the lowering of the flag at sundown. Taranto's **Holy Week Festival,** beginning the Sunday before Easter, has a ceremony steeped in medieval Spanish ritual; sheet-covered men carry papier-mâché statues and parade to all the churches.

BASILICATA

Mountainous and largely land-locked, Basilicata never attained the strategic importance of neighboring coastal regions, nor the economic prominence characteristically associated with booming port cities; as such, Basilicata is a land where foreigners rarely venture. Fortunately for those who do make the trip, its fascinating prehistoric caves, breathtaking vistas, colorful local culture, and smooth beaches retain a raw, untapped beauty. Basilicata is truly the hidden gem of Italy, its value known only to its inhabitants and astute Italian vacationers.

MATERA   ☎ 0835

Matera's claim to fame are the *sassi,* ancient homes carved directly in the rocky terrain. Until 1952, when the government declared the 7000-year-old homes unsafe and unsanitary, locals still inhabited these residences without the benefits of electricity or running water. Today, 50 years after the cliffs' inhabitants were moved to government-built suburban housing, trendsetters and professional firms started occupying *sassi,* sparking a wave of renovations. As restaurants, lavish hotels, and office buildings slowly creep into the cliffs, the once dismal dwellings have become quite swank. Thus, life comes anew to Matera, so beautiful and so oddly captivating that the city calls itself "The Heritage of Humanity." Riding this promise of enthusiasm and possibility, Matera has become the second-largest city in Basilicata, even earning the nickname "Capital of Nowhere." Despite the relative isolation of the city and the fact that it is the only provincial capital in Italy not connected by FS trains, Matera's extraordinary sights, inexpensive accommodations, and engaging local culture make a visit worth the effort.

▐ TRANSPORTATION

The train station, **Matera Centrale,** is in P. Matteotti. **FAL trains** run to Altamura (30min., M-Sa 13 per day 6:40am-8:59pm, €1.81) and Bari (1½hr., M-Sa 13 per day 6:03am-8:24pm, €3.62). **FAL buses** leave from P. Matteotti for Bari on Sunday (1¾hr., 6 per day 6:15am-2:05pm, €3.62), when train service is suspended. Buy tickets at the train station. **SITA buses** (☎0835 38 50 70) leave from P. Matteotti and run to: Altamura (30min., 3 per day 1:10-6:30pm, €1.29); Metaponto (1hr., 5 per day 8:15am-5:30pm, €2.63); and Taranto (1½hr., 6 per day M-Sa 6am-5pm, €5.16). There is reduced service on Sunday. Buy bus tickets at the ticket office across the street.

▐ ▐ ORIENTATION AND PRACTICAL INFORMATION

Matera's grottoes split into two small valleys that overlook a deep canyon in the **Parco della Murgia Materana.** From the **train** and **bus stations** at **Piazza Matteotti,** head down **Via Roma** or **Via Minzoni** to **Piazza V. Veneto,** the heart of the city and the entrance to the *sassi.* **Sasso Barisano,** the modern area located in the first valley, is straight ahead, through the stairway across from the Banco di Napoli. To reach the cavernous **Sasso Caveoso,** continue to the right on **Via del Corso,** which bears right into **Via Ridola,** and descend left at **Piazza Pascoli.** The more important *chiese rupestri* (rock churches) are on the other side of the ridge, opposite the Sasso Caveoso. The tourist office and most hotels offer a detailed map of the *sassi*.

The **APT Tourist Office** is at V. de Viti de Marco, 9. From the station, walk down V. Roma and take the second left. (☎ 0835 33 19 83, fax 33 34 52. Open M and Th 9am-1pm and 4-6:30pm, Tu-W and F-Sa 9am-1pm.) The city also has an **information office,** on V. Madonna della Virtù, the road along the ridge in the *sassi* district. (Open daily Apr.-Sept. 9:30am-12:30pm and 3:30-6:30pm.) In case of **emergency,** call ☎ 113 or an **ambulance** (☎ 0835 24 32 70). The **police** (☎ 0835 33 42 22) are on V. Minzoni. **Ospedale Madonna Delle Grazie** (☎ 0835 24 31) is on Cda. Cattedra Ambulante. For **Internet,** head to **Qui PC Net,** on V. Margherita, to the left of the Banco di Napoli. (☎ 0835 34 61 12. €1.40 per 15min., €4 per hr. Open daily 8am-1pm and 5-8:30pm.) The **post office** is on V. del Corso, off P. Veneto. (☎ 0835 25 71 11. Open M-F 8am-6:30pm, Sa 8am-noon.) **Postal Code:** 75100.

⌂ ACCOMMODATIONS

▓ **Sassi Hostel (HI),** V. S. Giovanni Vecchio, 89 (☎ 0835 33 10 09; hotelsassi@virgilio.it). From the station, take V. Minzoni to P. Veneto and V. S. Biagio to the church, where signs leading to the hostel appear on the right. Anything but primitive, the rooms in this well-run hostel are renovated *sassi*. Guests are invited to cavort amid prehistoric caves and fulfill their troglodyte fantasies. English, Spanish, and French spoken. All rooms have bath. Sheets and towels included. Curfew midnight. Dorms €16. AmEx/MC/V. ❷

Locanda di San Martino, V. S. Martino, 22 (☎ 0835 25 66 00; www.locandadisanmar-tino.it), offers the inimitable experience of sleeping inside what once was a neolithic temple. Located in the *sassi*, these luxurious rooms have TV, phone, A/C, and stylish bath. Single €65-105; doubles and suites €80-120. AmEx/MC/V. ❺

Il Piccolo Albergo, V. De Sariis, 11 (☎/fax 0835 33 02 01). Heading down V. Roma, take the 3rd left onto V. Lucana; V. De Sariis is on the left. 11 rooms have high ceilings and gorgeous wooden floors. Conveniently located with full amenities, including bath, TV, minibar, and A/C. Singles €55; doubles €80. AmEx/MC/V. ❹

Albergo Roma, V. Roma, 62 (☎ 0835 33 39 12), by tourist office. Currently undergoing renovations; reopens in 2005. 2004 prices: singles €21; doubles €36. ❷

Hotel San Domenico, V. Roma, 15 (☎/fax 0835 25 63 09). Über-modern decor and a swank, upscale bar lend a cosmopolitan atmosphere (the elevator alone speaks 3 languages). Convenient location. Wheelchair accessible, with A/C, TV, phone, and huge bath. Breakfast included. Singles €90; doubles €120. AmEx/MC/V. ❺

⎙ FOOD

Though small, Matera has managed to concoct several local specialties worth sampling, including *favetta con cicore* (soup of beans, celery, chicory, and croutons, mixed in olive oil) and *frittata di spaghetti* (pasta with anchovies, eggs, bread crumbs, garlic, and oil). Experience true Materan grit with *pane di grano duro*, made with extra-hard, local wheat, available at **Divella,** V. de Viti de Marco, 6, off V. Roma. (☎ 0839 33 18 64. Open M-Sa 8:15am-1:30pm and 5-8:30pm.) Fruit can be found at the **open-air market** off V. Minzoni near P. Veneto (open daily 9am-1pm).

▓ **Trattoria del Corso,** V. La Vista, 12 (☎ 0835 33 28 92), off P. Veneto near V. Manzoni. This local favorite serves up fantastic Basilicatan specialties and the kind of authentic charm you won't find at its pricier counterparts. *Primi* €4.50-6, *secondi* €6-9, cover €1.50. Open M-Th and Sa-Su noon-3pm and 7-11:30pm. AmEx/MC/V. ❸

PUGLIA, BASILICATA, CALABRIA

Ristorante Don Matteo, V. S. Biagio, 12 (☎0835 67 45 42), off P. Veneto, to the left of the *sassi*. Waiters greet diners at the bottom of the cliff-carved staircase. The nuanced flavors and the delicate *antipasto fritella contadina* are worth the less subtle prices. Casual dress, while welcome, may look out of place. *Antipasti* €10. *Primi* €8, *secondi* €10. Dessert €5. Open daily 1:30-3:30pm and 8:30-10:30pm. AmEx/MC/V. ●

Ristorante Osteria Arti e Mestieri La Stalla, V. Rosario, 73 (☎0835 24 04 55). From P. Veneto, take V. S. Biagio until the archway on the right; walk through, down the stairs, and follow signs to the restaurant. The perfect lunch break after trekking up those *sassi* stairs. Cool, rustic dining room. *Primi* €3-6, *secondi* €6-9. Open 11:30am-4pm and 7pm-12:30am. AmEx/MC/V. ●

Ristorante Pizzeria La Terrazzina, V. S. Giuseppe, 7 (☎0835 33 25 03), off P. Veneto, near Banco di Napoli. Savor immense portions of local delicacies in this beautifully renovated cave that doubles as wine cellar. Pizza €2.50-8. *Primi* €5-6, *secondi* €7-8. Cover €1.50. Open M and W-Su noon-3:30pm and 7pm-12:30am. AmEx/MC/V. ●

Trattoria Lucana, V. Lucana, 48 (☎0835 33 61 17), off V. Roma. Begin with the *orecchiette alla materana* (ear-shaped pasta with tomatoes and fresh vegetables; €5.86) and continue with the house specialty, *bocconcini alla lucana* (thinly sliced veal with mushrooms; €6.70). Service 10%. Cover €1. Open M-Sa 12:30-3pm and 8-10:30pm. Closed early Sept. AmEx/MC/V. ●

Gran Caffè, P. Veneto, 6. Behind an unassuming storefront lies a huge selection of pastries and fresh bread. No seating. Grab a sandwich, soda, and *cannoli* for less than €5 and enjoy them on the piazza's benches. Open daily 6am-11pm. Cash only. ●

Carpe Diem, V. Minzoni, 32/4 (☎0835 24 03 59), between the station and P. Veneto. Offers *tavola calda,* a stylishly mirrored interior, and focaccia with assorted toppings (€8 per loaf). Excellent sandwiches under €2. Open daily 7am-noon. Cash only. ●

◉ SIGHTS

ON THE WAY TO THE SASSI. The 7000-year-old homes lie in a maze of stone pathways, and a detailed map is necessary to negotiate them properly. To enter the heart of *sassi* zone, start from P. Veneto and head onto V. del Corso; immediately past the Chiesa di S. Francesco d'Assisi, turn left into P. Sedile. From there, V. Duomo leads to the beautifully restored **Puglian-Romanesque duomo.** Its towering spire and carved outer portals are certainly worth pausing to admire. Inside, the 15th-century carved choir stalls are just as intricate. *(Open daily 8am-1pm and 3:30-6pm.)* Retracing the path back to the Chiesa di S. Francesco d'Assisi, V. Ridola leads past the skeleton-and-skull-covered facade of the **Chiesa del Purgatorio.** The **Museo Ridola** looms on the right and is home to some of the region's finest archaeological treasures. Don't miss the exhibit on early 20th-century excavation techniques or the collection of prehistoric and Classical art housed in a 17th-century monastery. *(V. Ridola, 24. ☎0835 31 12 39. Open M 9am-2pm, Tu-Su 9am-8pm. €2.50, students 18-24 €1.25, under 18 or over 65 free.)* See human nature at its finest in the Museo Della Tortura, whose age-old implements were used for stretching, compacting, draining, and otherwise contorting the human body in order to break the spirit. *(V. S. Rocco, 147. Outside P. Veneto, down V. S. Biagio, and along the opposite side of the sassi. ☎0835 25 64 84. Open 9am-1pm and 3-8pm. €3, students €2, children €1.50.)*

THE SASSI. Little is known about the people who first built and inhabited the *sassi.* The dwellings themselves are carved in several styles from the soft limestone calcarenite. The oldest, inhabited around 7000 years ago, are the crumbling structures that line **Sasso Barisano** (along V. Addozio). The valley east of the duomo around **Sasso Caveoso** contains the second type of *sassi,* the simply carved nooks dating from around 2000 BC. The most elaborate *sassi*, and, at a little more than 1000 years old, some of the most recent constructions, are clustered near V. Bruno Buozzi (off V. Madonna delle Virtù near the duomo). Most of the 6th-century *chiese rupestri* (rock churches) remain unmodified, with remnants of some 12th-century frescoes. Until 1952, groups of up to 12 people still lived in these windowless caves, often sharing their dwellings with the family livestock. Local children roam the *sassi* offering tours of the caves to curious visitors; the organized ones are more enlightening. Try **Tour Service Matera,** P. Veneto, 42 (☎ 0835 33 46 33). For a comprehensive, self-guided tour, buy a book at any magazine stand. In the *sassi*, the **Cooperative Amici Del Turistica** offers information and tours in English, French, German, and Italian. The **Sassi by Night** tour is a good one. *(V. Fiorentini, 30. ☎ 0835 33 03 10. Open in spring and summer daily 8am-1pm and 4-9pm, in fall and winter 9am-noon and 4-7pm. €10 per person for groups of 4 or more.)* A public bathroom (€0.50) is near the bottom of the *sassi* area. *(Open daily 9am-6pm.)*

CHURCHES... WITH SASSI. Rock-hewn churches periodically punctuate the *sassi* along V. Bruno Buozzi. From P. V. Veneto, walk past the Museo Ridola on V. Ridola and bear left until reaching the end of the P. Pascoli; descend the stairs and head straight, until hitting V. Bruno Buozzi on the left. Or follow signs reading "Turistico Itinerario" and "Convicino di S. Antonio" from the bottom of V. Bruno Buozzi. Follow the path along the cliffs to reach the churches of **San Pietro Caveoso, Santa Maria d'Idris,** and **Santa Lucia alle Malve,** which preserve beautiful 11th-century Byzantine frescoes in their caves. *(Open daily 9:30am-1:30pm and 2:30-7pm. 1 church €2.10, 4 churches €4.20, all 7 churches €5.20.)* A nearby *sasso* is furnished as it was when 10 people and two horses shared its two small rooms. Tours of the cave are available in English. *(☎/fax 0835 31 01 18. Open daily 9am-9:30pm. €1.20.)* Farther along lies the multilevel complex of **Madonna delle Virtù** and **S. Nicola dei Greci,** which contains ancient frescoes, houses, and the frantic modern sculpture of famed artist Leoncillo. Informational tours are offered in English. *(Open daily 9am-9pm. €2.50, students €1.25.)*

PARCO DELLA MURGIA METERANA. The park straddles the ridge across the canyon from the *sassi* and offers some of the area's best **hiking.** The park entrance is off Str. Statale, down V. Annunziatella and then V. Marconi. The terrain, lush in some patches and bare in others, is odd and intriguing; over 150 rock churches dot the landscape, in addition to the strange *jazzi*, caves built by shepherds to shelter their flocks. The park was recently expanded, creating even more hiking options. The tourist office has information on private tour guides.

🎵 ENTERTAINMENT

At the end of June and beginning of July, Matera celebrates the ⬛**Festa di Santa Maria della Bruna,** which features numerous musical and cultural events, nightly fireworks displays, and open-air markets selling everything from power tools to psychic readings by exceedingly gifted parakeets. The revelry culminates with the **Assalto al Carro** on July 2. The *sassi* house an **International Sculpture Exhibition** from June to October in the churches of Madonna delle Virtù and San Nicola dei Greci.

🔼 DAYTRIPS FROM MATERA

ALTAMURA
Altamura is on the FAL line between Bari (1hr., 14 per day 6:03am-10:02pm, €2.63) and Matera (40min., 15 per day 5:08am-8:59pm, €1.70). Viale Regina Margherita runs from the station to the old city, where it becomes V. Federico di Svevia. Just after the old city,

V. Federico di Svevia splits into V. Pietro Colletta and V. Matera. The hospital (☎ 0803 108 11) is on Viale Regina Margherita; for the medical clinic, call ☎ 0803 10 82 01. The carabinieri (☎ 0830 14 10 14) are in P. S. Teresa, down V. N. Melodia from P. Duomo.

The urban center of Puglia's inland farm country, Altamura boasts a fantastic **Romanesque cathedral** and some rather unusual archaeological finds. The cathedral, located in P. Duomo in the old city, is immediately captivating with its rose window and what are perhaps the most exquisite and intricately decorated church portals in Puglia. Scenes from the life of Christ surround the main carving of the picturesque yet lugubrious *Cenacolo* (Last Supper). The Altamura **Archaeological Museum** displays an eclectic collection of relics from Greek and prehistoric tombs. At the entrance into the old city, turn left and continue on the road until signs for the museum appear. *(Open daily 9am-7:30pm. €2.20.)*

GRAVINA

Gravina is best reached from Altamura by FAL train (10min., 18 per day 7:08am-10:14pm, €1.03), while FS trains run to rural spots in the area. Museo Ettore Pomarici Santomasi is on V. Museo, 20. (☎ 080 325 10 21; www.fondazionesantomasi.it.) Open Tu-Su 9:30am-1pm. For the carabinieri, call ☎ 0803 26 42 72. The Ospedale Civile is on V. San Domenico (☎ 112 or 0803 10 81 11).

Gravina takes its name from the long, steep gorge over which it perches. This stunning ravine is one of the town's main highlights, as are the many historic, architecturally diverse buildings. Both train stations are at the end of the **Corso Aldo Moro** (on the other side of the tracks from the FAL station), which runs to the old city. The corso becomes **Via V. Veneto**, which turns into the tangled mass of roads that comprise most of the old city. Head downhill to reach P. Notar Domenico and the **Chiesa del Purgatorio,** decorated with statues of skeletons that recline with an eerie cheerfulness. The bears supporting the columns of the church represent the ancient dominance of the Roman Orsini family, once feudal lords of Gravina. Next to the church in a large palazzo, the archaeological museum **Ettore Pomarici Santomasi** huddles unobtrusively. Free admission includes tours of the collection of Lucanian grave relics, including some huge Greek *amphorae*. Next to the stations, the facade of **Chiesa di Madonna delle Grazie** bears a massive relief of an eagle spreading its wings. On C. Aldo Moro, heading away from the stations, turn left down V. Fontana La Stella to the stone bridge leading across the ravine for a spectacular view of the cliffs and the town.

METAPONTO   ☎ 0835

Much of Metaponto's charm is rooted in its split personality: while lonely Greek ruins set a somber and peaceful tone, powder-soft sands and the gleaming Ionian sea entice sensory revelry. Plan carefully, as Metaponto can feel like a ghost town during much of the year. However, from mid-July through August, campsites swell with city-dwellers escaping to the sea. The ideal time to visit is in July or September, when there are neither too many nor too few people around.

🚆🛈 TRANSPORTATION AND PRACTICAL INFORMATION. Metaponto is best reached by train. **Trains** run to: Bari (2hr., 11 per day 5:06am-9:34pm, €10.63); Reggio di Calabria (5hr., 12 per day 12:24am-7:07pm, €25.20); Rome (6hr., 9 per day 12:30am-9:34pm, €32.28); Salerno (3½hr., 7 per day 12:30am-5:35pm, €10.10); and Taranto (40min., 23 per day 5:06am-11:45pm, €3.60). Blue **SITA buses** run from the train station to Matera (1hr., 5 per day 7:05am-4:30pm, €2.63). Local Chiruzzi buses (☎ 0835 54 33 50) serve the immediate area. Bus #1 runs between the train station, the museum, and the *lido* (13 per day 5:05am-7:55pm, €0.70). Bicycle rental is available at the beach.

The town has four sections: **scalo** (train station), **borgo** (museum), **lido** (beach and hotels), and the Greek **ruins**. While *scalo, borgo*, and the ruins are all 1-2km apart, the *lido* is farther away. Both the beach and the ruins can be reached by a short bus ride from the station. In case of **emergency,** call ☎ 0835 74 19 97. The **post office** is near the Museo Archeologico, a 10min. walk straight ahead from the train station. (Open M-Sa 8am-1:15pm.) **Postal Code:** 75010.

▒ ▒ ACCOMMODATIONS AND FOOD. Most of Metaponto's accommodations line the beach, and fall into two categories: costly or camping. **Kammel Camping ❶,** V. Lido, 1, is at the end of V. Magna Grecia. The lively rhythms of the campground's *discoteca* invade the silence of the adjacent national forest. The site also provides tennis courts, game rooms, bars, a swimming pool, and a beach shuttle. (☎ 0835 74 19 26; www.kammel.it. Open July 21-Aug. 25. €8.50 per person, €8.50 per tent, €3.50 per car. Electricity €3.50. AmEx/MC/V.) **Camping Village Internazionale ❶,** on V. Magna Grecia, is less manicured than some of the surrounding sites, but still a good value. Bungalows are available for groups of four and five at a weekly rate. (☎ 0835 74 19 16. Open late May-Sept. €5-8 per person, €3-4 for children ages 2-6, €6-8 per tent, €3-5 per parking space. Bungalows range €259-724 per week. Prices vary seasonally.) Finding a cheap hotel on the *lido* isn't likely. A good value is **Hotel Residence Kennedy ❹,** Viale Jonio, 1, just off of P. Nord. Good-sized rooms have bath, A/C, TV, and fridge; some have kitchen facilities or a balcony. (☎/fax 0835 74 19 60; www.hrkennedy.it. Breakfast included. Singles €48-61; doubles €65-80. AmEx/MC/V.) Another option is the **Hotel Turismo ❹,** V. delle Ninfe, 5, with nice views outdoors but indoor decor as bland and impersonal as its name. All rooms have bath, TV, and A/C. (☎ 0835 74 19 17. Singles and doubles €68. AmEx/ MC/V.) **L'Oasi Ristorante Pizzeria ❸,** V. Lido, 47, is a good choice for a beachside lunch break, with tasty, cheap seafood and pizza. (☎ 0835 74 18 83. *Primi* €4-5, *secondi* €5-6. 4-course *menù* €16. Open daily noon-3pm and 7pm-midnight. MC/ V.) **Alimentari di Maria,** a mini-market off P. Nord, makes tasty *panini* for under €2. (Open daily 7am-6pm.) The scent of freshly baked bread entices hungry sunbathers to stop by **Macelleria 2000** (not to be confused with Mercato 2000), a butcher shop near the beach entrance at the end of P. Nord. Its tasty sandwiches or succulent roasted chicken (€5.50) can satisfy any hunger pang.

◙ SIGHTS. Most people go to Metaponto for the **beach,** and for good reason: the sand is as soft as sifted flour and the water a glittering turquoise. The drawback, of course, is massive congestion in the summer. If the crowds become unbearable, catch bus #1 to the *borgo* and see the area where the Greek mathematician **Pythagoras,** inventor of the Pythagorean theorem, taught until his death in 479 BC, and where Spartacus staged his famous slave revolt. Or stop by the **Museo Archeologico,** which displays magnificent jewelry, vases, and figurines—most from nearby ruins. Past the post office and down a lonely country road lie the ruins of the **Doric Tempio di Apollo Licius** and a **Greek theater** from the 6th century BC. It's another 5km to the **Tavole Palatine,** the ruins of a Greek temple of Hera and the best-preserved temple in Metaponto. (☎ 0831 74 53 27. Open M 9am-2pm, Tu-Su 9am-8pm. €2.50, ages 18-26 €1.25, under 18 or over 60 free.)

MARATEA ☎ 0973

A sprawling collection of small, tranquil towns on the water, Maratea is the only portion of Basilicata that touches the Tyrrhenian Sea. The natural landscape, running 30km along the coastline, boasts rock and sand beaches, creeks and caves, and pines, oaks, and olive trees. Wild rosemary, myrtle, and other blooms dot the surrounding mountains.

📠🔌 TRANSPORTATION AND PRACTICAL INFORMATION. Trains (☎ 097 387 69 06; ticket office open 7:15am-noon, 3:40-6pm, and 9-11pm) run from Stazione Maratea to: Cosenza (1¾hr., 17 per day 5:36am-10:41pm, €6.10); Naples (3hr., 13 per day 5:56am-11:10pm, €8.99); and Reggio di Calabria (3-4hr., 14 per day 5:36am-10:41pm). Somewhat erratic local buses run between the station, Fiumicello, and Porto. Though the main stop is down the road from the train station, don't hesitate to flag down a bus—they usually stop anywhere. Maratea Porto (4km) and Fiumicello (2km) can also be reached on foot from the train station. Exit the station, turn right, and continue down V. Profiti under the bridge. Turn left down the hill to Fiumicello. Porto is down the same road. Signs appear frequently along the way. From mid-May to October, Porto Turistico di Maratea (☎ 097 387 73 07), in Maratea Porto, rents out motorboats for €77.50. Cabmar taxis (☎ 097 387 00 84 or 033 790 15 79) are recommended if arriving at Maratea Station in the evening.

The **AAST Tourist Office,** V. Santa Venere, 40, is in P. Gesù, down the hill on V. Santa Venere. The staff has info on hotels and summer events. (☎ 097 387 69 08. Open daily in summer 8am-2pm and 3-8pm, in winter 8am-2pm as well as Tu and Th 3-6pm.) **Banco di Napoli,** V. S. Venere, 61, has an **ATM.** (Open M-F 8:35am-1:30pm and 2:50-3:55pm.) **Internet** is available at **Info Point,** V. S. Venere, 8/A, in Fiumicello. (☎ 0973 87 17 04. €5 for 30min., €9 per hr. Open daily 8:30am-1pm and 5-8pm.) A **post office** is in Maratea Porto, V. Porto, 27. (☎ 0973 87 67 11. Open M-Sa 8am-1:15pm.) **Postal Code:** 85046.

🍴🛏 ACCOMMODATIONS AND FOOD. The closer a hotel is to the water, the more expensive it is. Reservations are recommended in summer, particularly in August. Closest to the station and about a 10min. walk from the beach, **Hotel Fiorella ❸,** V. Santa Venere, 21, is on the hill on the right entering Fiumicello. The bus from the train station passes by the hotel; ask the driver where to exit. To walk from the station, continue down the curving V. Profiti and then take the stairs heading down on the left; follow to the bottom. The hotel has long white hallways and expansive rooms at a decent price. (☎ 0973 87 69 21, fax 87 65 14. July-Aug. singles €40; doubles €60. Sept.-June singles €30; doubles €50. Half pension €50-60, full pension €60-70. AmEx/MC/V.) **Hotel Settebello ❺,** V. Fiumicello, 52, is on the beach. Rooms have bath, shower, phone, and satellite TV; most also have a large seaside balcony. (☎ 0973 87 62 77; www.costadimaratea.com/settebello. Breakfast included. July-Aug. singles €85; doubles €112-115. Sept.-June singles €60-70; doubles €78-94. Half pension €57-84, full pension €70-97. Rooms with view €8-9 extra.) In Maratea Castrocucco, 8km down the coastal road from Maratea's port, **Camping Maratea ❶,** Località Castrocucco, 72, is both close to the sea and popular, so reserve early in summer. (☎ 097 387 75 80 or 387 16 80, fax 387 16 99. €4-8 per person, €6-10 with tent.) **Ristorante Le Fenice ❸,** V. Fiumicello, 13, past the tourist office toward the port, presents wonderfully fresh seafood (*tagliatelle al sugo di pesce* €8) and *al fresco* dining between bamboo screens. (☎ 0973 87 68 00. *Primi* from €6, *secondi* from €5.50. Open noon-3pm and 7-11:30pm. MC/V.)

🔆 SIGHTS. Maratea Centro is closest to the train station and has many secrets worth discovering, but if you came to Maratea to see the sea, **Fiumicello** (Santavenere) and **Maratea Porto** are closer to the water. Fiumicello melts down to the hillside in the form of small shops and restaurants along V. Santavenere until tumbling into the sea over a gorgeous beach. Maratea Porto's cove houses both modern boats and old fishing vessels, as well as an array of restaurants and shops. Watching over the coast from **Monte Biagio,** a 22m statue of *Il Redentore* (Christ the Redeemer) has stood with arms outstretched in benediction since 1963.

CALABRIA

Sometimes called the last great oasis of the Mediterranean, Calabria is an undiscovered land of inspiring history and unspoiled natural beauty. Though one of Italy's most under-developed regions, it is also the most under-appreciated. Two and a half millennia ago, when the northern cities that sniff at her today were small backwaters, Calabria was of worldwide importance, home to leading philosophers, artists, and athletes. Fortunately for local pride, traces of this illustrious past remain in abundance, from the Greek ruins at Locri to the Norman Castle at Cosenza. Many of the region's excavation sites remain untouched since antiquity, providing a view of the way the ancients lived—and a marked contrast to the more developed regions that have paved over their Greek and Roman heritage. The region also sports some of Italy's most beautiful beaches.

REGGIO DI CALABRIA   ☎ 0965

Though many regard the area as merely a departure-point for Sicily, Reggio and its environs actually comprise some of the finest landscapes in Italy. The provincial capital of Reggio di Calabria was one of the earliest and proudest Greek settlements on the Italian mainland, but it slid into neglect and disarray following centuries of raids and natural disasters. After a devastating 1908 earthquake, a new city arose from the rubble, crowded with designer stores and turn-of-the-century palaces but somewhat devoid of historical interest or charm. More inspired settings are very close at hand on the Tyrrhenian Coast to the north and the Ionian Sea to the east. The nearby towns of Scilla and Locri offer one of Italy's most attractive beaches and some fine archaeological treasures, respectively.

⌐ TRANSPORTATION

Flights: Aeroporto dello Stretto (☎ 0965 64 05 17), 5km south of town. Orange buses #113, 114, 115, 125, or 131 from P. Garibaldi outside Stazione Centrale (€0.90). Service to **Bologna, Florence, Milan, Rome,** and **Turin.**

Trains: Reggio's main train station is **Stazione Centrale** (☎ 0965 27 427), on P. Garibaldi at southern end of town. To: **Cosenza** (2½hr., 16 per day 12:05am-7:36pm, €11.60); **Naples** (4½hr., 14 per day 12:05am-10:25pm, €21.59); **Rome** (8hr., 14 per day 12:05am-10:25pm, €40.44); **Scilla** (30min., 18 per day, €2.10); **Tropea** (2hr., 11 per day 5:15am-8:40pm, €6.49).

Ferries: From the port, at the northern end of the city, boats and hydrofoils service **Messina** as well as the **Aeolian Islands** (Lipari, Salina, Vulcano). **FS** (☎ 0965 81 76 75), all the way to the left, against the water entering the port, shares hydrofoil service with **Ustica** (☎ 090 66 25 06 or 36 40 44), to the right of FS. FS office open daily 6:30am-8:15pm; Ustica's hours vary. **NGI** (☎ 335 842 77 84), across from Onda Marina bar to the right of the port entrance. Open M-F 12:20am-10:20pm, Sa 12:20am-8:20pm. **Meridiano** (☎ 0965 81 04 14) is on the corner of the water nearest the port entrance. Ferries run M-Sa 2:10am-11:50pm. Reduced service Su.

■ ❼ ORIENTATION AND PRACTICAL INFORMATION

Reggio's main artery is **Corso Garibaldi,** which runs parallel to the sea and to all the major sights. Facing away from **Stazione Centrale,** walk straight through **Piazza Garibaldi** to C. Garibaldi; a left turn leads to the heart of town. At the end of C. Garibaldi and down V. L. G. Zerbi is Reggio's **port,** from which hydrofoils and boats run to Messina and the Aeolian Islands. One block to the left of the station, the twin roads **Corso Vittorio Emanuele III** and **Viale Matteotti** trace the *lungomare*. City buses run continuously up and down C. Garibaldi and northward along the two roads. At its center, C. Garibaldi becomes a pedestrian route, perfect for an evening *passeggiata* past the many bars and designer outlets that line the street.

Tourist Office: APT booth (☎0965 271 20), at the central train station. Free **maps** as well as transportation and hotel information. Open M-Sa 8am-2pm and 2:30-8pm. **Main office,** V. Roma, 3 (☎0965 211 71 or 0965 89 25 12), has a wider variety of information and some English-speaking staff. Open M-F in the morning and M and W afternoons. **Branches:** airport (☎0965 64 32 91) and C. Garibaldi, 327 (☎0965 89 20 12). Open similar hours.

Currency Exchange: Banca Nazionale del Lavoro, C. Garibaldi, 431 (☎0965 85 11). Open M-F 8:20am-1:20pm and 2:35-4:05pm. **ATMs** line C. Garibaldi.

Emergency: ☎113. **Carabinieri** (☎112). **Police** ☎0965 539 91, on C. Garibaldi, near Stazione Centrale.

Pharmacy: Farmacia Centrale, C. Garibaldi, 435 (☎0965 33 23 32), is open M-F 8:30am-1pm and 5-8:30pm. **Farmacia Fata Morgana,** C. Garibaldi, 327 (☎0965 240 13), has the same hours.

Hospital: Ospedale Riuniti (☎0965 391 11), on V. Melacrino.

Internet: Sweet@Web, V. Giudecca, 35 (☎0965 211 34), with another branch at V. de Nava, 142 (☎0965 239 02). €3.60 per hr. Open M-F 10am-2pm and 4:30-8:30pm, Sa-Su 5-9pm. Discount for students and foreigners.

Post Office: V. Miraglia, 14 (☎0965 31 52 68). Bear left from P. Italia on C. Garibaldi. Open M-F 8:30am-6:30pm, Sa 8:30am-12:30pm. **Postal Code:** 89100.

ACCOMMODATIONS

Hotel Lido, V. 3 Settembre, 6 (☎0965 250 01, fax 89 93 93), near Stazione Lido and close to the beach. Offers modern rooms with unique decorations, each with large bath, A/C, TV, phone, and hair dryer. Reserve ahead in summer. Singles €40; doubles €80; triples and quads €100. AmEx/MC/V. ❹

Albergo Noel, V. Genoese Zerbi, 13 (☎0965 89 09 65, fax 33 00 44). With faux-wood paneling and loud bedspreads, the rooms are somewhat tacky, but location is the draw here—the port, beach, and museum are within blocks. Wheelchair accessible. Reserve ahead. Singles €27-30; doubles €37-40; triples €47-50. Cash only. ❸

Hotel Diana, V. Diego Vitrioli, 12 (☎0965 89 15 22) off C. Garibaldi and across from the duomo. While some of the rooms have amenities like TV, phone, and A/C, others are less appealing and you may find electrical, plumbing, or insect problems. Make sure to see a room before deciding to spend the night. Reserve 1 month ahead for Aug. Singles €27.50; doubles €55, with A/C €65. Cash only. ❸

FOOD

Chefs in Reggio serve *spaghetti alla calabrese* (with pepper sauce), *capocollo* (a ham spiced with local hot peppers), and *pesce spada* (local harpoon-hunted swordfish). Stock up at Dì per Dì, a **supermarket** opposite the train station on C. Garibaldi. (Open daily 8:30am-1:30pm and 5-8:30pm.) Bars along C. Garibaldi often offer baked goods, so sweeten the day with a few of the region's beloved *biscotti*.

Cordon Bleu, C. Garibaldi, 230 (☎0965 33 24 47). Despite chandelier lighting, shining marble interior, and a haughty French *nom,* this versatile joint serves cheap *tavola calda* goodies from €1. *Cannoli siciliani* €1.80. Upstairs seating €0.50 cover. Open daily 6:30am-11pm; food served 11am-9pm. MC/V. ❶

Le Palme, C. V. Emanuele III (☎0965 81 00 86), serves up seafood pizzas on a palm-lined patio along the *lungomare.* Pizza €4-7. *Primi* €9, *secondi* €10. Open daily noon-3:30pm and 7:30pm-2am. MC/V. ❸

Pizzeria Rusty, V. D. Romeo (☎0965 200 12), next to the museum. Double-folded Neapolitan slices the size of tables, priced by weight (€7.75 per kg), and *tavola calda* favorites such as *arancini* (€1.30) distinguish this tiny *rosticceria* from nearby ice cream-vending bars. *Calzoni* 1.30. Open M-Tu and Th-Su 9am-1:30pm and 6pm-midnight. ❶

La Pignata, V. Demetrio Tripepi, 122 (☎0965 278 41), up V. Giutecca from C. Garibaldi. Handsome dark-wood interior and sociable waiters create the perfect atmosphere for a little luxury at a very reasonable price. *Primi* from €6, *secondi* from €9. Cover €1.50. Open M-Sa 12:30-2:30pm and 7:30-10:15pm. AmEx/MC/V. ❸

🔆 SIGHTS

The preeminence Reggio di Calabria enjoyed in antiquity as a great Greek *polis* may have passed, but the ◪**Museo Nazionale** preserves the city's historical claim to fame with one of the world's finest collections of art and artifacts from *Magna Graecia* (Greater Greece). In the first-floor galleries, a wealth of *amphorae* and *pinakes* (wine jars and votive tablets) show scenes from mythology and daily life. The floor above the gallery has a large coin collection and a 2300-year-old novelty sarcophagus shaped like a huge, sandaled foot. Downstairs, treasures formerly submerged in the Ionian Sea, such as pottery, anchors, and broken statues comprise the **Sezione Subacquea.** If the Subacquea is the centerpiece, **I Bronzi di Riace** are the crowning jewels. Rescued from the depths of the sea in 1972, the Riace Bronzes are among the best (and arguably the most valuable) ancient Greek sculptures in the world; dating from the 5th century BC, they represent two nude male warriors in stunning detail. Muscular and assured, the bronzes share gallery space with the estimable **Head of the Philosopher,** which some point to as the Greek tradition's first lifelike portrait. A display before entering the gallery documents the bronzes' restoration process. (P. de Nava, on C. Garibaldi toward the Stazione Lido. ☎0965 81 22 55. Open daily 9am-7:30pm. Closed 1st and 3rd M of the month. €4, ages 18-25 €2, under 18 or over 65 free. Cash only.)

🎮 🎵 BEACHES AND ENTERTAINMENT

As the day cools, *Reggiani* mingle on the ◪**lungomare,** a long, narrow botanical garden stretching along the seaside that Italian author d'Annunzio immortalized as the "most beautiful kilometer in all of Italy." When they want to take a dip, travelers sprawl on the beach near **Lido Comunale.** Playgrounds, an elevated boardwalk, and monuments to the city's more famous citizens dot the *lungomare,* while the quiet beauty of a sunset behind the misty blue mountains of nearby Sicily provides a final natural touch to a pleasant afternoon swim. Calabrians finish the summer with the **Festival of the Madonna della Consolazione.** The four-day festival, celebrated in mid-September, concludes with an elaborate fireworks display.

🔳 DAYTRIPS FROM REGGIO DI CALABRIA

SCILLA

Scilla is accessible from Reggio by train (30min., 20 per day, €2.10) or by bus (20min., 12 per day, €1.29). This train station does not sell tickets, so purchase a round-trip ticket from Reggio or ask at nearby bars for regional train tickets. Buy bus tickets onboard.

PUGLIA, BASILICATA, CALABRIA

Walk along the beach and listen for mermaids singing; local legend has it that merfolk still dwell off the Scillan coast. Homer immortalized the town's great cliffs in *The Odyssey* as the home of the menacing Scylla, a terrible monster with six heads, 12 feet, and a fierce temper. The mythical creature devoured many a ship that steered away from Charybdis, a hazardous whirlpool in the straits where Sicily and Italy meet. Travelers today can expect a more hospitable welcome. Only 23km from Reggio, this fishing-village-cum-resort's languorous pace and distinctive geography (it is built directly into cliffs enclosing a sandy beach) can make the real world seem far away. Except, that is, for when the meteorological oddity *Fata Morgana* creates a natural magnifying glass out of the light over the sea, making the Sicilian city of Messina appear to be floating just over the water.

Scilla's most famous cliff now supports the 17th-century **Castello Ruffo**, evidence of the town's important historical role as a control base for the Straits of Messina. The cliffs have been valuable real estate to those bent on ruling the region for over 2000 years; everyone from the Italiots to Garibaldi himself has fought to take possession. Today, there isn't much to see at the castle besides the amazing view. (Open daily 9:30am-12:30pm and 4-7:30pm. €2.50, children €1.) Just down hill, 30m from the castle, **Chiesa di Maria S. S. Immacolata** is the largest and most impressive of Scilla's many churches. An enormous altarpiece and the bronze sculptured *Stations of the Cross* cannot contend with the beauty of the landscape, but are well worth the trip uphill. In August, Scilla celebrates its patron saint with the **Festa di San Rocco** and a grand fireworks display.

If Scilla proves enticing, spend the night at the seaside **Pensione Le Sirene ❸**, V. Nazionale, 57, a clean and cozy haven with 14 large rooms, sandwiched between the station and the beach. (☎0965 75 40 19; www.svagocalabria.com/pensionelesirene. Reserve ahead in summer. A/C €3 extra, €5 extra in Aug. Singles €30-42; doubles €45-50; triples €65; quads €85.) Unlike its mythical counterpart, Scilla does not devour its guests whole—they do the devouring. Ascend the stairs to **Vertigine ❷**, P. San Rocco, 14, to consume some specialty seafood with an epic view. (☎0965 75 40 15. *Primi* from €3.60, *secondi* from €5.20. Drinks from €1.29. Open daily noon-3pm and 7:30-10pm. AmEx/MC/V.) The cheapest meals are at **Pizzeria San Francesco ❷**, V. Cristoforo Colombo, 29, along the beach. This family-run establishment prides itself on its specialty, the *pizza stefania*—see it to believe it. (☎349 326 06 70. Pizza €3.50-6. Open noon-3pm and 7pm-midnight.)

LOCRI

From Reggio, trains (2hr., 23 per day, €5) run to and from Locri on the coast.

An easy and relaxing vacation from the urban energy of Reggio, **Locri** features the very best qualities of the Ionian Coast: expansive beaches and a wealth of ancient ruins. Between Bianco and Siderno, Locri is at the center of the coast's most pleasant and explorable beaches. The long, under-populated stretches of sand and stone allow for low-key afternoons lolling in the sun. Despite its location, Locri can hardly be called a "beach town." Instead, it contains the region's government offices, lodged in the grand **Comunale** building. With flowers, trees, and benches overshadowed by a WWI memorial, central **Piazza Re Umberto** is a tranquil spot to chill with card-playing old men in plaid shirts.

Located about 5km outside of town, **Locri Epizefiri** is a remarkable expanse of ancient ruins. Crumbling foundations and supports are a haunting testament to the preeminence of the settlement Locri Antica. Visitors can explore the **Cento Camere**, thought to be the commercial district of old, the presumed bank safe of **Tempio di Zeus**, and the Ionic **Tempio di Marasa**. The highlight of the site is the hillside **theater**, quietly abandoned to an overgrowth of weeds. Originally a stage for Greek tragedies, the theater has top-notch acoustics that might move sweet-voiced visitors to give impromptu performances. Evidence of Roman occupation of the area comes in the form of lower walls, which were used to transform the venue into a gladiator pit. Entrance to the ruins is only through the nearby **museum** (☎ 0964 39 04 33), which displays objects and maps of the site. Many of the more important statues discovered in the ancient city, including *Le statue dei Dioscuri*, excavated by archaeologist Paolo Orsi, have been removed to the national museum at Reggio di Calabria. Yet the museum showcases the more inaccessible ruins, such as *necropoli* urns and mirrors. (Museum open daily 9am-7:30pm. Closed 1st and 3rd M of the month. €2, EU residents 18-25 €1, EU residents under 18 or over 65 free. Ruins aren't always open, so call ahead.) There is a **Pro Loco Tourist Office** on V. M. di Savoia, one block to the left exiting the piazza in front of the station. (Open M-Sa 8am-8pm.) **Banco di Napoli** has a 24hr. **ATM** on V. Mileto. Turn right out of the station-front piazzas, then take the first left.

THE IONIAN COAST

Trains along the Ionian Coast often have erratic schedules and multiple connections, so allow ample travel time when planning an itinerary.

From Reggio to Riace, the Ionian Coast offers miles of marvelous beaches. White sands, rocks, and dunes cater to every taste and provide a contrast to the mountains visible in the distance. Though the ancient Greeks once made these shores as crowded as modern Tropea, now it is primarily locals who frequent these waters and relish their unexploited beauty. Even the more established sites at the villages of **Bovalino Marina, Bianco,** and **Soverato** are relatively unknown.

COSENZA   ☎ 0984

One of the most important cultural and industrial centers of Calabria, Cosenza is full of intrigue. From the plundered riches that King Alaric I supposedly buried in the city's Busento River in AD 410 to its Norman castle and 12th-century duomo, Cosenza's treasures mirror its unusual history. Though usually ignored by tourists due to its inland location far from the beaches, Cosenza has plenty to offer visitors, from its charming petite *centro storico* to its thriving nightlife.

⊏ TRANSPORTATION

Trains: Stazione Cosenza (☎ 0984 39 47 46), on V. Popilia, 4km north of the city center. Ticket office open daily 6:30am-8:25pm. **FS** (☎ 1478 880 88; available 7am-9pm) runs trains to: **Naples** (4½hr., 13 per day 4:20pm-10:30pm, €14.31); **Reggio** (2½hr., 16 per day, €17.46); **Rome** (6½hr., 14 per day 4:20am-10:30pm, €28.17). **Ferrovie della Calabria** sends trains to **Camigliatello** (1½hr., 2 per day, €1.91).

Buses: Autostazione (☎ 0984 41 31 24), on V. Autostazione. Where C. Mazzini ends in P. Fera, turn right on the marked sloping street. **Ferrovie della Calabria** regional blue buses for inland destinations leave from here and the train station; buy tickets opposite train ticket window. Ticket office open daily 6am-2:20pm and 4-7:30pm. To **Camigliatello** (9 per day, €1.91) and **San Giovanni** (2hr., 10 per day, €3).

Public Transportation: All orange **city buses** stop at P. Matteotti. Tickets (€0.77) are available at any magazine kiosk (main kiosk at V. Trieste with C. Mazzini, near P. dei Bruzi) and at most *tabacchi*. Buses **#4T, 22,** and **23** serve the old city, departing from P. Bruzi and stopping in P. Prefettura (every 30min. 5:30am-11pm). Buses **#15, 16,** and **27** run between P. Matteotti and the train station (every 7min. 5am-midnight). Reduced service Su. Routes posted on yellow hanging street signs in P. Matteotti and at all bus stops. Call ☎ 800 24 24 00 for info. **A word of caution:** these yellow schedules are the only way to tell which bus stop is which. Ask the driver where your stop is.

✦🛈 ORIENTATION AND PRACTICAL INFORMATION

The **Busento River** divides the city in two: the traffic-heavy new city, north of the Busento, and the relaxed old city, south of the river. **Corso Mazzini**, the main thoroughfare and shopping center, begins near the river at **Piazza dei Bruzi**, continues through the small **Piazza Kennedy**, and ends in **Piazza Fera**. To get to C. Mazzini, hop on any bus to **Piazza Matteotti** and, facing away from the bus stop, walk a block up C. Umberto into P. dei Bruzi. The bus station is on **Via Autostazione**, to the right off P. Fera at the end of C. Mazzini, where the *corso* splits seven ways. Cosenza's *centro storico* lies across the **Ponte Mario Martiri**, three blocks to the right from P. Matteotti when facing away from P. dei Bruzi. A labyrinth of multi-level medieval stone buildings, the old city is crossed with winding "roads," many of which are merely cobblestone staircases. The only discernible street, the narrow **Corso Telesio**, begins in the petite **Piazza Valdesi**, near the Busento, and climbs to the statue of the philosopher Telesio in the immaculate **Piazza Prefettura (Piazza XV Marzo)**.

In case of **emergency**, call ☎113, the **carabinieri** (☎112), or the **police** (☎0984 254 22), in P. dei Bruzi, behind the town hall. For an **ambulance**, dial ☎0984 68 13 21, or call the **Red Cross**, V. Popilia, 35 (☎0984 40 81 16). A **pharmacy** is at P. Kennedy, 7. (☎0984 241 55. Open M-F 8:30am-1pm and 4:30-8pm, 7am-1pm and 4:30pm-1am on alternate weeks.) **Farmacia Berardelli** is at C. Mazzini, 40. (☎0984 264 52. Open M-F 8:30am-1pm and 4:30-8pm. Posts after-hours rotation.) The hospital, **Ospedale Civile dell'Annunziata** (☎0984 68 11), is on V. Felice Migliori. For free **Internet**, head to **Casa delle Culture**, C. Telesio, 98. (Open M-Sa 9am-noon and 4-7pm.) The **post office**, V. Veneto, 41 (☎0984 221 62), is at the end of V. Piave, off C. Mazzini. (Open M-F 8am-4pm, Sa 8am-12:30pm.) **Postal Code:** 87100.

🛏 ACCOMMODATIONS

To reach **Hotel Grisaro ❸**, V. Monte Santo, 6, walk one block up C. Mazzini from P. dei Bruzi, then turn left on V. Trieste. V. Monte Santo is one block up on the right, marked by a bright sign. Rooms are spacious and comfortable, with balcony, TV, and fluffy bed. (☎0984 279 52, fax 278 38. Wheelchair accessible. Reserve ahead. Singles €28.50, with bath €36; doubles €52; triples €67; quads €78. MC/V.) Slightly more luxurious is **Hotel Excelsior ❹**, P. Matteotti, 14. High-ceilinged rooms all come with A/C, TV, phone, and a well-stocked bathroom. (☎0984 743 83, fax 743 84. Breakfast included. Singles €40; doubles €60. AmEx/MC/V.)

🍴 FOOD

Cosenza is a well-fed city. Its bounty of restaurants draws on the rich mushrooms and fresh *prosciutto* of the Sila forests, plentiful fish from the sparkling Tyrrhenian Sea, and the fruit of the region's orchards. For fresh, juicy produce, stop at **Cooper Frutta**, Viale Trieste, 25/29, a block from C. Mazzini, and pick up everything else from **Cooperatore Alimentare**, next door at Viale Trieste, 35. (Open M-Sa 7am-2:15pm and 4-8:30pm.) Take a picnic to nearby P. Vittoria and enjoy a peach, a loaf, and the old men playing *gioca tresete*, a local card game.

> **Taverna L'Arco Vecchio**, P. Archi di Ciaccio, 21 (☎0984 725 64). Take bus 4T to hillside village, or follow signs along V. Petrarca. Done up in elegant dark wood, this tasteful restaurant offers guests a range of salads (€6-8) and entrees in a subdued garden dining area. Marvelous location by the city's old arch. Large wine selection. Menu changes daily. Cover €1.50. *Primi* €5-8, *secondi* €5-11. Open M-Sa 1-3pm and 8-11pm. AmEx/MC/V. ❸

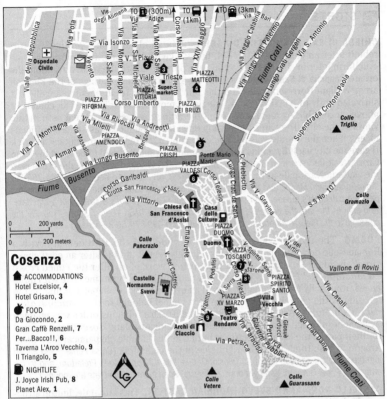

Cosenza

ACCOMMODATIONS
Hotel Excelsior, 4
Hotel Grisaro, 3

FOOD
Da Giocondo, 2
Gran Caffè Renzelli, 7
Per...Bacco!!, 6
Taverna L'Arco Vecchio, 9
Il Triangolo, 5

NIGHTLIFE
J. Joyce Irish Pub, 8
Planet Alex, 1

Gran Caffè Renzelli, C. Telesio, 46 (☎0984 268 14; www.grancafferenzelli.it), behind the duomo, proudly displays its 200 years of history with pictures and newspaper clippings. The Bandiera brothers, famous patriots of the Risorgimento, stopped by this mirror-and marble-trimmed cafe for a cup of coffee; an hour later Bourbon troops caught and killed them beneath the Valle di Rovina aqueduct. Find out if the cappuccino really is to die for. Mini pizza *rustica* €1.03. Gelato €2.60. Table service €0.52. Open M-F and Su 8am-midnight, Sa noon-midnight. Closed W in winter. Cash only. ❶

Il Triangolo, V. S. Quattromani, 22 (☎0984 225 08), down the road from P. Matteotti right before the bridge between the old and new cities. At this pizzeria's can't-miss F night dance parties, chipper old men foxtrot with ease and groups of young girls line-dance to pop music, all for the price of a calzone (€1.05) or sandwich (from €1.80). Pizza from €2.20. Open daily 9am-3pm and 6pm-last man standing. Cash only. ❶

Per...Bacco!!, P. dei Valdesi (☎0984 79 55 69; www.perbaccowinebar.it). Perfect for dinner on a warm summer night, this outdoor winebar/restaurant dishes up *Calabrese* specialties in a tree-lined piazza next to the river. Make sure to try one of their many varieties of *bruschetta* (€5). Live music Tu-F in summer. *Primi* €5, *secondi* €7-11. ❸

Da Giocondo, V. Piave, 53 (☎0984 298 10). Left off of C. Mazzini on V. Piave, then 2 blocks up on left. Decorated in city-themed artwork, this 3-room restaurant beams with irresistible local charm. Bow-tied waiters serve fresh fish, regional specialties, and tasty fruit desserts to complement a long wine list. *Primi* from €4, *secondi* from €5. Cover €2. Open M-Sa noon-3pm and 7-10pm. AmEx/MC/V. ❷

PUGLIA, BASILICATA, CALABRIA

👁 SIGHTS

CHIESA DI SAN FRANCESCO D'ASSISI. This small church's plain exterior, rebuilt after an earthquake in 1854, hides a lavish but somewhat worn Baroque cruciform interior. In the far right aisle, a portal leads to the main attraction, the ornate **Cappella di Santa Caterina,** which is graced by the paintings of the Flemish artist William Borremons. Behind the altar, a wooden tomb puts the angelic but shriveled body of a 500-year-old Franciscan monk on full display. The chambers above, accessible by a stairway from the adjoining sacristy, reveal astounding views of the city. They aren't generally open to the public, so ask church officials nicely. When the duomo was reconsecrated in 1222 after an earthquake, Frederick II gave the city a gilt **Byzantine crucifix** containing a splinter said to be from the True Cross. A skilled work in fine gold, the cross is truly exquisite. Now the cross is in the Galleria Nazionale at the Palazzo Arnone. Call ahead to see it. (☎0984 755 22. *Cross Ponte Mario Martiri, turn left up narrow C. Telesio to the duomo. Continue on C. Telesio just past the cathedral's facade, then turn right on V. del Seggio—yes, it's a street, not a staircase. Turn right at the top; the church is around the corner. Open Tu-Su 10am-7:30pm. Free. For the cross, go to the Palazzo Arnone on V. Gravina, but call ☎0984 79 56 39 ahead.)*

DUOMO. The duomo was erected in the middle of the 12th century with a Romanesque design, only to be almost entirely rebuilt in 1184 after an earthquake struck. Inside is Cosenza's second most prized work of art after the famed cross: *La Madonna del Pilerio,* a 12th-century painting in the Byzantine style with influences from Sicily and Campania. It is in an ornate Baroque chapel, the first on the left side of the church entrance. The next chapel belongs to the *Arciconfraternità della Morte* (Archbrotherhood of Death). This religious order was charged by ancient privilege to aid those condemned to death. Many *Cosentini* executed for their part in the Risorgimento are buried in this humble chapel near Isabella of Aragon, whose tomb is on the right side of the cathedral. *(Cross Ponte Mario Martiri into the old city, and head left up C. Telesio. Or take bus #22 or 23 to P. Prefettura, and facing away from P. del Governo, turn right down C. Telesio. Open mornings and late afternoons.)*

CASTELLO NORMANNO-SVEVO (NORMAN CASTLE). This fairy-tale, hilltop structure high above the city predates most of the *centro storico* and, in its ruined state, provides a silent, meditative testament to the city's tumultuous past. Originally built by the Saracens but refurbished by Frederick II after the *Cosentini* tried to overthrow him, the castle offers impressive views of the surprisingly compact city. Now serene and barely visited, with well-manicured grass and a few trees, the castle has been a barracks for the armies of three different monarchs, a prison, and a seminary. Earthquakes have destroyed many of the ornaments, but its flowered columns and long, high-ceilinged halls remain. *(Take bus #22 or 23 to P. Prefettura, and facing Teatro Rendano, walk up the stairs to the left of the theater about 200m, going left at the P. Archi di Ciaccio and continuing up the stairs opposite Taverna L'Arco Vecchio. Or take bus 4T to the elevated village and follow signs 10-15min. uphill. The climb is steep; bring water on hot days. Open daily 8am-8pm. Free.)*

TEATRO RENDANO. Calabria's most prestigious performance venue, this theater was constructed in 1895 and destroyed by WWII bombing. It has since been rebuilt to its former glory. Crimson, white, and gold, its plush interior has showcased the likes of José Carreras. Reservations for non-*Calabresi*—or unconnected *stranieri*—are extremely difficult to get during the opera season (Oct.-Dec.); seats for the theater season (Jan.-May) may be somewhat easier to come by. The Rendano also hosts regional performance groups during the summer, with readily available tickets. *(Behind the statue of Telesio in P. Prefettura. ☎0984 81 32 20. For plays, tickets may be available 10am-1pm and 5-8pm on day of performance, but availability can't be checked by phone. From €18. Student discounts.)*

PIAZZA TOSCANO. The piazza contains the ancient ruins of Cosenza, which excavators are still working to unearth. Like the skylight to an underground city, Plexiglass covers the original stone work, allowing visitors to view the remains of ancient buildings. Remnants of the artwork that once covered the stone walls are also on display. *(Directly behind the duomo.)*

VILLA VECCHIA. The public gardens at Villa Vecchia are off P. Prefettura from the road beside the palace. Their vegetation carpets heavy, lantern-lined stone ramps and spills out into a bench-lined enclosure. A demure young nymph remains eternally surprised at the appearance of visitors to her mossy fountain.

◧ NIGHTLIFE

Cosenza is the center of action for smaller neighboring towns. **Planet Alex,** P. XI Settembre, 12, off C. Mazzini, is a disco-pub in the new city that blasts DJ music until late. (☎0984 79 53 37. Open daily 6:30pm-3am.) Get a taste of the Emerald Isle in the *centro storico* at the **J. Joyce Irish Pub,** V. Cafarone, 19, a lively bar that's packed on the weekends. (☎0984 227 99. Open daily from 8pm. AmEx/MC/V.)

CAMIGLIATELLO AND SILA MASSIF ☎0984

"Its nature will amaze you," a billboard near Sila's train station proudly states. Indeed, the Sila wilderness is a breathtaking, untainted landscape of fertile green, home to lakes, mountain peaks, and woods that burst with wildflowers in the spring. Covering the widest part of the Calabrian peninsula, the Sila was once a huge forest, exploited from its earliest days to provide fuel and material for the buildings and fleets of Rome. Today the cutting of trees is rigidly controlled, and the area offers some of Italy's most spectacular natural settings and a wealth of activities to satisfy intrepid explorers. Camigliatello is the best base in the Sila, a resort town with many bus connections and access to hikes and ski slopes.

▤⚡ TRANSPORTATION AND PRACTICAL INFORMATION. FS trains run from Cosenza (1½hr., 2 per day 6:55am and 1:42pm, €1.70), but their schedules are fairly erratic, so **buses** from Cosenza **Autostazione** are usually the most reliable form of transport (40min., 9 per day 6:50am-7:05pm, €1.91). Find bus hours at the tourist office and buy tickets at Bar Pedace, the bar closest to the bus stop. **Maps** and information on Sila and surrounding attractions, events, and trails can be found at the **Pro Loco Tourist Office,** V. Roma, 5, uphill to the right from the train station and bus stop. (☎0984 57 81 59. Open daily 9am-1pm and 2-7pm.) **Banca Carime** is at V. del Turismo, 73. (☎0984 57 80 27. Open M-F 8:30am-1:20pm and 2:35-3:35pm.) For **medical emergencies,** call ☎0984 57 83 28. Camigliatello's **post office,** on V. Tasso, is at the intersection of V. del Turismo and V. Roma, next to Hotel Tasso. (☎0984 57 80 76. Open M-Sa 9am-1pm.)

▤◳ ACCOMMODATIONS AND FOOD. Hotel Meranda ❸, V. del Turismo, 29, offers modern rooms in a secluded, wooded area just off the main road. Facilities include an elegant restaurant/bar, *discoteca*, and video game room. (☎0984 57 80 22, fax 57 92 93. Doubles with half pension €34-60, with full pension €39-60. Extra bed €35-52.) **La Baita ❸,** V. Roma, 97, is 100m from the train station and just up the road on the right from the bus stop. The basic rooms are comfortable and include bath. (☎0984 57 81 97. Breakfast included. Singles €25, in Aug. and ski season €26; doubles €40/€47; triples €50/€57; quads €60/€68.) Buses run from Camigliatello to **La Fattoria ❶** campsite, 5km from Camigliatello, near a vineyard. (☎0984 57 83 64. Tent provided. €5.16 per person.)

Le Tre Lanterne ❸, V. Roma, 142, is a popular and friendly spot that specializes in *funghi porcini* (€9), or Sila-style mushrooms. (☎0984 57 82 03. Pizza from €3.50. *Primi* from €5, *secondi* from €8. Cover €1.50. Open Tu-Su 10:30am-3:30pm and 7-11:30pm. AmEx/MC/V.) Dine by lantern light at **Ristorante Hotel Lo Sciatore ❷**, V. Roma, 128, an upscale restaurant with a ski-lodge feel and extremely low prices, serving mushroom risotto and other *Calabrese* favorites. (☎0984 57 81 05. *Primi* from €4.50, *secondi* from €4. Wood-stove pizza from €2.60. Cover €1.60. Open daily 12:30-3pm and 7:30-10pm. AmEx/MC/V.) For a change of pace, try the *salumerie* that overflow with smoked cheeses, cured meats, and marinated mushrooms. Picnic grounds lie 10min. from the *centro*, up V. Tasso past the post office.

FESTIVALS AND ENTERTAINMENT. For a glimpse of traditional *Calabrese* culture, hop on the bus for **San Giovanni in Fiore**, 33km from Camigliatello, to view a 12th-century abbey, exhibitions of handicrafts at a museum, and traditional festivals (including the music and dancing of the world-renowned **Potato Festival**, held in November). Camigliatello is not much of a party town; local youth escape to nearby Cosenza for kicks at night; others remain for the blaring Eurotechno music, video games, foosball, and pool at **Le Bistro**, V. C. Alvaro, 68. (Internet €5 for 50min. Open Tu-Su 2:30pm-3am.)

OUTDOORS AND SKIING. Want snow? There's plenty of it at the **Tasso Monte Curcio Ski Trail**, 2km from town up V. Roma and left at Hotel Tasso. Go right at the fork in the road. In winter, minibuses leave for the trailhead from Camigliatello's bus stop. Buy tickets onboard. Though Tasso offers 35km of beautiful cross-country skiing, it has only two downhill trails that are 2km each. (☎0984 57 81 36 or 57 94 00. When snow is on the ground, lifts are open daily 8am-5pm. Round-trip lift ticket €4, weekends €5; full-day pass €15/€20.) Getting to the **Parco Nazionale di Calabria** (☎0984 57 97 57), 10km northwest, is more tricky; just two buses head into the park daily, in the morning and afternoon, at varying times. **Altipiani**, V. Corado, 20 (☎0984 57 81 54; www.inaltipiani.it), offers guided tours of the park in Italian to large groups. Arrange times and prices through reservation.

TROPEA ☎0963

Resounding with the crash of waves against imposing rock faces, the ancient buildings and rock-hewn grandeur of Tropea are the stuff of dreams. Poised at the edge of a severe precipice, the town's winding streets create a maze of hidden piazzas and dignified churches. Though emptied during the day when the beach's white sands beckon, these streets flood after sundown with a carnival-like procession of bronzed vacationers in skimpy designer wear, cradling creamy gelato cups that somehow never settle on their thighs. Tropea's traditional (if anomalous) dual claims to fame were its nobility and its red onions; the nobility has long since withered, but the onions remain as potent as the summer sun.

TRANSPORTATION AND PRACTICAL INFORMATION. Trains run from the Reggio train station (2hr., 10 per day). There are three direct returns to Reggio; all others change at **Rosarno**. As the station has no ticket office, buy tickets at **Valentour**, P. V. Veneto, 17 (☎0963 62 516; open M-F 9:30am-12:30pm and 4-9pm, Sa 9:30am-noon and 6-9pm, Su 6-9pm). **Autoservizi** (☎0963 611 29) operates convenient *pullmini* (little blue buses) that pick up passengers on V. Stazione every 30min. The vans (€0.80) travel 27 routes, going as far as 24km afield; they are often the easiest or only way to access some of the more remote attractions and accommodations around Tropea. For exact stops, ask the English-speaking staff at the **Pro Loco Tourist Office**, down V. Stazione at P. Ercole. (☎0963 614 75. Open

PUGLIA, BASILICATA, CALABRIA

daily 4:30-8:30pm.) **Banca Carime,** on V. Stazione, has an **ATM** and a **currency-exchange** machine. (Open M-F 8:20am-1:20pm and 2:35-3:35pm.) In case of **emergency,** call the **police** (☎113 or 0963 60 42 11) or the **carabinieri** (☎112 or 0963 610 18). For an **ambulance,** call ☎0963 613 66. The **post office** is on C. Rigna. (☎0963 612 90. Open M-F 8am-1:30pm, Sa 8am-12:30pm.) **Postal Code:** 89861.

⌐▢ ACCOMMODATIONS AND FOOD. The road to ▨**Da Litto (Hotel Hibiscus) ❷,** V. Carmine, 25, is a 10min. walk uphill along trafficked hairpin-curves, but if you call in advance, the hotel's friendly owners will be glad to pick you up. Each bungalow in the hotel's garden has a patio, kitchenette, and TV. (☎0963 60 33 42. Reserve in advance, and call the day before to confirm your reservation. Sept.-June €15 per person, July and late-Aug. €28, early-Aug. €38.) For camping by the sea, try the tree-shaded **Campeggio Marina dell'Isola ❶,** on V. Marina dell'Isola, at the bottom of the stairs that lead down to the beach. (☎0963 619 70, in winter 60 31 28; www.italiaabc.it/a/marinaisola. €8.50 per person, in winter €5. Tents provided. Cars €2.50. Electricity €2.50. Free hot showers. AmEx/MC/V.)

Tropea's sweet, red onions and pepper-hot cheeses spice up local dishes, along with such *Calabrese* wines as *Cirò* and the famous *Vecchio Amaro del Capo.* **Le Tre Fontane ❸,** in Largo Mercato, claims to have perfected the *fileya alla tropeana* (pasta with eggplant and tomato; €5). Tables flow into the small piazza with the three-headed fountain. (☎0963 614 19. *Primi* from €4.50, *secondi* from €7.50. Open daily noon-3pm and 7pm-midnight. AmEx/MC/V.) Head to the elegant **Pimm's Restaurant ❹,** Largo Migliarese, next to the lookout at the end of C. Emanuele, to dine to the tranquil sound of waves crashing over the shoreline. (☎0963 66 61 05. *Primi* from €8, *secondi* €10-18. Cover €2.50. Open in summer daily 12:30-2:30pm and 7:30-11pm; closed M in winter. MC/V.) **Ristorante Porta Vaticana ❸,** through the gate on V. Regina Margherita, serves enticing *risotto afrodite* (€7.50) in a softly-lit dining room guarded by two sturdy tree trunks. (☎0963 60 33 87. Cover €1.50. *Primi* from €5.70, *secondi* from €6.50. Open daily Feb.-Oct. noon-3pm and 7:30pm-midnight. MC/V.) En route to the beach, grab a made-to-order sandwich and a cool drink at the 60-year-old **Alimentari Pandullo Marco ❶,** Largo S. Michele, 20, on V. Stazione across from V. Umberto I.

▣▨ SIGHTS AND BEACHES. The gleaming **Santuario di Santa Maria dell'Isola** presides over the white cliffs at the edge of town. Though its image plasters

ON THE MENU

A SPOONFUL OF SUGA HELPS THE ONIONS G DOWN

Perhaps an onion cure wouldn' instantly have won the trust of th Banks children. Then again, the were British, not *Calabresi.* Th red cipolle onions that grow in Tro pea, famous worldwide for thei uniquely sweet flavor, also pos sess proven medicinal qualities First indicated by Pliny the Elder science has shown the onions to contain anti-influenza properties promote healthy circulation, lowe blood pressure, and even act as diuretics. Locals claim that the onions are most effective when munched raw, like an apple; nev ertheless, Tropean cooks utilize an impressive catalogue of cooked dishes and condiments with the onions as protagonists. *Marme lata di cipolla,* used like mustard to flavor meats and fish, is the favorite, although hosts of sauces creams, and marinades aren't fa behind. Hanging from strings a nearly every Tropean alimentari the onions are a steal at €1 pe kg. Combined with another Cala brian favorite, the *peperoncino* the vegetable is at its best, giving a spicy southern Italian flavor to an international favorite.

One crafty merchandiser a Gelateria Tonino on C. V. Eman uele, in Tropea, even created his own onion-flavored gelato; thoug unlikely to become a daily staple the novel taste of sweet onion and sugary cream almost makes one forget the health benefits.

postcards from Reggio to Cosenza, its sequestered beauty and historical significance warrant such pride. To honor the Madonna, townsmen take the church's *Holy Family* statues out to sea every August 15 in a procession of hundreds of small boats. The naval parade tours nearby towns before returning to a display of fireworks in the evening. (Sanctuary open daily 9:30am-noon and 3-8:30pm. No swimwear allowed. Church €1, museum and terrace €0.50.) Up the cliff is Tropea's graceful **Norman cathedral.** Besides some elegant polychrome marble work and several sword-bearing dead *Tropeani*, the interior houses two bombs that miraculously failed to destroy Tropea when an American warplane dropped them in 1943. To reach the **beach,** take a winding set of stairs down the cliffs at the end of V. Umberto (turn off V. Stazione to the left).

SICILY (SICILIA)

An enigmatic island of contradictions, Sicily's complex culture is born from a millennia of diverse influences. Sicily has either owned or been owned by every great Mediterranean empire since the arrival of the Phoenicians in 900 BC. Palermo and Solunto were founded as Phoenician cities at the same time that Carthage arose in North Africa, replacing the native Siculi and Sicany tribes from which Sicily derives its name. Greek dominance followed, and Sicily soon sported more Greeks and Greek temples than did Greece itself. Roman theaters, Arab mosques, and Norman cathedrals round out the remnants of the island's ancient diversity, giving way to more modern rule by Europe's largest empires. Yet the island's physical separation from the mainland is a literal reinforcement of residents' determined independence, assimilating foreign influences into a unique cultural pastiche that is perfectly at home on an island as diverse physically as it is historically. The crystal clear waters of the Tyrrhenian and Mediterranean Seas engulf pristine beaches and secluded rocky coves while the island's interior consists largely of panoramic plateaus and mountainous farmlands, all under the ominous shadow of the 3323m active volcano, Mt. Etna. Ancient Greeks lauded the golden island as the second home of the gods, but is better known to many of today's tourists as the home of The Godfather. While the Mafia remains an unspoken presence in Sicilian society, its power has weakened in recent years, and represents one minor element in the island's complex cultural tapestry. Home to chic resorts, archaeological treasures, and fast-paced urban cities, the island has plenty to offer every sort of traveler.

HIGHLIGHTS OF SICILY

BASK in the glow of Byzantine gold at Monreale Cathedral near Palermo. (p. 645.)

FLIT between visions of paradise as you choose a favorite Aeolian isle. (p. 655.)

SCALE famed Mt. Etna (p. 683) in the morning and party all night in Catania. (p. 683.)

COMMUNE with the sultry spendors of Pantelleria's azure-lapped shores. (p. 712.)

WITNESS Segesta's convergence of cultures, crowned by its perfectly preserved Greek temple. (p. 708.)

PALERMO ☎091

Simultaneously turbulent, exquisite, and intense, Italy's fifth largest city is a strangely alluring mix of beauty and decay. A gritty metropolis with over one million inhabitants, Palermo's pace of life dispels any myth of a sleepy Sicily, with its racing stream of cars, buses, and scooters setting the city's breakneck pace. Those who do opt to slow down and take it all in will be amply rewarded with its impressive sights, living relics of previous generations of Palermitano grandeur. While poverty, bombings, and centuries of neglect have taken their toll on much of Palermo, the city is currently on an upswing. The 1993 election of an anti-Mafia mayor brought an end to the mob's knee-bashing control, and with political cleanup underway, Palermo is now at work restoring its architectural treasures.

▛ TRANSPORTATION

Flights: Falcone Borsellino Airport at **Punta Raisi** (☎848 86 56 43), 30min. from central Palermo. Prestia & Comande (☎091 58 04 57) runs buses every 30min. from P. Castelnuovo (45min.) and Stazione Centrale (1hr., €4.65). Taxis (☎091 59 16 62) charge at least €30-50 and are parked outside the airport.

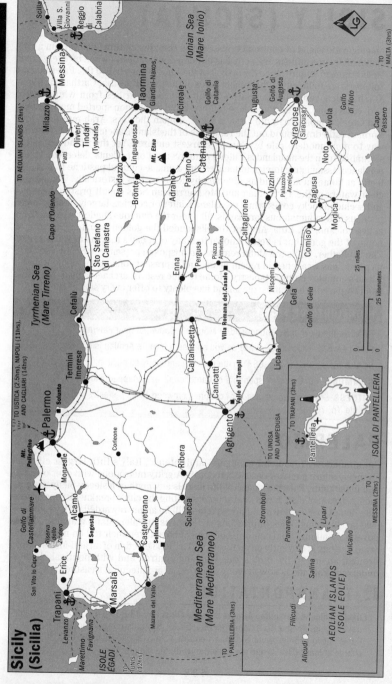

Sicily (Sicilia)

Scilla
Villa S. Giovanni
Reggio di Calabria

Ionian Sea (Mare Ionio)

TO MALTA (3hrs)

Messina
Taormina
Giardini-Naxos
Acireale
Golfo di Catania
Augusta
Golfo di Augusta
Syracuse (Siracusa)
Avola
Noto
Capo Passero
Golfo di Noto

Milazzo
Patti
Oliveri-Tindari (Tyndaris)
Linguaglossa
Mt. Etna
Randazzo
Bronte
Adrano
Catania
Paternò
Vizzini
Palazzolo Acreide
Ragusa
Modica
Comiso

TO AEOLIAN ISLANDS (2hrs)

Capo d'Orlando
Sto Stefano di Camastra
Enna
Pergusa
Piazza Armerina
Villa Romana del Casale
Niscemi
Gela
Golfo di Gela

Tyrrhenian Sea (Mare Tirreno)

Cefalù
Caltanissetta
Canicatti
Licata

Termini Imerese
TO USTICA (2.5hrs), NAPOLI (11hrs), AND CAGLIARI (14hrs)
Solunto
Palermo
Mt. Pellegrino
Monreale
Corleone
Ribera
Caltagirone

Sciacca
Agrigento
Valle dei Templi
TO LINOSA AND LAMPEDUSA

25 miles
25 kilometers

ISOLA DI PANTELLERIA
TO TRAPANI (3hrs)
Pantelleria
TO PANTELLERIA (3hrs)

Golfo di Castellammare
Riserva dello Zingaro
San Vito lo Capo
Erice
Segesta
Alcamo
Castelvetrano
Selinunte

Trapani
ISOLE EGADI
Levanzo
Marettimo
Favignana
Marsala
Mazara del Vallo

Mediterranean Sea (Mare Mediterraneo)

TO TUNIS (12hrs)

Stromboli
Panarea
Lipari
Vulcano
Salina
Filicudi
Alicudi
AEOLIAN ISLANDS (ISOLE EOLIE)
TO MESSINA (2hrs)

Trains: Stazione Centrale, in P. Giulio Cesare. At the foot of V. Roma and V. Maqueda. Ticket office (☎091 603 11 11) open 6:45am-8:40pm. **Luggage storage** available (see **Practical Information**). To: **Agrigento** (2hr., 14 per day 5:55am-8:20pm, €6.70); **Catania** (3½hr., 9 per day 5:55am-8:45pm, €14.10); **Messina** (3½hr., 14 per day 4am-8:45pm, €10.55); **Milazzo** (3hr., 15 per day 4am-8:45pm, €9.20); **Falcone Borsellino Airport** (40min., 23 per day 4:45am-10:10pm, €4.50); **Rome** (11hr., 9 per day 4am-8:45pm, €52.63); **Trapani** (2½hr., 10 per day 6:40am-8:40pm, €6.25).

Ferries and Hydrofoils:

Grimaldi Group (☎091 58 74 04), on the waterfront on V. Molo, off V. Francesco Crispi. These luxury ships have gyms and discos. Ticket office open M-F 8:45am-1pm and 2:15pm departure; Sa 9am-noon and 4:30pm departure; Su 4:30pm departure. Ferries to **Rome** (12hr.; Tu 10pm, Th 11pm, Su 6:30pm; €41-63) and **Genoa** (20hr.; summer 7 per week daily 8:30pm, check schedule for other months; €64-99).

Siremar, V. Francesco Crispi, 118 (☎091 58 24 03), on the last street before the waterfront, runs ferries to **Ustica** (2½hr.; M-Sa 9am, Su 8:15am; €10.60). Also runs hydrofoils June-Sept. (1¼hr., 2 per day, €17.80). Ticket office open daily 8:30am-1pm and 4-6:30pm.

Tirrenia (☎091 602 11 11), 100m after Grimaldi with the sea to the left. Open M-F 8:30am-12:30pm and 3:30-8:45pm, Sa 3:30-8:45pm, Su 5-8:45pm. Ferries to **Naples** (10hr., 8:45pm, €38-€55) and **Sardinia** (14hr., Sa 7pm, €42-€60).

Ustica (☎091 33 33 33) runs hydrofoils twice a day to the **Aeolian Islands.** Ticket office at end of Stazione Marittima. Open daily 9am-1pm and 5-7pm. All hydrofoils stop in **Alicudi, Filicudi, Lipari, Salina,** and **Vulcano** (3hr., 7am-4:45pm, €19.60-31.30). Schedule varies in winter.

Buses: All 4 lines run along V. Balsamo, by the train station. Facing away from the tracks, turn right; exit with McDonald's on the left and newspaper stands on the right; V. Balsamo is straight ahead, hidden by an army of buses. When purchasing tickets, ask exactly where your bus will be arriving and find out its logo.

Cuffaro, V. Balsamo, 13 (☎091 616 15 10). To **Agrigento** (2½hr.; M-Sa 7 per day, Su 3 per day; €6.90).

Segesta, V. Balsamo, 14 (☎091 616 90 39). Buses marked "Sicilbus," "EtnaTransport," or "Interbus." To: **Alcamo** (1hr.; M-F 10 per day 6:30am-8pm, Sa 8 per day 6:30am-8pm; €4.65, roundtrip €7.20); **Rome** (12hr.; from Politeama 6:30pm, from Stazione Centrale 6:45pm; €35, roundtrip €60.50); **Terrasini** (1hr.; M-Sa 6 per day 6:30am-8pm; €2.50, round-trip €4.10); **Trapani** (2hr.; M-F 26 per day 6:30am-9pm, Sa every hr.; €6.20). Reduced service Su.

SAIS Transporti, V. Balsamo, 16 (☎091 617 11 41). To **Corleone** (1¼hr., 5 per day 6am-6pm, €3.87).

SAIS, V. Balsamo, 16 (☎091 616 60 28), next door to SAIS. To: **Catania** (2½hr., M-Sa every hr. 5am-8:30pm, €11.82); **Catania Airport** (3¼hr., 8 per day, €11.93); **Messina** (3¼hr.; M-Sa every hr. 5am-8pm, Su every hr. 9am-7pm; €12.43); **Piazza Armerina** (1½hr., 8 per day 6:15am-8pm, €9.55).

Public Transportation: Orange **AMAT city buses.** Main terminal in front of Stazione Centrale, under dark green overhang. Tickets €1 per 2hr., €3.35 per day. Buy tickets from *tabacchi* or ticket booths. Pick up a free **transit map** from the tourist office or any AMAT info booth. Most bus stops are labeled and have route maps posted. Palermo also has the **Metropolitana** subway system, but it's usually faster to take a bus or even walk.

Taxis: Station office (☎091 616 20 01); **Autoradio** (☎091 51 27 27); **RadioTaxi** (☎091 22 54 55), in front of Stazione Centrale, next to the bus stop.

⚡ ORIENTATION

Palermo's newer half follows a grid pattern, but older sections to the south, near the **train station**, form a tangled knot. The train station dominates **Piazza Giulio Cesare,** from which two primary streets define Palermo's central axis. **Via Roma** begins directly across from the station and passes the post office. **Via Maqueda** is parallel to V. Roma and to the left from the front of the station and runs to the Teatro Massimo and **Piazza Verdi,** where it becomes **Via Ruggero Set-**

timo. After 300m, it runs into **Piazza Castelnuovo (Politeama)**, with the tourist office and Politeama. V. Ruggero Settimo becomes **Via della Libertà**, signaling the beginning of the new city and leading to the Giardino Inglese. Closer to the station, at Quattro Canti, **Via Vittorio Emanuele** intersects V. Maqueda, connecting **Piazza Independenza** to the sea. The parallel **Via Cavour** goes from **Piazza Verdi** toward the port.

> **SICILIAN STREET SMARTS.** Palermo shuts down at night and many of its streets are poorly lit. Knowing where to go and how to get there is essential, especially after dark. When possible, stay on the main streets of V. Roma, V. Maqueda, V. R. Settimo, V. della Libertà, or C. V. Emanuele—you may feel like the only pedestrian, but the stream of cars and scooters, which continues into the night, is reassuring. The areas behind the train station and around the port can be particularly dangerous after shops close in the evening. Daylight hours are safer, but still be cautious—don't flaunt cameras or wear a backpack, flashy jewelry, or a watch. Walk with a purposeful stride and avoid openly consulting maps.

TOURIST, LOCAL, AND FINANCIAL SERVICES

Tourist Office: P. Castelnuovo, 34, in the Banco di Sicilia building (☎091 605 81 11; www.palermotourism.com). Detailed **maps,** brochures, and the seasonal information packet, *Agenda.* Open June-Sept. M-Sa 8:30am-2pm and 3-7pm, Oct.-May M-F 8:30am-2pm and 2:30-6pm. Branches at the train station (☎091 616 59 14) and the airport (☎091 59 16 98; open daily 8:30am-midnight). Info kiosks in dark blue tents with maps scattered throughout the city and at the port.

Consular Services: UK, V. C. Cavour, 117 (☎091 32 64 12). Open daily 10am-noon. **US,** V. G. B. Vaccarini, 1 (☎091 30 58 57). Emergencies only. Open M-F 9am-12:30pm.

Currency Exchange: *Cambio* at the central post office and train station. **Banca Nazionale del Lavoro,** V. Roma, 201, and **Banco di Sicilia,** on V. R. Settimo, both open M-F 8:20am-1:20pm. **ATMs** can be found on V. Roma and V. Maqueda; the Bancomat 3-plus ATMs are newer and sometimes more reliable.

American Express: G. Ruggieri and Figli Travel, V. E. Amari, 40 (☎091 58 71 44). From P. Castelnuovo (Politeama), follow V. E. Amari toward the water. Cashes **traveler's cheques** for cardholders only. Ask for the red city map "Palermo in your pocket." Open M-F 9am-1pm and 4-7pm, Sa 9am-1pm.

Luggage Storage: In the train station at the end of track #8. €3 per bag for 12hr. Open daily 6am-midnight.

English-Language Bookstore: Libreria Feltrinelli, V. Maqueda, 395 (☎091 58 77 85), a few blocks before Teatro Massimo from the train station. An impressive selection of classics and bestsellers on the 2nd fl. Open Sept.-June M-Sa 9am-8pm, Su 10am-1:30pm and 5-8pm; July-Aug. M-Sa 9am-1pm, 4-8pm. **Mondadori Bookstore,** V. Roma, 287 (☎091 32 54 92). Not as many offerings as Feltrinelli, but still a decent selection. Internet €1.50 for 30min., €3 per hr. Open daily 9am-1pm and 4-8pm.

EMERGENCY AND COMMUNICATIONS

Emergency: ☎113. **Carabinieri** (☎112). **Ambulance** (☎118).

Police, V. Dogali, 29 (☎113 or 091 695 41 11).

Pharmacy: Lo Cascio, V. Roma, 1 (☎091 616 21 17). Look for green cross near the train station. Open daily 4:30pm-8:30am. **Di Naro,** V. Roma, 207 (☎091 58 58 69), on the right after C. V. Emanuele. Open M-F 8:30am-1pm and 4-8pm.

SICILY

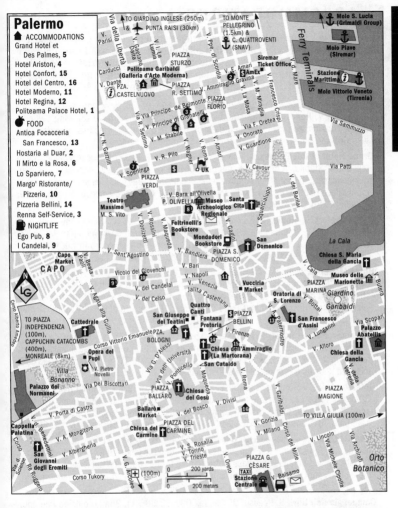

Palermo

🏠 ACCOMMODATIONS
Grand Hotel et
    Des Palmes, **5**
Hotel Ariston, **4**
Hotel Confort, **15**
Hotel del Centro, **16**
Hotel Moderno, **11**
Hotel Regina, **12**
Politeama Palace Hotel, **1**

🍴 FOOD
Antica Focacceria
    San Francesco, **13**
Hostaria al Duar, **2**
Il Mirto e la Rosa, **6**
Lo Sparviero, **7**
Margo' Ristorante/
    Pizzeria, **10**
Pizzeria Bellini, **14**
Renna Self-Service, **3**

🌙 NIGHTLIFE
Ego Pub, **8**
I Candelai, **9**

Hospital: Policlinico Universitario, V. del Vespro, 127 (☎091 655 11 11), or **Ospedale Civico,** V. C. Lazzaro (☎091 666 11 11; in case of emergency 606 22 43), near the train station.

Internet: Mondadori Bookstore (see English-language bookstores). Navigando Internet Point, V. della Libertà, 73 (☎091 34 53 32), down V. della Libertà from the Teatro Politeama, on the right after Giardino Inglese and before V. Notarbartolo. 8 computers. €3 per hr. Open M-Sa 10:30am-midnight, Su 4-11pm.

Post Office: V. Roma, 322 (☎091 160 or 753 11 11). Massive white-columned building 5 blocks up V. Roma past V. V. Emanuele. Open M-Sa 8am-6:30pm. Branch: Stazione Centrale (☎091 617 53 57), to the right of the station, beside the tracks. Open M-F 8am-6:30pm, Sa 8am-12:30pm. **Postal Code:** 90100.

SICILY

☞ ACCOMMODATIONS

Palermo is packed with places to stay at all levels of price and luxury, though the two sometimes have a less discernible relationship; always ask to see the room before accepting. V. Roma and V. Maqueda have high concentrations of budget accommodations, but the neighborhoods near the train station are dangerous at night. Women should be especially cautious when staying in this area.

▨ **Hotel del Centro,** V. Roma, 72, 2nd fl. (☎091 617 03 76; www.hoteldelcentro.it), 5 blocks up V. Roma from the station. Old-world-style rooms have towering ceilings, classy curtains, and cream-colored details. Bath, A/C, and TV. Breakfast included. Singles €48-62; doubles €72-85. Extra bed 35% more per person. MC/V. ❹

Grand Hotel et Des Palmes, V. Roma, 398 (☎091 602 81 11), between V. Pipe Granatelli and V. Stabile, in the *centro*. The peak of Palermitano grandeur, with sweeping marble staircases, stained glass windows, chandeliers, and Greek statues in the lobby. Large rooms have bath, A/C, and TV. Renovated in 2003. Breakfast included. Singles €100; doubles €185. AmEx/MC/V. ❺

Hotel Confort, V. Roma, 188 (☎091 32 43 62, fax 33 17 41). From the station, 2 blocks before V. V. Emanuele. Simply furnished rooms with dark wood-paneled walls, shared bath, and a location so central you'll want earplugs to drown out the noise. Lively TV lounge near front desk. Singles €25; doubles €39-45. Cash only. ❷

Hotel Moderno, V. Roma, 276 (☎091 58 86 83 or 58 82 60, fax 58 86 83), at V. Napoli. Although not as "moderno" as its name would lead you to believe, rooms are still nice and quiet—with somewhat plain decor. All but 3 have windows that open onto silent inner courtyard; bath, A/C, and TV included. Bar and communal TV room. Singles €55; doubles €75; triples €95; quads €105. AmEx/MC/V. ❹

Politeama Palace Hotel, P. R. Settimo, 15 (☎091 32 27 77; www.hotelpoliteama.it), beside the Politeama. Attractively located on P. R. Settimo and P. Castelnuovo. Bright, refined rooms with thick tapestry carpets offer bath, A/C, TV, and Internet. Breakfast included. Singles €140; doubles €190; triples €210. AmEx/MC/V. ❺

Hotel Ariston, V. M. Stabile, 139, 6th fl. (☎091 33 24 34). Take V. Roma 4 blocks past V. Cavour, or bus #122 from the station and get off before V. Amari. Between Teatro Massimo and the Politeama, above a small courtyard. 7 bright, modern rooms in minimalist style have bath, A/C, and TV. Reserve ahead. Singles €40; doubles €60. AmEx/MC/V. ❸

Hotel Regina, C. V. Emanuele, 316 (☎091 611 42 16, fax 612 21 69), at the intersection of V. Maqueda and C. V. Emanuele, across from the larger Hotel Centrale. Near the old city. Carved bureaus and glass globe lighting fixtures adorn pastel rooms. Be sure to triple-check your reservation before arriving. TV in lobby. Beach passes available. Singles €21, with bath €35; doubles €40/€50. AmEx/MC/V. ❷

Campeggio dell'Ulivi, V. Pegaso, 25 (☎/fax 091 53 30 21), 35min. outside Palermo. Take bus #101 from Palermo's central station to P. de Gasperi; then take bus #628 to V. Sferracavallo. Walk downhill a block and turn right on V. dei Manderini just after the post office. Campground is on the right. Neurotically clean facilities with free hot showers. Bungalows available. €6.50 per person, tent included. Cash only. ❶

☞ FOOD

The best restaurants in town are positioned between Teatro Massimo and Politeama. Palermo's bustling markets provide better budget opportunities than most supermarkets, and more interesting selections. **Ballarò** sprawls through the intricate streets behind V. Maqueda and C. V. Emanuele, while **Capo** covers the streets behind Teatro Massimo. **Vucciria** completes the trio in the area between C.

V. Emanuele and P. S. Domenico. All three are open Monday through Saturday during daylight. Saturday mornings are most chaotic. Try Palermitano specialty *cassata*, a sweet ricotta pastry.

■ **Lo Sparviero,** V. Sperlinga, 23/25 (☎/fax 091 33 11 63), 1 block toward P. Politeama from Teatro Massimo, off a small piazza. Shrouded in antique decor, this local secret serves classic Sicilian cuisine beneath a mounted ram's head. Varied salad options in large portions make interesting vegetarian choices (€4.50). Pizza from €4. *Primi* €5.50-8, *secondi* €6.50-13. Cover €1. Open daily 11am-6:30pm-midnight. AmEx/MC/V. ❷

■ **Antica Focacceria San Francesco,** V. A. Paternostro, 58 (☎091 32 02 64), in P. S. Francesco. This expansive *focacceria* has served delighted patrons in a secluded piazza since 1834. Behind the counter sits an infamous vat of *milza* (spleen). The brave can try it in a *panino* or with *maritata* cheese (€1.60), while the rest of us choose from the extensive menu, featuring both standard Italian fare and options from around the world. 19 salads from €3.60. *Primi* from €4, *secondi* €8-19. Cover €2. Open daily 12:30-3:15pm and 7:45-11:15pm. AmEx/MC/V. ❸

■ **Pizzeria Bellini,** P. Bellini, 6 (☎091 616 56 91), to the left of P. Pretoria in the shadow of the Teatro Bellini and the churches La Martorana and San Cataldo. Shaded outdoor seating among the ancient beauties of Palermo makes this restaurant an ideal and popular spot for a romantic meal. Pizza €4-7.50. *Primi* €6-8, *secondi* €7-13. Cover €1.50. Open daily noon-midnight. ❸

Margo' Ristorante/Pizzeria, P. Sant'Onofrio, 3 (☎091 611 82 30). Follow Vco. dei Giovenchi off V. Maqueda, opposite intersection of V. Maqueda and V. Bari. Upscale environment of rough-cut rock walls, tranquil music, and professional staff make eating a pleasure. Try specialty *ravioli di cernia, spada e crema di asparagi* (€8.50). Pizza €4-8. *Primi* €5.50-8.50, *secondi* from €8. Cover €2. Open Tu-Su 8pm-1am. AmEx/MC/V. ❸

Hostaria al Duar, V. Ammiraglio Gravina, 31 (☎0347 473 57 44 or 701 78 48), off V. Roma, 3 blocks toward the port. Terrific mix of Sicilian and Arabic flavors served on bright picnic tables. *Primi* from €3.50, *secondi* from €6.50; Tunisian *secondi* €2-6.20. Cover €1. Service 10%. Open daily 10am-3:30pm and 7pm-midnight. AmEx/MC/V. ❷

Il Mirto e la Rosa, V. Principe di Granatelli, 30 (☎091 32 43 53). Upscale vegetarian fare amid cathedral-like arches painted with flowers. Try *fettuccine al profumo d'estate* (in an aromatic sauce of tomatoes, pine nuts, peppers, garlic, and basil; €7). *Primi* from €7, vegetarian *secondi* from €5, modest-sized fish and meat *secondi* from €10. Open M-Sa 12:30-3pm and 7:30-11pm. AmEx/MC/V. ❷

Renna Self-Service, V. Principe di Granatelli, 29 A/B/C (☎091 58 06 61; rennass@tin.it). Fast-food joint as crowded as a high school cafeteria, except Renna doesn't skimp on taste or portions. *Primi* from €2, *secondi* from €3.40. Open M-Th and Sa noon-3:30pm and 7-10pm, F and Su noon-3:30pm. AmEx/MC/V. ❶

◉ SIGHTS

Ancient glory, centuries of neglect, and heavy WWII bombing have made Palermo a city of splendor and degradation, where the beauty of the past hides behind the face of urban blight. For much of the 20th century, corrupt politicians and Mafia activity diverted funds and attention from dilapidated landmarks, but the political changes of recent years have brought promising strides at cleaning and rebuilding.

■ **MONREALE.** Palermo's greatest treasure actually rests 8km outside the city. The extraordinary Cattedrale di Monreale is an example of the Sicilian take on Norman architecture, mixing Arabic and local styles on the northern template. The interior, however, is an unexpected masterpiece of Byzantine design. Its walls glisten with 6340 sq. m of golden mosaics, the largest display of Byzantine religious art outside the Hagia Sofia. The series of 130 panels depicts the massive Christ Panto-crator (Ruler of All) over the main altar, the mystical flavor of the locale empha-sized by the minimal light from the cathedral's small windows. Every few minutes, someone pays the €1 necessary to activate electric lighting in a portion of the church, and the sudden illumination never fails to startle. From the side entrance, the beginning of Genesis appears at the upper left of the central aisle. The two-tiered Old Testament narrative continues clockwise with images of Adam and Eve. The quiet, light-flooded **cloister** offers a contrast to the solemn shadows of the cathedral. Though seemingly empty, this courtyard contains one of the best and most unusual collections of Sicilian sculpture. Alternately plain and inlaid with Arabic tiles, 228 paired columns ring the interior. Each capital is unique, con-structed in Greco-Roman, Islamic, Norman, Romanesque, and Gothic styles. A bal-cony along the cathedral's apse looks over the cloisters and beyond to all of Palermo. Two doors down from the cloister is the entrance to tranquil **gardens.** *(Bus #389 leaves from Palermo's P. Indipendenza for Monreale's P. V. Emanuele. 30min., 3 per hr., €1. To get to P. Indipendenza, take bus #109 or 318 from Palermo's Stazione Centrale. Tour-ist info to the left of the church ☎091 640 44 13. Cathedral open daily 8am-6:30pm. Free admis-sion. Treasury open daily 9am-noon and 3:30-6pm. €1.50. Modest dress required. Cloister open M-Sa 9am-7pm. €4.50, roof access €1.55.)*

■ **CAPPELLA PALATINA.** This chapel, in the monstrous, towering conglomerate **Palazzo dei Normanni,** houses a smaller and more accessible version of the mosaics at Monreale. While one corner to the far left of the altar was designed by local arti-sans, Norman kings imported artists from Constantinople to cover every inch of the remaining interior with gold and azure surrounding solemn-faced saints. Locally crafted Arabic wall mosaics and ceiling designs complete the effect of cul-tural blending. Those who prefer this Christ Pantocrator over that of Monreale claim it is the softer and more compassionate of the two. Upstairs, guards lead tours of the **Sala di Ruggero,** or King Roger's Hall. *(Follow C. V. Emanuele to Palazzo dei Normanni; entrance on far right from P. Indipendenza. ☎091 705 48 79. Chapel open M-F 9-11:45am and 3-4:45pm, Sa 9-11:45am, Su 9-9:45am and 11:15am-12:45pm. Closed Easter M. Tours run M and F-Sa 9am-noon; otherwise by arrangement only. Call ahead.)*

■ **MUSEO ARCHAEOLOGICO REGIONALE.** Housed in a quiet palazzo in the town center, this museum features an impressive collection of Sicilian archaeological treasures. Most impressive are several fine Greek and Roman works, including a large section of the **Punic Temple of Himera,** and the 3rd-century-BC Greek *Ram of Syracuse.* Also not to be missed is the recently restored **Mosaico delle Quattro Sta-gioni,** depicting the four seasons in a haunting mosaic. Other temple remnants include fantastic renditions of Perseus beheading Medusa and Zeus courting Hera. *(Head away from the train station on V. Roma, and turn left onto V. Bara all'Olivella across from Teatro Massimo. P. Olivella, 24. ☎091 611 68 05 or 611 07 40. Open M and Su 8:30am-1:45pm, Tu-Sa 8:30am-6:45pm. €4.50, EU students €2, EU residents under 18 or over 65 free.)*

CAPPUCHIN CATACOMBS. Resembling the set of a horror movie, these murky subterranean chambers plunge you skull-first into the world of the grotesque. Over the course of 350 years, the Cappuchin friars preserved remains of over 8000 bodies. Attached to niches by wires and nails, grimacing, sneering skeletons at various stages of decomposition scream silently. The bodies are dressed in their finest and sorted by sex and profession. The highlight of this collection is the remains of a young girl, Rosalia, in a glass box. Alarmingly well-preserved, the child appears merely to be sleeping, on the cusp of life and an eternal dream. Sev-eral bishops and the painter Velázquez also inhabit these corridors. *(Take bus #109 or 318 from Stazione Centrale to P. Indipendenza. From there, hop on #327. Or, from C. V. Eman-*

uele, pass P. Indipendenza and turn right on V. Cappuccini, then right again on V. Il Pindemonte. P. Cappuccini, 1. ☎ 091 21 21 17. Open daily 9am-noon and 3-5:30pm; in winter daily 9am-noon and 3-5pm. €1.50.)

TEATRO MASSIMO. Constructed between 1875 and 1897 in a robust Neoclassical style, the **Teatro Massimo** is the largest indoor stage in Europe after the Paris Opera House. After undergoing 30 years of renovation, the theater reopened in grand Sicilian style (with trumpets and confetti) for its 100th birthday in 1997. Rumor has it that the restoration was prolonged by Mafia feuding, not by questions of artistry. (Incidentally, it was here that Francis Ford Coppola shot the climactic scene in *The Godfather Part III*.) Guided tours allow visitors to repose in the luxurious VIP guest box. Operas, plays, and ballets are performed here all year, while the **Festival della Verdura** brings famous international performers in late summer. In this period, shows move from the Massimo to nearby Villa Castelnuova. *(Across V. Maqueda from the Museo Archaeologico, 500m up V. Maqueda from the Quattro Canti intersection with C. V. Emanuele. ☎ 800 65 58 58 or 091 609 08 31, box office 091 605 35 55. Open Tu-Su 10am–4pm for 20min. tours in English, French, and German. Last tour 3:30pm. €3, under 18 or over 65 €2, school children €1, under 6 free. No entry during rehearsals.)*

PALERMO'S CATHEDRAL. As a part of their ongoing rivalry, the leaders of Palermo and Monreale tried to top each other by constructing the most beautiful church. Although many consider the mosaics in Monreale to be superior, Palermo's cathedral is still quite breathtaking. Continually renovated from the 13th through the 18th centuries, this structure's enormous exterior shows various styles butting heads. Arabic columns, Norman turrets, and an 18th-century dome crowd the facade and walls. Note the inscription from the Qur'an on the first left column before the entrance; in 1185 the Palermitano archbishop chose to plunk his cathedral down on top of a mosque, and this column was part of its stonework. The interior is dominated by stately, saint-lined arches and carved rock walls. Flying buttresses connect it to the former **archbishop's palace,** completed in 1460 and larger and more opulent than the church itself. *(On C. V. Emanuele. 091 33 43 76. Open daily 9:30am-5:30pm. Closed Su morning and during mass. Treasury and crypt open M-Sa 9:30am-5:30pm. €2.)*

QUATTRO CANTI AND LA FONTANA PRETORIA. The intersection of V. Maqueda and C. V. Emanuele forms the **Quattro Canti** (Four Corners). Each sculpted corner of this fantastic 17th-century piazza contains the statue of a season on the lower level, of a king of Spain (and thus, of the region) on the middle level,

THE LOCAL STORY

LA FAMIGLIA

Powerful because people owed them favors, strong because they supported one another, and feared because they did not hesitate to kill offenders, the Sicilian Mafia founded a brutal tradition that has dominated life since the late 19th century. The Mafia system has its roots in the *latifondi* (agricultural estates) of rural Sicily, where land managers and salaried militiamen protected their turf. Today Sicilians shy away from the topic, referring to the Mafia as *Cosa Nostra* (Our Thing).

At a grass-roots level, the Mafia has long controlled public works infrastructure, and for years farmers have lived in fear of land seizure and extortion. The Mafia was reported to have capitalized upon a drought in the summer of 2002 by stealing water from private wells and public water systems. Recent local resistance includes a farmers' group, Libera, that sells what it calls "anti-Mafia pasta," made from wheat grown on land seized from the Mafia by the government. Another jailed Mafia don's estate has been converted to a cooperative olive oil production site.

Since the mid-80s, Italian government efforts to curtail Mafia influence have met with some success. Dozens of members of Mafia dynasties like the Corleone, mythologized by *The Godfather* films, have been arrested, and in August 2002, Palermo police confiscated an estimated 500 million euros in Mafia property.

SICILY

and of one of the city's patron saints on the top level. Covered in soot and smog for decades, the sculptural works have recently benefitted from Palermo's city-wide restoration. P. Pretoria, down V. Maqueda, houses the oversized **Fontana della Vergogna** (Fountain of Shame) under Teatro Bellini. The fountain was given its name by irate churchgoers who didn't like staring at statues of monsters and nude figures as they left **Chiesa di San Giuseppe dei Teatini,** across the street. An even more shameful story explains its shameless size. In the early 16th century, a rich Florentine commissioned the fountain for his villa, sending his son to the Carrara marble quarries to ensure its safe delivery. In need of fast cash, the son sold the fountain to the senate of Palermo and shipped it to Sicily. *(630m down V. Maqueda from the train station.)*

PALAZZO ABATELLIS. Signs in P. Marina point toward this late 15th-century palazzo, which houses one of Sicily's best art museums, the **Galleria Regionale della Sicilia.** Dozens of religious panel paintings and sculptures from the Middle Ages through the Baroque period culminate with Antonello da Messina's unusual *Annunciation.* The massive and morbid fresco *The Triumph of Death* claims a room of its own on the lower level. *(V. Alloro, 4. From P. G. Cesare in front of train station, take V. Abramo Lincoln, then go left for 2 blocks on V. N. Cervello. ☎091 623 00 11. Open daily 9am-2pm, Tu-Th also 3-7:30pm. Ticket counter closes 30min. before museum. €4, EU students 18-25 €2, EU residents under 18 or over 65 free.)*

CHIESA DEL GESÙ (CASA PROFESSA). Nicknamed "Il Gesù," this green-domed church has a dazzling multicolored marble interior and surrealist ceiling paintings of the Last Judgment, depicting sworded figures beating the unworthy into Hell and a black-clad man waving a pastel flag with "Jesus" written across it. WWII bombing scarred its courtyard and the neighboring **Quartiere dell'Albergheria,** filled with condemned buildings and bomb-blackened facades. *(In P. Casa Professa, on V. Ponticello, across V. Maqueda. Open daily 7-11:30am and 5-6:30pm. No visits during mass.)*

OTHER CHURCHES. The famous **Santa Maria dell'Ammiraglio** ("La Martorana") was built for an admiral of Norman King Roger II. The Byzantine mosaics inside are the 12th-century equivalent of celebrity photos: Roger I stands with Jesus, and Admiral George admires the Mother of God. *(P. Bellini, a few steps from P. Pretoria. ☎091 616 16 92. Open M-Sa 8am-1pm and 3:30-5:30pm, Su 8:30am-1pm.)* Next door lies the smaller **Chiesa di San Cataldo,** dating from 1154, whose red domes and arches liken it to a mosque. *(Open M-F 9am-3:30pm, Sa 9am-12:30pm, Su 9am-1pm.)* Perhaps the most romantic spot in Palermo, the garden and cloister of the **Chiesa di San Giovanni degli Eremiti** (St. John of the Hermits), comes complete with fanciful bulbous pink domes designed by Arab architects. Gazebos and little fountains dot this vine-wreathed paradise. *(V. dei Benedettini, 3. Walk west from the train station on C. Tukory to Pta. Montalto and take a right. Open M-Sa 9am-7pm, Su 9am-1pm. €4.)*

PUPPETS. There are no small parts, only small actors. For 300 years, Sicilian-made puppets have taken the stage at the **Museo Internazionale delle Marionette,** offering a playful glimpse at Sicilian stage culture. Galleries also display puppets from across the globe; it's a small world, after all. *(V. Butera, 1. Follow signs from P. Marina. ☎091 32 80 60, fax 32 82 76. Open M-F 9am-1pm and 4-7pm. Closed 1 week in Aug. to celebrate Ferragosto, which falls on Aug. 15. €3, under 18 or over 65 €1.50. Demonstrations on request.)* Catch a puppet show at Vincenzo Argenti's **Opera dei Pupi.** Tall, armored puppets reenact the chivalric *Orlando Furioso.* *(V. P. Novelli, 1. ☎091 32 91 94. Shows daily 6pm. €7.75.)*

GARDENS. The city's fresh gardens and parks provide relief from Palermo's dense urbanity. The large and refined **Giardino Inglese** off V. della Libertà resembles a tropical paradise more than Hyde Park, harboring many a picnicker under its shady palms and marble busts. In summer, the park hosts free concerts. Down C. V. Eman-uele toward the port, the **Giardino Garibaldi** in P. Marina features enormous banyan trees, whose limbs and roots drip down from leaf to land. The large Parisian-style **Villa Giulia**, at the end of V. Lincoln, has white sand pathways, meticulous flower beds, and elaborate fountains. *(Open daily 8am-8pm.)*

MONTE PELLEGRINO. Monte Pellegrino, an isolated mass of limestone rising from the sea, is Palermo's principal natural landmark, separating the city from the beach at Mondello. Near its peak, the **Santuario di Santa Rosalia** marks the site where the young Palermitano *ragazza*, Rosalia, sought escape from a planned marriage and wandered into ascetic seclusion. After dying there, she appeared in an apparition to a woodsman many years later, and told him to carry her bones through the city in a procession. The procession is believed to have brought an end to the raging plague that was destroying the city. The real bones of Rosalia, the patron saint of Palermo, can be found in Palermo's cathedral, and are paraded around the city every year on July 15. (☎091 54 03 26. *Open daily 7am-7pm. Take bus #812 from P. Castelnuovo, runs every 1½hr.)*

◪◧ BEACHES AND NIGHTLIFE

Mondello Lido is a free beach for tourists. All registered hotels can provide tickets that must be shown at the entrance. Otherwise, beach-goers pay €8 to set up camp in the area near the Charleston—or sit for free directly on the shore-line. Palermo packs buses every weekend to seaside **Mondello**, a beach by day and playground of clubs and bars by night. Take bus #101 or 102 from the station to reach the Politeama and V. della Libertà, and then bus #806 in the same direction to reach Mondello; the beach is beyond a tree-filled area known as "La Favorita." Watch for the frequent vendors that wander around the sand with all types of goodies. *Ciambelle* (donuts caked in sugar; €1) are an essen-tial beach treat.

Nightlife centers around bars that are hard to find and even harder to stagger home from. For information on cultural events, pick up *Un Mese a Palermo*, a monthly brochure available at any APT office, or the far-from-redundant News-News. **Piazza Olivella**, in front of the Archaeological Museum, and **Via Candelai** are the two most popular nightlife hubs, and both are flooded by a mob of young *Palermitani* every night. **Ego Pub**, P. Olivella, 16, serves kebabs (€4.20) and horse meat salads (the ever-popular "piatto ego"; €4.70) to eager carni-vores by day and becomes a pub at the stroke of midnight. (☎328 281 68 01. Open nightly 5:30pm-3am.) **I Candelai**, V. Candelai, 65, also picks up around midnight with one of central Palermo's few dance floors. (☎091 32 71 51; www.candelai.it. Open daily in summer Th-Su 11pm-3am, in winter nightly 11pm-3am.)

USTICA ☎091

The crystal waters of Ustica have turned Sicily's first natural marine reserve into a bustling tourist port, with abundant outdoor and underwater activities to satisfy the adventurous. Hiking trails wind around the island's 9km scenic coastline, while guided tours explore such archaeological treasures as a prehistoric village and a necropolis. Perhaps the most spectacular attractions are the ancient arti-facts buried just below the water's surface, catalogued and labeled for divers to explore. Despite its distance from Palermo, the self-proclaimed "diving capital of the world" is a worthwhile and memorable destination.

▐▔ TRANSPORTATION

Ustica is accessible by ferry or hydrofoil from Palermo. **Siremar,** V. Capitano Vincenzo di Bartolo, 15 (☎091 844 90 02, fax 844 94 57), is open daily 9am-1pm and 3:30-7pm. It runs **hydrofoils** (1¼hr., 3 per day, €17.80) and **ferries** (2½hr., daily 5pm, €10.50) to Palermo. For public transportation on the island, orange **mini buses** run from Viale Cristoforo Colombo at the port to P. Vito Longo (every 30min., €.40). Hotel Clelia rents scooters for €20 per day (see **Accommodations**).

✦ ? ORIENTATION AND PRACTICAL INFORMATION

Tiny Ustica consists of two main piazzas with smaller streets branching out. **Via San Francesco al Borgo** leads from the hydrofoil port into **Piazza Umberto I,** which immediately turns into **Piazza Vito Longo**. To reach the town from the ferry port, take the road uphill and turn left at the fork. Though not an official tourist bureau, **Ostea Piccola Società Cooperativa,** V. S. Francesco al Borgo, offers information and advice on area hotels and restaurants, provides babysitting services, and has two computers with **Internet.** Ostea also provides guided tours, including walks to the prehistoric village and a boat tour. (☎091 844 81 12; www.ostea.it. Internet €1 for 15min., €2 for 30min., €4 per hr. Open daily Sept.-June 9:30am-1pm and 4:30-8pm, July-Aug. 10pm-midnight. Cash only.) A 24hr. **ATM** is at **Banco di Sicilia,** P. Capitano Vito Longo, 5. In case of **emergency,** call the **carabinieri** (☎091 844 90 49), the **hospital** (☎091 844 92 48), or contact **tourist medical assistance** (☎091 844 93 92). A **pharmacy** is in P. Umberto I. (☎091 844 93 82. Open M-F 8:30am-1pm and 5-8:30pm, Su 10:30am-1pm.) The **post office,** Largo Armeria, 13, is off P. Umberto I. (☎091 844 93 94. Open M-F 8am-1:30pm, Sa 8am-12:30pm.) **Postal Code:** 90010.

▐ ⌂ ACCOMMODATIONS AND FOOD

Though reasonable in the low season, accommodations in Ustica can be incredibly pricey in July and August (making the island a no-brainer for a summer daytrip). All price ranges listed here include seasonal variations. **Hotel Clelia ❸,** V. Sindaco, 29, offers some of the nicest rooms around; all sport cheery yellow walls, TV, A/C, minibar, phone, and hair dryer. (☎091 844 90 39. Breakfast included. Scooter rental available for €20 per day. Internet €4.80 per hr. Singles €32-80; doubles €56-140. Ages 5-11 50% discount. AmEx/MC/V.) **Albergo Giulia ❸,** V. San Francesco, 16, has 11 rooms equipped with TV, A/C, phone, minibar, hair dryer, and brightly tiled bathroom. (☎091 844 90 07. Singles €30-50; doubles €80-100. Cash only.) A 10min. walk from the center of town, **Albergo Grotta Azzurra ❺,** on Contrada San Ferlicchio, runs courtesy bus service to and from the port. The island's luxury hotel has soft blue rooms with a sea theme, a terrace dining room, and balconies, as well as a pool and private beach. (☎091 844 90 48. 2-week advance reservation required. Singles €97-161; doubles €138-231. AmEx/MC/V.)

    Ristorante Giulia ❹, under the same ownership as Albergo Giulia, serves some of Ustica's tastiest seafood, including *couscous con pesce*—a specialty worth its considerable price (€22). The *zuppa di lenticchie* (lentil soup; €6) is an Ustican favorite. (☎091 844 90 07. *Primi* from €6, all-fish *secondi* from €9. Open daily 8pm-1am. Cash only.) At **Trattoria da Umberto ❸,** P. della Vittoria, 7, a wooden overhang and looming trees provide abundant shade. The *pennette piccanti con capperi e olive* (pasta with capers and olives; €7) are a spicy house treat. (☎091 844 95 42. *Primi* €5-9, *secondi* €9-15. Open daily May-Sept. 12:30-3pm and 8:20-11pm. AmEx/MC/V.) **Mini Market Caminita,** P. Umberto I, 3, sells essentials. (☎091 844 94 74. Open M-Sa 8am-1pm and 4-8pm, Su 8am-1pm.)

👁 🎵 SIGHTS AND ENTERTAINMENT

The natural splendor of Ustica's marine reserve is easily accessible by marked **hiking trails.** Maps are available at Ostea (see **Practical Information**). **Boat tours** are a great way to see the fascinating, florescent grottoes dispersed around the coastline, among them the neon blue waters of ■**Grotta delle Barche** and **Grotta Azzurra,** a nautical graveyard filled with ancient vessels. Small boat owners advertise cheap rides that circumnavigate the island; find them at P. Umberto I or at the port. Set a price before embarking; women traveling alone should attempt to join a larger group before taking a tour. An hour-long trip costs about €5, a 2½hr. island tour and swim costs about €10. Professional tours run by **Ostea** offer a bit more flare and security for a slightly higher price. (☎091 844 81 12. Reservation required. 1hr. tour €7. 2½hr. island tour and swim €10-13. Cash only.) Ostea's **walking tours** of archaeological sights, including the prehistoric village and *necropoli*, run from €5. The island's most popular activity, **scuba diving** off rocky coasts, is quite affordable, with opportunities for day trips and long excursions. **Alta Marea,** on V. Cristoforo Colombo, runs dives from May through October. (☎347 175 72 55; www.altamareaustica.it. Boats leave port daily at 9:15am and 3:15pm. Single immersion €32, with wetsuit €52; 6 dives €174; 10 dives €210. Diving class €310.) Once submerged, see the ■**underwater archaeological remains** of Roman lead anchors and *amphorae*, part of Ustica's underwater archaeology experiment.

Entertainment on Ustica is straightforward: lounging in bars after a day outdoors. **John Bar,** P. Umberto I, 15, serves *tavola calda* favorites (from €1.30), including wurstel and steaming *calzoni*. Decadent *Iris* pastries come with cream, ricotta, *nutella*, and chocolate fillings. (☎091 844 90 23. Open daily 5:30am-1am.)

CEFALÙ ☎0921

The Sicilian proverb "good wine comes in small bottles" captures the timeless nature of little Cefalù, whose heavenly qualities were featured in the Academy Award-winning film *Cinema Paradiso*. Dominated by its grand duomo, Cefalù is a labyrinth of cobblestone streets curling around the base of Rocca, an enormous stone promontory. The city's aging terra-cotta and stone buildings cling to the water's edge, as crowds do to the social *lungomare*. Be aware, though, that Cefalù's charms do not come cheaply: the city's reputation as a beach resort and its proximity to Palermo allow *pensioni* to charge whatever they please.

THE LOCAL STORY

NO BONES ABOUT IT?

While mapping the Mediterranean, Ptolemy noted two islands northwest of Sicily, Ustica and Osteo'des. Ever since, geographers have sporadically insisted that neither island exists at all.

The most compelling evidence of either island's existence is the mythical explanation for the name Osteo'des, which has the word "bone" ("*os*") at its root. During the period of warfare against Syracuse, local lore contends, thousands of Carthaginian troops went unpaid and turned belligerent. Fearing disorder, the Cathaginian senate ordered the elimination of the rebels; feigning a military mission, they sent the troops out on a long sea voyage. When the ship reached Osteo'des, the 6000 mercenaries were forced off, doomed to starvation. Later, visitors found their skeletal remains.

Ustica unquestionably exists, but no island matches Osteo'des in location or description. Many scholars believe the two islands were, in fact, the same—mistakenly granted discreet identities by diverging accounts. But others insist that Ustica is too fertile to have been the scene of mass starvation; Osteo'des, they claim, once existed but has subsequently sunk, perhaps due to seismic activity. Whatever is true, the ghostly *doppelgänger* casts a shadow over the otherwise peaceful Ustica, and the florescent beam from its grottoes can come to take on a more ominous glow.

SICILY

▐ TRANSPORTATION

Cefalù is best accessed by train. From the intersection of V. Roma, V. Mazzini, and V. Matteotti, take V. A. Moro. The **train station** (☎0921 42 11 69), in P. Stazione, is 3 blocks ahead on the left. The station is open daily 4:30am-11:30pm. Tickets can be purchased at the station's bar. Trains depart to Messina (3hr., 12 per day 4:45am-9:47pm, €7.90); Milazzo (2hr., 15 per day, €6.95); Palermo (1hr., 34 per day 5:13am-10:20pm, €3.85); and Sant'Agata di Militello (50min., 12 per day 7:02am-9:16pm, €3.45). Spisa runs **buses** from the train station and the waterfront along P. Colombo to 26 towns (€1). The station bar's window and tourist office post schedules. **Taxis** are available from Kefautoservizi, in P. Stazione (☎0921 42 25 54), in P. Garibaldi (☎0921 422 158), or in P. del Duomo (☎0921 42 11 78).

▐ ORIENTATION AND PRACTICAL INFORMATION

From the **train station, Via Aldo Moro** curves down to the city's biggest intersection. To the left, **Via Roma** cuts through the center of the new city. Straight and to the left, **Via Matteotti** leads into the old city, changing at **Piazza Garibaldi** into the boutique-lined **Corso Ruggero. Via Cavour,** across the intersection from V. A. Moro, becomes the *lungomare.*

Tourist Office: C. Ruggero, 77 (☎0921 42 10 50, fax 42 23 86), in the old city. English-speaking staff has a vast supply of brochures, **maps,** hotel listings, and schedules. Open M-Sa 8am-7:30pm, Su 9am-1pm.

Currency Exchange: Banca S. Angelo (☎0921 42 39 22), near train station, at the corner of V. Giglio and V. Roma. Open M-F 8:30am-1:30pm and 2:45-3:45pm. A 24hr. **ATM** is at the **Banca di Sicilia** (☎0921 42 11 03 or 42 28 90), in P. Garibaldi.

Emergency: ☎113. **Carabinieri** (☎112). **Police** (☎113 or 0921 92 60 11).

First Aid: ☎0921 92 60 11. **Guardia Medica:** V. Roma, 15 (☎0921 42 36 23), in a modern yellow building in the new city, behind an iron fence. Open daily 8am-8pm.

Pharmacies: Dr. V. Battaglia, V. Roma, 13 (☎0921 42 17 89), in the new city. Open M-Sa 9am-1pm and 4:30-8:30pm. MC/V. **Cirincione,** C. Ruggero, 144 (☎0921 42 12 09). Open Sept.-July M-Sa 9am-1pm and 4:30-8:30pm. Call ahead in Aug.

Hospital: (☎0921 92 01 11) on Cda. Pietra Pollastra, outside the city limits.

Internet: Kefaonline, P. S. Francesco, 1 (☎0921 92 30 91), where V. Umberto meets V. Mazzini. €5 per hr. Open M-Sa 9:30am-1:30pm and 3:30-7:30pm. **Bacco On-Line,** C. Ruggero, 38 (☎0921 42 17 53), across from the tourist office. Wine store has 2 computers in back, so weather the slow connection with some red, white, or rosé. €2.50 for 30min. Open daily 9am-midnight.

Post Office: V. Vazzana, 2 (☎0921 42 15 28). In a modern concrete building on the right off the *lungomare,* 2 long blocks from P. Colombo. Open M-F 8am-7:30pm, Sa 8am-12:30pm. **Postal Code:** 90015.

▐ ACCOMMODATIONS AND CAMPING

▨ **Locanda Cangelosi,** V. Umberto I, 26 (☎0921 42 15 91), off P. Garibaldi. This centrally located *affittacamere* is the best deal in the city. Private residence has 4 large, simply furnished rooms, each with a balcony overlooking the *centro storico.* 2 shared baths. Laundry available €5 per load. Reserve ahead. Singles €30; doubles €40; triples €50. The owner also has 10 fully furnished apartments for €40-50 per night. ❸

Hotel Mediterraneo, V. A. Gramsci, 2 (☎/fax 0921 92 26 06 or 92 25 73), 1 block left from the station. 16 well-furnished rooms boast cloud-like beds, safe, A/C, TV, sparkling bath, and hair dryer. Buffet breakfast included. Singles €45-80; doubles €60-125; triples €80-145; quads €95-165. ❹

Hotel Riva del Sole, V. Lungomare, 25 (☎ 0921 42 12 30, fax 42 19 84). Classy waterfront hotel provides easy beach access and sea views. 28 doubles have A/C and TV. Restaurant, bar, and garden. June-Oct. half pension €86; full pension €96. Oct.-June with breakfast €99. AmEx/MC/V. ❺

Camping Costa Ponente (☎ 0921 42 00 85, fax 42 44 92), west of Cefalù on Cda. Ogliastrillo. A 45min. walk or short ride on the Cefalù-Lascari bus (€1) from P. Colombo. Campsite has pool, tennis court, and free hot showers. Sept.-June €5.50 per person, €4.50 per tent, €3.50 per car; July-Aug. €6 per person, €5 per tent, €4 per car. ❶

🍴 FOOD

Although many of the city's trattorias try to peddle overpriced tourist menus, excellent seafood can be found after little searching. Just off the *lungomare*, next door to the post office on V. Vazzana, a MaxiSidis **supermarket** sells basics, including bathing suits. (☎ 0921 42 45 00. Open daily 8:30am-1pm and 4:30-8:30pm.)

La Vecchia Marina, V. V. Emanuele, 73/75 (☎ 0921 42 03 88). In case the model ships and paintings of fishermen don't tip you off, seafood is the specialty at this excellent restaurant. Make a reservation in advance to get a table on the tiny terrace overlooking the harbor. *Primi* €5.20-8, *secondi* €7.75-10. Must order both a *primo* and *secondo*. Cover €1.60. Open M and W-Su noon-3pm and 7-11pm. AmEx/MC/V. ❹

Osteria la Botte, V. Veterani, 6 (☎ 0921 42 43 15), off C. Ruggero, 2 blocks past P. Duomo. An affordable gem among Cefalù's upscale restaurants. Intimate interior and candlelit exterior whisper of romance and history. *Primi* and *secondi* from €6.50. Cover €1.50. Open Tu-Su 12:30-3pm and 7:30-11:30pm. AmEx/MC/V. ❷

Gelateria di Noto, V. Bagno Cicerone (☎ 0921 42 26 54), where the *lungomare* meets the old town. More than 40 flavors of some of Sicily's best gelato, in a great location just off the beach. Go ahead and get the large cone (€1.80)—you'll probably even go back for seconds. Open daily 7am-3am. ❶

L'Arca di Noé, V. Vazzana, 7/8 (☎ 0921 92 18 73), across from the post office. An astounding variety of foods and decorations crowd wooden booths docked among nautical maps, anchors, and ropes. A ship-shaped bar and gelateria serve those on the run. Internet available. Pizza from €3.50. Open M-Sa 6am-3am. AmEx/MC/V. ❶

Pasticceria-Gelateria Serio Pietro, V. G. Giglio, 29 (☎ 0921 42 22 93). 1st left from the train station toward town. 30 gelato flavors, a dozen cakes, and piles of cookies make this sleek bar a sweet-tooth's dream. Marzipan €18 per kg. Open Sept.-July M-Tu and Th-Su 7am-1pm and 3-10pm; Aug. daily 7am-10pm. ❶

Ristorante-Pizzeria Trappitu, V. di Bordonaro, 96 (☎ 0921 92 19 72). Paintings, urns and a grinding mill wheel are conversations starters, but good food keeps mouths otherwise occupied. Impressive wine list enhances the traditional menu. *Primi* from €6.50, *secondi* €7-18.50. Open M-W and F-Su noon-3pm and 7pm-midnight. AmEx/MC/V. ❸

Al Porticciolo, V. di Bordonaro, 66 (☎ 0921 92 19 81), off C. Ruggero, near duomo. 2 locations on V. di Bordonaro make unique dishes like *pasta con le sarde* (sardines, fennel, raisins, and pine nuts; €7.50). Pizza from €3.50. *Primi* around €7, *secondi* €8-15. Cover €1. Open M-Tu and Th-Su noon-3pm and 7pm-midnight. AmEx/MC/V. ❸

Al Gabbiano, V. Lungomare G. Giardina, 17 (☎ 0921 42 14 95). Breezy eatery right above the water makes an ideal break from the beach. *Primi* from €4, *secondi* from €8. Open in summer daily noon-3pm and 7pm-1am; closed W in winter. AmEx/MC/V. ❷

👁 🏖 SIGHTS AND BEACHES

Tucked away in Cefalù's tiny streets is the city's magnificent **duomo**. It was constructed in AD 1131 after King Ruggero II promised to build a monument to the Savior if he lived through a terrible shipwreck. The dramatic, off-white structure combines Arabic, Norman, and Byzantine styles, a result of the craftsmen the king hired for its construction. Once a potential fortress with crenellated towers and firing outposts, it now only protects the king's body—and stunning Byzantine mosaics that cover the apse. A benevolent and enormous **Christ Pantocrator** mosaic surveys all who enter with glistening calm. (Open daily 8am-noon and 3:30-7:30pm. Modest dress required.) Stuffed alligator cases and ancient vases get equal footing in the chaotic **Museo Mandralisca**. Local Baron Mandralisca lived in the building and bequeathed his collection to the city. The 19th-century art connoisseur amassed an impressive array of medieval and early Renaissance Sicilian paintings by anonymous artists, including the centerpiece, the ▓**Ritratto di Ignoto** (Portrait of Unknown) by Sicilian 15th-century master Antonello da Messina. The image is inescapable in Cefalù, smirking at tourists from every postcard rack and hotel wall, but the real thing is surprisingly fresh and lively. For every good painting, however, there are a few hundred seashells, a shelf of old books, and a half-dozen lamps of questionable taste. (V. Mandralisca, 13, opposite the duomo. ☎0921 42 15 47. Open daily 9am-7pm. €4.15, €2.60 per person for groups of 10 or more.)

The massive **Rocca** (cliff) above Cefalù stands at the center of the city's history. Walls of medieval fortifications lace the edges, while crumbling cisterns and ovens line forgotten avenues. The **Tempio di Diana,** surrounded by pines and overlooking the city and sea, first served as a place of sea worship and later as a defensive outpost. (Take Salità Saraceni, a 20min. uphill hike. From P. Garibaldi, follow the signs for "Pedonale Rocca" from between the fountain and Banco di Sicilia, up V. G. Fiore to Vco. Macello. Use caution, as the path is slippery when wet. Gates close 1hr. before sunset.) Cefalù's most attractive **beaches, Mazzaforno** and **Settefrati,** lie west of town on Spisa's Cefalù-Lascari bus line. The popular **Attrezzata** is just off the *lungomare.* Crowded for good reason, the beach has white sand, turquoise shallows, and free showers. Most sections charge for an umbrella, chair and cabin, but the area closest to the old city is completely free. The seven stones jutting out from the waves are said to have been placed in memory of seven brothers who died here while trying to save their sister from pirates.

MILAZZO ☎090

Once upon a time, only one or two boats a day sailed from Milazzo's port. Now ferries and hydrofoils zip to the Aeolian Islands or to the Italian mainland every hour. Though this has created a hectic transportation hub out of a formerly sleepy town, Milazzo is nonetheless a worthwhile destination in itself, with affordable accommodations and unusual dining choices. If lacking in conventional tourist attractions, this port city is a pleasant gateway to calmer fronts, boasting ancient churches, a grand Arab-Norman castle, and antique charm in the old town.

🚆 🚌 TRANSPORTATION AND PRACTICAL INFORMATION. Trains run to Messina (40min., 19 per day, €2.65) and Palermo (2½hr., 12 per day, €9.20). **Giuntabus** (☎090 67 37 82 or 67 57 49) runs **buses** to Messina (45min., every hr. 14 per day, €3.10). Both city buses and Giuntabuses arrive in **Piazza della Repubblica** at the center of the **port.** The port and center are a 10min. orange bus ride from the **train station. Lungomare Garibaldi** runs the length of the port. Turn left down **Via Crispi**

and right into **Piazza Caio Duilio** and follow the yellow signs to the **tourist office,** P. C. Duilio, 20. (☎090 922 28 65. Open M-F 9am-noon and 3-6pm, Sa 9am-noon.) A **medical clinic** (☎090 922 16 95) is on V. F. Crispi.

ⅡⅭ ACCOMMODATIONS AND FOOD. At the family-run **Hotel Central ❷**, V. del Sole, 8, rooms have a cheery ambience and large, shared baths. (☎090 928 10 43. Singles €15-30; doubles €30-55. AmEx/MC/V accepted for long stays only.) Across the street is **Hotel California ❷**, V. del Sole, 9. Although nothing like the hotel of the Eagles' song, it has spacious, simple rooms and comfortable beds. (☎090 922 13 89. Singles €22; doubles with bath €45.) Those looking for an organic experience should check out the eco-friendly **Petit Hotel ❺**, directly across from the port. Paintings line rooms detailed with handmade tiles and equipped with bath, A/C, TV, phone, and organic bed linens. Their **restaurant ❹**, on a terrace overlooking the coast, satisfies every (organic) midnight craving. (☎090 928 67 84; www.petitho-tel.it. Singles €70-125; doubles €100-195; triples €130-245; quads €160-320.) Campgrounds at **Riva Smeralda ❶**, on Str. Panoramica, are 6km from town on Capo Milazzo and can be reached by bus from P. della Repubblica. (☎090 928 77 91. Free showers. €6-8.50 per person, €2.90-4.40 for a tent, €2.60-3.90 per car.)

Milazzo gears itself toward travelers on the go, but food doesn't necessarily have to be rushed. Attractive bars line the *lungomare,* and fruit vendors are along V. Regis in P. Natasi and at the intersection with V. del Sole. A large Girasole **super-market,** V. del Sole, 34, is a block away from Hotels Central and California. (Open M-Sa 10am-8pm. MC/V.) **Blue Pub ❶**, V. A. Manzoni, 4, carries 30 varieties of pizza in air-conditioned, turquoise Tex-Mex splendor. (☎090 928 38 39. Pizza from €3.60. Cover €1. Open daily 7pm-late.) For a relaxed, casual meal, **Ristorante Al Gambero ❷**, V. Luigi Rizzo, 5/7 (☎090 922 33 37), is a prime spot with a large, cov-ered patio overlooking the port. (Pizza from €3.50. *Primi* €5-6.50, *secondi* €8-13, Cover €1. Open 11am-4pm and 7pm-midnight; closed F in winter. AmEx/MC/V.)

◪ SIGHTS. Milazzo's fantastic **Arab-Norman Castello,** in the historic center, boasts foundations constructed over Greek, Roman, and Byzantine remains and the architectural input of numerous other civilizations, including a curving Aragonese wall. (Guided tours offered 6 per day; closed M. €3.10, under 18 or over 65 €1.60.)

AEOLIAN ISLANDS (ISOLE EOLIE)

Homer believed this unspoiled archipelago to be a home of the gods; residents deem them *Le Perle del Mare* (Pearls of the Sea). Every summer, boatloads of vis-itors experience the magic of the rugged shores and pristine landscapes of the Aeolians. Lipari, the central and largest island, has ancient ruins, a bustling port, and one of the finest archaeological museums in Italy. Visit nearby Stromboli for a spectacular color spectrum and a restless volcano, Panarea for inlets and elitism, Salina for sheer cliffs over cerulean waters, and Vulcano for corrosive mud baths and a crater. The raw wilderness of the more remote Filicudi and Alicudi harbors striking rock formations and tranquil isolation. Though affordable in the low sea-son, the islands experience an exponential price increase in July and August, and reservations for this period should be made no later than May.

▊ TRANSPORTATION

The archipelago lies off Sicily, north of Milazzo, the principal and least expen-sive embarkation point. **Trains** run to Milazzo from Messina (45min., 19 per day, €2.65) and Palermo (3hr., 12 per day, €9.20). **Giuntabus** (☎090 67 37 82 or 67 57

49) arrives at Milazzo's port from Messina (45min.; M-Sa 14 per day, Su daily; €3.10) and from the **Catania airport** (Apr.-Sept. daily 4pm, €10.33). From the Milazzo train station, the orange **AST bus** runs to the **seaport** (10min., every 30 min., €0.80). Ferries leave less frequently from Molo Bevellero in Naples. **Hydrofoils** and **ferries** run regularly in late July and August to Lipari from Messina (2½ hr., €16.50); Naples (5½hr., €74.90); Cefalù (3hr., €21.69); Palermo (4hr., €31.30); and Reggio Calabria (2-3hr., €17.50).

Hydrofoils run twice as fast and often as ferries, but for twice the price. Three hydrofoil and ferry companies serve the islands, all with ticket offices in Milazzo on V. dei Mille, directly across from the docks in the port. High season is July through August. Some travelers enlist the help of Aeolian residents, who pay less than tourists for tickets; be aware, however, that such activity can come with consequences. All holders of reduced fare tickets must prove residency, and failure to do so may result in fines that make the original ticket price look cheap.

Siremar, V. dei Mille, 18, in Milazzo, sends ferries and hydrofoils to the islands. (☎090 928 32 42, fax 928 32 43. Open daily 5:45am-6:30pm.) It also has offices in Lipari (☎090 981 21 93) and Naples (☎081 251 47 40). **Ustica,** V. dei Mille, 23 (☎090 928 78 21), in Milazzo, sends hydrofoils to the islands. It also has an office in Lipari (☎090 981 24 48). Ustica recently bought SNAV Lines, and some Ustica booths still say SNAV. **Navigazione Generale Italiana (NGI),** V. dei Mille, 26 (☎090 928 40 91, fax 928 34 15), in Milazzo; V. Ten. Mariano Amendola, 14 (☎090 981 19 55) at Porto Sottomonastero in **Lipari.** The following table lists ferry and hydrofoil info from Milazzo on Siremar and Ustica respectively. Schedules are subject to change, so call for definitive info. Both offices have convenient portable timetable booklets—just ask for an "orario."

TO	FERRY FROM MILAZZO		HYDROFOIL FROM MILAZZO	
	TIME	HIGH SEASON	TIME	HIGH SEASON
Vulcano	1½hr.	3 per day, 7am-6:30pm, €5.70	40min.	8 per day, 6:30am-7:30pm, €10.50
Lipari	2hr.	5 per day, 7am-6:30pm, €6.20	55min.	8 per day, 6:30am-7:30pm, €11.30
Salina	3hr.	2 per day, 7am-9am, €7.80	1½hr.	7 per day, 6:30am-7:30pm, €12.80
Panarea	4hr.	Daily (except Tu) at 2:30pm, Tu and Sa at 7am; €7.50	2hr.	5 per day, 7:50am-4:50pm, €13.30
Alicudi	6hr.	Daily (except Tu and Sa) at 7am, €11.70	3hr.	2 per day, 6:30am-2:30pm, €21.30
Filicudi	5hr.	Daily (except Tu and Sa) at 7am, Th at 2:30pm; €10.60	4½hr.	2 per day, 6:30am-2:30pm, €17.50
Stromboli	6hr.	Daily (except Tu) at 2:30pm, Tu and Sa at 7am; €9.90	2½hr.	5 per day, 7:50am-4:50, €16.20

LIPARI   ☎090

Centuries ago, wild-eyed pirates ravaged Lipari's shores. Today, boats and hydrofoils let loose packs of equally ravenous buccaneers looking for other kinds of treasures. They descend in swarms upon its beaches and wallow idly in its waves like listless merpeople; those who prefer the colors of the surrounding sea and mountains to neon umbrellas and speedos hike to nearby private beaches. Inexpensive hotels, divine sunbathing, and one of Italy's best archaeological museums make this an ideal launching pad for expeditions into the six neighboring islands.

⌐ TRANSPORTATION

Autobus Urso Guglielmo, V. Cappuccini, 9 (☎090 981 12 62 or 981 10 26), operates **buses** on most of the island. (Ticket office open daily 9am-7:30pm; tickets also available onboard.) Island tours (€3.62) depart daily 9:30, 11:30am, and 5pm. Reservation is required. **De. Sco.,** V. Stradale Pianoconte, 5, at the end of C. V. Emanuele closest to the hydrofoil docks, rents shiny scooters, lined up showroom-style. (☎090 981 32 88 or 368 753 55 90. Rental includes gas. €18-24 per day; Aug. €30-36. Open daily 8:30am-8pm. MC/V.) **Ditta Carbonaro Paola,** on C. V. Emanuele, 21, also rents scooters just steps away from De. Sco. (☎090 981 19 94. €15 per day; Aug. €25.) For **taxis,** call ☎090 988 06 16 or 339 577 64 37.

◼◼ ORIENTATION AND PRACTICAL INFORMATION

The **hydrofoil** and **ferry ports** are on either end of the promontory supporting the *castello* and museum. Restaurants and hotels cluster around **Corso Vittorio Emanuele II,** the main thoroughfare, and **Via Garibaldi,** which runs from the hydrofoil port around the base of the *castello* and is accessible by large stone stairs; C. V. Emanuele II ends at the docks. Maps can be purchased at *tabacchi* or bike rentals.

Tourist Office: AAST, C. V. Emanuele, 202 (☎090 988 00 95; www.netnet.it/aasteolie). From hydrofoil docks, turn right on V. Garibaldi, left on V. XXIV Maggio, right on C. V. Emanuele; office is 100m on the right. Info hub for all 7 islands. Ask for *Ospitalità in blu,* which contains helpful visitor information. Open July-Aug. M-F 8am-2pm and 4:30-9:30pm, Sa 8am-2pm; Sept.-June M-F 8am-2pm and 4:30-7:30pm.

Luggage Storage: At Ustica hydrofoil office. €3 per 12hr. Open 6:45am-8pm.

Currency Exchange: C. V. Emanuele is lined with banks and **ATMs.** Exchange money at **Banco Antonveneta** (☎090 981 21 18; open M-F 8:20am-1:20pm and 2:35-3:35pm), **Banco di Roma** (☎090 981 32 75; open M-F 8:30am-1:35pm and 2:50-4:10pm), or at the **post office** (cash only). Some of the smaller Aeolian islands have few or no ATMs, so get cash on Lipari before visiting them.

Laundry: Lavanderia Caprara Andrea, Vico Storione, 5 (☎090 981 31 77), off C. V. Emanuele. Wash and dry €4 per kg (min. 5kg). Open M-Sa 9am-1pm and 4:30-8:30pm.

Emergency: ☎113. **Carabinieri** (☎112 or 090 981 13 33). **Police** (☎090 981 27 57). Call ☎090 988 00 30 for non-emergencies. **Ambulance** (☎090 989 52 67). **First Aid** (☎090 988 52 67 or 981 10 10).

Medical Clinic: ☎090 988 52 26. Office 50m up V. Garibaldi from the waterfront, on the left under the Italian flag. Open M, W, and F 8:30am-1pm; Tu and Th 3:30-5:30pm.

Pharmacies: Farmacia Internazionale, C. V. Emanuele, 128 (☎090 981 15 83). Open in summer M-F 9am-1pm and 5-9pm; in winter 9am-1pm and 4-8pm. AmEx/MC/V. **Farmacia Cincotta,** V. Garibaldi, 60 (☎090 981 14 72). Open in summer M-F 9am-1pm and 5-9pm; in winter 9am-1pm and 4-8pm. 24hr. pharmacy list posted outside.

Hospital: Ospedale Civile di Lipari (☎090 988 51), on V. Santana. At southern end of C. V. Emanuele, descend the side street between scooter rental places and turn right on V. Roma. V. Santana is the 2nd left. Open daily 8am-8pm.

Internet: Internet Point, C. V. Emanuele, 185. Open daily in summer 9am-1pm and 5:30pm-midnight, in winter 9:30am-1:30pm and 4:40-9pm. 7 fast computers. €2 for 15min., €3 for 30min., €5 per hr. **Net C@fe,** V. Garibaldi, 61 (☎090 981 35 27). 2 computers in cafe. €3 for 30min., €5 per hr. Open daily 8am-3am; closed F in winter.

Post Office: Main branch for Aeolians (☎090 981 00 51), on C. V. Emanuele. Open M-F 8am-6:30pm, Sa 8am-12:30pm. **Postal Codes:** Canneto-Lipari 98052; Lipari 98055; all other islands 98050.

◼ ACCOMMODATIONS

Lipari reaches its saturation point in August, and prices rise as high as the temperatures. Reserve far ahead, even for early July. As soon as you step off of the hydrofoil exit ramp, you will be bombarded with offers for *affittacamere.* These are often the most affordable way to enjoy the islands, and some of the best deals are listed below. As always, ask to see the room before accepting and **always obtain a price quote in writing.** Also, prices are often fairly negotiable outside of August, so try to bargain your way to a better rate. Prices for private rooms are per person.

Casa Vacanze Marturano, V. Francesco Crispi, 97 (☎090 981 24 22 and 368 67 59 33; www.eoliearcipelago.it). Residences scattered on all 7 islands. Spacious rooms, most with shared kitchen and bath. Breakfast included in Panarea. Lipari and Salina €20-30. Vulcano, Panarea, Filicudi, Alicudi, and Stromboli €25-45. AmEx/MC/V. ❷

Casa Vittorio di Cassara, Vico Sparviero, 15 (☎/fax 090 981 15 23, 988 07 29, or 338 392 38 67), off V. Garibaldi, 78, at end of short stairway. Take V. Garibaldi from hydrofoil dock and U-turn at 1st possible left. From small alley, take 1st right. It's the yellow building with blue window frames. If it's locked, continue to the end of the street and turn right. At red iron gate, ring top left button. Ideal location near port and *centro*. Rooms with bath vary from intimate singles to 5-person penthouses. Some include kitchen and sea-view terrace. Rooms €15-40. Prices vary seasonally. Cash only. ❷

Pensione Enso il Negro, V. Garibaldi, 29, 3fl. (☎090 981 31 63, 981 24 73, or 368 66 52 83), 20m up V. Garibaldi from hydrofoil dock to the left, under a small doorway. Classy and comfortable, this hotel has elegant archways, wooden furniture, and painted tiles. 8 rooms have patio, fridge, A/C, and bath. 6 rooms are in a different location. Breakfast available. Singles €30-47; doubles €50-75. AmEx/MC/V. ❸

Hotel Rocce Azzurre, V. Maddalena, 69 (☎090 981 32 48, fax 981 32 47), on Porto delle Genti. Nestled in a quiet bay, this charming hotel has 33 rooms, all with bath and many with balcony. Breakfast included. Rooms €55-65. In Aug. half pension €100-110; full pension €120-130. AmEx/MC/V. ❺

Hotel Europeo, C. V. Emanuele, 98 (☎090 981 15 89), in the center of C. V. Emanuele and near both ports. Small, uninspiring rooms can be noisy at night. Top floor has external doors and a great view of the city. Apr.-July and Sept. €30; Aug. €40. Cash only. ❸

Baia Unci, V. Marina Garibaldi, 2 (☎090 981 19 09; www.campeggitalia.it/sicilia/baiaunci). Campgrounds near Canneto, 2km from Lipari. 10min. from beach. Self-service restaurant. Open Mar. 15-Oct. 15. €8-12 with tent. Cash only. ❶

🍴 FOOD

Legions of lovers have sprinkled sauces, garnished salads, and spiced meats with the island's *capperi* (capers), renowned for their aphrodisiacal powers. After following suit, complete a meal in style with local *Malvasia* dessert wine. Lipari's lip-smacking cuisine can get expensive, so head to **UPIM** supermarket, C. V. Emanuele, 212, for a budget meal. (☎090 981 15 87. Open M-Sa 8am-10pm. AmEx/MC/V.) Alimentari along C. V. Emanuele sell cheap fruit every day.

Da Gilberto e Vera, V. Garibaldi, 22-24 (☎090 981 27 56), has become famous nationwide for what may well be Italy's best sandwiches. Custom-made hot *panini* with any of Gilberto's ingredients: *prosciutto*, capers, fresh and dried tomatoes, olives, garlic, mint, etc. Also carries tons of picnic supplies, minus the basket. *Panini* €3.50. Open Mar.-Oct. daily 7am-4am; Nov.-Feb. 7pm-2am. AmEx/MC/V. ❶

La Cambusa, V. Garibaldi, 72 (☎349 476 60 61). Husband and wife team makes this trattoria feel like home. Cluster around outdoor tables with *Liparesi* or retreat indoors to enjoy authentic flavors of Sicily. Regulars rave about the pasta (from €5). Cover €1. Reservation recommended. Open daily noon-3pm and 7-11pm. Cash only. ❷

Ristorante Sottomonastero, C. V. Emanuele, 232 (☎090 988 07 20, fax 981 10 84). Tables are filled around the clock at this versatile bar-ristorante-pizzeria, which also specializes in Aeolian sweets. At night the action spills onto an outdoor patio. Pizza from €3.50. *Primi* from €5, *secondi* from €7. Cover €1.30. Open daily 7am-midnight; late July-Aug. 24hr. Kitchen open noon-2pm and 8:30-10pm. AmEx/MC/V. ❷

La Piazzetta (☎ 090 981 25 22, fax 981 25 11), off C. V. Emanuele, next to Subba (see below). Walls and menus boast signatures of its many famous satisfied customers, including Audrey Hepburn. The patio extending into a small piazza is almost as elegant as the lady herself. Pizza from €7.50. *Primi* from €7, *secondi* from €9.50. Open July-Aug. noon-2pm and 7:30-11pm; Sept.-June 7:30-11pm. MC/V. ❹

Pasticceria Subba, C. V. Emanuele, 92 (☎ 090 981 13 52). Pay by weight, in more ways than one, at the archipelago's oldest *pasticceria*. The *pasta paradiso*, an almond paste dumpling, is heavenly sweet. Large pastries from €1.55. Open daily May-Oct. 7am-1am; Nov.-Apr. 7am-midnight. Cash only. ❶

🔆 SIGHTS

Lipari's best sights—aside from its beaches—are all in the *castello* on the hill, where a gigantic **fortress** with ancient Greek foundations dwarfs the surrounding town. In the vicinity is the ◙**Museo Archeological Eoliano,** whose collection, explained in English and Italian, includes gigantic Liparite urns, galleries full of Greek and Sicilian red figureware pottery from the fourth and fifth centuries BC, and treasures of underwater exploration that range from Greco-Italic amphorae to the wreck of a 17th-century Spanish warship. The geological and volcanic section is devoted to the island's natural history. Walk up the stone steps to the right off V. Garibaldi; turn left at San Bartolomeo. (☎ 090 988 01 74. Museum open daily June-Aug. 9am-1:30pm and 4-7pm, Nov.-Apr. 9am-1:30pm and 3-6pm. Ticket office closes 1hr. early. €4.50, EU residents 18-25 €2, EU residents under 18 or over 65 free.) The Chiesa di San Bartolomeo, the town's cathedral, is on the same hill. Built in the 12th century, it was sacked and burned by Barbarossa the Turk in 1544. A new Baroque version, dedicated to St. Bartholomew, is done up in light blue hues and topped by a beautifully painted ceiling. Stratified Greek, Roman, and Stone Age **ruins** encircle the building; comprehensive charts show the process of excavation and the age of each structure. The park's centerpiece is a contemporary Ancient Greek-style **theater** that hosts performances. Ask at the tourist office for programs and ticket prices. (Both sites are across from the museum. Open daily 9am-1pm. Free.)

🔆 🌺 BEACHES AND FESTIVALS

From July to September, island bus tours (€2.58) run at 2pm from **Autobus Urso Guglielmo** (☎ 090 981 12 62 or 981 10 26), on V. Cappuccini. A better way to see the coastline is from the water, spending a leisurely day aboard a rented boat from the hydrofoil port. For still better views, take the Lipari-Cavedi bus to the gorgeous beaches of nearby **Canneto.** The pebbles are prickly and the sun scorching, so bring sunscreen and flip-flops. Rent a raft, kayak, or canoe along the beach at V. M. Garibaldi to explore the secluded coves flanking **Spiaggia Bianca** (€3-5 per hr., €13-20 per day). A few kilometers north at **Pomiciazzo,** white pumice mines line the road. Farther north at **Porticello,** people bathe at the foot of mines where flecks of stone float on the water's surface. A beach closer to the port is at **Porto della Gente.** From the docks, turn left on the *lungomare* and walk up the slight hill. Turn right up the stairs and take the first left away from the hotel. Turn right on the next road and follow it to the shore. These beaches provide stellar views of Salina, Panarea, and Stromboli. For the finest vista yet, take the Lipari-Quattropani bus to **Pianoconte** and head to **Monte S. Angelo.** The path to the mountain is tiny and thick with shrubbery, so ask for help or accept the fate of getting lost along the incline.

Summer fever reaches its breaking point (and surpasses the island's capacity) on August 24 with the **Festa di San Bartolomeo.** Processions, parties, and pyrotechnics take over in celebration. The quieter **Wine and Bread Festival** in mid-November features more delectable activities in the Pianoconte district.

VULCANO ☎090

Visitors can usually smell Vulcano long before they see it. The pungent island was once thought to be the home of the Greek god Vulcan, god of smiths, and of Aeolus, keeper of the winds—as well as the gate to Hell—though it is now best known for its volcanic craters and savage landscapes. The largest volcano is the active and heavily touristed Fossa di Vulcano. The great furnace currently lies benign, but geologists predict an eruption within the next 20 years. Black beaches, bubbling seas, and natural sulfuric mud spas may make Vulcano seem unfriendly, but these untamed natural phenomena usually end up winning over visitors.

▐ TRANSPORTATION

The island is accessible by **hydrofoil** and **ferry. Siremar** (☎090 985 21 49), atop a stone walkway at the Porto Levante intersection, runs hydrofoils to Lipari (10min., 8 per day, €2.60) and Milazzo (40min., 9 per day 7:20am-7:50pm, €10.40). **Ustica** (☎090 985 22 30), directly off the port next to Cantine Stevenson, runs hydrofoils to: Lipari (10min., 11 per day, €2.50); Milazzo (40min., 8 per day, €10.50); Palermo (4hr., 2 per day 7:40am-4:50pm, €31.30). **N.G.I. Biglietteria** (☎090 985 24 01) sells ferry tickets under a blue awning on V. Provinciale, just off P. Levante. Open daily 8:15am-noon, 5:15-6:30pm, 10:30-11:30pm. **Scaffidi Tindaro** (☎090 985 30 47) runs **internal buses** off the port on V. Provinciale, in front of Ritrovo Remigio. Rare buses (€1.85) run to Vulcano Piano. Catch a **taxi** from the port or call ☎339 579 15 76 or 347 813 06 31. Another option is **Centro Nautico Baia di Levante** (☎339 879 72 38 or 339 337 27 95).

◆ ▐ ORIENTATION AND PRACTICAL INFORMATION

Vulcano's casual atmosphere is manifested in the lack of posted street names and address numbers. Frequent directional signs and arrows, however, make this pedestrian island easily navigable. All ferries and hydrofoils dock at **Porto di Levante**, on the eastern side of **Vulcanello**, one of four volcanoes on the island. Facing away from the hydrofoil dock at the far left of the port, **Via Provinciale** heads left toward the largest volcano and the **Gran Cratere.** Straight ahead is **Via Porto Levante**, a semicircular road that loops through town and reconnects to the ferry docks. From the hydrofoil docks, V. Porto Levante splits in three directions at the small statue of Aeolus. The pharmacy is straight ahead, while the famed *acquacalda* and **Laghetto di Fanghi** are on the right. Continuing along to the left of the pharmacy, pass green pastures on the way to the black shoreline of **Sabbie Nere.**

Tourist Office: V. Provinciale, 41 (☎090 985 20 28 or 985 21 42), has info on *affitta-camere.* Open in summer daily 8am-1:30pm and 3-5pm. All other info at AAST in Lipari.

Bank: Banco Sicilia (☎090 985 23 35), 100m down from the port on V. Provinciale, has an **ATM.** Open M-F 8:30am-1:30pm and 2:45-3:45pm.

Currency Exchange: Ustica Office (☎090 985 22 30), at Porto di Levante.

Boat Rental: Centro Nautico Baia di Levante (☎339 879 72 38 or 337 27 95), in a shed on the beach behind Ritrovo Remigio, near the hydrofoil dock. 4-person motorboat €90-150 per day depending on style. Gas extra. Open daily 8am-10pm.

Scooter and Bicycle Rentals: *Noleggio* nemeses **Da Paolo** (☎090 985 21 12 or 338 139 28 09) and **Sprint da Luigi** (☎090 985 22 08 or 347 760 02 75), a block apart on V. Provinciale, have almost identical prices. Scooters per day in May €12.50-15; June €15.50-18; July-Aug. €25-30; Sept. €15.50. Bikes €5. Tandem bike €8 per hr., €20 per day, and minicar €15 per hr., €45 per day.

Emergency: Carabinieri (☎090 985 21 10). Police (☎090 985 25 77). First Aid (☎090 985 22 20).

Pharmacy: Farmacia Bonarrigo, V. Favaloro, 1 (☎090 985 22 44; in case of emergency 985 31 13), straight ahead of the port, at the far end of the small piazza where V. Provinciale breaks off. Open M-Sa 9am-1pm and 5-8pm, Su 9am-1pm. AmEx/MC/V. List of late-night pharmacies posted.

Post Office: At Vulcano Piano, down V. Provinciale. Open M-F 8am-1:20pm, Sa 8am-12:20pm. Postal Code: 98050.

ACCOMMODATIONS AND CAMPING

Hotel Torre, V. Favaloro, 1 (☎/fax 090 985 23 42), down V. Porto Levante from hydrofoil docks, near pharmacy. 8 enormous rooms come with bath, A/C, terrace, and kitchen; many offer extraordinary views. Good location near *acquacalda*. Cribs available. Doubles Oct.-Apr. €38; May €40; June-Sept. €50; Aug. €76. Extra person 35%. Solo travelers may receive low-season discount. Cash only. ❹

Residence Lanterna Bleu di Francesco Corrieri, V. Lentia, 58 (☎/fax 090 985 21 78), along V. Lentia, which breaks from V. Provinciale before the pharmacy. 1- or 2-room apartments are tranquil, if plain. All come with bath, A/C, kitchenette, and terrace. 400m from thermal and mudbaths. Breakfast €4. Oct.-Apr. singles €31; doubles €62; May-Sept. singles €45-70, doubles €86-136. Extra bed €13-19. AmEx/MC/V. ❹

Hotel Residence Mari del Sud (☎090 985 32 50; dipanesrl@tin.it), on V. Porto Ponente. Shorefront, resort-style hotel hosts activities ranging from diving lessons to Caribbean dance parties. Small rooms have TV, fan, and minibar. Breakfast included. Doubles €80-190. Half pension €55-110; full pension €82-137. AmEx/MC/V. ❺

Campeggio Togo Togo (☎090 985 23 03), at Porto Ponente, on opposite side of Vulcanello's isthmus neck, 1½ km from hydrofoil dock and adjacent to Sabbie Nere. Showers, tent, and hot water included. In summer, pizzeria and Internet. Open Apr.-Sept. Reserve ahead for Aug. €10 includes tent and light. Larger bungalow with TV and kitchenette. July-Aug. up to 4 people €83; Apr.-June and Sept. 1-7 €20 per person. ❶

FOOD

Granite and gelato are in abundance at the port, but venture off the main roads for a good meal. The aromatic *Malvasia* wine is a delight. Tridial Market, on V. Porto Levante in the piazza before the pharmacy, has essentials, plus a sandwich counter. (Open daily 8am-8:30pm.) An alimentari on V. Provinciale, toward the crater from the port, sells produce. (Open daily 8am-1pm and 5-8pm.)

Remigio, V. Porto Levante, 1 (☎090 985 20 85), at end of the hydrofoil docks. Popular with tourists and locals, this large bar sells hot and cold sandwiches made to order (€2). Delicious gelato and many, many desserts. Free baggage storage for patrons. Horseshoe *ciappe* €1.30. *Cassata* €2.20. Open daily 6am-2am. Cash only. ❶

Cafe Piazzetta (☎090 985 32 67), in Piazzetta Faraglione, down V. Provinciale from hydrofoil docks. Serves gelato and cocktails (€5.20), or order a more substantial pizza (from €5) or *Basiluzzo panino*, with tomato, cheese, lettuce, olive oil, salt, and oregano (€2.80). Live music June-Sept. evenings on the bamboo patio. Open daily Apr.-Sept. 7am-2am. Free baggage storage for patrons. AmEx/MC/V. ❶

Cantine Stevenson (☎090 985 32 47), on V. Porto Levante. Nightlife dive where locals lounge while listening to rousing classical music in a pub-like setting. Check out the 60-page wine list. Cocktails €5.50. Pizza €6.50. *Primi* from €6.50, *secondi* from €8. Dessert €4.50. Open daily 1pm-3am. MC/V. ❷

Ristorante-Bar Vincenzino, V. Porto Levante, 25 (☎090 985 20 16, fax 985 33 70), down hydrofoil docks, up V. Provinciale. Large, low-key restaurant/bar serves Aeolian specialties. *Gamberoni alla griglia* (grilled prawns) are an expensive treat at €18. *Primi* from €6.50, *secondi* from €7. Cover €1.50. Open daily 7am-10pm. AmEx/MC/V. ❸

◉ SIGHTS

Anyone visiting Vulcano for more than a day should tackle the 1hr. hike on a snaking footpath to the inactive ◪**Gran Cratere.** The summit rewards trekkers with unsurpassed views of the island, sea, and blackened volcanic landscape. The hike winds through bright yellow *fumaroli*, emissions of noxious smoke, and bizarre orange rock formations powdered with white dust. Between 11am and 3pm, the beaming sun transforms the volcano face into a furnace. Head out in the early morning or late afternoon, and bring a hat, sunscreen, sturdy climbing shoes, and plenty of water. Segments of the trail are quite strenuous and should be approached with caution. Obey the signs, and don't sit or lie down, as poisonous gases tend to accumulate close to the ground. Some travelers shave a good 30min. off their descent time by sprinting straight down the mountainside; this is an undeniable thrill, but the risk is a nasty spill. (Facing away from the water at the port, turn left on V. Provinciale and follow it until reaching a path with "Cratere" signs. The notices point to a dirt turn off 300m on the left.)

If everyone jumped into a radioactive mudpit, would you? The murky gray-brown of the Laghetto di Fanghi's water blends right in with the surrounding volcanic rock formations, but the putrid smell makes this natural spa impossible to miss. Undeterred, visitors by the hundreds spread gray sludge over their bodies for its allegedly curative effects (especially for arthritis). Therapeutic or not, the mud is radioactive and high in corrosive sulfuric acid, which can cause severe burning or blistering of the skin. Remove all silver and leather accessories, and keep the actual mud away from the eyes. If contact occurs, *immediately* rinse eyes with running water and a few drops of lemon juice from a nearby restaurant. (Up V. Porto Levante and to the right from the port. €1.50.) Directly behind the mud pits at the **acquacalda,** Vulcano's shoreline bubbles like a jacuzzi, courtesy of volcanic *fumaroli* beneath the surface. The sulfuric nature of the water has quite an effect on the human blood circulation, creating a heavenly sensation upon emerging—although the mercilessly corrosive acid tends to destroy bathing suits. This is not the place to display the latest in swimwear fashion. Disposable suits are available nearby for €5.

If sulfur burns and radioactive mud don't sound appealing, join carefree sunbathers on Vulcano's best beach, Sabbie Nere. Black sands curl up against white-crested waves, and colorful umbrellas form a rainbow of relaxation. (Follow V. Provinciale from the port, then take the road that veers to the left of the pharmacy. Continue along the pastures and past the Hotel Eolie until reaching the shore.)

STROMBOLI   ☎090

In Italian geology, "strombolic activity" refers to the most violent type of volcanic eruption. In keeping with its title, the aptly named island of Stromboli harbors the Aeolians' only active volcano—a fact that keeps residents few (around 370) and visitors many. Though the great Stromboli is always gurgling, the island itself keeps quiet until summer. Sporadic volcanic activity scares away all but the most determined visitors, cleaning out hotel rooms and turning the town into a deserted haven, if a dimly ominous one. The adventurous are drawn to nightly guided hikes up the mountain, but if the volcano's threat seems more intimidating than intriguing, renting a boat is also a great way to visit.

▐ TRANSPORTATION. Along the shorefront *lungomare*, **Siremar** (☎090 98 60 16; open daily 9am-1pm, 3-5:30pm, and 9-10pm), **Ustica** (☎090 98 60 03; open daily 8am-1pm and 3-8pm), and **N.G.I.** (☎090 98 30 03) run **ferries** and **hydrofoils** to the islands. **Boat rentals** are available from a number of companies at the port, including the **Società Navigazione Pippo.** (☎090 98 61 35 or 338 985 78 83. Boats from €60 per day; larger boats run up to €200; gas extra. Boat tours last 3hr. and depart 10:30am and 3:10pm daily; €20. Open daily 9am-noon, 2-8pm, and 9-10:30pm.)

▐▐ ORIENTATION AND PRACTICAL INFORMATION. On the calmer slopes of smoking Stromboli, the three villages of **Scari, Ficogrande,** and **Piscita** have melded into one stretch known as the town of Stromboli. From the ferry docks, the wide *lungomare* is on the right, continuing to the beach and two large hotels, while the narrow **Via Roma** heads from the ticket offices up to the town center. Twisting uphill to the left, V. Roma passes the **carabinieri** station (☎090 98 60 21) on the left, the island's only **ATM** next to the Alimentari da Maria, the **post office** (☎090 98 60 27; open M-F 8am-1:30pm, Sa 8am-12:30pm), and the **pharmacy** just before the piazza (☎090 98 67 13; open M-Sa 8:30am-1pm and 4-8:30pm, Sept.-May also 4-7:30pm), before finally reaching **Piazza San Vincenzo.** V. Roma then dips downhill, becoming **Via Vittorio Emanuele,** which runs past the **medical clinic** (☎090 98 60 97) and leads to the trail up the mountain. **Postal Code:** 98050.

▐▐ ACCOMMODATIONS AND FOOD. Unlike the more populated islands, the tourist deluge in Stromboli happens exclusively in August. In the low season, many *pensioni* close down and owners are reluctant to rent rooms for fewer than three nights. When hotels are solidly booked, *affittacamere* may be the best bet. Expect to pay between €20 and €30. Ask to see the room before paying, and don't be afraid to check for hot water and comfortable beds. From the main road, follow the small side street across from St. Bartholomew's church at the end of town to reach ▨**Casa del Sole ❷**, on V. D. Cincotta. Big dormitory rooms face a shaded terrace and shared kitchen, while the upstairs holds doubles painted in sea hues. Four bathrooms are downstairs. (☎/fax 090 98 60 17. Open Mar.-Oct. Dorm beds €22 per person; doubles €46. Prices vary seasonally.) **Pensione Brasile ❹**, up the street from Casa del Sole, offers simple white rooms and great home-cooked meals. (☎090 98 60 08; utenti.lycos.it/pensionebrasile. Breakfast included Apr.-June 15 and Sept.-Oct. €28. June 16-Sept. 7 half pension €47-60; full pension €60-73. MC/V.) **Pensione Villa Petrusa ❹**, off V. V. Emanuele, 10min. from the sea, has colorful gardens, a TV room and bar, and 26 comfortable rooms with large bath. (☎090 98 60 45. Breakfast included. Singles or doubles €30; in Aug. €50. Cash only.) **La Lampara B&B ❷**, V. V. Emanuele, 27, has five rooms decorated island-style, with brightly tiled floors, TV, and large bath. (☎090 98 64 09. Breakfast included. Rooms €20 per person; July €35; Aug. €45. AmEx/MC/V.)

Stuff a pre-hike knapsack snack at **Alimentari da Maria,** on V. Roma just before the church. (☎090 98 61 49. Open daily 8:30am-1pm and 4:30-8:30pm, Su 8:30am-1pm. MC/V.) In order to admire the volcano's explosive activity from solid ground, head to ▨**L'Osservatorio ❹**, in Punta Labronzo, the last establishment along V. V. Emanuele. The food is slightly overpriced, but the spectacular view of nighttime eruptions makes it well worth it. The restaurant is a serious trek away; bring a flashlight at night and wear sneakers. Taxis also depart for the restaurant from S. Bartolo every hour from 5-11pm. (☎090 98 63 60 or 337 29 39 42, fax 98 63 60. Pizza from €6.20. *Primi* from €7, *secondi* from €14. Cover €1.50. Open 9:30am-midnight. Cash only.) Locals say the best pizza on the island is **La Lampara ❸**, V. V. Emanuele, 27, on the left just after P. San Vincenzo. It shares management with La Lampara B&B. The freshly squeezed lemon *granite* (€2) are amazing, and the owner serves fish he caught himself. The *frittura di pesce misto* (mixed fried fish; €11) offers a nice sampling. (☎090 98 64 09, fax 98 67 21. Pizza from €5.50. *Primi* €6-10, *secondi* €10-14. Open Mar.-Nov. daily 6pm-midnight. AmEx/MC/V.) At the *rosticceria* **La Trottola ❷**, V. Roma, 34, delve into the *pizza Stromboli*, a cone-shaped creation bursting with mozzarella, tomatoes, and olives. (☎090 98 60 46. Pizza from €3.62. Open daily 8am-2pm and 4pm-midnight. MC/V.)

◙ SIGHTS. Strombolicchio, a gigantic rock with a small lighthouse, rises 2km in the distance from the black beach at **Ficogrande.** The ravages of the sea have eroded the rock from 56m to a mere 42m in the past century. Beachgoers should check out the small cove at the end of V. Giuseppe Cincotta, off V. V. Emanuele near Casa del Sole. Large rocks encircle the stretch of black sand.

At the ▧**volcano,** rivers of orange lava and molten rock spill over the slope, lighting the **Sciara del Fuoco** (Trail of Fire) at roughly 10min. intervals. The **Società Navigazione Pippo** (☎090 98 61 35), at the port, runs a boat trip for those wishing to view the volcano from the sea (1hr., 10pm, €15), although many visitors prefer to get a bit closer. An ordinance passed in 1990 made hiking the volcano without a guide illegal, and for good reason: a photographer was burnt to death after getting too close to the volcanic opening, and in 1998, a Czech diplomat, lost in the fog, walked off the cliff's edge. So if such an end is not in your stars, look into an escorted trip with ▧**Magmatrek,** on V. V. Emanuele (☎/fax 090 986 57 68; office open 10am-1pm and 4:30-6:30pm). This group once ran tours to the craters themselves, but new laws prohibit tours from going any higher than 450m. This still provides an impressive close-up view of the eruptions and is the most exciting way to see the volcano. The charismatic **Mario Zaia** (☎368 67 55 73), known as Zaza, is regarded as one of the most reliable volcano guides working today. (Helmets required and provided. All tours offered in English. Departures daily Mar.-June 3:30pm, July-Aug. 6pm, Sept.-Oct. 3:30pm; €13.50.) **Totem Trekking,** at P. S. Vincenzo, 4, rents equipment and supplies, as well as Internet access for €6/hr. (☎090 986 57 52. Open daily in summer 10am-1pm and 4:30pm-midnight, Dec. 15-Jan. 8 10am-1pm and 4:30-8pm. Call year-round to arrange rentals. AmEx/MC/V.)

 STOP IN THE NAME OF LAVA. Let's Go does not recommend, advocate, or take responsibility for anyone hiking Stromboli's volcano, with or without a guide. A red triangle with a black, vertical bar means "danger."

Those who choose to disobey the law (feigning ignorance of the four languages on the warning signs) and head up alone should coordinate to do the dangerous descent with a group. Take sturdy shoes, a flashlight, snacks, water, and warm clothes for the exposed summit. Don't wear contact lenses, as the wind sweeps ash and dust about unforgivingly. During the day only smoke is visible, so plan to reach the summit around dusk to nestle into a rock dugout and watch the brilliant lava bursts. Totem Trekking rents climbing shoes, daypacks, helmets, flashlights, and walking sticks. To reach the volcano, follow C. V. Emanuele from P. Vincenzo until reaching the large warning sign; bear right at the fork in the road. The path turns upward when a secluded stretch of beach comes into view and, after 400m, cuts between two white houses. Halfway up, the trail degenerates into a mire of volcanic rock. Follow the red, orange, and white rock markings *very* carefully; **do not attempt shortcuts** as it is very easy to get lost. Warning signs at the top ridge are sincere. The risk of walking off the edge is greater during spring and fall fogs. Above all, remember this golden rule: **when hiking down the volcano at night, use the same path you took up.**

⬛ ENTERTAINMENT. The plateau of **Piazza San Vincenzo** is Stromboli's geographic center and its most exciting 46 sq. m (besides the crater itself). Each night around 10pm, islanders flock to **Ritrovo Ingrid** for gelato (€1.55) and drinks. (☎090 98 63 85. Open daily Aug.-July 8am-1am, July-Aug. 8am-3am.) Its neighbor, **Ristorante-Pizzeria Il Conte Ugolino,** has a lovely seating area where people gather for conversation over food and drinks. The moon rising directly over the piazza is a magical sight, and from behind the church there's a great view of the volcano. (☎090 986 57 65. Cover €3. Service 15%.)

PANAREA   ☎090

As is apparent from the constant stream of white linen and Louis Vuitton luggage on the hydrofoil docks, petite Panarea is the island for chic repose. With simple white buildings and a beguiling elegance, Panarea attracts an older, upscale crowd seeking an understated place to relax—and those who can afford the privilege. In August, however, rambunctious youth overtake the *discoteche,* forcing its once-dignified waterside bars to pump up the volume and party well into the morning.

⬛⬛ ORIENTATION AND PRACTICAL INFORMATION. Panarea is accessible by **ferry** and **hydrofoil** (see **Aeolian Islands: Transportation**). The **Siremar** office is at the port. (Open M, Th, Sa 7am-11:30am; Tu-W, F, and Su 2-7:45pm and 2-6:30pm.) Panarea is a purely pedestrian island. Its only vehicles are bikes, scooters, and the golf carts that serve as taxis. All directional signs list distances by feet rather than kilometers, and street signs and numbers are very rare. The main road, **Via San Pietro,** runs past Chiesa San Pietro along an undulating stone path to **Punta Milazzese. Banca Antonveneta** has an **ATM** on V. S. Pietro, on the left from the port, and **Banca di Sicilia** has one on the patio of the Hotel Cincotta. Have a back-up plan in case ATMs don't work. The **post office** on V. S. Pietro **exchanges currency** and AmEx traveler's cheques. (☎090 98 30 28. Open M-F 8am-1:30pm, Sa 8am-12:30pm.) In case of **emergency,** call the **carabinieri** (July-Aug. ☎090 98 31 81; Sept.-June 981 13 33, in Lipari) or the **medical clinic** (☎090 98 30 40). A 24hr. **golf cart taxi** service is run by **Paola+Angelo** (☎333 313 86 10), on V. S. Pietro. Passage to the beach costs around €8. A **pharmacy** is at V. Iditella, 8. (☎090 98 31 48. Open in summer M-Sa 9am-1pm and 5-9pm, in winter M-Tu and Th-Su 9am-12:30pm.)

⬛ ACCOMMODATIONS. Hotels are small but costly, and prices peak in July and August. From the docks, turn left, follow the road past the ATM to the steps, and look for the manta ray symbol to spot ⬛**Hotel RAYA ❺,** on V. S. Pietro. From striking architecture to amazing views, all aspects of this hotel breathe island elegance. Its *discoteca* is famous on the island (see **Sights and Entertainment**), and service is coolly obliging. (☎090 98 30 13; info@hotelraya.it. Breakfast included. Economy singles €92-142; singles €186-278; doubles €236-440. AmEx/MC/V.) Turn right from the docks and climb stairs to the white and blue houses of **Da Francesco/Pasqualina ❹,** on V. del Porto. All 10 rooms have bath, fan, and sea view. A trattoria extends from the deck. (☎090 98 30 23. Breakfast included. Rooms €42-52 per person; with half pension €65-85. MC/V.) **Hotel Tesoriero ❹,** on V. S. Pietro, has the basics and more: bath, A/C, TV, and hair dryer, plus a bamboo-shaded terrace with sea view. (☎090 98 30 98 or 98 31 44; info@hoteltesoriero.it. Breakfast included. Doubles €78-150. Singles supplement €11-52. Extra bed 30% more. Half pension €60-100. AmEx/MC/V.) Attention to detail distinguishes **La Quartara ❺,** V. S. Pietro, 15, evident in the ornate and unique decor, with cream-colored canopy, balcony, A/C, TV, bath, hair dryer, and minibar. (☎090 98 30 27; www.quartarahotel.com. Breakfast included. Singles €70-220; doubles €130-300; with view €150-340. Singles supplement €36-100. Extra bed 20% more. Prices vary seasonally. Under 6 low season 50% discount.) Indulge in Mediterranean bliss with seaside pool and massages at **Hotel Cincotta ❺**, on V. S. Pietro next to Hotel Raya. Its light, airy rooms are finely stocked with bath, TV, minibar, and terrace with view. (☎090 98 30 14, fax 98 32 11. Breakfast included. Doubles €130-260; half pension €30 extra per person. Extra bed 20% more. Prices vary seasonally. AmEx/MC/V.)

◻ FOOD. Da Bruno **minimart** is on V. S. Pietro by the post office. (☎090 98 30 02. Open daily July-Aug. 7:45am-9pm, Sept.-June 8am-1pm and 4-9pm.) Locals line up at the **panificio** next door (☎090 98 32 84) for such savories as *biscotti*, focaccia, and pizza slices. (Open daily Sept.-July 6:30am-1:30pm and 5-8pm, Aug. 6:30am-9pm.) Near the port, at **Ristorante Da Pina ❹**, V. S. Pietro, 14, billowing swaths of gauze create an ethereal mood among the pillowed outdoor benches—guests don't sit, they lounge. *Gnocchi di melanzane* (with eggplants; €10) and *couscous di pesce e aragosta* (with fish and lobster; €10) are the irresistible house specials. (☎090 98 30 32 or 98 33 24, fax 98 31 47. *Primi* €10, *secondi* €15. Lobster €150 per kg. AmEx/MC/V.) Whenever a craving flares, find a cone of gelato (€2.50), snackable *panini* (€3.50), or a Sicilian sweet at **Ritrovo Naif ❶**, V. S. Pietro, open all night. (☎090 98 31 88; www.barnaif.com. Open in summer daily 24hr.; winter hours vary.)

◪◩ BEACHES AND ENTERTAINMENT. The few who seek out Panarea's beaches do so precisely because most others do not. Tiny and unencumbered by umbrellas, these are some of the more natural and intimate coves of the archipelago. From Punta Milazzese, three small beaches extend along the coastline; gradually changing from rocks to sand, the trio gives a wide spectrum of Aeolian shores. Two rights from the center of town lead to **Calcara** (also known as "Spiaggia Fumarole"), near the thermal springs at **Acquacalda**. Reach another beach by following V. S. Pietro's signs for **"Spiagietta Zimmari."** In a 30min. stroll along a scenic road alive with darting lizards and flowering cacti, rock gives way to sand in this perfect marriage between shore and sea. Arrive early to find an empty patch of sand, and stop by the supermarket before heading out, as Spiagietta Zimmari's only bar is pricey. For unobstructed views of coves and cliffs, embark on a boat tour with **Eolie Mare,** on V. Umberto I. The company also rents boats for private exploration. (☎090 98 33 28. Tour €50 for 2 people. Open daily 24hr.) For scuba diving, **Amphibia** has an office on the *lungomare*, up the stairs next to the hotel Da Francesco. (☎335 613 85 29. Office open daily May-Sept. 9am-1pm and 3-7pm. Single immersion €39, 3 dives €111, 6 dives €204. Wetsuit rental €17.)

Panarea comes alive in summer with disco fever. The spot to be is **Hotel RAYA**, V. S. Pietro, which pumps with energy and exclusivity until the first morning rays. Cover: €30-50. Three cocktails: €30. A party outfit that will get you past the door: €100. Chatting up Italian soccer players, Milanese banking heirs, and actresses from all over? Priceless. (☎090 98 30 13. Open July 23-Aug. 31. Hotel guests free.)

SALINA   ☎090

Though close to Lipari in both size and distance, Salina is far removed from its more developed neighbor. Untouched landscapes, stagnant villages, and the most dramatic beaches on the archipelago make this a tranquil paradise. With its vast variety of plants and flowers, Salina offers hiking, canoeing, and bicycling opportunities. The island's most astounding rock formations are at Semaforo di Pollara, chosen as the setting of Massimo Troisi's film *Il Postino*. Some of Sicily's best restaurants hide away on Salina's slopes, though the island's limited tourism has led to a dearth of budget accommodations.

▊ TRANSPORTATION. Porto Santa Marina is the main port of Salina, accessible by **hydrofoil** (30min., 10 per day, €5.30) and **ferry** (50min., 3 per day, €2.90) from Lipari. The smaller port of Rinella on the opposite side of the island receives hydrofoils (45min., €6) and ferries (90min., €3.40). **Ustica** (☎ 090 984 30 03) and **Siremar** (☎ 090 984 30 04) have offices on either side of the church of Santa Marina, in front of the port in P. S. Marina. Blue **C.I.T.I.S. buses**, V. Nazionale, 10 (☎ 090 984 41 50), in Malfa, stop at the church. Monthly schedules are posted at the Ustica office. **Buses** run to Pollara (40min., 7 per day 6:05am-5:15pm, €1.60) and Leni, Valdichiesa, Malfa, Gramignazzi, Rinella, and Lingua (12 per day 6:05am-8pm).

■ ☛ **ORIENTATION AND PRACTICAL INFORMATION.** The main road, **Via Risorgimento**, runs parallel to the *lungomare*. **Rent scooters** from **Motonoleggio Bongiorno Antonio**, V. Risorgimento, 240, in Santa Marina. Facing away from the hydrofoil docks, turn left up the road that curves uphill. Turn right up the first side street just before a row of parked scooters to reach the office. Caution: Salina's roads are extremely narrow and curvy, and locals drive with a notorious and reckless abandon, so leave driving to the experts. If you do drive, then absolutely wear a helmet. (☎ 090 984 34 09 or 984 32 64. Scooters €8-8.50 per hr., €26-31 per day. Mountain bikes €2.50-3.50 per hr., €8-10.50 per day. Gas extra. Open daily in summer 8:30am-8pm; in winter 8:30am-1:30pm. AmEx/MC/V.)

In case of **emergency,** call the **carabinieri** (☎ 090 984 30 19), **police** (☎ 090 984 31 28), or **first aid** (☎ 090 984 40 05). The **Farmacia Comunale,** V. Risorgimento, 211, is at the bottom of the street. (☎ 090 984 30 98. Open M 5:30-8:30pm, Tu-F 9am-1pm and 5:30-8:30pm, Sa 9am-1pm.) **Banco di Sicilia,** V. Risorgimento, 158-160, cashes **traveler's checks, exchanges money,** and has an **ATM.** (☎ 090 984 33 65. Open M-F 8:30am-1:30pm.) **Salina Computer,** on V. Risorgimento, 110, has **Internet** and is open daily 8:30am-1pm and 3-8:30pm. (☎ 090 984 34 44. €6 per hr.) The **post office,** at V. Risorgimento, 130, exchanges American Express **traveler's cheques.** (☎ 090 984 30 28. Open M-F 8am-1:30pm, Sa 8am-12:30pm.) **Postal Code:** 98050.

■ ☛ **ACCOMMODATIONS AND FOOD.** Restaurants crowd Santa Marina, the dockside town, but most accommodations are farther afield. By the port consider **Pensione Mamma Santina ❹,** V. Sanità, 40, which offers first-rate rooms painted in melon hues. Guests mingle on the terrace, and the owner/chef (recently featured in *Cucina Italiana*) has been known to give cooking lessons to inquisitive onlookers. (☎ 090 984 30 54; www.mammasantina.it. Rooms €60-90 per person. Half pension €25 extra per person. €30 surcharge for use of a double as a single. AmEx/MC/V.) Salina's only true budget accommodations, **Campeggio Tre Pini ❶,** V. Rotabile, 1, maintains neat, terraced campsites that drop down to the sea, as well as a market, bar, and restaurant. (☎ 090 980 91 55, in winter 980 90 41. Take the bus or hydrofoil to Rinella, and confirm destination with driver. Reserve July-Aug. €6-8 per person, €8-11 per tent.)

As always, the cheapest way to eat is a cold lunch: assemble a beach picnic at any alimentari on V. Risorgimento. But given Salina's cuisine, it is almost inexcusable not to indulge in a fine meal. An exerting but richly rewarded 15min. uphill walk leads to ▧**Ristorante da Franco ❹,** V. Belvedere, 8. Climb the hill from Mamma Santina, then veer right on V. Belvedere just before the main road. Promising "courtesy, hospitality, and quality" from "the best of nature," the restaurant offers award-winning and supremely fresh local specialties, not to mention the best views in Salina. The chef-owner is a familiar face in the international foodie press. (☎ 090 984 32 87. *Primi* from €9.30, *secondi* from €13. Homemade wine €9.30. Open daily noon-2pm and 7:30pm-midnight. Closed Dec. 1-20. AmEx/MC/V.) At night, **Ni Lausta ❸,** V. Risorgimento, 188, packs gabby patrons into the bar downstairs. Evening diners go upstairs for *pasta modo mio,* or "pasta my way," an oft-changing pasta dish, in the relaxed terrace garden. (☎ 090 984 34 86. Lunch *menù* €20, dinner *menù* €35. Open 1-3pm and 6pm-midnight, bar closes at 3am. MC/V.)

SICILY

SICILY

⬛🏵 SIGHTS AND FESTIVALS. Seeing Salina's finest sight involves a 1hr. bus ride from Santa Marina to the striking ⬛**Pollara,** a beach 100m straight down from the town's cliffs in the middle of a half-submerged volcanic crater. The trip, though fast-paced and precipitous, is worth every twist and turn. Black sand, crumbling boulders, and raked sandstone walls create the rough crescent of land that hugs impossibly blue water. To the far right, a natural rock archway bursts from the water and suns itself against a cliff. On the other side of the island, **Valdichiesa** rests at the base of **Monte Fossa delle Felci,** the highest point of the Aeolians. Trails lead from the town 962m up the mountain. For less aerobic activity, relax at **Malfa's** luxurious beach, which offers equally tantalizing views—here, of the huge sulfur bubbles known as *sconcassi.* The first Sunday in June, the population of Salina heads to Pollara for the **Sacra del Cappero,** often numbering 1000 celebrators. Each restaurant and volunteering family brings its own special dish where the *cappero* (caper) is key. Visitors are invited to contribute their own treats, which is an easy way to make friends and get in with the locals.

FILICUDI AND ALICUDI   ☎090

Overlooked by most visitors to the Aeolian Islands, the remote Filicudi and Alicudi are the archipelago's two best kept secrets. Largely undeveloped outside of the port areas, these two islands offer an understated escape from their more fast-paced neighbors. Each is named for the dense plants that grace its cliffs—Filicudi after the fern, and Alicudi after the heather. Outside the summer rush, both islands are left solely to their 400 inhabitants; those who do venture to these rugged refuges discover lands beyond the frontiers of tourism, where many of the rooms for rent are from fishermen, and the quickest way to plug into nature is a sheer drop from cliffs into the sea.

⬛🔢 TRANSPORTATION AND PRACTICAL INFORMATION. The islands are connected by infrequent **ferries** and **hydrofoils** to Milazzo (see **Aeolian Islands: Transportation,** p. 655) and Lipari. Filicudi's transportation center is **Filicudi Porto,** on the southern peninsula. Stone steps in Filicudi lead from the dock into the hills. Only 2½km across, Alicudi is populated on the eastern and central slopes and all but deserted in the south. In case of **emergency** on either island, call the **carabinieri** (☎090 988 99 42) or **first aid** (☎090 988 99 61), although there are no **hospitals** on either island. Filicudi's **post office** (☎090 98 80 53) is uphill to the right of the port and Alicudi's is at the port, although the latter is rarely open. Filicudi has an **ATM** next to the Siremar office at the port. There are **no ATMs** in Alicudi, and credit cards are not accepted at the ticket offices, so bring extra cash for your return trip.

⬛⬛ ACCOMMODATIONS AND FOOD. Even reaching accommodations in Filicudi can be an adventure. Its two nicest hotels are perched atop the cliff directly over the port. The island's only paved road reaches it eventually, but the most direct route (though not necessarily the easiest) is a steep 15min. climb up staggered rock steps. Most hotels will drive you from the port, so ask before you arrive. To walk, the ascent begins at the right after exiting the dock, just before Hotel Phenicusa. At the top, ⬛**Hotel La Canna ❹,** V. Rosa, 43, has thoughtfully decorated rooms with bath, TV, and A/C. Shared features include a relaxing terracotta terrace, Internet, a **restaurant ❸** serving typical Aeolian fare and seafood specialties, and a pool with bar. (☎090 988 99 56, fax 988 99 66. Breakfast included. Restaurant open 12:30-1:30pm and 8:15-9:30pm. Doubles €60-124. Half pension €52-92; full pension €72-112. MC/V.) Hotel-restaurant **Villa La Rosa ❹,** V. Rosa, 24, is the social center of the island. A bar, mini-supermarket, video arcade, and *dis-*

coteca are among its considerable amenities. The ornate rooms all boast large bath, minibar, fan, and a terrace slung with a hammock. (☎ 090 988 99 65, fax 988 92 91. Half pension €45-70; full pension €61-86. MC/V.) **Hotel Club Phenicusa** ❹ is more securely grounded by the port. Every room has a balcony facing either mountains or the sea. (☎ 090 988 99 46; www.capocalava.com. Breakfast included. €34-75; half pension €57-98, full pension €67-108. View of sea €8-10 extra, depending on season. Half or full pension required July-Aug. AmEx/MC/V.) The ever-busy **Da Nino Sul Mare** ❹, on V. Porto, serves hungry beachgoers both waterfront snacks and full-out meals. (☎ 090 988 99 84. *Primi* €9, *secondi* €12. Open 8am-midnight. MC/V.) Da Nino also rents motorbikes (€30 per day) and boats (€90-230 per day). Filicudi has a small **supermarket,** located further along V. Porto.

🖭 🎿 **SIGHTS AND HIKING.** Exploring by water is a great way to see the islands' charms from a distance. Contact **I Delfini** (☎/fax 090 988 90 77), on V. Pecorini in Pecorini Mare, a village near the port, for boat, moped, and scuba diving rentals. The lack of developed towns and related activity makes Filicudi ideal for outdoor exploration and hiking. A thick tangle of cacti, fruit trees, and flowers drapes over verdant slopes and rocky terraces. A hike up **Fossa delle Felci** (774m) opens onto a rewarding vista of **La Canna,** a rock spike that rises 71m out of the sea. Some sandy beaches, including the **Grotta del Bue Marino,** stretch before enchanting caves, while more crystalline waters shimmer around the rocky beach in **Pecorini Mare.** Alicudi's rocky beaches offer privacy and seclusion, and nude sunbathing is the norm in the areas farther from the port.

EASTERN SICILY

MESSINA ☎ 090

Messina is a transportation hub if ever there was one; better air conditioning and a duty-free shop would turn this fast-paced town into an airport. While its role as a major port and the main commercial connection between Sicily and the mainland has brought prosperity, Messina has also weathered nonstop invasions, plagues, and earthquakes. Despite all obstacles, the town maintains its dignity in points of historical interest and beauty such as the duomo, the tall and allegorical clock tower next door, and the church of Santa Maria Annunziàta dei Catalani.

FROM THE ROAD

CARO DIARIO

The sheer cliffs grow more rugged with each passing island. Time here seems measured by the beat of wave against rock. I can see why Homer was enamored; my imagination, too, is captured. Finally I've made it to Filicudi.

For the Greeks, the Aeolians represented the edge of an empire and the border of the unknown. Aeolus, Keeper of the Winds, held court in Lipari; giants and Lotus Eaters comprised his dissident subjects. Though hardly undiscovered, the islands are the stuff of legends, the very basis of the Western literary imagination.

To truly experience the remote beauty of Filicudi, it's necessary to take to the road. The island has no gas station, but as in the rest of Sicily, *motorini* rule the roads. My guide and I speed along the twisting mountain paths on our own *motorino,* wind peeling away the thick July heat. My guide seems unable to tear his eyes from the landscape: indeed, the love of the Aeolians' residents for each jutting peak, for the white curl of waves against rocky shores, runs deep.

The Portals of Hell may no longer open from the depths of Vulcano, and perhaps the Keeper of the Winds has abdicated his throne in favor of still more solitary shores. But I almost cannot believe there isn't some fabulous creature lurking along the coast, or three sultry sirens perched atop a rock splitting the crystal waters.

—Alexie Harper

SICILY

⌐ TRANSPORTATION

Trains: Stazione Centrale FS (☎090 67 97 95 or info 147 88 80 88), in P. della Repubblica. Call ahead; schedules change frequently. To: **Naples** (7hr., 11 per day, €21.59); **Palermo** (3½hr., 12 per day, €10.55); **Rome** (9hr., 17 per day, €41.37); **Syracuse** (3½hr., 9 per day, €8.19); **Taormina** (40 min., 21 per day, €2.05). Trains to the west stop in **Milazzo** (45min., €2.35), the main port of the Aeolian Islands.

Buses: Messina has 4 bus carriers, many of which serve the same routes.

AST (☎090 66 22 44, ask for "*informazioni*"). Ticket office in an orange minibus in P. Duomo across from the cathedral. Serves small and less touristed areas all over Sicily and southern Italy.

SAIS, P. della Repubblica, 6 (☎090 77 19 14). Ticket office is behind the trees, across from far left tip of the FS station. To: **Catania airport** (1-2hr., 6 per day, €6.97); **Catania** (1½hr., 9 per day, €6.20); **Florence** (12½hr.; 1 per week, Su; €50); **Naples** (22hr., 3 per week., €25); **Palermo** (1½hr., 8 per day, €12.39).

Interbus, P. della Repubblica, 6 (☎090 66 17 54), has blue offices left of the train station, beyond the line of buses. To: **Giardini Naxos** (1½hr., 9 per day, €2.50); **Naples** (1 per week, Su; €22); **Rome** (2 per day, €30); **Taormina** (1½hr., 12 per day, €2.50).

Giuntabus, V. Terranova, 8 (☎090 67 37 82 or 67 57 49), 3 blocks up V. I Settembre, left on V. Bruno, right on V. Terranova. To **Catania Airport** (Apr.-Sept. daily 4pm, €10.33) and **Milazzo** from Terranova (45min.; M-Sa 14 per day 6am-6pm, Su 1 per day; €3.10).

Ferries: Meridiano (☎347 910 01 19 or 641 32 34), on the waterfront 300m from the FS station. To **Reggio** (40min.; M-Sa 12 per day, Su 1 per day; €1.50).

Hydrofoils: From Messina Marittima, the waterfront wing of Stazione Centrale, **FS** sends hydrofoils to **Reggio** (25min., 12 per day, €2.60) and **Villa San Giovanni** (30min., 2 per hr., €1). **Ustica** (☎0903 640 44), has offices in a blue building on the waterfront side of C. V. Emanuele, 2km north of the train station off C. Garibaldi. Hydrofoils to: **Aeolian Islands** (2hr., June-Sept. 3-6 per day for each destination); **Lipari** (40min., 6 per day, €16.50); **Panarea** (1¾hr., 3 per day, €19.10); **Salina** (1¼hr., 4 per day, €19.10).

Public Transportation: Orange **ATM buses** leave either from P. della Repubblica or from the bus station, 2 blocks up V. I Settembre from the station, on the right. Purchase tickets (€0.90 for 1½hr.) at any *tabacchi* or newsstand. Detailed bus info on yellow-bordered signs outside the bus station. Bus **#79,** which stops at the duomo, museum, and aquarium, can only be taken from P. della Repubblica.

Taxis: Radiotaxi Jolly (☎090 65 05), to the right of the duomo.

◢◣ ☷ ORIENTATION AND PRACTICAL INFORMATION

Messina's transportation center is **Piazza della Repubblica,** in front of the **train station,** home to the tourist office and headquarters for several bus lines. **Via G. la Farina** runs in front of the train station. Beyond the highrises to the left, **Via Tommaso Cannizzaro** leads to the center of town, meeting palm-lined **Viale San Martino** at **Piazza Cairoli.** Enter P. della Repubblica from the train station. At the far right end begins **Via I Settembre,** which intersects **Corso Garibaldi.** C. Garibaldi runs along the harbor to both the hydrofoil dock and **Corso Cavour.**

Tourist Office: AAPIT, V. Calabria, 301 (☎090 67 42 36), on the right corner facing P. della Repubblica from train station. Well-staffed, with a deluge of **maps** and info on Messina, the Aeolians, and Reggio Calabria. Open M-Sa 8:30am-6:30pm.

MIDNIGHT MESSINA. Women should not walk alone in Messina at night, and no one should roam the streets near the train station or the harbor after 10pm. Stay near the more populated streets around the duomo and the university. Be wary of pick-pockets and purse-snatchers, and keep money in a secure place.

Currency Exchange: F. lli. Grosso, V. Garibaldi, 58 (☎090 77 40 83). Open M-F 8:30am-1pm, Sa 8:30am-12:30pm.

ATMs: Outside the train station and to the right. Also at V. T. Cannizzaro, 24, and **Banco di Napoli** on V. Emanuele facing the port.

English-Language Bookstore: Libreria Nunnari e Sfameri, V. Cannizzaro, 116 (☎090 71 04 69). University bookstore stacks 4 shelves with classics—brush up on Shakespeare and Faulkner. Open M-F 8:30am-1pm and 4-8pm, Sa 8:30am-1pm. MC/V.

Emergency: ☎113. **Carabinieri** (☎112). **Ambulance** (☎118).

Medical Clinic: V. Garibaldi, 242 (☎090 34 54 22).

Pharmacy: Farmacia Abate, Viale S. Martino, 39 (☎090 637 33, for info on all pharmacies in town 71 75 89). From the train station take V. del Vespro 4 blocks and turn left. All pharmacies open M-F 8:30am-1pm and 4:30-8pm. Late-night rotations posted.

Hospital: Ospedale Piemonte (☎090 222 43 47), on Viale Europa.

Internet: Internet Point, V. Maddalena, 117 (☎090 77 05 00). 5 fast computers for €3 per hr. Open daily 8am-11pm. **Stamperia,** V. T. Cannizzaro, 170 (☎090 640 94 28; stamperi@tin.it). €5.16 per hr. Open M-F 8:30am-1:30pm and 3:30-8pm.

Post Office: ☎0906 68 64 15. In P. Antonello, off C. Cavour and across from Galleria. Open M-Sa 8:30am-6:30pm. There is also a branch next to the train station on V. Stazione with the same hours. **Postal Code:** 98100.

ACCOMMODATIONS

Messina is perennially more fly-by than stop-over. Its handful of hotels caters not to cost-conscious travelers but to deep-pocketed businessmen. Cheaper hotels are found in the shady neighborhood by the station; be careful at night.

Hotel Mirage, V. N. Scotto, 3 (☎090 293 88 44). Turn left from the train station, pass buses, and continue under the *autostrada* bridge onto V. N. Scotto. Mission-style simplicity in white rooms with tall windows. Curfew midnight. Singles €25; doubles €40, with bath €55; triples €65. MC/V. ❷

Hotel Touring, V. N. Scotto, 17 (☎090 293 88 51), a few steps from Hotel Mirage. Mirrors and marble-lined halls lead to sparsely decorated rooms with dark wood furniture, armoirs and sundry posters. Payphone outside lobby. Curfew 1:30am. Singles €25, with bath and TV €40; doubles €40/€50, with A/C €68. Cash only. ❷

Hotel Cairoli, Viale S. Martino, 63 (☎090 67 37 55). From the train station, walk 4 blocks up V. del Vespro and left 1 block. A white and blue sign is prominent over the doorway. Small rooms are plain and often sparsely furnished, but they come with A/C, TV, and phone. Ask at front desk for a free breakfast coupon at the bar around the corner. Singles €34-40, €46 with bath; doubles €50, €80 with bath. AmEx/MC/V. ❸

The Royal Palace Hotel, V. T. Cannizzaro, 224 (☎090 65 03; reservation.rph@framonhotels.it). Sophisticated rooms with bath, TV, and A/C smartly service a professional clientele. Fancy **restaurant** ❺ downstairs. Breakfast €11. Lunch or dinner €27.50. Singles €84.70-112.20; doubles €119-159. AmEx/MC/V. ❺

FOOD

Restaurants and trattorias cluster in the area around V. Risorgimento, reached by following V. Cannizzaro two blocks past P. Cairoli. Messina is hooked on swordfish—baked, fried, or stewed (*pesce stocco*). Eggplants and olives combine to form *caponata*, a dish of fried eggplant, onion, capers, and olives in a red sauce. For dessert, *cannoli* and sugary *pignolata* are both decadent. At **Osteria del Campanile** ❸, V. Loggia dei Mercanti, 9-13, behind the duomo, locals flood the sidewalk tables and subdued dining room for *fettuccine salmonate* (€6.20) and other simple but reliable staples. (☎/fax 090 71 14 18. *Primi* from €5.20, *secondi* from €6.20. Open M-Sa noon-3pm and 5-11:30pm. AmEx/MC/V.) Art-deco splendor garnishes **Osteria Etnea ❷**, V. T. Cannizzaro, 155-57, near the university. Delicious signature pasta and fish dishes (from €3.10) like *spaghetti etnea* (€4.65) have a flare of their own. (☎090 71 80 40. Cover €1.55. Open M 8-11:30pm, Tu-Sa 12:30-4pm and 8-11:30pm, Su 12:30-4pm. AmEx/MC/V.) Follow V. I Settembre away from the duomo one block and turn right to reach **Pizza e Coca ❷**, V. C. Battisti, N47. This is your red-checkered, breadbox-sized, cheap-as-anything Little Italy-style pizzeria—in the real Italy. (☎090 67 36 79. *Bruschetta* €3. Pizza from €4, family size from €12. Takeout and delivery available. Open daily noon-2am, Su 5pm-midnight.)

◉ SIGHTS

Though Messina has lost many of its monuments to both natural and man-induced calamities, the town still features a number of great sights. Churches on the outskirts of town, such as Montalto, offer sweeping vistas of the city and port.

PIAZZA DEL DUOMO. Bright flagstones and shady trees provide a relaxing respite from the bustling city that surrounds this central piazza. The great **duomo,** built in Norman times and dedicated in 1197 to the Virgin Mary, dominates the square with an enormous sandstone face that can be blinding in the afternoon sun. The surprisingly long nave rolls past 14 niche sculptures of saints and sweeping tile floors to arrive at a massive altar dedicated to Madonna della Lettera, the city's patron saint. A statue of Archbishop Angelo Paino to the left of the altar commemorates the tireless efforts of the man who rebuilt the duomo twice, first after the earthquake of 1908 and again after WWII bombing destroyed half of the church. **Il Tesoro** (the Treasury), a modern two-story museum, houses the church's most valuable possessions, including gold reliquaries, chalices, and candlesticks. The highlight is the ornate *Manta d'Oro* (Golden Mantle), a special cover decorated with precious stones and jewels used to drape the picture of the Madonna and Child in the church's altar. It is on display after being locked away for three centuries and emerges from the church each year for an annual festival (see **Entertainment**). Plans for the ◙campanile began in the early 16th century, and at 90m, it was intended to be the highest in Sicily. After being struck by lightning in 1588, restorations continued until 1933, when the tower acquired its prominent clock. The structure displays man's progression from base being to noble creature, as well as an astrological wheel. At noon, a creaky recording of the *Ave Maria* booms and a gigantic lion lets out a mechanized roar. Below the clock tower, ancient myth and local lore meet in stone at the **Fontana di Orione,** designed by Angelo Montorsoli, a pupil of Michelangelo, in 1547. The intricate fountain glorifies Orion, the mythical founder of Messina. *(Duomo open daily 7am-7:30pm. Guided tours of Treasury in English, French, and German. Treasury open M-Sa 9am-1pm. €2.58, under 18 or over 65 €1.55.)*

MUSEO REGIONALE. A converted spinning mill houses whatever was salvaged from the monastery of St. Gregory and churches throughout the city after the devastating earthquakes of 1894 and 1908. Galleries around a quiet courtyard display the development of the rich Messinese artistic tradition. Among more notable pieces are *The Polyptych of the Rosary* (1473) by local master Antonello da Messina; Andrea della Robbia's terra-cotta *Virgin and Child;* and Caravaggio's life-sized *Adoration of the Shepherds* (1608) and *Resurrection of Lazarus* (1609). Just past the entrance, bronze door panels detail the story of the Madonna della Lettera. *(Take bus #8 or 79 from the station or P. Duomo to P. Museo. ☎090 36 12 92. Museum open Oct.-May Tu-Sa 9am-2pm and Su 9am-1pm; June-Sept. Tu, Th, and Sa 3-7pm.*

Ticket office closes 30min. early. €4.50; EU residents 18-25 €2; EU residents under 18 or over 65 and students of literature, philosophy, or art free.)

PORT. The port is more than a place to catch a hydrofoil: Messina's history and character largely center on its former naval prowess. The enormous **La Madonnina,** a 6m tall golden statue, surveys the city from a 60m column across the water in the port's center. On the city side, the gleaming **Fontana di Nettuno** by Montorsoli graces the intersection of V. Garibaldi and V. della Libertà. The muscular marble god stands over the monsters Scylla and Charybdis, extending one arm to calm the seas. The port is dangerous after dark, so make this a daytime excursion.

CHIESA DELLA SANTISSIMA ANNUNZIÀTA DEI CATALANI. Known as "Catalani" because it was given to the guild of Catalan merchants in the 16th century, this church was built between 1150 and 1200 over the remains of a pagan temple and then rebuilt after its front section collapsed in a flood in the Middle Ages. Islamic and Byzantine influences are apparent in the archways and layout. *(On V. Garibaldi.)*

🎵 ENTERTAINMENT

The **Festa di Madonna della Lettera** on June 3 celebrates Messina's guardian. Parades throughout the city culminate at the duomo, where the *Manta d'Oro* is restored to the altar for one day every year. Messina overflows with sightseers and approximately 150,000 white-robed pilgrims during the nationally celebrated **Ferragosto Messinese** festival August 13-15. During the first two days of Ferragosto, one of Italy's most important holidays, two huge human effigies called Mata and Grifone zoom around city in the *Processione dei Giganti* (Procession of the Giants).

TAORMINA   ☎ 0942

Legend has it that Neptune wrecked a Greek boat off the eastern coast of Sicily in the 8th century BC and that the sole survivor, so inspired by the spectacular scenery onshore, founded Taormina. Historians tell a different tale: the Carthaginians founded Tauromenium at the turn of the 4th century BC, only to have it wrested away by the Greek tyrant Dionysius. Disputed origins aside, Taormina's beauty is uncontested; its pines and mansions crown a cliff above the sea. Disoriented, fanny-packed foreigners, hearty backpackers, and elite VIPs all come for a glimpse of what millions of photographic flashes and hyperbolic statements can't seem to dull: a vista that sweeps dizzily from boiling Etna to the straits of Messina.

MESSINA IN STRAITS

Sicily has long prided itself on its physical and cultural separation from the rest of Italy. The isolated island, however, may soon face a significant sort of integration into the mainland: Prime Minister Silvio Berlusconi has set construction of the world's largest suspension bridge, connecting Sicily to the southern tip of Italy, to commence in 2005. The bridge is expected to promote development and employment in two of the poorest regions in Italy.

But many Italians don't see it that way. Controversy concerning the bridge has spawned an anti-bridge campaign spearheaded by a number of political and environmental groups. Campaign supporters, fearful of potential Mafia influence in its construction, are also worried that such a bridge would destroy the area's delicate ecosystem and natural beauty. Ironically, this could help to destroy the very tourism that bridge proponents hope to increase. Furthermore, protesters argue that a bridge would triple crossing costs for locals and leave a projected 3,000 ferry and hydrofoil operators out of work.

Even logistics of the bridge itself are under debate: many claim that the bridge is not only impractical but impossible, citing the seismic activity constantly causing Sicily to inch towards the mainland. Despite these objections, however, construction is due to conclude in 2012.

TRANSPORTATION

Taormina is accessible by bus from Messina or Catania. Although **trains** from Catania and Messina are more frequent than buses, the train station lies far from Taormina, at the base of Giardini-Naxos. **Buses** run from the train station to **Taormina** (every 30min. 7:35am-11pm, more frequently in the summer) and **Giardini-Naxos** (7:50am-11:20pm, more frequently in the summer).

Trains: ☎0942 89 22 021. At the bottom of Giardini-Naxos's hill. To: **Catania** (50min., 25 per day 1:20am-8:16pm, €3.05); **Messina** (40min., 22 per day 4:02am-11:40pm, €2.84); **Syracuse** (2hr., 11 per day 4:30am-8:09pm, € 6.70).

Buses: Interbus (☎0942 62 53 01). Ticket office off C. Umberto, at the end of V. Pirandello (open daily 6:20am-11:45pm.) **CST** (☎0942 23 301) offers *Etna Tramonto,* a sunset trip up the volcano (July-Aug. M and W 3:45pm, Sept. M and W 3:15pm, Oct. M and W 2:15pm; €55). To: **Catania** (M-Sa 12 per day 6:30am-9:45pm, Su 12 per day 6:30am-6pm; €3.80, round-trip €6.20) and **Messina** (M-Sa 10 per day 6:30am-7:20pm; Su 8:50am, 12:30, 6pm; €2.50, round-trip €4.10). Same bus runs to **Giardini-Naxos** and **train station** (dir: Recanti or Catania; M-F every 30min. 6:50am-midnight; €1.20, round-trip €2). Also to **Gole Alcantara** (M-Sa 4 per day 9:30am-6:30pm, Su 9:30am; round-trip €4.30) and **Isola Bella, Mazzaro,** and **Spisone** (M-Sa 14 per day 6:30am-7:40pm, Su 4 per day 8:40am-5:40pm; €1.50, round-trip €2). Pick up a helpful paper schedule at the Taormina bus terminal. **SAT,** C. Umberto, 73 (☎0942 24 653; www.sat-group.it), operates day-long tours to Mt. Etna.

Moped and Car Rental: Cundari Rent, Viale Apollo Arcageta, 12 (☎0942 247 00), around corner from post office at the end of C. Umberto. Scooters €25 per day, €149 per week. 14+. Cars from €55 per day (larger cars cost more), and from €265 per week. 21+. Gas extra. Open daily 8:30am-1pm and 4-8pm. 10% *Let's Go* discount.

ORIENTATION AND PRACTICAL INFORMATION

To reach the city from the **train station,** hop on the blue **Interbus** that makes the trip uphill (10min., every 30min. 5am-11pm, €1.30). Cars are not allowed on Taormina's steep and narrow streets; automobiles can park in a small lot at the base of **Via Pirandello.** From the bus depot, a short walk left up V. Pirandello leads to the town's main street, **Corso Umberto.** Beginning under a stone archway, the boutique-lined road runs left through four principal piazzas. Small stairways and sidestreets wind downhill to a variety of more affordable restaurants, shops and bars.

Tourist Office: AAST (☎0942 232 43, fax 249 41), in P. Corvaja, off C. Umberto across from P. V. Emanuele. Friendly staff provides several pamphlets and a generic **map;** the turquoise fold-out "SAT Sicilian Airbus Travel" map is more helpful, as is the CST map, both available at the tourist office. Accurate and detailed maps are also posted on high brown signs throughout the city. Open M-Sa 8:30am-2pm and 4-7pm.

Currency Exchange: Dozens of banks and **ATMs** line C. Umberto and V. Pirandello; so do many currency exchange offices, including **Rocco Frisono,** C. Umberto, 224 (☎0942 248 06), between P. Sant'Antonio and P. Duomo. Open M-Sa 9am-1pm and 4-8pm.

American Express: La Duca Viaggi, V. Don Bosco, 39, 2nd fl. (☎0942 62 52 55), in P. IX Aprile. Mail held. Open M-F Apr.-Oct. 9am-1pm and 4-7:30pm, Nov.-Mar. 9am-1pm and 2-6pm.

Emergency: ☎113 or 0942 61 11 11. **Police** (☎112 or 0942 232 32).

Pharmacy: Farmacia Ragusa, P. Duomo, 9 (☎0942 24 104). Posts the weekly rotation for late-night pharmacies. Open M-Tu and Th-Su 8:30am-1pm and 5-8:30pm.

First aid: ☎0942 62 54 19 or 57 92 97.

Hospital: Ospedale San Vincenzo (☎0942 57 92 97), in P. S. Vincenzo.

Internet: Internet Cafe, C. Umberto, 214 (☎0942 62 88 39). Sports a large number of fast computers at €2 for 20min., €5 per hr., plus a Western Union money transfer station. Open daily 9am-8pm.

Post Office: ☎0942 73 230. On P. Sant'Antonio at the very top of C. Umberto near the hospital. Cashes traveler's checks. Open M-Sa 8am-6:30pm. Postal code: 98039.

ACCOMMODATIONS

Taormina's popularity as a resort town makes cheap accommodations difficult to find. Those on a tight budget should consider staying in a hostel, or in nearby Mazzarò, Spisone, or Giardini-Naxos (p. 677). Hike down steep trails to Mazzarò and Spisone or take the bus or cable cars; service stops around 1:30am.

■ **Taormina's Odyssey Youth Hostel,** Traversa A di V. G. Martino, 2 (☎0942 245 33). A 15min. walk from the intersection of C. Umberto and V. L. Pirandello. Take V. C. Patrizio to V. Cappuccini. When it forks, veer right onto V. Fontana Vecchia. There should be signs to follow. Renowned among backpackers as a first-class hostel. Friendly English-speaking employees, clean rooms, lockers and a great price make this social hostel well worth the hike. 28 dorm-style beds, 1 double. €15-18 per person. Reserve ahead in summer. Cash only. ❷

La Campanella, V. Circonvallazione, 3 (☎0942 233 81, fax 62 52 48). Ascending 3 flights of rough-hewn stone stairs to reach the entrance can be daunting, but it makes the view of Taormina from the top even more worthwhile. Bright sitting room, courtyard, and comfortable rooms. Breakfast included. Singles €60; doubles €80. Cash only. ❹

Hotel Villa Nettuno, V. Pirandello, 33 (☎0942 237 97, fax 62 60 35). Walk up stone steps toward the hotel's sign. Charming, vibrant inn, complete with an ornate parlor and a beautifully maintained garden. Ask for a room with a sea view at no extra charge. Reserve ahead in summer. Singles €40; doubles €74. AmEx/MC/V. ❸

Pensione Svizzera, V. L. Pirandello, 26 (☎0942 237 90; www.pensionesvizzera.com), 3min. from the bus station. Pricey, but worth every euro. Glorious sea views, palm-laden patio, and seaside garden terrace. All rooms with bath and TV. Breakfast buffet included. Reservation recommended May-Sept. Closed Jan. 10 through Feb. 20. Prices vary seasonally: singles €60-90; doubles €80-120; triples €110-125; quads €125-140. AmEx/MC/V. ❺

Inn Piero, V. Pirandello, 20 (☎0942 231 39), near base of C. Umberto after gas station, in 2 buildings overlooking the sea. Less expensive than most of its neighbors, Piero offers affordable accommodations in a great location. Small, neat rooms have bath. Breakfast included. 15% discount on ground-floor restaurant. Reserve in summer. Singles €35-50; doubles €70-80. Student discount 10%, except in Aug. AmEx/MC/V. ❸

FOOD

Taormina's restaurants are of consistently high quality; prices tend to vary, though so shop around for the best deals. An **SMA** supermarket, V. Apollo Arcageta, 21, is at the end of C. Umberto, near the post office. (Open M-Sa 8:30am-1pm and 4:30-8:30pm.)

La Cisterna del Moro, V. Bonifacio, 1 (☎0942 230 01), off of C. Umberto. With incredible food served on a flower-filled terrace, this pizzeria/pub is a fantastic compromise between casual pizza joint and formal restaurant. The affordable pizza (€5-8) will leave you smiling, and the stunning view will keep you around long after dessert. Open noon-3pm and 7pm-midnight (later in the summer). AmEx/MC/V. ❷

Trattoria da Nino, V. Pirandello, 37 (☎0942 212 65), between the bus station and the town center, is the real Sicily. Trust the polyglot charmer Nino to guide you through the extensive menu in this tiny restaurant. For dessert the *macedonia* is a show-stopper. *Primi* €3-8, *secondi* €5-10. Discount for students and with *Let's Go*. Open noon-3pm and 6:30-11pm. AmEx/MC/V. ❷

Bella Blu, V. Pirandello, 28 (☎0942 242 39; www.paginegialle.it/bellablu). The sign outside boasts, "Probably the best view in Taormina." Or the most unique: cable cars gliding down the mountain between clusters of cypress trees provide a tranquil backdrop for sharing thick, gooey pizza (€4.50). *Primi* from €4.50, *secondi* from €6.50. Cover €1.50. Open daily 11am-5pm and 6pm-11pm. AmEx/MC/V. ❷

Gastronomia la Fontana, V. Constantino Patricio, 28 (☎0942 234 78), at the end of V. Pirandello, up the hill and left at the Arco Capuccini. Follow the smell of rotisserie chicken and lasagne to this cluttered takeout spot. Pizza from €3 (or by the slice for €1), *panini*, and savory snacks including *cipolline* and *arancine* (€1-1.50). Open daily July noon-3pm and 6-11pm, Aug. noon-3pm and 6pm-1am; Tu-Su Sept.-June noon-3pm and 6-11pm.

🔵 SIGHTS

The wonderfully preserved, 3rd-century **Greek theater** is Taormina's greatest treasure. It offers an unsurpassed view of Etna, whose sultry smoke and occasional eruptions rival even the greatest Sophoclean tragedies when it comes to drama. In ancient times, the cliffside arena seated 5000 spectators; that same number packs in annually for the summer-long festival **Taormina Arte.** (☎0942 231 23. From P. V. Emanuele, walk up V. Teatro Greco. Open daily 9am-1hr. before sunset. €4.15, EU residents €2, EU residents under 18 or over 65 free.) From P. V. Emanuele, take C. Umberto to reach the **duomo.** This 13th-century structure, rebuilt during the Renaissance, takes center stage in Taormina today. The Gothic interior shelters paintings by Messinese artists and an alabaster statue of the Virgin Mary displayed over marble floors. A two-legged female centaur, Taormina's mascot, crowns the fountain out front. (Opening hours vary; inquire at Museo Sacra, next door.) Behind the tourist office, the **Chiesa di Santa Caterina** protects a small theater, the **Roman Odeon.** The short walk down V. di Giovanni leads to Taormina's peaceful public gardens, the **Villa Comunale.** Filled with people relaxing under shady palms during summer's greatest heat, the gardens look out over Giardini-Naxos below and Etna in the distance. A trek to the **piccolo castello** offers an escape from boisterous crowds. V. Circonvallazione, which runs parallel to and above C. Umberto, leads to a small stairway that snakes up the mountainside to the castle.

🎵 🔵 ENTERTAINMENT AND BEACHES

While action-packed Giardini-Naxos plays host to the area's wildest nights, in summer Taormina also stays up well past its bedtime. A large variety of chic bars line C. Umberto and its side streets. Don't miss ▩**Cafe Marrakech,** P. Garibaldi, 2 (follow signs from C. Umberto). This exotic bar's cocktails (from €6) and Turkish coffees (€5-6) seduce party-goers both indoors and under Arabic tents outside. (☎0942 62 56 92. Open Tu-Su 5pm-3am.) **Mediterraneo,** V. di Giovanni, 6, packs in a lively crowd that devours crepes and cocktails. (☎0942 233 98.) Don't miss live music Wednesdays. The lively **O'Seven,** P. Largo La Farina, 6, off C. Umberto near V. Teatro Greco, serves beer (from €3) and drinks in a casual pub-like atmosphere. (☎0942 240 40. Open daily 11am-3am. AmEx/MC/V.) The **Casanova Pub,** V. Paladini, 2, off C. Umberto before P. Garibaldi, serves pizza (from €6.50), beer (from €5), and cocktails (from €6) in a spacious interior and casual outdoor setting. (☎0942 239 45. Open daily 10am-7am. AmEx/MC/V.)

Every summer brings **Taormina Arte,** a theater, ballet, music, and film extravaganza. Past performances have attracted the likes of Jose Carreras, Bob Dylan, and Ray Charles. (☎0942 62 87 49; www.taormina-arte.com. Box office at C. Umberto, 19.) The **Galleria Gagliardi** debuts the latest in art at C. Umberto, 187a. Exhibits change every 15 days. (☎0942 62 89 02. Open 10am-1pm and 5-10pm.)

Cable cars zip along the *funivia* from V. Pirandello to the **beach** in a breezy ride (☎0942 236 05. In summer every 15min. M 9am-1am, Tu-Su 8am-1am; €1.60, €2.70 round-trip). At the popular **Lido Mazzarò,** lounge chair rentals (€7.50) from **Lido La Pigna** include shower, parasol, and changing area—or just enjoy the view while drinking a cafe on the terrace upstairs. A 15min. walk to the right, shallow, sparkling waters flow around the tiny **Isola Bella,** a nature preserve 100m offshore. The strong-stomached can travel the narrow, winding route by bus to **Castelmola,** the highest point in Taormina, complete with a medieval castle and regal panoramas.

GIARDINI-NAXOS ☎0942

Now the eastern coast's ultimate beach town and a watering hole for throngs of tourists, Giardini-Naxos was in 734 BC the first Greek colony in Sicily. Naxos enjoyed moderate success until an alliance with Syracuse in its 5th-century BC war for independence against Athens resulted in the colony's utter devastation. Today the modern town has more *giardini* (gardens) than ancient remains, with fertile slopes, shady palms, and wild flowers clinging to volcanic cliffs.

🚉🛈 TRANSPORTATION AND PRACTICAL INFORMATION. Only 5km away from Taormina, Giardini-Naxos shares a train station with its neighbor. **Interbus** runs from Giardini to the **train station** and Taormina's **bus station** (☎0942 62 53 01; in summer 40 per day 7:35am-11:35pm, €1.30). Signs throughout town point the way to the helpful **AAST Tourist Office,** V. Tysandros, 54, along the *lungomare.* (☎0942 510 10. Open M-F 8:30am-2pm and 4-7pm, Sa 8:30am-2pm.) In case of **emergency,** call the **carabinieri** (☎112) or **first aid** (☎0942 539 32). **Post offices** are at V. Erice, 1 (☎0942 510 90), and Lungomare Naxos, 151 (☎0942 57 11 90).

🛏🍴 ACCOMMODATIONS AND FOOD. As in Taormina, hotels here fill up in July and August, though prices are better; reserve far ahead in summer. Beachfront hotels crowd V. Tysandros, varying considerably in quality and price—better deals can be found on nearby V. Naxos. Just one block from the beach, the **Hotel Costa Azzurra ❸,** V. Naxos, 35, offers bright, spacious rooms at an unbeatable price. (☎0942 514 58. Singles €30-35; doubles €46-60. AmEx/MC/V.) **Hotel Villa Mora ❸,** V. Naxos, 47, combines privacy with direct access to the beach. Though small, all rooms have bath, TV with CNN, and a fan; some have A/C. (☎/fax 0942 518 39; www.hotelvillamora.com. Breakfast included. Open Mar.-Dec. Singles €40-50; doubles €68-80. MC/V.) **Pensione Otello ❸,** V. Tysandros, 62, along the *lungomare,* has tiny, no-frills rooms and cramped showers. (☎0942 510 09. Singles €35 per person. Aug. €40 per person.) **Arathena Rocks Hotel ❹,** V. Calcide Eubea, 55, is a pleasure to the senses with bright, carpeted hallways and decorated doors. Sunbathe by the pool or watch the waves crash against the rocky beach from the balcony. Pick-up and drop-off service to and from Taormina available. (☎0942 513 49; www.hotelarathena.com. Breakfast included. Singles €58, with half pension €70; doubles €104/€128. MC/V.)

Buy necessities at Sigma **supermarket,** V. Dalmazia, 31, down from the central bus stop. (Open M-Sa 8:30am-1pm and 4:30-8:30pm, Su 8:30am-1pm.) Located at the tip of Giardini-Naxos's port, **Angelina ❷,** V. Calcide Eubea, 2, serves its seafood seaside. Lively regulars also enjoy the extensive menu (try the *Maccheroni alla "Angelina"*) and equally impressive wine shelf. (☎/fax 0942 51 477. *Primi* from

€5, *secondi* from €8. Open daily noon-4pm and 6:30pm-midnight. AmEx/MC/V.)
Trattoria-Pizzeria Nettuno ❷, V. Tysandros, 68, offers seafood, pasta, and wood-fired
pizza in a breezy atmosphere. Make sure to check out the considerable list of specials, which changes weekly. (☎/fax 0942 57 12 76. Pizza from €4. *Primi* €4-6,
secondi €8-11. Cover €1. Open M-W and F-Su noon-4pm and 6pm-midnight.
AmEx/MC/V.) The touristy **Ristorante-Pizzeria Lido da Angelo ❷,** V. Umberto, 523,
serves pizza (from €4) and seafood classics on a patio over a private beach.
(☎0942 519 02. Entrees from €6. Cover €1. Open daily 8:30am-4pm and 6:30pm-
midnight. AmEx/MC/V.)

◪ ◩ SIGHTS AND ENTERTAINMENT. Excavations in the 1960s unearthed
traces of a **Greek city** built of solidified lava blocks, founded in the shadow of the
volcano. Visit the traces of the fortress ruins, now overgrown with wildflowers, to
escape the city bustle. The nearby **Museo Archeologico** records the ancient city's
earliest days and includes an inscribed ceramic cup, the colony's earliest surviving
writing. (☎0942 510 01. Open 9am-7pm; €1, under 18 or over 65 free.)

Beach by day, fluorescent-lit pub promenade by night, Giardini-Naxos offers
ample entertainment options for wiling away the hours in between. Around 11pm
during the summer, busloads of glitzed-up revelers head to pubs, restaurants, and
flashy *discoteche.* The party starts 20m from the bus stop at pizzeria/karaoke bar
Mister Roll II, V. Jannuzzo, 31. (☎0942 65 30 87. Open daily 8:30pm-5am; closed Tu
in winter.) The disco-happy should hang a left to **Cabana,** V. Jannuzzo, 1. Follow
back-lit palm trees and the neon blue cursive sign to this striking but not overbear-
ing complex, complete with rotating techno, oldies, Latin, international pop music,
and a piano bar and restaurant before 1am. (☎0942 65 30 29. Cover €13. Open in
summer 11:30pm-dawn.) Farther left, a poorly lit but well-trafficked road leads
down to the all-night *lungomare* party at V. S. Naxos/V. Tysandros, a hyper-sen-
sory experience with live music, popcorn and cotton candy vendors, whizzing pre-
teen in-line skaters, and people, people, people.

CATANIA   ☎095

Though beset with some of the island's worst traffic and pollution, Catania still
earns its status as a Sicilian treasure. From the stately grace of its piazzas to the
ancient history lingering around Greek and Roman remains, the city merges tradition with youthful revelry, as university students funnel into its numerous cafes
and bars. Leveled repeatedly, sometimes by invaders but most often by nearby Mt.
Etna, Catania has been rebuilt several times since its founding as a Greek colony
in 729 BC. After the monstrous 1693 earthquake, G. B. Vaccarini recreated the city
with his Baroque piazzas and duomo. Later, the virtuoso composer Vincenzo Bellini introduced another type of harmony: the opera.

▐ TRANSPORTATION

Flights: Fontanarossa (☎095 34 05 05). Take the *alibus* from train station or pay about
€20 for the 15min. cab ride. 1 flight daily to Malta with **Air Malta,** C. Sicilia, 71 (☎095
34 53 11).

Trains: ☎095 53 27 19. In P. P. Giovanni XXIII. To: **Agrigento** (4hr., 7 per day 5:55am-
7:20pm, €9.20); **Enna** (1½hr., 7 per day 5:55am-7:20pm, €4.60); **Florence** (12hr.,
17 per day 3:15am-10:07pm, €43); **Messina** (2hr., 20 per day 3:15am-9:25pm,
€5.05); **Palermo** (3½hr., 10 per day 3:15am-7:20pm, €11.25); **Rome** (10hr., 14 per
day 3:15am-10:07pm, €33.47); **Syracuse** (1½hr., 11 per day 6:10am-8:53pm,
€4.65); **Taormina/Giardini-Naxos** (1hr., 23 per day 3:15am-9:25pm, €3.05).

Buses: All companies are on V. D'Amico, across the city bus-filled piazza in front of the train station. Service is significantly reduced on Su, so weekend travelers may wish to take a train instead. **SAIS Trasporti** (☎095 53 62 01) serves **Agrigento** (3hr., 13 per day 6:45am-9pm, €10) and **Rome** (14hr.; 7:50, 9pm; €40, under 26 or over 60 €35). **SAIS Autoline** (☎095 53 61 68) to: **Enna** (1½hr.; M-Sa 7 per day 6:40am-9:25pm, Su 3 per day 9am-8pm; €6); **Messina** (1½hr.; M-Sa 25 per day 5am-10:30pm, Su 6 per day 7am-10:30pm; €7); **Palermo** (3hr., 16 per day 5am-10:30pm, €12). **Interbus** and **Etna** (☎095 53 27 16) both run to: **Brindisi** (8hr.; 10:30am, 10pm; €35.57); **Noto** (2½hr.; 2, 5:45pm; €5.60); **Ragusa** (2hr., 11 per day 6am-8pm, €6.20); **Taormina/ Giardini-Naxos** (1hr., 10 per day 7:15am-7:45pm, €4).

Ferries: La Duca Viaggi, P. Europa, 1 (☎095 722 22 95). Walk up V. Africa from train station. Ferry tickets to **Malta** (high season €85.22).

Public Transportation: AMT buses leave from train station in P. Papa Giovanni XXIII. **Alibus** goes to the airport and **#27** to the beach. Tickets (€0.77) valid for 1½hr. are sold at *tabacchi* and newsstands.

Scooter Rental: Hollywood Rent by Motoservice, P. Cavour, 12 (☎095 44 27 20). Scooters and bikes from €30, motorcycles from €50, cars from €50. Rates subject to change without notice. Open M-Sa 8am-1pm and 4-8pm.

✈ 🛈 ORIENTATION AND PRACTICAL INFORMATION

Via Etnea, running from the duomo to the Giardini Bellini, is Catania's chic main street. From the **train** and **bus stations** in the waterfront **Piazza Giovanni XXIII, Corso Martiri della Libertà** heads west into the city center, changing into **Corso Sicilia** in **Piazza della Repubblica**—and later bisecting V. Etnea at **Piazza Stesicoro,** under the watchful eye of a pigeon-covered Bellini monument. A right on V. Etnea leads to budget accommodations, fashionable boutiques, the post office, and the gardens; the Teatro Bellini and city's Technical University cluster around the duomo to the left. Though Catania is notorious for petty thievery, travelers can enjoy it if they are cautious. At night stick to the populated and well-lit areas along V. Etnea, and always be wary of staged distractions.

Tourist Office: AAPIT, V. Cimarosa, 10 (☎095 730 62 79 or 730 62 22), near the Giardini Bellini. From V. Etnea, turn on V. Pacini before the post office and follow signs. English-speaking staff offers brochures on city, region, and Etna. Open M-F 8am-8pm, Sa-Su 8am-2pm. **Branches** at station (☎095 730 62 55) and airport (☎095 730 62 66 or 730 62 77). Same hours as downtown office.

Budget Travel: CTS, V. Ventimiglia, 153 (☎095 53 02 23, fax 53 62 46), off P. della Repubblica. Useful info on travel in Sicily, Italy, and beyond. Open M-F 9:30am-1pm and 4:30-7:30pm, Sa 9:30am-12:30pm.

American Express: La Duca Viaggi, P. Europa, 1 (☎095 722 22 95), up V. Africa from train station. Mail held for 1 month. Open M-F 9am-1pm and 4-7:30pm, Sa 9am-noon.

Emergency: ☎113. **Carabinieri** (☎112). **Police** (☎095 53 13 33).

Ambulance: ☎095 37 71 22 or 38 21 13. **Medical clinic,** C. Italia, 234 (☎095 37 71 22).

Pharmacy: Crocerossa, V. Etnea, 274 (☎095 31 70 53). Open daily 8:30am-1pm and 4:30-8pm. AmEx/MC/V. **Croceverde,** V. G. D'Annunzio, 43 (☎095 44 16 62), at the intersection of C. Italia and C. della Provincia.

Hospital: Ospedale Garibaldi (☎095 759 11 11), in P. Santa Maria del Gesù.

Internet: Internet Caffetteria, V. Penninello, 44 (☎095 31 01 39), has 10 computers, cappuccino, sandwiches, and email to combat hunger and homesickness. €1 for up to 30min., €2 per hr. Open M-F 10am-9pm, Sa 10am-1:30pm, and 5-10pm.

Post Office: V. Etnea, 215 (☎095 715 51 11), in the big building next to Giardini Bellini. Open M-Sa 8am-6:30pm. **Postal code:** 95125.

ACCOMMODATIONS

Though a plethora of posh stores lining the streets suggests high hotel prices, many *pensione* near V. Etnea are affordable. Reserve early for summer.

Hotel Gresi, V. Pacini, 28 (☎095 32 27 09, fax 095 715 30 45; www.siciliaholi-day.net), off V. Etnea before Villa Bellini and post office. Decorated hallways lead to an inviting salon, breakfast room, and spacious social bar. Clean rooms with gorgeously painted ceilings all have bath, A/C, TV, and phone. Breakfast €5. Singles €45; doubles €70. AmEx/MC/V. ❹

Agorà Youth Hostel, P. Curro, 6 (☎095 723 30 10; http://agorahostel.hypermart.net). Find fountain in the corner of P. Duomo opposite the train station and follow the diagonal street for 3 short blocks before making a left. Tempermental hot water and electrical outlets are well compensated for by price and central location. Night owls will enjoy the bar and restaurant on the ground floor, while light sleepers might want to spend a couple of extra euros for a low-priced *pensione* further from the train station. 2 computers with Internet. (€4 per hr.) Breakfast included. Dorms €16. ❷

Hotel Ferrara, V. Umberto, 66 (☎095 31 60 00, fax 31 30 60), off V. Etnea across from the gardens. Stately wooden entrance leads to high-ceilinged, rosy rooms which vary in noise and light levels but are all clean and comfortable. Singles €33, with bath €49; doubles €49/€60; triples €71/€81; quads €97/€108. Cash only. ❸

Hotel Mele, V. Leonardi, 24 (☎/fax 095 32 75 42), off V. A. d. Sanguiliano near P. Bellini, above the Iguana Pub (2 floors up). If you can get past the skeletons and cobwebs of the haunted house-themed nightclub below, this *pensione* is an excellent deal. Spacious rooms furnished with quirky antiques make you feel like you're spending a night in a haunted mansion. Singles €20; doubles €35. Cash only. ❷

Pensione Rubens, V. Etnea, 196, 3rd fl. (☎095 31 70 73, fax 715 17 13), above the Thai Consulate. Amicable owners and attractive, well-kept rooms make this a comforting home away from home. All rooms have bath, A/C, TV, and phone. Reserve ahead in summer. Singles €45; doubles €70. Extra bed €15. AmEx/MC/V. ❸

FOOD

When *Catanesi* ring the dinner bell, chances are they'll enjoy local favorites like eggplant- and ricotta-topped *spaghetti alla norma*, named for Bellini's famous opera. Another hit is the fresh and glistening *masculini*, or anchovies, rumored to have aphrodisiacal powers. The marketplace off P. del Duomo and V. Garibaldi features excitable vendors advertising fresh fish, fruit, and traditional sweets. The action runs in the morning and early afternoon (M-Sa). An SMA **supermarket** is at C. Sicilia, 50. (☎095 32 60 699. Open M-Sa 8:30am-8:30pm.) **Bar Savia** , V. Etnea, 304, across from Bellini Gardens, serves the best *granite di gelsi* (mulberry slushies, €1.60) in town. (Open M-Sa 8am-9:30pm.) Perhaps the best deal, however, is the *arancina*—an extremely filling meat-stuffed fried rice ball that can be bought for €1.30 at any bar with a sign reading "Tavola Calda."

Trattoria Rosso Pomodoro, V. Coppola, 28 (☎095 250 00 10), off V. Biondi near Teatro Bellini, has an understated, inviting atmosphere and superior cuisine. Displays impressive *antipasto* buffet. Specialty mixed seafood dish €8. *Primi* from €4, *secondi* from €4.50. Cover €1.50. Open Tu-Su noon-2pm and 7pm-midnight. AmEx/MC/V. ❷

SICILY

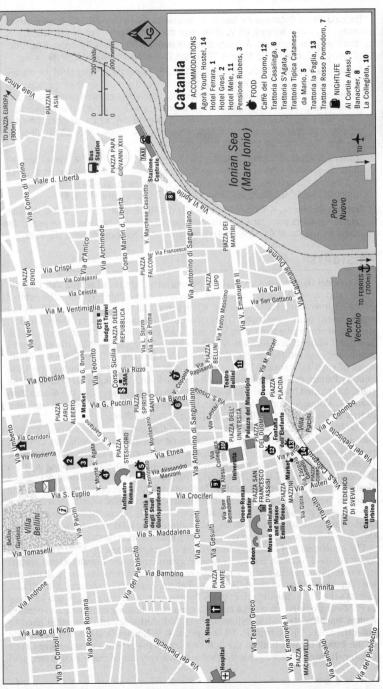

Catania

ACCOMMODATIONS
Agorà Youth Hostel, **14**
Hotel Ferrara, **1**
Hotel Gresi, **2**
Hotel Mele, **11**
Pensione Rubens, **3**

FOOD
Caffè del Duomo, **12**
Trattoria Casalinga, **6**
Trattoria S'Agata, **4**
Trattoria Tipica Catanese da Mario, **5**
Trattoria la Paglia, **13**
Trattoria Rosso Pomodoro, **7**

NIGHTLIFE
Al Cortile Alessi, **9**
Banacher, **8**
La Collegiata, **10**

Trattoria Tipica Catanese da Mario, V. Penninello, 34 (☎095 32 24 61; www.catani-acity.com/trattoriamario), off V. Etnea near the amphitheater. Fish is the specialty at this family-run restaurant. *Al fresco* dining in summer. *Primi* from €4, *secondi* from €6. Cover €1.50. Open M-Sa 11am-3:30pm and 7pm-midnight. AmEx/MC/V. ❷

Trattoria la Paglia, V. Pardo, 23 (☎095 34 68 38), brings the bustling air of the market-place indoors, near P. del Duomo. Don't be surprised if you end up sharing a table with strangers; this popular pit-stop makes every effort to pack in as many customers as possible. Tired of tomatoes? Trade red sauce for black with *spaghetti al nero di seppia* (with squid ink, €4.65). Make sure to come during the day, as the shoppers from the market make this place especially lively. *Primi* from €4, *secondi* from €5.50. Open M-Sa noon-4pm and 7pm-midnight. AmEx/MC/V. ❷

Trattoria S'Agata, V. Monte S. Agata, 11-13 (☎095 31 54 53), off V. Etnea. Turn left after the Stefanel store in P. Stesicoro. Catanese charm accompanies the food. Check out their risotto varieties. Wood-bound menus in many languages list *primi* and *secondi* (from €7). Cover €2. Open daily noon-3pm and 7-10pm. AmEx/MC/V. ❸

Trattoria Casalinga, V. Biondi, 19 (☎095 31 13 19). Popular with the locals, this little restaurant offers *primi* for €5 and *secondi* for €7. Planned full *menùs* are perfect for larger groups. Cover €1. Open daily noon-4pm and Tu-Su 8pm-midnight. MC/V. ❸

🄶 SIGHTS

In **Piazza del Duomo,** Giovan Battista Vaccarini's little lava **Fontana dell'Elefante** (1736) commands the city's attention. Vaccarini carved his elephant (the symbol of the city) without visible testicles. When the statue was unveiled, horrified *Catanesi* men, who construed from this omission an attack on their virility, demanded corrective measures. Vaccarini's acquiescence was, well, monumental. Residents claim that visitors may attain citizenship by smooching the elephant's nether regions, but the height of the pachyderm's backside precludes the fulfillment of such aspirations. The other buildings on the piazza, including the 18th-century **Palazzo del Municipio** on the left and the former **Seminario dei Chierici** on the right, are striped black and white to mirror the duomo's side. Visit the **Museo Diocesano,** V. Etnea, 8, next to the duomo, to see priestly vestments several centuries old. (☎095 28 16 35. Open Tu-Su 9am-12:30pm and 4-7:30pm.)

The 1950 restoration of the **duomo** revealed glimpses of its interior predating its Baroque makeover. Restorators discovered stumps of old columns and tall, pointed arches of the original three apses. In the Norman **Cappella della Madonna,** on the right, the sparkling walls surround a beautiful Roman sarcophagus and a 15th-century statue of the Virgin Mary. The body of Catania's beloved priest, the Beato Cardinal Dusmet, lies nearby, his bronze head and bony fingers protruding from his vestments. To the right of the main door is **Bellini's tomb,** guarded by a life-size marble angel. The words and music from his *Sonnambula* are inscribed above the tomb and translate as "Ah, I didn't think I'd see you wilt so soon, flower." (Hours vary; closed to visitors during mass. Modest dress required.)

The centerpiece of Catania's restoration efforts rests just up V. Etnea. Marked by an ethereal fountain and tall, crooked cyprus trees, the **Giardini Bellini** sprawl over several small hills and around tiny ponds. Sunday afternoons find half the city strolling here, gelato in hand. Below an elegant Victorian bandstand, a small plot displays the day's date in perfect grass figures, replanted daily. A few blocks away in P. Stesicoro, modern streets cradle a sunken pit holding ruins of a 2nd-century **Roman amphitheater,** with visible tunnels that gladiators and monsters used to enter the arena. Uphill from P. del Duomo, at V. V. Emanuele 260, lies the entrance to the **Roman Theater,** built in the 2nd century on the grounds of an earlier Greek theater. Its arched passageways, lined with the remains of marble columns, spill out into the similar but smaller **Odeon,** with another entrance around the back. Mt. Etna's 1669 eruption coated the marble of both theaters with lava. (☎ 095 715 05 08. Open daily 9am-1:30pm and 3-7pm. €2, €1 for EU residents.)

🎵 ENTERTAINMENT

Teatro Massimo (Bellini), V. A. di Sanguiliano, 233, mesmerizes audiences in a sumptuous setting. Sink into plush red seats for a symphony or wait for the thrill of opera (Jan.-June). Student discounts are available for all tickets; contact the tourist office. (☎ 095 715 09 21. Box office open M 9:30am-12:30pm, Tu-F 5-7pm.) The AAPIT's free monthly bulletin *Lapis,* available at bars and the tourist office, details Catania's hot nightlife, movies, concerts, and festivals.

Participants in the nightly *passeggiata* circulate the P. del Duomo and swarm near Teatro Bellini. Cafes pulsate with life on weekends, drawing a sometimes raucous crowd. Local university students and urban thirty-somethings frequent neighborhood watering holes. In the late evening, university students swarm the streets near P. Università. **La Collegiata** is a student favorite, with live music and large crowds (open 7pm-4am).

Try **Al Cortile Alessi,** V. Alessi, 30, for courtyard dining under swaying nespola trees. (Open Tu-Su 8pm-last person leaves. AmEx/MC/V.) **Caffè del Duomo,** across from the elephant fountain, offers gelato and coffee for a nice low-key night in Catania's main piazza. (☎ 095 715 05 56. Open daily 5:30am-3am.) From the *centro,* locals drive to the dance floor of **Banacher,** V. XXI Aprile S.S., 114, a 15min. taxi ride from Catania's center. Lights keep the dancing crowds captive until 5am at what is reputed to be Europe's largest outdoor disco. (☎ 095 27 12 57. Open Tu-Su 10pm-3am.) Weekend summer crowds also scooter 20min. away to **Aci Castello,** a nocturnal destination for people seeking *passeggiate,* seaside bars, and general mayhem beside the ruins of a Norman castle.

This side of Catania's coast is far from the city chaos but still subject to Etna's fury; huge, black boulders line the jagged shore, hurled there by eruptions of yore. Previous tectonic activity created a series of nearby islands that are now marine reserves, including the **Island of the Cyclops** of Odyssian fame. Catania's biggest feast day honors the city's patron **Sant'Agata.** Fireworks and non-stop partying in the first five days of February salvage the city from winter gloom. The crowded beach **La Plaja** has a charming view of a nearby power plant. (Take bus #427, which runs June-Sept.) Farther from the port is the more rugged **La Scogliera,** with fiery cliffs and a bathing area. (Take bus #334 from P. del Duomo; 30min.)

🚌 DAYTRIP FROM CATANIA

MOUNT ETNA
An AST bus leaves from Catania's central train station at 8:15am for a 2hr. ride to Rifugio Sapienza. The bus leaves Etna at 4:30pm (times subject to change; round-trip €4.80). In case of emergency, call ☎ 0942 53 17 77.

The lava-seared wilderness of Mt. Etna is one of Italy's most compelling natural settings. Etna's history of volcanic activity is the longest documented of any volcano—the first recorded eruption was in 1500 BC, though it was probably active long before that. Europe's largest active volcano (at 3350m), it has long held sway over the residents of eastern Sicily: The Greek poet Hesiod envisioned Etna as the home of Typhon, the last monster conceived by Earth to fight the gods before the dawn of the human race. The ancients also claimed its fires were the home of Vulcan, the gods' blacksmith. Apparently Typhon's aggressions aren't over yet: a 1985

ALWAYS TIME TO LEAVE

Dominique di Salvo has been fascinated by volcanoes since she was a girl, so 28 years ago, she traded her native Paris for the simmering setting of Mt. Etna. When the volcano erupted in summer 2002, destroying her restaurant, di Salvo wasn't ready to give in.

LG: How many people live on Mt. Etna?
A: Three. There are three of us who live here at 2000m: my husband, my son, and me. Other people come only to work.
LG: And you're not afraid?
A: Not at all. This is not like Pompeii that has explosions. No, Etna is not like Pompeii or Vesuvius. Here, lava takes a long time to come down the mountain.
LG: Your restaurant was destroyed by an eruption recently, is that correct?
A: Yes, I said it was safe for people, but not for buildings. I am working in this restaurant while I rebuild mine, and when other restaurants in the area have been destroyed, the owners come to work in mine. We help each other out when an eruption occurs.
LG: What if Etna erupts again?
A: There is always time to leave. Most people who die [here] do so from heart problems or asthma. This happens to people who don't know that at 2000m, or 3000m, people don't feel that well. This is a problem of mountains, not Etna.

eruption destroyed much of the summit tourist station, and eruptions in 2001 and 2002 sent lava rolling down slopes at 100m per hour. The volcano continues to emit ash and smoke plumes, causing discomfort for area residents.

From Rifugio Sapienza (1900m), where the AST bus stops, a 3hr. hike to the aptly named **Torre del Filosofo** (Philosopher's Tower, 2920m) gives a broad and contemplative view of the looming peaks and Etna's steaming craters. Anyone with sturdy shoes can take a 30min. jaunt exploring the crater in front of the parking area. From the Philosopher's Tower, a 2hr. hike leads to the **craters** themselves. **Valle del Bove,** Etna's first volcanic crater, is on the way down. While the view of the hardened lava, huge boulders, and unearthly craters is incredible, the trail is so difficult and the volcanic activity so unpredictable that sightseers are only allowed access by guided tour. On a certified tour, hikers can hold molten rocks heated by subterranean activity or watch guides burn newspapers on exposed rifts in the rock. Those who brave the trip should take precautions: carry water and bring warm clothing, as winds are ferocious and pockets of snow linger even in mid-July. Travelers not wishing to hike can take an off-road shuttle up to Philosopher's Tower for €42 (includes a guided tour of the nearby craters).

CST, C. Umberto, 99-101, runs tours to 3000m (☎0942 62 60 88; csttao@tiscalinet.it. June-Aug. M and W 3:45pm, Sept. 3:15pm, Oct. 2:15pm; €55) and to 2000m (year-round Tu and Th 8am, €25). Also try **Gruppo Guide Alpine,** V. Etna, 49 (☎095 91 41 41). **SAT,** C. Umberto, 73, operates day-long tours from Taormina. (☎0942 24 653; www.sat-group.it. Bus tours for Etna leave M 8:30am, €28; tours of the crater area in bus and jeep available Tu and Th 3pm, €65.)

After an intense hike, campers can curl up at **Camping La Timpa,** V. Santa Maria la Scala, 25, in the countryside of Acireale. They offer **bungalows ❸** and **camping ❶.** (☎095 764 81 55; www.campingla-timpa.it. €4.50-7.30 per person, €2 per car. Doubles €45; triples €50; quads €55. Prices rise substantially during high season.)

CENTRAL SICILY

ENNA ☎0935

Dubbed *l'ombelico della Sicilia* (the navel of Sicily), Enna is an isolated city of ancient charms, worn stone streets, churches in a multitude of architectural styles, and some of the most beautiful, far-reaching views in

Sicily. At night, the intimate piazzas spring to life with revelers whose strolls inevitably lead them to railings overlooking dramatic mountainsides. But for the best view in town, walk the short distance to the towers of the Castello di Lombardia. On clear days, the imposing silhouette of Etna shimmers in the distance.

▣ TRANSPORTATION

Enna is accessible by both bus and train, but taking the bus sidesteps the 8km uphill hike into town from the train station.

Trains: ☎ 0935 50 09 10. Buses connect the train station to the town center (M-Sa 6 per day 6:25am-8:55pm, €1.29). To: **Agrigento** (2hr., 7 per day 7:16am-8:40pm, €5.45); **Catania** (1¼hr., 7 per day 6:13am-8:12pm, €4.65); **Palermo** (3hr., 6 per day 7:16am-8:40pm, €7.50).

Buses: All buses depart from the bus station on V. Diaz, a short walk uphill from P. Matteotti. **Interbus** (☎ 0935 50 23 90) and **SAIS** (☎ 0935 50 09 02) are under one roof, with an additional Interbus office (☎ 0935 50 31 41) on V. Roma by the tourist office. Regional buses also make various stops throughout the city. To: **Catania** (2hr.; M-Sa 6 per day 6:20am-6:15pm, Su 7:15am, 5:15, and 6:15pm; €5.94) continuing to **Noto, Ragusa,** and **Syracuse; Palermo** (2hr., 9 per day, €7.75); **Piazza Armerina** (35min., 11 per day 7am-9:45pm, €2.70).

Taxis: In P. Scelfo (☎ 0935 50 09 05). In P. V. Emanuele (☎ 0935 50 09 06).

◪ ▨ ORIENTATION AND PRACTICAL INFORMATION

The **bus station** lies just outside Enna's central historic district. **Via Vittorio Emanuele** runs from the station to **Piazza Matteotti,** where **Via Roma** branches in two directions. V. Roma passes straight past **Piazza Vittorio Emanuele** and the duomo, toward the Castello di Lombardia. The right fork of V. Roma cuts an arc through residential areas to the **Torre di Federico II.** Beware of V. Roma's disordered addresses; every location often has two sets of street numbers, and very often neither is correct. Ask for directions to prevent confusion.

Tourist Offices: AAPIT, V. Roma, 411-413 (☎ 0935 52 82 28). Info on Enna province. Open M-Sa 8:30am-1:30pm and 3-7pm. For info on the city, transportation, and lodgings, head to **AAST,** P. Cloajanni, 6 (☎ 0935 50 08 75, fax 26 119), beside Hotel Sicilia. English and French spoken. Open M-Sa 8am-2:15pm, W also 2:45-6:15pm.

Currency Exchange: Banks line V. Roma between P. V. Emanuele and P. Umberto I. Currency exchange also available at the post office.

ATM: In P. Umberto I, on V. Roma.

Emergency: ☎ 113. **Ambulance** (☎ 118).

Police: ☎ 0935 52 21 11. **Carabinieri** (☎ 112 or 0935 50 12 67) in P. Europa.

First Aid: ☎ 0935 45 245. **Medical Clinic** (☎ 0935 50 08 96) open daily 8pm-8am.

Pharmacy: Farmacia del Centro, V. Roma, 315 (☎ 0935 50 06 50), posts the late-night rotation schedule, as does **Farmacia Librizzi,** P. V. Emanuele, 21 (☎ 0935 50 09 08). Open 9am-1pm and 4-8pm.

Hospital: Ospedale Umberto, V. Trieste, 54 (☎ 0935 45 111).

Internet: Ciemme, V. Lombardia, 31 (☎ 0935 50 47 12, fax 50 67 35), next to the castle, has 4 speedy computers. €2.50 per hr. Open daily 9am-1pm and 4-8pm.

Post Office: V. Volta, 1 (☎ 0935 56 23 12). Take a left off V. Roma just before the AAPIT office and walk to the right of the "Provincia" building. Open M-F 8am-7pm, Sa 8am-12:30pm. **Postal Code:** 94100.

♠ ACCOMMODATIONS

Enna is short on accommodations, though a bed and breakfast lies nearby in Calascibetta, accessible by bus. **Affittacamere da Pietro ❸**, Cda. Longobardo da Pietro, is 4km from Enna. To get there, follow the bed and breakfast signs from V. Roma or take the bus for Calascibetta and ask to be dropped off at the Affittacamere da Pietro. All 18 rooms have bath and TV. (☎ 0935 336 47 or 340 276 576 36. Singles €30; doubles €45. Cash only.) Right in the heart of town, just up V. Roma from the AAPIT office, **Hotel Sicilia ❺**, P. Colajanni, 7, has luxurious, elegantly decorated rooms complete with bath, TV, hair dryer, antique furniture, and Botticelli reproductions. Breakfast buffet is included, served on a terrace with nice views. (☎ 0935 50 08 50. Singles €62; doubles €91; triples €110. AmEx/MC/V.)

♦ FOOD

Enna's relaxed character extends to its dining, making eating out an enjoyable and lengthy affair. Restaurants cluster along Viale Marconi behind V. Roma and P. Crispi. Find basic supplies at the Sigma **supermarket** right before the castle at V. Lombardia, 21. Picnickers can also investigate V. Mercato Sant'Antonio, lined with alimentari, fruit stands, and bakeries. Watch the action outside the duomo from the tiny **Bar del Duomo ❶**, in P. Mazzini, while munching selections from their rows of perfect cookies. (☎ 0935 24 205. Open M and W-Su 6am-midnight.) Or satisfy a sweet tooth in style at **Caffè Roma ❶**, V. Roma, 312. Delectable goodies and gelato (€1.30) served in a posh interior. (☎ 0935 50 12 12. Open daily 6am-11pm.) The flower-covered terrace of ◪**Ristorante La Fontana ❷**, V. Vulturo, 6, in the intimate P. Crispi, overlooks the valley and offers a lovely meal setting. Try the *spaghetti alla donna concetta* (€6.20), a house specialty. (☎ 0935 25 465. *Primi* from €4.65, *secondi* from €7.80. Cover €1.04. Open daily noon-3:30pm and 7-11pm. AmEx/MC/V.) Feast on fantastic food and watch pedestrians stroll from the elegant stone and wood dining room of **San Gennaro da Gino ❷**, Viale Marconi, 6. Start with the extensive *antipasto* buffet and finish off with delicious *panna cotta* (€3). Piano bar nights are Tuesday and Friday. (☎ 0935 24 067, fax 50 61 91. Pizza from €3.10. *Primi* €6-7, *secondi* €6-10. Cover €1.50. Open daily 12:30-3pm and 8pm-12:30am. AmEx/MC/V.) Head to the mirror-lined walls and refined decor of **Ristorante Pizzeria Ariston ❷**, V. Roma, 353, for a proper indoor meal. (☎ 0935 260 38. Additional entrance on V. Vulturo. Pizza from €4. *Primi* from €6.50, *secondi* from €6. Cover €1.30. Open M-Sa 12:30-2:30pm and 7:30-10:30pm. AmEx/MC/V.)

♦ SIGHTS

Although grass and vines have overrun its enclosed courtyards, the thick walls and towers of the **Castello di Lombardia** attest to a time when residents of Enna were more engaged in defending their environment than enjoying it. These days, however, visitors can guiltlessly savor a view of the entire province and, on clear days, Mt. Etna, from ◪**La Pisana,** the tallest of the castle towers. The Swabians constructed the castle, named for a Lombardian siege, in the Norman period. (From the duomo, V. Roma curves uphill and becomes V. Lombardia before ending at the Castello. ☎ 0935 50 09 62. Open daily Apr.-Oct. 8am-8pm, Nov.-Mar. 8am-5pm, though gates often stay open later.) One of the city's other architectural marvels is the **Torre di Federico II**, which concealed Sicilian defenders during WWII. A tunnel runs from the *torre* to the castle at the other end of town. The entrance is visible from within the tower. Adjacent to the castle, a natural **fortress** also offers excellent views of the city. The weeping Demeter supposedly mourned the loss of her daughter Persephone to Hades at the **Rocca di Cerere,** on the path below the *Castello*. (*Rocca di Cerere* on the path leading up to left of the castle. Turn left on V. IV Novembre for public gardens. Open daily 9am-8pm. Free.)

Though more than a dozen religious fraternities throughout the city have their own churches, all participated in creating the curious ⚅**duomo,** which combines as many architectural styles as there are brotherhoods. Construction began in the early 14th century, but the cathedral was remodeled throughout the 15th and 16th centuries, resulting in a stylistic potpourri. The eclecticism extends to the church's interior, which juxtaposes Gothic doors, medieval walls, Renaissance paintings, and gilded Baroque flourishes. The sacrilegious stretch out on wooden pews to appreciate the marvelous wood-paneled ceiling. (Open daily 9am-1pm and 4-7pm.) The **Museo Alessi,** in the rectory immediately behind the cathedral on V. Roma, matches the schizophrenic spirit of the duomo with its own varied collection. Ancient coins and pottery share space with oil paintings and the church's treasures, which include a fine silver model cathedral. On the ground floor is a stunning gold crown, depicting the story of Christ's ascension, which adorns the head of the Madonna during the annual Festa della Madonna (see **Entertainment**). (☎0935 50 31 65. Open daily 8am-8pm. €2.60, students or over 60 €1.50.)

🎜 ENTERTAINMENT

Every July 2, Enna celebrates the **Festa della Madonna** with the procession of three enormous votive statues through the streets of the city, followed by fireworks, music, and traditional *mastazzoli* (apple cookies). The party continues through the summer with the feasts of **Sant'Anna** and **Madonna di Valverde** on the last Sundays of July and August respectively. Every Easter, the brothers of each fraternity don hoods and capes and parade through the streets. Processions of a speedier sort take place at the **Autodromo di Pergusa** (☎0935 256 60, fax 258 25), which hosts **Grand Prix** auto races from March through October. The most important race is the Formula 3 in May. Otherwise, the Autodromo acts as an all-purpose arena, hosting everything from motorcycle races to dog shows.

PIAZZA ARMERINA   ☎0935

Perched in the Erei Mountains, the medieval city of Piazza Armerina shows few signs of time's passing. Traditional Sicilian music still echoes off the green-domed duomo and King Martino's *Castello Aragonese*, and many streets are little more than twisting stone staircases. But the foothills below contain the city's real attraction, the famed Villa Romana and its remarkably intact ancient mosaics, which are among the largest and most beautiful in the world.

🖭🎝 **TRANSPORTATION AND PRACTICAL INFORMATION. Buses** run to Piazza Armerina from Caltanissetta (1hr., 4 per day 7:40am-6pm, €4.10); Enna (35min., 8 per day 5:45am-5:10pm, €2.70); and Gela (1hr., 5 per day 7am-7:05pm, €3.40). Buses arrive at the city's northern end in **Piazza Senatore Marescalchi.** Facing away from the **Interbus** office, walk two short blocks before turning left on **Via D'Annunzio,** which quickly becomes **Via Chiaranda,** then **Via Mazzini,** and finally arrives at **Piazza Garibaldi,** the historic center. The **tourist office,** V. Cavour, 1, is in the courtyard of a palazzo just off P. Garibaldi. (☎0935 68 02 01. Open M-F 9am-1pm and Tu-Th 3-6pm.) In P. Garibaldi, **Farmacia Quattrino** posts the night-shift rotations. (☎0935 68 00 44. Open M-F 9am-1pm and 4-8pm.) In case of **emergency,** call the **carabinieri** (☎0935 68 20 14) or **first aid** at ☎112.

🖬🖿 **ACCOMMODATIONS AND FOOD.** For the best budget accommodations, follow the yellow signs to ⚅**Ostello del Borgo ❷,** Largo S. Giovanni, 6, a renovated 14th-century monastery on V. Umberto. This gem offers 20 rooms with dignified furniture and good beds. All private rooms include bath and toiletries; dorms have cramped but clean showers and toilets down the hall. Request a room on the second or third floor to avoid a rude awakening as the staff prepares breakfast. Internet on one fast computer for €2 per hr. (☎ 0935 68 70 19; www.ostellodelborgo.it. Wheelchair accessible. Buffet breakfast included. Dorms €15; singles €43; doubles €57; triples €75; quads €91. AmEx/MC/V.) **Hotel Villa Romana ❹**, V. De Gasperi, 18, offers posh, beautifully furnished rooms with full amenities, including bath, TV, A/C, and phone. Three restaurants and two bars round out this three-star splurge. (☎/fax 0935 68 29 11; www.piazza-armerina.it/hotelvillaromana. Breakfast included. Singles €60; doubles €85; triples €115; quads €125. AmEx/MC/V.)

A mere handful of restaurants sprinkle the streets of Piazza Armerina's historic district, though more options are available in other areas. **Ristorante Pizzeria Pepito ❸**, V. Roma, 140, serves Italian comfort food with a distinctly Spanish flair. Enjoy specialties such as *agnello al forno* (baked lamb €10) in either the casual downstairs or the more formal upstairs dining room, the latter with impressive views of the gardens across the street. (☎ 0935 68 57 37. *Primi* €6-7, *secondi* from €7. Cover €1. Open M and W-Su noon-3pm and 7-midnight. AmEx/MC/V.) Savvy locals head to **Ristorante Pizzeria da Toto ❷**, V. Mazzini, 29, near P. Garibaldi, for pizza and *insalata capricciosa* (an elaborate salad of mixed Sicilian ingredients €3.60) served swiftly in a comfortable ambiance. (☎/fax 0935 68 01 53. Pizza €4-5. Cover €1.05. Open Tu-Su noon-3:30pm and 6pm-midnight. AmEx/MC/V.)

◪ **SIGHTS.** A fertile valley 5km southwest of town shelters the ◪**Villa Romana del Casale.** This remarkable site, known locally as "I Mosaici," is thought to have been constructed at the turn of the 4th century, but a 12th-century landslide kept it mostly hidden for another 800 years. In 1916 famed archaeologists Paolo Orsi and Giuseppe Culterra unearthed 40 rooms of extraordinary stone mosaics—and there are rooms that have yet to be excavated. Glass walls and ceilings shade the mosaics for protection but still allow for a sense of what the villa would have looked like at the height of its glory. Guidebooks from nearby vendors explain the finer points of the villa's construction and history. Enter first through the **baths**, then pass into a large **hall** on the left to find a mosaic depicting a chariot race; the flying legs, at the left, are all that remain of the driver, believed to have been Maximenius Herculeus, co-ruler of the western half of the Roman Empire with Diocletian. Max's great wealth, fondness for the hunt, and side business as an importer of exotic animals are part of the tiles' tale. One of the largest rooms shows the dramatic capture of bulls, tigers, and lions, while the floor of the enormous **Triclinium** depicts the Battle of the Giants and the Feats of Hercules. The **Salle delle Dieci Ragazze** (Room of Ten Girls) showcases ten bikini-clad beauties in what is probably the most famous of the villa's mosaics. While the **Cubicolo Scena Erotica** is not quite as scandalous as its title suggests, the bare tush and intimate kiss depicted still make it the raciest mosaic at the villa. A room off the great hall illustrates the battle between Odysseus and Polyphemus, though the artist fudged the finer narrative details, generously allowing the Cyclops three eyes instead of one. (☎ 0935 68 00 36. Buses run to the villa 6 times per day 9am-5pm, the last return is 5:30pm. Buses leave from P. Marescalchi or Hotel Villa Romana. Bus info, V. Umberto, 6. ☎ 0935 856 05. The 5km walk is well marked with signs pointing to I Mosaici. Bring lots of water—the sun can be brutal. Villa and ticket office open daily 8am-6:30pm. €4.50, ages 18-25 €2, under 18 or over 65 free.)

SOUTHERN SICILY

SYRACUSE (SIRACUSA)   ☎ 0931

Mixing baroque beauty with archaeological jewels, Syracuse combines the relics of an ancient Mediterranean powerhouse with the beauty of a seaside Sicilian town. At its peak in the ancient world, Syracuse cultivated a worthy selection of great contributors to Western culture, including Theocritus, Archimedes, and the Greek lyric poet Pindar. After conquests by the Romans and Arabs, the city's fortunes waned and it receded from the spotlight. Yet Syracuse has elegantly stepped into the 21st century to become the flower of modern Sicily, as the stunning ruins of the Temple of Apollo and history-rich duomo sit comfortably beside more contemporary structures.

⌐ TRANSPORTATION

Trains: ☎ 0931 67 964. On V. Francesco Crispi, between Ortigia and the Archaeological Park. To: **Catania** (1½hr., 11 per day 4:50am-7:45pm, €4.23); **Florence** (14hr., 12 per day 4:50am-8:40pm, €45.76); **Messina** (3hr., 9per day 4:50am-7:45pm, €8.26); **Milan** (16hr., 11 per day 4:50am-8:40pm, €49.78); **Noto** (30min., 9 per day 5:20am-8:30pm, €2.65); **Ragusa** (2hr., 4 per day 5:20am-5:35pm, €5.73); **Rome** (12hr., 11 per day 4:50am-8:40pm, €37.70); **Taormina** (2hr., 10 per day 4:50am-7:45pm, €6.82); **Turin** (20hr., 8 per day 4:50am-8:40pm, €49.63). **Luggage storage** available (see **Practical Information**).

Buses: AST (☎ 0931 44 92 11 or 44 92 15), next to the post office on Ortigia, left after stone bridge. Little service on weekend. To: **Gela** (4hr.; 6:30am, 1:30pm; €7.23); **Piazza Armerina** (3hr., 7am, €7.23); **Ragusa** (3hr., 9 per day 5:30am-7:15pm, €5.42). **Interbus,** V. Trieste, 40 (☎ 0931 66 710), 1 block from P. delle Poste toward center of Ortigia, 2nd street to left after stone bridge. To: **Catania** (M-F 20 per day 5:45am-8pm, Sa-Su 5 per day 6:30am-6:30pm; €4.10); **Noto** (1hr., 11 per day 7:05am-8:30pm, €2.50); **Palermo** (3hr.; 3 per day 6am-2:30pm; €13.40, €18.50 round-trip).

Local Transportation: Orange **AST buses** depart from P. delle Poste. Buses #21 and 22 run past Fontane Bianche every 2-3 hours; buses #23 and 24 do as well but much less frequently. Tickets (€0.77) are sold in *tabacchi.*

Taxis: ☎ 0931 697 22 or 609 80. From the train station to Ortigia costs about €8.

◆ ▪ ORIENTATION AND PRACTICAL INFORMATION

Ponte Umbertino connects the island of Ortigia to mainland Syracuse. On the mainland, **Corso Umberto I** links the bridge to the **train station** and passes through **Piazza Marconi,** from which **Corso Gelone** passes through town to the **Archaeological Park.** C. Umberto continues past **Foro Siracusano** to the train station.

Tourist Office: APT, V. S. Sebastiano, 43 (☎ 0931 48 12 00). From the station, take V. F. Crispi to V. Catania, which becomes C. Gelone after the tracks. Turn right on Viale Teocrito after 10min., then left on V. S. Sebastiano; the office is 150m down on the left, across from the catacombs. Useful tourist **map** includes a mini-guide. English spoken. Open daily 8:30am-1:30pm and 3-6:30pm.

AAT Office: Ortigia, V. Maestranza, 33 (☎ 0931 46 42 55). After crossing Ponte Umbertino, turn right through P. Pancali to uphill C. Matteotti. Turn left onto V. Maestranza at the fountain in P. Archimede; office is in courtyard of the palazzo across from the pharmacy. Open M-F 8am-2pm and 2:45-5:30pm, Sa 8am-2pm.

Luggage Storage: In train station. Open daily 7am-1pm and 3-7pm for deposit and pickup; €3.90 per 24hr.

English-Language Bookstore: Libreria Gabo, C. Matteotti, 38 (☎ 0931 662 55). Classic novels and travel guides. Also offers Internet access on 3 computers for €4 per hr. Open M-Sa 9am-1pm and 4:30-8:30pm, Su 4:30-8:30pm.

Emergency: ☎ 113. **Carabinieri** (☎ 0931 44 13 44). **Police** (☎ 0931 49 51 11).

First aid: ☎ 0931 48 46 39. From P. Archimede in Ortigia, turn down V. Maestranza; take 1st left onto V. S. Coronati. Open daily 8am-8pm.

Pharmacy: Mangiafico Farmacia, C. Matteotti, 53 (☎0931 656 43). Open M-Sa 8:30am-1pm and 4:30-8pm. MC/V.

Hospital: Ospedale Generale Provinciale (☎0931 72 41 11), a beige brick monstrosity on V. Testaferrata, off the end of C. Gelone.

Internet: PC Service di Michele Pantano, V. dei Mergulensi, 35 off P. Archimede (☎0931 48 08 48). 1 computer, with fast connection. €0.08 per min., €4.80 per hr. Open M-F 4-8pm, Sa-Su 9am-1pm.

Laundry: Lavenderia ad Acqua, C. Umberto, 13, near the bridge to Ortigia. €3-5 per load, depending on size. Open M-Sa 8:30am-8:30pm, Su 4-8pm.

Post Office: P. delle Poste, 15 (☎0931 48 93 10), on Ortigia. Turn left after crossing the bridge. Offers **currency exchange.** Open M-Sa 8am-7:40pm. **Postal Code:** 96100.

♠♠ ACCOMMODATIONS AND CAMPING

Many budget accommodations have staked out the area between the station and the bridge to Ortigia. While prices are good, the quality is not stellar. This area is run-down and visitors, especially women, should avoid walking alone at night. Ortigia's few options are more expensive but of higher quality.

B&B Artemide, V. Vittorio Veneto, 9 (☎/fax 0931 690 05 or 338 373 90 50; www.bedandbreakfastsicily.com), keeps 3 bright, quiet rooms furnished with antiques. All have bath, A/C, and color TV. Cots available for children. Reserve early in summer. Singles €50; doubles €70; triples €90. AmEx/MC/V. ❹

Pensione Bel Sit, V. Oglio, 5, 5th fl. (☎0931 602 45, fax 46 28 82). Follow signs from C. Gelone, close to the train station. Large, simply furnished rooms with colorful bed-spreads have fan and airy windows; some with bath. Upstairs rooms also have A/C and TV. Reserve 1 week ahead for July-Aug. Singles €20; doubles €34. Cash only. ❷

Hotel Posta, V. Trieste, 33 (☎0931 218 19; bookinghotelposta@hotmail.com). A classy joint near the waterfront with excellent service and large, comfortable rooms with bath, A/C, and TV. Singles €70-75, in winter €50; doubles €95/€75. AmEx/MC/V. ❺

Hotel Archimede, V. F. Crispi, 67 (☎0931 46 24 58, fax 46 20 40), near the train station. Comfortable and beautifully decorated, with efficient, professional staff. All rooms with bath, A/C, and TV. Breakfast included. Singles €35-50; doubles €50-75; triples €70-90; quads €90-120. AmEx/MC/V. ❷

Hotel Centrale, C. Umberto I, 141 (☎0931 605 28, fax 611 75), near the train station, is a great value. Staff is friendly; clean rooms, some with views, have sink and A/C. Shower and toilet in hallways. Singles €17, with view €18; doubles €26, with bath €35; triples with bath €37. Cash only. ❷

Fontane Bianche, V. dei Lidi, 476 (☎0931 79 03 33), 20km from town, near the beach. Take bus #21 or 22 (€0.77) from P. delle Poste in Ortigia. Showers included. Open May-Sept. €6 per person in high season, €4.50 in low season; €4 per tent. ❶

♠ FOOD

While hotel prices can run fairly high, restaurants are affordable. On the mainland, the area around the station and the archaeological park offers some of the best deals. Ortigia has an **open-air market** on V. Trento, off P. Pancali, as well as several budget options on V. Savoia and V. Cavour.

▨ **Trattoria Del Forestiero,** C. Timoleonte, 2 (☎0931 46 12 45 or 335 843 07 36), on the mainland. From the start of C. Gelone, take V. Agatocle to P. Euripede; restaurant is on the far side at start of C. Timoleonte. Walk ten minutes out of touristy Ortigia and you'll

Siracusa

🏠🏕 ACCOMMODATIONS

B&B Artemide, 13
Fontane Bianche, 1
Hotel Archimede, 2
Hotel Centrale, 3
Hotel Posta, 6
Pensione Bel Sit, 4

🍎 FOOD

Al Ficodindia, 9
Il Gattopardo Trattoria, 8
Trattoria Kalliope, 11
La Siciliana, 7
Spaghetteria do Scogghiu, 10
Trattoria Del Forestiero, 5
Trattoria Pescomare, 12

find better food at half the price at this lively local favorite. Try their specialty, a pizza *forestiero*. Pizza from €2.50; takeout available. *Primi* from €3.10, *secondi* from €4.20. Cover €1.10. Open M and Th-Su noon-3:30pm and 7-11:30pm. ❶

🍴 **Spaghetteria do Scogghiu,** V. D. Scinà, 11, a tiny street off P. Archimede, in Ortigia. An impressive selection of spaghetti—over 20 varieties—in a busy, hole-in-the-wall restaurant in the center of Ortigia. *Primi* and *secondi* from €5.50. Cover €1.50. Open Tu-Su noon-3pm and 6:30pm-midnight. ❷

Trattoria Pescomare, V. Saverino Landolina, 6 (☎0931 210 75), in Ortigia near P. Duomo. Tucked into a romantic courtyard under twisting vines and the soft glow of intertwined lighting fixtures, Pescomare serves a refreshing variety of salads and starters, but specializes in fish (from €7). Open Tu-Sa noon-3pm and 7pm-1am. AmEx/MC/V. ❷

La Siciliana, V. Savoia, 17 (☎0931 689 44 or 74 91 04), in Ortigia, by Hotel Gran Bretagna. A casual trattoria within 2 blocks of the bridge to the mainland. Seafood *antipasto* €5. *Primi* and *secondi* from €6. Cover €1. Open Tu-Su noon-3pm and 7pm-midnight. AmEx/MC/V. ❸

Il Gattopardo Trattoria, V. Cavour, 67 (☎0931 219 10), draws a hip, college-aged crowd. Leopard-lined walls pay homage to the trattoria's namesake. Kitchen specializes in traditional Sicilian fare, especially *pizza alla norma*. *Primi* and *secondi* €5. Open M-Sa 10am-1pm and 8-11pm. Cash only. ❶

Trattoria Kalliope, V. d. Consiglio Regionale, 26 (☎0931 46 00 08). In a small piazza filled with statues and jazz music, Kalliope serves up appetizing pasta and seafood dishes in a casual, outdoor environment. *Primi* from €5, *secondi* from €7. Cover €1. Open noon-3pm and 7pm-midnight, closed Tu. ❷

Al Ficodindia, V. Arezzo, 7/9 (☎338 131 25 16), off V. Cavour in Ortigia. An *antipasto* buffet (€4.15) features typical Sicilian kitchen specialties. Try the house favorite, *linguine al cartoccio*, with calamari and shrimp cooked in white wine with traditional Sicilian flavoring. Accommodates large numbers in pleasant setting. Pizza from €2.50. *Primi* €5-7, *secondi* around €7. Open M-Tu, Th-Su noon-3pm and 7:30pm-midnight. ❷

👁 SIGHTS

MAINLAND SYRACUSE

🏛 **ARCHAEOLOGICAL PARK.** Syracuse's three centuries as a strategic city on the on the Mediterranean left behind a collection of immense monuments. The Greek ruins are the most impressive, but Roman remains also attest to a rich heritage. Two theaters, an ancient quarry, and the world's largest altar (all listed below) share a fenced compound, visited with a single ticket. Walk through the gauntlet of souvenir stands to reach the ticket office. *(Follow C. Gelone to V. Teocrito; park entrance down V. Augusto to the left; follow the frequent signs. Park open daily in summer 9am-2 hours before sunset; in winter 9am-3pm. Ticket office open daily in summer 9am-6pm, in winter 9am-2pm. €4.50, EU residents 18-25 €2, EU residents under 18 or over 65 free.)*

GREEK THEATER. Seated in a theater row that was carved into the hillside in 475 BC, it's easy to understand why Syracuse became such a successful Greek colony. If the 15,000 spectators watching Aeschylus's original production of *The Persians* got bored, they could lift their eyes over the now-ruined scenic building to scan green fields, colorful flowers, the sparkling sea—and oncoming attackers, as Syracuse's location was spectacularly strategic. Original Greek inscriptions line the walls along the mid-level aisles, and the track for the *deus ex machina*, a large crane that made the gods "fly," is still in place around the orchestra. *(Closes early during theater season—May and June. Accessible with the same ticket for the archaeological park and quarry.)*

PARADISE QUARRY. The floral valley next to the theater derives its name from the gardens that line the base of large, chalky cliffs. These quarries provided most of the characteristic gray stone that built old Syracuse. Two large artificial caves were cut into the walls, the **Orecchio di Dionigi** (Ear of Dionysius) and the **Grotta dei Cordari** (Ropemakers' Cave). The latter is closed to the public for safety reasons, but visitors can still experience the Orecchio di Dionigi, which is famous for the echoes that ricochet off its walls. Legend claims the tyrant Dionysius put his prisoners here so he could eavesdrop on their conversations. Though the acoustics are still impressive, no subversive plots can be heard here now—just the boisterous explanations of tour guides. *(Open daily from 9am to 2hr. before sunset.)* Outside this area lies **Ara di Ierone II** (the altar of Hieron II, 241-215 BC), once used for public sacrifices. At 198m by 23m, it is the world's largest altar. Up the hill and through the other gate is a 2nd-century Roman **amphitheater.** Visitors can see the tunnels through which gladiators and their prey entered the arena floor.

MUSEO ARCHEOLOGICO PAOLO ORSI. Named for the most famous archaeologist in Sicily, this museum has an overwhelming collection of over 18,000 objects from prehistory through ancient Greece and early Christianity (40,000 BC-AD 600). From the introductory room at the museum's core, hallways branch into chronologically arranged, maze-like galleries that wind through time and space. Exquisite *kouroi* torsos, grimacing Gorgons, elegant vases, and Pygmy elephant skeletons rest in dimly-lit galleries. Otherworldly inhabitants populate gigantic urns and rough tombs in the museum's large garden. *(Viale Teocrito, 66. ☎0931 46 40 22. Open Tu-Sa 9am-2pm and 3-6pm, Su 9am-2pm. Ticket office open Tu-Sa 9am-2pm and 3-5pm, Su 9am-1pm. €4.50, EU residents 18-25 €2, EU residents under 18 or over 65 free.)*

CATACOMBA DI SAN GIOVANNI. Dating from AD 415-460, this subterranean maze has over 20,000 tombs carved into the walls of what used to be a Greek aqueduct. No corpses linger—only ghostly frescoes, an occasional sarcophagus, and a few wall-carvings. The 4th-century **Cripta di San Marziano,** the crypt of the first bishop of Syracuse, lies below the **Chiesa di San Giovanni** next door. *(Across from tourist office on V. S. Giovanni, off V. Teocrito from C. Gelone. Mandatory guided tours every 15-20min., Tu-Su 9:10am-12:30pm and 2:30-5:30pm. €3.50, under 15 or over 65 €2.50, school groups €1.50 per person. MC/V.)*

SANTUARIO DELLA MADONNA DELLE LACRIME. For three days in 1953, a small mass-produced statuette of the Madonna reputedly began to weep in the home of the Iannuso family, on V. degli Orti. Since then the number of pilgrims grew so large that the commanding spire of the **Basilica Madonna delle Lacrime** was built in 1994 on the competition-winning plans of Frenchmen Michel Arnault and Pierre Parat. Pilgrim or not, a stop at the sanctuary to admire the impressive architecture will be well worth it. The **Museum of Lacrymation** and the **Museum of Liturgy** complement the basilica; timetables placed outside of the sanctuary tell the statue's tale. *(☎0931 214 46; www.madonnadellelacrime.it. Both museums open daily 9am-12:30pm and 4-6pm. Sanctuary open 7am-9pm. Sanctuary free. Museum of Lacrymation €1.55, Museum of Liturgy €1, both museums €2.)*

MUSEO DEL PAPIRO. Long before the printing press and tell-all autobiographies, papyrus scrolls promised the quickest path to earning a place in eternity. The museum, created to promote research on antique and contemporary uses of papyrus, displays pages from the ancient *Egyptian Book of the Dead*, with spells to facilitate entry into the afterlife. Special attractions include invocations (translated into Italian) to the Eater of Souls and the Snake that Rises. There's also an entrancing video on papyrus's history and a collection of texts and woven objects. *(V. Teocrito, 66, near Orsi museum. ☎0931 616 16. Open Tu-Su 9am-1pm. Free.)*

SICILY

ORTIGIA

Across Ponte Umbertino, Ortigia offers a bustling pace and more selective restaurants and nightlife than the mainland. Before rescuing Sicily from barbary, the Greeks landed in Ortigia, using the island as a point of embarkment for their attack on the mainland. At the end of the bridge, the fenced-in ruins of the **Tempio di Apollo** gleam white in the setting sun. Dating from 575 BC, it is the oldest peripteral (columns on all sides) Doric temple in Sicily. The island flourished in the Baroque period, leaving today's smattering of elegant churches and the **Palazzo Impellizzeri,** V. Maestranza, 22. *Siracusani* glide with an air of casual entitlement onto the island's streets and piazzas during the long summer evening's *passeggiate*.

DUOMO. The 18th-century exterior of the cathedral looks like the standard Baroque compilation of architectural fancies. The interior is anything but. A 5th-century BC Temple of Athena first stood on the site, and rather than demolishing the pagan structure, architects incorporated it into their construction. Fluted columns line the interior, recalling the structure's Classical origins. Large, shiny letters proclaim this the first Christian church in the West. Legend has it that the temple became a church with the arrival of St. Paul. The first chapel on the right is dedicated to St. Lucia, the light-bearer and Syracuse's patron saint. Catch a glimpse of her left arm in the elaborate glass reliquary. Hidden from view above the reliquary is a masterpiece of Sicilian silver work, a life-sized statue of Lucia that parades through the streets on her feast day (see **Entertainment**). Lest people forget how she died, silversmiths thoughtfully included a dagger protruding from her throat, the punishment dealt the saint by the pagan government of AD 304. *(Down V. Minerva from P. Archimede. Open daily 8am-noon and 4-7pm. Modest dress required.)*

FONTE ARETUSA. This ancient pond fed by a "miraculous" fresh-water spring near the sea overlooks Pta. Grande. *Siracusani* believe that the nymph Arethusa escaped the enamored river god Alpheus by diving into the sea and that the goddess Diana rescued her by transforming her into this fountain. The river surfaces here at the Fonte Aretusa. *(P. Aretusa. From P. Duomo, walk down V. Picherale.)*

🔄 ENTERTAINMENT

Siracusani, like all Italians, fall prey in summer to powerful ancestral instincts that force them from the cities to the beaches. **Fontane Bianche** is one such beach, well populated and with many discos. The campground there ensures a place to sleep when buses stop running. Take bus #21 or 22 (30min., every 2-3 hours,€0.77). In Ortigia, nightlife consists of a grand tour of the island, stopping at any of several bars along the way. Check out **Troubador,** off P. S. Rocco, or the nearby **Buio** ("darkness"). True to its name, this club sees the most action after sunset. In summer, the Ortigia hotspot is **La Grotta Aretusa,** behind the Fonte Aretusa. Patrons drink or play pool and video games in a mossy natural grotto. (Open M and W-Su 6:30pm-last person leaves. Cave open after 6pm.) In May and June, the city stages **classical Greek drama** in ancient amphitheaters. The APT office has details. Tickets for **Istituto Nazionale del Dramma Antico** are available at the theater box office, in the Archeological Park. (☎0931 221 07; www.indafondazione.org. Open M-F 10am-6:30pm.) At the **Festa di Santa Lucia,** December 13, men shoulder the silver statue of the city's patron saint in a 6hr. procession from the duomo to S. Lucia al Sepolcro on the mainland. After a week, the statue returns to the duomo December 20.

▶ DAYTRIP FROM SYRACUSE

NOTO

Interbus buses leave from Syracuse (1hr., 11 per day 7:05am-8:30pm, €2.50). Ticket office opposite bus stop in Bar Efirmedio. Noto can also be reached by train (30min., 9 per day 5:20am-8:30pm, €2.65). The station is a 15min. walk from town.

A haven of Baroque unity, Noto is a pleasure to the eyes. After a 1693 earthquake shook Sicily's shore, the noble Landolina and Nicolaci families made Noto their favorite renovation project, restoring its architectural elegance with monumental staircases, chubby *puti* moldings, and pot-bellied balconies. Noto has a slower pace than coastal towns, making it a calm and educational retreat from frenzied tourist destinations. Toward the city center from C. V. Emanuele and up four flights of giant-sized steps stands the immense **Chiesa di San Francesco all'Immacolata**, built in 1704 and currently closed for renovation, which houses one of the bloodiest crucifixes in Sicily. On C. V. Emanuele, stop at the **Teatro Comunale Vittorio Emanuele** to gaze up at its gorgeously painted balconies and bright red drapes. (Open M-Sa 8:30am-1:30pm and 3-8pm. €1, show tickets from €8-€20.) From C. V. Emanuele, turn right on V. Niccolaci for a view of the balconies of the **Palazzo Niccolaci,** supported by cherubs, griffins, and sirens. **La panoramica dal Campanile** affords a matchless view of the city from the top of the **Chiesa di San Carlo** (€1.50, under 18 €1). Decent **beaches** are 7km away at **Noto Marina.** Buses depart from the Giardini Pubblici. (July-Aug. M-Sa 8:30am, 12:45pm; €1.20.)

To reach the **APT Tourist Office** from the bus stop at the **Giardini Pubblici** (Public Gardens), cross the paved way with the fountain on the right. Turn left through the tunnel of low hanging trees and pass under the **Porta Nazionale** (built in 1838) onto **Corso Vittorio Emanuele.** The tourist office is in the garden's Villetto Ercole, behind the Fontana d'Ercole. Enter the garden through the gate and head to the back behind the fountain. Once there, grab a **free map.** (☎0931 57 37 79. Open Sept.-Apr. M-Sa 8am-2pm and 3:30-6:30pm, Apr.-Sept. daily 8am-2pm and 3:30-6:30pm.) To reach the town center from the **train station,** follow the road leading uphill and to the right until it ends, then walk through the park for a block. A left turn here and five minute walk will put you at the far end of the town's main street, C. V. Emanuele, and the Tourist Office will be on your right.

Call to reserve one of three well-furnished rooms (two with A/C) at ▥ **Centro Storico ❸,** C. V. Emanuele, 64. This tiny hotel is run by a welcoming family and has an eclectic feel. (☎0931 57 39 67; chrislibra@jumpy.it. €7-30 per person for at least 2 people.) Other rooms are available on a weekly or monthly basis at V. Fratelli Bandiera, to the right and up a flight of stairs. (☎0931 83 58 75. Rooms €20; €5 extra for kitchen.) Amazing views from a beautiful old building more than compensate for the strict rules and stiff management at **Il Castello Youth Hostel ❶,** V. Fratelli Baniera, 1. (☎0931 57 15 34. Dorms €14.25, must show HI membership.) **Trattoria al Buco ❷** tempts with homemade pasta and fish. (☎0931 83 81 42. Cover €0.70. *Primi* from €4, *secondi* from €5.50. Open M-F and Su noon-3:30pm and 7pm-midnight, Sa 7pm-midnight. AmEx/MC/V.) Big eaters fill up on somewhat bland but inexpensive cuisine at **Trattoria del Carmine ❶,** V. Ducezio, 1, a crowd-pleaser with three dining rooms. (*Primi* and *secondi* from €5. Open 12:30-3:30pm and 7pm-midnight. AmEx/MC/V.) **Pasticceria La Vecchia Fontana ❶,** C. V. Emanuele, 150, scoops up sinfully rich gelato, plus pastries and sandwiches. (☎0931 83 94 12. Open M and W-Su 6am-1am. Cups €1.10-1.80.) Just down the road, at C. V. Emanuele, 125, is **Caffè Sicilia ❶,** one of Noto's classic bars and a long-time attraction for ice cream aficionados and wine connoisseurs. Also popular is its selection of gourmet sweets. (☎0931 83 50 13. Open Tu-Su 8am-11pm.)

RAGUSA ☎ 0932

Settled deep in Sicily's interior, Ragusa is distant even from its nearest neighbors and distinct in every way. The language spoken here has little to do with Italian, and the lethargic pace of the sweltering town sets it apart from its Sicilian brethren. Expect the narrow streets to be all but deserted during residents' daily afternoon siesta. Part of the town's charm derives from its curious construction, which divides Ragusa into two distinct sections. The picturesque older area, *Ragusa Ibla*, and the more modern *Ragusa Superiore*, which was built entirely after the earthquake of 1693, are separated by a breathtaking valley—one of the city's many spectacular natural features. This combination of antique buildings and wide vistas makes Ragusa the retreat that time forgot, but travelers should not.

▐ TRANSPORTATION

The **train station** is at the Ragusa Superiore end of V. Roma, in P. del Popolo, behind the bus stop. Trains run to: Caltanissetta (5hr., 5 per day 4:08am-8:20pm, €8.75); Gela (1¼hr., 6 per day 4:08am-8:20pm, €4.25); Palermo (7hr., 6 per day 4:08pm-8:20pm, €17.60); and Syracuse (2hr., 6 per day 6:05am-6:30pm, €5.85). **Buses,** in P. del Popolo, at the Ragusa Superiore end of V. Roma, run to: Catania (2hr; M-F 5 per day 8am-7pm, Sa 2 per day 5:30am and 2pm; €6.20); Gela (1½hr.; M-Sa 9:45am, 4:15pm; €3.87, €6.20 round-trip); Noto (1½hr.; M-Sa 8 per day 6:50am-7:15pm; €3.87, round-trip €6.20); Palermo (4hr.; M-F 4 per day 5:30am-5:30pm, Sa-Su 3:15 and 5:30pm; €10.59); and Syracuse (2hr.; M-Sa 8 per day 6:50am-7:15pm; €5.42, round-trip €8.78). Connections to Agrigento and Enna run via Gela. Buy tickets at **Bar Puglisi** across the street. (Open M-Sa 5am-10pm, Su noon-10pm.)

◀▚ ▐ ORIENTATION AND PRACTICAL INFORMATION

The **train** and **bus stations** are in **Piazza del Popolo** and nearby **Piazza Gramsci.** To reach **Ragusa Superiore,** the new center, from either of these piazzas, turn left on **Viale Tenente Lena,** walk through **Piazza Libertà** on V. Roma and across **Ponte Senatore F. Pennavaria,** the first of three bridges crossing the **Vallata Santa. Corso Italia,** off V. Roma, goes downhill for several blocks, passing the post office in **Piazza Matteotti** before becoming **Via XXIV Maggio.** It ends at Chiesa di Santa Maria della Scala. Here, stairs and roads wind down to **Ragusa Ibla,** the lower and older section.

The **AAPIT Tourist Office,** V. Capitano Bocchieri, 33, is in Ragusa Ibla, beyond the duomo and behind a small entryway with flags above the door. The helpful English-speaking staff provides brochures, **maps,** and other useful information. (☎ 0932 22 15 29, fax 62 34 76. Open M-F 9am-1:30pm, Tu 6-8pm, Sa-Su 9:30am-1pm.) In case of **emergency,** call ☎ 113, the **police** (☎ 112, 0932 62 10 10 or 62 47 77), an **ambulance** (☎ 118), **first aid** (☎ 0932 62 14 10 or 62 16 92) or the **medical clinic** (☎ 0932 62 39 46) in P. Igea. The **Ospedale Civile** (☎ 0932 24 51 84) is on V. di Vittorio in a peach building. A **post office** (☎ 0932 23 21 11) is in P. Matteotti, two blocks down C. Italia from V. Roma. (Open M-Sa 8am-6:30pm. Closes at noon last day of the month.) *Fermoposta* services are at V. Ercolano. **Postal Code:** 97100.

▌ ACCOMMODATIONS

From the train station, cross P. del Popolo to V. Sicilia. Turn right and pass the gas station to find **Hotel Jonio ❷,** V. Risorgimento, 49. The best deal in town, these plain rooms all have TV and bath. (☎ 0932 62 43 22, fax 22 91 44. Breakfast included. Singles €30, with half pension €41; doubles €48/€70; triples €66. AmEx/MC/V.) A fancier option, **Mediterraneo Palace ❺,** is across the bridge from the train station, at

SICILY

V. Roma, 189. Despite the odd fisherman's tarp that shields the hotel's entrance from the brutal sun, this Palace exemplifies comfort and modernity. Spacious rooms all have pay TV, minibar, A/C, and bath, some with bath massage. (☎0932 62 19 44. Singles €90; doubles €118. Wheelchair accessible. AmEx/MC/V.) Escape the city and head to campsite **Baia del Sole ❶**, on Lungomare Andrea Doria, in Marina. Tumino buses run from P. Gramsci in Ragusa to P. Duca degli Abruzzi in Marina (25min.; 13 per day 6am-8:30pm; €2.30, €3.40 round trip). Keeping the water on the right, walk 1km from the main piazza on the *lungomare*. Hot showers are available from 7-9am and 5-7pm. (☎0932 23 98 44. €10 per tent.)

🍴 FOOD

Visitors to Ragusa should try the town's specialty *panatigghie*, thin but savory pastries filled with the unlikely trio of cocoa, cinnamon, and ground meat. Purchase **grocery** essentials at SMA, a short walk from the station on Viale Sicilia. (☎0932 62 43 42. Open M-Sa 8:30am-8pm.)

   La Valle, V. Risorgimento, 70 (☎0932 22 93 41; www.lavalle.it). Tasty no frills pizza and pasta options can be boxed up for take-out or eaten in the quirky mint-green dining room. A colorful if slightly confusing menu presents pizza from €4. *Primi* from €5, *secondi* from €6. Cover €2. Open M and W-Su noon-3pm and 7pm-midnight. AmEx/MC/V. ❷

   Iblantica, C. XXV Aprile, 36 (☎0932 68 32 23), in the heart of Ragusa Ibla. Serves the best cuisine of the old city. *Primi* from €4.20, *secondi* from €6.20. The fish of the day is a steal at €4.15. Cover €1.30. Open M-Sa 7-11:30pm. AmEx/MC/V. ❷

   Ristorante Orfeo, V. S. Anna, 117 (☎0932 62 10 35), off V. Roma in the *centro,* serves Sicilian specialties in a classy atmosphere. The aesthetically-conscious dining room sports unique table decorations. Fresh fish from €7.50. *Primi* from €7, *secondi* from €7.50. Cover €2.30. Service 10%. Open M-Sa noon-3pm and 7-10pm. AmEx/MC/V. ❸

   Pizzeria La Grotta, on V. G. Cartia, 8 (☎0932 22 73 70), 2nd right off V. Roma walking away from the bridge. Original variations on standard *tavola calda* fare, including 31 *panini* choices. Wacky creations like pizza topped with french fries or nutella are wildly popular with the kiddies. Pizza slices €1.30. Open M-Tu and Th-Su 5:30pm-2am. ❶

👁️ 🎵 SIGHTS AND ENTERTAINMENT

The hilltops of Ragusa Superiore and Ragusa Ibla offer fantastic views of the countryside. Ragusa Ibla, the ancient section, is accessible by a steep but lovely 10min. hike down from the church at the bottom of C. Italia (V. XXIV Maggio) or by catching the #1 or 3 bus (€0.77) from P. del Popolo. The buses return to the newer Ragusa Superiore from Largo Camerina, one block from the cathedral in Ibla. The stairs at S. Maria offer a stellar view, crowned by a monastery and the 18th-century dome of **San Giorgio,** which glows an unearthly turquoise at night. (Modest dress required.) The road to the left after the set of tricky steps to P. Repubblica circumvents the town, passing abandoned monasteries and lush farmland. P. del Duomo di San Giorgio sits at the top of the city. C. XXV Aprile runs downhill from the piazza, passes two churches, and ends at the **Giardino Ibleo.** Ragusa Superiore's **Museo Archeologico,** below Ponte S. Pennavaria, displays pottery from the nearby Syracusan colony of Camarina. (☎0932 62 29 63. Open daily 9am-1:30pm and 4-7:30pm. €2, ages 18-25 €1, under 18 or over 65 free.)

   During the summer, Italians pack their swimsuits, rev up their Vespas, and spend the weekend baking their bodies and splashing in the crystal blue waters at 🏖️**Marina di Ragusa. Autolinee Tumino** (☎0932 62 31 84) runs buses to Marina from P. Gramsci (25min.; 13 per day, last bus returns at 9:15pm; €2.30, round-trip €3.40).

Ask the bus driver for a schedule with return times. In the piazza, grab a cup of Marina's best gelato for the road at ☒**Delle Rose ❶** (€1.30 per scoop). Since 1990 Ragusa Ibla has played host to the annual **Ibla Grand Prize,** an international piano, voice, and composition competition that runs from late June to early July. Performances are held in the theater of the **Palazzo Comunale.**

AGRIGENTO   ☎0922

For a city that incorporates majestic Greek monuments and medieval churches with equal aplomb, Agrigento remains surprisingly under-appreciated. Visitors are treated to some of the Mediterranean's most impressive Greek ruins—a series of ancient Doric temples, some of which are remarkably intact. The fantastic juxtaposition of this relic-filled valley and the town's complex of urban high-rises creates a surreal scene straight out of one of local celebrity Luigi Pirandello's plays. Although Agrigento today takes great pride in its modernity, traces of its storied past still linger in the winding cobblestone streets and notably friendly populace—not to mention the fine museums.

▐ TRANSPORTATION

Trains: In P. Marconi, below P. Aldo Moro. Ticket office open M-Sa 6:30am-8pm. To **Catania** (3¼hr.; 12:20, 7:45pm; €9.20) via **Enna** (2hr., €5.73) and **Palermo** (2hr., 10 per day 4:50am-8:05pm, €6.70).

Buses: From P. V. Emanuele, buses are to the left in P. Roselli. **Cuffaro** runs buses to **Palermo** (M-Sa 7 per day 7am-6:30pm, €6.71) and back to **Agrigento** (M-Sa 7 per day 5:45am-8pm); schedules and information available at the bar down from the SAIS offices in P. Roselli. **SAIS Trasporti,** V. Ragazzi, 99 (☎0922 59 59 33), behind the ticket office, runs buses to: **Caltanissetta** (1hr., M-Sa 14 per day 4:30am-7:15pm, €4.13); **Catania** (2¾hr., 11 per day, €9.81); and the **airport.** Indirect transport to **Rome** and **Messina.** All buses run with reduced service Su.

Public Transportation: Orange **TUA buses** depart from the train station. Ticket (€0.80) valid 1½hr. Buses #2 and 2/ run to the beach at San Leone; #1/, 2, 2/, 3, and 3/ run to the Valle dei Templi; #1/ runs to Pirandello's house. Tickets available at any *tabacchi* (there's one in the train station).

Taxis: At train station, in P. Marconi (☎0922 266 70). In P. Aldo Moro (☎0922 218 99). A trip to the temples should run about €8 on the meter—but make sure it's running.

▟▛ ORIENTATION AND PRACTICAL INFORMATION

Agrigento's **train station** is in **Piazza Marconi,** also the main stop for all city buses. Walk up the stairs to find the town's lively park-like central square, **Piazza Aldo Moro.** From P. Aldo Moro, the posh **Via Atenea** leads to the *centro storico.* At the far side of P. Aldo Moro is **Piazza Vittorio Emanuele,** containing the post office, just beyond which is the **bus station.** The temples are a bus ride (#1, 1/, 2, 2/, 3, or 3/) or a long walk away, below the town.

Tourist Office: AAPIT kiosk in the train station and **AAST,** in P. Aldo Moro, in the center of the square. Both offices have English-speaking staff and provide **maps** and brochures. Open M-F 8am-1pm and 3-7pm, Sa 8am-1pm; AAST only open in summer. Another summer office is in **Valle dei Templi,** adjacent to parking and bar. English spoken. Open daily 8:30am-1pm and 3pm-sunset.

Emergency: ☎113. **Carabinieri,** P. Aldo Moro, 2 (☎0922 59 63 22). **First Aid** (☎0922 40 13 44).

Pharmacy: Farmacia Averna Antonio, V. Atenea, 325 (☎ 0922 260 93). Open M-F 9am-1:30pm and 5-8:30pm. **Farmacia Dr Patti,** V. Atenea, 129 (☎ 0922 205 91). Open M-F 9am-1:30pm and 5-8:30pm. Both post late-night and weekend rotations.

Hospital: Ospedale Civile (☎ 0922 49 21 11), on S. Giovanni XXII.

Internet: Libreria Multimediale, V. Celauro, 7 (☎ 0922 40 85 62), off V. Atenea, 2 blocks from P. Aldo Moro. 1 computer; €1 for 15min., €3 per hr. Open M-Sa 9:30am-1pm and 4:30-8pm. **Michele Lorgio Fotografo,** V. Cesare Battisti, 11 (☎ 0922 296 60), off V. Atenea from P. Aldo Moro, has one slow computer. €3.70 for 30min., €6 per hr. Open M-Sa 9am-1pm and 5-8pm.

Post Office: P. V. Emanuele (☎ 0922 59 51 50, fax 229 26). Call in the morning for inquiries. Open M-Sa 8am-7pm. **Postal Code:** 92100.

🏠 🏕 ACCOMMODATIONS AND CAMPING

🏨 **Hotel Belvedere,** V. S. Vito, 20 (☎/fax 0922 200 51). Follow clearly marked signs from train station. Friendly staff hosts guests in colorful rooms with fan and telephone. Some rooms overlook a small garden. Breakfast €3. Singles €35, with bath €49; doubles €43/€64; triples €76/€96. 5% discount with *Let's Go*. Cash only. ❸

Hotel Bella Napoli, P. Lena, 6 (☎/fax 0922 204 35), off V. Bac Bac. Take V. Atenea 500m uphill and turn right after the sign for Eden Bar. Cheerful yellow hallways lead to clean, pastel-toned rooms. Rooftop terrace overlooks the valley. Rooms have bath, A/C, and TV. Breakfast €3. Singles €35; doubles €65; triples €80. MC/V. ❸

Antica Foresteria Catalana, P. Lena, 5 (☎/fax 0922 204 35). Next door to Hotel Bella Napoli and under the same management, Catalana offers larger rooms with high slanting ceilings and more luxurious decoration. Some with balcony, all with bath, A/C, and TV. Breakfast €3. Singles €45; doubles €75; triples €100. MC/V. ❹

Hotel Concordia, V. S. Francesco d'Assisi, 11 (☎ 0922 59 62 66), at the end of V. Pirandello, just after the basilica. Rooms are noisy, cramped, and somewhat bland, but the hotel's convenient central location and low price have their own merits. Pay extra for a room with bath to avoid the trek to the basement for a shower. Singles €18, with bath and TV €25; doubles €40/€45. AmEx/MC/V. ❷

Camping Nettuno (☎ 0922 41 62 68), on the beach at V. l'Acquameno by the bus stop. Take bus #2 or 2/ from the train station. Reasonable market, restaurant, bar, and pizzeria. Showers €0.50. €5 per person, €5 per tent, €2.50 per car. ❶

🍴 FOOD

Plenty of alimentari line V. Pirandello, and the small stairways tucked off V. Atenea lead to authentic, inexpensive trattorias. Indulge a sweet tooth at the candy stalls along V. della Vittoria. The town specialty is *torrone*, a nut-filled cream-colored nougat. The *Sette Soli*, a smooth local wine, nicely complements most meals.

🍴 **Trattoria Atenea,** V. Ficani, 32 (☎ 0922 202 47). From P. Aldo Moro turn right just beyond the Stefanel store. Locals recommend this restaurant for its huge portions and no-frills atmosphere. Especially tempting is the house special, *cavatelli della casa*. Extensive seafood offerings include *calamari* (squid) and *gamberi* (shrimp). *Primi* €3.62, *secondi* €5.16. Cover €1.29. Open M-Sa noon-3pm and 7-10pm. ❷

🍴 **Manhattan Trattoria/Pizzeria,** Salita M. degli Angeli, 9 (☎ 0922 209 11), up steps off V. Atenea. Don't expect to fold your slice in half New York style—the food here is typically Sicilian. Sit inside or on terraced steps leading to the street. The chef's specialty seafood ravioli and tortellini options are especially good (€6-7). Pizza from €3.50. Fish €10-11. Cover €1.50. Open noon-3pm and 7-11pm. AmEx/MC/V. ❷

Pizzeria Miriana, V. Pirandello, 6 (☎ 0922 228 28), at the start of V. Pirandello off P. Aldo Moro. Quick, satisfying food among locals for those on the go. Friendly cooks serve pizza by the slice (€1) and *panini* from €1.55. Open M-Sa 8am-10pm. ❶

Trattoria de Paris, P. Lena, 7 (☎ 0922 254 13), beside Hotel Bella Napoli. Serenity rules in this spacious establishment, perfect for a quiet lunch away from the bustling V. Atenea. Fresh fish €7.70. *Primi* €4.10, *secondi* €5.10. Service 10%. Open M-Sa noon-3pm and 7:30-10:30pm, Su noon-3pm. AmEx/MC/V. ❷

La Corte degli Sfizi, Cortile Contarini, 4 (☎ 0922 200 52), off V. Atenea. Classic Sicilian dishes served in a peaceful, bamboo-enclosed garden. Dinner *menù* €14-16. *Primi* €4.15, *secondi* €4.65. Cover €1.55. Service 20%. Open M and W-Su 11am-3:30pm and 4:30pm-late. AmEx/MC/V. ❸

👁 SIGHTS

🌑 VALLE DEI TEMPLI. Planted on a lesser ridge below Agrigento's hilltop perch, the five elevated temples are a picture-perfect tribute to the indomitability of paganism. Having survived the ravages of time, earthquakes, vicious Punic Wars, and the rise of Christianity, the temples are today official World Heritage Landmarks. As sunlight transitions to moonlight, the temples cast tall, eerie silhouettes across the countryside; once it's dark, they're illuminated by concealed lighting. Since the temples close at night, however, this is a view which must be admired from afar. From the entrance, a wide avenue heads uphill along the ridge, first passing the **Tempio di Ercole.** One row of solid, squat columns is all that remains of the earliest of the temples. Farther along, the perfectly intact pediment and columns of the **Tempio della Concordia** have lent themselves to many an idyllic vacation photo. With its walls and 34 columns intact, this temple remains one of the best preserved. Erected in the mid-5th century BC from limestone, it owes its survival to its early use by the archbishop of Agrigento for Christian rituals. The road through the valley ends at the 5th-century BC **Tempio di Giunone,** with its elegant columns and partially extant pediment. To the left during the ascent, holes in the ground mark an early Christian burial site. Across the street lies the entrance to the eternally unfinished **Tempio di Giove Olimpico.** Had Carthaginian troops not interrupted its construction in 406 BC, it would have been one of the largest Greek temples ever built. The toppled jigsaw of partitioned columns and walls has challenged archaeologists for years, but the temple's most interesting sight is the gigantic *telamones,* 8m sculpted male figures intended to have encircled the temple, holding up the roof and entablature. One of these massive men has been reconstructed at the site. At the far end of the path, past the Tempio di Giove, stand four lone columns of the long since destroyed **Tempio di Castore e Polluce.**

The **Museo Nazionale Archeologico di San Nicola,** 1km uphill from the parking lot, has a fabulous collection of red and black figureware vases, terra-cotta votive figures, and funerary vessels from the area's necropolis. Escape from the sun and go indoors to see an upright *telamon,* as well as model projections of how a completed Tempio di Giove Olimpico might have looked. The **Chiesa di San Nicola** near the museum displays the sarcophagus of Phaedra, one of the most impressive 3rd-century works of art. *(Valle dei Templi is several kilometers from the city. Starting on V. F. Crispi, it's a 30min. walk from the train station to the entrance, following signs downhill and left at the lower intersection. Or take bus #1/, 2, 2/, 3, or 3/ from train station; buses stop in a dirt carpark with a snack bar. Make sure to bring lots of water, sunscreen, light clothes, and good walking shoes, as there is no break from the relentless Agrigento sun. Visiting when the park first opens or right before it closes is a good way to avoid both heat and crowds. Temples open 8:30am-7pm. €4.50, EU students 18-25 €2, EU residents under 18 free or over 65. Museum open M and Su 9am-1pm, Tu-Sa 9am-7pm. €4. Combined ticket for temples and museum €6.)*

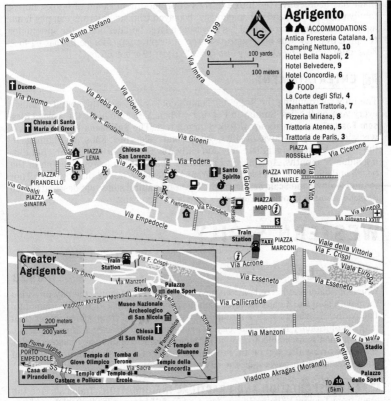

CHIESA DI SANTA MARIA DEI GRECI. Built atop a 5th-century BC Greek temple, the church is the most interesting medieval building in Agrigento. The interior features a Norman ceiling, original Doric columns, and 14th-century frescoes of a strangely wizened Christ child. *(Follow the signs up the hill from V. Bac Bac off V. Atenea. The church has been under restoration for several years, but is expected to reopen in 2005 with a plexiglass floor to showcase the excavated Greek temple beneath the church.)*

CHIESA DEL PURGATORIO (S. LORENZO). The legendary craftsman Serpotta employed all of his wizardry to make this church's stucco sculptures look like marble. The statues of the Virtues were intended to help parishoners stay out of purgatory by reminding them of its unpleasantries. Church elders did a thorough job; it's pretty hard to ignore all the reminders of eternal damnation, including the unusual skull and crossbones on the confessional and the countless depictions of roasted sinners. To the left of the church, underneath a sleeping lion, lies the 5th-century BC entrance to a network of Greek underground aqueduct channels which run the length of the city but are not open to the public. *(In P. Purgatorio off V. Atenea in the centro storico. Open M-Sa 10:30am-1pm and 4-8pm. €1.50.)*

CASA NATALE DI LUIGI PIRANDELLO. Thespians searching for dramatic inspiration in the town that bored playwright **Luigi Pirandello** need not search long to find traces of their idol—the man has achieved all but mythical status here. His birthplace has been converted into a fairly self-promoting museum of books, notes, family photographs, and conspicuously displayed trinkets. Pilgrims can pay homage to Pirandello personally at his **gravesite;** a large boulder marks the spot under the pine tree that was his greatest source of inspiration. *(Take the TUA bus #1 to P. Kaos.* ☎ *0922 51 11 02. Open daily 9am-7pm.* €2, under 18 or over 65 free.)

🎵 ENTERTAINMENT

The hills surrounding the Valle dei Templi come alive with the sound of music every year on the first Sunday in February, when Agrigento hosts the **Almond Blossom Festival,** an international folk-dancing fest. The **Settimana Pirandelliana,** a week-long outdoor festival of plays, operas, and ballets in P. Kaos, pays homage to the town's beloved son in late July and early August. (Info ☎ 0922 23 561.) But during summer months, *Agrigentini* primarily abandon the town in search of the beach and nightlife at **San Leone,** 4km from Agrigento by bus #2. Just be careful not to tumble down the **Scala dei Turchi,** the beautiful natural steps that descend to **Lido Rossello,** another popular beach, after a night of carousing.

WESTERN SICILY

MARSALA   ☎ 0923

When Garibaldi and his red-shirted devotees landed in Marsala, the city provided them with men and means, making itself the proud launchpad of the Risorgimento. Today, the air wavers with hot and dusty *scirocco* wind from Africa rather than with revolutionary fervor. The city is best known for its sweet *Marsala* wine, which gained fame thanks to British enthusiast John Woodhouse; it also contains several worthwhile sights, including the ruins of a Carthaginian warship of Marsala's ancient predecessor, the city of Lilybaeum.

⊟ 🖝 TRANSPORTATION AND PRACTICAL INFORMATION. Trains service the town from Trapani (30min., 14 per day, €2.65). **AST buses** (☎ 0923 23 222) run from Trapani (30min.; 3 per day 6:50am-2:10pm; €2.60, round-trip €4.20; return to Trapani, 5 per day 7am-5pm). **Salemi buses** (☎ 0923 98 11 20) run from Palermo (2½hr.; M-Sa 17 per day 6:15am-8:45pm, Su 5 per day 10:30am-8:45pm; return to Palermo M-Sa 17 per day 5:15am-6pm, Su 5 per day 7:30am-6pm). For a **taxi,** call ☎ 0923 71 29 92. From the **train station,** a right facing V. A. Fazio and then a slight left onto **Via Roma** leads to the *centro storico.* V. Roma turns into **Via XI Maggio** and then **Via Veneto.** The **Pro Loco Tourist Office** is at V. XI Maggio, 100, before Palazzo Comunale and the duomo. (☎ 0923 71 40 97; www.prolocomarsala.org. Open M-Sa 8am-8pm, Su 9am-noon.) In case of **emergency,** call the **carabinieri** (☎ 112 or 0923 95 10 10), **police** (☎ 0923 71 88 11), **first aid** (☎ 0923 95 14 10), or **medical clinic** (☎ 0923 78 23 43). A **pharmacy,** one block from Pro Loco at V. XI Maggio, 114, posts the late-night rotation. (☎ 0923 95 32 54. Open M-F and Su 9am-1:30pm and 4:30-8pm.) The main **post office** is at V. Garibaldi, 5, across the street from the duomo. (Open M-F 8am-6:30pm, Sa 8am-12:30pm.) Another is closer to the station at V. Roma, 167. (☎ 0923 95 10 52. Open 8am-2pm.) **Postal Code:** 91025.

🍴🛏 ACCOMMODATIONS AND FOOD. Marsala has few budget lodgings, so travelers may wish to visit as a daytrip from nearby Trapani. The tourist office provides a pamphlet of hotels. Those planning to spend a few nights should check out **Hotel Garden ❸,** V. Gambini, 36. The gritty train station neighborhood

SICILY

and drab exterior belies a sparkling interior, complete with marble, mirrors, and shared bath. Tidy rooms have TV, fan, and woven rugs. (☎0923 98 23 20. Singles €35, with bath €40; doubles €51, with bath €55. AmEx/MC/V.) Comfortable beds are also available at **New Hotel Palace ❾**, V. Lungomare Mediterraneo, 57. A courtyard envelops a pool and succession of refined rooms with bath, A/C, and TV. (☎0923 71 94 92; www.newhotelpalace.com. Singles €80-90; doubles €130-150. AmEx/MC/V.) **Hotel Acos ❹**, V. Mazara, 14, has 35 rooms, as well as a bar, restaurant and parking. (☎0923 99 91 66; www.acoshotel.com. Breakfast €5. Singles €40-52; doubles €57-130.)

The self-sufficient should head to Gerardi, a gourmet **supermarket** at P. Mameli, 14, through Pta. Garibaldi. (☎0923 95 22 40. Open M-Sa 8am-2pm, 4:30-8:30pm.) The expansive and aromatic **Trattoria Garibaldi ❷**, P. Addolorata, 5, across from the sanctuary of Maria S. S. Addolorata, serves typical Italian fare and vegetarian omelettes. (☎0923 95 30 06. *Primi* from €4.50, *secondi* from €6. Cover €1. Open M-F noon-3pm and 7:30-10pm, Sa 7-10pm, Su noon-3pm. AmEx/MC/V.) **E & N Cafe ❶**, V. XI Maggio, 130, serves delectable *cannoli* (from €1.30) to crowds until late. (☎0923 95 19 69. Open daily in summer 7:30am-2am, in winter 7:30am-11pm. MC/V.) Facing the cathedral's main door, head left through Pta. Garibaldi into P. Garibaldi; take the first right and look for a sign several blocks down, on the corner with V. Sabilla, for **Nuova Trattoria da Pino ❷**, V. San Lorenzo, 27. *Antipasto* buffet and seafood specialties are served in a serene atmosphere on loud tablecloths. Try the *spaghetti vongole gamberi* (€6), the chef's recommendation. (☎0923 71 56 52. *Primi* from €4.50, *secondi* from €5. Service 10%. Open M-Sa 1-3:30pm and 8pm-midnight, Su 8pm-midnight. AmEx/MC/V.)

◉ ⬛ SIGHTS AND ENTERTAINMENT. The **Museo Archeologico Regionale Baglio Anselmi** guards the famed **Carthaginian warship**. This now-skeletal vessel sank in the devastating final battle of the First Punic War (241 BC), in which Rome defeated Carthage, establishing its naval supremacy. The few wooden planks, preserved for over 2000 years in underwater sand off Marsala, are the largest existing portion of this type of ship. Across the hall, other galleries display objects from Lilybaeum and the isle of Motya, including pottery and two life-size male sculptures. (Follow V. XI Maggio through its portal end to P. della Libertà. Facing the bright pink cinema, take Viale Nazario Sauro slightly left, continuing right at its end; the museum is on Lungomare Boeo. (☎0923 95 25 35. Open M-Tu, Th, Sa-Su 9am-1:30pm; W, F 9am-1:30pm and 4-6:30pm. €2, under 18 €1, EU residents over 65 free.)

Visitors can walk through the wine-scented halls of the **Cantine Florio,** the oldest and most famous of the Marsala wine production areas, built in 1833. There is an *enoteca* at the far end of the facilities. (Take V. Francesco Crispi toward the water from the main intersection of V. Roma next to the train station. At the end, turn left and follow Lungomare Mediterraneo until reaching the painted "Florio" sign. ☎0923 78 11 11. Free tours daily July-Sept. 11am and 3:30pm; call to arrange a tour Oct.-June. *Enoteca* open 9am-12:45pm and 3-5:45pm.) On the way back, stop by the **Fontana del Vino** (Fountain of Wine), where a wine-loving lady drinks gustily with a barrel-bearing donkey. The piazza around the fountain, with a brick pattern that mimics the Union Jack, is a subtle poke at the British presence in Marsala.

Down V. XI Maggio and left down V. Sauro, the **Chiesa di San Giovanni** conceals the **Grotta della Sibilla** (reached through a trapdoor), where an ancient oracle spent 28 years preaching to believers through a hole in the ceiling. Early Christians staked out the cave in the 4th century, hence the frescoes of fish and doves; St. Paul is said to have baptized converts in the pool here, and a statue of St. John covers the reclusive sibyl's grave. (Open daily 10am-2pm and 5-7pm.) Just behind the duomo at V. Garraffa, 57, the **Museo degli Arazzi** (Flemish Tapestry Museum) con-

SICILY

tains eight 16th-century Flemish tapestries that illustrate scenes including Titus's war against the Jews in AD 66-67. The tapestries were brought to Sicily by the King of Spain in 1594. The museum also provides info on Marsala's various churches. (☎0923 71 29 03. Open Tu-Sa 9am-1pm and 4-6pm, Su 4-6pm. €1.50, students €0.50.) A few steps down from P. Repubblica and the duomo, the **Museo Civico** houses several of the thousand red shirts, as well as Garibaldi's own rather snazzy uniform. (In the San Pietro complex. Open Tu-Su 9am-1pm and 4-8pm.)

The ◼**Marsala DOC Jazz Festival** jams it up with music and wine in the last two weeks of July, and has attracted jazz greats such as Charlie Parker, Omar Sose Octec, and Vasquez y Puente Celeste. The festival's emblem colorfully depicts a mellowed-out bass player strumming his six-foot wooden bottle of Marsala.

TRAPANI ☎0923

Between two stretches of *lungomare*, ancient rooftops span the length of Trapani's old city, harboring packs of roaming wild dogs and scores of tourists. Just below the horizon, colorful fishing boats and massive ferries plow through the waves. Reliable transportation and extensive lodgings make Trapani a good base for adventures to Segesta's temple, the Egadi Islands, Erice's medieval streets, San Vito's beaches, and the natural splendor of the Lo Zingaro reservation.

▐ TRANSPORTATION

Flights: Vincenzo Florio Airport (☎0923 84 25 02), in Birgi en route to Marsala, 16km outside of Trapani. Buses from P. Malta are timed to coincide with flights. Daily flights to Rome and Pantelleria. Not a heavily used airport.

Trains: ☎0923 89 20 21. In P. Stazione. Ticket office open daily 6am-7:50pm. To: **Castelvetrano** (1.5hr., 15 per day 4:35am-8:30pm, €4.25); **Marsala** (30min., 14 per day 4:35am-8:30pm, €2.65); **Palermo** (2hr., 11 per day 5am-7:30pm, €6.25).

Buses: AST (☎0923 210 21). Main station in P. Malta behind the train station. To: **Erice** (45min.; M-Sa 11 per day 6:40am-7:30pm, Su 4 per day 9am-6pm; €1.80, round-trip €2.90); **Marsala** (M-Sa 6:50am, 12:50, 2:10pm; €2.60); **San Vito Lo Capo** (1½hr.; M-Sa 11 per day 7am-8:30pm, Su 4 per day 8am-7:15pm; €3.20). **Segesta** (☎0923 21 754) runs buses to local towns and to **Rome** (15hr., 5:30pm, €38).

Ferries: *Traghetti* (ferries) and *aliscafi* (hydrofoils) leave for the **Egadi Islands** (Levanzo, Favignana, and Marettimo), **Ustica, Pantelleria,** and **Tunisia.** Ferries leave from Stazione Marittima across from P. Garibaldi, and hydrofoils depart from a dock further up V. A. Staiti, about 150m toward the train station. Tickets for sale from the travel agents along V. A. Staiti and from ticket booths on the docks. Chart below shows high-season (June-Aug.) times and rates; low-season frequency and prices are lower. Sea transport schedules alter due to poor weather. Schedules are available at all ticket offices and at tourist office.

Ustica (☎0923 222 00; www.usticalines.it), in a yellow booth at the hydrofoil dock. AmEx/MC/V.

Siremar (☎0923 54 54 55; www.siremar.it), with ticket offices at a blue and white striped waterfront booth at the hydrofoil dock and in Stazione Marittima. Open M-F 6:15am-noon, 3-7pm, and 9pm-midnight; Su 3-3:30pm, 5:15-6:45pm, and 9pm-midnight. AmEx/MC/V.

Tirrenia (☎0923 54 54 55; www.tirrenia.it), in Stazione Marittima. Open M 6:30am-1pm and 3-6pm, Tu 9am-1pm and 4-9pm, W-F 9am-1pm and 3-6pm, Sa 9am-noon. AmEx/MC/V.

DESTINATION	COMPANY	DURATION	FREQUENCY	PRICE
Favignana (Egadi Islands)	Siremar (ferry)	1hr.	3 per day	€3.20
Favignana (E.I.)	Ustica (hydrofoil)	20min.	10 per day	€5.30
Favignana (E.I.)	Siremar (hydrofoil)	25min.	10 per day	€5.30

DESTINATION	COMPANY	DURATION	FREQUENCY	PRICE
Levanzo (E.I.)	Siremar (ferry)	1hr.	3 per day	€3.20
Levanzo (E.I.)	Siremar (hydrofoil)	20min.	10 per day	€5.30
Levanzo (E.I.)	Ustica (hydrofoil)	20min.	10 per day	€5.30
Marettimo (E.I.)	Siremar (ferry)	3hr.	1 per day	€6.60
Marettimo (E.I.)	Siremar (hydrofoil)	1hr.	4 per day	€11.60
Marettimo (E.I.)	Ustica (hydrofoil)	1hr.	2 per day	€10.50
Pantelleria	Siremar (ferry)	5½hr.	midnight daily	€20.60
Pantelleria	Ustica (hydrofoil)	2½hr.	1:35pm daily	€34
Ustica via Favignana	Ustica (hydrofoil)	2½hr.	3 per week	€19
Cagliari (Sardinia)	Tirrenia (ferry)	11½hr.	Tu 9pm	€38.21
Tunis, Tunisia	Tirrenia (ferry)	8½hr.	M 10am	€51.38

Public Transportation: Orange **SAU buses** have main terminal at P. V. Veneto, down V. Osorio from the station and right on V. XXX Gennaio, and straight to the water. Office on left when facing water. Posts schedules of all routes. Tickets (€0.60) sold at *tabacchi*.

Taxis: ☎ 0923 228 08. In P. Umberto, outside the train station. ☎ 0923 232 33. In V. A. Staiti, near the port.

◀▚ 🛈 ORIENTATION AND PRACTICAL INFORMATION

Trapani sits on a peninsula two hours west of Palermo by bus or train. The old city began at the outer tip of the hook, growing backward from the peninsula until it tripped and spilled new wider streets and cement high-rises onto the mainland. The **train station** is in **Piazza Umberto,** with the **bus station** just to the left in **Piazza Malta.** From the train station, **Via Osorio** passes the **Villa Margherita Gardens** to end at the perpendicular **Via XXX Gennaio.** A right on this road leads to **Piazza V. Veneto** and the local city bus depot. A left goes down to **Via A. Staiti,** which runs along the port. The **tourist office** is at the end of **Corso Italia,** off V. XXX Gennaio. From P. V. Veneto, **Via Garibaldi** becomes **Via Libertà** and moves into the old city. **Corso Vittorio Emanuele** in the older section of town runs all the way to the **Torre di Ligny.**

Tourist Office: AAPIT (☎ 0923 290 00; www.apt.trapani.it), in P. Saturno, up V. Torrearsa from the port. Staff provides **maps,** help with lodgings, and info on attractions in and around town. Pick up a *Trapani Hotels* guide. Open M-Sa 8am-8pm, Su 9am-noon.

Currency Exchange: Banks line many of the city's streets, including C. Italia. They generally have better rates than the train station. The post office also changes money and traveler's checks. **ATMs** are at Stazione Marittima in the old city and along V. M.V. Scontrino in front of the train station.

Emergency: Police (☎ 113 or 0923 59 02 98), P. V. Veneto. **Carabinieri,** V. Orlandini, 19 (☎ 0923 271 22). **First Aid,** P. Generale Scio, 1 (☎ 0923 296 29). **Ambulance** (☎ 0923 80 94 50).

Pharmacy: Viale Margherita, 9, next to P. V. Veneto. All pharmacies open Su-F 9am-1:30pm and 4:30-8pm. After-hours schedule posted. Look for bright green cross.

Hospital: Ospedale Sant'Antonio Abate (☎ 0923 80 91 11), on V. Cosenza, far northeast of the city center.

Internet: Phone & Internet di Ferrante Paolo, V. Regina Elena, 26/28 (☎ 0923 288 66, fax 43 74 76), across from Stazione Marittima, has 4 speedy computers. €2.50 for 30min., €5 per hr. Open M-Sa 9am-1pm and 4-8:30pm. **Point Phone Calls and More,** C. V. Emanuele, 15-18 (☎ 0923 59 38 60), has 3 fast computers. €1 for 20 min., €3 per hr. Open daily in summer 9am-1pm and 5-9pm, closed Su afternoon and Th morning; in winter closed Sa-Su.

SICILY

Post Office: P. V. Veneto, 3 (☎0923 43 44 04). From the train station, turn right on V. M. V. Scontrino and left through the small fountain park. Continue left on V. Fardella, with iron-fenced public gardens on the left; it's on the left after Palazzo del Governo. **Currency exchange,** booth #18. Open M-Sa 8am-6:30pm. **Postal Code:** 91100.

♠♠ ACCOMMODATIONS AND CAMPING

▨ Albergo Moderno, V. Genovese, 20 (☎0923 212 47, fax 233 48). From P. S. Agostino on C. V. Emanuele, turn right on V. Roma and left on V. Genovese. Light blue walls bring the sea indoors, while balconies look over the *centro storico*. Large rooms have bath and TV. Reception 24hr. Singles €25; doubles €35; triples €45. AmEx/MC/V. ❷

Hotel Vittoria, V. F. Crispi, 4 (☎0923 87 30 44, fax 298 70), off P. V. Emanuele, near train station. 65 large, luxurious rooms offer modern atmosphere, some with view of the rocky coast. Inviting communal area has a bar and TV. Breakfast €5. Singles €53; doubles €79; triples €106. AmEx/MC/V. ❹

Pensione Messina, C. V. Emanuele, 71, 4th fl. (☎/fax 0923 211 98). A slightly run-down courtyard and stairs lead to an eclectic mix of mirrors and statues in this tiny, 9-room hotel. Bright, high-ceilinged rooms are largely unexceptional, but location and price couldn't get any better. All rooms have balcony and sink. Shared bath. Breakfast €3.50. Singles €18-20; doubles €30-35. Extra bed 35%. Cash only. ❷

Nuovo Albergo Russo, V. Tintori, 4 (☎0923 221 66, fax 266 23), off C. V. Emanuele. 35 rooms are somewhat standard but comfortable and centrally located. All come with bath, A/C, and TV. Breakfast €3. Sept.-June singles €40; doubles €70; triples €95. July-Aug. and Easter week singles €42; doubles €80; triples €108. AmEx/MC/V. ❹

Campeggio Lido Valderice (☎0923 57 34 77), on V. del Detince, in seaside town of the same name. Take bus for Bonegia or San Vito Lo Capo (€3.20). Follow flower-lined road opposite bus stop and perpendicular to the highway, and turn right at its end. Well-shaded campground near beaches. Hot showers €0.60. €4.90 per person, €4.50 for small tent. €8.30 for campers (light provided), €2 per car. AmEx/MC/V. ❶

▯ FOOD

In Trapani, couscous, a North African mainstay, is prepared with fish and touted as a Sicilian specialty. Bakeries carry *biscotti con fichi*, the Italian Fig Newton. The old city has many *alimentari*, as well as a daily fish and fruit **market** along the northern *lungomare* at the intersection of V. Maggio and V. Garibaldi

▨ Pizzeria Calvino, V. N. Nasi, 71 (☎0923 214 64), 100m from the duomo. Loaded with gooey cheese, their pizza is widely considered the best in town; there's a line out the door every night. 30 delicious varieties. Order to go or reserve 1-2hr. ahead for a table. Delivery available. Pizza from €3.50. Open M and W-Su 7pm-12:30am. MC/V. ❶

▨ Trattoria da Salvatore, V. N. Nasi, 19 (☎0923 54 65 30), 1 street toward the port from C. V. Emanuele. Family-run restaurant serves regional pastas like *busiata con sarde* (with sardines; €4.15) to a regular local crowd. Feuds over soccer matches on the overhead TV are as spicy as the house couscous (€7.50). Menu changes daily. *Primi* from €4-5, *secondi* €7-8. Cover €1.30. Open M-Sa 12-3:20pm and 6:30-11pm. AmEx. ❷

Panineria Spaghetteria Poldo, P. Cucatelli, 8 (☎347 03 23 231), off V. Turretta near the ferry station. Don't let the orange and yellow walls turn you off—Poldo has some of Trapani's best food, serving Sicilian specialties and *panini* (€1.50-4) until late into the night. *Primi* from €6, *secondi* from €7. Cover €1. Open daily 9am-5am. ❸

Pizzeria Mediterranea di Mario Aleci, Viale Duca d'Aosta, 15 (☎0923 54 71 76), off C. V. Emanuele. Long tables draped in plastic under an open-air lattice provide ample space for evenings with *la famiglia*. So many varieties of pizza (€3.85-5.95), and they're all scrumptious. Open daily 7pm-midnight. Cash only. ❷

Taverna Paradiso, Lungomare Dante Alighieri, 22 (☎0923 87 37 51). This classy, blues-playing tavern serves seafood and drinks in a romantic villa-like interior, complete with vine-covered stone walls and cherub sculptures. *Primi* from €9, *secondi* €9-13. Cover €3. Open M-Sa 12:30-3:30pm and 7:30-10:30pm. AmEx/MC/V. ❹

👁 SIGHTS

Delicate stone statues blend into the gray exterior of this 17th-century Baroque **Chiesa del Purgatorio,** in the heart of Trapani's old city. Inside, 20 nearly life-sized wooden sculptures, known as *I Misteri,* depict the passion and crucifixion of Christ. Every year on Good Friday, the sculptures are dressed in gold and silver and paraded around the city for 24 hours of celebration; each requires the strength of 14-30 men. The sculptures' 18th-century artists constructed the Roman soldiers to resemble powerful Spanish conquistadors, reflecting Spanish dominance in Sicily at the time. Several statues damaged in WWII have since been reconstructed to better resemble the Romans. (1 block up V. D. G. Giglio from P. Garibaldi, across from Stazione Marittima; follow signs from the port. Open daily 9am-noon and 4-7pm.)

The main attraction in the modern part of town is the enormous and lavishly decorated **Sanctuario dell'Annunziata.** This church houses a 14th-century statue of the Madonna of Trapani. Legend has it that a boat carrying the statue got caught in a storm; the captain promised God that if he survived, he would leave it as a gift to the first port at which he arrived. In the same complex is the **Museo Nazionale Pepoli,** which features a collection of local sculpture and painting, coral carvings, and folk-art figurines, including a frightening portrayal of Herod's baby hunt. (Take SAU buses #24, 25, or 30 from P. V. Emanuele, 2 blocks to the right of the train station. Sanctuario ☎0923 53 91 84; museum ☎0923 55 32 69 or 53 12 42. Sanctuario open M-Sa 7am-noon and 4-7pm, Su 7am-1pm and 4-7pm; museum open M-Sa 9am-1:30pm, Su 9am-12:30pm. Call to confirm hours. €2.50, 18-25 €1, under 18 or over 65 free.)

The picturesque **Torre di Ligny,** at the end of a wide jetty off a promontory, is visible from both of Trapani's ports. By day, the rock walls of the tower seem outcroppings of the rocky surf, as the identically-colored brick fortress rises over boulders spilling out into the sea. By night, the northern coastline appears as a vision of bright lights reflecting off shimmering waters. The tower houses the **Museo di Preistoria/ Museo del Mare,** with shells, prehistoric artifacts, and underwater excavation pieces. (☎0923 223 00. Open M-Sa 9:30am-noon, Su 10:30am-12:30pm. €1.55.) At the

"CUSCUS OGGI"

Arab and North African influences are found all over western Sicily but nowhere are they more evident than in the cuisine. One item that's sure to grace the menu of any restaurant in Trapani or Favignana is *cuscus con pesce.* It may be spelled *cuscus, kuskus, kuscous,* or the English couscous, but it always means the same thing: rice-like semolina pellets, the hard wheat middlings used to create pastas, served in a spicy fish sauce composed of tomatoes, parsley, and garlic.

Couscous has long been a mainstay in North African food and it is for this reason that Trapani, closer to Tunisia than to mainland Italy, has adopted it to create a fish-based Sicilian specialty. *Cuscus con pesce* is a quirkier menu item than most; it's often twice the price of the other *primi* on the menu due to the unusual ingredients and extra preparation required. Beware the €5 couscous—it is likely a watered-down version served with a broth instead of fresh fish. Many restaurants in Favignana and Pantelleria only offer the dish a few nights a week, usually signaled by a sign posted outside the restaurant. So as you are wandering the streets of Trapani, keep your eyes peeled for a telltale sign reading "Cuscus Oggi" (couscous today), and you've found your restaurant.

cusp of the old and new cities, the **Villa Margherita's** gardens offer a delightful change of pace from cobblestone and cement. Banyan trees, palms, and fountains surround flower-lined avenues. Playgrounds and statuary complete the peaceful picture. Each July, the gardens host the **Luglio Musicale Trapanese,** a festival of opera, ballet, and cabaret that draws national and international stars to the temporary stage amid shady trees. Other concerts happen virtually every other month as well. (☎0923 214 54. Shows 9pm. Info booth inside park gates.)

▶ DAYTRIPS FROM TRAPANI

RISERVA DELLO ZINGARO

Bus tickets available in San Vito at Mare Monti, V. Amadeo, 15 (☎0923 97 22 31; info@sanvitomaremonti.com). Buses depart from P. Marinella (M, W, F at 8am; return M, W, F at 7pm; €8, reservation required). Bluvacanze, V. Savoia, 13 (☎0923 62 10 85), runs excursions (M, W, F 9am, return 4pm; €15).

For shade and seclusion, escape 10km from San Vito to the Riserva dello Zingaro, Italy's first nature reserve, complete with rare Bonelli's eagles, mountain trails, and prehistoric caves. An unfinished four-lane highway came perilously close to marring the isolation of the pristine reserve, but a 1981 environmental rally halted the highway in its tracks. Once in the reserve, follow the yellow brick road to successive secluded pebble beaches that stretch along the coastline. Due to entrances on both sides of the reserve, the middle two beaches offer the most privacy. Camping is illegal and motor vehicles are prohibited, but the hiking is superb.

SEGESTA

Tarantola buses (☎0924 310 20) leave from P. Malta in Trapani for Segesta (4 per day 8am-5pm, return 4 per day 7:10am-6:35pm; €3.10, round-trip €4.75). Temple open 9am-7pm; ticket office 9am-6pm. €4.50, EU residents 18-25 €2, EU residents under 18 or over 65 free.

The extraordinary ■**Doric temple** at Segesta is one of the best-preserved relics of ancient Greek architecture. Isolated and untouched, it dominates a landscape of sudden valleys and lush vineyards of this former Trojan colony. Roam among the 5th-century BC columns or take a liliputian seat on a pedestal to contemplate their dignified tranquility. A wealth of multicultural ruins, including a Greek theater, a castle, and a mosque, cluster nearby around Monte Barbaro. Taking the bus (every 30min., €1.20) is worth it to avoid the steep uphill trek in the midday sun, but the 25min. walk to the top is quite pleasant on cooler days. The **Greek theater** carved into the top of the hill has a 4000-person capacity and holds performances from mid-July to August every other year. Ask at the Trapani tourist office for details. Neighboring the theater is the first **mosque** discovered in Sicily, built in the 12th century during Norman rule. A Christian lord destroyed it to construct his **castle** on the same site in the next century, which he abandoned a half-century later. The temple and theater are best appreciated in the morning and late afternoon, when temperatures are lower and the light brings out the stone's golden and silver hues.

ERICE   ☎0923

With a magical castle, ancient ritual temples, and mysterious fogs, Erice could be Italy's Camelot. Once upon a time, the town was powerful and wealthy, as evident in its meticulously crafted stone streets and medieval dwellings. Myth holds that fertility goddesses dwelled on the mountain, and cults to the Phoenician Tanit-Astarte, the Greek Aphrodite, and the Roman Venus all sought sanctuary on its cliffs. The only magic in effect today is Erice's gradual transformation into a resort, comfortably accommodating tourists who stage their own disappearing act from more populated towns nearby.

■ TRANSPORTATION AND PRACTICAL INFORMATION. The **bus** from Trapani departs from P. Malta to Erice/Montalto (40min.; M-Sa 11 per day 6:40am-7:30pm, last return to Trapani 8:30pm; Su 4 per day 9am-6:50pm, last return to Trapani 7:30pm; €2.90 round trip). Buses stop on **Via Conte Pepoli,** which leads up to the **Balio Gardens.** From there, **Via Nasi** runs to **Piazza San Cataldo** and **Piazza San Domenico.** The **AAST Tourist Office,** near **Piazza Umberto** on V. Guarrasi, 1, provides colorful town **maps** and brochures. (☎0923 86 93 88. Open M-F 8am-2:30pm.) An **ATM** is on **Via Vittorio Emanuele,** near P. Umberto.

■ ACCOMMODATIONS AND FOOD. Hefty hotel prices make Erice more affordable as a daytrip, but weary overnighters should certainly try **La Pineta ❹,** Viale N. Nasì. In their own natural wonderland, 23 cottages have bath, TV, minibar, and terrace. (☎0923 86 97 83; www.lapinetaerice.it. Breakfast included. Open July-Aug. Singles €50-70; doubles €80-115; triples €114-155; quads €145-185. Half pension €60-85. AmEx/MC/V.) Alternatively, the cheerful and immaculate accommodations at **Albergo Edelweiss ❺** have the feel of a mountain lodge. (Cortile P. Vincenzo, 9, off P. S. Domenico. ☎0923 86 94 20; a.edelweiss@libero.it. Breakfast included. All rooms with bath. Singles €61; doubles €82.63; triples €103; quads €110. MC/V.)

Erice's restaurants are charming, but prices make them less of a fairy-tale than a reality-bite. A short odyssey through the town's back alleys leads to **Ristorante Ulisse ❸,** V. Santa Lucia, 2, serves excellent pizza and Sicilian specialties amid refreshing A/C. Follow signs from the city entrance nearest the bus stop. (☎0923 86 93 33 or 53 12 15. Cover €2. Pizza from €4.50. *Primi* and *secondi* from €6.50. Open daily noon-3pm and 8-11pm. AmEx/MC/V.) At **La Vetta ❸,** V. G. Fontana, 5, off P. Umberto I, savor regional couscous and *busiati* (both €7), Sicilian pasta hand-rolled into a narrow tube. (☎0923 86 94 04. Pizzas from €4.50. *Primi* €7, *secondi* from €6. Cover for restaurant €2, for pizzeria €1.50. Open M-W and F-Su noon-3:30pm and 7:30pm-midnight. AmEx/MC/V.) The Balio Gardens, up Viale Conte Pepoli from the bus stop, have stone benches carved directly into the hillside which survey the whole valley, making them ideal for an enchanting picnic. Stock up on supplies at **Salumeria Bazar del Miele,** V. Cordici, 16, which sells Sicilian cooking. (☎0923 86 91 81. Open daily 9:30am-8pm. AmEx/MC/V.) For dessert, snack on sweets at the **Antica Pasticceria del Convento ❷,** V. V. Emanuele, 14, in P. S. Domenico. The freshly-made cookies come in all shapes and colors (€12 per kg). Try the famous *belli e brutti ma buono* ("pretty and ugly but tasty") sweets, made with almond paste. (☎0923 86 93 90. Open daily 9am-1pm and 3:30pm-3am.) **Pasticceria Tulipano ❶,** V. V. Emanuele 10-12, bakes fancy pastries, among them *morbido a coco* (€20 per kg), an almond-coconut candy specific to Erice. Quick meals from the *tavola calda* include pizza and pasta, enjoyable among the shaded outdoor tables. (☎0923 86 96 72. Open daily 7:30am-midnight. AmEx/MC/V.)

■ SIGHTS. Erice fits an impressive number of sights inside its surrounding 8th-century BC **Elymian walls.** Towering upon a hill, the vine-covered **Castello di Venere** (Norman Castle) was built on the site of several ancient temples to fertility goddesses. Though it served as a prison until 1940, its more ominous legacy is the hollow tub standing against the wall farthest from the entrance, likely once used for human sacrifice. Inquire at the tourist office about guided tours. Next to the castle is a Spanish-style **Torre Medievale,** and at the castle's base, the ◙**Giardini del Balio** spread swaying green boughs over stone benches and fountain. The views from the gardens and the castle are incomparable, with most of the western country-side, the Egadi Islands, Pantelleria, and occasionally Etna and Tunisia peeking over the horizon. Throughout Erice, 61 churches await exploration, all accessible by joint €0.50 ticket. The 14th-century **Gothic duomo** features delicate stonework in its large windows, and its **bell tower** offers broad views. (Open daily 10am-6pm. Duomo €1; including bell tower €2.) In P. Umberto, the **Museo Comunale di Erice,** inside the library, houses a small but varied collection primarily relating to the city's sacred fertility goddesses. (Open M-Sa 8:30am-7:30pm, Su 9am-1pm. Free.)

EGADI ISLANDS (ISOLE EGADI)

Inhabited since prehistoric times, the Egadi Islands offer some of the best outdoor adventures in Sicily. Lying just off the coast of Trapani, the archipelago of Favignana, Levanzo, and Marettimo is easily accessible by ferry or hydrofoil (for ferry details, see p. 704). Favignana is the largest and most modern of the trio, with plenty of beaches—and enough tourists to pack them. In the tiny port towns of Levanzo and Marettimo, mules and sheep share plains with cacti, while rugged cliffs climb high in all directions. To really get to know the islands, dedicate at least an entire day to each, as the finest beaches and most intriguing discoveries lie far from the ports. And stop by the ATM in Trapani or Favignana before leaving, as there aren't any on Levanzo or Marettimo.

FAVIGNANA ☎ 0923

Favignana's ample and appealing beaches make it a summer playground for Italians enamored of island living. They build summer homes on the shoreline, while short-term vacationers arrive eager for a tan and expecting the modern conveniences its sisters lack. Crowded but laid-back, it's ideal for pitching a tent on the shore or roughing it (resort style) on the glorious beaches.

E⁊ TRANSPORTATION AND PRACTICAL INFORMATION. Siremar (☎0923 92 13 68) and Ustica (☎0923 92 12 77) both run **hydrofoils** to the island from Trapani (25min., 20 per day 6:30am-8:20pm, €5.30). Siremar also runs **ferries** from Trapani to Favignana (1hr., 3 per day 7am-5:15pm, €3.20). Island **buses** are necessary to reach the more remote and beautiful beaches. Tarantola buses (☎0923 92 19 44 or 31 020) run from Porto Florio: **Line 1** (8 per day 8am-4:50pm) to Calamone (5min.), Lido Burrone (8min.), Cala Azzurra (15min.); **Line 2** (8 per day 7:45am-7pm) to Calamone and Cala Rotonda (13min.); **Line 3** (6 per day 8:30am-5:40pm) to Cala Rossa (7min.), Lido Burrone, and Calamone. Buy tickets (€0.60) at *tabacchi*. Francesca e Rocco, Traversa Calamoni, 7, runs minibus excursions around the island, available 24hr. (☎348 586 0676. €8 per person, 5-person min.) **Noleggio Isidoro,** V. Mazzini, 40, rents **bikes** and **scooters.** (☎347 323 30 50. Bikes €3 per day, scooters €15 per day. Open daily 7am-8pm.)

Hydrofoils and ferries drop passengers off at **Florio Porto.** From there, **Via V. Emanuele** leads to **Piazza Europa** and then to **Piazza Madrice,** which contains the tourist office and many of the island's businesses. **Via Garibaldi** breaks off of V. V. Emanuele, becoming **Via Libertà** as it heads to the countryside. The most beautiful beaches are about 1km away. A **Pro Loco Tourist Office,** P. Madrice, 8 (☎0923 92 16 47), provides brochures, schedules, and **maps** (€1) of Favignana and other islands. (Open in summer M-Sa 9am-1pm and 4-8pm, Su 9am-1pm; in winter 10am-noon). **Banco di Sicilia,** P. Madrice, 12, next to Pro Loco, has an **ATM** and **currency exchange.** (☎0923 92 13 47. Open M-F 8:20am-1:20pm and 2:50-3:50pm.) In case of **emergency,** the **carabinieri** (☎0923 92 12 02) are in V. S. Corleo, near P. Castello, and **first aid**

(☎0923 92 12 83) is off V. Calamoni. **Farmacia Barone** is at P. Madrice, 64. (☎347 110 77 16. Open daily 8:30am-12:30pm and 5-8pm.) **Farmacia Dottore Abramo** is at P. Europa, 41. (☎0923 92 16 66. Open M-W and F-Su 8:30am-12:30pm and 5-8:30pm.) Both post late-night rotations. The **post office** is at V. G. Marconi, 3, off P. Madrice. (☎0923 92 12 09. Open M-F 8am-1:30pm, Sa 8am-12:30pm.) **Postal Code:** 91023.

SICILY

☐☐ ACCOMMODATIONS AND FOOD. Raw and rural, Favignana has better camping than hotel options. However, the **Casa Vacanze Mio Sogno ❷**, V. Calamoni, 2, is a real steal. This *affittacamere*, couched in a castle-like structure, offers independent rooms with bath, kitchenette, TV, and patio, arranged around a small garden. Reserve ahead in summer. (Take V. Libertà and turn left on V. Dante. ☎0923 92 16 76. €21-40 per person.) Far from the *centro*, **Camping Village Miramare ❶**, on Prov. Punta Sottile, offers a wide range of accommodation options, and its sports activities create a lively scene. (Take bus #2 or the establishment's shuttle from the city center. ☎0923 92 22 00 or 92 13 30; www.egadi.com/miramare. Open Apr.-Oct. €10.50 per person. Hot showers included. Call ahead for shuttle. Bungalow with breakfast. Doubles €42-91.50; triples €62-137.50; quads €73-163. Half pension doubles €92.70-126.70; triples €139-190; quads €172-230. MC/V.)

Tuna is a big part of Favignana's culinary tradition. A variety of tuna products are on sale at the **Antica Tonnara di Favignana ❶**, V. Nicotera, 6 (☎/fax 0923 92 16 10 or 333 455 94 72; AmEx/MC/V) and at **La Casa del Tonno ❶**, V. Roma, 12 (☎0923 92 22 27; open daily 8:30am-noon and 4-10:35pm; AmEx/MC/V). Stock up for a languorous day at the beach at **San Paolo Alimentari**, V. Mazzini, 24. (☎0923 92 16 80. Open M-Tu and Th-Sa 8am-1pm and 5-8pm, W 8am-1pm.) A fruit and vegetable **open-air market** sits at the intersection of V. Libertà and V. Di Vita until sunset. The comfortable ⬛**La Bettola ❸**, V. Nicotera, 45, at P. Castello, serves fish fresh out of the water on cool indoor tables and an outdoor patio. (☎/fax 0923 92 19 88; www.isoleegadi.it/labettola. *Primi* €7-8, *secondi* €10. Cover €1.50. Open daily 1-2:30pm and 8-11pm, closed Th in winter. AmEx/MC/V.) For more of Favignana's favorite fish, head to **Trattoria-Pizzeria da Franco ❹**, V. V. Emanuele, 30, where tuna pizza is served late into the night. (☎347 119 43 90. Pizza around €6. *Primi* €11-12, *secondi* €9-10. Cover €1.60. Open daily 10am-3pm and 5pm-1am. AmEx/MC/V.) **Ristorante Aegusa ❸**, V. Garibaldi, 17, down the road from hotel of the same name, offers three Sicilian specialty meals of the day on a cool sea of blue and yellow tables. (☎0923 92 24 30. *Primi* from €6.50, *secondi* from €10. Cover €3. Open daily 8-10am, 1-2pm, and 8-10:30pm. AmEx/MC/V.)

☐☐ BEACHES AND SIGHTS. The island's most popular beaches are the **Lido Burrone, Calamone, Cala Rossa**, and **Cala Azzurra. Lido Burrone** is best equipped, with places to change and shower. Both **Cala Azzurra** and the rocky **Cala Rossa** are touted as the most beautiful. All beach areas can be reached by the public **Tarantola buses** (€0.60; see **Transportation**). The tip of the island around **Cala Rotonda** and **Galera** makes a gorgeous boat trip but is difficult to access from land. With stints as a prison, an Arab lookout tower, and a Norman fortress, the **Castello di Santa Caterina** is a formidable sight on a hill overlooking the city. Funky cafe by day and lively bar by night, ⬛**Camarillo Brillo**, V. V. Emanuele, 18, is a favorite haunt of youth marooned on the island, offering nightly live music. Come for the tunes and stay for the Sicilian wine bar. (Open daily Easter-Sept. 8am-3am.)

LEVANZO ☎0923

Levanzo's town is little more than a row of whitewashed, blue-shuttered buildings hugging the cliffs on the port. The two bars directly above the docks serve as the island's social center. The **Ustica hydrofoil office** is directly on the dock, while the

Siremar office is up a clearly-marked alley off the *lungomare*. Right from the harbor is **⬛Albergo Paradiso ❹**, which keeps the island's best rooms, each with bath, many with sea view. The hotel's cozy restaurant serves traditional and regional specialties. (☎/fax 0923 92 40 80. Reserve for Aug. by mid-Mar. July-Aug. Half pension €75; full pension €85. Open Mar.-Nov. AmEx/MC/V.) Head down the *lungomare* to visit the island's primary attraction, the **Grotta del Genovese**, a cave containing 14,000-year-old Paleolithic incisions and slightly younger ochre-grease paintings of tuna fish rituals and dancing men (€5, ages 5-11 €3). The tour guide **Natale Castiglione,** in the ceramics shop Grotta del Genovese, offers information on the site. (☎0923 92 40 32; nacasti@tin.it. Tour reservation required at least 1 day in advance. Boat or jeep excursions €13. Open 10am-1pm and 3-6pm.) A few kilometers along the coastal road to the left of the town, secluded grottoes and beaches await. The crystal-clear water between the rounded rock beach and the neighboring island has a ripping current when the winds pick up, so snorkel carefully.

MARETTIMO   ☎0923

The most physically remote of the Egadi Islands, Marettimo is equally distant in spirit. Pristine white cubic buildings line the curve of the port, the island's gateway to a calmer, more soothing way of life. Because there are few roads, a boat is the best way to see Marettimo's most intriguing caves; rent one from the port. Beyond the village, the only intrusion into the island's rugged environment is an outstanding set of stone hiking trails crossing the island. The 2½hr. hike to **⬛Pizzo Falcone** (686m), the highest point on the Egadi Islands, starts at the sea road, past the Siremar office and Il Pirate. Prime time to arrive at the peak in summer is around 6pm, for a view of the sun setting over the wilderness. Along the way, snuggled between dramatic cliffs and greenery, stand the **Case Romane**, ruins dating back to Roman domination. To the right of the little village and past an arc of beach sand at **Punta Troia,** a 17th-century **Spanish castle** tops the cliff. According to local legend, when a prince chose to marry one of two princess sisters over the other, the rejected princess threw her sister off the edge of the cliff. The heartbroken prince then tossed the offending sister down the same route, following her fall with his own. Locals say that at sunset, the ghosts of the two lovers find each other again at the castle.

A few piazzas connect the town's maze-like streets. A **cultural center** on V. Scalo Vecchio, along the docks lined by fishing boats, has information on all three islands. (Open 8am-noon and 3-8pm.) Ask about private room rentals (€49-59 per person) at **Il Pirate ❹,** and dine in its **trattoria ❹,** which serves fresh seafood. Full meals run about €20. (☎0923 92 30 27) **Marettimo Residence ❺,** the last establishment along the town and visible from the hydrofoil docks, rents bungalows with bath, kitchenette, and patio. (☎0923 92 32 02 or 92 35 00; Internet available. Prices per week: 1 bedroom €450-1150; 2 bedrooms €600-1400. AmEx/MC/V.)

PANTELLERIA   ☎0923

Unlike its disco-saturated sisters, Pantelleria's main attraction is its natural beauty and tranquil isolation. Seduced by the island's subtle magic, celebrities from Giorgio Armani to Sting have constructed *dammusi*, Arab-influenced dwellings unique to the island, all along its coasts. Visitors come to Pantelleria for hot springs, thickly wooded mountains, terraced hillsides, and the Mediterranean's best capers (found growing wild along the island's roads). They come to ride along winding mountain roads, shaped by additional curves mandated by Mussolini during WWII when it was a military base threatened by air attack. But above all, they come to linger. After just a couple of minutes, it's easy enough to see why.

⌐ TRANSPORTATION

Pantelleria is surprisingly expansive. Almost all tourists rent a car or scooter, and consequently public travel resources like buses are few and far between. The midnight ferry from Trapani may save money on a night's hotel, but if spending the night struggling to curl up in a straight-backed ferry chair doesn't sound appealing, opt for the hydrofoil and relax on the noon return ferry instead.

Airport: ☎ 0923 91 11 72. Flights from the largest Italian cities service the airport, including Rome, Venice, Milan, Palermo, and Catania. (14 departures per day 9:45am-6:45pm.) **Air Sicily** (☎ 0923 91 22 13).

Ferries: Ustica hydrofoil tickets for sale at **Agenzia Minardi,** V. Borgo Italia, 15 (☎ 0923 91 15 02), on the *lungomare*. Open daily 7:30am-1pm and 6-10:30pm (2½hr., 8:30am, €34); also available at **La Cossira** (☎ 0923 91 10 78), left of Hotel Khamma, where V. Catania meets the *lungomare*. Open daily 9am-1pm and 5:30-7:30pm. **Siremar,** V. Borgo Italia, 65 (☎ 0923 91 11 04), on the waterfront, runs ferries to **Trapani** (5hr., €20.60-23). Open M-F 6:30am-1pm, 5-6:30pm; Sa-Su 6:30am-1pm.

Island Buses: Infrequent buses run weekdays from P. Cavour to the airport and the 5 island towns of Khamma-Tracino, Scauri-Rekale, Bukkuram, Sibà, and Bugeber (€1). Check schedule posted outside the tourist office.

Scooter and Car Rental: Autonoleggio Policardo, V. Messina, 31 (☎ 0923 91 28 44; noleggiopolicar@tiscalinet.it), off the port, up the street to the right after the giant fenced-in scooter lot. Scooters €15-21 per day; in Aug. €40 per day. Cars 21+. €26 per day, €126 per week; €55 per day in Aug. Open daily 8am-8pm.

✴ ⁊ ORIENTATION AND PRACTICAL INFORMATION

Ferries and **hydrofoils** arrive at the northwestern tip of the teardrop-shaped island. The town of Pantelleria borders the curved **port.** The town's main street, **Via Borgo Italia,** changes to **Lungomare Paolo Borsellino** and stretches from the docks to the private sailboat moorings. At the end of Lungomare P. Borsellino beneath the **Castello, Piazza Almanza** becomes **Piazza Cavour.** Most services are located here, including the tourist office. Roads at either end of the *lungomare* lead along the coast to other towns. Facing away from the water, the road to the left goes to **Bue Marino, Gadir, Lago Specchio di Venere,** and **Arco dell'Elefante.** The right road leads to the **airport,** the **Sesi, Scauri town,** and **Rekale.** An inland road above and to the right of the southwestern sea highway, past the Agip gas station, leads to **Sibà** and **Montagna Grande.** Get a road map from the Pro Loco office before going on any excursions.

Tourist Office: Pro Loco (☎ 0923 91 18 38), in P. Cavour in the corner of municipal building closest to Banco di Sicilia. Look for the language flags. Lots of brochures, free **maps,** bus schedules, and help finding lodgings. Open M-Sa 9:30am-1pm.

Currency Exchange: Banca Nuova (☎ 0923 91 27 32), up V. Catania from the *lungomare*. Open M-Sa 8:20am-1:20pm and 2:40-3:40pm; Su 8:20-11:50am. **ATM** here, and across the street at **Monte dei Paschi di Siena** and **Banco di Sicilia,** in P. Cavour across from the municipal building.

Carabinieri: V. Trieste, 13 (☎ 0923 91 11 09).

First Aid: P. Cavour, 21 (☎ 0923 91 02 55), on the far right side of the Municipal building (opposite Banco di Sicilia). Open M-F and Su 8am-8pm, Sa 10am-8pm.

Pharmacy: Farmacia Greco, P. Cavour, 26 (☎ 0923 91 13 10). Open M-Sa 8:30am-1pm and 4:30-8pm.

Hospital: ☎ 0923 91 11 10.

Internet: Internet Point Da Pietro, V. Dante, 7 (☎0923 91 13 67). Open daily 9:30am-2pm, 4:30-9pm. €6 per hr.

Post Office: V. Verdi, 2 (☎0923 69 52 11), behind the municipal building and across from Banco di Sicilia, off P. Cavour. **Exchanges currency** and **traveler's checks.** Open M-F 8am-1:30pm and Sa 8am-12:30pm. **Postal Code:** 91017.

■ ACCOMMODATIONS

Most visitors stay in *dammusi*, square-shaped, domed dwellings of Arab descent unique to the island. Their white roofs and one-meter-thick black lava stone walls keep the interior cool, and cisterns catch rainwater from tubes that run from the roof. The classic *dammuso* is whitewashed inside and simply furnished, with a sleeping alcove and several niches for storage. There are over 3000 *dammusi* on Pantelleria, and nearly every resident rents one out or knows someone who does. The town of Pantelleria also has reasonable *affittacamere*. Room quality varies considerably, and finding a place often requires perseverance. For both *dammusi* and rooms, it's best to inquire at the bars lining the beach or the tourist office and look for flyers advertising rooms. Many *dammusi* require a minimum four-day stay and cost about €25 per night. Be ready to haggle. Follow the sea road 10km west from Pantelleria town to Scauri's port, where 14 *dammusi* are for rent from ⚄**La Vela ❷**, in Scauri Scalo. All have kitchen, bath, and terrace. Small beach, brilliant purple bougainvillea, bamboo-shaded porches, and a restaurant with sea view should seal the deal. (☎0923 91 18 00 or 91 65 66. Reserve 4 months ahead for July and Aug. €20-30 per person. Cash only.) **Hotel Khamma ❸**, Lungomare Borgo Italia, 24, enjoys a central location and sea views at the end of the docks. Its polished rooms have bath, TV, A/C, phone, and minibar. (☎0923 91 25 70. Breakfast included. 7-night min. stay in Aug. Reserve far ahead. Singles €39-57; doubles €67-103; triples €88-134. AmEx/MC/V.) Go native but don't forego modern luxuries at **Hotel Cossyra Mursìa ❹**, along the road from Pantelleria town to Scauri, before the *sesi*. This resort-style hotel overlooking the sea has rooms fashioned to resemble *dammusi*, with a large deck with three swimming pools, TV lounges, a piano bar, tennis courts, archery ranges, scuba diving excursions, and an acclaimed restaurant. (☎0923 91 12 17; www.mursiahotel.it. Bed and breakfast double €100-106. Half pension double €116-170; single room add €8. Open Mar.-Oct. AmEx/MC/V.)

■ FOOD

Arab domination in the 8th century turned Pantelleria away from fishing to the cultivation of its rich volcanic soil. A local specialty, *pesto pantesco*, is a sauce of tomato, capers, basil, and garlic, eaten with pasta or on *bruschetta*. The local *zibbibo* grape yields the island's yellowish grape jelly and the amber *passito* and *moscato* dessert wines. A SISA **supermarket** in Pantelleria sits above the *lungomare*. Hike up the stairs at the 90-degree bend of the *lungomare*, passing the Banco Nuova sign on the right. (Open M-Tu and Th-Su 8:30am-1pm and 6-8:30pm, W 8:30am-1pm. MC/V.) ⚄**Ristorante-Pizzeria Castiglione ❸**, V. Borgo Italia, 24, along the *lungomare*, serves 39 kinds of pizza from a wooden stove (takeout available, starting from €4-6) in a chic, modern dining room. Fish *secondi* are a particularly good deal. (☎0923 91 14 48. *Primi* €6-8, *secondi* €8. Cover €1. Open daily noon-2pm, 7:30pm-midnight. Oct.-May closed W. AmEx/MC/V.) **La Pergola ❸**, in Località Suvaki between Pantelleria town and Scauri, after the *sesi* monuments, creates a summery atmosphere with bright yellow tablecloths and a large garden. The trattoria serves couscous and local specialties year-round. (☎0923 91 84 20. Open 8-

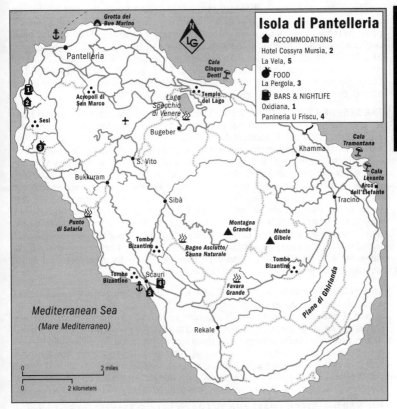

Isola di Pantelleria

🏠 ACCOMMODATIONS
Hotel Cossyra Mursìa, **2**
La Vela, **5**

🍴 FOOD
La Pergola, **3**

🍺 BARS & NIGHTLIFE
Oxidiana, **1**
Panineria U Friscu, **4**

11:30pm.) **Trattoria il Fabbiano ❷**, V. Triste, 5, serves no-frills Italian comfort food in a simple modern dining room. Its affordable *primi* (€4-5) are one of the best deals in town. (☎0923 91 19 09. Open daily 9am-3pm and 6pm-midnight.)

🔆 SIGHTS

Pantelleria's sights are like a long yield bond—greater payoffs for a less hurried investment. Don't plan to hit more than two destinations in a day. Pantelleria's bus system is notoriously unreliable, not infrequently leaving travelers waiting in the sun for half a day; furthermore, many inland and coastal sights are a good hour's walk from the scattered bus stops. Relief comes in the form of motorized transportation, an absolute necessity for most destinations inland and to the south.

▧ BAGNO ASCIUTTO AND MONTAGNA GRANDE. Far from the port near the inland town of Sibà is a natural rock sauna and the summit of Pantelleria's highest mountain. Signs guide through and beyond Sibà to the sauna; the last 10min. or so must be traveled on foot. Inside, visitors lie face down in a deep, low cave. Bring water and a towel and be prepared to leave and reenter several times—the oven-like heat is hard to stand. Farther along the sauna path, at the foot of Monte Gibele, the **Favara Grande** is a *fumarole* (crater) that emits clouds of hot

SICILY

smoke. Most of the trails that leave from the asphalt road are short but pretty hikes, and a shady picnic area in a pine grove near the summit is the perfect place to relax after a *bagno asciutto* ("dry bath," or sauna). If the midday heat is already enough, head to ◼Montagna Grande just for the view. The road past Sibà leads almost to the top, with fantastic views stretching for miles in every direction. Watch out for the lush Ghirlanda Plain. *(To get to Sibà, take the Sibà bus from P. Cavour. M-F 4 per day 6:40am-7:40pm. Both the Bagno and the mountain are clearly marked. By car or scooter, follow signs from Pantelleria town for Sibà.)*

THE SESI AND PUNTO DI SATARIA. The Bronze Age people who inhabited Pantelleria 5000 years ago left behind the *sesi*, dome-shaped funerary monuments built around 1800 BC. Tunnels in the *sesi* gave access to the womb-shaped chambers that stored kneeling corpses. Many gave been torn down for building material, but the largest remaining congregation of *sesi* forms a cemetery with 70 tombs. *(On the road from Pantelleria to Scauri. Look for a sign indicating the "zona archeologica" to the left, past the Hotel Cossyra Mursìa.)* Farther down the sea road from the *sesi* is the **Punto di Sataria.** Stairs lead down to a cave once thought to be the home of the nymph Calypso, with whom Ulysses resided for seven years of his Odyssey. The 40°C (104°F) water in the thermal pools, only a jump away from the much cooler sea, is believed to cure aching joints. *(Portions of this site may be blocked off due to falling rocks. Buses to Scauri-Rekale pass both sites, so ask the driver where to exit. Be sure to ask about return times. Buses depart Pantelleria M-F 5 times per day 6:40am-2pm. By car or scooter, follow the road from Pantelleria to Scauri.)*

LO SPECCHIO DI VENERE (THE MIRROR OF VENUS). Legend has it that Venus used this lake as a mirror before her dates with Bacchus, a fan of Pantelleria for its strong *zibbibo* wine. Mere mortals may also be lured by a glimpse down into this startlingly aquamarine pool, fringed with firm white mud and sunken into a bowl of green hillside. Sulfur springs warm the water and enrich the mud. Local practice recommends letting the sun dry the therapeutic mud to a white cake on the skin and then taking a long swim through the warm waters to wash it off. *(From P. Cavour take the bus to Bugeber; ask driver where to exit and ask about return times. Buses depart Pantelleria M-F 7:50am and 2pm. By car or scooter, head to Bugeber and follow signs for the turn-off.)*

THE NORTHEASTERN COAST AND THE ARCO DELL'ELEFANTE. In the shadow of the imposing black rock structures lining the coast, visitors crowd the best swimming holes off Pantelleria, located in three small inlets along the northeastern coast. The first, Gadir, is one of the more popular *acquacalda* spots on the island. Cement encloses the bubbly natural pool next to the sea. Even better swimming is down the coast at **Cala di Tramontana** and **Cala di Levante,** unscathed by the omnipresent concrete that rings the island. Perfect for sunbathing, these twin coves are actually one, split by a rocky outcropping. Cala di Levante offers a view of the ◼Arco dell'Elefante, off to the right. The unofficial symbol of the island, the unusual rock formation looks like a large elephant guzzling up the surf. *(All 3 inlets are on the Khamma-Tracino bus line. Buses leave P. Cavour M-F 6 per day 6:40am-5:20pm. Check return times. By car or scooter, follow signs for Khamma and Tracino, then signs for coastal roads.)*

IL PIANO DI GHIRLANDA. Surrounded by its own crumbled lip, this fertile crater makes a beautiful 2hr. hike from Tracino. On the way, scope out the farming terraces where peasants, working out of small, utilitarian *dammusi*, tend fruit orchards and caper fields. Follow signs to the **Byzantine tombs** at Gabbiana; surrounded by a vineyard, these tombs mark the final resting place of a family of four from the early Middle Ages, carved deep into the rock. *(By car, take road leading out of Tracino's P. Perugio. Or take Tracino bus to the Byzantine tombs, then follow signs to trails.)*

◪ BEACHES AND BOAT TOURS

Though surrounded by leagues of turquoise water and carved into dramatic rock formations, Pantelleria's choicest bathing options are not sandy beaches. The closest things to a beach are the pebble-filled coves. Swimming areas around the coast are rated on maps by a three-point scale charting difficulty of access. Rocky coves and swimming grottoes abound but require a trek. The swimming closest to Pantelleria is **Grotta del Bue Marino,** 2km to east, along the *lungomare* to the right of town when facing the water. Snorkelers hug its coast, sunbathers drape over volcanic rock, and some hurl themselves off cliffs into the sea below. **Use extreme caution:** water is shallow in places, and the bottom is lined with jagged rocks.

A 🛥boat tour is the best, fastest, and most relaxing way to see Pantelleria. Skimming over liquid glass waters provides an excellent glimpse of hidden caves, colorful marine life, and volcanic remains. Passengers slip in demurely with mask and flippers, or dive recklessly off top decks for an unrivaled *bagno dolce.* Boats also offer a view of some of Pantelleria's greatest, and otherwise inaccessible, rock formations, including Cinderella's Slippers, *L'Arco dell'Elefante,* and *I Cinque Denti* (The Five Teeth). The boats lining the ports offer diverse advantages: smaller ones can nudge into tiny crevices between rocks, but their larger cousins provide bamboo shade, napping cushions, and space for children—or grown-ups—to play. **Adriano Minardi,** V. Borgo Italia, 15 (☎/fax 0923 91 15 02), runs tours of the island. Expect to pay about €25-30 for any service at sea.

◪ NIGHTLIFE

Pantelleria's most obvious nightlife is at the port, where *Panteschi* take 24hr. *passagiate* near several interchangeable bars. **Tikirriki,** V. Borgo Italia, 5/7 (☎0923 91 10 79) and **Il Goloso,** V. Borgo Italia, 35 (☎0923 91 18 14), both serve until about 2am and have canopied tables outside by the water. Twelve kilometers away in the town of Scauri is the lively **Bar-Panineria U Friscu,** C. da Scauri, 54, on the western seaside road from Pantelleria, where music blasts until very late. The only disco open during the summer is **Oxidiana,** on the western seaside road heading out of Pantelleria, on the left just before Hotel Cossyra Mursia; look for a huge electronic scrolling banner that reads "Tutte le Sere." Come mid-summer to pack the pod seats and multi-level outdoor dance floor. (☎0923 91 23 19. Open July-Sept. 15.)

SARDINIA (SARDEGNA)

An old Sardinian legend says that when God finished making the world, He had a handful of dirt left over, which he threw into the Mediterranean and stepped on, creating the island of Sardinia. The contours of His divine foot formed some of the world's most spectacular landscapes. Haphazard, rough-hewn coastlines, tiny rivers, rolling hills, and mighty mountain ranges today sustain about a million people, sometimes described as too sturdy to be Italians. D. H. Lawrence sought respite from the "deadly net of European civilization" that plagued him even in the outermost reaches of Sicily and found his refuge among the wild horses and pink flamingos of this untamed island. When the vanity of cultivated mainland Italy starts to wear thin and one more Baroque facade or crammed piazza threatens to send you flying into the face of an oncoming Fiat, Sardinia is just the cure.

The feudal civilizations of warring shepherd-kings that settled here 3500 years ago left about 8000 scattered *nuraghi* ruins. These gutted cone-shaped towerhouses, which are unique to Sardinia, were built with stone blocks and assembled without mortar. Shuffled between the Phoenicians and the Carthaginians, Sardinia got a break when the Romans claimed the island and made it an agricultural colony. But by the 13th century, it was again a stomping ground for the Pisans, the Aragonese, the newly united Spanish, and the *Piemontesi*. Only decades ago, *padroni* (landlords) controlled the land and farmers toiled under a system akin to serfdom. It was from this war-torn and exploited land that Vittorio Emanuele, Italy's first king, began his campaign to unify Italy in 1861. Sardinia's history, cuisine, and language render it a cultural anomaly and curiosity among the Italians and Europeans who flock to the crystal clear waters along its sparkling coastline. With dependable bus and train systems making all parts of the island easily accessible, travelers seek out secluded mountains of the interior well as miles of beaches. The growing tourist industry, however, has not changed Sardinia all that much, and visitors are inevitably transformed by this unconventional and beautiful territory. It is one of the last quiet and barely touristed refuges left in all of Europe.

HIGHLIGHTS OF SARDINIA

UNCOVER the once-secret retreat of Cala Gonone, with its archaeological wonders, striking mountains, and picturesque harbor. (p. 756.)

VACATION like the rich and famous on one of Europe's hottest beaches, Costa Smeralda. (p. 743.)

VIEW Orgosolo's incomparable activist murals, sheltered in the mountains near Nuoro. (p. 754.)

VISIT Cagliari's Museo Archeologico to learn about Sardinia's first cultures. (p. 724.)

▛ TRANSPORTATION

FLIGHTS. Flights on *Alitalia* link Alghero, Cagliari, and Olbia to major Italian cities. Though flights are faster than water travel, exorbitant fares discourage most air travelers.

FERRIES. The cheapest way to Sardinia is by ferry to Olbia from Civitavecchia, Genoa, or Livorno; expect to pay €20-75 each way, depending on the company, season, boat speed, and departure time (night trips, fast ferries, and summer

Sardinia (Sardegna)

SARDINIA

CORSICA (FRANCE)

TO GENOA (7-19hrs)

TO GENOA (6-13hrs)

Bonifacio

Santa Teresa di Gallura
Budelli
Spargi
Isola Maddalena
La Maddalena
Caprera

Capo Testa

Palau

Costa Paradiso

Arzachena

Costa Smeralda

Golfo Aranci

Olbia

Golfo di Olbia

TO CIVITAVECCHIA (3½hrs) AND LIVORNO (7hrs)

Asinara

Cala d'Oliva

Fornelli

Golfo dell' Asinara

Stintino

Porto Torres

Castelsardo

Sassari

Oschiri

Grotta di Nettuno

Fertilia

Alghero

Chilivani

Coghinas R.

Ozieri

Siniscola

Capo Caccia

Teneo R.

Sardinian Sea (Mare di Sardegna)

Bosa

Macomer

Nuoro

Tirso R.

Dorgali

Orosei

Cala Gonone

Cuglieri

Oliena

Golfo di Orosei

S. Caterina

Orgosolo

Putzu Idu

S'Archittu

Sinis Peninsula

Sórgono

Tonara

Fonni

▲ *Monti del Gennargentu*

San Giovanni di Sinis

Cabras

Is Aruttas

Torre Grande

Tharros

Oristano

Aritzo

Arbatax

TO CIVITAVECCHIA (11hrs) AND LIVORNO (16½hrs)

Golfo di Oristano

Lanusei

Arborea

Isili

Jerzu

Barumini

Sanluri

Guspini

Costa Verde

Mannu R.

Villaputzu

Tyrrhenian Sea (Mare Tirreno)

Bugerru

Domusnovas

Iglesias

Assemini

Cagliari

TO GENOA (20hrs)

Portoscuso

Carlo Forte

Calasetta

Carbonia

Isola di San Pietro

Sant' Antioco

Solanas

Costa Rei

Villasimius

Golfo di Cagliari

TO CIVITAVECCHIA (15½hrs)

Isola di Sant'Antioco

Pula

Nora

Capo Boi

Capo Carbonara

Santa Margherita di Pula

TO NAPOLI (15½hrs)

Capo Teulada

Capo Spartivento

Mediterranean Sea (Mare Mediterraneo)

TO TRAPANI (12hrs)

TO PALERMO (13½hrs)

0   20 miles

0   20 kilometers

ferries cost more). The cheapest fares are for daytime *posta ponte* (deck class) slots on slow-moving boats, but most ferry companies require that *poltrone* (reserved armchairs) be sold to capacity before they open *posta ponte*. In the price ranges below, the low number is the low-season *poste ponte* fare, and the high number is the high-season *poltrone* fare. Expect to pay €10-20 more for a *cabina* with a bed, and an extra €5-15 depending on the season, duration, and taxes. Travelers with cars, mopeds, animals, or children should arrive 1½hr. before departure; everyone else should arrive 45min. early. Vehicles can cost €50-120, depending on the length of the voyage and the season. The ferry schedule chart below is for summer service. All winter ferries sell at lower prices and run overnight.

Tirrenia (☎ 199 12 31 99 or 081 317 29 99 for reservations; www.tirrenia.it) has offices in most city harbors, including: **Cagliari** (☎070 66 60 65), **Civitavecchia** (☎076 658 19 25 or 658 19 26), **Genoa** (☎010 269 69 81), and **Olbia** (0789 20 71 00). There are also Tirrenia offices in **Livorno** (☎0586 42 47 30), on Calata Addis Abeba–Varco Galvani; **Naples**, Rione Sirignano, 2 (☎081 251 47 63). **Palermo** (☎091 602 11 11), on Calata Marinai d'Italia; **Porto Torres**, V. Mare, 38 (☎079 518 10 11).

Sardinia Ferries (☎019 21 55 11; www.sardiniaferries.com). Offices in **Livorno**, at the Stazione Marittima (☎0586 88 13 80), and in **Civitavecchia** (☎0766 60 07 14), at Calata Laurenti.

Moby Lines has offices in **Olbia's** (☎0789 279 27, or 0565 27 60 77) and in **Livorno's** Stazione Marittima (☎0586 89 99 50), or V. Veneto, 24 (☎0586 82 68 23), and in **Genoa** (☎010 254 15 13).

Grand Navi Veloci (☎010 20 94 59, fax 550 92 25 for reservations) has offices in: **Genoa,** V. Fieschi, 17 (☎010 550 91); **Livorno** (☎0586 40 98 04); **Milan** (☎0289 01 22 81); **Olbia** (☎0789 20 01 26); and **Porto Torres** (☎0795 160 34), in the Porto Industriale, by the water.

Linea dei Golfi (www.lineadeigolfi.it) has offices in **Cagliari** (☎070 65 84 13), **Olbia** (☎0789 246 56). Ferries from Piombino and Livorno to **Olbia** (€16.50-35), and **Piombino** (☎0565 22 23 00).

Enermar (www.enermar.it) has offices at **Genoa's** port (☎ 199 76 00 03) and **Palau** (☎ 199 76 00 01).

ROUTE	COMPANY	DURATION	FREQUENCY	PRICE
Civitavecchia-Olbia	Tirrenia (unità veloce)	4hr.	2-3 per day, 8:30am	€27.63-45.54
Civitavecchia-Olbia	Tirrenia (traditional)	8hr.	1 per day, 11pm	€16-25.15
Civitavecchia-Cagliari	Tirrenia (traditional)	14½hr.	1 per day, 6:30pm	€22.91-40.28
Genoa-Olbia	Tirrenia (traditional)	13¼hr.	July-Aug. 1 per day, 6pm	€33.92-64.78
Genoa-Porto Torres	Tirrenia (traditional)	10hr.	1 per day, 9pm	€33.92-64.78
Naples-Cagliari	Tirrenia (traditional)	16hr.	1-2 per week, 7:15pm	€19.36-40.80
Palermo-Cagliari	Tirrenia (traditional)	13½hr.	1 per week, 5pm	€20.39-38.21
Trapani-Cagliari	Tirrenia (traditional)	10hr.	1 per week, Su midnight	€20.39-38.21
Civitavecchia-G. Aranci	Sardinia Ferries	7-10hr.	3 per day in summer	€26-70-44.70
Livorno-Golfo Aranci	Sardinia Ferries	5-8hr.	3 per day in summer	€26.70-44.70
Olbia-Livorno	Moby Lines	10hr.	2-3 per day	€20-46
Bonifacio-S. Teresa	Moby Lines	1hr.	10 per day in summer	€8-12
Genoa-Palau	Enermar	12hr.	1 most days	€35-59
Genoa-Olbia	Grand Navi Veloci	8-10hr.	1 per day	€42-77
Genoa-Porto Torres	Grand Navi Veloci	11hr.	1-3 per day	€31-74
Piombino-Olbia	Linea dei Golfi	6½hr.	July-Aug. 6-14 per week	€16.50-35

CAGLIARI ☎070

Since the Phoenicians founded the ancient port town of Korales over two millennia ago, strings of civilizations have competed for domination of Sardinia's capital and largest city. In the 11th century, after defeating the Genoese, the Pisans built the fortified town of *Castrum Kolaris*, which became one of the most important artistic and cultural centers on the Mediterranean. Cagliari maintains the energy of a modern European cultural enclave, with chic boutiques, the island's largest university, and cafes serving espresso-sipping students. Civilizations converge in the city, where cobblestoned streets snake around ancient monuments in the 13th-century Castello district and a vast Roman amphitheater still stages theatrical and musical performances. After a day of sightseeing the sparkling green water and bright sands of Il Poetto beckon just minutes away, offering one of the best beaches in all of Sardinia.

▆ TRANSPORTATION

Flights: ☎070 210 51. In the village of Elmas. ARST buses run from the airport 8km to the city terminal at P. Matteotti (30min., 24 per day 6:25am-12:10am, €0.67).

Trains: FS (☎147 88 80 88), in P. Matteotti. Open daily 6:10am-8:45pm. 24hr. ticket machines. To: **Olbia** (4hr., 6:32pm, €12.95) via **Oristano** or **Macomer; Oristano** (1½hr., 16 per day 5:40am-9:57pm, €4.55); **Porto Torres** (4hr., 2:30 and 4:28pm, €12.95); **Sassari** (4hr., 6:49am and 4:28pm, €12.10).

Ferrovie della Sardegna (☎070 58 02 46), in P. Repubblica. Info office open daily 7:30am-8:45pm.

Buses: There are 3 bus stations that serve Cagliari.

ARST, P. Matteotti, 6 (☎070 409 83 24). Office open M-Sa 8-8:30am, 9am-2:15pm, and 5:30-7pm, Su 1:30-2:15pm and 5:30-7pm. When office is closed, buy tickets on bus. Serves local towns, including **Villasimius** (15 per day 5am-8:10pm, €2.89) and **Arbatax** (10:25am-3pm, €7.64). Also runs to **airport** (10min., 24 per day 6:10am-8:45pm, €0.67).

PANI (☎070 65 23 26) ticket booth in Stazione Marittima. Office open M-Sa 8am-2:15pm and 5:30-7pm, Su 1:30-2:15pm and 5:30-7pm. Buses leave from front of Stazione Marittima to: **Nuoro** (3½hr., 4 per day 5:30am-6:15pm, €11.31); **Oristano** (1½hr., 4 per day 5:30am-6:15pm, €5.84); **Sassari** (3hr., 7 per day 5:30am-7pm, €12.60-13.43).

FMS (☎800 04 45 53 or 078 14 00 78), on Viale Colombo, runs to **Calasetta** and **Sant'Antioco** (both 2hr., 2 per day 10am-4pm). Buy tickets at newsstand across from Farmacia Spanno on V. Roma. Buy tickets 1 day ahead if traveling on Su.

Ferries: Tirrenia (☎070 66 60 65 or 800 82 40 79), in Stazione Marittima. **Luggage storage** available (see **Practical Information**). Open M, W, F 8:30am-7pm, Tu and Th 8:30am-6:50pm, Sa 8:30am-6pm, Su 4-8pm.

Car Rental: Ruvioli, V. dei Mille, 9 (☎070 65 89 55; info@ruvioli.it). Major credit card required. Web reservations preferred. From €63 per day, from €303 per week. 21+. Open daily 9:30am-1pm and 4:30-7pm. Pick up the car at the **airport branch** (☎070 24 03 23). Open daily 8:30am-9pm. AmEx/MC/V. **Auto assistance** (☎070 684 88 74; www.autoassistance.it), in Stazione Marittima, rents cars (from €62), motor scooters (€31-45), and a few old mountain bikes (€10 per day). Insurance included. 21+. Open M-F 9am-1pm and 3-7pm. AmEx/MC/V.

Local Buses: ☎070 200 83 18. Orange **CTM buses** run from P. Matteotti. Tickets sold in in park across from ARST station. €0.77 per 1½hr., €1.29 per 2hr., €2.17 per day. **Buses P, PQ,** and **PF** go to **Il Poetto** 5:20am-10:50pm, last return 11:25pm.

Taxis: Radiotaxi Quattro Mori (☎070 40 01 01).

✈ 🛈 ORIENTATION AND PRACTICAL INFORMATION

Via Roma greets new arrivals to town, stretching between the **harbor, Stazione Marittima,** and the PANI bus stop on one side and outdoor cafes on the other. At one end of V. Roma, **Piazza Matteotti** contains the **train station,** the **ARST station,** and the tourist office. Across from P. Matteotti, **Largo Carlo Felice** climbs the steep hill leading to **Piazza Yenne,** then heads to the Castello district, the historic center of town. Merchants converge on the terraces of the Bastione di S. Remy for a **flea market** on Sunday morning and a smaller daily ■**flea market** in P. del Carmine, where visitors hone their bargaining skills and find quality antiques for low prices.

Tourist Office: ☎ 070 66 92 55. P. Matteotti, in park across from the train and bus stations. English-speaking staff has substantial info on local sights. Open summer M-Sa 8:30am-1:30pm and 2:30-7:30pm. Hours subject to change in winter.

Budget Travel: CTS, V. Cesare Balbo, 12 (☎ 070 48 82 60). Info on student discounts and packages. Open M-F 9am-1pm and 4-7:30pm, Sa 9am-1pm. **Memo Travel,** V. Pitzolo, 1/A (☎ 070 40 09 07). Open M-F 9am-1pm and 4-7:30pm, Sa 9am-1pm.

Luggage Storage: At Stazione Marittima. Free. Open Sa-Su 7am-7pm.

English-Language Bookstore: Libreria della Costa, V. Roma, 65 (☎ 070 65 02 56). Sizable collection of classics and bestsellers. Open M-Sa 9am-8:30pm, Su 10am-1:30pm and 5-9pm. AmEx/MC/V.

Laundry: Lavanderia Self-Service, V. Sicilia, 20 (☎ 070 56 55 21 or 349 433 11 20), off V. Bayle. Wash €3.50 per 6kg, dry €3.50 for 20min. €0.50 discount 8-10am and 2-4pm. Open daily 8am-10pm; last wash 9pm.

Emergency: ☎ 112. **Police** (☎ 070 40 40 40). **Ambulance** (☎ 118). **First Aid** (☎ 070 50 29 31).

Pharmacy: Farmacia Dr. Spano, V. Roma, 99 (☎ 070 65 56 83). Open in summer M-F 9am-1pm and 4:50-8:10pm, Sa 9am-1pm; in winter M-F 9am-1pm and 4:30-7:50pm, Sa 9am-1pm.

Hospital: V. Ospedale, 46 (☎ 070 66 32 37), by the Chiesa di S. Michele.

Internet: Mail Boxes Etc., V. Trieste, 65/B (☎ 070 67 37 04), near the post office. 2 computers with fast connection. €1.50 for 15min., €5 per hr. **Fax** and UPS service available. Open M-F 9am-1pm and 4-7:30pm. MC/V.

Currency Exchange: Banca di Roma, P. Yenne at the corner of C. V. Emanuele II. **ATM** outside. Open M-F 8:25am-1:35pm and 2:50-4:10pm, Sa 8:25-11:55am.

Post Office: V. Carmine, 27 (☎ 070 603 11). Take V. Sassari from P. Matteotti. *Fermoposta,* phone cards, and **currency exchange.** Open M-F 8:10am-6:40pm, Sa 8:10am-1:20pm. **Postal Code:** 09100.

▌ ACCOMMODATIONS

To reach **Hotel Jack Vittoria ❹,** V. Roma, 75, cross V. Roma from the train station or ARST station and turn right. Founded in 1938 and still one of Cagliari's loveliest hotels, the 20 majestic rooms have Venetian chandeliers and A/C, and most have bath and TV. Check-in is on the third floor. (☎/fax 070 66 79 70. Breakfast €5. Reserve ahead. Singles €40-50; doubles €66-75; triples €101. Cash only.) The best budget option in town is **Albergo Palmas ❷,** V. Sardegna, 14. Cross V. Roma and turn right. Take the first left on Largo Carlo Felice and a right on V. Sardegna. The accommodating management and an excellent location round out 14 simple rooms, all with balcony. (☎ 070 65 16 79. Shared bath. Reception on the second floor. Reservation recommended. Singles €23; doubles €31-38. AmEx/

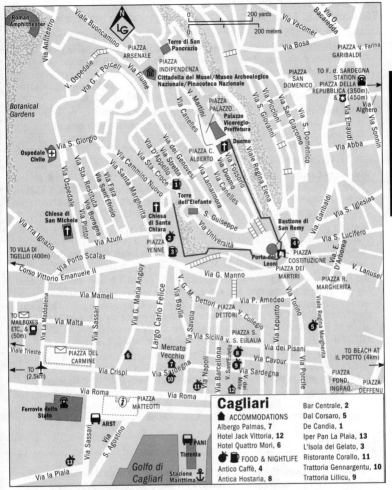

Cagliari

⌂ ACCOMMODATIONS
Albergo Palmas, **7**
Hotel Jack Vittoria, **12**
Hotel Quattro Mori, **6**

🍴 🏠 FOOD & NIGHTLIFE
Antico Caffè, **4**
Antica Hostaria, **8**

Bar Centrale, **2**
Dal Corsaro, **5**
De Candia, **1**
Iper Pan La Plaia, **13**
L'Isola del Gelato, **3**
Ristorante Corallo, **11**
Trattoria Gennargentu, **10**
Trattoria Lillicu, **9**

MC/V.) Set back from the port, close to P. Yenne, the handsome **Hotel Quattro Mori ❹**, V. G. M. Angioy, 27, offers 42 rooms with marble floors and dark wood furnishings. Rooms have bath, A/C, TV, and fridge. (☎070 66 85 35; www.hotel4mori.it. Breakfast €8. Reservation recommended. Singles €57; doubles €73; triples €95. AmEx/MC/V.)

🍴 FOOD

Along V. Sardegna, many small shops sell fruit, cheese, and bread. Try **Mini Market La Marina,** V. Sardegna, 43, which also has a heavenly bakery. (Open M-Sa 7:30am-2pm and 4:30-8:30pm. MC/V.) The colossal **Iper Pan La Plaia,** V. la Plaia, 15, is the mother of all **grocery stores.** (Open M-W and Sa 9am-9pm, Th-F 9am-9:30pm, Su 9am-2pm and 5-9pm.) On Sunday mornings, explore the **market** on the far side of the stadium in Borgo S. Elia for fresh fruit and seafood. The many cafes that line V. Roma and Largo Felice are perfect places for a breakfast pastry, a *panino* for lunch, a cup of espresso, and great people-watching.

▨ **Trattoria Lillicu,** V. Sardegna, 78 (☎070 65 29 70). Run by the same family for 80 years, Lillicu serves classic Sardinian dishes like *lacetti di agnelle* (lamb; €6.50) and deftly prepared seafood. A wide selection of vegetable *antipasti* are available either fresh, grilled, or pickled. *Primi* €6.50-11.50, *secondi* €6-13. Cover €1.55. Reservations recommended. Open M-Sa 1-3pm and 8-11pm. AmEx/MC/V. ❸

▨ **Antica Hostaria,** V. Cavour, 60 (☎070 66 58 70, fax 66 58 78). This beautiful restaurant sports Art Nouveau decor and tuxedo-clad waiters, and starts meals off with a sparkling *aperitif.* Try house favorite *fregola con arselle* (tiny semolina pasta in clam broth; €8) or veal in *vernaccia* sauce (€8). *Primi* €3-15, *secondi* €8-18. Cover €2. Open M-Sa 12:45-3pm and 8-11pm. AmEx/MC/V. ❸

Ristorante Corallo, V. Napoli, 4 (☎070 66 80 27), just off V. Roma. At tables set with complimentary fresh vegetables (radishes, celery, lettuce), enjoy *gnochetti* in a variety of sauces (from €3) or delicious seafood. Suckling pig is a specialty on Sundays. *Primi* €6-9.50, *secondi* €6.50-9.50. Open M-Sa 1-3pm and 8-11pm. AmEx/MC/V. ❸

Trattoria Gennargentu, V. Sardegna, 60 (☎070 65 82 47). Join locals in this casual salumeria-restaurant for *spaghetti alle arselle e bottarga* (with baby clams and ground fish eggs; €7) and zesty *salsiccia arrosta* (roasted sausage; €8). *Primi* €3.50-8.50, *secondi* €5-11. Cover €1.55. Open M-Sa 12:30-3pm and 8-11pm. AmEx/MC/V. ❷

Dal Corsaro, Viale Regina Margherita, 28 (☎070 66 43 18; www.dalcorsaro.com). Prices are high, but the food and atmosphere here are the height of elegance. Meals include complimentary *aperitif,* miniature homemade sorbet, and inventive versions of regional specialties. Order the award-winning *minstre'e cocciula e fregolina sarda* (in a clam broth; €10) and receive a commemorative engraved plate. *Primi* €10-18, *secondi* €15.50-35. Open M-Sa 1-4pm and 8pm-midnight. AmEx/MC/V. ❺

Bar Centrale, P. Yenne, 4 (☎070 65 78 75), fills with chatty locals and a young teen crowd on summer evenings. *Panini* from €2. Cocktails from €5. Open daily 7:30am-3am. Cash only. In the adjoining **L'Isola del Gelato** (☎070 65 98 24), a waterfall in the wall feeds a river running beneath the transparent floor. Over 120 gelato flavors and 16 creamy mousses make this a wildly popular gelateria. Cups from €1, giant 5-scoop cup €3. Open Mar.-Nov. daily 9am-2am. Cash only. ❶

🔘 SIGHTS

MUSEUMS. Although the menacing spear above the entrance recalls the building's original purpose, today the **Cittadella dei Musei** at P. Arsenale houses a modern complex of research museums that includes the ▨**Museo Archeologico Nazionale.** The extensive collection of Sardinian artifacts from the Nuraghic era to the Byzantine includes Mycenean pottery from 1600 BC Barumini, the largest of Sardinia's *nuraghi*, jewelry and coins from the Punic Phoenician Age, Roman glass works and mosaics, and a 1000-year-old army of tiny bronze figurines. Comprehensive explanations in English and Italian use the artifacts to narrate the history of Sardinian occupation. The entire second floor of the museum devotes itself to the archaeological history of Cagliari from the Nuraghic to the Roman age. *(Take V. Buoncammino to P. Arsenale and pass under the Torre di S. Pancrazio to the Arsenale. ☎070 65 59 11. Open Tu-Su 9am-8pm. Wheelchair accessible. €4, students 18-25 €2, under 18 or over 65 free.)* The **Pinacoteca Nazionale,** in the complex with the archaeological museum, displays medieval and Baroque religious paintings and altarpieces. The labyrinthine museum is built around the remains of a 16th-century fortification, visible on the ground floor and discovered during reconstruction of the Citadel in 1966. (☎070 66 24 96 or 67 40 54. Open Tu-Su 9am-8pm. Wheelchair accessible. €2, students 18-25 €1, under 18 or over 65 free. Both museums €5, students €2.50.)

▨ **DUOMO (CATTEDRALE DI SANTA MARIA).** The Pisans constructed this massive **Gothic cathedral** during the second half of the 13th-century, dedicating it to the Virgin Mary and St. Cecilia. The duomo is modeled after the one in Pisa (p. 465) and filled with art by Pisan masters: the pulpits on either side of the main door, carved in 1162, are by Gugliemo, and the four wrestling lions at the base of the altarpiece are by Pisano. The ornate wooden balcony to the left, in front of the altar was constructed for the Piemontese king, who refused to sit among the people for fear of regicide. Steps descend below the altar to the sanctuary, carved into the rock in the early 17th century. Colorful marble inlays conceal 179 niches housing the remains of about 200 martyred saints from Cagliari. The sanctuary also contains two funerary monuments to the Savoyard Royal Family and the large marble sarcophagus of Cagliari archbishop Signore Francesco de Esquivel. (P. Palazzo, 4. ☎070 166 38 37. Open M-F 8am-12:30pm and 4:30-8pm, Su 8am-1pm and 4-8pm. Free. Modest dress required.)

BASTIONE DI SAN REMY. Approaching **Piazza Costituzione,** sightseers are dwarfed by an enormous arch and a staircase that seems to be carved into the hillside. Climb up the graceful though graffiti-covered double stairway to the terraces of the 19th-century *bastione* for a spectacular view of Cagliari below. Take particular note of the **Golfo degli Angeli,** the pink flamingos, and the **Sella del Diavolo** (Devil's Saddle), a massive rock formation. The *bastione* divides the modern city and the medieval Castello district. For a stroll through medieval Cagliari, start at the top of the *bastione* and follow the narrow streets past Aragonese churches and Piemontese palaces, then stop at the Pisan wall that runs along the hill.

ROMAN AMPHITHEATER. Constructed after the Carthaginians succumbed to the Roman juggernaut in 238 BC, this amphitheater conforms beautifully to the natural slope of the rocky landscape. Though it once held 10,000 spectators, it lost its downhill side to the Pisans who used the wall as a quarry to build their monuments in the 13th century. Underground cages held ferocious animals in the days when the arena hosted gladiatorial combats. Today, summer performances in the theater (see **Entertainment**) are just a little more civilized. (V. Fra Ignazio. ☎070 56 25 96. 30min. guided tours given Apr.-Oct. 1 Tu-Su 10am-1pm and 3-6pm; last tour 5:30pm. €4, students €2.)

PALAZZO VICEREGIO. Constructed by the Aragonese in 1216 and later used as a seat for Spanish and Savoyard viceroys, this beautiful palace maintains its original Pisan marble floor and 18th-century furnishings. Portraits inside are by such Sardinian masters as Giovanni Marghinotti. The palace serves as Cagliari's provincial seat. (Next to the duomo in P. Palazzo. Open daily 9am-2pm and 4-7pm. Free.)

LA TORRE DELL'ELEFANTE. Built by the Pisans in 1307 and designed by Sardinian architect Giovanni Capula as a key point in the castle's defense system, the tower takes its name not from its gigantic stature but from a small stone elephant, carved by Guantino Gavillin, on a ledge 10m above ground. Climb the tower's four steep flights of wooden stairs for views of the town and sea. (At the intersection of V. Università and V. Cammino Nuovo, just above P. Yenne. Open in summer Tu-Su 9am-1pm and 3:30-7:30pm, in winter 9am-5pm. €2, students €1.)

BOTANICAL GARDENS. Peaceful footpaths wind past more than 500 plant species, many unique to Sardinia. Also on the grounds is a Roman cave used to transport water from the adjacent Punic-Roman cistern. (V. Fra Ignazio, 11. Take V. S. Ignazio da Laconi to University. ☎070 675 35 01. Open daily May-Aug. 8am-1:30pm and 3-7pm, Sept.-Apr. 8am-1:30pm. €2, students €1, under 6 or over 60 free.)

SARDINIA

VILLA DI TIGELLIO. Positioned on a commercial street amid modern buildings, the 2nd- to 3rd-century ruins are named for Sardinian poet Tigellio Ermogene, former inhabitant and friend to Caesar. The villa holds the remains of an ancient thermal bath. *(On V. Tigellio, off C. V. Emanuele. No entrance, but good views from the street.)*

BEACHES

Il Poetto, Cagliari's most popular stretch of beach, spans 10km from the Devil's Saddle to the Margine Rosso (Red Bluff). The beach was famous for its pure white sands until the government dumped several tons of coarse brown sand on top to prevent erosion. Locals claim it's ugly, but only because their gorgeous **Villasimus** and **Chia** allow them to have high standards. And despite the brown sand, the crystal waters are still beautiful. Behind Il Poetto, the salt-water **Stagno di Molentargius** (Pond of Molentargius) provides a habitat for flamingos. *(City buses P, PQ, and PF run to the beaches. 20min., €0.77).* To avoid crowded areas, hold off for a few stops after hitting the beach area. For more private sunning and swimming, head to **Cala Mosca,** smaller and surrounded by dirt paths. A 4.3km circular trail leaves from the road to the left of Il Poetto, dropping first into the isolated **Cala Fighera,** then continuing uphill past the ruins of towers and a cistern from the Punic-Roman age. Alternatively, take city bus #5 to Stadio Amsicora, then bus #11 to the beach.

ENTERTAINMENT AND NIGHTLIFE

The **Roman Amphitheater** continues to dazzle spectators with theater, dance performances, opera, and concerts in July and August. Most shows start at 9:30pm and cost €8-50. Buy tickets at the amphitheater from 7pm on performance nights or at the **box office,** Viale Regina Margherita, 43. (☎070 65 74 28. Open M-F 10am-1pm and 5-11pm, Sa 10am-1pm, Su when there's a show.) **Outdoor movies,** mostly dubbed American films, are screened in July and August around 9pm at the Marina Piccola off Spiaggia del Poetto. Buy tickets (€4) at the Marina.

Most bars and clubs in the city are open from 9pm to 5am, but shut down in the summer when students hit the beaches and the dancing moves outdoors. The older crowd at **De Candia,** V. De Candia, 1, sways under Eastern-inspired DJ music and colorful cocktails, including *assenzio* (absinthe) lightened with burnt sugar. The bar is positioned on a terrace on top of the Bastione de San Remy. (☎070 65 58 84. Cocktails €5.50-8. Open daily 7am-4am.) Join the famous faces plastered to the walls at the **Antico Caffè,** P. Costituzione, 10/11, who have come for delicious desserts like crepes (€3.50-6) and sinful ice-cream sundaes (€4-7) for over 150 years. Call to reserve a table outside. (☎070 65 82 06. Service 20%. Open daily 7am-2am. AmEx/MC/V.) To dance the night away, either find a ride or rent one—most *discoteche* are 15-20km outside of Cagliari, on the beaches. The best night to go out is Friday. On the first of May, Sardinians flock to Cagliari for the **Festival of Sant'Efisio,** honoring a deserter from Diocletian's army who saved the island from the plague but couldn't save himself from a beheading. A costumed procession escorts his effigy from the capital down the coast to the small church that bears his name.

SASSARI ☎079

Founded as the first free town of Sardinia in 1294, Sassari held onto its medieval walled-town layout until the late 1800s, despite expansions led by the ruling Pisans, Genoese, Aragonese, and Austrians. It has since become the island's second largest city and the home to its first university, popularly called "Culleziu," built by the Jesuits from 1559 to 1605. The university's presence has bolstered Sassari's cultural life, crowding its streets with bookstores, museums, tiny restaurants and shops, and plenty of students. Largely bypassed by the waves of tourism that have hit the rest of the island, Sassari is a culturally unique and interesting modern city to explore. With an interesting history and the vibrancy of a present-day commercial center, Sassari is in many ways representative of modern Sardinian life.

▐▀ TRANSPORTATION

Trains: ☎079 26 03 62. In P. Stazione, 1 block from P. Sant'Antonio. Take bus #8 from P. d'Italia. Tickets (€0.57) available at bars around town. **Luggage storage** available (see **Practical Information**). To: **Alghero** (35min., 11 per day 6:09am-8:55pm, €1.81); **Cagliari** (3½hr., 7 per day 7:06am-6:50pm, €12.10); **Olbia** (2hr., 6 per day 7:06am-8:35pm, €5.60); **Porto Torres** (20min., 9 per day 5:58am- 6:45pm, €1.25).

Buses:

ARST (info ☎079 263 92 06 or 236 92 03). Buses depart from V. Italia in the public gardens, and the bus station on V. XXV Aprile, just in front of the train station, to **Castelsardo** (1hr., 11 per day 7:20am-7:45pm, €2.01); **Nuoro** (1¾hr., 2 per day 9:35am and 2:50pm, €6.30-7.64) and **Porto Torres** (35min., 1-2 per hr. 5:20am-10pm, €1.19). Buses run to **Fertilia Airport** (40min., 5 per day 7:25am-7:30pm, €1.76, departures only from the bus station). Tickets sold at Tonni's Bar, C. M. Savoia, 11, and at the ticket office at the bus station.

FDS (☎079 24 13 01), with buses leaving from V. XXV Aprile, serves the local area. Tickets are sold on C. Vico, where the bus stops. Destinations include **Alghero** (50min., 13 per day 5:50 am-8:15pm, €1.50) and **Castelsardo** (1hr., daily 11:35am, €1.10).

PANI (☎079 23 69 83, fax 267 7560), with buses leaving from V. XXV Aprile. Office open M-F 5:30-6:35am, 8:30am-2:15pm, and 5-7:15pm, Sa-Su 5:30-6:35am, 9-9:30am, noon-2:15pm, and 5-7:15pm, or around the time of bus departures. Buses to: **Cagliari** (3-4hr., 7 per day 6am-7:15pm, €13.43); **Oristano** (2¼hr., 4 per day 6:36am-7:15pm, €7.18); **Nuoro** (2½hr., 6 per day 6:36am-7:15pm, €6.77); **Torralba** (40min.-1hr., 6 per day 6:36am-7:15pm, €2.32).

Taxis: RadioTaxi (☎079 26 00 60). Available 24hr.

Car Rental: Avis, V. Mazzini, 2 A/B (☎079 23 55 47). From €72 per day. 21+. Under 25 pay more. Open M-Sa 8:30am-12:30pm and 4-7pm. AmEx/MC/V. **Eurorent,** V. Roma, 56 (☎079 23 23 35). Fiats or other small "Class B" vehicles from €60 per day. 21+. Credit card required. Open M-Sa 8:30am-1pm and 4-7pm.

▐▓▌ ▐ ORIENTATION AND PRACTICAL INFORMATION

All buses stop in the **giardini pubblici** before heading to the **bus station**. Since these gardens are close to Sassari's attractions, get off at **Via Italia** in the park. **Emiciclo Garibaldi** lies ahead, a small semi-circular piazza, past **Via Margherita di Savoia**. To reach the town center, head straight through Emiciclo Garibaldi onto **Via Carlo Alberto**, which spills into **Piazza Italia**. To the right, **Via Roma** runs to the tourist office and the Museo Sana. To the left lies **Piazza Castello**, packed with people and restaurants, 200m from **Corso Vittorio Emanuele**, a major thoroughfare cutting through the historic town center.

Tourist Office: V. Roma, 62 (☎079 23 17 77), a few blocks to the right of P. d'Italia when facing the provincial administration building. Go through the gate and the doorway on the right. English-speaking staff provides **maps** and bus and train schedules. Open M-Th 9am-1pm and 4-6pm, F 9am-1:30pm.

Budget Travel: CTS, V. Manno, 35 (☎079 20 04 00, fax 234 585), assists with student accommodations. Open M-F 9:30am-1pm and 4:30-7pm, Sa 9:30am-1pm.

Currency Exchange: Banca Commerciale D'Italia, P. D'Italia, 22-23, has an **ATM** outside. Open M-F 8:20am-1:20pm and 2:35-4:05pm, Sa 8:20am-11:50pm. Many other banks around the piazza and around town.

Luggage Storage: ☎079 26 03 62. In the train station. €4 per 12hr. Open daily 6:50am-8:50pm.

English-Language Bookstore: Demetra di Sassari, V. Cavour, 16 (☎079 201 31 18). Selection on 3rd fl. of mostly ancient and British classics. Open daily 9am-8:30pm. MC/V. **Gulliver Librerie,** V. Portici Crispo, 4 (☎079 23 44 75). Also mostly ancient and British classics. Open M-Sa 9am-9pm, Su 9am-1pm and 4-9pm. AmEx/MC/V.

Emergency: ☎113. **Police** (☎079 283 05 00), V. Coppino, 1.

Ambulance: Red Cross, C. Vico, 4 (☎079 23 45 22).

Hospital: Ospedale Civile, V. Montegrappa, 82/83 (☎079 206 10 00).

Pharmacy: Simon, V. Brigata Sassari, 2 (☎079 23 11 44). Posts a list of late-night pharmacies. Open M-F 5pm-1am, Sa 8:30pm-1pm, Su 8:30pm-M 9am. There's another pharmacy down the street, and several others in town.

Internet Access: Dream Bar, V. Cavour, 15 (☎079 23 75 57). 4 computers. €2.60 for 30min., €5.20 per hr. Open M-Sa 9am-9:30pm. Cash only.

Post Office: V. Brigata Sassari, 13 (☎079 282 12 67), off P. Castello. Open M-F 8:15am-6pm, Sa 8:15am-1pm. **Currency exchange,** phone cards, and *fermoposta*. **Postal Code:** 07100.

ACCOMMODATIONS

Sassari has several nice options both within and outside the city limits. **Il Gatto e la Volpe ❷,** Caniga Località Monti di Tesgia, 23, is a funky oasis in the countryside, 5km from the city. Its five rooms have unique color schemes, and some have terrace, kitchenette, and bath. Dynamic young owners Marcello and Luigi do their best to accommodate, offering beach and archaeological excursions, sailing trips, and mountain bike rentals (€11 per day). Call for free pick up from the bus station. (☎079 318 00 12 or 328 692 32 48. Internet and shared kitchen. Breakfast included. Reserve ahead. Rooms €22. Apartments with kitchen €25 for 2, €30 for 1. Extra beds available. Cash only.) Pricier but inside the city, **Frank Hotel ❹,** V. Armando Diaz, 20, is a quiet hotel with lovely rooms and nice management. All rooms have bath, A/C, phone, minibar, and TV. (☎/fax 079 27 64 56. Buffet breakfast included. Singles €47-49; doubles €67. AmEx/MC/V.) **Hotel Leonardo da Vinci ❹,** V. Roma, 79, is a gorgeous luxury option, replete with oriental rugs, imported granite floors, and hallways lined with chandeliers. The enormous rooms have bath, A/C, phone, minibar, TV, and hair dryer. (☎079 28 07 44; www.leonardodavincihotel.it. Buffet breakfast €12. Parking available. Singles €74-78; doubles €100; triples €123. AmEx/MC/V.)

FOOD

A covered **market** occupies P. Mercato, down V. Rosello from V. V. Emanuele. (Open M-F 8am-noon, Sa 8am-1pm.) Multimarkets **supermarket** is on the corner of V. Cavour and V. Manno. (☎079 23 72 78. Open M-Sa 8am-9pm.)

Trattoria La Vela Latina, Largo Sisini, 3 (☎ 079 23 37 37), in a piazza off V. Arborea. Owner Francesco loves his guests as much as they love his food. Flavorful horse or donkey meat (€10) could win over the most timid of eaters. For something less adventurous, try high-quality *brodo di pesce fresco* (stew of fish, grains, and spices; €8). *Primi* €6-10, *secondi* €7-13. Open M-Sa 1-2:30pm and 8-10:30pm. AmEx/MC/V. ❸

Ristorante Trattoria L'Assassino, V. Ospizio Cappucini, 1 (☎079 23 50 41). Facing away from the statue of Tola, walk straight. At the end of the street, turn right. Comfortable local favorite serves all the *Sardi* specialties. Fill up on tender tripe, horse, or roast suckling pig that falls off the bone. 3-course *menù* from land or sea €20. *Primi* €3.50-8, *secondi* €5-11. Open M-Sa 1-3pm and 8-11pm. Cash only. ❷

Trattoria Da Antonio, V. Arborea, 2/B (☎079 23 42 97), behind the post office. This wood-paneled find is a meat lover's heaven, with a few items available for vegetarians. Ask the waitstaff to recommend horse, donkey, and tentacled creatures. Meat dishes €5-10. Cover €1. Open daily 1-3pm and 8:30-11pm. MC/V. ❷

Il Senato, V. Alghero, 36 (☎079 27 77 88). Elegant, splurge-worthy restaurant, reputedly among Sardinia's best. Ingredients are first-rate. Don't miss the *dolce della suocera* (€4), the "mother-in-law cake" with ricotta, almond, and caramelized sugar crust. *Primi* €7-10, *secondi* €8-13. Open M-Sa 1-2:20pm and 8-11pm. AmEx/MC/V. ❹

◉ ♫ SIGHTS AND ENTERTAINMENT

Museo Giovanni Antonio Sanna, V. Roma, 64, is an informative and well-presented archaeological museum that gives multilingual guidebooks to visitors. Artifacts dating from the Neolithic to the Middle Ages, including arrowheads, tools, ceramics, Nuraghic bronze statuettes, and Romanesque sculptures, detail the island's history chronologically. (☎079 27 22 03. Open Tu-Su 9am-8pm. €2, ages 18-25 €1, EU citizens under 18 or over 65 free.) From the center of town, walk down C. V. Emanuele from P. Castello and turn left on V. al Duomo to P. Duomo to reach Sassari's duomo, **Cattedrale di San Nicolò.** Reconstructed in Gothic Catalán style in 1480, only the bell tower remains of its 13th-century Romanesque structure. The impressive facade, covered with statues and engravings, conceals an unremarkable white interior, though some recently uncovered early frescoes fill the side chapels. (Open daily 8:30am-noon and 4-7:30pm. Free. Modest dress required.)

The lavish **Sardinian Cavalcade,** on the third week in May, is Sardinia's most notable folk festival. The party includes a parade of costumed emissaries from local villages, a horse exhibition, singing, and dancing. On August 14th, **I Candelieri** brings worker's guilds carrying enormous candles through the streets. The festival, dating back to the Middle Ages, is one of the oldest and most colorful on the island. Each guild has its own costume, and the candles are bedecked with flowers and streamers. If it weren't for the ◪**University Pub,** V. Amendola, 49/A, Sassari would be devoid of a hip youth scene. A favorite among locals, the subdued pub offers dirt-cheap drinks (beer from €1.60) and overflows with students when school's in session. Request (but don't inhale) the cannabis beer (€4) or the mysterious Sardinia Island mixed drink (€5.70), whose contents are strong but secret. (☎079 20 04 23. Open Sept.-July M and W-Su 8:30pm-1am.)

▷ DAYTRIP FROM SASSARI

CASTELSARDO

Take an ARST bus (1hr., 11 per day 7:20am-7:45pm, €2.01) or FDS bus (1hr., daily 11:35am, €1.10) from Sassari. From P. Pianedda, follow V. Nazionale uphill to the walled historic center. Buses are few and far between. Open July-Aug. daily 9am-midnight, Sept.-July M-Sa 9am-midnight. Castle and museum €2.

Castelsardo's striking location atop a lofty crest and its proximity to sandy beaches make it a popular stop along the Costa Paradiso. Renowned across the island for its beauty, the town boasts quiet waters and cool breezes. Crowning the village is a large and stunningly well-preserved **castle,** erected when the Republic of Genoa founded the medieval village in 1102. The **wicker museum** inside is fairly dull but provides access to the castle's rooftop terrace, which gives panoramic views of the town's streets—now filled with women selling woven baskets.

ALGHERO ☎ 079

Vineyards, ruins, and horseback rides are all a short trip away from Alghero's charming palm-lined parks and cobbled streets. Also known as *Barcelonetta*, the city has changed hands between everyone from native Sardinians to the *Aragonese* and the *Genovese;* a distinctly Spanish flare still makes itself felt. In addition to Italian, a dialect of Catalán chimes in the streets, left by Pere I of Aragon after his 14th-century conquest. The architecture and cuisine also reflect this influence: peek inside S. Francesco or nibble on *paella* for proof.

┌─ TRANSPORTATION

Flights: ☎ 079 93 50 39 or 93 52 82. Airport near Fertilia, 6km north of the city. Domestic flights year-round, charter flights to European destinations in summer.

Trains: FDS (☎ 079 95 07 85) on V. Don Minzoni, in the northern part of the city. Take **AP** or **AF bus** from in front of Casa del Caffè in the park (3 per hr.), or walk 1km along port. Open daily 5:45am-9pm. Buy tickets at **FS stand** in the park and ride the bus to the station for free. **Luggage storage** available (see **Practical Information**). To **Sassari** (40min.; 11 per day 6:01am-8:47pm; €1.81, €3.10 round-trip). Reduced service Su.

Buses:

ARST (☎ 800 86 50 42) and **FDS** (☎ 078 95 04 58). Tickets for both available at stand in the public gardens (☎ 079 95 01 79). Blue buses depart from V. Catalogna, next to park. To: **Bosa** (1½hr., 4 per day 6:35am-7:30pm, €2.89-3.72); **Porto Torres** (1hr., 9 per day 4:45am-8:45pm, €2.32); **Sassari** (1hr., 1-2 per hr. 5:35am-7pm, €2.58).

FS runs orange **city buses** (☎ 079 95 04 58). Buy tickets (€0.57) at *tabacchi*. Buses run from V. Cagliari (front of Casa del Caffè) to the airport (20min., 6 per day 5:45am-8:30pm). **Line AF** runs between Fertilia and V. Cagliari (Alghero's *giardini*), stopping at the port (every 40min. 7:10am-9:30pm, return from Fertilia 7:50am-9:50pm). **AP** (from Viale della Resistenza) runs to train station (every 40min. 6:20am-9pm). **AO** (from V. Cagliari) heads to the *lido* (beach) and the hospital (2 per hr. 7:15am-8:45pm). **AC** (from V. Liguria) runs to **Carmine** (2 per hr. 7:15am-8:45pm).

Taxis: On V. Emanuele (☎ 079 97 53 96) across from the BNL bank, or at the airport (☎ 079 93 50 35).

Car Rental: Avis, P. Sulis, 9 (☎ 079 97 95 77), or Fertilia airport (☎ 079 93 50 64). Cars from €60 per day with unlimited mileage. 25+. Credit card required. Open M-F 8:30am-1pm and 4-7pm, Sa 8:30am-1pm. AmEx/MC/V. **Europcar** (☎ 079 93 50 32; www.europcar.it). From €70 per day, including insurance. 150km max. per day. Open daily 8am-11pm.

Bike/Moped Rental: Cycloexpress di Tomaso Tilocca (☎/fax 079 98 69 50; www.cicloexpress.com), at the harbor near the intersection of V. Garibaldi and V. Spano. Road bikes €8-10 per day, mountain bikes €7-13 per day, tandems €15 per day, electric scooters €15 per day, motor scooters €23-50 per day. Open M-Sa 9am-1pm and 4-8:30pm, Su 9am-1pm. AmEx/MC/V.

◧ ❓ ORIENTATION AND PRACTICAL INFORMATION

ARST buses stop at the corner of **Via Catalogna** and **Via Cagliari**, on the waterfront one block from the **port**. The tourist office, in **Piazza Porta Terra**, lies diagonally across the small park, on the right beyond the easily visible towers of the *centro storico*. The **train station** is a hike from the town center but accessible by local orange buses (lines AF and AP). To walk from the station, follow **Via Don Minzoni** until it becomes **Via Garibaldi** along the waterfront.

Tourist Office: P. Porta Terra, 9 (☎079 97 90 54; www.infoalghero.it), on the right from the bus stop, toward the old city. Multilingual staff offers an indexed street **map,** tours of the city, and daytrips to local villages. Open Apr.-Oct. M-Sa 8am-8pm, Su 10am-1pm; Nov.-Mar. M-Sa 8am-2pm.

Horseback Riding: Club Ippico Capuano (☎079 97 81 98, 338 326 48 79, or 338 169 33 97), 3km from Alghero on Str. Villanova. Daily guided excursions. Pick-up service from Alghero; €5 per carload. Reserve 2-3 days ahead. €15.50 per hr., day with picnic €51.65, weekend trip €129. Open year-round.

Currency Exchange: Banca Nazionale del Lavoro, V. Emanuele, 5 (☎079 98 01 22), across from the tourist office, has a 24hr. **ATM.** Open M-F 8:20am-1:20pm and 3-4:30pm, Sa 8:20-11:50am. Currency exchange also at the **post office.**

Luggage Storage: In train station. €1 per day.

English-Language Bookstore: Mondolibro, V. Roma, 50 (☎079 98 15 55), has a decent collection. Open daily 9:30am-1pm and 5pm-midnight. AmEx/MC/V.

Emergency: ☎113. **Carabinieri** (☎112). **Police,** P. della Mercede, 4 (☎113 or 97 20 00). **Ambulance** (☎118). **First Aid** (☎079 99 62 33).

Pharmacy: Farmacia Puliga di Mugoni, V. Sassari, 8 (☎079 97 90 26). Posts late-night rotation schedule. Open May-Oct. M-Sa 9am-1pm and 5-9:30pm, Feb.-Apr. M-Sa 9am-1pm and 4:30-8:30pm, Nov.-Jan. 9am-1pm and 4-8pm. AmEx/MC/V.

Hospital: Ospedale Civile (☎079 99 62 00), on V. Don Minzoni in Regione la Pietraia.

Internet Access: Bar Miramar, V. Gramisci, 2 (☎079 973 10 27). 2 computers. €1.60 for 15min., €5 per hr. Open daily 8am-1pm and 2:30pm-12:30am. Cash only.

Post Office: V. Carducci 33/35 (☎079 972 02 31), has *fermoposta* and **currency exchange.** Open M-F 8:15am-6:15pm, Sa 8:15am-1pm. **Postal Code:** 07041.

■■ ACCOMMODATIONS AND CAMPING

▨ **Hostal del'Alguer (HI),** V. Parenzo, 79 (☎/fax 079 93 20 39 or 079 93 04 78), in Fertilia. From the port, take bus AF to Fertilia; turn right and walk down the street. Hostel is on right. Personable owners offer 100 beds, bike rental, bar, pool tables, and info on attractions. Internet and phone available in lobby. Breakfast included. Lunch or dinner €8. Reception daily 7-10am, noon-2:30pm, and 3:30pm-midnight. 4- to 6-bed dorms €13; family rooms with 2 beds €16-18. HI card required. ❶

▨ **Hotel San Francesco,** V. Machin, 2 (☎/fax 079 98 03 30; www.sanfrancescohotel.com). Walk straight from the tourist office and take 3rd right. 20 simple, clean rooms in this 4th-century church cloister have bath, A/C, TV, phone, and beautiful stone walls. Enjoy breakfast on a terrace encircling the church courtyard. Breakfast included. Reservation required June-Aug. Singles €45-55; doubles €73-90. MC/V. ❸

Bed and Breakfast MamaJuana, Vco. Adami, 12 (☎339 136 97 91; www.mamajuana.it), on a side street in the heart of the old town, parallel to V. Roma. 4 eclectic medieval rooms are spruced up with antique furniture and lovely paintings, plus bath and TV. Housekeeping for extra fee. Breakfast included at a nearby cafe. Check-in 6-8pm. Singles €30-50; doubles €50-75. Cash only. ❸

Hotel La Margherita, V. Sassari, 70 (☎079 97 90 06, fax 97 64 17), near the intersection of P. Mercedes. 53 spacious rooms with A/C, phone, and TV in a central location; some have balcony. Rooftop terrace is good for socializing and sunbathing. Breakfast included. Singles €45-60; doubles €75-95; triples €115-130. AmEx/MC/V. ❹

La Mariposa (☎079 95 03 60; www.lamariposa.it), V. Lido, 22. Campground near the beach, 1.5km from Alghero toward Fertilia, offers restaurant, bar, market, bike rental, diving excursions, and beach access. Laundry €5 per load. Reservation recommended in summer. Open Mar.-Oct. €7-10.50 per person, ages 3-12 €4.80-5; €3-8 per tent; €2-4 per car; Apr.-June tents and cars free. 4-person bungalows €44-75. Hot showers €0.50. AmEx/MC/V. ❶

◘ FOOD

On V. Sassari, near the tourist office, a **market** offers fresh produce every morning. On Wednesday, the **open-air market** on V. de Gasperi floods with crowds. (Take the *linea mercato* bus from V. Cagliari.) Stop by the **Antiche Cantine del Vino Sfuso,** C. V. Emanuele, 80, a *cantina sociale* that serves decent, inexpensive wine for a mere €1 per L. (Open M-Sa 8:30am-1pm and 4:30-8pm. MC/V.) A SISA **supermarket** is at V. Sassari, 49. (Open M-Sa 8am-9pm, Su 8am-1:30pm and 5-8:30pm.)

■ **Al Tuguri,** V. Maiorca, 113 (☎/fax 079 97 67 72; www.altuguri.it). Delicious variations on traditional cuisine earn elegant Tuguri its stellar reputation. Exceptional 5-course *menùs* (with meat, fish, or vegetarian dishes; €26-28) with each day's market selection. Reservation recommended. *Primi* €8.50-9.50, *secondi* €8.50-16. Open M-Sa 12:30-2pm and 8-10:30pm. MC/V. ❹

Ristorante da Ninetto, V. Gioberti, 4 (☎079 97 80 62). From P. Porta Terra, take V. Simon and turn right on V. Gioberti. Snug restaurant housed in an 8th-century *frantoio* (olive press) with arched stone ceilings. Savory fare includes a fresh fish selection and homemade *seadas* (honey-sweetened fried cheese; €4). *Primi* €6-18, *secondi* €10-20. Open daily 12:15-2:30pm and 7:15pm-midnight. AmEx/MC/V. ❹

Trattoria Maristella, V. Kennedy, 9 (☎079 97 81 72). Slightly removed from the historic center, this local haunt serves some of the best fish in town. Come for laid-back meals at exceptional value. Try the *fregola con cozze e vongole* (*semolina* pasta cooked with seafood; €8). *Primi* €6.50-8, *secondi* €7-12.50. AmEx/MC/V. ❸

Osteria Taverna Paradiso, V. Umberto, 29 (☎079 97 80 01). Stone-vaulted ceilings and good meat and fish make for charming dining in the *centro storico.* Try the cheese platter (€7.25-8.30) for dessert. 3-course daily *menù* €13.50-22.50. *Primi* €6.20-10.50, *secondi* €7.20-13. Open daily noon-2:30pm and 7:30pm-midnight. MC/V. ❸

◉ SIGHTS

A leisurely walk through the *centro storico* reveals tiny alleys, half-hidden churches, and ancient town walls. The old city is hard to navigate without a map, so stop by the tourist office before heading inside. The **Torre di Porta Terra** dominates the entrance to the town near the public gardens. It was financed by the Jewish community in the 15th-century and consequently is known as the **Torre degli Ebrei** (Jewish Tower). Heading down V. Roma, turn left on V. Principe Umberto to see the **Teatro Civico,** built in the 19th-century, and the **Palazzo Machin,** a classic example of Gothic-Catalán architecture. Alghero's **duomo, La Cattedrale di S. Maria,** on V. Roma at the end of V. P. Umberto, was begun in 1552 and took 178 years to construct, resulting in a stunning, motley Gothic-Catalán-Renaissance facade. Rebuilt in the 19th-century, the cathedral has Gothic choirs, a mosaic of John the Baptist, and the original *Porta Petita* (small door) from the Catalán structure. A right turn from V. Roma onto V. Carlo Alberto reveals the **Chiesa di San Francesco.** First built in the 13th-century, the church collapsed in 1593 and was rebuilt during the Renaissance. The heavy Neoclassical facade conceals a graceful Gothic presbytery and a beautiful marble altar. (Open M-F 7:30am-noon and 5-6:20pm, Su 5-7:30pm. Free. Modest dress required.) Heading away from the harbor, V. Carlo Alberto arrives at the beautiful **Chiesa di San Michele** at P. Ginnasio, built between 1661 and 1675 and dedicated to the patron saint of Alghero. V. Carlo Alberto ends at Piazza Sulis and the **Torre dello Sperone,** where French soldiers were imprisoned in 1412 after failing to capture the Catalán fortress. In the 19th-century, Sardinian patriot Vincenzo Sulis was a prisoner here.

The countryside around Alghero is filled with spectacular nature reserves, inland mountains, and cliffs plunging into the sea, making it a popular destination for trekking and bicycling. Inquire at the tourist office for a comprehensive list of itineraries. One of the most popular parks, the **Le Prigionette Nature Reserve**, lies at Porto Conte, off the Fertlia-Porto Conte highway on the road to Capo Caccia. Buses heading toward the Grotte di Nettuno pass by the reserve three times daily. Bike and hiking paths wind through mountains and valleys filled with wild horses, ending in panoramic cliffs and peaks. The forestry house at the park entrance supplies good **maps** and advice. (☎079 94 90 60. Open M-F 8am-4pm, Sa and Su 9am-5pm.) **FDS buses** also lead directly to **Porto Conte** (30min.; every hr. 7:10am-11:30pm, last return midnight; €0.88), where a dirt road leads to **Punta Giglio Reserve.** The rough road is a difficult but popular route for bikers, ending after 3km at a limestone peak on Punta Giglio. The point offers one of the most impressive views in the region, as well as several WWII barracks to explore. The seaside highways heading away from Alghero around the Porto Conte and Capo Caccia area are also popular for biking and quite safe thanks to low traffic levels.

🎵 🎭 ENTERTAINMENT AND NIGHTLIFE

Alghero comes alive at night, with people streaming through the cramped streets of the *centro storico* and pouring onto the promenade through the early morning hours. (Hostelers beware: the last bus to Fertilia is at 11:30pm.) Locals in search of warm evening breezes and decent bands head to the open-air bars along **Lungomare Dante.** Both locals and tourists also find amusements aplenty at **Poco Loco,** V. Gramsci, 8, heading inland from Lungomare Dante past P. Sullis. Famed for its pizza-by-the-meter (€17-27; half-meter also available), Poco has many attractions—six late-night bowling lanes, Internet (€5.20 per hr.), and great live music on summer weekends. (☎079 97 31 034. Live music F-Sa 11pm. Beer from €2; cocktails €5.50. Open in summer daily 8pm-3am or later. MC/V.) Overlooking the water, **Bar El Trò,** Lungomare Valencia, 3, has live music or DJs spinning after 11:30pm. (☎079 973 30 00. Cocktails €6.50. Open daily May-Oct. 9pm-6am; Nov.-Apr. 8:30pm-6am.) On weekends, over 2000 dancers jam the three floors at **Discoteca Il Ruscello,** Località Angeli Custodi, 57, 2km from Alghero on the road to Fertilia. (☎/fax 079 95 31 68. Open daily July 16-Aug. 24 12:30-6am; Aug. 25-July 15 F-Su 12:30-6am. Cover €20, includes 1 drink. AmEx/MC/V.)

🔲 DAYTRIP FROM ALGHERO

GROTTE DI NETTUNO

FDS buses (☎079 95 01 79) run to Capo Caccia (50min.; 3 per day 9:15am-5:10pm, last return 6:05pm; €1.76). Or take the frequent and pleasant Navisarda Grotte di Nettuno ferry boat tour. Boats (☎079 97 62 02, 95 06 03, or 97 89 61) leave Alghero's Bastione della Maddalena (1hr.; June-Sept. 8 per day 9am-5pm; Apr.-May and Oct. 9, 10am, and 3pm; round-trip €10, under 13 €6).

The Duke of Buckingham dubbed the 🔲**Grotte di Nettuno** "the miracle of the gods." These majestic caves, discovered by fishermen in the 18th century, have been around for 60 to 70 million years and today are one of Sardinia's most frequented tourist destinations. Be careful not to bump your head—one cubic centimeter of stalactite took 100 years of dripping rainwater to form. Well-run 30min. tours are conducted in Italian, French, English, and German. The caves are in **Capo Caccia,** a steep promontory that juts out from **Porto Conte.** Built in 1954, the steep **Escala del Cabirol** provides access to the grotto by land for those brave enough to walk down the 632 steps that plunge to the sea between massive white cliffs. (☎079 94 65 40. Open daily Apr.-Sept. 9am-7pm, Oct. 10am-4pm, Nov.-Mar. 9am-1pm. Groups admitted every hr. €8, under 12 €4.) ARST buses to Capo Caccia stop along the way at the **■Nuraghi di Palmavera** (☎079 95 32 00, fax 98 87 65), 3km past Fertilia, where a central tower surrounded by 50 huts forms a limestone complex dating from 1500 BC. The **S.I.L.T. cooperative** (☎079 95 32 00) offers tours in English, French, German, and Spanish. (Nuraghi open daily Apr.-Oct. 9am-7pm, Nov.-Mar. 9:30am-4pm. €2.10, with guided tour €3.60. Group and student discounts.)

PORTO TORRES   ☎079

Founded in 27 BC, the village of Turris Libissonis served as one of the Roman Empire's principal ports along the trading routes between Sicily and Africa. Today the Roman ruins and Romanesque 12th-century church are worth a brief glimpse. Dominated by industrial zones and port bustle, however, Porto Torres is of best use to visitors as an access point to more memorable coastal areas.

■ TRANSPORTATION. Trains (☎079 51 46 36), on V. Fontana Vecchia near the port, are synchronized with ferries, running to Sassari (20min., 1-2 per hr. 5:40am-9:50pm, €1.25) and continuing to Olbia. **ARST buses** (☎079 263 92 00 or 800 86 50 42) run from the port and along C. V. Emanuele. Reduced service Su. Tickets are available in **Bar Acciaro,** C. V. Emanuele, 38, and the bar **Green Point,** on the port. Buses run to: Alghero (1hr., 7 per day 6:05am-10:05pm, €2.32); Fertilia Airport (40min., 8:15am and 2pm, €1.55); and Sassari (35min., 1-4 per hr. 6:05am-10pm, €1.19). **Taxis** (☎079 51 40 52) are on C. V. Emanuele.

■■ ORIENTATION AND PRACTICAL INFORMATION. Porto Torres has one major thoroughfare, **Corso Vittorio Emanuele,** which leaves from **Piazza Colombo** where the buses stop and runs perpendicular to the sea from the port. From the train station, take a right onto **Via Fontana Vecchia** and then a quick left onto **Via Eleanora d'Arborea,** which ends at C. V. Emanuele. The **Pro Loco Tourist Office,** V. Roma, 3, is in **Piazza Garibaldi,** the first left off of C. V. Emanuele when coming from P. Colombo. The staff provides **maps,** bus schedules, and info on local sights, beaches, and excursions. (☎079 504 19 97. Open July-Sept. M-F 8am-noon and 4-8pm, Sa 8am-1pm; Oct.-Apr. M-Sa 9am-1pm.) Farther up the street, the **BNL** bank, C. V. Emanuele, 18/20, has an **ATM** outside. (Open M-F 8:30am-1:30pm and 2:45-4:15pm, Sa 8:30am-noon.) In case of **emergency,** call the **carabinieri** (☎079 50 24 32) or an **ambulance** (☎079 50 80 70). **Farmacia Rubatiu,** C. V. Emanuele, 73, is down the block from the bank. (☎079 51 40 88. Open M-Sa 9:15am-1pm and 5-8:30pm.) The **post office** is at V. Ponte Romano, 83, before the baths. (Open M-F 8:15am-1:15pm and Sa 8:15am-12:45pm.) **Postal Code:** 07046.

■■ ACCOMMODATIONS AND FOOD. Centrally located on the water just off of P. Colombo, **■Hotel Elisa ❹** offers guests spacious rooms with nice wooden furniture, a popular restaurant, and four generations of family experience. All 26 rooms have bath, TV, phone, hair dryer, and fridge, and most have balcony or windows with sea views. (☎079 51 32 60, fax 51 37 86. Breakfast buffet included. Singles €44-49; doubles €68-73; triples €86-93. AmEx/MC/V.) To reach **Albergo Royal ❸,** V. S. Satta, 8, from the port or bus stop, walk up C. V. Emanuele away from the water until reaching a yellow "Albergo Royal" sign hanging overhead. Turn left and walk 300m along V. Petronia and then follow the signs. The enormous rooms have simple but comfortable decor. All come with bath, TV, and some with balcony and A/C. (☎079 50 22 78. Singles €25-35; doubles €50-65. Cash only.)

In the morning, an **outdoor market** is at the intersection of V. Delle Vigne and V. Sacchi. A SISA **supermarket** is on V. Mare, 24. (☎079 50 10 24. Open daily 8am-8:30pm. AmEx/MC/V.) Locals and visitors flock to **Piazza Garibaldi ❷**, P. Garibaldi, 13 (☎079 50 15 70), a bright two-floor restaurant with outdoor seating and tasty pizza (€3.00-8-50) and late-night drinks. (Beer from €1. Open daily 11am-2am. AmEx/MC/V.) Head to **Trattoria La Tana ❷**, V. Cavour, 26, off C. V. Emanuele for traditional *gnochetti alla sarda* (€4) or a nice fillet of horse (€9) in the casual and comfortable dining room. (☎079 50 22 46. Pizza €2.50-6. *Primi* €3-4.50, *secondi* €5.50-10.50. Open in summer daily noon-4pm and 7pm-midnight, closed Tu in winter.) For sandwiches, pizza, or pasta on the go, try **Poldiavolo ❶**, in P. XX Settembre, where the food is popular and prepared quickly. The friendly owner piles his *panini* with everything from veal to vegetables. (Pizza €3.70-6.50. *Panini* €3.50. Open daily noon-midnight. Cash only.)

◐◖ SIGHTS AND BEACHES. The ruins of the **Roman Thermal Baths** attest to the wealth and success of Turris Libissonis as a grain port for the Romans. Popularly referred to as **Palazzo Re Barbaro**, the ruins were believed to be the ancient seat of Sardinian Governor Barbaro (slayer of local saints Gavino, Proto, and Gianuario) until excavations turned up the three traditional bath chambers. The baths are accessible from the museum **Antiquarium Turritano**, V. Ponte Romane, 99, which houses ancient Roman artifacts, including mosaics and pottery. (Open 9am-8pm. €2.50, students €1.50. Guided visits in English available M-Sa 9:30am-1pm and 3:30-7:30pm. €5, students €3.) The town also boasts the 12th-century **Basilica di San Gavino**, the largest and oldest Romanesque-Pisan church in Sardinia.

Soak up some rays at the two **beaches** along Porto Torres's shore. Though framed by the industrial port in the background, **Spiaggia Lungo Scoglio**, 250m from the port, is family-friendly, complete with a metal dolphin diving over a rock that juts out of the water. **Spaggia di Balai**, about 10min. down Lungomare Balai, is larger and more secluded, separated from the road by a small, grassy park.

PALAU   ☎0789

Situated on the luminous waters of Sardinia's northern coast, Palau is both a gorgeous destination and a centrally located base from which to explore Costa Smeralda and La Maddalena. Palau's most famous inhabitant is the *roccia dell'orsù*, an enormous rock that the tireless mistral winds have carved into the shape of a bear. It was an object of intrigue even in Homer's day, now immortalized in his *Odyssey* with a warning of the ferocious *Lestrigoni* people that lived around it. Palau is now a heavily touristed town composed of modern buildings painted in typically Sardinian pastel shades. The real attraction is the incomparable coastline nearby.

▐◪ TRANSPORTATION AND PRACTICAL INFORMATION. The port end of **Via Nazionale**, Palau's single major thoroughfare, contains a white building that houses a bar, ferry ticket offices, and a newsstand that sells ARST bus tickets (buses stop outside). **ARST buses** run to Olbia (14 per day; €2.32 to the *centro*, €2.58 to the port) and Santa Teresa di Gallura (7 per day 7:55am-9:25pm, €1.72). **EnerRmaR** (☎199 76 00 02) and **Saremar Ferries** (☎0789 70 92 70) serve the island of La Maddalena (15min.; 3 per hr. 7:15am-2am; round-trip €5.80, under 12 €2.20, cars €8.40-16.80, bicycles free). **Centro Servizio Autonoleggio**, V. Nazionale, 2, rents cars. (☎0789 70 85 65. 20+. From €45 per day, including insurance and unlimited mileage. Open 24hr. AmEx/MC/V.)

Palau's **tourist office**, V. Nazionale, 96, slightly uphill from the center of town, offers info on beaches, outdoor activities, and tours of neighboring islands. (☎/fax 0789 70 95 70. Open M-Sa 8am-1pm and 3:30-7pm, Su 8:30am-1pm.) **Banca di**

SARDINIA

Sassari, V. Roma, 9, has **currency exchange** and **ATMs** in front. (Open M-F 8:20am-1:20pm and 2:30-3:30pm, Sa 8:20am-12:30pm.) In case of **emergency,** dial ☎113, contact the **carabinieri** (☎112), call the **medical clinic** (☎0789 70 93 96), or contact the **hospital** in Olbia (☎0789 52 20). **Farmacia Nicolai** is at V. Delle Ginestre, 19. (☎0789 70 95 16, for urgent needs, 329 953 46 93. Open M-Sa 9am-1pm and 5-8pm. AmEx/MC/V.) The **post office** is in a piazza at the intersection of V. Garibaldi and V. La Maddalena. (☎0789 70 85 27. Open M-F 8:15am-1:15pm, Sa 8:15am-12:45pm.)

⌐⌐ ACCOMMODATIONS AND FOOD. Accommodations in Palau are often prohibitively expensive. **Hotel La Roccia ❹,** V. dei Mille, 15, has a lobby built around an enormous boulder, and themed rooms, such as "Il Faro" (the lighthouse). All 22 rooms have balcony, bath, A/C, phone, and TV. (☎0789 70 95 28; www.hotellaroccia.com. Breakfast €8-10. Call ahead for reservations. Single €45-80; doubles €75-125. Extra bed additional 35%. AmEx/MC/V.) **Hotel del Molo ❹,** on V. dei Ciclopi, 25, has a pleasant staff and 14 quiet, air-conditioned rooms, all with bath, TV, phone, and fridge, some with balcony and charming sea view. (☎0789 70 80 42. Breakfast €4. Singles €35-92; doubles €55-115; triples €81-155. AmEx/MC/V.) Among the attractive camping options, **☒Acapulco ❶,** Loc. Punta Palau, has a private beach, a bar with nightly piano music (live singer July-Aug.), a pizzeria, and a restaurant. It also arranges underwater spear-fishing and excursions to La Maddalena Archipelago. (☎0789 70 94 97; www.campingacapulco.com. Open Mar. 1-Oct. 15. Reserve ahead in summer. Adults €8-16.50, children ages 4-12 €5.50-11, tent and hot shower included. Bungalows with mandatory half pension €38-54. 4-person caravans €52-89. Set of 2 towels €6. Electricity €2.50. AmEx/MC/V.) **☒Baia Saraceno,** Loc. Puna Nera, 1, also offers picturesque camping facilities 500m outside Palau. White stucco bungalows, restaurant, pizzeria, and a bar are interspersed among trees along the coastline. The facility arranges water sports and trips to nearby islands. (☎078 970 94 03; www.baiasaraceno.com. Adults €8-16.50, children €5.50-11. Bungalows with half pension €38-54; bungalows with kitchen €62-115; 4-person caravan €52-89. Electricity €2.50. AmEx/MC/V.)

Numerous *panaterie* and alimentari line V. Nazionale, and a **market** every Friday (8am-1pm) crowds the harbor with fresh cheeses, meats, clothing, and crafts. The friendly waitstaff of **☒L'Uva Fragola ❶,** P. V. Emanuele, 2, serve a variety of crisp, refreshing salads (€5.50-10.50), spaghetti (€4.50-7), and 39 types of creative pizzas (€3.56-8.00) with toppings like octopus and egg. Savor a homemade dessert at the bright green tables. (☎0789 70 87 65. Cover €1. Open daily noon-3pm and 7-11pm. MC/V.) **Ristorante Robertino ❸,** V. Nazionale, 20, is pleasant restaurant with flavorful pastas (spaghetti with shellfish; €11) and delicious fresh fish. (☎0789 70 96 10. *Primi* €5.50-12, *secondi* €8-16. Cover €1.55. Open Tu-Su 1-2:30pm and 8-10:30pm. MC/V.) **Ristorante Il Covo ❸,** V. Sportiva, 12, serves seafood and traditional, meat-heavy Sardinian cuisine at reasonable prices. The homemade *tagliolini* pasta with cuttlefish ink, fish eggs, and zucchini (€9) is an intriguing winner. (☎0789 70 96 08. Pizza €5.80-8. *Primi* €6.80-10, *secondi* €5-14.50. 4-course Sardinian dinner €30. Cover €1.90. AmEx/MC/V.)

◎ SIGHTS. Little **Spiaggia Palau Vecchia** is the beach to the left of the port when facing the water, and down the stairs. Its shores are shaded most of the day, and therefore not the best for tanning purposes. The **Roccia dell'Orsù** is Palau's trademark curiosity. **Caramelli buses** run to the rock at **Capo d'Orso** (15min.; 5 per day 7:30am-6pm, last return 6:20pm; €0.62) from the port, 3km from town along V. Capo d'Orso. Caramelli also runs to **Porto Pollo** (30min.; 5 per day 8:15am-7:20pm, last return 7:55pm; €1.19), a beautiful beach dotted with Mediterranean scrub and colorful seaweed just under the water. Several private boat companies run all-day tours of the archipelago (see **La Maddalena: Sights,** p. 738).

LA MADDALENA ARCIPELAGO ☎0789

Corsica and Sardinia were once joined by a massive land bridge; La Maddalena, Caprera, and the 50-plus smaller islands that surround them are its fragmented remains. Tourists cram the major streets, tasting treats at the many *pasticcerie*, and then move on to the calm, white sand beaches. But tourism has not spoiled the islands; the entire archipelago is a national park, and commercial development is strictly regulated. Italian patriots mob La Maddalena for their own reasons: their national hero, the unifier Giuseppe Garibaldi, made the nearby island of Caprera his home while he was in exile. With white sands, crystal clear waters, and miles of roads for biking, La Maddelena is a paradise for beach bums, backpackers, and outdoor adventurers.

TRANSPORTATION AND PRACTICAL INFORMATION

EneRmaR (☎199 76 00 02) and Saremar (☎0789 70 92 70) run **ferries** between Palau and La Maddalena (15min., 3 per hr. 7:15am-2am, €2.90, €8:40-16:80 per car, bicycles free). For **taxi service,** call ☎0789 73 65 00 or 72 20 80. Rent **bikes** and **motor scooters** at **Nicola,** V. Amendola, 18. (☎0789 73 54 00. Bikes €10 per day. Motor scooters €20-50. Half-day rates available. Open daily 8am-8pm.)

A **tourist office** is in P. des Geneys, on the waterfront. (☎0789 73 63 21. Open May-Oct. M-Sa 9am-1pm and 4:30-6:30pm.) A **Banco di Sardegna,** on V. Amendola off P. XXIV Febbraio, has **currency exchange** and a 24hr. **ATM.** (Open M-F 8:20am-1:20pm and 2:35-4:05pm.) In case of **emergency,** call the **carabinieri** (☎0789 73 70 04 or 73 69 43), an **ambulance** (☎0789 73 74 97), or the **hospital** (☎0789 79 12 00). The **Farmacia Russino** is at V. Garibaldi, 5. (☎0789 73 73 90. Open M-F and Su 9am-1pm and 5-8:30pm.) **Patsi Net Internet Point,** V. Montanara, 4, has fast connections. (☎0789 73 10 55, fax 72 19 19. €6 per hr. Open daily 9am-2pm and 6-11pm. AmEx/MC/V.) A self-service **laundromat,** Azzura Lavanderia, is at V. Dei Mille, 3. (☎389 97 240 27. Wash €3.50 for 6kg, dry €5. Open M-Sa 9am-1pm and 4:30-8pm. Cash only.) A **post office** is in P. Umberto, 1. (☎0789 73 75 95. Open M-F 8:15am-6:15pm, Sa 8:15am-noon.) **Postal Code:** 07024.

ACCOMMODATIONS AND FOOD

Hotel Arcipelago ❹, V. Indipendenza 11, is a good deal, though it's a 20min. walk from the town proper. From P. Umberto, follow V. Mirabello along the water until reaching the intersection with the stoplight. Turn left here, then turn right at Ristorante Sottovento onto V. Indipendenza. Continue uphill, taking the first left on a branch of the main road. The hotel is around the corner from the grocery store. Twelve rooms come tastefully furnished with wooden furniture and paintings, and all have TV, phone, large bath, and nice views. (☎0789 72 73 28. Breakfast included. Reservation required July-Aug. Singles €43-55; doubles €53-82; triples €77-110. V.) Next door, **Hotel La Conchiglia ❹,** V. Indipendenza, 3, offers seven comfortable rooms, all with bath, TV, phone, A/C, and fridge. Friendly manager Andrè and family give excellent advice on local attractions. (☎0789 72 80 26. Breakfast included. Singles €40-70; doubles €60-90. AmEx/MC/V.)

Pick up the basics at the Dimeglio **supermarket,** V. Amendola, 6. (☎0789 73 90 05. Open M-Sa 8:30am-1pm and 3-8pm, Su 9am-1pm. MC/V.) The true find, **Ristorante il Mirto ❹,** in Località Punta della Gatta, lies about 7km from the city,

SARDINIA

though €14 taxi fare is worth it. This authentic Sardinian trattoria serves traditional *primi* such as hearty ravioli and a tender roast suckling pig *secondo*. The
staff is attentive and accommodating. (☎0789 73 90 56. Reservation recommended in summer. *Primi* €10-12, *secondi* €8-18. Open noon-3pm and 7:30pm-
midnight. Cash only.) Young and hip locals flock to ◪**Garden Bar ❸**, V. Garibaldi,
61, for its tasty, varied cuisine, friendly owner, and couches at the tables
upstairs. (☎0787 73 88 25. Pizza €3.50-7.50. *Primi* €5-13, *secondi* €5-20. Open
daily 11am-1:30am. MC/V.) Get to **Il Forno di Benatti ❶**, V. Principe Amadedeo, 28,
for a slice of *focaccia sarda* (€1 per kg) before savvy locals snap it up. An enormous variety of pizza slices, thick and laden with toppings, are available to go.
(☎0789 73 70 60. Other focaccia €0.50 per serving. Pizza €0.90-1.30. Open M-Sa
7:30am-2:15pm and 3-8pm. Cash only.)

🏖 🏝 BEACHES AND ISLANDS

The little islands surrounding La Maddalena are paradises of uninhabited natural
beauty. Their national park status protects them from development and curbs
the activity of tourists who bathe in the sparkling coves. Some claim that these
waters, radiating in brilliant shades of green and blue, are the clearest in the
world. Some spots have been closed off altogether, such as the forested island
Budelli and its beach, **Spiaggia Rossa**. Fortunately, the nearby island **Razzoli** has
equally magnificent swimming holes, and sightseers can still set out to islands
such as ◪**Santa Maria**, with its long, white sand cove, by boat. Santa Maria's **lighthouse**, a 20min. stroll from the beach down a labeled trail, looks out over the surrounding islands, including nearby ◪**Spargi**. The waters in Spargi's **Cala Verde**
bay shimmer in stunning shades of green. On Spargi's western side, lovers
canoodle on the shores of the pristine **Cala dell'Amore**. Around **Cala Corsara**,
windswept rock formations reward the adventurous with spectacular vistas.
Lacking a private yacht or powerboat, the only way to visit the archipelago is on
an all-day **boat tour**. Companies like ◪**Delfino Bianco di Ulisse** (☎347 366 36 28 or
0789 73 86 66) send ticketsellers to the docks mornings and evenings. Packing up
to 100 people, the cruises are fun and informative, as guides point out the garish
or whimsical rock formations along the way. Tours cost €25-30 and typically
include a pasta lunch and two or three 2hr. stops at beaches along the way, often
at Spargi's Cala Corsara and **Cala Santa Maria.** Most boats leave between 10 and
11am and return between 5 and 6pm. Purchase tickets one day ahead. Private
tours are also available.

Buses run from La Maddalena to Caprera's Punta Rossa (6 per day 9:42am-
1:15pm, last return 6:40pm), giving travelers access to beaches along the eastern
peninsula. Sunbathers fill the shores of Spiaggia del Relitto, whose wide strip of
white sand and expansive swimming cove have made it one of Caprera's largest
and most popular beaches. To reach it, follow the main road through Caprera to
Punta Rossa and turn left on the dirt path after the beach Due Mare, following it
for 1km. Visitors can rent chairs (€10) and umbrellas (€3) or explore the rugged
coastline in paddle boats and kayaks (€10 per hr.), available along the beach daily
9am-7pm. If Caprera doesn't satiate the quest for the perfect panorama, bike or
motor La Maddalena's **Panoramica dei Colmi,** about 25km of paved road circling the
island. The road passes by marvelous sea views and attractive beach destinations,
including **Cala Lunga** and the watersport-friendly **Cala Spalmatore.**

The tiny and secluded ◪**Cala Coticcio** is a postcard-perfect cove with fine sand
and crystal-clear water. It's easiest to reach by boat; on foot, turn left at the first
street after the Casa di Garibaldi and climb the hill for 4km. Then follow the steep
rocky trail marked with gray arrows for 30min. and take a left at the fork.

SANTA TERESA DI GALLURA ☎0789

Perched on a hilltop on the sea, it is not immediately clear to new arrivals that Santa Teresa is in fact near water. But as soon as you crest the hill in the middle of town, the sight of the strikingly blue sea is breathtaking. The little town is a lovely launching point for exploring coves, inlets, and the Capo Testa, a peninsula of wind-sculpted granite with magnificent beaches. Santa Teresa boasts its own sandy beach, Rena Bianca, from which the hazy shores of Corsica are visible.

▐ TRANSPORTATION

ARST buses (☎0789 55 30 00) depart from V. Eleonora d'Arborea, in the parking lot across the street from the port office, and run to: Olbia (1¾hr., 6 per day to town and airport 6:10am-8:50pm, €3.72); Palau (40min., 12 per day 6:10am-8:50pm, €1.76); Sassari (3hr., 5 per day 5:15am-7:15pm, €5.83). Buy tickets at **Baby Bar** on V. Nazionale, 100m from the bus stop. **Saremar** (☎0789 75 41 56) runs **ferries** to Bonifacio, Corsica (1hr., 8-10 per day 8am-8:30pm, €9-12 including port tax for Corsica). Tickets are available at the office on V. del Porto. Open daily 9am-12:30pm and 2-10:30pm. For ferry details, see p. 720.) For a **taxi**, call ☎0789 75 42 37, 75 44 07, or 74 10 24.

✳ ▐ ORIENTATION AND PRACTICAL INFORMATION

The ARST bus stop is at the far end of the parking lot that is across the street from the post office. Facing the post office, turn right, head to the intersection, and turn right on **Via Nazionale.** Head for the church at the end of the street, in **Piazza San Vittorio,** and turn right again to reach **Piazza Vittorio Emanuele.** The tourist office is on the opposite side of the piazza.

Tourist Office: P. V. Emanuele, 24 (☎0789 75 41 27). Provides help with accommodations and lists rooms for rent. Ask about horse, moped, and boat rentals. Open June-Sept. M-Sa 8:30am-1pm and 3:30-7:30pm, Su 9am-noon and 5-7pm; Oct.-May M-Sa 8am-1pm and 3:30-6:30pm.

Boat Tours: Consorzio delle Bocche, P. V. Emanuele, 16 (☎0789 75 51 12), offers tours of the archipelago. Daily full-day tour 9:15am-5:30pm. Lunch included. €35, ages 4-12 €18. Office open daily 10am-1pm and 6pm-12:30am.

Horseback Riding: Scuola di Turismo Equestre/Li Nibbari (☎337 81 71 89), in Marazzino, 4km from town. Guided excursions €18 per hr.

Scuba Diving: No Limits Diving Center, V. del Porto, 16 (☎/fax 0789 75 90 26), offers guided excursions (€35-50). AmEx/MC/V.

Car Rental: GULP (Hertz), V. Nazionale, 58 (☎0789 75 56 98; info@gulpimmobiliare.it). 25+. €50-150 per day, €260-600 per week, insurance included. Open M-Sa 8am-1pm and 5-7:30pm. AmEx/MC/V.

Scooter and Bike Rental: Global Noleggio, V. Maria Teresa, 50 (☎0789 75 50 80 or 338 295 61 06; www.globalinformation.it). Motor scooters €18-50 per day, mountain bikes €8-20 per day. Open daily 9am-1pm, 3-8pm, and 9pm-midnight. AmEx/MC/V.

Emergency: ☎113. **Ambulance** (☎118). **Police** (☎112), on V. Nazionale.

Medical Clinic: ☎0789 75 40 79. On V. Carlo Felice. Open 24hr.

Pharmacy: P. S. Vittorio, 2 (☎0789 75 53 38). Open daily June-Aug. 9am-1pm and 5-8:30pm; reduced hours in low season. List of late-night pharmacies posted.

Internet Access: Happy Phone, V. Imbriani, 1 (☎0789 75 43 17), behind the tower. 4 computers. €1 for 10min., €5 per hr. Open M-Sa 9am-1pm, 4-8pm, and 9pm-midnight; Su 10am-1pm and 4-8pm.

Post Office: ☎0789 73 53 24. On V. d'Arborea, near the bus stop. Open M-F 8:05am-12:45pm, Sa 8am-12:30pm. **Postal Code:** 07028.

ACCOMMODATIONS

Hotel Moderno, V. Umberto, 39 (☎0789 75 42 33, fax 75 92 05), centrally located off V. Nazionale. 16 comfortable rooms sport patterned bedspreads, bright bath, A/C, and balcony with chairs. Friendly staff. Buffet breakfast included. Open Apr.-Sept. Singles €38-55; doubles €62-100. MC/V. ❸

Hotel Bellavista, V. Sonnino, 8 (☎/fax 0789 75 41 62), 2 blocks past P. V. Emanuele, close to the beach. Airy rooms all have large tiled bath; many have balcony with fantastic sea view. Breakfast €4. Singles €31-33; doubles €49-58; triple €60. MC/V. ❸

Hotel Marinaro, V. G.M. Angioy, 48 (☎0789 75 41 12; www.hotelmarinaro.it). Spacious and modern, with colorful decor and elegant dining room with outdoor seating. All rooms equipped with bath, A/C, TV, and phone; some with terrace. Breakfast €8. Half pension required in Aug. Singles €45-75, with half pension €60-90; doubles €75-100/ €90-150; triples €85-125. AmEx/MC/V. ❹

Pensione Scano, V. Lazio, 4 (☎0789 75 44 47). Small, bright rooms share large baths. Trim wooden furniture and paintings decorate the halls. Breakfast included. Singles €23; doubles with bath €45. Half pension €36-68. MC/V. ❷

FOOD

Alimentari line V. Aniscara, off P. V. Emanuele. A fruit and clothing **market** by the bus station opens Thursday morning and runs until the early evening. The SISA **supermarket,** on V. Nazionale next to Banco di Sardegna, has picnic supplies. (Open M-Sa 8am-1pm and 4:30-8pm, Su 9am-noon. MC/V.)

Papè Satan, V. Lamarmora, 22 (☎0789 75 50 48). Look for the sign off V. Nazionale. Neapolitan family cooks pizza in a traditional brick oven. Try the devilishly rich *pizza alla Papè Satan* with cream, butter, mozzarella, and prosciutto (€7.50) or the *quattro stagioni* (€8) with anchovies. Cover €2. Open daily noon-2:30pm and 7pm-midnight. ❷

Ristorante Azzurra, V. Graziani, 9 (☎0789 75 47 89). Friendly staff serves delicious fish and homemade pasta like *tagliatelle* with clams, tuna eggs, and tomatoes (€8.50). *Primi* €7-13, *secondi* €6-16. Open daily noon-2pm and 7-11:30pm. AmEx/MC/V. ❸

Da Thomas, V. Val d'Aosta, 22 (☎0789 75 51 33). Enjoy fresh fish and a menu full of shellfish treats on a relaxed outdoor patio, away from the madding crowds. *Primi* €6-14, *secondi* €7-14. Open daily 12:30-3pm and 7:30-11pm. AmEx/MC/V. ❸

Griglieria Paldo, V. Garibaldi, 4 (☎0789 75 58 60). This pub-turned-restaurant, serving a variety of decent grilled meats, retains its colorful mosaic decor and casual atmosphere. Pasta €6.50-10. Cover €1.80. Open daily noon-3pm and 5pm-2am. MC/V. ❷

SIGHTS AND BEACHES

Long before tourists discovered it, Santa Teresa was home to **Lu Brandali,** one of the largest and least disturbed prehistoric villages in the region. From V. Nazionale, turn right on an unlabeled dirt road across from SISA. From here, a narrow path leads to a massive Sardinian **Tomba di Giganti,** communal village graves used between the 14th and 10th centuries BC. Due to their enormous dimensions and stone construction, the tombs were believed in later years to hold legendary giants. Overgrown trails wind uphill past the old village dwellings and a pair of towers before culminating at the ruins of a *Nuraghe*. The village is not very well labeled, so stop by the tourist office for historical information on the site.

V. XX Settembre leads toward the sea. As the road forks, bear left and continue past Hotel Miramar to reach **Piazza Libertà**. The Argonese **Tower of Longonsardo** (c. 1358-1577), on the ruins of an ancient **nuraghe**, is framed by a sea backdrop. Corsica's shore is visible through the mist. (Open daily 10am-12:30pm and 4-7pm. Entrance €1.50.) Walk down the stairs to reach **Spiaggia Rena Bianca,** a popular white sand beach in a swimming cove. (Chair rental €5, with umbrella €15. Paddle boats €10 per hr., kayaks €5-8 per hr. Open daily 8am-7pm. Cash only.)

Some of the town's most notable attractions lie 3km away, at the rugged peninsula **Capo Testa**. Take the **Sardabus** from the post office (10min.; 5 per day; €0.67, round-trip €1.24) or by bike or on foot along **V. Capo Testa**, off V. Tibula from V. Nazionale. The bus stops at **Spiaggia Rena di Ponente**, where two seas meet to form long beaches ideal for water sports. (Deck chair rental €6; umbrella €6. Single canoes €5 per hr., doubles €8 per hr.; windsurfers €12 per hr.) From the beach, a gated dirt road leads 25min. to the remote and stunning ◪**Valley de la Luna.** Once an international hippie community, it holds abandoned fire rings, rock paintings, and carved posts, and is ringed by granite trails great for exploring. V. Capo Testa continues for 2.5km along the peninsula to a picturesque abandoned **faro** (lighthouse). Steps cut into the rock below the lighthouse lead to a **watchtower.**

◪ NIGHTLIFE

Groove's Cafe, V. XX Settembre, 2, has a funky second floor with cushioned chairs and outdoor balcony seating—perfect for nodding along to house and acid jazz after 11pm. (Cocktails €5-7. Open daily 6am-4am. Cash only.) On the other side of the piazza, **Bar Conti,** V. Regina Margherita, 2, caters to a more upscale tourist crowd with multi-colored drinks. DJs spin music upstairs on the dance floor. (☎ 0789 75 42 71. Beer from €2, cocktails from €7. Open daily 8am-3am.)

OLBIA   ☎ 0789

As the closest port to the mainland, Olbia is a major transportation hub. Its main industry is housing and feeding the thousands of tourists coming through the port and airport daily. Located a short distance from the Golfo Aranci and some of the most beautiful beaches on the Mediterranean on the Costa Smeralda, it serves well as a launching pad for other, more interesting locations. For new arrivals, take a breath and take a quick stroll past the shops and restaurants, then head elsewhere.

▉ TRANSPORTATION

Flights: Olbia airport is served by **Meridiana** (☎ 199 11 13 33). Local bus #2 runs from the airport to the city center (€0.55).

Trains: FS (☎ 0789 224 77) on V. Pala, just off of C. Umberto. Service to: **Sassari** (2hr., 3 per day, €5.90) with connections to **Alghero, Cagliari, Oristano,** and **Porto Torres** (2¼hr., 2:08pm, €7.05).

Buses: ARST station, C. Umberto, 64 (☎ 0789 211 97), in the heart of the city. To: **Palau** (1hr., 14 per day 4:20am-11:15pm, €2.32); **Porto Cervo** (1hr., 5 per day 6:25am-4pm, €2.70) **Santa Teresa di Gallura** (2hr., 7 per day 6:45am-8:15pm, €3.72); and **Sassari** (3hr., 6:15am and 8:05pm, €7.64). Buy tickets at the ticket office in the station. **Sun Lines:** V. Pozzo, 23 (☎ 0789 508 85), the airport (☎ 348 260 98 81), and Stazione Marittima (☎ 0789 20 80 82), runs shuttle service to Porto Cervo and Palau from the airport, Stazione Marittima, and P. Crispi (4 per day, €12).

Ferries: Tirrenia (☎ 0789 246 91), in Stazione Marittima. (See chart, p. 720.)

SARDINIA

Car Rental: Avis, V. Ghiberti, 14 (☎0789 539 60; www.avisautonoleggio.it) off of V. Aldo Moro. Cars from €61.30 per day, including insurance and taxes. 21+. Open daily 8am-11pm. AmEx/MC/V. Many rental companies also have airport offices.

Taxi: At the airport (☎0789 691 50) and in the city center (☎0789 227 18).

✳🛈 ORIENTATION AND PRACTICAL INFORMATION

Ferries arrive at **Stazione Marittima,** 1km east of the city center on **Viale Isola Bianca.** ARST buses run from Stazione Marittima to the **ARST station** on **Corso Umberto,** Olbia's main street. **Piazza Margherita** is at the intersection of C. Umberto and **Viale Regina Elena,** which runs to **Piazza Crispi. Viale Umberto** is at the end of C. Umberto and runs along the water. At C. Umberto's other end is **Via G. D'Annunzio,** which becomes **Viale Aldo Moro** and has many shops and snack bars.

Tourist Office: V. Piro, 1 (☎0789 214 53), just off C. Umberto. Helpful, English-speaking staff provides free **maps** and information on accommodations and transportation. Open M-F 8:30am-2pm and 3:30-6pm, Sa 8:30am-2pm.

Emergency: ☎113. **Carabinieri** (☎0789 212 21). **Ambulance** (☎0789 55 22 01).

Hospital: V. Aldo Moro (☎0789 55 22 00).

Pharmacy, C. Umberto, 134 (☎0789 213 10). Open M-Sa 9am-1pm and 5pm-8:20pm.

Internet Access: InterSmeraldo, V. Porto Romano, 8/B (☎0789 253 66). 9 fast computers in a pleasantly air-conditioned room. Fax service available. €2.50 for 30min., €5 for 1hr. Open M-Sa 10am-11pm, Su 5-11pm. Cash only.

Currency Exchange: Banca Intesa, across C. Umberto from the ARST station, has an ATM. Open M-F 8:30am-1:30pm and 2:45-4:15pm, Sa 8:30am-noon.

Post Office: V. Bari, 7 (☎0789 20 74 00). Take V. Acquedotto from C. Umberto to the intersection of V. Acquedotto and V. Bari. Open M-Sa 8am-1pm. **Postal Code:** 07026.

♟🏠 ACCOMMODATIONS AND FOOD

Olbia lacks budget accommodations, so if that's what you're looking for, either ask about *agriturismo* options at the tourist office or head elsewhere. For those who can afford it, Olbia does have some splendid, albeit expensive, options. **Hotel Centrale ❸,** C. Umberto 85, is the best deal in town. Centrally located, all rooms are clean with private bath. Some have A/C and balconies as well. (☎0789 230 17. Reception on the 2nd fl. Singles €40; doubles €60. AmEx/MC/V.) **Hotel Cavour ❹,** V. Cavour, 22, in the heart of Olbia, has 21 clean rooms with A/V, bath, and fridge. (☎0789 20 40 33. Singles €45-60, with half pension €66-81; doubles €70-85, with half pension €112-127. AmEx/MC/V.) With a homey restaurant on the first floor, **Hotel Terranova ❺,** V. Garibaldi, 3, lets recently renovated rooms with A/C, bath, and TV. (☎0789 223 95. Wheelchair accessible. Breakfast included. Singles €60; doubles €80. AmEx/MC/V.)

The many restaurants along C. Umberto advertise overpriced tourist menus, and cater to a mostly foreign crowd. Head down the little sidestreets for better, less pricey restaurants. The Super Pan **supermarket,** P.Crispi, 2, is perfect for stocking up on supplies. (☎0789 263 82. Open M-Sa 8:30am-9pm, Su 8:30am-1:30pm.) **Gelateria Smeralda ❶,** C. Umberto, 124, has the best gelato in town. Try the purple local specialty *mirto* (myrtle) for a change of pace. (☎0789 264 43. Cones from €1, *maxi* size €3. Open M-Sa 4pm-midnight. Cash only.) Just off C. Umberto, **Pizzeria Il Pomodoro ❷,** V. Sassari, 10, serves decent pizzas at reasonable prices. Try the *San Felice* (with salmon and shrimp) for €8. (☎0789 288 80. Pizza €3.10-8.

Open M and W-Su 7:30-11:30pm. AmEx/MC/V.) **Il Gambero ❷**, V. Lamamora, 15, near the train station, is a nice alternative to the tourist-targeted fare on C. Umberto. The *pennette al piccolo mare* (€6) makes good use of one of Olbia's best assets: fresh seafood. The Sardinian specialty dessert *seadas* (€3.50) is a must. (☎0789 238 74. *Primi* €4.50-7, *secondi* €4-12. Open daily 12:30-4:30pm and 7:30-10:30pm. AmEx/MC/V.) Set in an old-fashioned stone house, **Da Paolo ❸**, V. Cavour, 15, serves delicious victuals in a lively family atmosphere. Browse the restaurant-owned shop next door for some Sardinian products. (☎0789 216 75. *Primi* €6.50-10, *secondi* €6.50-14. Open M-Sa 12:30-3:30pm and 7:30-11pm, Su 7:30-11pm. AmEx/MC/V.)

COSTA SMERALDA ☎0789

A jutting peninsula between the Golfo di Arzachena and the Golfo di Cugnana, Costa Smeralda was once a barely inhabited, underdeveloped tract of land. In the 1960s, a consortium transformed the coast into the exclusive playground for the rich that it is today. With stunning hills, quiet beaches, and sightings of the rich and famous, Costa Smeralda is the new black of European vacationing, and worth a visit, most likely as a day trip from a more affordable location.

Costa Smeralda boasts some of the most lovely and secluded ■**beaches** in the world. Many are privately owned, but even those available to the public are pristine and worth the trek. Most are accessible only by pedestrian dirt roads that connect them to the main roads. Along **S.P. 94** there are small parking areas and dirt tracks that lead to glorious beaches. The beaches of Costa Smeralda are not only a must-see for travelers to Sardinia, but for any traveler to the Mediterranean region.

Spiaggia Capriccioli boasts shimmering water, miles of white sand, and even fewer people than many of the other beaches. From Porto Cervo, take **S.P. 59** toward Olbia and take a left onto S.P. 94, following the signs for Cala Volpe. Continue following signs for Cala Volpe (do not turn right and continue on S.P. 94) until you can go no further. From this point, take the dirt track on the left for Spiaggia Capriccioli, and the one on the right for Spiaggia La Celvia, where emerald water is framed by white sand and trees, and sailboats bob lazily in the sea. **Spiaggia Rena Bianca**, further south along the coast in the direction of Olbia, leads toward other great beaches, including **Spiaggia di Cala Razza di Juncu, Spiaggia di Cala Petra Ruja,** and **Spiaggia di Liscia Ruja,** all dotting the coast one after another. The crystal waves and white sands are perfectly edenic. All are accessible from tracks off of S.P. 94, starting about 1.5km north of the junction with **S.P. 73** coming from Olbia, and about 2km south of the junction with S.P. 59, from Porto Cervo.

ARST buses run from Porto Cervo and Baia Sardinia to Arzachena and Olbia (1hr., 5 per day 9:25am-8:05pm, €2.70). Otherwise, there is no public transportation on the peninsula. Some beaches are within walking distance, but for most, car, bicycle, or scooter rental is a must. **S.S. 125**, the main highway between Olbia and Arzachena, cuts just to the south of Costa Smeralda. S.P. 59 makes a loop around the peninsula, stops in most major towns, and junctions with S.P. 125. From Olbia take S.S. 125 to S.P. 59 and follow the signs for Porto Cervo and Baia Sardinia. Once on the peninsula, take S.P. 59 from either Baia Sardinia or Porto Cervo and follow the signs to Abbiadori (to the southeast), then take S.P. 94 to many of the beaches along the coast. From Olbia take S.S. 125 for 7km, take a right onto S.P. 73 and go for another 7km, and then take a right onto S.P. 94.

The ARST bus stop in Porto Cervo is at the uphill end of V. della Marina, the main street. Follow V. della Marina downhill to the water and the famous **Piazzetta,** filled with high-end boutiques, famous restaurants, and ultra-chic people. In Baia Sardinia, ARST buses stop near **Piazza Centrale** at the center of town. From the stop, turn left and walk downhill 50m to the piazza. The nearest **AAST tourist office** to Costa Smeralda is in Arzachena, on V. Dettori just off of Viale Costa Smeralda, the main street in town and has info on accommodations. (☎0789 824 64. Open M-Sa 9am-1pm and 3:30-6:30pm, Su 9am-1pm.) ARST buses stop in several places on V. Costa Smeralda; simply ask the driver for the nearest one to V. Dettori.

If you want to stay close to the action, head to **Villaggio Camping Cugnana ❶**, Loc. Cugnana on S.P. 125, equidistant to Olbia and Costa Smeralda. It boasts clean bungalows, all with bath and some with kitchen and A/C. Take the ARST bus from either Olbia or Arzachena and ask the bus driver to stop at Villaggio Camping Cugnana or call for driving directions. (☎0789 331 84. 2 person bungalows €260-585 per week; 4 person bungalows €450-920 per week. €155 refundable security deposit for all bungalows. Camping €8-16.20 per adult, children 4-12 €7-9.60, tent included. Open Apr. 1-Sept. 30. AmEx/MC/V.) Most of the world-class restaurants of Costa Smeralda are beyond the reach of budget travelers, though there are some snack bars with slightly more affordable fare—on the whole you're better off packing a lunch. The towns of Porto Cervo and Baia Sardinia are the only points on the peninsula accessible by public transportation.

ORISTANO   ☎0783

This modest-sized city's charm reveals itself in the church festivals that color its streets, in Sardinia's largest duomo, and in the small, active historical center preserved amid the surrounding commerce. In the 7th century, the inhabitants of Tharros repelled invasion after invasion until a band of merciless Moorish pirates forced them to abandon their homes. With nowhere else to go, they set up camp around nearby Oristano, which soon became an important independent commercial port under the rule of Eleanora of Arborea, one of Sardinia's most important saints. Today the city is a base for exploring the natural and historical splendor of the nearby Sinis Peninsula and its enticing Phoenician and Roman ruins at Tharros, the awe-inspiring arch at S'Archittu, and the beaches of Is Aruttas.

▐ TRANSPORTATION

Trains: ☎0783 89 20 21 for schedules. In P. Ungheria, 1km from the town center. **Luggage storage** available (see **Practical Information**). To: **Cagliari** (1-2hr., 16 per day 4:50am-9:24pm, €4.55); **Macomer** (1hr., 10 per day 5:40am-9:25pm, €2.90); **Olbia** (2½hr., 2 per day 1:20pm and 7:48pm, €8.85) via **Ozieri, Chilivani,** or **Macomer.** To get to **Sassari,** connect via Macomer or Chivilani.

Buses: PANI, V. Lombardia, 30 (☎0783 21 22 68). Ticket office inside Bar Blu, on V. Lombaridia. Open daily 7am-10pm. To: **Cagliari** (1½hr., 4 per day 8:55am-9:34pm, €5.84); **Nuoro** (2hr., 4 per day 7:05am-7:50pm, €5.84); **Sassari** (2¼hr., 4 per day 7:05am-7:50pm, €7.18). **ARST,** on V. Cagliari 102, runs local routes (☎0783 711 85 or 800 86 50 42). **Luggage storage** available. Ticket office open daily 7:30am-2pm and 4:30-6pm. To: **Cagliari** (2hr., 7:10am and 2:10pm, €5.94); **Putzu Idu** (dir: Su Pallosu; 50min., 7 per day 7am-6:18pm, €1.76); **San Giovanni di Sinis** (July-Oct.; dir: Is Aruttas; 40min.; 5 per day 9am-7:05pm, last return 7:45pm; €1.45); **Santa Caterina** (dir: Scano Montiferro; 40min., 8 per day 7:50am-7:05pm, €1.76).

Taxis: At P. Roma (☎0783 702 80) and at the train station (☎0783 743 28). Available 7am-1pm and 3-8:30pm. For 24hr. service, call ☎336 81 35 85.

Car Rental: Avis, V. Liguria, 17 (☎0783 31 06 38). Cars €49-121. Insurance included. 25+. Open M-F 9am-1pm and 4-7:30pm, Sa 9am-noon. AmEx/MC/V.

Scooter Rental: Marco Moto, V. Cagliari, 99/101 (☎0783 31 00 36). Rents mountain bikes €8.50 per day, scooters €44-75 per day, and scooters with sidecars €100 per day. Insurance and helmet included. Open M-F 8:30am-1pm and 3:30-8pm, Sa 8:30am-1pm. AmEx/MC/V.

Bike Rental: Ciclosport Cabella, V. Busachi, 2/4 (☎/fax 0783 727 14). Large selection of beautiful mountain and road bikes. Extremely knowledgeable staff. Open M-F 9am-1pm and 4-8pm, Sa 9am-1pm and 5-8pm. Mountain and city bikes €8 per day, road bikes €20 per day. AmEx/MC/V.

◼ 🛈 ORIENTATION AND PRACTICAL INFORMATION

To get to the city center from the **ARST bus station**, take the exit nearest to the ticket office and turn left. Continue past the duomo and head straight onto **Via De Castro**, which spills into **Piazza Roma**, the heart of the city. From the **train station**, follow **Via Vittorio Veneto**, the street farthest to the right, to **Piazza Mariano**. Then take **Via Mazzini** to P. Roma. From the **PANI station** on **Via Lombardia** on the other side of town, face Blu Bar and turn right. At the end of the street, turn right on **Via Tirso**, left on **Via Cagliari**, and left on **Via Tharros**, which leads directly into P. Roma.

Tourist Office: Pro Loco, V. Ciutadella de Minorca, 8 (☎/fax 0783 706 21). **Maps** and info on local festivals. Open daily 9am-noon and 4:30-7:30pm. **EPT**, P. Eleonora, 19. Info on Oristano and province, lodgings, events, sights, and excursions. Open M-F 9am-1pm and 5-6:30pm.

Currency Exchange: Banca Nazionale del Lavoro, Banca di Napoli, Credito Italiano and **ATMs** are in P. Roma. All open M-F 8:20am-1:20pm and 3-4:30pm, Sa 8:20-11:50am.

Luggage Storage: In the train station. €1.55 per day. Open daily 6am-7:30pm. Also at ARST station. €1.55 per day. Open daily 6am-7:50pm.

Emergency: ☎113. **Red Cross** (☎0783 21 03 11). **Medical Clinic** (☎0783 743 33). **Ambulance** (☎336 81 34 90).

Pharmacy: V. Umberto, 49/51 (☎0783 603 38). Open M-F 9am-1pm and 5-8:20pm.

Hospital: ☎0783 31 71. On V. Fondazione Rockefeller.

Internet Access: Internet Point, V. Cagliari, 288 (☎0783 701 44), outside of ARST bus station, across the street to the left. 6 computers with fast connection. €4.20 per hr. Open M-F 9:30am-1pm and 3:30-8:30pm. Cash only.

Post Office: V. Mariano, 4 (☎0783 36 80 15). **Currency exchange** and **fax** available. Open M-F 8:15am-6:30pm, Sa 8:15am-1pm. **Postal Code:** 09170.

🏠 🏕 ACCOMMODATIONS AND CAMPING

Oristano caters primarily to travelers on their way to the beaches, and low competition maintains high prices. For info on attractive *agriturismi* and bed and breakfasts, ask at the tourist office or call the **Posidonia Society,** V. Umberto, 64, in Riola, 10km from Oristano. (☎/fax 0783 41 16 60; www.sardegnaturismo.net. Open year-round daily 9am-1pm and 4-7pm.)

ISA, P. Mariano, 50 (☎/fax 0783 36 01 01). From ARST station, take exit nearest to the ticket office, turn left, then right on V. V. Emanuele. Walk through P. D'Arborea and adjoining P. Martini, then follow V. Lamarmora to the end. Turn right, then immediately left, and follow signs. Hotel with luxurious Sardinian marble floors (made from the spines of fish) and oriental rugs. All rooms have bath, A/C, TV, phone, and minibar; some have spacious balcony. Central location. Breakfast €6. Singles €40-60; doubles €65-90; triples €75-93. AmEx/MC/V. ❹

Piccolo Hotel, V. Martignano, 19 (☎0783 715 00). From the ARST station, take exit nearest to ticket office, turn right and continue across P. Mannu. Head down the street to the left and take 1st left. Turn right at the end. Small hotel on a quiet street in the historic center. 10 rooms with bath, some with TV and balcony. Spacious and tastefully decorated with antiques. Breakfast €2.58. Singles €32; doubles €53. Cash only. ❸

Antonella Bed and Breakfast, V. Sardegna, 140 (☎0783 738 63). Follow V. Tirso out of P. Roma; turn right on V. Sardegna. 3 huge rooms on the outskirts of the historic center, run by the friendly Antonella, share a balcony and clean bath. Kitchen facilities available. Breakfast included. Singles €25; doubles €46. Cash only. ❷

Marina di Torregrande (☎/fax 0783 222 28), on V. Stella Maris, 150m from the beach and 100m out of Torre Grande toward Oristano (7km). Orange local buses leave from V. Cagliari in front of ARST station (10min., 2 per hr. 7:30am-12:30am, €0.80). Facilities include a pizzeria, bar, and market with fresh produce. Check-in 9am-noon and 4-7pm, though office is usually staffed all day. Open May-Sept. Free parking and hot showers. €4.50-5.50 per person, €2.60-3.50 per child; 6.60-9.10 per tent; bungalows with bath €42-65. Electricity €1.60. Cash only. ❶

🏠 FOOD

The Euro-Drink **market,** P. Roma, 22, sells inexpensive basics and Sardinian products like *mirto* and *seadas.* (Open M-Sa 8am-1:30pm and 5-9pm. MC/V.) A SISA **supermarket** is on V. Amiscora, 26. (Open M-Sa 8am-8pm. MC/V.)

Ristorante Craf da Banana, V. De Castro, 34 (☎0783 706 69). Slightly more expensive than other restaurants near the center, but far more stylish, with low-arched brick ceilings and fine cuisine. Owner Salvatore cooks a delicious ravioli and fettucine *della casa* with a meaty wild boar sauce (€7). *Primi* €6-7, *secondi* €8-13. Reservation recommended. Open M-Sa noon-3pm and 8-11pm. AmEx/MC/V. ❷

Trattoria Da Gino, V. Tirso, 13 (☎01782 714 28). Locals love the traditional cooking and family feel. Follow a savory *spaghetti alla bottarga* with delicious fresh fish or meat. *Primi* €4-10, *secondi* €7.50-12. Open M-Sa 12:30-3pm and 8-11pm. MC/V. ❷

Pizzeria La Grotta, V. Diego Contini, 3 (☎0783 30 02 06), off P. Roma. A bright restaurant serving the best brick-oven pizza in town in lots of creative varieties. A popular favorite is *alla carciofi freschi e bottarga* (with artichoke hearts and fish eggs; €7.30). Pizza €2.80-8.20. Open daily 7:30pm-12:30am. AmEx/MC/V. ❷

Ristorante Il Faro, V. Bellini, 25 (☎0783 700 02; www.ristoranteilfaro.net). As Dad and son chat with customers at this elegant, renowned restaurant, Mom cooks up unique renditions of Sardinian specialties like *pecora* (lamb) with potatoes and onions (€16) with the highest-quality ingredients, though such innovation doesn't come cheap. *Primi* €10-15, *secondi* €10-20. 4-course *menù* €35. Cover €3. Reservation recommended. Open M-Sa 12:45-2:45pm and 8-10:45 pm. AmEx/MC/V. ❺

👁 🎵 SIGHTS AND ENTERTAINMENT

The pastel **Chiesa di San Francesco,** the largest duomo in Sardinia, was first built in 1250 but heavily restructured in the 19th century, leaving little of the original interior intact. A notable remnant is the gruesome wooden crucifix draped with the emaciated and tortured body of Christ. Constructed by a 16th-century Catalán teacher, the cross was once attributed to Nicodemus; it was said that such a vivid depiction could only have been captured by an eyewitness. The sacristy houses a 16th-century polyptych of *St. Francis Receiving the Stigmata* and Nino Pisano's 14th-century marble statue of San Basilio. (In P. E. d'Arborea at the end of V. de Castro. Open daily. Mass Su 9am. Free.) Once a fortified entrance to the medieval city, the 13th-century **Tower of San Mariano II** dominates P. Roma. On summer evenings, young *Oristanesi* gather in this piazza and the adjoining C. Umberto to flirt, sip Ichnusa (Sardinian beer) and chatter away on their *telefonini*. The collection of Nuraghic, Punic, Phoenician, and Roman artifacts at **Antiquarium Arborense,** unearthed at Tharros, includes urns, cups, and earthenware of all shapes and sizes, some dating as far back as 5000 BC, as well as a tabletop model of the ancient port of Tharros. (In P. Corrias, near P. E. d'Aborea. ☎ 0783 79 12 62. Wheelchair accessible. Open M, W, and F-Sa 9am-2pm and 3-8pm, Tu and Th 9am-2pm and 3-11pm. €3, students €1.) In its synthesis of Lombard and Pisan influences the 12th-century **Basilica of Santa Giusta** is typically Sardinian. (V. Manzoni, 2, on the road to Cagliari, 3km out of town. ☎ 0783 35 92 05. Open daily 7:30am-12:30pm and 4-7:30pm. Free.) To get there, take the ARST bus (dir: Arborea; 5min.; every hr. 6:15am-8:05pm, last return 9:30pm; €0.67) and get off at the first stop. **Maneggio Ippocamo,** in Rimedio, leads day-long horseback tours. (☎ 333 479 49 55. Discounts for groups of 5 or more. Open M-Sa 9am-6pm. Tours €100. Lessons €15 per hr.) To arrange vineyard and gastronomic tours, hikes, and tours of the Sinis Peninsula, contact the **Posidonia Society** (see **Practical Information**).

Oristano comes alive for the annual **Sartiglia,** on the last Sunday of *Carnevale* and the following Tuesday (usually in March). The citizens of Oristano don traditional finery (horseback riding gear, expressionless masks, and small top-hats) and ride on horseback through the streets. One of the festive days is sponsored by the *falegnami* (woodworkers) and the other by the *contadini* (farmers). At the Sartiglia's climax, riders charge down the street on horseback, trying to pierce six-inch metal stars with their spears. The more stars they hit, the better the upcoming harvest.

◤ DAYTRIP FROM ORISTANO

SINIS PENINSULA

From July-Aug., reach Tharros by taking the ARST bus to San Giovanni di Sinis (dir: Is Aruttas; 40min.; 5 per day 9am-7:05pm, last return 8:15pm; €1.45). Ruins open daily 9am-7pm. €4. ARST buses run to: S'archittu (30min.; 8 per day 7:10am-7:10pm, last return 7:10pm; €1.45); Is Aruttas (July-Aug. 50min.; 5 per day 9am-7:05pm, last return 8:15pm; €1.45); Putzu Idu (dir: Su Pallosu; 1hr.; 7 per day 7am-6:18pm, last return 7:07pm; €1.76). Take local orange bus and follow locals to Torregrande's coarser sands (15-20min., Sept.-June 1-2 per hr. 6am-7:10pm, €0.88).

Visiting Oristano and skipping the Sinis Peninsula is like visiting Italy without trying the pasta. Tranquil beaches, stark-white cliffs, rolling country hills, and ancient ruins, all within an easy day's drive, make the trip unforgettable. Public transportation is infrequent, so try to rent a moped or a car. The peninsula's southern tip, a narrow finger of land rising into a hill 17km west of Oristano contains the ruins of the ancient Phoenician and Roman port of **⬛Tharros.** Civilizations pile on top of each other here, with Roman cobblestone roads threading between the ruins of varying eras. A Nuraghic village dates to the 16th century BC; two **temples,** the Roman-style "Temple K" and a Hellenic temple later reconstructed by Romans (utilizing its original base), date to the 1st and 3rd centuries BC, respectively. Also among the ruins are Roman baths with still-intact chambers, Punic-Roman defensive walls, an AD 300 Roman aqueduct, and a Phoenician shrine. Two white columns rise above the rest of the ruins, framed by the blue sea in the background, creating a stunning backdrop. A 16th-century Spanish watchtower crowns the hill and offers expansive views from the top. (Open daily 9am-1pm and 4-7pm. €2, ages 6-15 €1.) A dirt road continues past Tharros and culminates at a lighthouse on the **Capo San Marco,** the tip of the peninsula where the Phoenicians first landed. Strips of white-sand beach line this road. The little beach town of **San Giovanni,**

FROM THE ROAD

CHEWING THE FAT

have been chatting with Efisio at
a cafe. We're talking about Sardinia and how tourism is affecting
the lives of country folks such as
himself. After finishing off his
espresso, he grabs his cellular
phone, has an abrupt conversation in Sard, and begins to get up.
"We go hunt pig," he says
decidedly.

After having been told, not
asked, what I was doing that afternoon, I wonder how one hunts
pigs. Pigs live in pigpens, and root
around in the mud. They don't
seem difficult to hunt. They just
sort of stand there. It dawns on
me, as Efisio and I enter his rust-
covered truck, that my friend's
weak command of English has
misled me. Surely we're going to
his farm to *slaughter* pigs.

My stomach turns. I've never
seen an animal slaughtered, and
I'm not interested in having this be
the first time. But it is too late.
We're already speeding down dirt
roads through the dry, rocky countryside of Sardinia.

Off we go with Efisio's pals,
through stunning country seemingly untouched by human hands.
We abruptly pull off the dirt road.
They lift the flatbed tarp. Bows,
arrows, and spears. Ah, I get it.
We're not hunting pigs. We're
hunting boars.

I get a two-minute explanation.
Shoot arrows at a boar to make
him angry and get him to charge.
When he charges, grab the spear
and make a circle, and stick him

1.5km from Tharros, boasts a **Basilica Paleocristiana**,
a Byzantine style church built in AD 470 in the form
of a Greek Cross. Dedicated to St. John the Baptist,
the church was damaged by Arabian raids and
restored by a Cabras resident in 1838; it remains one
of the most revered churches on the island.

When crossing the bridge that connects the mainland to the peninsula, get an eyeful of the **Stagno di
Cabras**, the source of most of the island's characteristic *bottarga* (fish roe). The community of Cabras runs
the park covering the bottom of the peninsula, with a
tourist office in San Giovanni, on the road to Tharros,
offering helpful **maps** of the area. (Open daily 10am-
1:30pm and 3-7:30pm.) Two kilometers up the coast
from Tharros, the **Parco di Seu** is a dark green promontory dotted with rosemary and honeysuckle, where
mapped dirt paths lead through pinewood forests and
along the rocky coast. Here, another tourist center
offers information on the park's vegetation and the
surrounding coastline. (☎347 894 85 86. Open daily
10am-1:30pm and 3-7:30pm.) About 4km up the coast
stretches the secluded beach of ◙**Is Aruttas,** accessible
by bus from San Giovanni. With famous fine white-
quartz sand, an endless stretch of Sardinia's clear blue
water, and no town for miles around, this is the place
to disappear from civilization. Heading back to
Oristano, the bus from Is Aruttas passes by the little
inland town of **San Salvatore**, with a sanctuary built in
1780. Every year between the end of August and the
first Sunday in September, thousands of young bare-
footed men in white frocks run with the statue of their
patron saint from Chiesa Maggiore in Cabras 6km to
the San Salvatore sanctuary. This tradition simulates a
legendary attempt in 1506 by a group of men to
recover the statue after Moors stormed the village.

Farther up the coast from Is Aruttas, the shallow,
sloping waters of ◙**Putzu Idu** are dotted with bobbing
boats and bathers. The beach town hosts a number of
diving companies, such as **Diving Club Putzu Idu**
(☎0783 537 12) and organizations that lead kayaking
and trekking excursions. On the same bus line,
slightly to the north of the peninsula and off the road
to Cagliari, **Santa Caterina di Pittinuri** is a sleepy seaside town where people lounge on ◙**S'Archittu,** a
massive, naturally-formed limestone arch, and leap
15m into the waters of a beautiful rocky inlet.

BOSA ☎0785

Glowing with cheery pastels, Bosa is a charming
coastal town with the vibrancy of a large city. Home
to artists looking for inspiration and others just looking to get away from it all, Bosa is blessedly undiscovered by the crowds that swamp resorts nearby.

Though the twisting stone streets and valleys of goat herds seem forgotten by time, the newer Bosa Marina one kilometer away boasts a lengthy *lungomare*, beautiful beaches, an assortment of seaside bars, and a hostel.

TRANSPORTATION. Buses run from Bosa to **Piazza Palmiro Togliatti** in Bosa Marina (5min., 22 per day, €0.67). Additionally, buses from **Alghero** or **Oristano** often continue to Bosa Marina. **ARST buses** run from Bosa to **Oristano** (1½hr., 6 per day 5:10am-4:20pm, €4.44) and **Sassari** (2hr., 5 per day 6:20am-6pm, €4.44). Buy tickets from the *tabacchi*, V. Alghero, 7A. **FDS buses** run to **Alghero** (1½hr., 6:35am and 3:40pm, €5) and **Nuoro** (1¾hr., 4 per day 6:06am-7:31pm, €5.10) Buy tickets at the FDS office in P. Zanetti. (Open in summer daily 5:30-8:30am, 9:30am-1pm, and 1:05-3:20pm; in winter 5:30-8:30am and 9:30am-7:35pm.) For a **taxi**, call ☎0785 37 41 62 or 336 81 18 00.

ORIENTATION AND PRACTICAL INFORMATION. Bosa, the city proper, home to the *centro storico*, lies on either side of the **River Temo**, about 1km inland. **Bosa Marina** is across the river and 1km from the centro on the beach. Buses stop in Bosa's **Piazza Angelico Zanetti,** from which **Via Azzuni** leads to **Piazza Gioberti** at the base of the *centro storico*. The **Pro Loco Tourist Office,** V. Azuni, 5, the intersection of V. Francesco Romagna and V. Azuni, has friendly English-speaking guides with great **maps** and information on both the town and surroundings. (☎0785 37 61 07. Open M-Sa 10:30am-1pm and 5:30-8:30pm.) For **currency exchange,** head to **Unicredit Banca,** at the corner of V. Lamarmora and V. Giovanni XXIII. (☎0785 37 31 18. Open M-F 8:20am-1:20pm and 2:35-4:05pm, Sa 8:20am-12:45pm.) In case of **emergency,** dial ☎113 or call the **Red Cross** (☎0785 37 38 18) or **carabinieri** (☎0785 37 31 16). **Internet Web Copy,** P. IV Novembre, 12, has five computers with fast connection (€6 per hr.) and **fax** services. (Open M-Sa 8:30am-1pm and 5-9pm.) **Euroservice,** V. Azuni, 23, rents cars, motor scooters, and bikes. (☎0785 37 34 79. 18+ for car or scooter. Cars from €64 per day; scooters €18-44 per day; bikes €10 per day. Insurance included. Open M-Sa 9am-1pm and 5-8pm.) The **post office,** V. Pischedda, 1, also has currency exchange. (☎0785 37 31 39. Open M-F 8:15am-6:30pm, Sa 8:15am-12:45pm.) **Postal Code:** 08013.

ACCOMMODATIONS. Bosa Marina is home to a well-run **Youth Hostel ❶,** at V. Sardegna, 1. From P. Palmiero Togliatti, take V. Sassari to V. Grazia

when he gets close enough. I have no idea how I got myself into this, but nod and follow along.

We walk into the woods. Efisio stops, grabs my arm, and points. He's excited, and wants me to shoot an arrow. I have no idea what I'm shooting at, but release my arrow. It rips through the woods and lodges in a tree trunk. I'm proud that I shot an arrow without injuring myself, but while I'm admiring my work, Efisio has sent a few arrows toward the boar and everyone is grabbing their spears. I do the same.

As the beast comes charging from the woods, I instinctively run backward. All I know is that some ugly thing with horns is not happy, and is going to try his best not to end up wrapped up in cellophane at the supermarket. I would do the same in his position.

The men begin to close around each other, and as it approaches they use all their force and shove their spears deep into the boar's back and chest. It squeals and twitches and flails for what seems like 10 minutes. Then all of a sudden, quiet.

Efisio waves me over. I look around and realize that I am a good 200 feet from the rest of them, holding my spear upside-down, ready to do harm to nothing in particular. I walk over. Efisio's buddies are gutting the animal, and on the ground next to it is its tongue that has already been cut out. We sit around, have a few drinks, a few laughs, and a few bites of tongue. All in a day's work, at least in Sardinia.

-Yaran Noti

Deledda and turn right. After two blocks, turn left and look for the hostel at the end of the street. Close to the beach, the hostel has clean rooms, a bar open until midnight, and a nice staff. (☎/fax 0785 37 50 09. Breakfast €3. Dinner €10.33. 50 beds. 6- to 8-bed dorms €13, including sheets and hot water; doubles available by reservation. Half pension €20.66. Cash only.) Also in Bosa Marina, the friendly **Hotel Al Gabbano ④**, on Viale Mediterraneo, offers large, comfortable rooms directly across from the beach, all with bath, TV, A/C, phone, and fridge, and most with balcony. (☎0785 37 41 23, fax 37 41 09. Restaurant downstairs. Buffet breakfast €5.20. Beach chair and umbrella included. Singles €45-58; doubles €58-78. AmEx/MC/V.) In Bosa, the lavish **Bed and Breakfast Loddo Gonaria ❷**, V. Martin Luther King, 5, is reminiscent of a mansion. Repose in six enormous rooms decorated with antique headboards and chandeliers, and enjoy home-made honey and jam for breakfast. (From the bus stop, follow V. D. Manin, turn right at the river onto Lungo Temo De Gasperi and follow it to V. M. L. King; it's 50m down on the right. (☎0785 37 37 90. Breakfast included. Rooms €22-30. Cash only.) **Albergo Perry Clan ❷**, V. Alghero, 3, in Bosa, offers 12 rooms with bath and A/C. From the bus stop, follow V. D. Manin and take first right on Viale Giovanni XXIII; the hotel is on the left after P. Dante Alighieri. (☎0785 37 30 74. Singles €20; doubles €40. Cash only.)

🞆 **FOOD.** Head to SISA **supermarket**, P. Gioberti, 13, for fresh produce and groceries. (☎0785 37 34 23. Open M-Sa 8am-1pm and 5-8pm.) Couched in a medieval building in the *centro storico*, **Ristorante Borgo Sant'Ignazio ❷**, V. S. Ignazio, 33, serves traditional cuisine like lobster *in salsa bosana* (with onions and tomatoes; €9) and *azada di gattucio* (€8), a relative of shark. (☎0785 37 46 62. *Primi* €6-10, *secondi* €8-14. Open in summer daily 12:30-3:30pm and 7:30-10:30pm. AmEx/MC/V.) The satisfying **Ristorante Barracuda ❷**, Viale Repubblica, 17, serves fresh, savory seafood on a casual outdoor patio. (☎0785 37 41 50. *Primi* €6.50-14.50, *secondi* €9.50-15.50. Open daily 12:30-4pm and 8pm-midnight. Closed W in winter. Cash only.) **Sa Pischedda ❷**, V. Roma, 8, prepares fantastic *razza alla bosana*, a garlicky sautéed flat fish, and cooks delicious brick-oven pizza. (☎0785 37 30 65. Pizza €3-8, dinner only. *Primi* €7.50-10, *secondi* €7.50-17. Open daily 12:30-3pm and 7:30pm-midnight. AmEx/MC/V.) For creamy, tasty gelato, try **Ice Dream**, in P. IV Novembre. Homemade and rich with flavor, the gelato is the best in town. (☎0785 374 35. Cones from €1.50. open daily 10am-11pm. Cash only.)

🞆🞅 **SIGHTS AND BEACHES.** Walk around Bosa's **Quartiere Sa Costa** and inhale the history. The town's panoramic **Castello Malaspina**, a 15min. hike uphill through the *centro storico*, dates from 1112 and still holds the early 14th-century **Chiesa Nostra Signora Regnos Altos,** which contains frescoes painted in the manner of the Tuscan school. (☎333 544 56 75. Castle and church open daily 9:30am-1:30pm and 5:30-8:30pm. €2, under 12 €1.) Bosa's principal museum, **Casa Deriu,** C. V. Emanuele II, 59, exhibits the original furnishings, tapestries, and family portraits from the wealthy Deriu family's 19th-century home. The third floor holds a collection of ceramics, prints, and paintings by renowned *Bosano* Melkiorre Melis, a leader in the applied and plastic arts. (Open Tu-Su noon-1pm and 7:30-11:30pm. €3, students €1.) Across the river, 2km into the valley along V. S. Antonio, stands the Romanesque **Chiesa di San Pietro.** Built in 1062, this heavy stone church is one of Sardinia's oldest, and displays Medieval stone carvings unearthed from sarcophagi nearby. (Open daily 9:30am-1:30pm and 5:30-8:30pm. €1.)

Ten kilometers north of Bosa on the road to Alghero stands the Torre Argentina, overlooking peaceful beaches. A long stretch of sandy beach filled with local families awaits in Bosa Marina, with a *lungomare* lined with bars and its very own **Aragonese Tower.** (Open occasionally; check with tourist office.) The **Bosa Diving Center** (☎ 0785 37 56 49; www.bosadiving.it), V. Colombo, 2, in Bosa Marina, offers a range of popular activities, including: hour-long guided snorkeling tours (€24 per person, night tours €29); scuba trips (single immersion €31-41, 2 dives €57-74, night dives €35-40; higher prices include equipment costs); group treks along the coast (€33); river boat rides with exceptional views of the city (€6); and sea trips to nearby grottoes and beaches (2hr., €13). Call for more info.

NUORO   ☎ 0784

Though set against a dramatic mountain backdrop, the architecture of this provincial capital is distinctly modern. A few parts of Nuoro are lively during the day, but the town is relatively small and acts as a transportation hub for the rest of the province. For travelers who are coming through, Nuoro offers several museums and some small, winding streets to explore. Its most attractive quality is undoubtedly its proximity to more interesting destinations in the surrounding countryside.

▐ TRANSPORTATION

Trains: ☎ 0784 301 15. On V. Lamarmora in P. Stazione. Buy tickets M-Sa 7:30am-7pm. To **Cagliari** (3½-5hr., 6 per day 5:45am-6:51pm, €10.80) via **Macomer.**

Buses: The following bus companies serve Nuoro:

ARST (☎ 0784 29 41 73). Buses stop at the ARST station on V. Toscana between V. Sardegna and V. Santa Barbara. Tickets available at the bar in the ARST station (open M-Sa 6:30am-9pm), at Il Gusto Macelleria next door, and at bars along the street. To: **Cagliari** (2:05 and 7:10pm, €9.50); **Dorgali** (1hr., 6 per day 6:53am-7pm, €2.01); **Olbia** (7 per day 5:30am-8:50pm, €7.64); **Oliena** (30min., 13 per day 6:53am-7:45pm, €0.80); **Orgosolo** (30min.; 8 per day 5:50am-6:30pm, last return 7:40pm; €1.45).

PANI, V. B. Sassari, 15 (☎ 0784 368 56). From P. Stazione walk up V. Stazione and follow it to the right. Ticket office open 9am-noon, 5-7:30pm, and 30min. before each departure. Buses to: **Cagliari** (3½hr., 4 per day 6:52am-7:31pm, €11.31); **Oristano** (2hr., 4 per day 6:52am-7:31pm, €5.84); **Sassari** (2½hr., 6 per day 5:52am-7:31pm, €6.77).

F. Deplanu (☎ 0784 29 50 30) runs buses from the ARST station to the **Olbia airport** (1½hr., 5 per day 5:45am-5pm, €9.30) and to the **Alghero airport** (2¾hr., 2 per day, €12.39). Buses are scheduled around plane arrivals and departures.

Local Transportation: Buy tickets (€0.57) for the local buses at newsstands, *tabacchi,* or in the train station. **Bus #4** runs from P. V. Emanuele, through the center of town, to the train station and the hospital (3 per hr.), while **E6** runs in the opposite direction, stopping at the train station on its way through town to P. V. Emanuele.

Car Rental: Autonoleggio Maggiore, V. Convento, 32 (☎/fax 0784 304 61). Affiliated with National Car Rental. €72.64 per day. 23+. Open M-F 8:30am-1pm and 3:30-7pm, Sa 8am-1pm. AmEx/MC/V.

Taxis (☎ 368 90 94 71). From P. Stazione. One of the only in the area, so call ahead.

▐ ▐ ORIENTATION AND PRACTICAL INFORMATION

From the ARST station, turn right on **Viale Sardegna.** When you reach Piazza Sardegna, take a right onto **Via Lamarmora** and follow it to **Piazza delle Grazie** and the center of town. To get to the tourist office from P. delle Grazie, turn left and follow **Via**

IV Novembre uphill to P. Italia. Facing the PANI bus stop, turn left and take **Via B. Sassari** to **Piazza Italia,** and the tourist office. **Via Roma** leads from P. Italia to **Piazza San Giovanni** and the town's social hub, **Piazza Vittorio Emanuele. Corse G. Garibaldi** is a major street with shops and cafes that runs out of P. V. Emanuele.

> **Tourist Office: EPT,** P. Italia, 19 (☎ 0784 320 37), on street level in summer and on the 4th fl. in winter. Enthusiastic staff has brochures and hiking info. Ask about nature excursions and *agriturismo* options. Open in summer M-Sa 8:30am-1:30pm and 3:30-8pm, Su 9:30am-1:30pm; in winter Tu-W 9am-1pm.

> **Emergency:** ☎ 113. **Ambulance** (☎ 118). **Carabinieri** (☎ 112).

> **Medical Clinic** (☎ 0784 24 02 49).

> **Hospital: Ospedale San Francesco** (☎ 0784 24 02 37), on the highway to Bitti.

> **Internet Access: Informatica 2000,** C. Garibaldi, 156 (☎ 0784 372 89, fax 23 50 87). 2 computers with fast connection. €1 for 10min., €2.50 for 30min., €5 per hr. **Fax** service also available. Open M-F 9am-8pm, Sa 9am-1pm.

> **Post Office:** P. Crispi, 8 (☎ 0784 24 52 96), off V. Dante. Open M-F 8:15am-6:30pm, Sa 8:15am-12:45pm. **Currency exchange** €2.58 per transaction. **Postal Code:** 08100.

ACCOMMODATIONS

Inexpensive hotels are rare in Nuoro and campgrounds are in distant towns; if you plan to stay in the area head to the smaller hamlets in the hills. Convenient *agriturismo* options include **Testone ❸** (☎ 0784 23 05 39 or 329 411 51 68. Rooms €42.) **Il Portico ❸,** V. M. Bua, 13, off the northern end of P. V. Emanuele near P. Mazzini, is a pleasant little hotel with a prime central location. All the rooms have bath; some have balcony. (☎ 0784 375 35, fax 25 50 62. Reception M-Sa 12:30-3pm and 8-11pm. Singles €40; doubles €55. AmEx/MC/V.) To reach **Hotel Ristorante Grillo ❺,** V. Mons. G. Melas, 14, turn right out of the ARST station on Viale Sardegna, then right on V. Lamarmora. Follow it for 750m into the center of town, then turn right on V. A. Manozini after the church and right on V. Convento; the hotel is ahead on the corner. This establishment offers attentive family management and 46 airy, comfortable rooms with bath, A/C, TV, and phone. The **restaurant ❹** downstairs is very popular. (☎ 0784 386 68 or 386 78; www.grillohotel.it. Breakfast included. Singles €66; doubles €92; triples €120; quads €140. Half pension €65-82; full pension €91-98.) **Hotel Sandalia ❹,** V. Einaudi, 14, along the road to Cagliari and Sassari, is a 20min. walk from the center. From the ARST station, go as far as V. Lamarmora and turn left; the hotel is at the top of the hill and marked with a large sign. All rooms are modern and come equipped with bath, A/C, TV, and phone. (☎/fax 0784 383 53. Singles €55; doubles €75; triples €80; quads €85. AmEx/MC/V.)

FOOD

For provisions, head to ⬛**Mercato Civico,** P. Mameli, 20, off V. Manzoni, which has vegetables, fruit, cheese, and meat, fresh from the Sardinian farms nearby. Go early to get the choicest picks. Prices aren't really labeled, so brush up on your bargaining skills. (Open M-Sa 7am-1:30pm and 4:30-8pm, July-Aug. closed Sa afternoon.) A quality bakery, **Antico Panifico,** V. Ferraciu, 71, off P. delle Grazie, sells hot rolls fresh from its wood-burning oven, a Sardinian *pane carasau,* and scrumptious *panzerotti* (from €1.75) filled with cheese, tomato, and a choice of eggplant, mushroom, or ham. (Open M-Sa 8am-8pm.)

■ **Canne Al Vento,** V. Repubblica, 66 (☎ 0784 20 17 62), a 10min. walk down V. Lamarmora from P. delle Grazie, past the train station. Flowers brighten a lovely room where guests dine on classic *culurgiones* (ravioli stuffed with potatoes, cheese, and mint; €7) or heaping platters of *arrosto misto* (mixed grilled meats; €10). *Primi* €5.25-9, *secondi* €5.25-12. Open M-Sa 12:30-3pm and 8-10:30pm. AmEx/MC/V. ❷

Ristorante Tascusi, V. Apromonte, 15 (☎ 0784 372 87). Owner Gianfranco does the cooking at this local favorite. Chat while he prepares delicious *malloreddus al sugo di cinghiale* (pasta shells in wild boar sauce; €5.25). Brick-oven pizza €3-7. *Primi* €4.65-8, *secondi* €6-13. Open M-Sa noon-3pm and 7:30pm-midnight. MC/V. ❶

Da Giovanni, V. IV Novembre, 9, 2nd fl. (☎ 0784 305 62). A local favorite that appears simple, but one taste of *bocconcini alla vernaccia* (beef in white wine sauce; €7.78) confirms the cuisine is fantastic. *Primi* €7-8, *secondi* €7-10.30. Open M-F noon-4pm and 7:30-11pm, Sa noon-4pm. AmEx/MC/V. ❷

La Pasticceria Artigiana, V. L. Rubeddu, 8 (☎ 0784 355 42). From P. Italia, take V. Corrasi to V. Torres. Turn left on V. Torres, right on V. delle Frasche, right on V. Floris, and V. Rubeddu is the next right. Best homemade Sardinian pastries in the area. A bag of 20 pastries runs about €5. Open M-Sa 8:30am-1pm and 4:15-8pm. Cash only. ❶

SARDINIA

◎ 🎵 SIGHTS AND ENTERTAINMENT

All the cool kids gravitate toward P. V. Emanuele—nicknamed *giardini*—to sit, talk, and smoke in the evenings. A more mature crowd proves that such *laissez-faire* loitering is ageless, converging upon C. Garibaldi to do much of the same.

■ **MUSEO DELLA VITA E DELLE TRADIZIONI POPULARI.** Sardinia's largest ethnographic museum contains an extensive collection of traditional costumes, hand-woven rugs, musical instruments, sweets, and jewelry from around the island. The pieces are arranged in a series of white stucco houses circling a flowered courtyard, a reconstruction of a typical Sardinian village. One house is possessed by lurid carnival masks shaped like devils, donkeys, pigs, cows, and goats. (*V. Antonio Mereu, 56.* ☎ *0784 25 60 35. Open Oct.-June daily 9am-1pm and 3-5pm; July-Sept. 9am-8pm. €5, students €2, under 18 or over 60 free.*)

MUSEO ARTE NUORO. This striking white building houses imaginative contemporary art that employs a mixture of standard and folkloric images and themes. The middle two floors maintain a permanent collection of works by 20th-century Sardinian painters, while the first and fourth floors display rotating exhibits by modern artists. (*V. S. Satta, 15.* ☎ *0784 25 21 10. Open Tu-Su 10am-1pm and 4:30-8:30pm. €3, students €2, under 18 or over 60 free.*)

MONTE ORTOBENE. A gargantuan bronze statue of Christ the Redeemer, the town's symbol, beckons intrepid hikers to the peak of this hill, where a shady park and dynamic views await. Follow a 50m trail from the tourist office to the bronze *Il Redentore*, dating from 1905. From the bus stop on Monte Ortobene, walk 20m down the road to see Monte Corrasi, which dwarfs the neighboring town of Oliena. (*Take the orange ATP bus #8 from P. V. Emanuele 7km to the summit (15 per day 8:15am-8pm, last return 8:15pm; €0.55). Or hike the 4.5km trail Il Solitudine; start behind Chiesa della Solitudine at the beginning of V. Ortobene and follow the red/white blazes marked "Trail 101." Beware wild boars and mountain goats, both of which can be dangerous to humans, roam the hills.*)

SACRA DEL REDENTORE. On August 29, Nuoro celebrates the **Sacra del Redentore** (Feast of the Redeemer), a spartan religious procession during which the townsfolk attend a service at the 16th-century **Chiesa del Monte,** atop Monte Ortobene (open only for the holiday). The Sunday preceding the somber occasion offers far more lively revels, consisting of choral performances, folk dancing, and a colorful parade of merry-makers in traditional costume.

▶ DAYTRIP FROM NUORO

ORGOSOLO
Take an ARST bus (40min.; 8 per day 5:50am-6:30pm, last return 7:40pm; €1.45) from the ARST station in Nuoro.

The bus ride alone merits a trip to picturesque ▨ **Orgosolo,** but the town itself—with spare architecture and a sleepy, shaded piazza—is a paragon of Sardinian mountain beauty. The allure of Orgosolo's vistas is enhanced by its famed Picasso-like murals, which adorn the buildings along C. Repubblica and its surrounding alleyways. Artists from around the globe created these works, some of them polit-ical, others depicting scenes from daily Sardinian life. The Milanese anarchist group *Gruppo Dioniso* created the first mural in 1969, and Francesco del Casino, a teacher from Siena, reinvented the mural-painting as an ongoing project in 1975. His works focus on social and political issues, including imperialism, fascism, and commercialism. Artists continue to make new murals focused on such modern themes as terrorism and Sardinian independence.

The town **tourist office,** P. Caduti in Guerra, next to the second bus stop, dis-tributes helpful city **maps** and information on the murals and local attractions. (Open in summer daily 7am-7pm.) For a place to stay, exit the bus at the third stop and follow signs to the **Hotel Sa'e Janna ❹,** V. E. Lussu, 17, a family-run establishment offering 35 enormous rooms with bath and balcony. The breezy top-floor rooms have the best mountain views. (☎0784 40 12 47. Singles €39; doubles €49; triples €70. Half pension €44-49.50, full pension €88. AmEx/MC/V.) The **restaurant ❷** downstairs serves *cavallo* (horse; €6.80) and other tradi-tional homemade dishes. *(Primi* €4-5.50, *secondi* €5.20-6.80. AmEx/MC/V.) More of del Casino's less-political paintings decorate the cozy **Petit Hotel ❷,** V. Mannu, 9, off C. Repubblica. Backtrack from the bus stop at the small park (keeping the police station to the right), then head up the incline on the left and follow the signs. Eighteen quiet rooms all have bath, dark wood furniture, and flower-decked balconies. (☎/fax 0784 40 20 09. Breakfast €5. Singles €28; dou-bles €40; triples €57; quads €67. AmEx/MC/V.)

To eat a traditional meal in the mountains, contact **Cultura e Ambiente,** a local organization that operates excursions into the hills and organizes lunches in a field behind its restaurant, **Supramonte ❸,** in Località Sarthu Thithu, 3km uphill from town. Busloads of tourists arrive daily to devour smoked meats, roasted *por-chetto,* cheese, fresh fruits and vegetables, and pastries off wooden platters. Four pastors grow, prepare, and serve the meals. (☎0784 40 10 15 or 349 177 58 72; www.supramonte.net. Conducted for groups, but individuals may call ahead to join. Transportation provided on request. Lunch €18. Call for group rates.) The group also runs the clean, panoramic **Camping Supramonte ❶.** (Hot showers free. €3 per person, €4 per tent; bungalows with bath €20. AmEx/MC/V.)

DORGALI   ☎0784

Nestled in mountains and ringed by pastures, pint-sized Dorgali offers visitors relaxation and quiet among friendly locals. Crafts have given residents a creative respite from farming and the town has gradually developed into a community of artisans. Since the tourism boom hit Sardinia in the 60s, travelers have trekked to

Dorgali to admire the ceramic, weaving, and woodworking shops that line its main street. Though roads connect it to nearby Cala Gonone and magnificent archaeological and natural sights, Dorgali maintains its isolated, traditional charm.

TRANSPORTATION AND PRACTICAL INFORMATION. ARST buses stop at V. Lamarmora, 59, across from the *carabinieri*, and at the intersection of V. Lamarmora and C. Umberto. Buy tickets at the bar at the intersection of V. Lamarmora and C. Umberto. The schedule is posted at the tourist office. Buses run to: Cala Gonone (20min., 10 per day 6:20am-7:45pm, €0.67); Nuoro (45min., 9 per day 6:05am-7:50pm, €2.01); and Olbia (3hr., 2 per day 6:35am and 5:25pm, €7.64). **Via Lamarmora,** which runs uphill from the bus stop, and **Corso Umberto** (perpendicular to V. Lamarmora) are the major streets, with shops, bars, and a few restaurants. **Via Roma** descends to **Viale Kennedy,** which runs along the bottom of town. The **Pro Loco Tourist Office,** V. Lamarmora, 108, offers info on Dorgali, Cala Gonone, and surrounding attractions. (☎0784 962 43. Open M-F May-Sept. 9am-1pm and 4-8pm, Oct.-Apr. 9am-1pm and 3:30-7pm.) In case of **emergency,** call ☎113, the **carabinieri** (☎0784 961 14), an **ambulance** (☎118 or 0784 942 66), or contact the **medical clinic** (☎0784 965 21). The hospital, **Ospedale Civile San Francesco** (☎0784 24 02 37), is in Nuoro, on the highway toward Bitti. **Currency exchange** and **ATMs** are available at **Banca Intensa** (open M-F 8:20am-1:25pm and 2:35-4pm, Sa 8:20-11:50am), at the intersection of V. Lamarmora and V. Fleming and at the post office. **Farmacia Mondula,** V. Lamarmora, 55, at the intersection with V. Sardegna, posts the late-night rotation. (Open M-Tu and Th-Su 8:30am-1pm and 4:30-8pm.) The **post office** is at the corner of V. Lamarmora and V. Ciusa, across the street from the bus stop. (☎0784 947 12. Open M-F 8am-noon.) **Postal Code:** 08020.

ACCOMMODATIONS AND FOOD. Accommodations in Dorgali are generally less expensive than those in neighboring beach resorts. Ask the tourist office for a list of *agriturismi*. Dorgali's best deal, ▧**Bed and Breakfast ❷,** V. Azzuni, 5, keeps four pristine rooms, all with bath, in the center of town. (☎/fax 0784 963 35. Breakfast included. Singles €20-25; doubles €40. French and German spoken, but no English. Cash only.) Just off V. Lamarmora is the family-managed **Hotel S'Adde ❸,** V. Concordia, 38, which keeps attractive rooms with bath, A/C, and phone. (☎/fax 0784 94 44 12. Wheelchair accessible. Parking available. Breakfast €6. Singles €35-45; doubles €56-60; triples €75-80. AmEx/MC/V.) Surrounded by gardens and fruit trees, **Il Querceto ❹,** V. Lamarmora, 4, 10min. downhill from the town center, is reminiscent of a countryside retreat. The 29 enormous rooms all have tiled bath, A/C, satellite TV, and large balcony. (☎0784 965 09; www.ilquerceto.com. Breakfast included. Singles €47-58; doubles €74-194; triples €105-138; quads €128-164. AmEx/MC/V.)

Locals crowd the lunch tables at ▧**Ristorante Colibri ❸,** V. Gramsci, 14. From V. Lamarmora take V. Cerere, which becomes V. Gramsci, to the intersection with V. Flores, to chat over plates of scrumptious game and the local specialty *penne alla dorgalese* (with hot pork sauce; €6.50). Finish a great meal with a glass of *mirta*, a licorice-flavored local specialty. (☎0784 960 54. *Primi* €6.50-7, *secondi* €9.50-10.50. Cover €2. Open daily July-Aug. 12:30-3pm and 8-10pm, in winter closed Su. Cash only.) For a small town, Dorgali has no shortage of snack bars, but the brick-oven pizzas at **Il Giardino ❶,** V. E. Fermi, on the road to Cala Gonone, are a slice above the rest. Try the delicious *giardino*, laden with grilled veggies (€7), a bountiful salad (€8), or an international selection of beers (from €2). The house ▧tiramisu (€3) is the best dessert in town. (☎0784 942 57. Pizza €3.50-7.50. *Primi* €4.50-8, *secondi* €6-13. Open M and W-Su noon-3pm and 7pm-midnight. Wheelchair accessible. AmEx/MC/V.) **Deiana**

Dolci Sardi ❶, V. Africa, 3, off P. Francetta, downhill from V. Lamarmora, serves handmade Sardinian sweets. (☎0784 950 96. Pastries €7.50-22 per kg. Open M-Sa 8:30am-1pm and 4-8pm. Cash only.)

🗋 SHOPPING. Dorgali's craft stores are at the heart of its appeal. Tourists wander the tiny streets observing practiced artists weave, mold, and bake their wares. Stores display the handmade filigree jewelry, *tappeti* (wool and cotton weavings), carvings, and pastries along V. Lamarmora and its side streets; many showrooms are next door to the owner's workshop. Serafina Senette and her mother weave beautiful *tappeti* at **Il Tapetto di Serafina Senette**, P. G. Asproni, 22. (☎0784 952 02. Open daily 8:30am-1pm and 4:30-8pm. Cash only.) At **Il Loddo**, V. Lamarmora, 110, owners sell their ceramics, handcrafted and painted in attractive original designs. (☎0784 967 71. Open M-Sa 9:30am-1pm and 4-8pm; Aug. also open Su. MC/V.) Dorgali is also known for its red wine, round, heavy, and very flavorful. Ask for a sample at many of the *enoteche* around town.

🏃 OUTDOORS. Dorgali is an ideal base from which to explore some of Sardinia's natural and archaeological treasures. The reputable agency **Coop Ghivine** (V. Lamarmora, 69/E) leads hiking, boating, geological, archaeological, cultural, and gastronomic excursions throughout the Gennargentu range and the Golfo di Orosei. (☎349 442 55 52; www.ghivine.com. Call ahead to arrange a meeting with the staff. Daytrips €40 per person, including lunch.)

CALA GONONE   ☎0784

Nestled on the sea and surrounded on three sides by mountains, Cala Gonone was once only accessible by boat. Now, a tunnel connects this once quiet town to Dorgali, transforming much of Cala Gonone into an upscale resort. Quickly becoming one of Sardinia's most popular tourist destinations, the area has mountains to scale, archaeological wonders to explore, a postcard-perfect harbor sheltered by limestone cliffs, and secluded sandy beaches—including the famed Cala Luna— still best reached by boat or on foot.

📧 TRANSPORTATION AND PRACTICAL INFORMATION. Buses depart from the tourist office, at the intersection of Viale Del Bue Marino and Viale C. Colombo. **ARST buses** run to: Dorgali (20min., 10 per day 6:40am-8:10pm, €0.67); Nuoro (45min., 9 per day 6:05am-7:25pm, €2.01); and Olbia (3hr., 6:35am and 5:25pm, €7.64). Buy tickets at Bar La Pinetta on Viale Colombo. **Fratelli Deplano** (☎0784 29 50 30) runs buses to **Olbia Airport** (2½hr.; 8, 10am, and 1:30pm; €7.64). Purchase tickets onboard. Viale C. Colombo leads downhill to the harbor; **Lungomare Palmesare** and **Lungomare S'Abbe Durche** run along the seafront. The **tourist office,** on Viale del Bue Marino, offers info on accommodations and boat schedules to beaches and attractions. (☎0784 936 96. Open daily Apr.-June and Sept. 9am-1pm and 3:30-7pm, July-Aug. 9am-10pm.) An **ATM** is outside the yellow building in the center of the port. In case of **emergency,** call ☎113, the **medical clinic** at ☎0784 934 66, or the **carabinieri** at ☎0784 961 14. An **Internet point** is at V. Cristoforo Colombo, 5. (☎0784 92 00 15. €3 for 15min., €6.50 per hr. Open M-Sa 10am-1pm and 5-9pm. Cash only.) The **post office,** at the corner of Viale C. Colombo and V. Cala Luna, has **currency exchange.** (Open M-F 8:15am-1:15pm and Sa 8:15am-12:45pm, last day of the month 8:15am-noon.) **Postal Code:** 08020.

🍴 ACCOMMODATIONS AND FOOD. One of Cala Gonone's oldest hotels, **Hotel Marimare ❹**, P. Giardini, 12, looms large over the town, sitting right in the center of the harbor. Luxurious amenities such as a rooftop solarium and a generous breakfast buffet only sweeten the 35 sunny rooms, all with bath, A/C, Internet, TV, and phone. (☎0784 931 40; www.htlmiramare.it. Singles €40-67; doubles €70-120. Half pension €54-82; full pension €64-92. AmEx/MC/V.) The simple **Piccolo Hotel ❷,** V. Cristoforo Colombo, 32, is an excellent value, with 13 bright rooms, clean baths, and seaview balconies. (☎0784 932 35 or 932 32. Breakfast €2.50. Singles €21-41; doubles €31-51. Extra bed 30%. Cash only.) ⚑**Camping Villaggio Calagonone ❶,** V. Callodi, 1, just off Viale C. Colombo, is a gorgeous four-star village, set back from the harbor in a mountain-ringed pine grove. Site amenities include a restaurant, pizzeria, market, bar, and recreational facilities such as a pool, tennis and basketball courts, and a barbecue area. (☎0784 931 65. Reception daily 8am-8pm. Gates open 7am-11pm for cars. Adults €11-16, children ages 2-12 €6-9. Electricity €2-3. Tent, parking, and hot showers free. Campers for 2 €26-48, with toilet €31-54; for 4 €46-82/€48-88. Bungalows for 4 with shower €54-115. MC/V.)

Most restaurants in town are either associated with hotels or dish out perfunctory tourist fare. Next to the post office, **Ristorante Self-Service L'Anphora ❶,** V. Cala Luna, is a cafeteria-style restaurant offering a huge variety of dishes, including fresh sea bass baked with mushrooms (☎0784 930 67. Pizza €2.50-2.70. *Panini* from €1.60. *Primi* €4-7, *secondi* €3.50-8. Takeout available. Open in summer daily 8:30am-11pm. AmEx/MC/V.) **Il Pescatore ❸,** V. Acqua Dolce, 7, serves flavorful favorites like mixed *antipasti* (€12 per person) and *spaghetti allo scoglio,* with shellfish; €9. (☎0784 831 74. *Primi* €6.50-9, *secondi* €6-23. Open daily 12:30-3pm and 8-11:30pm. MC/V.)

⚑🏊 **BEACHES AND OUTDOORS.** Cala Gonone is ideally positioned to allow access to both stunning beaches and adventure-sport venues. V. Bue Marino leads 3km along the waterfront, passing long stretches of beach before arriving at the resplendent **Cala Fuili.** ⚑**Cala Luna,** famed for its crystal clear waters and tropical backdrop, is accessible by boat or foot. Sheltered by limestone cliffs, the isolated cove has maintained its pristine beauty despite the boatloads of tourists that visit daily. To reach Cala Luna, hike a strenuous 1½hr. on the 4km trail that departs from Cala Fuili. Alternatively, **Consorzio Trasporti Marittimi** sells ferry tickets to Cala Luna at its white booth on the port. (☎0784 933 02, ticket booth 933 05. 8 per day 9am-5pm, last return 6:30pm; adult round-trip €8.50-16, ages 4-12 €4.50-8.) Consorzio also runs ferries to the elusive **Bue Marino.** The most famous of the deep grottoes carved into the mountainside between Cala Fuili and Cala Luna, Marino is accessible only by sea. (Ferry fees include guided tour. Bue Marino: adult round-trip €13-18, ages 4-12 €8. Bue Marino and Cala Luna: adults €18-25, ages 4-12 €11-15.) Tour guides lead visitors through cave chambers that conceal natural curiosities, including the dripping stalactites of the "Lamp Room," and the "Mirrors Room," in which a large pool of water reflects off the cave walls in a rainbow of colors, owing to variances in mineral composition. (30min. tours offered in Italian, English, and French. 8 per day, 10 in Aug., 9:30am-5:30pm. €7.)

Prima Sardegna, V. Lungomare Palmasera, 32, rents cars (€55-72 per day), mountain bikes (€16-21), and single and double kayaks (€24/€42). Its guides also lead excursions by boat, bike, or foot to natural and archaeological sites for €30-160 per person, depending on trip and duration. (☎0784 933 67 or 333 576 21 85; www.primasardegna.com. Open daily 9am-1pm and 4-8pm. AmEx/MC/V.) **Dolmen Servizi Turistici,** V. Vasco de Gama, 18, arranges biking, trekking, archaeological, and cultural tours, and rents mountain bikes and scooters at comparable prices. (☎347 068 56 04 or 347 881 66 40; www.sardegnadascoprire.it. Info booth at port. Office open daily 9am-1pm and 4-8pm. Info booth open daily 8:30am-11pm. AmEx/MC/V.) Many booths along the port provide private daily boat rentals. People interested in **scuba diving** should head to **Argonauta Diving Club,** V. dei Lecci, 10, behind the campground. (☎0784 93 046; www.argonauta.it.)

SARDINIA

APPENDIX

LOCAL CONDITIONS

TEMPERATURE AND CLIMATE

°CELSIUS	-5	0	5	10	15	20	25	30	35	40
°FAHRENHEIT	23	32	41	50	59	68	77	86	95	104

To convert from °C to °F, multiply by 1.8 and add 32. For a rough approximation, double the Celsius and add 25. To convert from °F to °C, subtract 32 and multiply by 0.55. For a rough approximation, subtract 25 from Fahrenheit and cut it in half.

AVERAGE TEMPERATURE AND PRECIPITATION											
	JANUARY			APRIL			JULY			OCTOBER		
	°C	°F	cm/in.	°C	°F	cm/in.	°C	°F	cm/in.	°C	°F	cm/in.
Florence	10/2	50/35	6.4/2.5	19/8	66/46	7.1/2.8	31/17	87/62	3.4/1.3	21/10	69/50	10.3/4
Milan	6/-4	42/25	5.2/2	17/5	63/40	12.5/5	28/15	82/59	6.4/2.5	18/6	63/43	8.4/3.3
Rome	14/3	56/38	8.1/3.2	19/7	66/45	5.6/2.2	30/17	86/62	1.8/0.7	22/11	73/52	12/4.6
Venice	6/-1	42/31	5.6/2.2	16/8	61/46	7.3/2.9	27/18	81/63	6.8/2.7	18/9	64/48	7.7/3

INTERNATIONAL CALLING CODES

To call internationally from anywhere in Italy without a calling card, dial the international access number ("00") + country code (for the country you are calling) + number. For operator-assisted and calling card calls, dial the international operator: ☎170. For directory assistance, dial ☎12.

TELEPHONE CODES			TELEPHONE CODES	
Australia	61		Monaco	377
Austria	43		New Zealand	64
Canada	1		Slovenia	386
France	33		South Africa	27
Germany	49		Spain	34
Greece	30		Switzerland	41
Ireland	353		UK	44
Italy	39		US	1

TIME ZONES

Italy is 1hr. ahead of Greenwich Mean Time (GMT), 6hr. ahead of US Eastern Standard Time (EST), 9hr. ahead of Vancouver and San Francisco time, 9hr. behind Sydney time, and 11hr. behind Auckland time. From the last Sunday in March to the last Sunday in September, Italy switches to Daylight Savings Time and is 2hr. ahead of GMT but still 6hr. later than EST.

MEASUREMENTS

Italy uses the metric system. Below are metric units and their English system equivalents.

ENGLISH TO METRIC	METRIC TO ENGLISH
1 inch (in.) = 2.54cm	1 centimeter (cm) = 0.39 in.
1 foot (ft.) = 0.30m	1 meter (m) = 3.28 ft.
1 yard (yd.) = 0.914m	1 meter (m) = 1.09 yd.
1 mile (mi.) = 1.61km	1 kilometer (km) = 0.62 mi.
1 ounce (oz.) = 28.35g	1 gram (g) = 0.035 oz.
1 pound (lb.) = 0.454kg	1 kilogram (kg) = 2.202 lb.
1 fluid ounce (fl. oz.) = 29.57ml	1 milliliter (mL) = 0.034 fl. oz.
1 gallon (gal.) = 3.785L	1 liter (L) = 0.264 gal.
1 acre (ac.) = 0.405ha	1 hectare (ha) = 2.47 ac.
1 square mile (sq. mi.) = 2.59 sq. km	1 square kilometer (sq. km) = 0.386 sq. mi.

ABBREVIATIONS

ABBREVIATIONS		ABBREVIATIONS	
Corso	C.	Porta	Pta.
Contrada	Cda.	San, Santo, Santa	S.
Di, Del, Dei, Della, Delle	d.	Strada	Str.
Locanda	Loc.	Via	V.
Piazza	P.	Vicolo	Vco.

FESTIVALS AND HOLIDAYS

Italians work 35hr. per week, take 2hr. lunch breaks, close some businesses on Mondays, take elaborate coastal vacations for a month each summer—and still manage to amass dozens of holidays. Many celebrations have religious origins, but they're not all that pious. **Carnevale** energizes Italian towns in February during the 10 days before Lent. During **Scoppio del Carro,** held in Florence on Easter Sunday, Florentines set off a cart of explosives in keeping with medieval tradition. The fantastic Sienese **Palio** on July 2 and August 16 transforms the Piazza del Duomo into a horse-racing track and divides the city in support of the 12 *contrade* (teams). Festivals in smaller towns are quirkier and offer more unadulterated local charm, such as the mouth-watering victuals in Cortona (p. 438) and drunken revelry in Gubbio (p. 487). For a complete list of festivals, write to the **Italian Government Tourist Board** (p. 9) or visit www.italiantourism.com/tradition.html.

DATE	FESTIVAL	LOCATION
Jan. 6, 2005	Epifania (Epiphany)	Nationwide
Feb. 6-13, 2005	Festa del Fiore di Mandorlo (Almond Blossom)	Agrigento (p. 702)
late Feb.-early Mar.	Carnevale	Venice (p. 302)
Feb. 27- Mar 1, 2005	Sartiglia (Race & Joust)	Oristano (p. 747)
Mar. 21-27, 2005	Settimana Santa (Holy Week)	All over Italy
Mar. 25, 2005	Venerdi Santo (Good Friday)	All over Italy
Mar. 27, 2005	Pasqua (Easter)	All over Italy
Apr. 25, 2005	Giomo della Liberazione (Liberation Day)	All over Italy
May 1, 2005	Festa dei Lavoratori (Labor Day)	All over Italy

DATE	FESTIVAL	LOCATION
May 1-4, 2005	Sagra di Sant'Efisio (Festival of St. Efisio)	Cagliari (p. 726)
May 7-8, 2005	Festa di Calendimaggio	Assisi (p. 495)
May 7-8, 2005	Festa di S. Nicola	Bari (p. 603)
Sa before 1st Su in May	Festa di S. Gennaro	Naples (p. 555)
May 8, 2005	Sagra del Pesce (Festival of Fish)	Camogli (p. 186)
May 8, 2005	Ascensione (Feast of the Ascension)	All over Italy
May 15, 2005	Corsa dei Ceri (Candle Race)	Gubbio (p. 489)
May 15, 2005	Festa della Matricola (Graduation Feast)	Bologna (p. 356)
May 29, 2005	Palio della Balestra (Crossbow Contest)	Gubbio (p. 490)
June	Calcio Fiorentino (Soccer Games)	Florence (p. 421)
June 15, 2005	Corpus Christi	All over Italy
June 18, 2005	Giostra del Saraceno (Joust of the Saracen)	Arezzo (p. 436)
June 24, 2005	Festa di S. Giovanni (Feast of St. John)	Florence (p. 421)
June 26, 2005	Gioco del Ponte (Battle of the Bridge)	Pisa (p. 467)
late June	Mostra Internazionale del Nuovo Cinema (International New Cinema)	Pesaro (p. 513)
late June-early July	S. Maria della Bruna (Feast of the Dark Madonna)	Matera (p. 623)
late June-mid-July	Spoleto Festival	Spoleto (p. 501)
June-July	Ravenna Festival	Ravenna (p. 382)
July	Umbria Jazz Festival	Perugia (p. 485)
July 2, 2005	Festa della Madonna (Feast of the Virgin Mary)	Enna (p. 687)
July 12, 2005	Palio della Balestra (Crossbow Contest)	Lucca (p. 461)
mid-July	Palio Marinaro (Boat Race)	Livorno (p. 470)
July 16, 2005	Festa del Redentore (Feast of the Redeemer)	Venice (p. 300)
July 25, 2005	Giostra del Orso (Joust of the Bear)	Pistoia (p. 455)
late July-early Aug.	Settimana Musicale (Music Week)	Siena (p. 432)
late July-late Aug.	Taormina Arte	Taormina (p. 676)
late July-early Aug.	Settimana Pirandelliana	Agrigento (p. 702)
Aug. 7, 2005	Torneo della Quintana (Joust of the Quintana)	Ascoli-Piceno (p. 522)
Aug. 14-15, 2005	Sagra della Bistecca (Steak Feast)	Cortona (p. 441)
Aug. 15, 2005	Ferragosto (Feast of the Assumption)	All over Italy
Aug. 16, 2005	Palio	Siena (p. 460)
Aug. 28-29, 2005	Sagra del Redentore (Feast of the Redeemer)	Nuoro (p. 753)
late Aug.-early Sept.	Venice International Film Festival	Venice (p. 302)
early Sept.	Festival MareMusica a Minori|	Salerno (p. 596)
early Sept.	D'ouja d'or Wine Festival	Asti (p. 158)
Sept. 13, 2005	Luminara (parade of the Volto Santo)	Lucca (p. 461)
Sept. 18, 2005	Palio di Asti	Asti (p. 158)
Sept. 19, 2005	Festa di S. Gennaro	Naples (p. 555)
Nov. 1, 2005	Ogni Santi (All Saints' Day)	All over Italy
Nov. 2, 2005	Giorno dei Morti (All Souls' Day)	All over Italy
Nov. 21, 2005	Festa della Madonna della Salute (Festival of the Virgin, Patron of Good Health)	Venice (p. 302)
Dec. 24, 2005	Le Farchie di Natale (Christmas Eve)	All over Italy
Dec. 25, 2005	Natale (Christmas Day)	All over Italy
Dec. 26, 2005	Festa di S. Stefano	All over Italy

THE ITALIAN LANGUAGE

PRONUNCIATION

VOWELS

There are seven vowel sounds in standard Italian. **A**, **i**, and **u** each have one pronunciation. **E** and **o** each have two pronunciations, one open and one closed, depending on the vowel's placement in the word, the stress, and the regional accent. Below is their approximate pronunciation.

VOWEL PHONOLOGY	
a:	a as in father (casa)
e: closed	ay as in bay (sera)
e: open	eh as in set (sette)
i:	ee as in cheese (vino)
o: closed	o as in show (sono)
o: open	aw as in awful (bocca)
u:	oo as in moon (gusto)

CONSONANTS

C and G: Before **a**, **o**, or **u**, **c**, and **g** are hard, as in cat and goose or as in the Italian word colore (koh-LOHR-eh), "color," or gatto (GAHT-toh), "cat." Italians soften **c** and **g** into **ch** and **j** sounds, respectively, when followed by **i** or **e**, as in English cheese and jeep or Italian ciao (chow), "goodbye," and gelato (jeh-LAH-toh), "ice cream."

CH and GH: H returns **c** and **g** to their "hard" sounds in front of **i** or **e** (see above): chianti (ky-AHN-tee), the Tuscan wine, and spaghetti (spah-GEHT-tee), the pasta.

GN and GLI: Pronounce **gn** like the **ni** in onion, thus bagno ("bath") is "BAHN-yoh." **Gli** is like the **lli** in million, so sbagliato ("wrong") is said "zbal-YAH-toh."

SC and SCH: When followed by **a**, **o**, or **u**, **sc** is pronounced as **sk**. Scusi ("excuse me") yields "SKOO-zee." When followed by an **e** or **i**, **sc** is pronounced **sh** as in sciopero (SHOH-pair-oh; strike). **H** returns **c** to its hard sound (sk) before **i** or **e**, as in pesche (PEHS-keh; peaches), not to be confused with pesce (PEH-sheh; fish).

Double consonants: When you see a double consonant, hold it for a long time and stress the preceding vowel; failing to do so can lead to confusion. For example, penne all'arrabbiata is "short pasta in a spicy red sauce," whereas pene all'arrabbiata means "penis in a spicy red sauce."

STRESS

In Italian, stress generally falls on the next-to-last syllable. An accent indicates when it falls on the last syllable: città (cheet-TAH) or perché (pehr-KEH).

GENDER AND PLURALS

Italian nouns fall into two genders, masculine and feminine. The singular masculine ending is usually **o**, as in uomo, and the feminine is usually **a**, as in donna. Words ending in an **a** in the singular (usually feminine) end with an **e** in the plural; mela (MEH-lah), "apple," becomes mele (MEH-leh). Words ending with **o** or **e** take an **i** in the plural: conto (KOHN-toh), "bill," is conti (KOHN-tee), and cane (KAH-neh), "dog," becomes cani (KAH-nee). Words with a final accent, like città and caffè, and words that end in consonants, like bar and sport, do not change in the plural. Adjectives agree with their noun in gender and number. They are formed by adding the gender and number ending to the root.

APPENDIX

PHRASEBOOK

ENGLISH	ITALIAN	PRONUNCIATION
GENERAL		
Hello/So long (informal)	Ciao	chow
Good day/Hello	Buongiorno	bwohn-JOHR-noh
Good evening	Buonasera	BWOH-nah-SEH-rah
Good night	Buonanotte	BWOH-nah-NOHT-teh
Goodbye	Arrivederci/ArrivederLa (formal)	ah-ree-veh-DEHR-chee/ah-ree-veh-DEHR-lah
Please	Per favore/Per piacere	pehr fah-VOH-reh/pehr pyah-CHEH-reh
Thank you	Grazie	GRAHT-see-yeh
How are you?	Come stai/Come sta (formal)?	COH-meh STA-ee/stah
I am well	Sto bene	stoh BEH-neh
You're welcome/May I help you?/Please	Prego	PREH-goh
Excuse me	Scusi	SKOO-zee
I'm sorry	Mi dispiace	mee dees-PYAH-cheh
My name is...	Mi chiamo...	mee kee-YAH-moh
What's your name?	Come ti chiami?	COH-meh tee kee-YAH-mee
Yes/No/Maybe	Sì/No/Forse	see/no/FOHR-seh
I don't know	Non lo so	nohn loh soh
I have no idea	Boh!	boh
Could you repeat that?	Potrebbe ripetere?	poh-TREHB-beh ree-PEH-teh-reh
What does this mean?	Cosa vuol dire questo?	COH-za vwohl DEE-reh KWEH-stoh
I understand	Ho capito	oh kah-PEE-toh
I don't understand	Non capisco	nohn kah-PEES-koh
I don't speak Italian	Non parlo italiano	nohn PAHR-loh ee-tahl-YAH-noh
Do you speak English?	Parla inglese?	PAR-lah een-GLEH-zeh
Could you help me?	Potrebbe aiutarmi?	poh-TREHB-beh ah-yoo-TAHR-mee
How do you say...?	Come si dice...?	KOH-meh see DEE-cheh
What do you call this in Italian?	Come si chiama questo in italiano?	KOH-meh see kee-YAH-mah KWEH-stoh een ee-tahl-YAH-no
this/that	questo/quello	KWEH-sto/KWEHL-loh
more/less	più/meno	pyoo/MEH-noh
TIME		
At what time...?	A che ora...?	ah keh OHR-ah
What time is it?	Che ore sono?	keh OHR-eh SOH-noh
It's noon	È mezzogiorno	eh MEHD-zoh-DJOHR-noh
midnight	mezzanotte	MEHD-zah-NOT-eh
now	adesso/ora	ah-DEHS-so/OH-rah
tomorrow	domani	doh-MAH-nee
today	oggi	OHJ-jee
yesterday	ieri	ee-EH-ree
right away	subito	SU-bee-toh
soon	fra poco/presto	frah POH-koh/ PREH-stoh
after(wards)	dopo	DOH-poh
before	prima	PREE-mah
late/later	tardi/più tardi	TAHR-dee/pyoo TAHR-dee
early	presto	PREHS-toh

late (after scheduled arrival time)	in ritardo	een ree-TAHR-doh
daily	quotidiano	kwoh-tee-dee-AH-no
weekly	settimanale	seht-tee-mah-NAH-leh
monthly	mensile	mehn-SEE-leh
vacation	le ferie	leh FEH-ree-eh
weekdays	i giorni feriali	ee JOHR-nee feh-ree-AH-lee
Sundays and holidays	i giorni festivi	ee JOHR-nee fehs-TEE-vee
day off (at store, restaurant, etc.)	riposo	ree-POH-zo

DIRECTIONS AND TRANSPORTATION

Where is...?	Dov'è...?	doh-VEH
How do you get to...?	Come si arriva a...?	KOH-meh see ahr-REE-vah ah
Do you stop at...?	Si ferma...?	SEE FEHR-mah
...at the center of town	in centro	een CHEHN-troh
...at the consulate	al consolato	ahl kohn-so-LAH-toh
...at the hospital	all'ospedale	AH-los-peh-DAH-leh
...at the post office	all'ufficio postale	AH-loo-FEE-choh poh-STAH-leh
...the station	la stazione	lah staht-zee-YOH-neh
near/far	vicino/lontano	vee-CHEE-noh/lohn-TAH-noh
turn left/right	gira a sinistra/destra	JEE-rah ah see-NEE-strah/DEH-strah
straight ahead	sempre diritto	SEHM-preh DREET-toh
here	qui/qua	kwee/kwah
there	lì/là	lee/lah
the street address	l'indirizzo	leen-dee-REET-soh
the telephone	il telefono	eel teh-LEH-foh-noh
street	strada, via, viale, vico, vicolo, corso	STRAH-dah, VEE-ah, vee-AH-leh, VEE-koh, VEE-koh-loh, KOHR-soh
large, open square	piazzale	pee-yah-TZAH-leh
stairway	scalinata	scah-lee-NAH-tah
beach	spiaggia	spee-YAH-geeah
river	fiume	fee-OO-meh
toilet, WC	gabinetto	gah-bee-NEH-toh
Take the bus from/to...	Prenda l'autobus da/a...	PREN-dah LAOW-toh-boos dah/ah...
What time does the... leave?	A che ora parte...?	ah keh OHR-ah PAHR-teh
From where does the... leave?	Da dove parte...?	dah DOH-veh PAHR-teh
...the (city) bus	...l'autobus	LAOW-toh-boos
...the (intercity) bus	...il pullman	eel POOL-mahn
...the ferry	...il traghetto	eel tra-GHEHT-toh
...hydrofoil	...l'aliscafo	LA-lee-scah-foh
...the plane	...l'aereo	lah-EHR-reh-oh
...the train	...il treno	eel TREH-noh
the ticket office	la biglietteria	lah beel-yeht-teh-RI-ah
How much does it cost?	Quanto costa?	KWAN-toh CO-stah
I would like to buy...	Vorrei comprare...	voy-RAY com-PRAH-reh
...a ticket	...un biglietto	...oon beel-YEHT-toh
...a pass (bus, etc.)	...una tessera	OO-nah TEHS-seh-rah
one-way	solo andata	SO-lo ahn-DAH-tah
round-trip	andata e ritorno	ahn-DAH-tah eh ree-TOHR-noh
reduced price	ridotto	ree-DOHT-toh

student discount	lo sconto studentesco	loh SKOHN-toh stoo-dehn-TEHS-koh
The train is late	Il treno è in ritardo	eel TRAY-no eh een ree-TAHR-doh
the arrival	l'arrivo	la-REE-voh
the departure	la partenza	la par-TENT-sah
the track or train platform	il binario	eel bee-NAH-ree-oh
the flight	il volo	eel VOH-loh
the reservation	la prenotazione	la preh-no-taht-see-YOH-neh
the entrance/the exit	l'ingresso/l'uscita	leen-GREH-so/loo-SHEE-tah
I need to get off here	Devo scendere qui	DEH-vo SHEN-der-eh qwee

EMERGENCY		
I lost my passport/wallet	Ho perso il passaporto/portafoglio	oh PEHR-soh eel pahs-sah-POHR-toh/por-ta-FOH-lee-oh
I've been robbed	Sono stato derubato/a	SOH-noh STAH-toh deh-roo-BAH-toh/tah
Wait!	Aspetta!	ahs-PEHT-tah
Stop!	Ferma!	FEHR-mah
Help!	Aiuto!	ah-YOO-toh
Leave me alone!	Lasciami stare!/Mollami!	LAH-shah-mee STAH-reh/MOH-lah MEE
Don't touch me!	Non mi toccare!	NOHN mee tohk-KAH-reh
Go back to where you came from!	Vai a quel paese!	VAH-ee ah KWEL pa-EH-zeh
I'm calling the police!	Telefono alla polizia!	tehl-LEH-foh-noh ah-lah poh-leet-SEE-ah
military police	carabinieri	CAH-rah-been-YEH-ree
municipal police	polizia	poh-lee-TZEE-yah
Go away, moron!	Vattene, cretino!	VAH-teh-neh creh-TEE-noh

MEDICAL		
I have... allergies	Ho... delle allergie	OH... DEHL-leh ahl-lair-JEE-eh
...a cold	...un raffreddore	oon rahf-freh-DOH-reh
...a cough	...una tosse	OO-nah TOHS-seh
...the flu	...l'influenza	linn-floo-ENT-sah
...a fever	...una febbre	OO-nah FEHB-breh
...a headache	...mal di testa	mahl dee TEHS-tah
My foot/arm/booty hurts	Mi fa male il piede/braccio/culo	mee fah MAH-le eel PYEHD-deh/BRAH-cho/COO-loh
I'm on the pill	Prendo la pillola	PREHN-doh lah PEE-loh-lah
(3 months) pregnant	incinta da tre mesi	een-CHEEN-tah (dah TREH MEH-zee)
the blood	il sangue	eel SAHN-gweh
the appendix	l'appendice	lap-EHN-dee-cheh
a gynecologist	un ginecologo	oon jee-neh-KOH-loh-goh

HOTEL AND HOSTEL RESERVATIONS		
hotel/hostel	albergo/ostello	alh-BEHR-goh/os-TEHL-loh
Hello? (answering phone)	Pronto?	PROHN-toh
Do you speak English?	Parla inglese?	PAHR-lah een-GLEH-zeh
Could I reserve a single room/double room (for the second of August)?	Potrei prenotare una camera singola/doppia (per il due agosto)?	poh-TREH-ee preh-noh-TAH-reh oo-nah CAH-meh-rah SEEN-goh-lah/DOH-pee-yah (pehr eel DOO-eh ah-GOH-stoh)
Is there a bed available tonight?	C'è un posto libero stasera?	cheh oon POHS-toe LEE-ber-oh sta-SER-ah
with bath/shower	con bagno/doccia	kohn BAHN-yo/DOH-cha
Is there a cheaper room without a bath/shower?	C'è una stanza più economica senza bagno/doccia?	cheh oo-nah STAN-zah pyoo eko-NOM-ika senzah BAHN-yo/DOH-cha
open/closed	aperto/chiuso	ah-PEHR-toh/KYOO-zoh
sheets	i lenzuoli	ee lehn-SUO-lee

the blanket	la coperta	lah koh-PEHR-tah
the bed	il letto	eel LEHT-toh
heating	il riscaldamento	eel ree-skahl-dah-MEHN-toh
How much is the room?	Quanto costa la camera?	KWAHN-toh KOHS-ta lah KAM-eh-rah
I will arrive (at 2:30pm)	Arriverò (alle due e mezzo)	ah-ree-veh-ROH (ah-leh DOO-eh MED-zoh)
Certainly	Certo!	CHAIR-toh
We're closed during August	Chiudiamo ad agosto	kyu-dee-AH-moh ahd ah-GOH-stoh
We're full	Siamo al completo	See-YAH-moh ahl cohm-PLAY-toh
We don't take telephone reservations	Non si fanno le prenotazioni per telefono	nohn see FAHN-noh leh preh-noh-tat-see-YOH-nee pair teh-LEH-foh-noh
You'll have to send a deposit/check	Bisogna mandare un anticipo/un assegno	bee-ZOHN-yah mahn-DAH-reh oon ahn-TEE-chee-poh/oon ahs-SAY-nyoh
What is that funny smell?	Che cos'è quest'odore strano?	keh kohz-EH kwest-oh-DOOR-eh STRAH-noh?

RESTAURANTS

food	il cibo	eel CHEE-boh
wine bar	l'enoteca	len-oh-TEK-ah
breakfast	la colazione	lah coh-laht-see-YO-neh
lunch	il pranzo	eel PRAHND-zoh
dinner	la cena	lah CHEH-nah
coffee	il caffè	eel kah-FEH
appetizer	l'antipasto	lahn-tee-PAH-stoh
first course	il primo	eel PREE-moh
second course	il secondo	eel seh-COHN-doh
side dish	il contorno	eel cohn-TOHR-noh
dessert	il dolce	eel DOHL-cheh
bottle	la bottiglia	lah boh-TEEL-yah
waiter/waitress	il/la cameriere/a	eel/lah kah-meh-ree-EH-reh/rah
the bill	il conto	eel COHN-toh
cover charge	il coperto	eel koh-PEHR-toh
tip	la mancia	lah MAHN-chee-yah

AMORE

I have a boyfriend/girl-friend	Ho un ragazzo/una ragazza	oh oon rah-GAHT-soh/oo-nah rah-GAHT-sah
Let's get a room	Prendiamo una camera	prehn-DYAH-moh oo-nah CAH-meh-rah
Oh, I'm leaving tomorrow	Oh, vado via domani	Oh VAH-doh vee-ah doh-MAH-nee
Voluptuous!	Volutuoso/a!	VOL-oot-oo-OH-zhoh/zhah
To be enamoured of	Essere innamorato/a di	Eh-seh-reh een-am-mo-rah-to/ta dee
Just a kiss	Solo un bacio	SOH-loh oon BAH-chee-oh
Are you single?	Sei celibe?	SEY CHEH-lee-beh
You're cute	Sei carino/a (bello/a)	SEY cah-REEN-oh/ah (BEHL-loh/lah)
I love you, I swear	Ti amo, te lo giuro	tee AH-moh, teh loh DJOO-roh
I'm married	Sono sposato/a	soh-noh spo-ZA-to/ta
You're quite a babe	Sei proprio un figo/una figa	SEY PROH-pree-yo oon FEE-goh/oona FEE-gah
She dances poorly, why don't you dance with me?	Lei balla male, perchè non balli con me?	LEY BAHL-lah mal-eh, pehr-KEH nohn BAHL-lee con meh
I only have safe sex	Pratico solo sesso sicuro	PRAH-tee-coh sohl-oh SEHS-so see-COO-roh
Leave her alone, she's mine	Lasciala stare, è mia	LAH-shyah-lah STAH-reh, eh mee-ah
Leave right now!	Vai via subito!	vai VEE-ah SOO-beet-oh
I'll never forget you	Non ti dimenticherò mai	nohn tee dee-men-tee-ker-OH mah-ee
heterosexual/straight	etero (sessuale)	EH-teh-roh (ses-SOOAH-leh)

APPENDIX

bisexual	bisessuale	bee-sehs-soo-AH-leh
gay	gay	GAH-ee
lesbian	lesbica	LEH-sbee-cah
transvestite	travestito/a	trah-veh-STEE-toh/tah

AT THE BAR		
May I buy you a drink?	Posso offrirle qualcosa da bere?	POHS-soh ohf-FREER-leh kwahl-COH-zah dah Beh-reh
I'm drunk	Sono ubriaco/a	SOH-noh oo-BRYAH-coh/cah
Let's go!	Andiamo!	Ahn-dee-AH-moh
I don't drink	Non bevo	nohn BEH-voh
Cheers!	Cin cin!	cheen cheen
Do you have a light?	Mi fai accendere?	mee fah-ee ah-CHEN-deh-reh
No thank you, I don't smoke	No grazie, non fumo	noh GRAH-zyeh nohn FOO-moh
Do you have an ashtray?	Hai un portacenere?	ah-ee oon pohr-tah-CHEH-neh-reh
I was here first!	C'ero io prima!	CHEH-roh EE-oh PREE-mah
Do you believe in aliens?	Credi negli extraterrestri?	CREH-dee neh-lyee ehx-trah-teh-REH-stree
I feel like throwing up	Mi viene di vomitare	mee VYE-neh dee voh-mee-TAH-reh
a beer	una birra	OO-nah BEER-rah
glass of wine	bicchiere di vino	bee-KYE-reh dee VEE-noh
liter of wine	litro di vino	LEE-troh di VEE-noh

MENU READER

PRIMI	
pasta aglio e olio	garlic and olive oil
pasta all'amatriciana	in a tangy tomato sauce with onions and bacon
pasta all'arabbiata	in a spicy tomato sauce
pasta alla bolognese	in a meat sauce
pasta alla boscaiola	egg pasta, served in a mushroom sauce with peas and cream
pasta alla carbonara	in a creamy sauce with egg, cured bacon, and cheese
pasta alla pizzaiola	tomato-based sauce with olive oil and red peppers
pasta alla puttanesca	in a tomato sauce with olives, capers, and anchovies
gnocchi	potato dumplings
ravioli	square-shaped and often stuffed with cheese or vegetables
tagliatelle	thin and flat, these are the northern version of fettuccini
polenta	deep fried cornmeal
risotto	rice dish, comes in nearly as many flavors as pasta sauce

PIZZA	
alla capriciosa	with ham, egg, artichoke, and more
con rucola (rughetta)	with arugula (rocket for Brits)
marinara	with red sauce and no cheese
margherita	plain ol' tomato, mozzarella, and basil
pepperoni	bell pepper
polpette	meatballs
quattro formaggi	with four cheeses
quattro stagioni	four seasons; a different topping for each quarter of the pizza, usually mushrooms, *prosciutto crudo*, artichoke, and tomato

SECONDI	
animelle alla griglia	grilled sweetbreads

SECONDI

asino	donkey (served in Sicily and Sardinia)
bistecca	steak
cavallo (sfilacci)	horse (a delicacy throughout the South and Sardinia)
coniglio	rabbit
cotoletta	breaded veal cutlet with cheese
cozze	mussels
gamberi	prawns
granchi	crabs
manzo	beef
osso buco	braised veal shank
polpo	octopus
prosciutto	smoked ham, available cured (*crudo*) or cooked (*cotto*)
salsiccia	sausage
saltimbocca alla romana	slices of veal and ham cooked together and topped with cheese
seppia	cuttlefish, usually served grilled in its own ink
speck	smoked raw ham, lean but surrounded by a layer of fat
tonno	tuna
trippa	tripe (chopped, sautéed cow intestines, usually in a tomato sauce)
vitello	veal
vongole	clams

CONTORNI

broccoletti	broccoli florets
cavolo	cabbage
cipolla	onion
fagioli	beans (usually white)
fagiolini	green beans
funghi	mushrooms
insalata caprese	tomatoes with mozzarella cheese and basil, drizzled with olive oil
insalata mista	mixed green salad
lattuga	lettuce
melanzana	eggplant
tartufi	truffles

ANTIPASTI

antipasto rustico	assortment of cold appetizers
bresaola	thinly sliced dried beef, served with olive oil, lemon, and *parmigiano*
bruschetta	crisp slices of garlic-rubbed, baked bread, often with raw tomatoes
carpaccio	extremely thin slices of lean, raw beef
crostini	small pieces of toasted bread usually served with chicken liver or mozzarella and anchovies, though other toppings abound
fiori di zucca	zucchini flowers filled with cheese, battered, and lightly fried
supplì	fried rice ball filled with tomato, meat, and cheese

FRUTTA

anguria/cocomero	watermelon
arancia	orange
ciliegia	cherry
fragola	strawberry
lampone	raspberry
pesca	peach

prugna	plum
uva	grape
DOLCI	
cannoli	Sicilian tube pastries filled with sweet ricotta
cassata siciliana	sponge cake, sweet cream, cheese, chocolate, and candied fruit
gelato	Italian-style ice cream
granita	ice-based fruit or coffee slushee
macedonia	fruit salad
panna cotta	flan
sfogliatelle	sugar-coated layers of crunchy pastry with ricotta
tiramisù	marscapone, eggs, and lady fingers dipped in *espresso*
PREPARATION	
al dente	firm to the bite (pasta)
al forno	baked
al sangue	rare
al vino	in wine sauce
alla griglia	grilled
ben cotta/o	well done
cruda/o	raw
fresca/o	fresh
fritta/o	fried
non troppo cotta/o	medium rare
piccante	spicy
ripieno	stuffed

APPENDIX

ART AND ARCHITECTURE GLOSSARY

abbazia/badia	abbey; acquired prominence during medieval monasticism
anfiteatro	amphitheater, a circular or elliptical building with tiered seating used for contests or spectacles
architrave	the lowermost part of an entablature, resting directly on top of a column
arco	arch, a structure invented by the Romans
apse	a semicircular, domed niche projecting from the altar end of a church
baldacchino	stone or bronze canopy supported by columns over the altar of a church
basilica	a rectangular building with aisle and apse, but no transept; used by ancient Romans for public administration and by Christians as churches
battistero	a baptistry, usually a separate building near the town's duomo where the town's baptisms were performed; some have spectacular front doors
campanile	a bell tower, usually freestanding
cappella	chapel, a smaller religious edifice than a church, in private estates or homes
castrum	the ancient Roman military camp; many Italian cities were originally built on a rectilinear plan with straight streets, the chief of which was called the decumanus maximus
Cenacolo	"Last Supper"; a depiction of Christ at dinner on the evening before his crucifixion, often found in the refectory of an abbey or convent
chancel	the space around the altar reserved for clergy and choir
chiaroscuro	the balance between light and dark in a painting, and the painter's ability to show the contrast between them
chiesa	church; some incorporate elements from earlier structures, such as temple columns
cloister/chiostro	a courtyard; generally a quadrangle with covered walkways along its edges, often with a central garden, forming part of a church or monastery

condottiere	a leader of mercenary soldiers in Italy in the 14th and 15th centuries, when wars were almost incessant
cornice	a decorated, sculpted band that crowns a wall
cosmati work	mosaic on marble, found in early Christian churches
cupola	a dome; invented by the Romans; in the Renaissance, it acquired more than one layer for structural support
deposition	a depiction of the dead body of Christ being removed from the cross
diptych	a painting in two parts or panels
duomo	cathedral; the official seat of a diocesan bishop of the Roman Catholic Church, and usually the most notable church of an Italian town
forum	in Roman antiquity, a square containing municipal buildings and/or markets; smaller towns have one forum, larger cities can have several
fresco	a painting made on wet plaster that bonds to the wall when it dries; it requires extremely swift brushwork and no mistakes; developed in the Renaissance
frieze	a band of decoration; architecturally, this can also refer to the middle part of an entablature (everything above the columns of a building) between the architrave and the cornice
grotesque	painted, carved, or stucco decorations of fantastic, distorted human or animal figures, named for the grotto work from Nero's buried Golden House
in restauro	under restoration; a key term in Italy
Latin Cross	a cross with the vertical arm longer than the horizontal arm
intarsia	inlay work, usually of marble, metal, or wood
loggia	a covered gallery or balcony
lunette	a semicircular frame in a ceiling or vault, holding a painting or sculpture
mausoleum	a large tomb or building with places to entomb the dead above ground
mithraeum	a temple to the Roman god Mithras, god of light
nave	central body of a church, starting from the apse and often intersecting the transept
nuraghe	cone-shaped tower-houses built of stone and assembled without mortar
palazzo	an important building of any type, not just a palace
Pietà	a depiction of the Virgin mourning the dead Christ
pietra serena	gray to bluish stone commonly used in Renaissance constructions
pilaster	a rectangular column set into a wall as an ornamental motif
polyptych	altarpiece with more than three panels
presepio	nativity scene
putti	(sing. *putto*) the little nude babies that flit around Renaissance art occasionally and Baroque art incessantly
reliquary	holding place for a saint's relics, usually the bones, but often much stranger body parts including organs, hair, eyeballs, and fingernails
sinopia drawing	a red pigment sketch made on a wall as a preliminary study for a fresco
sottoportico	street or sidewalk continuing under a building (like an extended archway)
stigmata	miraculous body pains or bleeding resembling Christ's crucifix wounds
terme	ancient Roman baths and, consequently, social centers
telamoni	large, often sensual, statues of men used as columns in temples
tessera	one of the small colored pieces of stone or glass used in making mosaics
transept	in a cruciform church, the arm of the church that intersects the nave or central aisle (i.e., the cross-bar of the T)
travertine	a light-colored marble or limestone, used in the Colosseum and the facade of St. Peter's Basilica, among other structures
triptych	a painting in three panels or parts
trompe l'oeil	literally, "to fool the eye," a painting or other piece or art whose purpose is to trick the viewer, as in a flat ceiling painted so as to appear domed
tufa	a soft stone composed of volcanic ash (*tufa* in Italian)

INDEX

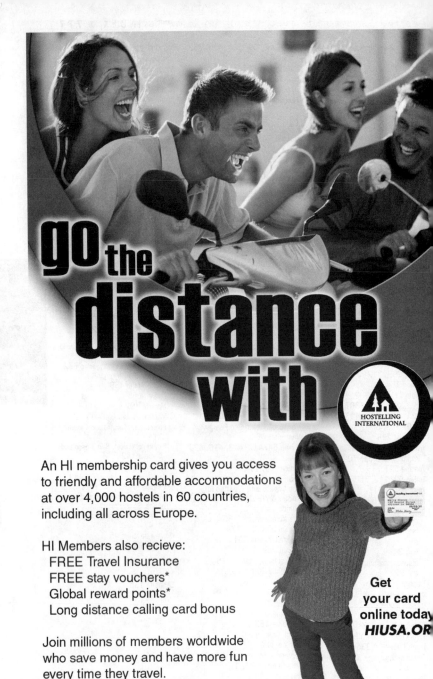

go the distance with

HOSTELLING INTERNATIONAL

An HI membership card gives you access to friendly and affordable accommodations at over 4,000 hostels in 60 countries, including all across Europe.

HI Members also recieve:
  FREE Travel Insurance
  FREE stay vouchers*
  Global reward points*
  Long distance calling card bonus

Join millions of members worldwide who save money and have more fun every time they travel.

*at participating hostels

Get your card online today
HIUSA.OR

CATCH
YOUNG MONEY!

YOUNG MONEY is the premier lifestyle and money magazine for young adults. Each issue is packed with cutting-edge articles written by the nation's top college journalists.

Whether your goal is to save money, make more cash or get ahead in your career path, YOUNG MONEY will help you make smarter financial decisions. So subscribe now. It's one decision you will never regret.

Subscribe Online TODAY and Receive Your **FREE ISSUE**
www.youngmoney.com

your life. *right now.*

LONG ON WEEKEND. SHORT ON CASH.

The fastest way to the best fare.

ORBITZ
AND GO!™

©2004 Orbitz, LLC

ABOUT LET'S GO

GUIDES FOR THE INDEPENDENT TRAVELER

At Let's Go, we see every trip as the chance of a lifetime. If your dream is to grab a machete and forge through the jungles of Brazil, we can take you there. If you'd rather bask in the Riviera sun at a beachside cafe, we'll set you a table. We write for readers who know that there's more to travel than sharing double deckers with tourists and who believe that travel can change both themselves and the world—whether they plan to spend six days in London or six months in Latin America. We'll show you just how far your money can go, and prove that the greatest limitation on your adventures is not your wallet, but your imagination. After all, traveling close to the ground lets you interact more directly with the places and people you've gone to see, making for the most authentic experience.

BEYOND THE TOURIST EXPERIENCE

To help you gain a deeper connection with the places you travel, our researchers give you the heads-up on both world-renowned and off-the-beaten-track attractions, sights, and destinations. They engage with the local culture, writing features on regional cuisine, local festivals, and hot political issues. We've also opened our pages to respected writers and scholars to hear their takes on the countries and regions we cover, and asked travelers who have worked, studied, or volunteered abroad to contribute first-person accounts of their experiences. We've also increased our coverage of responsible travel and expanded each guide's Alternatives to Tourism chapter to share more ideas about how to give back to local communities and learn about the places you travel.

FORTY-FIVE YEARS OF WISDOM

Let's Go got its start in 1960, when a group of creative and well-traveled students compiled their experience and advice into a 20-page mimeographed pamphlet, which they gave to travelers on charter flights to Europe. Four and a half decades later, we've expanded to cover six continents and all kinds of travel—while retaining our founders' adventurous attitude toward the world. Our guides are still researched and written entirely by students on shoestring budgets, experienced travelers who know that train strikes, stolen luggage, food poisoning, and marriage proposals are all part of a day's work. This year, we're expanding our coverage of South America and Southeast Asia, with brand-new *Let's Go: Ecuador*, *Let's Go: Peru*, and *Let's Go: Vietnam*. Our adventure guide series is growing, too, with the addition of *Let's Go: Pacific Northwest Adventure* and *Let's Go: New Zealand Adventure*. And we're immensely excited about our new *Let's Go: Roadtripping USA*—two years, eight routes, and sixteen researchers and editors have put together a travel guide like none other.

THE LET'S GO COMMUNITY

More than just a travel guide company, Let's Go is a community. Our small staff comes together because of our shared passion for travel and our desire to help other travelers see the world. We love it when our readers become part of the Let's Go community as well—when you travel, drop us a postcard (67 Mt. Auburn St., Cambridge, MA 02138, USA) or send us an e-mail (feedback@letsgo.com) to tell us about your adventures and discoveries.

For more information, visit us online: www.letsgo.com.

MAP INDEX

MAP LEGEND

Symbol	Label	Symbol	Label	Symbol	Label
✈	Airport	∴	Ancient Ruin	M	Metro Station
✛	Hospital	🚌	Bus Station	🏛	Museum	‧‧‧‧	Pedestrian Zone
🚓	Police	🚂	Train Station	🏨	Hotel/Hostel	—	International Border
✉	Post Office	⬠	Arch/Gate	⛺	Camping	– – –	Regional Border
(i)	Tourist Office	⚓	Ferry Landing	🍎	Food		Park
$	Bank/ATM/Exchange	✝	Church/Cathedral	🍺	Nightlife		Beach
⚑	Embassy/Consulate	✡	Synagogue	🏖	Beach		
▪	Point of Interest	🏰	Castle	💻	Internet Cafe		Water
℞	Pharmacy	⛰	Mountain	🛍	Shopping	Ⓝ	The Let's Go compass always points NORTH.
🎭	Theater	♨	Hot Springs	☎	Phone Office		